# FIFTY-ONE LANDMARK ARTICLES

# IN MEDICINE

# The JAMA Centennial Series

# FIFTY-ONE LANDMARK ARTICLES IN MEDICINE
## The JAMA Centennial Series

Edited by

Harriet S. Meyer, MD

Contributing Editor, JAMA

George D. Lundberg, MD

Editor, JAMA

AMERICAN MEDICAL ASSOCIATION

Chicago

Library of Congress Cataloging-in-Publication Data

Main entry under title:

Fifty-one landmark articles in medicine.

   ''This book is a collection of articles published weekly in
the *Journal of the American Medical Association* from July 3, 1983,
through August 10, 1984, as part of THE JOURNAL's Centennial
celebration. Each chapter consists of a landmark article that
was originally published in THE JOURNAL and a commentary
prepared for the Centennial Series by a current author. The
oldest article first appeared on August 30, 1884, and the most
recent on August 5, 1968'' — Pref.

   Includes index.

   1. Medicine — Addresses, essays, lectures.
2. Journal of the American Medical Association.
I. Meyer, Harriet S. II. Lundberg, George D.
III. American Medical Association. IV. JAMA.
[DNLM: 1. Medicine — collected works. WB 5 F469]
R111.F6 1985      610      85-11204
ISBN 0-89970-197-3

Printed in the United States of America

# The Journal of the American Medical Association.

## PUBLISHED WEEKLY.

Vol. I.
No. 1.

SATURDAY, JULY 14, 1883.

Annual Subscription, $5.00.
Single Copies, 10 Cents.

## CONTENTS.

# Journal of the American Medical Association.

## Editor: N. S. DAVIS, M.D., LL.D.

THE Official Organ of the American Medical Association. Published weekly in the place of the annual volume of Transactions that was formerly issued. It contains thirty-two pages of reading matter each week, distributed in the following departments: Original Matter; Editorials; Editorial Summary of Progress; Correspondence, Domestic and Foreign; Proceedings of Societies; Association News and Miscellany.

The JOURNAL has a wide circulation, going to all members of the Association and many subscribers in every State and Territory.

### Subscription Price, Five Dollars Per Annum.

Address,

## Journal American Medical Association,

65 RANDOLPH STREET, CHICAGO, ILLINOIS.

# Contents

# Foreword

This book is a collection of articles published weekly in the *Journal of the American Medical Association* from July 3, 1983, through August 10, 1984, as part of THE JOURNAL's Centennial celebration. Each chapter consists of a landmark article that was originally published in THE JOURNAL and a commentary prepared for the Centennial Series by a current author. The oldest article first appeared on August 30, 1884, and the most recent on August 5, 1968.

All authors of current perspectives were asked to comment on the background of the landmark article, its importance to its time, and its influence today; authors accomplished these ends in a variety of ways. We think that what the articles lack in uniformity they make up for in elan.

We gleaned candidate landmark articles from several sources: nominations by members of the *JAMA* staff and editorial board; entries in the work *A Medical Bibliography: Garrison and Morton* (third edition, 1976); and a list of most cited *JAMA* articles, provided by the Institute for Scientific Information in Philadelphia. We excluded articles published after 1969, because we thought it would be difficult to assess the historic impact of any article less than 15 years old.

The editorial board and staff members then rated the landmark potential of each of the 150 articles on the resulting list, and their votes, combined with some editorial judgment, resulted in our final selection. Readers of THE JOURNAL provided two additional articles (chapters 22 and 51 of this book).

It is well to review the past, for, as soon as a disease is elucidated or a cure discovered, the efforts and suffering therefrom are fast forgotten; as Dr. Bean writes in chapter 4, "We today who go careless and carefree are a forgetful people." Tortuous paths, insights clear to most of us only retrospectively, and remedies taken for granted fill these pages.

Also emergent are the major forms of medical discovery. The *experiment* illustrates enterprise and deduction at their best, in early efforts at transplantation (chapter 5), transmission of disease in animals as a first step in the hunt for an etiology (chapters 6 and 9), and the isolation in the laboratory of thyroxine (chapter 13). Clinical experiments take dramatic forms, including self-experimentation (chapter 26) and the willful infection of volunteers with yellow fever (chapter 4) and hepatitis (chapter 49).

While laboratory criteria are today more and more the staple of nosology, investigations into "new" diseases such as toxic shock syndrome and acquired immunodeficiency syndrome harken back to a time when the *case description* was prime in the elucidation of disease. Representative in this collection are the pioneer descriptions of dermatitis herpetiformis (chapter 1), tularemia (chapter 20), regional enteritis (chapter 23), atypical pneumonia (chapter 30), diffuse collagen disease (chapter 34), and the battered child syndrome (chapter 46).

The increasingly sophisticated *therapeutic trial* evolves in the pages of this collection, with the "Sippy diet" for ulcer (chapter 12), the Rubin test for fallopian tube patency (chapter 14), a diet for pernicious anemia (chapter 21), early antimicrobial trials (chapters 27, 33, 36, and 37), and nitrogen mustard derivatives in leukemia (chapter 40).

Toward the end of the collection emerges the *epidemiologic investigation,* exemplified by the landmark numbers of subjects in Hammond and Horn's study of smoking and disease (chapter 43) and the longevity of follow-up thanks to union records in the study of asbestos exposure and lung cancer (chapter 47).

Perhaps no advance is so bold as the first attempt at a new surgical procedure. However logical, much depends on its early success, especially if it is a radical or new solution, such as ductus arteriosus ligation (chapter 31) or the Blalock-Taussig shunt (chapter 38). A split-second decision may come into play, as in the first successful pneumonectomy (chapter 24). These and other *surgical series* in this collection exemplify the qualities Dr. Baue describes in the latter chapter:

the availability of appropriate technology . . . trained and experienced surgeons familiar with what has been done and what might be done, the courage to move beyond what is known, and serendipity — the right patient at the right time for an epochal event to occur.

Our contributors often place their topics in a social context. War can spur medical advances — the elucidation of yellow fever, the testing of chloroquine therapy for malaria. Events outside the medical sphere come into play — a suspected bootlegging (chapter 17), the sons of Presidents Calvin Coolidge and Franklin Roosevelt (chapter 27). Our medical knowledge and our laws are often out of phase. Dr. Shaw notes in chapter 15 that the actor Charlie Chaplin was convicted on a paternity charge, despite blood type evidence incompatible with guilt. In discussing the Harvard committee report on "irreversible coma" (brain death), Dr. Joynt writes, "It has made physicians into lawyers, lawyers into physicians, and both into philosophers" (chapter 50). How greatly out of step medical knowledge and society can be is perhaps best illustrated by the experience of Dr. Denslow Lewis, whose article, "The Gynecologic Consideration of the Sexual Act," appeared in THE JOURNAL 84 years after he first sought its publication (chapter 51).

The personal is an outstanding part of these articles, as the many names recognizable as eponyms and textbook authors attest. It is exciting that several of the perspective authors knew those on whose work they write. Many of the LANDMARK ARTICLE authors are still alive, and one contributes a perspective in these pages; two (Dr. Burrill Crohn and Dr. C. Henry Kempe) contributed letters illuminating their original work shortly before they died. Compelling persons, without whom it is hard to conceive of advances ever occurring, include Dr. Maxwell Finland (as Dr. Petersdorf notes in chapter 33) and Dr. Harvey Cushing — whose talents as a draughtsman will also be evident in chapter 3, along with his elegance of language — a feature, sadly, more common in yesterday's articles than today's.

It is hoped that these articles will inspire readers in more than one way. At opposite poles of a single process are the beauty of fulfilled prediction and the groping from a misleading clue to a correct solution. Both are the realization of the promise of the scientific method; as Gill and Jenkins write, it depends on

the importance of careful observation and logical follow-up at each step, the power of simple experimental approaches when used imaginatively, and balanced judgment and restraint in interpreting experimental data [chapter 48].

\*   \*   \*   \*   \*

Dr. Kempe has written in another context, "We are, in a way, one big family." That is exemplified in the efforts that have gone into this collection, and we wish especially to thank Drs. M. Therese Southgate and Lester King for their editorial and historical counsel; Marlene Hinsch, Cheryl Iverson, and JoAnne Weiskopf for supervising the production of the series; James Zrimsek for copy editing; Bonnie Van Cleven for seeing the series into book form; Micaela Sullivan and the staff of the AMA Library for bibliographic support; Sharon Iverson for enormous secretarial support; Sue Baugh for preparing the index; our esteemed contributors; and the entire staff and editorial board of THE JOURNAL, whose names appear on our masthead.

*H.S.M.*
*G.D.L.*

Chapter 1

⸺❧ T H E ❧⸺

# Journal of the American Medical Association.

EDITED FOR THE ASSOCIATION BY N. S. DAVIS.

PUBLISHED WEEKLY

| VOL. III. | CHICAGO, AUGUST 30, 1884. | NO. 9. |

# Dermatitis Herpetiformis

by Louis A. Duhring, M.D., of Philadelphia, Pa.

Read in the Section on Practice of Medicine and Materia Medica, of
American Medical Association, May, 1884.

Under the name Dermatitis Herpetiformis I propose to place a number of cases of skin disease that I have encountered from time to time. These cases at present are for the most part nameless, having been regarded and diagnosed, either as peculiar manifestations of one or another of the commoner and well-known diseases, as eczema, herpes, or pemphigus, or, in some cases, as undescribed diseases. From these remarks it will be inferred that the disease is rare, and such in a measure is the fact. At the same time I have met with a sufficient number of cases during the last fifteen years, to warrant the view that the disease is worthy of a special description and a name. I first recognized the affection as being peculiar as far back as 1871, but with the few cases observed at that time was at a loss to classify or to treat them satisfactorily. Since this date I have encountered a number of other cases illustrating the same and other varieties of the disease. In the first edition (1877) of my Treatise on Skin Diseases, I made no allusion to the subject, for the reason that my mind was not clear as to the relation that the several cases I had encountered bore one to another, nor that they were really all merely different manifestations of the same pathological process. In the light, however, of a number of marked cases that have now been under observation for a period of years, and of others that have been more recently noted, the statement may be made that, dissimilar as they may in some cases at first sight appear, they all represent varieties of one and the same disease, for which I propose the name "dermatitis herpetiformis."

In the present communication attention will be directed to the principal features of the disease, describing more particularly its symptoms and natural course. On another occasion cases illustrating the several varieties will be brought forward.

It may be premised here that dermatitis herpetiformis

includes what Hebra[1] designated first herpes impetiginiformis and afterwards "impetigo herpetiformis;" that is to say, that the cases of Hebra constitute one of the varieties of the disease it is proposed to call dermatitis herpetiformis. And here it may be remarked that this name must not be confounded with the "dermatitis circumscripta herpetiformis" of Neumann, a term introduced by this author a few years ago to designate lichen planus, which at that time he supposed to be an undescribed disease. It may be added that this term is now no longer used by Neumann.

In the second edition of my Treatise on Skin Diseases (1881) p. 276, under the title "impetigo herpetiformis," will be found an abstract of Hebra's description of the disease he so named.

His account may be summarized as follows: It is a rare and grave form of skin disease, of which, at the date of his report, he had seen but five examples, four of which terminated fatally. The disease is characterized by the formation of yellowish pustules, arranged in groups or in an annular form, which tend to run together and to dry into yellowish, greenish, or brownish crusts, beneath which a red, excoriated, moist surface exists. On the periphery of the lesions and patches new groups and rings of pustules form. The course of the disease was similar in every case. Each outbreak of pustules was preceded by malaise, chills, fever, and systemic disturbance. The disease occupied all regions, with preference for the anterior surface of the trunk and the flexor surfaces of the thighs.

Single cases, under different names,[1] were before this

---

[1] Wiener *Med. Wochensch.* No. 48, 1872; see also *Lancet*, March 23, 1872.

[1] Wiener *Med. Wochensch.*, No. 48, 1872; The *Lancet*, March 23, 1872; Atlas der Hautkrankheiten, Heft ix, Tafeln 9 und 10. Wien, 1876.

date reported by Bærensprung,[2] Neumann,[3] Auspitz,[4] and Geber.[5] Heitzmann[6] has more recently also reported a case with the name impetigo herpetiformis. As supplementary to Hebra's description, I gave my own experience with hitherto undescribed varieties of the disease in the following language: "*Within the last ten years I have from time to time met with cases, occurring in both sexes, representing other phases of the disease than heretofore described. In some cases the lesions were vesicular and bullous,[7] in others pustular; in still others, and in the majority of cases, bullous and pustular combined, or these lesions appearing alternately,—the disease being at one time vesicular and bullous, at another time pustular. In all instances the disposition to group or to extend about the periphery was more or less marked. A varied amount of constitutional disturbance, with violent itching, was always present. The disease manifested a disposition to constant recurrence, in the form of repeated attacks, extending in the majority of cases over years, and was but little influenced by treatment. None of the cases occurred in pregnant women; nor in any case has the disease proved fatal. The disease is liable to be confounded with eczema, ecthyma, and pemphigus, according as the lesions happen to be vesicles, pustules, or blebs. The etiology and pathology of the disease are both obscure. In some cases it possesses many features in common with pemphigus; . . . . . other cases, however, manifest but little disposition to the formation of blebs. It is therefore evident that the process is capable of appearing in the form of various lesions, and that the true impetigo herpetiformis represents but one variety of the disease. More information is needed before the disease can be assigned its proper place in classification.*"

These words, written four years ago, give a brief account of the disease which is the subject of this communication, and portray its important features. The description is succinct, but it embraces the leading points, and, it may be added, agrees with the views I hold at the present time.

It will be seen from this discription that the name impetigo herpetiformis is altogether inappropriate to express the condition in other and equally important varieties of the disease. The cases that fell under Hebra's observation were for the most part instances of the pustular variety, and he therefore regarded the name he selected as proper; but to call a vesicular or bullous disease "impetigo," with our present ideas of nomenclature, is of course most confusing. Because of the multiformity of the lesions manifested in the several varieties, which will be shown may exist, therefore I think the term dermatitis more suitable, allowing as it does all varieties of this most protean affection to come under its title. The

adjective herpetiformis expresses the chief characteristic of the disease, and as in Hebra's cases of the pustular variety, has been present in all of my cases. The disease is unquestionably herpetic, especially in its typical and commonest manifestation, that is, the lesions tend to be vesicular and to occur in small groups or clusters. And for this reason it has on several occasions occurred to me that the affection ought to be regarded as a herpes, an observation that was also made by Hebra, and by the other reporters of cases mentioned. All of these observers recognized its herpetic character.

The name herpes pruriginosus, it might be suggested, or herpes chronicus (as proposed by Neumann) would seem suitable and would answer well for most of the cases observed, itching being always a marked and constant symptom. At the same time, if this term were adopted, our present definition of herpes would require to be changed, and we should be obliged to regard pustular and bullous lesions as manifestations of herpes, an admission which would be confusing, or even disastrous in its results.

For these reasons I think the name now introduced preferable. That such a protean disease as I have intimated exists, and that these varied cutaneous manifestations are all but forms of one pathological process, there can be no doubt, and I shall elucidate this point by describing the several important varieties, which, as in the case of eczema, are based upon the predominance of certain lesions. Before doing this, however, I may refer to certain symptoms common to all forms of the disease, to which no particular allusion has as yet been made. In severe cases prodromata are usually present for several days preceding the cutaneous outbreak, consisting of malaise, constipation, febrile disturbance, chilliness, heat, or alternate hot and cold sensations. Itching is also generally present for several days before any sign of efflorescence. Even in mild cases slight systemic disorders may precede or exist with the outbreak. This latter may be gradual or sudden in its advent and development. Not infrequently it is sudden, one or another manifestation breaking out over the greater part of the general surface diffusely or in patches in the course of a few days, accompanied by severe itching or burning.

A single variety, as for example, the erythematous or the vesicular, may appear, or several forms of lesion may exist simultaneously, constituting what may very properly be designated the multiform variety. The tendency is, in almost every instance that I have observed, to multiformity. There is, moreover, in almost every case a distinct disposition for one variety, sooner or later, to pass into some other variety; thus, for the vesicular or pustular to become bullous, or *vice versa*. This change of type may take place during the course of one attack or on the occasion of a relapse; or, as is often the case, it may not show itself until months or years afterward. I have notes of several cases where, during a period of from two to five years, the erythematous, vesicular, and bullous varieties were all in turn manifested. Permit me, however, again to state that not only multiformity of lesion, but irregularity in the order of develoment, is the rule, whether during an attack or later in the course of the disease.

Itching, burning or pricking sensations are always

[2]Atlas der Hautkrankheiten, Tafel 8. Berlin, 1867.
[3]Lehrbuch der Hautkrankheiten, III. Auflage, Wien, 1873, p. 173.
[4]Archiv für Derm. und Syph., II. Heft, 1869, p. 246.
[5]Jahresb. des K. K. Allg. Krankenhauses zu Wien, Jahrg. 1871.
[6]Archives of Dermatology, January, 1878.
[7]In Hebra's fifth case the disease was characterized by vesicles and blebs, from which circumstance he was inclined to regard the disease as a variety of herpes, and designated it "herpes impetiginiformis." Lancet, March 23, 1872.

present. When the eruption is profuse they are intense, and cause the greatest suffering. As in the case of eczema, before and with each outbreak they become most violent, abating in a measure only with the laceration or rupture of the lesions.

The disease is rare, but is of more frequent occurrence than I formerly supposed. I have encountered fifteen cases, during a period of as many years, drawn from hospital, dispensary and private practice. All, with one exception, were adults, including both sexes in about equal proportion. The natural history is interesting. The process is in almost all instances chronic, and is characterized by more or less distinctly marked exacerbations or relapses, occurring at intervals of weeks or months. The disposition to appear in successive crops, sometimes slight, at other times severe, is peculiar. Relapses are the rule, the disease in most cases extending over years, pursuing an obstinate, emphatically chronic course. All regions are liable to invasion, including both flexor and extensor surfaces, the face and scalp, elbows and knees, and palms and soles. Excoriations and pigmentation, diffuse and in localized areas, are in old cases always at hand in a marked degree. The pigmentation is usually of a mottled, dirty-yellowish or brownish hue, and is persistent. I have seen it as pronounced as in chronic pediculosis corporis.

The more important forms of the disease may now be considered.

## DERMATITIS HERPETIFORMIS (ERYTHEMATOSA).

The erythematous variety manifests itself in patches or as a diffuse efflorescence, as an erythema or superficial inflammation, usually of an urticarial or erythema-multiform-like type. The urticarial element may be marked, the skin showing a disposition to acute œdematous infiltration in a diffuse form. Urticarial complication, rather than urticaria, is suggested by the condition of the skin; in like manner, a resemblance to diffuse erythema multiforme may be noted. At times the patches, whether discrete or confluent, are circumscribed, and later, by their coalition, show irregularly-shaped, marginate outlines, as in erythema multiforme. The color varies with the shape, being at first bright-red, but soon becoming deep-red or violaceous, mottled, and tinged with yellowish hues. The variegation is usually pronounced in the later stages of the process, at which period more or less diffuse pigmentation is also present. Together with the erythematous inflammation there may form maculopapules, or circumscribed or diffuse flat infiltrations, variable as to size and shape; also vesico-papules, the process now bearing a resemblance to the first stage of herpes iris. It will thus be noted that the eruption, in its general aspect and course, is much like that of erythema multiforme. In severe cases the outbreak is preceded by and accompanied with malaise, chilliness or slight febrile disturbance. The itching is generally violent, the disease differing in this respect from erythema multiforme.

Its course is variable. It may continue for days or weeks, or, as is usually the case, it may pass into the multiform variety, to be described later. It may be the first manifestation, or it may follow other varieties as a relapse.

As a variety, it is not as clearly defined as the vesicular, bullous or pustular, in some cases it appearing to be but the first manifestation of one of the first-mentioned forms. But it is important that its features be described, for the reason that it is liable to be met with as a clinical picture, and may readily be confounded with other diseases, notably, urticaria, erythema multiforme or eczema. I recall two cases where the diagnosis was at first difficult, and it was not until other manifestations appeared on the skin that the true nature of the process became evident.

## DERMATITIS HERPETIFORMIS (VESICULOSA).

The vesicular variety is that most frequently met with. It is characterized by variously sized, varying from a pin-head to a pea, flat or raised, irregularly shaped or stellate, glistening, pale-yellowish or pearly, usually firm or tensely distended vesicles, as a rule, unaccompanied by areolæ. In their early stages they can be seen only with difficulty, and are liable to be overlooked in the examination. Sometimes they can only be detected or seen to advantage in an oblique light. This observation I have repeatedly noted, and arises from the fact of the lesions being flat, translucent and without areolæ. In size they vary extremely, large and small being formed side by side, and in this respect they differ from the vesicles of eczema. Here and there papules, papulo-vesicles, vesico-pustules and small blebs will sometime be encountered. Concerning their distribution, the eruption as a whole is disseminate, the lesions existing scattered more or less profusely over a given region, as, for example, the neck or the back, but they are for the most part aggregated in the form of small clusters or groups of two, three or more; or there may be patches here and there as large as a silver dollar, upon which a number will be seated. When in close proximity they incline to coalesce, as in herpes zoster, forming multilocular vesicles or small blebs. Where this occurs they are generally slightly raised and are surrounded with a pale or distinctly reddish areola, which shows forth the irregular, angular or stellate outline of the lesion. At this stage, moreover, the little cluster will generally present a "puckered" or "drawn up" appearance, indicative of its herpetic nature.

The eruption is usually profuse, sometimes to the extent of the upper extremities, trunk and thighs being well covered. It may attack any region, the neck, chest, back, abdomen, upper extremities, and thighs all being especially liable to invasion.

The most striking symptom is the itching. Not infrequently burning is also complained of. Itching, however, predominates, and is in all cases violent or even intense. Patients state that it is altogether disproportionately in excess of the amount of eruption. It is, moreover, a persistent itching, causing the sufferer to scratch constantly. It generally precedes the outbreak, and does not abate until the lesions have been ruptured. Old sufferers, familiar with the natural course of the process, have informed me that they can obtain no relief until the lesions have been ruptured. From my observation I should say that the itching was both more severe and more lasting than in vesicular eczema. The vesicles make their appearance slowly, so that several days, or a week, may be required for their complete development. Notwithstanding that scratching is indulged in in the early stages of the disease, excoriations are not prominent, owing to the fact that the walls of the lesions are tough, and do not rupture, and that they incline to re-fill immediately on being evacuated.

The diagnosis in some cases is attended with difficulty, on account of the resemblance to vesicular eczema. I recall the embarrassment experienced in the classification of the earlier cases encountered, and the provisional diagnoses of "vesicular eczema?" made at the time. But the irregularity in the size and form of the vesicles; their angular or stellate outline; their firm, tense walls, with no disposition to rupture, and their herpetic character, will all serve to aid in the diagnosis. In some cases the constitutional disturbance and the magnitude of the eruption, as regards profusion, distribution, and multiformity, showing a more formidable disease than eczema, will also be striking. The itching and burning will usually be found to be more continuous and intenser than in eczema. The obstinacy of the disease to the ordinary treatment of eczema, moreover, must also soon become apparent, the usual milder remedies so frequently of service in acute vesicular eczema, being of little or no benefit in this disease. Finally, the tendency to repeated relapses, and the chronicity of the affection, must strike the observer as peculiar. This variety cannot be confounded with herpes zoster, herpes iris, or pemphigus. Its relations to the "herpes gestationis" of some authors will not be considered in this paper, further than to state that in my opinion they are probably one and the same disease. On a future occasion I shall deal more at length with this point.

## DERMATITIS HERPETIFORMIS (BULLOSA).

In the bullous variety the lesions are more or less typical blebs, tense or flaccid, rounded or flat, usually the former, filled with a serous or cloudy fluid, seated upon a non-inflammatory or slightly inflamed base. In size they vary from a pea to a cherry or walnut, and are for the most part irregular or angular in outline. They incline to group in clusters of two or three, the skin between them in this event being reddish and puckered. Sometimes in immediate proximity—almost contiguous—will exist one, two or three, or a part of a circle of small, pin-head sized, flat, whitish pustules. Vesicles of all sizes, flat or raised, are also generally found near by or disseminated over the affected surface. As in the other varieties, all regions may be attacked, especially the trunk, upper extremities and thighs. In several cases I have seen the greater part of the general surface invaded most profusely, in which event the lesions are usually smaller than where comparatively few exist. They incline to appear in crops at irregular intervals, as in the other varieties. The lesions are generally ruptured in the course of a few days and then crust over with a yellowish, greenish or brownish crust. They are accompanied by burning and itching, which may be very severe. They bear resemblance to those of pemphigus vulgaris, with which of course they may be readily confounded, but they are more herpetic in character. They differ in that they incline to group, and have a more inflammatory herpetic aspect, the type of which picture is seen in herpes zoster. Moreover, around and near the bleb will usually be found vesicles and pustules, the latter often in close proximity, the whole manifestation being quite different from that of pemphigus.

The pustular variety is generally less clearly defined than the vesicular, because the lesions are often intermingled with vesicles, vesico-pustules and blebs. In typical cases the pustules are acuminate, rounded or flat, tense or flaccid, usually the former, and vary in size from a pin-point to a pea or silver quarter-dollar. Vesicles and blebs in some cases precede the pustules. The smallest lesions are generally flat, or on a level with the surrounding skin, and, as stated, are frequently not larger than a pin-point or pin-head. Larger pustules, the size of a pea, are generally rounded or acuminate, and are surrounded by a reddish inflammatory areola. Later they incline to flatten, and to increase in size by spreading peripherally, and drying in the centre.

Sometimes they are seated on a slightly raised base. When fully matured they generally present an "angry" appearance, the skin immediately around them having a "puckered" look, from the fact that the pustule itself is irregular in outline, as sometimes is the case in herpes zoster.

They incline to form in groups of two, three or more, and moreover, often appear in patches of two or more groups. Such an arrangement is generally met with on the trunk. The grouping is further peculiar, in that a central pustule will often be immediately surrounded by a variable number of smaller pustules, sometimes in a circinate form, as in herpes iris.

In other localities, however, no such peculiarity occurs, the lesions being discrete, and even disseminate. The pustules are usually opaque, and of a whitish color; sometimes they are yellowish, though they are seldom so yellowish as in pustular eczema. Not infrequently slight hæmorrhagic exudation occurs, as in the later stages of herpes zoster, giving them a reddish, bluish or brownish hue. They are generally accompanied by sensations of heat, pricking or itching; in some cases these symptoms precede for several days the eruption. They pursue a slow course, from one to two weeks being usually necessary for their full development; in other cases their maturation occurs more rapidly. In some cases, together with the pustules are found vesicles and blebs of various shapes and sizes, and these often form immediately by the side of, or in close proximity to, the pustules. Papules and papulo-vesicles may also be present. In a given area, say of a few square inches, as for example upon the abdomen, there may exist all of these lesions in various stages of evolution. This multiformity is striking, and presents a curious and peculiar mixture of lesions. The attacks last from two to four weeks, after which there generally follows a comparative respite of from one to six weeks. The disease may thus be kept up indefinitely, the outbreaks being at one time slight, at another time severe.

Sometimes it has preceded other varieties; in other cases it has followed the bullous variety; while in some instances that have been under observation for a long period, it has at intervals of months alternated between the vesicular and bullous varieties. After what has been previously said, it need scarcely be stated that this variety is identical with the "impetigo herpetiformis" of Hebra, although in but few of the cases observed by me have the symptoms been so pronounced as in Hebra's experience, if I may judge from the portraits in his Atlas of Skin

Diseases. The account given by me relates to the disease as I have encountered it. Hebra's account has been already given, and need not be repeated here. The difference of experience concerns chiefly the severity of the process. Thus, in none of my cases has it proved fatal, while it will be remembered four out of five of Hebra's cases died, and according to Kaposi[1] (Hebra's successor), ten out of eleven cases observed by him have perished. Finally, I have observed it to occur about as often in men as in women, and also in the latter apart from pregnancy. Hebra, on the other hand, met with it only in women, and, moreover, only during the parturient state.

Concerning the constitutional symptoms, they may be stated to vary with the gravity of the attack. Usually, however, they are more marked than in the other varieties, rigors and alternate paroxysms of heat and cold being especially noticeable. It is the most serious phase of the disease.

## DERMATITIS HERPETIFORMIS (PAPULOSA).

The papular variety is in my experience rarer than any other form. I have met with only two cases, one in an adult, the other in a boy, and in both of these the eruption was scanty. It is characterized by the formation of small or large pea-sized, irregularly-shaped, usually firm, reddish or violaceous papular lesions, occurring for the most part in groups of two or three, scattered here and there over the affected surface. They are of variable size, large and small ones not infrequently existing side by side, and are as a rule ill-defined, being neither acuminate nor flat, but resemble the papular infiltrations sometimes met with in abortive herpes zoster. They are of an acute or subacute inflammatory type, and, as stated, bear resemblance to abortive herpetic lesions, and also to certain phases of chronic relapsing papular eczema. Their surfaces are generally excoriated, from scratching, and may be covered with blood-crusts, or with slight, adherent, thin epidermic scales.

The itching is severe, so much so that comparatively few lesions may so torment the patient as to interfere with the night's rest.

Ill-defined papulo-vesicles are also met with here and there, as in the case sometimes of papular eczema. The lesions pursue a slow, chronic course, lasting from one to two or four weeks, when they gradually disappear, leaving more or less pigmentation. Relapses are the rule at longer or shorter intervals.

As I have intimated, this variety bears a close resemblance to chronic papular eczema, and the earlier cases encountered by me were so diagnosed, but the irregularity in the size and form of the lesions; the disposition to group; the usually slow evolution of the lesions; the tendency to appear in crops at irregular intervals; the chronicity of the process; and the extreme obstinacy to local and internal treatment, are all peculiar. It is the mildest phase of the disease.

## DERMATITIS HERPETIFORMIS (MULTIFORMIS).

This may be regarded in the light of clinical variety, one that is eminently useful from a practical standpoint.

It is a variety of the disease in the same sense that eczema rubrum is a variety of eczema. It is important to consider it for the reason that it is a picture which may at any time show itself in the course of the disease. It is a phase not infrequently met with, and on account of the great mixture of lesions and the difficulties presented in diagnosis, is worthy of special description. The multiform variety consists of erythematous, sometimes slightly raised, urticarial patches of variable size and outline, often confluent, of a reddish or violaceous, yellowish, dusky, sometimes variegated, color, not unlike that of erythema multiforme. In addition, there often exist more or less well-defined, irregularly shaped or rounded, maculo-papules and flat infiltrations, papules and vesico-papules, all in various stages of evolution. Small blebs and pustules, pin-point sized or larger, may also be present, though with the vesicular element predominating it is not usual to meet blebs or pustules of large size nor in numbers. As the disease is in an early or late stage of its existence, will pigmentation and excoriations be slight or marked. Briefly, then, to recapitulate, there exists a mixture of lesions, with no single type predominating, calling to mind in its behavior eczema, although it is far more capricious and protean. It must also be remembered that the process may at any period change its type, such an occurrence usually taking place with an exacerbation or a relapse. Thus, the vesicular variety may exist for a variable period, to be followed in a few weeks or months by an attack of blebs, or it may be pustules, or by a mixture of the blebs and pustules. This mingling of several varieties is a marked and peculiar feature of the disease, giving a very striking dermatological picture, different from that seen in any other disease of the skin.

In conclusion, permit me to summarize by saying that I have endeavored to show:

1. The existence of a distinct, well-defined, rare, serious, inflammatory disease of the skin, manifestly of an herpetic nature, characterized by systemic disturbance, a great variety of primary lesions, by severe itching and burning, and by a disposition to appear in repeated successive outbreaks.

2. That the disease is capable of exhibiting itself in many forms, all having a tendency to run into or to succeed one another irregularly in the natural course of the process.

3. The principal varieties are the erythematous, papular, vesicular, bullous and pustular, which may occur singly or in various combinations.

4. That it is a remarkably protean disease.

5. That the pustular variety is the same manifestation as the disease described by Hebra under the name "impetigo herpetiformis," this being the only form hitherto described.

6. That the several other and equally important forms are worthy of special remark.

7. That the term "dermatitis herpetiformis" is sufficiently comprehensive and appropriate to include all varieties of the process.

8. That it may occur in both sexes, and in women independent of pregnancy.

9. That it usually pursues a chronic, variable course, often lasting years, and is exceedingly rebellious to treatment.

---

[1] Pathologie und Therapie der Hautkrankheiten, 2te Auflage, Wien, 1883.

July 8, 1983
(*JAMA* 1983;250:217-221)

# Dermatitis Herpetiformis Elucidated*

John B. Kalis, MD, Frederick D. Malkinson, MD, DMD

The early 19th century marked the birth of dermatology as a specialty in Europe. Postgraduate training in dermatology was available only in the European capitals. When Louis Duhring returned to his native Philadelphia after two years of specialty training in London, Paris, and Vienna, he established a private practice and a public dispensary devoted to the diagnosis and treatment of skin disorders. Duhring's keen clinical sense, pragmatic approach, clarity of prose, and thorough knowledge of the literature soon gained him local recognition. In 1873, he was appointed as a lecturer on skin disorders at the University of Pennsylvania, Philadelphia. In 1875, at the age of 35 years, he was appointed the first professor of dermatology at the University of Pennsylvania, a post he held for 35 years. His excellent textbooks, widely read here and in Europe, and his establishment of dermatitis herpetiformis (DH) as a distinct disease entity soon led to his recognition as one of this country's most renowned dermatologists.

In his original article, Duhring[1] described a group of patients with a chronic, pruritic, pleomorphic disease. He named this disorder "dermatitis herpetiformis" because of the herpetiform grouping of the more typical lesions and emphasized its diverse forms of presentation. Duhring's excellent clinical observations were the first to establish DH as a major distinct dermatosis, and, in many details, his perceptive descriptions of its signs and symptoms are as valid now as they were then. Before the publication of Duhring's article, many cases of DH had been described under a wide variety of confusing names. Through astute observations and the careful evaluation of previous reports, Duhring recognized the overall similarity of these seemingly diverse disorders. Between 1884 and 1897, he published 18 additional articles on the subject of DH. Only much later on did the

observations of others reveal that he had erroneously included among his cases the unrelated disorders of impetigo herpetiformis, herpes gestationis, and, perhaps, bullous pemphigoid.

Since 1884, but largely in the past 35 years, considerable progress has been made in the treatment of DH as well as in our knowledge of its immunologic aspects and pathogenesis. In addition, a number of other conditions associated with DH have been recorded. This commentary will review these various advances.

### Clinical Aspects

The prevalence of DH is unknown, but it is an uncommon disease, as Duhring emphasized. It occurs most frequently in whites and it seems to be rare in blacks. It may develop at any age but is most common in the second to fourth decades of life. Men are affected somewhat more often than women. As Duhring noted, the primary lesion is usually a vesicle; however, erythematous papules, persistent, edematous erythematous plaques, and, rarely, bullae may also occur. A herpetiform grouping of lesions is often but by no means invariably present. Excoriations are common, and scarring, when it occurs, is usually secondary to the trauma of vigorous scratching. Postinflammatory hyperpigmentation is also a frequent finding.

The lesions are symmetrically distributed, principally over the extensor surfaces, and are often widespread. Common sites of involvement include the elbows, knees, buttocks, sacrum, shoulders, posterior nuchal area, and scalp. The face, especially at the hairline, the shoulders, and the axillary folds may be affected. Oral mucous membrane lesions have been uncommonly reported but, in a certain percentage of patients, may have been overlooked.[2]

The major symptom of DH is pruritus, which can be of variable severity but is usually exceedingly intense. It has a notable burning quality that is of diagnostic importance.[1] A prodrome of burning or itching may precede, by eight to ten hours, the eruption of individual lesions or

From the Department of Dermatology, Rush-Presbyterian-St Luke's Medical Center, Chicago.

*A commentary on Duhring LA: Dermatitis herpetiformis. *JAMA* 1884;3:225-229.

groups of lesions. The patients invariably obtain symptomatic relief by forceable rupture of the vesicles.[1] Systemic symptoms are usually absent; if present, they are mild, in some contrast to the emphasis accorded them by Duhring.[1]

Dermatitis herpetiformis usually follows an eminently chronic course and persists for decades. Spontaneous exacerbations and remissions, with the latter occasionally lasting for months to two or more years, are characteristic. The occurrence of increased disease activity has been attributed to febrile illnesses, menses, and the use of oral contraceptives.[3,4] Long-term mitigation of disease severity and even permanent remissions occasionally occur in later years. The oral administration of potassium iodide frequently induces exacerbations of DH. Potassium iodide patch tests (up to 50% in petrolatum), applied to uninvolved skin sites, may produce clinical blisters in patients with untreated active disease, although the histopathological findings often differ from those seen in spontaneous DH lesions.[5]

### Histopathology

The histopathology of early nonvesicular lesions in DH may be diagnostic. It is characterized by variable numbers of eosinophils, polymorphonuclear leukocytes, and fibrin present in the dermal papillae and a perivascular lymphohistiocytic infiltrate in the upper and middle dermis. Characterization of the round cells in the infiltrate suggests a predominance of B cells in early lesions, followed later by a predominance of T cells.[6]

As the inflammatory process evolves with microabscess formation, a subepidermal separation results from necrosis in the tips of the dermal papillae. The overlying basement membrane is often but not invariably preserved.[7] The characteristic site of early blister formation occurring just below the basal lamina has also been shown by electron microscopy. In newly arising vesicles, the blister is multilocular, but later it becomes unilocular, at which time it is difficult to distinguish it diagnostically from other subepidermal blistering disorders.

### Gastrointestinal Manifestations

In the 1960s, DH was found to be associated with the small-bowel microscopic characteristics of gluten-sensitive enteropathy (GSE).[8,9] The current belief is that the etiology of DH may be inextricably linked to this associated gastrointestinal (GI) tract disorder. Although milder, the histopathological changes in GSE accompanying DH are similar to those found in adult celiac disease. They may also be found in the relatives of patients with DH, suggesting the presence of a genetic factor. The most common area of gut involvement is the proximal small intestine. Biopsy specimens show variable degrees of villous flattening and abnormalities of surface epithelial cells, elongation of the epithelial crypts, and a lymphocyte–plasma cell infiltrate, containing few neutrophils or eosinophils, present in the lamina propria. Uniform strict criteria for the diagnosis of small-bowel disease have not been established, but it is generally held that virtually all patients with DH have GSE. Biochemical evidence for the malabsorption of fat, D-xylose, lactose, glucose, folate, and vitamin $B_{12}$ may be found. The GSE of DH is indistinguishable from ordinary GSE, except for more severe histopathological and clinical findings in the latter. Malabsorption symptoms are present in 4% to 38% of patients with DH. The enteropathy is reversible on a strict gluten-free diet.[9]

Gastric abnormalities such as achlorhydria, hypochlorhydria, and gastric atrophy have been noted in many patients with DH. Gastric parietal cell antibodies and, rarely, pernicious anemia may also be found.[10]

### Immunology and Immunopathology

The most constant and virtually diagnostic laboratory finding in DH is a granular deposition of IgA in the papillary tips in perilesional and normal-appearing skin[11,12] as well as in unaffected buccal mucosa.[13] This disease feature has enormously increased the accuracy of diagnosis of DH. IgA deposition is persistent, unvarying in intensity over time, and rarely altered by therapy. The IgA deposited in the skin can bind a secretory component produced by GI tract epithelial cells, which suggests that it originates from plasma cells in the wall of the small intestine.[14] However, IgA deposits are not found in the gut lining. The IgA in the skin is commonly associated with the deposition of C3, C5, and properdin. This finding is consistent with alternate complement pathway activation. IgG and IgM may also occasionally be found in the papillary dermis along with IgA. Immunoelectron microscopic examination suggests that the IgA deposits are closely associated with dermal microfibrillar bundles.[15] However, the exact binding site for IgA is unknown. The diagnostic significance of the deposition of IgA in the papillary dermis of patients with DH is apparent from the results of a long-term study of 16 IgA-negative patients with clinical features suggestive of DH; an alternative diagnosis was subsequently established in 13 cases.[16]

The presence of IgA in the skin suggests either the occurrence of antibody formation to a specific skin antigen or the deposition of antigen-antibody complexes specifically or nonspecifically bound to the skin. To date, however, extensive investigations have failed to establish definitively either of these possibilities.

A circulating antibody with specificity for localization in the dermal papillary tips is essentially never demonstrable in the serum of patients with DH.[17] Antireticulin antibodies, which may cross-react with gluten and trap circulating gluten-antigluten antibodies in the dermal papillae, have been described in approximately 20% of patients with DH.[18] These antibodies are generally of the IgG or IgA class. They are also found in certain other diseases characterized by bowel mucosal damage, however. Likewise, IgA-, IgG-, and, later, IgM-class antibodies to gliadin, a constituent of gluten, have been reported in some patients with DH, indicating again that gut wall damage and increased permeability to certain antigens may enhance antibody formation.[19] Attempts to detect gluten in the skin of patients with DH by direct immunofluorescence microscopy have been unsuccessful.[10,19] However, gliadin has been shown to bind in vitro to reticulinlike fibers in human dermis and other tissues,[19] and serum gluten levels are elevated in patients with DH.[20]

The incidence of circulating immune complexes and their importance in DH are controversial. Circulating IgA complexes have been identified in 30% to 40% or more of patients with DH,[21,22] especially after wheat feeding.[23] Defective reticuloendothelial clearance of immune complexes has also been found in DH.[24] This suggests that circulating IgA immune complexes may provide the link between the pathological changes in the skin and gut. However, neither the level of immune complexes nor the severity of the clearance defect correlates well with disease activity.[21,24]

Postulates on the pathophysiology of DH have attempted to explain blister formation on immunologic grounds.[17] Subepidermal blister formation in DH is secondary to the destruction of the papillary dermis, and this, presumably, is enzymatic in origin. Polymorphonuclear leukocytes contain serine proteinases and collagenase. It is possible that the chemotactic complement components, generated by alternate pathway activation by IgA in the skin, may induce infiltration of the dermis by granulocytes, which then release these enzymes with resultant papillary dermal destruction. Such a hypothesis, although attractive, fails to explain either the absence of pathological changes in normal skin, which also shows deposition of IgA and complement, or the persistence of IgA in the skin of most patients who are in natural remission or have responded to a gluten-free diet (see next section). It should also be emphasized that early blister formation may occur in the absence of the polymorphonuclear cell infiltrate. Clearly, other factors in addition to IgA bound in the papillary dermis are required for blister formation.

In addition to antireticulin and antigliadin antibodies and circulating immune complexes, other autoantibodies and immunologic abnormalities have been described in DH. Antigastric parietal cell, antithyroid microsomal, anti-smooth-muscle, and antinuclear antibodies may be found in up to 50% of cases. Rarely, a decrease in serum C3, C4, and IgM levels may occur.[25,26]

## Histocompatibility Antigens

An increased incidence of DH occurs in persons with the histocompatibility antigens HLA-B8 and Dw3-Drw3. Although the frequency of these antigens in patients with DH ranges up to 80% to 90%, increases in their prevalence have also been found in such diseases as systemic lupus erythematosus (SLE), pernicious anemia, Sjögren's disease, and celiac disease, all of which have a presumed immunologic basis. Despite the presence of the associations, the occurrence of DH in multiple family members is rare, and not all patients with DH have these antigens. This suggests that the relevant immune-response gene may be in linkage disequilibrium with HLA-B8.

Anti-serum samples obtained from the mothers or multiparous wives of patients with DH have shown the presence of certain surface B-cell antigens associated with ordinary GSE and with DH.[27] These antigens appear to be distinct from the HLA antigens. It has been postulated that two sets of genes, determining the presence of the HLA complex and the B-cell surface

antigens, respectively, may act in concert to form a binding site for gluten protein, which then initiates an exaggerated immunologic response to gluten.[17]

## Associated Diseases

As previously stated, DH has been associated with other diseases having a presumed immunopathogenic origin. A wide variety of thyroid disorders has long been known to be associated with DH, and these may occur in a considerable percentage of patients. Variations in thyroid function have also been claimed to precipitate the disease onset or exacerbations or both. The concurrence of DH and pernicious anemia has also been recorded. Systemic lupus erythematosus, Raynaud's phenomenon, glomerulonephritis, vitiligo, diabetes mellitus, and atopic dermatitis all occur more frequently in patients with DH than in the normal population.[28]

In addition to the GSE seen in DH, ulcerative colitis may rarely be found. Several cases of a DH-like eruption, a nonspecific colitis, polyarthritis, and pyoderma gangrenosum have also been reported.[29]

There have also been occasional reports of intestinal lymphoma[30] and gastric carcinoma in patients with DH. Overall, however, there are no firmly established data demonstrating that patients with DH have a generally increased risk of malignant neoplasms.

## Differential Diagnosis

Because of the pleomorphic character of the DH eruption and the frequent accompanying excoriations, the disease may be confused with neurotic excoriations, prurigo, scabies, papular urticaria, and transient acantholytic dermatosis. Subcorneal pustular dermatosis and impetigo herpetiformis must also be considered in the differential diagnosis. The correct diagnosis can be made by careful clinical examination, histopathological study, and immunofluorescence microscopy. Subepidermal blistering disorders such as bullous erythema multiforme, herpes gestationis, linear IgA disease, chronic bullous dermatosis of childhood (CBDC), vesiculobullous eruptions of SLE, and bullous pemphigoid may be more difficult to differentiate from DH. Except for bullous erythema multiforme, in which immunofluorescence microscopy findings are restricted to superficial dermal blood vessels, these diseases require brief special comment.

Herpes gestationis is a pruritic, papulovesicular disease of pregnancy or the immediate postpartum period that was previously thought to be a variant of DH because of its close clinical resemblance to that disorder. On direct immunofluorescence microscopy, a linear deposition of C3 and, in some cases, of IgG is found at the dermoepidermal junction, rather than a granular deposition of IgA in the papillary dermis. A circulating herpes gestationis factor is often found in the serum of patients with this disease. This HG factor is an IgG anti-basement membrane antibody that is deposited in the lamina lucida.[31,32] Ultrastructurally, blister formation follows degenerative and necrotic changes in the epidermal basal cell layer rather than occurring below the basement membrane.[32]

In certain patients satisfying the clinical and histopathological criteria for DH, immunofluorescence microscopy reveals only a homogeneous or granular linear pattern of IgA deposition along the basement membrane zone. This differs from the granular pattern typically seen in the papillary dermis in DH.[12] These patients make up a distinct group that usually lacks gluten-sensitive enteropathy and, compared with patients with DH, has a somewhat lower or even normal frequency of HLA-B8 or HLA-Dw3 antigens.[33,34] Moreover, a circulating IgA anti-basement membrane antibody, absent in DH, may be present in patients with linear IgA disease.[17] Immunoelectron microscopy has localized the deposition of IgA to the lamina lucida or the subbasal lamina region.[15]

Chronic bullous dermatosis of childhood is a pruritic bullous eruption that, clinically and histopathologically, may resemble DH or bullous pemphigoid.[35] Unlike DH occurring in childhood, CBDC is usually a self-limited disorder. Like patients with linear IgA disease, CBDC cases usually show linear IgA deposition at the basement membrane zone on direct immunofluorescence microscopy, circulating IgA anti–basement membrane zone antibodies, and normal jejunal biopsy specimens.[36,37] Chronic bullous dermatosis of childhood is, therefore, considered by some to be a variant of linear IgA disease occurring in childhood.

A vesiculobullous eruption with histopathological and clinical findings closely resembling DH has recently been described in patients with SLE.[38,39] This eruption may or may not occur during a systemic exacerbation of SLE and is nonpruritic. Microscopically, the lesions show neutrophilic papillary microabscess formation, and the blister site is subepidermal. Leukocytoclastic vasculitis has also been noted in some patients.[39] Direct immunofluorescence microscopy of perilesional skin shows the deposition of linear IgG at the dermoepidermal junction (the lupus band) and, often, IgM, IgE, IgA and/or C3 at the dermoepidermal junction as well. It is obviously important to distinguish cases of this form of bullous SLE from the occasional case of concomitant DH and SLE.

Bullous pemphigoid is a subepidermal blistering disease in which tense bullae occur on erythematous or normal-appearing skin. On direct immunofluorescence microscopy, a linear deposition of IgG and C3 is usually found along the dermoepidermal junction. The immunoglobulin deposition has been localized to the lamina lucida of the basal lamina by immunoelectron microscopy. Also, a circulating anti–basement membrane zone antibody is often present in the serum samples of patients with bullous pemphigoid.

A congenital disease with the clinical findings of DH often present at birth has been shown to be a form of epidermolysis bullosa.[40]

With the exception of linear IgA disease, none of the previously mentioned disorders shows IgA deposition on direct immunofluorescence microscopy of biopsy specimens taken from normal skin sites.

## Therapy

Before the introduction of oral sulfapyridine treatment,[41] oral inorganic arsenical compounds were the principal form of therapy for DH. Because of the associated toxicity of these compounds and the risks for long-term occurrence of premalignant and malignant lesions, many other medications had also been used. These included ionizing radiation, UV radiation, autohemotherapy, intravenous sodium cacodylate, autogenous vaccines from stool, sedatives, cowpox vaccination, and antibiotics. Costello[41] clearly showed that sulfapyridine, but no other sulfonamide developed up to that time, produced dramatic clinical improvement or complete remission in patients with DH.[41] So striking was the treatment response that, for a time, such drug therapy was widely used as a diagnostic procedure for DH. Continuous sulfapyridine therapy was required for this long-lasting disorder, but drug doses well below those exerting antibacterial actions were highly effective. In later years, only sulfonamides possessing a pyridine ring were found to be effective for DH. In the early 1950s, the sulfone compounds, diasone and dapsone, were also shown to be extremely efficacious, although, again, continuous therapy was required for disease suppression.[42-44] Among current drug therapies, dapsone given orally is generally considered to be the treatment of choice for DH. New lesions cease to appear and the pruritus is often relieved within 24 to 36 hours after therapy is begun. Discontinuation of dapsone therapy results in the exacerbation of symptoms and signs, usually within 24 to 48 hours.

The mechanism of action of the sulfones is unknown. It is probably not caused by their antimicrobial effects because, like sulfapyridine, they may totally suppress disease manifestations in extremely small dosages (25 to 50 mg/day). The sulfones — and sulfapyridine — are known to be effective for several other dermatoses characterized microscopically by accumulations of polymorphonuclear leukocytes at disease sites. The anti-inflammatory effect of sulfones as well as of certain sulfonamides may be at least partly related to their inhibition of the myeloperoxidase-$H_2O_2$-halide–mediated cytotoxic system found in polymorphonuclear leukocytes.[45]

A gluten-free diet has been shown to be effective in reducing the required dapsone dosage over periods of months to years or, in many cases, in eventually replacing dapsone as the sole means of therapy.[9] The effectiveness of the diet is clearly related to the strictness with which the patient adheres to it.[46] Remission of the disease from a gluten-free diet may not be seen for six months to several years after the initiation of therapy but may persist, with dietary maintenance, indefinitely. Reversal of the jejunal villous architectural abnormalities and improvement in small-bowel function also occur on a gluten-free diet, although this is not seen with dapsone therapy. After many years, a gluten-free diet is occasionally followed by some diminution of IgA deposition in the skin,[46] but it is more regularly associated with a substantial reduction in antireticulin and antigluten antibody titers.[47] The reintroduction of gluten into the diet usually results in the exacerbation of DH and the accompanying enteropathy over a two-week to several-month period. Overall, where patient compliance is eminently good, a gluten-free diet alone is the treatment of choice for DH, although initially combined drug treatment may be needed for a rapid response.

When a gluten-free diet is unacceptable to the patient and in patients in whom therapy with dapsone or sulfapyridine is contraindicated because of the potential or regularly occurring side effects of these drugs, colchicine may be given. The therapeutic response to this drug is variable but may be impressive, especially if patients can tolerate the higher drug dosages.[48] In some cases, however, a gradual escape from therapeutic response may occur. Dermatitis herpetiformis responds unpredictably to corticosteroids given for systemic effects, but the persistent nature of the disease usually obviates long-term therapy with these agents because of the anticipated incidence of serious side effects. Overall, in this eminently chronic disease, which may endure from years to decades, no curative therapies are currently available. Nevertheless, complete and continuous disease control can be achieved in almost all patients with sulfapyridine or sulfone therapy alone, a strict gluten-free diet alone, or a suitable combination of drug and dietary treatment.

### References

1. Duhring LA: Dermatitis herpetiformis. *JAMA* 1884;3:225-229.
2. Fraser NG, Kerr NW, Donald D: Oral lesions in dermatitis herpetiformis. *Br J Dermatol* 1973;89:439-450.
3. Haim S, Friedman-Birnbaum R: Hormonal factors in dermatitis herpetiformis. *Dermatologica* 1972;145:199-202.
4. Katz SI: Dermatitis herpetiformis. *Int J Dermatol* 1978;17:529-535.
5. Haffenden GP, Blenkinsopp WK, Ring NP, et al: The potassium iodide patch test in dermatitis herpetiformis in relation with a gluten-free diet and dapsone. *Br J Dermatol* 1980;102:313-317.
6. Reitamos S, Reunala T, Kontinnen YT, et al: Inflammatory cells, IgA, C3, fibrin and fibronectin in skin lesions in dermatitis herpetiformis. *Br J Dermatol* 1981;105:167-177.
7. Riches DJ, Martin BGH, Seah PP, et al: The ultrastructure changes in the skin in dermatitis herpetiformis after withdrawal of dapsone. *Br J Dermatol* 1976;94:31-37.
8. Marks J, Shuster S, Watson AJ: Small bowel changes in dermatitis herpetiformis. *Lancet* 1966;2:1280-1282.
9. Fry L, McMinn RMH, Cowan JD, et al: Effect of gluten-free diet on dermatological intestinal and haematological manifestations of dermatitis herpetiformis. *Lancet* 1967;1:557-561.
10. Katz SI, Hall RP, Lawley TJ, et al: Dermatitis herpetiformis: The skin and gut. *Ann Intern Med* 1980;93:857-874.
11. Cormane RH: Immunofluorescent studies of the skin in lupus erythematosus and other diseases. *Pathol Eur* 1967;2:170-180.
12. Fry L, Seah PP: Dermatitis herpetiformis: An evaluation of diagnostic criteria. *Br J Dermatol* 1974;90:137-146.
13. Harrison PV, Scott DG, Cobden I: Buccal mucosa immunofluorescence in coeliac disease and dermatitis herpetiformis. *Br J Dermatol* 1980;102:687-688.
14. Unsworth DJ, Leonard JN, Payne AW, et al: IgA in dermatitis-herpetiformis skin is dimeric. *Lancet* 1982;1:478-479.
15. Yaoita H: Identification of IgA binding structures in skin of patients with dermatitis herpetiformis. *J Invest Dermatol* 1978;71:213-216.
16. Fry L, Walkden V, Wojnarowska F, et al: A comparison of IgA positive and IgA negative dapsone responsive dermatoses. *Br J Dermatol* 1980;102:371-382.
17. Katz SI, Strober W: The pathogenesis of dermatitis herpetiformis. *J Invest Dermatol* 1978;70:63-75.
18. Seah PP, Fry L, Hoffbrand AV, et al: Tissue antibodies in dermatitis herpetiformis and adult coeliac disease. *Lancet* 1971;1:834-836.
19. Unsworth DJ, Leonard JN, McMinn RMH, et al: Anti-gliadin antibodies and small intestinal mucosal damage in dermatitis herpetiformis. *Br J Dermatol* 1981;105:653-658.
20. Lane AT, Huff JC, Weston WL: Detection of gluten in human sera by an enzyme immunoassay: Comparison of dermatitis herpetiformis and celiac disease patients with normal controls. *J Invest Dermatol*

1982;79:186-189.
21. Hall RP, Lawley TJ, Heck JA, et al: IgA-containing circulating immune complexes in dermatitis herpetiformis, Henoch-Schönlein purpura, systemic lupus erythematosus and other diseases. *Clin Exp Immunol* 1980;40:431-437.
22. Zone JJ, LaSalle BA, Provost TT: Circulating immune complexes of the IgA type in dermatitis herpetiformis. *J Invest Dermatol* 1980;75:152-155.
23. Zone JJ, LaSalle BA, Provost TT: Induction of IgA circulating immune complexes after wheat feeding in dermatitis herpetiformis patients. *J Invest Dermatol* 1982;78:375-380.
24. Lawley TJ, Hall RP, Fanci AS, et al: Defective Fc-receptor functions associated with the HLA-B8/DRw3 haplotype. *N Engl J Med* 1981;304:185-192.
25. Fraser NG, Dick HM, Crichton WB: Immunoglobulins in dermatitis herpetiformis and various other skin diseases. *Br J Dermatol* 1969;81:89-95.
26. Mohammed I, Holborow EJ, Fry L, et al: Multiple immune complexes and hypocomplementaemia in dermatitis herpetiformis and coeliac disease. *Lancet* 1976;1:487-490.
27. Mann DL, Katz SI, Nelson DL, et al: Specific B-cell antigens associated with gluten-sensitive enteropathy and dermatitis herpetiformis. *Lancet* 1976;1:110-111.
28. Davies MG, Marks R, Nuki G: Dermatitis herpetiformis: A skin manifestation of a generalized disturbance in immunity. *Q J Med* 1978;186:221-248.
29. Perry HO, Brunsting LA: Pyoderma gangrenosum: A clinical study of 19 cases. *Arch Dermatol* 1957;75:380-386.
30. Gjone E, Norday A: Dermatitis herpetiformis, steatorrhea and malignancy. *Br Med J* 1970;1:610.
31. Katz SI, Hertz KC, Yaoita H: Herpes gestationis: Immunopathology and characterization of the HG factor. *J Clin Invest* 1976;57:1434-1441.
32. Yaoita H, Gullino M, Katz SI: Herpes gestationis: Ultra-structure and ultrastructural localization of in vivo-bound complement. *J Invest Dermatol* 1976;66:383-388.
33. Lawley TJ, Strober W, Yaoita H, et al: Small intestinal and HLA types in dermatitis herpetiformis patients with granular and linear IgA skin deposits. *J Invest Dermatol* 1980;74:9-12.
34. Leonard JN, Haffenden GP, Ring NP, et al: Linear IgA disease in adults. *Br J Dermatol* 1982;197:301-316.
35. Esterly NB, Furey NL, Kirschner BS, et al: Chronic bullous dermatosis of childhood. *Arch Dermatol* 1977;113:42-46.
36. Marsden RA, Skeete MVH, Black MM: The chronic acquired bullous disease of childhood. *Clin Exp Dermatol* 1979;4:227-240.
37. Chorzelski TP, Jablonska S: IgA linear dermatosis of childhood (chronic bullous disease of childhood). *Br J Dermatol* 1979;101:535-542.
38. Penneys NS, Wiley HE: Herpetiform blisters in systemic lupus erythematosus. *Arch Dermatol* 1979;115:1427-1428.
39. Hall RP, Lawley TJ, Smith HR, et al: Bullous eruption of systemic lupus erythematosus. *Ann Intern Med* 1982;97:165-170.
40. Anton-Lamprecht I, Schnyder UW: Epidermolysis bullosa herpetiformis Dowling-Meara. *Dermatologica* 1982;164:221-235.
41. Costello MJ: Sulfapyridine in the treatment of dermatitis herpetiformis. *Arch Dermatol* 1947;56:614-622.
42. Esteves J, Brandao FN: Au sujet de l'action des sulfamides et des sulfones dans le maladie du Duhring. *Treb Soc Portuguesa Dermatol Venereol* 1950;8:209.
43. Cornbleet T: Sulfoxone (diasone) sodium for dermatitis herpetiformis. *Arch Dermatol* 1951;64:684-687.
44. Kruizinga EE, Hamminga H: Treatment of dermatitis herpetiformis with diaminodiphenylsulphone (DDS). *Dermatologica* 1953;106:383-394.
45. Stendahl O, Molin L, Dahlgren C: The inhibition of polymorphonuclear leukocyte cytotoxicity by dapsone: A possible mechanism in the treatment of dermatitis herpetiformis. *J Clin Invest* 1978;62:214-220.
46. Fry L, Leonard JN, Swain F, et al: Long term follow-up of dermatitis herpetiformis with and without dietary gluten withdrawal. *Br J Dermatol* 1982;107:631-640.
47. Ljunghall K, Scheynius A, Jonsson J, et al: Gluten-free diet in patients with dermatitis herpetiformis. Effect on the occurrence of antibodies to reticulin and gluten. *Arch Dermatol* 1983;119:970-974.
48. Silvers DN, Juhlin EA, Berczeller PH, et al: Treatment of dermatitis herpetiformis with colchicine. *Arch Dermatol* 1980;116:1373-1374.

Oct 5, 1889
(*JAMA* 1889;13:478-483)

## Chapter 2

# Diagnosis and Treatment of
# Abscess of the Antrum

*Read before the Section of Laryngology and Otology, at the Fortieth
Annual Meeting of the American Medical Association, at Newport,
June, 1889.*

by J. H. Bryan, M.D.,
of Washington, D.C.

The antrum is that triangular-shaped cavity in the superior maxilla, sometimes found extending into the malar bone forming a second cavity. It is lined by mucous membrane continuous with that of the nose, and it is occasionally thrown into folds forming partial septa, a fact of considerable clinical importance. It varies in size according to the age and sex of the individual, being small in children, and larger in the male than in the female. It diminishes in size in old age and after the loss of the teeth.

Of the surgical affections of the antrum, suppurative inflammations play the most important part. Until within recent years abscess of the antrum was regarded as rather an uncommon affection, but we now know that it exists much more frequently than was formerly supposed. It occurs generally after the second dentition; although there is one case recorded by P. B. Pedley,[1] of a girl 8 years of age, where the abscess was due to caries of a temporary canine tooth.

Among the causes of abscess of the antrum may be enumerated: 1. traumatism; 2. the acute infectious diseases, such as measles scarlet fever and smallpox; 3. syphilis; 4. an extension of the inflammation from the lining membrane of the nose; 5. extension of the inflammatory process from the suppurating pulp of a tooth resulting from dental caries. Authorities differ as to the most common of these causes. Zuckerkandle, for example, believes that it is more often due to an extension of the inflammation from the nose; while others regard disease of the teeth the principal factor in the etiology. I am of the opinion that the form of inflammation of the antrum characterized by a sero-mucous secretion, and known as *hydrops antri*, is the result of an extension of a

catarrhal inflammation of the nose. On the other hand, that form which is more chronic in character, and is accompanied by a mucopurulent secretion, is the result of an extension from the teeth.

The under surface of the antrum is separated from the alveolar process by a thin lamella of bone, which is formed with the development of the permanent teeth; occasionally, however, it is absent, and the roots of the teeth are then likely to extend into the antral cavity. Its floor is in close relation to the roots of the first and second molar teeth; and when the cavity is unusually developed the roots of the first and second bicuspid teeth are brought in contact with it. Lying in such close proximity to the floor of the maxillary sinus, the teeth when diseased are likely to transmit the septic process there, and set up a suppurative inflammation.

The symptoms of this affection vary with the intensity of the inflammation. In a few cases there is distension of the walls of the superior maxilla and swelling of the cheek of the affected side; pain in the infra-orbital region, and at the inner angle of the orbit; tenderness on pressure over the canine fossa, and occasionally a crepitating sensation imparted to the fingers, due to a springing of the distended walls of the antrum; a narrowing of the field of vision, due to pressure on the floor of the orbit, a symptom, according to Ziem, much more frequently associated with affections of the ethmoid cells, and a valuable point in the differential diagnosis between abscess of the antrum and of the ethmoid cells. In some cases there is a discharge of fetid pus from the nose, generally unilateral and of long standing. Long continued secretions of pus from the nose, especially when confined to one side and associated with caries of the molar teeth, should always direct our attention to the antrum as the source of the trouble. A suppurative inflammation of the

---

[1]Lancet, Feb. 16, 1889.

nose is an extremely rare affection. Stoerk has described such a disease, occurring as an epidemic among the Gallician Jews.[2] It may, however, occur from infection, as for example, from gonorrhœal poison.

There are four possibilities, after eliminating wounds, and inflammations following the acute exanthemata that may give rise to pus in the nasal chambers: 1. foreign bodies, including nasal polypi; 2. diseases of the bones; 3. secretion of pus from the antrum of Highmore; 4. secretion of pus from the frontal sinus and from the anterior ethmoid cells. The secretions from the anterior ethmoidal cells may enter the middle meatus, along with those from the frontal sinus, through the infundibulum, while the secretions from the posterior cells find their way into the pharynx along with those from the sphenoidal sinus.

If the pus should continue to flow after the removal of the polypi, or foreign body, we are then likely to have either an abscess of the maxillary sinus, of the frontal sinus, or of the ethmoid cells. Occasionally it is difficult to differentiate between these, for in each case pus is found in the middle meatus extending along the inferior border of the middle turbinated bone. When this body is sufficiently contracted, which can be accomplished by an application of a 20 per cent. solution of cocaine, the middle meatus will be brought into full view, and pus found in the hiatus semi-lunaris. If it is not possible to bring about the contraction of this body by cocaine, then the hypertrophied or swollen tissue should be destroyed by means of the cautery, or chromic acid. The opening of the frontal sinus will be found just below and in front of the ostium maxillare in a funnel-shaped depression—the infundibulum. Owing to the close proximity of these two openings it is very difficult to discover from which the pus flows. Hartmann, of Berlin, has suggested the following device to ascertain the source of the secretions: After drying the parts thoroughly with absorbent cotton, he drives a blast of air through the affected nostril by means of a Politzer air-bag. By this procedure he claims to be able to aspirate the pus from the sinus and thus discover its source. Another point in the differential diagnosis is that abscess of the maxillary sinus is of comparatively frequent occurrence, while that of the frontal sinus is rare.

The most positive means of differentiating between these two affections, is by making an exploratory puncture, as suggested by Moritz Schmidt.[3] He places a small pledget of cotton saturated with a 20 per cent. solution of cocaine under the inferior turbinated body, about its middle, and allows it to remain in until the parts are thoroughly anæsthetized; then raising the end of the turbinal body, he pierces the thin wall of the antrum with a sharp-pointed and curved syringe. The point of the instrument should be not too fine, so that it will bend or break when making the puncture. There is no pain following the operation and it is entirely devoid of danger. This little instrument should be employed in all doubtful cases, and its use will, I think, tend to prove that the affection is much more common than is generally supposed. The indications for treatment are to let out the

pus and drain and disinfect the cavity until the inflammation subsides. If the abscess should point anywhere it should be evacuated at that place.

A great deal has been written recently with regard to the surgical treatment of these cases, and it is interesting to note the tendency on the part of modern surgeons to deviate from the well-tried practice that has stood for nearly a century, and to return to the original suggestion of John Hunter, and the practice of Jourdain—to evacuate these abscesses through the nose.

For nearly a century the practice has been to enter the antrum from the mouth. The operation that has met with the most favor is that known as Cooper's—through the alveolar process. In case a molar tooth is present it should be extracted and the opening enlarged; or if, as frequently happens, the tooth has been extracted at some previous time, the alveolar process should be perforated at that point. This is best done by means of a small trephine, attached to a surgical engine, or to the electric motor. The instrument should be directed slightly forwards and inwards. This operation has the advantage: 1. that of draining the antrum at it most dependent part, and that the cavity can be readily cleansed by syringing; 2. that it can be performed without the aid of an anæsthetic—a few drops of a 4 per cent. solution of cocaine injected into the gum being sufficient to completely anæsthetize the parts. Its disadvantages are: 1. the liability of food and bacteria from the mouth to enter the sinus and assist in keeping up the suppuration; 2. the occasional necessity of extracting a sound tooth.

If the front wall of the antrum should bulge forward in the canine fossa, then the operation known as Desault's should be performed—resecting a small piece of bone from the fossa. Other surgeons have opened the antrum through this fossa by means of a trocar, and Fergusson recommended an ordinary carpenter's gimlet.

Another operation through the mouth is that devised by Bertrandi, who opened the antrum through the hard palate, when a slight bulging of that bone showed a tendency on the part of the abscess to open at that point.

Hartmann, of Berlin, revived, in 1884, a method proposed by Jourdain in the early part of the present century, of washing out and disinfecting the antrum through its natural opening, the ostium maxillare, in the middle meatus. This procedure is also recommended by Stoerk, and they claim to have cured a number of cases in this way. The disadvantages of this procedure are great and the results so uncertain that it will never be generally used; for the antral opening in the middle meatus is situated so far above the floor of that cavity that it cannot be thoroughly drained, and it would be impossible to wash out through a tube of small calibre the thick colloid secretions that are so often found in these abscesses.

The antrum is a pneumatic extension of the nasal chamber and communicates normally with it. When for any reason this communication is shut off the operation that would restore its natural condition would seem the most rational one to select. Jourdain opened this sinus through the infundibulum, in the middle meatus; but this operation never became popular, because, owing to the high situation of the point selected for making the opening, it was difficult to perform it. It is, moreover, not

[2]Krankhieten des Kehlkopfes, p. 161.
[3]Berl. Klin. Wchschr., Dec. 10, 1888.

unattended with danger, owing to the possibility of wounding the floor of the orbit.

Mikulicz advises that the antrum be opened through the lateral wall of the nose at a point where it is thin and easily perforated.[4] He uses a special instrument for the purpose, which consists of a sharp, double-cutting knife attached to a handle bent at a blunt angle. It has a flange, so as to prevent its being shoved in too deep. The parts having been thoroughly anæsthetized with cocaine, the instrument is passed into the nose, and when about the middle of the inferior meatus, it is turned outward and by firm pressure is made to penetrate the thin wall of the sinus. By a to and fro movement the opening can be made as large as desired.

This operation has the advantage of draining the cavity at its floor, and the opening being easily accessible it can be readily syringed out; the secretions pass through the nose, instead of into the mouth, and there is little danger of the entrance of foreign particles into the antrum to keep up the suppuration. This operation is, however, not practicable: 1. when the nasal chambers are of abnormally small calibre; 2. when there is a deflected septum; and 3. when there is marked hypertrophy of the inferior turbinated body. The principal disadvantage of the operation is that it leaves a ragged edge in the wall of the antrum, against the margins of which the nasal secretions are caught, and becoming dried and hardened may cause an ulceration when an attempt is made to remove them.

The local treatment is very important, the successful issue of the case depending largely upon the solutions used, and the care with which they are applied. The cavity should be irrigated or syringed gently with mild disinfecting and stimulating lotions daily until all suppuration has ceased, when the main opening may then be allowed to close.

The fetor that almost invariably accompanies these conditions is best overcome by means of a solution of permanganate of potash, after which the cavity should be syringed with a weak solution of common salt and carbolic acid. If the solutions are applied through an opening in the alveolar process, great care should be exercised not to drive them too forcibly against the roof of the cavity, for by so doing distressing pain may be produced in the eye.

This treatment will, in many cases, be all that is required; but in the more obstinate forms of inflammation the local application of the peroxide of hydrogen will be found very efficacious; or, better still, glycozone, a mixture of the peroxide of hydrogen and glycerine. In this preparation we have the combined effect of the glycerine, which abstracts water from the lining membrane of the cavity and keeps it constantly flushed, and the peroxide, which destroys its septic contents and, at the same time, stimulates the inflamed membrane to healthy action. The following are notes of four interesting and instructive cases that have come under my observation:

*Case 1.*—Mrs. E. presented herself for treatment March 3, 1887, giving the following history: She has had frequent attacks of coryza, and for a number of years has suffered from hay fever. Two years ago she had consider-

able trouble with the second molar tooth in the upper jaw on the left side, which the dentist broke in attempting to remove it, leaving the roots in the gum, and they, from time to time, have caused her pain. About a week prior to consulting me she caught a severe cold at a funeral; since then she has suffered intense pain in the face and in the ear; for several days there has been a watery discharge from the nose. Examination: The left side of the face is very much swollen, and there is some distention of the anterior wall of the superior maxilla; pressure upon the affected side of the face is very painful and gives a crepitating sensation to the fingers; the nose is tightly blocked on the left side, the right side partly open; the first and second biscupid teeth are absent on the left side, the roots of the second molar remaining and deeply imbedded in the gum; the remaining teeth are in good condition; secretions from the nose are watery in character; examination of the left ear shows a small fistulous opening in external auditory canal just under the annulus tympanicus, about midway of its anterior inferior quadrant, but having no connection with the middle ear: mt. normal in color; hd. $\frac{24}{24}$.

On March 4th I perforated the antrum through the canine fossa by means of an ordinary trocar and inserted a Knapps mastoid drainage tube, small size. There was a profuse muco-purulent flow following the operation. The cavity was washed out with a warm solution of common salt and carbolic acid. After the third syringful had been injected the solution passed out of the nose. There was little or no odor present. This treatment was pursued daily for ten days, when the secretions ceased entirely. The drainage tube caused some irritation in the cellular tissue of the cheek, and was removed at the end of the seventh day. Two days after the operation the nose opened on both sides, so that a rhinoscopic examination could be made. The mucous membrane of the left side was deeply congested and very sensitive, the mildest applications causing paroxysms of sneezing. There was also an ulceration of the septum about the size of a silver three-cent piece, laying bare the cartilage. By the use of detergent sprays the inflammatory condition subsided, and the application of a solution of nitrate of silver (gr. v, ad, $\frac{7}{5}$ j) to the ulcer caused it to heal, completely covering the cartilage.

*Case 2.*—Mr. _____, U.S.N., presented himself in the spring of 1888, complaining of a nasopharyngeal catarrh of long standing, and stated that he was sceptical as regards a cure. He complained principally of a profuse secretion of the nose, and when in the reclining position the secretions dropped into his throat, causing him great annoyance.

On examination the inferior turbinals on both sides were markedly hypertrophied, so much so that no satisfactory examination of the upper part of the nasal chambers could be made. The septum was slightly deviated to the left in its upper part. The vault of the pharynx was bathed with a white secretion, but there was no swelling or hypertrophy in this region. The hypertrophied tissue was reduced on both sides by means of the galvano-cautery and chromic acid. The left middle turbinal body was then found enlarged, leaving only a fissure between it and the deflected septum. Pus was found in this fissure and in the middle meatus, reappearing as soon

---

[4]Archiv. für Klin. Chir., Berl., xxiv, 626.

as it was wiped away with absorbent cotton.

Upon further inquiry he stated that in 1867 he had some trouble with the second molar tooth in the upper jaw on the left side. The nerve was killed and the tooth filled without removing the dead pulp. After suffering for two years with frequent small abscesses around the tooth the filling and the decomposed tissue were removed. He dates the nasal discharge from six months after the first filling was put in. He has never had any pain in the face, but it is somewhat fuller on the affected side. The nasal discharge has been constant and very annoying.

Being unable to decide whether there was an abscess of the ethmoid cells, complicating the antral condition, the case was referred to Prof. Harrison Allen, who diagnosed an abscess of the maxillary sinus. At this point my relations to the case terminated, for he was transferred to his attending physician, Dr. Rixey, U. S. N., through whose courtesy I am allowed to continue the report of the case.

The second molar tooth was extracted and found badly ulcerated at its roots, the opening in the alveolar process was enlarged and the cavity syringed with warm, disinfecting solutions, bringing away a great quantity of very fetid pus and mucus. The treatment has been carefully carried out under Dr. Rixey's direction with marked improvement in his condition. Although there is some secretion still, sufficient to require the cavity to be washed out once a day, he is comparatively comfortable. He wears a gold tube in the alveolar opening, covered by a plate, so as to prevent any of the secretions passing into the mouth.

*Case 3.*—Mrs. P., admitted Sept. 10, 1888, complaining of a fetid discharge into the mouth through an opening left by a recently extracted tooth. She gave the following history: For a number of years she has been afflicted with nasal catarrh, for which she received treatment from numerous physicians without any benefit. About three years ago the secretions from the left side of the nose became so profuse that her life has been a burden. She frequently complained of toothache, and a week ago she had the second molar tooth on the left side extracted. Since then the nasal secretions have greatly diminished, but a great quantity of foul pus is passing constantly into the mouth. She complains of constant nausea and loss of appetite, and is obliged to mop the gums constantly, so as not to swallow the pus. There has never been any swelling of the face, and the patient does not recall having had any tenderness on that side of the face. Present condition: She has an anxious expression; complexion sallow; tongue furred; pus was observed flowing freely from the opening in the gum; a probe passed readily into the antrum; no swelling or pain on pressure on the affected side of face. Examination of the nose shows a collection of thin pus in the middle meatus along the lower border of the middle turbinal on the left side; the right side shows no abnormal condition.

The opening into the antrum was enlarged and the cavity syringed with a solution of permanganate of potash. Immediately there came from the left side of the nose a great quantity of fetid and dark green pus, partly fluid and some of thicker consistency. The odor was almost unbearable. The cavity was washed out daily with a solution of common salt and carbolic acid for nearly three weeks, when the discharge ceased entirely and the opening into the antrum was allowed to close.

*Case 4.*—Capt. _____, U. S. A. First seen Feb. 1, 1889. Complained of nasal catarrh, from which he has been suffering for a number of years. When a cadet at West Point the nerve of the left second molar tooth was killed. Two years later the tooth broke off and a piece of raw cotton was taken out of it in a very fetid condition. He never had any trouble with his nose prior to that time. There has always been more or less pain in the left side of the face since the tooth was filled. About two years ago the secretion of pus from the nose became very annoying, dropping back into the pharynx when he is in the reclining position.

Examination shows the left side of the face to be somewhat fuller than the right. There is a suffusion of the conjunctiva of the left eye which has existed for some time. The second molar tooth in the upper jaw on the affected side is absent; the other teeth are in good condition. There is a thin purulent secretion from the left side of the nose, which is most abundant in the middle meatus; it recurs rapidly after removal. The mucous membrane on the affected side of the nose deeply congested. The alveolar process was opened by means of a small trephine, 3 mm. in diameter, attached to a surgical engine, the gum having been previously anæsthetized by the injection of a few drops of a 4 per cent. solution of cocaine. The cavity was readily reached, and it was then syringed out with a warm solution of bicarbonate of soda. A great quantity of fetid pus, mixed with a thick yellow colloid mucus, came out through the nose. There was some bleeding following the operation, but that soon ceased. The antrum was washed out daily for ten days with a solution of common salt and carbolic acid, when the odor ceased, but with little effect on the quantity of secretion of pus. The treatment was then changed to a solution of boracic acid, with no marked improvement following. One application of a solution of bichloride of mercury (1-2500) was made, but owing to the severe pain it caused it was not tried again. I then used a solution of the peroxide of hydrogen with some benefit, but as the improvement was not as rapid as could be desired I was advised to try glycozone. Each application was followed for several hours afterwards by a profuse watery discharge from the nose. The improvement, after the use of this application, was marked from the outset, and in ten days after its first application all suppuration had ceased, the opening in the alveolar process was allowed to close, and the patient was discharged cured.

My experience with glycozone is limited, and I can only judge of its efficacy in this one case; but it seems to me to possess advantages that we have long been in need of in treating these chronic abscesses of the maxillary sinus.

DR. J. O. ROE said: It is my opinion, based on my own experience, that abscess of the antrum is more often caused by diseases in the nose than by diseases of the teeth. I can now recall eight cases of abscess of the antrum that have come under my care. In four of these cases the abscess was caused by, or associated with, nasal polypi, and there was no disease of the teeth. In three of the other cases the disease was associated with, and apparently caused by, dental caries. In two of the four cases associated with nasal polypi the abscess was not suspected before the polypi were removed, the fetid discharge being attributed to retained secretion that had become decomposed. In every case there was more or less nasal disease. In the study of these cases I concluded that the nasal difficulty had a marked influence in the production of the disease in the antrum; first by the irritation in the nose, causing a turgescence of the lining membrane of the interior of the antrum; secondly, by the direct extension of the disease from the nose into the antrum over the continuous surface, and thirdly, by closure of the nasal opening into the antrum by the disease in the nose, thereby causing a retention of the discharge excited by the congestion or disease in the antrum.

DR. LIPPINCOTT was under the impression that purulent disease of the antrum was frequently due to morbid conditions of the teeth. Abscess of the orbit not infrequently has for its *raison d'etre* a suppuration process originating in the antrum; and in a large proportion of orbital abscesses arising in this way the primary cause has been dental caries.

DR. E. FLETCHER INGALS, of Chicago, had treated several cases of the kind. One had been cured after about three weeks' treatment, having been washed out repeatedly with peroxide of hydrogen through the normal opening into the nasal cavity. However, he had three cases under observation where every form of treatment had been inefficient in checking the purulent discharge. They had worn tubes in the alveolar process for periods of five, three and two years respectively, and in neither did there appear to be any dead bone, as the discharge was not offensive. He thought that an opening at least 8 mm. in diameter should be made, to allow the introduction of a tube and free discharge.

DR. DALY, of Pittsburg, President, said he had had some experience in the disease of the antrum referred to in the paper just read, and had written a paper upon a series of such cases, which he read before the American Laryngological Association some eight years ago. He was in the habit of opening the antrum through the alveolar process. A surgical engine is not necessary for this. He had once gone into the antrum through the socket of a tooth by means of a small bevel-pointed screw-driver belonging to a gun case. It ought to be borne in mind, however, that the operation is not without danger. One of the brightest men that has ever adorned the American medical profession died a day or two following an operation on his antrum—a man whose teachings have since become regarded as revelations made far in advance of his time and profession. I refer to the late Dr. Beard, of New York. The surgeon who operated on Dr. Beard gave me, shortly after, an account of the operation, which was done with his customary care and skill. The opening was large and made into the antrum by means of the dental engine. Within twenty-four hours after the patient had a chill and other symptoms of septic infection, and died, creating an irreparable loss to the medical profession. The after treatment is necessary to be continued with the utmost care and asepticism for a long time, and not among the least useful and efficient cleanser is one that is nearly always at the hand of the patient, wherever he may be. I refer to soap and water. The third case upon which I operated went to the far West after a few weeks' care, having with him a prescription for an antiseptic fluid which was ordered to be used several times a day. The patient lost the bottle, or broke it, and as a *dernier ressort* used soap and water, found it efficient and continued it until the discharge ceased at the end of six months. He has for eight years remained quite well.

DR. D. BRYSON DELAVAN, of New York, referred to a case of abscess of the antrum which had resisted a great variety of treatments at skillful hands, in which the application of the galvano-cautery to the mucous membrane of the middle turbinated body of the affected side was followed by marked temporary relief.

DR. BRYAN agreed with all that had been said, and further stated that the obstinacy of these cases was, he thought, largely due to incompletely washing out the cavity, leaving septic matter between the partial folds of mucous membrane, which is sufficient to start up the inflammation again after it had apparently subsided.

July 15, 1983
(JAMA 1983;250:400-404)

*Landmark Perspective*

# Abscess of the Antrum—Pioneer Rhinology*

Byron J. Bailey, MD

It is both an honor and a challenge to review and comment on the landmark publication entitled "Diagnosis and Treatment of Abscess of the Antrum," by Joseph H. Bryan, MD, published in the Oct 5, 1889, issue of THE JOURNAL. Bryan's original manuscript was presented to those assembled at the Section of Laryngology and Otology at the 40th Annual Meeting of the American Medical Association, which was held in June 1889.

The great significance of this publication is apparent when it is placed in the context of the location and time of its publication. European physicians were providing most of the advances in rhinology. The brief period between 1886 and 1893 is the interval during which physicians began to become aware of the frequent need for surgical intervention in the management of chronic sinus infection. In 1886, Mikulicz[1] published his important work in Germany, recommending the transnasal, surgical management of chronic maxillary sinus infection, and, in 1893, an American physician, George Walter Caldwell[2] described the approach to the maxillary antrum via the canine fossa, an operation that has remained important to the present day.

The report by Bryan emphasizes the key elements of diagnosis, the variety of manifestations, and the contemporary medical management of sinusitis, but its chief importance rests in the emphasis given to the need for surgical therapy in the event of persistent maxillary sinus abscess.

A review of several historical conditions and dates serves to illuminate the context of the setting in which this contribution was provided.

### Historical Perspectives—1889

In 1889, Benjamin Harrison had just been elected the President of the United States by the vote of the Electoral College after failing to win a majority of the popular vote, and Queen Victoria reigned over the British Empire. The Republic of Brazil was founded in this hemisphere. The population of the United States had grown to approximately 62,000,000 people. It was the year of the tragic Johnstown flood, in which 2,000 people lost their lives, and the year in which the "great land rush" had opened the Oklahoma Indian Territory for settlement.

In the world of commerce, Bell's telephone was beginning to be seen as more than a curiosity, Edison's electrical light was celebrating its tenth birthday, and the first automobiles powered by internal combustion engines had been produced independently by Daimler and Benz two years previously.

It was an exciting time in the area of medical science generally, as advances in pharmacology, surgery, and anesthesia were expanding the therapeutic options available to physicians.

In Germany, Ferdinand Cohn had established the foundation for the science of bacteriology in 1872, and, five years later, Robert Koch published his fundamental postulates for determining the etiology of specific infectious diseases. Progress was rapid, and by 1885, Louis Pasteur was able to report the successful use of a vaccine to prevent rabies in a young boy.

In 1889, Joseph Hammond Bryan, MD (1857-1935), was an otolaryngologist in private practice in Washington, DC. He had been graduated from the University of Virginia, Charlottesville, and received further medical training at the University of the City of New York.

At the time, otolaryngology and ophthalmology were specialties that were often practiced conjointly. They were, to some degree, leading the transition from general medicine and general surgery toward an era of specialization. In large cities, eye and ear hospitals were emerging and were viewed as resources where patients might obtain the best medical care for problems involving these anatomic regions. Bryan was one of four physicians who founded the Episcopal Eye, Ear, and Throat Hospital of Washington, DC.

Dr Bryan seems to have been a scholarly reader and author, and his work reflects familiarity with the most current publications and concepts from Europe and the United States. Between 1883 and 1898, Bryan published 18 articles, most of which dealt with various aspects of sinus infection and surgical management of diseases of the paranasal sinuses.

Practitioners of this relatively new specialty had begun to organize into professional societies, and we note that this was the 40th Annual Meeting of the Section of Laryngology and Otology of the AMA, making it the most senior specialty organization still in existence today. The American Otological Society had been founded 21 years previously, and the American Laryngological Association had been organized ten years previous to this publication. It would be another seven years before the organization of the American Academy of Ophthalmology and Otolaryngology and the American Laryngological, Rhinological, and Otological Society.

Bryan was a fellow of the American College of Surgeons and a member of the AMA and the American Otological Society. In 1891, he became a member of the American Laryngological Association, in which he subsequently served as librarian (1894) and president (1902).

Although he was beyond the usual age for military

---

From the Department of Otolaryngology, University of Texas Medical Branch, Galveston.

*A commentary on Bryan JH: Diagnosis and treatment of abscess of the antrum. JAMA 1889;13:478-483.

service, Bryan enlisted in the US Army Medical Corp during World War I and subsequently became chief of the Eye, Ear, Nose, and Throat Service at the Walter Reed General Hospital, Washington, DC.

It was noted that, "while his prime consideration was the profession of medicine, he developed many lay connections because of his loyal public spirit, kindly nature, firm convictions, sense of justice, and personal philosophy."[3]

Bryan died on Feb 3, 1935, at the age of 78 years, after suffering a cerebral hemorrhage.

The trend toward specialization was viewed with alarm by some and actively opposed by many others. One of the foremost critics of the evolution of specialization was Sir William Osler, who spoke out against specialty development with great vigor and eloquence on many occasions. Among his most serious attacks are the following:

No more dangerous members of our profession exit than those born into it, so to speak, as specialists. Without any broad foundation in physiology or pathology, and ignorant of the great processes of disease, no amount of technical skill can hide from the keen eyes of colleagues defects which too often require the arts of the charlatan to screen from the public.[4]

Two years later, Osler stated: "There are, in truth, no specialties in medicine, since to know fully many of the most important diseases a man must be familiar with their manifestations in many organs."[5]

Osler pursued his comments along these lines with later statements such as the following: "By all means, if possible, let [the young physician] be a pluralist, and — as he values his future life — let him not get early entangled in the meshes of specialism."[6] He then went further to say: "The incessant concentration of thought upon one subject, however interesting, tethers a man's mind in a narrow field."[7]

### Rhinology in 1889

We must recall that the field of rhinological diagnosis and treatment was in its infancy at the time of this publication. There were no effective antibiotic agents, roentgenographic studies were not to be introduced for another seven years, and anesthesia provided limited opportunities for performing complex operative procedures.

On a more fundamental level, a review of standard textbooks of that day indicates the serious lack of understanding of the pathophysiology of sinus infections and even lack of awareness of the importance of this group of disorders. Examples of this are numerous on review of these textbooks, and one finds that the typical reference book of the day may contain more than 100 pages on diseases of the nasal cavity, without making a single reference to any pathological conditions involving the paranasal sinuses. The illustrations in these textbooks show pathological changes in the nasal cavity in great detail, while presenting only a sketchy outline of the maxillary antrum, almost as if it were a "twilight zone" either too complex to comprehend or too unimportant to merit careful depiction. It was not until about 1900 and thereafter that standard textbooks in otolaryngology began to deal with diseases of the paranasal sinuses in more than a superficial and passing manner.

The earliest awareness of the need to remove irreversibly and chronically diseased tissue from the maxillary antrum began to appear during the 1890s. In the textbook by E. B. Gleason, *A Manual of the Diseases of the Nose, Throat and Ear,* correlation of persistent, unilateral, purulent nasal drainage with chronic paranasal sinus infection (usually involving the maxillary antrum) was described in the following manner: "A discharge of pus from one nostril, especially if periodic in character, which smells and tastes fetid to the patient, should always excite the suspicion of disease of the antrum. Upon inspection, the pus will be found flowing from beneath the middle turbinated body."[8]

It is somewhat surprising, therefore, to note the emphasis that Bryan places on the significance of maxillary sinusitis when he states that, "of the surgical affections of the antrum, suppurative inflammations play the most important part." During the 1880s, abscess of the antrum was regarded as an uncommon problem, but today we see chronic maxillary sinusitis frequently. The maxillary sinus continues to be the region most often involved in paranasal sinusitis, and infection remains as the most frequent indication for surgical treatment. The frequency of pediatric sinusitis apparently was underestimated by the physicians of that time. It seems that a single case report of maxillary sinusitis in a girl 8 years of age was worthy of a report in *Lancet* that same year. Today, we recognize the rather common occurrence of acute sinusitis in children and note that chronic sinusitis and complications of sinusitis in the pediatric age group are not rare.

Ludwig Grunwald[9] of Munich states in the preface to his book published in 1900:

The subject of nasal suppurations has not yet been treated in detail by any author. I was induced to attempt the task by the conviction that the importance of purulent nasal discharge as a symptom is very far from being appreciated by the public, and that this indifference is to some extent shared by the profession. Yet, it is a symptom which is common to various conditions, some quite trivial, and others threatening life.

In addition it was my object to show that this symptom in the great majority of cases depend[s] upon local (or circumscribed) disease, which, as a rule, requires surgical treatment for its cure.

Grunwald also states a few pages later that "to Ziem belongs the credit of having shown that a large proportion of cases of nasal suppuration are due to localized diseases, more especially of the accessory sinuses." A review of Ziem's publications indicates that between 1889 and 1893, he published four articles correlating the presence of maxillary sinusitis with parotid swelling, iritis, peritonsillar abscess, and metastatic abscesses in distant sites.

While Bryan attributes a disproportionate importance to the relationship between maxillary sinusitis and dental infection, it seems that he is due a great deal of credit for the originality of his observations in regard to the significance of primary infection of the maxillary sinus.

The etiologic factors for maxillary sinusitis are listed by Bryan as trauma, "the acute infectious diseases, such as measles, scarlet fever, and smallpox," syphilis, spread of nasal infection, and extension of dental infection. Comparing these observations with the current textbook emphasis, one notes that there has been a shift toward increasing importance of viral nasal infection and allergic rhinitis as the two major factors predisposing to maxillary sinusitis.

Obviously, the incidence of smallpox, measles, scarlet fever, and syphilis has been diminished by global immunization programs and antibiotic therapy. Today, the major bacterial offenders are the ubiquitous staphylococci and streptococci, with an increasing importance being given to infections caused by *Hemophilus influenzae.* These tremendous changes in emphasis on etiology cause us to wonder how different these factors will be in the year 2083. The differentiation proposed by the author's suggestion that acute maxillary sinusitis is a disease arising from nasal infection while chronic maxillary sinusitis results from dental infection has not been borne out by subsequent investigation. Dental sources probably account for less than 10% of the cases of maxillary sinusitis, either acute or chronic. Factors that produce obstruction of the sinus opening (eg, allergic rhinitis, polyps, septal deviation) seem to be the primary consideration in the case of chronic or recurrent sinusitis today. The reference to "inflammation of the antrum characterized by a sero-mucous secretion, and known as *hydrops antri*" may refer to infection of the sinus in association with a viral upper respiratory tract infection or might indicate an awareness of allergic rhinosinusitis, but we are not given sufficient detail to be certain.

In Wright's[10] textbook, *A Treatise on Diseases of the Nose, Throat, and Ear,* published in 1902, chapter 21 is entitled "Diseases of the Accessory Sinuses" and was written by Sir St Clair Thomson. Thomson states that the causes of sinusitis are not well determined but that they may be either primary or secondary. He notes that sinusitis is seen in conjunction with influenza, pneumonia, enteritis, measles, scarlatina, smallpox, and meningitis with fairly high frequency. Less common etiological factors are diphtheria, erysipelas, glanders, mumps, and gonorrhea. Even less commonly, sinusitis is seen in conjunction with acute rheumatism, acute peritonitis, and "contracted kidney." Poisoning with mercury, phosphorous, and lead are described as predisposing factors, as are "diving into the water, feet foremost," and inserting probes or cannulas into healthy sinuses. Thomson also indicates that most chronic sinusitis follows several episodes of acute sinusitis.

Thomson, who practiced in London, also quotes another article by Joseph H. Bryan[11] and describes him as one of the authorities who has pointed out the frequency with which sinus infections are associated with ophthalmologic complications. Thomson then goes on to state that "the study and general recognition of the latent form (chronic sinusitis) dates from the year 1886, when attention was particularly directed to it by Ziem."

### The Role of Dental Infection

Further along in his article, Bryan returns to the importance of the dental origin of sinus infection. This emphasis was common in other reports of the period, and while it is possible to accept this concept, the overstatement may have been related to the difficulty of examining the nasal cavity carefully. The overemphasis on the association between dental and sinus infection may have accounted for the prevalent and standard surgical practice of the time — approaching the interior of the maxillary sinus surgically through a carious, infected tooth for the purpose of draining the infection. An effort was made to extract the tooth to gain access to the antrum; the surgeon enlarged the opening by means of various surgical instruments of the day. The popularity of this approach probably served to delay the acceptance of more appropriate procedures that provide access to the sinus by opening through the lateral wall of the nose or the canine fossa.

We recall that dentists of that time were engaged primarily in the extraction of teeth and that dental hygiene for the general public, preventive dental care, and restorative dentistry were in their infancy. It is possible that dental caries and infection were so advanced and widespread in the adult population that they did account for a much higher percentage of the sinus infections seen by physicians.

### Description of Symptoms and Findings

Bryan's description of the symptoms and physical findings is of high quality, and, characteristic of the period, there is a predominance of careful observation and literary excellence over factual scientific reporting. Bryan groups under the heading of symptoms and signs of sinusitis the following features: (1) "distention" of the walls of the maxilla (which might describe a number of different pathological conditions, including mucocele, osteomyelitis, and subperiosteal abscess), (2) swelling of the cheek (which might include all of the previously mentioned conditions plus cellulitis), (3) tenderness on pressure in the canine fossa, and (4) narrowing of the field of vision (possibly secondary to orbital cellulitis or abscess, rather than pressure, and not necessarily a key point in differentiating maxillary sinusitis from ethmoid sinusitis).

His description did not include such common symptoms and signs as the following: (1) perennial or seasonal nasal obstruction, (2) posterior and anterior nasal drainage, (3) associated obstructive septal deviation, (4) fever, and (5) malaise.

### Differential Diagnosis

Bryan elaborates the differential diagnostic possibilities for purulent nasal discharge after trauma and nasal infection, and these are of interest. He refers first to the possibility of nasal "foreign bodies, including nasal polypi," indicating that there was little understanding of the pathophysiological process associated with nasal polyposis.

Grunwald,[9] of Munich, provided broader insight into this area in his textbook, *A Treatise of Nasal Suppuration,* when he stated: "My own view is that polypi in a majority of all cases are almost as good as pathognomonic of empyemata of the accessory cavities, or focal suppuration in the nasal passages." Thus, it seems that physicians at the time associated the presence of polyps in the nasal cavity with chronic suppuration rather than with allergic rhinitis, which is believed to be the more common etiologic correlate today.

Bryan further states that another cause for similar signs and symptoms is related to "diseases of the bones," a rather cryptic statement that may refer to the presence of exposed bone secondary to necrosis of the overlying mucosa or to a secondary osteomyelitis as a complication of persistent sinusitis. These pathological conditions were sometimes believed to be the cause of dental infections and in other instances were seen as the result of dental infection. Grunwald,[9] having had more experience with maxillary sinus surgery, describes the presence of exposed bone at the time of antrotomy and deals with this subject more extensively.

Infection involving the frontal and ethmoid sinuses is also noted to be a distinctive diagnostic possibility that might be confused with maxillary sinusitis in some patients.

While Bryan alludes to the concept of allergic rhinitis, contemporary authors explored the state of this concept in more detail. For example, Morell MacKenzie[12] described the excellent clinical investigations reported by Blackley in 1873, in which he was the first to document the relationship between minute amounts of pollen and the symptoms of nasal congestion and rhinorrhea. He conducted these experiments on himself and showed that the pollen from grasses and flowers were capable, by themselves, of provoking an attack of allergic rhinitis. Previous to that time, a wide range of factors had been implicated, including the following: (1) the "nervous temperament" of the patient, (2) the pursuit of higher education (one series reported that allergic rhinitis was present in 49 of 59 patients with advanced education and concluded that it was a disease of the educated class), (3) heat (the episodes were more prevalent in the summertime), (4) light (more patients were afflicted during the time of the year when the days were longer), (5) excessive ozone in the atmosphere, and (6) overexertion.

Morell MacKenzie advised treatment by avoiding exposure to pollen, and he must have been popular with his patients, at least those who could afford to follow his therapeutic regimen, which included the following advice: "a sea voyage is probably the most perfectly satisfactory step that can be taken," "take up residence at the seaside," and, further, "remain indoors during the whole of the hayfever season." For those who could not afford this therapy, he recommended plugging the nose with cotton wadding. The common remedies of the day included zinc and asafetida pills, belladonna, and quinine.

Bryan believed that persistent, purulent rhinorrhea after polypectomy was an indication of the likelihood of sinus abscess and went on to describe the problems of differentiating the exact sinus involved. Being aware that the frontal, maxillary, and anterior ethmoidal sinuses all drain into the same small area, he advised the following diagnostic steps that were "state of the art" in 1889 and remain in use in modified form today: (1) the use of cocaine solution to shrink the middle turbinate and permit visualization of the middle meatus area so that the source of the pus can be distinguished precisely, (2)

excision of excessively hypertrophic turbinates, and (3) pressure displacement of pus from the involved sinus by means of a forced flow of fluid past the sinus ostia.

Finally, Bryan concludes appropriately that it is known that abscess of the antrum occurs frequently, while frontal sinus abscess is rare. He recommends that if all else fails, one should fall back on the rules of statistical probability.

As "the most positive means" of diagnosing antral abscess, Bryan recommends an exploratory puncture as suggested by Moritz Schmidt. After topical cocaine anesthesia, a sharp-pointed and curved syringe is introduced through the thin wall of the antrum and the contents are aspirated. He may be forgiven for falling victim to his enthusiasm when he states that "there is no pain following the operation and it is entirely devoid of danger," and he was basically correct in proposing (1) that diagnostic puncture be used in all doubtful cases, (2) that purulent sinusitis would be found to be "much more common than generally supposed," (3) that treatment should be instituted "to let out the pus and drain and disinfect the cavity until the inflammation subsides," and (4) that if the abscess points at a particular spot, that area should be the area of evacuation.

## Major Significant Observations

The most significant features of this article relate to Bryan's impressions concerning the need to move away from the evacuation of antral abscesses in the mouth and back "to the original suggestion of John Hunter, and the practice of Jourdain—to evacuate these abscesses through the nose." Today, the most common surgical procedure to establish maxillary sinus drainage is the creation of a permanent nasoantral window in the region of the inferior meatus of the lateral wall of the nasal cavity. For almost a century now, this technique has remained in favor.

Bryan's article marks the beginning recognition of the need for surgical intervention in the case of chronic, purulent infection of the maxillary sinus. At the time of his writing, operations on the maxillary antrum were held in low regard in the United States, and maxillary surgery had barely begun to emerge in Europe, as recorded by Grunwald.

Apparently, the creation of an opening between the nose and the maxillary sinus through the inferior meatus was first described by the English surgeon, Gooch,[13] who died in 1780 and whose original contribution was noted by Adelmann. The procedure of nasoantral fenestration did not gain favor until it was reintroduced and popularized by Mikulicz[1] in 1886 and strongly endorsed by Krause, another prominent German surgeon.

It was probably on the basis of observations by surgeons during the period from 1886 to 1893 that there developed a growing awareness of the concept of surgical excision of irreversibly damaged sinus mucosa. Prolonged infection was noted to produce ulcerative, proliferative, and polypoid changes in the sinus lining that could not be managed by any technique short of removal.

The nasoantral approach to the maxillary sinus is extremely limiting in terms of the visibility and access to the antrum with surgical instruments. It is likely that these deficiencies led to the development of a more radical antrostomy technique to gain improved visualization and access to the maxillary sinus.

It remained for Henri H. Luc[14] of France and George W. Caldwell[2] of the United States to develop and report independently on their experience with the canine fossa radical antrostomy. These pioneer surgeons have been rewarded for their efforts by the crediting of this common surgical procedure to them, and it bears their eponym in current medical practice.

After 1900, the Caldwell-Luc operation rapidly replaced the practice of the preceding century, ie, the drainage of the maxillary antrum into the mouth (Cooper's operation) by a surgical approach through the alveolar process after the extraction of a molar tooth.

Bryan indicated his perceptiveness in surgical matters by his emphasis on the aggressive local treatment by irrigation and cleansing of the diseased area, which he described as "very important."

At one point in the article, Bryan falls victim to a common literary error. He describes the procedure in question and recommends that an opening be made "about the size of a silver three-cent piece." This comment should serve to remind all authors to avoid any description of size other than that using the metric system or a description that involves a comparison not likely to become obsolete.

Bryan's comments concerning the long-term morbidity associated with retained dental roots and dental fragments remain an important admonition. These fragments act as a foreign bodies and serve to form the nidus of a chronic infection that will defy cure until the offending marterial is removed.

In case 3, Bryan describes a patient with nasal secretions "so profuse that her life has been a burden." Most of us have experienced a mild sinus infection with prompt recovery and we remember the event as nothing more than a minor inconvenience, but it is important to remember that patients who suffer chronic sinusitis have symptoms and debilitation that are not comparable in degree or in kind. These patients are deserving of our most effective medical and surgical efforts, and, in fact, they must have these if they are to return to a complete state of health.

The section involving the discussion of the article is also worthy of comment. The comments offered by Dr Roe indicate his awareness of some of the pathophysiological features of chronic sinus infection as they relate to the spread of infection from the nasal cavity to the sinuses. Dr Daly described his treatment of a famous physician of the time who died one day after exploration of the antrum as a result of septicemia, calling to mind the potentially fatal sepsis against which we protect our patients today with antibiotics whenever any instrumentation or operation involving the paranasal sinuses is undertaken. The rich blood supply and direct venous drainage to the cavernous sinus must remain ever in our minds as we work in this area. Dr Ingals described the good results that he had obtained from irrigation of the natural ostium, and this technique has withstood the test of time and continues to be a useful adjunct for refractory

cases even today. Dr Delavan emphasized the important principle of surgical management of associated obstructive lesions to establish adequate drainage from the maxillary sinus. The article lacks a clear elaboration of the importance of the surgical removal of all irreversibly diseased mucosa from the maxillary sinus in the presence of chronic infection, although this importance is implied.

---

It has been, for me, a stimulating and satisfying experience to prepare this review. The opportunity to take a close look at the careful and innovative work of many pioneer physician-scientists has served to restore an appropriate perspective and appreciation for the abilities of these men. Dr Bryan and the prominent physicians who discussed his article have made important contributions that have benefited all of us who practice in the specialty today. By a coincidence involving two of the discussants of the article, it was Dr Delavan who wrote so eloquently the following words as he paid tribute to Dr Ingals on his death in 1918:

For accurate knowledge, calm reasoning, and wise judgment, he had no superior. Indeed, with rare exceptions there was no one who equalled him in professional ability, versatility, and breadth of view. Strong for the right, fearless in expressing it, and of indomitable patience and industry, the success of his life, measured by what he accomplished, is an inspiring story. To his influence, far beyond that of any other, is due the present advanced position of laryngology in the northern, middle section of the United States, while his contributions to our specialty have permanently enriched it.[15]

The contributions of Dr Bryan and others during the last two decades of the 19th century have provided the foundation for advances that benefit all of us today. We are deeply in the debt of these outstanding early otolaryngologists.

### References

1. Mikulicz J: Zur Prioritätsfrage der osteo plastichen Resection am Fusse. *Arch Klin Chirurgie* 1886;33:220-225.
2. Caldwell GW: *NY Med J* 1893;58:526-528.
3. The American Laryngological Association: *1878-1978: A Centennial History.* Los Angeles, Westland Printing Co, 1978, p 13.
4. Osler WH: Remarks on specialism. *Boston Med Surg J* 1892;126:457.
5. Osler WH: The army surgeon. *Med News* 1894;64:318.
6. Osler WH: Internal medicine as a vocation. *Med News* 1897;71:660.
7. Osler WH: Chauvinism in medicine. *Montreal Med J* 1902;31:684.
8. Gleason EB: *A Manual of Diseases of the Throat & Ear.* Philadelphia, WB Saunders Co, 1907.
9. Grunwald L: *A Treatise on Nasal Suppuration,* Lamb W (trans). New York, William Wood & Co, 1900.
10. Thomson S: Diseases of the accessory sinuses, in Wright J (ed): *A Treatise on Diseases of the Nose, Throat, and Ear.* Philadelphia, Lea Brothers and Co, 1902, chap 21.
11. Bryan JH: The relation of the accessory cavities to diseases of the eye. *JAMA* 1899;33:1197-1203.
12. MacKenzie M: *A Manual of Diseases of the Throat and Nose.* New York, William Wood & Co, 1884, vol 2.
13. Gooch, quoted by Adelmann, in Grundwald L: *A Treatise on Nasal Suppuration,* Lamb W (trans). New York, William Wood & Co, 1900, p 224.
14. Luc H: *Bull Med Soc France,* 1897, vol 13, part 2.
15. Delavan DB: Ephraim Fletcher Ingals. *Trans Am Laryngol Assoc* 1918;40:185-194.

# Chapter 3

# A Method of Total Extirpation of the Gasserian Ganglion for Trigeminal Neuralgia*

## By a Route Through the Temporal Fossa and Beneath the Middle Meningeal Artery.

by Harvey Cushing, M.D.,

Associate in Surgery, The Johns Hopkins University.
Baltimore.

Of the many diseases which, on therapeutic grounds, are supposed to occupy a border-line position between the provinces of the physician and surgeon, perhaps no one more than intractable epileptiform neuralgia illustrates so well the dictim of that renowned Philadelphian and friend of many doctors, Benjamin Franklin, to the effect that "he is the best physician who knows the worthlessness of the most medicines."

Granting the premise in all cases of true tic douloureux, the neuralgia quinti major of Henry Head, in which all three divisions of the trigeminal nerve are affected, that surgical measures alone can with any degree of certainty be depended on to afford relief from this horrible affliction and that the removal of the Gasserian ganglion must ultimately be contemplated, it is to be regretted that this final procedure should generally be regarded as one hazardous in its performance and uncertain in its permanent effects. Two factors may be held responsible for the ill repute in which the ganglion operation at present stands; in the first place the considerable attendant mortality, ordinarily placed at 20 per

cent., and secondly the impression which is prevalent regarding the possibility of recurrence of the neuralgia, an impression which has been occasioned by the reports of cases in which incomplete operations have been performed with a subsequent return of pain.

Almost without exception descriptions of the operation relate in apalling fashion the severity of the hemorrhage which has ensued during one step or another of the procedure, and which has in most instances precluded the possibility of a total extirpation. Granting an equal familiarity with the surgico-anatomic relations of the ganglion semilunare, especially those referable to its dural envelope, the successful accomplishment of its removal, whatever the method employed, will depend entirely on the degree with which an operator may avoid a bloody wound, since a clean dry field is almost a *sine qua non* for the manipulations, which even on the cadaver offer considerable difficulty. The objective point of the operation is necessarily located at the bottom of a close-walled operative well whose depth varies from 5 to 8 cm., and blood-staining even in comparatively slight amount will obscure the ganglion and be incompatible with its complete removal. Consequently, under circumstances which have demanded that the operation be conducted in two or three sittings with periods of tamponade of from two to five days, with possible preliminary ligation of the

*Presented at a meeting of the College of Physicians of Philadelphia, April 20, 1900. The subject was illustrated by dissections and photographs of cases. In the present communication the operative procedure alone is discussed. The description of cases with the anatomic and physiologic questions relative to them will be published subsequently.

carotid and almost without exception leaving wounds which have required drainage, there is little occasion for surprise that many operators have contented themselves with division of the second and third branches—N. maxillaris and N. mandibularis—and random removal of the adjoining portion of the ganglion with the aid of blunt hooks or the curette. It has been a not infrequent experience at the hands of those who have been careful enough to submit to histologic examination the tissues removed, under such circumstances, from the supposed site of the ganglion, to find that no ganglionic structure whatever was demonstrable, and that recurrences should be recorded in such instances is no occasion for disparagement of the operation.

Apparently, heretofore in but few cases, notably by Keen[1] and Krause,[2] and Coelho's[3] case and in a few others, has the ganglion been removed *in toto* and as a recognizable entity worthy of histologic study. Relative to photographs of the ganglia removed by Krause and Doyen,[4] Marchant[5] has commented on the necessity of microscopic examination of the tissues removed in confirmation of their presumed ganglionic character. The experience of finding no ganglionic elements in such material has occurred even to operators as skillful as Dr. Keen.[6]

Whether after complete extirpation of the ganglion a continuance or recurrence of painful stimuli of the central system of neurons may follow, must remain a matter of temporary uncertainty, since observations on such conditions have only held over a period of very few years. It is certain, however, from physiologic knowledge of the process of nerve repair, that there can be no peripheral regeneration of the lower system of sensory neurons after the ganglion has been removed, such regeneration as always occurs after division or evulsion of the individual roots and possibly after incomplete removal of the ganglion itself. Experimental evidence,[7] in the case of the spinal cord, goes to show that division of the central axons of peripheral sensory neurons does not preclude the possibility of physiologic regeneration between a spinal ganglion and the cord. This same principle is applicable to the cerebral sensory ganglia, and in consequence by analogy with the spinal cord it is evident that the simple division of the sensory root of the fifth nerve—N. trigeminus—which procedure has been proposed as an alternative for the removal of the ganglion itself, would be inefficient. The degenerative changes found by Dr. Spiller in the sensory root of one of my cases has aroused a suspicion of possible recurrence of the pain; in this case, however, one in which there was a return of neuralgia a few weeks after two earlier peripheral operations, there has been no sensation of pain whatever since the operation nine months ago. (Cf. Case 1.)

In view of the foregoing data, I believe that it may with propriety be stated:

1. That the probability of non-recurrence bears a direct relation to the degree of entirety with which the ganglion has been removed.

2. That the satisfactoriness of the operation is commensurate with the degree of preservation of the ganglion during its removal and the consequent possibilities of a histologic identification of its elements.

3. That the evolution of the operation must be in the direction of avoidance of hemorrhage which will interfere with the manipulations necessary to successfully liberate the ganglion.

## OPERATIVE METHODS IN GENERAL.

A variety of methods more or less familiar have been proposed, by means of which the ganglion may be approached, the two most widely quoted being associated with the names of Hartley and Krause and of William Rose. The fact that Rose, in his original operation,[8] excised the superior maxilla in order to reach the ganglion only emphasizes the terrible nature of the malady which made justifiable such a mutilating procedure undertaken for its relief. In the subsequent development of the operative method by what is known as the *pterygoid route*, which Rose[9] and his followers have adopted, the ganglion is approached from below by a trephine opening at the roof of the zygomatic fossa. If for no other reason than that the ganglion can hardly be removed *in toto* from such a situation, this route should be abandoned, and its uncertainties are evidenced by descriptions of methods by which this structure may be broken up with a curette and thus destroyed.

The methods proposed by Doyen,[10] Quénu,[11] Poirier[12] and other French surgeons with an approach by what is known as a combined *temporo-sphenoidal route*, also

1. Keen, W. W., and W. G. Spiller: Remarks on Resection of the Gasserian Ganglion, with a Pathological Report on Seven Ganglia. Am. Jour. of the Med. Sci., Vol. cxvi (1898), p. 503.

2. Krause, Fedar: Die Neuralgie des Trigeminus nebst der Anatomie und Physiologie des Nerven. Leipzig, Verlag von F. C. W. Vogel, 1896.

3. Coelho, Sabino; Ablation du ganglion de Gasser avec arrachement protubérantiel du trijumeau dans un cas de névralgie faciale rebelle. Revue de Chir., T. xix., Mai, 1899, p. 623.

4. Doyen, E.: L'extirpation du Ganglion de Gasser. Archives provinciales de Chirurgie. T. iv., Juli, 1895, p. 429.

5. Marchant, Gérard et Henri Herbert: De la résection du ganglion de Gasser dans les névralgies faciales rebelles. Revue de Chirurgie. T. xvii, 1897, p. 287. These writes say in a foot-note, p. 295: "Nous aimerions malgré tout, voir figurer, dans ces observations, a coté de la photographie, le résultat de l'examen histologique. Un ganglion arraché, tordu ou broyé par les mors de la pince est en général assez altéré dans sa forme et peut donner lieu a de certaines illusions. Nous ne pouvons nous empêcher de penser que dans un cas (Dennetiers, *Societe de Chirurgie*, 15 juillet, 1896), ou, d'après son aspect, la partie enlevée ressemblait tant bien que mal a un ganglion, l'examen histologique le plus consciencieux n'a pu déceler la présence d'aucune cellule ganglionnaire. Il en fut de même dans deux cas de Keen.

6. Keen, W.W.: Remarks on Operation on the Gasserian Ganglion with the report of five additional cases. Am. Jour. of the Med. Sci., Jan., 1896, Vol. cxi, p. 59. Case 2.

7. Baer, Dawson, and Marshall: Regeneration of the Dorsal Root Fibers of the Second Cervical Nerve within the Spinal Cord. Jour. of Exp. Med., Baltimore, Vol. iii, 1899, No. 1.

8. Rose, Wm.: Removal of the Gasserian Ganglion for Severe Neuralgia. The Lancet, Nov. 1, 1890, Vol, ii, p. 914.

9. Rose, Wm.: The Lettsonian Lectures on the Surgical Treatment of Trigeminal Neuralgia. Lecture ii. The Lancet, Feb. 6, 1892, Vol. 1, p. 295.

10. On Extirpation of the Gasserian Ganglion. Ref. Annals of Surgery, Vol. xxiii (1896), p. 69.

11. Quénu et Sibileau: Bull. Ac. Med., 10 Jan., 1894; indorsed by Tichonowitch, Centralblatt für Chir., 24 März, 1900, S. 322.

12. Poirier, P.: Reséction du Ganglion de Gasser; arrachement protubérantiel du trijumeau. Gaz. d. Hôp., Par., 1896, ixix, 808-810.

possess some of the disadvantages of the method of Rose, for though the exposure is better, the ganglion is approached from below through the bloody area of the pterygoid plexus with necessary ligation of the internal maxillary artery, and after location of the inferior maxillary nerve—N. mandibularis—the roof of the zygomatic fossa is rongeured away to the foramen ovale and an attempt made to remove the ganglion by using this nerve as a guide to its position. Personal experience with this operative method, though limited to the cadaver, has demonstrated that it is exceedingly difficult to remove the ganglion from this situation in a satisfactory degree of preservation, and furthermore, as will be seen, the blood-supply to the ganglion is almost entirely from below and is especially abundant in the neighborhood of the foramen ovale, consequently the difficulties of this method during life must be considerable. Jacob[13] has recently described an operation in which the infraorbital branch—N. infraorbitalis—of the superior maxillary nerve is first located at the floor of the orbit, the skull trephined and the ganglion approached and identified by means of this nerve in much the same way that the inferior maxillary nerve is utilized in the last described procedure, but inasmuch as these nerves are accessible and plainly recognizable within the skull, it seems unnecessary to demand any such preliminary extracranial sign-post to the seat of operation.

The fact, however, that French surgeons since Doyen have clung to the temporo-sphenoidal route, gives evidence that its possibilities are deserving of consideration, but inasmuch as the great majority of operators have followed the lead of Hartley[14] and of Krause[15] by way of the temporal fossa to the ganglion, doubtless their method should be considered as fraught with less danger and as offering better chances of a successful outcome than any other heretofore described, and it is noteworthy that practically by this method alone in an occasional instance has it been possible to completely extirpate the ganglion. There are many difficulties arising, chiefly from hemorrhage, which those who have seen or attempted this operation of Hartley and Krause will remember but too vividly. In the first place, the Wagner osteoplastic flap in the temporal region must be so taken that it includes the sulcus arteriosus in the anterior inferior angle—angulus sphenoidalis—of the parietal bone which lodges the middle meningeal artery, and consequently the vessel, owing to the frequent depth of the sulcus, is quite commonly lacerated and is the occasion of delay long before the real operative seat is reached. Again, when the ganglion is approached, the operator is so far—measuring on the curve of the skull—from the cavum Meckelii in which the ganglion lies, that an amount of elevation of the brain and underlying dura is necessary, which is

incompatible with the preservation of the artery at its lower fixed point, namely, at the foramen spinosum. Hence Krause finds it essential to attempt a preliminary double ligation of the vessel after its emergence from this foramen. This is a difficult procedure, and is not uncommonly unsuccessful, and hemorrhage from the meningeal under any circumstances is an unpleasant thing with which to deal.

Disadvantages other than the obligation of dealing with this arterial bugbear arise from the necessary degree of retraction which is essential for a satisfactory exposure of the deeper parts of the ganglion when this high temporal method is employed. On one occasion, in a left-sided case, a consequent aphasia was noted and in most of the earlier operations undertaken by this method no attempt was made to remove more than the outer portion of the ganglion. Had it been deemed necessary on all occasions to expose and liberate the sensory root proximal to the ganglion, I am certain that the employment of this high temporal route would have been found frequently impossible and always attended by grave difficulties.

Even by the method which I have used, in which there is required but slight elevation of the brain, there has been invariably an associated retardation of the pulse. This is illustrated by the accompanying ether chart, which presents characteristics almost identical with that seen on all four occasions in which I have operated.

Victor Horsley[16] has proposed and carried out an operation by this route in which the dura is immediately opened and the temporal lobe itself retracted, leaving the dura covering the middle fossa in place against the bone. Few operators could handle the brain thus freed of its support without injury, and after considerable experience with the removal of the ganglion from above, even when the calvarium and brain have been removed, I have found that greater difficulties are encountered, in spite of the exposure, in freeing it from the dural envelope than will be met with when the approach is from the side, as in the operation to be described.

THE DIRECT INFRA-ARTERIAL METHOD.

The method of enucleation which the writer, with some hesitation, proposes to describe makes use of the paramount advantage of the Hartley-Krause operation, namely that of exposure of the ganglion by the temporal route. The trephine opening through the fossa temporalis, however, is sufficiently low so that the extradural manipulations may be conducted *underneath the arch made by the middle meningeal vessel*, which is retracted with the dura and yet remains uninjured at its two fixed points, namely, at the foramen spinosum of the temporal bone and at the sulcus arteriosus of the parietal. Under this arch with but slight elevation of the temporal lobe the entire ganglion and its sensory root may be exposed. The method may be said to give the maximum of exposure with the minimum of cerebral compression and injury of blood-vessels. The operation, therefore, differs only in its

13. Jacob, O.: Un procédé de resection du ganglion de Gasser. Revue de Chir., T. xix, (1899), p. 29.

14. Hartley, Frank.: New York Med. Jour., March 19, 1892. Subsequently—Intracranial Neurectomy of the Fifth Nerve. Annals of Surg., Vol. xvii, 1893, p. 511.

15. Krause, Fedar: Resection des Trigeminus innerhalb der Schädelhöhle. Verhandlungen der Deutchen Gessellschaft für Chir., Berlin, June, 1892, p. 199.

16. Horsley, Victor: The Various Surgical Procedures devised for the relief or cure of Trigeminal Neuralgia. British Med. Jour., Vol. ii., 1891, p. 1249.

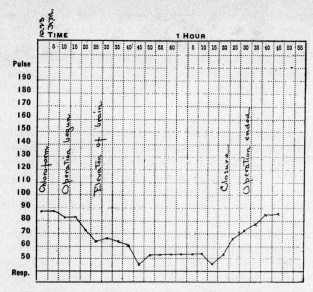

Ether chart of Ganglion Case, showing "five minute" pulse-rate during operation, in illustration of compression pulse due to slight elevation of temporal lobe.

details from that proposed by Hartley and Krause; it is, however, upon detail that the success of this, supposedly one of the most delicate of surgical procedures, depends.

*Anatomic Notes.*—There are certain anatomic features which must be taken into consideration in this particular operative method, or indeed in any method: in the first place, concerning the dural envelope which encloses the ganglion as well as the intracranial portion of its three peripheral branches.[17]

As commonly described, the dura splits and encloses

---

17. It is superfluous to say that an operation on the ganglion by any route should not be undertaken without perfect familiarity with its anatomic relations, and it is important that this familiarity should be gained by way of the particular method of approach selected. Only after a great number of operations at the autopsy table can one satisfactorily train his reflexes to appreciate the degree of force which it is necessary to apply at the edge of the ganglionic dural sheath in order that it may be split and the ganglion exposed by lifting away its superior covering, and similarly the force which may be applied in the subsequent elevation of the ganglion and its four branches from the underlying dura to which it has been left attached. For this procedure the only instrument which is requisite is a blunt dissector of proper shape, and in the possibilities offered by the one selected, the operator should train himself. Only after repeated operations on fresh cadavers possessing skulls of various indices did the writer feel justified in dealing with the ganglion at the operating-table and confident of removing it *in toto*. To satisfactorily free the entire ganglion is a delicate procedure and familiarity with the crackling sensations mparted to the hand while liberating it from its dural envelope can not be overvalued. I know of no operation which could be undertaken without such preliminary experience with equal rashness. I have found the experience gained from practice on ordinary anatomic material to be unsatisfactory. The toughening of the dried dura and altered consistency of the ganglion and brain imparts, through the dissecting instrument, sensations markedly different from those which are given by fresh tissues. I have performed this particular operation on autopsy subjects about thirty times, and have removed the ganglion in a number of other ways, invariably in a much less perfect state of preservation. It is extraordinary how much easier it is to remove the ganglion through an opening in the temporal fossa by this method than it is through an open calvarium after the brain has been removed.

the ganglion in a double layer as it lies in the cavum Meckelii. This fibrous envelope is closely adherent to the ganglion, and experience has shown that the point at which the layers are most easily separated is at the area of dural attachment about the superior maxillary nerve, where it enters the foramen rotundum. This is the first point at which the simple elevation of the dura is resisted and, by careful blunt dissection, working between this point and that of its second attachment at the foramen ovale, it is found to be a comparatively easy matter to split the enclosing envelope between these two points and to elevate the upper layer of the ganglionic sheath, leaving the ganglion entirely exposed and lying attached to the basal layer of its sheath in the ganglionic fossa. There is, however, in addition to the thick dural layer of the envelope thus elevated, a second, thinner layer of transparent fibrous tissue which overlies and is attached firmly to the ganglion, extending backward over the sensory root—N. trigeminus—but which does not cover the three peripheral divisions as does the rest of the sheath. An attempt has been made to show this second layer in Fig. 2, after its separation from the ganglion, and I am ignorant as to whether this has been heretofore described. After elevation of the main dural sheath and exposure of the three peripheral branches this thin second layer is left intimately adherent to the ganglion, binding it and the sensory root to the underlying tissues. I believe this to be the chief obstacle to evulsion of the ganglion *in toto*, as it is ordinarily attempted.

The importance during the operation of leaving the ganglion attached to the underlying portion of its sheath, and of not elevating it until the final step, is due partly to the fact that it is much less difficult to free it from the underlying surface of dura and bone below than from the elastic cerebral surface, as will be emphasized later, and furthermore because the blood-supply of the structure comes almost entirely from beneath. The chief supply ordinarily comes from a branch of the meningeal soon after its entrance into the skull, and consequently the third division—N. mandibularis—is often the most bloody one to liberate. A small branch usually comes from the carotid and passes over the sixth nerve—N. abducens—to the under surface of the ganglion. Another common branch is a small radicle of the ophthalmic to the first division; another by way of the foramen ovale is the lesser meningeal, and occasionally a branch appears through the foramen rotundum from the internal maxillary artery.

Relative to the middle meningeal artery, it not infrequently happens that the vessel communicates with the lacrimal artery by an anastomotic branch through the outer angle of the sinus sphenoidalis. Occasionally the latter artery may derive, in this way, its main origin from the meningeal, or vice versa the meningeal from the lacrimal. Under these circumstances it can be seen that the vertical extent of the arch under which we must work is somewhat narrowed. Such an anomaly was met with in Case 4 of my series; it nevertheless did not seriously encroach the field of view.

Another factor may occasionally interfere with the view of the ganglion, one which has been encountered especially in skulls with a broad cephalic index, and this

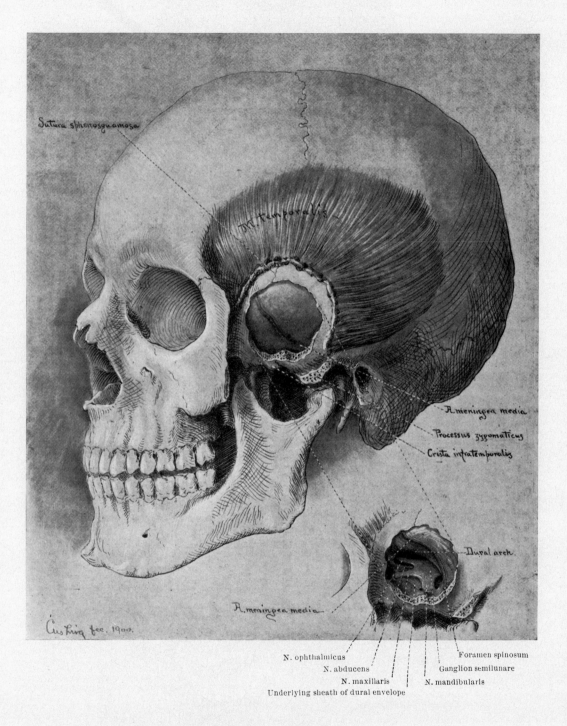

FIG. I.—Showing relations of the middle meningeal artery to the operative foramen before and after elevation of the dura and exposure of the ganglion.

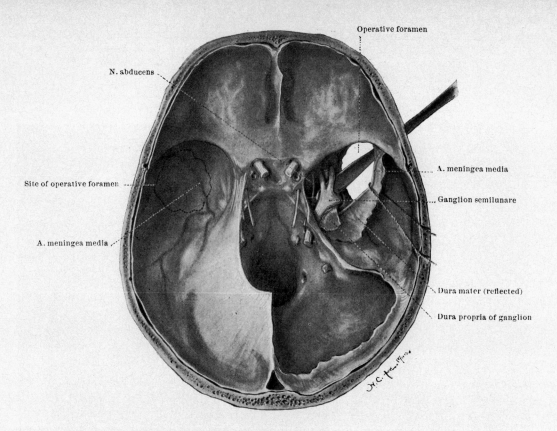

N. abducens

Site of operative foramen

A. meningea media

A. meningea media

Ganglion semilunare

Dura mater (reflected)

Dura propria of ganglion

FIG. II.—Showing on the right, after reflection of the dura, the ganglion and its intracranial branches liberated from their dural envelope and elevated by the blunt dissector introduced through the operative foramen; on the left, the dura in situ and the relation of the operative foramen to the ganglion and middle meningeal artery.

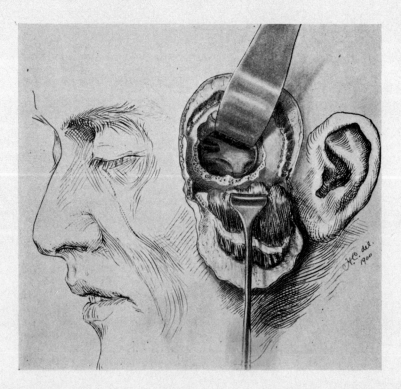

FIG. III.—Sketch from cadaver of the field of operation: showing situation of the incision, retraction of temporal muscle over displaced zygomatic arch, osseous foramen and final exposure of ganglion under meningeal arch.

is the more embarrassing since the ganglion in such brachycephalic cases may lie from 1 to 1½ cm. deeper than usual. This obstruction consists of a bony prominence which, in slight degree, is present in all skulls, but at times is sufficiently developed to partly hide the ganglion when viewed from the side and to ward off the curved blunt dissector in its approach to the ganglion. This process, apparently unnamed,[18] is more or less developed in all skulls and is roughly indicated by the elevation at the lower rim of the operative foramen in the drawings that accompany this paper. This process is situated to the outer side and slightly anterior to the foramen ovale on the greater wing of the sphenoid between the row of sphenoidal foramina and the sutura sphenosquamosa. In Case 2, a patient with a markedly brachycephalic skull, it was necessary to chisel off the top of this prominence before the ganglion could be attacked. A similar and still more developed bony protection renders the ganglion operation in dogs almost impossible.

Underlying the lower sheath of the ganglionic envelope posteriorly there is usually to be made out a dense triangle of fibrous tissue which partly covers the foramen lacerum and under the anterior edge of which the carotid artery emerges. Over the artery and close to the edge of this ligamentous structure, and consequently near to the inner edge of the ganglion, the sixth nerve—N. abducens—passes. It is in this situation, on account of the diminished likelihood of injuring the sinus cavernosus, which is only expressed farther forward, that I have preferred to attack the ganglion and its sensory root when it becomes necessary during the process of liberation to pry the structure outward in order to free the attachments of its inner border. I have been able in this way to avoid injury of the sinus and to remove the first division— N. ophthalmicus—by freeing it from behind forward, though I have invariably caused a paralysis—fortunately only temporary—of the sixth nerve. Injury to the sinus, however, is not such a calamity as is usually presumed. An interpretation of its character is given in Spalteholz' Handatlas der Anatomic (Zweite Auflage, 1899, Bd. ii, S. 397 und 441), which is much less startling to an operator than the manner in which it is usually depicted as resembling the other cranial sinuses.

DESCRIPTION OF THE OPERATION WITH DISCUSSION OF THE VARIOUS STEPS.

1. *Formation of muscle flap and exposure of the temporal fossa.*—A horseshoe-shaped skin incision is made in the temporal region, its base about 4 cm. in breadth, corresponding to the zygomatic arch, and its convexity reaching about 5 cm. above it, but slightly higher than the level of the pinna of the ear. (Cf. Fig. 3.) The incision, therefore, needs to be much lower and may be considerably smaller than that for the Wagner osteoplastic procedure as adopted by Hartley and Krause. This skin flap is turned downward, some branches of the temporal artery being divided in the process, until the underlying temporal fascia is exposed well on to its attachments to the zygomatic arch and the posterior or

temporal border of the malar bone. An incision is then made through the temporal fascia concentric with and just inside of the skin incision, and at the base of the skin flap it is carried along the middle of the outer surface of the zygomatic arch through the periosteum down to the bone. The periosteum is then elevated from the bony arch, leaving the masseteric attachment at its lower edge uninjured, and the zygomatic processes of the malar and temporal bones (Cf. Fig. 1) are divided with heavy forceps as in the resection of a rib. An incision concentric with the skin incision is then carried down through the temporal muscle, and the muscle is scraped away from the bony wall of the temporal fossa, to which it has no attachment in this situation, and retracted downward together with the resected portion of the zygoma and into the space which this bony arch formerly occupied. (Cf. Fig. 3.) In this way the lower portion of the temporal fossa of the skull, as far down as the attachment of the external pterygoid muscle below the infratemporal crest, is well exposed.

*Discussion of Step.*—The one deformity consequent to the operative method via the temporal route follows upon the incision through the temporal fascia, namely, the division of the branches of the facial nerve which supply the occipito-frontalis muscle. As a result, there is a post-operative inability to elevate the eyebrow on the affected side. This paralysis, however, is not apparent during expressional rest except in old individuals in whom there may be some resultant smoothing out of the cutaneous wrinkles on that side. This deformity is well shown in the photograph of one of Krause's patients. (Op. cit. S. 44, Abbildung 14.) I have found that it is necessary to temporarily resect the zygoma in order to satisfactorily retract the temporal muscle. A downward displacement of the bone, of only a centimeter or two, is all that is required to make room for the muscle, which otherwise would arch up over the zygoma and prevent proper exposure of the lowest portion of the fossa temporalis. It is easier to preserve than to detach the bony fragment, on account of the firm attachment of the masseter. This is not a necessary detail, however, and perhaps it would be advantageous to remove it. A new zygoma in one of my cases has reformed after excision, and possibly in this case there is less post-operative deformity since the atrophy of the temporal and masseter muscles shows less plainly than in the other cases in which the arch of the replaced zygoma seems unduly prominent on account of the sunken fossæ above and below it.

2. *Exposure and elevation of dura as far as the ganglionic sheath.*—With a mallet and gouge, a small trephine opening is made through the most prominent portion of the exposed great wing of the sphenoid, and with rongeur forceps this opening is enlarged to a diameter of about 3 cm., its lower margin being carried well down and possibly including the ridge between the temporal and zygomatic fossa—the crista infratemporalis. The uninjured middle meningeal artery runs on the dura thus exposed, across the opening in the bone as the diameter of its circle. (Cf. Fig. 1.) The dura, with this vessel, may then be easily lifted, almost bloodlessly, from the base of the middle fossa until the first point of firm dural attachment at the foramen ovale is reached.

*Discussion of Step.*—It has seemed unnecessary to the writer to attempt to make an osteoplastic flap even were it possible to deal with it in this deep situation, for the reason that the opening to be made through the skull is so small and afterclosure of the wound so well protected. It is possible, indeed

---

18. One might presume to call this the processus fasciei cerebrallis ossis sphenoidalis according to the His nomenclature.

that new bone is subsequently formed to cover the defect, since the slight pulsation of the flap which is apparent for some time after the operation ultimately disappears. It is well to make the first opening in the bone at the upper part of the proposed area of removal, since, it is easeier to bite away the bone with the rongeur forceps in a downward direction, and furthermore, because as the base is approached the sphenoidal wing becomes much thicker—occasionally 5-6 mm.—and consequently is less easily penetrated with the mallet and chisel. Care must be taken in the use of the gouge, since the bone is at times exceedingly thin and one or two strokes with the mallet will carry the instrument through. Additional care is necessary for the middle meningeal artery is usually exposed by the first small opening in the skull. It ordinarily runs beneath the most prominent part of the wing of the sphenoid and squamous portion of the temporal bones, which have been uncovered, and this is naturally the point selected for the primary opening.

It is important in view of preservation of the ganglion and avoidance of possible injury to the deeper vessels that no fragments of bone be allowed to fall down between the skull and dura, since at a later stage of the operation, when it is necessary to firmly press pledgets of gauze against the ganglion to check the bleeding from its underlying arterioles, these spiculæ may, as occurred in one of my cases, be firmly driven into its substance. By a similar accident one of them might be driven into the sinus. Occasionally the prominence, which has been described above, as present on the floor of the fossæ, may be of sufficient size to later interfere with a satisfactory approach to the foramen ovale. This may then be chiseled off or the floor of the fossa rongeured away so as to include it. In the drawings, I have not made the trephine opening quite low enough. It should be carried down so as to include the crista infratemporalis, which therefore should not be shown preserved as in Fig 1.

3. *Elevation of dura with meningeal artery and exposure of upper surface of ganglion.*—By careful blunt dissection with the proper instrument, and by working at the dural attachment about the foramen rotundum and in the line between this point and the foramen ovale, where it is again firmly attached, the edge of the dural envelope which encloses the ganglion and its peripheral intracranial branches may be split, and by careful elevation the entire upper surface of the stellate structure be exposed well back on to the sensory root, the ganglion being left in its bed still adherent to the underlying portion of the envelope.

*Discussion of Step.*—This procedure should be attended with but little hemorrhage, since the blood-supply, as heretofore stated, is from below. It is of importance that *the ganglion should not be elevated in this maneuver*, since it is advisable to postpone what degree of hemorrhage is unavoidable as long as possible, and furthermore because it is much easier to elevate the overlying dural sheath from the ganglion if its attachments to the unyielding base have remained uninjured. This entire procedure is carried on under the arch made by elevating the temporal lobe and its overlying dura and artery. A simple spatula of about 2¼ cm. in width, which can be bent at the proper angle, makes the most satisfactory retractor for these structures. (Cf. Fig. 3).

4. *Liberation and extraction of ganglion and its branches.*—After the exposure of the upper surface of the ganglion and before division of any of the peripheral branches, these three nerves with the ganglion and trigeminal root should be liberated from the attachments to the base. (Cf. Fig. 2, right side). This is readiy accomplished by working with the blunt dissector in the crotches between the second and third divisions and also along each side of the nerves. After the ganglion and the second and third divisions have been liberated and can be lifted up by the dissector, it is necessary to free the superior and internal edge of the trigeminal root and first division. It is well to conduct these manipulations as near as possible to the sensory root, since that is the safest point and one at which there is less likelihood of injuring the cavernous sinus and sixth nerve. The ganglionic structure may thus be completely liberated (as shown in Fig. 2) without division or laceration of a single branch. With a firmly locking pair of hemostatic forceps—I have used Kocher's—the structure may then be grasped just back of the site of the true ganglion on the trigeminal root; the three peripheral divisions are in turn held up with a blunt nerve hook and divided with scissors close to their foramina; the sensory root is then evulsed by means of the previously attached pair of forceps.

*Discussion of Step.*—This part of the operation is the most difficult and the one in which preliminary training on the cadaver is found most essential. The degree of force necessary to separate the ganglion without injuring it, for if lacerated or torn away from its roots its extraction becomes most uncertain, can only be learned by experience which should hardly be gained at the expense of the patient. The operator's reflexes should have become familiarized with the crackling sensations imparted to the hand on separating the adhesions at one point or another during the process of liberation. The bleeding which follows on the maneuver, especially about the foramen ovale, is sometimes very annoying but ordinarily may be checked in a few minutes by the pressure of a pledget of gauze. It would naturally be supposed that the proximity of the meningeal and its fixed point at the foramen spinosum would be an embarrassment, especially when an attempt is made to liberate the third division by insinuating the elevator under the posterior border of the nerve—N. mandibularis—between it and the artery. This I have not found to be the case.

I do not see how the third and fourth nerves can be injured in this procedure; the sixth, however, lies very near the ganglion, has always been seen and, I must confess, injured in each of my four cases. This, however, has fortunately occasioned only temporary symptoms, the resulting internal strabismus having disappeared in each case in the course of a few weeks. In one instance I felt certain that I tore the nerve across; if so it must have regenerated. There has also resulted in all of my cases a temporary paralysis of the sympathetic with contracted pupil. This has invariably disappeared much earlier than the motor paralysis of the abducens. As stated above, it is well in the liberation of the first division—N. ophthalmicus—to free the nerve at the ganglionic end and to strip it out from behind forward if it is desired to remove it at all, else the cavernous sinus may be injured. This accident, however, is by no means such a calamity as it is credited with being. The sinus is not an open canal, as usually believed, but made up of compartments in which local thromboses may occur readily and promptly, and thus hemorrhage be controlled by a few moments of pressure. Bleeding from the small ganglionic arteries about the foramen ovale may be much more annoying. On one occasion I accidentally plunged the dissector directly into the sinus anterior to the ophthalmic border of the true ganglion. The profuse momentary hemorrhage ceased after a few moments of pressure with some gauze. The trigeminal sensory if properly extracted invariably comes away from the pons where it is loosely attached. I have never seen any evidence of shock consequent upon this procedure such as Horsley describes in his single case.

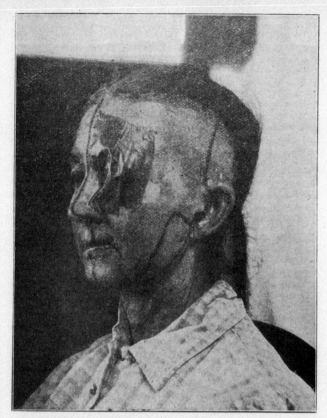

Fig. 4. Photograph of Case 4, taken on the tenth day in illustration of a method of protecting the eye.

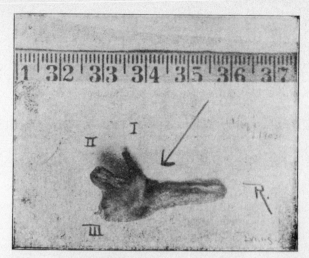

Fig 6. Tissues removed from Case 2. (Dr. Spiller). The arrow indicates the direction of application of the evulsing forceps, whose imprint shows upon the ganglion. Photograph taken from specimen after hardening in formalin, and high lights as in Fig. 5, from reflection of fresh tissues do not appear.

Fig. 5. Specimen from Case 1. (Dr. Spiller). Photograph was taken from the fresh tissue and consequently shows points of high light. The first division (I), (N. ophthalmicus) was removed as a separate piece after extraction of the ganglion and other branches. The tissue was placed in Muller's fluid one half hour after removal.

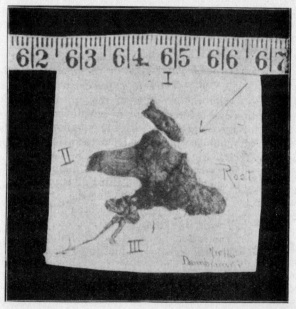

Fig. 7. Specimen from Case 3. (Dr. Spiller). The arrow points to the line of impress of the evulsing forceps. The third division (N. mandibularis) is considerably lacerated as an unsuccessful attempt was made to evulse this from the foramen ovale instead of dividing the root as usual. Shreds of the motor root can be seen distinct from the rest. The first division (N. ophthalmicus) was torn away from the ganglion during its elevation and was removed from the wall of the sinus after extraction of the ganglion. Photographs taken after hardening in formalin.

5. *Closure and Dressing.*—The zygoma and flap of skin, muscle and fascia are replaced. The zygomatic arch in my first case, as stated, was removed, and in one of the later ones wired in position. This is an unnecessary detail inasmuch as the masseter is paralyzed and the resected portion of the bone when replaced remains in position. The temporal muscle and fascia are secured in place by fine interrupted sutures at the upper curve of the incision, and a few sutures are taken in the divided periosteum and fascia over the replaced zygomatic arch. In applying the dressing the eye is covered by a large sheet of rubber protective which bridges across from the nose and forehead to the malar prominence of the cheek and prevents the pressure of the bandage against the eye. In none of my four cases has the wound been drained, and in none has there been failure to obtain healing by primary union: the resulting scar has been very slight (Cf. Fig. 4), and in one instance hardly to be detected. An

Fig. 8. Specimens from Case 4. (Dr. Barker). A spicule of bone is shown driven firmly into the ganglion, which was not removed in a good state of preservation. The sensory root (R), (N. trigeminus) tore away from the ganglion during extraction and was subsequently removed. Photograph taken after hardening in formalin.

unsightly scar, such as is shown in many photographs of cases, would almost deter a surgeon from the operation.

I have not found it necessary to suture the lids as has been advocated, in treatment of the eye. In fact, I should think the local reaction resultant to this procedure would be detrimental in case there was an ensuing keratitis, which apparently is at times unavoidable. The simple protective method which has been used is shown in the accompanying photograph of one of the patients. The eye is thus kept moist, protected from dust and the patient may deemly see through the covering. A Buller shield answers the same purpose.

It is not the writer's intention on this occasion to take up the physiologic aspects of the four cases which have been operated on, nor to report the histories in any detail, except in so much as they may be of value in interpreting the pathologic lesions, to be described by Drs. Barker and Spiller. The physiologic question relative to disturbances of taste and of secretory activity in the trigeminal area, the consideration of the post-operative areas of sensory anesthesia, the discussion of so-called trophic changes consequent on removal of the ganglion, and similar topics, must be left to a subsequent communication in spite of the fact that they doubtless represent the most interesting side of the Gasserian ganglion question, and one which is second only in importance to its pathologic aspect. The photographs show that in each instance the ganglion and intracranial roots have been completely removed and the resulting anesthesia has been absolute over the entire area of trigeminal sensory distribution in consequence. The completeness of the post-operative anesthesia may be regarded as an index of the totality of the extirpation.

It will be noted that the ganglia of the first two cases examined by Dr. Spiller were removed during a period of extreme exacerbation of the neuralgia. In Dr. Barker's cases the operation was performed during a period of comparative freedom from pain. Brief summaries of the histories preceding the operative period are as follows:

CASE 1.—James W., 63 years of age, entered the hospital Aug. 2, 1899. He had been a sea captain by profession until the onset of his right-sided neuralgia, from which he had suffered for ten years. The pain occurred originally in the third division of the trigeminus. In July, 1896, and again in June, 1897, two peripheral operations with evulsion of the infraorbital and inferior dental nerves had failed to give him more than a few weeks of respite from pain. For the two years before entrance he had been bed-ridden, and his sufferings had had no remission. At the time of operation his extreme paroxysms occurred every minute and a half on an average, and with only slight relief during the intervals. His chief point of radiation of pain was just below the outer corner of the mouth. From there the pain spread into the territory of all three divisions of the N. trigeminus during the paroxysms, to terminate at a point near the parietal eminence. The ganglion is shown in the accompanying photograph (Fig. 5).

CASE 2.—W. E., 55 years of age, entered the hospital Dec. 17, 1899. He had been a business man until neuralgia interrupted his activities. He had suffered from pain, which appeared primarily in the distribution of the infraorbital branch, for twelve years. In 1892 the infraorbital nerve was evulsed, with relief for several months. On the return of pain, the inferior dental became involved, and subsequently the supraorbital region and pain finally extended to the territory innervated by the suboccipital nerves. His sufferings for several months before entrance were such that he had been in confinement and, on admission to the hospital, he was practically maniacal. His chief pain point from which the paroxysms radiated was situated in the right nasolabial fold. His sufferings were continuous, with exacerbations every few moments, or consequent on the slightest peripheral stimulus. The ganglion and branches are shown in the accompanying photograph (Fig. 6).

CASE 3.—A. D., 38 years of age, a shoemaker by trade, entered the hospital in January, 1900, having suffered from trifacial neuralgia for only two years. The onset was attributed to exposure and pain, and was at first limited to the supraorbital area. One year later the infraorbital region became involved and soon the whole territory of the third division, the pain during the paroxysms extending into the suboccipital region. In March, 1899, by peripheral operations, I evulsed an inch or two of the inferior dental and infraorbital nerves, which showed the usual histologic changes after being removed. After relief for eight months the pain returned—November, 1899—with renewed vigor. The paroxysms at the time of entrance were not frequent nor very severe. The pain spread downward from the supraorbital division into the territory supplied by the second and third branches. The patient was operated on during this interval of comparative freedom. The ganglion is shown in Fig. 7.

CASE 4.—Elizabeth R., 60 years of age, had suffered for seven years from left-sided tic-douloureux, which originated in the superior maxillary branch of the trigeminal nerve, and was attributed to exposure. The definite point of origin of her paroxysms had always been situated near the ala of the nose. In August, 1897, 5 cm. of the infraorbital nerve was evulsed (Cushing) from the floor of the orbit. The nerve histologically showed the usual degenerative changes. Relief ensued for sixteen months, after which interval, with the return of pain the first and third divisions became invaded. In June, 1899, the regenerated nerve from the same situation was again evulsed (Mitchell) with subsequent relief for only four months. In January, 1900, the ganglion and roots were removed in toto, though with considerable difficulty and not in a good state of preservation. (Cf. Fig. 8.) The operation was performed during a period of comparative freedom from pain.

July 22/29, 1983
(JAMA 1983;250:529-531)

# Cushing and Trigeminal Neuralgia*

Donald J. Dalessio, MD

This article, published on April 28, 1900, was presented at a symposium in Philadelphia only eight days earlier, on April 20, 1900. One might observe that it thus seems to achieve a goal of rapid publication unknown in our "modern times." The article was one of a series of eight published by THE JOURNAL in two successive issues, climaxed by a go-with editorial on tic douloureux. All of the articles had been presented at a *Symposium on the Fifth Nerve and its Neurological and Surgical Relations* given before the College of Physicians of Philadelphia. Presumably, the editor of THE JOURNAL then had a lively interest in the trigeminal nerve, for this concentration of articles on the diseases of a single cranial nerve is striking. Neither before nor since has tic douloureux been covered in such detail in THE JOURNAL.

The article is the work of the young Harvey Cushing (H. C.), aged 31 years, who was then finishing four years of general surgery residency at The Johns Hopkins Hospital, under the direction of William S. Halsted, the most prestigious surgeon of that time. H. C.'s titles during those four years included assistant resident surgeon, resident surgeon, assistant in surgery, and associate in surgery.

To appreciate the impact and excellence of H. C.'s work, it is important to review briefly some historical landmarks in the development of surgery. It was only 24 years previously that Joseph Lister attended an International Congress in Philadelphia to espouse his concepts of antisepsis. Lister suggested that germs caused disease and could be killed using carbolic acid. To that end, wounds were bathed in it, dressings were soaked in it, and it was sprayed about the operating theater during surgical procedures.

Asepsis, a related concept, was derived from antisepsis but was designed to prevent wound contamination, and it was this concept that caught on in the decade between 1885 and 1895. During these years, steam was first used to sterilize surgical dressings. Soon thereafter, sterilization of instruments and gowns became the norm.

The surgical scrub was introduced—a radical concept; one washed before operations as well as afterward.

In about 1890, Halsted introduced the use of sterile rubber gloves, but it was not until 1895 that they were used regularly by a few modern surgeons, as much for their protection as for the health of the patient.

Nor was surgical diagnosis much advanced. In 1886, Fitz[1] presented his study of appendicitis and characterized it as a clinical entity, causing much excitement. Cholecystotomy was attempted at about the same time, and surgery for inguinal hernia was proposed, undertaken, and rapidly developed.

It was also about this time that the new Johns Hopkins Hospital was dedicated (May 6, 1889). A remarkable faculty of young men had been accumulated as staff, including William Osler, age 39; William Welch, age 38; W. S. Halsted, age 33; and J. Kelly, only 31.[2] Thus was founded a faculty without peer, but perhaps more importantly, the hospital was organized into units, with a head or chief in charge of each service. It was into this stimulating atmosphere that Cushing came in October of 1896, fresh from his experiences at the Harvard Medical School and the Massachusetts General Hospital.

### Halsted and Cushing

At least initially, there seems to have been no major affinity between Halsted and Cushing, nor would such be expected, since Halsted was surgical chief and Cushing an assistant resident. Nevertheless, by March of 1897, Halsted had invited H. C. to become his surgical resident in succession to Joseph C. Bloodgood. This was not accomplished with ease, however, for Bloodgood[3] stayed on in the residents' rooms for another 12 months to finish his monograph on hernia.

This inconvenience notwithstanding, H. C.'s work continued apace. He is credited with having been the first surgeon in this country to remove the spleen in Banti's disease (splenic anemia), the patient having been referred to him by Osler. He was occupied with appendicitis, work on local anesthesia, using cocaine infiltration to affect nerve blocks, and, eventually, care of the sick and wounded from the Spanish American War who began to arrive at Hopkins in late summer of 1898; he published an article on the surgery for intestinal perforation evoked by typhoid fever.[4]

---

From the Department of Medicine, Division of Neurology, Scripps Clinic and Research Foundation, La Jolla, Calif.

*A commentary on Cushing H: A method of total extirpation of the Gasserian ganglion for trigeminal neuralgia. *JAMA* 1900;34:1035-1041.

On the ice in Bernese Oberland, Switzerland, December 1900. Hugo Kronecker, with cane, is on left; Cushing is on right. Reprinted with permission of Yale Medical Library.

As the new century approached and his training was ending, Cushing began to make plans to study for a period in Europe. His work under Halsted had become progressively more independent, owing in part, to Halsted's health, which was not then robust. Cushing has provided insights into his relationship with Halsted:

I saw relatively little of him during my three years as Resident, less and less as he perhaps began to feel that I might be entrusted with the bulk of the routine work. A great deal of this was of course major surgery and the assistance was very poor. There was at the time a rotation service for house officers who were only on surgery for four months; and as Young soon was side-tracked into urology, there was no one of any experience to give anaesthesia for prolonged cases like breast cases or for serious conditions such as intestinal strangulations and the like. It was owing to this that I took up local anaesthesia without getting much moral support from the 'Professor.' I little realized at the time the reasons for this.

He had few private patients, indeed was too difficult of access and too much away to build up a consulting practice. . . . We sometimes went out of town with him to operate, less often in private houses in Baltimore. An operating trunk was prepared for these occasions and a large part of the staff would go along — most elaborate performances they were, for which he charged prodigious fees.

He stood the summer heat badly and usually went away sometimes for six months at a stretch. . . . Under this regime I became perhaps a little too independent and his letters hint that I may have been too prone to put myself on paper. I can understand better now how this must have annoyed him and I think it was true in the case of all of his assistants that when they began to write he was ready to let them go.

I sensed this in time and felt that I had better get away. I had

spoken to him the year before of an ambition to go and work with Kocher in whose *Verletzungen der Wirbelsäule* I had become interested through my studies of a case of haematomyelia. He did not know Kocher but went on to Berne that summer (1899), passed some time there, and became greatly attached to him, regarding him, I believe, as the leading surgeon on the Continent. They were very much alike in their surgical methods and had a common bond of interest in the goitre question.

Kocher, however, was a man of prodigious and incessant industry, whereas Halsted took things very easily, not to say lazily, in the eyes of his juniors. This, I am now quite sure, was due to ill health during the period of my residency and I lament that at the time I did not fully appreciate it. There is a series of notes apparently written in the spring of 1900 from 1201 Eutaw Place — quill-pen notes which show something of his irregularities under which I must have fretted considerably.[5(p160)]

H. C. was abroad for fourteen months in 1900 and 1901, having departed America without any real commitment yet that he would specialize in neurological surgery. His year in Europe would change that. He was perhaps most influenced by Theodor Kocher and Hugo Kronecker in Berne, where he studied the effects of cations on nerve-muscle preparations,[6] and the relationships of intracranial pressure to multiple variables, including the systemic pressure. Subsequently, he visited C. J. Sherrington in Liverpool, where, for a month, he participated in cortical localization experiments on three apes, studies that further enhanced his growing interest in brain surgery.

### Return From the Continent

Yet, Cushing returned from Europe in August of 1901 to an uncertain future. He was not even sure if there would be a place for him in Halsted's Surgical Clinic.

My return to Baltimore was largely due to pressure brought to bear by Welch and Osler. After long delay, I was finally given an appointment one afternoon at Eutaw Place, the 'Professor' [Halsted] receiving me in his dressing-gown and slippers. He suggested that I *take up and teach orthopaedics,* which I could not very well do without displacing Baer to whom I felt somewhat responsible. So in a small way I started in with some work at the Church Home and Infirmary; and finally in the distribution of the teaching which we juniors usually arranged among ourselves Finney suggested that I take over the course in operative surgery which previously he had been giving on the cadaver.[5(p204)]

Shortly thereafter, however, he was assigned to the Neurological Clinic. As he reported in a note to his father:

Besides this I will have, after all the backing and filling, the neurological side of the Clinic. Inasmuch as this was what really brought me back here according to a proposition from Dr. Halsted six months ago I rather hung on to it. I must work in the neurological dispensary mornings with Dr. Thomas and try to learn something in general about nerve cases — then I will have entry into the wards to see the house cases and one clinic a week with the 4th year surgical group on this material and a chance to operate on them once a week. Should I ever have any patients (I have one now with a boil and am worried to death about him. Curious isn't it? Have had a series of 16 on that leg of mine and regard them with indifference), I can take them to one of the private hospitals here, the Church Home or the Union Protestant Infirmary where most of the younger men do their work.[5]

## The First *JAMA* Article

The manuscript under review represents, then, Cushing's second major neurological publication. (The first, published in 1898, reported on two cases of hematomyelia.[7]) It is intensely and minutely descriptive, as its title implies, and the method of extirpation of the gasserian ganglion consumes most of the text. The operative procedure itself is set down in exhaustive, meticulous detail.

The article contains an interesting figure of an "ether chart" that graphs the pulse rate during the procedure, which lasted for 95 minutes. Cushing notes that the pulse rate falls as the trigeminal ganglion is manipulated; subsequently, he relates this phenomenon to vagotonia. No other vital signs are graphed. Indeed, none were available. In fact, the use of the sphygmomanometer in surgery was introduced by Cushing himself, when he returned from Europe in 1901, toting an early model.

Comment should also be made on the excellence of the drawings in this report, which are Cushing's own work. His articles were always copiously illustrated. Whenever possible, the pathological findings were presented pictorially. After his long treatise on operative technique, H. C. describes four cases briefly and advises that the fuller description of the patients, their outcomes, and certain anatomic and physiological questions regarding trigeminal neuralgia would be published subsequently.

## The Second *JAMA* Article

True to his word, in 1905, Cushing did publish a report of 20 cases of operation for trigeminal neuralgia, in THE JOURNAL, volume 44.[8]

This was, and is, a masterful manuscript. Each patient is described in detail, with the reasons for surgery, the operation itself, and the outcome. H. C. reviews the complications of each operation carefully. Photographs of the patients are emphasized, showing relative zones of hypesthesia and anesthesia; one photograph is taken with the light deliberately angled overhead to emphasize the atrophy of temporal and masseter muscles produced when the motor root was sectioned. H. C. describes in detail his understanding of the anatomic and physiological consequences of the removal of the gasserian ganglion and advances some plausible remarks regarding the etiology of trigeminal neuralgia (still a favorite armchair topic of neurologists and neurosurgeons). One reads this article with a sense of developing awe, realizing that the author is writing with such precision about a clinical syndrome, lacking any neuroradiological techniques, when even leukocyte counts were unique and a major laboratory undertaking, and before regular use of transfusions. Yet, much of the material is as apt today as it was then, and the clinical descriptions are still worthy of careful study.

The method of presentation of this latter article in volume 44 of THE JOURNAL also deserves editorial comment. As far as I can tell, this was a single manuscript, but it is presented on pages 773, 860, 920, 1002, and 1088. At the end of each section reads the phrase "to be continued," and at the beginning of the next section, reference is made to the previous ending. Thus, the article reads a little like the magazine series of the day. One can imagine physicians waiting expectantly for the new *JAMA* to arrive so that Cushing's latest exploits could be digested!

## Total Extirpation Rapidly Abandoned

Yet, despite the brilliance of H. C.'s work, this operation — *total* extirpation of the gasserian ganglion — rapidly fell into disuse. In 1901, Spiller and Frazier[9] published their work, showing that trigeminal neuralgia could be consistently relieved by dividing the sensory root, preserving motor function and making the total extirpation of the ganglion an unnecessary and superfluous procedure.[9] The Frazier-Spiller operation became the norm and still remains the last resort of the modern neurosurgeon, although with more modern techniques, including radiofrequency rhizotomy, with or without glycerol, and posterior decompression of the trigeminal nerve, it is rarely required any longer.

Shortly after H. C.'s second article on trigeminal neuralgia was published, the Hunterian Laboratory of Experimental Medicine was completed, and H. C. became the director of the laboratory until 1912. Much of his work then was devoted to experiments on the pituitary gland. In 1912, his first major monograph appeared, *The Pituitary Body and Its Disorders,* which described the gland in the detail for which he became famous and included 50 case reports as well as experimental observations on the anatomy and physiology of the gland.

With the publication of the monograph, Cushing became the acknowledged leader of neurosurgery; shortly thereafter, he departed Hopkins to become professor of surgery at Harvard and surgeon in chief at the Peter Bent Brigham Hospital. His star was ascending rapidly; in short order, he was the most famous surgeon in America.

## References

1. Fitz RH: Perforating inflammation of the vermiform appendix: With special reference to its early diagnosis and treatment. *Trans Assoc Am Phys* 1886;1:107.

2. Bordley J, Harvey AM: *Two Centuries of American Medicine.* Philadelphia, WB Saunders Co, 1976.

3. Bloodgood JC: Operations on 459 cases of hernia in the Johns Hopkins Hospital from June 1889 to January 1899. *Johns Hopkins Hosp Rep* 1899;7:223-567.

4. Cushing H: Laparotomy for intestinal perforation in typhoid fever: A report of four cases, with a discussion on the diagnostic signs of perforation. *Johns Hopkins Hosp Bull* 1898;9:257-269.

5. Fulton JF: *Harvey Cushing: A Biography.* Springfield, Ill, Charles C. Thomas Publisher, 1946.

6. Cushing H: Concerning the poisonous effect of pure sodium chloride solutions upon the nerve-muscle preparation. *Am J Physiol* 1901;6:77-90.

7. Cushing H: Hematomyelia from gunshot wounds of the spine: A report of two cases, with recovery following symptoms of hemilesion of the cord. *Am J Med Sci* 1898;115:654-683.

8. Cushing H: The surgical aspects of major neuralgia of the trigeminal nerve: A report of twenty cases of operation on the gasserian ganglion, with anatomic and physiologic notes on the consequences of its removal. *JAMA* 1905;44:773-778, 860-865, 920-929, 1002-1008, 1088-1093.

9. Spiller WG, Frazier CH: The division of the sensory root of the trigeminus for the relief of tic douloureux. *Univ Penn Med Bull* 1901;14:341-352.

Feb 16, 1901
(*JAMA* 1901;36:431-440)

## Chapter 4

# The Etiology of Yellow Fever

## An Additional Note*

Walter Reed, M.D.,
Surgeon, United States Army.

Jas. Carroll, M.D., and Aristides Agramonte, M.D.,
Acting Assistant-Surgeons, U.S. Army.

At the Twenty-eighth Annual Meeting of the American Public Health Association,[1] held in Indianapolis, Ind., Oct. 22-26, 1900, we presented, in the form of a preliminary note, the results of our bacteriologic study of yellow fever, based on cultures taken from the blood in eighteen cases, at various stages of the disease, as well as on those which we had made from the blood and organs of eleven yellow fever cadavers. We also recorded the results obtained from the inoculation of eleven non-immune individuals by means of the bite of mosquitoes (culex fasciatus, Fabr.) that had previously fed on the blood of patients sick with yellow fever. We were able to report two positive results, in which the attack of yellow fever followed the bite of a mosquito within the usual period of incubation of this disease.

In one of these cases all other sources of infection could be positively excluded. From our several observations we drew the following conclusions: 1. Bacillus icteroides (Sanarelli) stands in no causative relation to yellow fever, but, when present, should be considered as a secondary invader in this disease. 2. The mosquito serves as the intermediate host for the parasite of yellow fever. Since the publication of our preliminary note, we have continued our investigations, especially as regards the means by which yellow fever is propagated from individual to individual, and as to the manner in which houses become infected with the contagium of this disease. The results already obtained are so positive and striking that, with the permission of Surgeon-General Sternberg, we have concluded to present to this Congress an additional note, in which we will record these later observations. We desire to here express our sincere thanks to the Military

Governor of the Island of Cuba, Major General Leonard Wood, U. S. V., without whose approval and assistance these observations could not have been carried out.

In order to exercise perfect control over the movements of those individuals who were to be subjected to experimentation, and to avoid any other possible source of infection, a location was selected in an open and uncultivated field, about one mile from the town of Quemados, Cuba. Here an experimental sanitary station was established under the complete control of the senior member of this Board. This station was named Camp Lazear, in honor of our late colleague, Dr. Jesse W. Lazear, Acting Assistant-Surgeon, U. S. A., who died of yellow fever, while courageously investigating the causation of this disease. The site selected was very well drained, freely exposed to sunlight and winds, and, from every point of view, satisfactory for the purposes intended.

The personnel of this camp consisted of two medical officers, Dr. Roger P. Ames, Acting Assistant-Surgeon, U. S. A., an immune, in immediate charge; Dr. R. P. Cooke, Acting Assistant-Surgeon, U. S. A., non-immune; one acting hospital steward, an immune; nine privates of the hospital corps, one of whom was immune, and one immune ambulance driver.

For the quartering of this detachment, and of such non-immune individuals as should be received for experimentation, hospital tents, properly floored, were provided. These were placed at a distance of about twenty feet from each other, and were numbered 1 to 7 respectively.

Camp Lazear was established Nov. 20, 1900, and from this date was strictly quarantined, no one being permitted to leave or enter camp except the three immune members of the detachment and the members of the

*Read at the Pan-Am. Med. Cong., held in Havana, Cuba. Feb. 4-7, 1901.
1. Phila. Med. Jour., Oct. 27, 1900.

Board. Supplies were drawn chiefly from Columbia Barracks, and for this purpose a conveyance under the control of an immune acting hospital steward, and having an immune driver, was used.

A few Spanish immigrants recently arrived at the Port of Havana, were received at Camp Lazear, from time to time, while these observations were being carried out. A non-immune person, having once left this camp, was not permitted to return to it under any circumstances whatever.

The temperature and pulse of all non-immune residents were carefully recorded three times a day. Under these circumstances any infected individual entering the camp could be promptly detected and removed. As a matter of fact only two persons, not the subject of experimentation, developed any rise of temperature; one, a Spanish immigrant, with probably commencing pulmonary tuberculosis, who was discharged at the end of three days; and the other, a Spanish immigrant, who developed a temperature of 102.6 F. on the afternoon of his fourth day in camp. He was at once removed with his entire bedding and baggage and placed in the receiving ward at Columbia Barracks. His fever, which was marked by daily intermissions for three days, subsided upon the administration of cathartics and enemata. His attack was considered to be due to intestinal irritation. He was not permitted, however, to return to the camp.

No non-immune resident was subjected to inoculation who had not passed in this camp the full period of incubation of yellow fever, with one exception, to be hereinafter mentioned.

### OBSERVATIONS.

Having thus sufficiently indicated the environment of Camp Lazear and the conditions under which its residents lived, we will now proceed to a narration of the observations thus far made at this experimental station. At the time these inoculations were begun, the several tents were occupied as follows: Tent No. 1 by 1 immune and 1 non-immune; No. 2 by 1 immune and 2 non-immunes; No. 3 by 2 immunes; No. 4 by 3 non-immunes; No. 5 by 3 non-immunes; No. 6 by 2 non-immunes; and No. 7 by 1 non-immune.

For the purpose of experimentation subjects were selected as follows: from Tent No. 2, 2 non-immunes, and from Tent No. 5, 3 non-immunes. Later, 1 non-immune in Tent No. 6 was also designated for inoculation.

CASE 1.—Private John R. Kissinger, Hospital Corps, U. S. A., aged 23, a non-immune, occupant of Tent No. 2, with his full consent, was bitten at 10.30 a. m., Nov. 20, 1900, by a mosquito—C. fasciatus—that had bitten a severe case of yellow fever on the fifth day, eleven days previously; another severe case, on the third day, six days before, and a third severe one on the third day, three days before. As Kissinger had not absented himself from Columbia Barracks for a period of more than thirty days, it was considered safe to inoculate him without waiting for his period of incubation to pass.

Nov. 23, 1900, Kissinger was again bitten by the same mosquito. The result of both inoculations was negative. The mosquito, therefore, was incapable of conveying any infection on the eleventh or fourteenth day after it had bitten a severe case of yellow fever on the third day of the disease. This insect had been kept at ordinary room temperature and died November 26, 1900.

Dec. 5, 1900, at 2 p. m., twelve days after the last inoculation. Kissinger was again bitten by five mosquitoes—C. fasciatus— two of which had bitten fatal cases of yellow fever, on the second day, fifteen days before; one a severe case on the second day, nineteen days previously, and two a mild case on the third day, twenty-one days before.

The record of temperature and pulse, taken every three hours, following this inoculation, showed that the subject remained in his usual state of health during the following three days, except that on December 8, on the third day, Kissinger had slight vertigo, upon rising, which soon passed away. At 4.30 p. m.—commencement of fourth day—he complained of frontal headache; otherwise he felt well and partook of supper with appetite; at 9 p.m., temperature was 98.4 F., pulse 90; at 11.30 p. m., he awoke with a chill, his temperature 100 F., pulse 90; he complained of severe frontal headache and backache; his eyes were injected and his face suffused. December 9 at 3 a. m., his temperature was 102 F., pulse 102; he had violent headache and backache with nausea and vomiting. He was then removed to the yellow fever wards. His subsequent history was that of a case of yellow fever at moderate severity. Albumin appeared in the urine on the fourth day, increased to one-fifth by volume on the sixth day and disappeared on December 22. Granular casts were present in considerable numbers from the fourth to the eighth day. The conjunctivæ were jaundiced on the third day. The diagnosis of yellow fever in this case was made by Drs. Juan Guitéras, Carlos Finlay, W. C. Gorgas, and A. Diaz Albertini, the board of yellow fever experts of the city of Havana, who saw the patient on several occasions during his illness. (See Chart I.) The period of incubation in this case was 3 days, 9½ hours.

CASE 2.—John J. Moran, aged 24, an American, non-immune occupant of Tent No. 2, with his full consent, was bitten at 10 a. m., Nov. 26, 1900, by a mosquito—C. fasciatus—which twelve days before had bitten a case of yellow fever of moderate severity, on the third day of the disease. This insect had also bitten a well-marked case of yellow fever—second day—ten days previously.

November 29, at 2.20 p. m., Moran was again bitten by the same mosquito. The result of both of these inoculations was negative. This insect was, therefore, incapable of conveying the infection fifteen days after having bitten a case of yellow fever of moderate severity on the third day, and thirteen days after it had bitten a well-marked case of this disease on the second day. This mosquito had been kept at room temperature. Moran's case will be again referred to when we come to speak of the infection of a building by means of contaminated mosquitoes.

CASE 3.—A Spanish immigrant, aged 26, a non-immune occupant of Tent No. 5, with his full consent, was bitten at 4 p. m., Dec. 8, 1900, by four mosquitoes—C. fasciatus—which had been contaminated as follows: one by biting a fatal case of yellow fever, on the third day, seventeen days before; one a severe one, on the third day, eighteen days before; one a severe case, on the second day, twenty-two days before, and one a case of moderate severity, on the third day, twenty-four days previously.

The record of temperature and pulse, taken every three hours after the inoculation, shows no rise of temperature above 99 F. until 6 p. m., December 13, on the sixth day, when 99.4 F. is recorded; pulse 68. The subject, who was of a very lively disposition, retained his usual spirits until noon of the 13th, although he complained of slight frontal headache on the 11th and 12th. He took to his bed at noon of the 13th, the fifth day, complaining of increased frontal headache and a sense of fatigue. At 9 p. m., his temperature was 98.2 F., pulse 62.

December 14, at 6 a. m., temperature was 98 F., pulse 72, and he still complained of frontal headache and general malaise. Profuse epistaxis occurred at 7.45 a. m.; at 9 a .m., temperature was 99.6 F.., pulse 80; at 1.15 p. m., temperature was 100 F., pulse 80, and he complained of a sense of chilliness, with frontal headache increased, and slight pain in the back, arms and legs; at 3 p. m., temperature was 100 F., pulse 80; at 4.15 p. m., temperature 100.7 F., pulse 68; his face flushed and eyes congested. He was removed to the yellow fever wards. A trace of albumin was found in the urine passed at 3.30 p. m.,

when the patient took to his bed; if reckoned to the onset of fever, it was 5 days and 17 hours.

CASE 4.—A Spanish immigrant, aged 27, a non-immune occupant of Tent No. 5, with his full consent, was bitten at 10 a. m., Nov. 26, 1900, by a mosquito—C. fasciatus—which had bitten a severe case of yellow fever, on the second day, ten days

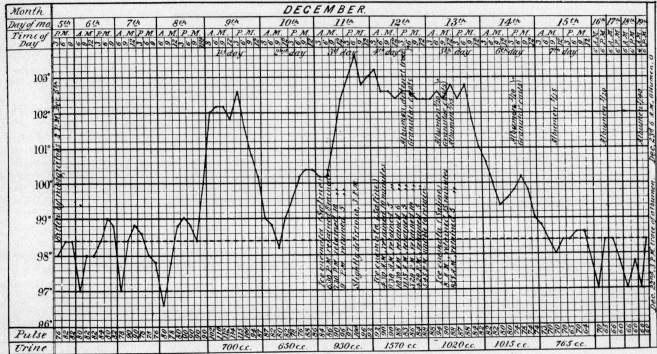

Yellow fever, produced by the bite of *Culex fasciatus*
Period of incubation, 3 days 9½ hours.

Chart I.

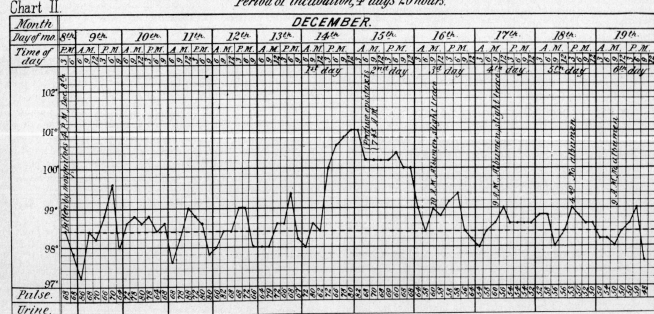

Yellow fever, produced by the bite of *Culex fasciatus.*
Period of incubation, 4 days 20 hours.

Chart II.

December 15; a few hyaline cases were present. He was seen at this time by the Havana board of experts and the diagnosis of mild yellow fever confirmed. (See Chart No. 2.)

The period of incubation in this case was four days and twenty fours, counting from the time of inoculation to the hour

before. Three days later, November 29, he was again bitten by the same insect. December 2, after an interval of three days, he was again bitten by the same insect, and also by a second mosquito—C. fasciatus—which, twelve days before, had been contaminated by biting a fatal case of yellow fever on the third day. No unfavorable effects followed any of these attempted inoculations. The first-mentioned mosquito, therefore, was incapable of conveying any infection on the seventeenth day after biting a severe case of yellow fever on the second day; the other also failed to infect on the twelfth day after biting a fatal case of yellow fever on the third day. Both of these mosquitoes had been kept at ordinary room temperature.

December 9, after an interval of seven days, the subject was again bitten, at 10.30 a. m., by one mosquito—C. fasciatus—which had been infected nineteen days before by biting a fatal case of yellow fever on the second day of the disease. He remained in his usual health until 9 a.m., December 12, the third day, when he complained of frontal headache; his temperature was 98.8 F., pulse 96. This headache continued during the entire day. At 6 p.m., temperature was 99 F., pulse 94; at 9 p. m., temperature 99 F., pulse 84; at 9.30 p. m., temperature 99.4 F., pulse 82. Severe headache and backache was complained of; his eyes were injected and his face suffused. The following morning he was sent to the yellow fever wards. Urine passed at 4.20 p. m., December 15, the third day, gave a distinct trace of albumin. Many hyaline casts were present on the same date. The conjunctivæ were jaundiced on the third day.

The patient was seen by the board of experts on December 14, and the diagnosis of yellow fever made. (See Chart No. 3.)

The period of incubation in this case was 3 days, 11½ hours.

CASE 5.—A Spanish immigrant, aged 26, a non-immune occupant of Tent No. 5, with his full consent, was bitten at 10 a.m., Nov. 26, 1900, by a mosquito—C. fasciatus—that had bitten a well-marked case of yellow fever, on the third day, twelve days before. November 29 he was again bitten by the same insect. December 2 he was for the third time bitten by two mosquitoes—C. fasciatus—both of which had bitten a well-marked case of yellow fever, on the third day, eighteen days before. As no bad results followed any of these inoculations, it follows that these mosquitoes were incapable of conveying any infection eighteen days after they had bitten a well-marked case of yellow fever on the third day. Both of these insects had been kept at room temperature.

December 11, after an interval of nine days, the subject was again, at 4:30 p.m., bitten by the same mosquitoes, four in number, that had been applied to Case 3, three days prior to this time, with positive results.

The record of temperature and pulse, taken every three hours following the inoculation, showed no change till December 13, the second day, at 9 a.m., when the temperature was 99 F., and the pulse 78. From this hour till 6 p.m. the temperature varied from 99.2 to 99.6 F. The subject complained of frontal headache, slight in degree, during the entire day. At 9 p.m. his temperature was 98.4 F., pulse 62.

December 14, the third day, he complained of slight frontal headache during the entire day, and was indisposed to exertion. From 6 a.m. to 6 p.m. the temperature averaged 99.2 F., and the pulse varied from 64 to 90; at 9 p.m. it was 98.4 F., the pulse 78. December 15, the fourth day, at 6 a.m., temperature was 98.2 F., pulse 78. He still had frontal headache. At 9 a.m., temperature was 99.2 F., pulse 80; at 12, noon, the former was 99.2 F., the pulse 74. The subject now went to bed, complaining of headache and pains throughout the body. At 2 p.m., the temperature was 100 F., the pulse 80; eyes much congested; face flushed. At 6 p.m. his temperature had risen to 102 F., and the pulse to 90. He was then transferred to the yellow fever wards. Albumin appeared in the urine at 7:30 a.m., December 17. Bleeding from the gums and roof of the mouth occurred on the sixth and seventh days of his illness.

This case was examined by the board of experts on the 16th and 19th, and the diagnosis of yellow fever made.

Albumin disappeared on the sixth day, the temperature falling to normal on this date, and remaining near this point till

December 23, the ninth day of sickness, when a relapse occurred, attended with bleeding from the gums on December 24 and 25, with the appearance of red blood cells and pus cells in the urine in moderate numbers. Fever subsided on December 26, and the urine became normal on December 29. (See Chart iv.)

The period of incubation in this case, if reckoned from the time of inoculation to the hour when the patient took to his bed, was 3 days, 19½ hours.

The four patients whose histories we have given above were also examined by a number of physicians of Havana, among whom we may mention Dr. Bango, of "La Covadonga," Dr. Sanchez, of "La Benéfica," and Dr. Moas, of "La Purissima Concepcion," by all of whom the diagnosis of yellow fever was confirmed. Let us now rapidly review the circumstances attending these cases of experimental yellow fever, in order to emphasize certain points of interest and importance in connection with their occurrence. (We omit any reference to the clinical histories.)

It should be borne in mind that at the time when these inoculations were begun, there were only 12 non-immune residents at Camp Lazear, and that 5 of these were selected for experiment, viz., 2 in Tent No. 2, and 3 in Tent No. 5. Of these we succeeded in infecting 4, viz., 1 in Tent No. 2 and 3 in Tent No. 5, each of whom developed an attack of yellow fever within the period of incubation of this disease. The one negative result, therefore, was in Case 2—Moran—inoculated with a mosquito on the fifteenth day after the insect had bitten a case of yellow fever on the third day. Since this mosquito failed to infect Case 4, three days after it had bitten Moran, it follows that the result could not have been otherwise than negative in the latter case. We now know, as the result of our observations, that in the case of an insect kept at room temperature during the cool weather of November, fifteen or even eighteen days would, in all probability, be too short a time to render it capable of producing the disease.

As bearing upon the source of infection, we invite attention to the period of time during which the subjects had been kept under rigid quarantine, prior to successful inoculation, which was as follows: Case 1, fifteen days; Case 3, nine days; Case 4, nineteen days; Case 5, twenty-one days. We further desire to emphasize the fact that this epidemic of yellow fever, which affected 33.33 per cent. of the non-immune residents of Camp Lazear, did not concern the 7 non-immunes occupying Tents No. 1, 4, 6 and 7, *but was strictly limited to those individuals who had been bitten by contaminated mosquitoes.*

Nothing could point more forcibly to the source of this infection than the order of the occurrence of events at this camp. The precision with which the infection of the individual followed the bite of the mosquito left nothing to be desired in order to fulfill the requirements of a scientific experiment.

The epidemic having ceased on Dec. 15, 1900, no other case of yellow fever occurred in this camp until we again began to expose individuals to inoculation. Thus fifteen days later we made the following observation:

CASE 6.—A Spanish immigrant, aged 27, a non-immune occupant of Tent No. 6, with his full consent, was bitten at 11 a.m., Dec. 30, 1900, by four mosquitoes—C. fasciatus—that had been contaminated seventeen days previously by biting a mild case of yellow fever on the first day of the disease (Case 4). These insects had been kept at a temperature of 82 F.

The subject remained in his normal condition until the evening of Jan. 2, 1901, the third day, when he complained of frontal headache. At 6 p.m., his temperature was 99 F., pulse 64. He slept well, but still complained of headache on the following morning, January 3. He partook sparingly of breakfast, and afterward lay on his bed, being disinclined to exert

by the board of experts on the second and seventh days of his attack, and the diagnosis of yellow fever confirmed. (See Chart v.)

The period of incubation in this case was three days, 22½ hours. The subject had remained in strict quarantine for twenty-two days preceding his inoculation.

In considering the character of the attacks and the course of the disease in these five cases of experimental

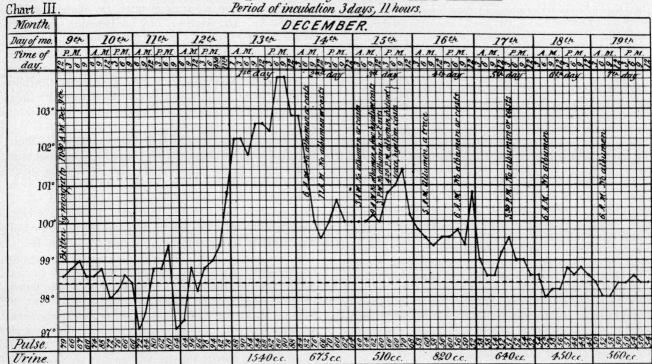

Yellow fever produced by the bite of Culex fasciatus.
Chart III.
Period of incubation 3 days, 11 hours.

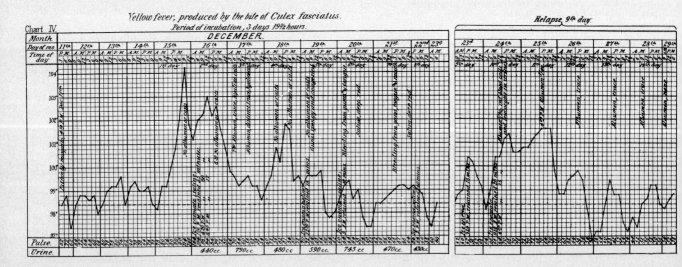

Yellow fever; produced by the bite of Culex fasciatus.
Chart IV.
Period of incubation, 3 days 19½ hours.
Relapse, 9th day.

himself. At 9 a.m., the temperature was 99 F., the pulse 96; at 10:30 a.m., temperature 100 F., pulse 80. A sense of chilliness and sharp frontal headache was complained of, and at 3 p.m. his temperature was 100.8 F., his pulse 89, and his eyes were congested and face flushed. He was removed to the yellow fever wards. A specimen of urine passed at midnight, January 4, contained a distinct trace of albumin. Slight bleeding from the gums occurred on the fifth and sixth days. The patient was seen

yellow fever, it must be borne in mind that these infected individuals were all young men, in good general physical condition and placed amid excellent hygienic surroundings. Further, it must not be forgotten that, upon the earliest manifestation of an approaching infection, they were each and all put to bed at once, and were even carried to the yellow fever wards while occupying the same bed. In other words, these men were kept at absolute rest from the first inception of the disease. Just what bearing this may have had on the subsequent course of the fever, we can not say, but since so much stress is laid on absolute rest of the patient by those having most experience in the treatment of yellow fever, the influence of this enforced rest, in our cases, upon the subsequent course of the attack, was doubtless of much importance. We reserve a consideration of the clinical side of these cases for a future report.

In our opinion the experiments above described conclusively demonstrate that an attack of yellow fever may be readily induced in the healthy subject by the bite of mosquitoes—C. fasciatus—which have been previously contaminated by being fed with the blood of those sick with yellow fever, provided the insects are kept for a sufficient length of time after contamination before being applied to the person to be infected.

Our observations do not confirm Finlay's statement that the bite of the mosquito may confer an abortive attack of yellow fever, when applied to the healthy subject two to six days after it has bitten a yellow fever patient. We have always failed to induce an attack, even of the mildest description, when we have used mosquitoes within less than twelve days from the time of contamination, although the insects were constantly kept at summer temperature. We could cite instances where we have applied mosquitoes at intervals of two, three, four, five, six, nine, and eleven days following the contamination of the insect with the blood of well-marked cases of yellow fever, early in the disease, without any effect whatever being produced by the bite. Thus in one case no result followed the bite of fourteen mosquitoes which four days previously had been contaminated by biting a case of yellow fever on the first day. Again, seven days later, or eleven days after contamination, the surviving seven of these insects failed to infect an individual. On the seventeenth day after contamination, however, the bite of four of these mosquitoes—all that remained of the original fourteen—was promptly followed by an attack of yellow fever in the same individual. These insects had been kept, during the whole of this time, at an average temperature of 82 F.

Our observations would seem to indicate that after the parasite has been taken into the mosquito's stomach, a certain number of days must elapse before the insect is capable of re-conveying it to man. This period doubtless represents the time required for the parasite to pass from the insect's stomach to its salivary glands, and would appear to be about twelve days in summer weather, and most probably about eighteen or more days during the cooler winter months. It follows, also, that our observations do not confirm Finlay's opinion that the bite of the contaminated mosquito may confer immunity against a subsequent attack of yellow fever. In our experience, an individual may be bitten on three or more occasions by contaminated mosquitoes without manifesting any symptoms of disturbance to health, and yet promptly sicken with yellow fever within a few days after being bitten by an insect capable of conveying the infection.

## ACQUIREMENT OF THE DISEASE.

Having shown that yellow fever can be conveyed by the bite of an infected mosquito, it remains to inquire whether this disease can be acquired in any other manner. It has seemed to us that yellow fever, like the several types of malarial fever, might be induced by the injection of blood taken from the general circulation of a patient suffering with this disease. Accordingly we have subjected four individuals to this method of infection, with one negative and three positive results. Reserving the detailed description of these cases to a subsequent occasion, we may state that in one of the positive cases, an attack of pronounced yellow fever followed the subcutaneous injection of 2 c.c. of blood taken from a vein at the bend of the elbow, on the first day of the disease, the period of incubation being three days and twenty-two hours; in the second case, 1.5 c.c. of blood, taken on the first day of the disease, and injected in the same manner, brought about an attack within two days and twelve hours; while in our third case, the injection of 0.5 c.c. of blood taken on the second day of the disease, produced an attack at the end of forty-one hours.

In the case mentioned as negative to the blood injection, the subsequent inoculation of this individual with mosquitoes already proved to be capable of conveying the disease, also resulted negatively. We think, therefore, that this particular individual, a Spanish immigrant, may be considered as one who probably possesses a natural immunity to yellow fever.

It is important to note that in the three cases in which the injection of the blood brought about an attack of yellow fever, careful cultures from the same blood, taken immediately after injection, failed to show the presence of Sanarelli's bacillus.[2]

Our observations, therefore, show that the parasite of yellow fever is present in the general and capillary circulation, at least during the early stages of this disease, and that the latter may be conveyed, like the malarial parasite, either by means of the bite of the mosquito, or by the injection of blood taken from the general circulation.

## CAN YELLOW FEVER BE PROPAGATED IN ANY OTHER WAY?

We believe that the general consensus of opinion of both the medical profession and the laity is strongly in favor of the conveyance of yellow fever by fomites. The origin of epidemics, devastating in their course, has been frequently attributed to the unpacking of trunks and boxes that contained supposedly infected clothing; and hence the efforts of health authorities, both state and national, are being constantly directed to the thorough disinfection of all clothing and bedding shipped from ports where yellow fever prevails. To such extremes have efforts at disinfection been carried, in order to prevent

---

2. A fourth case of yellow fever, severe in type, has been produced by the subcutaneous injection of 1 c.c. of blood taken from the general circulation on the second day of the disease, the period of incubation being three days and one hour. The patient from whom the blood was obtained was an experimental case which was in turn produced by the injection of blood—0.5 c.c.—derived from a non-experimental case of fatal yellow fever. As "controls," Cases 1, 4, 6 and 7 of this report were also injected subcutaneously with 1 c.c. of the same blood without manifesting any symptoms whatever. The blood which produced this fourth case of yellow fever, when transferred at the same time to bouillon tubes in considerable quantities, gave no growth whatever.

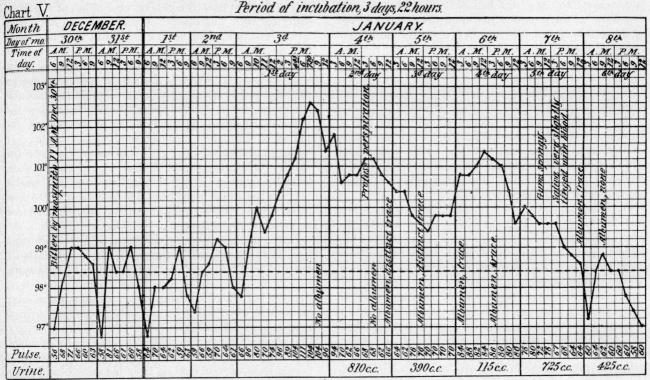

**Chart V.**

*Yellow fever, produced by the bite of Culex fasciatus.*
*Period of incubation, 3 days, 22 hours.*

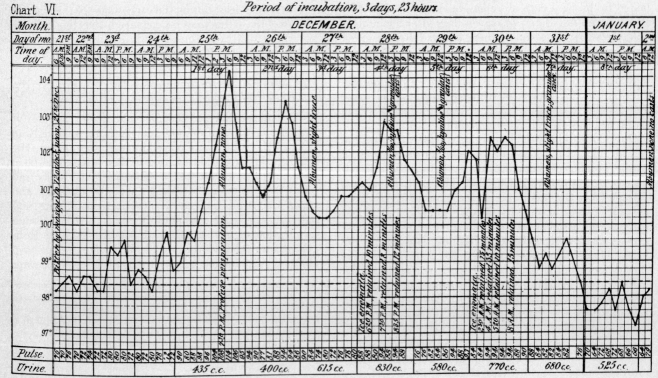

**Chart VI.**

*Yellow fever, produced by the bite of Culex fasciatus.*
*Period of incubation, 3 days, 23 hours.*

the importation of this disease into the United States, that, during the epidemic season, all articles of personal apparel and bedding have been subjected to disinfection, sometimes both at the port of departure and at the port of arrival; and this has been done whether the articles have previously been contaminated by contact with yellow fever patients or not. The mere fact that the individual has resided, even for a day, in a city where yellow fever is present, has been sufficient cause to subject his baggage to rigid disinfection by the sanitary authorities.

To determine, therefore, whether clothing and bedding, which have been contaminated by contact with yellow fever patients and their discharges, can convey this disease is a matter of the utmost importance. Although the literature contains many references to the failure of such contaminated articles to cause the disease, we have considered it advisable to test, by actual experiment on non-immune human beings, the theory of the conveyance of yellow fever by fomites, since we know of no other way in which this question can ever be finally determined.

For this purpose there was erected at Camp Lazear a small frame house consisting of one room 14x20 feet, and known as "Building No. 1," or the "Infected Clothing and Bedding Building." The cubic capacity of this house was 2800 feet. It was tightly ceiled within with "tongue and grooved" boards, and was well battened on the outside. It faced to the south and was provided with two small windows, each 26x34 inches in size. These windows were both placed on the south side of the building, the purpose being to prevent, as much as possible, any thorough circulation of the air within the house. They were closed by permanent wire screens of .5 mm. mesh. In addition sliding glass sash were provided within and heavy wooden shutters without; the latter intended to prevent the entrance of sunlight into the building, as it was not deemed desirable that the disinfecting qualities of sunlight, direct or diffused, should at any time be exerted on the articles of clothing contained within this room. Entrance was effected through a small vestibule, 3x5 feet, also placed on the southern side of the house. This vestibule was protected without by a solid door and was divided in its middle by a wire screen door, swung on spring hinges. The inner entrance was also closed by a second wire screen door. In this way the passage of mosquitoes into this room was effectually excluded. During the day, and until after sunset, the house was kept securely closed, while by means of a suitable heating apparatus the temperature was raised to 92 to 95 F. Precaution was taken at the same time to maintain a sufficient humidity of the atmosphere. The average temperature of this house was thus kept at 76.2 F. for a period of sixty-three days.

Nov. 30, 1900, the building now being ready for occupancy, three large boxes filled with sheets, pillow-slips, blankets, etc., contaminated by contact with cases of yellow fever and their discharges were received and placed therein. The majority of the articles had been taken from the beds of patients sick with yellow fever at Las Animas Hospital, Havana, or at Columbia Barracks. Many of them had been purposely soiled with a liberal quantity of black vomit, urine, and fecal matter. A dirty "comfortable" and much-soiled pair of blankets,

removed from the bed of a patient sick with yellow fever in the town of Quemados, were contained in one of those boxes. The same day, at 6 p.m., Dr. R. P. Cooke, Acting Assistant-Surgeon, U. S. A., and two privates of the hospital corps, all non-immune young Americans, entered this building and deliberately unpacked these boxes, which had been tightly closed and locked for a period of two weeks. They were careful at the same time to give each article a thorough handling and shaking in order to disseminate through the air of the room the specific agent of yellow fever, if contained in these fomites. These soiled sheets, pillowcases and blankets were used in preparing the beds in which the members of the hospital corps slept. Various soiled articles were hung around the room and placed about the bed occupied by Dr. Cooke.

From this date until Dec. 19, 1900, a series of twenty days, this room was occupied each night by these three non-immunes. Each morning the various soiled articles were carefully packed in the aforesaid boxes, and at night again unpacked and distributed about the room. During the day the residents of this house were permitted to occupy a tent pitched in the immediate vicinity, but were kept in strict quarantine.

December 12, a fourth box of clothing and bedding was received from Las Animas Hospital. These articles had been used on the beds of yellow fever patients, but in addition had been purposely soiled with the bloody stools of a fatal case of this disease. As this box had been packed for a number of days, when opened and unpacked by Dr. Cooke and his assistants, on December 12, the odor was so offensive as to compel them to retreat from the house. They pluckily returned, however, within a short time and spent the night as usual.

December 19 these three non-immunes were placed in quarantine for five days and then given the liberty of the camp. All had remained in perfect health, notwithstanding their stay of twenty nights amid such unwholesome surroundings.

During the week, December 20-27, the following articles were also placed in this house, viz.: pajamas suits, 1; undershirts, 2; night-shirts, 4; pillow-slips, 4; sheets, 6; blankets, 5; pillows, 2; mattresses, 1. These articles had been removed from the persons and beds of four patients sick with yellow fever and were very much soiled, as any change of clothing or bed-linen during their attacks had been purposely avoided, the object being to obtain articles as thoroughly contaminated as possible.

From Dec. 21, 1900, till Jan. 10, 1901, this building was again occupied by two non-immune young Americans, under the same conditions as the preceding occupants, except that these men slept every night in the very garments worn by yellow fever patients throughout their entire attacks, besides making use exclusively of their much-soiled pillow-slips, sheets and blankets. At the end of twenty-one nights of such intimate contact with these fomites, they also went into quarantine, from which they were released five days later in perfect health.

From January 11 till January 31, a period of twenty days, "Building No. 1" continued to be occupied by two other non-immune Americans, who, like those who preceded them, have slept every night in the beds formerly occupied by yellow fever patients and in the nightshirts used by these patients throughout the attack, without change. In addition, during the last fourteen nights of their occupancy of this house they have slept, each night, with their pillows covered with towels that had been thoroughly soiled with the blood drawn from both the general and capillary circulation, on the first day of the disease, in the case of a well-marked attack of yellow fever. Notwithstanding this trying ordeal, these men have continued to remain in perfect health.

The attempt which we have therefore made to infect "Building No. 1," and its seven non-immune occupants, during a period of sixty-three days, has proved an absolute failure. We think we can not do better here than to quote from the classic work of La Roche.[3] This author says: "In relation to the yellow fever, we find so many instances establishing the fact of the nontransmissibility of the disease through the agency of articles of the kind mentioned, and of merchandise generally, that we can not but discredit the accounts of a contrary character assigned in medical writings, and still more to those presented on the strength of popular report solely. For if, in a large number of well authenticated cases, such articles have been handled and used with perfect impunity—and that, too, often under circumstances best calculated to insure the effect in question—we have every reason to conclude, that a contrary result will not be obtained in other instances of a similar kind; and that consequently the effect said to have been produced by exposure to those articles, must—unless established beyond the possibility of doubt—be referred to some other agency.

The question here naturally arises: How does a house become infected with yellow fever? This we have attempted to solve by the erection at Camp Lazear of a second house, known as "Building No. 2," or the "Infected Mosquito Building." This was in all respects similar to "Building No. 1," except that the door and windows were placed on opposite sides of the building so as to give through-and-through ventilation. It was divided, also, by a wire-screen partition, extending from floor to ceiling, into two rooms, 12x14 feet and 8x14 feet respectively. Whereas, all articles admitted to "Building No. 1" had been soiled by contact with yellow fever patients, all articles admitted to "Building No. 2" were first carefully disinfected by steam before being placed therein.

On Dec. 21, 1900, at 11.45 a.m., there were set free in the larger room of this building fifteen mosquitoes—C. fasciatus—which had previously been contaminated by biting yellow fever patients, as follows: 1, a severe case, on the second day, Nov. 27, 1900, twenty-four days; 3, a well-marked case, on the first day, Dec. 9, 1900, twelve days; 4, a mild case, on the first day, Dec. 13, 1900, eight days; 7, a well-marked case, on the first day, Dec. 16, 1900, five days—total, 15.

Only one of these insects was considered capable of conveying the infection, viz., the mosquito that had bitten a severe case twenty-four days before; while three others—the twelve-day insects—had possibly reached the dangerous stage, as they had been kept at an average temperature of 82 F.

At 12, noon, of the same day, John J. Moran—already referred to as Case 2 in this report—a non-immune American, entered the room where the mosquitoes had been freed, and remained thirty minutes. During this time he was bitten about the face and hands by several insects. At 4.30 p.m., the same day, he again entered and remained twenty minutes, and was again bitten. The following day, at 4.30 p.m., he, for the third time, entered the room, and was again bitten.

CASE 7.—On Dec. 25, 1900, at 6 a.m., the fourth day, Moran complained of slight dizziness and frontal headache. At 11 a.m. he went to bed, complaining of increased headache and malaise, with a temperature of 99.6 F., pulse 88; at noon the temperature was 100.4 F., the pulse 98; at 1 p.m., 101.2 F., the pulse 96, and his eyes were much injected and face suffused. He was removed to the yellow fever wards. He was seen on several occasions by the board of experts and the diagnosis of yellow fever confirmed. (See Chart 6).

The period of incubation in this case, dating from the first visit to "Building No. 2," was three days and twenty-three hours. If reckoned from his last visit it was two days and eighteen hours. There was no other possible source for his infection, as he had been strictly quarantined at Camp Lazear for a period of thirty-two days prior to his exposure in the mosquito building.

During each of Moran's visits, two non-immunes remained in this same building, only protected from the mosquitoes by the wire-screen partition. From Dec. 21, 1900, till Jan. 8, 1901, inclusive—eighteen nights—these non-immunes have slept in this house, only protected by the wire screen partition. These men have remained in perfect health to the present time.

December 28, after an interval of seven days, this house was again entered by a non-immune American, who remained twenty-five minutes. The subject was bitten by only one insect. The following day he again entered and remained fifteen minutes, and was again bitten by one mosquito. The result of these two visits was entirely negative. As the mortality among the insects in this room, from some unknown cause, had been surprisingly large, it is possible that the subject was bitten by insects not more than thirteen days old, in which case they would probably not infect, since they had been kept for only five days at a temperature of 82 F., and for eight days at the mean temperature of the room, 78 F.

Be this as it may, nothing can be more striking or instructive as bearing upon the cause of house infection in yellow fever, than when we contrast the results obtained in our attempts to infect Buildings No. 1 and No. 2; for whereas, in the former *all* of seven non-immunes escaped the infection, although exposed to the most intimate contact with the fomites for an average period of twenty-one nights each; in the latter, an exposure, reckoned by as many minutes, was quite sufficient to give an attack of yellow fever to one out of two persons who entered the building—50 per cent.

Thus at Camp Lazear, of 7 non-immunes whom we attempted to infect by means of the bites of contaminated mosquitoes, we have succeeded in conveying the disease to 6, or 85.71 per cent. On the other hand, 7 non-immunes whom we tried to infect by means of fomites, under particularly favorable circumstances, we did not succeed in a single instance. Out of a total of 18

---

3. R. La Roche: Yellow Fever, vol. ii, p. 516, Philadelphia.

non-immunes whom we have inoculated with contaminated mosquitoes, since we began this line of investigation, 8, or 44.4 per cent., have contracted yellow fever. If we exclude those individuals bitten by mosquitoes that had been kept less than twelve days after contamination, and which were, therefore, probably incapable of conveying the disease, we have to record eight positive and two negative results—80 per cent.

## CONCLUSIONS.

1. The mosquito—C. fasciatus—serves as the intermediate host for the parasite of yellow fever.

2. Yellow fever is transmitted to the non-immune individual by means of the bite of the mosquito that has previously fed on the blood of those sick with this disease.

3. An interval of about twelve days or more after contamination appears to be necessary before the mosquito is capable of conveying the infection.

4. The bite of the mosquito at an earlier period after contamination does not appear to confer any immunity against a subsequent attack.

5. Yellow fever can also be experimentally produced by the subcutaneous injection of blood taken from the general circulation during the first and second days of this disease.

6. An attack of yellow fever, produced by the bite of the mosquito, confers immunity against the subsequent injection of the blood of an individual suffering from the non-experimental form of this disease.

7. The period of incubation in thirteen cases of experimental yellow fever has varied from forty-one hours to five days and seventeen hours.

8. Yellow fever is not conveyed by fomites, and hence disinfection of articles of clothing, bedding, or merchandise, supposedly contaminated by contact with those sick with this disease, is unnecessary.

9. A house may be said to be infected with yellow fever only when there are present within its walls contaminated mosquitoes capable of conveying the parasite of this disease.

10. The spread of yellow fever can be most effectually controlled by measures directed to the destruction of mosquitoes and the protection of the sick against the bites of these insects.

11. While the mode of propagation of yellow fever has now been definitely determined, the specific cause of this disease remains to be discovered.

Aug 5, 1983
(*JAMA* 1983;250:659-662)

# Walter Reed and Yellow Fever*

## William B. Bean, MD

Yellow fever was a disease of unknown cause, curious, almost haphazard spread, short duration, and, often, a high fatality rate. It died out soon after a frost and did not appear in cool climates or high elevations. Some thought filth caused its spread — that it arose in the fetid, reeking decay around docks. Others believed it to be imported, mainly by ships from tropical lands. It rarely attacked nurses, doctors, or hospital attendants. The very mystery increased the sickening fear it created. It brought business to a halt. People fled from it if they could. Thus, when the manner of its spread was learned and could be stopped, it was stripped of its lethal secrets. We today who go careless and carefree are a forgetful people.

The article reprinted in this issue of THE JOURNAL was the classic contribution of the Yellow Fever Board appointed by Surgeon General Sternberg and headed by Dr Walter Reed. One member, Lazear, died of yellow fever, which developed under circumstances that are still uncertain. Another, Carroll, had a severe attack, which left him a strangely embittered man. Agramonte, a Cuban physician presumably immune to yellow fever, was the fourth member of the board.

### Insect Vectors

History abounds in the attribution of disease to various insects, ticks, lice, bedbugs, flies, and mosquitoes — unfortunately, largely educated guesses or speculation. Beaupurthuy, Nott, and, in particular, Charles Finlay were convinced that a mosquito might transmit yellow fever. In 1879, the American yellow fever study team, with Chaille, Sternberg, Rudolph Matas, and others, had gone to Cuba to investigate endemic yellow fever. The Memphis Epidemic of 1878 had produced much panic and fear. Their report gave the best available account of the natural history of yellow fever. It led Finlay, an eager Scottish-French physician in Havana, to abandon his idea

From the Department of Medicine, College of Medicine, University of Iowa, Iowa City.

*A commentary on Reed W, Carroll J, Agramonte A: The etiology of yellow fever: An additional note. *JAMA* 1901;36:431-440.

that it arose from alkaline earth. He suggested that the mosquito transmitted it, and he selected the *Culex fasciatus,* now called *Aedes aegypti,* which was correct. For 20 years he tried to prove his idea. Unfortunately, no one had been trained in experimental medicine. Finlay did not control his subjects or keep them from other mosquito bites or exposure to yellow fever. He did not produce a case, and he was wrong in saying that an infected mosquito, biting a person, could induce immunity without causing clinical yellow fever. He thought erroneously that a mosquito biting a victim with mild yellow fever would transmit a mild form of the disease and, thus, one might receive almost a free ride to immunity. Later, Gorgas and Guiteras found, to their horror, that this idea was wrong, and they and their subjects had great misfortune when three of their eight experimental subjects with yellow fever died, including the heroic Clara Maass. They all had received prompt and efficient medical care and support.

Finlay's main idea was exactly right. He watched the board's experiments closely. He supplied the eggs from which the Reed Board raised their own mosquitoes for experimental purposes. With the demonstration of the transmission by mosquitoes, Finlay, hitherto a source of merriment and derision with his alarming stutter and muttonchop whiskers, became a hero overnight.

Sir Patrick Manson, a British physician working in the Orient, was the first to demonstrate that the mosquito might transmit a human infection. The parasitic organism that produces filariasis could be found in mosquitoes that had bitten patients who had it. The biting had to take place at night because of the curious habit of filaria of entering the bloodstream only at night. Manson did not consider patient-mosquito-new patient spread but thought the mosquito was sickened or poisoned by the filaria and died, falling into water. When the water was drunk, the next victim was infected.

In the later 1880s in Galveston, Tx, Dr George Dock tried to produce *malaria* with mosquitoes. Unfortunately, he selected the highly prevalent *A aegypti,* which transmits yellow fever but not malaria. If he had chosen the appropriate mosquito, he might have antedated Ross' work by approximately ten years. In 1898, Ross demonstrated that the parasite of malaria is picked up by the mosquito, ultimately settles in the salivary glands, and, thus, transmits the parasite of malaria to the next victim or experimental subject. The Yellow Fever Board knew about Ross' work. Thus, the mosquito was in the air, so to speak.

In the fall of 1898, when the war with Spain was over, the Typhoid Fever Board, consisting of Walter Reed, E. O. Shakespere, and Victor Vaughan, had demonstrated that flies, feces, fingers, and filth rather than impure water or milk were the major methods of transmission of camp typhoid fever in new recruits of an army raised suddenly without knowledge of or interest in field sanitation. All the camps had soldiers from towns, villages, and cities where typhoid fever was a common summer and fall event. No large unit avoided an outbreak. More than five times as many American soldiers died of typhoid fever than died because of any military effort of Spaniards or Cubans. This Reed Board also made the capital observation that typhoid fever might break out in a camp where none had existed in the past and everybody was well. It was discovered that well persons, sometimes without any history of typhoid fever, might harbor in their alimentary canal virulent typhoid organisms. Since hygienic measures were crude at best, the environment teemed with virulent typhoid organisms.

These lessons were immediately taken to heart by Leonard Wood, the military surgeon who had risen suddenly from the rank of captain to major general. He was the civil governor-general with headquarters in Havana. With most military and other medical experts, he believed that strict sewage disposal and pure water — scrubbing the city of Havana clean — would wipe out both typhoid and yellow fever.

### Yellow Fever: Early Investigations

Typhoid fever was practically eliminated. Malaria occurred but not with an alarming incidence; it could be treated. Suddenly, in the summer of 1900, yellow fever broke out in its usual erratic fury, not only affecting the Spanish immigrants but many of Wood's headquarters staff and other officers, all living in immaculate quarters. Many died. George Miller Sternberg, the army surgeon general, a truly distinguished bacteriologist and the world's greatest authority on yellow fever, knew that something would have to be done. He appointed Reed as chairman of the Yellow Fever Board. From Walter Reed's letters, particularly to Gorgas and to Professor Barringer at the University of Virginia as well as in records left by Hurd, superintendent of Johns Hopkins Hospital, it is clear that Sternberg's earlier unsuccessful efforts to transmit yellow fever by mosquitos and his realization that Finlay had failed to prove his hypothesis made him urge Walter Reed to leave the mosquito hypothesis alone.

In 1898, Sanarelli, a well-trained Italian bacteriologist working in South America, announced that he had found *the* cause of yellow fever, a bacterium he called *Bacillus icteroides,* the "jaundice-producing bacillus." In Wash-

ington, Sternberg directed Reed and Carroll to see if they could verify Sanarelli's observations. They could not. The *B icteroides* was the lowly hog cholera bacillus with which Reed had become familiar when Welch was studying it in 1890. That year, Reed had a sabbatical at the Johns Hopkins Hospital. It took Carroll and Reed a year to correct this error, although the US Marine Hospital (later the Public Health) Service stoutly defended Sanarelli, even after the convincing work of the Reed Board. The Marine Hospital officials did not change their opinion until several years later. Sanarelli's dangerous experiments on patients without any sign of consent were vigorously attacked by William Osler when the studies of Reed and Carroll were reported to the Association of American Physicians.

The epidemiology of outbreaks of yellow fever was difficult to study accurately. An admitted yellow fever epidemic closed down all business activity. Its existence was frequently denied by officials until it had reached crisis proportions. The history of yellow fever was summarized in LaRoche's two-volume treatise, which Walter Reed had studied thoroughly. Almost every idea or bit of evidence had something to contradict it.

Two points that were important in making more plausible a study of the mosquito as a possible vector came from Henry Rose Carter and from Walter Reed's observation of yellow fever breaking out in an isolated military prison where there was no possible direct contamination with yellow fever. There, the disease developed in two of a small group of prisoners a short time after they were incarcerated. Carter, Reed's fellow alumnus of the University of Virginia, had been puzzled by the fact that ships at sea that had left a port where an epidemic was raging might be free of the disease, perhaps for weeks, when, only then, it would break out on board. In some way, the ship harbored the cause. Carter's studies in small Mississippi towns demonstrated that when someone, perhaps returning from a visit to New Orleans, came down with yellow fever when there was no local epidemic or case, the next cases in family or friends occurred three or more weeks after the first victim took sick. He concluded that in some way the environment had become infected and that this infection, whatever it was, took a period to attain the necessary virulence to produce the disease. He had discussions with Reed, Lazear, and other members of the board who were thoroughly familiar with this puzzling problem.

Jefferson Randolph Kean, another Virginia alumnus and a close friend of Walter Reed, was an important link in the chain of events that led to the ultimate demonstration of the mosquito's role in transmitting yellow fever and, particularly, what could be done to prevent the spread of the disease. His name does not appear on any of the articles, and, thus, his important role has been overlooked or forgotten. The studies set forth in the Feb 16 article were greatly facilitated when Kean, working near General Leonard Wood's headquarters, persuaded Reed to request that Wood finance the establishment of an experimental yellow fever camp. It was named Camp Lazear. Wood also provided funds for a reward for volunteers.

Lazear had been directly responsible for raising the mosquitoes. His pocket notebook had records of each mosquito raised from eggs obtained from Finlay, each kept in a separate test tube. After Lazear's death, Reed had the evidence showing which victim had been bitten on which day of the disease, how long the mosquitoes were kept until they bit volunteers, and whether and how soon the volunteers contracted yellow fever, if they did. Yellow fever had been transmitted by mosquitoes in elegant, foolproof experiments. Blood taken from a victim early in the course of the disease and injected into a volunteer produced yellow fever. Almost a year later, at the suggestion of Welch at Johns Hopkins, the work of Loeffler and Frosch on hoof and mouth disease, demonstrating the ultrafiltrate transmission, was repeated by the Reed Board. The actual experiments were performed by Carroll, demonstrating that an ultrafiltrate of blood produced the disease. Although rabies was a viral disease in which the method of transmission was well recognized, viruses were not understood at the time. The yellow fever virus was not discovered until two decades after the Reed Board completed its work.

### The Reed Studies

When the studies were begun, Walter Reed was in the maddening position of realizing that the yellow fever that killed Lazear and almost killed Carroll did not prove anything, since there were other possible exposures and no effort had been made to keep away from autopsies, avoid patients with yellow fever, or avoid bites by stray mosquitoes. Dean's case was the one clear example in the preliminary report, impressive but hardly a proof.

Several things were critically necessary in the experiments. Volunteers had to have complete information about the risk they undertook. It is obvious that volunteering to do something that may cause death is itself heroic. One of the curious ironies of fate was that the Americans who volunteered, unless they contracted yellow fever or had exposed themselves to the filth of yellow fever victims, were not given the yellow fever medal established by a grateful Congress some ten years after the experiments. Several soon volunteered again and did acquire yellow fever from mosquitoes, which demonstrated that they were not immune. Spaniards and most of the American volunteers received $100 in gold for volunteering and, if they contracted yellow fever, another $100 in gold. Many more wished to volunteer than could be accepted into the experiments. All knew that they would contract yellow fever if they stayed in Havana.

Kean was responsible for inaugurating the mosquito cleanup campaign that Gorgas followed some months later, at first reluctantly and then zealously. The significance of the Yellow Fever Board studies related in the Feb 16 article was that they cleared up critical omissions from the preliminary report. Neither Lazear nor Carroll had experimentally controlled and produced yellow fever. Dean's case was one example but an impressive one. Reed and his colleagues knew that there were many things critical to the proper conduct of the kind of experiments necessary. They could find no animals in which the disease would develop, so volunteers had to

be found. They had to have complete information about the risk, which was obvious to everyone in Havana. Perhaps because they had splendid and prompt medical attention, there were no fatalities in more than 20 volunteers who contracted yellow fever. Careful inspection of the fever charts in the article indicates that they were copies from the usually sloppy hospital charts or from nurses' notes and records. (Many of these originals are in the Reed archives in the Health Sciences Library of the School of Medicine, University of Virginia, Charlottesville.)

Walter Reed knew that yellow fever had occurred in a prison where there was no one with yellow fever and surmised that the disease must have come in some other way than by contact — an important additional clue. The principal findings of the experiments reported in the *JAMA* article were as follows:

1. The mosquito could pick up the poison from a victim only during the first two or three days of the disease. (We now know that, thereafter, the viremia is over.)

2. The infected mosquito had to live for at least 12 days before its bite became infectious, a finding completely missed by Finlay. Then, if the person bitten was not immune, there was an incubation period averaging about five days. The natural disease lasted five days to a week, often producing jaundice and rendering the blood incoagulable. (Liver damage interfered with vitamin K–promoted production of prothrombin.) If the person survived, the immunity was about as good as any immunity we know.

3. Blood taken from a victim of yellow fever early in the disease and injected into a volunteer would produce yellow fever. This was a capital observation. Later, the board found that a filtrate of blood forced through a porcelain filter that no microscopic cell or bacterium could penetrate produced the disease. It was sterile to bacteriologic methods but contained the yellow fever poison, just as whole blood did. The ultrafiltrate was infectious. Thus, the fact that the disease was produced in a human being with a filterable virus was established.

Perhaps the most heroic persons involved in the studies were those who slept in the filth, bedclothes, and blankets of those who had died of yellow fever. This conjures up a hauntingly disagreeable and offensive kind of self-sacrifice. The average volunteer must have been certain that black vomit and contaminated bedclothes were much more likely to contain the poison than the fragile little mosquito (although it did produce a sting and swelling out of proportion to its tiny size). Who could imagine that such a creature could transmit anything that would produce such a frightful and frequently fatal disease?

Fortunately, the significance of the observations was recognized much earlier by Kean than it was by Gorgas. At about the time of the publication of the *JAMA* article, Kean was acting sanitary officer of Havana. He instituted the program of putting kerosene on cisterns and emptying every conceivable water-holding object in this tropical city, a major undertaking. Inspectors were responsible for any case of yellow fever that might occur in their territory.

## Publication and Outcome

The publication of Reed's article in THE JOURNAL, which was described in a perceptive and commendable editorial in the Feb 16 issue, could give no idea of Reed's own reaction to the publication, which had disturbed and vexed him considerably. He was still smarting from the fact that the preliminary report had been published by Gould in the *Philadelphia Medical Journal* without the corrections he had sent and without his having the opportunity to look at galley proofs. Reed worried that the way the article was written might have suggested that permission was obtained from only two of the three subjects, whereas it had been obtained from each one. What he disliked about the publication of the article in *JAMA* was that the organization had been changed, the headings rearranged, and the article subjected to substantial editorial changes without any communication with the authors. Reed naturally wanted to have the article published rapidly, since he had a suspicion that Durham and Myers, two English observers who had spent time in Havana during the early stages of the yellow fever studies and then went to South America to study another epidemic, might scoop him in publishing the mosquito idea. However, no such thing occurred.

Publishers and printers and even editors sometimes seem to be natural enemies of those who perform experiments and prepare articles. That, however, is but one side of the coin. Sternberg himself was anxious to have the results of the Reed Board when the evidence had become scientific demonstration rather than suggestive testimony and a large element of hope. Sternberg, a world-reknowned bacteriologist, distinguished scientist, and great innovator in changing the direction and emphasis of the Army Medical Corps, saw the contributions of the Reed Board succeed, contrary to his expectations and beliefs. He published a statement to the effect that he had suggested that Major Reed test the mosquito hypothesis. The information we have bearing on this suggests that he had told Reed to leave the mosquito alone, since he had made tests of it and found the idea worthless. Details found in Reed's letters to Gorgas were deleted from Gorgas' book *Sanitation in Panama*, published in 1915. The letters do describe the dwindling and disappearance of yellow fever from Havana when Kean's rules and regulations were enforced by Gorgas with the utmost vigor. For the first time in a century and a half, a month went by and then almost a year without a single death caused by yellow fever, and Gorgas was responsible for the sanitation that made the Panama Canal possible.

Thus, Walter Reed, who was to die in November 1902, lived long enough to know that the studies gave public health authorities a means of preventing the occurrence of the disease, although the cause had not been isolated. It was a poison of infinitely small size that somehow must multiply before it could do its harm. Two major universities recognized the immense importance of the work. Reed received an honorary Master of Arts degree from Harvard and an LLD from the University of Michigan. Walter Reed had hoped for and expected as reward the supreme honor of the Medical Corps: the position of surgeon general; but this was not to be. Exhausted by the experiments, always short of money, appalled by the studies of Guiteras and Gorgas, who produced eight cases of yellow fever with three deaths, plagued by the daily routine of examining boards, and even charged erroneously by the personnel officers with being absent from duty (on a board!) without leave, Reed was depressed in mind, body, and estate.

Although he was in the true sense the founder of modern and ethical clinical experimentation, Walter Reed was aware that duty and virtue are their own and often only reward. He was mindful that the Harvard faculty knew what it was about when his honorary MA diploma bore the citation, "Walter Reed, medical graduate of Virginia, the military surgeon who in Cuba designed and carried out those experiments which have given man control of that fearful scourge, yellow fever."

This essay is based on a collection of the letters, papers, and writings of Walter Reed of approximately 14,000 pages and an unpublished biography of 1,300 pages with 270 pages of notes, bibliographies, and sources in the Claude Moore Health Sciences Library, University of Virginia, Charlottesville. Dr Bean is the author of *Walter Reed: A Biography* (Charlottesville, University of Virginia Press, 1982).

Nov 14, 1908
(*JAMA* 1908;51:1662-1667)

## Chapter 5

# Results of the Transplantation of Blood Vessels, Organs and Limbs*

Alexis Carrel, M.D.

From the Rockefeller Institute for Medical Research.
New York.

### INTRODUCTION.

The idea of replacing diseased organs by sound ones, of putting back an amputated limb or even of grafting a new limb on a patient having undergone an amputation, is doubtless very old. The performance of such operations, however, was completely prevented by the lack of a method of uniting vessels, thus re-establishing a normal circulation through the transplanted structures. The feasibility of these grafts depended on the development of the technic.

The history of vascular surgery is too well known to need repetition. It recently reached the active stage of its development with the experiments of Murphy in Chicago and of Payr in Gratz. Murphy united the arteries by invagination and suture, while Payr used a magnesium tube. The remarkable experiments performed in 1903 by Hoepfner with the method of Payr gave an illustration of what could be obtained in vascular surgery by a proper method.

Finally a very simple method of circular structure was developed, which has given excellent results and has been extensively used in experimental work. It appears that vessels sutured under certain conditions heal very easily, and that no thrombosis occurs as long as the operation is aseptic and the union of the vascular ends accurate. The results are durable, the circulation being maintained through the anastomoses for more than a year in several cases, and in one instance for nearly three years. The examination of the anatomic results shows that the scar of the severed vessels is, in many cases, so small that, after a few months, it is hardly discernible. There is no modification of the caliber of the vessel at the level of the anastomoses. Slight faults of technic may lead to obliterative thrombosis, but when the vessels are of sufficient caliber, accidents seldom occur. Therefore, this method of anastomoses can be employed for more complicated operations, the transplantation of vessels, organs, anatomic regions, and limbs.

### I. TRANSPLANTATION OF VESSELS.

A segment of an artery or vein can be transplanted between the cut ends of an artery or a vein, between two regions of the circulatory apparatus, and even between a serous cavity and a vessel. For instance, in some cases of ascites it would be useful to establish a permanent drainage of the peritoneal cavity by suturing a piece of a valvular vein between the peritoneum and a large vein.

Ruotte cut the saphenous vein and sutured its peripheral end to the peritoneum in a case of chronic ascites. The ascites disappeared.

The graft of a segment of vein between branches of the portal vein and the vena cava would act as a substitute for Talma's operation. However, the main application of the vascular transplantations will be, probably, the re-establishment of the circulation through an artery of which a segment has been accidentally or surgically destroyed. The ideal method would be to transplant between the cut ends of the artery a fresh segment of human artery. But this is not easily practical. Therefore, I attempted to determine whether or not a segment of vein, or a segment of artery preserved in cold storage or

---

* Read in the Section on Surgery and Anatomy of the American Medical Association, at the Fifty-ninth Annual Session, held at Chicago, June, 1908.

°Because of lack of space, the article is here abbreviated by the omission of all of the pictures and part of the text. The complete article appears in the Transactions of the Section and in the author's reprints.

an artery from an animal of another species can be used safely.

*The Transplantation of a Segment of Artery.*—This was performed for the first time in 1896 by Jaboulay. He thought that this method could be applied to the treatment of aneurisms, but the anastomoses were imperfect and in every case thrombosis occurred. Nine years later Hoepfner performed successfully the transplantation of segments of arteries by using the method of Payr, and in a remarkable series of experiments demonstrated the possibility of transplanting arteries without the occurrence of thrombosis. In 1905, in Chicago, and afterward in New York, I applied to the transplantation of arteries the circular suture and found that this method gives excellent results, even when the vessels are of different caliber. The transplantation of a segment of artery on an artery of another animal of the same species is ordinarily successful when the vessels are of sufficient size and the anastomoses are performed correctly. After a few months the transplanted segment has absolutely the same appearance as the normal vessel. The histologic examination of transplanted arteries shows that the wall does not undergo marked modification. Wood has studied the vessels during the seventy days following the operation. The elastic and muscular fibers of the media remain normal. There is a little increase of the interstitial connective tissue. The intima is sometimes a little thickened.

The remote results are excellent. A dog, into whose aorta a segment of aorta from another dog had been transplanted, was living and in good health nine months after the operation, and the femoral pulse was normal. These results show that segments of fresh arteries transplanted from an animal on another animal of the same species remain practically normal from a physiologic and histologic standpoint.

*Transplantation of Veins.*—Unfortunately this operation would not be very practical on man, for it is difficult to get fresh pieces of human arteries. If the veins could act as a substitute for arteries, the problem of the treatment of large wounds or of resection of arteries would be solved, for it is always possible to get venous material from the patient himself. The first attempt of transplantation of a segment of jugular vein into the carotid artery of a dog was made by Gluck in 1898, but thrombosis occurred. In 1903 Exner performed six experiments of the same character, but in all cases thrombosis took place. He thought the failure was due to the poor nourishment of the transplanted vessels, resulting from disturbance of the vasa vasorum. In the same year Hoepfner, using the magnesium tubes of Payr, made ten transplantations of veins on arteries, with constant negative results.

In 1905 I succeeded with Guthrie in transplanting segments of jugular veins into the carotid artery and found that the vein quickly undergoes structural changes, consisting chiefly of the thickening of its wall. Stich and Makkas observed the same results. Watts succeeded also in transplanting segments of jugular on the carotid. I obtained excellent results in the transplantation of the vena cava into the aorta, operations which had been attempted by Goyanes in Spain. From all these experiments it is possible to know the anatomic evolution of a piece of vein transplanted on an artery.

The transplantation is often successful, but much less constantly successful than the transplantation of arteries on arteries. Thrombosis occurs more frequently, due, perhaps, to the difference of caliber of the vessels generally used, jugular vein and carotid artery. The approximation of the intimas is difficult, fibrin deposits itself on the foldings of the vein, and can produce, under certain conditions, obliterative thrombosis. When the artery and the vein are of the same caliber, the results are much better. I performed twice the transplantation of the vena cava into the aorta and in both cases the healing was perfect. It is probable that the results of the venous transplantations could be as good as those of the arterial transplantation if the caliber of the vessels were similar.

A segment of vein transplanted into an artery undergoes immediately very marked change. Its lumen is dilated, but its wall becomes thicker and stronger. No aneurism has ever been observed. It seems, on the contrary, that the vein adapts itself to its arterial functions, and reacts against the increased blood pressure by thickening its wall. The anatomic changes begin very soon after the operation. Fourteen days after the operation Guthrie and myself found the wall of the transplanted segment very much thickened. The thickening was produced mainly by an increase of the connective tissue of the adventitia and the interstitial tissue of the muscular coat. This very considerable thickening does not always happen.

The remote results are excellent. Eight months after the operation, I extirpated the carotid artery of a dog into which a segment of jugular had been transplanted. The lumen of the vein was dilated, but its wall was very thick and strong. There was no stenosis or dilatation of the anastomoses. The intima of the vein had in the neighborhood of the anastomoses a scar-like appearance.

These experiments show that a vein can adapt itself to the arterial functions. But it seems that the transplantation of veins on arteries is less safe than the transplantation of arteries on arteries.

*Transplantation of Preserved Arteries.*—Therefore, it would be very important to find a method of preserving tissues outside of the body for a few days or a few weeks. I attempted to use the influence of the cold for preserving the vessels. Therefore, segments of arteries were aseptically extirpated and preserved in cold storage slightly above the freezing point. Concerning the nature of the preservative fluid and the optimum temperature, no definite technic has yet been adopted.

The actual method consists of extirpating the vessels under rigid asepsis, of washing them in Locke's solution and of immediately placing them in a glass tube, which contains, on a small piece of absorbent cotton, a few drops of Locke's solution. The tube is sealed and put into an ice box, the temperature of which is constantly between 0 and 1 C. Some vessels have been preserved also in tubes filled with Locke's solution. The vessels undergo very little gross anatomic changes during the first weeks. Afterward they became less elastic. The periadventitial connective tissue acquires a soapy consistency. However, from a histologic standpoint, the muscle fibers remain ordinarily normal, even after one month.

Arterial segments were transplanted after having been kept in the refrigerator from one to thirty-five days. The occurrence of thrombosis was observed mainly at the beginning of the use of the method. Clinical and histological examinations of the results were made from five days to one year and a half after the operation. The gross anatomic changes of the vessels are ordinarily very slight. But the wall presents generally marked histologic lesions. These lesions seem to depend on the nature of the preservative used and the length of time spent in the refrigerator. A fragment of carotid artery transplanted into a dog after twenty-four hours of cold storage in salt solution, showed a complete destruction of the muscle elements five days after the operation. In another case very little change of the muscle fibers was observed after eighteen days.

The following observation shows that a segment of artery preserved in cold storage for ten days acts as a living vessel probably for an indefinite period of time. On Feb. 26, 1907, a segment of carotid was extirpated from the body of a dog thirty-five minutes after death and preserved in a tube of Locke's solution in cold storage. On March 6 this segment was transplanted into the left carotid artery of a dog. On May 3, 1907, we examined, with Dr. Crile, the neck of this dog, and found that the transplanted segment had the same appearance as the other parts of the artery. On May 15, 1908, the neck of the dog was opened again. The left carotid artery appeared to be entirely normal. By a careful dissection one of the anastomoses was exposed. There was no induration of the wall at its level. The only evidence of the suture was a very narrow dark line on the adventitia. The transplanted segment was altogether similar to the other parts of the carotid.

The carotid artery and the transplanted segment were extirpated. When the carotid was empty and retracted itself, the transplanted segment became very apparent, because it did not contract itself. It had evidently lost all its elasticity. The intima was smooth and glistening. The location of the anastomoses was marked merely by a slight difference in color. There was no evidence of scar, from a gross anatomic standpoint. The intima was thickened, and, in a point where the media was a little thinner, presented a patch of greater thickness. The cellular tissue of the adventitia was also increased. The media was very much modified. Its internal portion had undergone hyaline degeneration. The external part was composed of fibers, of which it was difficult to say if they were connective or muscular. The elastic framework had entirely disappeared. It must be noticed that in spite of the lack of elastic tissue, the vessel has not undergone any dilatation and was apparently normal. A few other animals into which segments of vessels preserved in cold storage were grafted demonstrate that the remote results of this operation may be excellent.

These observations show that a vessel transplanted after having been kept in cold storage for a few days or weeks can functionate normally for a long time. The anatomic results are excellent, for the vessel, in spite of deep histologic changes, is not a dead but a living structure.

Other methods of preservation of vessels have been tried, but with little success. I transplanted segments of arteries which had been frozen for several days. The immediate results were sometimes apparently excellent. But, ultimately, in all cases except one, obliteration, atrophy and absorption of the vessel occurred after a few days, weeks or months.

The transplantation of devitalized arteries has been attempted by Levin and Larkin in New York, but in almost every case thrombosis occurred. However, after the transplantation of a segment of aorta fixed in formalin into the aorta of a dog, excellent circulation was observed. Histologic examination ten days after the transplantation showed that the wall was composed of amorphous tissue in which the elastic framework was seen to be very well preserved. In another case of Levin and Larkin, twenty days after the operation, the wall of the vessel was completely amorphous and surrounded by dense connective tissue. A similar experiment has been performed in St. Louis by Guthrie, who obtained an excellent functional result, but no histologic examination of the vessel has yet been published.

I found also that it is possible to use peritoneum as a substitute for the arterial wall.

*Transplantation of Arteries Between Animals of Different Species.*—It is generally believed that a piece of tissue transplanted from one animal into another of different species undergoes cytolysis and disappears. It is not always true. There are several varieties of heteroplastic transplantations according to the zoologic distance which separates the host and the owner of the transplanted tissue. If a piece of tissue is transplanted from an animal to another and very different animal—from the mouse to the lizard, for instance—cytolysis occurs. But if the owner of the tissue and the host belong to more closely related zoologic sections, as, for instance, the guinea-pig and the rabbit, the graft does not undergo any cytolysis, but gradually disappears by atrophy. A few vessels are formed, but the vascularization is much less developed than it happens when the animals are of a same species. Nevertheless, as it has been shown by Cristiani, grafts between animals of different species, as guinea-pig and rabbit, can take. But these grafts are less vascularized than normally. These facts led me to attempt heteroplastic transplantation of blood vessels, with the view that between animals as closely related as cat and dog, or man and monkey, the vessel would not undergo any cytolysis, but would stand the serum of the other animal, and, perhaps, adapt itself to its new conditions of life.

Heteroplastic transplantations of vessels have been performed by Hoepfner in Berlin several years before my experiments. But the results were absolutely negative. Nevertheless, in December, 1906, I presented before the American Physiological Society a cat into which a segment of carotid artery of a dog had been grafted. The femoral pulse was normal. An exploratory laparotomy was performed afterward and the transplanted segment found almost normal. To-day, one year and seven months after the operation, the femoral pulse is still normal. At the same time, Stich and Makkas transplanted successfully segments of arteries from rabbit and cat to dog, and from man to dog. Afterward Guthrie successfully grafted onto a dog the arteries of a rabbit and cat.

The anatomic evolution of the vessels will be divided artificially into three periods: before the twentieth day, from the twentieth day to the seventieth day, and after the seventieth day. During the first two weeks the transplanted segment remained normal from a gross anatomic standpoint. The muscular fibers are normal. The interstitial connective tissue is slightly increased. Generally, the intima is free from a thrombus. In a case of transplantation of human vessel on dog, I found the intima completely covered by a thin layer of fibrin. Stich has observed the same disposition. This layer does not interfere with the circulation, but isolates the transplanted vessel from the blood. Wood has found that twenty days after the operation the lesions of the elastic fibers are already marked, while the muscle fibers are still normal.

The lesions are more marked on rabbits' than on cats' vessels, when transplanted on dogs. From the twentieth to the seventieth days, the vessel undergoes a more or less marked dilatation of its lumen. The lesions are characterized by a progressive and complete disappearance of the elastic framework, by a diminution in the number of the muscle fibers, an increase of the interstitial connective tissue, and a thickening of the intima. Nevertheless, the endothelium may persist. Fifty-two days after the operation Stich saw the endothelium covering the anastomosis.

In another case, where the wall was covered partially by a parietal thrombus, the intima was lined by endothelial cells. Wood found that seventy days after the operation all the elastic tissue had disappeared. Afterward the lesions seem to go on slowly. After six months I found the carotid artery of a dog, transplanted on a cat, very much dilated. The intima was smooth, and there was no evidence of the anastomoses. They could be approximately located only by the beginning of the dilatation. No elastic fibers could be detected. The media was deeply modified. Its internal part had in part undergone hyaline degeneration. The external part was composed of connective tissue and a few fibers, presenting the histologic reaction of muscle fibers. The adventitia was thickened.

This shows that the vessel does not undergo any cytolysis. Slowly the elastic fibers disappear, the lumen becomes dilated, the connective tissue increases, and the muscle fibers, which at first remain normal, diminish in number, and finally are almost completely resorbed. The vessel is progressively transformed into a tube formed almost exclusively of connective tissue. But this tube is made of living tissue and can act as an artery for one year and a half, at least.

## II. THE TRANSPLANTATION OF ORGANS.

The transplantation with the re-establishment of the circulation by vascular anastomoses permits the graft of a whole organ, like the kidney or the spleen. As regards glands like the thyroid, parathyroid and ovaries, the action of which on the organism is efficient even when the volume of glandular tissue is small, the graft of pieces of tissues by simple implantation is sufficient.

In 1905 I succeeded with Guthrie in extirpating and replanting the thyroid gland with reversal of the circulation. Eleven days after the operation the wound was opened and the circulation of the gland was found going on. The animal is still alive and the anatomic examination of the gland will be made later.

The brilliant results obtained by Halsted in the transplantation of the parathyroid, and by Bush and Schmieden in the transplantation of the suprarenals, show that the graft of these small bodies by simple implantation is efficient. Nevertheless, it would be possible also to graft the parathyroids with immediate re-establishment of the circulation by using the method of transplantation in mass.

I attempted to develop a method of transplantation in mass of the suprarenal glands on cats. A first cat was killed and both suprarenals extirpated with the corresponding segments of the aorta and vena cava. On a second cat the aorta and vena cava were transversely severed a few centimeters below the kidneys, the anatomic specimen was placed into the abdominal cavity, and the ends of the aortic and caval segment united to the ends of the aorta and vena cava. The circulation was immediately re-established into the suprarenals. Four experiments were performed. On two animals the glands were found degenerated or atrophied. Two others are still living, more than six months after the operation, and will be examined later. It is probable that the glands are resorbed.

The transplantation of the ovaries is so successful by simple implantation that a complicated vascular operation seems to be necessary. This question was almost completely settled several years ago, chiefly by the experiments of Knauer and also Foa.

In 1907 Guthrie obtained excellent results on chickens and observed offsprings from the grafted animals. The clinical applications of Knauer, experiments by Morris and many others are too well known to be discussed again.

The spleen of dogs is favorably disposed from an anatomic standpoint for transplantation. The operation is very simple. The spleen is extirpated, washed out with Locke's solution and immersed in a jar full of the same solution. Afterward the spleen is removed from the jar, placed in the abdominal cavity and the peripheral ends of the splenic vessels are united to the central ends. The nerves are sutured and organ suspended by suture of the gastrosplenic pedicles.

The operation is easy when the animal is of large size. Several months ago I performed this operation twice only, on a medium-sized dog and also on a large dog. Both animals recovered uneventfully and are in good health.

The transplantation of the intestines consists of extirpating a loop of intestine from an animal and of substituting it for a loop of intestine of another animal. Anastomosis of the vessels is performed. The intestine almost immediately takes on its normal color, and strong peristaltic movements appear. Then the continuity of the gut is re-established by two intestinal anastomoses. I performed this operation only twice. In each case infection occurred. The postmortem examination showed gaseous cysts under the peritoneal coat of the transplanted loop of intestine. It is probable that during the period of anemia the microbes of the intestine penetrate the wall. In this case a successful transplantation of the intestine will be probably unrealizable, or, at least, exceedingly difficult.

In 1902 the first attempt of transplanting a kidney was made by Ullmann. The same year I performed several transplantations of the kidneys on dogs. Septic complications occurred in every case. In 1905 Floresco published a few cases of the transplantation of the kidney in the lumbar region. Guthrie and I examined for the first time the functions of a transplanted kidney and found that they are not very different from the normal.

The transplantation in mass of the kidneys consists of extirpating from a first animal both kidneys, their vessels and the corresponding segments of the aorta and vena cava, their nerves and nervous ganglia, their ureters and the corresponding part of the bladder; of placing this anatomic specimen into the abdominal cavity of a second animal whose normal kidneys have been previously resected and the aorta and vena cava cut transversely; and of suturing the vascular segments between the ends of the aorta and vena cava, and of grafting the flap of bladder onto the bladder of the host. In every case the re-establishment of the renal functions was observed. These functions were determined by the character of the urines and the general condition of the animals.

The secretion of urine may begin as soon as the arterial circulation is re-established. In several cases clear urine flowed from the ureters while the flap of bladder was being grafted onto the host. More often no urine was seen flowing from the ureters immediately after completion of the operation. But the secretion always began during the first twenty-four hours. In some cases the amount of urine during the first twenty-four hours was more than 100 c.c. However, a cat urinated only 25 c.c. during the first twenty-four hours; the second day the amount of urine passed was only 16 c.c.; this urine was highly concentrated and contained much urea. In all the experiments the urinary secretion went on as long as the animal lived. Every cat urinated abundantly every day, but the animals presented sooner or later some complication, which modified in some measure the renal functions.

As is to be expected after an operation as complex as the transplantation in mass, various accidents occurred; hydronephrosis, intestinal compression by peritoneal adhesions, volvulus, phlegmon, puerperal infection, compression of the renal veins by organized hematoma of the connective tissue, which were the direct or indirect causes of death in these animals. It is well known that several of the complications, especially the compression of the renal veins, produce grave renal lesions of their own.

In some cases there was a little albumin during the first days ranging from 0.50 to 0.25 for 1,000 c.c. In other cases the albumin disappeared about one week after the operation.

The general condition of the animal can be used, in some measure, to indicate the perfection of the urinary

elimination. One cat was in excellent health until the twenty-ninth day after the operation. Then gastrointestinal symptoms appeared, and death occurred on the thiry-first day after the operation.

In another case, on the eighteenth day after the transplantation albumin appeared in the urine and a direct examination of the kidneys was made to ascertain the cause. The general condition was little affected by the operation and the albumin disappeared on the twenty-first day, but reappeared again a little later. On the thirty-fifth day the animal was very weak and emaciated. She died on the thirty-sixth day of acute calcification of the arteries.

We can conclude from these results that the functions of the kidneys re-established themselves after the transplantation.

The histologic examination of the transplanted kidneys showed that the organs presented some lesions, very slight in some cases, and more marked in others. The lesions belonged to two classes: hydronephrosis and subacute interstitial nephritis. Nephritis is not a necessary complication of the transplantation, for it was completely absent in some cases. It is possibly due to secondary causes.

The transplantation in mass of the kidneys permits of an almost ideal reconstruction of the urinary apparatus after a double nephrectomy. However, it is a complex operation, and the animal is exposed to many complications. The method called "simple transplantation" exposes the kidney to ureteral or vascular troubles, but it is practically harmless for the animal itself. This operation consists simply of dissecting a kidney, cutting the renal vessels and ureter a few centimeters below the hilus, implanting the organ on the same, or another animal, and of anastomosing its vessels to the renal vessels of the host.

I performed the double nephrectomy and the replantation of one kidney in five dogs. The secretion of the urine remained normal as long as no ureteral complication occurred. The conditions of the kidneys were excellent. A little more than two months after the operation, the location of the anastomoses of the renal vein could not be detected. The anastomosis of the renal artery was seen as a small and indistinct line on the intima.

The remote results of this operation are excellent. On February 6 the left kidney of a middle-sized bitch was extirpated, perfused with Locke's solution and put into a jar of Locke's solution at the temperature of the laboratory. The ends of the vessel were prepared for anastomoses, and afterward the kidney was replaced into the abdominal cavity. The circulation was re-established after suture of the vessels and the ends of the ureter united. The animal made an uneventful recovery. Fifteen days afterward the right kidney was extirpated. The animal remained in perfect health. The urine did not contain any albumin. It is generally of low density. To-day the animal is in perfect condition.

This observation demonstrates definitely that an animal can live in normal condition after both kidneys have been extirpated and one replaced. It removes also, without need of further discussion, the objections of the experimenters who claim that the section of the renal nerves, the temporary suppression of the renal circulation, or the perfusion of the kidneys produce necessarily dangerous and even fatal lesions of this organ.

## III. TRANSPLANTATION IN MASS OF THE AURICLE, THE EXTERNAL AUDITORY CANAL, PART OF THE SCALP, LYMPH GLANDS OF THE NECK AND PARTS OF THE COMMON CAROTID ARTERY AND EXTERNAL JUGULAR VEIN FROM A DOG TO ANOTHER DOG.

By using the method of transplantation in mass it becomes possible to perform the transplantation of a whole anatomic region, with its main artery and vein. The limits of the anatomic specimen must be approximately those of the field of distribution of the main artery. But, on account of the collateral circulation, it would be impossible to transplant a very much larger region. For instance, the whole scalp can probably be transplanted successfully if the vascular connections are re-established on one side only.

I succeeded in transplanting the auricle, the external auditory canal, part of the scalp, the lymph glands of the neck, and parts of the common carotid artery and external jugular vein from a dog to another dog.

The auricle and the transplanted tissues were in normal condition. The temperature of both auricles, normal and transplanted, were about the same. The transplanted ear was as thin and glossy as the normal one. Except for the difference of color, it could not have been seen that the ear did not belong to the dog.

## IV. THE TRANSPLANTATION OF LIMBS.

The transplantation of a limb from one animal to another of the same species is a problem very much simpler than the transplantation of a gland. It presents some difficulties, merely from a surgical standpoint. The anatomic structures of a limb are resistant and do not undergo autolytic modification after a short time of anemia. Besides, it is well known, from a clinical standpoint, that the circulation of a limb can be stopped completely for several hours by an Esmarch bandage without further occurrence of any lesions or nervous troubles. It is permitted also to suppose that structures, such as skin, muscles, vessels, bones, etc., are not very sensitive to slight modifications in the composition of the serum, and that after transplantation the blood of their new owner would not be toxic for them. Besides, it is almost certain that the new limb would have no harmful influence on his host, as may happen after a transplantation of the kidneys. Therefore, there is apparently no reason why the leg or the arm of an animal or of a human being could not be transplanted successfully on another animal of the same species or another human being.

In April, 1907, I found that a thigh, extirpated from the fresh cadaver of a dog, and transplanted onto another dog, could begin to heal in a very satisfactory manner.

This case demonstrated that it is possible to re-establish the circulation into a transplanted thigh and to obtain cicatrization of the anatomic structures. The union of the vascular anastomoses was excellent and the circulation of the limb constantly normal. Therefore, it was probable that, by using a little better technic, definitive results could be obtained.

A few other operations were performed, but in every case breaking of the bone suture or infection occurred. Nevertheless, by using more careful asepsis in the transplantation of the leg from one fox terrier to another, the new leg united to its host by first intention.

This experiment is the first example of successful grafting of a new limb on an animal. It demonstrates that the leg, in spite of the change of owner, remains normal. After a short period of edema and of high temperature, due perhaps to secondary causes, the new leg assumed the same appearance as the normal one. The temperature of the new foot did not differ from that of the other posterior foot. The healing of the cutaneous incision occurred normally, and the appearance of the skin was the same above and below the circular incision—that is, on the normal and transplanted part of the limb. No trophic troubles occurred. The cicatrization of a small exploratory incision made on the transplanted foot became slightly infected. Nevertheless, it healed rapidly, and the cicatrization was so perfect that the scar was not discernible on the twenty-second day. The normal and new tibias were strongly united by a fibrous callus. The question of the regeneration of nerves, and of the re-establishment of the functions, has still to be studied.

## V. CONCLUSIONS.

It is proved that the remote results of the transplantation of fresh vessels can be perfect, and that arteries, kept for several days or weeks outside of the body, can be transplanted successfully, and that after more than one year the results remain excellent. It has been shown, also, for the first time, that transplanted kidneys functionate, that an animal, having undergone a double nephrectomy and the transplantation of both kidneys from another animal, can live normally for a few weeks, and that an animal which has undergone a double nephrectomy and the graft of one of his own kidneys can recover completely and live in perfect health for eight months, at least. Finally, it has been demonstrated that a leg extirpated from a dog and substituted for the corresponding leg of another dog, heals normally.

Fig. 1.—Arteriovenous anastomosis of the common carotid artery and the internal jugular vein of a dog; fifteen days after operation.

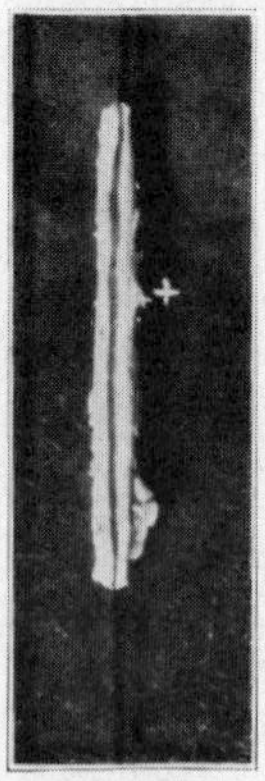

Fig. 2.—Arterio-arterial anastomosis of the central end of the left carotid artery to the peripheral end of the right carotid; one year after the operation. Scar almost invisible.

Fig. 3.—Transplantation of a segment of aorta into the abdominal aorta; eight days after operation.

Fig. 4.—Transplantation of a segment of carotid into the carotid artery; three months after operation.

Fig. 5.—Segment of external jugular vein transplanted on carotid artery; fifteen days after the operation.

Fig. 6.—Segment of external jugular vein transplanted on carotid artery; eight months after operation.

Fig. 7.—Segment of carotid preserved in cold storage for ten days and transplanted into the carotid artery; fifteen months after the operation. Anastomosis completely invisible.

Fig. 8.—Transplantation of a fresh segment of carotid of dog into the abdominal aorta of a cat. The transplanted segment is very much dilated; the anastomoses are invisible.

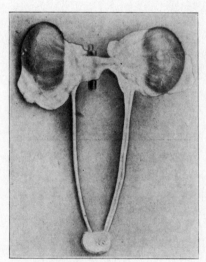

Fig. 9.—Kidneys, segment of aorta and vena cava, ureters and part of the bladder extirpated from first cat.

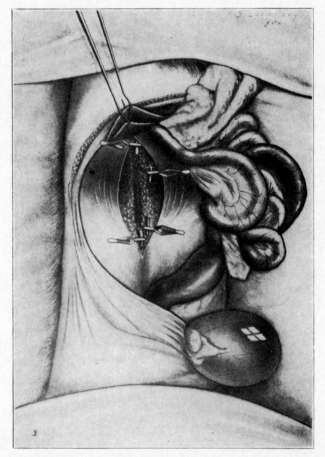

Fig. 10.—Second animal ready for the reception of the anatomic specimen (Fig. 9). The aorta and vena cava have been cut and their ends are ready for the anastomoses.

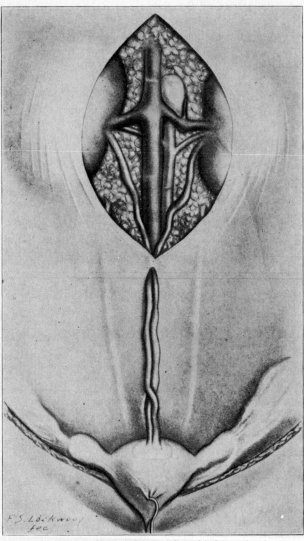

Fig. 11.—Specimen showing the transplanted kidneys after healing of the aortic and caval anastomoses and of the sutute of the flap of the bladder.

Fig. 12.—Cat looking at piece of meat on the twenty-first day after the double nephrectomy.

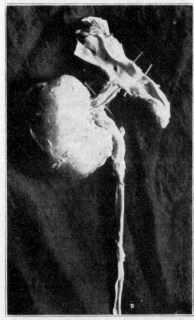

Fig. 13.—Replanted kidney, two months after the operation. The aorta and renal artery have been opened longitudinally. The scar of the arterial anastomosis, located a few millimeters from the bifurcation of the renal artery, has become almost completely invisible.

Fig. 14.—Extirpation of both kidneys. Replantation of one kidney; four months after the operation.

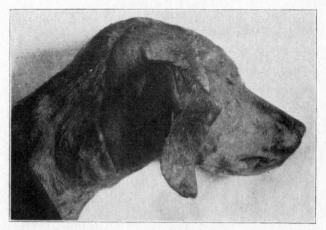

Fig. 15.—Transplantation of the auricle, scalp, cartilaginous auditory canal, etc.; three weeks after the operation.

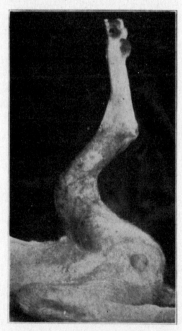

Fig. 16.—Transplantation of the leg from one dog onto another. The new leg has united by first intention and the scar is visible; twenty-two days after operation.

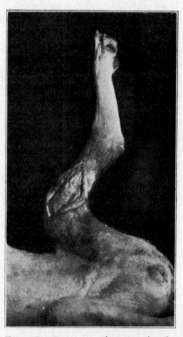

Fig. 17.—Specimen showing the fibrous callus uniting the tibia of the new leg to the upper part of the tibia of the host.

Aug 19, 1983
(*JAMA* 1983;250:954-957)

# Vascular Anastomosis and Organ Transplantation*

James D. Hardy, MD

I am particularly privileged to be invited to write a companion piece on the occasion of the republication of Carrel's *JAMA* article of 1908. On a sunny Sunday morning in 1935-1936, as a premed freshman sitting on the terrace of the Pi Kappa Alpha fraternity house at the University of Alabama in Tuscaloosa, I turned to the rotogravure section of the *Birmingham News-Age Herald* and saw there a photograph and write-up of Alexis Carrel and Charles A. Lindbergh with their perfusion apparatus, by means of which they had kept a chicken's heart alive for an extended period, I think for months. This article made a memorable impression on me, and I still have it in my collection of memorabilia denoting times, places, and events. How the world turns, now almost 50 years later.

The ultimate dimensions of the field of blood vessel anastomosis and organ transplantation, in which Carrel was the major pioneer, have proved to be enormous. Moreover, in this penetrating publication, he foresaw early and stated clearly much of what has since come to pass, often 40 to 80 years later. Carrel never performed clinical surgery after his house officer days, choosing to devote himself almost completely to research. And herein lies the basis of his prodigious experimental achievements.

The first requirement for blood vessel and, thus, whole-organ transplantation was the perfection of a dependable technique for vascular anastomosis. A variety of techniques had previously been employed, with little success, before the report of Dörfler[1] of Wissenberg, Germany, in 1899. Previous investigators had believed that to pierce the intima with the needle and suture would result in thrombosis, and, thus, they had sutured adventitia and media but had avoided the intima.

This resulted in a high incidence of thrombosis. Dörfler, in contrast, using fine, round needles and fine silk, included all layers in the suture line and achieved considerable success, and this technique was gradually accepted as the standard. Carrel knew of others working in the field of vascular anastomosis while he was still in France and experimenting there in his native country. For example, he worked under Jaboulay in Lyon and knew of the early work of Briau, another of Jaboulay's pupils. And there were still others. Therefore, it should be realized that Carrel did not discover or invent vascular surgery, but he made it the central theme of his work, and, in due course, by relentless and disciplined research and imagination, he made himself its foremost scientist and champion. This achievement probably accounted for the fact that it was he alone who was awarded the Nobel Prize for this and related work in 1912 at the age of 39 years.

## BLOOD VESSEL TRANSPLANTATION

The studies that Carrel made, first in France and then with Guthrie et al[2] at the University of Chicago and finally at the Rockefeller Institute in New York, generated many publications. The article under discussion herein was a survey of some of the work he had done. Carrel had gone to the Rockefeller Institute in 1906.

**Vessel Transplants, "LeVeen Shunt," and Portacaval Shunts.**—In his introduction to the "Transplantation of Vessels," Carrel (p 944) notes the following:

A segment of an artery or vein can be transplanted between the cut ends of an artery or vein, between the two regions of the circulatory apparatus, and even between a serous cavity and a vessel. For instance, in some cases of ascites it would be useful to establish a permanent drainage of the peritoneal cavity by suturing a piece of valvular vein between the peritoneum and a large vein.

Thus, the possible clinical use of vein grafts was fully documented, and a "LeVeen shunt" for ascites was

From the Department of Surgery, University of Mississippi Medical Center, Jackson.

*A commentary on Carrel A: Results of the transplantation of blood vessels, organs and limbs. *JAMA* 1908;51:1662-1667.

proposed by this visionary almost 60 years earlier. He stated that "Ruotte cut the saphenous vein and sutured its peripheral end to the peritoneum in a case of chronic ascites. The ascites disappeared." Carrel further states that "the graft of a segment of vein between the branches of the portal vein and the vena cava would act as a substitute for Talma's operation." He also apparently foresaw extra-anatomic arterial bypasses.

**Blood Vessel Storage.**—But notwithstanding the previously mentioned possibilities, Carrel wrote as follows: "However, the main application of vascular transplantations will be, probably, the re-establishment of the circulation through an artery of which a segment has been accidentally or surgically destroyed." Carrel then proceeded to explore the transplantation of blood vessels stored in Locke's solution in the refrigerator. Vessels were transplanted in the same animal, between two animals of the same species, and between animals of different species. As will be seen later, in connection with whole-organ transplantation, Carrel realized that the greater the degree of genetic disparity between partners, the smaller the degree of long-term success.

### Transplantation of Arteries

As we have seen, Carrel was well aware of previous arterial experiments by others, most notably by Jaboulay in 1896. Jaboulay had thought that this method could be applied to replacement of aneurysms. Carrel fully established that arterial transfer in animals could be made routinely successful.

However, no precise clinical use of the technique of artery storage and subsequent transplantation was made until 1948, when Gross et al[3] first used aortic homografts to bridge long segments of coarctation of the thoracic aorta in children. I well remember the excitement at the time. My chief in cardiothoracic surgery sought immediately to learn how Dr Gross had stored his homografts, only to find that this information would soon be made available in an early issue of *Surgery, Gynecology and Obstetrics.* After this use of human homografts to bridge long coarcted segments in the thoracic aorta in 1948, Dubost of Paris and his team replaced an abdominal aortic aneurysm with a homograft in 1952, and the rest is history. For the first time, a serviceable method for the management of aortic aneurysms was available. In time, homografts gave way to the excellent fabric grafts in use today.

Thus, the perfection of arterial suture and subsequent transplantation of arteries was, in my judgment, Carrel's single most important contribution, for it has prolonged countless lives of patients with a wide variety of arterial pathological conditions. This alone would have rendered the Nobel Prize well deserved.

### Transplantation of Veins

Carrel did much work with vein transplantation, and he perceived and fully described in 1908 many of the facts that have been repeatedly "discovered" since. He realized that few arteries can be sacrificed without major problems, and he pointed out that "if the veins could act as a substitute for arteries, the problem of the treatment of large wounds or of resection of arteries would be solved, for it is always possible to get venous material from the patient himself."

In 1905, Carrel and Guthrie succeeded in transplanting segments of jugular veins into the carotid artery and found that "the vein quickly undergoes structural changes, consisting chiefly of the thickening of its wall. Stich and Makkos observed the same results." Thus, Carrel was fully aware that veins become adjusted to arterial pressures, the so-called arterialization of veins that he carefully documented, and he stated that "no aneurism has ever been observed." In view of these original and explicit recordings of the dependability of vein autotransplants, it is remarkable that only in the last 15 to 20 years have surgeons in general felt firm confidence that vein grafts can be looked on as safe and, indeed, often preferable to other materials when a vein of sufficient diameter and length is available.

### Transplantation of Preserved Arteries

A major interest of Carrel's, running through years of his work, was the search for an optimal method for long-term storage of arterial grafts. He found early that arterial segments could be kept in the refrigerator for 35 days and then transplanted successfully. With such information in the literature, one can only smile at the great concern in 1948 that cold storage of the aorta harvested from a fresh cadaver for even 24 to 48 hours might be too long. As pointed out by Edwards and Edwards[4] in their fine little monograph on Carrel, the new investigator beginning arterial transplantation research would do well to check first to see if Dr Carrel did not publish the proposed research at the turn of the century.

### Artery Transplants Between Different Species: Xenografts

It is generally believed that a piece of tissue transplanted from one animal into another of different species undergoes cytolysis and disappears. It is not always true. There are several varieties of heteroplastic transplantations according to the zoologic distance that separates the host and the owner of the transplanted tissue. If a piece of tissue is transplanted from an animal to another and very different animal—from the mouse to the lizard, for instance—cytolysis occurs. But if the owner of the tissue and the host belong to more closely related zoologic sections, as, for instance, the guinea-pig and the rabbit, the graft does not undergo any cytolysis, but gradually disappears by atrophy.

Here, precisely, are described the basic elements of the pathology of graft rejection when transplants are performed across minor as compared with major genetic disparities—the very essence of allograft and xenograft transplantation rejection.

### THE TRANSPLANTATION OF ORGANS

Clearly, the seminal early blood vessel work of Carrel and Guthrie at Chicago and thereafter of Carrel in New York paved the way for whole-organ transplantation. The idea of organ transplantation had been prominent in blood vessel research circles in Europe even before Carrel came to the University of Chicago in 1904 and was assigned to work with Charles C. Guthrie in George N. Stewart's laboratory.

## Kidney

Carrel and Guthrie transplanted the kidney in cats, both short-term allografts and long-term autografts with considerable success, definitely establishing this procedure as a clinical possibility — although in point of fact, Ullman[5] had transplanted the kidney in 1902. They found that as soon as the vascular anastomoses had been completed and circulation reestablished, the ureters became active and urine secretion began promptly in some instances. In most of the other animals, the secretion of urine began within the first 24 hours. These workers clearly established that innervation was not necessary for good renal perfusion or for renal or ureteral function.

The fact that cats could survive at times for several weeks on one or both allotransplanted kidneys was widely noted and unquestionably gave much impetus to national and international interest in the future of renal transplantation in humans. Carrel had transplanted kidneys in dogs while still in France, but sepsis had resulted in a poor result in every case.

Had modern transplanters been thoroughly familiar with this 1908 publication, many questions again solved laboriously in the laboratory during the 1940s and 1950s would have been avoided.

## Transplantation of Other Organs

Included also in this article are transplantations of thyroid, adrenals, spleen, intestine, and limbs. The endocrine allotransplants do not seem to have been stressed by having to provide the entire support of the recipient, but early survival of the transplants was demonstrated. The intestinal transplant animals all died of infection, but here it was well demonstrated that the allotransplants promptly regained normal color and peristalsis.

The *limb transplants* are of particular interest. Carrel writes:

The transplantation of a limb from one animal to another of the same species is a problem very much simpler than the transplantation of a gland. It presents some difficulties, merely from a surgical standpoint. The anatomic structures of a limb are resistant and do not undergo autolytic modification after a short time of anemia. Besides, it is well known, from a clinical standpoint, that the circulation of a limb can be stopped completely for several hours by an Esmarch bandage without further occurrence of any lesions or nervous troubles. It is permitted also to suppose that structures, such as skin, muscles, vessels, bones, etc., are not very sensitive to slight modifications in the composition of the serum, and that after transplantation the blood of their new owner would not be toxic for them.

Herein Carrel presents a knowledge that the blood of an unrelated donor is usually "*toxic*" to an allograft, but he is somewhat mistaken in supposing that whole-limb tissue is not susceptible to allograft rejection. However, he had already demonstrated in blood vessel experiments that vascular allografts could exhibit long-term survival, and certainly bone allografts are clinically useful.

He and Guthrie definitely established the technical feasibility of limb transplantation in the dog.

## Heart Transplantation

For some reason, Carrel does not discuss heart transplantation in this 1908 article, although he and Guthrie had reported heart allotransplantation to the neck vessels in the dog in 1905.[6] The heart beat actively for about two hours before failing because of what the investigators thought was thrombosis. This in itself was a striking achievement and was generally well known when, in the 1950s, heart transplantation came under active investigation in many laboratories, including our own.

## ORGAN TRANSPLANTATION IN HUMANS

Looking back, it is interesting to speculate as to why the remarkably explicit pioneer laboratory work of Carrel and others in the early 1900s did not lead to earlier application in humans. In the case of blood vessel grafts, the field simply awaited the advent of blood vessel surgery in general (needles, sutures, techniques, and general interest), arteriography, the presence of one versed in cardiovascular surgery in humans (Gross), the clear moral imperative for using such a graft to bridge an otherwise uncorrectable coarcted segment of the thoracic aorta, doubtless a knowledge of the pioneer work of Carrel and Guthrie, and the courage to use the briefly preserved aortic homograft in man. Gross' aortic grafts were clearly successful, and this modality was promptly accepted for the carefully selected patients in whom it was required.

With whole-organ transplants, the reasons for the long delay were patently many and complex, but some of these come readily to mind. First, there is a vast moral and psychological gulf between laboratory investigation in animals and clinical investigation in humans. When an animal experiment fails, another animal is immediately available without concern; when a human transplant fails, the resulting dimensions are immeasurably larger.

### The Kidney

As Carrel had clearly perceived, the blood of the recipient of an allograft is "toxic" to the graft and, in most instances, will produce rejection in due course. Skin allografts had long been used in humans because their rejection would not be fatal to the new host. In contrast, in view of the increasingly clear analysis of self *v* nonself as especially delineated by Medawar and his group, surgeons were reluctant to transplant the kidney in humans until blood dialysis was fully available. Peritoneal dialysis was somewhat effective but, all too often, peritonitis set in. Therefore, not until the Kolff kidney was available in the late 1940s and early 1950s was a planned formal effort initiated to transplant kidneys in humans, most notably in Boston and in Paris. Basic, too, was immunosuppression, using both drugs and radiation. Murray et al[7] showed early that kidney transplantation between identical (isologous) twins was successful, proving clearly that when the immunologic rejection reaction was avoided, kidney transplantation in humans was successful. It remained for innumerable investigators and investigations to improve immunosuppression until today, approximately 70% to 80% of kidneys from good-match cadaver donors can be expected to be successful at one year, with a gradual but slow attrition rate thereafter.

Kidney autotransplants performed for one reason or another are routinely successful clinically.

## Other Organs

The current article makes no mention of lung or liver transplants. They performed gut transplants in animals, with little success because of infection, and modern gut allotransplants in humans have enjoyed little success, largely because of rejection but doubtless with elements of infection as well. However, gut autotransplants have, with the further development of microsurgery, become successful in the management of a variety of clinical situations such as replacement of the esophagus.

## Heart Transplantation

Heart transplantation, first performed to the neck vessels of the dog by Carrel and Guthrie,[6] is not mentioned in the current article. Extensive orthotopic heart transplantation studies after the advent of a practical heart-lung machine in 1954 led to increasing success in animals.[8] The first heart transplant in man was performed by Hardy and colleagues in 1964.[9] The heart of a large chimpanzee was readily inserted, functioned immediately, but gradually failed at about two hours owing in considerable measure to the advanced metabolic deterioration of the recipient preoperatively. There was no gross or microscopic evidence of hyperacute rejection. The second — and the first successful — heart transplant in man was performed by Barnard et al in 1967.[10] The most experienced heart transplant group now achieves a one-year survival rate for human heart allotransplants that is almost 80%.[11]

In summary, by any standard, Carrel's superb, sustained, and disciplined investigations such as those outlined in his accompanying article set in motion a host of scientific advances that have greatly benefited mankind.

## References

1. Dörfler J: Über Arteriennaht. *Beitr Klin Chir* 1899;25:781-825.
2. Guthrie CC, Harbison SP, Fisher B: *Blood Vessel Surgery and Its Applications.* Pittsburgh, University of Pittsburgh Press, 1959.
3. Gross RE, Bill AH Jr, Pierce EC II: Methods for preservation and transplantation of arterial grafts: Observations on arterial grafts in dogs: Report of transplantation of preserved arterial grafts in nine human cases. *Surg Gynecol Obstet* 1949;88:689-701.
4. Edwards WS, Edwards PD: *Alexis Carrel: Visionary Surgeon.* Springfield, Ill, Charles C Thomas Publisher, 1974.
5. Ullman E: Experimentelle Nierentransplantation. *Wien Klin Wochenschr* 1902;15:281.
6. Carrel A, Guthrie CC: The transplantation of veins and organs. *Am Med* 1905;10:1101.
7. Murray JE, Merrill JP, Harrison JH: Renal homotransplantation in identical twins. *Surg Forum* 1955;6:432-436.
8. Lower RR, Stofer RC, Shumway NE: Homovital transplantation of the heart. *J Thorac Cardiovasc Surg* 1961;41:196-204.
9. Hardy JD, Kurrus FD, Chavez CM, et al: Heart transplantation in man. *JAMA* 1964;88:1132-1140.
10. Barnard C: The operation: A human cardiac transplantation: An interim report of a successful operation performed at Groote Schuur Hospital, Cape Town. *S Afr Med J* 1967;41:1271-1274.
11. Hunt SA, Stinson EB: Cardiac transplantation. *Annu Rev Med* 1981;32:213-220.

## Chapter 6

# The Transmission of Acute Poliomyelitis to Monkeys[*]

### Simon Flexner, M.D., and Paul A. Lewis, M.D.

#### New York

Poliomyelitis or infantile paralysis prevailed in epidemic form along the Atlantic seaboard in the summer of 1907. About that time it appeared in Austria and Germany. In the summer of 1909 the disease reappeared as a focalized epidemic in Greater New York and had, by that time, spread widely throughout the United States and Europe.

The cause and mode of dissemination of the disease are unknown; and hence there exists no intelligent means of prevention. While the severity and fatality of the disease fluctuate widely, its effects are always so disastrous as to make it of the highest medical and social importance.

In spite of many thorough studies of the spontaneous disease in man, our knowledge of causation and prevention has not been advanced; it may be hoped that it will be advanced by the opportunity for fundamental study opened up by the successful transmission of the disease to lower animals.

In May, 1909, Landsteiner and Popper[1] published a report of two successful inoculations of monkeys with the spinal cord obtained from two fatal cases of poliomyelitis. The injections were made into the peritoneal cavity. One monkey became paralyzed in the lower extremities and died on the sixth day after inoculation; the other was killed on the nineteenth day. In both, lesions of the spinal cord similar to those in man existed. The disease could not be transferred to other monkeys. Our efforts to transmit the disease to lower animals were first made in 1907, at which time cerebrospinal fluid obtained by lumbar puncture was introduced into the spinal canal and peritoneal cavity in monkeys and other animals. We were limited to this fluid, as we did not secure material from a fatal case. The results were negative. Since September of this year we have secured suitable material

Transmission of M. A. virus through monkeys. The virus is being transmitted further. The abbreviation M. signifies monkey.

from two cases of poliomyelitis in human beings. For the material from one we are indebted to Dr. Ridner, of Lake Hopatcong, N. J., and for the other to Dr. Le Grand Kerr, of Brooklyn.

Dr. Ridner's patient died on the fifth or sixth day after the appearance of the paralysis, which affected the lower extremities. The lumbar cord was obtained in a sterile condition, twenty-six hours after death, and a portion was inoculated into monkeys about twelve hours later.[2] The entire spinal cord was obtained from Dr. Kerr's case twelve hours after death, and inoculation into monkeys

---

[*]From the Laboratories of the Rockefeller Institute for Medical Research.

1. Landsteiner and Popper: Ztschr. f. Immunitätsforsch., Orig., 1909, ii, 377.

2. No reference will be made in this preliminary report to other varieties of animals employed.

was made four hours later. In Dr. Kerr's case, in which death occurred on the fourth day, the lesions were diffuse throughout the cord. Paralysis had been very extensive. The gross and microscopic lesions were characteristic in both cases.

In order to favor the transmission of the disease to monkeys, the brain was chosen as the site of inoculation, which was made under ether anesthesia through a small trephine opening. After the operation, the animals were at once lively and normal. The injected material consisted at first of emulsions in salt solution of the spinal cord from the children and later of emulsions of the spinal cord of monkeys developing the paralysis. An effort was made to enrich the inoculating material by incubating it in celloidin sacs placed in the peritoneal cavity of monkeys and rabbits. At the present time we wish merely to record the series of successful experiments which we have conducted with the spinal cord obtained from the case of Dr. Ridner and designated M. A. The accompanying chart will show at a glance what has been accomplished up to date with the M. A. virus. We may mention here that the microscopic study of the spinal cord from the affected monkeys has shown, without exception, lesions similar to those of poliomyelitis in man. In some cases the lesions in the cords of monkeys could be detected by the naked eye.

The chart shows unmistakably that by employing the intracranial method of inoculation it is possible to carry the virus of epidemic poliomyelitis successfully through a series of monkeys. It is highly probable that the transmission may be carried on indefinitely. Should this expectation prove well founded, the outlook for securing a fuller understanding of the nature of this disease will be immeasurably improved.

It should incidentally be mentioned that not only is the spinal cord active, but the cortex of the brain also (Monkey 24). A delayed or unsuccessful inoculation may be converted into a successful infection by reinoculation with an active virus (Monkey 8).

It has long been supposed that epidemic poliomyelitis is an infectious disease. Its mode of spread certainly points to that view. A single successful inoculation with human virus could not establish the view, because the result might be due to a transferred toxic body. But now that successive transfer of the active agent of the disease has been accomplished, any doubt of its infectious origin can hardly be longer maintained.

The experiments with the virus of poliomyelitis are being continued, as is the search for additional evidences of its micro-organismal nature.[3] The complete protocols of the experiments here summarized and still other experiments will be published in a forthcoming issue of the *Journal of Experimental Medicine.*

---

3. A thorough search for bacteria by cultural and other methods was made in 1907, and again this year, but none that could be viewed as the causative agent has been discovered.

# The Transmission of Epidemic Poliomyelitis to Monkeys

## A Further Note*

Simon Flexner, M.D., and Paul A. Lewis, M.D.

New York

In a previous communication[1] we presented in the form of a chart the results secured up to that time in producing poliomyelitis in monkeys by injecting intracerebrally a virus, denominated M.A., obtained from the spinal cord of a child suffering from epidemic infantile paralysis. The virus had been passed successively through three generations of monkeys and is still being transmitted.

We desire in this communication to present the results in the form of a chart[2] obtained up to this time with the second virus, denominated K. It is, in our opinion, desirable that the facts thus far secured relating to this virus be published, since they extend considerably the previous observations.

*From the Laboratories of the Rockefeller Institute for Medical Research.

1. THE JOURNAL A. M. A., Nov. 13, 1909, liii, 1639.

2. In the chart M. signifies monkey.

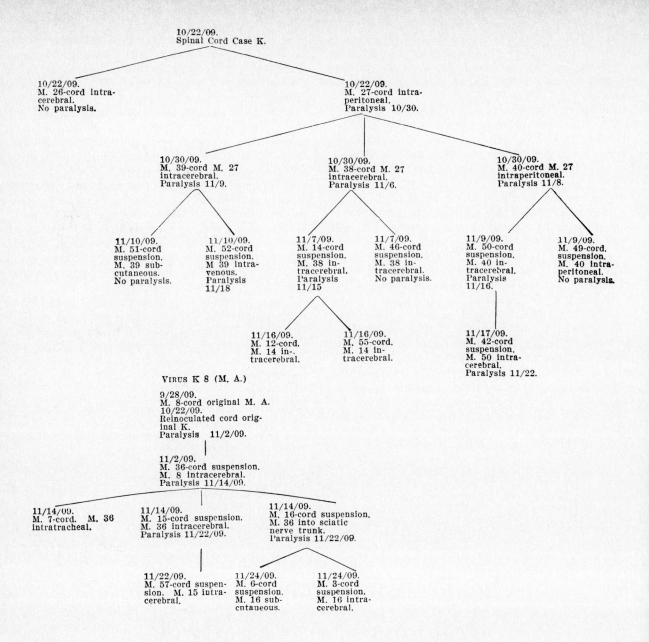

10/22/09.
Spinal Cord Case K.

10/22/09.
M. 26-cord intra-
cerebral.
No paralysis.

10/22/09.
M. 27-cord intra-
peritoneal.
Paralysis 10/30.

10/30/09.
M. 39-cord M. 27
intracerebral.
Paralysis 11/9.

10/30/09.
M. 38-cord M. 27
intracerebral.
Paralysis 11/6.

10/30/09.
M. 40-cord M. 27
intraperitoneal.
Paralysis 11/8.

11/10/09.
M. 51-cord
suspension.
M. 39 sub-
cutaneous.
No paralysis.

11/10/09.
M. 52-cord
suspension.
M 39 intra-
venous.
Paralysis
11/18

11/7/09.
M. 14-cord
suspension.
M. 38 in-
tracerebral.
Paralysis
11/15

11/7/09.
M. 46-cord
suspension.
M. 38 in-
tracerebral.
No paralysis.

11/9/09.
M. 50-cord
suspension.
M. 40 in-
tracerebral.
Paralysis
11/16.

11/9/09.
M. 49-cord.
suspension.
M. 40 intra-
peritoneal.
No paralysis.

11/16/09.
M. 12-cord.
M. 14 in-.
tracerebral.

11/16/09.
M. 55-cord.
M. 14 in-
tracerebral.

11/17/09.
M. 42-cord
suspension.
M. 50 intra-
cerebral.
Paralysis 11/22.

Virus K 8 (M. A.)

9/28/09.
M. 8-cord original M. A.
10/22/09.
Reinoculated cord orig-
inal K.
Paralysis   11/2/09.

11/2/09.
M. 36-cord suspension.
M. 8 intracerebral.
Paralysis 11/14/09.

11/14/09.
M. 7-cord.   M. 36
intratracheal.

11/14/09.
M. 15-cord suspension.
M. 36 intracerebral.
Paralysis 11/22/09.

11/14/09.
M. 16-cord suspension.
M. 36 into sciatic
nerve trunk.
Paralysis 11/22/09.

11/22/09.
M. 57-cord suspen-
sion.   M. 15 intra-
cerebral.

11/24/09.
M. 6-cord
suspension.
M. 16 sub-
cutaneous.

11/24/09.
M. 3-cord
suspension.
M. 16 intra-
cerebral.

In the first place, it can now be affirmed that the virus of poliomyelitis cannot be very difficult of transmission to monkeys under the conditions leading to the development of the lesions and symptoms characteristic of epidemic poliomyelitis in man, since both specimens of human cord furnishing the original virus have sufficed for the transmission of the disease successively.

In the next place, it can now be stated that it is not absolutely essential that the virus be introduced into the brain, but that successive transmission is possible by way of the peritoneal cavity (Monkeys 27 and 40), by intravascular injection (Monkey 52), and by intraneural injection (Monkey 16). The lesions in the monkey in which the virus was introduced into the sheath of the sciatic nerve developed first on the side inoculated and later extended to the opposite side of the spinal cord.

On the other hand, it cannot yet be affirmed that still other avenues do not exist for the entrance of the virus into the central nervous system. Additional observations are required and are, indeed, in process of being made,

before the statement can be ventured that infection does not occur by way of the skin, the respiratory passages and the digestive tract.

The conclusions to be drawn from the experiments related are to the effect that the virus of epidemic poliomyelitis is readily transmissible from man to monkeys and from monkey to monkey, by way of the brain, the peritoneal cavity and the circulation, and that, however transmitted successfully, it becomes established in the spinal cord and medulla, where it sets up characteristic lesions which are followed by equally characteristic effects that exhibit themselves as the usual symptoms of infantile paralysis in human beings.

Moreover, it can now be stated that this experimental form of poliomyelitis in monkeys is a severe and very often a fatal disease, and when recovery from the disease takes place there persist residues of paralysis which resemble the paralytic effects also persisting in human subjects of poliomyelitis.

Aug 12, 1983
(JAMA 1983;250:808-810)

# The Virus of Poliomyelitis*

## From Discovery to Extinction

### Jonas Salk, MD

Gustavson[1] defined science as that body of knowledge obtained by techniques that enable us to place limiting values on our preconceptions. A review of what we now know about poliomyelitis reveals a list of preconceptions that have been modified with the help of techniques developed to examine them. When ideas are transformed in this way, it is oftentimes difficult to understand why we thought as we did previously.

It was once believed that (1) poliomyelitis was not an infectious disease, (2) the virus reached the CNS via nerve pathways and not via the bloodstream, (3) the virus was strictly neurotropic, unlikely of cultivation in nonneural tissue, and (4) the prevention of the disease could not be accomplished by a noninfectious virus vaccine because it was also believed that (5) the process of infection was required for inducing effective and durable immunity.

The scientific investigation of these and other questions began in 1909 with the successful transmission to monkeys of the causative agent of poliomyelitis by Flexner and Lewis[2,3] and by Landsteiner and Levaditi.[4] They demonstrated, using spinal cord tissue of paralyzed children, that the lesions seen in humans with paralytic poliomyelitis could be reproduced in monkeys. Such effects were induced by virus introduced into the bloodstream and did not require direct inoculation into the CNS or via nerve pathways. These observations anticipated the later discovery that in humans, the virus multiplies in the digestive tract and gains access to the CNS via the bloodstream. This also provided the conceptual foundation for the prevention of the paralytic disease through the establishment in the bloodstream

of an antibody barrier to virus invasion of the CNS.

From then until now, our knowledge about all aspects of poliomyelitis has grown and limiting values have been and continue to be placed on our preconceptions about the disease, means for its prevention, and its eventual eradication from the human population. When this is achieved, the scientific method, with its appropriate technology, will have revealed its continuing value in the evolving science of preventive medicine and its practice in the maintenance of the public health.

#### The Causative Agent

After the discovery of the causative agent of poliomyelitis in 1909, it was not until 1931 that Burnet and Macnamara[5] recognized the existence of more than one antigenic variety. Similar observations were made by Paul and Trask[6] in 1933, and, by 1949, three immunologic varieties were identified by Bodian and associates[7] and Kessel and Pait.[8]

The discovery in 1949 by Enders and colleagues[9] that the viruses of poliomyelitis could be propagated in cultures of nonneural tissue not only made possible the development of a source of virus for vaccinologic studies but brought evidence to bear on the question of whether polioviruses were strictly neurotropic. This discovery reinforced the developing hypothesis that polioviruses multiply in nonneural tissue and only thereafter are disseminated from the primary site of multiplication in the gastrointestinal (GI) tract and to a secondary site in the CNS and that the virus could be intercepted before invasion of the CNS by an antibody barrier in the bloodstream.

The presence of virus in the bloodstream before the onset of paralysis, both in experimental animals and in humans, was reported by Bodian[10] and by Horstmann.[11] Bodian[12] also demonstrated the interception of virus, before invasion of the CNS, by administering low levels

From The Salk Institute for Biological Studies, San Diego.
*A commentary on Flexner S, Lewis PA: The transmission of acute poliomyelitis to monkeys. *JAMA* 1909;53:1639, and Flexner S, Lewis PA: The transmission of epidemic poliomyelitis to monkeys: A further note. *JAMA* 1909;53:1913.

of antibody to cynomolgus monkeys and chimpanzees fed virus that causes paralysis when given orally. Hammon et al[13] reduced the incidence and severity of paralysis in children by passive administration of relatively small amounts of antibody before exposure or early in the incubation period of infection. This confirmed that the virus could be blocked and paralytic poliomyelitis in humans could be prevented by the presence of antibody in the serum.

### Immunization

Among the earliest reports on attempts to prevent poliomyelitis by active immunization in monkeys and humans were those of Brodie and Park[14] and of Kolmer[15] in the early 1930s.

Morgan,[16] more than a decade later, demonstrated that a formaldehyde-treated suspension of CNS tissue from monkeys containing a type 2 strain of poliomyelitis virus induced the formation of antibody; resistance to intracerebral challenge was demonstrated in monkeys vaccinated with type 1 virus similarly prepared. Howe[17,18] demonstrated antibody formation in chimpanzees and in human subjects given gamma globulin followed by a noninfectious vaccine.

Koprowski and associates[19] fed human subjects an attenuated infectious preparation of type 2 virus, which had been propagated in the CNS of rodents; an antibody repsonse was induced along with evidence of virus multiplication in the GI tract.

Two different theoretical approaches to inducing durable immunity to poliomyelitis have been pursued: (1) noninfectious forms of the poliovirus administered by injection and (2) attenuated forms administered orally.

### Noninfectious Poliovirus Vaccine

The necessary conditions for destruction of infectivity with retention of antigenicity had to be established and safeguards provided for ensuring the absence of infectious virus.[20] After extensive studies in animals and in human subjects,[21-24] a nationwide field trial of a noninfectious poliovirus vaccine was undertaken in 1954 by Dr Thomas Francis, Jr[25] (initiated and organized by the National Foundation for Infantile Paralysis and conducted by medical and health authorities in conjunction with many volunteer organizations and the American public). A year later, approximately 45 years after the virus of poliomyelitis was first isolated by Flexner and Lewis and by Landsteiner and Levaditi, a noninfectious poliovirus vaccine became available for general use. (See pp 361-373.)

The noninfectious virus vaccine, by creating an antibody barrier to virus invasion of the CNS and pharynx, has been shown to be effective for protection of the individual and the community.[26] In those countries in which it has been used widely, the disease has been eradicated and the circulation of naturally occurring virus has been eliminated.[27]

In the subsequent years, experimental and experiential evidence has revealed that the minimum requirement for immunity to paralysis is the presence of antibody in the serum or immunologic memory or both, ie, a state of immunologic hyperactivity, which is irreversible and,

therefore, durable for life.[28] It was apparent from the outset that the critical factor for effectiveness is the quantity of antigen contained in the vaccine requiring care in production and in standardization.[29] Progressive improvement in these respects occurred in the 1960s and 1970s, with developments in cell culture technology and improved means for vaccine standardization.[30,31]

### Attenuated Infectious Poliovirus Vaccine

The objective of immunization against poliomyelitis by means of avirulent viruses is to imitate what nature does . . . to provide long-lasting immunity by means of one or more inoculations or feedings of small amounts of the three immunologic types of virus. . . . Poliomyelitis viruses which are candidates for immunization of human beings must be as free of paralytogenic capacity in human beings and as harmless in other respects as the special 17D strain of yellow fever virus.[32]

The Sabin strains of attenuated poliovirus were selected and introduced for use in the United States in 1961 (earlier in other countries). (See Chapter 45.) Their effectiveness is now well established. However, an associated risk exists in the use of the live attenuated poliovirus vaccine.[33] The use of a noninfectious form of poliovirus vaccine has been suggested as a way of avoiding this risk.[27]

Under certain conditions in tropical and subtropical areas, another need exists where the live attenuated virus vaccine fails to immunize a considerable portion of vaccinated children and has little or no influence on the dissemination of wild viruses, unless the vaccine can be administered in mass campaigns in a period of a few days and repeated again at an appropriate interval. Where this can be done, dramatic effects have been observed.[34] Where this is not feasible, other approaches are being explored. In such regions, a suitably potent and standardized noninfectious vaccine, incorporated with diphtheria-pertussis-tetanus vaccine, has been formulated to induce immunity to paralytic poliomyelitis after the first dose. Such a procedure induces durable immunity since, as noted previously, the minimal requirement for immunity to paralysis is the irreversible induction of immunologic memory, and this can be induced by a single dose of a suitably formulated and appropriately standardized noninfectious poliovirus vaccine.[35]

### The Future

The brevity of the articles by Flexner and Lewis has had the effect of demanding equal brevity in highlighting the significance of their discoveries as these unfolded in the three quarters of a century since their reports appeared. They initiated a process that will end at some time in the future with the extinction from the human population of the virus they identified. Might we expect that this could be achieved by the centenary of their discovery?

The story of polio is unusual among human diseases. It is caused by an agent that did not reveal the extent to which it was present in the human population until unmasked by improvement in hygienic conditions. Even before its fearsome qualities could be fully revealed, means for immunization were developed. Through the expeditious and judicious use of science and technology, the world will have been spared more crippling than would otherwise have occurred.

Although poliovirus vaccines have been available for almost three decades and great effort has been expended to extend their use, it is estimated that approximately 500,000 cases per year are still occurring, especially in the developing countries in which adequate immunization programs have not yet been established. The limiting factor is in part developmental and economic and in part the need for political will. This reveals, once again, that all of the problems of man cannot be solved in the laboratory.

Nevertheless, continued advances in the laboratory now make possible the production of noninfectious poliovirus vaccine in continuously propagating cells without the need for monkeys. This, together with reduction in the number of vaccine administrations required for inducing the desired effect, brings within the range of economic and practical feasibility the applica-

tion of poliomyelitis vaccination, either in a noninfectious or an infectious form, in regions of the world in need of a simple and appropriate regimen for immunization against poliomyelitis and other childhood diseases as part of a wider program for extending health for children the world over. The prospects for the future are as promising as our ability to learn how to use more effectively and efficiently the knowledge and the skills we now possess. Although scientists customarily leave to others the application of their findings, it is necessary to recognize a special responsibility to see our work through to completion when there is something that we know that is not known to others.

The story of poliomyelitis will reveal the way in which preconceptions about the cause of the disease and about the requirements for immunization were tested, refuted, or disproved by careful observation and experimentation. There remains now to test, refute, or disprove the prediction that poliomyelitis can be eradicated and the viruses extinguished from the human population.

## References

1. Gustavson RG: Pitcairn-Crabbe lecture. University of Pittsburgh, spring 1958.
2. Flexner S, Lewis PA: The transmission of acute poliomyelitis to monkeys. JAMA 1909;53:1639.
3. Flexner S, Lewis PA: The transmission of epidemic poliomyelitis to monkeys: A further note. JAMA 1909;53:1913.
4. Landsteiner K, Levaditi C: Experimental infantile paralysis. C Rend Soc Biol 1909;67:787-790.
5. Burnet FM, Macnamara J: Immunological differences between strains of poliomyelitis virus. Br J Exp Pathol 1931;12:57-61.
6. Paul JR, Trask JD: A comparative study of recently isolated human strains and a passage strain of poliomyelitis virus. J Exp Med 1933;58:513-529.
7. Bodian D, Morgan IM, Howe HA: Differentiation of types of poliomyelitis viruses: III. The grouping of 14 strains into three immunological types. Am J Hyg 1949;49:234-245.
8. Kessel JF, Pait CF: Differentiation of three groups of poliomyelitis virus. Proc Soc Exp Biol Med 1949;70:315-316.
9. Enders JF, Weller TH, Robbins FC: Cultivation of the Lansing strain of poliomyelitis virus in cultures of various human embryonic tissues. Science 1949;109:85-87.
10. Bodian DA: Reconsideration of the pathogenesis of poliomyelitis. Am J Hyg 1952;55:414-438.
11. Horstmann DM: Poliomyelitis virus in blood of orally infected monkeys and chimpanzees. Proc Soc Exp Biol Med 1952;79:417-419.
12. Bodian DA: Experimental studies on passive immunization against poliomyelitis: II. The prophylactic effect of human gamma globulin on paralytic poliomyelitis in cynomolgus monkeys after virus feeding. Am J Hyg 1952;56:78-89.
13. Hammon WM, Coriell LL, Stokes J Jr: Evaluation of Red Cross gamma globulin as a prophylactic agent for poliomyelitis. JAMA 1952;150:739-760.
14. Brodie M, Park WH: Active immunization against poliomyelitis. Am J Public Health 1936;26:119-125.
15. Kolmer JA: Vaccination against acute anterior poliomyelitis. Am J Public Health 1936;26:126-135.
16. Morgan IM: Immunization of monkeys with formalin-inactivated poliomyelitis viruses. Am J Hyg 1948;48:394-406.
17. Howe HA: Duration of immunity in chimpanzees vaccinated with formalin inactivated poliomyelitis virus. Fed Proc 1952;11:471-472.
18. Howe HA: Antibody response of chimpanzees and human beings to formalin-inactivated trivalent poliomyelitis vaccine. Am J Hyg 1952;56:265-286.
19. Koprowski H, Jervis GA, Norton TW: Immune responses in human volunteers upon oral administration of a rodent-adapted strain of poliomyelitis virus. Am J Hyg 1952;55:108-126.

20. Salk JE, Gori JB: A review of theoretical, experimental, and practical considerations in the use of formaldehyde for the inactivation of poliovirus. Ann NY Acad Sci 1960;83:609-637.
21. Salk JE, Bennett BL, Lewis LJ, et al: Studies in human subjects on active immunization against poliomyelitis: 1. A preliminary report of experiments in progress. JAMA 1953;151:1081-1098.
22. Salk JE, Lewis LJ, Bennett BL, et al: Antigenic activity of poliomyelitis vaccines undergoing field test. Am J Public Health 1955;45:151-162.
23. Salk JE: Vaccination against paralytic poliomyelitis: Performance and prospects. Am J Public Health 1955;45:575-596.
24. Salk JE: Considerations in the preparation and use of poliomyelitis virus vaccine. JAMA 1955;158:1239-1248.
25. Francis T Jr, Korns RF, Voight RB, et al: An evaluation of the 1954 poliomyelitis vaccine trials: Summary report. Am J Public Health 1955;45:1-63.
26. Salk JE: Preconceptions about vaccination against paralytic poliomyelitis. Ann Intern Med 1959;50:843-861.
27. Salk J, Salk D: Control of influenza and poliomyelitis with killed virus vaccines. Science 1977;195:834-847.
28. Salk JE: Persistence of immunity after administration of formalin-treated poliovirus vaccine. Lancet 1960;2:715-723.
29. Salk J, van Wezel AL, Stoeckel P, et al: Theoretical and practical considerations in the application of killed poliovirus vaccine for the control of paralytic poliomyelitis. Dev Biol Stand 1981;47:181-198.
30. van Wezel AL, van Steenis G, Hannik CA, et al: New approach to the production of concentrated and purified inactivated polio and rabies tissue culture vaccines. Dev Biol Stand 1978;41:159-168.
31. Petricciani JC, Salk PL, Salk J, et al: Theoretical considerations and practical concerns regarding the use of continuous cell lines in the production of biologics. Dev Biol Stand 1982;50:15-25.
32. Sabin AB: Avirulent viruses for immunization against poliomyelitis, in International Poliomyelitis Congress: Poliomyelitis—Papers and Discussions Presented at the Third International Poliomyelitis Conference. Philadelphia, JB Lippincott Co, 1955, pp 186-194.
33. Salk D: Eradication of poliomyelitis in the United States: I. Live virus vaccine-associated and wild poliovirus disease: II. Experience with killed poliovirus vaccine: III. Poliovaccines—practical considerations. Rev Infect Dis 1980;2:228-273.
34. Sabin AB, Ramon-Alvarez M, Alvarez-Amezquita J, et al: Live, orally given poliovirus vaccine: Effects of rapid mass immunization on population under conditions of massive enteric infection with other viruses. JAMA 1960;173:1521-1526.
35. Salk J, Stoeckel P, van Wezel AL, et al: Antigen content of inactivated poliovirus vaccine for use in a one- or two-dose regimen. Ann Clin Res 1982;14:204-212.

May 28, 1910
(*JAMA* 1910;54:1768-1769)

## Chapter 7

# Removal of Neoplasms of the Urinary Bladder

## A New Method, Employing High-Frequency (Oudin) Currents Through a Catheterizing Cystoscope*

Edwin Beer, M.D.

Surgeon to Montefiore Home; Assistant Visiting Surgeon to Belle-
vue Hospital; Assistant Adjunct Surgeon to Mount Sinai
Hospital; Junior Surgeon to the New York
Neurological Institute; Cystoscopist to
the German Hospital
New York

This brief preliminary report is written with the object of calling the attention of the profession to a new and simple method of destroying new growths of the urinary bladder. Even though my experience is not extensive, limited as it is to two large papillary growths, still the observations made leave no doubt in my mind that the Oudin current, employed as I have employed it, will prove effective in the cure of benign papillomata, as well as useful in malign tumors, papillomatous or not, both as a hemostatic and as a cauterizing agent.[1] My experiences also suggest the usefulness of these currents in many other conditions both in the bladder and in other parts, e. g. tuberculous ulcers of the bladder, prostatic hypertrophy, growths in the urethra, etc.

In March, 1908, I hit on the idea of using the high-frequency current as I now use it. Expert electric manufacturers told me I could not obtain the effects I desired through a water medium; that an air gap was necessary. Moreover, that if I used the current as I intended, it would burn out my cystoscope. Others who had experience with these currents in skin conditions were equally pessimistic. Despite these opinions I ordered from the manufacturer a thoroughly insulated cable, No. 6 French caliber, so that it could be introduced readily through the catheter tunnel of a Nitze catheterizing cystoscope. My experimental work was confined to the removal of skin warts through a water medium. I soon convinced myself of the efficacy of this therapy, despite the absence of an air gap. I also tested my Nitze cystoscopes and found that they stood the test perfectly. They were not burned out and I could readily see what was going on at the end of the electrode though very rarely an insignificant variation in the intensity of the light occurred.

Through the courtesy of Dr. A. G. Gerster, I was able to try out this new method in an inoperable tumor of the bladder in a woman of 81. In a second case, that of woman of 66, I employed this method also. Both patients were troubled with hematuria. In the second case the bleeding was very active, while in the first case it was moderate when the treatment was begun. As my experiences in these cases were highly satisfactory, I hasten to lay them before the profession, that others may avail themselves thereof.

### TECHNIC, ETC.

*Instruments*—1. I employed the Oudin current derived from a Wappler machine, placing the rheostat

---

*From the First Surgical Service of Mount Sinai Hospital.
1. In early cases of malignant disease a complete destruction may be possible

vertically so that one-half the resistance was thrown into the circuit. The spark gap in the muffler was approximately 1/10—⅛ inch.

2. Nitze, double-catheter cystoscope was used. In one catheter tunnel, I placed the electrode introducing it just as one introduces a catheter while to the other catheter tunnel I attached a tube for irrigation.

3. The electrode was a simple 6-ply cable of copper wire thoroughly insulated with rubber and cut off squarely at the vesical end. It measured No. 6 French and was made for me by the Wappler firm.

*Application*—The applications were made directly to the growth, the electrode being pushed a short distance in among the villi under the guidance of the eye and then the current was turned on for fifteen to thirty seconds at various points. The bladder was distended with distilled water. Experience may show that some other medium is preferable in view of the fact that ionization with magnesia appears particularly effective in removal of skin papillomata.

## EFFECTS AND RESULTS

The immediate visible effects are very striking. No spark is seen even when the full current is thrown on without any resistance. While the current is on gas is generated quite freely and is seen bubbling out of the growth. If the point of application is superficial we can readily see a blanching of the tissues about the point of application; and at the spot where the electrode's point rested, the tissues are blackened—carbonized. As the electrode is withdrawn from the growth, very frequently it is found to be adherent to the villi, and as it is pulled on, the whole tumor moves with the electrode, which finally comes away with a piece of the tumor well baked to its vesical end.[2] This is only rarely followed by bleeding and a reapplication of the current at the same spot controls this bleeding. The great heat generated melts the insulating rubber at the end of the electrode so

that one has to cut it off squarely from time to time, to prevent the wires from protruding freely and injuring the bladder wall.

In the second case the very first application of the current controlled the bleeding to such an extent that cystoscopy, which had been almost impossible, owing to the excessively rapid clouding of the medium from the arterial bleeding, became fairly easy. Eight applications at one sitting to various parts of the growth, aggregating in all four minutes, controlled the bleeding. In the first case, the hematuria was equally well controlled, but the result was less striking than in Case 2, in which the severe hemorrhage ceased at once and intensely bloody urine gave way to normal yellow urine.

Such applications of fifteen to thirty seconds seem to cause a very well-marked necrosis, which is in part due to the heat engendered. Other factors probably contribute to the final result. How much ionization, electrolysis and other factors contribute, I cannot state as yet. By making applications at eight to twelve different points in the two large tumors treated, a total necrosis of all the villous outgrowths followed with absolute cessation of hematuria. Gradually during three to five weeks the dead tissue separated from the healthy and the tumors were expelled in small masses, as the mucous membrane gradually grew in around the base of the dead tissue.[3] No ulcers were visible at any time.

The treatment caused no more discomfort than an ordinary cystoscopy. The bladder mucous membrane was but little affected by the application though some congestion and trigonitis developed in the vicinity of the growths.

At some future date, I shall report these cases in full, which is hardly necessary for this preliminary note.

116 West Fifty-eighth Street.

---

2. These fragments have been used for microscopic examination.

3. If the flat base of the growth remains after the sloughing of the necrotic villi, these small areas must be treated in turn directly, to produce a cure. To avoid perforating the bladder, shorter application of fifteen seconds should be used here, such as I used in Case 1.

Sept 9, 1983
(*JAMA* 1983;250:1326)

# Bladder Cancer Control*

Gerald P. Murphy, MD, DSc

Edwin Beer made many contributions to the study of bladder cancer. We are indebted to him for the summary of his work at the Mount Sinai Hospital published in 1935.[1]

Looking back in that volume on his contributions to the control of bladder cancer, Beer felt that the first advance in operative therapy had been introduced by Billroth in 1874. At the time, urologic surgeons relied on either blind transurethral manipulation or lateral perineal incisions for the removal or excision of bladder tumors. Billroth often employed a suprapubic incision and first removed a bladder tumor under direct visual control. Despite the proven validity in this approach, by 1885 only nine bladder tumors had been removed in this way, according to a review by Antal that was cited by Beer in 1935.[1]

Beer believed that the operative approach to removal of bladder cancer was developing according to two schools in the 1890s, both of which he saw as influencing his work. In England and America, the perineal and urethral routes had the most proponents, whereas in Austria, Germany, and France the suprapubic approach had numerous followers. The snaring of bladder polyps with the Nitze cystoscope had been achieved with limited success only in females, using the technique devised by Howard Kelly of Baltimore.[2]

Beer's description in the accompanying article, published on May 28, 1910, was unquestionably a "first." He developed the first successful transurethral removal under direct vision of a bladder tumor. Two patients are described in the article. A high-frequency current was derived from an Oudin resonator, which was attached to an ordinary x-ray machine. With the aid of Rheinhold Wappler's engineering skill, underwater endoscopic fulguration and destruction of the bladder tumor were achieved.[1] This achievement is amply chronicled in the article in THE JOURNAL and represents a fundamental extension to cancer control. Until this time, there was no other way to deal with superficial bladder tumors or, indeed, invasive inoperable ones. In a recent review by Brendler and Ferber[3] on the history of urologic surgery at New York's Mount Sinai Hospital, Reed Nesbit is quoted as saying, "The development of this technique by its brilliant discoverer marked one of the greatest advances in the history of urology: it led not only to radical changes in the therapeutic management of bladder tumors, but also paved the way for subsequent electro-resection methods by proving that high-frequency current could be employed effectively under water." Young[4] and others quickly adapted this technique to bladder cancer and other areas.

Concurrent with the development of electroresection was the adaptation of endoscopic radium seed insertion both by Young[5-7] and Kelly[8] of Baltimore. Transvesical, transrectal, and transurethral approaches were advocated at this time by Young and Frontz.[5]

The field was so developed by Beer that in 1918 Young[7] proposed that the "benign papilloma" of the bladder should be routinely treated by endoscopic fulguration. They further believed that additional tumors might appear later, and that these should also be treated by fulguration, since an ultimate cure by this means was feasible. This viewpoint, with slight modification, is still held by many today. However, even Young[7] recognized that endoscopic resection of a wide area of the bladder wall could be achieved but might not have lasting beneficial effect. Interstitial therapy and other surgical approaches were developed as a result. Efforts at the prevention of bladder recurrence included the instillation of trichloroacetic acid, applied through ureteral catheters directly to the neoplasm.[1] As advocated by E. Joseph and Lowsley and Kirwin,[9] the instillation of 50% phenol following transurethral resection was employed. Some of these adjuvant techniques, including instillation of formaldehyde solution for troublesome hemorrhage in advanced cases of bladder cancer, are used even today.

One could continue a review of the additional therapeutic approaches introduced in the course of the therapy of bladder cancer. One, however, is hard put to find a more significant single contribution than Beer's.[1] Without transurethral removal of neoplasms using the technique devised, urology would have been limited to the diagnostic approach to bladder cancer rather than an approach that was both diagnostic and therapeutic.

Edwin Beer occupies a significantly honored and hallowed place in urologic oncology for his seminal contribution.

## References

1. Beer E: *Tumors of the Urinary Bladder.* Baltimore, William Wood & Co, 1935.
2. Harvey AM: Pioneers in urology: James R. Brown, Howard A. Kelly. *Johns Hopkins Med J* 1974;134:291-302.
3. Brendler H, Ferber WLF: Early days of urology at Mount Sinai. *Urology* 1974;3:246-250.
4. Young NH: The employment of the high-frequency current for the extraction of calculi incarcerated in the lower end of the ureter. *J Urol* 1918;2:35-38.
5. Young HH, Frontz WA: Some new methods in the treatment of carcinoma of the lower genito-urinary tract with radium. *Trans Am Urol Assoc* 1917;11:20-58.
6. Young HH: The use of radium in cancer of the prostate and bladder: A presentation of new instruments and new methods of use. *JAMA* 1917;68:1174-1177.
7. Young HH: Recent progress in the treatment of cancer of the prostate, seminal vesicles and bladder. *South Med J* 1918;11:120-129.
8. Kelly HA: Two hundred and ten fibroid tumors treated by radium. *Surg Gynecol Obstet* 1918;27:402-409.
9. Lowsley OS, Kirwin TJ: *Clinical Urology,* ed 3. Baltimore, Williams & Wilkins Co, 1956, vol 2.

From the Roswell Park Memorial Institute, Buffalo.
*A commentary on Beer E: Removal of neoplasms of the urinary bladder. *JAMA* 1910;54:1768-1769.

Chapter 8

# The Relation of Blood Platelets to Hemorrhagic Disease

## Description of a Method for Determining the Bleeding Time and Coagulation Time and Report of Three Cases of Hemorrhagic Disease Relieved by Transfusion*

From the Hunterian Laboratory of Experimental Pathology, Johns Hopkins University

### W. W. Duke, M.D.
Kansas City, Mo.

It is my purpose in this paper to report three cases and experiments which furnish additional evidence to show that the blood platelets play a part in stopping hemorrhage, and that one type of hemorrhagic disease may be attributed to an extreme reduction in the number of platelets. The cases possibly explain the relief which sometimes follows transfusion in hemorrhagic disease. It is my purpose also to describe a method for studying hemorrhage called the bleeding time, and to describe briefly a simple method for determining the coagulation time.

In the cases there was marked hemorrhagic diathesis, a normal coagulation time, and almost an absence of platelets. Transfusion was performed in each case. After transfusion there was a marked increase in the number of platelets and remarkable relief of hemorrhage. When the platelet counts returned to their previous low level, hemorrhages returned. Later in the course of the disease in two of the cases, the platelet count rose spontaneously and this rise also was followed by relief of hemorrhage. The cases are reported to show the marked dependence of pathologic hemorrhage in this type of disease on the reduced numbers of platelets. The experiments are reported briefly to show that platelet counts reduced experimentally by benzol are not associated with changes in the coagulability of the blood which account for the hemorrhages of the condition and suggest that this type of hemorrhagic diathesis is due directly to the lack of platelets.

### A METHOD FOR DETERMINING THE BLEEDING TIME

A small cut is made in the lobe of the ear. At half-minute intervals the blood is blotted up on absorbent paper. This gives a series of blots of gradually decreasing size. Each blot represents one-half minute's outflow of blood. The rate of decrease in the size of the blots shows the rate of decrease of the hemorrhage. The cut should be made of such a size that the first half minute's outflow of blood makes a blot 1 or 2 cm. in diameter. The total duration of such a hemorrhage is called the bleeding time.

Figure 1 (A, B, C) was made from cuts of different size. These sets of blots show that within certain limits the duration of a hemorrhage does not depend on the size of the cut. If these figures represent capillary hemorrhages it is evident that a large number of capillaries will stop bleeding as rapidly as a small number.

The normal bleeding time varies from one to three minutes.

The bleeding time is slightly delayed (five to ten minutes) in severe anemia (Fig. 2).

Great delays in the bleeding time were found in, (1)

---

*Read in the Section on Practice of Medicine of the American Medical Association, at the Sixty-first Annual Session, held at St. Louis, June, 1910.

cases in which the platelet count was excessively reduced (ten to ninety minutes—Fig. 3), (2) cases in which the fibrinogen content of the blood was excessively reduced (ten minutes to twelve hours), and (3) experimental animals in which both platelets and fibrinogen were reduced.

It is remarkable that the bleeding time is independent of the coagulation time. The bleeding time was normal in several cases of jaundice in which the coagulation time was very much delayed. Two of these patients died of pathologic hemorrhage. It was also normal in a patient with hemophilia, who had a slight delay in the coagulation time and pathologic hemorrhage. The bleeding time was found to be normal in several types of purpura

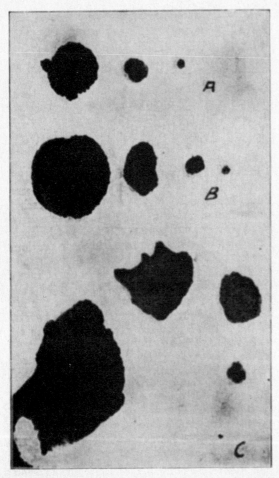

Fig. 1.—Normal bleeding times: A, from small cut; B, from larger cut; C, from very large cut.

hemorrhagica in which the platelet counts were normal. It is difficult to explain why these patients had hemorrhage into the tissues, from mucous membranes, and from operation wounds, and at the same time had normal bleeding from ear-pricks.

The bleeding time, then, in types of disease associated with low platelet counts, or with a reduced quantity of fibrinogen shows a tendency to prolonged hemorrhage. In these types of disease, a delayed bleeding time is a more reliable indication of hemorrhagic diathesis than hemorrhagic symptoms, for such symptoms usually depend on general and local causes. The latter are, of

course, not constant. In the cases reported in this paper the bleeding time was invariably delayed when pathologic hemorrhage was evident, and was often considerably delayed before hemorrhage began.

The method is apparently of no value in determining the tendency to bleed in jaundice and hemophilia, and in the types of purpura hemorrhagica which have normal platelet counts.

## A SIMPLE METHOD FOR DETERMINING THE COAGULATION TIME[1]

The apparatus consists of a slide on which are mounted two 5 mm. disks. One disk is covered with the blood to be tested. The other is covered with normal blood. The two drops of blood should be of about the same depth. The slide is then inverted over a glass nearly full of water kept at 40 C. and is covered with a warm, damp cloth. The coagulation time is determined by holding the slide in a vertical position for a moment. When the end point is reached the drop does not hang, as in Figure 4 a, but retains the contour of a perfect sphere (Fig. 4 b). The end point appears sharply and is easily determined.

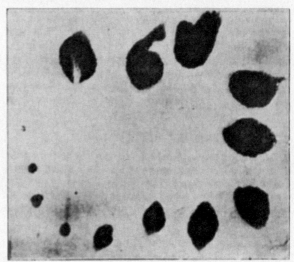

Fig. 2.—Slightly delayed bleeding time. From a case of secondary anemia.

The normal coagulation time by this method varies from five to seven minutes. A very shallow drop clots one to two minutes sooner than a very deep one. The normal blood can be used for a control, or can be used for obtaining a comparative time.

If simply the comparative time is desired, the temperature of the water may be allowed to vary between 35 and 40 C., and the glass may be covered with the hand instead of a damp cloth. A delay of two minutes can be easily determined by this method.

## PLATELET COUNTS

Wright's method[2] was used in making the platelet counts. According to this method the blood is drawn up in a 1-100 pipette, mixed with a solution of cresyl blue

1. This method is a modification of Hinman and Sladen's slide method (Johns Hopkins Hosp. Bull., 1907, xviii, 207). The principle was first used by Milian.
2. Wright and Kinnicut: Tr. Assn. Am. Phys., May, 1910.

**TABLE 1.—CASES OF HEMORRHAGIC DISEASE IN WHICH THE PLATELET COUNT, COAGULATION TIME AND BLEEDING TIME WERE DETERMINED**

| Disease. | No. of Cases. | Symptoms. | Plate Count. | Coag. Time. | Fibrinogen Content of Blood. | Bleeding Time. | Other Diseases which may Give Similar Blood and Similar Symptoms |
|---|---|---|---|---|---|---|---|
| Idiopathic purpura hemorrhagica. | 3 | Purpura, spontaneous hemorrhages. | Below 20,000 . | Normal .. | .................... | 60 min. + | Penicious anemia, lymphocytic leukemia, nephritis, typhoid fever. |
| Aplastic anemia ............. | 2 | Ecchymoses, epistaxis...... | Low ............ | Normal .. | Nor. in experimental aplastic anemia. | Delayed. | |
| Chronic Ulcerative colitis. | 1 | Melena ................ | 20,000 to 30,000 | Normal .. | .................... | 10-20 min. | |
| Chloroform poisoning .... | Dogs, 3 | Bleeding from gums and operation wounds | Normal or slightly reduced. | Normal .. | Excessively reduced | Hours ..... | Phosphorus poisoning, hemorrhagic smallpox. |
| Jaundice.................. | 2 | Hemorrhage after operation | Abundant in smears. | 30 min... 40 min... | | 1-2 min... | |
| | 1 | Purpura hemorrhagica | 350,000......... | 8 min. .. | Probably normal in jaundice. | 3 min...... | |
| | 8 | No symptoms ................ | Abundant in smears | Nor. or delayed. | .................... | 1-3 min... | |
| Hemophilia................ | 1 | Bleeding from wound; hematoma in knee. | 350,000......... | 9 min. ... | Normal in hemophilia. | 2. min..... | |
| Purpura simplex .......... | 2 | Purpura........................ | Abundant in smears. | Normal.. | .................... | Normal... | |
| Henoch's purpura ....... | 1 | Purpura, intestinal crisis, melena. | 275,000......... | Normal.. | .................... | Normal... | |
| | 1 | Purpura, urticaria, angioneurotic edema. | 300,000......... | Normal.. | .................... | Normal... | |
| Nephritis.................. | 4 1 | Epistaxis ................ Ecchymoses................ | Abundant in smears. | Normal... | .................... | Normal... | |

**TABLE 2.—DETAILED FINDINGS IN CASE 1**

| Date. | Platelet Counts. | Plates in Stained Blood Smears. | Bleeding Time. (Minutes.) | Coagulation Time. | Urine. | Stools. | Epistaxis. |
|---|---|---|---|---|---|---|---|
| May 8 ................ | 6,000............ | 1-2 per smear .... | 47 | 5 minutes.......... | Smoky ......... | Tarry ......... | Moderate. |
| May 9 ................ | None seen ......... | None seen ......... | 90 | 5 minutes.......... | Smoky ......... | Tarry ......... | Moderate. |
| May 10 ................ | 3,000............ | | | 5 minutes.......... | Smoky ......... | Tarry ......... | Moderate. |
| May 11 ................ | | 2 per smear....... | 50+ | 4½-5 minutes..... | Smoky ......... | Tarry ......... | Extreme. |
| (Transfusions). | | | | | | | |
| May 12 ................ | 123,000............ | 1-3 in each field. | 3 | 4½ minutes ....... | Clear.......... | Tarry ......... | None. |
| May 13 ................ | | 1 in 3-4 fields .... | 3 | .................... | .............. | Yellow........ | None. |
| May 14 ................ | | | 30 | .................... | Clear.......... | .............. | None. |
| May 15 ................ | | 3 per smear ....... | 40 | .................... | Clear.......... | Occult blood. | Slight. |
| May 16 ................ | | 1 per smear ....... | 50 | 5 minutes.......... | .............. | .............. | Moderate. |
| May 17 ................ | 1,500............ | 3 per smear ....... | 50 | .................... | Clear.......... | Fresh blood. | Moderate. |
| (Spontaneous increase in the number of platelets). | | | | | | | |
| May 18 ................ | | | | .................... | | Occult blood. | None. |
| May 19 ................ | | 1-6 per field ...... | 2 | .................... | .............. | .............. | None. |
| May 23 ................ | | | 2 | 5 minutes.......... | Clear.......... | No blood..... | None. |
| May 24 ................ | 84,000............ | 3-8 per field ...... | 4 | .................... | .............. | .............. | None. |

BLOOD EXAMINATION
May 8, R. C., 3,264,000; Hbg., 50%; W. C., 5,000
May 10, R. C., 3,260,000; Hbg., 50%.
May 11, R. C., 2,700,000; Hbg., 40%; W. C., 7,000
May 12, R. C., 3,600,000; Hbg., 46%
May 14, R. C., 3,500,000; Hbg.
May 16, R. C., 3,444,000; Hbg., 55%; W. C., 6,000
May 24, R. C., 5,000,000; Hbg., 70%; W. C., 2,400

and potassium cyanid and counted by the red cell technic. The red cells are laked by this solution and the leukocytes and platelets are stained. This is a great advantage, for the platelets can be easily recognized and can be counted with a high dry lens. The counts made by this method are uniformly lower than those made by Pratt's method.[3] This method, however, gives constant results if care is used in the technic. The normal count, according to Wright and Kinnicut, varies from 250,000 to 400,000.

### REPORTS OF CASES[°]

CASE 1.—*Summary.*—Acute purpura hemorrhagica. Purpura; spontaneous hemorrhages; practical absence of platelets; delayed bleeding time; normal coagulation time. This case is of interest in showing relief of hemorrhage, both after the rise in the platelet count following transfusion, and after a spontaneous rise in the count which occurred later in the disease.

*History.*—S. M., a man aged 20, Armenian, tailor, was admitted to Massachusetts General Hospital May 8, 1909, complaining of epistaxis. The family history is negative for hemorrhagic disease. The patient has always been strong and well, and has had no serious illnesses. He has never had prolonged epistaxis, spontaneous ecchymoses, joint trouble, urticaria, nor abdominal crises. His digestion has always been good. For three weeks before admission to the hospital he had been feeling run down, and had had slight sore throat. For five days he had been troubled with persistent epistaxis. He noticed that his urine was high-colored, his stools black, and that he was covered with purpuric rash. There was nothing further of importance in the history.

*Examination.*—The patient was a well-developed and well-nourished young man, pale and weakened by loss of blood. A small amount of blood was then oozing from the border of his gums, and nasal mucous membranes. Scattered over his entire body, including the soles of his feet, mucous membranes, tongue and scleræ, were fine muscular purpuric blotches, 1 to 5 mm. in diameter. In places, especially on the lower extremities, they were confluent, and covered areas 2 to 3 cm. in diameter. Retinæ were free from hemorrhage. There were a few mucous râles at the lung apices, and a soft systolic blow at the base of the heart. The spleen edge was palpable just below the costal margin. There were no telangiectases on his skin or mucous membranes. Blood-smears showed almost a total absence of blood-plates, 6,000 by count. On the following day the counts were even lower. The bleeding time was forty minutes. The coagulation time was normal.

The course of disease can be followed by the chart (Fig. 5). During the first four days in the hospital there was an almost constant oozing of blood from the nose, which could be controlled for only short periods of time by packing. The stools and urine each day contained considerable blood.

*Transfusion.*—On May 11, the patient lost over a pint of blood from the nose, and his condition became so critical that he was transfused at 2 a. m. by Dr. F. T. Murphy. An Armenian friend of about the same age was donor. That a large amount of blood was given by transfusion was evident from the improvement in the patient's general condition, color, and pulse, and

3. Pratt, J. H.: A Critical Study of the Various Methods Employed for Enumerating Blood Platelets, THE JOURNAL A. M. A., Dec. 30, 1905, p. 1999.

4. I wish to express my thanks to Dr. F. T. Murphy, Dr. Hugh Cabot, Dr. L. A. Conner and Dr. R. D. McClure for permission to report these cases, and to Dr. J. H. Wright for his kind assistance in making the platelet counts.

from the rise in the pulse-rate of the donor.

*Course of Disease.*—The platelet count, taken six hours after transfusion, was 123,000. The bleeding time had dropped to three minutes. The coagulation time was practically unchanged. Epistaxis had stopped before this time, and the packing had been removed from the nose. The urine was then free from blood. The stools on the following morning were light yellow, but contained a small amount of occult blood. No fresh purpuric spots appeared and the ones present began to fade, disappearing completely in five days. Thirty-six hours after transfusion it could be seen from stained smears that the

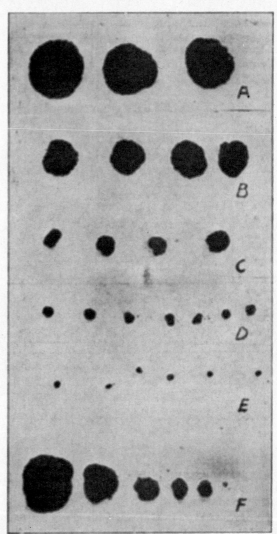

Fig. 3.—Great delay in bleeding time. From Case 1. Platelet count 3,000, coagulation time normal. The blots in Series A were taken immediately after the ear was pricked; Series B, 20 minutes; C, 40 minutes; D, 60 minutes, and E, 80 minutes later. The bleeding time at this time was 90 minutes. Series F, showing a normal bleeding time, was taken after the transfusion. Platelet count was then 110,000.

platelets were decreasing rapidly in number, and on the third day one could be found only after prolonged search. At this time the bleeding time was again delayed. The day following this the patient's nose began to bleed and fresh blood appeared in the stools. Since the onset of the disease the patient had had an irregular temperature, varying from 99 to 103 F. This came to normal, except for slight remissions, on May 20. Apparently the disease had run its course, for at this time plates reappeared in the blood (80,000), and hemorrhage from ear-pricks would last for only three minutes. There was no further epistaxis or melena. Convalescence was uneventful, and since then the patient has continued his vocation without symptoms.

*Differential Counts.*—Made on May 8, 9, 12, 15, 23. Polymorphonuclear neutrophils made up from 80 to 86 per cent. of the cells. The remainder were lymphocytes with an occasional mast-cell and eosinophil. Only one blast was seen.

*Red Cells.*—Moderate variation in size. Shape normal. Moderate amount of achroma and polychromatophilia. An occasional stippled cell.

*Coagulation Time.*—The comparative method was used. The temperature was kept constant at 40 C. My blood, which had a coagulation time of five to six minutes, was used as a control. Usually several determinations were made and the average taken.

*Platelet Counts.*—Pratt's method was used in making the platelet counts on May 8, 9 and 10. The other determinations were made by Wright's method. The variations in the platelet count were so marked that estimations from stained cover-glass preparations of the blood proved satisfactory. Smears were looked over carefully with oil immersion lens on the days mentioned, and the number seen per smear or field averaged.

*Retraction of Clot.*—The clot was non-retractile after standing forty-eight hours on May 11 and 16. It retracted normally on May 12 and May 23.

*Bleeding Time.*—Determined by the method described. As a rule several determinations were made and the times averaged.

*Urine.*—Normal except that it contained a sediment of red cells and a slight trace of albumin on May 8 to 11. It contained no sugar, bile, peptone, albuminose, or nucleoproteid.

*Stools.*—May 8 to 12, rather copious, soft and black; from May 13 to 16, soft and light yellow (milk diet). Guaiac test was faintly positive on May 13 and 14; strong on May 15. On May 17, the stools were brown and soft and mixed with about 50 c.c. of fresh blood and a little mucus. On May 18, the stools gave the guaiac test. May 19 to 23, the guaiac test was negative. No parasites or ova were found.

The patient was seen eleven months after his illness and was then apparently strong and healthy. White count 4,700. Polymorphonuclears, 66 per cent.; lymphocytes, 34 per cent.; hemoglobin, 85 per cent. Plates 240,000. Bleeding time one minute.

CASE 2.—*Summary.*—Chronic ulcerative colitis; melena; reduced platelet count; delayed bleeding time; normal coagulation time. The bleeding time was normal after the rise in the platelet count following transfusion. The melena was slightly increased by transfusion. The case is of interest in showing a difference between the curative influence of transfusion in normal and in pathologic hemorrhage. Although the general tendency to hemorrhage (shown by the shortened bleeding time) was markedly diminished by transfusion, hemorrhage from the intestinal ulcers was increased. The case shows the difficulty of judging the tendency to abnormal hemorrhage by hemorrhagic symptoms alone.

*History.*—A. C., American, a boy aged 8, was admitted to Massachusetts General Hospital Nov. 15, 1909, complaining of weakness and diarrhea. The family history is negative for hemorrhagic disease. The patient's early life was normal. He had had no serious acute illnesses. After the age of 2 he suffered almost continually from diarrhea. He developed slowly, was always thin, and never strong enough to go to school. After the age of 4, there were four periods of a month or less in which the stools contained considerable blood, and the patient became pale and weak. He bled excessively from a trivial cut once. He never had ecchymosis on slight injury, joint disturbance, nor other evidence of hemorrhagic disease. For a month before admission to the hospital, the diarrhea was more severe, the stools contained blood, and the boy was becoming pale and weak.

*Examination.*—The patient was poorly developed, thin and pale, skin clear. Except for evidence of anemia, there was nothing of interest on physical examination. There were no telangiectases on the skin or mucous membranes, and no

jaundice. Blood-smears showed a scarcity of the plates. Counts varied from 20,000 to 30,000. The bleeding time was twenty minutes. The coagulation time was normal.

During the first two and one-half weeks in the hospital a prominent symptom was diarrhea. The patient had from eight to thirty stools a day, which consisted mostly of thin pus, and often contained a small amount of blood and mucus. The patient's temperature varied from 98 to 103 F.

*Transfusion.*—On November 3 the patient was transfused by Dr. Hugh Cabot, preparatory to cecostomy. The child's father was donor. Following transfusion there was improvement in general condition and color. The temperature came to normal, and the pulse-rate dropped from 150 to 110.

*Course of Disease.*—The platelet count, taken two hours after transfusion, was 90,000, and the bleeding time was two minutes. The coagulation time was unchanged. The amount of blood in the stools, however, was increased. In interpreting this result it must be borne in mind that the patient had an extensive chronic ulcerative colitis (proved by autopsy), a condition which may cause melena when the blood is normal. The increase following transfusion was thought to be due to overfilling of the blood-vessels. Cecostomy was performed on the following day without excessive hemorrhage. As in the previous case, the platelets introduced by transfusion disappeared rapidly, and in a few days the count reached its former low level. The bleeding time again became delayed. The melena continued. The boy gradually became anemic, febrile, and died about a month later of septicemia.

*Autopsy.*—Chronic ulcerative colitis and enteritis. Extensive inflammatory thickening of the intestinal walls. Chronic pleuritis. Hyperplasia of mesenteric lymph-nodes. Streptococcus obtained from heart blood.

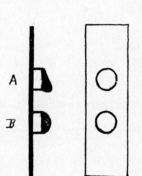

Fig. 4.—Instrument for determining the coagulation time.

DETAILED FINDINGS IN CASE 2

| Date. | Platelet count. | Bleeding time (min.). | Coagulation time. |
|---|---|---|---|
| 10/26 | 32,000 | 20 | Normal |
| 10/28 | 23,000 | 20 | .......... |
| 10/30 | 22,000 | 20 | Normal |
| 11/ 2 | 20,000 | 20 | 5 min. |
| (Transfusion). | | | |
| 11/ 3 | 89,000 | 3 | 5 min. |
| 11/ 4 | 72,000 | 2½ | .......... |
| 11/ 6 | 25,000 | 3 | Normal |
| 11/ 8 | ........ | ... | .......... |
| 11/ 9 | 25,000 | 10 | .......... |
| 11/13 | ........ | 10 | .......... |

BLOOD EXAMINATION

| | | | |
|---|---|---|---|
| 10/15, R. C | ..............3,600,000 | Hbg., 42% | White Counts, 3,700 |
| 10/19, R. C | ..............1,600,000 | Hbg., 20% | White Counts, 3,100 |
| 10/31, R. C | ..............1,224,000 | Hbg., 15% | White Counts, 4,700 |
| 11/ 2, R. C | ..............1,200,000 | Hbg., ..... | White Counts, ....... |
| 11/ 3, morning | ..........3,280,000 | Hbg., 70% | White Counts, 3,800 |
| 11/ 3, afternoon | ........3,416,000 | Hbg., ..... | White Counts, 2,200 |
| 11/ 4, | ................................ | Hbg., 85% | |
| 11/ 9, | ................................ | Hbg., 90% | |
| 11/13, | ....................3,600,000 | Hbg., 70% | |

*Differential Counts.*—Polymorphonuclear neutrophils varied from 40 per cent. to 60 per cent. The remainder were lymphocytes with an occasional mast-cell and eosinophil. No blasts seen.

*Red Cells.*—Moderate variation in size. Shape normal. Moderate amount of achroma and polychromatophilia. No stippling.

*Coagulation and Bleeding Time.*—Determined as in Case 1. The platelets were counted by Wright's method.

*Retraction of Clot.*—On October 26 there was a very slight retraction of the clot after twenty-four hours; on November 3 and 4 a moderate amount of retraction; on November 9 no retraction.

*Urine.*—Normal.

*Stools.*—Eight to thirty a day, throughout the patient's illness. Small in amount and of pea-soup consistency. Stools contained considerable pus, a small amount of food residue and mucus. During the first few days, after admission, they contained considerable fresh blood. For ten days before transfusion they contained very little blood. After transfusion the stools were port-wine in color and contained considerable blood. Melena continued until death. Stools contained no parasites or ova. Cultures taken frequently showed only the colon bacillus.

CASE 3.—*Summary.*—Chronic purpura hemorrhagica[5]: Ecchymoses; purpura; hemorrhages from mucous membranes; low platelet count; delayed bleeding time; relief of hemorrhage for three days followed transfusion; relief of hemorrhage after a spontaneous rise in the platelet count.

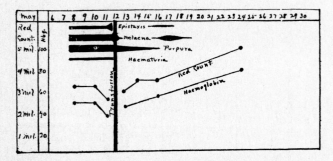

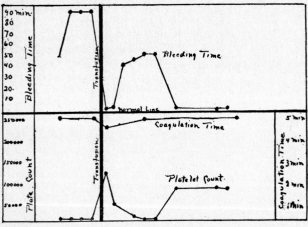

Fig. 5.—Chart of Case 1.

*History.*—Georgiana ———, American, a girl aged 3, was admitted to New York Hospital Oct. 3, 1909, complaining of epistaxis. The patient's parents, and three brothers and sisters are living and well. There is no history of hemophilia in the family. The patient has had no acute illnesses. She has had prolapse of the rectum several times. Since the age of 19 months, she has been subject to nose bleed, and ecchymosis following slight injury. Four months before admission to the hospital, symptoms were more severe, and at one time she became pale and weak from epistaxis and bleeding from a small cut on the head. She improved somewhat after this, and for the following two months there was little bleeding. Two days before

---

5. This case has been reported in another connection by Pool and McClure, Annals of Surgery, September, 1910.

she came to the hospital, epistaxis began again and continued until admission to the hospital.

*Examination.*—The patient was a moderately developed and nourished little girl. She was pale and rather weak from loss of blood. On the right shoulder, cheek, and lower extremities were several small ecchymoses. There were no telangiectases. The physical examination was otherwise unimportant. Epistaxis continued almost without ceasing for five days, and the child became almost pulseless.

*Transfusion.*—She was transfused on October 7 by Dr. R. D. McClure. The patient's father was donor.

*Course of Disease.*—Transfusion improved the patient's pulse—volume and color, but owing to bronchopneumonia which developed at about the same time, her condition remained serious for a few days. The temperature, which had ranged from 98 to 102 F., began to decrease and reached normal about a week later. The pulse-rate immediately dropped from 160 to 120 and a few days later to 90, where it remained. There was no bleeding for three days after transfusion. On the fourth day there was slight epistaxis, and hemorrhage from the vagina and transfusion wounds. Later, she had slight epistaxis and melena, as marked on the chart, and a fine petechial rash which followed straining at stool.

*Blood Examinations.*—August 8—red cells 2,300,000, hemoglobin 34 per cent. Other estimations showed about the same ratio between the red count and hemoglobin. The white count varied from 16,000 to 21,000. Blood smears on some occasions showed an excess of lymphocytes (71 per cent.), but usually polymorphs predominated. The red cells showed polychromatophilia and moderate variation in size. There were no blasts. The coagulation time was about normal (Boggs' instrument). The urine was not remarkable.

For five weeks after leaving the hospital the patient had no further bleeding. During the sixth week, however, she had prolapse of the rectum with bloody stools. One week later, she noticed that ecchymoses followed slight injuries. When seen at this time, (Nov 24, 1909), her color and general health were fairly good. On her head, elbow and legs, were several small ecchymoses. Blood plates, as determined from stained smears and counting chamber, were extremely scarce. The bleeding time was about sixty minutes. The coagulation time was normal. The clot was firm and non-retractile. The white count was 7,000; polynuclears, 45 per cent.; lymphocytes, 55 per cent.; hemoglobin, 90 per cent. The patient was seen again four months later (April 7, 1910). She had been free from hemorrhagic symptoms for some time. Plates were then abundant in stained smears, and hemorrhage from ear pricks would last for from five to ten minutes. The hemoglobin was 85 per cent.

Platelet counts were not made in this case at the time of transfusion. It seems probable, however, that, as in the previous cases, the relief of hemorrhage, after transfusion, was associated with an increase in the platelet count.

## COMMENT

A review of the cases shows a striking dependence of hemorrhagic diathesis on the reduced number of platelets. In Cases 1 and 2 the platelet counts before transfusion were 3,000 and 20,000; the bleeding times were, respectively, ninety and twenty minutes. After transfusion the counts were 110,000 and 89,000, and the bleeding time in each case was three minutes. After the disappearance of these platelets, apparently introduced into the patients' circulation by transfusion, the bleeding times were again delayed (forty minutes and twenty minutes). In Cases 1 and 3 the bleeding times (forty minutes and one hour) came to normal after spontaneous rises in the platelet counts.

As to spontaneous hemorrhages, there was complete relief in Cases 1 and 3 for three days after transfusion and after spontaneous rises in the platelet counts. In Case 2 intestinal hemorrhage was slightly increased by transfusion, in spite of the fact that the general tendency to bleed (shown by the shortening of the bleeding time) was less marked. This apparently contradictory result may be accounted for by the fact that intestinal hemorrhage in this case was not entirely pathologic hemorrhage, but was due largely to bleeding from intestinal ulcers. The increase after transfusion may have followed the more complete filling of the blood-vessels.

In each of the cases the coagulation time of the blood bore no relation either to the platelet count or to hemorrhagic symptoms. The coagulation time was practically the same before and after transfusion, and before and after the spontaneous rises in the platelet count.

Other cases of hemorrhagic disease with a reduced number of platelets (twenty) have been reported by Denys, Hayem, Ehrlich, Helber, Bensaude and Rivet, Coe, Pratt and Selling. In one case reported by Bensaude and Rivet[6] there was a low count (6,000) during a hemorrhage crisis. During a remission in the disease the count was 161,000. Coe[7] has attached more importance to the relationship between the reduced number of platelets and hemorrhage than other observers. In one of his cases, the most severe epistaxis occurred when the platelets, estimated from stained smears, were almost absent. Previously they had been present, but in diminished number. In another case of purpura hemorrhagica, platelets, frequently estimated from smears, were almost absent during two hemorrhagic periods, and were present during remissions.

The reported cases differ in etiology. Many belong to the group known as idiopathic purpura hemorrhagica. Some of the cases were evidently symptomatic. One of Pratt's cases[8] accompanied nephritis. The platelet count was 9,000. Benzol poisoning was the etiologic agent in Selling's cases. The clinical condition was aplastic anemia. In one of his cases the platelet count was 2,500. In Case 2 reported in this paper, the hemorrhagic diathesis may have been secondary to ulcerative colitis. Platelet counts may also be low in lymphocytic leukemia, pernicious anemia, and early typhoid fever, and in each disease purpura hemorrhagica is a recognized complication.

The data leads one to believe that a reduced number of platelets is not simply a phenomenon accompanying some types of hemorrhagic disease, but rather that it may be the direct cause of hemorrhagic diathesis in several diseases.

## EXPERIMENTAL WORK

Experimental work seemed desirable to determine whether the hemorrhagic diathesis was due directly to the lack of platelets, or whether it was due to an

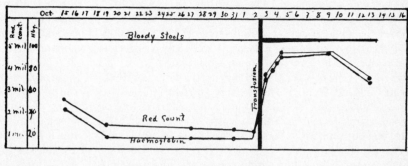
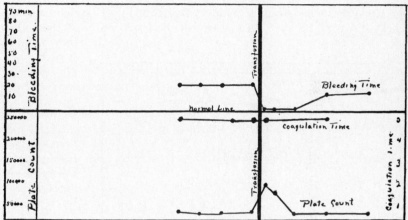

Fig. 6.—Chart of Case 2.

abnormal coagulability of the blood which might accompany a reduced number of platelets. It seemed desirable also to know to what extent the platelet count must be reduced to cause hemorrhage.

In benzol poisoning we have a condition simulating idiopathic purpura hemorrhagica. Santessin[9] has reported cases and experiments in which hemorrhages were produced by benzol. Selling's cases[10] of a similar nature clinically, had very low platelet counts. He has found[11] that subcutaneous injections of benzol in animals reduces the platelet count. This reduction is thought to be due largely to the aplastic condition of the bone-marrow caused by the poison.

My experiments were performed mainly on dogs, and, according to a method suggested by Dr. Selling. Benzol was given daily for six to twelve days. The platelet count would usually rise at first, but later would fall and continue low for a number of days after the injections of benzol had been stopped. In several instances the count

6. Arch. gén de méd., 1905, I, 193.

7. Coe, J. W.: The Treatment of Purpuric Conditions and Hemophilia, THE JOURNAL A. M. A., Oct. 6, 1906, p. 1090.

8. Osler's Modern Medicine, 1908, iv.

9. Santessin: Arch. f. Hyg., 1897. xxi, 336; Skand. Arch. f. Physiol., 1900, x, 1.

10. Selling: Bull. Johns Hopkins Hosp., 1910, xxi, 32.

11. Unpublished experiments which will appear in the Journal of Experimental Medicine.

was reduced to 30,000. The white count was usually high even in the late stages of the poisoning.

The results[12] support a conclusion which might be drawn from this series of cases, namely, that when other conditions are normal, moderately low platelet counts are not associated with hemorrhagic diathesis. The platelet counts, after transfusion, in Cases 1 and 2 were only one-third of the normal, and yet there was no evidence of pathologic hemorrhage. The bleeding time was only moderately delayed (ten to twenty minutes) in Case 2, when the platelet counts varied from 20,000 to 30,000. The tendency to bleed in Cases 1 and 3 was extreme only during the practical absence of platelets. In the experimental work the platelet counts in dogs and rabbits were reduced from the normal (200,000 to 600,000) to from 50,000 to 75,000 without the appearance of hemorrhagic diathesis. Only a more extreme reduction (to 30,000) caused a delay in the bleeding time, and hemorrhages into the organs. There is an analogy between this observation and the observations of Whipple and Hurwitz on chloroform poisoning.[13] They found that, when other conditions are normal, a moderate reduction

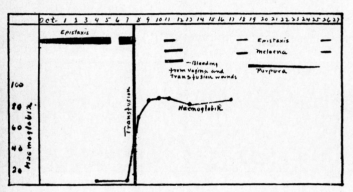

Fig. 7.—Chart of Case 3.

in the quantity of fibrinogen does not cause hemorrhagic diathesis. In their experiments hemorrhage was prolonged only when the reduction was extreme. It seems likely, then, that both platelets and fibrinogen play a striking rôle in the control of hemorrhage. Either one may be moderately reduced without symptoms, but after an extreme reduction there is a tendency to bleed.

The experiments failed to show abnormalities in the coagulability of the blood accompanying low platelet counts, which account for prolonged hemorrhage. The coagulation time was normal, or slightly shortened when the platelet count was as low as 30,000. The quantity of fibrinogen was normal or slightly increased (0.55 per cent. to 0.65 per cent.); furthermore, the fibrinogen present was all convertible into fibrin, and the fibrin examined in a number of ways had a normal microscopic appearance.

The serum in one instance was examined by Professor Howell, and found to contain thrombin. The only

abnormality in the clot noted was diminished retractibility, a peculiarity shown by Hayem and others to be associated with and probably due directly to a lack of platelets. Normal plasma deprived of platelets in various experimental ways clots quickly, but does not retract from the sides of the vessel containing it, and extrude serum.

The hemorrhagic diathesis is explained, possibly, through investigations on experimental thrombi. In a bleeding vessel, there are conditions suitable for the formation of a thrombus, that is, injured intima and a flowing stream of blood. Platelets, although they have little, if any, influence on the clotting of still blood, play a striking rôle in the formation of thrombi. The investigations of Hayem, Eberth and Schimmelbusch, Welch, Pratt, and others, have shown that after trauma to a blood-vessel platelets are the first element to adhere to the injured intima, and that within a few minutes they are massed in great numbers at the injured point. Later, leukocytes, fibrin, and red cells are included in the process, and a plug is formed consisting of masses of each of these elements. The investigations of J. H. Wright[14] show more clearly the rôle which the thrombus plays in stopping hemorrhage. His experiments were made by puncturing vessels with a needle. The resulting thrombi were likewise made up largely of platelets, and were evidently a factor in plugging the opening. An absence of platelets would lead to abnormality in the formation of thrombi, and might be a cause of prolonged hemorrhage. Pratt has laid more emphasis than other observers on the rôle which red cells play in thrombus formation. The failure of erythrocytes in carrying out this function explains, possibly, the delayed bleeding time noted in severe anemia.

CONCLUSIONS

The question now arises whether the facts admit the conclusion that an extreme reduction in the number of platelets is a cause of hemorrhagic diathesis, or whether the low platelet count must be considered a phenomenon which is sometimes found in hemorrhagic disease. The facts are as follows:

1. In the cases of hemorrhagic disease summarized, evidently differing in nature and etiology (acute and chronic idiopathic purpura hemorrhagica, chronic ulcerative colitis, aplastic anemia, nephritis), the constant features associated with the tendency to bleed were the reduced number of platelets, and the modification of the clot probably dependent on it, namely diminished retractility.

2. In the cases reported in this paper, relief of the tendency to bleed followed not only the rises in the platelet count occurring at a remission in the disease, but followed also the rise brought about by transfusion. In the latter case, the tendency to bleed returned when the platelets disappeared.

3. Experiments in which the platelet count was reduced by benzol failed to show an abnormality in the coagulability of the blood, which accounts for the hemorrhages of benzol poisoning.

12. A complete report of results will be made later.

13. Unpublished experiments which will appear in the Journal of Experimental Medicine.

14. Personal communication.

4. The structure and the mode of formation of experimental thrombi suggests, from an anatomic standpoint, that platelets play a rôle in stopping hemorrhage.

It may be permissible to mention two more points of interest suggested by the cases.

None of the patients showed so marked a tendency to bleed after transfusion as before, even after the platelet counts had dropped to their previous low level. In Cases 1 and 2, the bleeding times were ninety minutes and twenty minutes before transfusion. On the fifth day after transfusion, when the count was again low, the bleeding times were only half as long, fifty minutes and ten minutes. The spontaneous hemorrhages in Cases 1 and 3 were never so severe after as before transfusion. Since anemia is associated with a delayed bleeding time, this relief might be accounted for by the rise in the red count. In interpreting the beneficial results following transfusion, this point should always be considered.

In each of the cases, the platelets introduced by transfusion disappeared rapidly. It is granted that these platelets may have been destroyed prematurely by the disease from which the patient suffered, or by processes analogous to hemolysis, etc. The uniform rapidity in the rate of disappearance, however, suggests that platelets are short-lived bodies. This interpretation is supported by the results obtained from the study of transfusion in benzol poisoning. In this case also, platelets introduced by transfusion disappear rapidly. It is also supported by results, to be reported later, which show that the normal rate of formation of platelets is probably extremely rapid, and may amount to as much as one-fourth of the entire number in the body per day. The evidence suggests strongly that platelets disintegrate or are utilized by the body in enormous numbers, and that the count is kept constant under a given set of conditions by a correspondingly rapid rate of formation.

The type of hemorrhagic disease described in this paper can be sharply differentiated from other types of disease, such as hemophilia, melena neonatorum, purpura simplex, Henoch's purpura, etc., which are due to other abnormalities. To this type of disease belong the so-called idiopathic purpura hemorrhagicas, and some cases of symptomatic purpura. The latter will probably be found most frequently in aplastic anemia, pernicious anemia, lymphocytic leukemia, typhoid fever and intestinal diseases. The symptoms may be mild, or may be so severe and acute that the patient bleeds to death in a few days. In mild cases, purpura may not appear. The only demonstration of the disease may be (as in Case 2) excessive hemorrhage from a local lesion.

The diagnosis is easy. If the platelet count is reduced to a sufficient degree to cause hemorrhage, the fact may be determined by examining carefully made cover-glass preparations. The absence of retractility of the clot is considered by Hayem and his pupils characteristic of the condition, and is of diagnostic import. A point which I have found of value in following the cases and also in the diagnosis is the marked delay in the bleeding time.

Transfusion gives good results in the treatment of the disease. In addition to replacing blood, it stops hemorrhage for a few days, and may tide the patient over a serious crisis. The treatment is probably applicable to the symptomatic as well as to the idiopathic types of disease, and may be useful in the treatment of some cases of typhoid hemorrhage.

In concluding, I wish to acknowledge my indebtedness to Dr. E. H. Whipple, of the department of pathology, to Professor W. H. Howell of the department of physiology, and to Dr. L. Selling for their kind assistance in the experimental work.

2928 Forest Avenue.

---

## ABSTRACT OF DISCUSSION

Dr. J. H. Pratt, Boston: There seems to be some relation between the blood platelets in the blood and purpura hemorrhagica. Normally, the number of blood platelets is about 450,000 to the cubic millimeter. In simple purpura I found the platelet count was greatly reduced; in one fatal case it fell as low as 7,000. This patient had continuous hemorrhages from the lips and mouth. The platelet count was made 3 times on different days, and the largest number of platelets found was 16,000. In a case of mild purpura hemorrhagica there were 105,000 platelets per cm. The only other condition in which I have found very low platelet counts is lymphatic leukemia. The relation between purpura and the coagulation time is less clear. Wright asserted that purpura was due to delay in the coagulation time and that the treatment of the disease consisted in reducing the coagulation time to the normal by the administration of calcium chlorid or calcium lactate. I found the records of the Johns Hopkins Hospital and the Massachusetts General Hospital those of 34 cases of purpura in which the coagulation time of the blood had been determined. The average coagulation time of the blood in this series of cases was 5½ minutes, which is within the normal limits. In only a few cases did I find a delay in the coagulation. I have seen a patient with purpura bleeding to death from the mucous membrane when the coagulation time was normal. Over the lobe of the ear at the site of the puncture a thick, moist clot formed, but blood continued to ooze from the wound for a long time. I believe that Dr. Duke's method of determining the "bleeding time" will be found to have great clinical value. In the case I have just cited in which the coagulation time was normal the bleeding time was doubtless greatly increased.

Dr. W. W. Duke, Kansas City, Mo.: Transfusion must be done by the direct method. Defibrinated blood is free from platelets and therefore in itself would not increase the count. There is a special indication for transfusion preparatory to operation in this condition. In addition to the usual results which follow transfusion, the tendency to bleed is diminished.

Sept 2, 1983
(*JAMA* 1983;250:1210-1214)

# W. W. Duke and His Bleeding Time Test*

## K. M. Brinkhous, MD

The 1910 article by Duke[1] on platelets and bleeding has been judged by history to be one of the outstanding contributions to the science and practice of medicine during the first half of this century. In this article, Duke made two tremendous contributions. First, he firmly established with excellent data for the times that platelets are needed for hemostasis and that thrombocytopenia is associated with purpura and other hemorrhagic manifestations. The important role of platelets in the formation of thrombi had already been established in the 1880s by the work of Eberth and Schimmelbusch, Bizzozero, and Hayem. However, the origin of the platelets was uncertain. Hayem erroneously believed they were derived from red cell precursors, a view Osler gently ridiculed with the statement: "I have spent many weary hours over them, but I never caught one 'blushing.' "[2] In 1905, Wright demonstrated the platelet derivation from the megakaryocyte. Spaet,[3] in a short history of platelets, points out that they were known as "blood dust." The idea of platelets as dust appropriately connotes the uncertain clinical importance assigned to circulating platelets at the time. Although there had been a few case reports of thrombocytopenia in the literature before 1910, it was Duke's article that gave credibility to the importance of platelets in hemorrhagic disease. Second, Duke described the original bleeding time (BT) test in this article. To this day, the test, along with its modifications, is used to provide an index of platelet function.

This commentary will focus on two themes: (1) the circumstances and background that led Duke to make this important contribution to medicine and (2) the basic biologic mechanisms reflected in the BT test and the importance assigned to BT testing today.

### Biographical Sketch

Duke was born on Oct 18, 1882, in Lexington, Mo. He received the PhB degree from Yale University in 1904 and the MD degree from Johns Hopkins University in 1908. He was listed in many biographical volumes during his life and later.[4] In all these listings, the first year after receiving the MD degree is unaccounted for. Yet, this must have been the year in which he did much of the work for his 1910 article. Circumstances point to his being a worker for this period and perhaps longer in the Hunterian Laboratory of Experimental Pathology, Johns Hopkins Medical School, the director of which was Dr George H. Whipple.[1,5,6] He was a postgraduate student at the Massachusetts General Hospital (MGH) in 1909 and 1910, where he met the pathologist John Homer Wright, already well known for his study of megakaryocytes. He also spent some time at the New York Hospital. Being a peripatetic physician in training with work in many institutions was part of the times. He continued his travels during the period 1910 to 1912, attending the Universities of Vienna, Berlin, and Tübingen. He established his practice in internal medicine in Kansas City, Mo, in 1912, with an appointment at the University of Kansas as professor of experimental medicine, 1914 to 1918. He wrote several other articles on platelets and hemorrhage in the period from 1912 to 1915, after which time his attention was given over largely to the new field of allergy. He was a prolific writer and continued to publish many articles and books, several of which emphasize foci of infection in relation to teeth and tonsils. He died at the age of 63 years.

From the Department of Pathology, University of North Carolina at Chapel Hill.

*A commentary on Duke WW: The relation of blood platelets to hemorrhagic disease. *JAMA* 1910;55:1185-1192.

## The Prepared Mind

Pasteur is often quoted on the importance of the "prepared mind" for the making of significant contributions. Duke was 27 years old at the time his most important article was published. So the period of Duke's training in preparation for the 1910 article encompasses his medical student days at Johns Hopkins and the period immediately after graduation. Johns Hopkins at the time was the center of ferment in medical education and experimental and clinical medicine. One expectation for the school and the medical student is reflected in a quotation from William Henry Welch, dean and professor of pathology: ". . . with provision for as intimate, prolonged, personal contact of the student with the subject of study as he finds in the laboratory."[7] In his medical student days, Duke took advantage of Welch's provision in a literal fashion. He became student assistant to William H. Howell, professor of physiology and author of the widely used textbook of physiology of the day. From this association, three substantial articles (1906 to 1908) were published in the *Journal of Physiology* and the *American Journal of Physiology*. Duke lists in his biographical sketch[4] his contribution as "co-discoverer physiology of heart beat in relationship to the potassium and calcium content of the blood." While in Howell's laboratory, Duke was undoubtedly exposed to the increasing interest and excitement about blood coagulation as well as to Howell's historic interest in the megakaryocyte. Howell gave this giant cell of the bone marrow its name in 1890,[2] even before it was recognized as the mother cell of the platelet. Howell's contributions to coagulation, often written with student assistants, are well known even today, particularly his discovery of heparin.

Whipple was studying liver necrosis in dogs when Duke, who had just received the MD degree, became associated with him in the Hunterian Laboratory. Whipple had observed that the animals had lost their blood fibrinogen and that the bleeding from skin-puncture wounds was long.[8] Normal platelet counts and long BT on these animals were reported in Duke's 1910 article. In other experiments, Duke[6] showed that dogs with a low platelet count of 36,000 to 38,000/cu mm had a long BT. At Duke's request, Howell tested the blood samples from thrombocytopenic animals with a long BT and found that thrombin was actively generated. From this, Duke concluded that the BT test was not a test for blood clotting.

With this laboratory background at Johns Hopkins, it was natural for Duke to look for clinical counterparts of what he had been studying in the laboratory. At MGH, he received help from Wright, whose platelet-counting method he had been using in his experimental work.[1] Two of the three cases of thrombocytopenia reported in the 1910 article were from MGH; one was from New York Hospital. So Duke was both fortunate and wise in the choice of the persons with whom he worked. Three of them are recognized as giants in the history of medical research—the physiologist William Henry Howell and two pathologists, George Hoyt Whipple, a Nobel laureate, and John Homer Wright.

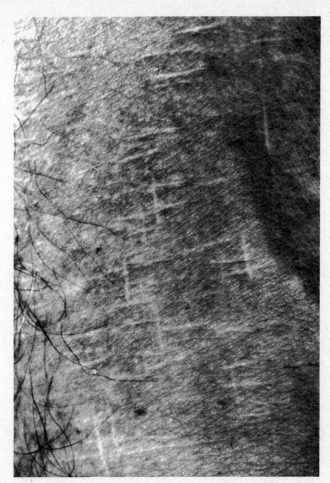

Scars on forearm of man subjected to multiple bleeding time determinations.

## The Bleeding Time Test

Over the years, there have been many modifications of the BT test to make it more sensitive and reproducible. Three of these have been widely adopted: (1) use of the forearm as the site of the test instead of the ear lobe, as was used by Duke, (2) use of a sphygmomanometer cuff (40 mm Hg) to increase the venous pressure in the forearm, and (3) use of a template method to control the length and depth of the incision. The first two modifications were introduced in 1935 by Ivy and colleagues.[9] Thus modified, the test became known as the "Ivy BT." Duke[1] recognized the importance of the size of the incision, as did most subsequent workers. Devices were developed to attain a standard incision by Tocantins[10] and, more recently, by Mielke et al[11] and the Babsons.[12] The effects of many other variables on the test have been studied, including different skin sites, local temperature and blood flow, rate of bleeding from the wound, type (lancet or knife) and direction of wound, and number of incisions per test to obtain reliable results.[13] Scarring seems to be somewhat more discernible with transverse wounds (Figure). Another variable is the effect of the air interface with the exuding blood. A "thrombogenic" layer of proteins is deposited at this interface, triggering platelet activation, adhesion, and aggregation. This variable is controlled in the saline BT test.[14] The BT test, despite much effort to develop an ex vivo substitute, still remains firmly entrenched as an almost indispensable member of the panel of screening tests for hemostatic or platelet function.[12]

## The Hemostatic Plug

Stoppage of blood flow from the BT wound is dependent on the formation of the hemostatic plug, sometimes called a "wound thrombus" to distinguish it from the simpler platelet or white thrombus occurring in intact vessels. Time-lapse studies of the morphological structure of the BT wound display a rapidly changing scene.[15] Within seconds, activated platelets are observed to form aggregates at the sites where blood leaves the cut vessels. It is known that under optimal conditions, activation time is in milliseconds.[16] The platelets in these extravascular aggregates exhibit interdigitating pseudopodia, concentration of granules centrally, degranulation, and evidence of secretion. The aggregates quickly evolve into large, complex masses with the appearance of clear, greatly expanded balloonlike vesicles at the periphery. The evolution of these extravascular platelet aggregates in the hemostatic plug follows the stereotyped pattern of aggregate formation in vitro in clotting blood[17] rather than that observed with platelet adhesion and white thrombus formation in a vessel. Fibrin soon appears at the periphery of the wound and at the periphery of the aggregates, and, in time, it stabilizes the platelet aggregates by forming in the interstices between individual platelets. Platelet fibrinogen is believed to be the source of the intra-aggregate stabilizing fibrin network. Blood continues to flow until the ends of the severed vessels are occluded with a platelet thrombus. Its histogenesis has been technically difficult to determine, but it appears that, as the enlarging extravascular platelet aggregate sticks to collagen at the edge of the cut vessel, the intraluminal platelets are activated as they arrive in the flowing blood. An occlusive platelet thrombus forms that is a continuum of the wound thrombus. With this, bleeding stops. Many platelets are consumed in this whole process, yet only a few are involved in constructing the intravascular plug. The stability of the hemostatic plug can be tested with a secondary BT method.[14,18]

## Pathophysiological Basis of a Long BT

A normal BT reflects the prompt formation of an effective hemostatic plug. A prolonged BT implies a defective hemostatic plug and is caused by three main factors: (1) thrombocytopenia, (2) thrombocytopathy, and (3) deficient platelet-binding proteins needed for normal platelet function. Thrombocytopenia was demonstrated by Duke[1] in his original article to cause a long BT. Platelet counts of less than 100,000/$\mu$L result in a prolonged BT.[19] The predictable shortening of BT with platelet transfusion is directly related to the increased platelet count.[20] Platelet volume may be a factor in addition to platelet number. For example, small platelets in near-normal numbers as in Wiskott-Aldrich syndrome may be responsible for a long BT.[20] One could infer from recent data[21] that large platelets could compensate in part for reduced numbers to give a normal BT.

Thrombocytopathy may be either genetic or acquired. Glanzmann's thrombasthenia and Bernard-Soulier syndrome are examples of the genetic type of thrombocytopathy. As to acquired thrombocytopathy, the most common today seems to be drug induced, the aspirin platelet defect. This defect is caused by inhibition of cycloxygenase, the platelet enzyme needed for thromboxane production and related platelet aggregation. The aspirin defect develops within hours after ingestion of the drug and consistently causes a moderate prolongation of the BT, with return to normal in four days.[20] Use of a postaspirin BT procedure increases the sensitivity of the test.[22]

Disorders of platelet-binding proteins causing a long BT may also be genetic or acquired. Congenital afibrinogenemia and von Willebrand's (vW) disease are examples of genetic disorders. Examples of the acquired disorders are the hypofibrinogenemias associated with disseminated intravascular clotting, severe liver disease,[1] or defibrinogenation with snake venom enzymes. Other examples of acquired disorders are the autoimmune vW syndrome[23] and inhibitor vW disease,[24] with neutralization of indigenous or administered plasma vW factor, respectively.

## Hemostatic Plug Formation as a Receptor-Mediated Reaction

Defective hemostatic plug formation with normal platelet counts and long BT is caused by either thrombocytopathy or a platelet-binding protein deficiency. Mechanistically, these two general causes of a long BT are related because of the nature of the process by which platelets are activated and aggregated. An extraordinary variety of platelet-activating agents have been identified, including thromboxanes, thrombin, collagen, adenosine diphosphate (ADP), and specific lipids. Each activation-aggregation reaction acts through identified or putative glycoprotein (GP) membrane receptors.[25] Hemostatic plug formation can thus be viewed as the result of receptor-mediated reactions. Theoretically, it should be possible to analyze the quantitative and qualitative aspects of each reaction that contributes to hemostatic plug formation, assess its relative importance, and predict the results of the BT test. This state of affairs has not yet arrived, although it may not be far away. It is estimated that as many as 1,000 articles on platelets are published yearly, providing new insights into platelet function. The pathologies of two receptor-mediated reactions, one with fibrinogen, the other with vW factor, are indicative of the developing state of the art.

In the case of fibrinogen, it was shown years ago that external fibrinogen is an absolute requirement for ADP to aggregate platelets.[26] Today this reaction of ADP, fibrinogen, and platelets is viewed as consisting of multiple steps. Adenosine diphosphate with calcium ion first induces a fibrinogen receptor in the platelet membrane, followed by fibrinogen binding to platelets with formation of intraplatelet bridges and aggregation. The receptor has been identified as membrane GPs[27-29] known as the GP IIb/IIIa complex. Lack of either the receptor or fibrinogen results in a long BT. The receptor complex is missing in Glanzmann's disease[28] and may be inactivated in some forms of autoimmune thrombocytopenic purpura.[30] Indirect evidence suggests that the defect in the hemostatic plug is different in Glanzmann's disease, with receptor deficiency, and in congenital afibrinogenemia, with platelet-binding protein deficiency. In the former, with lack of receptor, fibrin is present but aggregates are missing.[31] In the latter, with lack of fibrinogen, platelet aggregates develop in abundance and in bizarre, giant forms but without the fibrin component.[32] Drugs such as ticlopidine hydrochloride may inhibit fibrinogen-platelet binding.[33]

In the case of vW factor, the platelet receptor[25] seems to be a single GP, GP Ib, which is deficient in Bernard-Soulier disease. Gram-negative organisms may inactivate this receptor protein,[34] and it is suggested that this mechanism could contribute to a long BT in sepsis. The platelet-binding or aggregating protein, vW factor, is part of the factor VIII macromolecular complex and is lacking in severe vW disease.[35] Several years ago, it was observed that transfusions of high-potency factor VIII concentrates in vW disease can normalize the platelet-aggregating vW factor activity of plasma but, unlike cryoprecipitate, do not correct the prolonged BT defect.[36] This enigma, the dissociation between the vW factor platelet-aggregating activity of plasma and the BT correction, has not been completely resolved. One hypothesis is that only the highest–molecular-weight (mw) multimers of the factor VIII complex contribute to formation of an effective hemostatic plug and, hence, a normal BT. The multimeric composition of the complex is ordinarily identified by immunoelectrophoresis, a time-consuming and expensive procedure. A recent discovery is that, with use of the two "activators," ristocetin and botrocetin, of the vW factor reaction with platelets, an index of the qualitative multimeric composition of the factor VIII complex can be obtained rapidly.[37] Ristocetin is active with the higher-mw multimers. Botrocetin is active with a full range of multimeric forms and could correlate with the values for factor VIII–related antigen. Thus, in variant vW disease type II with a long BT and lack of the high-mw multimers, the ristocetin test is weak or negative, but the botrocetin test is positive.[37,38]

## Prospects for the Future

Will the BT test continue to survive the test of time and remain an important method of evaluating platelet function in the years ahead? For an indication of the future, one might look at another global test for hemostatic integrity, the whole-blood clotting time. While important only a few years ago, today it has been supplanted by a triad of screening tests, the partial thromboplastin time, the prothrombin time, and the thrombin clotting time. As the intricacies of the fibrin clotting mechanism were more fully understood, more reliable information than that furnished by the whole blood clotting time was obtained by better methodology. The platelet hemostatic function has been more refractory to analysis than has been the fibrin clotting system. With the rapid progress now being made in platelet research, one should anticipate the importance of BT test receding as better and perhaps simpler methodologies become available. In thrombocytopenia,

a platelet count furnishes more precise information than the BT test.[19,20] Simple testing in a matter of seconds is now possible for qualitative and quantitative assessment of vW factor and its antibody inhibitor for diagnosis of vW disease and vW syndrome.[39,40] Simple and rapid testing for the integrity of the fibrinogen-GP IIb/IIIa reaction seems to be available through the thrombin clotting time as an index for fibrinogen and through ADP aggregation of platelets as an index of receptor function. Nevertheless, BT testing is still performing a valuable function in many clinical conditions such as the bleeding tendency in uremia with a normal platelet count[41] and with antibiotic therapy.[42] For the present, the BT test is not only surviving but is actually doing well, despite the onslaught of sophisticated research findings.

## On Citations

Thus, it is not surprising that this pivotal article by Duke on the BT test is consistently cited in the current literature each year, as documented in the *Science Citation Index*. An interesting sidelight is that many references to this article are wrong, all of them citing volume 14 instead of 55, indicating that the error was handed down from year to year, from author to author. With a little sleuthing and the data of the *Science Citation Index*, one can readily construct the tree of these perpetuated erroneous references. Such trees should be useful in emphasizing the importance of correct bibliographic citations.

This study was supported in part by grant HL-01648 from the National Institutes of Health. Margaret L. Gulley, junior medical student, University of North Carolina, Chapel Hill, assisted with the bibliographic studies. The author expresses his appreciation to John R. O'Brien, MD, Portsmouth and South East Hampshire District Pathology Service, St Mary's General Hospital, Portsmouth, United Kingdom, for the gift of the illustration.

## References

1. Duke WW: The relation of blood platelets to hemorrhagic disease: Description of a method for determining the bleeding time and coagulation time and report of three cases of hemorrhagic disease relieved by transfusion. *JAMA* 1910;55:1185-1192.
2. Brinkhous KM, Shermer RW, Mostofi FK (eds): *The Platelet.* Baltimore, Williams & Wilkins Co, 1971, p 388.
3. Spaet TH: Platelets: The blood dust, in Wintrobe MM (ed): *Blood Pure and Eloquent.* New York, McGraw-Hill Book Co, 1980, pp 549-571.
4. Debus AG: *World Who's Who in Science.* Chicago, Marquis Who's Who Inc, 1968, p 490.
5. Corner GW: *George Hoyt Whipple and His Friends.* Philadelphia, JB Lippincott Co, 1963.
6. Duke WW: The rate of regeneration of blood platelets. *J Exp Med* 1911;14:265-273.
7. Flexner S, Flexner JT: *William Henry Welch and the Heroic Age of American Medicine.* New York, Viking Press, 1941, p 303.
8. Whipple GH, Sperry JA: Chloroform poisoning: Liver necrosis and repair. *Johns Hopkins Hosp Bull* 1909;20:278-289.
9. Ivy AC, Shapiro PF, Melnick P: The bleeding time in jaundice. *Surg Gynecol Obstet* 1935;60:781-784.
10. Tocantins LM: The bleeding time. *Am J Clin Pathol* 1936;6:160-171.
11. Mielke CH Jr, Kaneshiro MM, Maher IA, et al: The standardized normal Ivy bleeding time and its prolongation by aspirin. *Blood* 1969;34:204-215.
12. Babson SR, Babson AL: Development and evaluation of a disposable device for performing simultaneous duplicate bleeding time determinations. *Am J Clin Pathol* 1978;70:406-408.
13. Bowie EJW, Owen CA Jr: The bleeding time. *Progr Hemost Thromb* 1974;2:249-271.

14. Copley AL, Lalich JJ: Bleeding time, lymph time, and clot resistance in men. *J Clin Invest* 1942;21:145-152.

15. Wester J, Sixma JJ, Geuze JJ, et al: Morphology of the early hemostasis in human skin wounds: Influence of acetylsalicylic acid. *Lab Invest* 1978;39:298-311.

16. Born GVR: Platelets in haemostasis and thrombosis, in Rotman A, Meyer FA, Gitler C, et al (eds): *Platelets: Cellular Response Mechanisms and Their Biological Significance.* Chichester, England, John Wiley & Sons Inc, 1980, pp 3-15.

17. Rodman NF Jr, Painter JC, McDevitt NB: Platelet disintegration during clotting. *J Cell Biol* 1963;16:225-241.

18. Borchgrevink CF, Waaler BA: The secondary bleeding time: A new method for the differentiation of hemorrhagic diseases. *Acta Med Scand* 1958;162:361-374.

19. O'Brien JR: The bleeding time in normal and abnormal subjects. *J Clin Pathol* 1951;4:272-285.

20. Harker LA, Slichter SJ: The bleeding time as a screening test for evaluation of platelet function. *N Engl J Med* 1972;287:155-159.

21. Thompson CB, Jakubowski JA, Quinn PG, et al: Platelet size as a determinant of platelet function. *J Lab Clin Med* 1983;101:205-213.

22. Stuart MJ, Miller ML, Davey FR, et al: The post-aspirin bleeding time: A screening test for evaluating haemostatic disorders. *Br J Haematol* 1979;43:649-659.

23. Meyer D, Frommel D, Larrieu MJ, et al: Selective absence of large forms of factor VIII/von Willebrand factor in acquired von Willebrand's syndrome: Response to transfusion. *Blood* 1979;54:600-606.

24. Sarji KE, Stratton RD, Wagner RH, et al: Nature of von Willebrand factor: A new assay and a specific inhibitor. *Proc Natl Acad Sci USA* 1974;71:2937-2941.

25. Phillips DR, Jennings LK, Berndt MC: Studies of inherited bleeding disorders to identify platelet membrane glycoproteins involved in adhesion and aggregation, in Sheppard JR, Anderson VE, Eaton JW (eds): *Membranes and Genetic Disease.* New York, Alan R Liss Inc, 1982, pp 151-163.

26. Brinkhous KM, Read MS, Mason RG: Plasma thrombocyte-agglutinating activity and fibrinogen: Synergism with adenosine diphosphate. *Lab Invest* 1965;14:335-342.

27. Leung LLK, Kinoshita T, Nachman RL: Isolation, purification, and partial characterization of platelet membrane glycoproteins IIb and IIIa. *J Biol Chem* 1981;256:1994-1997.

28. Howard L, Shulman S, Sadanandan S, et al: Crossed immunoelectrophoresis of human platelet membranes. *J Biol Chem* 1982;257:8331-8336.

29. Bennett JS, Vilaire G, Cines DB: Identification of the fibrinogen receptor on human platelets by photoaffinity labeling. *J Biol Chem* 1982;257:8049-8054.

30. van Leeuwen EF, van der Ven JTM, Engelfriet CP, et al: Specificity of autoantibodies in autoimmune thrombocytopenia. *Blood* 1982;59:23-26.

31. Cohen I, Gerrard JM, White JG: Ultrastructure of clots during isometric contraction. *J Cell Biol* 1982;93:775-787.

32. Rodman NF Jr, Mason RG, Painter JC, et al: Fibrinogen—its role in platelet agglutination and agglutinate stability. *Lab Invest* 1966;15:641-656.

33. Verstraete M: A pharmacological approach to the inhibition of platelet adhesion and platelet aggregation. *Haemostasis* 1982;12:317-336.

34. Cooper HA, Bennett WP, Kreger A, et al: The effect of extracellular proteases from gram-negative bacteria on the interaction of von Willebrand factor with human platelets. *J Lab Clin Med* 1981;97:379-389.

35. Hoyer LW: The factor VIII complex: Structure and function, in Menache D, Surgenor DM, Anderson H (eds): *Hemophilia and Hemostasis.* New York, Alan R Liss Inc, 1981, pp 1-26.

36. Blatt PM, Brinkhous KM, Culp HR, et al: Antihemophilic factor concentrate therapy in von Willebrand disease: Dissociation of bleeding-time factor and ristocetin-cofactor activities. *JAMA* 1976;236:2770-2772.

37. Brinkhous KM, Read MS, Fricke WA, et al: Botrocetin (venom coagglutinin): Reaction with a broad spectrum of multimeric forms of factor VIII macromolecular complex. *Proc Natl Acad Sci USA* 1983;80:1463-1466.

38. Howard MA, Salem HH, Thomas KB, et al: Variant von Willebrand's disease type B—revisited. *Blood* 1982;60:1420-1428.

39. Brinkhous KM, Read MS: Use of venom coagglutinin and lyophilized platelets in testing for platelet-aggregating von Willebrand factor. *Blood* 1980;55:517-520.

40. Brinkhous KM, Culp HR: Quantitation of von Willebrand factor and an antibody inhibitor. *Thromb Res* 1976;8(suppl 2):125-132.

41. Mannucci PM, Remuzzi G, Pusineri F, et al: Deamino-8-D-arginine vasopressin shortens the bleeding time in uremia. *N Engl J Med* 1983;308:8-12.

42. Weitekamp MR, Aber RC: Prolonged bleeding times and bleeding diathesis associated with moxalactam administration. *JAMA* 1983;249:69-71.

Jan 21, 1911
(JAMA 1911;56:198)

## Chapter 9

# Transmission of a Malignant New Growth by Means of a Cell-Free Filtrate*

### Peyton Rous, M.D.

#### New York

A tumor of the chicken, histologically a spindle-celled sarcoma, has been propagated in this laboratory since October, 1909,[1] and in the past few months has developed extreme malignancy.[2] From a bit inoculated into the breast muscle of a susceptible fowl there develops rapidly a large, firm growth; metastasis takes place to the viscera; and within four to five weeks often the host dies. The behavior of the new growth has been throughout that of a true neoplasm, for which reason the fact of its transmission by means of a cell-free filtrate assumes exceptional importance.

### EXPERIMENTS

For the first experiments on the point use was made of ordinary filter-paper and the ground tumor suspended in Ringer's solution. It was supposed that the slight paper barrier, which allows the passage of a few red blood-cells and lymphocytes, would suffice to hold back the tumor and render the filtrate innocuous. Such has been the experience of other workers with mouse and dog tumors. But in the present instance characteristic growths followed the inoculation of small amounts of the watery filtrate, and followed also the inoculation of the fluid supernatant after centrifugalization of a tumor emulsion.

These results led to more critical experiments, which will be here detailed. Tumors of especially rapid growth and young, well-grown, barred Plymouth Rock fowls were used throughout.

EXPERIMENT 1.—Tumor material from the breast of Chicken 92 (tumor generation 6 A) was ground with sterile sand, suspended in a considerable bulk of Ringer's solution, and shaken for twenty minutes in a machine. The sand and tumor fragments were separated out by centrifugalization in large tubes for five minutes at 2,800 revolutions per minute. Of the supernatant fluid a little was pipetted off, and this centrifugalized anew for fifteen minutes at over 3,000 revolutions per minute. From the upper layers sufficient fluid for inoculation was now carefully withdrawn. The pure-bred fowls were injected in one breast with 0.2 c.c. of the fluid, in the other with a small bit of tumor tissue. All developed sarcoma at the site of this latter inoculation, and in seven the same growth slowly appeared at the point where the fluid had been injected.

EXPERIMENT 2.—Tumor from Chicken 90 (tumor generation 6 A) was ground, suspended, and shaken as before. But after one centrifugalization the fluid was passed through a Berkefeld filter No. 2 (coarse). Before filtration, it was pinkish-yellow, cloudy; afterwards, faintly yellow, limpid. Nine fowls were inoculated with 0.2 c.c. of the filtrate in each breast, and twenty-two more received filtrate in one breast, a bit of tumor in the other. Of the nine, one slowly developed a sarcoma in each breast, and later microscopic growths were found in its lungs. Of the twenty-two receiving both filtrate and tumor, five developed sarcoma where the filtrate had been injected, and these five showed especially large growths from the tumor bit.

The Berkefeld filter employed was later found slightly pervious to *Bacillus prodigiosus*.

EXPERIMENT 3.—The filtrate was similarly prepared except that a small Berkefeld filter (No. 5 medium), impermeable to *Bacillus prodigiosus*, was used. As before, the filtration was done at room temperature. Fowl 124 (generation 7 A) furnished the material. Twenty chickens were inoculated in each breast with the filtrate, but none have developed tumors.

EXPERIMENT 4.—In this experiment the material was never allowed to cool. About 15 gm. of tumor from Chicken 140 (generation 7 B) was ground in a warm mortar with warm sand, mixed with 200 c.c. of heated Ringer's solution, shaken for thirty minutes within a thermostat room, centrifugalized, and the fluid passed through a filter similar to that used in Experiment 3. Both before and after the experiment, this filter was found to hold back *Bacillus prodigiosus*. The filtration of the fluid was done at 38.5 C., and its injection immediately followed. In four of ten fowls inoculated with the filtrate only

* From the Laboratories of the Rockefeller Institute for Medical Research.

1. Jour. Exper. Med., 1910, xii. 696.

2. Rous, Peyton: Metastasis and Tumor Immunity: Observations with a Transmissible Avian Neoplasm, THE JOURNAL A M. A., Nov. 19, 1910, p. 1805.

(0.2 to 0.5 c.c. in each breast) there has developed a sarcoma in one breast; and though the growths required several weeks for their appearance their enlargement is now fairly rapid. Pieces removed at operation have shown the characteristic tumor structure.

## CHARACTERS OF THE TUMOR

As has been pointed out, the special significance of these results lies in the growth's identity as a tumor. The original sarcoma was found as a unique instance in a flock of healthy fowls; and, though susceptible normal chickens and others with the tumor have since been kept together in close quarters for long periods, no instance suggesting a natural infectivity of the growth has occurred. When inoculated, it is at first a local disease, very dependent on the good health of the host. At this time intercurrent illness of the fowl will check the nodule's growth or even cause it transiently to disappear. For long the sarcoma could be transferred only to fowls of the same pure-bred variety in which it arose, and this only in an occasional individual; but like many tumors, it has gained on repeated transplantation a heightened malignancy, and the power to grow in other varieties of the same animal. Yet in these it does not do well; and it has not been successfully transplanted to other species.

Histologically, the growth has always consisted of one type of cells, namely, spindle-cells in bundles, with a slight, supporting, connective tissue framework. The picture does not in the least suggest a granuloma; and cultures from the growth remain sterile as regards bacteria. At the edge of the invading mass there is often practically no cellular reaction, but lymphocytes in small number may be present, as is common with tumors in general. Metastasis takes place early, through the blood-stream, and the secondary nodules have the same character as the primary. Several instances of the sarcoma's direct extension into vessels have been encountered. The secondary growths are distributed especially to the lungs, heart and liver, and in the last organ are sometimes umbilicated. The host becomes emaciated, cold and drowsy, and shortly dies.

Transplantation experiments with the tumors resulting from the filtrate are at present under way. The tumor of Experiment 2, which arose in the fowl that received filtrate alone, has already been successfully transplanted.

Sixty-Sixth Street and Avenue A.

Sept 16, 1983
(JAMA 1983;250:1447-1449)

# The Rous Sarcoma Virus*

Henry C. Pitot, MD, PhD

Francis Peyton Rous was a pathologist who received his clinical training as a medical student under William Osler at the Johns Hopkins Medical School and his training in pathology with Warthin at the University of Michigan and with Schmorl in Dresden, Germany. Like many physicians of that time, he contracted the occupational disease of pathologists, tuberculosis, first as a medical student during an autopsy; the resultant tuberculous axillary gland was later excised. Following his postgraduate training in pathology, pulmonary tuberculosis developed, which necessitated a period in the New York Adirondack Mountains for recovery.

Rous had initially desired to be a botanist or a writer and, in fact, had given evidence of these inclinations during his early teens. After the death of his father, his mother rejected the idea of joining her family in Texas; instead, she chose to stay in Baltimore, where there were excellent educational opportunities for her two daughters and son, Peyton. As circumstances would have it, he entered Johns Hopkins University on a scholarship and then went to the Medical School. After his training in pathology and his bouts with tuberculosis, he had an opportunity to work at the Rockefeller Institute in New York under Simon Flexner in the then relatively embryonic field of cancer research. This decision was opposed by some of his influential friends, one of whom told him, "Whatever you do, don't commit yourself to the cancer problem."[1]

### Then

Medical science in the 19th century had seen the dramatic discovery of the infectious nature of disease. However, at the time of the publication of the first description of the successful (and later demonstrably reproducible) transmission of a solid tumor by a cell-free filtrate,[2] many allegedly carcinogenic agents — noncellular, bacterial, or protozoan — had been described by medical and biological scientists.[3] Several years earlier, Ellerman and Bang[4] had demonstrated that a leukemia in chickens was transmissible by some subcellular component. However, this discovery excited no great interest in relation to cancer research, since leukemias at that time were not regarded as necessarily related to cancer.[1]

The year before the initial publication of the cell-free transmission of this sarcoma,[2] Rous[5] published a description of the chicken sarcoma and its transplants, the tumors from which the cell-free filtrates were obtained. The original sarcoma was found to occur spontaneously in a Plymouth Rock chicken of "pure blood." Direct transplantation, originally to blood relatives and later in the same strain of chickens, proved fairly easy, and the primary tumors metastasized rapidly, resulting in the death of the hosts within four to five weeks. Possibly because of the rapid growth of the neoplasm, Rous attempted the transmission of the tumor by cell-free filtrates. His attempt to transmit the neoplasm by cell-free extracts, a procedure that had previously been tried with negative results in many carcinomas and sarcomas, indicated the scientific curiosity of Peyton Rous.

His first description of the cell-free transmission of the sarcoma, published in THE JOURNAL in 1911,[2] was soon followed by a more complete description published in the *Journal of Experimental Medicine*.[6] These now classic findings were contrary to the then-current views about cancer, and medical opinion in general remained skeptical despite the fact that a number of investigators confirmed Rous' findings within the next few years (eg, Fujinami's description of a sarcoma in 1915). In fact, for years afterwards, pathologists refused to consider that the discovery was even relevant to the problem of cancer. The fact that Fibiger's studies (for which he received the Nobel Prize in 1927) on the causation of stomach cancer in rats by a parasitic worm, published shortly after Rous' articles,[2,6] were later found to be incorrect did not enhance the idea of the infectious nature of neoplasia.[7] Even when Shope[8] in 1932 demonstrated a viral causation for a papilloma in rabbits, skepticism continued. It was not until 1951 and the discovery of Gross[9] that leukemia could be transmitted in mice by inoculation of newborn animals with cell-free extracts of the neoplasm from mice of the AKR strain that medical scientists and investigators seriously began to consider the possibility that viruses could be a

---

From the McArdle Laboratory for Cancer Research, Medical School, University of Wisconsin, Madison.

*A commentary on Rous P: Transmission of a malignant new growth by means of a cell-free filtrate. *JAMA* 1911;56:198.

significant cause of cancer, at least in lower animals if not in the human being.

## Now

Today, the scientific fruits of Dr Rous' publication of Jan 1, 1911, are truly remarkable. The impact of this discovery in the field of cancer research has few peers in the scientific literature of oncology, and the ramifications of a number of the discoveries that resulted from Rous' work have had far-reaching effects in such fields as genetics, molecular biology, virology, and even botany. Fortunately, the scientific community recognized the importance of Rous' contributions by awarding him, together with Charles Huggins, the Nobel Prize in Physiology or Medicine in 1966.

Following the demonstrated significance of viruses in the induction of tumors in animals in the early and mid-1950s, Temin and Rubin[10] showed in 1958 that cultured cells from chick embryos could be infected with the Rous sarcoma virus, such infection resulting in foci of morphologically changed or transformed cells. This seminal discovery was at the forefront of numerous subsequent demonstrations of viral, chemical, and radiation-induced focal transformation in cultured cells. In 1964, on the basis of studies on chicken cells transformed by the Rous sarcoma virus in cell culture, Temin[11] proposed that the replication of and the transformation induced by Rous sarcoma virus involved a stable DNA intermediate. This proposal required the then heretical process of RNA acting as a template for the synthesis of DNA.

Just as with Rous' original finding, published in 1911, Temin's proposal met with skepticism and, at times, even open ridicule. The validity of Temin's proposal was proved by him and his associate, Mizutani,[12] and almost simultaneously by Baltimore[13] in 1970 when they announced the discovery of an enzyme, present in the virion of the Rous sarcoma virus, that catalyzed the synthesis of DNA from an RNA template.

The enzyme, known as an RNA-directed DNA polymerase (or, colloquially, as reverse transcriptase), has now been purified and characterized from several sources and its activity demonstrated in all known RNA oncogenic viruses, which are today termed *retroviruses.*[14] In addition to our greater understanding of the nature of cell transformation from knowledge of the intracellular function of reverse transcriptase, the enzyme has become invaluable for transcribing RNA molecules into DNA copies, which are then used in recombinant DNA studies, especially in higher organisms.

Even before the dramatic demonstration of reverse transcriptase by Temin and Mizutani[12] and by Baltimore,[13] Huebner and Todaro[15] proposed that cells of all vertebrate species contain genomes of RNA tumor viruses, termed *virogenes,* which are vertically transmitted from parent to offspring and contain oncogenes. Although genetic evidence for the virogene concept was demonstrated for a specific leukemia-susceptible strain of mice, the AKR strain of mice,[16] little evidence was found at that time for generalizing this hypothesis. At about the same time that Huebner and Todaro proposed the virogene-oncogene hypothesis, Temin[17] proposed the protovirus hypothesis, suggesting that, within normal cells, precursors of retroviruses (protoviruses) occurred that could give rise through transcription and reverse transcription to a DNA molecule that could be incorporated into the genome. Almost prophetically, Temin also theorized that such protoviruses might be similar to "controlling elements" (today termed *transposons*) that occur in maize, bacteria, and *Drosophila.*

Evidence to support both of these theories was soon reported. Following the demonstration of the physical and genetic structure of the genome of the Rous sarcoma virus, Erikson and colleagues[18] identified the product of the gene, termed *src,* whose presence in the virus was required for transformation to the neoplastic state. They showed that this gene product was a protein kinase and, most important, that normal cells possess an almost identical enzyme, transcribed from a cellular gene whose coding sequences were almost identical with those of the viral *src* gene. Since then, genes responsible for transformation have been found in virtually all highly oncogenic RNA viruses. Such genes have been termed *onc* genes. Their cellular homologues, remarkably conserved in normal cells throughout evolution, have also been described.[19]

The present findings tend to support both the oncogene and protovirus hypotheses. The structures of the transforming genes of the highly oncogenic retroviruses are different from their cellular homologues in that most of the latter, like cellular genes in eukaryotes, possess introns — large segments of DNA inserted into the coding region of the gene itself — such introns having no known informational content, and that cellular *onc* genes are not linked to virogenes. The recent demonstration that cellular *onc* genes may be transfected into susceptible cells and transform them from a low to a high level of malignancy[20] underscores the importance of such genes in the conversion of normal to neoplastic cells, probably not only when they are in viruses but also as a result of other carcinogenic agents, such as chemicals and radiation.

## The Future

These are exciting times in basic cancer research and in biology in general. Rous died in 1970 before he could fully see and appreciate the fruits of his discovery, first announced in THE JOURNAL.[2] Although his studies and discoveries were immediately directed toward an understanding of the neoplastic transformation, his work was that of a naturalist in the truest sense. The ramifications of his findings are numerous today and promise to be extended much further in the future. Surely his article, published in THE JOURNAL in 1911, marked the beginning of a new era in biology that, like so many important discoveries, took years to be appreciated and exploited. In a sense, the future can be described by excerpts from a letter written by Rous in 1962[21]: "It's a dreamy life without any dreams other than itself . . . like a bee asleep in a corolla . . . that bee seems to have waked up."

Professor Howard Temin, PhD, read the manuscript critically before its submission for publication, and Ilse Riegel, PhD, helped in its preparation.

# References

1. Andrewes CH: Francis Peyton Rous 1879-1970. *Biogr Mem Fellows R Soc* 1971;17:643-662.

2. Rous P: Transmission of a malignant new growth by means of a cell-free filtrate. *JAMA* 1911;56:198.

3. Wolff J: Die Lehre von der Krebskrankheit von den ältesten Zeiten bis zur Gegenwart. Jena, East Germany, G. Fischer, 1907, vol 1, pp 519-721.

4. Ellerman V, Bang O: Experimentelle Leukämie bei Hühnern. *Z Hyg Infekt* 1909;63:231.

5. Rous P: A transmissible avian neoplasm. (Sarcoma of the common fowl.) *J Exp Med* 1910;12:696-705.

6. Rous P: A sarcoma of the fowl transmissible by an agent separable from the tumor cells. *J Exp Med* 1911;13:397-410.

7. Clemmensen J: Johannes Fibiger – gongylonema and vitamin A in carcinogenesis. *Acta Pathol Microbiol Scand* 1978;270:1-55.

8. Shope RE: A transmissible tumor-like condition in rabbits. *J Exp Med* 1932;56:793-800.

9. Gross L: Spontaneous leukemia developing in C3H mice following inoculation, in infancy, with AK-leukemic extracts, or AK-embryos. *Proc Soc Exp Biol Med* 1951;76:27-32.

10. Temin HM, Rubin H: Characteristics of an assay for Rous sarcoma virus and Rous sarcoma cells in tissue culture. *Virology* 1958;6:669-688.

11. Temin HM: The participation of DNA in Rous sarcoma virus production. *Virology* 1964;23:486-494.

12. Temin HM, Mizutani S: RNA-dependent DNA polymerase in virions of Rous sarcoma virus. *Nature* 1970;226:1211-1213.

13. Baltimore D: RNA-dependent DNA polymerase in virions of RNA tumour viruses. *Nature* 1970;226:1209-1211.

14. Gallo RC: RNA-dependent DNA polymerase in viruses and cells: Views on the current state. *Blood* 1972;39:117-137.

15. Huebner RJ, Todaro GJ: Oncogenes of RNA tumor viruses as determinants of cancer. *Proc Natl Acad Sci USA* 1969;64:1087-1094.

16. Kozak CA, Rowe WP: Genetic mapping of the ecotropic murine leukemia virus–inducing locus of BALB/c mouse to chromosome 5. *Science* 1979;204:69-71.

17. Temin HM: Malignant transformation of cells by viruses. *Perspect Biol Med* 1970;14:11-26.

18. Erikson RL, Purchio AF, Erikson E, et al: Molecular events in cells transformed by Rous sarcoma virus. *J Cell Biol* 1980;87:319-325.

19. Bishop JM: Oncogenes. *Sci Am* 1982;246:81-92.

20. Cooper GM: Cellular transforming genes. *Science* 1982;217:801-806.

21. Huggins C: Peyton Rous: In memoriam 1879-1970. *Perspect Biol Med* 1970;13:465-468.

Dec 7, 1912
(*JAMA* 1912;59:2015-2020)

# Chapter 10

# Clinical Features of Sudden Obstruction of the Coronary Arteries

James B. Herrick, M.D.

Chicago

Obstruction of a coronary artery or of any of its large branches has long been regarded as a serious accident. Several events contributed toward the prevalence of the view that this condition was almost always suddenly fatal. Parry's writings on angina pectoris and its relation to coronary disease, Jenner's observations on the same condition centering about John Hunter's case, Thorvaldsen's tragic death in the theater in Copenhagen with the finding of a plugged coronary, sharply attracted attention to the relation between the coronary and sudden death. In Germany Cohnheim supported the views of Hyrtl and Henle as to lack of considerable anastomosis, and as late as 1881 lent the influence of his name to the doctrine that the coronary arteries were end-arteries; his Leipsic necropsy experience, as well as experiments on dogs, forced him to conclude that the sudden occlusion of one of these vessels or of one of the larger branches, such as the ramus descendens of the left coronary, meant death within a few minutes. Others emphasized the same view.

No one at all familiar with the clinical, pathologic or experimental features of cardiac disease can question the importance of the coronaries. The influence of sclerosis of these vessels in the way of producing anemic necrosis and fibrosis of the myocardium, with such possible results as aneurysm, rupture or dilatation of the heart, is well known. So also is the relation of the coronaries to many cases of angina pectoris, and to cardiac disturbances rather indefinitely classed as chronic myocarditis, cardiac irregularities, etc. It must be admitted, also, that the reputation of the descending branch of the left coronary as the artery of sudden death is not undeserved.

But there are reasons for believing that even large branches of the coronary arteries may be occluded—at times acutely occluded—without resulting death, at least without death in the immediate future. Even the main trunk may at times be obstructed and the patient live. It is the object of this paper to present a few facts along this line, and particularly to describe some of the clinical manifestations of sudden yet not immediately fatal cases of coronary obstruction.

Before presenting the clinical features of coronary obstruction, it may be well to consider certain facts that go to prove that sudden obstruction is not necessarily fatal. Such proof is afforded by a study of the anatomy of the normal as well as of the diseased heart, by animal experiment and by bedside experience.

The coronaries are not so strictly end-arteries, i. e., with merely capillary anastomoses, as Cohnheim and others thought. By careful dissections, by injection of one artery from another, by skiagraphs of injected arteries and by direct inspection of hearts made translucent by special methods, there is proof of an anatomic anastomosis that is by no means negligible.

Jamin and Merkel's† beautiful stereoscopic skiagrams show the remarkably rich blood-supply of the heart, with occasional anastomoses between vessels of considerable size. The possibility of injection of one coronary artery from the other is admitted even by those who deny that

---

†Jamin and Merkel: Die Koronararterien des menschlichen Herzens in stereoskopischen Röntgenbildern, Jena, 1907. Extensive bibliographies are contained in the articles by Thorel (Lubarsch-Ostertag's Ergebnisse, ix, Abt 1), and in Amenomiya Virchows Arch. f. path. Anat., 1910, cxcix, 187). I repeat only some of the more important references and add new ones.

such injection proves more than a capillary non-functioning anastomosis. Amenomiya,[1] by injecting hearts of young persons, showed naked-eye anastomoses in the subepicardial tissue. He feels that Hirsch and Spalteholz[2] have nearly cleared up the question as to the relation between the heart muscle and disease of the coronary artery from the anatomic standpoint. Hirsch says that in dogs the anastomosing vessels are functionally competent, and Spalteholz says that in man the vessels are nearly the same as in dogs, rich in anastomoses even in those of considerable caliber. The latter investigator, by a method of injection and treatment of the heart so as to make the muscle transparent, shows to the naked eye that there are anastomoses of considerable size.

Among others who are on record as believing that there are non-negligible anastomoses may be mentioned Haller, Huchard, Orth, Michaelis, Langer, Legg, West. All recognize, however, that there are individual differences, and also that though the heart may show rich anastomoses, these are not necessarily functional, i. e., that an artery which anatomically is not a terminal artery may yet be such functionally.

But there is proof not only of anatomic connection between the two coronaries, but that in certain instances, at least, such connection is of functional value. Experiments on lower animals and the clinical experiment of disease of the coronaries with autopsy findings show this.

Much of the earlier experimental work on the lower animals, obstructing the coronary arteries by ligatures, clamps or artificial emboli, gave promptly fatal result. Among those who worked along this line and reached these conclusions may be mentioned Erichsen (1842), Panum (1862), von Bezold, Samuelson (1880), Cohnheim and Schulthess-Rechberg (1881), G. Sée, Roche-Fontaine and Roussy (1881), Bettelheim (1892), Kronecker, and, to some extent, Michaelis. The work of Cohnheim[3] attracted particular attention and his conclusions as to end-arteries, irreparable injury, and cessation of the beat of both sides of the heart within two minutes from the time of shutting off the coronary circulation confirmed and elaborated the conclusions of the earlier experimenters, and was in turn confirmed by the French writers just named, by Bettelheim and others.

But soon dissent was heard from various quarters as to many of Cohnheim's results, and among other things as to the sudden death following the ligations. Michaelis found that the injury from ligation in rabbits was not so serious or irreparable as in dogs. Fenoglio and Drouguell, in 1888, found that some dogs might live. Porter showed that after ligation of one or two large branches of the coronary artery a dog might live hours or days. More than half his animals lived after ligation of the descending branch of the left coronary. Von Frey, at the

Congress for Internal Medicine in 1891, said that he doubted the sudden stopping of the heart as Cohnheim taught; he believed that clearly the greater weight should attach to these observations in which the ligation was borne without harm; and that the stopping of the heart was not a necessary consequence of the obstruction of a large coronary branch. Hirsch in eight dogs and two apes had no sudden deaths from ligation. Bickel,[4] under Orth and Amenomiya, had a dog live nineteen days after the ligation of the descending branch of the left coronary; he killed two dogs, one on the eighth and the other on the seventeenth day after ligation. Kölster ligated smaller branches; his dogs lived, and when killed at intervals of several weeks showed the progressive changes of fibrosis of the myocardium. Imperfect technic, by which damage was done to the heart muscle and pneumothorax produced, is offered as a partial explanation, at least, for the more rapidly fatal results obtained by Cohnheim and others. Miller and Matthews[5] call attention to the better results where ether as an anesthetic is employed rather than curare or other drug. With ether they were able to ligate large branches, many of their dogs living several weeks.

Experimentally, then, sudden death, even late death, is not a necessary consequence of obstruction of even large branches, such as the descending branch of a coronary artery.

There are numerous autopsy observations, frequently with helpful clinical history, that show directly or by inference the existence of efficient anastomoses, and the ability of the heart at times to survive the obstruction of a coronary or some large branch. Some of these instructive cases may be mentioned. Pagenstecher, on account of an accident, ligated the descending branch of the left coronary artery and the patient lived five days. Thorel has seen hearts with complete obstruction of the artery, with fibrous or calcified myocardium, and yet no symptoms during life, the patient dying of some other disease. I have seen the descending branch completely occluded with an extensive fibrous area in the interventricular septum and at the apex, the latter aneurysmally dilated, where the process was clearly one of long standing. West[6] cites several cases in which at autopsy complete obstruction of one coronary was found, yet the patients had long survived this serious lesion.

Chiari, in a 32-year-old nephritic, found a sclerosed right coronary plugged by a thrombus, with resulting scattered patches of myomalacia cordis in the areas supplied by this artery. A portion of this thrombus had become detached and had embolically plugged the left coronary, resulting in sudden death. From the symptoms and the autopsy findings the thrombus in the right artery had formed at least two days before. The fact that the softened patches in the myocardium were scattered, with normal tissue between, and that the heart functionated fairly well until the left artery also was obstructed, leads Chiari to infer that anastomoses must exist between the

---

1. Amenomiya: Ueber die Beziehungen zwischen Koronararterien und Papillarmuskeln im Herzen, Virchows Arch. f. path. Anat., 1910, cxcix. 187.

2. Hirsch and Spalteholz: Koronararterien und Herzmuskel, Deutsch. med. Webnschr., 1907, No. 20.

3. Cohnheim and Schulthess-Rechberg: Ueber die Folgen der Kranzarterienverschliessung für das Herz, Virchows Arch. f. path. Anat., 1881, lxxxv, 503.

4. Cited by Amenomiya (See Note 2).

5. Miller and Matthews: Effect on the Heart of Experimental Obstruction of the Left Coronary Artery, Arch. Int. Med., June, 1909, p. 476.

6. West: Tr. Path. Soc., London, 1882, xxxiv, 67.

right and left coronaries. Merkel[7] drew the same inference as to anastomoses from the patchy character of the lesions in the heart of a woman of 76 years, there being normal muscle between the softened areas. The left coronary was the seat of the obstruction. He also saw in a man of 37 the left coronary closed, with nourishment through the right artery. Dock[8] in a case of gradual occlusion of the right coronary artery was able to demonstrate a direct opening of the finger branches of the left coronary into the end of the right.

Spalteholz says that we all know cases of stoppage of large vessels without large infarcts resulting. Recklinghausen and Fujinami found this condition in man, as Hirsch had in dogs and monkeys; i. e., smaller infarcts than the distribution of the vessel would lead one to expect. Galli saw complete closure of the entrance to the right coronary artery yet no change in the myocardium. By injection he found a round-about anastomosis between the right and left coronary arteries. Samuelson cites the case of a patient living five hours after obstruction, Huber one of a patient living several days. Aschoff and Tawara[9] saw a patient live fourteen days, "with nearly complete infarction of the parietal wall of the left ventricle." In several cases of angina pectoris cited by Huchard[10] the patients lived many hours after the onset of the final attack, which autopsy showed was due to a thrombotic closure of an artery. Osler refers to the fact that the patient may live for some time after obstruction. Krehl expressly states that in man the more or less sudden occlusion of an entire coronary artery, or at least a large branch, such as the descending branch, is compatible with a continuance of life.

One may conclude, therefore, from a consideration of the clinical histories of numerous cases in which there has been careful autopsy control, from animal experiments and from anatomic study, that there is no inherent reason why the stoppage of a large branch of a coronary artery, or even of a main trunk, must of necessity cause sudden death. Rather may it be concluded that while sudden death often does occur, yet at times it is postponed for several hours or even days, and in some instances a complete, i. e., functionally complete, recovery ensues.

The clinical manifestations of coronary obstruction will evidently vary greatly, depending on the size, location and number of vessels occluded. The symptoms and end-results must also be influenced by blood-pressure, by the condition of the myocardium not immediately affected by the obstruction, and by the ability of the remaining vessels properly to carry on their work, as determined by their health or disease. No simple picture of the condition can, therefore, be drawn. All attempts at dividing these clinical manifestations into groups must be artificial and more or less imperfect. Yet such an attempt is not without value, as it enables one the better to understand the gravity of an obstructive accident, to

differentiate it from other conditions presenting somewhat similar symptoms, and to employ a more rational therapy that may, to a slight extent at least, be more efficient.

The variations in the results are to be accounted for in part by variations in the freedom with which anastomosing branches occur. Presumably, too, symptoms will vary with the vessel or branches occluded. It is conceivable that with occlusion of the right coronary the symptoms might be different from those following obstruction of the left artery; systemic edema might be a consequence of the former condition and pulmonary edema of the latter. These points are, however, by no means settled either by experimental or clinical observation. The condition of the remaining vessels as to patency and presence of sclerosis must play an important part in deciding how much they are capable of doing in the way of compensatory nutrition to the anemic myocardium; the strength of the heart itself, as determined, perhaps, by old valvular or myocardial disease, would also have its influence. And presumably a sudden overwhelming obstruction, with comparatively normal vessels, would be followed by a profounder shock than the gradual narrowing of a lumen through sclerosis which has accustomed the heart to this pathologic condition and has perhaps caused collateral circulation through neighboring or anastomosing vessels to be compensatorily increased. The influence of the vessels of Thebesius is also not to be overlooked in this connection; compensatory circulation through these accessory channels may be of considerable importance in nourishing areas of heart muscle poorly supplied by sclerotic or obstructed arteries.

Attempts to group these cases of coronary obstruction according to clinical manifestations must be more or less unsatisfactory, yet, imperfect as the groups are, the cases may be roughly classified.

One group will include cases in which death is sudden, seemingly instantaneous and perhaps painless. Krehl[11] has emphasized the peculiarities of the sudden death of this type, the lack of terminal respiratory agony, of distortion of the features, of muscular contractions.

A second group includes those cases in which the attack is anginal, the pain severe, the shock profound and death follows in a few minutes or several minutes at the most.

In a third group may be placed non-fatal cases with mild symptoms. Slight anginal attacks without the ordinary causes (such as walking), perhaps some of the stitch pains in the precordia, may well be due to obstruction of small coronary twigs. Such an interpretation of these phenomena is, however, only a surmise based on the fact that other causes for the pains are lacking and that the patchy fibrosis of the myocardium that is later found at autopsy may have originated in obstruction of the sclerotic vessels; and such obstruction in small vessels may well have produced symptoms differing chiefly in degree from those caused by obstruction of larger arteries of the heart.

In a fourth group are the cases in which the symptoms

7. Merkel, H.: Ueber den Verschluss der Kranzarterien des Herzens, Festschrift für Rosenthal, Leipsic, 1906.

8. Dock, George: Notes on the Coronary Arteries, Ann Arbor, 1896.

9. Aschoff and Tawara: Die heutige Lehre von deu pathologisch-anatomischen Grundlagen der Herzschwäche, p. 56, Jena, 1906.

10. Huchard: Traité clinique des maladies du coeur, Second Edition, p. 560.

11. Krehl: Der Vetschluss der Kranzarterien; in Nothnagel's System, xv, 369.

are severe, are distinctive enough to enable them to be recognized as cardiac, and in which the accident is usually fatal, but not immediately, and perhaps not necessarily so. It is to the clinical features of this group that attention is directed in what follows.

By way of introduction, I give in outline the history of a case, experience with which acutely attracted my attention to this subject.

CASE 1.—*History.*—A man, aged 55, supposedly in good health, was seized an hour after a moderately full meal with severe pain in the lower precordial region. He was nauseated and, believing that something he had just eaten had disagreed with him, he induced vomiting by tickling his throat. The pain continued, however, and his physician was called, who found him cold, nauseated, with small rapid pulse, and suffering extreme pain. The stomach was washed out and morphin given hypodermically. The pain did not cease until three hours had passed. From this time the patient remained in bed, free from pain, but the pulse continued rapid and small, and numerous râles appeared in the chest. When I saw him twelve hours from the painful attack his mind was clear and calm; a moderate cyanosis and a mild dyspnea, were present. The chest was full of fine and coarse moist râles; there was a running, feeble pulse of 140. The heart tones were very faint and there was a most startling and confusing hyperresonance over the chest, the area of heart dulness being entirely obscured. The abdomen was tympanitic. The urine was scanty, of high specific gravity, and contained a small amount of albumin and a few casts. The temperature was subnormal, later going to 99 F. Occasionally there was nausea and twice a sudden projectile vomiting of considerable fluid material. This condition remained with slight variations up to the time of death, fifty-two hours after the onset of the pain, though at one time the râles seemed nearly to have disappeared. A few hours before death the patient described a slight pain in the heart region, but said it did not amount to much. A remarkable circumstance, and one that occasioned surprise in those who saw the patient and who realized from the almost imperceptible pulse and the feeble heart tones how weak the heart must be, was the fact that he frequently indulged in active muscular effort without evident harm. He rolled vigorously from side to side in the bed, sat suddenly bolt upright, or reached out to take things from the table near by; and once, feeling a sudden nausea, he jumped out of bed, dodged the nurse and ran into the bathroom, where he vomited; and yet he seemed none the worse for these exertions.

*Necropsy* (Dr. Hektoen).—The heart was of normal size, but both coronary arteries were markedly sclerotic, with calcareous districts and narrowing of the lumen. A short distance from its origin the left coronary artery was completely obliterated by a red thrombus that had formed at a point of great narrowing. The wall of the left ventricle showed well-marked areas of yellowish and reddish softening, especially extensive in the interventricular septum. At the very apex the muscle was decidedly softer than elsewhere. The beginning of the aorta showed a few yellowish spots, these areas becoming less marked as the descending part was reached. An acute fibrinous pericardial deposit, which showed no bacteria in smears, was found over the left ventricle. (The pericarditis probably explains the slighter pain complained of a few hours before death.) There was marked edema of the lungs. In other respects the anatomic findings were those of health.

A colleague personally related to me the case of a man of 60 who three days after a severe anginal seizure, felt well enough to walk on the street, though with some dyspnea. He died suddenly on the fifth day. The obstruction in the left coronary, and the muscular

softening found at autopsy were similar to those in the case just described.

Since my attention has been called to this condition, I have seen five other cases that I am convinced were instances of coronary thrombosis, the patients living many hours after the accident, though no autopsy control confirms this opinion. All were men beyond 50. In all there was some evidence of peripheral arteriosclerosis; all had had previous anginal attacks. In all the final attack was described as the severest and most prolonged in the experience of the patient. Morphin alone had given relief. In all the sudden development of a weak pulse, with feeble cardiac tones, was a striking feature; the pulse was generally rapid. Dyspnea and cyanosis varied in degree. Râles, moist and dry, were usually present. Emphysema was present to a moderate degree in two of the five. Only one patient left his bed after the attack. His pulse showed great improvement as to quality and rate, though dyspnea, râles, edema of the legs, albumin, increased area of cardiac dulness, etc., showed failure of the heart muscle. From the time of the seizure, i. e., the time of the obstruction, to death was in one case three days, in one seven, in two twelve, and in one, twenty days.

One of these cases is, it seems to me, a typical one of this sort and, though necropsy is lacking, I venture to give the history.

CASE 2.—The patient was a man of 65, of exemplary habits. His health had been good up to three years before, when he noticed at times a tight feeling in the precordia on walking. For the past three months typical anginal seizures often compelled him to stop after walking two or three blocks. Three days before he had had a moderately severe angina. Thirty-six hours before I first saw him, in the night he made a noise, awakening his wife. For a few seconds he was, perhaps, unconscious. He complained of unbearably severe pain in the upper stomach region; the pain did not radiate. He was nauseated and belched gas freely. His physician saw him inside of twenty minutes and gave sodium bicarbonate, which was vomited. The pain continuing, a hypodermic injection of morphin was necessary. The patient was pale, covered with cold sweat and had a small, rapid pulse. His appearance was that of collapse. His distress seemed to him largely abdominal.

When I saw him his color had returned and he was ruddy-cheeked. He complained of extreme weakness. His mind was clear. There was a little cyanosis, and respiration was somewhat labored. There were numerous râles in the chest. The pulse was 110 and small. The heart tones were faint; there was no murmur. The heart was a trifle enlarged, as it had been for some years. The area of cardiac flatness was decidedly small on account of overlying lung. The liver dulness was but a narrow band along the costal margin; the edge of the liver could be palpated. No spleen could be made out. The urine contained a distinct ring of albumin and a few granular and hyaline casts. There was a doubtful faint trace of bile. On digalen and nitroglycerin there seemed to be some improvement in the quality of the pulse.

At a second visit the condition was much the same. There had been a few periods of more marked oppression in breathing, with some increase in cyanosis and weakness of the pulse.

At a third visit, Oct. 19, 1910, it was learned that the patient had had a bad night, with severe attacks of dyspnea. The pulse had been but barely perceptible at the wrist and beat 120 to the minute. At 5 a. m. both the physician and the patient himself had felt that death was at hand. The patient had rallied, however, and when I saw him was conscious, with very feeble pulse of 110, and barely perceptible heart tones. He was extremely weak. Breathing was of the Cheyne-Stokes type. The patient seemingly dozed during apnea, yet answered questions. What I took to be a faint pericardial friction could be made out over the lower left sternal border. The patient said he was not in pain. He declared that he obtained relief from swallowing orange juice, which he repeatedly sipped. He remained in this condition for sixteen hours longer. From the onset of his severe anginal attack to death was seven days.

The instructive case of Professor Panum is described by Fraentzel.[12] For a few weeks Panum had noticed dyspnea and a tight feeling on going up stairs. May 1, 1885, coming home in the wind, he stopped often, and on reaching home had a sudden, severe, tearing pain in the precordia, running out to the left arm and fingers. The pulse became rapid, small and irregular. The patient broke out into a profuse sweat. He was nauseated and induced vomiting by tickling his throat. The physical findings are not accurately known. The mind was clear to the last. Death occurred suddenly about fourteen hours after the onset of symptoms. At the necropsy both upper lobes of the lungs and the middle lobe were found emphysematous. The left coronary artery was atheromatous, narrowed, and a white soft thrombus was attached to the wall. The musculature of the left ventricle was degenerated and softened and had ruptured just to the left of the septum.

Engelhardt[13] describes the case of a man of 51 in whom, after a thrombosis of the left coronary artery with suddenly developing gastric and abdominal symptoms, there was an illness of eight days, with fever, meteorism, vomiting, oppression, and then in a tachycardial attack rupture of the anterior wall of the left ventricle, with hemopericardium. Death twelve hours after the rupture. The symptom-complex resembled the picture of the abdominal-pectoral vascular crises (Pal).

A study of cases of this type shows that nearly all are in men past the middle period of life. Previous attacks of angina have generally been experienced, though, as shown by my first case, the fatal thrombosis may bring on the first seizure. The seizure is described by patients who have had previous experience with angina as of unusual severity, and the pain persists much longer. In some instances there has been no definite radiation of the pain, as to the neck or left arm, though this may have been a feature of other anginal attacks, and the pain, as in these two cases, may be referred to the lower sternal region or definitely to the upper abdomen. Cases with little or no pain have been described. In Chiari's case pain is not referred to, the patient though with slow, irregular and weak pulse being out of bed. The obstruction of the right coronary was, as Chiari says, "so to speak, latent." Thorel also refers to a painless case. Some of Huchard's cases with obstruction did not show anginal pain. Nausea and vomiting, with belching of gas, are common. There may be tympany. Ashy countenance, cold sweat and feeble pulse complete the picture of collapse. The attention of the patient and the physician as well may, therefore, be strongly focused on the abdomen, and some serious abdominal accident be regarded as the cause of the sudden pain, nausea, collapse. The cardiac origin may be the more easily overlooked when there has been no previous typical angina, and when, as may happen (Case 1), there is no arteriosclerosis manifested peripherally and no enlargement of the heart to be made out.

Cohnheim found that in dogs the pulse after obstruction was slow. This may be so in the thrombotic obstruction of disease in man. In Hammer's case[14] the pulse dropped from 80 to 8 per minute, the patient living thirty hours from the onset of the symptoms that marked the closure of the right coronary opening. A rapid pulse is frequently seen however. The pulse may be irregular. A striking feature has been its weakness. In two patients I have seen a rapid, thready, almost imperceptible, radial pulse, of such a quality that if met with in pneumonia or typhoid fever it would have warranted one in presaging death within a few minutes or hours. Yet one patient lived forty hours and another four or five days with a pulse of this quality. Blood-pressure is low. The heart tones have been feeble—in fact, often startlingly feeble. Feeble contraction of the weakened, anemic heart muscle accounts for the weak pulse and the weak tones. Still another reason for the faint tones is found in the acute emphysema—*Lungenschwellung* and *Lungenstarrheit* of von Basch—by which condition the heart sounds are obscured by overlapping air-containing lungs. This also makes it difficult to map out the outlines of the heart and, coupled with the feeble apex impulse, may make such an examination for the size of the heart very unsatisfactory.

Dyspnea and cyanosis have been variable, at times much less than one would expect from the character of the accident and the quality of the heart's action. Râles, dry and moist, have been present in many cases, in some, as in my first case, largely moist, diffuse, not very large. Here there was a moderate amount of thin, frothy, slightly blood-tinged fluid expectorated, as in edema of the lungs, which condition was found at the autopsy. I mention this because some, with Cohnheim, contended that the conditions for edema would not be produced by coronary obstruction, as both right and left heart ceased beating simultaneously. Others, e. g., Samuelson, Bettelheim and Michaelis, found edema. My case shows such edema. Possibly the right heart may have remained relatively stronger than the left after the accident, and so Welch's condition for edema has been presented.

The weakness of the heart and the low blood-pressure will account for the scanty urine and the trace of albumin. A palpable liver may likewise owe its enlargement to passive congestion.

Nearly always the mind is clear—at times unusually clear—until toward the last. Some patients seem conscious, as is so common in angina, that they are face to face with death, but in none that I have seen has there been uncontrollable fear or the restlessness of fright. The seriousness of the accident seemed to be realized, but there was no panic. Perhaps the relief from the agony of the initial pain causes an unnatural mental calmness.

General weakness has been marked in some cases, in

---

12. Fraentzel: Krankheiten des Herzens, Berlin, 1892, iil, 51.

13. Engelhardt: Ein Fall von Herzruptur, Deutsch. med. Wchnschr., xxxv, 1919, No. 19, p. 838.

14. Hammer: Wien. med. Wchnschr., 1878, No. 5.

others not. One patient showed for more than a week an asthenia comparable to that of the terminal stage of pernicious anemia or Addison's disease. He hesitated to move in bed for the further reason that even turning on the side caused him the sensation as though the heart were giving out. Even slight movement caused some pain. His case is representative of the type of status anginosus. Obrastzow regards this as the usual manifestation of coronary thrombosis. My experience shows that such obstruction may be followed by a complete cessation of pain for hours, and even to the time of death. Some of these patients of the latter type will, if permitted, move freely or even get out of bed.

The occurrence of a serofibrinous exudate over the area of myocardial softening, with roughening of the pericardium, has been noted in several instances. This may explain a later precordial distress, as in Case 1. A fine pericardial friction, therefore, occurring several hours or a few days after the initial pain, may be confirmatory evidence of coronary obstruction. Osler[15] concluded, in one of his cases of angina, that the attack was probably associated with acute infarct of the ventricle, "as a pericardial rub was detected the next day." Dock[8] recognized this pericarditis *intra vitam* in one of his cases and found it post mortem over the softened area. In one of Leyden's cases in which the patient lived five days from the onset of symptoms of dizziness, faintness, small pulse, there was found myomalacia cordis, and especially at the apex, where a softened area reached to the surface, there was pericarditis; cloudy fluid was in the pericardial sac. This was almost certainly a case of coronary obstruction, though the occluding lesion is not described. This pericarditis is in keeping with some of the experimental work on lower animals, e. g., that of Bickel, who in his dogs killed nineteen and seventy days after ligation found localized pericarditic adhesions over the area representing the myocardial softening.

Death is the result in nearly all of these cases. Yet it may be delayed for many days. More than this, there is, as has been shown by reference to experimental work, no intrinsic reason why some patients with obstruction of even large branches of the coronary artery may not recover. Experimental animals sometimes do. And, as already said, mild cases must occur, and one cannot pretend to say where the dividing line should be drawn between the mild obstruction of a coronary branch, whose recovery means a few fibrous patches in the myocardium, and the more serious one that in a few days is to lead to rupture of the heart or is to produce an extensive weakened fibrous area that will ultimately yield in cardiac aneurysm. Death may then be caused by rupture, by sudden asystole, or by gradual giving out of the weakened heart muscle—by "ingravescent systole," as Balfour[16] styles it—a mode of death occupying from half an hour to a week, illustrated by one of his cases in which death occurred one week after the obstruction, which was found post mortem. In one instance in which I

believe the anginal seizure was thrombotic a dilatation of the heart, with orthopnea, dropsy, etc., followed the seizure. Death here was, as in cardiac failure, from other causes. Some of the dogs of Miller and Matthews died in this way several weeks after the ligation of the coronary. In cases in which the heart slowly wears out in the course of a few days, Cheyne-Stokes respiration, general asthenia, urinary scantiness, with mental apathy and exhaustion may be present.

Emphasis ought to be laid on the resemblance of some of these cases to surgical accidents. The sudden onset with pain over the lower sternal and epigastric region, the nausea and vomiting, the tympany, the feeble pulse, ashy color, cold sweat and other signs of collapse make one think of such conditions as gall-bladder disease, acute hemorrhagic pancreatitis, perforation of gastric or duodenal ulcer, hemorrhage into the adrenal capsule, etc. The dyspnea, hyperresonant thorax, obscured heart tones, may suggest pneumothorax or diaphragmatic hernia. In my first case, while the diagnosis made was that of cardiac accident, there were so many disquieting features that surgical counsel was called to make sure that some surgical accident, such as those enumerated, had not been overlooked. Details as to differential diagnosis need not be given. Where there is arteriosclerosis, enlarged heart, a history of previous angina, typical radiation of the pain to the neck and arm, the diagnosis will not be so difficult as where these suggestive aids are lacking. The bilateral character of the emphysema, the persistence of breath sounds, often with râles, the failure of the heart to be dislocated, will help exclude pneumothorax and diaphragmatic hernia. The absence of blood from the vomitus, the absence of peritonitic tenderness, a study of the temperature, the leukocytes, etc., will help in excluding subdiaphragmatic accidents.

Obrastzow[17] calls particular attention to this resemblance to surgical accidents which my own experience corroborates. Engelhardt's case also illustrates this point.

If these cases are recognized, the importance of absolute rest in bed for several days is clear. It would also seem to be far wiser to use digitalis, strophanthus or their congeners than to follow the routine practice of giving nitroglycerin or allied drugs. The hope for the damaged myocardium lies in the direction of securing a supply of blood through friendly neighboring vessels so as to restore so far as possible its functional integrity. Digitalis or strophanthus by increasing the force of the heart's beat, would tend to help in this direction more than the nitrites. The prejudice against digitalis in cases in which the myocardium is weak is only partially grounded in fact. Clinical experience shows this remedy of great value in angina, and especially in cases of angina with low blood pressure, and these obstructive cases come under this head. The timely use of this remedy may occasionally in such cases save life. Quick results should also be sought by using it hypodermically or intravenously. Other quickly acting heart remedies would also be of service.

122 South Michigan Avenue.

15. Osler: Lumleian Lectures on Angina Pectoris, Lancet. London. March 12 and 26, and April 9, 1910.

16. Balfour: Clinical Lectures on Diseases of the Heart, Edition 3, 1898, pp. 316 and 328.

17. Obrastzow and Straschesko: Zur Kenntniss der Thrombose der Koronararterien des Herzens, Ztschr. f. klin. Med., 1910, lxii, 116.

Oct 7, 1983
(*JAMA* 1983;250:1763-1765)

# Obstruction of the Coronary Arteries— Herrick's Vision*

J. Willis Hurst, MD

Herrick carefully leads his readers paragraph by paragraph to the conclusions he wishes to teach. Accordingly, I will discuss his classic article paragraph by paragraph.

**Paragraph 1.**—Herrick sets the stage by pointing out that the prevailing view in 1912 was that sudden occlusion of a coronary artery meant death in a few minutes. This view was supported by autopsy studies, by experimental work on dogs, and by famous physicians of the time. Herrick also points out that several famous persons believed that the coronary arteries were end arteries and were not capable of anastomosing with other vessels.

Herrick then states that such concepts are incorrect.

**Paragraph 2.**—Herrick emphasizes the importance of sclerosis of the coronary arteries and lists all the complications of the disease that we know today, including chronic myocarditis, which we now call "ischemic cardiomyopathy." He points out that disease of the left anterior descending coronary artery deserves its reputation of causing sudden death.

Herrick makes certain, as he emphasizes that sudden obstruction of a coronary artery may not cause death, that no one assumes that he does not appreciate the seriousness of the disease.

**Paragraph 3.**—Herrick emphasizes that there are reasons for doubting the prevailing views and that he intends to present facts to prove that even large branches of the coronary arteries can be occluded without resulting in death in the immediate future. He also tells the readers that he will describe the clinical features of the disorder to guide them in their day-to-day work.

From the Department of Medicine, Emory University School of Medicine, Atlanta.

*A commentary on Herrick JB: Clinical features of sudden obstruction of the coronary arteries. *JAMA* 1912;59:2015-2020.

**Paragraphs 4 Through 8.**—Paragraphs 4 through 8 deal with a question that raged at the time: Are the coronary arteries end arteries or not? Are they able to form anastomotic connections that are larger than capillaries? Herrick then gives data, both experimental and clinical, that he believes prove that anastomotic connections do develop and that in certain instances such connections are of functional value.

**Paragraphs 9 Through 15.**—Paragraphs 9 through 15 contain Herrick's analysis of the experimental and clinical data that led him to believe that sudden obstruction of a coronary artery can occur without immediate death.

He points out that famous earlier workers concluded that sudden obstruction of a coronary artery caused sudden death in experimental animals. Dissent occurred because other workers found that sudden obstruction of a coronary artery did not always cause death and that results varied according to the experimental animal that was used.

Herrick indicated that there were many autopsy studies that showed "directly or by inference the existence of efficient anastomoses, and the ability of the heart at times to survive the obstruction of a coronary or some large branch." The best proof was when Pagenstecher ligated the descending branch of the left coronary artery and the patient lived five days. The patient had been in an accident. Herrick goes on to give examples of obstruction of a coronary artery, but he does not always state the nature of the obstruction. He does, however, include an example of coronary thrombosis.

He again states in paragraph 15 that sudden obstruction of a coronary artery is serious, that it can lead to sudden death but does not invariably do so.

**Paragraphs 16 Through 38.**—The content of paragraph 16 intrigues me because of my own personal interest. Herrick points out the many variables that influence the clinical manifestations of coronary obstruction. What he states is still true today. He then makes his case for the creation of subsets of the condition. He states:

All attempts at dividing these clinical manifestations into groups must be artificial and more or less imperfect. Yet such an attempt is not without value, as it enables one the better to understand the gravity of an obstructive accident, to differentiate it from other conditions presenting somewhat similar symptoms, and to employ a more rational therapy that may, to a slight extent at least, be more efficient.

Herrick's capacity to think is shown in paragraph 17, where he writes:

And presumably a sudden overwhelming obstruction, with comparatively normal vessels, would be followed by a profounder shock than the gradual narrowing of a lumen through sclerosis which has accustomed the heart to this pathologic condition and has perhaps caused collateral circulation through neighboring or anastomosing vessels to be compensatorily increased.

He then describes the characteristics of four subsets of patients with sudden obstruction of the coronary arteries and presents the clinical data related to two cases. In case 1 he states that the obstructed artery was blocked by a red thrombus. He also relates that a colleague had seen a similar patient. He states that he had seen five other patients who lived many hours after what he thought was coronary thrombosis, but he did not have autopsy proof of the presence of a "red thrombus."

He also describes other case reports in which a white thrombus was found at autopsy.

He highlights in paragraph 37 that the attention of the patient and the physician may be focused on the abdomen and that some serious abdominal accident may be regarded as the cause of sudden pain, nausea, or collapse. He lists the abdominal disorders that are often thought to be present, such as "gall-bladder disease, acute hemorrhagic pancreatitis, perforation of gastric or duodenal ulcer, hemorrhage into the adrenal capsule, etc." He describes what we now call "completed infarct," right ventricular and left ventricular infarcts, and many other currently appreciated clinical features of myocardial infarction.

**Paragraph 39.**—Herrick's comments in the last paragraph show that his predictions were not always correct. Here, to give the practitioner some method of dealing with the serious consequences of sudden obstruction of the coronary arteries, he champions the use of digitalis rather than nitrates. He has no data on the subject but reasons that digitalis would, by increasing the force of contraction, increase the "supply of blood through friendly neighboring vessels so as to restore so far as possible [the] functional integrity" of the myocardium. Admittedly, the value of digitalis in patients with myocardial infarction is still debated today, but, during the last decade, the beneficial role of nitrates has gained in popularity compared with the use of digitalis.

### Herrick's Impact

Herrick, who saw clearly and wrote beautifully, taught us three things in his 1912 article on sudden obstruction of the coronary arteries.

• The coronary arteries are capable of anastomosing with other neighboring vessels. Herrick labeled these collateral vessels "friendly vessels." He concluded that the collateral vessels were larger than capillaries. Any coronary arteriographer knows that now, but Herrick knew it before arteriography was dreamed of.[1-3]

• Herrick pointed out the wisdom of creating a taxonomy consisting of subsets of coronary disease in which the characteristics of the subset are carefully defined so that therapy can eventually be linked to the specific subset. We have made progress in this area. A simple clinical taxonomy includes asymptomatic disease, sudden death, stable angina, unstable angina, Prinzmetal's angina, prolonged myocardial ischemia without evidence of infarction, and prolonged myocardial ischemia with evidence of infarction (the latter is further divided into evolving infarct, completed infarct, complicated infarct, and uncomplicated infarct).[4] Obviously, the subsets can be further refined by considering the results of the ECG and radionuclide stress tests, coronary arteriography, and left ventriculography. The failure to understand the analysis of coronary disease according to subsets results in the lay press' and many physicians' failure to understand that the treatment of coronary disease can seldom be stated in general terms. For example, there are subsets of coronary disease that are benefited by coronary bypass surgery and other subsets that are not.

• Before Herrick's article, the prevailing view was that sudden obstruction of a coronary artery led to death within minutes. He cited examples in which the sudden obstruction was caused by coronary thrombosis. He pointed out that death did not always occur immediately and that patients could live for hours, days, months, or years. He furthermore gave the possible scientific reasons why such variability in survival could occur. There appear to be several pathophysiological pathways to the development of myocardial infarction, and these mechanisms are being actively studied today.[5-7]

The impact of Herrick's brilliant presentation in 1912 was minimal. Herrick was disappointed with the reception the profession gave his views on the subject of sudden obstruction of coronary arteries. Richard Ross, in his address on Herrick at the annual meeting of the American Heart Association in November 1982, quoted Howard Means' account of the comments of my friend, Worth Daniels, on Herrick's 1912 presentation. He wrote:

Dr. Worth B. Daniels of Washington asked Dr. Herrick to what he had attributed the long lag between the 1912 paper and the general ability of the profession to make the diagnosis of obstruction of the coronary arteries. Herrick replied, "You know I've never understood it. In 1912 when I arose to read my paper at the Association, I was elated, for I knew I had a substantial contribution to present. I read it, and it fell flat as a pancake. No one discussed it except Emanuel Libman, and he discussed every paper read there that day. I was sunk in disappointment and despair."[8]

The failure to hear a clear voice is common when little can be done about a problem. Widespread interest seems to depend on the ability of physicians at large to change the direction of a patient's clinical course. In other words, there is a tendency to ignore new information until the information can be used to alter treatment in a favorable way. As a rule, a few persons keep working until an idea or concept is moved from the intellectual arena to the practical arena.

Many years passed, and as they passed, more and more physicians began to diagnose coronary thrombosis. The ECG was introduced into day-to-day practice, and later the measurement of cardiac enzymes was used to diagnose myocardial infarction. Even today, however, patients along with physicians may assume that the pain of coronary obstruction may be "indigestion" and are surprised to discover it is caused by ischemia of the heart.

A debate still exists as to whether coronary thrombosis is the cause or the result of infarction and whether it is always present in myocardial infarction. The debate as to the frequency of thrombosis identified at angiography and the frequency of thrombosis found at autopsy in patients with myocardial infarction is an important one and is not settled. New subsets of infarction include evolving infarction and completed infarct, and, as Herrick

suggested, different treatment may be indicated in the two different subsets.

Today, intracoronary streptokinase infusion,[9,10] coronary angioplasty,[11] and coronary bypass surgery[12] are available to apply or not to apply to patients with "sudden obstruction of the coronary arteries." Such patients are labeled as having an evolving infarction when the diagnosis is made within a few hours of the onset of chest pain. Accordingly, numerous physicians are interested in whether the obstruction is caused by atheromatous plaques alone, atheromatous plaques plus thrombosis, or coronary spasm with or without thrombosis and atheromatous plaques, since the pathogenesis of the infarct might determine the method and success of treatment.

Herrick's views are undoubtedly studied more now than they were when his article was published. The excitement we feel now was started when an elated Herrick walked to the podium in 1912. Few heard him then, but many people hear him now.[13]

## References

1. Kirk ES, Jennings RB: Pathophysiology of myocardial ischemia, in Hurst JW (ed): *The Heart,* ed 5. New York, McGraw-Hill Book Co, 1982, pp 976-1008.

2. Gregg DE, Patterson RE: Functional importance of the coronary collaterals. *N Engl J Med* 1980;303:1404-1406.

3. Kirk ES, Hirzel HO: The critical role of coronary collateral blood flow in the pathophysiology of myocardial infarction, in Kaltenbach M, Lichtlen P, Balcon R, et al (eds): *Coronary Heart Disease.* Stuttgart, West Germany, Georg Thieme Verlag, 1978, pp 11-21.

4. Hurst JW, King SB III, Walter PF, et al: Atherosclerotic coronary heart disease: Angina pectoris, myocardial infarction, and other manifestations of myocardial ischemia, in Hurst JW (ed): *The Heart,* ed 5. New York, McGraw-Hill Book Co, 1982, pp 1009-1149.

5. Ridolfi RL, Hutchins GM: The relationship between coronary artery lesions and myocardial infarcts: Ulceration of atherosclerotic plaques precipitating coronary thrombosis. *Am Heart J* 1977;93:468-486.

6. DeWood MA, Spores J, Notski R, et al: Prevalence of total coronary occlusion during the early hours of transmural myocardial infarction. *N Engl J Med* 1980;303:897-902.

7. Mathey DG, Kuck KH, Tilsner V, et al: Nonsurgical coronary artery recanalization after acute transmural myocardial infarction. *Circulation* 1981;63:489-497.

8. Means JH: *Association of American Physicians: Its First 75 Years.* New York, McGraw-Hill Book Co, 1961, p 316.

9. Rentrop P, Blanke H, Karsch KR, et al: Acute myocardial infarction: Intracoronary application of nitroglycerin and streptokinase. *Clin Cardiol* 1979;2:354-363.

10. Rentrop P, Blanke H, Karsch KR, et al: Selective intracoronary thrombolysis in acute myocardial infarction and unstable angina pectoris. *Circulation* 1981;63:307-317.

11. Gruentzig AR: Technique of percutaneous transluminal coronary angioplasty, in Hurst JW (ed): *The Heart,* ed 5. New York, McGraw-Hill Book Co, 1982, pp 1904-1908.

12. Hurst JW, King SB III, Logue RB, et al: Value of coronary bypass surgery: Controversies in cardiology: Part 1. *Am J Cardiol* 1978;42:308-329.

13. Hurst JW: The Canterbury tales and cardiology. *Circulation* 1982;65:4-6.

Jan 30, 1915
(*JAMA* 1915;64:425-426)

# Chapter 11

# Sodium Citrate in the Transfusion of Blood[*]

Richard Weil, M.D.

New York

Blood mixed in proper proportions with a solution of sodium citrate does not clot, owing to the well-known fact that the calcium salts are no longer available for coagulation. Such blood may be kept for many days in the ice-box, without losing its oxygenating function. After one week the cells show little change under the microscope, and very slight reduction in the resistance to toxic physical or biologic agencies. After a few days there is merely some tinging of the supernatant fluid. Experimentally, I have found that guinea-pigs or dogs may be practically exsanguinated, and can then be rapidly restored by venous transfusion of citrated blood, even if the blood is several days old. No unpleasant reactions occur. Human patients have been treated in the same way, receiving in various cases amounts ranging from 10 to 350 c.c. of citrated blood. The blood was used fresh in some instances; and in others, it was from three to five days old. Such injections are perfectly well borne and produce no apparent disturbance of any kind except a transient rise of temperature and polyuria.

The method is simple. Blood is aspirated from a vein and is at once well mixed with sodium citrate in 10 per cent. solution in water, in the proportion of 1 c.c. of solution to 10 c.c. of blood. Exceptionally one encounters blood which requires slightly more or less citrate proportionately. Preliminary tests, 0.1 c.c. of the solution to 0.5 c.c., 1 c.c. and 2 c.c. of blood, respectively, being used, enable one to determine rapidly the requisite proportions in any individual instance. If the mixture is made in the syringe, in cases in which not more than 50 c.c. are to be transfused, the transfer can be made directly from donor to donee. If larger amounts are to be used, the blood is expelled into a flask, from which the injecting syringes are filled. In drawing the blood, it is convenient to use a three-way stop-cock which communicates with the needle, with a 10 c.c. syringe containing the citrate, and with a large aspirating syringe.

The same method has been used for direct transfusion in dogs. The needles are introduced into the veins of donor and donee, and are both connected by a T-shaped tube with a syringe. An accessory syringe permits of the injection of the citrate solution into the tubing between the syringe and the donor's needle. The blood is alternately aspirated and expelled, the direction of the current being controlled by two stop-cocks. The apparatus is very simple, and requires the help of only one assistant.

A possible objection is based on the influence of the sodium citrate on the coagulation time of the donee. This has been tested for me in a series of cases by Dr. Beck of the General Memorial Hospital. The figures indicate that the introduction of large amounts of 20 per cent. sodium citrate solution do not lower the coagulation time in the least. In fact 5 gm. of sodium citrate reduces the coagulation time by one-half. The tests have been made on blood aspirated from the vein immediately before, and ten minutes after the injection. It gradually returns to normal.

The uses of this method require little discussion. For the frequent injection of small amounts of blood, it offers obvious advantages. For the direct transfer of large amounts, it may be compared with the method introduced by Satterlee and Hooker. It has, however, the obvious advantage that sodium citrate is always easily obtainable, which is not the case with hirudin. The fact that the blood can be kept on hand for some days may be of value in cases of threatened hemorrhage, as in gastric ulcer, or typhoid. Indeed, its effect on coagulation time indicates its use in hemorrhagic conditions. Essentially, the method is similar to the old method which relied on the use of defibrinated blood. It is, however, simpler than this, and avoids the effects attributed to the presence of fibrin ferment in the defibrinated blood. The possible disadvantages connected with its use can be determined only by prolonged observation.

In selecting the blood to be transfused, it has been customary to mix the serum and the cells of donor and donee in varying proportions, in order to avoid the dangers resulting from agglutination or hemolytic effects. I have found it quite satisfactory to use the following method for the purpose: The citrated bloods of the two individuals are mixed in narrow tubes as follows, three tests being made: One c.c. of each; 0.1 c.c. of one, to 0.9 c.c. of the other, and vice versa. After incubation for one hour, agglutination may easily be determined. Hemolysis is disclosed by the color of the upper layer, if the cells have settled sufficiently; if not centrifugation is required. This method is much less elaborate than that at present in use, but has the advantage that it preserves the natural conditions.

---

[*]From the General Memorial Hospital.

970 Park Avenue.

Oct 14, 1983
(*JAMA* 1983;250:1902-1904)

# Preserving Blood*

### Herbert A. Perkins, MD

More than 11 million pints of blood are deposited in blood banks in the United States each year, and the resulting components are generally available in the quantity needed. Physicians can order blood transfusions with as little effort as they order aspirin tablets. It was not always that easy. Weil's[1] article on the use of citrate to collect blood for transfusion provided the basis for establishment of blood banks, but the story began long before his work and it continues to evolve at an ever-accelerating rate.

Blood banks could not be established, of course, until means to store blood were developed. Two things were required: maintaining the blood in a liquid state and preserving the ability of the red cells to circulate and function in the recipient after transfusion. Unless transfused red blood cells are viable, they leave the circulation of the recipient almost immediately. Adult red cells in the circulation have lost their nuclei, but they are still capable of the complex reactions required for membrane integrity. They derive their energy from adenosine triphosphate (ATP) synthesized by the glycolytic cycle. Current red cell preservative solutions are intended to provide optimal amounts of glucose, phosphate, and adenine for the generation of ATP. Anticoagulation is accomplished by binding calcium to citrate. In the almost 70 years since Weil's article, no better or safer anticoagulant has been discovered.

### The Background for Weil's Work

The story of blood transfusion begins in 1616 with Harvey's report on the circulation of the blood. The first transfusion of blood into a human being was done by Denys in Paris in 1667, using the blood of a lamb. The first patient escaped with his life, but a subsequent recipient died, and transfusion fell into disrepute.

The era of blood transfusions into human patients really began in 1818 when the English physician and obstetrician, Blundell, reported the resuscitation of a moribund patient by transfusion of human blood. Further studies by Blundell and confirmation by others permanently established blood transfusions as an effective form of therapy, but the complexity and dangers of the procedure drastically limited its use.

Initial attempts to collect blood for transfusion withdrew donor blood into syringes or basins using a variety of cannulas. The blood was then transfused as fast as possible (before it could clot) into a donor vein using a funnel or syringe. Many of the efforts of the almost 100 years between Blundell and Weil were devoted to inventing complicated devices in an attempt to simplify a most difficult procedure. Considerable impetus to transfusion therapy was given in 1902 by Carrel with his method of direct anastomosis of blood vessels, approximating endothelial linings. This approach, uniting a donor artery to a recipient vein, eliminated clotting problems, but it was awkward and was soon replaced by a technique that substituted cannulas and connecting tubing. Either of these approaches had the distinct disadvantage that there was no way of determining the amount of blood transferred from donor to recipient.

This concern led to a further adaptation in which a syringe was attached via a T-connection to the tubing connecting donor and recipient veins. Temporary clamps or valves ensured that the blood went in the desired direction. Quantitation of transfused blood was again possible, but coagulation was again a major problem. Attempts to avoid clotting made serial use of large numbers of small syringes and required three to four persons to carry out the procedure.[2] This was the situation when Weil began his studies.

Attempts to keep the blood liquid had begun within a few decades of Blundell's report. Deliberate defibrination of blood was used for many years and was defended as safe by a number of transfusionists, but continuing controversy suggests that undesirable side effects were

From the Irwin Memorial Blood Bank of the San Francisco Medical Society.

*A commentary on Weil R: Sodium citrate in the transfusion of blood. *JAMA* 1915;64:425-426.

seen. Weil's article comments on the dangers of infusing fibrin ferment (activated clotting factors) into the patient. Presumably he was aware that this could potentiate intravascular coagulation.

Further attempts to overcome coagulation consisted of addition of chemicals including sodium bicarbonate, sodium phosphate, and ammonia.[3] Oxalate was tested in dogs in 1891, and in 1908-1909, Lespinasse used hirudin, peptone, and sodium citrate, rejecting them all on the grounds that they were too toxic.[4]

### The Weil Article (and Others)

In 1914, four independent investigators proved that citrate was, indeed, a safe anticoagulant under appropriate conditions. This discovery was rated by DeGowin et al[5] as "perhaps next in importance to the discovery of" the ABO blood groups in the development of transfusion therapy. (See also Chapter 15.)

The first report of a successful transfusion of citrated blood into a human patient was from Albert Hustin[6] in Belgium, published in May 1914. DeBakey[3] wrote that he had a copy of the progress notes of the recipient showing that the citrated blood had been transfused in March 1914. The second case report was from Luis Agote in Argentina,[7] and reference to this appeared in the *New York Herald* on Nov 14, 1914. Agote's case report was printed in January 1915; Weil[1] and Richard Lewisohn[8] published during the same month.

The four reports give no indication that the investigators had all been stimulated to try citrate by the same previous publications. Hustin referred to the "well-known" work of Gengou on sodium citrate, but Lewisohn stated that he had been unable to find any reference to the use of citrate in contemporary publications and that he had discovered Hustin's report in the Belgian literature only after his work was done. Lewisohn also credits Weil with describing his findings at a Dec 17, 1914, meeting of the Academy of Medicine. Weil's brief report casts no light on the stimuli that led him to investigate citrate. Rosenfield[9] believes that the report of Agote's work in the *New York Herald* prompted Lewisohn and Weil to rush into print. Clearly, however, their work must have been done when they saw that news item.

All four of these investigators began their studies because of the problems with clotting that occurred with the direct blood transfusion techniques in use. Hustin and Agote showed only that citrate could be safely used to delay coagulation of donor blood long enough so that direct transfusion could be easily accomplished. Hustin's technique was not very practical, since he was of the opinion that donor blood must be diluted with large volumes of both sodium citrate and dextrose to achieve sufficient prolongation of coagulation. Lewisohn made further contributions. He was concerned about previous reports of citrate toxicity. Recognizing that some patients would require transfusion of large volumes of blood, he carefully determined the minimum concentration of citrate required to keep blood from clotting for several hours. By the time of Lewisohn's second more complete report,[2] he had given 22 patients transfusions in the relatively brief period of two months.

Weil went one giant step beyond the others. He showed that blood collected into sodium citrate could be safely transfused and would be effective after storage for several days. Guinea pigs and dogs were practically exsanguinated and then rapidly restored with citrated blood that, in some experiments, was several days old. Weil also gave human patients blood stored up to three to five days in volumes of 10 to 350 mL. It was the ability to store blood for transfusion, not the easing of problems of direct transfusion, that made the use of citrate so important.

### Who Was Weil?

Richard Weil was born in New York City on Oct 15, 1876. He received his AB from Columbia University in 1896 and graduated from the College of Physicians and Surgeons in 1900. Postgraduate education was obtained in New York, Vienna, and Strasbourg. He joined the faculty of Cornell Medical College in 1905 and eventually became the head of its Department of Experimental Medicine. He also became a member of the staffs of the German Hospital, Mount Sinai Hospital, and the Huntington Fund for Cancer Research. His article on citrate for blood transfusion was from the General Memorial Hospital (now Memorial Center for Cancer and Allied Diseases).

Weil contributed more than 60 articles to the literature on clinical and experimental medicine, primarily in areas related to the serology of cancer and general problems of immunity, but his most practical contribution and the one for which he is best known was the article under discussion. Weil died of influenzal pneumonia in 1917, only a couple of years after that publication.

### Early Progress in the Use of Citrate

The studies of Weil were rapidly followed by further advances. In an article accepted for publication on Sept 15, 1915, Rous and Turner[10] carefully explored means to prolong the in vitro survival of red blood cells, making the extremely important observation that addition of dextrose to the citrate allowed blood to be stored far longer without spontaneous hemolysis. They attributed the benefit to an osmotic effect, since the role of glycolysis in preserving red cell viability was not yet recognized. Using exchange transfusion in rabbits, Rous and Turner showed that red cells stored for two weeks in glucose-citrate solution remained in the circulation, while cells stored for three weeks were rapidly lost.

Oswald Robertson, a medical officer in the US army during World War I, employed the solutions recommended by Rous and Turner to store blood on ice as long as 26 days before transfusion into wounded soldiers of the British Expeditionary Force. In 1918, he reported on 22 transfusions, concluding that results were identical to those seen with direct transfusions.[11] Robertson had proved the feasibility of blood banks, but 20 years passed before the first permanent blood bank was established.

### The Slow Years

Despite Robertson's report, the use of citrate remained controversial, and the only attempt to establish a blood bank in the 1920s was by Yudin in the USSR, who used cadaver blood. Cadaver blood has had limited use in the Soviet Union and has never been found to be a practical or useful source in this country.

The controversy over citrate was prompted in large part by the frequency of febrile reactions when citrated blood was used. The cause was bacterial pyrogens in the citrate solution. Although the febrile effect of some intravenous solutions had been recognized before 1914, the role of bacterial pyrogens was not established until the work of Florence Siebert in 1923.[12] Long after her reports, febrile transfusion reactions continued because of pyrogens in the reused transfusion sets. This problem was not eliminated until the introduction of disposable plastic tubing in the 1950s.

Another form of citrate toxicity undoubtedly resulted from administration of excessive quantities of citrate, causing depression of the recipient's ionized calcium. Although Salant and Wise[13] had shown as early as 1917 that transfused citrate disappeared rapidly, the Krebs cycle, which provides a mechanism whereby almost all cells of the body can dispose of excess citrate, was not described until 1937. Arguments about citrate toxicity continue today, even though cardiac standstill during massive transfusion was shown to result from hypothermia (caused by rapid transfusion of refrigerated blood) rather than hypocalcemia.[14]

### The First Blood Bank

Despite the controversies about the use of citrate, the use of blood transfusions continued to accelerate. At Mount Sinai Hospital in New York, the number of transfusions was doubling every five years.[9] The major obstacle remaining to delay the formation of blood banks was the absence of sterile blood containers prefilled with citrate and dextrose. Glucose cannot be autoclaved in sodium citrate without turning to caramel. Robertson avoided that problem by autoclaving the solutions separately and combining them just before blood collection.[11]

The first permanent blood bank, started in 1937 by Fantus[15] at Cook County Hospital, used sodium citrate without glucose. Fantus recommended donating blood for autotransfusion one to two weeks before delivery or surgery and claimed that his citrated blood was good for three to four weeks. However, his evidence was lack of in vitro hemolysis; he had no data on the viability of his stored cells. See also Chapter 28.)

### Further Improvements in Citrate Solutions

Loutit, Mollison, and Young[16] took the next major step during the early years of World War II. They demonstrated that if they lowered the pH of the citrate-dextrose solution by an appropriate ratio of citric acid to sodium citrate, the acidified citrate-dextrose (ACD) solution could be autoclaved without turning the sugar to caramel. They further showed that the viability of the ACD red cells was better than that of citrate-dextrose red cells. Acidified citrate-dextrose solution was quickly accepted worldwide with agreement that blood could be stored in it at refrigerator temperature for at least 21 days and still maintain acceptable red cell viability.

Acidified citrate-dextrose solution remained the standard anticoagulant-preservative solution for the next 30 years. Gibson et al[17] improved it somewhat by adding phosphate and raising the pH slightly to produce citrate-phosphate-dextrose solution (CPD). Only within the last few years has an important advance been made by adding adenine to the CPD solution; this prolongs the permissible storage of red cells from 21 to 35 days.

The development of a technique whereby a sterile collecting bottle containing ACD solution could be manufactured and sold on a wide scale, coupled with the demands for plasma of World War II, led to development of blood banks at an explosive rate. When the war ended, the demand was reduced, but civilian blood banks were here to stay.

Weil, Lewisohn, Hustin, and Agote undoubtedly believed that their goals were important, but they could hardly have predicted the size and variety of the services that resulted from their work. Instead of being rare events with the complexity of a surgical operation, blood collection and transfusion have become easily available procedures. Blood can now be waiting for the patient who needs it and in whatever quantities are necessary. The separation into components would not be a total surprise to the early users of citrate as an anticoagulant, since they frequently let their diluted blood settle to decrease the volume of the transfused red cells, but they could hardly have predicted protein fractions and hemapheresis. Nevertheless, modern blood banks owe Weil and his colleagues a great debt

### References

1. Weil R: Sodium citrate in the transfusion of blood. *JAMA* 1915;64:425-426.

2. Lewisohn R: Blood transfusion by the citrate method. *Surg Gynecol Obstet* 1915;21:37-47.

3. Kilduffe RA, DeBakey M: *The Blood Bank and the Technique and Therapeutics of Transfusions.* St Louis, CV Mosby Co, 1942, p 30.

4. Keynes G (ed): *Blood Transfusion.* Baltimore, Williams & Wilkins Co, 1949, p 37.

5. DeGowin EL, Hardin RC, Alsever JB: *Blood Transfusion.* Philadelphia, WB Saunders Co, 1949, p 2.

6. Hustin A: Note sur une nouvelle méthode de transfusion. *Bull Soc R Sci Med Nat Brux* 1914;72:104-111.

7. Agote L: Nuevo procedimiento para la transfusion de la sangre. *An Inst Modelo Clin Med* 1915;1:25.

8. Lewisohn R: A new and greatly simplified method of blood transfusion. *Med Rec* 1915;87:141-142.

9. Rosenfield RE: Early twentieth century origins of modern blood transfusion therapy. *Mt Sinai J Med* 1974;41:626-635.

10. Rous P, Turner JR: The preservation of living red cells in vitro: I. Methods of preservation. *J Exp Med* 1915;23:219-237.

11. Robertson OH: Transfusion with preserved red blood cells. *Br Med J* 1918;1:691-695.

12. Seibert FB: Fever-producing substance found in some distilled waters. *Am J Physiol* 1923;67:90-104.

13. Salant W, Wise LE: The action of sodium citrate and its decomposition in the body. *J Biol Chem* 1917;28:27-58.

14. Boyan CP: Cold or warmed blood for massive transfusions. *Ann Surg* 1964;160:282-286.

15. Fantus B (ed): Blood preservation. *JAMA* 1937;109:128-131.

16. Loutit JF, Mollison PL, Young IM: Citric acid-sodium citrate-glucose mixtures for blood storage. *Q J Exp Physiol* 1943;32:183-202.

17. Gibson JG II, Rees SB, McManus TJ, et al: A citrate-phosphate-dextrose solution for the preservation of human blood. *Am J Clin Pathol* 1957;28:569-578.

May 15, 1915
(*JAMA* 1915;64:1625-1630)

## Chapter 12

# Gastric and Duodenal Ulcer

## Medical Cure by an Efficient Removal of Gastric Juice Corrosion

Bertram W. Sippy, M.D.

Chicago

Favored by unusual clinical facilities, I have gradually evolved and established in practice a method of treating gastric and duodenal ulcers. The method is based on well-recognized principles underlying the healing of ulcer. Old and established facts of physiology are largely utilized. The results of treatment are far beyond early expectations.

The treatment consists essentially in accurately protecting the ulcer from gastric juice corrosion until healing of the ulcer takes place.

After an experience of twelve years in applying the principle involved in the treatment, I am convinced that the vast majority of cases of gastric, and more particularly duodenal, ulcer now treated surgically, and with indications commonly accepted as justifiable, can be readily and more quickly cured by the management advocated.

As I understand the ulcer problem, the principles involved in treatment are centered about these important and fundamental questions:

1. What are the causes of peptic ulcer?

2. What retards or prevents the healing of peptic ulcer?

3. What can we as physicians and surgeons do to promote the development of granulation tissue essential to the healing and final cicatrization of peptic ulcer?

For half a century it has been recognized that a peptic ulcer develops in approximately the following manner: A circumscribed area of the mucous membrane or wall of the stomach or adjacent duodenum, through malnutrition or necrosis, loses its normal resistance to the peptic action of the gastric juice and becomes digested. The resulting defect is an ulcer.

The recent work of Dr. E. C. Rosenow renders it probable that hematogenous bacterial (streptococcus) invasion is the most common factor in the production of the local malnutrition and necrosis. Undoubtedly, local

defects of malnutrition and necrosis from whatever cause would practically always undergo rapid repair, without serious clinical symptoms, in the absence of gastric juice corrosion.

All present knowledge tends to substantiate the belief that has existed for many years, namely, that an ulcer of the stomach or duodenum would heal approximately as rapidly as an ulcer located elsewhere in the body, if its granulating surfaces were not subjected to the digestive action of the gastric juice.

The digestive action of the gastric juice is due to the solvent action of pepsin or albuminous substances that have been properly permeated by hydrochloric acid. Pepsin is practically inert in alkaline and neutral mediums. It acts slightly in the presence of a combined acid medium, but combined acids are incapable of preparing albumins properly for the action of pepsin. A free acid, such as hydrochloric acid, is required to permeate the albumin and prepare it for the full action of the peptic ferment. Pepsin exerts no appreciable solvent or digestive action on the raw and exposed surfaces of a gastric or duodenal ulcer in the absence of free hydrochloric acid.

The principle involved in the treatment advocated consists essentially in efficiently shielding the ulcer from the corrosive effect of the gastric juice. This is accomplished by maintaining an accurate neutralization of all free hydrochloric acid, thus rendering the digestive action of the gastric juice inert from 7 a. m. until about 10:30 p. m., or during the entire time that food and the accompanying secretion are present in the stomach. In addition, it is accurately determined whether an excessive night secretion is present. If so, this is removed each night until the irritability of the gastric glands has subsided. This applies almost entirely to cases of duodenal and pyloric ulcer that have been associated with stagnation of food and secretion for one or two months, and longer. Such cases almost invariably are attended by a more or less copious continued secretion during the night, which should be removed by aspiration two or three times each night, if necessary. Usually after three or four days of accurate control of free acidity the excessive night secretion disappears. Subsequently the normal quantity (about 10 c.c.) of gastric juice present in the stomach during the night is left undisturbed.

The neutralization of hydrochloric acid is accomplished by frequent feedings and the use of alkalies in carefully regulated but adequate quantities. Experience in applying the method to all types of individuals under widely varying conditions has abundantly demonstrated that the corrosive or digestive action of the gastric juice can be thus practically annulled until healing of the ulcer is accomplished. The conditions for the healing of peptic ulcer thus obtained are rendered as ideal as they can be made to be in the light of our present knowledge and understanding.

It will be impossible to give the details of the management in this paper. Briefly stated, the patient remains in bed for from three to four weeks. Unless some serious complication is present, some or all of his regular work may be done at the end of four or five weeks. A wide variety of soft and palatable foods may be given. The following plan of diet has been found most adaptable: Three ounces of a mixture of equal parts milk and cream are given every hour from 7 a. m. until 7 p.m. After two or three days soft eggs and well-cooked cereals are gradually added, until at the end of about ten days the patient is receiving approximately the following nourishment: 3 ounces of the milk and cream mixture every hour from 7 a. m. until 7 p. m. In addition, three soft eggs, one at a time, and 9 ounces of a cereal, 3 ounces at one feeding, may be given each day. The cereal is measured after it is prepared.

Cream soups of various kinds, vegetable purées and other soft foods, may be substituted now and then, as desired. The total bulk at any one feeding while food is taken every hour should not exceed 6 ounces. Many of the feedings will not equal that quantity. The patient should be weighed. If desired, a sufficient quantity of food may be given to cause a gain of 2 or 3 pounds each week.

A large variety of soft and palatable foods may be used, such as jellies, marmalades, custards, creams, etc. The basis of the diet, however, should be milk, cream, eggs, cereals and vegetable purées. Lean meat is not given during the period of accurate observation, since it interferes with the tests for occult blood in the stool and aspirated stomach contents.

The acidity is more easily controlled by feeding every hour and giving the alkalies midway between feedings. The acidity may, however, be controlled by feeding every two, three and four hours. I have maintained complete control of the free hydrochloric acidity in several cases by feeding three times daily. In most cases, however, the plan of feeding every hour is best.[1]

1. Further details relative to management may be found in my articles on Treatment of Gastric Ulcer, Pyloric Obstruction, etc., published in 1911 in Volume III, Handbook of Practical Treatment, edited by Musser and Kelly.

It is only fair to state that the views expressed and the methods described[1] in 1911 were as radical as I then dared publish in a handbook for the use of practitioners. Since that time numerous slight modifications of procedure, some of which were then on trial and others of later development, have become thoroughly established in my practice.

The uncomfortable preliminary starvation period serves no purpose when the acidity is controlled and has, therefore, been entirely abandoned. Slightly larger doses of alkalies than were then advised were then being regularly employed. The practice of maintaining an absolutely accurate control of the free hydrochloric acidity during the entire time that food and the accompanying secretion are present in the stomach has become thoroughly established. This requires the administration of varying quantities of alkalies, corresponding to individual cases. Also, in addition to giving an alkaline powder midway between feedings, the powders are continued every half hour after the last feeding, until 10 p. m. In all cases of pyloric obstruction from duodenal and pyloric ulcer it has been found advisable to empty the stomach of all remaining food and secretion at about 10:30 p. m., thus removing the stimulus to an excessive night secretion. In most cases a short time after treatment is begun the stomach will be found empty at that time. The management of excessive night secretion has already been described.

Cases of stomach ulcer unassociated with stagnation of food and secretion are usually controlled by feeding every hour and giving a powder containing 10 grains each of heavy calcined magnesia and sodium bicarbonate, alternating with a powder containing 10 grains of bismuth subcarbonate and 20 or 30 grains of sodium bicarbonate, midway between feedings. Cases of pyloric and duodenal ulcer that have been associated with stagnation of food and secretion longer than two months almost invariably require larger quantities of alkalies.

Heavy calcined magnesia has approximately four times the neutralizing power of sodium bicarbonate. Since its neutralizing effect is prolonged compared with that of sodium bicarbonate, and for other reasons, calcined magnesia should be used between as many feedings as possible. An uncomfortable diarrhea usually prevents its exclusive use as a neutralizer. Other stable alkalies similar in action to calcined magnesia are being carefully tested.

In a few cases of duodenal ulcer with high grade obstruction it has required the equivalent of 100 grains of sodium bicarbonate every hour, midway between feedings, and three doses with intervals of one-half hour after the last feeding, at 7 or 8 p. m., to neutralize all the free hydrochloric acidity.

The average length of time that a patient with peptic ulcer should be under the accurate control and observation of the physician is about four weeks. During this period, if observations have been carefully and intelligently conducted, the finer points essential to a complete diagnosis of peptic ulcer, including such conditions and complications that may attend the ulcer, will have been determined, and the patient will have learned how to manage himself accurately. Thus the gratifying results to be obtained by the management advocated are secured.

It has been my experience that in the management of no other serious disease is it so easily possible to obtain the intelligent cooperation of all classes of patients. The reasons are probably of this nature: The things required of the patient during the after-management are straightforward and relatively simple; the sufferings of the patient before treatment have often been so severe that he usually requires no further stimulus to do his part. Fortunately, the most accurate cooperation is usually secured from patients who have long suffered from the obstructive type of duodenal or pyloric ulcer.

The nonobstructive type of gastric ulcer requires relatively little attention to details compared with the obstructive type of duodenal and pyloric ulcer. The dosage of alkali required to control the acidity is smaller, and it is seldom, if ever, necessary to remove the remaining food and secretion at bedtime.

Ideal conditions for the healing of peptic ulcer are maintained when the aspirated stomach contents show absence of free hydrochloric acid during the entire time that food and the accompanying secretion are present in the stomach, and all excessive night secretion is controlled.

Experience has shown that when the free acidity is found controlled late in the afternoon and just previous to taking the powders or feedings, the acidity is likely to be controlled at all other times during the feeding hours.

It is not difficult to determine the amount of alkali required between feedings to control accurately all free acidity. If not controlled the first few days by giving the usual amount, then the dose is gradually increased until the acidity is regularly found controlled.

It should be understood that the presence of free hydrocholoric acid now and then for a few minutes each day does not seriously interfere with the healing of the ulcer. Such short periods during which corrosion of the ulcer may be possible are as nothing compared with the duration of corrosion to which duodenal and pyloric ulcers are subjected after gastro-enterostomy. In the ordinary surgical treatment of these conditions such ulcers are subjected to the corrosive action of the gastric juice during the whole period of normal stomach digestion, which occupies many hours each day. The majority of pyloric and duodenal ulcers treated by gastro-enterostomy show few symptoms after the operation, and such ulcers probably usually heal in the course of time, the same as the majority of the nonobstructive type of gastric ulcers usually heal without treatment. In either case, however, the conditions for healing are far from ideal.

As will be more clearly stated later, the symptoms of pyloric and duodenal ulcer after gastro-enterostomy and the symptoms of the usual nonobstructive type of gastric ulcer without treatment are approximately the same. Other things being equal, the conditions for healing are approximately the same. Both are subjected to the same duration of gastric juice corrosion. The very great tendency for peptic ulcer to heal, if the hindrance to healing is removed to only a moderate degree, is responsible for the recoveries that occur when gastro-enterostomy is performed for an ulcer located at the outlet of the stomach, causing stagnation of food and secretion.

While the symptoms may be controlled and healing accomplished in the majority of all cases of uncomplicated peptic ulcer by applying the usual or Leube type of medical management; while operative procedure successfully performed, such as gastro-enterostomy and pyloroplastic operations, may be infinitely superior to the Leube and other types of medical management in general use when applied to cases of pyloric obstruction, all types of medical and surgical treatment now in common use accomplish relatively little toward protecting the ulcer from gastric juice corrosion when compared with what may be easily, comfortably and safely accomplished by applying the accurate medical management which I have established and advocated.

In order that it may be known that the statements made in this paper are based on adequate clinical evidence, I feel justified in saying that at the Presbyterian Hospital I have under my medical management from twenty-five to thirty and more private cases of peptic ulcer at all times. Fully 70 per cent. of these cases are of the duodenal or pyloric type, presenting abnormal retention of food and secretion, varying from the slightest to the highest grades. The results obtained by such management are almost beyond belief.

Pyloric obstruction due to spasm of the pylorus, resulting in the retention of food and secretion from one meal to the next during the daytime, and until 3 or 4 o'clock in the morning, and even until the next morning at breakfast-time, disappears at once under the influence of such management.

Pyloric obstruction, even of the highest grade, and of long duration, as evidenced by the presence of vigorous peristaltic waves, showing through the abdominal wall, history of vomiting food eaten the day before for many months, the aspiration of food eaten twelve or more hours before, and the presence of abundant sarcinae, often rapidly disappears, so that at the end of ten days' or two weeks' management, seven hours after the largest and coarsest kind of a motor meal is given the stomach is found empty.

As unbelievable as it may seem, cases of duodenal ulcer recurrent for years, that have finally developed a high grade pyloric obstruction due to actual anatomic narrowing from indurated, infiltrated and edematous tissue, have yielded completely to the management.

The explanation for such astonishing results is probably as follows: The active more or less annular ulcer at the pyloric or duodenal outlet is embedded in edematous tissue infiltrated with round cells, and other products of inflammation of varying grades. Under the management advocated, the greatest hindrance to healing having been removed, healing and cicatrization of the ulcer begin more or less rapidly, the round cells and other exudative products disappear, the infiltrated tissue grows thinner in all directions, and when healing of the ulcer takes place, notwithstanding the tendency of scar tissue to contract, the opening through the pylorus or duodenum becomes gradually larger instead of smaller. Whatever the explanation, I have accumulated indisputable evidence that the size of the opening through the tissue that is causing the obstruction gradually becomes larger. Recorded observations of such cases now extend over a period of eight years. The early cases of pyloric obstruction due to actual tissue narrowing observed were treated thus medically instead of surgically, because other diseased conditions were present, rendering surgical intervention unusually hazardous.

As a result of the encouraging outcome in these cases, during the past four years, cases have been purposely selected for such investigative work. The results were so uniformly good that within the past two years a constantly increasing number of cases of that type have been treated thus by medical management, without being subjected to surgical operation. Up to the present time our experience is that none has failed to show that the obstruction yields in the course of a few weeks' or months' management, during all of which time, except the first four or five weeks, the patient is on his own responsibility, so far as treatment is concerned, and doing practically all his regular work.

Roentgen-ray studies of cases of pyloric obstruction after gastro-enterostomy have convinced me that very much the same thing occurs after gastro-enterostomy. As the ulcer heals, the food passes more and more through the pylorus. Since the conditions for healing of a pyloric or duodenal ulcer after gastro-enterostomy are not so favorable as they are under accurate medical management, as advocated, the opening up of the obstruction does not take place as rapidly, and perhaps not as completely.

In the light of all present knowledge, the development of granulation tissue leading to the healing and final cicatrization of peptic ulcer is promoted by a given type of medical or surgical treatment directly proportionate to the influence exerted by that treatment on the duration and intensity of gastric juice corrosion.

The serious defect in the Leube, Lenharz and all other types of medical management, in general use the world over, lies in the lack of accurate knowledge of what is actually being accomplished while the patient is under treatment. As a rule, if pain and other symptoms are well controlled, no attempt is made to determine accurately how much, if any, the duration or intensity of gastric juice corrosion is reduced. Pain of ulcer may be entirely absent when the aspirated stomach contents show varying, even high, grades of free hydrochloric acidity. The peptic corrosion that occurs when a small quantity of free hydrochloric acid is present is approximately as great as when a high degree of free acidity exists. Unquestionably, the lack of accurate control of the free acidity of gastric secretion is responsible for such failures as occur when the various types of medical management in general use are applied to the treatment of peptic ulcer.

When death, jejunal ulcer and serious complications, the result of faulty technic, are excluded, the failures that occur when surgical treatment is applied are attributable to the same lack of efficient control of gastric juice corrosion. Gastro-enterostomy, when successfully performed, usually causes the stomach to empty itself of food and secretion in approximately normal time, but never appreciably earlier than the physiologic limit of normal time.

In 15 per cent. of a series of eighty cases tested by me after gastro-enterostomy, considerable food and secretion were recovered seven hours and as long as twelve hours after the ingestion of a motor meal consisting of ordinary food containing vegetables.

Ulcers of the stomach and duodenum are corroded as long as food and free hydrochloric acid secretion are present in the stomach. When gastro-enterostomy is performed for a duodenal or pyloric ulcer that is causing stagnation of food and secretion, the healing of the ulcer is benefited only proportionate to the number of minutes or hours that the duration of peptic corrosion is thereby reduced.

It must be remembered that after gastro-enterostomy, food and secretion continue to pass through the pylorus proportionate to the size of the opening that exists through the strictured area of the pylorus and duodenum. Only a small fraction of 1 per cent. of all cases of pyloric and duodenal ulcer for which gastro-enterostomy is now regularly performed are near the danger point of starvation because of the narrowness of the opening at the outlet. The average case has lost only moderately in weight. Such loss of weight as does occur is nearly always due to voluntary restrictions in diet because of pain, and not because the opening is actually narrowed to such a degree that sufficient nourishment is unable to pass through.

Any one sufficiently interested to study accurately cases after gastro-enterostomy by means of the Roentgen ray will easily demonstrate to himself that food and secretions are pushed through the pyloric orifice proportionate to the size of the opening at that outlet. When Roentgen-ray meal of the consistency of food is used, the musculature is seen to force the stomach contents against the pyloric outlet with such persistent vigor that none can doubt that the major portion of all food and secretion passes through the pyloric outlet within a short time after gastro-enterostomy is performed. In every case after gastro-enterostomy, unless the pylorus is occluded by operative procedure, a sufficient quantity of gastric juice is poured through the pyloric outlet to keep the ulcer constantly bathed in the corrosive secretion until the stomach has emptied itself of food and secretion.

A duodenal ulcer after gastro-enterostomy is placed in no more favorable conditions for healing than attend the usual untreated stomach ulcer located distant from the pylorus, or for other reasons unassociated with stagnation of food and secretion. The duration of corrosion in both instances equals that of the normal digestion period, which is several hours each day. The symptomatology of a duodenal ulcer after gastro-enterostomy is similar to that of the ordinary untreated stomach ulcer unassociated with stagnation of food and secretion.

That a duodenal ulcer treated by gastro-enterostomy usually heals in the course of time, and meanwhile is likely to cause but few serious symptoms, is consistent with the probable fact that the majority of stomach ulcers, located, as they are, on the lesser curvature or posterior wall and distant from the pylorus, usually give rise to few serious symptoms and heal without treatment.

Probably only such stomach ulcers as are located at or

very near the pylorus, or that penetrate to or beyond the peritoneal coat, or become unusually large, or cause hemorrhage, or develop malignancy, produce serious symptoms.

If the commonly accepted conception of peptic ulcer is correct, namely, that the digestive action of the gastric juice constitutes the greatest hindrance to healing that is amenable to medical and surgical control, then it must follow that the healing of peptic ulcer is promoted most by that type of management which reduces to the greatest degree the duration and intensity of gastric juice corrosion.

No operative procedure as yet devised enables the stomach to empty itself of food and secretion appreciably earlier than normal time. Hence no operative procedure except excision of the ulcer or pyloric occlusion with gastro-enterostomy for duodenal and pyloric ulcer results in protecting a peptic ulcer from the corrosive effect of the gastric juice during the several hours each day occupied by normal stomach digestion. My experience has demonstrated beyond question that it is entirely possible and remarkably easy to exercise practically absolute control over peptic activity for many months, and, if necessary, for years.

The gratifying results to be obtained by applying the treatment or the principles involved in the treatment to cases ordinarily regarded as absolutely intractable to medical management, including such cases as gastro-enterostomy and other surgical procedure legitimately applied have failed to relieve, demonstrate that there can be no lack of incentive for the internist to develop a technic in the medical management of peptic ulcer that is as accurate and painstaking as that required of the surgeon in performing gastro-enterostomy or pyloroplastic operations.

In my service at the Presbyterian Hospital, surgical procedure in the treatment of peptic ulcer is limited to the following complications and conditions that attend ulcer:

1. Perforation.
2. Perigastric abscess.
3. Secondary carcinoma.

When, after careful study of the case, there is a reasonable reason for suspecting that a carcinoma is developing at the seat of an ulcer, if no contraindication exists, the ulcer-bearing area should be widely resected, with due regard to lymphatic distribution.

4. Hour-glass or other rare deformity of the stomach that is causing serious symptoms.

In very exceptional cases the history or Roentgen-ray examination may give evidence of a large, deep excavated ulcer, and justify an attempt to excise the ulcer, or perforate it with a cautery, and then lessen its size by suture.

5. Foci of infection about the roots of teeth, in the tonsils and elsewhere in the body are sought and removed.

Rosenow's contribution to the etiology of peptic ulcer is of the utmost importance relative to the recurrence of ulcer and the prophylactic treatment of the disease.

It is manifestly useless to talk about the end result of any form of treatment of peptic ulcer when the patient harbors an alveolar abscess. An abscess about the root of a tooth may be responsible for recurrences of ulcer extending over a period of years.

6. Hemorrhage of serious nature from peptic ulcer is a direct result of corrosion of blood vessels by the gastric juice. Such corrosion is impossible when the digestive action of the gastric juice is annulled by accurate medical management.

Since serious bleeding practically never occurs after the first week of medical management, as outlined, surgical treatment is considered only in connection with patients who are bleeding when first seen, or within the first week after treatment is begun.

The results of surgical intervention when instituted for the control of serious hemorrhage at the time it is occurring are admittedly not encouraging.

I have subjected relatively very few cases to surgical operation for the control of hemorrhage.

7. Pyloric obstruction of high grade due to actual cicatricial narrowing that fails, under the influence of accurate medical management, to yield sufficiently to allow a motor meal to pass in normal time.

Operative experience shows that of all cases of duodenal and pyloric ulcer presenting definite clinical evidence of obstruction at the outlet, less than 10 per cent. are found at operation to be associated with an actual tissue narrowing of serious grade.

I differentiate two clinical types of pyloric obstruction resulting from ulcer:

1. Pyloric obstruction due to conditions easily removable by two weeks of the accurate medical management advocated. More than 90 per cent. of all cases of pyloric obstruction due to ulcer are of this type.

2. Pyloric obstruction due to anatomic narrowing from infiltrated tissue, some of which may be cicatricial tissue in varying stages of development.

The probable cause of the first is pyloric spasm, inflammatory swelling, and at times, perhaps, a local peritonitis.

If at the end of two weeks of accurate medical management, during which the acidity is properly controlled both night and day, a full motor meal is given and 100 c.c. or more of food is found at the end of seven hours, an actual anatomic tissue narrowing exists, in practically all cases, unless nausea or some other condition is interfering temporarily with the motor power.

I formerly subjected such cases to gastro-enterostomy.[2] As previously stated, with reasons given, I am now convinced that unless the opening is so very narrow that death from starvation is threatened, the size of the opening will practically always increase—if both day and night corrosion is accurately controlled. Experience to date and the method has shown that as yet none has failed to open up sufficiently to allow the stomach to empty itself of a full meal in seven hours.

When the pyloric outlet is large enough to permit the stomach to empty itself of a full meal within the limit of normal time, it is useless to perform gastro-enterostomy for peptic ulcer at the pyloric outlet or elsewhere. When an ample pyloric outlet exists, the healing of peptic ulcer

---

2. Musser and Kelly, iii.

can be hastened only by such means as can bring about a reduction of the duration of gastric juice corrosion to a shorter period than that occupied by normal stomach digestion. No operative procedure accomplishes this except when a duodenal or pyloric ulcer is treated by gastro-enterostomy, combined with pyloric occlusion.

The medical management advocated accurately protects the pyloric and duodenal ulcer from gastric juice corrosion, and thus renders gastro-enterostomy combined with pyloric occlusion unnecessary. Gastro-enterostomy combined with pyloric occlusion is not without mortality when performed by those most expert. The mortality of such and all other operative procedures when performed by the rapidly increasing number of those who conscientiously attempt to imitate the expert is known best by those who through persistent endeavor have finally acquired a skill that is attended by a low mortality.

The medical management of peptic ulcer the world over is today practically the same as that advocated by Leube, Riegel and others of twenty-five years ago. Such medical management is efficient, to a certain degree. The general tendency for a peptic ulcer to heal if Nature is aided but slightly is responsible for the cures that can be brought about by it. The majority of all uncomplicated ulcers heal under its influence. No doubt many cases of duodenal ulcer can be cured by it.

If no more accurate means of medical management are at hand, surgical treatment has a very wide field of usefulness in the management of peptic ulcer. It may legitimately be applied only to such conditions and complications of peptic ulcer as are mechanically relievable or removable, and with reasonable safety to the patient.

The old and generally accepted belief that gastric juice corrosion is the most important influence that retards the healing of ulcer receives confirmation from the results that are obtained by all methods of treatment that have contributed to the healing of ulcer.

If the commonly accepted conception relative to gastric juice corrosion is correct, the number of cases of peptic ulcer now generally considered legitimately operable may be enormously reduced by the careful application of the method of medical treatment advocated.

The striking results to be obtained by applying the principle of accurately protecting the ulcer from gastric juice corrosion would seem to be the best evidence yet produced in substantiation of the old corrosion theory of peptic or digestive ulcer.

For the purpose of lessening the great confusion that has attended the problem relative to the treatment of peptic ulcer since the days of the first successful gastro-enterostomies, I recommend the application of earnest thought to the three fundamental questions, as stated in the beginning of this article. It is only by persistent effort directed toward a rational solution of these essential questions that the greatest progress in the treatment of peptic ulcer is to be attained:

1. What are the causes of peptic ulcer?

2. What retards or prevents the healing of peptic ulcer?

3. What can we as physicians and surgeons do to promote best the development of granulation tissue essential to the healing and final cicatrization of peptic ulcer?

122 South Michigan Avenue.

Oct 28, 1983
(JAMA 1983;250:2198-2202)

# Bertram W. Sippy and
# Ulcer Disease Therapy*

## Geoffrey M. Zucker, MD, Charles B. Clayman, MD

This issue of THE JOURNAL reprints Bertram W. Sippy's article on "Gastric and Duodenal Ulcer: Medical Cure by an Efficient Removal of Gastric Juice Corrosion." That such commemoration is appropriate can be appreciated only when Sippy's role in the history of peptic ulcer disease is recognized. From our present perspective, it is hard to imagine the confusion and conflict surrounding the etiology, pathogenesis, and treatment of ulcers that existed at the end of the 19th century. Both in America and Europe, differing theories existed as to the nature of the illness and its treatment. Sippy's report was the culmination of years of observation and clinical practice, and by virtue of the force of his personality, his perseverance, and the correctness of his therapy, his name is remembered to this day.

### Brief History of Ulcer Disease

The historical beginnings of the understanding of ulcer of the stomach and duodenum are obscured in antiquity. One of the earliest comments is by Gaius Pliny (AD 23-79), who also gave its cure: "Receits for the paine of stomacke and loines: also for the infirmities of the rein's. If there be an ulcer growne in the stomacke, drinke the milke of an asse or cow, and it will heale it."[1]

Pliny's advice notwithstanding, knowledge of diseases

From the Department of Internal Medicine, Cooley-Dickinson Hospital, Northampton, Mass (Dr Zucker); the Section of Gastroenterology, Department of Medicine, Northwestern University Medical Center, and the Division of Scientific Publications, American Medical Association, Chicago (Dr Clayman).

*A commentary on Sippy BW: Gastric and duodenal ulcer: Medical cure by efficient removal of gastric juice corrosion. JAMA 1915;64:1625-1630.

of the digestive system among the ancients and through the Dark Ages was limited to acquaintance with symptoms. With the Renaissance began studies of anatomy and, hence, knowledge of structure and, occasionally, pathology of the stomach and duodenum. Autopsies led to the recognition of gastric ulcer by Galen, while methods of treatment were given by Celsus. The digestive capacity of gastric juice was recognized by John Hunter,[2] who asked, "Why does the stomach not digest itself?" The term "peptic ulcer" had arisen from the assumption that the lesion resulted from the process of digestion. The first complete description of the morbid anatomy and symptoms of gastric ulcer was that of Matthew Ballie of London, who, in 1793, published his observations in *Morbid Anatomy of Some of the Most Important Parts of the Human Body*. While Ballie presented a drawing in 1799 showing a duodenal ulcer in association with multiple gastric ulcers, he and most of his contemporaries and successors paid most attention to lesions in the stomach. Such attention to and emphasis on gastric ulcers continued throughout the 19th and early part of the 20th centuries, while duodenal ulcer disease was believed to be a rarer variant, uncommonly recognized during life.

Outstanding contributions during the first half of the 19th century were those of Abercrombie[3] and Cruveilhier.[4] In France, Cruveilhier first clearly distinguished between ulcer and cancer of the stomach; because of his classic descriptions of gastric ulcer, the term "round ulcer of Cruveilhier" was often used to describe a benign ulcer well into the late 19th century.

While Cruveilhier virtually ignored duodenal ulcer, John Abercrombie[3] of Edinburgh wrote in 1828: "The leading peculiarity of disease of the duodenum, so far as we are at present acquainted with it, seems to be that food is taken with relish and the first state of digestion is not impeded, but the pain begins about the time when the food is passing out of the stomach, or two to four hours after a meal." Like Cruveilhier,[4] he advocated the use of dietary modification, and milk in particular: "The food must be in very small quantity and of the mildest quality, consisting chiefly or entirely of farinaceous articles and milk. . . . In the more advanced stages . . . benefit may be obtained by some internal remedies such as oxide of bismuth, lime water and nitric acid." While the outstanding achievement in physiology of this period was made by William Beaumont (1833), especially his work with gastric juice and the physiology of digestion, others, such as Virchow (1853), Rokitansky (1839), and Brinton (1856), theorized on the pathogenesis of ulcer disease. The importance of trauma and irritation of the gastric mucosa by hot or cold foods, violent vomiting, hemorrhage, and mucosal injuries from coarse foods served as the basis for a mechanical origin for ulcer. Virchow originated the theory that vascular occlusion and infarction of small areas of gastric mucosa were a possible etiologic factor. Such infarctions from a variety of embolic or thrombotic causes would then lead to digestion of the affected necrotic tissue. As early as 1880, Cohnheim stated that formation of the ulcer depends on chemical factors. Shortly thereafter, Riegel,[5] in 1886, attributed hyperchlorhydria to the development of chronic ulcer. Later, in 1903, he stated:

As soon as food enters the stomach, the secretion of gastric juice is stimulated and since in ulcer an abnormally high secretion of hydrochloric acid usually occurs, the ulcer and the sensory nerves that are at its base are irritated either by the acid directly or by the peristaltic movement of the stomach.

To this day, discussion of the mechanism of ulcer pain relates to this statement.

The role of hyperchlorhydria in the pathogenesis of ulcer disease was by no means uniformly accepted. Böttcher, in 1874, was the first to demonstrate bacteria in the marginal tissue of ulcers, and later, E. C. Rosenow postulated that hematogenous bacterial invasion (often from carious teeth) was the most common factor in the production of local (ie, gastric) malnutrition and necrosis. However, the discovery of gastric acid analysis by intubation of the stomach by Kussmaul (1869) and the creation of the gastric pouch by Pavlov laid the stage for the recognition of the role of gastric juice, and hyperchlorhydria in particular, in the genesis of peptic ulcer. By 1906, Frank Billings[6] would write:

Chronic ulcer of the stomach and duodenum, frequently termed round, perforating or peptic ulcer, follows nutritional disturbance of a limited area of the mucosa which results in the destruction of this circumscribed region by gastric juice. The gastric juice is the destructive agent and, therefore, plays the most important role in the causation of ulcer of the stomach and duodenum.

Although Billings recognized other factors as potentially contributory, he clearly attributed the active role in ulcer formation to gastric juice. Similar recognition on the continent was soon forthcoming, and in 1907, A. W. Mayo Robson[7] also wrote of hyperacidity in ulcer disease. At the same time, Sir Berkeley Moynihan,[8] one of the greatest surgeons of his time, would write: "It is not improbable that the gastric ulceration is the primary condition, duodenal ulcer being secondary, and caused, it may well be, by the digestion of the duodenal mucosa by the hyperacid gastric juice." Although such men as Sir Arthur Hurst still doubted these ideas, more and more work attested to their importance.

## Treatment

In the history of the treatment of ulcer, the name of Cruveilhier is outstanding. Eighteen hundred years after Pliny advocated milk as the cure for ulcer disease, Cruveilhier formalized principles that were followed into Sippy's day. These include the observations, first, that ulcer of the stomach is curable, second, that dietary hygiene is of importance in treatment and prevention of recurrence, and last, that a milk diet produced healing. The addition of milk powder to the milk to make it more nutritious was suggested by Riegel. Complicated and graduated dietetic programs also cited by Riegel were developed by Leube, Lenhartz, Ewald, and others. Every physician had his own program, some incorporating supplements of olive oil, brandy, or even "nutrient enemas." Strict bedrest was the rule for at least a month or two, often combined with a period of preliminary starvation for several days before therapy was begun. Antacid preparations of alkalies and bismuth salts had been used in the treatment of gastric disturbances; their beginnings are lost to us. Ewald advised use of alkalies combined with rhubarb and cane or milk sugar every hour in small doses. Bouveret administered from 8 to 14 g of bicarbonate of soda per day.[9] Belladonna or atropine was sometimes used, and, occasionally, morphine. Treatment of abdominal pain was often worse than the cause[8]: leeches and poultices to the area and, if necessary, arsenic, silver nitrate, carbolic acid, cannabis indica, cocaine, or hydrocyanic acid taken internally. Bleeding complications were often handled in a like manner. Ulcers were frequently brought to the physician's attention when either bleeding or persistent vomiting had supervened. When symptoms abated, recurrences would follow. There were no objective means to diagnose ulcers or follow up their response to treatment. It is no wonder that the majority of physicians experienced in the treatment of ulcer disease at the start of the 20th century recommended surgery.

Although experiments on animals had been performed for years, the first successful partial gastrectomy was performed by Billroth in 1881, in a case of carcinoma of the stomach. In the same year, one of Billroth's assistants, Wolfler, performed the first gastroenterostomy, also done for cancer of the stomach. Five years later, Heineke and Mikulicz independently performed and described the first pyloroplasty. Thus, within a period of five years were described the three principal types of operations on the stomach used for the next 50 years. Although many variations and modifications have been made, the principles of drainage and removal of acid-stimulating or secreting portions of the stomach are still unchanged. The favorable outcomes seen by the surgeons for their treatment of ulcer disease, both benign and malignant, led to a rapid rise in the popularity of surgical intervention. By 1899, Elliot Joslin,[10] in one of the rare articles presenting a comparative, statistical analysis of various medical regimens with surgical therapy, stated: "The mortality of 8%, and the failure of medical treatment to effect a lasting cure in 60% of the patients indicates the need of surgical intervention in other than emergency cases of this disease." With the background of aseptic surgery then practiced, tremendous strides were made by three pioneer surgeons—Moynihan in England and W. J. and C. H. Mayo in this country. The teachings of these surgeons revised the concepts of the incidence, pathological types, symptoms, and treatment of peptic ulcer, particularly duodenal ulcer. By the start of World War I, both gastroenterostomy and gastric resection were widely practiced for gastric and duodenal ulcer disease. Vagotomy and a drainage procedure were introduced by L. R. Dragstedt just after World War II.

In 1895, the roentgen ray was developed. Within two years, Cannon published his monograph on the first practical plan for visualization of the digestive tract. This led rapidly to the development of knowledge of the motor function of the gastrointestinal (GI) organs and then of ulcer diagnosis. With this background and the almost simultaneous rise of abdominal surgery, two of the most important factors in the development of modern ulcer diagnosis and treatment were established.

### Bertram Welton Sippy (1866-1924)

Bertram W. Sippy was born in Richland County, Wisconsin, Oct 30, 1866. His family had settled there two generations before, having come from Ohio by wagon, passing through Chicago. The original Sippy is said to have come to this country from France as a stowaway with Lafayette.[11] Reared on a farm until the age of 17 years, Bertram attended the county school and high school, then studied for two years at the University of Wisconsin. At the age of 21 years, he entered Rush Medical College, Chicago, from which he graduated in 1890. Courageously overcoming the handicap of a prolonged illness during his senior year, he won by competitive examination second place in the group of eight successful candidates in the Cook County Hospital intern examinations. In 1892, in an effort to gain funds for further training in Vienna, Dr Sippy obtained appointment as division surgeon for the Northern Pacific Railroad at Missoula, Mont. Sippy worked there for three years. The following 18 months were spent at the University of Vienna, where his determination to devote his life to internal medicine crystallized. Returning to Chicago in 1898, he secured a service at the Cook County Hospital and began teaching at Rush Medical College. Dr Sippy's first important contribution to the medical literature, "Splenic Pseudoleukemia," published in 1899, resulted from an exhaustive clinical and pathological study of a case of splenomegaly with anemia that he discovered in the wards of the County Hospital. The recognition accorded him by Osler[12] and others was most gratifying. A neurological article appeared in 1902 and one on the diagnosis of influenza in 1903.[13,14] The first articles on GI topics were published in 1904. It was here that Sippy's

interests flowered. In 1906, Sippy published an excellent dissertation on the diagnosis of esophageal lesions.[15] A chapter on diseases of the esophagus appeared in the 1912 *Handbook of Practical Treatment,* edited by Musser and Kelly.[16] "Diseases of the Esophagus" was written for Billings'[17] *Forchheimer's Therapeusis of Internal Diseases,* published in 1915. Of the various topics discussed, two are particularly important: strictures, both benign and malignant, and idiopathic dilation of the esophagus (in cardiospasm).

Sippy recognized the dangers of blind bouginage and seized on the principle of guided force, using a silk thread to create a track along which metal dilating bougies could then be passed. Once a piano wire had been placed over the thread, the dilating bougies could be safely passed and the structure opened. His device, with little modification, is used by gastroenterologists to this day.

Dr Sippy was one of the first American physicians to be interested in cardiospasm. In 1904, at the meeting of the Association of American Physicians in Washington, DC, there were three papers on achalasia. Dr Sippy exhibited a dilated esophagus obtained at autopsy and x-ray films of two other cases. This seems to be the first roentgenologic description of the disorder. In addition, he devised a pneumatic balloon dilator with a special introducer, the use of which afforded his patients much relief. Once again, versions of this device are still used in the treatment of achalasia.

Dr Sippy's name is remembered by today's physicians primarily for his treatment of peptic ulcer, a lesion still imperfectly understood. As his 1915 article illustrates, Sippy's style of writing was as clear and forceful as his personality and his mode of practice. He recommended an intelligent and systematic search in every case, placing special emphasis on detailed history. Points in the history were discussed to the most minute detail—so much so that on completion, one had an idea of what the major complicating problems were and what the diagnosis was. In diagnosing these lesions, the presence or absence of blood in the GI tract was important. The patient's stools were sent to the laboratory for testing for occult blood. In addition, each patient underwent fluoroscopy of the stomach and duodenum with Dr Sippy in attendance. Thus, the history, physical examination, laboratory procedures, and x-ray were all used in making a diagnosis.

Once a diagnosis of ulcer was made, all efforts were directed at its healing, meaning strict neutralization of gastric acidity. As Sippy's article demonstrates, this could be done by frequent milk-cream feedings and chemical neutralization with alkali salts, such as a "30-30 test powder," consisting of 30 grains (2 g) each of calcium carbonate and sodium bicarbonate, or bismuth subnitrate or calcined magnesia. Sippy's method of relieving nocturnal ulcer pain involved aspiration of the stomach with an Ewald tube, which he performed regularly at 4:30 PM and 9:30 PM three times per week himself and at other times with the assistance of his younger colleagues. The volume of gastric content so obtained was measured, as were the free and total acidities. Failure of the volume to decrease on treatment often meant that surgery was advised. On the basis of literally thousands of such observations, Dr Sippy concluded that the pain of peptic ulcer occurred only if at least 50 mL of gastric content was present with "an adequate supply of free acidity." This term was never defined precisely, but it was assumed to be in the neighborhood of 40 clinical units. "Necessary for the production of distress or pain of peptic ulcer is an adequate degree of free hydrochloric acidity acting on nerves sufficiently sensitive to be irritated by the degree of acidity present."[18] Thus, Sippy's conclusions were the same as those reached by Riegel in 1903 and Moynihan in 1910, that the pain of ulcer was caused by the acid irritation of the nerve endings rather than to the contraction of the stomach.

Sippy[19] realized that gastric acid neutralization had far-reaching therapeutic consequences:

1. Pyloric obstruction is influenced as described.
2. The pain is completely controlled.
3. Excessive night secretion is controlled.
4. Hemorrhage ceases, occult blood disappears from the stool.
5. Perforation has not been known to appear after the second day of management on our service.
6. The penetrating type of ulcer is rapidly influenced; the defect as shown by the roentgen ray relatively rapidly disappears. If the defect is not definitely influenced during the first two weeks of treatment, cancer is thereby suggested or the defect is due to an old cicatrix or the conditions for healing are not good. If a skilled surgeon is available, the patient should be operated on.
7. Ulcers of the stomach and duodenum that have failed to heal after gastro-enterostomy and other surgical procedures are relieved at once of the distress symptoms and eventually healing has taken place in many instances.
8. Healing of ulcer occurs. Necropsies on patients that have died of . . . intercurrent diseases . . . have shown that the ulcer was healing or healed.

Sippy's program was not without its drawbacks. The calcium powder in this dosage was constipating. It was necessary to balance this effect with magnesium salts. Cases of scurvy were reported, since the diet was deficient in vitamin C. Instances of the milk alkali syndrome were encountered, usually in patients with kidney damage or in the elderly.

As a result of his success in the medical treatment of peptic ulcer, Sippy[20] was able to narrow the previously wide indications for surgical treatment to a relative few.

1. Perforation.
2. Perigastric abscess.
3. Secondary carcinoma. . . .
4. Hour-glass or other rare deformity of the stomach that is causing serious symptoms. . . .
5. Foci of infection about the roots of teeth, in the tonsils and elsewhere in the body are sought and removed. . . .
6. Hemorrhage of a serious nature from peptic ulcer is a direct result of corrosion of blood vessels by the gastric juice.
7. Pyloric obstruction of high grade due to actual cicatricial narrowing that fails, under the influence of accurate medical management, to yield sufficiently to allow a motor meal to pass in normal time.

Operative experience shows that of all cases of duodenal and pyloric ulcer presenting definite clinical evidence of obstruction at the outlet, less than 10 per cent are found at operation to be associated with an actual tissue narrowing of serious grade.

Sippy had tremendous influence on the thinking of his day on the subject of ulcer. Sippy's[18] paper read before the Association of American Physicians followed one by William J. Mayo on chronic duodenal ulcer. Judging from the discussion, the physicians present were more impressed by the surgical paper than by the medical, but Dr Mayo concluded with the following comment, "In view of the discussion, I should perhaps change my title to 'The Surgical Treatment of Non-Healing Duodenal Ulcers'; and fully agree that those cases that have a chance to get well under medical treatment should be given an opportunity to do so." Although not all surgeons were as diplomatic as William Mayo and many did not readily accept Sippy's ideas, Dallas Phemister, chief of surgery at the University of Chicago, would turn over some of his patients for medical treatment before considering surgery (Walter L. Palmer, MD, oral communication, March 1983). Sippy's students and assistants became his advocates and disciples, and, in the years to come, Ralph Brown, Sara Jordan, and Walter Palmer, among others, continued to teach and practice what he had realized.

### Medical Therapy After Sippy

In 1917, Dragstedt[21] cited Sippy's medical treatment for peptic ulcer, and by 1935, Eusterman and Balfour[22] of the Mayo Clinic acknowledged that "Sippy deserves the credit for reviving interest in the medical treatment of ulcer at a time when enthusiasm for such treatment had reached a low ebb." Sippy's influence continued to grow after his death in 1924. To this day, his principles of gastric acid neutralization as essential for healing of peptic ulcer and his indications for surgical intervention remain valid. Although science has strengthened the clinician's armamentarium, the end points of therapy are the same—no acid, no ulcer. Not only has this dictum served the test of time, but careful, endoscopically-monitored double-blind studies have documented the superiority of an antacid regimen over placebo.[23]

More recently, other means of influencing acid production have been used instead of chemical neutralization of gastric acid. The once-popular anticholinergic drugs have received some recent reevaluation, and antidepressants (with both anticholinergic and $H_2$-receptor antagonist activity) have been tried. The $H_2$-receptor antagonists are increasingly popular and are considered to be as effective as an antacid regimen in the healing of duodenal ulcers.[24] Sucralfate, an aluminum salt of sucrose sulfate, acts by the binding to the surface of ulcers in the stomach and duodenum, thereby covering the ulcer crater and providing an effective barrier against gastric juice. This agent may be as effective as cimetidine and is certainly superior to placebo.[25,26]

The role of prostaglandins has been studied in the regulation of gastric mucosal blood flow and acid secretion. Separate from and unrelated to their inhibition of gastric secretion, prostaglandins exhibit a "cytoprotective" effect wherein the mucosa is protected from inflammation caused by noxious agents.[27] Clinical trials are under way to assess the efficacy of synthetic analogues of prostaglandin E1 and E2 in the healing of peptic ulcer. If successful, this will represent an instance wherein beneficial influence of a cellular factor has been achieved.

Finally, it may be that we are ready to deal with the questions raised by Dr James B. Herrick on the occasion of Sippy's death[11]:

I do not know whether his theory is correct or his management of the condition the best. Time will tell. But Bertram Sippy's life was one of useful service. . . . He stimulated, in Chicago and the whole country, internists, surgeons, physiologists, pathologists, to a more enlightened reconsideration of the whole question of ulcer and other gastrointestinal disease.

We wish gratefully to acknowledge the insights provided by Walter L. Palmer, MD.

## References

1. Pliny G: *The Historie of the World* (commonly called *The Natural Historie*), Holland P (trans). London, Adam Islip, 1601, vol 2, p 329.

2. Hunter J: On digestion of the stomach after death, in *Philosophical Transactions of the Royal Society*. London, 1772, vol 62, p 447.

3. Abercrombie J: *Pathological and Practical Researches on the Diseases of the Stomach,* ed 3. Philadelphia, Casey Lea & Blanchard, 1938, p 320.

4. Cruveilhier J: *Anatomie Pathologique,* 1829-1835, vol 10 and 20; 1835-1842, vol 38. *Arch Gen Med* 1856;7:149, 442.

5. Riegel F: Diseases of the stomach, in Stockton CG (ed): *Nothnagel's Encylopedia of Practical Medicine*. Philadelphia, WB Saunders Co, 1905.

6. Billings F: Etiology and diagnosis of gastric and duodenal ulcer. *Alabama Med J,* 1906, pp 544-551.

7. Robson AWM: The Hunterian lecture on duodenal ulcer and its treatment. *Br Med J* 1907;1:248-254.

8. Moynihan B: Duodenal ulcer, in *The Practitioner*. London, John Briss, 1907, vol 76, p 249.

9. Riegel F: Diseases of the stomach, in Stockton CG (ed): *Nothnagel's Encyclopedia of Practical Medicine*. Philadelphia, WB Saunders Co, 1905, p 634.

10. Joslin E: *Gastric Ulcer at the Massachusetts General Hospital. Am J Med Sci* 1899;118:167-183.

11. Brown R, Brown EVL: Memorial from the Institute of Medicine of Chicago: Bertram Welton Sippy, 1866-1924, in *Bertram Welton Sippy, M.D*. Aransas Press, Tex, Biography Press, 1974.

12. Osler W: On splenic anemia. *Am J Med Sci* 1900;119:54-73.

13. Sippy BW: Lesions of the conus medullaris and cauda equina: A contribution to the study of spinal localization. *JAMA* 1902;38:1195-1203.

14. Sippy BW: The diagnosis of influenza. *Chicago Med Rec* 1903;24:334-343.

15. Sippy BW: Diagnosis of esophageal lesions. *Ann Surg* 1906;13:858-869.

16. Sippy BW: Diseases of the esophagus, in Musser JH, Kelly AOJ (eds): *A Handbook of Practical Treatment*. Philadelphia, WB Saunders Co, 1912, vol 3, pp 316-327.

17. Sippy BW: Diseases of the esophagus, in Billings F (ed): *Forchheimer's Therapeusis of Internal Diseases*. New York, D Appleton & Co, 1915, vol 3, p 52.

18. Sippy BW: Gastric and duodenal ulcer: Medical cure by an efficient removal of gastric juice corrosion. *Trans Assoc Am Physicians* 1915;30:129-148.

19. Sippy BW: Relative value of medical and surgical treatment of gastric and duodenal ulcer. *JAMA* 1922;79:26-29.

20. Sippy BW: Gastric and duodenal ulcer: Medical cure by an efficient removal of gastric juice corrosion. *JAMA* 1915;64:1625-1630.

21. Dragstedt LR: Contributions to the physiology of the stomach. *JAMA* 1917;68:330-333.

22. Eusterman G, Balfour D: *The Stomach and Duodenum*. Philadelphia, WB Saunders Co, 1935, p 18.

23. Peterson WL, Sturdevant RAL, Frankl HD, et al: Healing of duodenal ulcer with an antacid regimen. *N Engl J Med* 1977;297:341-345.

24. McCarthy D: Peptic ulcer: Antacids or cimetidine? *Hosp Pract,* 1979, pp 52-64.

25. Marks IN, Lucke W, Wright J, et al: Ulcer healing and relapse rates after initial treatment with cimetidine or sucralfate. *J Clin Gastroenterol* 1981;3(suppl 2):163-165.

26. McHardy G: A multicenter double-blind trial of sucralfate and placebo in duodenal ulcer. *J Clin Gastroenterol* 1981;3(suppl 2):147-152.

27. Robert A: Cytoprotection by prostaglandins. *Gastroenterology* 1979;77:761-767.

June 19, 1915
(*JAMA* 1915;64:2042-2043)

## Chapter 13

# The Isolation in Crystalline Form of the Compound Containing Iodin, Which Occurs in the Thyroid

## Its Chemical Nature and Physiologic Activity[*]

E. C. Kendall, Ph.D.

Rochester, Minn.

During the past twenty years, investigation has firmly established, among other things, the following two facts: (1) The thyroid contains some substance capable of producing marked physiologic effects, and (2) iodin is a constant constituent of normal and pathologic glands. These two facts are emphasized because most of the controversies concerning the thyroid have arisen from attempts to explain the relation between the physiologic activity and the presence of iodin.

It is obvious that no final conclusions could be arrived at until either some substance possessing physiologic activity had been isolated in pure form and shown to be a normal constituent of the gland, or until the compound containing iodin had been isolated in pure form and its physiologic activity determined.

Last December I[1] reported the separation from the thyroid of a preparation containing 60 per cent. of iodin. The present paper is a summary of the results thus far obtained. In brief, the compound containing iodin, the presence of which, as a normal constituent of the thyroid, was foretold by Baumann[2] nineteen years ago, has been isolated in pure crystalline form, and further, it has been shown that this compound is the substance in the thyroid which is responsible for the physiologic activity of the gland.[3]

Previous investigation has shown that the compound containing iodin is firmly held as a constituent of the thyroid proteins. Hence separation of this compound must be preceded by a breaking down of the proteins into the simpler constituents of which they are composed. Baumann attempted this hydrolysis, using 10 per cent. sulphuric acid, but no satisfactory cleavage of the molecule resulted. The hydrolysis which has been successful was accomplished with sodium hydroxid in alcohol as a medium for carrying out the process.

A large number of compounds are obtained by this splitting up of the protein, but they are separated into two groups by the addition of acid. Those compounds insoluble in acid are designated Group A, and those soluble Group B.

The total iodin in the gland is found to be divided almost equally between the two groups. By further hydrolysis of the A group the compound containing iodin has been separated in pure crystalline form. Its exact formula cannot now be stated, but it appears to be di-iodo-di-hydroxy-indol. It crystallizes in microscopic needles that melt around 220 C. It is very insoluble in alcohol, ether, water, acids and sodium carbonate. Dilute hydrochloric acid dissolves 1 part in about 200,000. It is readily soluble in dilute alkali and ammonia.

No definite substance possessing physiologic activity has been isolated from the B group, but it is known to be a complex mixture containing amino-acids. The iodin in B is in organic combination, but the nucleus to which it is

[*] From the Mayo Clinic.

1. Kendall, E. C.: A Method for the Decomposition of the Proteins of the Thyroid, with a Description of Certain Constituents, Jour. Biol. Chem., 1915, xx, 501.

2. Baumann, E.: Ueber das normale Vorkommen von Jod im Thierkörper, Ztschr. f. physiol. Chem., 1895-1896, xxi, 319.

3. The physiologic activity referred to is the production of the so-called hyperthyroid symptoms, tachycardia, increase in metabolism with loss of weight and increase in nervous irritability. Some other constituents of the gland possess physiologic activity, but of minor importance.

attached is unknown.

The thyroid having been separated into several different constituents, it seemed desirable to test each one for its possible physiologic activity. It was found that the typical effects of administration of desiccated thyroid—a rapid increase in pulse rate and vigor, increase in metabolism with loss of weight, and increase in nervous irritability—are all produced by the A constituents.

The next step showed that in A, containing about 5 per cent. of iodin, the effects produced are directly proportional to the amount of iodin present. And finally, in the purification of A and the separation of the iodin compound in crystalline form, the same typical effects were produced through all the various stages of purity, up to and including the crystalline compound containing 60 per cent. of iodin.

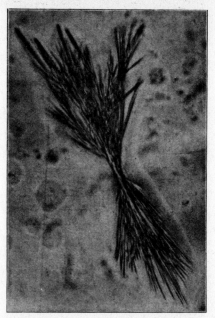
Crystals of the iodin-containing compound which occurs in the thyroid.

In testing B for physiologic activity, it was found that no apparent effects are produced when B is given experimentally to a normal animal or human being, but that a considerable degree of activity is manifest when B is given to patients suffering from cretinism, myxedema and certain conditions of the skin. However, no toxic effects have been produced by the administration of B, even in large amount.

This nontoxic effect of B is in strong contrast to the action of A. Although both A and B contain iodin, it has been shown that the toxicity of A is in direct proportion to its iodin content, but B iodin given in equal amount produces no apparent effect.

As previous investigators have pointed out, it is not iodin per se that is necessary. This work shows that it is the iodized indol that produces the physiologic activity. The actual amount of the crystalline iodin compound necessary to produce marked effect is exceedingly small. A total of 11 mg. (one-sixth grain), given in divided doses during a period of fourteen days to a cretin weighing 40 pounds, increased the pulse rate from 90 to 140. A total of 30 mg. (one-half grain), given in divided doses over a period of eighteen days to a woman weighing 112 pounds, increased the pulse rate from 75 to 130. Not only in rate but also in apparent vigor of the beat the cardiogram of a heart, after administration of the iodin compound, simulates a cardiogram of a patient with exophthalmic goiter.

What, then, is the relation of this iodin compound and the symptoms of exophthalmic goiter? Pathologic investigation has shown that the severity and duration of the symptoms are accompanied by definite histologic changes in the thyroid. It has been shown that in the severest forms of exophthalmic goiter the parenchyma is far more active than in the normal gland.

Analysis of 137 thyroids from exophthalmic goiter cases showed that, in those glands having a thin, watery secretion, the iodin content was very low, but as the secretion became thicker and less diffusible, the percentage of iodin increased.

These results point to two functions of the thyroid: One function is the manufacture of the iodin compound, and the other that of acting as a reservoir for this compound. We have no means at present of measuring the manufacturing capacity of the gland, but we do know that it is greatly increased in exophthalmic goiter. The reservoir capacity of the gland is obviously proportional to the iodin content. The total amount of iodin in the severest form of exophthalmic goiter averaged 7 mg., and the total iodin in glands in which the secretions had become thick and less diffusible was 35 mg. That is, the reservoir capacity had increased 500 per cent., and when it is known that 1 mg. a day of the pure crystalline iodin compound will produce marked toxic symptoms in a normal person, the important rôle played by the iodin compound in the production of symptoms of exophthalmic goiter is evident.

The separation in pure form of the iodin compound is the first necessary step in the further study, not only of pathologic conditions, but also of the normal physiology of the gland.

SUMMARY

1. By an alkaline alcoholic hydrolysis, the thyroid proteins are broken into many simpler constituents. These may be separated into two groups: the acid insoluble compounds are designated Group A; those acid soluble, Group B.

2. From Group A a pure crystalline compound, containing 60 per cent. of iodin, has been isolated. It appears to be di-iodo-di-hydroxy-indol.

3. Group B contains iodin in some unknown form of combination. It is a mixture containing amino-acid complexes and a low molecular weight.

4. Administration of A produces in the dog and in the human being a rapid increase in pulse rate and vigor, and increase in metabolism and nervous irritability. This physiologic activity is produced by the compound containing iodin in all stages of purity up to and including its crystalline form.

5. Given in excess, toxic symptoms are produced. The amount of the iodin compound required to produce toxic effects is exceedingly small.

6. In exophthalmic goiter two abnormal conditions exist. First, the secreting capacity of the gland is greatly increased and, second, the reservoir capacity of the gland is greatly decreased. The iodin compound plays an important role in the production of the symptoms of exophthalmic goiter.

7. The constituents of Group B produce no toxic symptoms, but in cases of cretinism, myxedema and certain skin conditions, they exert physiologic activity.

Oct 21, 1983
(JAMA 1983;250:2047-2048)

# The Isolation of Thyroxine*

Martin L. Nusynowitz, MD

How fitting that on Christmas day, 1914, while the armies of Europe were locked in mortal combat, there was isolated the substance that would be the salvation of unnumbered thousands afflicted with hypothyroidism, bringing to them life and well-being. On that day, Edward C. Kendall crystallized and isolated thyroxine, enabling the determination of its chemistry.[1] Within 12 years, Harrington and Barger[2] were able to delineate its structure and synthesize the hormone.

Kendall's accomplishment was the capstone of more than 40 years of work on hypothyroidism. In 1871, Fagge[3] described spontaneous cretinism and speculated on the appearance of the disease occurring in adults, and three years later, Gull[4] first described adult myxedema.

Although thyroid extirpation experiments in animals were occurring about this time, the association between Gull's disease and the thyroid gland was not well established until two Swiss surgeons, Reverdin and Kocher,[5,6] reported on the effect of thyroidectomy in humans. Substitution therapy, by one means or another, was a natural consequence of these observations, culminating in 1892 in the observation that oral administration of thyroid gland constituted satisfactory treatment.[7,8] Several years later, Magnus-Levy[9] showed that total catabolism was increased in patients with exophthalmic goiter and by the ingestion of thyroid gland in normal persons. He thereby established the basis of the pathophysiology of both hypothyroidism and thyrotoxicosis. Shortly thereafter, Baumann[10] discovered that iodine was a normal constituent of the thyroid, and in 1907, Marine[11] demonstrated that iodine was necessary for normal thyroid function.

It was Kendall's great discovery, published in *JAMA* in 1915, that unequivocally established that the crystalline compound isolated contained 60% iodine and had the full physiological activity of the entire gland. This proved the essentiality of iodine to the hormone. Indeed, this characteristic, unique to thyroid hormone, enabled later investigators to apply radiotracer technology to the study of thyroid physiology and pathology when radioiodine became available some decades later.[12,13]

The consequences of Kendall's observations and the work based on them have been central in providing a model for the workings of all of the endocrine glands and for the prevention, diagnosis, and treatment of thyroid disease. Kendall's crystallization of the thyroid hormone, soon to be named "thyroxine," enabling its subsequent characterization and synthesis, has had astounding practical results. There is probably no other drug, and certainly no other hormone, that is as inexpensive, easy to take, or as effective as thyroxine; the mortality and morbidity of hypothyroidism are totally reversible by the ingestion of a nickel's worth (one tablet) daily. As has been shown recently, this disorder is exceedingly common and should be diligently sought out[14,15]; indeed, screening programs for congenital forms are inherent in good medical practice. Unfortunately, the advantages possessed by thyroxine have led to its abuse in the treatment of obesity and other disorders for which it is not indicated.

Finally, Kendall's research set the pattern for investigation into the hormones: isolation from glandular extracts, purification, demonstration of physiological properties,

---

From the Division of Nuclear Medicine, Department of Radiology, University of Texas Medical Branch, Galveston.

*A commentary on Kendall EC: The isolation in crystalline form of the compound containing iodin, which occurs in the thyroid. *JAMA* 1915;64:2042-2043.

determination of structure, and synthesis devolved from and were based on this work. In 1950, Kendall was awarded the Nobel Prize in medicine for much of the basic chemical research that led to the synthesis of the steroid hormones. Undoubtedly, these achievements were in no small measure based on his earlier work with thyroxine, the publication of which graced the pages of this journal.

## References

1. Kendall EC: The isolation in crystalline form of the compound containing iodin, which occurs in the thyroid. *JAMA* 1915;64:2042-2043.

2. Harrington CR, Barger G: Thyroxine III: Constitution and synthesis of thyroxine. *Biochem J* 1927;21:169-183.

3. Fagge CH: On sporadic cretinism, occurring in England. *Med Chir Trans* 1871;54:155.

4. Gull WW: On a cretinoid state supervening in adult life in women. *Trans Clin Soc Lond* 1874;7:180.

5. Reverdin JL: *Rev Med Suisse Rom* 1882;2:539.

6. Kocher T: Ueber Kropf exstirpation und ihre Folgen. *Arch J Klin Chir* 1883;29:254.

7. Mackenzie HWG: A case of myxoedema treated with great benefit by feeding with fresh thyroid glands. *Br Med J* 1892;2:940.

8. Fox EL: A case of myxoedema treated by taking extract of thyroid by the mouth. *Br Med J* 1892;2:941.

9. Magnus-Levy A: Ueber den respiratorischen Gewechsel unter dem Einfluss der Thyreoiden sowie unter verschiedenen pathologisch-en Zustaenden. *Berl Klin Wchnschr* 1895;32:650.

10. Baumann E: Der Jodgehalt der Schilddruessen von Menschen und Thieren. *Z Physiol Chem* 1896;22:1.

11. Marine D: On the occurrence and physiological nature of glandular hyperplasia of the thyroid (dog and sheep), together with remarks on important clinical (human) problems. *Johns Hopkins Hosp Bull* 1907;18:359.

12. Hertz S, Roberts A, Evans RD: Radioactive iodine as an indicator in the study of thyroid physiology. *Proc Soc Exp Biol Med* 1938;38:510.

13. Hamilton JG, Soley MH: Studies in iodine metabolism of the thyroid gland in situ by the use of radio-iodine in normal subjects and in patients with the various types of goiter. *Am J Physiol* 1939;127:557.

14. Dos Remedios LV, Weber PM, Feldman R, et al: Detecting unsuspected thyroid dysfunction by the free thyroxine index. *Arch Intern Med* 1980;140:1045-1049.

15. Nusynowitz ML: Screening tests and the free thyroxine index. *Arch Intern Med* 1980;140:1017.

# Chapter 14

# Nonoperative Determination of Patency of Fallopian Tubes in Sterility

## Intra-uterine Inflation With Oxygen, and Production of an Artificial Pneumoperitoneum

## Preliminary Report*

### I. C. Rubin, M.D.

#### New York

The value of oxygen in conjunction with the roentgen ray as an aid in the diagnosis of obscure abdominal conditions has been demonstrated in a number of recent publications. No ill effects have accompanied or followed the pneumoperitoneum produced by inflation of the abdominal cavity with oxygen gas. The tolerance of the peritoneum for oxygen even in large volume, and the fact that its presence can be detected by fluoroscopy and roentgenography have led to its use as a diagnostic procedure in determining patency of the fallopian tubes. If the gas injected into the uterus under certain measurable pressure would pass into the fallopian tubes, it ought to reach the general peritoneal cavity. In patients with patent fallopian tubes the gas would establish an artificial pneumoperitoneum identical with that produced when injected by direct abdominal puncture. In patients with occluded tubes no such result could be obtained.

Accordingly, experiments were carried out on extirpated uteri with the adnexa intact. In the first experiment it was readily seen that oxygen passed into the uterine opening of the tubes and then escaped through the fimbriated end. When the tubes were ligated or were occluded by pathologic processes, this did not follow. After determining the amount of gas required for our purposes, the first clinical application of the intra-uterine oxygen inflation was made, Nov. 3, 1919, at Mount Sinai Hospital. It was successful in proving the patency of the fallopian tubes in this first patient. The abdomen became visibly distended and the pneumoperitoneum was confirmed by the roentgenographic examination. The symptoms associating the gas inflation by way of the uterus were the same as those described for the method by direct abdominal puncture.

Encouraged by the result of the first trial, I tested it out in a series of thirty-five cases of sterility in which there were different clinical histories and physical findings. In this first series it was our endeavor to find out the limits of application, the quantity of gas to be employed, the time and rate of flow, and the reliability of the oxygen injected as a diagnostic procedure. In the second series of twenty cases, estimations were made on pressure. This has proved a valuable adjunct. Altogether, fifty-five patients were examined by means of oxygen inflation of the uterus. There were absolutely no untoward symptoms or sequelae. The patients with two exceptions were ambulatory, and were allowed to go home from within a few minutes to a half hour after examination. Two cases were from the hospital wards. The patients were all followed up and carefully examined for complications, none of which have to the present writing appeared.

In some cases the result confirmed our clinical diagnosis of probably closed or patent tubes. In a number of cases the tubes were proved to be open when we had reason to suspect they were closed by disease, while in others the tubes were demonstrated to be occluded when we had believed them to be normal. The method had practically the value of an exploratory laparotomy for purposes of determining the continuity of the lumen of the fallopian tubes. The two possible dangers, namely, embolism and infection, are more theoretical than actual.

Embolism from oxygen introduced into the uterus in a stream of discrete bubbles never occurs, and infection need never occur if the cases are not acute and are properly selected. In fifty-five cases which form the basis of this preliminary report, there were no symptoms even suggestive of a possible peritoneal irritation, although some of them had presented gross pathologic conditions before the examination was made. These questions, with the case histories, will be more fully discussed in a future communication.

---

* From the Second Gynecological Service and X-Ray Department of Mount Sinai Hospital.

261 Central Park West.

ept 4, 1920
*JAMA* 1920;75:661-667)

# The Nonoperative Determination of Patency of Fallopian Tubes

## By Means of Intra-uterine Inflation With Oxygen and the Production of an Artificial Pneumoperitoneum*

I. C. Rubin, M.D.

New York

The determination of patency of fallopian tubes has itherto been possible only by direct inspection and alpation obtained by laparotomy. Physician examination was wholly inadequate because it still left the uestion of patency a matter of speculation. This is specially true when, as in certain intances, the tubes are ealed tight at their fimbriated end, although no distension of the lumen is present. In other instances it is hard o diagnose occlusion of the tube due to hydrosalpinx vhen the walls are flaccid. Some tubes are closed by dhesions secondary to a peritonitis that arises outside of he gynecologic domain. No matter how clear the history, he question as to whether such a tube is patent or not is lways a matter of doubt. The same holds true in cases in vhich the tube may be occluded by a tumor.

It is often not possible to distinguish whether a mass in ither lateral fornix is due to disease of the tube or the vary. Even in the presence of a bilateral mass, the tubes 1ay nevertheless be patent despite suspicions directed gainst them. I have seen a patient who refused peration, although the surgeon assured her that she had •us tubes and would not only be sterile, but would emain an invalid. I have since established that her tubes re patent by the use of intra-uterine oxygen inflation. In er case the ovaries were undoubtedly at fault.

An accurate knowledge of the anatomic patency of the tubes is admittedly important in formulating prognosis and therapy of female sterility. If we are aware that a patient is sterile because her fallopian tubes are closed, plastic operations on the cervix, curettage, dilatation and opotherapy will obviously be useless. Indeed, the disease in the tubes is often clinically manifest after an operation on the cervix, as evidenced by a rise of temperature, pain, tenderness and swelling to one or both sides of the uterus developing within a short time after the operation. The patient may in all innocence charge this to the surgeon, when in reality it is simply a lighting up of an old latent infection. The impossibility of fecundation in unsuccessful cases is due to obstruction in some portion of the tube, either at the uterine ostium, along its lumen, or at the fimbriated end. In the presence of a small cornual polyp blocking the uterine insertion of the tubes, or occlusion by salpingitis isthmica nodosa, hydrosalpinx or some malformation within the tube lumen (complete spurs, blind canals, etc.), any operation on the lower uterine portion must result in failure.

### INCIDENCE OF STERILITY DUE TO DISEASE OF THE TUBES

It is well to remember, as Giles states, that practically 11 per cent. of female sterilities is due to tubal disease. In women under 24 years of age it is higher, reaching 14.4 per cent. Add to these 4.4 per cent. of cases due to blocking of the fallopian tubes by peritonitis, and we have an average incidence of 15 per cent. of cases of sterility due to pathologic tubes. For convenience we will not include tumor formations and malformations. It will then be seen that one out of six or seven women owes her sterility to closed tubes.

*From the Second Gynecological Service and the Roentgen-Ray epartment of Mount Sinai Hospital.

*Read before the Section on Obstetrics, Gynecology and Abdominal urgery at the Seventy-First Annual Session of the American Medical ssociation, New Orleans, April, 1920.

*Owing to lack of space, this article is abbreviated in THE JOURNAL y the omission of several illustrations. The complete article appears in e Transactions of the Section and in the author's reprints.

Here it may be mentioned that, in certain cases in which no gross physical abnormality can be elicited by examining the woman (2 per cent. of cases) and the potency of the male partner is established by the finding of live spermatozoa in the cervix and fundus uteri, a congenital atresia of the tubes or of some part of the lumen may be the real cause of the sterility. One naturally hesitates to subject such a woman to an exploratory laparotomy, so that a method whereby patency of the tube could be demonstrated without surgical means is eminently desirable.

### INTRA-UTERINE OXYGEN INFLATION
#### AS A METHOD OF DIAGNOSIS

This I believe has been effected by the combination of oxygen with fluoroscopy and roentgenography. It is possible to determine whether the tubes are patent or otherwise by inflating the uterus with oxygen and in normal cases filling the peritoneal cavity with a measured quantity of oxygen. The artificial pneumoperitoneum establishes definitely the patency of the fallopian tubes. In a preliminary report I pointed out that the peritoneum tolerates the oxygen introduced by way of the uterus and fallopian tubes equally as well as by direct abdominal puncture. There is no doubt, however, that the result is the same whether the peritoneum is filled with oxygen through the abdominal wall by puncture or through the uterine cavity without puncture. For general abdominal diagnosis at least a liter to a liter and a half of gas is necessary. For the specific purpose of establishing the fact of open fallopian tubes the amount of oxygen need not exceed 300 c.c., and in the last of my cases tested by this method about 150 c.c. would be the average volume used.

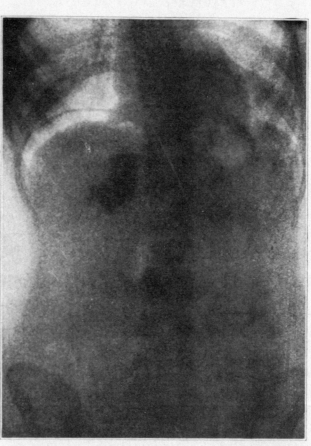

Fig. 4.—Pneumoperitoneum: 250 c.c. of oxygen injected into the peritoneal cavity by way of the uterus and fallopian tubes. Diaphragm visible on the right side, not on the left. Slight downward displacement of the liver.

In one case from Dr. H. Lilienthal's service I injected oxygen by way of the fallopian tubes for the diagnosis of a possible perinephric abscess complicating an operation for acute perforative appendicitis. An abdominal sinus at the site of the appendix incision was proved to communicate with the peritoneal cavity because most of the oxygen escaped through it. Bubbles of gas were seen to form through the moisture at the sinus opening, and this leakage prevented the formation of an enclosed pneumoperitoneum.

*The small volume of oxygen has the advantage of enabling us to examine the patient in the office without the necessity of her going to bed for twenty-four hours or more.* Symptoms of phrenic irritation are decidedly less, and the patients may go about their daily work. When a greater amount of oxygen is injected, the patient is more comfortable in a moderate Trendelenburg posture. This causes the oxygen to rise to the pelvis, and the excursions of the diaphragm are less hampered by the column of oxygen.

In the first patient in whom I injected oxygen through the uterus I did not measure the quantity but allowed it to pass into the peritoneal cavity till a moderate amount of visible distention resulted. The fluoroscopic and roentgenographic pictures were the same as described by Stein and Stewart, who introduce the oxygen through a trocar or needle thrust into the abdominal wall. This patient was allowed to go home one hour after the examination and advised to lie down in a bed with the foot elevated. She was reexamined at the end of the third day, and a small amount of oxygen was still present below the diaphragm. The estimated amount she must have received was from 2 to 2.5 liters.

In the next thirty-two cases of sterility examined by intra-uterine oxygen inflation it was endeavored to establish several points: (1) the tolerance of the patient for the method as a diagnostic procedure; (2) the possible danger of infection; (3) the danger of embolism; (4) the diagnostic reliability of the findings and interpretation and (5) the minimum volume of oxygen necessary to produce the pneumoperitoneum which could be seen by fluoroscopic examination.

1. *Tolerance of the Patient.*—The patients stood the examination with very slight discomfort. At most it was like the pain produced in some patients by the introduction of a uterine sound. Nervous women complained more from fear than actual pain, because the vast majority of the patients made no complaint during the injection. The passing of the oxygen into the peritoneal cavity is painless. Uniformly there is some sense of pressure about the diaphragm within five or ten minutes and slight "sticking" sensations in one or both shoulders.

A half liter of oxygen causes very moderate symptoms. A liter of oxygen is followed by greater epigastric oppression and shoulder pains. When more than a liter is used, the symptoms are proportionately increased. When from 100 to 200 c.c. are injected, the symptoms are very slight and do not interfere with the patient's daily routine.

2. *Possible Dangers of Peritoneal Infection.*—There are no pelvic symptoms after the gas inflation. In no case was there evidence suggestive of peritoneal irritation. Not a single one of the symptoms characteristic of peritoneal infection was noted. There was no nausea or vomiting, pains, rigidity or tenderness, or rise in temperature or pulse rate. The patients were all closely observed. They were followed through three or four menstrual periods to note any late sequel of the oxygen test.

3. *Possible Dangers of Embolism.*—In no instance were there symptoms suggestive of air embolism. This question gave me some concern in first contemplating the method. By actual experiment on the dog I found that the animal tolerated 350 c.c. of oxygen introduced directly into the leg vein without any symptoms attending the injection or following it. The rate of oxygen flow was the same as employed in my sterility patients. As 350 c.c. is the very maximum amount required, I felt that the accident of embolism from oxygen could be disregarded. I have since learned that a number of army surgeons use this method of intravenous oxygen injection for therapeutic purposes, especially in pneumonia.

4. *Diagnostic Reliability of the Findings and Interpretation.*—When an artificial pneumoperitoneum was produced, it was conclusive in proving the patency of the genital canal from the external end to the internal abdominal end. This, however, could result when only one tube was patent and the other closed, as well as when both tubes were actually patent. For practical purposes in the consideration of sterility it suffices that one fallopian tube is patent. Future observations may make it possible for us to draw definite conclusions on the question of unilateral or bilateral patency, and, if unilateral, which side is open or closed. At this time I am not prepared to present data on this point.

When an artificial pneumoperitoneum does not result from the intra-uterine oxygen inflation, the probability is that there is some obstruction in the genital canal above

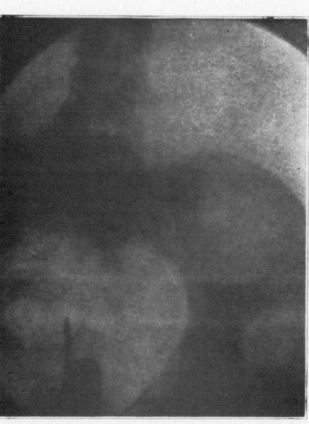

Fig. 7.—Case of ablated tubes. Bilateral salpingo-oophorectomy two years before. Speculum and intra-uterine cannula in situ. Large Thomas pessary also visible. Oxygen injected by syringe (40 c.c. used). Uterine cavity, transversely pear-shaped, plainly visible.

the internal os. It may be at the uterine ostium of the fallopian tubes, along their course, or at the fimbriated end. Whether this be by uterine cornual polypi occluding the opening as a ball valve or inspissated mucus in the tubal lumen, or agglutination of the plicae of the endosalpinx or a sealing over of the fimbria, the result will be the same. One negative result is not enough to establish nonpatency. In such an instance the test is repeated once or twice, a little more gas being used each time. If in the repeated tests the oxygen fails to pass through, we may conclude that the patient is sterile because of this mechanical blockade. Occasionally, however, when the stenosis operates like a ball valve, as in the case of a polyp at either uterine horn, the greater pressure by the increased gas volume may succeed in forcing the oxygen through, and then a pneumoperitoneum would result. In such an event, however, the test would still have a certain diagnostic value and might serve to indicate the proper therapeutic measure to be adopted to overcome this difficulty. Inspissated mucus at the uterine end of the tube would have the same effect, and here, too, the negative result is significant of a mechanical cause of sterility.

These results I am able to demonstrate on the extirpated uterus with adnexa attached. In one case[1] I had the opportunity to confirm by operation the clinical findings as obtained by the oxygen test:

This was a patient, aged 27, who had been married twelve years and had three children, the youngest of whom was 2 years old. Since the birth of the youngest child she believed herself pregnant twice; each time an abortion was performed. She complained of pains in the pelvis and prolonged menstrual flow. Examination by Dr. H. N. Vineberg, attending gynecologist, disclosed a moderate cystic enlargement of the right adnexa, which was slightly tender, the left side being apparently normal. The uterus was enlarged about 100 per cent. The temperature was normal, the pulse, 80. A diagnosis of diseased adnexa on the right side was made. As inflation of this uterus under a pressure of 190 failed to produce an artificial pneumoperitoneum, I felt that the left tube was also diseased and closed. Laparotomy in this case, performed six days after the oxygen injection,

---

1. In another case, in which the condition was diagnosed as multiple fibroids, the oxygen failed to produce an artificial pneumoperitoneum. At operation both tubes were closed (double hydrosalpinx).

revealed an old standing pelvic peritonitis; both tubes were closed at the fimbriated end, that on the right side being moderately distended, while the left tube was but slightly swollen. They were both embedded in adhesions, in which the ovaries were also slightly involved. The inflation with oxygen was attended by no pain or discomfort. There had been no fresh lighting up of the process. The patient made an absolutely uneventful recovery from the operation.

While I should not advocate the use of this method in frank inflammatory conditions, this one experience has a definite value, in demonstrating its safety of application. On the specimen removed by operation I was able to repeat the oxygen injection and to corroborate the findings both as to the intra-uterine pressure and as to patency. When the pressure reached 190, the oxygen began to regurgitate through the external os. By tightening the latter around the cannula, the pressure rose to 210 and then fell slightly as the gas escaped along the sides of the instrument. This greater pressure failed to force the oxygen through the tubes or to distend them.

In order to see whether the stream of oxygen bubbles might force infective material into the peritoneal cavity, I opened the clubbed end of one of the pus tubes and repeated the oxygen injection in the same way as before. Again the same findings; no pus escaped into the basin of water into which the tube was immersed. The explanation for this is that the intramural portion of the tube lumen, normally only about 1 or 2 mm. in diameter, becomes plugged in pathologic conditions with pus or mucus. In addition, the swelling of the endosalpinx as well as that of all the coats of the tube results in practically obliterating the lumen of the tube and shutting it off from the uterine cavity. While in certain rare cases a large hydrosalpinx or pyosalpinx drains into the uterus, in the majority of cases the uterine end of the tubes remains occluded and resists the usual pressure to which the oxygen is subjected in testing for patency. When the fimbriated ends are clubbed, there is absolutely no danger of forcing them open. It requires many times the pressure necessary for the practical application of the method. Besides, the external os acts as a safety valve, allowing the oxygen to escape as soon as a certain pressure is reached.

As far as introducing infective material from the uterine cavity into normal tubes and thence into the peritoneum is concerned, several factors make that highly improbable. One is that the cavity of the body of the uterus is in most cases free of infection. Pus or mucus, if present, is more likely to descend from infected tubes. When the uterine discharge is frankly purulent, the method is not to be used. Against this theoretical objection is the practical fact that in none of the seventy cases has there been such an occurrence.

In the nonpatent cases one may also use thorium or bromid as a control. The citrate thorium solution or sodium bromid solution may be injected into the uterus,

and under obturation the roentgenogram may be made. I did this a few times in the earlier experiments, but have been able to dispense with it in my later work.

### TECHNIC

The technic of the procedure is very simple. The instruments needed for the intra-uterine injection are (1) a metal cannula (Keyes-Ultzman type) perforated at the tip by several small apertures (Fig. 9); (2) a tenaculum (bullet) forceps; (3) a uterine sound; (4) a dressing forceps; (5) a bivalve vaginal speculum (Graves type), and (6) an oxygen tank connected with a water bottle. The rubber stopper is perforated at three points through which bent glass connecting tubes pass into the bottle; one of these glass tubes connected with the oxygen tank dips down below the water level. The two other glass tubes dip down for 1 or 2 inches, and do not reach the water level. One of these is attached by rubber tubing to a mercurial manometer and the other is attached in the same way to the metal cannula. In order to determine the volume of oxygen gas released from the tank, it is allowed to pass through the water bottle in a stream of discrete bubbles. These should not exceed 300 per minute. The actual amount per minute can then be measured by displacing an equivalent quantity of water from a graduated bottle into another.

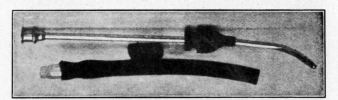

Fig. 9.—*a*, Keyes-Ultzmann cannula perforated at the tip by several small apertures with urethral rubber tip for obturation of the external os of the cervix; *b*, a piece of rubber tubing with glass connecting tube originally used in the apparatus (this is not absolutely necessary).

It will then be seen that for example, the gas displaces from 200 to 250 c.c. of water per minute. The same rate is then maintained in the intrauterine injection. The water bottle that is connected with the oxygen tank contains hot boiled water or some mild antiseptic solution.

The cervix is exposed by means of the speculum; the vagina is carefully wiped clean and the cervix is cleansed dry and painted with tincture of iodin. If there is any uncertainty regarding the direction of the uterine cavity, it may be determined by passing the sound. The cervix is steadied with tenaculum forceps grasping its anterior lip. The oxygen, which has been released from the tank and regulated, is now allowed to pass from the water bottle through the glass and rubber connecting tubing to which the metal cannula is attached. By pinching the rubber tubing near the cannula one can make sure that all the joints are air tight. The mercury immediately rises in this case. If there is some leakage between the oxygen source and the cannula, the pressure will be negative. This is a very important point to be observed. Having made certain of the pressure, the air valves in the manometer are opened and the catheter is then inserted into the uterine cavity to a point well beyond the internal os. This is done so that there is no immediate escape back along the cervical canal and out into the vagina. The rubber urethral tip, placed ordinarily from 1½ to 2 inches away from the cannula tip, is then fitted into the external os, insuring better obturation. This is not essential in the nulliparous intact cervix, but is required in the irregular patulous external os resulting from previous operations or from lacerations attending childbirth. The air valves are now closed. Within a few seconds after the oxygen enters the uterine cavity, the pressure as noted in the mercury manometer will rise; within from one half to three quarters of a minute in the patent cases the mercury reaches its maximum point. It then fluctuates for a few seconds or drops rather sharply from 10 to 30 points, maintaining the last level more or less for the rest of the time. There may be a slight audible escape of oxygen from the external os in the cases of patent tubes, but as a rule there is none till the cannula is removed, when slight regurgitation is present.

In the nonpatent cases, the pressure usually rises steadily for three quarters of a minute to a minute or longer, and then drops sharply as the gas regurgitates into the vagina. As the time required for sufficient oxygen to pass into the abdomen where it can be detected by fluoroscopic examination is one and a half minutes, the cannula is not withdrawn till this time limit is reached. If the pressure reaches 200 mm. in one minute, it is well to open one of the air valves (needle valve) to prevent it from mounting higher. In all our patent cases this high level was not reached.

The intra-uterine gas pressure has been a valuable adjunct in checking up the time required for the gas to pass through the tubes and reach the peritoneal cavity. In our earlier cases we had decided on a three-minute interval as being necessary. In that time from 750 to 850 c.c. were released from the oxygen tank. We had no way of telling when the gas actually passed through the fallopian tubes. The symptoms were naturally accentuated. The pneumoperitoneum was excessive. A liter of oxygen was not necessary when a quarter of a liter was just as valuable for the purposes of establishing the fact of patency. With the manometer attached to the water bottle we can decide, knowing the rate of flow beforehand, how much we wish to inject into the abdomen. From the moment the pressure falls, we allow the gas to flow for from one-half to one minute, and can estimate the quantity used with reasonable accuracy, allowing for an error of 50 c.c., which for practical purposes is

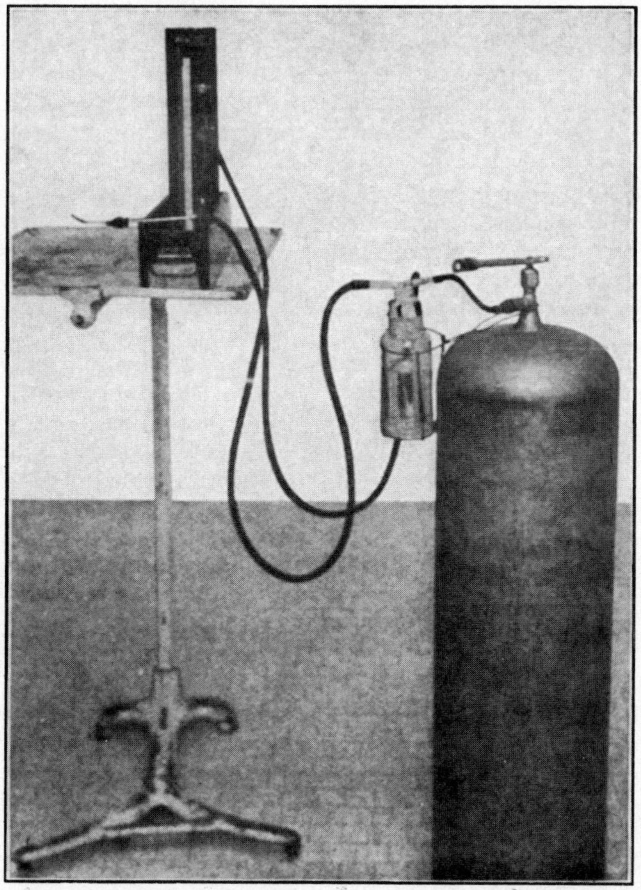

Fig. 10.—The apparatus set together. The same rate of flow of oxygen as previously determined by displacing water is maintained before and during the intra-uterine oxygen inflation. The mercurial manometer may be of the standard type, as illustrated here, or it may be of the Tycos type, and can then be inserted directly into the rubber stopper of the water bottle.

unimportant.

Various types of pressure devices were tried to estimate intra-uterine gas pressure. The mercury manometer of the standard type was finally adopted. For this advice I am indebted to Dr. Arthur J. Bendick, associate roentgenologist to Mount Sinai Hospital. This was particularly important, because of the theoretical possibility of air embolism resulting from too great pressure which might force the oxygen into the blood vessels. In none of the first group of cases, in spite of the absence of accurate control, did such an accident occur. It has been clearly demonstrated that oxygen, as used in this method, does not cause embolism.

In the first group, ten patients were reexamined two or three times because they had had minimal amounts of oxygen. Most of these were found to have patent tubes when a sufficient volume of oxygen under pressure was injected. When the pressure test was adopted, it became unnecessary to repeat the examination in the negative cases except when in a nervous patient it had to be interrupted. This happened in one case; and on reexamination the patient, being reassured, submitted to the complete test. She then proved to have patent fallopian tubes. It is a good rule to repeat the test at least once in the nonpatent cases in order to check up the result of the first examination.

In the positive patent cases, the pressure need not exceed 40 mm. The average pressure is from 60 to 80; occasionally the pressure rises to 100 or more before the oxygen will pass through the uterine ostium of the fallopian tubes. When the pressure reaches 150 or more, the likelihood is that the tube lumen is closed completely or stenosed, but not necessarily in every case. A pressure of 200 is tolerably certain to be due to closed tubes. *Fluoroscopy, however, should always be employed to check up the partially stenosed cases, as sometimes oxygen will succeed in escaping into the abdomen, though the pressure required to force it in is comparatively high.*

While the pressure gage as studied in the second series of thirty-seven cases is an excellent indication of patency of the fallopian tubes, it is well always to examine the patient with the fluoroscope. It occasionally happens that with the greater pressure a slight amount of gas succeeds in entering the peritoneal cavity and reaching the subphrenic space on the right or left side, where it can be detected by the roentgen ray.

In the positive cases, that is, when the tubes are patent, the oxygen will be seen as a clear space below the diaphragm, most often on both sides, but occasionally on one side only. The space varies, depending on the volume of oxygen injected. In the average case in which from 150 to 250 c.c. is used, this clear space below the diaphragm varies between one-quarter to 1 inch in depth. The diaphragm appears as a transverse septum above the dense liver shadow on the right side and over the pale stomach margin on the left. It is unmistakable, and is readily seen when the patient breathes deeply. In all our cases in which we have made roentgenograms the finding was always confirmatory. Stout patients require a somewhat greater amount to allow for the density of the abdominal wall.

The whole examination is complete within five minutes. When the minimum volume of oxygen has been used, that is, from 100 to 150 c.c., the symptoms are negligible. There is the slightest discomfort around the diaphragm, and slight sticking pains referred to one or both shoulders. The patient dresses herself and is able to go home with comfort, and performs her duties as though she had had a simple cystoscopy. When, however, more gas has been used, the symptoms may be somewhat annoying. In such cases it is well for the patient to lie down for a few hours on reaching home, with the foot of the bed elevated (moderate Trendelenburg posture).

In the negative cases, that is, when the tubes are occluded, no artificial pneumoperitoneum results. These patients have no discomfort after examination, and have none of the referred pains in the shoulders or about the diaphragm.

In none of the cases are there pains in the pelvis following the intra-uterine oxygen injection. A little bloody oozing for a few minutes follows a withdrawal of the cannula, particularly in cases just before or just after the menstrual period. It is well, therefore, to make the examination about ten days after the menstrual period.

### RESULTS OF EXAMINATION

Altogether seventy cases were examined by the method of intra-uterine oxygen inflation; thirty-three without the control of the manometer, and thirty-seven with the manometer. In the first group various quantities of gas were used to establish particularly the minimum amount required to produce an artificial pneumoperitoneum without, however, the annoying symptoms which would destroy the usefulness of the method as a diagnostic aid. Various types of sterility cases were tested. Some were primary sterilities, the marriage dating back from one to twelve years or more and in which no operations were performed either to relieve the condition or for tubal, ovarian or uterine disease. Some of the patients had had one or several curettages for the relief of sterility; some for alleged miscarriages. A few had had one child and became relatively sterile for a number of years. A few cases in which it was definitely known that one or both tubes were ablated on account of pyosalpinx were used as

controls to check up the diagnostic value of the method. A few patients had had plastic operations on the cervix for the cure of primary sterility.

### INDICATIONS FOR THE APPLICATION OF THE METHOD

The method is indicated:

1. In all cases of primary sterility in which all factors except that of tubal disease may be excluded. Here it has a definite prognostic as well as diagnostic value.

2. In cases of primary sterility in which the patient is known to have passed through a pelvic infection of gonorrheal origin.

3. In cases of primary sterility in which the patient had peritonitis of appendicular origin.

4. In cases of relative sterility in which the patient had a pelvic infection following childbirth or abortion, particularly when induced.

5. In cases of one child, sterility without the definite history of pelvic infection.

6. In cases in which it had been necessary to remove one whole tube and part of another for hydrosalpinx or pyosalpinx (conservative surgery).

7. After unilateral ectopic pregnancy to determine the patency of the residual tube.

8. After cases of salpingostomy for the cure of sterility of tubal origin to demonstrate the success of the operation which was calculated to effect open tubes.

9. After sterilization by tube ligation to test the patency of the tied or severed tubes.

10. After multiple myomectomy to make certain that at least the uterine ostium of the tube has been left intact.

### FINDINGS IN SEVENTY CASES IN WHICH EXAMINATION WAS MADE FOR PATENCY OF FALLOPIAN TUBES

| | | | | |
|---|---|---|---|---|
| First Series: Cases examined without pressure control | | | | 33 |
| A. Absolute sterility | | | 25 | |
| (a) Patients previously operated on | | 8 | | |
| Tubes proved patent | 5 | | | |
| Tubes proved nonpatent | 3 | | | |
| (b) Patients not previously operated on | | 17 | | |
| Tubes proved patent | 10 | | | |
| Tubes proved nonpatent | 7 | | | |
| B. Relative sterility | | | 8 | |
| (a) Patients previously operated | | 4 | | |
| Tubes proved patent | 1 | | | |
| Tubes proved nonpatent | 3 | | | |
| (b) Patients not operated on | | 4 | | |
| Tubes proved patent | 3 | | | |
| Tubes proved nonpatent | 1 | | | |
| Second Series: Cases examined with pressure control | | | | 37 |
| A. Absolute sterility | | | 10 | |
| (a) Patients previously operated on | | 8 | | |
| Tubes proved patent | 2 | | | |
| Tubes proved nonpatent | 6 | | | |
| (b) Patients not operated on | | 5 | | |
| Tubes proved patent | 5 | | | |
| Tubes proved nonpatent | 0 | | | |
| B. Relative sterility | | | 27 | |
| (a) Patients previously operated on | | 15 | | |
| Tubes proved patent | 12 | | | |
| Tubes proved nonpatent | 3 | | | |
| (b) Patients not operated on | | 12 | | |
| Tubes proved patent | 9 | | | |
| Tubes proved nonpatent | 3 | | | |

The method is not to be used in the presence of any acute subacute pelvic infection, nor in the presence of purulent diseased bartholinian glands, urethra, vagina or cervix.

The causes of sterility are too often obscure and undetermined. It appears, however, that at least the mechanical factor of patency should be possible of determination in most cases. The method of intrauterine oxygen inflation with the production of an artificial pneumoperitoneum obviates the necessity of surgical exploration and is especially serviceable in the obscure cases.

261 Central Park West.

---

## ABSTRACT OF DISCUSSION

Dr. John O. Polak, Brooklyn: Dr. Rubin suggests a most ingenious method to establish the patency of the tubes. It is, of course, along the same lines as the introduction into the uterus and tubes of argyrol under pressure, and the use of thorium. I have used both these methods and have discarded them, as they gave very little information, except pictorial. I am not convinced that it is a safe procedure to inflate the uterus and tubes under the pressure necessary to introduce oxygen into the peritoneal cavity by way of the tube and produce pneumoperitoneum. Again, the irritability of different uteri must be considered. In some women simple manipulation of the cervix or the introduction of anything into the cervix will cause most severe uterine reaction and no one has ever told us how to select the individual case. That of itself would prohibit the general use of this method, although it certainly has very many apparent advantages. When sterility exists, we can do a great deal by a proper investigation of the forces that produce sterility. Among 687 sterile women examined, 400 had tubal disease. In many of these cases of one-child sterility, the woman denies infection, yet she has had a parametritis, a pelvic peritonitis and a perisalpingitis. It is only in the straight gonococcal cases, without any mixed infection, that regeneration is possible. In sterility the two chief causes outside of the male, are endocervicitis and the infections involving the tube either from the inside or the outside. We can follow that up very well by the aspiration of the ejaculated semen at different periods after copulation and at different locations, and if we find living spermatozoa in the uterus, it is reasonable to suppose the existence of a tubal or ovarian condition which justifies abdominal section. With such a history it would be safer to do abdominal section than to inflate the tubes or uterus with gas.

Dr. Isador C. Rubin, New York: The objections raised by Dr. Polak are not unknown to me. These were the very objections we had, but they were overruled by actual experimentation. About the irritability of the uterus, the vast majority of these patients tolerated the method very well. One very nervous woman could not stand the method on first trial, but she did on second trial. The method is no more of a procedure so far as the tolerance of the patient is concerned than is cystoscopy. The bladder is no more irritable to the introduction of a cystoscope than the uterus is to a sound. Of course, there are cases in which you will not use that method, but even in these cases the method is absolutely safe. Of the safety of the method I am thoroughly convinced. I do not recommend it in cervices pouring out pus, or when there is much fever, not when there is pelvic infection. There are cases in which it is impossible even to go in for the spermatozoa, because the method is not tolerated by the uterus. As soon as the inflation reaches the point where the pressure overcomes the tight slit in the uterine end of the tube, the pressure drops from 60 or 80 to 40 or 30 or even 20. The amount of pressure required is not so enormous. It is surprising how much the uterus can stand. The cervix acts as a safety valve. I feel that the method has a scope.

Nov 4, 1983
(*JAMA* 1983;250:2366-2368)

# The Rubin Test*

Edward C. Hill, MD

The introduction of a foreign object or material through the cervical canal into the uterine cavity was considered a dangerous thing to do at the time that Isidor Rubin[1] first thought that it might be a way of demonstrating tubal patency. Even such a simple procedure as sounding the uterus was judged by many eminent gynecologists of that day to be a violation of acceptable medical practice. The endometrial cavity was considered sacrosanct.

Nevertheless, Rubin was concerned because, other than by laparotomy, there was no reasonably good method to determine whether the tubes were open or closed. The conscientious physician was extremely reluctant to recommend abdominal surgery for this sole purpose because of the grave risks involved.

Female infertility in those days was considered to be primarily a problem of cervical obstruction. The Pozzi operation, a type of tracheloplasty, was in vogue if there was, on pelvic examination, no clinically obvious adnexal disease. Tubal obstruction was thought to be responsible for female infertility in less than 15% of patients. Yet, it was generally acknowledged that the fallopian tubes could be obstructed without any clinical manifestation of tubal disease.

Before the turn of the century, the diagnosis of infectious endometritis was frequently made and was based on microscopic observations of premenstrual and menstrual endometrium showing the presence of an acute inflammatory infiltrate. Not until Hitschmann and Adlers[2] discovered that polymorphonuclear leukocytes were to be found in the endometrium during the course of normal menstrual cycles did the medical profession accept the fact that the uterine cavity was, except in complications of pregnancy and acute gonorrhea, generally free of bacterial infection. This acceptance came slowly.

From the Department of Pathology, Massachusetts General Hospital, Boston, and the Department of Obstetrics and Gynecology, University of California at San Francisco.

*A commentary on Rubin IC: Nonoperative determination of patency of fallopian tubes in sterility. *JAMA* 1920;74:1017, and Rubin IC: The nonoperative determination of patency of fallopian tubes. *JAMA* 1920;75:661-667.

## Rubin's Work

In the early 1900s, urologists were using a radiopaque silver salt solution (Collargol) in diagnostic cystography. Rubin was 31 years of age in 1914 and working in the laboratory of Professor Ernst Wertheim at the Frauenklinik II in Vienna. He embarked at this time on a study to determine whether Collargol could be used to show the uterine cavity and fallopian tubes roentgenographically. First, he injected this solution into the uteri of rabbits and female cadavers. His initial reports[3,4] on this technique suggested that this method could be used to show submucous fibroids as well as patency of the fallopian tubes. Unknown to Rubin, and working independently, W. H. Cary[5] of New York City, was developing the same technique. His publication reporting this work appeared in the *American Journal of Obstetrics and Diseases of Women and Children*. It preceded Rubin's by a few months and was the first description of hysterosalpingography (HSG).

Collargol, however, had serious drawbacks. It caused peritoneal irritation when the tubes were patent; patients complained of severe colic, and there was fear of obstruction of normally patent tubes due to inspissation and the irritant qualities of the solution.

Subsequent trials with thorium nitrate, sodium bromide, and sodium iodide were carried out with similar undesirable side effects. Rubin abandoned this as a diagnostic method.

As Rubin pointed out in his preliminary report in THE JOURNAL, oxygen was at that time being introduced by needle puncture into the peritoneal cavity as a contrast medium in abdominal roentgenography.[6] It was well tolerated. Rubin reasoned that, if introduced into the abdomen through the uterus, oxygen would not carry infectious material into the peritoneal cavity; it was rapidly absorbed when compared with the radiopaque solutions, and it would leave no chemical residue to block the tubes. Rubin thought that the introduction of an oxygen pneumoperitoneum by tubal insufflation and its demonstration by fluoroscopy and roentgenography would serve to prove tubal patency. His preliminary experiments on surgically excised, intact uteri and tubes proved that it was feasible, and he then proposed to carry it out in a living subject.[7]

Rubin received the support of Dr Hiram N. Vineberg, his colleague and mentor at Mount Sinai Hospital in New York City, who said: "The idea is entirely new to me, but I have confidence in you. I hope your preliminary work has been adequately prepared and that you will undertake the test clinically with all due precautions for the patient's safety. I shall stand behind you."[7] With this, the first examination by uterotubal insufflation took place in the X-ray Department of the hospital on Nov 3, 1919. Oxygen was passed through a water bottle and into the uterus via a cervical cannula without pressure monitoring. The amount of gas introduced was roughly estimated by counting the number of bubbles per minute seen in the water bottle. The insufflation was continued until there was visible distention of the patient's abdomen, subsequently confirmed by fluoroscopy and abdominal roentgenograms. The patient was comfortable while maintaining the recumbent position but experienced considerable epigastric distress and severe shoulder pain when she assumed the upright position. She was kept in bed at home but was able to come to the X-ray Department three days later for another roentgenographic examination of the abdomen. This showed a small amount of residual gas beneath the diaphragm and, thus, patency of the tubes. She conceived within two months of this event, being delivered of a full-term, normal infant. Eighteen months later she had her second child.

Rubin performed the test on 54 additional infertile patients, and these were the basis for his preliminary report. On April 29, 1920, he gave his definitive report before the Section on Obstetrics, Gynecology, and Abdominal Surgery of the American Medical Association. Despite the doubts expressed by Dr Polak, the professor of obstetrics and gynecology at the Long Island College of Medicine, the method described by Rubin was enthusiastically adopted by the medical profession. A number of reports by others[8-11] soon appeared in the literature. Modifications in the apparatus, the gas used, and interpretation of findings followed. Carbon dioxide was substituted for oxygen because it was absorbed more rapidly from the peritoneal cavity and caused less discomfort. There was also less danger from gas embolization. Auscultation of the abdomen was substituted for roentgenography. A safety valve at 200 mm Hg was attached to the apparatus to avoid excessive pressures, and a kymograph was attached to the machine to record the pressures. After the publication by Furniss,[9] the procedure came to be known as the "Rubin test." It became firmly established as the only definitive office method of testing for tubal patency in the infertile female patient.

By submitting questionnaires to various colleagues, Rubin[1] recorded 80,376 tubal insufflations before 1940. There were 190 pelvic infections among this group, only 27 of which were severe, for a morbidity rate of 0.0024%. The Rubin test was thoroughly proved to be a safe and effective method, and it was widely adopted in England[12] as well as the United States.

The test had its drawbacks, however, the most serious of which were a number of false results, indicating tubal obstruction when it was not present. This was ascribed to either tubal spasm or a ball-valve effect of endometrial tissue at the uterotubal junction. Moreover, the results gave no indication as to the site of obstruction when nonpatency was proved. False results were minimized by repeating the test two or three times, preferably in the early proliferative phase of the cycle, when the endometrium was still relatively thin, and smooth-muscle relaxants were used to overcome tubal spasm.

The passage of gas through the uterus and fallopian tubes proved to be therapeutic as well as diagnostic. In a personal series reported in 1947, Rubin[1] recorded 590 pregnancies in 3,200 infertile patients. In 65% of these conceptions, tubal insufflation was the only treatment.

Hysterosalpingography was also being developed during this interval, and both iodized oils (Lipiodol)[13] and water-soluble radiopaque dyes (Salpix)[14] were found to be more acceptable than those previously tried. Rubin[1] considered tubal insufflation and HSG as competitive, citing a number of reasons for using his method.

Miller,[15] in an interpretation and evaluation of tubal patency tests, pointed out that gas insufflation and HSG were not competitive but complementary. He used HSG to follow up the Rubin test, if necessary, to localize the area of obstruction and allow a better selection of cases for salpingostomy. This became the standard of practice of the medical profession.[16]

## The Rubin Test Today

In recent years there has been, in some quarters, a trend away from tubal insufflation in favor of moving directly to HSG as a method of evaluating the tubal factor in the investigation of female infertility.[17] Those who do so rationalize it on the basis of the false results of the Rubin test and the advantages of HSG. By and large, these are clinicians whose clientele have a relatively high rate of tubal infections causing obstruction. Hoffman[18] reports that the popularity of the Rubin test has waned to the point that only 20 insufflation units were sold in 1978 by the nation's largest manufacturer of this type of medical equipment. At the same time, he points out the value of tubal insufflation, stating that it "deserves better than it has received from its detractors."

In a recent symposium on advances in the diagnosis and treatment of infertility,[19] tubal insufflation was not mentioned as a part of the diagnostic examination of the infertile woman. In fact, the debate concerned whether HSG should precede laparoscopy as the primary procedure. The consensus was that HSG and laparoscopy are not competitive but complementary procedures. In their practical guide for physicians, Hammond and Talbert[20] recommend only HSG in the evaluation of the tubal factor. This is also the method of Hulka,[21] who states that HSG should be performed on all infertile patients as part of the initial assessment. Tubal insufflation is not even considered as an alternative.

In practices in which the incidence of tubal infections is low, the Rubin test continues to be used as a screening method.[22] Those who support this approach do so because of concern regarding the complexity and expense of HSG, the possibility of anaphylactic reaction to the dye, and the slight but definite risk of irradiation.

The etiologic factors in female infertility are multiple, and tubal obstruction, although serious, may play no causal role in the case of any one person. The Rubin test is remarkably utilitarian and, when properly performed, observing the appropriate indications and contraindications, is safe. It is an effective screening method. The thoughtful and careful physician, through the use of this technique, thoroughly proved since its first performance by Rubin more than 60 years ago, can immediately recognize the patient whose infertility is not related to tubal disease. He can then concentrate his efforts toward other possibilities, thus saving his patient the time, expense, discomfort, and risk of the more complex procedures.

Isidor Rubin died on July 8, 1958, while attending an international cancer congress in London,[23] but the Rubin test is not dead.

### References

1. Rubin IC: *Uterotubal Insufflation.* St Louis, CV Mosby Co, 1947.

2. Hitschmann F, Adlers L: Der Bau der Uterusschleimhaut des geschlechtsreifen Weibes mit besonder Beruckstigung der Menstruation. *Monatsschr Geburtschilfe Gynaekol* 1908;27:1.

3. Rubin IC: Rontgendiagnostik der Uterustumoren mit Hilfe von intrauterinen Collargolinjektionen. *Zentralbl Gynaekol* 1914;38:658.

4. Rubin IC: X-ray diagnosis in gynecology with the aid of intrauterine Collargol injection. *Surg Gynecol Obstet* 1915;20:435.

5. Cary WH: Note on determination of patency of fallopian tubes by the use of Collargol and x-ray shadow. *Am J Obstet Dis Women Child* 1914;69:462.

6. Stein A, Stewart WA: Roentgen examination of the abdominal organs. *Ann Surg* 1919;70:95.

7. Rubin IC: The beginnings of uterotubal insufflation. *J Mt Sinai Hosp* 1943;10:231.

8. Dickinson RL: Tubal patency test and unsealing by simple air-filled pipette. *Am J Obstet Gynecol* 1922;4:159.

9. Furniss HD: The Rubin test simplified. *Surg Gynecol Obstet* 1921;33:567.

10. Peterson R: X-ray after the inflation of the pelvic cavity with carbon-dioxide gas. *Surg Gynecol Obstet* 1921;33:154.

11. Rongy AJ, Rosenfeld SS: Transuterine insufflation: A diagnostic aid in sterility. *Am J Obstet Gynecol* 1922;3:496.

12. Sharman A: Some lessons from 4,000 uterotubal insufflations. *Br Med J* 1954;1:239.

13. Rutherford RN: Therapeutic value of repetitive lipiodol tubal insufflations. *West J Surg* 1948;56:145.

14. Rubin IC, Myller E, Hartman CG: Salpix. *Fertil Steril* 1953;4:357.

15. Miller NF: An interpretation and evaluation of tubal patency tests. *JAMA* 1945;129:243-246.

16. Pauerstein CJ: *The Fallopian Tube: A Reappraisal.* Philadelphia, Lea & Febiger, 1974.

17. Wentz AC: An overview of female infertility, in Givens JR (ed): *The Infertile Female.* Chicago, Year Book Medical Publishers, 1979, pp 15-25.

18. Hoffman JJ: Tubal factor in infertility, in Givens JR (ed): *The Infertile Female.* Chicago, Year Book Medical Publishers, 1979, pp 345-358.

19. Gomel V: Impact of microsurgery in gynecology, in Insler V, Bettendorf G (eds): *Advances in Diagnosis and Treatment of Infertility.* New York, Elsevier North-Holland Inc, 1980, pp 277-284.

20. Hammond MG, Talbert LM: *Infertility: A Practice Guide for the Physician.* Chapel Hill, NC, Health Sciences Consortium Inc, 1981.

21. Hulka JF, in Hammond MG, Talbert LM (eds): *Infertility: A Practical Guide for the Physician.* Chapel Hill, NC, Health Sciences Consortium Inc, 1981.

22. Taymor ML: *Infertility.* New York, Grune & Stratton Inc, 1978.

23. Speert H: *Obstetrics and Gynecology in America: A History.* Chicago, American College of Obstetricians and Gynecologists, 1980.

Aug 27, 1921
(*JAMA* 1921;77:682-683)

## Chapter 15

# Medicolegal Application of Human Blood Grouping

### Reuben Ottenberg, M.D.

Adjunct Physician, Mount Sinai Hospital; Instructor in Bacteriology, Columbia University College of Physicians and Surgeons
New York

Although the inheritance, according to definite mendelian principles, of group-specific substances in human blood has been known for ten years, the application of this information to medicolegal questions has not yet been made. It is my object in the present paper to present the possibilities of this practical application and to define the instances in which it can be used.

The term iso-agglutination describes the agglutination of red blood cells by contact with blood serum derived from another individual of the same species. Landsteiner, in 1901, showed that this is a normal phenomenon in all human blood, and reduced its occurrence to a definite law. With regard to the behavior of their serum and red blood cells, all human beings, without regard to race, sex or state of health, fall into one of three groups. In the first group the red cells are not agglutinable by any other human serum, while the serum is found to agglutinate the red cells of all persons not belonging to the first group. In the second group, the red cells are agglutinated by the serum of the first and third groups, while the serum agglutinates the cells of the third group only. The third is the obverse of the second group, its red cells being agglutinated by serum of the first and second groups, its serum agglutinating only cells of the second group. Landsteiner correctly concluded that the phenomena were due to the presence of two kinds of specific agglutinin, of which one was present in the serum of the second group; another in the serum of the third group; and both in the serum of the first group. Landsteiner tested blood of mothers and their new-born children and found that these were frequently different from each other.

Descatella and Sturli the following year confirmed Landsteiner's findings. Among 155 persons examined by them were four who did not fit in any of Landsteiner's three groups, their cells being agglutinated by the serum of all other groups, while their serum contained no agglutinin whatever. This fourth group was, however, only definitely recognized and named as such in 1907 by Jansky. These workers showed that the group peculiarities are permanent throughout life for each individual. They also made the important observation that in embryologic development, the specific agglutinability of the red cells (called agglutinogen) appears first and is usually present at birth, while the specific agglutinative power of the blood serum (called agglutinin) which is to characterize the individual through life may be absent at birth and may not appear for months.

If we represent the two red cell agglutinogens by A

TABLE 1.—GROUPING OF HUMAN BLOOD, ACCORDING TO JANSKY[°]

| Group | Serum | Red Blood Cells |
|---|---|---|
| I | Agglutinates cells of the three other groups; contains agglutinins $\alpha$ and $\beta$ | Inagglutinable; contain no agglutinogen |
| II | Agglutinates cells of Groups III and IV; contains agglutinin $\beta$ | Agglutinated by serum of Groups I and III; contain agglutinogen A |
| III | Agglutinates cells of Groups II and IV, contains agglutinin $\alpha$ | Agglutinated by serum of Groups I and II; contain agglutinogen B |
| IV | No agglutinative effect; contains no agglutinin | Agglutinated by serum of Groups I, II and III; contain agglutinogens A and B |

[°]The grouping according to Jansky is logical and has priority. It has been adopted officially by the American Association of Immunologists and by the American Association of Pathologists and Bacteriologists. The groupings of von Dungern and Hirschfeld and of Moss differ only in terminology. The reader must keep this in mind in going over the literature.

## TABLE 2.—HEREDITARY CONSTITUTION OF RED CELLS OF THE FOUR GROUPS OF HUMAN BLOOD

GROUP I

| NA | NA |
| NB | NB |

GROUP II

| 1 | | 2 | |
|---|---|---|---|
| A | A | A | na |
| NB | NB | NB | NB |
| Pure | | Hybrid | |

GROUP III

| 1 | | 2 | |
|---|---|---|---|
| NA | NA | NA | NA |
| B | B | B | nb |
| Pure | | Hybrid | |

GROUP IV

| 1 | | 2 | | 3 | | 4 | |
|---|---|---|---|---|---|---|---|
| A | A | A | na | A | A | A | na |
| B | B | B | B | B | nb | B | nb |
| Pure | | Partial Hybrid | | Partial Hybrid | | Full Hybrid | |

## TABLE 3.—LIMITATION OF OFFSPRING

| Unions of I and I | give only I |
|---|---|
| Unions of I and II }<br>Unions of II and II } | give only I and II |
| Unions of I and III }<br>Unions of III and III } | give only I and III |

and B and the corresponding serum agglutinins by $\alpha$ and $\beta$, we can then schematically show the grouping of human blood according to Jansky as in Table 1.

In 1908 I noticed that the groupings were hereditary and followed Mendel's law, but was unable fully to work out the mechanism of inheritance. In 1910 came the important work of von Dungern and Hirschfeld. They showed that the susceptible substance is present in both parents, and occurs in most of the children; while, when a particular substance (A or B) is present in only one parent, some of the children inherit it; when neither parent has a particular one of these substances, no child ever shows it. In other words A as an inherited character is dominant over the character not A, while B is dominant over not B, and the two pairs of unit characters, A and Not A, B and Not B, are inherited independent of each other. Medicolegally then, if A or B is present in a child's blood, one of the alleged parents must possess it.

Let us now turn to consider the mechanism of heredity of these blood properties.

The quality A is dominant to Not A, and B to Not B. The qualities Not A and Not B are not mere blanks, but are definite qualities of red cells associated, respectively, with the development in the serum of agglutinins; and von Dungern and Hirschfeld showed that the inheritance of the paired qualities A and Not A, B and Not B, have no relation to each other. Thus, if we compared A and Not A with Black and White, B and Not B could be represented by some entirely different and independent pair of characters, like Tall and Short.

Now with regard to the inheritance of A and Not A, there are for each individual three possibilities:

1. Either both of his parents are A and the individual

## TABLE 4.—INSTANCES IN WHICH THE CHILD MUST BE ILLEGITIMATE, OR NOT THE CHILD OF THE SUPPOSED FATHER

| Known Mother | Supposed Father | Child | | |
|---|---|---|---|---|
| I | I | II | III | IV |
| I | II | | III | IV |
| I | III | II | | IV |
| II | I | | III | IV |
| II | II | | III | IV |
| III | I | II | | IV |
| III | III | II | | IV |

is pure A and can transmit to his offspring only the quality A, since all of his germ cells must carry that quality.

2. Or both of his parents are Not A and the individual is pure Not A and can transmit only Not A.

3. Or one parent is A, the other Not A, and the individual is a hybrid, A-Not A, and (according to the mendelian law) his germ cells in equal numbers carry the properties A and Not A, even though the red cells of the individual himself show (because of the dominance of that quality), only A.

With regard to the inheritance of B or Not B, exactly the same three possibilities exist.

If we represent apparent or dominant qualities by capital letters, recessive ones by small letters, and abbreviate Not A, Not B, to NA, NB, na, nb, we can then represent the hereditary constitution of the four classes of human blood as in Table 2.

It is clear at once that Group I (the most numerous group representing over 40 per cent. of the community) can never be hybrid. Group II (the next most numerous, representing about 40 per cent. of the community) can be hybrid only with regard to its dominant quality A, so that there are two kinds of persons belonging to Group II, pure A-A, transmitting only A to offspring, and hybrid, A-Not a, transmitting these two quantities to offspring in equal numbers. The same is true for Group III (from 12 to 15 per cent. of the community); it can be hybrid only with regard to its dominant quality B. Group IV, on the other hand, (the rarest of the groups, only 2 to 5 per cent. of the community) has four possibilities. It may be pure with regard to both dominant qualities A and B, or pure with regard to one, while hybrid with regard to the other, or hybrid with regard to both.

A detailed analysis[1] of the offspring resulting from unions of persons belonging to the various groups shows that in certain instances the possible kind of offspring are sharply limited. These are tabulated in Table 3.

The unions tabulated in this chart comprise over 80 per cent of all unions, and are the instances in which under certain circumstances deductions of medicolegal value may be drawn.

On the other hand, all unions containing a member of

---

1. The full data on which these conclusions are based are published in a paper which will appear in a forthcoming number of the Journal of Immunology.

Group IV and unions of II and III may give rise to offspring of any of the four groups.

Suppose, then, that the blood of a child and the alleged parents have been tested, what conclusions can be drawn? If the child's blood is the correct group for the alleged parents, then we can say that the child *could* be their offspring, not that it of necessity must be. But, on the other hand, if the child's group is wrong for the two asserted parents, then one can say with absolute certainty that the child must have a parent other than one of those asserted.

The commonest instance, of course, is that of disputed paternity. Here we can readily tabulate the instances in which it is possible to be sure that the child is illegitimate or is not the child of an asserted father (Table 4). It is noticeable that Group I is absent from the third column of Table 4 because a child of Group I can be the offspring of any combination of parents.

The same kind of evidence (Table 4) can be used, either to prove the illegitimacy of the offspring or (circumstances being reversed) to prove the innocence of a correspondent asserted to be the father of a given child.

Likewise, in the rarer cases of disputed maternity or of alleged substitution of one child for another, Table 4 shows the instances in which it can be stated with certainty that the child is spurious; i. e., a child of one of the groups in the third column cannot be the offspring of the parents on the corresponding lines in the first two columns.

In practice, of course, it may be difficult to obtain the consent of all three parties (or at times four), to the blood test. The test can be easily done with a few drops of blood obtained from a painless prick with a small needle. In view of this, and the importance of the questions often at issue, it seems as though some legal means could be devised by which the persons concerned could be compelled to allow the examination at the hands of a representative of the court.

15 West Eighty-Ninth Street.

March 25, 1922
(*JAMA* 1922;78:873-877)

# Medicolegal Application of Human Blood Grouping

## Second Communication

Reuben Ottenberg, M.D.

New York

In 1910, von Dungern and Hirschfeld[1] discovered that the substances A and B present in human red blood cells (on whose presence or absence the so-called blood grouping depends) are inherited according to Mendel's law. They studied 348 persons belonging to seventy-two different families. (The families were those of university professors or members of their research institute, and each family is identified in their article.)

They observed that:

1. A never occurs in a child if not present in one of the parents; the same is true of B.

2. When one of these substances is present in both parents, it occurs in most of the children.

3. When only one parent has one of these particular substances, some of the children inherit it.

4. When a particular substance is absent from both parents, no child ever has it.

They were forced to the conclusion that Mendel's law holds for these blood qualities, on the supposition that they were dealing with two pairs of unit characters—A and Absent A, B and Absent B. They found their facts explicable only on the assumption that the presence of A is dominant over its absence (or "not A") and the

1. Von Dungern and Hirschfeld: Ztschr. f. Immunitätsforsch, Orig. **6:** 284, 1910.

presence of B over its absence (or "not B").

This conclusion was further fully supported by numerous other considerations which the analysis of their data afforded. They close by saying: "The fact that the demonstrable substances A and B in the blood cells can never appear in the children, if absent in both parents, is forensically available."

## ILLUSTRATIVE FAMILIES

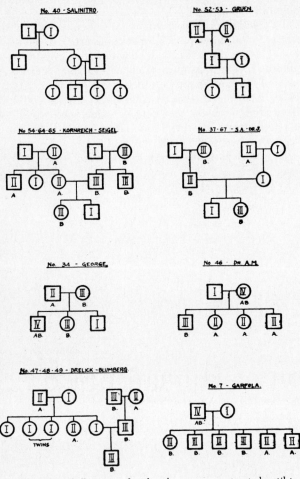

In this chart of illustrative families, by an error not noted until too late for correction, the square and the circle representing father and mother in the second generation of Family 37-67 were reversed.

The facts of von Dungern and Hirschfeld have never been questioned. In two families on which I had previously reported, and in eight subsequently examined, there was not a single exception to their rules. When, therefore, in 1921 the subject again became of interest to me, I wrote an article in which are explicitly worked out the special conditions under which the observations of von Dungern and Hirschfeld could be applied in a medicolegal case.

In this article[2] the A B terminology, used by von Dungern and Hirschfeld, is translated into the four blood group terminology of Jansky, which is more familiar to American readers and has been officially adopted[3] by the American Association of Immunologists, the Society of American Bacteriologists and the Association of Patholo-

2. Ottenberg, Reuben: J. Immunol. **6:**363 (Sept.) 1921.
3. Isohemagglutination, J. A. M. A. **76:**130 (Jan. 8) 1921.

### TABLE 1.—OBSERVATIONS OF FAMILIES IN WHICH BOTH PARENTS WERE IN GROUP I

| Family No. | Name | Source | Individuals | Age of Child | Group | Agglutinable Substances |
|---|---|---|---|---|---|---|
| 14 | Zanker | Mount Sinai Hospital | Father | ..... | I | — — |
| | | | Mother | ..... | I | — — |
| | | | Harold | ..... | I | — — |
| 17 | Mazzola | Mount Sinai Hospital | Father | ..... | I | — — |
| | | | Mother | ..... | I | — — |
| | | | Samuel | ..... | I | — — |
| 22 | MacGruder | Vanderbilt Clinic | Father | ..... | I | — — |
| | | | Mother | ..... | I | — — |
| | | | Earl | 8 yrs. | I | — — |
| | | | Gladys | 7 yrs. | I | — — |
| | | | Ruby | 3 yrs. | I | — — |
| | | | Hilda | 2 yrs. | I | — — |
| | | | Baby | 2 mos. | I | — — |
| 25 | Liebert | Presbyterian Hospital | Father | ..... | I | — — |
| | | | Mother | ..... | I | — — |
| | | | Robert | ..... | I | — — |
| 26 | Demos | Presbyterian Hospital | Father | ..... | I | — — |
| | | | Mother | ..... | I | — — |
| | | | Tony | ..... | I | — — |
| 39 | Breslow | Acquaintance | Father | ..... | I | — — |
| | | | Mother | ..... | I | — — |
| | | | Diana | 6 yrs. | I | — — |
| 40 | Salinitro | Acquaintance | Maternal grandfather | | I | — — |
| | | | Maternal grandmother | | I | — — |
| | | | Their son | | I | — — |
| | | | Their daughter | ..... | I | — — |
| | | | Her husband | ..... | I | — — |
| | | | Grandchildren ... | | | |
| | | | Rose | 13 yrs. | I | — — |
| | | | Louis | 12 yrs. | I | — — |
| | | | Marian | 7 yrs. | I | — — |
| | | | Adele | 9 yrs. | I | — — |
| 42 | Sokol | Nursery and Child's Hospital | Father | ..... | I | — — |
| | | | Mother | ..... | I | — — |
| | | | Child | ..... | I | — — |
| 43 | Tiedemann | Nursery and Child's Hospital | Father | ..... | I | — — |
| | | | Mother | ..... | I | — — |
| | | | Child | ..... | I | — — |
| 59 | Wolff | Personal | Maternal grandfather | | I | — — |
| | | | Maternal grandmother | | I | — — |
| | | | Father | ..... | I | — — |
| | | | Mother | ..... | I | — — |
| | | | Robert | 6 yrs. | I | — — |
| | | | James | 3 yrs. | I | — — |
| 53 | Gruen (The paternal grandparents are family 52 Table 2) | Personal | Father (Toby) | ..... | I | — — |
| | | | Mother | ..... | I | — — |
| | | | Dorothy | 14 yrs. | I | — — |
| | | | Robert | 8 yrs. | I | — — |
| 59 | Klaw (Maternal grandparents, see No. 56, Table 5) | Personal | Father | ..... | I | — — |
| | | | Mother (Alma) | ..... | I | — — |
| | | | Stanley | 3 yrs. | I | — — |

gists and Bacteriologists.[4] A short report[5] giving the conclusions of this article was published in THE JOURNAL, Aug. 27, 1921.

4. To refresh the memories of readers, A and B are the substances in human red cells which make them susceptible to agglutination by the human serum agglutinins $\alpha$ and $\beta$.

The red cells of Group I have neither A nor B.
The red cells of Group II have A.
The red cells of Group III have B.
The red cells of Group IV have A and B.
The serum of Group I has $\alpha$ and $\beta$.
The serum of Group II has $\beta$.
The serum of Group III has $\alpha$.
The serum of Group IV has neither $\alpha$ nor $\beta$.

The A B terminology here used is that of von Dungern and Hirschfeld. In many textbooks the A and B are reversed, the letter B being used for Group II agglutinogen and the other letters changed accordingly. The final result is the same.

5. Ottenberg, Reuben: Medicolegal Application of Human Blood Grouping, J. A. M. A. **77:**682 (Aug. 27) 1921.

## TABLE 2.—OBSERVATIONS OF FAMILIES IN WHICH BOTH PARENTS WERE IN GROUP II

| Family No. | Name | Source | Individuals | Age of Child | Group | Agglutinable Substances |
|---|---|---|---|---|---|---|
| 4 | Hatenback | Nursery and Child's Hospital | Maternal grandmother | | II | A — |
| | | | Mother | ..... | II | A — |
| | | | Father | ..... | II | A — |
| | | | Child | 3 yrs. | I | — — |
| 12 | Sinsheimer | Mount Sinai Hospital | Father | ..... | II | A — |
| | | | Mother | ..... | II | A — |
| | | | Joseph | ..... | II | A — |
| 19 | Auslander | Acquaintance | Father | ..... | II | A — |
| | | | Mother | ..... | II | A — |
| | | | Donald | ..... | II | A — |
| | | | Brother | ..... | II | A — |
| 31 | Appel | Acquaintance | Father | ..... | II | A — |
| | | | Mother | ..... | II | A — |
| | | | Judith | 15 yrs. | II | A — |
| 33 | Dr. F. | Acquaintance | Father | ..... | II | A — |
| | | | Mother | ..... | II | A — |
| | | | Arthur | 18 yrs. | II | A — |
| | | | Harold | 17 yrs. | II | A — |
| | | | Thelma | 15 yrs. | II | A — |
| 41 | McLean | Nursery and Child's Hospital | Father | ..... | II | A — |
| | | | Mother | ..... | II | A — |
| | | | Girl | 10 yrs. | II | A — |
| 51 | Schaeffer | Nursery and Child's Hospital | Father | ..... | II | A — |
| | | | Mother | ..... | II | A — |
| | | | Child | ..... | II | A — |
| 52 | Gruen (Grandchildren, see No. 53, Table 1) | Personal | Father | ..... | II | A — |
| | | | Mother | ..... | II | A — |
| | | | Toby | 33 yrs. | I | — — |
| 62 | Michaels | Acquaintance | Maternal grandfather | | II | A — |
| | | | Maternal grandmother | | II | A — |
| | | | Moses (their son) | 23 yrs. | I | — — |
| | | | Esther (their daughter) | 35 yrs. | I | — — |
| | | | Mrs. Marlow (married daughter) | ..... | II | A — |
| | | | Mr. Marlow (her husband) | ..... | II | A — |
| | | | Bernice (grandchild) | 4 yrs. | II | A — |
| 61 | Benjamin | Acquaintance | Father | ..... | II | A — |
| | | | Mother | ..... | II | A — |
| | | | Jewel | 19 yrs. | II | A — |
| | | | John | 14 yrs. | II | A — |

## TABLE 3.—OBSERVATIONS OF FAMILIES IN WHICH BOTH PARENTS WERE IN GROUP III

| Family No. | Name | Source | Individuals | Age of Child | Group | Agglutinable Substances |
|---|---|---|---|---|---|---|
| 16 | Wilson | Mount Sinai Hospital | Father | ..... | III | — B |
| | | | Mother | ..... | III | — B |
| | | | Thomas | ..... | I | — — |
| 32 | Berkelheimer | Acquaintance | Father | ..... | III | — B |
| | | | Mother | ..... | III | — B |
| | | | Sadie | 24 yrs. | III | — B |
| | | | Isidor | 23 yrs. | III | — B |
| 55 | J. H. | Personal | Father | ..... | III | — B |
| | | | Mother | ..... | III | — B |
| | | | Zillah | 27 yrs. | III | — B |
| | | | Hannah | 25 yrs. | III | — B |
| | | | Arthur | 20 yrs. | III | — B |
| | | | Rosalind | 16 yrs. | III | — B |

## TABLE 4.—OBSERVATIONS OF FAMILIES IN WHICH PARENTS WERE IN GROUPS I AND II

| Family No. | Name | Source | Individuals | Age of Child | Group | Agglutinable Substances |
|---|---|---|---|---|---|---|
| 3 | Wolf | Acquaintance | Father | ..... | I | — — |
| | | | Mother | ..... | II | A — |
| | | | Louis | 13 yrs. | I | — — |
| | | | Joseph | 9 yrs. | I | — — |
| | | | Beatty | 7 yrs. | I | — — |
| | | | Samuel | 5 yrs. | II | A — |
| 6 | Smith | Vanderbilt Clinic | Father | ..... | I | — — |
| | | | Mother | ..... | II | A — |
| | | | Ruth | 5 yrs. | II | A — |
| | | | Roberta | 2½ yrs. | II | A — |
| 8 | Pearl | Mount Sinai Hospital | Father | ..... | II | A — |
| | | | Mother | ..... | I | — — |
| | | | Ruth | ..... | II | A — |
| 9 | Block | Mount Sinai Hospital | Father | ..... | I | — — |
| | | | Mother | ..... | II | A — |
| | | | Mamie | ..... | II | A — |
| 10 | Piermont | Mount Sinai Hospital | Father | ..... | II | A — |
| | | | Mother | ..... | II | A — |
| | | | August | ..... | I | — — |
| 15 | Cohen | Mount Sinai Hospital | Father | ..... | II | A — |
| | | | Mother | ..... | I | — — |
| | | | Harry | ..... | II | A — |
| 20 | Millner | Acquaintance | Father | ..... | II | A — |
| | | | Mother | ..... | I | — — |
| | | | Selma | 11 yrs. | II | A — |
| | | | Toby | 9 yrs. | II | A — |
| 21 | Rudd | St. Luke's Hospital | Father | ..... | II | A — |
| | | | Mother | ..... | I | — — |
| | | | Child | ..... | I | — — |
| 27 | Gambieri | Presbyterian Hospital | Father | ..... | I | — — |
| | | | Mother | ..... | II | A — |
| | | | Maud | 14 yrs. | II | A — |
| 28 | Pauli | Presbyterian Hospital | Father | ..... | II | A — |
| | | | Mother | ..... | I | — — |
| | | | Daughter | ..... | II | A — |
| | | | Daughter | ..... | II | A — |
| | | | Daughter | ..... | I | — — |
| 30 | Adler | Acquaintance | Father | ..... | II | A — |
| | | | Mother | ..... | I | — — |
| | | | Daughter | ..... | II | A — |
| 29 | Respoli | Vanderbilt Clinic | Father | ..... | I | — — |
| | | | Mother | ..... | II | A — |
| | | | Irene | 14 yrs. | I | — — |
| | | | Amelio | 12 yrs. | II | A — |
| | | | Concetta | 10 yrs. | II | A — |
| | | | James | 7 yrs. | I | — — |
| | | | Susan | 3 yrs. | I | — — |
| 35 | Silverson | Acquaintance | Father | ..... | I | — — |
| | | | Mother | ..... | II | A — |
| | | | Daughter | 12 yrs. | I | — — |
| | | | Son | 8 yrs. | I | — — |
| 47 | Dreliek (Grandchild, see No. 48, Table 5) | Acquaintance | Father | ..... | II | A — |
| | | | Mother | ..... | I | — — |
| | | | Frieda } Twins | 15 yrs. | I | — — |
| | | | Lillian } | 15 yrs. | I | — — |
| | | | Rebecca | 17 yrs. | II | A — |
| | | | Sadie | 23 yrs. | I | — — |
| | | | Mrs. Blumberg | 27 yrs. | I | — — |
| 64 | Kornreich (Grandchild, see No. 65, Table 6) | Acquaintance | Father | ..... | I | — — |
| | | | Mother | ..... | II | A — |
| | | | Martin | 16 yrs. | II | A — |
| | | | Lena | 25 yrs. | I | — — |
| | | | Mrs. F. Siegel | 28 yrs. | II | A — |
| 66 | May | Personal | Father | ..... | II | A — |
| | | | Mother | ..... | I | — — |
| | | | Marjorie | 15 yrs. | I | — — |
| | | | Betty | 10 yrs. | II | A — |
| | | | James | 7 yrs. | I | — — |
| 67 | S. A. (Paternal grandparents of No. 37, Table 5) | Personal | Father | ..... | II | A — |
| | | | Mother | ..... | I | — — |
| | | | Herbert | ..... | I | — — |

## TABLE 5.—OBSERVATIONS OF FAMILIES IN WHICH PARENTS WERE IN GROUPS I AND III

| Family No. | Name | Source | Individuals | Age of Child | Group | Agglutinable Substances | |
|---|---|---|---|---|---|---|---|
| 5 | Hearn | Vanderbilt Clinic | Father | ...... | III | — | B |
| | | | Mother | ...... | I | — | — |
| | | | Fred | 8 yrs. | III | — | B |
| | | | Vincent | 3½ yrs. | III | — | B |
| | | | Maynard | 2½ yrs. | I | — | — |
| | | | Charles | 1 yr. | I | — | — |
| 11 | Fuchs | Mount Sinai Hospital | Father | ...... | III | — | B |
| | | | Mother | ...... | I | — | — |
| | | | Jacob | | I | — | — |
| 18 | Dubrow | Mount Sinai Hospital | Father | | I | — | — |
| | | | Mother | ...... | III | — | B |
| | | | Sidney | | I | — | — |
| 23 | W.B. | Dr. N. Rosenthal | Father | | III | — | B |
| | | | Mother | ...... | I | — | — |
| | | | Daughter | ...... | III | — | B |
| | | | Daughter | ...... | III | — | B |
| 24 | Schmitt | Presbyterian Hospital | Father | | III | — | B |
| | | | Mother | ...... | I | — | — |
| | | | Child | ...... | I | — | — |
| 36 | Mikulet | Acquaintance | Father | | I | — | — |
| | | | Mother | ...... | III | — | B |
| | | | William | 11 yrs. | I | — | — |
| 37 | Dr. J. (Paternal grandparents No. 67, Table 4) | Personal | Maternal grandfather | | I | — | — |
| | | | Maternal grandmother | | III | — | B |
| | | | Mother, Dorothy A. (=Mrs. A.) | ...... | III | — | B |
| | | | Father, Herbert A | ...... | I | — | — |
| | | | George | ...... | I | — | — |
| | | | Amy | 3 yrs. | III | — | B |
| 38 | Dr. L. S. | Acquaintance | Father | | III | — | B |
| | | | Mother | ...... | I | — | — |
| | | | Abraham | 3 yrs. | III | — | B |
| 48 | Blumberg (Grandparents; see No. 47, Table 4 and No. 49, Table 6) | Acquaintance | Father | | III | — | B |
| | | | Mother | ...... | I | — | — |
| | | | Ruth | 3 yrs. | III | — | B |
| 54 | Siegel (Grandchildren, see No. 65, Table 6) | Personal | Father | | I | — | — |
| | | | Mother | ...... | III | — | B |
| | | | Fred | 30 yrs. | III | — | B |
| | | | Louis | 23 yrs. | III | — | B |
| 56 | Ash (Daughter=mother of No. 56, Table 1) | Personal | Paternal grandfather | | I | — | — |
| | | | Paternal grandmother | | III | — | B |
| | | | Alma, daughter | | I | — | — |
| | | | Edward, their son | ...... | III | — | B |
| | | | Mrs. A., his wife | ...... | I | — | — |
| | | | Mark | 3 yrs. | III | — | B |

## TABLE 6.—OBSERVATIONS OF FAMILIES IN WHICH THERE WERE UNIONS CONTAINING A MEMBER OF GROUP IV, OR UNIONS OF GROUPS II AND III

| Family No. | Name | Source | Individuals | Age of Child | Group | Agglutinable Substances | |
|---|---|---|---|---|---|---|---|
| | | | *Parents of Groups I and IV* | | | | |
| 7 | Garfola | Vanderbilt Clinic | Father | ...... | IV | A | B |
| | | | Mother | ...... | I | — | — |
| | | | Julia | 17 yrs. | III | — | B |
| | | | Daniel | 13 yrs. | III | — | B |
| | | | Michael | 8 yrs. | III | — | B |
| | | | Tony | 6 yrs. | III | — | B |
| | | | Salvator | 5 yrs. | II | A | — |
| | | | Charles | 3 yrs. | II | A | — |
| 46 | Dr. A. M. | Personal | Father | ...... | I | — | — |
| | | | Mother | ...... | IV | A | B |
| | | | Phillip | 20 yrs. | III | — | B |
| | | | Sarah | 24 yrs. | II | A | — |
| | | | Dorothy | 22 yrs. | II | A | — |
| | | | Abraham | 26 yrs. | II | A | — |
| | | | *Parents of Groups II and III* | | | | |
| 34 | George | Vanderbilt Clinic | Father | ...... | II | A | — |
| | | | Mother | ...... | III | — | B |
| | | | Ormond | 6 yrs. | IV | A | B |
| | | | Lillian | 2 yrs. | III | — | B |
| | | | Herbert | 2 mos. | I | — | — |
| 49 | Blumberg (Grandchild, No. 48, Table 5) | Acquaintance | Father | ...... | III | — | B |
| | | | Mother | ...... | II | A | — |
| | | | Son | 33 yrs. | III | — | B |
| 65 | Siegel (Grandparents, No. 54, Table 5 and No. 64, Table 4) | Acquaintance | Father (Fred) | ...... | III | — | B |
| | | | Mother (née Kornreich) | ...... | II | A | — |
| | | | Betty | 6 yrs. | III | — | B |
| | | | Erwin | 3 yrs. | I | — | — |
| | | | *Parents of Groups II and IV* | | | | |
| 2 | Wisler | Personal | Paternal grandmother | | III | — | B |
| | | | Father | ...... | IV | A | B |
| | | | Mother | ...... | II | A | — |
| | | | Son | 6 yrs. | II | A | — |
| | | | Son | 3 yrs. | IV | A | B |
| 13 | Wolfson | Mount Siani Hospital | Father | ...... | II | A | — |
| | | | Mother | ...... | IV | A | B |
| | | | Lilly | | II | A | — |
| 44 | Leichterman | Nursery and Child's Hospital | Father | ...... | II | A | — |
| | | | Mother | ...... | IV | A | B |
| | | | Child | ...... | IV | A | B |
| 45 | Lapidus | Mount Sinai Hospital | Father | ...... | IV | A | B |
| | | | Mother | ...... | II | A | — |
| | | | Dorothy | ...... | II | A | — |
| 60 | Schaap | Acquaintance | Father | ...... | II | A | — |
| | | | Mother | ...... | IV | A | B |
| | | | Daughter | 9 yrs. | II | A | — |
| | | | *Parents of Groups III and IV* | | | | |
| 1 | Hinchliffe | Personal | Father | ...... | IV | A | B |
| | | | Mother | ...... | III | — | B |
| | | | Joseph | 4 yrs. | IV | A | B |

Early in this year there appeared an article by Dr. J. A. Buchanan.[6] It contained eight charts, none of which is identified as representing an actual family. From the context, however, and the opinions expressed by the author, it seems necessary to assume that some of the charts are based on actual observation. The author, however, does not present the data on which he relies in condemning as incorrect the conclusions of von Dungern and Hirschfeld and myself.

As no data have been recorded[7] since the original publication of von Dungern and Hirschfeld, I wish to present briefly sixty-seven additional families (255 persons). Twenty-six of these families were examined in various hospitals in the last two years as a part of hospital routine, incident to blood transfusion, and the results were kindly furnished to me by the men in whose laboratories the tests had been made.[8] The remaining families were examined by myself. The accompanying tables represent all the families examined, numbered in their original order from one to sixty-seven.

In my previous papers, I stated that when both parents were in Group I, all the children must be in Group I. In Table 1 are all of the families examined in which both parents were in Group I.

In my previous papers, I stated that when both parents belong to Group II, there can be only two possible kinds of children—Group II and Group I. In Table 2 are all fam-

6. Buchanan, J. A.: Medicolegal Application of the Blood Group, J. A. M. A. **78**:89 (Jan. 14) 1922.

7. In the Helsingfors Letter (J. A. M. A. **77**:1668 [Nov. 19] 1921) the correspondent, describing the Congress of Northern Pathologists, held in Stockholm, August 29 and 30, says: "Jervell of Christiania had continued examinations started by von Dungern and Hirschfeld in 1910 in regard to the iso-agglutinins and the corresponding receptors, and the agglutinogens A and B. . . . He was able to confirm the earlier findings."

8. I am indebted to Dr. Humphries, Dr. Famulener, Dr. Mandlebaum and Dr. Astrowe.

ilies examined in which both parents were of Group II.

Likewise, it was stated that when both parents were of Group III the children would all be III or I (Table 3).

In my previous papers it was stated that when the parents were of Group I and II, the children would all belong to Group I or II (Table 4).

Likewise it was stated that, when the parents were of Groups I and III, the children would all belong to one of these two groups (Table 5).

"All unions containing a member of Group IV, and unions of II and III may give rise to offspring of any of the four groups" (Table 6).

On going over the families, one sees several which bring out in a striking way the mechanism of inheritance. Thus, the Garfola family (Table 6, Family 7), in which all the children belong to groups different from those of the parents, can be explained only on von Dungern and Hirschfeld's hypothesis. The two agglutinogens A and B, combined in one parent and absent from the other, appear separately in the children. The same phenomenon occurs in the Dr. A. M. family (Table 6, Family 46). The reverse occurs in the George family (Table 6, Family 34), in which the two agglutinogens, only one of which is represented in each parent, are combined in one of the children.

In the case of the Garfola family, the examination occurred in such a way that one of the tests of a scientific theory, i. e., its ability to foretell as yet unascertained facts, could be put to a trial. I visited and tested the mother and the three youngest children in the morning, and on finding that the mother was in Group I (no A or B) and the children either in Group III (substance B) or in Group II (substance A), was able to say definitely that the father must be in Group IV (A B), because, as the mother had neither of the two dominant substances present in the children, the father must have both of them. The blood of the father was obtained the evening of the same day and the prediction verified. Analogous predictions could have been made under suitable circumstances in many of the families.

No fact has at any time been observed by me which fails to conform to the theory of von Dungern and Hirschfeld or to the conclusions of my previous papers. It is worth pointing out that for medicolegal purposes it is not necessary to employ or even to understand the mendelian theory. One can simply state the accumulated evidence at present available (consisting of 603 persons in 139 families), thus: Substance A, which is nothing but susceptibility of the red blood corpuscles to agglutination by any Group III serum, and Substance B (susceptibility to Group II serum) never appear in a child unless present in one of the parents. From this all the inferences presented in my previous paper may be derived.

Unless Buchanan publishes his data, it will not be possible to consider his opinions critically. It is, however, necessary to discuss his paper because of the importance of correcting any mistaken impression which it may have conveyed.

Buchanan's difficulties arise primarily from omission to consider the work of previous investigators. He says:

Moss demonstrated in 1909 that three agglutinins and three agglutinogens are necessary to permit the existence of four

blood groups. The work of Moss remains uncontradicted. . . . In my investigation of the inheritance of the blood groups I have discarded the use of a and b and A and B.

As a matter of fact, the existence of $\alpha$, $\beta$, A and B, first postulated by Landsteiner, the discoverer of the blood groups in 1901, has been recognized by practically all of the large number of workers in the field except Moss. The three agglutinin idea was never put forward by Moss as a fully developed theory but only as a suggestion. The facts presented by Moss in 1909 in no way contradict Landsteiner's theory, and exact confirmation of the actual existence of the two agglutinins with two corresponding agglutinogens was published in 1902 by Descatello and Sturli, in 1920 by Koeckert, in 1921 by Schutze, in 1920 by Unger, and in 1921 by Hooker and Anderson.[9] Indeed, the demonstration of these substances is so easy that for years it has been a class exercise in the course on immunology in the College of Physicians and Surgeons, New York, in which course I have had the pleasure of acting as assistant.

Buchanan's opinions can only be explained as due to a misinterpretation of the work of von Dungern and Hirschfeld. Neither they nor I ever implied that "the blood group of the child must be evident in the parents." On the contrary, their explanation exactly and completely accounts for those instances (of which they present a number and of which seventeen others occur in my table) in which the child's group is different from that of either parent. Inspection of Buchanan's charts (his Figures 1 and 8), on the basis of which he claims that a child would have been falsely declared illegitimate, shows that such would not have been the case; his instances definitely belong, according to the observations of von Dungern and Hirschfeld as tabulated by me, among those in which no conclusions as to legitimacy can be made.

Students of genetics do not agree with him that the character of inheritance can never be ascertained without a study of three generations. In the investigations in which the mechanism of inheritance was originally discovered by Mendel, it was necessary to observe three generations. But since the nature of mendelian dominance and recessiveness has been understood there have been numerous instances in which two generations have given all the possible combinations, and it has been easy to identify the mendelian nature of an inherited character by inspection.[10] However, a number of three generation families are presented herewith, and all bear out the previous conclusions, which had been based principally on two generation data.

## CONCLUSION

The facts submitted fully support von Dungern and Hirschfeld's conception of the heredity of the blood groups, and its medicolegal application.

15 West Eighty-Ninth Street.

9. Hooker and Anderson: J. Immunol. 6:419 (Nov.) 1921: an experimental study so complete that it will probably remain the conclusive word on the subject.

10. The only combination of parents absent from the data of von Dungern and Hirschfeld and myself is IV IV, the rarest of all possible combinations.

Dec 23, 1922
(*JAMA* 1922;79:2137-2139)

# Medicolegal Application of Human Blood Grouping

## Third Communication: Sources of Error in Blood Group Tests, and Criteria of Reliability in Investigations on Heredity of Blood Groups

Reuben Ottenberg, M.D.

Adjunct Physician, Mount Sinai Hospital
New York

Since 1907, when I did the first transfusion recorded in which tests for blood compatibility were made,[1] I have performed many thousand blood group tests. Occasionally I have had to correct my own errors as well as those of others. Experience with successive generations of hospital interns has taught me that, in spite of the simplicity of the test, most beginners will make mistakes in grouping unless specifically taught about certain sources of error.

The subject is particularly important at present because: (1) Blood transfusion is being increasingly used; (2) the group test will probably be employed in the near future in medicolegal work, and (3) Buchanan's recent articles[2] denying the correctness of all the preceding work on the heredity of the blood groups make it necessary for some other person to do an extensive piece of investigation.

### WHAT IS THE BEST TECHNIC?

A number of different methods are in use. Any of them will give correct results in the hands of an expert who is acquainted with all the sources of error.

1. The test tube method is the oldest. It has the disadvantages that it is wasteful of serum and that readings are more difficult to make than with other methods, so that weak agglutination can be overlooked.

2. The modified Wright capillary pipet method has the disadvantage of requiring too much glassware and too much expertness.

3. The hanging drop method and the use of hollow ground slides are "to be avoided, since the red corpuscles may sink to the bottom of the depression and simulate a massive agglutination where none is present"—an opinion which I have held for a long time and which was independently reached by Learmouth.[3]

4. The open slide method of Vincent[4] is the method of choice. The technic is extremely simple. One drop of serum is placed on a slide, and into it is allowed to fall one drop of the cell emulsion. (This is better than platinum loopfuls of serum and cells, because with the latter the amount is rather too small.) The slide is tilted and rotated gently, so that the cells are uniformly distributed; this is repeated every couple of minutes.

1. Ottenberg, Reuben: Ann. Surg., April, 1908, p. 506.
2. Buchanan, J. A.: Medicolegal Application of the Blood Group, J. A. M. A. **78:** 89 (Jan. 14) 1922; **79:** 180 (July 15) 1922.
3. Learmouth: J. Genetics **10:** 141, 1920.
4. Vincent, Beth: A Rapid Macroscopic Agglutination Test for Blood Groups, and Its Value in Testing Donors for Transfusion, J. A. M. A. **70:** 1219 (April 27) 1918.

Agglutination is easily seen with the naked eye in from one to ten minutes at room temperature. The microscope is not needed and should not be used. Genuine agglutination is always visible to the naked eye. The observations should never be extended for longer than fifteen minutes.

The method has the added advantage that the dried tests can be kept, according to the suggestion of Culpepper and Ableson,[5] as permanent records. If the slides are not moved after the first ten or fifteen minutes, the artefact of agglutination due to drying does not occur. To prevent their chipping off, the dried specimens should be painted with a layer of collodion.[6]

## SOURCES OF ERROR IN THE TESTS

*Deteriorated Serums.*—The agglutinative power of serums gradually diminishes, no matter how they are kept. Different specimens vary, some deteriorating very rapidly, others hardly at all. Sealed samples kept on the ice retain their strength for long periods. None of the known methods of preserving serums is entirely satisfactory.

These facts suggest two essential precautions which can be demanded in all authentic work: (1) Every test must be done in duplicate with two different serums of each test group (II and III). (2) Test serums must be shown to be active at the time of the tests. This must be controlled by using them against known Group II and Group III cells within at most a few days of the tests.

*The Use of Serums Originally Weak.*—Agglutinative serums vary greatly in strength. A test serum must be shown not only to be of the correct group, but also to be highly potent before it is accepted for use.

*Hemolysis.*—Hemolysin never occurs in serum without the corresponding agglutinin. Complete hemolysis can hardly be overlooked and may usually be regarded as the equivalent of agglutination in assigning the group. When hemolysis occurs, agglutination can nevertheless be demonstrated, either by first inactivating the serum and washing the red cells or by keeping the test from the start at icebox temperature.

The chief danger is partial hemolysis combined with weak agglutination, in which case the two can obscure each other.

*Incubation at 37 C.*—Because it favors hemolysis, incubation in a warm atmosphere should not be practiced.

*Drying.*—Nonspecific agglutination, due probably to increased salt concentration, can occur if the mixture is allowed to become partly dried. This is easily avoided by ending the observations in ten, or at most fifteen, minutes.

It is possible, although I have not seen it happen, that, if test serums are kept in open tubes, they may in time become sufficiently concentrated to produce this false agglutination. As Karsner and Koeckert[7] have shown, the use of dried and then redissolved serum is to be condemned.

*Settling of Cells.*—This is one of the commonest sources of mistakes. It can occur with any method. The cells settle to the bottom in a compact sheet, which, if only slightly stirred, looks like massive agglutination. The remedy is thorough mixing before results are read; this will make a smooth emulsion of merely settled cells, while it will accentuate real agglutination.

*Use of the Microscope.*—The microscope is, in my opinion, a source of error. Rouleaux formation is sometimes hard to distinguish from fine agglutination. In every instance in which the doubt has been raised by microscopic examination and settled by examination of the person's serum as well as cells, the naked eye observation has proved correct, the microscopic, confusing.

*Too Thick a Cell Emulsion.*—The red cells do not need to be washed for agglutination tests (unless hemolysis is also to be tested for). Unless blood is drawn from a vein in order to get serum, the emulsion is most easily obtained by pricking the finger and expressing about 5 drops of blood into a cubic centimeter of 3 per cent. sodium citrate. The emulsion should be diluted with 0.9 per cent. saline solution to about 2.5 per cent. strength, i. e., about half as dense as the sheep-cell emulsion ordinarily used in the Wassermann test. If the emulsion is much too dense, some of the cells may remain unagglutinated and mask the agglutination of the others. I pointed this out in 1911,[8] and I have seen actual mistakes in transfusion cases due to this fact.

*Undeveloped Group Characters.*—The group characteristics are not fully developed in all young infants. Occasionally they are imperfectly developed in older children. (This has no relation to the so-called "subgroups" which have been claimed to exist on the basis of posttransfusion reactions, but for whose existence there is no real evidence.)

On account of this possibility of undeveloped group characters, the serum as well as the cells must be examined in children and, in all cases of doubt, in adults. It is also on this account that it is so essential to repeat the tests if a second or third transfusion is done in a child.

*Auto-Agglutination.*—This is an exceedingly rare phenomenon. It occurs only at a low temperature. It is easily detected and ruled out as a source of error if only the possibility of its occurrence is kept in mind. It is on account of this that the control test of a drop of cell emulsion with saline solution, or, if possible, with a drop of the patient's own serum, should always be examined.

## HOW TO AVOID INCLUDING CASES OF ILLEGITIMACY WHEN COLLECTING DATA ON HUMAN HEREDITY

No one knows how common or rare secret illegitimacy is. There is no absolute method of preventing the

5. Culpepper, W. L., and Ableson, M.: J. Lab. & Clin. Med. 6: 276 (Feb.) 1921.

6. I showed the dried records of the last twenty families examined in my recent heredity study (Medicolegal Application of Human Blood Grouping, J. A. M. A. 78: 873 [March 25] 1922), all mounted on cardboard, to bring out the family relationships, at the meeting of the American Association of Immunologists in Washington, May 1, 1922. These are now deposited with Prof. T. H. Morgan in the department of zoology at Columbia University.

7. Karsner, H. T., and Koeckert, H. L.: Influence of Desiccation on Human Normal Isohemagglutinins, J. A. M. A. 73: 1207 (Oct. 18) 1919.

8. Ottenberg, Reuben: J. Exper. Med. 13: 425 (April) 1911.

accidental inclusion of an illegitimate child or even of a family of such children in statistics on heredity. This is one of the difficulties of the study of human heredity. The best resource which I can suggest is the following rule: No family should be examined until the mother fully understands the object of the examination. If she then makes any objection, no matter on what grounds, the examination should not be made, or the results should not be considered.

## LITERATURE OF THE QUESTION OF HEREDITY

The present communication is written as the result of the recent articles of Buchanan.[2] In these articles Bu-

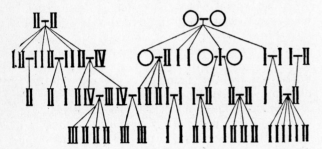

Keyne's family, fifty-nine individuals, tested in four generations. Circles represent persons who could not be examined.

chanan, aside from his claims as to his own work, makes so many misleading statements concerning the literature that it would be unfair to readers if I omitted to correct him.

Thus, he tries to convey the impression that authors other than himself have failed to confirm the hereditary nature of the blood group. He says:

The interesting studies of Learmouth show that the old theory of the two specific substances for the blood group and the mendelian inheritance of the blood are at variance. The blood group is either not hereditary or the laboratory experiments concerning the specific substances responsible for the blood groups are being misinterpreted.

Actually Learmouth,[3] both in general and in specific detail, comes to exactly the opposite conclusion, agreeing precisely with me—or rather I with him, since his article preceded my recent one.

Learmouth had forty families with 101 children, 181 persons in all. There was only one exception, a Group II child from Group I parents; and he himself suggests illegitimacy as the explanation.

Regarding this exception, I cannot do better than quote Keynes,[9] who says, with regard to it:

There are three possible explanations of this (1) The observations were at fault; (2) the putative father was not the real father; (3) the mendelian theory of inheritance is wrong. The mendelian theory is established on so firm a basis that, in the absence of more numerous exceptions, (3) may be rejected. There is no reason for supposing that the observations were inaccurate; and we are therefore brought to the conclusion that in such a case the child is illegitimate.

Keynes himself contributes another family of fifty-nine persons in four generations. It does not show any variation from the results that were to be anticipated. As the family is the largest yet recorded, I reproduce the pedigree in the accompanying chart (reversing the I's and IV's to correspond to the Jansky terminology).

Buchanan says further:

My findings are in accordance with the results of studies of the blood group in families that have been published.

Far from this being true, Buchanan's findings flatly contradict those of every other author who has written on the subject—of von Dungern and Hirschfeld,[10] in Heidelberg; Jervell,[11] in Christiania; Learmouth,[3] in Liverpool; Keynes,[8] in Oxford; Weszecsky,[12] in Czeckoslovakia; Tebbutt and McConnel,[13] in Australia, and myself,[6] in New York.

As it is incredible that a law of heredity which holds true in almost a thousand cases and in such diverse places should not hold in Minnesota, and improbable that Buchanan should have encountered so large a number of illegitimacies, it follows that his wrong conclusions must rest on his own mistakes.

## PREDICTION OF REMAINING PARENT GROUP

| Known Children in Group | One Parent Known to Be in Group | The Other Parent Must Be in Group |
| --- | --- | --- |
| II | I | II or IV |
| II | III | II or IV |
| III | I | III or IV |
| III | II | III or IV |
| IV | I | IV |
| IV | II | III or IV |
| IV | III | II or IV |
| II and III | I | IV |
| II and III | II | III or IV |
| II and III | III | II or IV |
| II and IV | I | IV |
| II and IV | II | III or IV |
| II and IV | III | II or IV |
| III and IV | I | IV |
| III and IV | II | III or IV |
| III and IV | III | II or IV |
| II, III and IV° | I | IV |
| II, III and IV | II | III or IV |
| II, III and IV | III | II or IV |

°This combination of children (II, III and IV) has not yet been described in the literature. Its occurrence would depend on occasional "crossing" in the chromosomes, as was pointed out to me by Dr. M. Gichner of Baltimore.

One other misleading statement of Buchanan's must be mentioned. He says:

The incorrectness of the statement of Ottenberg that he could foretell the parents by studying the children resulting from

9. Keynes, Geoffrey: Blood Transfusion, Oxford Medical Publications, 1921, p. 90.

10. Von Dungern and Hirschfeld: Ztschr. f. Immunitätsforsch. u. exper. Therap. 6: 284, 1910.

11. Helsingfors Letter, J. A. M. A. 77: 1668 (Nov. 19) 1921.

12. Weszescky: Biochem. Ztschr. 107: 159, 1920. The author concludes that the mendelian inheritance described by von Dungern and Hirschfeld holds, but his charts present two anomalous cases.

13. Tebbutt, A. H., and McConnel, S. V.: M. J. Australia 1: 201 (Feb. 25) 1922.

unions of Groups IV and I is shown in the seventy-second family of von Dungern and Hirschfeld, the twenty-ninth and thirty-eighth families of Learmouth, and the Tink family of my own investigation.

Of course, I never made any such statement. The one instance in which I foretold—and correctly—the group of the father after knowing that of mother and children is described in my recent article clearly enough that anyone should understand it. Buchanan's choice of instances from Learmouth and from von Dungern and Hirschfeld is peculiarly unfortunate, since by coupling their cases with his own Tink family he suggests that their families, like his, are anomalous. This is not the case. Learmouth's twenty-ninth family consists of parents in Groups I and IV and six children in Group IV, his thirty-eighth family, of parents also in Groups I and IV and four children in Group IV. Von Dungern and Hirschfeld's seventy-second family consists of parents in Groups I and IV, three children in Group IV and one in Group I. These all conform to the laws of heredity as first fully described by von Dungern and Hirschfeld.

Buchanan fails to understand that, from the nature of the case, it is never possible to say from the children alone what the parents must be; but, knowing the children and one parent, one can sometimes state what the other parent must be.

The instances in which it is possible to predict the remaining parent, (the children and one parent being known), are implied, but not tabulated, in my previous papers. They are presented in the accompanying table.

In making such predictions, children of Group I are disregarded since, showing only recessive qualities, they can arise from any combination of parents. Thus, if additional children of Group I occurred in any of the foregoing families, the prediction as to the remaining

parent would not be altered. If the reader wishes to amuse himself by studying the appended family of Keynes, he will find that there are eight cases in which the one parent being suitably chosen as known, and the children being known, it would have been possible to make a correct prediction as to the other parent. The same is true of the two families of Learmouth and the one of von Dungern and Hirschfeld cited above.

## SUMMARY

1. The best technic for the tests is the open slide method.

2. The sources of error are: (1) deteriorated serums; (2) weak serums; (3) hemolysis; (4) incubation at 37 C.; (5) drying; (6) settling of cells; (7) microscope observation; (8) dense cell emulsions; (9) undeveloped group characters, and (10) autoagglutination.

3. On account of these, the following precautions must be observed: (a) Every test must be done in duplicate, using different sets of test serums. (b) Test serums must be shown to be active at the time of the tests. (c) Wherever there is the possibility of doubt, both serum and cells of the individual must be tested. (d) The cell emulsion without addition of test serum must also be examined.

4. In studies of human heredity, the accidental inclusion of cases of illegitimacy can best be avoided if the mother of each family fully understands the object of the examinations and consents to them.

5. Buchanan's failure to confirm the hereditary nature of the blood groups is apparently the result of errors of observation. He disagrees with all other authors, who are unanimous in their findings and have recorded almost a thousand cases.

15 West Eighty-Ninth Street.

# Paternity Determination*

## 1921 to 1983 and Beyond

### Margery W. Shaw, MD, JD

D r Reuben Ottenberg's three articles published in THE
JOURNAL in 1921 and 1922 are remarkably prescient.
The reader will find his articles easier to follow by
mentally translating blood groups I, II, III, and IV to O, A,
B, and AB, respectively.

Although Ottenberg contributed much family data to
analyze the inheritance of the ABO system, he and other
scientists at that time were laboring under the false
assumption that there were two loci for the ABO blood
groups that segregated independently. Thus, some of
the predictions he made in the last Table of the third
article[1] are erroneous: an O parent cannot have an AB
child. This would, of course, be possible under the
two-locus hypothesis. For example, AABB times aabb
would necessarily yield all AaBb children with the
phenotype AB. Perhaps the reason he and others made
this error was because there were so few AB matings
available for study (the population frequency of the AB
phenotype is approximately 4%). It was not until 1925
that Bernstein conclusively demonstrated the single-
locus, three-allele system for the Mendelian inheritance
of the ABO blood group.

In the first article, Ottenberg states: ``. . . if the child's
[blood] group is wrong for the two asserted parents,
then one can say with absolute certainty that the child
must have a parent other than one of those asserted.
The commonest instance, of course, is that of disputed
paternity.''[2] The remainder of this commentary will deal
with the medicolegal aspects of paternity testing 62 years
after Ottenberg's suggestion. In addition, I will make
some predictions about the determination of paternity in
the future.

### Medicolegal Aspects

After the discovery of the inheritance pattern of the
ABO blood groups in 1925, the MN system was

elucidated in 1927 and the Rh system was added in 1940.
These three systems could exclude a wrongly accused
male 50% of the time. By 1975, fifty-seven genetic
polymorphisms were available and it was possible to
achieve a probability of exclusion of 99% without the use
of the complex HLA locus.[3] The HLA system is the single
most powerful test available today; HLA alone is disposi-
tive in about 90% of the cases.[4]

As they traditionally have been when faced with new
scientific evidence, the courts were reluctant to allow the
jury to consider blood group test results in disputed
paternity cases. In a 1931 bastardy proceeding in
Pennsylvania, the appellate court granted a new trial
because blood tests purported to show that the accused
man could not have been the father.[5] But in 1936, the
Pennsylvania Superior Court refused to order the mother
and child to have blood tests performed,[6] and a New
York court did not require the alleged father to submit to
blood tests since ``it would furnish no satisfactory proof
of defendant's paternity.''[7]

The most celebrated court case on blood grouping
and paternity was that of Charlie Chaplin in California in
1946.[8] Although the tests indisputably established that he
could not be the father, the court ordered him to pay
child support! The court would not allow the blood
group evidence to be conclusive unless the legislature
had recognized it as such, thus allowing the jury to weigh
the blood group test results along with the other
evidence presented by Ms Berry in determining paternity.

In 1950, William J. Brennan, now a US Supreme Court
Justice but then a judge of the New Jersey Superior
Court, summarized the contemporary legal status of
blood typing:

The value of blood tests as a wholesome aid in the quest for
truth in the administration of justice . . . cannot be gainsaid. . . .
Their reliability as an indicator of the truth has been fully
established. The substantial weight of medical and legal
authority attests their accuracy, not to prove paternity, and not
always to disprove it, but ``they can disprove it conclusively in a

From the Institute for the Interprofessional Study of Health Law, the
University of Texas Health Science Center at Houston.

*A commentary on Ottenberg R: Medicolegal application of human
blood grouping. *JAMA* 1921;77:682-683; *JAMA* 1922;78:873-877; and
*JAMA* 1922;79:2137-2139.

great many cases provided that [the tests] are administered by specially qualified experts."[9]

Two years later, the American Medical Association endorsed the use of ABO, MN, and Rh tests for use by the courts[10] and another judge announced in a legal opinion: "For a court to declare that these tests are not conclusive would be as unrealistic as it would be for a court to declare that the world is flat!"

Today, blood group and other genetic tests are used by the courts as conclusive evidence to exclude paternity. Title IV-D of the federal Social Security Act requires that states receiving federal support for aid to dependent children attempt to locate fathers of both legitimate and illegitimate children in order to enforce child support.[12] This has resulted in a massive number of paternity determinations paid for by the state. Not surprisingly, the courts and legislatures have responded quickly by accepting new scientific evidence as it becomes available. In fact, the Iowa Supreme Court has held that indigent fathers have no right to counsel in paternity disputes because the accuracy of blood tests has approached mathematical certainty.[13] The court believed that the risk of error in a paternity action is not seriously affected by the presence or absence of counsel.

### Present and Future

As an example of the recent trend in rapid assimilation of new scientific developments, let us examine the status of HLA "tissue-typing" tests. As recently as 1975, no American court had allowed HLA test results to be admitted into evidence. But as of May 1982, 17 state legislatures had rewritten their statutes to allow HLA evidence to show a "likelihood of paternity" in addition to paternity exclusion. If only a "preponderance of evidence" is necessary in a civil action and if a man has not been excluded when the probability of exclusion is better than 99.6%, then it is more likely than not that he is the biological father. Six other states have introduced bills to allow HLA evidence and five state courts found HLA tests admissible where the statute is silent. Only three states have upheld statutes disallowing evidence of the likelihood of paternity.[14]

The calculations required to determine likelihood of paternity are more complicated than the calculations of the probability of exclusion of paternity. However, a computer program called PATTEST has been written to simplify the interpretation of test results.[15] Seldom is a large battery of tests required. Only in those cases in which HLA does not exclude the alleged father are blood group and other tests performed. In addition to the battery of 23 blood groups, there are many genetic polymorphisms for hemoglobin, red cell and white cell enzymes, and serum proteins.[3]

Perhaps the most exciting discovery applicable to paternity testing is the existence of restriction endonuclease fragment-length polymorphisms (RFLPs). The restriction endonuclease enzymes recognize unique "strings" of nucleotides in the DNA and snip the DNA into fragments wherever these strings occur. By the use of a number of such enzymes, the DNA can be literally "chopped" into many small pieces. Because individuals differ in their DNA sequences, it is possible to identify many unique sites in the DNA that vary from person to person. Family studies can trace the inheritance patterns of the RFLPs in the same way that any other Mendelian character can be traced.[16] In 1978, one RFLP locus was reported to be near the human betaglobin gene.[17] By 1981, seventeen more RFLPs were found.[18] More than 100 such DNA polymorphic sites have now been identified! (Mark Skolnick, PhD, oral communication, 1983.) The ability to discover others is virtually limitless, depending only on time and money constraints and the availability of other restriction endonuclease enzymes that will recognize different "strings" in the DNA. Already more than 200 such enzymes have been described. Although RFLP research has been primarily directed toward mapping the human genome, it could also be applied to paternity testing.

In conclusion, I predict that with the application of computers and DNA sequence polymorphisms, it will become possible to be certain of the identity of the biologic father of any person unless the alleged father has an identical twin. This prediction should be technically and economically feasible by the end of this century. Furthermore, for purposes of inheritance and intestate succession, it should be possible to determine paternity even if the father is deceased, by extensive genetic testing of the paternal relatives. Motherhood has always been a biologic certainty; now fatherhood will be as well. We will have come one step closer to equality of the sexes.

### References

1. Ottenberg R: Medicolegal application of human blood grouping: Third communication: Sources of error in blood group tests, and criteria of reliability in investigations on heredity of blood groups. *JAMA* 1922;79:2137-2139.
2. Ottenberg R: Medicolegal application of human blood grouping. *JAMA* 1921;77:682-683.
3. Shaw MW, Kass M: Illegitimacy, child support, and paternity testing. *Houston Law Rev* 1975;13:41-62.
4. Terasaki PI: Resolution by HLA testing of 1,000 paternity cases not excluded by ABO testing. *J Fam Law* 1977-1978;16:543-557.
5. *Commonwealth v Zammarelli,* 17 Pa D & C 299 (1931).
6. *Commonwealth v English,* 186 A 298 (Pa 1936).
7. *In re Swahn's Will,* 285 NYS 234 (1936).
8. *Berry v Chaplin,* 169 P2d 442 (Cal 1946).
9. *Cortese v Cortese,* 76 A2d 717 (NJ 1950).
10. Davidsohn I, Levine R, Weiner AS: Medicolegal applications of blood grouping tests. *JAMA* 1952;149:699-706.
11. *Ross v Marx,* 90 A2d 545 (NJ 1952).
12. 42 USC §§651-660 (1976).
13. *Hamilton v Snodgrass,* 325 NW2d 740 (Iowa 1982).
14. Admission of HLA test results approved by Kansas court. *Fam Law Rep* 1982;8:1113.
15. Chakraborty R, Ferrell RE: Correlation of paternity index with probability of exclusion and efficiency criteria of genetic markers for paternity testing. *Forensic Sci Intl* 1982;19:113-124.
16. Botstein D, White RL, Skolnick MH, et al: Construction of a genetic linkage map in man using restriction fragment length polymorphisms. *Am J Hum Genet* 1980;32:314-331.
17. Kan YW, Dozy AM: Polymorphism of DNA sequence adjacent to human beta-globin structural gene: Relationship to sickle mutation. *Proc Natl Acad Sci* 1978;75:5631-5635.
18. Skolnick MH, White R: Strategies for detecting and characterizing restriction fragment length polymorphisms (RFLPs). *Cytogenet Cell Genet* 1982;32:58-67.

Feb 10, 1923
(*JAMA* 1923;80:368-373)

Chapter 16

# Roentgenography of Urinary Tract During Excretion of Sodium Iodid*

Earl D. Osborne, M.D.
Charles G. Sutherland, M.B. (Tor.)
Albert J. Scholl, Jr., M.D.
and
Leonard G. Rowntree, M.D.

Rochester, Minn.

There is need of a simple and painless method of depicting the urinary tract, bladder, kidneys and ureters. By the use of catheters and various opaque mediums, success has been attained so far as the bladder, ureters and pelves of the kidney are concerned. Cystography and urography, while of great importance, are not without drawbacks and limitations. The use of the urethral or ureteral catheter is subject to obvious objections from both the physician's and the patient's standpoint. Technically, ureteral catheterization is at times very difficult, and it often subjects the patient to excruciating pain and occasionally to serious reactions. While pyelography may clearly delineate the renal pelves, it may fail to reveal the outline of the kidney itself. In surgical and medical diseases of the kidney, information concerning the size and location of these organs is of paramount interest. In nephritis, for example, it would be of decided value to be able to ascertain definitely during the patient's life whether his kidney is large, small or contracted, or of normal size. While the kidneys may be clearly outlined by inducing a pneumoperitoneum, and possibly by injecting air locally into the renal regions, these procedures, for obvious reasons, are not likely to be practiced generally.

It occurred to one of us (L. G. R.) that if, in roentgenography of the urinary tract, advantage could be taken of the fact that sodium iodid, after its introduction into the body, is normally excreted in the urine, roentgenograms of the kidneys, ureters and bladder might be secured without the need of catheterization.

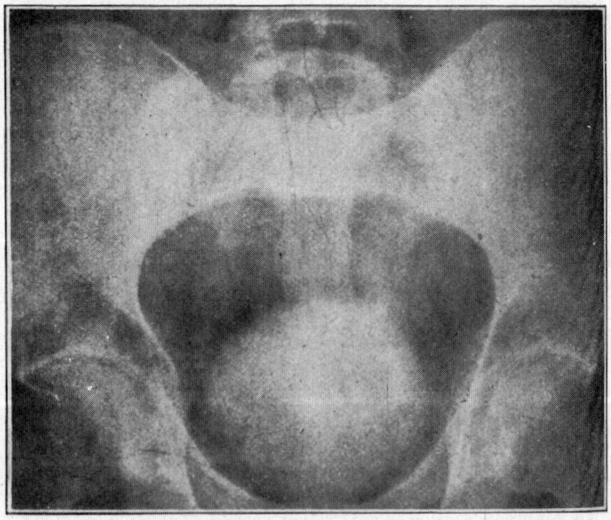

Fig. 1.—The patient received 200 c.c. of a 10 per cent. solution of sodium iodid intravenously. The roentgenogram made two hours later revealed a perfect outline of the full bladder.

An ideal opportunity for the clinical testing of this idea presented itself in the section on dermatology and syphilology of the Mayo Clinic, where one of us (E. D. O.) was utilizing intravenously from 50 to 250 c.c. of a 10 per cent. solution of sodium iodid in the study of the pharmacology and therapeutics of iodids. This circumstance made possible an immediate and direct clinical study, eliminating the necessity of carrying out time-consuming preliminary investigations on animals.

*From the Division of Medicine, Mayo Clinic.

The patients were informed of our interest in this problem, and many of them volunteered to undergo the roentgen-ray studies.

## THE INTRODUCTION OF VARIOUS MEDIUMS IN THE URINARY TRACT

Voelcker and Lichtenberg,[1] in 1906, were the first to report the use of an opaque roentgenographic medium, injected into the pelvis of the kidney for the purpose of determining the pelvic outline. Colloidal silver, the medium suggested by them, was dirty and expensive, and it often caused severe reactions. In 1915, Burns[2] reported very satisfactory results with thorium nitrate. Various other chemical compounds were suggested, but none were satisfactory. The proprietary preparations were

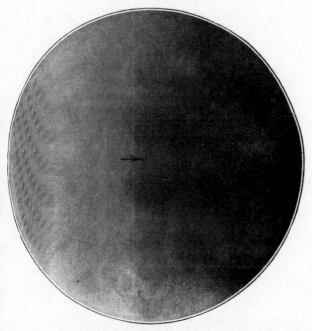

Fig. 2.—The patient received 135 c.c. of a 10 per cent. solution of sodium iodid intravenously. The roentgenogram made one and one-half hours later contained shadows of the pelvis, the major calices and a portion of the ureter on both sides.

expensive and often caused marked reactions. The work of Braasch and Mann[3] has demonstrated that practically all the silver compounds, when retained in the pelvis of the kidney or injected under pressure, produce areas of cortical necrosis. In some instances, it has been possible to find definite deposits of the metal in the renal cortex. Praetorius,[4] who suggested the use, as a medium, of a preparation claimed to contain colloidal silver iodid, cites twelve deaths, previous to 1917, from the use of colloidal

silver. Later, Schüssler[5] and Barreau[6] reported severe reactions from the use of the preparation claimed to contain colloidal silver iodid.

Fig. 3.—The patient received 100 c.c. of a 10 per cent. solution of sodium iodid intravenously. The roentgenogram made one hour later contained a definite outline of the pelvis of a left kidney, with the ureter from 4 to 6 cm. distant from the kidney hilus.

Kelly and Lewis,[7] in 1913, were the first to suggest the use of an iodid as a medium. They recommended silver iodid emulsion. Sodium iodid as a medium in roentgenography was introduced by Cameron[8] in 1918. The striking lack of toxicity of sodium iodid has long been known, but not fully appreciated. Enormous doses have been used clinically by syphilologists in the treatment of syphilis. Experimentally, the lack of toxicity of the iodids was illustrated recently by Weld,[9] who found that toxic effects did not follow the administration intravenously of 50 c.c. of a 25 per cent. solution to dogs weighing 6 kg. Weld suggested the use of sodium bromid, which is now generally used for depicting the renal pelves and ureters in urologic examinations at the Mayo Clinic. Sodium bromid causes fewer reactions than sodium iodid, but

1. Voelcker, F., and Lichtenberg, A.: Pyelographie (Roentgenographie des Nierenbeckens nach Kollargolfüllung), München, med. Wchnschr. **53:** 105-107, 1906.

2. Burns, J. E.: Thorium, a New Agent for Pyelography, Preliminary Report, J. A. M. A. **64:** 2126-2127 (June 26) 1915.

3. Braasch, W. F., and Mann, F. C.: Effects of Retention in the Kidney of Media Employed in Pyelography, Am. J. M. Sc. **152:** 336-347 (Sept.) 1916.

4. Praetorius, G.: Pyelographie mit kolloidalem Jodsilber ("Pyelon"), Ztschr. f. Urol. **13:** 159-168 (April) 1919.

5. Schüssler, H.: Zur Pyelographie mit "Pyelon," München. med. Wchnschr. **67:** 750-751 (June 28) 1920.

6. Barreau, E.: Zur Frage der Pyelographie, Ztschr. f. Urol. **15:** 134-144, 1921; Ueber Pyelon, ibid. **15:** 507, 1921.

7. Kelly, H. A., and Lewis, R. M.: Silver Iodide Emulsion—a New Medium for Skiagraphy of the Urinary Tract, Surg., Gynec. & Obst. **16:** 707-708. 1913.

8. Cameron, D. F.: Aqueous Solutions of Potassium and Sodium Iodids as Opaque Mediums in Roentgenography, Preliminary Report. J. A. M. A. **70:** 754-755 (March 6) 1918; A Comparative Study of Sodium Iodid as an Opaque Medium in Pyelography, Arch. Surg. **1:** 184-214 (July) 1920.

9. Weld, E. H.: The Use of Sodium Bromid in Roentgenography, J. A. M. A. **71:** 1111-1112 (Oct. 5) 1918; Toxicity in Pyelographic Mediums, Report of a Death Following the Use of Thorium Nitrate, J. Urol. **3:** 415-426 (Oct.) 1919. Renal Absorption with Particular Reference to Pyelographic Mediums, Med. Clin. N. America **3:** 713-731 (Nov.) 1919.

does not give such clear roentgenographic outlines. Sodium bromid, like sodium iodid, is of such low viscosity that it often runs from the pelvis and ureter before the roentgenogram is completed.

### METHOD OF ADMINISTRATION OF SODIUM IODID

*Intravenous Administration.*—The method of intravenous administration of sodium iodid has been employed in the section on dermatology and syphilology since 1918. The patient is first given 15 grains (about 1 gm.) of potassium iodid by mouth, three times a day for two days, in order to determine whether there is an idiosyncrasy to the drug. If no symptoms of acute iodism occur, the intravenous injection of a 10 per cent. solution is begun, the third day. Various dosages have been

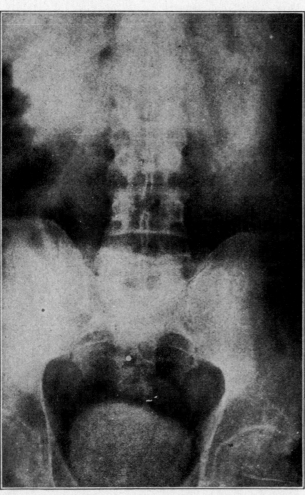

Fig. 4.—The patient received 100 c.c. of a 10 per cent. solution of sodium iodid intravenously. The roentgenogram made one and one-half hours later revealed a perfect outline of a full bladder, and an outline of the pelvis of the left kidney with a suggestion of the calices and the ureter for a distance of from 3 to 4 cm. below the hilum of the kidney. The right kidney area was obscured by gas in the colon.

employed, ranging from 5 to 20 gm. of a 10 per cent. solution of chemically pure sodium iodid. As Osborne has pointed out, 10 gm. may be given to practically every patient without untoward symptoms, provided the injection is not too rapid, that is, not completed in less than four or five minutes. With a dose of more than 10 gm.,

symptoms appear, probably due to osmotic changes resulting from large amounts of the hypertonic salt solution. It would seem that 10 gm. is a fair dose for the average routine case. Naturally, the usual contraindications to iodids apply here; that is, patients with tuberculosis, adenomatous thyroids, exophthalmic goiter and marked debility are not good subjects for this form of treatment. Generally speaking, our results following the intravenous administration of sodium iodids may be summarized thus:

1. Satisfactory roentgenograms of the bladder were secured in practically every case with doses of from 5 to 20 gm. intravenously.

### TABLE 1.—IODIN IN THE URINE AFTER SODIUM IODID INTRAVENOUSLY

| | Sodium Iodid, 5 Gm. | | | Sodium Iodid, 10 Gm. | | | Sodium Iodid, 20 Gm. | | |
|---|---|---|---|---|---|---|---|---|---|
| | Iodin Excreted | | | Iodin Excreted | | | Iodin Excreted | | |
| Time After | Urine, C.c. | Per Cent. | Mg. per 100 C.c. | Urine, C.c. | Per Cent. | Mg. per 100 C.c. | Urine, C.c. | Per Cent. | Mg. per 100 C.c. |
| 15 min. | 9.5 | 1.2 | 5.6 | 43.0 | 1.2 | 2.5 | 55.0 | 0.5 | 1.6 |
| 30 min. | 17.5 | 3.5 | 8.5 | 21.5 | 1.9 | 7.8 | 40.0 | 0.6 | 2.8 |
| 45 min. | 16.5 | 2.9 | 7.4 | 21.5 | 2.5 | 10.0 | 26.0 | 0.5 | 3.8 |
| 1 hr. | 14.0 | 2.0 | 6.3 | 22.5 | 2.7 | 10.2 | 25.5 | 1.0 | 7.0 |
| 2 hrs. | 77.5 | 8.8 | 4.9 | 95.0 | 8.7 | 7.7 | 146.0 | 8.4 | 9.8 |
| 3 hrs. | 54.0 | 5.4 | 4.4 | 106.0 | 5.2 | 4.2 | 104.0 | 7.7 | 12.7 |
| 4 hrs. | 43.0 | 6.4 | 6.2 | 93.0 | 2.5 | 2.2 | 133.0 | 10.4 | 13.3 |
| 6 hrs. } | ..... | .... | ....... | 25.0° | 1.9 | 5.9 } | | | |
| 7 hrs. } | 218.0 | 16.5 | 3.2 } | .... | .... | ...... } | 225.0 | 15.6 | 11.8 |
| 8 hrs. | ..... | .... | ....... | 102.0 | 8.7 | 7.2 | | | |
| 18 hrs. | 490.0 | 19.5 | 1.6 | 473.0 | 17.6 | 3.2 | 375.0 | 23.4 | 10.5 |
| 24 hrs. | 245.0 | 10.0 | 1.7 | 590.0 | 6.6 | 0.9 | 151.0 | 8.1 | 7.5 |
| 48 hrs. | 1055.0 | 14.7 | 0.59 | 965.0 | 15.5 | 1.4 | 1080.0 | 13.9 | 1.2 |
| 72 hrs. | 960.0 | 2.8 | 0.12 | 1005.0 | 4.6 | 0.3 | 1030.0 | 3.7 | 0.6 |
| 96 hrs. | 995.0 | 0.5 | 0.02 | 1120.0 | 0.3 | 0.02 | 975.0 | 0.1 | 0.01 |
| 120 hrs. | 1010.0 | Trace | ....... | 945.0 | Trace | ....... | 950.0 | Trace | |
| In 24 hrs. | | 76.2 | ....... | | 59.5 | ....... | | 76.2 | |
| In 48 hrs. | | 90.9 | ....... | | 75.0 | ....... | | 90.1 | |
| In 72 hrs. | | 93.7 | ....... | | 79.6 | ....... | | 93.8 | |
| In 96 hrs. | | 94.2 | ....... | | 79.9 | ....... | | 93.9 | |

°Approximately four fifths of this specimen was lost.

2. Ten gram doses of sodium iodid intravenously gave fair roentgenograms of the kidneys and ureters in approximately 50 per cent. of the cases, and occasionally of the liver and spleen.

3. The best roentgenograms of the upper urinary tract and of the spleen and liver were secured with the use of large doses, that is, from 15 to 20 gm.

The time elapsing between the administration of the sodium iodid and the taking of the roentgenogram is of vital importance. Table 1 shows the amount and concentration of iodin in the urine at varying intervals following the intravenous administration of 5, 10, and 20 gm. doses of a 10 per cent. solution of sodium iodid. The highest point of concentration following a dose of 5 gm. is in the second fifteen minute interval, when 8.5 mg. of iodin was excreted in each cubic centimeter of urine. With a dose of 10 gm., this amount rose to 10.2 mg. of iodin for each cubic centimeter of urine during the third fifteen minute interval, and following the 20 gm. dose, to 12.7 mg. during the second hour and 13.3 mg. during the third hour. From these data, it is seen that the roentgenograms should be taken one-half hour, one hour and two or three hours after doses of 5, 10, and 20 gm., respectively. Our best results have been obtained by following this procedure, based on an actual determination of the rate of excretion of sodium iodid.[10]

*Administration by Mouth.*—It was at first thought that roentgenograms of the urinary tract, following administration of sodium iodid by mouth, would be of no value because of the shadows cast by the drug in the stomach and in the small intestine. The contrary has been shown, however, when the proper technic is employed and attention is paid to the time interval between the administration of the iodid and the making of the roentgenogram. Satisfactory roentgenograms have been obtained at one and two hour intervals following a single large dose of 10 gm. of sodium iodid. This method,

TABLE 2.—URINARY EXCRETION OF IODIN AFTER SODIUM IODID BY MOUTH

| | Sodium Iodid, 1 Gm. | | | Sodium Iodid, 5 Gm. | | | Sodium Iodid, 20 Gm. | | |
|---|---|---|---|---|---|---|---|---|---|
| | | Iodin Excreted | | | Iodin Excreted | | | Iodin Excreted | |
| Time After Before | Urine, C.c. Sample | Per Cent. Trace | Mg. per 100 C.c. ....... | Urine, C.c. Sample | Per Cent. Trace | Mg. per 100 C.c. ....... | Urine, C.c. Sample | Per Cent. Trace | Mg. per 100 C.c. |
| 1 hr. | 59.0 | 5.3 | 0.76 | 77 | 7.3 | 4.03 | 296 | 10.9 | 6.34 |
| 2 hrs. | 46.0 | 8.6 | 1.58 | 52 | 7.1 | 5.60 | 122 | 6.2 | 8.42 |
| 3 hrs. | 52.0 | 7.1 | 1.29 | 119 | 9.9 | 3.51 | 63.5 | 1.6 | 4.24 |
| 4 hrs. | 45.5 | 6.3 | 1.32 | 212 | 6.8 | 1.35 | | | |
| 6 hrs.⎫ | | | | 365 | 18.5 | 2.14 | 252 | 4.4 | 2.97 |
| 10 hrs.⎭ | 300 | 24.0 | 0.75 | 226 | 11.0 | 2.06 | 886 | 30.9 | 5.9 |
| 24 hrs. | 470 | 26.7 | 0.53 | 433 | 23.7 | 2.32 | 734 | 23.6 | 5.4 |
| 48 hrs. | 910 | 12.6 | 0.13 | 843 | 12.1 | 0.61 | 1120 | 14.2 | 2.1 |
| 72 hrs. | ...... | .... | ....... | 895 | 2.4 | 0.10 | 955 | 5.7 | 0.8 |
| 96 hrs. | ...... | .... | ....... | 990 | 0.4 | 0.01 | 885 | 0.2 | 0.04 |
| 20 hrs. | ...... | .... | ....... | 1120 | Trace | Trace | 1060 | Trace | Trace |

however, is not applicable to routine cases because of the local gastric upset following the ingestion of such large amounts of the salt. Our best results have been obtained by administering 3 gm. of sodium iodid hourly for three hours and taking the roentgenograms from one hour to two hours after the last dose. The rationale of this procedure is shown in Table 2. The urinary concentration of iodin following the oral administration of sodium iodid becomes highest during the one hour to three hours after the ingestion of from 1 to 5 gm. of the salt.

The patient is prepared in the routine manner for roentgen-ray examination of the urinary tract. At 8 a. m. he is instructed to take the first powder, consisting of 3 gm. of the sodium iodid, well diluted in from one to two glasses of water. He is instructed to empty the bladder at this time and not to pass more urine until the examination is completed. At 9 a. m. and at 10 he repeats the procedure, and at 11 the first roentgenogram is made, after which he is instructed to void as much urine as possible. This is measured and a second roentgenogram is made. It may be that the administration of large doses of sodium iodid will yield uniformly better results, but such has not been our experience. The employment of less

10. These data and those dealing with the oral administration have been taken from work already published and work now in the process of publication by Osborne on the general subject of the pharmacology and therapeutics of iodids (Osborne, E. D.: Iodin in the Cerebrospinal Fluid, with Reference to Iodid Therapy, J. A. M. A. **76:** 1384-1386 (May 21) 1921; Contributions to the Pharmacology and Therapeutics of Iodids, ibid. **79:** 615-617 (Aug. 19) 1922; Contributions to the Pharmacology and Therapeutics of Iodids, II, to be published).

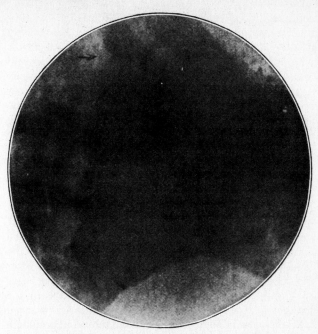

Fig. 5.—The patient received 100 c.c. of a 10 per cent. solution of sodium iodid intravenously. The roentgenogram made one hour later contained a definite shadow of the pelvis of the left kidney and the ureter for a distance of from 4 to 6 cm. below the hilum of the kidney. There was also a definite suggestion of the major calices.

than 3 gm. for each dose has not yielded satisfactory results except in a few instances.

In case the bladder alone is to be studied, the administration of a single dose of from 3 to 5 gm. of sodium iodid, without previous preparation, is all that is necessary. In this case the patient should be instructed not to void and the roentgenogram should be taken three hours after the ingestion of the drug. Results following the oral administration of sodium iodid may be summarized thus:

1. Very satisfactory roentgenograms were secured of the kidneys, pelves of the kidney, ureters and bladder in approximately 50 per cent. of cases, with repeated doses.

2. In a few cases the liver and spleen were also strikingly outlined.

3. Uniformly excellent results were obtained in the roentgenography of the bladder, following the repeated doses and after a single dose.

### ROENTGENOLOGIC TECHNIC

In the first studies the technic routinely employed in the examination of the kidneys, ureters and bladder was used. Preliminary control roentgenograms were made before the administration of the sodium iodid. Plates 5 by 7 inches were used, without intensifying screens, one roentgenogram being made of each kidney area and one of the bladder area. A medium focus, standard Coolidge tube was used, with 60 kilovolts, 50 milliamperes, an average distance of 67.5 cm. from the target to the plate, and the time was varied from two to eight seconds according to the thickness of the patient. An aluminum compression cap, 12.5 cm. in diameter, fitted over the bottom of the cone, was clamped down as far as could be comfortably borne by the patient. Fairly satisfactory roentgenograms of thin, normal and even moderately stout subjects were obtained by this technic. The plates were marked with the patient's registration number and with the number of hours intervening since the administration of the sodium iodid. In some cases a series of roentgenograms was made at varying intervals after the administration. Another series of studies was made using duplitized films in intensifying screens, varying the kilovoltage and milliamperage according to the thickness of the subject, with uniformly better results, particularly in stout subjects. Control films were also made. Still another series was made using 14 by 17 inch duplitized films in intensifying screens with the Potter-Bucky diaphragm. A single film was made in a few cases; in the majority, two films were made, one high, to include the complete kidney area, and the other to include the bladder area. In this series, many films were made after the subjects had held the urine the allotted time; after they had emptied the bladder and the amount voided had been measured, a second film was made and marked with the amount voided. When actual retention occurred,

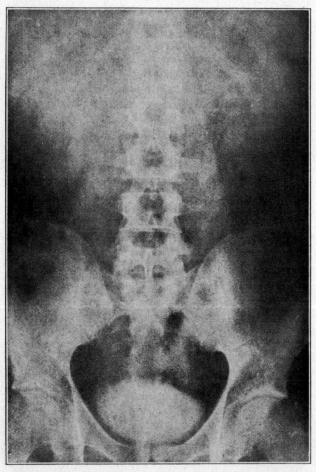

Fig. 6.—The patient received 100 c.c. of a 10 per cent. solution of sodium iodid intravenously. The roentgenogram made one hour later revealed a definite shadow of the partially filled bladder. The density of the kidneys, the spleen and the lower margin of the liver appeared to be increased over the normal. The pelves of both kidneys and the ureters for a distance of from 4 to 6 cm. from the hilum of the kidney were definitely outlined. On the right, there was a suggestion of the lower major calices.

it was depicted in the roentgenogram. The best uniform results were obtained with the Potter-Bucky diaphragm technic.

## INTERPRETATION OF THE RESULTS

In some of the films and plates, because of gas in the colon or because of the thickness of the patient, it was not possible positively to identify the kidney and other solid organs. On the majority of the films and plates, the shadows of the kidneys, the lower margin of the liver and the spleen were sharply outlined, and it was our impression that, comparing the control plates and films with those made after the administration of the sodium

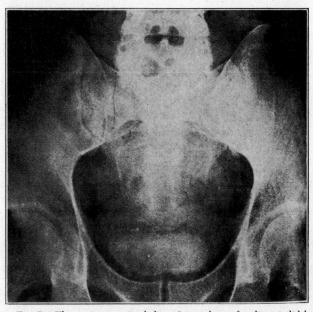

Fig. 7.—The patient received three 3 gm. doses of sodium iodid by mouth. Roentgenograms were made two hours after the last dose, and a shadow of the full bladder was obtained. The patient voided 125 c.c. of urine, and a roentgenogram was made which revealed retention that had not been suspected clinically. Further clinical study revealed the existence of a cord bladder.

iodid, there was a slight increase in the density of the shadow cast by these organs in the second plates and films of the series.

The pelvis of the kidney filled with iodid solution to varying degrees and the ureters could be traced in a number of instances, while in a few there was even a suggestion of the calices. In all of the plates and films the bladder was distinctly outlined and, as we have mentioned, retained iodid solution could be seen in patients with urinary retention. Obviously, only some of the better plates are shown in the accompanying illustrations.

## COMMENT

The method described offers numerous possibilities in the field of research, not only with regard to the urinary tract, but also with regard to other systems, organs and tissues. We are firmly convinced that this investigation will serve as a stepping stone in other fields of study. The method affords an approach to the study of the physiology of the bladder, its form and position under varying degrees of distention, and the phenomena associated with distention and with emptying. It should also prove of decided value in the study of pathologic conditions of the bladder, such as diverticula, tumor and diseases secondary to disturbances in its innervation, or to obstruction in the lower urinary tract, such as stricture and enlarged prostate. In the study of the kidneys, the success of the method is only partial. It will be of assistance in a limited way, especially in determining the size, shape and position of these organs. It is too early and our results are too uncertain to determine whether the method has any value in the study of the liver and spleen.

Much is offered by this method in the study of the vascular system. Under the fluoroscope, the cephalic vein has the appearance of a steel wire, from the point of injection of the iodid at the elbow to the juncture of the cephalic vein with the subclavian. This has been noted following the use of 10 and 20 per cent. solutions of sodium iodid. In all probability, with variations in the technic, important results will be obtained with regard to the venous returns and the peripheral arterial circulation. In the study of aneurysm and of arteriovenous anastomosis, it should also be of value.

## CONCLUSIONS

1. By the method described, it is possible to obtain roentgenograms of the urinary tract during the excretion of sodium iodid following its intravenous or oral administration.

2. The method uniformly gives excellent and accurate shadows of the urinary bladder and renders reliable information relative to its size, shape and location.

3. It has been partially successful in depicting the renal pelves and the ureters in a limited number of cases.

4. In a number of cases it assists in revealing the kidney itself through intensifying the renal shadow.

5. It has been proved a success in revealing the existence of residual urine in the bladder and in furnishing approximate information of the amount, thus

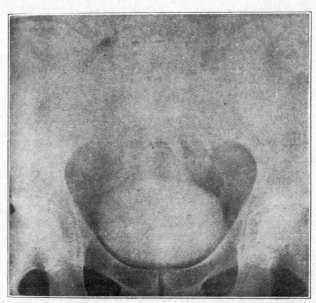

Fig. 8.—The patient received one dose of 5 gm. of sodium iodid by mouth, and a roentgenogram was made three hours after the ingestion of the drug. A perfect outline of the full bladder was revealed.

eliminating the necessity of catheterization and its attendant dangers of infection.

6. Oral administration of the drug will prove satisfactory for routine use in making roentgenograms of the bladder, while for shadows of the ureters and kidneys intravenous injection of large doses of sodium iodid is desirable.

Nov 25, 1983
(*JAMA* 1983;250:2854-2855)

# Intravenous Urography*

## John A. Evans, MD

The article by Osborne and colleagues entitled "Roentgenography of Urinary Tract During Excretions of Sodium Iodid" that appeared in THE JOURNAL Feb 10, 1923, is medically of considerable historical importance in that it was the first attempt to provide a simple, safe, practical intravenous (IV) method of visualizing the kidneys, ureters, and bladder. Visualization of these structures by retrograde ureteral catheterization had been achieved some years earlier in 1906 by Voelcker and von Lichtenberg.[1] However, instrumentation was required — not invariably successful, even as today — and the contrast media used at that time were irritating and even toxic if absorbed. Therefore, retrograde pyelography, despite its limitations, was the only means of demonstrating renal anatomy and, at this time, was only partially successful.

An IV method or, even better, an oral method of roentgenographically visualizing the upper urinary tract would be a great contribution to the diagnosis and treatment of urinary tract disease. Credit for the initial attempt to provide such a method must go to this group of Mayo Clinic physicians. The importance of their studies at that time went far beyond their own modest accomplishments in that it demonstrated the clinical feasibility of IV urography and stimulated further research efforts to find a more effective IV urographic agent. Final success in achieving this objective was not to be realized until 1929, when Moses Swick,[2] working at that time in von Lichtenberg's urologic hospital in Berlin, published his researches on Uroselectan (iodomethamate sodium). Swick's work was, therefore, the fulfillment of the early efforts of the Mayo Clinic group to find a "simple and painless method of depicting the urinary tract, bladder, kidneys and ureters."

### Development of IV Urography

The initial attempt at IV urography had been suggested by Rowntree, who, aware that sodium iodid given IV was normally excreted in the urine, believed it could be used as a roentgenographic contrast medium for studying the urinary tract. The clinical opportunity to test this suggestion quickly presented itself when it was found that Osborne, in the section of dermatology and syphilogy, was using IV doses of 50 to 250 cc of a 10% solution of sodium iodid in a study of the pharmacology and therapeutics of iodids. Patients were, therefore, readily available for urinary tract roentgenography. The amount and concentration of iodin in the urine at varying

intervals after the IV administration of 5-, 10-, and 20-g doses of a 10% solution of sodium iodid were charted From these data, based on the actual determination o the rate of excretion of sodium iodid, it was evident tha the best roentgenograms should be taken 30 minutes one hour, and two to three hours after the IV injection of 5-, 10-, and 20-g doses. The results of these studie are interesting. The larger doses produced severe reactions. Successful visualization of the bladder wa consistently obtained. This in itself was an achievement since it provided the means of studying both bladde structure and function under normal and pathologica conditions. Neurogenic bladder, diverticula, outle obstruction, prostatic enlargement, and bladder tumor were some of the conditions that were now demon strated without resorting to catheterization with it attendant risks in a preantibiotic era.

Adequate visualization of the calyces, renal pelves and ureters proved much less successful. The 10-g IV doses of sodium iodid produced only fair studies of the kidneys in 50% of cases. The best studies were obtained with the 15- to 20-g doses. It was also noted that with the higher doses, liver and spleen were better visualized However, with the higher doses, severe reactions were frequent. Despite the reactions and the inadequacies o the roentgenograms by today's standards, these investi gations proved to be a benchmark in the historica development of IV urography. Some of the observation: are interesting in historical retrospection. In a number o cases, the authors comment on the intensification of the renal shadow as well as those of the liver and spleen or the "second plates and films" of the examination. Thi: may well be the first observation of a nephrogram effec during IV urology.

In 1929, with the introduction of Uroselectan as an IV contrast agent, opacification of the renal parenchyma was reported by von Lichtenberg and Swick.[3] Furthe observations on opacification of the renal parenchyma were subsequently reported by Wesson and Fulmer[4] ir 1932 and by Wilcox[5] in 1935. In 1938, Robb and Steinberg,[6] in their classic article on IV angiography, also commented on opacification of the renal parenchym: during their studies. Soon the terms *nephrogram* and *nephrography* came into general use. The nephrogram': mechanism was studied by Weems and Florence[7] and deemed to be the result of the concentration of the contrast medium in the tubular system as a result o glomerular filtration. The nephrogram during the early years was of limited diagnostic importance because o the relatively poor opacification achieved with the smal amounts of contrast medium used. Later, Weems and associates[8] as well as Vesey and co-workers,[9] using better contrast media, improved the diagnostic value o

From the Department of Radiology, New York Hospital–Cornell Medical Center, New York.
*A commentary on Osborne ED, Sutherland CG, Scholl AJ Jr, et al: Roentgenography of urinary tract during excretion of sodium iodid. *JAMA* 1923;80:368-373.

the nephrogram.

In 1954, Evans and associates[10] combined bolus IV nephrography with tomography and coined the term *nephrotomography*. This technique, using high volumes of concentrated contrast media, ushered in the modern era of excretory urography. Later, Schnecker et al[11] substituted drip infusion for the bolus injection, thus simplifying the technique and converting nephrotomography into a routine urographic procedure. In uroradiology today, the nephrotomogram as a component of routine IV urography is of considerable diagnostic value in that it provides excellent visualization of the functioning renal parenchyma as well as the calyces and renal pelvis. As a result, many diseases of the renal parenchyma are now easily diagnosed by excretory urography. Furthermore, the bolus injection of IV contrast media has again become popular because of the recent introduction of digital subtraction angiography. This latter technique has the potential of playing an important role in evaluating renovascular hypertension, studying renal blood flow, and improving the resolution of renal parenchymal masses.[12] The future of digital urography remains to be determined. The modern urogram, however, has resulted in a substantial reduction in the need for retrograde pyelography.

In their clinical investigations, Osborne and associates, working with sodium iodid as a radiopaque agent for visualizing the urinary tract, also tried the oral as well as the IV administration of this drug. Despite the shadows cast by the drug in the stomach and intestines, satisfactory roentgenograms of the kidneys, ureters, and bladder were said to have been obtained in 50% of cases, with repeated doses. These results were observed by administering 3 g of sodium iodid hourly for three hours and taking roentgenograms from one to three hours after the last dose. The roentgenographic quality of the studies by today's standards would be unacceptable. The oral ingestion of the salt produced local gastric irritation and upset, which precluded the oral administration as a practical method of visualizing the kidneys. In the historical development of IV urography, Swick,[13] in describing his researches, also tried the oral administration on dogs of one of the iodine compounds furnished him by Professor Benz, a chemist who was collaborating with Swick in studying radiopaques for visualizing the urinary tract. The agent tried was not absorbed and thus failed to visualize the kidneys. Interest in an oral urographic medium was quickly abandoned after the successful clinical experiments with Uroselectan. However, because of the occasional fatality after IV urography, one in 75,000 examinations,[14] a nontoxic oral radiopaque providing satisfactory visualization of the urinary tract would be a highly desirable addition to the presently available urographic media.

## Predictions

Perhaps the most interesting and prophetic observation in The Mayo group's clinical investigations using sodium iodid as a contrast medium for excretory urography was the statement, "Much is offered by this method in the study of the vascular system." Their fluoroscopic observations allowed them to follow the contrast medium from the point of injection at the antecubital fossa to the junction of the cephalic vein with the subclavian vein. This was a striking observation at the time and led the authors to make this amazingly prophetic statement: "In all probability, with variations in the technic, important results will be obtained with regard to the venous returns and the peripheral arterial circulation. In the study of aneurysm and of arteriovenous anastomosis, it should also be of value." Thus, the advent of cardiovascular radiology was anticipated and predicted some 15 years before the epochal article by Robb and Steinberg on venous angiocardiography, which initiated and introduced the roentgenologic visualization of the cardiovascular system in humans. Today, this amazing prediction of 60 years ago has culminated in the specialty field of cardiovascular radiology involving therapeutic as well as diagnostic applications.

Radiology as a medical specialty is currently experiencing dramatic advances in imaging technology. Within the past few years, major advances have taken place in (1) diagnostic ultrasound, (2) computed tomography, (3) digital radiography, and the latest of the exciting technological advances, (4) nuclear magnetic resonance. The next decade, however, may see excretory urography, which has used conventional roentgenographic techniques for the past several decades, replaced by the new technique of digital urography. Despite the recent dramatic technological imaging achievements, IV urography introduced 60 years ago by Osborne, Sutherland, Scholl, and Rowntree and made clinically feasible through the researches of Swick remains the most contributory of uroradiological examinations.

### References

1. Voelcker F, von Lichtenberg A: Pyelographie (Röntgenographie des Nierenbeckens nach Kollargolfüllung). *München Med Wochenschr* 1906;53:105.
2. Swick M: Darstellung der Niere und Harnwege im Röntgenbild durch intravenöse Einbringung eines neuen Kontraststoffes, des Uroselectans. *Klin Wochenschr* 1929;8:2087-2089.
3. von Lichtenberg A, Swick M: Klinische Prüfung des Uroselectans. *Klin Wochenschr* 1929;8:2089-2091.
4. Wesson MB, Fulmer CC: Influence of ureteral stones on intravenous urograms. *AJR* 1932;28:27-33.
5. Wilcox LF: Kidney function in acute calculous obstruction of the ureter: Some observations of kidney and ureter function in acute calculous obstruction of the ureter based on excretory urography. *AJR* 1935;34:596-605.
6. Robb GP, Steinberg I: Visualization of the chambers of the heart, the pulmonary circulation and the great blood vessels in man: A practical method. *AJR* 1939;4:1-17.
7. Weems HS, Florence TJ: Nephrography. *AJR* 1947;57:338-341.
8. Weems HS, Olnick HM, James DF, et al: Intravenous nephrography: A method of roentgen visualization of the kidney. *AJR* 1951;65:411-414.
9. Vesey J, Dotter CT, Steinberg I: Nephrography, simplified technic. *Radiology* 1950;55:827-833.
10. Evans JA, Dubilier W Jr, Monteith JC: Nephrotomography: A preliminary report. *AJR* 1954;71:213-223.
11. Schencker B, Marcure RW, Moody DL: Simplified nephrotomography: The drip infusion technique. *AJR* 1965;95:283-290.
12. Hillman BJ, Ovitt TW, Capp MP: The potential impact of digital video subtraction angiography (DVSA) on screening for renovascular hypertension. *Radiology* 1982;142:577-579.
13. Swick M: The discovery of intravenous urography: Historical and developmental aspects of the urographic media and their role in other diagnostic and therapeutic areas. *Bull NY Acad Med* 1966;42:128-151.
14. Hartman GW, Hattery RR, Witten DM, et al: Mortality during excretory urography. *Mayo Clin Experience* 1982;139:919-922.

Sept 8, 1923
(*JAMA* 1923;81:819-821)

# Chapter 17

# An Ovarian Hormone

## Preliminary Report on Its Localization, Extraction and Partial Purification, and Action in Test Animals*

Edgar Allen, Ph.D. and Edward A. Doisy, Ph.D.

St. Louis

The fact that double ovariectomy abolishes the cyclic changes which normally occur in the genital tract of female mammals demonstrates that these changes are due to some influence from the ovaries. That this influence is hormonal in nature is indicated by the maintenance of cyclic changes by autotransplantation of the ovaries to other sites in the body.[1] Many attempts have been made to localize the seat of production of an internal secretion in definite ovarian structures. The follicles, the corpora lutea[2] developing in them after ovulation, and the interstitial tissue[3] have all been cited as possible sources, and many different ovarian preparations have been used clinically in the belief that therapeutic effects were being secured from accompanying hormones.

But there appears to be no conclusive evidence of either a definite localization of the hypothetic hormone or of the specific effect claimed for the commercial ovarian extracts in wide clinical use. The recent reviews of Frank[4] and of Novak[5] may be cited to illustrate the well founded skepticism concerning the activity of commercial preparations. The reason for this distrust is the absence of any suitable test for the activity of ovarian extracts. Without a practicable test, the search for any hormone is obviously a very haphazard and uncertain task. With a suitable test it has been relatively easy to establish the seat of production of the ovarian hormone of estrus, to observe its effect on animals, and to study methods for its extraction and preliminary purification.

### THE TEST METHOD

In 1917, Stockard and Papanicolaou[6] described an exact method for following estrual changes in the living guinea-pig. This method has been applied to the correlation of estrual phenomena in the genital organs of the rat[7] and the mouse.[8] During the anabolic phase of the cycle in these rodents, the epithelium of the vagina grows to a considerable thickness and a cornified layer similar to that in the epidermis develops. During the catabolic phase, the outer layers of this epithelium degenerate and are removed by leukocytic action. These changes provide a definite succession of cell types in the vaginal lumen, each one characteristic of a certain phase of the cycle. Thus the microscopic examination of vaginal smears is a reliable indicator of the estrual condition of the living animal.

*From the Departments of Anatomy, Biologic Chemistry and Surgery, Washington University Medical School, St. Louis, with the assistance of Byron F. Francis, Harry V. Gibson, Leroy L. Robertson, Cleon E. Colgate and William B. Kountz.

1. Marshall, F. H. A.: The Physiology of Reproduction, 1922, p. 320.

2. Fraenkel, Ludwig: Die Function des Corpus Luteum, Arch. f. Gynäk. **68:** 438, 1903.

3. Marshall and Runciman: On the Ovarian Factor Concerned in the Recurrence of the Oestrous Cycle, J. Physiol. **49:** 17 (Dec. 22) 1914.

4. Frank, R. T.: The Ovary and the Endocrinologist, J. A. M. A. **78:** 181 (Jan. 21) 1922.

5. Novak, Emil: An Appraisal of Ovarian Therapy, Endocrinology **6:** 599 (Sept.) 1922.

6. Stockard, C. R., and Papanicolaou, G. N.: Existence of a Typical Oestrous Cycle in the Guinea-Pig, with a Study of Its Histological and Physiological Changes, Am. J. Anat. **22:** 225 (Sept.) 1917.

7. Long, J. A., and Evans, H. M.: The Oestrous Cycle in the Rat and Its Associated Phenomena, Mem. Univ. California **6:** 1922.

8. Allen, Edgar: The Oestrous Cycle in the Mouse, Am. J. Anat. **30:** 297 (May) 1922; Racial and Familial Cyclic Inheritance and Other Evidence from the Mouse Concerning the Cause of Oestrous Phenomena, Am. J. Anat., to be published.

9. This has recently been checked in the rat (Long and Evans, Footnote 7) and in the mouse (Allen, Footnote 8).

Since these cyclic phenomena in the genital tract cease after double ovariectomy,[9] their induction by the injection of ovarian extracts constitutes a positive test for the efficiency of those extracts. The estrual cycle of the mouse and the rat is of four to six days' duration, and this short period makes them especially suitable for test animals.

## LOCALIZATION OF THE HORMONE OF ESTRUS

From the results of an earlier investigation by one of us[8] on the estrual cycle in the mouse, it was concluded that the corpora lutea of estrus[10] and the interstitial tissue could be excluded as possible sources of the hormone of estrus and that this was produced in the follicles. Among earlier workers, Frank[4] reported very briefly inducing uterine hyperemia in two normal virgin rabbits by the injection of liquor folliculi. Although his results appear to be positive, the ovaries were not removed from his test animals, and one cannot be quite sure that the changes described were not caused by the activity of the ovaries. Previously, Frank and several writers mentioned by him (especially Hermann[11]) had reported similar results from the injection of material obtained from the corpus luteum and the placenta (Hermann spayed some of his test animals). Consequently, this test does not seem to be specific for the hormone of estrus.

## PRELIMINARY EXPERIMENTS

Our first experiments were carried out with liquor folliculi from hog ovaries, which are a readily available source for the isolation of the contents of the follicles. Since the estrual cycle in the sow is of three weeks' duration,[12] and large follicles are present in the ovaries during only a part of this time, only one in every three or four ovaries is a profitable source of liquor folliculi.[13] A selection is made of ovaries containing follicles larger than 5 mm. in diameter. The follicular contents (liquor folliculi, follicle cells and occasional ova) are aspirated through a hypodermic needle into a suction bottle. At least 100 c.c. of readily workable material can be obtained from one pound of carefully selected ovaries.

In the first series of experiments, nine mice and rats were prepared for use as test animals by double ovariectomy. A week later they were given three injections at intervals of five hours of liquor folliculi aspirated from large follicles. These injections were made subcutaneously with the expectation that slow absorption from this region would be more closely comparable to the secretion of the hormone in normal animals. From forty to forty-eight hours after the first injection, all of the animals receiving liquor folliculi were in full estrus, as determined by microscopic examination of the smears. As a check on these results, the animals were killed and the uterus and vagina of each studied histologically. They were in a typical estrual condition as described for these rodents.[14]

Since the liquor aspirated from the follicles contains follicle cells and some ova, tests were next made with centrifugated liquor and Berkefeldt filtrate. Positive results in these experiments showed that the hormone is extracellular and present in the liquor folliculi. Realizing that liquor folliculi with its large protein content would be unsuitable for continued injections into patients and test animals, we began the preparation of extracts.

## METHOD OF EXTRACTION

Fresh liquor folliculi is added to a double volume of 95 per cent. alcohol and allowed to stand until the proteins are coagulated (about twenty-four hours). The coagulum is filtered off. The filtrate, which is practically protein free, contains the active constituent. Further extraction of the coagulated protein with boiling alcohol yields an additional amount of the hormone. The alcohol is distilled off (the hormone being thermostable), and the residual aqueous suspension extracted with ether. The ether extract is evaporated, and the solids are dried in a vacuum desiccator. The residue is dissolved in a minimal quantity of ether, and a double volume of acetone is added. To insure completeness of separation, the solution and precipitation are repeated twice. The precipitate, which consists of lipoids (lecithin and cephalin), shows no activity in the test animal. The combined filtrates are evaporated, and the residue is dried. By boiling out the solid material with 95 per cent. alcohol, the active substance is obtained free from protein but contaminated with a little fatty material. The alcohol is evaporated off, and the minute yield of oily residue taken up in purified corn oil or emulsified in dilute sodium carbonate. This constitutes a partially purified preparation of this follicular hormone, the subcutaneous injection of which produces no ill effects in our test animals.

A few points of chemical interest may be added. This hormone seems to be stable toward dilute alkali when boiled with it in alcoholic solution. The active substance resembles the neutral fats somewhat in that it is soluble in alcohol, acetone, chloroform and ether and it may be extracted from aqueous mediums by both ether and chloroform. Strongly acidic or basic groups seem to be absent, since it can be extracted with ether from either dilute acid or alkali. Most of our better preparations fail to give the biuret reaction, thus indicating the absence of protein and polypeptids.

## ACTION IN TEST ANIMALS

Further animal experiments have confirmed our early results, and we are now in a position to make the following preliminary announcement concerning this follicular hormone and its action:

1. From one to three injections of this extract into spayed animals produce typical estrual hyperemia, growth, and hypersecretion in the genital tract and growth in the mammary glands. These changes include

---

10. The distinction is clearly drawn here between the corpora lutea of estrus and those of pregnancy. Only nonpregnant animals were referred to in the earlier paper.

11. Hermann, E.: Ueber eine wirksame Substanz im Eierstocke und in der Placenta, Monatschr. f. Geburtsh. u. Gynäk. **41:** 1 (Jan.) 1915.

12. Corner, G. W.: The Ovarian Cycle in Swine, Science **53:** 420 (April 29) 1921.

13. This may be one reason for the conflicting reports of the therapeutic value of commercial extracts from ovaries unselected as to follicular development.

14. Stockard and Papanicolaou (Footnote 6). Long and Evans (Footnote 7). Allen (Footnote 8).

thickening and cornification in the vaginal walls, which constitutes a test easily followed in the living animal. After a time the effect of these injections wears off and typical degenerative changes set in. This hormone seems to be an efficient substitute for the endocrine function of the ovaries of the nonpregnant animal. It is probable that its alternate presence and absence in the circulation is sufficient to explain the mechanism of estrual phenomena in the genital tract in the absence of pregnancy.

2. While these spayed animals are in a condition of artificially induced estrus, they can be mated with normal vigorous males. They experience typical mating instincts, the spayed females taking the initiative in the courtship and showing no aversion to advances by the male. Successful copulation occurs, followed, as in normal animals, by the formation of typical vaginal plugs. Since these animals will copulate only when in estrus, the conclusion seems justified that this follicular hormone is the cause of estrual or mating instincts.

---

15. The attainment of sexual maturity is defined here as the opening of the vaginal orifice at the appearance of the first estrus.

16. Allen, Edgar: Ovogenesis During Sexual Maturity, Am. J. Anat. 31: 441 (May) 1923. It is tentatively suggested that the development of the follicles in the immature ovary is restrained by the nutritional demands of rapid prepubertal body growth which limit the amount of nutriment necessary for the full development of the follicles and their contained ova.

3. Several injections of active extracts were made into animals immediately after weaning, at an age of from to 4 weeks. They became sexually mature[15] in from two t four days, at least twenty to forty days before the usua time of the attainment of puberty. These experiment were controlled by uninjected litter sisters which did no prematurely attain to puberty. From these experiments i is concluded that the attainment of sexual maturity involving possibly the development of the secondar sexual characters, is brought about by a hormone fron the follicles, although the consummation of their matura tion is in some way restrained.[16]

4. So far we have obtained only negative results from our extracts of corpora lutea and commercial extracts o ovaries, corpora lutea, and ovarian residue from three o the largest firms manufacturing biologic products.

5. It is probable that this hormone is produced unde the influence of maturing ova by their follicle cells. Sinc it is obtained from the ovaries of hogs and cattle an produces results in the mouse and rat, it is not specie specific. It is probably produced in all ovaries as their ov mature, and therefore is probably common to all femal animals.

The details of the experimental evidence for th foregoing statements will be published at an early dat Tests of the therapeutic value of this hormone are no being carried on.

Nov 18, 1983
(*JAMA* 1983;250:2684-2688)

# Allen and Doisy's 'An Ovarian Hormone'*

## Arthur T. Hertig, MD

The term *hormone* was first coined in 1904 by W. M. Bayliss and C. H. Starling "for the active substances secreted into the blood stream or tissue fluids by the ductless or endocrine glands."[1] Adrenaline was the first hormone to be obtained in pure form from the medulla of the adrenal gland; watery extracts were obtained in 1894 by G. Oliver and E. H. Schafer; subsequently, J. J. Abel and A. C. Crawford in 1897 isolated an ester of the hormone — assumed to be the hormone itself — whereas in 1901, J. Takamine and B. Aldrich apparently succeeded in obtaining adrenaline itself in crystalline form, although it was shown later to be mixed with noradrenaline, a closely related hormone.[1]

In 1902, Bayliss and Starling had discovered secretin, which is elaborated by the intestinal mucosa when stimulated by hydrochloric acid from the stomach. The hormone, thus obtained, when injected into the bloodstream, directly stimulates the pancreas.[1]

In 1914, E. C. Kendall succeeded in isolating thyroxin, the active constituent of thyroid secretion (see Chapter 13). Kendall and C. R. Harrington determined the structure of this pure substance in 1926, followed in 1928 by the synthesis of thyroxin by Harrington and C. Barger.[1]

Insulin was isolated by F. G. Banting and C. H. Best in J. R. MacLeod's laboratory in 1922. J. B. Collip of parathyroid fame assisted in the work by purification and standardization of insulin. It is of interest that much previous work had been done by others in attempting to isolate insulin by eliminating the digestive ferments of the pancreas. In fact, C. K. Drinker stated that the year before the discovery by Banting, Best, and MacLeod, a third-year student at Harvard Medical School had suggested the same experiment, but it was turned down by his teachers as being beyond his efforts and abilities.[1]

Thus, four hormones had been isolated before 1923,

when Allen and Doisy did their classic but preliminary work, republished in this issue, on the estrus hormone. Although Allen had worked primarily on the estrus cycle in the mouse, he found that the liquor folliculi of the hog ovary yielded a more abundant supply of this fluid. He injected it into ovariectomized mice and rats and caused resumption of their estrus cycles. This was the first time that a precise source of the estrus hormone had been proved. Before that time, it was known that ablation of the ovaries caused cessation of the estrus cycle in rodents and that subsequent surgical implantation of this organ into the abdominal musculature resulted in resumption of that cycle. It was thought prior to Allen and Doisy that the corpus luteum was the source of the estrus hormone. Incidentally, the basis of the so-called Allen-Doisy test for estrogen — the appearance of the estrus cycle in immature mice when injected with liquor folliculi — is the direct result of this classic, landmark work by these two investigators.[2,3]

The exact morphological basis for following the estrus cycle in the guinea pig had been worked out by Stockard and Papanicolaou[4] in 1917. Both of these investigators were anatomists. Although Dr "Pap" later became world famous for his test for cancer done initially on human vaginal smears, he was for years primarily interested in the endocrine changes and their morphological counterparts in the mammalian estrus-menstrual cycle. It was because of these continuing interests in collaboration with Herbert Traut — a gynecologist then at Cornell Medical School — that the Papanicolaou vaginal smear of exfoliated cells from the genital tract led to the now worldwide test for cancer. More of this aspect will be discussed later in relation to the various applications to and effects of estrogens on various branches of medicine.

### Biographical Notes

To return to Allen and Doisy, it is of great interest and importance how these two brilliant and dedicated investigators happened to combine their talents in what proved to be epochal research. Allen was 31 years old and Doisy 29 at the time the accompanying LANDMARK ARTICLE was published. (The article is No. 4 and No. 14 in

From the Departments of Comparative Pathology, New England Regional Primate Research Center, Harvard Medical School, Southborough, Mass; and the Department of Pathology, Harvard Medical School, Boston.

*A commentary on Allen E, Doisy EA: An ovarian hormone: Preliminary report on its localization, extraction and action in test animals. *JAMA* 1923;81:819-821.

their respective bibliographies.) Allen was an anatomist-endocrinologist, whereas Doisy was (and still is) a biochemist. Both were in their respective departments at Washington University in St Louis and in relatively low academic ranks. Both were born in the Middle West: Allen in Canyon City, Colo, and Doisy in Hume, Ill. Both were promoted in 1923 to professorships and chairmanships of their respective departments; Allen went to the University of Missouri in Columbia, whereas Doisy stayed in St Louis but transferred to St Louis University. Thus were received the rewards of early scholarship by these young men!

In a delightful autobiography published in 1976 and written when he was aged 82 years, Doisy[5] tells of how he and Edgar Allen happened to engage in collaborative research. They met in the medical school library in 1920, Allen a "well-built young man with white hair" of 28 years who asked Dr Doisy about something in one of Abderhalden's publications. This chance meeting led to a mutual and long-lasting friendship involving such things as respective spouses, first-born babies, and bridge games. They moved to south St Louis in 1920 and lived one block apart; Doisy had a Model T Ford, but Allen had no car. Thus, Allen rode to work with Doisy. The two young men planned various things, including faculty-student baseball games. In 1922, Doisy was asked to help Allen on some of his work with the estrus cycle of the mouse; specifically, Doisy was to prepare extracts of ovarian tissue, although it wasn't convenient at the time for the biochemist. Nevertheless, the extracts were prepared even though Doisy was then intensely interested in and preoccupied with blood buffers, uric acid, and the preparation of insulin. (The latter helped to save the lives of two patients when no insulin was available in St Louis. It will be recalled that insulin as a new hormone had just that year, 1922, been isolated in Toronto.) Because the injection of sow's liquor folliculi produced vaginal cornification in the mouse, Doisy realized its great scientific importance and so prepared extracts of liquor folliculi, corpora lutea, whole ovaries, and other products.

When Allen moved to the University of Missouri in 1923, collaboration became more difficult but did not cease entirely. Nor did Doisy give up his interest in the estrus hormone. Indeed, he and his associates crystallized that hormone and presented the data — with slides of the crystallized homone, later to be called "Theelin" — at the 13th International Physiological Congress in August 1929. An interesting sidelight on this presentation concerns the last-minute success in the preparation of the crystals *after* the abstract of the article had been submitted. Doisy was allowed to change the abstract and thus secure credit, in print, for the isolation of the first female sex hormone!

The meeting of the 13th Congress was a most happy occasion for Doisy personally as well as scientifically. Dr Doisy had studied with Professor Otto Folin at Harvard on a scholarship granted by the Chicago Harvard Club and obtained his PhD in 1920. As was reported at the congress, "Dr Folin appeared to be 'pleased' and a friend of Doisy's remarked. 'I guess Harvard did not make a mistake when you received your degree.' "

The congress abstract (No. 39 in Doisy's bibliography) was published in 1929 in the *Proceedings of the Society for Experimental Biology and Medicine;* the definitive article was published in 1930 (item No. 40 in the bibliography).

The task of isolating and purifying the estrus hormone was not all smooth sailing. Aschheim and Zondek[6] in 1927 had reported that the urine of pregnant women possessed estrogenic activity. This led to an extensive collaborative effort of pregnant patients with Doisy's laboratory. Dr Doisy's Model T Ford was pressed into service, with a hired driver. The latter, on his urine-collecting rounds, was stopped for some traffic violation; the officer thought he had stopped a bootlegger. (This was 1927 — remember Prohibition?) The driver protested this allegation and offered the policeman a drink; the cop sniffed of one opened bottle and said, "My God, it *is* urine! Your job is bad enough without getting pinched for it — drive on!"

Although Doisy and his co-workers actually crystallized the estrogenic hormone, Dr Allen continued his brilliant investigations on the physiological properties of the estrogenic hormone in collaboration with Doisy and many other colleagues. This research resulted in some 25 articles, of which he was the senior author in 23. This sustained research effort involved many different test animals, including the mouse, hen, monkey, and human. A classic is Allen's[7] Carnegie monograph (No. 29 in his bibliography) on the menstrual cycle of the monkey, *Macacus rhesus,* now *Macacus mulatta.*

This classic monograph, together with George W. Corner's equally classic Carnegie monograph published in 1923,[8] firmly established that the common Indian monkey possessed a menstrual cycle comparable to that of the human female. The experimental monkeys had an incidence of 50% ovulation.[7] Ovulation occurred on the tenth to 14th day of the cycle computed from the beginning of the last menses[7] but had been stated somewhat differently by Corner as occurring 12 to 14 days before the onset of the next expected flow. Thus, these data are comparable to those of human ovulation, which occurs 12 to 16 days before the next expected menstruation; in a classic 28-day cycle, ovulation occurs at about midcycle. This is the fertile period normally, or, in the rhythm method of contraception, the "unsafe period." Corner cites earlier workers — Frankel (1903), Ancel and Villemin (1907), and Schröeder (1914) — all of whom *suggested* that ovulation in the human female occurs about 10 to 15 days before the onset of menstruation. Incidentally, these suggestions and later verified data are borne out by the work of myself and my colleague Dr John Rock, in our recovery of 34 human fertilized ova from 211 patients of proved fertility.[9]

It was not long after Allen and Doisy's work on the estrus hormone of the ovarian follicle that Corner and Willard Allen published their classic work on the isolation of progestin from the corpus luteum of the sow and its effect on the menstrual and pregnant cycle of the rabbit.[10,11]

Although Allen and Doisy continued their collaborative researches until 1927, Allen continued his researches with colleagues at Missouri and later at Yale and elsewhere until his untimely death at sea in 1943, aged 53 years, "while performing duties in the service of his country." The *Journal of Biology and Medicine* dedicated its volume 17, No. 1, to Edgar Allen's memory. The following is quoted from that dedication.

This number is dedicated to the memory of Edgar Allen, Professor of Anatomy and Chairman of the Department of Anatomy at Yale University School of Medicine, who died February 3, 1943, while performing duties in the service of his country. Professor Allen's pioneer studies on the female sex hormone and on the physiology of menstruation brought him international fame; and his organizational capacities, personal integrity, and spontaneous friendliness made him an outstanding leader among scientists. His effervescent enthusiasm furnished encouragement and incentive to many engaged in scientific endeavor and endeared him to those with whom he was associated. Some who were closely associated with him have contributed the papers in this issue as a tribute to one whose work exemplified the vigorous growth of experimental endocrinology and morphology and one who has contributed to these fields some of their most vital concepts.

Edward A. Doisy continued to work with his own colleagues for some years on female sex hormones (folliculin, Theelin [estrone], Theelol [estriol]) and other substances related to female reproduction. In the meanwhile, he became interested in vitamin K, the vitamin essential for the normal clotting of blood. His first article on that subject was published in 1937, regarding recovery of anemia caused by lack of that vitamin (No. 80 in his bibliography); there were 17 subsequent articles. He and co-workers isolated and characterized both K and $K_2$. Edward A. Doisy received and shared the 1933 Nobel Prize in 1944 with Henrik Dam of Denmark. The citation read "for his [Dam's] discovery of vitamine K and the other half to Doisy for his discovery of the chemical nature of vitamine K."[1] Dr Doisy, in characteristically modest fashion, did not mention this prestigious award in his autobiography referred to previously.

The extensive ramifications in medicine of Allen and Doisy's work will be summarized only briefly under the following categories: (1) the vaginal smear of exfoliated cells from female genital cancers, (2) the effect of endogenous and exogenous estrogens on human target tissues, and (3) oral contraceptives and their effect on social and world population problems.

### Exfoliative Cytology and Its Relationship to Cancer

As noted earlier, Stockard and Papanicolaou[4] in 1917 published their precise work on the estrus cycle of the guinea pig as mirrored in the vaginal smear and histological examinations of the vagina. (The effect of this publication on Allen and Doisy's work has already been alluded to.) Dr Herbert F. Traut, a gynecologist at Cornell, became a collaborator of Dr Pap and furnished vaginal smears from patients on the gynecologic wards. The beautifully color-illustrated results of that collaboration were presented as a demonstration before the American Association of Anatomists in New York City in April 1940 (when Norway was invaded). I was there and noted the general lack of interest in this beautiful work — supposedly because the exfoliated cells were pathological. The consensus of remarks heard personally was, "Yes, these pretty cells are there in the vaginal smear, but where do they come from and what is their meaning?" (Dr Traut answered this question at the time but told Hertig some years later, "I don't know but all these vaginal smears came from women with genital cancer." Conversation regarding this demonstration was held with Herbert Traut in 1956 when I was a visiting professor in the Department of Obstetrics and Gynecology at the University of California Medical School in San Francisco.) The first definitive article on this subject was published in 1941.[12]

In any event, Dr Pap's findings were not generally taken seriously by either clinicians, anatomists, or pathologists. Herewith is a brief résumé of the history of the vaginal smear in Boston, about which I had personal knowledge.

1. The vaginal smear technique was introduced to Boston at the Massachusetts General Hospital in the mid-1940s by the late Dr Maurice Fremont-Smith, an internist.

2. The late Mrs Ruth Graham became the cytotechnician and soon became a recognized expert in this new and burgeoning field; she was encouraged also by the late Joe Vincent Meigs, clinical professor of gynecology at Harvard Medical School.

3. The American Cancer Society in April 1947 hosted a seminar on the subject at the old Sommerset Hotel that was attended, among others, by Dr Tracy B. Mallory, pathologist at Massachusetts General Hospital. An ardent disciple (name forgotten) of J. Earnest Ayer of Montreal accused pathologists of "getting on the band wagon and stealing credit for this new technique." Dr Mallory, in a characteristic low, almost inaudible voice as though talking to himself, replied, "I don't know a single pathologist who is the least interested in this technique."

4. Dr Meigs persuaded me to join the newly formed "Intersociety Cytology Council," which met regularly in New York and was attended by Dr Pap himself as well as many other persons of different disciplines. The late Dr Paul Fletcher was the secretary and really the driving force behind this infant organization. He took meticulous notes at its meetings and dictated them "on the spot." He was a dynamic and energetic obstetrician-gynecologist from St Louis University, where Dr Doisy was. (It was my sad duty to write Paul's obituary in 1963.[13] He died at the young age of 59 years.)

5. At the annual 1956 meeting of the council in Cleveland, the struggling organization was almost destroyed over a silly jurisdictional dispute concerning categories of memberships. Some of the MDs wanted to make second- and third-class citizens out of the pure cytologists who really did all the fundamental work and the cytotechnicians who did and still do the lion's share of the actual work in cytology laboratories. Dr Pap pleaded, with tears in his eyes and a choked voice, for unity and common sense, but to no avail. Dr Lew Sheffey of Philadelphia succeeded Hertig as president and the latter resigned from the council soon thereafter.

One does not need to elaborate on the present extent and value of diagnostic exfoliative cytology nor the number of patients — male and female — it has benefited.

It is, however, a magnificent, though stormy, chapter in diagnostic medicine, and it all grew out of an anatomist-endocrinologist's interest in the vaginal manifestations of the estrus cycle of the guinea pig!

### The Effect of Endogenous and Exogenous Estrogens on Human Target Tissues

In 1963, Gore and I[14] contributed chapter 10, "Estrogenic Lesions of the Ovary" to Grady and Smith's *The Ovary*. The following is quoted from the summary.

In summary, the common factor in all estrogenic ovarian lesions is active cortical stroma, either the stroma proper or thecal cells presumably derived from the cortical stroma. Nevertheless, the site of origin of estrogen within the normal ovary has not yet been determined. Nor is there at this time an easy, inexpensive technique for assessing estrogens. Practically, examination of the vaginal smear for cornified cells seems to be the most useful technique. It seems that estrogenic lesions are often associated with unusual endometrial activity, ranging from hyperplasia to carcinoma. As this relationship is not inevitable or completely accepted, unusual endometrial activity cannot be used to indicate estrogenic lesions of the ovary.

Estrogenic lesions include cortical stromal hyperplasia and thecomatosis as well as granulosa-theca cell tumors. In addition, active cortical stroma is seen in a variety of tumors, cystadeno-fibroma, primary and metastatic carcinoma, and Brenner tumor. It is probable that gynandroblastoma and the ovary of the Stein-Leventhal syndrome should also be included.

The chapter is well-illustrated; the bibliography has 85 references and is a good summary of what was known at that time (1963) about estrogenic lesions of the ovary. More modern references are in the works by Scully[15] and the British authors Fox and Langley.[16]

In practical terms, the relationship of estrogen both exogenous and endogenous to carcinoma of the endometrium is pertinent at this juncture. The best summary of this much debated subject is by Ziel.[17]

Data reported since 1975 indicate that the natural hormone estrogen may act as a carcinogen when unopposed by an adequate amount of progesterone. Carcinogenesis may proceed when estrogen is present at a low level for a long time or when it is present at a high level for a short time. It is generally accepted that 3 groups of women have been at risk of developing cancer from exogenous estrogen exposure: 1) women who took sequential oral contraceptives; 2) postmenopausal women who received estrogen replacement therapy; 3) girls with ovarian dysgenesis who received unopposed therapy at puberty. Similarly, 4 groups of women appear to be at risk of developing cancer from endogenous estrogen sources: 1) women with granulosa-cell or theca-cell ovarian tumors; 2) anovulatory women; 3) obese postmenopausal women; 4) women with liver disease. The falling incidence of endometrial cancer associated with diminished estrogen sales is the final proof of an association of estrogen exposure with development of disease.

I was one of three consulting pathologists who independently examined approximately 100 curettings from a series collected at the Kaiser-Permanente Medical Center in Los Angeles and that resulted in a report by Gordon et al in 1977.[18] Ziel and Finkle[19] had previously published an article on this series reporting a strong relationship between estrogen use and subsequent endometrial cancers.

### Oral Contraceptives

The validity and usefulness of oral contraceptives began in 1953 with the fundamental work of Pincus and Chang.[20] They demonstrated that a number of synthetic compounds related to progesterone actively inhibited ovulation in mated rabbits when given by mouth. The efficacy of these compounds was proved clinically by Pincus et al[21] in 1958, based on presumptive evidence by Rock et al[22] in 1957 that the basal body temperature of patients so treated indicated that they had not ovulated. It was soon found that these synthetic progestins had small amounts of estrogen, which led to the formulation of the "pill" that contained both female sex hormones in their composition.

The international compendium of all information up to 1977 concerning human reproduction — its fundamental physiology, its historical background, its societal impact, contraception, population control, and financial costs — was initiated by the Ford Foundation with the collaboration of the Rockefeller Foundation and the International Development Research Center of Canada.[23] This was a two-year study and involved the integrated effort of 165 worldwide and eminent scholars in their respective fields. It was spearheaded by Roy O. Greep, internationally acclaimed endocrinologist. It has a 36-page summary with 20 recommendations for research and its funding. There are 41 essays on scientific data alone. There is one paragraph from Greep's preface to the volume of 622 pages worth quoting:

There is a goodly degree of timeliness to the present survey. Reproductive endocrinology is rounding out its first half century of meaningful experimentation. The total annual support of reproductive research over that period has grown from virtually nothing to somewhere in the neighborhood of $120 million. With these gains in activity it seemed an appropriate time to take an inventory of where the field stands, how it is progressing, what its needs are, and how further progress might be more effectively gained.

That the female sex hormones — estrogens and progestins — have played an outstanding role during the half century since Allen and Doisy's LANDMARK ARTICLE of 1923 hardly needs emphasis.

---

In conclusion, if any readers are interested in the innumerable ramifications of estrogen and the other sex hormones, all one has to do is to read the several editions of *Sex and Internal Secretions*. The first, by Edgar Allen,[24] was published in 1932, nine years after the publication of the accompanying LANDMARK ARTICLE.

The second edition, bigger and, of course, heavier, was much more sophisticated and thorough and had 28 contributors — a literal "who's who" of world-famous endocrinologists.[25]

The third edition, now a two-volume set, edited by the late William C. Young[26] of Kansas and published in 1961, is again a compilation of 28 authors, many the same as in prior editions. It has a stirring foreword by George W. Corner and a most moving biography of Edgar Allen himself by W. C. Young. One thing is worth recording from that biography, since it concerns the accompanying LANDMARK ARTICLE. Just before the 1923 meeting of anatomists, Allen found that the substance in follicular fluid caused cornification in the mouse vagina. He had no abstract prepared, but at the meetings he merely mentioned his accepted abstract "Ovogenesis During Sexual Maturity," then spent most of the allotted time telling about the cornifying effect of the follicular hormone on the vagina of the spayed mouse. Thus, this was the first oral announcement about the effect of the follicular hormone; the first written is in the accompanying LANDMARK ARTICLE.

These three volumes are both monuments to Edgar Allen and beacons to guide future researchers in the field of female reproductive physiology.

And so, the tiny flame kindled by Stockard and Papanicolaou in 1917 was fanned into a blaze in 1923 by the synergistic inspiration, persistence, and dedication of Edgar Allen and Edward A. Doisy. This blaze has become a conflagration — controlled, of course — that has spread to all areas of comparative and human medicine.

"Doing easily what others find difficult is talent, doing what is impossible for talent is genius."[27]

## References

1. Schuck H, Sohlman R, Osterling A, et al: Hormones and vitamines, in The Nobel Foundation (ed): *Nobel: The Man and His Prizes.* Amsterdam, Elsevier Publishing Co, 1962, pp 225-245.

2. Allen E, Doisy EA: An ovarian hormone: Preliminary report on its localization, extraction and action in test animals. *JAMA* 1923;81:819-821.

3. Allen E, Doisy EA: The induction of a sexually mature condition in immature females by injection of ovarian follicular hormone. *Am J Physiol* 1924;69:577-588.

4. Stockard CR, Papanicolaou GN: Existence of a typical oestrus cycle in the guinea-pig, with a study of its histological and physiological changes. *Am J Anat* 1917;22:225.

5. Doisy EA: An autobiography. *Ann Rev Biochem* 1976;45:1-9.

6. Aschheim S, Zondek B: Hypophysenvarderlappenhormone und ovarialhormone im harn non Schwangeren. *Klin Wochenschr* 1927;6:1322.

7. Allen E: The menstrual cycle of the monkey, *Macacus rhesus*: Observations on normal animals, the effects of removal of the ovaries and the effects of injections of ovaries and placental extracts into spayed animals. *Contrib Embryol* 1927;19:1-44.

8. Corner GW: Ovulation and menstruation in *Macacus rhesus. Contrib Embryol* 1923;15:73-101.

9. Hertig AT, Rock J, Adams EC: A description of 34 human ova within the first 17 days of development. *Am J Anat* 1956;98:435-493.

10. Corner GW, Allen WM: Physiology of the corpus luteum: II. Production of a special uterine reaction (progestational proliferation) by extracts of the corpus luteum. *Am J Physiol* 1929;88:326.

11. Allen WM, Corner GW: Physiology of corpus luteum III: Normal growth and implantation of embryos after early ablation of the ovaries, under the influence of extracts of the corpus luteum. *Am J Physiol* 1929;88:340.

12. Papanicolaou GN, Traut HF: The diagnostic value of vaginal smears in carcinoma of the uterus. *Am J Obstet Gynecol* 1941;42:193-206.

13. Hertig AT: In memoriam, Paul Franklin Fletcher, M.D., 1903-1962.

*Acta Cytologica* 1963;7:274-275.

14. Hertig AT, Gore H: Estrogenic lesions of the ovary, in Grady HG, Smith DE (eds): *The Ovary,* monograph 3, in International Academy of Pathologists: *Monographs in Pathology.* Baltimore, Williams & Wilkins Co, 1963, pp 175-208.

15. Scully RE: *Tumors of the Ovary and Maldeveloped Gonads,* fascicle 16, series 2. Washington, DC, Armed Forces Institute of Pathology, 1979.

16. Fox H, Langley FA: *Tumors of the Ovary.* London, William Heinemann Medical Books Ltd, 1976.

17. Ziel HK: Estrogen's role in endometrial cancer. *Obstet Gynecol* 1982;60:509-515.

18. Gordon J, Reagan JW, Finkle WD, et al: Estrogen and endometrial carcinoma: An independent pathology review supporting original risk estimate. *N Engl J Med* 1977;297:570.

19. Ziel HK, Finkle WD: Increased risk of endometrial carcinoma among users of conjugated estrogens. *N Engl J Med* 1975;293:1167.

20. Pincus G, Chang MC: The effects of progesterone and related compounds on ovulation and early development in the rabbit. *Acta Physiol Latinoam* 1953;3:177-183.

21. Pincus G, Rock J, Garcia CR, et al: Fertility control with oral medication. *Am J Obstet Gynecol* 1958;75:1333-1346.

22. Rock J, Garcia CR, Pincus G: Synthetic progestins in the normal human menstrual cycle. *Recent Prog Horm Res* 1957;13:323-346.

23. Greep O, Koblinsky MA, Jaffe FS: The female reproductive system, in *Reproduction and Human Welfare: A Challenge to Research.* Cambridge, Mass, MIT Press, pp 79-164.

24. Allen E (ed): *Sex and Internal Secretions,* ed 1. Baltimore, Williams & Wilkins Co, 1932.

25. Allen E: *Sex and Internal Secretions,* ed 2. Baltimore, Williams & Wilkins Co, 1939.

26. Young WC (ed): *Sex and Internal Secretions,* ed 3. Baltimore, Williams & Wilkins Co, 1961.

27. Amiel HF, quoted by Davidoff H (ed): *The Pocket Book of Quotations.* New York, Pocket Books Inc, 1942.

Jan 26, 1924
(*JAMA* 1924;82:301-302)

## Chapter 18

# The Etiology of Scarlet Fever[*]

### George F. Dick, M.D.
### and
### Gladys Henry Dick, M.D.

#### Chicago

Owing to the constancy with which hemolytic streptococci of one kind or another have been found associated with scarlet fever, they have long been considered as a possible cause of the disease. Attempts to prove their causal relation have encountered many obstacles, chief of which has been the failure to produce experimental scarlet fever.

#### TYPES OF STREPTOCOCCI

The hemolytic streptococci associated with scarlet fever do not all show the same cultural characteristics. They may be divided into two groups according to their effect on mannite. In a series of 100 cases studied in 1922 and 1923, hemolytic streptococci were found in all; 16 per cent. of these strains fermented mannite, and 84 per cent. did not ferment mannite.

In 1923, we[1] reported experimental scarlet fever produced with one of the strains that fermented mannite. This strain was isolated from a case of scarlet fever. It produced experimental scarlet fever. It was isolated from the experimental disease, and again grown in pure culture. All of Koch's laws were thus fulfilled except that one which requires that the organism be constantly present in the disease. In order to meet this requirement, it was necessary to learn whether or not experimental scarlet fever could be produced with a strain of hemolytic streptococcus that did not ferment mannite.

#### INOCULATION OF SCARLET FEVER

Two volunteers were chosen. One showed an entirely negative skin test with the filtrate of the streptococcus previously used.[2] The other showed a positive skin test. A hemolytic streptococcus that did not ferment mannite was isolated from the throat of a scarlet fever patient. Part of a forty-eight hour culture of this organism was swabbed on the tonsils of each volunteer.

The volunteer who showed a negative skin test remained well. She had no sore throat, no fever and no rash. The volunteer who showed a positive skin test developed scarlet fever.

This was a woman, aged 22. Thirty-four hours after inoculation, she complained of generalized aching. At the end of forty-one hours, her temperature by mouth was 100.4 F. She felt nauseated and vomited twice; forty-six hours after inoculation, a faint scarlatinal rash appeared. The temperature, at this time, had reached 102. During the day, the rash became more marked. By evening, it had become intense, and the temperature had risen to 102.8. The leukocyte count was 22,400, with 91 per cent. polymorphonuclear leukocytes. The next day, the rash was still marked. The highest temperature was 101.2. On the morning of the fifth day of the disease, the temperature was normal. The rash was still present. At the time of the highest temperature, the urine showed a trace of albumin. During convalescence, it was normal. Recovery was uneventful. On the twentieth day of the disease, there was a typical desquamation on the hands, and beginning desquamation on the feet.

#### CONCLUSION

Since the streptococci used in these experiments have fulfilled all the requirements of Koch's laws, it may be concluded that they cause scarlet fever.

[*]From the John McCormick Institute for Infectious Diseases.

1. Dick, G. F., and Dick, Gladys H.: Experimental Scarlet Fever, J. A. M. A. **81:** 1166 (Oct. 6) 1923.

2. Dick, G. F., and Dick, Gladys H.: A Skin Test for Susceptibility to Scarlet Fever, this issue, p. 265.

Dec 9, 1983
(*JAMA* 1983;250:3097-3099)

# The Historical Role of the Dick Test*

Gene H. Stollerman, MD

The contemporary medical student who reads in 1983 the brief *JAMA* article that was written by the Dicks[1] some 60 years ago could well wonder why it was selected by the current editors of THE JOURNAL as a historical highlight of modern medicine. After all, scarlet fever is now a relatively rare and not serious disease. It is no more dangerous an affliction than is a nonscarlatinal streptococcal infection of comparable severity. Indeed, the scarlatinal rash actually may be diagnostically helpful in signaling the cause of an acute pharyngitis or, indeed, in flagging an outbreak of such infections. With the advent of antibiotics, this erstwhile feared and dramatic disease has been dropped almost universally from the list of quarantinable contagious diseases by local health authorities. The rash that is produced by the streptococcal erythrogenic toxin is now likely to be regarded as a clinical curiosity of some theoretical interest because of its uncertain pathogenesis.

### The Beginnings of Streptococcal Research

Transporting ourselves back a century, however, we can readily recreate the confusion that followed Pasteur's[2] discussion of puerperal sepsis in 1879, when he correctly recognized a chain-forming coccus as an organism related to the disease, an organism named *Streptococcus pyogenes* a few years later by Rosenbach.[3] Within one year of Pasteur's report, these bacteria were found to be present in the blood of patients dying of scarlet fever.[4] Before the 19th century came to a close, the search for the causative "virus" resulted in ten patients being inoculated with material obtained from the oral secretions of a patient who had an attack of scarlet fever. Such efforts were, however, abandoned when complications such as "nephritis" and other systemic reactions occurred in recipients.[5]

As early as 1903, in the same year that Schottmüller[6] demonstrated the hemolysis of red cells on a blood agar plate by pathogenic streptococci, a remarkable attempt

at immunization against scarlet fever was made. Gabritschewsky[7] injected killed scarlatinal streptococci, together with the broth in which they were grown, into humans, and scarlet fever developed in some, thus preceding by 20 years the observations of all other investigators! The use of this whole culture–killed vaccine was investigated by numerous European workers who reported a notable decrease in the incidence of scarlet fever in vaccinated children compared with nonvaccinated controls.[8]

Schottmüller's identification of hemolytic streptococci was, however, causing confusion about scarlet fever at the same time that it was helping to sort out the varied and ubiquitous streptococci. By 1919, Brown[9] had further classified hemolytic reactions into the alpha, beta, and gamma terminology, but the study of biochemical and cultural characteristics still could not be correlated with pathogenicity. It was obvious that hemolytic streptococcal pharyngitis did not always cause scarlet fever. Dochez and associates[10] began a systematic attempt in 1919 at an immunologic classification of $\beta$-hemolytic streptococci. Employing prospective animal experiments and serological agglutination methods, they studied a great number of strains and succeeded in identifying many different antigenic types among hemolytic streptococci that were isolated from human infections. These methods did not provide a conclusive answer about scarlet fever, but they did help to spawn Rebecca Lancefield's[11] serological classification of these organisms.

The early 20th century was intensely oriented toward producing horse antisera for many exotoxins, notably diphtheria, and a horse serum actually *was* prepared by Moser and von Pirquet[12] against scarlatinal streptococci. This serum agglutinated some strains of scarlatinal streptococci in higher titers than hemolytic streptococci isolated from other sources. The horse serum prevented the development of local and systemic reactions if given before the injection of humans with Gabritschewsky's vaccine. The serum even seemed to ameliorate the course and the symptoms of scarlet fever.[4] Because, however, streptococci were still not accepted as the

From the Department of Medicine, Boston University School of Medicine.

*A commentary on Dick GF, Dick GH: The etiology of scarlet fever. *JAMA* 1924;82:301-302.

cause of scarlet fever, the streptococcal vaccine was no longer used in its prophylaxis.

### The Dicks' Toxin and Antitoxin

The work of the Dicks, then, was a renewed attempt at immunization against streptococcal disease, but this time with the extracellular products of the organism. This stimulus resulted from their production of scarlet fever in humans experimentally with the hemolytic streptococcus. By 1924, Dochez and Sherman[13] also had published in THE JOURNAL their production of an antiscarlatinal horse serum that was designed to neutralize the presumed toxic moiety of scarlet fever. Schultz and Charlton[14] and Mair[15] had established that serum from persons who have had scarlet fever could blanch the rash of the disease (Schultz-Charlton reaction). Dochez was also able to produce this "extinction phenomenon" by using horse antiserum prepared against *Streptococcus scarlatinae*. Antisera prepared from other hemolytic streptococci did not blanch the rash.

The Dicks'[16] studies, published in 1924, unequivocally demonstrated the presence of an erythrogenic toxin in the blood broth cultures of *S scarlatinae*. They described a skin test analogous to the Schick test; they were able to neutralize the toxic filtrate in vitro and in vivo by the use of convalescent serum and showed that susceptible persons could be immunized by repeated doses of toxin until skin reactivity became negative. In the decade after 1924, numerous attempts were made to produce immunity against scarlet fever,[8] most of which involved graded toxin injections into susceptible persons followed by reversal of the Dick test.

### The Stimulus to Rheumatic Fever Research

During this era, the relationship of rheumatic fever to streptococcal infection was becoming increasingly evident. The possibility that erythrogenic toxin might play a role in the pathogenesis of rheumatic fever was investigated by Alvin Coburn. He noted the high incidence of a Dick-negative reaction among rheumatic children who did not have scarlet fever and surmised that these children probably had had frequent infections with erythrogenic streptococcal organisms and thus were immune to the rash of scarlet fever. In an attempt to reduce the incidence of scarlet fever as a possible form of prophylaxis against rheumatic fever, Coburn and Pauli[17] embarked on experiments in the 1930s that employed active and passive immunization with scarlatinal New York 5-toxin and antitoxin. They produced reversal of skin sensitivity but did not decrease the incidence of streptococcal infections nor the development of subsequent rheumatic disease in the group studied compared with suitable controls. A decade later, Jackson[18] verified this work by again showing that immunization with Dick toxin protects against the rash of scarlet fever but not against invasion by streptococci. The concept of type-specific immunity to streptococcal M-serotypes was just emerging from Rebecca Lancefield's[11] work on the bacteriology and immunology of the organism. The remaining story of the control of rheumatic fever is modern history.[19]

Interest in erythrogenic toxin has subsequently waned with some revival in its investigation when the concept was established that temperate bacteriophage infection could induce the production of an exotoxin by the infected bacterium. Toxigenic diphtheria strains were shown to be bacteriophage infected, and the role of similar infection in the production of scarlatinal toxin was also implicated.[20]

In the past decade, largely as a result of the studies of Kim and Watson,[21] scarlatinal toxin has been highly purified and has been shown to comprise at least three distinct polypeptides, A, B, and C, each antigenically distinct. These substances have most of the biologic properties that have also been characteristic of gram-negative polysaccharide endotoxins. Like endotoxin, the erythrogenic toxins activate most of the cellular and humoral components of acute inflammation. From animal studies, it seems to be necessary to sensitize the host to small doses of the erythrogenic toxins before a strong erythrogenic reaction occurs (often followed by desquamation). When stronger antigenic stimulation occurs, however, immune protection against the toxin's effects prevents any reaction. Such experiments seem to fit the clinical fact that scarlet fever is usually not observed in infants nor in very young children until they have had their initial streptococcal infection. Older children and adults become sensitized and then progressively more immune and this is reflected by increased incidence of negative reaction to the Dick test as well as increasing rarity of the clinical disease with age.[22]

Oddly enough, current interest in erythrogenic toxin has centered on what was once considered a rare clinical event — scarlet fever occurring from staphylococcal infections. It had long been recognized that staphylococcal infections that were associated with staphylococcal abscesses could cause the classic scarlatinal rash apparently because of a staphylococcal erythrogenic toxin similar to that of hemolytic streptococci.[23] The prevalence, however, of the "toxic shock syndrome"[24] in women who use vaginal tampons and its association with the occurrence of a large burden of staphylococcal growth in such a medium has again aroused interest in the pathophysiology of erythrogenic toxins.

We have come a long way from the era when scarlet fever was a feared infection and an ominous precursor of the scarlatinal "Nachkrankheiten" of Bela Schick[25] — scarlatina, glomerulonephritis, and rheumatic fever. Ironically, however, we still know neither the specific antigens of the latter two streptococcal sequels nor the complete story of the pathophysiological implications of erythrogenic toxins.

The Dick test may now be but a historical oddity, but its impact on the research of its time was unmistakably important, and the cellular physiology of the erythrogenic polypeptides of streptococci and staphylococci may yet hold promise for new insights into cellular processes of inflammation.

Many of the historical studies cited were originally brought to my attention by the diligent library research of F. A. Gill, MD,[26] when he completed a thesis under my preceptorship as a senior medical student in 1960. This thesis became a valuable resource in subsequent reviews of the history of streptococcal infections and rheumatic fever.[19] My own reviews of the early history of scarlet fever depended heavily on the famous review of the literature by Arthur L. Bloomfield[27] in 1952.

# References

1. Dick GF, Dick GH: The etiology of scarlet fever. *JAMA* 1924;82:301-302.

2. Pasteur L: Etologie du charbon. *Bull Acadde Méd Par* 1879 2s;8:1222-1234.

3. Rosenbach FJ: *Mikro-organismen bei den Wund-infections-krankheiten des Menschen.* Wiesbaden, Germany, Bergmann, 1884.

4. Dochez AR: Etiology of scarlet fever, in *Harvey Lecture Series 20.* Philadelphia, JB Lippincott Co, 1924-1925, vol 20, pp 131-155.

5. Stickler JW: Scarlet fever reproduced by inoculation: Some important points deducted therefrom. *Med Rec NY* 1899;16:363-366.

6. Schottmüller H: Die Artunterscheidung der fur den Menschen pathogenen Streptokokken durch Blutagar. *MMW* 1903;1:849-909.

7. Gabritschewsky G, cited by Gill FA: A review of past attempts and present concepts of producing streptococcal immunity in humans. *Q Bull* (Northwestern University Medical School) 1960;34:326-339.

8. Thomson D, Thomson R: The role of the streptococci in scarlet fever. *Ann Picket-Thomson Res Lab* 1930;6:1-470.

9. Brown JH: The use of blood agar for the study of streptococci, monograph 9. New York, Rockefeller Institute of Medical Research, 1919.

10. Dochez AR, Avery OT, Lancefield RC: Studies of the biology of streptococcus: I. Antigenic relationships between strains of *Streptococcus hemolyticus. J Exp Med* 1919;30:179-213.

11. Lancefield RC: Specific relationship of cell composition to biological activity of hemolytic streptococci, in *Harvey Lecture Series 36.* Lancaster, Pa, Science Press, 1940-1941, pp 251-290.

12. Moser P, von Pirquet C: Zur Theorie der Inkubationszeit. *Wien Klin Wochenschr* 1903;16:1244-1247.

13. Dochez AR, Sherman L: Significance of *Streptococcus hemolyticus* in scarlet fever and the preparation of a specific antiscarlatinal serum by immunization of the horse to *Streptococcus hemolyticus-scarlatinae. JAMA* 1924;82:542-544.

14. Schultz W, Charlton W: Serologische Beobachtungen am Scharlachexanthem. *Z Kinderheilkd* 1918;17:328-333.

15. Mair W: An immunity reaction in scarlet fever. *Lancet* 1923;2:1390-1393.

16. Dick GF, Dick GH: Prevention of scarlet fever. *JAMA* 1924;83:84-86.

17. Coburn AF, Pauli RH: Studies on the immune response of the rheumatic subject and its relationship to activity of the rheumatic process. *J Clin Invest* 1935;14:763-768.

18. Jackson RT: Active immunisation against *Streptococcus scarlatinae. Irish J Med Sci* 1941;6:260-266.

19. Stollerman GH: *Rheumatic Fever and Streptococcal Infection.* New York, Grune & Stratton Inc, 1975, chap 1, pp 1-20.

20. Zabriskie JB, Read SE, Fischetti VA: Lysogeny in streptococci, in Wannamaker LW, Matsen JM (eds): *Streptococci and Streptococcal Diseases: Recognition, Understanding and Management.* New York, Academic Press Inc, 1972, pp 99-118.

21. Kim YB, Watson DW: Streptococcal exotoxins, in Wannamaker LW, Matsen JM (eds): *Streptococci and Streptococcal Diseases: Recognition, Understanding and Management.* New York, Academic Press Inc, 1972, pp 33-50.

22. Rantz LA, Boisvert PL, Spink WW: The Dick test in military personnel, with special reference to the pathogenesis of the skin reaction. *N Engl J Med* 1946;225:39.

23. Stevens FA: The occurrence of *Staphylococcus aureus* infection with a scarlatiniform rash. *JAMA* 1927;88:1957-1958.

24. Reingold AL: Nonmenstrual toxic shock syndrome: The growing picture. *JAMA* 1983;249:932.

25. Schick B: Über die Nachkrankheiten des Scharlach. *Jahrb Kinderheilk* 1907;65:132-135.

26. Gill FA: A review of past attempts and present concepts of producing streptococcal immunity in humans. *Q Bull* (Northwestern University Medical School) 1960;34:326-339.

27. Bloomfield AL: A bibliography of internal medicine: Scarlet fever. *Stanford Med Bull* 1952;10:114-129.

Feb 23, 1924
(*JAMA* 1924;82:613-614)

# Chapter 19

# Roentgenologic Examination of the Gallbladder

## Preliminary Report of a New Method Utilizing the Intravenous Injection of Tetrabromphenolphthalein*

Evarts A. Graham, M.D.
and
Warren H. Cole, M.D.

St. Louis

The revolutionary effect on the diagnosis of gastrointestinal conditions which was made possible by the use of the opaque meal has given rise repeatedly to the idea that if, by some means, an opaque substance could be safely introduced into the gallbladder so that its contour could be seen with the roentgen ray, the diagnosis of many obscure and doubtful cases of cholecystitis might be made easy and accurate. To fulfil the necessary practical requirements, the opaque substance must be something that is excreted into the bile after being injected either subcutaneously or intravenously or after being given by mouth; and, furthermore, it must be devoid of toxic

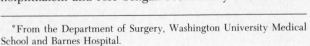

Fig. 1.—Gallbladder shadow in a 5.25 kilogram dog, twenty-four hours after intravenous injection of 1.5 gm. of tetrabromphenolphthalein with 0.3 gm. of calcium hydroxid.

effects when used in the concentrations necessary for the shadow of gallbladder to be seen. The extensive use of various dyes in the search for a test of liver function has revealed the fact that certain ones are excreted almost entirely into the bile, as, for example, tetrachlorphenolphthalein and rose bengal. Preliminary tests of intra-

*From the Department of Surgery, Washington University Medical School and Barnes Hospital.

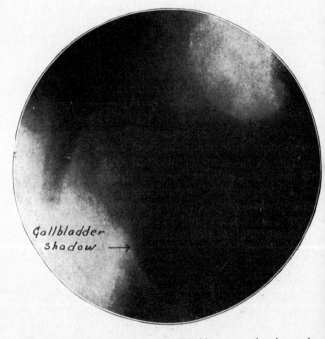

Fig. 2.—Appearance of a human gallbladder, twenty-four hours after intravenous injection of 5 gm. of tetrabromphenolphthalein with 1 gm. of calcium hydroxid. The patient weighed 130 pounds (59 kg.).

venous injections of the sodium salt of tetrachlorphenolphthalein into experimental animals failed to reveal satisfactory roentgen-ray shadows of the gallbladder. Because of the similarity of chemical structure, it was thought that tetra-iodophenolphthalein would also be excreted into the bile and might cast a satisfactory shadow because of its iodin content. Roentgen-ray shadows of the gallbladder were revealed, but the substance seemed to be too toxic to permit its extensive use in man. Accordingly, it was felt that tetrabromphenolphthalein might be a suitable compromise between the toxic iodin compound and the less opaque chlorin compound. The experimental results with this substance were satisfactory so far as toxicity was concerned but in some instances the shadows of the gallbladder were not so definite as was desired.

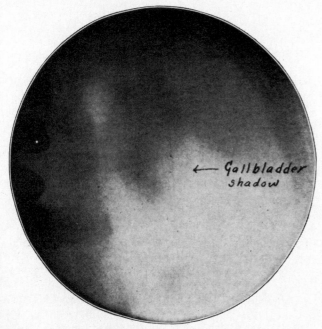

Fig. 3.—Appearance of same gallbladder as in Figure 2, thirty hours after injection: The shadow has become less distinct as the substance has begun to leave the gallbladder.

It was therefore decided to try the calcium salt instead of the sodium salt of tetrabromphenolphthalein. This substance, when injected intravenously, has given definite and cleanly cut shadows of the gallbladder both in experimental animals and in human subjects. No untoward effects have been observed in the human subject with the concentrations used. This preliminary report is made merely to introduce the method. As yet, our observations have been too few to permit conclusions based on the interpretation of what should constitute the normal shadow and the precise interpretation of deviations from the normal shadow. It is possible, also, that some other substance will prove to have advantages over calcium tetrabromphenolphthalein. Further work is now in progress along this line.

METHOD

A dose of 0.25 gm. of the dye per kilogram of body weight was found sufficient to cast a shadow of the gallbladder, when injected intravenously into a rabbit or dog with 0.05 gm. of calcium hydroxid per kilogram. A shadow could likewise be obtained by combining the dye with twice as much strontium hydroxid as calcium hydroxid.

A dose of 0.1 gm. per kilogram, when injected into a human subject, was found sufficient to cast a shadow. At present, 6 gm. has been the largest dose used. Six grams of tetrabromphenolphthalein is mixed with 1.2 gm. of calcium hydroxid, ground in a mortar with a few cubic centimeters of water, and dissolved in from 325 to 350 c.c. of distilled water. Addition of calcium lactate was found to produce a more stable solution and slightly increase its solubility. Therefore, a solution of 2 gm. of calcium lactate in a few cubic centimeters of water is added. The solution has been sterilized by heating it to the boiling point under a flame, and heating in a water bath at from 95 to 100 C. for fifteen minutes. Occasionally, a small amount of the calcium salt precipitates on the bottom of the receptacle. This dissolves readily on the addition of a small amount of water or saline solution, after the clear solution is decanted off. The solution is filtered and given intravenously by the gravity method, similar to an arsphenamin injection. The solution is introduced slowly. Usually from twenty-five to thirty minutes is consumed in the injection, so that symptoms, if present, can be detected early. Roentgenograms of the gallbladder region are taken at intervals of several hours, beginning three hours after the injection. The patient is instructed to lie on his right side when lying down, but is encouraged to walk around or sit up one or two hours after the injection.

TOXICITY

Increasing the dose above 0.25 gm. per kilogram of body weight was found toxic to an animal. Occasionally a hematuria resulted before death. A dose of 0.35 gm. per kilogram is usually fatal instantaneously.

As yet, only a few patients have been injected. All of these weighed 130 pounds (59 kg.) or more and received a dose of from 5 to 6 gm., which is approximately 0.1 gm. per kilogram. Only one suffered any symptoms. When she had received 4.75 gm., or 0.079 gm. per kilogram, she complained of vertigo and slight nausea. Each of these symptoms disappeared in an hour. Slight variation in pulse and blood pressure are recorded, but no more than what might be explained by emotion and an increase in body fluid. None suffered hematuria or albuminuria.

RESULTS

As stated, definite and distinct shadows of the gallbladder are obtained on exposure to the roentgen ray. Up to date, shadows have been obtained on all patients who presumably had a normal gallbladder. It is more difficult to obtain a shadow of a pathologic gallbladder. We believe, however, that this fact will be almost as much aid in diagnosis as a good shadow, since we feel that virtually all normal gallbladders can be made to cast a shadow if proper methods are used. Effort is being made by us to devise methods that will withhold the dye in the biliary system for a longer time, and in a greater concentration.

Dec 2, 1983
(JAMA 1983;250:2977-2982)

# The Graham-Cole Test*

## The Oral Cholecystogram Today

Harold G. Jacobson, MD, Wilhelm Z. Stern, MD

The pioneer efforts of Graham and Cole to produce a radiological examination of the gallbladder were prompted by a desire to enhance and refine the diagnosis of gallbladder disease beyond that achieved by history and physical examination.

It is interesting to consider the background of the period in which the Graham-Cole test was designed. The specialty of radiology was not yet in formal existence (the American Board of Radiology was not organized until 1934). Drs Graham and Cole were not even radiologists (see Chapter 24). Both men, being members of the Department of Surgery at Washington University School of Medicine, undoubtedly felt ill at ease about exploring or removing a gallbladder without first ascertaining its pathological state. The hazards of surgery, particularly those of anesthesia, were, of course, much greater than they are today, so that proper indications for surgery were paramount.

In addition to its relevance for surgeons, the article by Graham and Cole[1] was important to the disciplines of general practice, internal medicine, gastroenterology, and, of course, radiology, all of which deal with the common problem of gallbladder disease.

The cumbersome pioneer technique of February 1924 entailed an intravenous (IV) drip infusion of a mixture of 5 to 6 g of tetrabromphenolphthalein and 1 to 1.2 g of calcium hydroxide, dissolved in 325 mL of distilled water. Roentgenograms were obtained at intervals of several hours, resulting in adequate demonstration of the gallbladder up to 24 hours, with the image becoming increasingly less distinct thereafter.

From this initial procedure, the current radiological examination of the gallbladder stimulated the development and introduction of improved contrast agents, but without any alteration in the basic physiological principles advanced by Graham and Cole. As a result, it was not too long before the updated Graham-Cole test became "king" in the diagnostic armamentarium used for the detection of gallbladder disease, and it has been steadfastly so for half a century. It is interesting that Graham and Cole were able to predict the diagnostic importance of nonvisualization as suggesting a pathological disorder.

The unchallenged status of oral cholecystography came to an end in the late 1970s, when the introduction of ultrasonography established its clinical usefulness in the evaluation of the biliary tract, particularly the gallbladder. However, a place still exists for the current radiological studies of the gallbladder, yet still applying the principles of the Graham-Cole test (examination).

### Pharmacologic Principles of Oral Cholecystography

The most widely used contrast agent during the past 40 years has been iopanoic acid (Telepaque), a triiodinated compound excreted primarily via the liver. Three grams (six tablets) is ingested in the evening, and roentgenograms of the gallbladder area are obtained approximately 14 hours later during the following morning. A moderate degree of diarrhea is commonly experienced by the patient, but serious complications are rare, occurring principally in persons with hepatorenal disease. The efficacy of the study necessarily requires free (unobstructed) transit of the ingested opacifying agent into the small bowel, adequate intestinal absorption, and sufficient hepatic excretion into the biliary tract. Disturbances in any of these mechanisms will result in nonvisualization of the gallbladder, which, in the instance of a normal gallbladder, would give a false-positive result. Other extraneous factors that may interfere with opacification of the normal gallbladder are peritonitis, pancreatic insufficiency, and recent abdominal surgery.[2]

Iopanoic acid is soluble in fat but relatively insoluble in water. In the liver, it is conjugated to form a glucuronide ester that is water soluble.[3] In the past, instructions for patients called for a fat-free supper on the evening before the examination, with the rationale that fat would evacuate the contrast medium accumulating in the gallbladder. However, recent experimental and clinical

From the Department of Radiology, the Albert Einstein College of Medicine at the Montefiore Medical Center, Bronx, NY.

*A commentary on Graham EA, Cole WH: Roentgenologic examination of the gallbladder: Preliminary report of a new method utilizing the intravenous injection of tetrabromphenolphthalein. *JAMA* 1924;82:613-614.

evidence has demonstrated the important role of bile salts in the intestinal absorption and hepatic excretion of iopanoic acid.[4] It is, therefore, considered important that the patient have a meal containing fat at the time iopanoic acid is ingested to ensure an adequate *entero-hepatic recirculation of bile salts*—an action stimulated by intake of fat. It has been observed for a long time that in a number of persons with normal gallbladders, as often as 25% of the time, visualization of the gallbladder is poor or does not occur on the first day of the study.[5] However, on the second day, a repeated study after a second dose of iopanoic acid will demonstrate a normally functioning gallbladder. This apparent inconsistency in evaluating the status of the gallbladder may be remedied by giving divided doses of iopanoic acid spread out over a 48-hour period. It has been suggested that the inadequate opacification of the gallbladder on the first day may be due to an absence of circulating bile salts, caused by a diet low in fat or by persons being deprived of food, whether willfully or unwittingly.

Water should not be withheld after the evening meal, since iopanoic acid has a uricosuric effect.[6] Indeed, dehydration should be avoided before any radiological study in which contrast medium is given.

Conjugated iopanoic acid is excreted by the liver into the biliary tract and passes into the gallbladder if the cystic duct is patent, thereby permitting its visualization radiologically. Poor opacification of the gallbladder in patients with cholecystitis was attributed in the past to inability of the diseased gallbladder to absorb water and concentrate the opacifying medium. Experimental work by Lasser[3] and colleagues has shown, however, that in the inflamed gallbladder, *reabsorption of iopanoic acid* occurs, accounting for diminished opacification. Reabsorption does not occur in persons with normal gallbladders.

### Conduct of the Examination

**Preliminary Roentgenogram.**—Although some authorities do not believe a preliminary film to be necessary,[6] most radiologists obtain a preliminary film of the right upper quadrant, unless a recent plain film is available. Ten percent to 20% of biliary calculi are radiopaque[5]; they may be obscured by the contrast-filled gallbladder, and their demonstration on the preliminary film may obviate the need for cholecystography. Calcification of the gallbladder wall ("porcelain gallbladder") is a sequel of chronic cholecystitis and may be a precursor for the development of carcinoma of the gallbladder (in approximately 25% of cases). "Milk of calcium bile," associated with obstruction of the cystic duct, is also best studied by examination with plain films, in upright and horizontal-beam projections; the opaque bile in such instances will gravitate to the dependent portion of the gallbladder. When communication with the small bowel has occurred or if emphysematous cholecystitis is present, the gallbladder will be filled with gas. Fissuring of opaque calculi may suggest the presence of gas in the calculus, arranged, on occasion, in a triradiate pattern ("Mercedes-Benz sign"), permitting recognition on plain films.[7]

The standard oral cholecystogram, performed the morning after the oral ingestion of the contrast medium (iopanoic acid), includes at least three projections: posteroanterior prone, left anterior oblique prone, and posteroanterior erect. Small radiolucencies within the opacified gallbladder constitute the most frequent problem in interpretation. These may be caused by radiolucent calculi, polyps, papillomas, and overlying intestinal gas. Various techniques have been used to separate the image of the gallbladder on the film from overlying bowel.[2] These include the horizontal-beam film (right side down), cranial or caudal tilt of tube of 25°, fluoroscopy with graded compression and spot films, air insufflation of the hepatic flexure of the colon (which has a contiguous positional relationship to the gallbladder[8]), barium swallow for assessment of gallbladder-duodenal relationship, and laminography. No single technique is uniformly applicable, and problem cases must be handled individually.

In instances of poor opacification of the gallbladder, rapidly acting oral cholecystographic agents (eg, ipodate calcium) may be administered, usually to advantage, augmenting opacification of the gallbladder within about four hours. A day of hospitalization may thus be saved.[4]

Unless the presence of calculi is definitely established, a cholagogue (usually containing considerable fat) is administered and a final roentgenogram is obtained 30 to 60 minutes later. While European authors have written extensively about gallbladder "dyskinesia" (relating to incomplete or even no obvious emptying of the gallbladder), American radiologists generally have not attached the same importance to gallbladder dynamics. Small calculi obscured by excessive contrast in the gallbladder, on occasion, are identified after the fatty meal; the cystic and common bile ducts are also frequently delineated.[5]

### Interpretation

The most common abnormalities of the gallbladder diagnosed radiologically are impaired or absent opacification of the gallbladder and cholelithiasis. If the previously mentioned extrinsic causes of nonopacification (eg, malabsorption, hepatic disease) can be excluded, inadequate or absent opacification strongly suggests gallbladder disease (usually chronic cholecystitis) or cystic duct obstruction or both. The appearance of iopanoic acid in the bowel may be of diagnostic help: a particulate pattern is associated with nonabsorbed iopanoic acid, while conjugated iopanoic acid (excreted by the liver) produces a smooth coating of the bowel. In the latter instance, nonopacification of the gallbladder indicates intrinsic disease of that structure. Similar reasoning applies to the use of sodium tyropanoate.[9]

Calculi must be differentiated from air bubbles, and errors are frequently made in this regard. On films obtained with the horizontal beam, small calculi may "layer out" or float in the middle portion of the gallbladder (Fig 1). The specific gravity of bile is increased by the contrast medium and the same calculi may not float when reexamined without contrast (eg, by ultrasound).

Persistent, excessively dense opacification of the gallbladder is encountered, on occasion, 24 to 36 hours after oral cholecystography. Such opacification is associ-

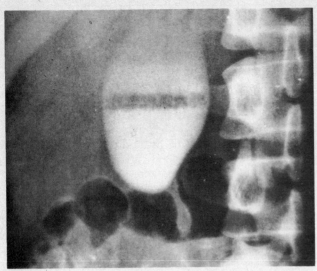

Fig 1.—Layering of biliary calculi. Oral cholecystogram in upright position shows radiolucent layer of biliary calculi in midportion of gallbladder. Level of layering determined by specific gravity of calculi relative to contrast-laden bile.

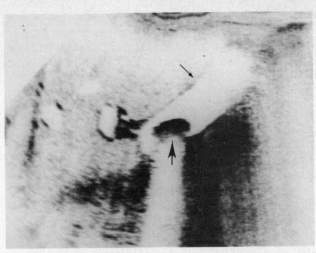

Fig 2.—Calculus of gallbladder demonstrated on sonography. Sagittal sonogram of right upper quadrant of abdomen, 7 cm to right of midline, shows fluid-filled gallbladder as anechoic area (small arrow). In dependent portion of gallbladder, note strongly echogenic focus (large arrow), accompanied by sharply demarcated acoustic shadow, characteristic of calculus.

Fig 3.—Complementary roles of oral cholecystography and ultrasonography in demonstrating multiple gallbladder calculi. Left, Longitudinal ultrasonogram of gallbladder shows several small echogenic foci in its dependent portion (arrows). Right, Oral cholecystography shows multiple, small radiolucencies indicating presence of biliary calculi (courtesy of Dr Ruth Rosenblatt).

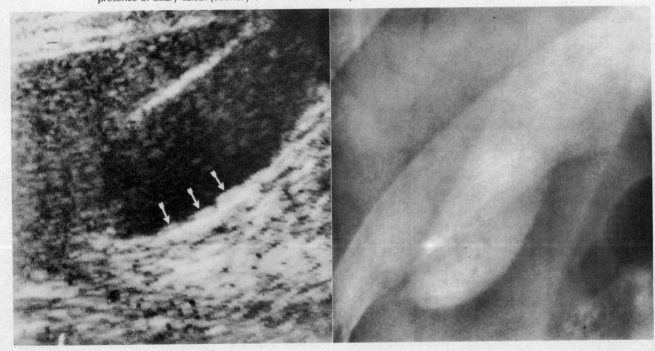

ated with intrinsic gallbladder disease (eg, acalculous cholecystitis or papillomatosis). However, this radiological feature is not necessarily pathological; it may be caused by enterohepatic recirculation of conjugated iopanoic acid.[10] Of interest is the increase in size of the gallbladder that may be present in diabetic patients[11] and in persons after vagotomy.

**Noncalculous Lesions of the Gallbladder.**—The most common cause of a solitary polypoid mass in the gallbladder is a cholesterol polyp. This lesion has no glandular elements, being composed largely of macrophages laden with cholesterol esters.[12] The differential diagnosis includes inflammatory polyp, mucosal adenoma, and unusual benign lesions (eg, hamartoma, heterotopic pancreatic rest). Carcinoma of the gallbladder is often infiltrating and invasive rather than being initially seen as an isolated polypoid mass. Since carcinoma occurs principally in chronically diseased gallbladders with stones, verification of carcinoma via oral cholecystography is rarely accomplished.[12]

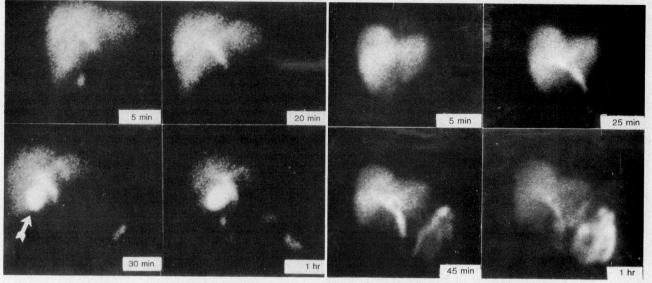

Fig 4.—Cholescintigraphy. Left, Normal biliary tract. Serial scans after intravenous administration of technetium Tc 99m diisopropyl iminodiacetic acid show normal accumulation of radioactivity in common bile duct and gallbladder (arrow). Right, Acute cholecystitis. Serial scans show normal common bile duct without radioactivity in gallbladder, consistent with cholecystitis and cystic duct obstruction (courtesy of Dr Heidi Weissmann).

The term *adenomyomatosis* refers to hyperplasia of the gallbladder wall, which can be diffuse, segmental, or localized. When the process is well established, intramural "diverticula" develop (Aschoff-Rokitansky sinuses), which opacify on oral cholecystography.[12] Aschoff-Rokitansky sinuses may serve as a nidus for the development of calculi. An hourglass deformity of the opacified gallbladder is a radiological sign of segmental adenomyomatosis. The localized type most commonly is initially seen in the fundus of the gallbladder as an umbilicated filling defect (adenomyoma) with an opacified center, often accompanied by fundal diverticula. The "phrygian cap" gallbladder, generally considered a normal variant, may predispose to fundal diverticulosis.[13]

The term *hyperplastic cholecystoses* was suggested by Jutras to include the entities of adenomyomatosis, cholesterolosis (strawberry gallbladder), neuromatosis, lipomatosis, fibromatosis, and hyalinocalcinosis (calcified gallbladder).

**Other Radiological Methods for Examination of the Gallbladder.**—Intravenous cholangiography (IC), developed by Wise[14] in the late 1950s, was useful in the diagnosis of acute cholecystitis, often associated with cystic duct obstruction. Opacification of the common bile duct without opacification of the gallbladder during IC was characteristic of obstruction of the cystic duct. Unfortunately, the procedure has been accompanied frequently by adverse effects, often of serious consequence. As a result, a considerable decrease in its use has occurred, and in a number of centers, this procedure has been discarded. It is still used, on occasion, for evaluation of the common bile duct after cholecystectomy.

Another radiological diagnostic modality is intraoperative study of the gallbladder via a cholecystostomy or through a transhepatic approach.[15]

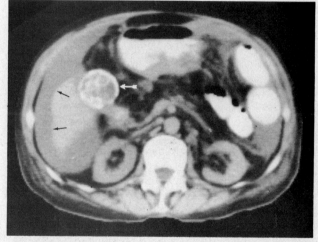

Fig 5.—"Porcelain" gallbladder with calculi demonstrated on computed tomography shows calcification of gallbladder wall (white arrow) with several calcified calculi in its lumen. Liver is surrounded by ascites (black arrows). Contrast medium (diatrizoate meglumine) is present in upper gastrointestinal tract (courtesy of Dr David Frager).

### The Emergence of Ultrasonography

This method of examination promises to be and, in fact, is held by many to be the new "gold standard" of examination of the gallbladder. With the refinement of gray-scale ultrasonography in the past five years, a steady increase in the use of this modality has occurred. The advantages of ultrasonography include (1) absence of side effects from contrast medium, (2) ability to perform the study in the presence of various disorders already present (eg, liver disease, jaundice, malabsorption, pregnancy), (3) establishment of the diagnosis within one hour rather than 16 hours, and (4) absence of ionizing radiation. It must be emphasized that the

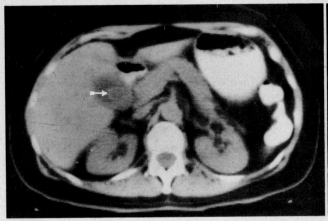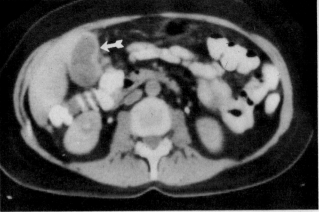

Fig 6. — Gallstone with thickening of gallbladder wall demonstrated on computed tomography. Left, Faintly calcified calculus is observed in center of gallbladder (arrow). Right, After intravenous administration of contrast (in addition to oral contrast), thickening of gallbladder wall is demonstrated (arrow), consistent with chronic cholecystitis (courtesy of Dr David Frager).

satisfactory performance of ultrasonography demands, as a general rule, greater skill than is required in accomplishing the radiological examinations.

The diagnostic accuracy of ultrasonography in the detection of gallbladder calculi is very high (Fig 2) and at least on a par with or even superior to oral cholecystography. In difficult cases, the two modalities can complement each other (Fig 3). It has been determined from such correlative studies that the rate of accuracy of oral cholecystography, previously believed to be in the range of 98%, is actually lower. False-positive study findings are extremely rare, but the incidence of false-negative results of oral cholecystography in persons with strongly suggestive clinical symptoms and signs of gallbladder disease does not permit the complete exclusion with confidence of the presence of cholelithiasis and particularly small calculi.

Ultrasonographic study of the gallbladder may be difficult in obese patients when the gallbladder occupies a high position (under the ribs) or when it is overlapped by gas. Ultrasonic nonvisualization in a fasting patient can occur when the gallbladder is thickened and contracted from chronic cholecystitis or when its lumen is filled by calculi or neoplasm rather than by liquid bile. Biliary sludge, generally recognized on ultrasound as a layer of low-amplitude, nonshadowing echoes in the dependent portion of the gallbladder, may occasionally give misleading pseudotumoral appearance of neoplasm (pseudotumor).[16]

Cholecystosonography is used as an emergency procedure in the study of acute cholecystitis.[17] The demonstration of gallstones in association with edematous thickening of the gallbladder wall is highly suggestive, but not pathognomonic, of acute cholecystitis. The gallbladder wall may be thickened in ascites and hypoalbuminemia or even when the viscus is contracted. Currently, the preferred method for diagnosis of acute cholecystitis is cholescintigraphy after IV administration of technetium Tc 99m diisopropyl iminodiacetic acid. Visualization of the common bile duct without visualization of the gallbladder is characteristic of acute cholecystitis in such

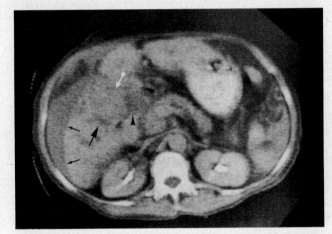

Fig 7. — Carcinoma of gallbladder demonstrated on computed tomography. After intravenous administration of contrast, irregularly lucent gallbladder containing or almost replaced by a mass of increased density is noted (white arrow). Findings are highly suggestive of carcinoma of gallbladder. Ascites is present lateral to liver (small black arrows). Thin, radiolucent rim (large black arrow), representing either fat or ascitic fluid, separates gallbladder from right lobe of liver. Radiolucent image medial to gallbladder is dilated bile duct (arrowhead), probably common hepatic duct (courtesy of Dr Mark Goldman).

studies (Fig 4), although here, too, the possibility of occasional false-positive study findings (caused by chronic cholecystitis) has been reported.[18,19]

In this connection, limitation of space precludes any major discussion of radionuclide cholescintigraphy, which images the gallbladder and the rest of the hepatobiliary system, and consideration of the efficacy of computed tomography (CT).

Cholescintigraphy, using such radionuclide agents as technetium Tc 99m iminodiacetic acid, demonstrates its major (and exciting) role in the diagnosis of acute cholecystitis by its evaluation of patency of the cystic duct quickly, effectively, and, in general, accurately (Fig 4). Other contributions include evaluation of liver function and anatomic delineation (mass lesions may be identified).

Computed tomography may be of major importance in selected instances in the diagnosis of disorders of the gallbladder. However, its limited availability, expense in purchase and operation, relative efficacy (when compared with ultrasound), and use of radiation establish CT as being of limited value in diagnosis of gallbladder disease. However, instances do abound wherein CT and ultrasound are complementary and, on occasion, CT solely (of the imaging modalities) establishes the diagnosis (see Figs 5 through 7 for examples of special instances in which CT was diagnostic).[20]

For a detailed evaluation of noncalculous lesions (eg, small polypoid masses, hyperplastic cholecystosis including adenomyomata or Rokitansky-Aschoff sinuses or both), cholecystography remains a superior diagnostic modality to ultrasonography. The assessment of medical therapy for cholesterol calculi, ie, the determination of size of calculi, is also easier with oral cholecystography.[6] As a primary procedure for detection of gallstones, oral cholecystography (the Graham-Cole test) is gradually being displaced by ultrasound but remains an important complementary study. The Graham-Cole test has, however, remained the cornerstone for the highly accurate diagnosis of disorders of the gallbladder for well over half a century and still retains its importance in many instances despite the introduction of and highly effective use of ultrasonography.

## Conclusion

Radiological examination of the gallbladder served as the ``gold standard'' in the diagnosis of gallbladder disease for 50 years. Few diagnostic modalities have enjoyed the complete confidence of the medical profession for so long a period. Given the widespread prevalence of gallbladder disease, it is most appropriate for THE JOURNAL to honor the epochal manuscript by Graham and Cole written in 1924. These pioneers of an outstanding achievement are appropriately honored by their contribution being designated a LANDMARK ARTICLE in JAMA's centennial series.

The pharmacologic principles, the methodology of the examination, and the problems in interpretation in modern oral cholecystography are briefly described. While radiological examinations of the gallbladder are now being increasingly replaced by ultrasonography (and, in some special instances, by radionuclide scanning and CT), oral cholecystography still remains a valuable complementary procedure in difficult cases.

*Sic transit gloria mundi.*

## References

1. Graham EA, Cole WH: Roentgenologic examination of the gallbladder. Preliminary report of a new method utilizing the intravenous injection of tetrabromphenolphthalein. *JAMA* 1924;82:613-614.

2. Shapiro JH, Stern WZ, Jacobson HG: Oral cholecystography: A review of techniques. *AJR* 1959;82:1003-1010.

3. Lasser EC: Pharmacodynamics of biliary contrast media. *Radiat Clin North Am* 1966;4:511-519.

4. Berk RN, Leopold GR: Present status of imaging of the gallbladder. *Invest Radiol* 1978;13:477-489.

5. Rosenbaum HD: An evaluation of oral cholecystography. *JAMA* 1974;229:76-79.

6. Berk RN: The biliary tract. Refresher course at annual meeting of American Roentgen Ray Society, San Francisco, March 1981.

7. Meyers MA, O'Donohue N: The Mercedes-Benz sign: Insight into the dynamics of formation and disappearance of gallstones. *AJR* 1973;119:63-70.

8. Jacobson HG, Shapiro JH, Stern WZ, et al: Positional relationship of the gallbladder and hepatic flexure. *Am J Digest Dis* 1956;1:294-300.

9. Muhletaler CA, Gerlock AJ, Amberg JR, et al: Radiographic appearance of the nonabsorbed (unconjugated) and conjugated sodium tyropanoate (bilopaque) in the bowel. *Invest Radiol* 1982;17:506-509.

10. Banner P, Bleshman MH, Speckman JM: Persistent gallbladder opacification after iopanic acid cholecystography: Diagnostic implications for acalculous cholecystitis. *AJR* 1979;132:51-54.

11. Bloom AA, Stachenfeld R: Diabetic cholecystomegaly. *JAMA* 1969;208:357-359.

12. Ochsner SF: Solitary polypoid lesions of the gallbladder. *Radiat Clin North Am* 1966;4:501-510.

13. Jutras JA, Levesque HP: Adenomyoma and adenomyomatosis of the gallbladder. *Radiat Clin North Am* 1966;4:483-500.

14. Wise RE: *Intravenous Cholangiography.* Springfield, Ill, Charles C Thomas Publisher, 1962.

15. Schein CJ, Stern WZ, Jacobson HG: *The Common Bile Duct.* Springfield, Ill, Charles C Thomas Publisher, 1966.

16. Fakhry J: Sonography of tumefactive biliary sludge. *AJR* 1982;139:717-719.

17. Cooperberg P, Golding RH: Advances in ultrasonography of the gallbladder and biliary tract. *Radiat Clin North Am* 1982;20:611-633.

18. Schuman WP, Mack LA, Rudd TG, et al: Evaluation of acute right upper quadrant pain: Sonography and 99m Tc-PIPIDA cholescintigraphy. *AJR* 1982;139:61-64.

19. Weissmann HS, Frank MS, Bernstein LH, et al: Rapid and accurate diagnosis of acute cholecystitis with 99m Tc-HIDA cholescintigraphy. *AJR* 1979;132:523-528.

20. Toombs BD, Sandler CM, Conoley PM: Computed tomography of the nonvisualizing gallbladder. *J Comput Assist Tomogr* 1981;5:164-168.

April 25, 1925
(*JAMA* 1925;84:1243-1250)

## Chapter 20

# Tularemia*

### Edward Francis, M.D.

Surgeon, United States Public Health Service
Washington, D. C.

Tularemia occurs in nature as a very fatal bacteremia of various rodents (especially rabbits) and is due to *Bacterium tularense;* it is transmissible to man as an accidental infection by the bite of an infected blood-sucking insect or tick, or by the lodgment on his hands of the blood or internal organs of an infected rodent, as in the case of market men, cooks, hunters or laboratory workers.

Among the few diseases of man that have been discovered in the last fifteen years is tularemia. It is the only disease of man that has been elucidated from beginning to end by American investigators alone. These investigators have worked in widely separated states, and in most instances each made his first contribution while in ignorance of the work of the others.

The first observations of each were characterized by the nature of the work for which he was especially trained; thus, a serologist first noted the presence of antitularense amboceptors in his own blood after a febrile attack, and in the blood of his attendant while dissecting infected rodents in his laboratory. A clinician first described the symptoms and course of the disease in a group of six cases occurring in his practice, which he differentiated as due to the bite of a blood-sucking fly found on horses. Finally, a bacteriologist isolated the causative organism from a human case in which the site of infection was the eye.

In consequence of these circumstances, a variety of names or synonyms sprang up, according to the conditions under which the disease was first encountered by each, and we find plaguelike disease of rodents, deer-fly fever, *Bacillus tularense* infection of the eye, rabbit fever and glandular type of tick fever.

### SYNONYMS AND HISTORY

*Plaguelike Disease of Rodents.*—McCoy,[1] in 1911, described what he called "a plaguelike disease of rodents," prevalent among the California ground squirrels but first observed in squirrels received from Tulare County, Calif. McCoy and Chapin,[2] in 1911, discovered the causative organism of the disease and named it *Bacterium tularense.*

McCoy and Chapin, in 1912, reported complement fixation and agglutination of *Bacterium tularense* by the serum of Chapin and of a laboratory attendant, both of whom were extensively engaged in handling or dissecting infected rodents in the laboratory.

It is a matter of record that shortly previous to testing his own serum in 1911, Dr. Chapin had a febrile attack which kept him off duty for twenty-eight days. In the light of present knowledge it seems certain that what to McCoy and Chapin was a puzzling circumstance (the presence of antitularense amboceptors in the serums of two laboratory workers) was the first proof on record of two unrecognized human cases of tularemia identified serologically.

*Deer-Fly Fever.*—In Utah, the disease in man was for several years popularly known as "deer-fly fever" owing to the belief that the infection was due to the bite of the blood-sucking fly *Chrysops discalis,* commonly found on horses. This belief found expression in a paper published by Pearse,[3] in 1911, in which he described six cases, which constitute the first reported human cases of tularemia differentiated clinically.

---

*The disease is named tularemia on account of the presence in the blood of the causative organism, Bacterium tularense. This organism was so named by McCoy and Chapin, who discovered it in 1912 as the cause of a fatal epidemic among the ground squirrels in Tulare County, Calif. Tulare County was so named because that region was once covered with extensive marshy beds of the reed tule, a large variety of bulrush.

1. McCoy, G. W.: A Plaguelike Disease of Rodents, Bull. 43, Hyg. Lab., U. S. P. H. S., April, 1911.

2. McCoy, G. W., and Chapin, C. W.: Bacterium Tularense, the Cause of a Plaguelike Disease of Rodents, Bull. 53, Hyg. Lab., U. S. P. H. S., January, 1912; Further Observations on a Plaguelike Disease of Rodents with a Preliminary Note on the Causative Agent Bacterium Tularense, J. Infect. Dis. 10: 61-72, 1912.

3. Pearse, R. A.: Insect Bites, Northwest Med., March, 1911.

Belief in the agency of the deer-fly was crystallized into demonstration, in 1919 and 1920, when I[4] isolated *Bacterium tularense* from seven human cases and seventeen jack rabbits in Utah, and named the disease tularemia; Mayne and I[5] proved the deer-fly *Chrysops discalis* to be a transmitter of the infection in laboratory animals.

So slow had been the diffusion of printed knowledge on this subject from California to Utah, or from Utah to California, that it required ten years for the identity of the California rodent disease and the Utah human disease to become recognized.

*Bacillus Tularense Infection of the Eye* (Vail,[6] 1914); *Bacillus Tularense Conjunctivitis* (Sattler,[7] 1915); *Conjunctivitis Tularensis* (Lamb,[8] 1917).—Three cases of tularemia occurred in the practices of three ophthalmic surgeons of Cincinnati. The bacteriologic diagnosis in these three eye cases was made by Wherry and Lamb,[9] who isolated *Bacterium tularense* on culture medium from guinea-pigs into which eye scrapings had been injected. They also isolated the organism from two dead wild rabbits collected in nature near the residence of Sattler's patient.

Vail's case is the first human case of tularemia on record to be diagnosed bacteriologically.

*Rabbit Fever.*—A man (E. N.) working in the Washington, D. C., market went to his physician, Dr. J. Lawn Thompson, in 1921, for treatment for what he informed the physician was "rabbit fever," adding that "rabbit fever" was well known among market men. This patient's serum agglutinated *Bacterium tularense* in a dilution of 1:320 at the Hygienic Laboratory. This was the first case of tularemia to be reported for the eastern United States.[10]

*Glandular Type of Tick Fever.*—Dr. H. E. Lamb of Gooding, Idaho, in a paper read before the South Idaho District Medical Association, in April, 1923, used the phrase "glandular type of tick fever" to describe cases which were encountered in practice by himself and Dr. J. H. Cromwell. At that time they considered these cases as a type of Rocky Mountain spotted fever, and added that about 10 per cent. of their cases of "tick fever" (fever following a tick bite) had been of the glandular type without eruptions; that the glands in some cases suppurated, while in others they did not, and that these patients were very sick and had fever for several weeks.

The interpretation is justified that these cases of the glandular type of tick fever were tularemia, especially since the serum of a similar case sent to the Hygienic Laboratory, in 1924, by Dr. R. M. Johnson of Billings, Mont., agglutinated *Bacterium tularense* in a dilution of 1:320.

Parker, Spencer and I,[11] reporting in May, 1924, had demonstrated the infection in the common wood tick of Montana, *Dermacentor andersoni* Stiles, collected in nature from vegetation, and in the heart blood of a snowshoe rabbit; also in ticks collected from the horse, mountain goat, woodchuck, mountain rat and Columbian ground squirrel.

## GEOGRAPHIC DISTRIBUTION IN MAN AND RODENTS

So far as is now known, tularemia is confined to the United States. It has been authentically reported from thirteen states and the District of Columbia, extending from the Pacific to the Atlantic coast—California, Utah, Wyoming, Idaho, Colorado, Ohio, Indiana, Tennessee, North Carolina, Montana, New Mexico, Virginia, West Virginia and the District of Columbia.

*California.*—McCoy and Chapin, in 1911 and 1912, described tularemia as a plaguelike fatal epizootic of the California ground squirrel. Although the infection has prevailed among those squirrels until the present time, no human case has been reported from California other than two laboratory cases contracted while the patients were dissecting infected rodents in the U. S. Public Health Service laboratory at San Francisco in 1911. The blood serums of these two patients gave complement fixation and agglutination of *Bacterium tularense*.

*Utah, Wyoming, Idaho and Colorado.*—There has existed in Utah, at least since 1908, a human disease known locally as deer-fly fever. What I believe to be the first clinical reference to human cases of tularemia is contained in a paper read before the Utah State Medical Association, Salt Lake City, Oct. 3, 1910, by Dr. R. A. Pearse,[3] Brigham City, Utah. Dr. Pearse refers to six cases, which occurred in the month of August, caused by the bites of a fly, on the exposed parts of the body (neck, ear, cheek, wrist, ankle and hand). After an incubation of from two to five days, the glands that drained the bitten area became markedly swollen and went on to suppuration in about half the cases. In all the cases the site of the fly bite progressed from a red infiltration to complete breaking down of the tissues and sloughing, resulting in a punched-out circular ulcer about one-fourth inch in diameter and one-eighth inch in depth. Most of the patients had severe chills during the incubation period. The temperatures ranged from 98 to 104 F. The duration of the disease was from one to four weeks, and the severity varied "from slight malaise to death."

In 1919 and 1920, I[4] studied seven cases of deer-fly fever near Fillmore, Millard County, Utah, and found them positive for tularemia, clinically, culturally and serologically. These cases occurred in June, July and August during the seasonal prevalence of the fly *Chrysops discalis*. The sites of the fly bites were the neck, temple, ear, and posterior surface of the lower third of the thigh. In all cases, suppuration occurred in the glands draining the bitten area. All patients had fever; one died on the twenty-sixth day of illness. I heard of perhaps two dozen other cases in the general community in which I worked. From seventeen jack-rabbits, sick or dead, in the community I isolated *Bacterium tularense*, thus establishing the great resorvoir of infection.

Dr. C. E. Harris[12] of Basin, Wyo., published a paper, in 1924, giving his experience with the disease. In a personal communication, Dr. Harris informed me that he and Dr. E. W. Croft have seen about 200 cases of tularemia in the past few years.

4. Francis, Edward: Deer-Fly Fever; a Disease of Man of Hitherto Unknown Etiology, Pub. Health Rep. **34:** 2061-2062 (Sept. 12) 1919; The Occurrence of Tularemia in Nature, as a Disease of Man, Pub. Health Rep. **36:** 1731-1738 (July 29) 1921.

5. Francis, Edward; and Mayne, Bruce: Experimental Transmission of Tularemia by Flies of the Species Chrysops Discalis, Pub. Health Rep. **36:** 1738-1746 (July 29) 1921.

6. Vail, D. T.: Bacillus Tularense Infection of the Eye, Ophth. Rec. **23:** 487, 1914.

7. Sattler, Robert: Bacillus Tularense Conjunctivitis, Arch. Ophth. **44:** 265, 1915.

8. Lamb, F. W.: Conjunctivitis Tularensis, with Report of a Case, Ophth. Rec. **26:** 221-226 (May) 1917.

9. Wherry, W. B., and Lamb, B. H.: Infection of Man with Bacterium Tularense, J. Infect. Dis. **15:** 331-340, 1914. Wherry, W. B.: A New Bacterial Disease of Rodents Transmissible to Man, Pub. Health Rep. **29:** 3387-3390, 1914. Wherry, W. B., and Lamb, B. H.: Discovery of Bacterium Tularense in Wild Rabbits, and the Danger of Its Transfer to Man, J. A. M. A. **63:** 2041 (Dec. 5) 1914.

10. Lake, G. C., and Francis, Edward: Six Cases of Tularemia Occurring in Laboratory Workers, Bull. 130, Hyg. Lab., U. S. P. H. S., 1922, p. 81.

11. Parker, R. R.; Spencer, R. R., and Francis, Edward: Tularemia Infection in Ticks of the Species Dermacentor Andersoni Stiles, in the Bitterroot Valley, Montana, Pub. Health Rep. **39:** 1057-1073 (May 9) 1924.

12. Harris, C. E.: Tularemia, Med. Sentinel **32:** 6 (Jan.) 1924.

Personal communications have been received from a number of physicians; to these I shall refer briefly. Dr. T. B. Beatty, state health commissioner of Utah, informed me of a fly-bitten patient whom he had in 1914 near Tremonton, Utah. Dr. R. B. Stevens of Fillmore, Utah, saw eight cases in 1919. Dr. Charles Stuart Moody of Menan, Idaho, reported three cases in 1923. Dr. D. Homer Junkin of Idaho Falls, Idaho, wrote that fourteen cases were reported by the Idaho Falls Medical Society, in October, 1921, of which he had five. July 25, 1924, Dr. Junkin forwarded to the Hygienic Laboratory a specimen of serum taken on the twenty-first day of illness from a fly-bitten patient; this serum agglutinated *Bacterium tularense* in a dilution of 1:160.

*Ohio.*—Three cases of tularemia in which the site of infection was the left eye occurred in the practices of three ophthalmic surgeons of Cincinnati, named above. A peculiar coincidence is that all three of these patients had the infection in the left eye. In none of them was there any involvement of the right eye or of the glands of the right side of the head and neck. The only records of eye cases of tularemia other than these three are in the patient of Dr. F. C. Hodges reported below from West Virginia, and the cases mentioned under Arizona.

CASE 1.—The first human case of tularemia on record to receive bacteriologic confirmation was one that occurred in 1913 in the ophthalmic practice of Dr. Vail. The patient applied for treatment, November 24, having been ill three days, and presented ten discrete ulcers of the conjunctiva of the left eye; there were fever and glandular enlargement on the left side, involving the preauricular and anterior cervical regions; the clinical diagnosis was glandular farcy, or glanders. Scrapings from a conjunctival ulcer were injected intraperitoneally into a male guinea-pig, by Wherry and Lamb, and, after several animal passages, *Bacterium tularense* was isolated from guinea-pigs on coagulated egg medium. How the ocular infection occurred is unknown; the patient was a meat cutter in a cheap restaurant; presumably, he handled infected rabbits.

CASE 2.—The second case was likewise one with unilateral involvement of the left conjunctiva, and occurred in 1914 in the ophthalmic practice of Dr. Sattler. The patient was the wife of a farmer residing on the M farm in Ohio County, southern Indiana, and applied to Dr. Sattler for treatment within twenty-four hours after the onset of symptoms in the left eye; he found her with a temperature of 104 F. and with seven very small ulcers of the left conjunctiva. The next day there was excessive prostration, high fever and painful glandular enlargement of the preauricular, cervical and submaxillary regions of the left side. October 9, some of the secretion of the left eye was injected intraperitoneally, by Wherry and Lamb, into a guinea-pig, from which *Bacterium tularense* was isolated on coagulated egg yolk medium.

How the ocular infection occurred remains a speculative assumption, but the fact remains that the patient had prepared rabbit meat for the table, and that Wherry and Lamb isolated *Bacterium tularense* on culture medium from guinea-pigs inoculated with material obtained from two wild rabbits found dead in November, 1914, 4 miles from the M farm on which the patient resided.

CASE 3.—The third case was also one in which the site of infection was the left conjunctiva, and occurred in 1916 in the ophthalmic practice of Dr. Lamb. The patient was a young colored girl, who, two days before the onset of illness, had prepared some rabbits for dinner. November 15, she had a chill and headache, and on the following day had pain and swelling in the left eye; the conjunctiva of the lower lid was the site of six or seven small, deep ulcers, filled with necrotic plugs; the left preauricular gland was enlarged and tender. November 20, four small ulcers appeared on the conjunctiva of the upper lid, and the glands of the neck were exquisitely tender. November 16, pus from the eye was inoculated intraperitoneally, by Wherry and Lamb, into a guinea-pig, from which *Bacterium tularense* was isolated on coagulated egg yolk medium. The preauricular gland proceeded to suppuration.

*Indiana.*—The patient in Case 2, reported from Ohio, resided at the time of her infection in Ohio County, Ind. Two cotton tail rabbits found dead 4 miles from her residence were found by Wherry and Lamb to be infected with *Bacterium tularense.*

*Washington, D. C.*—Three cases have occurred in Washington following the dressing of rabbits offered for sale in the local market.

CASE 4.—E. N., a patient of Dr. J. Lawn Thompson, was a market man who, in November and December, 1921, worked at a rabbit stand, skinning rabbits and pulling out the internal organs. At this time he suffered an attack of fever and prostration, accompanied by a marked painful enlargement of the axillary glands of one arm, which continued for a month but did not suppurate. Strangely, he diagnosed his own case, calling it "rabbit fever," and stated that the condition was well known among market men. The physician did not suspect the true condition of his patient until six months later, June 29, 1922, when his blood serum was sent to the Hygienic Laboratory for agglutination of *Bacterium tularense;* agglutination was complete in a dilution of 1:320.

CASE 5.—Mrs. C. S., a patient of Dr. J. Russell Verbrycke,[13] Dec. 8, 1923, dressed two rabbits bought in the Washington market and fried them for supper; they were eaten by the family of four. December 13, she had a sudden onset of fever and headache. December 23, the patient still had fever, was jaundiced, and manifested a slight resistance of the upper abdomen on both sides, which led to the diagnosis of acute choledochitis and cholangeitis, and it was decided to operate. December 24, the gallbladder was exposed but gave no evidence of disease. December 30, the blood serum, collected December 29, was sent to the Hygienic Laboratory and fund to agglutinate *Bacterium tularense* in a dilution of 1:80. The patient died on the night of December 30, on the seventh day after operation and the eighteenth day of illness.

Microscopic sections of the patient's liver and spleen showed the typical lesions of tularemia. *Bacterium tularense* was recovered on culture medium from guinea-pigs, rabbits and white mice inoculated with a piece of the patient's spleen.

CASE 6.—Mr. A., a patient of Dr. William J. G. Thomas, was a market man who, in November and December, 1923, was engaged at a rabbit counter, dressing and selling rabbits. About December 1, he became ill with fever and prostration, but persisted at work under difficulty until Feb. 11, 1924, when he first consulted his physician. At this time he presented an enlarged gland in his right epitrochlear region, and three enlarged glands in the right axilla. Blood serum, collected, February 11, was tested at the Hygienic Laboratory and found to agglutinate *Bacterium tularense* in a dilution of 1:320.

*Tularemia in Market Rabbits.*—I[14] examined the dressed rabbits in the Washington, D. C., market for evidence of tularemia in the months of November, December and January months embracing the "open season," at which time wild rabbits are unprotected by the game laws and consequently are offered for sale in large numbers. In these investigations, examination was confined to the liver, because this organ was the most readily obtainable of the three (spleen, liver and lymph glands) in which the lesions are readily seen by gross

13. Verbrycke, J. R.: Tularemia, with Report of a Fatal Case Simulating Cholangeitis, with Postmortem Report, J. A. M. A. **82:** 1577-1581 (May 17) 1924.

14. Francis, Edward: Tularemia in the Washington, D. C., Market, Pub. Health Rep. **38:** 1391-1396 (June 22) 1923; Mil. Surgeon **53:** 164 (Aug.) 1923.

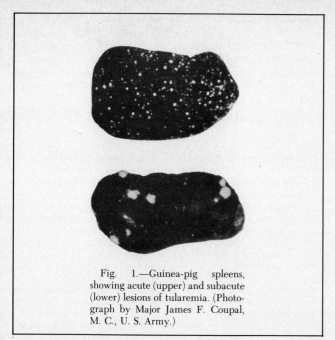

Fig. 1.—Guinea-pig spleens, showing acute (upper) and subacute (lower) lesions of tularemia. (Photograph by Major James F. Coupal, M. C., U. S. Army.)

examination. In December, 1922, 914 livers from the Washington market were examined at the Hygienic Laboratory, of which seven were studded over with small foci of necrosis suggesting tularemia. These seven were injected separately into guinea-pigs, causing death on about the fifth day with typical lesions in the lymph glands, liver and spleen (Fig. 1) from which cultures of *Bacterium tularense* were obtained. Two of the seven livers were from rabbits shipped from Tennessee; the source of the other five was not determined. In December, 1923, one infected liver was similarly obtained from the market, having arrived from Tennessee. In December, 1924, again, one infected liver was obtained, and this rabbit, likewise, had been shipped from Tennessee.

*Tennessee.*—In the account of tularemia in the Washington market, it is shown that the places of shipment of two infected rabbits found in December, 1922, were Greenville, Tenn., and Shouns, Tenn.; the place of shipment of one found in December, 1923, and another found in December, 1924, was Greenville, Tenn.

*North Carolina.*—Dr. Lucius G. Gage of Charlotte, N. C., reported[10] that his patient (Mrs. W.), while cleaning some quail, Dec. 27, 1921, stuck a sharp point of a wing bone into the middle finger of her left hand, after which she turned to a pan full of rabbits and manipulated them. This was followed by an attack of fever, which lasted about a month and was accompanied by suppuration of the glands at the elbow, adenitis of the axilla, and marked scarring at the site of infection on the finger. The patient's serum was submitted to the Hygienic Laboratory in May, 1922, and found to agglutinate *Bacterium tularense*.

*Montana.*—Parker, Spencer and I,[11] in 1924, by investigations made in the Public Health Service Laboratory located at Hamilton, Mont., demonstrated the infection in the common wood ticks of Montana, *Dermacentor andersoni* Stiles. These ticks were collected from the horse, the mountain goat, the woodchuck, the mountain rat and the Columbian ground squirrel; also in unfed ticks collected from vegetation, and from the heart blood of a snowshoe rabbit. Tularemia is evidently present in the rodents of Montana, and the wood tick transmits the infection among rodents, and to man. A case of human infection due to tick bite was reported in 1924 by Dr. R. M. Johnson of Billings, Mont.; his patient came from near the southern boundary of Montana, was bitten on the leg by a tick, and three weeks later (July 5, 1924) his serum was forwarded to

the Hygienic Laboratory and found to agglutinate *Bacterium tularense* in a dilution of 1:320.

*New Mexico.*—Ten cases occurred during the first week of August, 1924, in the vicinity of Carlsbad, N. M., and were investigated by Dr. T. B. H. Anderson of the U. S. Public Health Service. The investigation was made at the request of the Bureau of Biological Survey, U. S. Department of Agriculture, on account of reports received in that bureau that jack-rabbits were dying about Carlsbad in numbers sufficient to suggest tularemia.

Dr. Anderson reported that the onset of illness in these ten cases occurred about two or three days after the patients had cut up jack rabbits for chicken and hog feed and for fish bait, in a community where there was a heavy mortality among jack-rabbits.

He reported that the symptoms were a sudden onset with chills, fever and general body pains; that about two or three days later, swelling and tenderness of the glands draining the infected points on the fingers were noted, and were followed within a couple of days by one or more ulcers on the fingers. Enlargement of the epitrochlear or axillary glands was noted in all cases; six of these proceeded to suppuration. One patient who, previous to and during his attack of tularemia, was the subject of a chronic heart lesion, died at the end of the fourth week of illness. The clinical diagnosis of anthrax had been incorrectly made, in these cases as the result, probably, of the severity of the ulcers at the site of infection on the hands. Against a clinical diagnosis of anthrax one should have noted the presence of suppuration of the axillary glands, which does not occur in anthrax, and the fact that anthrax does not occur in nature as a fatal disease of jack-rabbits.

Blood serum was taken from two patients and forwarded to the Hygienic Laboratory to be tested for agglutination of *Bacterium tularense*, with the result that one serum taken forty-four days after the onset of illness caused complete agglutination in a dilution of 1:1,280, while the other serum, taken forty-nine days after the onset of illness, caused complete agglutination in a dilution of 1:320.

*Virginia.*—CASE 7.—The first case to be reported from Virginia was that of Mrs. A. M., a patient of Dr. Turner S. Shelton of South Richmond, who states[15] that three weeks before the onset of illness his patient stuck a needle in her finger, which remained sore, and that eight days before sickness began, she dressed a rabbit which the cat had caught. She first felt ill, Nov. 23, 1924, and on the next day had a chill followed by a temperature of 104 F., with nausea and vomiting. In about five days, the case resembled typhoid fever; there was some tenderness of the axillary glands and soreness of the right index finger. The blood culture and the Widal test were negative. December 5, her blood serum was sent to the Hygienic Laboratory, and it was found to agglutinate *Bacterium tularense* in a dilution of 1:160; a second sample of serum, December 17, agglutinated the organism in a dilution of 1:2,560. The titer, December 26, was 1:1,280, and, February 10, was 1:640.

CASE 8.—C. W., a patient of Dr. O. C. Brunk of Richmond, Nov. 27, 1924, went hunting, and during the day his hands became badly scratched by briars; at the end of the day he dressed five rabbits. On the night of November 29 he had a hard chill, and on the next day his physician found him with a temperature of 103 F., severe headache, and pains in the back and epigastrium; and on the dorsal surface of each thumb there was an area of infection, with signs of pus beneath the scab. During the subsequent ten days his temperature was irregular, at times 99.5 and again 103 F.; he complained of pains in the arms, and the axilla of the right arm showed definite glandular

15. Shelton, T. S.: Tularemia, J. A. M. A. **84:** 1019 (April 4) 1925.

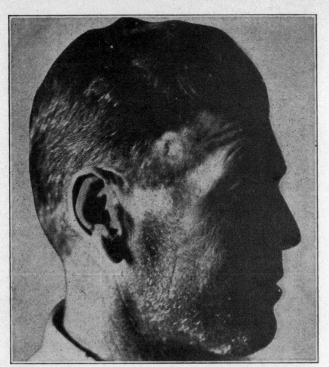

Fig. 2.—Appearance of patient after recovery from tularemia; bitten on temple by the fly Chrysops discalis.

enlargement. Throughout his illness there was great prostration and frequent sweats. The infection on the thumbs resulted in two punched-out ulcers. After eleven days his fever subsided, but he still complained of being very tired, on the slightest exertion. By December 23, the patient seemed to have recovered entirely. December 18, the patient's blood serum was sent to the Hygienic Laboratory; it agglutinated *Bacterium tularense* in a dilution of 1:320.

*Tularemia in Rabbits.*—These two cases of tularemia in man point plainly to infection of the rabbits about Richmond, Va., one patient having dressed a rabbit which the cat had caught and the other having dressed five rabbits at the end of a day's hunt.

*West Virginia.*—CASE 9.—The first case to be recognized in West Virginia was Mr. C. W., a patient of Dr. F. C. Hodges of Huntington. The patient was a dresser of game and chickens in the Huntington market. The first day of the "open season" for rabbits was Nov. 15, 1924, and on this date rabbits were first offered for sale in the market and were first dressed by the patient. November 20, the patient called a physician on account of a red papule on the middle finger of the left hand; the second, third and fourth fingers were swollen; the lymph glands in the left axilla were enlarged and tender; the temperature was 103 F., and continued high for seven days, accompanied by delirium; the patient was confined to bed for thirty-six days, during which time the left axillary glands suppurated and discharged pus; "lumps" appeared on the skin of the left arm and forearm, and one appeared over the dorsal region of the spine; greenish pus, obtained by incision of the "lumps," was free from organisms in smears and repeatedly failed to give growth when inoculated to glucose broth, glucose agar and Sabouraud's medium.

Early in the disease there was an ulcerated condition of both lids of both eyes, which gradually healed after two weeks.

March 20, 1925 (four months after the onset of the illness), the temperature was 99.3 F., pulse 100, red blood cells 4,208,000, white cells 12,900; hemoglobin 68 per cent. and blood Wassermann reaction negative. Blood serum collected March 16, 1925, and tested at the Hygienic Laboratory,

agglutinated *Bacterium tularense* in a dilution of 1:640.

*Arizona.*—The following letter, brown with age, was recently found in a forgotten file by Dr. Frederick G. Novy of Ann Arbor, Mich., who marked it "tularemia" and sent it to me. In the light of present knowledge, it constitutes the very first description of cases of tularemia, of which three were eye infections.

Phoenix, Territory of Arizona, Sept. 19, 1907.

Dr. Frederick G. Novy,
Ann Arbor, Mich.

Dear Doctor:

There have been during the summer several individuals in this locality who have suffered from an infection as a result of skinning and dressing wild rabbits. They were of the so-called "jack" variety. Three of these persons have had their primary lesion in or about the eye. Small abscesses formed in the lids and on the bulbar conjunctiva as well. In one case the cornea was involved. The preauricular gland being involved, as well as the anterior cervical and the submaxillary. At the onset there were chills, profuse sweating and an elevation of temperature of from 2 to 5 degrees, with rapid pulse, lasting several days. The glands suppurated and all were evacuated. In one case a nodular condition of the lids still remains. There were no deaths; in fact, the illness was not profound. In one instance the infection took place in the foot, and others in the hands, etc. The adjacent lymphatics, of course, being involved.

Yours very truly,     ANCIL MARTIN, M.D.

## SYMPTOMS AND COURSE OF TULAREMIA

Case histories and notes have been recorded for forty-nine cases, of which fourteen were caused by fly bite in Utah and Idaho, one was caused by tick bite in Montana; ten patients had cut up jack-rabbits for hog feed, chicken feed and fish bait in New Mexico; ten had dressed wild cottontail rabbits for food in Ohio, Washington, D. C., North Carolina, Virginia and West Virginia, and fourteen were laboratory workers who had performed necropsy on infected guinea-pigs or rabbits in laboratories in San Francisco, Washington, D. C., Hamilton, Mont., and London, England.

Two clinical types of symptoms are encountered in analyzing these cases.

Of thirty-five cases in which the patients were fly-bitten, tick-bitten or hand cut up jack-rabbits or dressed cottontail rabbits, thirty-three were of the glandular type, with enlarged glands and an evident local site of infection; in only two of the thirty-five was there a record of absence of enlarged glands or absence of a local site of infection.

Fourteen cases of infection of laboratory workers were free from enlarged glands or local site of infection, and to the clinician they simulated typhoid fever and were therefore of the typhoid type.

*Glandular Type.*—Incubation: The incubation period has not been determined with certainty except in eight cases, in which it was two, two, two, three, five, five, eight and nine days, with an average of four and one-half days. Considering the probable incubation period in other cases, I would put the most common incubation period at from two to five days.

Onset and Symptoms: The onset is sudden, often occurring while the patient is at work, and is manifested by headache, chills, bodily pains, vomiting, prostration and fever. In cases which are caused by fly bites or tick bites, or in which there is some other evident site of infection, contracted from manipulating the internal organs of wild rabbits, the patients complain, within forty-eight hours after the onset, of pain in the area of the lymph glands which drain the site of infection; and on examination these glands are found to be tender and slightly

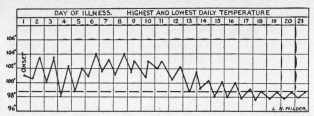

Fig. 3.—Temperature in a human case of tularemia (laboratory infection).

enlarged; only the regional glands are involved and not those of other parts of the body. The glandular pain precedes by about twenty-four hours any definite reference by the patient to the site of infection, which now becomes manifest as a painful, swollen, inflamed papule, which speedily breaks down, liberating a necrotic core or plug and leaving an ulcer about one-fourth inch in diameter, with raised edges and having a punched-out appearance (Fig 2). The fever lasts from two to three weeks, and may reach a height of 104 F.; there may be a transient remission to about normal on the third and fourth days, after which the temperature rises again and does not fall to normal until the end of two or three weeks (Fig. 3); or there may be daily remissions, almost to normal, suggesting a septic type of fever.

There is redness of the skin overlying the enlarged and tender lymph glands, and this redness may be continuous to the site of infection, or red streaks may be visible on an extremity. In about half the cases the lymph glands proceed to suppuration, and after the inflammation has subsided an abscess ruptures through a soft, thin spot in the skin. In the other half of the cases the glands do not break down but remain hard, palpable and rather tender for two or three months, gradually returning to normal.

The normal blood count is not sufficiently changed in any particular to be of diagnostic importance, although in many cases the leukocyte count has been somewhat increased.

Agglutinins for *Bacterium tularense* are absent from the blood during the first week of illness, but appear in the second week, reaching their height at the end of the third or fourth week. They then begin to decline, but persist in considerable titer for several years. Agglutination is a point of great diagnostic value and makes possible the differentiation of tularemia from typhoid fever and other infections during the febrile period.

Convalescence is slow; it is rare for a patient to be at work again at the end of a month; usually the second month is spent lying about the house, owing to weakness on exertion, and during the third month only half-time work is performed. The patients finally recover without evident complications, although some have not entirely returned to normal for six months or even a year.

Death is rare, and yet, of seven cases which I studied in Utah, one patient, who was fly-bitten on the right side of the neck, died on the twenty-sixth day of illness with a complicating pneumonia of the right upper lobe. Of ten cases reported by Anderson, from Carlsbad, N. M., one patient, who previous to and during his attack of tularemia had a chronic heart lesion, died at about the end of the fourth week of illness. Of three cases reported from Washington, D. C., one patient died on the eighteenth day of illness and on the seventh day after an exploratory abdominal incision. With better recognition of the disease by physicians, some deaths, which otherwise would be ascribed to typhoid fever or septic infection, may be recorded as due to tularemia.

*Typhoid Type.*—Laboratory Infections: Twelve of fourteen cases of tularemia occurring in laboratory workers who had performed necropsy on infected guinea-pigs or rabbits did not show any evident site of infection or enlargement of lymph glands, but in all other respects the symptoms were the same as those of the glandular type. Two English patients showed moderate involvement of the cervical glands. These cases occurred in four laboratories, located at San Francisco; Washington, D. C.; London, England, and Hamilton, Mont.

McCoy and Chapin,[2] in 1912, made the first reference to laboratory cases of this infection. They reported complement fixation and agglutination of *Bacterium tularense* by the serums of Chapin and a laboratory attendant, both of whom were extensively engaged in handling or dissecting infected rodents in the laboratory at San Francisco.

The Public Health Service records show that ninety-four days after beginning work with tularemia animals in the laboratory, Dr. Chapin was granted twenty-eight days' leave of absence, beginning March 1, 1911, on account of sickness, the nature of which could not be diagnosed. The illness was accompanied by fever, was unaccompanied by glandular enlargement or other local lesion, and incapacitated this officer for all duty. No absence from duty on the part of the laboratory attendant can now be recalled by Dr. Chapin. Shortly after returning to duty, Dr. Chapin discovered the positive findings in his own serum and in the serum of his attendant. In the light of present knowledge it seems certain that what to McCoy and Chapin was a puzzling circumstance (the presence of antitularense amboceptors in the serums of two laboratory workers) was the proof of two unrecognized human cases of tularemia identified serologically.

Lake and I[16] reported that all six men who, during 1919, 1920 and 1921, were intimately connected with the laboratory investigations of tularemia which the Public Health Service was conducting, contracted this disease. Such a record of morbidity among investigators of a disease is probably unique in the history of experimental medicine. Fortunately, there were no fatalities. Two of the men contracted the disease in the field laboratory in Utah, where they were compelled to work under primitive conditions; the other four contracted the infection in the Hygienic Laboratory at Washington, D. C. Two of the men were physicians, with years of experience in working with infectious diseases and materials; one was a highly trained scientist, and the other three were experienced laboratory assistants.

Ledingham and Fraser[17] reported that in the Lister Institute of Preventive Medicine, London, England, three of the personnel who were conducting laboratory experiments with the infection in guinea-pigs contracted the disease in 1922. The carrying of the infection by animal passage habitually proved so dangerous that "by a brave discretion" it was given up by the institute. The source of infection in this instance was a culture of *Bacterium tularense* that had been sent to the Lister Institute from the Hygienic Laboratory at Washington, D. C.

In the Public Health Service Laboratory located at Hamilton, Mont., two physicians and one attendant, who performed necropsy on infected animals or removed them from the dissection boards, contracted the disease in 1924. All were well aware of the danger to laboratory workers, and took unusual precautions against infection.

## AGGLUTINATION TESTS

The definite diagnosis of tularemia in fourteen laboratory workers rested finally on the agglutination of *Bacterium tularense* by their blood serum in each

16. Lake, G. C., and Francis, Edward: Six Cases of Tularemia Occurring in Laboratory Workers, Pub. Health Rep. **37:** 392-413 (Feb. 24) 1922.

17. Ledingham, J. C. G., and Fraser, F. E.: Tularemia in Man from Laboratory Infection, Quart. J. Med. **17:** 365-382, 1923-1924.

instance. The fever in each was such as to suggest typhoid, but the only records of positive Widal tests were in two patients who had received three injections of single typhoid vaccine; a slightly positive Widal reaction is recorded in these cases.

The laboratory cases afforded an unusual opportunity to study the early appearance of agglutinins and their long persistence. Both phases of agglutination are shown in the accompanying tables.

## PORTAL OF ENTRY IN LABORATORY WORKERS

Two of three laboratory cases occurring in England gave moderate evidence of pain, tenderness and swelling localized in the cervical glands, but otherwise there was an absence of local lesions.

None of the eleven laboratory cases occurring in America showed any evident site of infection or enlarged

TABLE 1.—*Agglutination Titers of Laboratory Cases for Bacterium Tularense Early in Tularemia*

| Case | Time in Days | Titer 1 to | Case | Time in Days | Titer 1 to |
|---|---|---|---|---|---|
| R. R. P.° | 7 | 0 | R.† | 14 | 10 |
| | 14 | 640 | | 46 | 80 |
| | 21 | 1,280 | | 470 | 320 |
| B.† | 7 | 0 | C. W. P. | 19 | 320 |
| | 14 | 160 | | | |
| | 406 | 160 | R. R. S.° | 21 | 640 |
| | | | | 28 | 1,280 |
| S.† | 6 | 0 | | 200 | 640 |
| | 12 | 40 | | | |
| | 403 | 80 | S. S. M.° | 28 | 1,280 |

°Hamilton, Mont., case.
†Lister Institute case.

glands. It is difficult to account for this absence. The portal of entry of the infection in laboratory workers is unknown. All of them had either performed necropsy on infected animals or removed the animals from the dissection boards. Presumably, infected tissue and blood found lodgment on their hands, and then the infection either penetrated the skin or found its way to the mouth and was swallowed. If it penetrated the skin of the hand, one would expect a local lesion or glandular enlargement of the arm, or both; if it found entrance to the mouth, one might expect glandular enlargement of the neck. To support the view that the infection in these cases penetrated the unbroken skin of the hands, we know that guinea-pigs on the normal skin of which infected spleen juice is placed die acutely of typical tularemia, in the absence of any clipping of the hair or rubbing of the skin or of any possibility that the infection might have gained entrance to the animal's mouth. We know that, in culture mediums, cystin is a requirement of growth of the organism, and that the cystin content of the skin is high; hence the possibility must be considered that the cystin of the skin supplies conditions for growth of the organism and subsequent penetration of the skin.

The mechanism of infection of laboratory workers is discussed by Ledingham and Fraser of England, with special reference to one of their three cases. Their third patient, S., dated his infection from one exposure only,

while performing a necropsy on a chloroformed guinea pig and passing the virus to another. He remembered distinctly that the animal had coughed in his presence during anesthesia. Nine days later the illness set in. This was his sole association with tularemia. The view is expressed that a droplet respiratory infection might explain such cases.

## INSECT TRANSMISSION

The only animals yet found infected in nature are the ground squirrels of California and Utah, and the jack rabbits, snowshoe rabbits and cottontail rabbits of several states, but not domestic rabbits raised in rabbitries. These rodents, which constitute the great reservoir of infection manifest, when dying, the characteristic bacteremia, thus affording the necessary condition for ready transfer by blood-sucking insects and ticks.

Transmission from rabbit to rabbit in nature is by the rabbit tick *Haemaphysalis leporis-palustris* Packard, and by the rabbit louse *Haemodipsus ventricosus* Denny,[18] neither of which bites man, but they transfer the infection throughout the year and perennially from rabbit to rabbit.

Transmission to man is by (1) the blood-sucking fly *Chrysops discalis* (deer-fly)[5] commonly found on horses in Utah and in the adjoining states; this fly, after biting

TABLE 2.—*Titers of Laboratory Cases, Showing the Persistence of Agglutinins in the Blood Serum of Long-Recovered Patients in Washington, D. C.*

| Case | Onset | 1921 | 1922 | 1923 | 1924 | 1925 |
|---|---|---|---|---|---|---|
| G. O. L. | Oct. 23, 1920 | Aug. 5=320 | 6-27=320 | 3-1=160 | 2-22= 80 | 1-31=8 |
| G. W. O. | April 9, 1921 | Aug. 5=160 | 6-27=160 | ........... | 4-16=160 | 1-31=8 |
| C. W. P. | July 17, 1921 | Aug. 5=320 | 6-27=160 | ........... | 4-16= 80 | 1-31=8 |
| E. F. | Aug. 23, 1919 | Jan. 19=100 | 6-29= 40 | 3-1= 40 | 4-15= 40 | 1-31=4 |

an infected rabbit, bites man on an exposed part of the body; (2) the wood tick *Dermacentor andersoni* Stiles, commonly found in Montana and in the adjoining states; the virus is capable of surviving the winter in this tick and of being transmitted from stage to stage as the tick develops.

Under laboratory conditions, transmission has been effected among white mice by the mouse louse *Polyplax serratus* Burm[19] and the common bedbug, *Cimex lectularius;*[20] from guinea-pig to guinea-pig by the biting stable fly *Stomoxys calcitrans;*[21] from ground squirrel to ground squirrel by the squirrel flea *Ceratophyllus acutus.*[1]

18. Francis, Edward; and Lake, G. C.: Experimental Transmission of Tularemia in Rabbits by the Rabbit Louse Haemodipsus Ventricosus (Denny), Pub. Health Rep. 36: 1747-1753 (July 29) 1921.

19. Francis, Edward; and Lake, G. C.: Transmission of Tularemia by the Mouse Louse Polyplax Serratus (Burm), Pub. Health Rep. 37: 96-100 (Jan. 20) 1922.

20. Francis, Edward; and Lake, G. C.: Transmission of Tularemia by the Bedbug, Cimex Lectularius, Pub. Health Rep. 37: 83-95 (Jan. 20) 1922.

21. Wayson, N. E.: Plague and Plaguelike Disease: A Report on Their Transmission by Stomoxys Calcitrans and Musca Domestica, Pub. Health Rep. 29: 3390-3393, 1914.

## NONCONTAGIOUSNESS

No instance has been reported of the spread of the infection from man to man by mere contact or by the bite of insects which previously have bitten a patient. Dr. C. E. Harris, however, reported a case of direct transmission to a mother who, while dressing an ulcer and an opened gland on the neck of her son, pricked her thumb with a safety pin, resulting in a severe infection of the thumb; typical fever and prostration, with rather early suppuration of the epitrochlear and axillary glands, but without red streaks on the arm, followed.

## IMMUNITY

The only instance that has been reported of a second attack in man was in a laboratory worker engaged daily in performing necropsies, without gloves, on laboratory animals in the Hygienic Laboratory, Washington, D. C.[16] The second attack developed two years and five months after the first attack; there was a papule engrafted on a crack on the finger from which *Bacterium tularense* was isolated by guinea-pig inoculation. There was also a lymphadenitis involving the epitrochlear and axillary glands of the same arm, but an absence of fever or other notable constitutional symptoms.

The long persistence of agglutinins in the blood of recovered patients may be an indication of their immunity.

Susceptible laboratory animals (guinea-pigs, rabbits and white mice) have exhibited no evidence of immunity in our laboratory; all have died with the single exception of one rabbit, which survived a severe attack.

## DIAGNOSIS

Knowledge of at least the name of a disease must precede its diagnosis; a physician cannot be expected to diagnose a disease of which he has never heard. Glandular farcy was suspected in the first Cincinnati eye case on account of the glandular enlargements, and led to the inoculation of conjunctival scrapings into a male guinea-pig. Anthrax was suspected in the cases at Carlsbad, N. M., probably on account of the severity of the ulcers on the fingers, and they were so reported in the news items to THE JOURNAL. Typhoid is the diagnosis on the hospital records of a case in Washington, D. C., the temperature chart of which appears in Figure 3; this was a case of laboratory infection in which there was no evident site of infection or glandular enlargement. The suspicion of typhoid fever is common in cases of tularemia, especially of the typhoid type. Septic infection was the physician's diagnosis in a Washington, D. C., market case in which the site of infection was on the finger and was followed by glandular enlargement in the epitrochlear and axillary regions. Cholangeitis was the diagnosis in a Washington, D. C., case which manifested jaundice, fever and slight resistance of the upper abdomen, without glandular enlargement or a local lesion.

In an endemic focus in Utah and the adjoining states, a person presenting a fly bite on an exposed part of the body in June, July or August, with inflammation of the adjacent lymph glands and with fever and prostration, at once arouses the suspicion of tularemia.

Tick-bitten patients in Montana and the adjacent states with consequent glandular enlargements and fever, but without the eruption of spotted fever, suggest tularemia.

In a person who has dressed or cut up wild rabbits, as in the case of a market man, cook or hunter, and who develops a sore on the hand accompanied by inflamed glands of the cervical epitrochlear or axillary regions, together with fever and marked illness, tularemia should be borne in mind, and the appropriate tests should be made. These cases usually develop in the months of November, December and January, when wild rabbits become a common article of food offered in the markets.

Laboratory workers who are engaged in dissecting guinea-pigs, rabbits and mice artificially infected with *Bacterium tularense*, and who present a sudden onset of fever without glandular enlargements and without an evident site of infection, should immediately consider tularemia.

When a patient gives a negative Widal test in spite of the insistence of the physician that his case simulates typhoid, inquiry should elicit whether the patient has manipulated the internal organs of a rabbit; if so, the blood serum should be tested for agglutination of *Bacterium tularense*.

A fatal epizootic in wild rabbits should direct attention to tularemia, which will be evidenced by a spotted condition of the spleen especially, and also of the liver of dead or sick rabbits. Natural infection has never been reported in domestic rabbits bred in rabbitries and sold for food or for laboratory purposes.

## LABORATORY TESTS

*Agglutination.*—The blood serum of a patient suffering from tularemia agglutinates *Bacterium tularense*, just as the serum of a typhoid patient agglutinates *Bacillus typhosus;* this is a very reliable and practical test.

Agglutinins are absent from the blood during the first week of illness, but blood taken in the second week has always reacted positively in our cases. The agglutinin titer reaches its maximum at the end of the third or fourth week, when a decline in titer begins. Persistence of agglutinins in the blood of patients who have recovered is, however, a notable and fortunate occurrence, in that the serum of patients, although recovered for several years, is of great diagnostic value.

Serum is collected under ordinary sterile conditions, as for the Wassermann test; but if the serum cannot be collected sterilely no phenol (carbolic acid) or tricresol should be added, but an equal amount of undiluted pure neutral glycerin should be added as a preservative. At least 0.5 c.c. of serum is required for a test; a somewhat larger quantity is preferable.

Suspected serum or tissues may be sent to the Director, Hygienic Laboratory, Twenty-Fifth and E streets, N.W., Washington, D. C., for diagnosis.

*Animal Inoculations.*—Pus from the site of the fly bite or tick bite, or other site of infection, or from the patient's suppurating glands, or tissue from a wild rabbit's spotted spleen or liver should be injected subcutaneously into the abdomen of guinea-pigs or rabbits; such material should first be rubbed in a mortar, suspended in salt solution, and strained through coarse gauze. Within a week the animals should die, presenting a gray, granular caseation of the enlarged lymph glands of the groin, and great numbers of small white foci of necrosis, studded over the enlarged spleen, especially, and over the liver.

Material from the dead animal's glands, spleen and liver, when rubbed on the shaven, abraded skin of another guinea-pig or rabbit, should likewise cause its death within a week with the same typical lesions of the lymph glands, spleen and liver, and thus the infection may be propagated for an indefinite number of passages through guinea-pigs or rabbits. Cultures of *Bacterium tularense* may be obtained by inoculation from the blood, spleen or liver of these animals to coagulate egg yolk or serum glucose cystin agar[22] on which mediums the organism grows as a small, nonmotile, gram-negative rod, while on plain agar no growth will take place. The bacteriologic diagnosis of tularemia should not be

expected from cultural inoculations, or from smears made direct from the patient. In severe cases the patient's blood injected intraperitoneally into these animals will likewise cause the infection and death of the animals.

More reliance should be placed on the gross pathologic evidence of the disease in guinea-pigs or rabbits than on direct microscopic findings in the patient or animal.

Spleens of infected guinea-pigs or rabbits, if dropped into pure glycerin and placed in the icebox, will remain virulent for at least a month, thus affording a means of shipping live virus for the purpose of identification.

Workers who are engaged in performing necropsies of infected animals should wear rubber gloves and observe all other precautions to avoid infection. In spite of all such precautions, however, cases have occurred among laboratory workers.

### TREATMENT

The treatment is symptomatic. Rest in bed is most important. Those who have had most experience with the enlarged glands do not advise excision or even incision until a very evident soft, thin place appears in the skin overlying the glands. No preventive vaccine or curative serum has been perfected.

---

22. Francis, Edward: The Amino-Acid Cystine in the Cultivation of Bacterium Tularense, Pub. Health Rep. **38**: 1396-1404 (June 22) 1923; Mil. Surgeon **53**: 169 (Aug.) 1923.

# Tularemia Revisited*

## Jay P. Sanford, MD

The retrospectroscope is a marvelous instrument. To place Dr Francis' LANDMARK ARTICLE into perspective, it seemed most appropriate to review the sections on tularemia in current representative textbooks of internal medicine and infectious diseases.[1-4] These texts generally present history, etiology, epidemiology, pathogenesis, clinical manifestations, diagnosis, treatment, and prevention. Contrast this with the subtitles in Francis' article: "Synonyms and History," "Geographic Distribution in Man and Rodents," "Symptoms and Course," "Agglutination Tests," "Portal of Entry," "Insect Transmission," "Non-contagiousness," "Immunity," "Diagnosis," "Laboratory Tests," and "Treatment." After reading the current texts and then rereading Francis, the déjà vu is most striking.

The synthesis of the original observations of a serologist, a clinician, and a bacteriologist that Francis reports in his 1925 article based then on 49 cases provides most of the information that is needed to diagnose tularemia in 1983. The causative bacterium of the "plague-like disease of rodents" prevalent among California ground squirrels from Tulare, Calif, was discovered by McCoy and Chapin[5] in 1911 and named *Bacterium tularense*. In working with infected rodents, Chapin had a febrile attack and subsequently found his serum to have antitularense antibodies. Thus, from the very beginning, the laboratory hazard of *Francisella tularensis* was apparent. In Utah in 1911, Pearse[6] described six cases of an illness that occurred in August caused by the bites of a fly. After an incubation of two to five days, the glands that drained the bitten area became markedly swollen and went on to suppuration in three patients. The site of the fly bite progressed from a red infiltration to a punched-out circular ulcer. Most patients had severe chills during the incubation period. Temperatures varied from 37 to 40 °C (98 to 104 °F). The duration of disease was one to four weeks. In 1907, Dr Martin of Phoenix,

Territory of Arizona, wrote to Dr F. G. Novy at the University of Michigan:

There have been during the summer several individuals . . . who have suffered from an infection as a result of skinning and dressing wild rabbits. . . . Three of these persons have had their primary lesion in or about the eye. . . . The pre-auricular gland being involved . . . In one instance infection took place in the foot, and others in the hands, etc. The adjacent lymphatics, of course, being involved.[7]

From an awareness of the laboratory isolation of *B tularense* both from rodents as well as from three cases of conjunctivitis in Cincinnati and deer fly fever, Francis[8] isolated *B tularense* from seven human cases of deer fly fever in Utah and named the disease *tularemia* in 1921.

From the 49 reported cases, he noted tularemia to occur across the United States from the Pacific to the Atlantic.[7] Clinically, he characterized the disease as initially seen as a glandular type with an incubation period of two to five days, the onset being sudden. Manifestations included headache, chills, bodily pains, vomiting, prostration, and fever. Within 48 hours of onset, pain developed in the area of regional lymph nodes. The site of the bite became inflamed and ulcerated. Agglutinins appeared in the second week. One patient experienced a complicating pneumonia and died; however, death was rare. A second type was described as typhoidal, being encountered especially as a laboratory infection. Additionally, the oculoglandular form was described. Transmission was shown to involve blood-sucking insects, including the deer fly (*Chrysops discalis*) and the wood tick, as well as direct contact with infected tissues. No instances of person-to-person transmission by mere contact were observed.

### Now

**Epidemiology.**—Between 1927 and 1948 in the United States, 22,812 cases of tularemia were reported, with a case fatality of 7.7%.[9] Subsequently, it has been shown that tularemia is not limited to the United States but rather is ubiquitous in the northern hemisphere between 30° and 71° north latitude, being reported in 1925 in Japan and in 1928 in Russia.[10] In the decade from 1972 through 1981, the number of cases of human

From the Uniformed Services University of the Health Sciences, Bethesda, Md.

*A commentary on Francis E: Tularemia. *JAMA* 1925;84:1243-1250.

tularemia varied from 129 to 288 per year. Approximately 100 species of wild mammals, nine species of domestic animals, 25 species of birds, and several species of fish and amphibians have been found to be naturally infected.[10] Vertebrate animals are designated "reservoirs," but in the true sense they are rarely reservoirs, since the majority of them become sick and either die or recover with loss of the organism. Ticks are not only important vectors but serve as reservoirs, since the organism can be transmitted transovarially. There are now a number of cases, especially in children, acquired by cat bite.[11] This probably reflects mechanical transmission from the infected teeth or claws after contact with an infected rabbit. *Francisella tularensis* can survive in water and mud. A few human cases have been traced to contaminated water.[12]

**Clinical Manifestations.**—Authors continue to classify forms of tularemia based on portal of entry. Six forms are now described: ulceroglandular, glandular, oculoglandular, oropharyngeal, typhoidal, and pneumonic. The oropharyngeal form occurs after ingestion of inadequately cooked meat.[13] Clinical features include exudative or membranous pharyngitis with cervical adenitis. Pneumonic tularemia is most common in laboratory workers and is most severe, with the highest mortality.[14] Symptoms include dry cough, pleurisy, dyspnea, and, rarely, cyanosis. About one fourth of patients have extensive roentgenographic involvement but few symptoms or signs. On physical examination, diffuse, generalized moist rales (two thirds) are most commonly noted. Pleural rubs are also commonly observed (40%). Roentgenographically, the most frequent findings are bronchopneumonia, hilar adenopathy, pleural effusion, consolidation, and "ovoid densities."[15] Unilateral or bilateral pleural effusion is common.

**Diagnosis.**—Demonstration of serum agglutinins remains the most reliable means of diagnosis. Half of patients are initially seen with a titer against *F tularensis* of 1:160 or greater (a level considered diagnostic). Another half demonstrate a rising titer during the course of three weeks. The result of an intradermal tuberculin-type test with killed organisms is positive early in more than 90% of patients.[16] Unfortunately, the antigen is not generally available.

**Treatment.**—The major advance since Francis' initial review has been the advent of the antibiotic era. Streptomycin sulfate is and remains the drug of choice; 0.5 g intramuscularly (IM) every 12 hours for ten days will eradicate organisms. With streptomycin therapy, there is usually marked clinical improvement in 48 to 72 hours. Kanamycin sulfate (15 mg/kg/day IM) or gentamicin (3.0 mg/kg/day IM) are also effective but offer no substantial advantages over streptomycin.[17] Tetracycline hydrochloride and chloramphenicol are effective in controlling the acute symptoms; however, unless treatment consists of 2.0 g daily for 15 days, relapses are common.[18]

**Prevention.**—Killed vaccines were developed that were not effective. A live attenuated vaccine has been developed that reduces the incidence of typhoidal tularemia, and while it does not prevent ulceroglandular disease, it reduces the severity.[19] This vaccine remains investigational primarily for use by workers in laboratories. The efficacy for prevention of naturally acquired disease is unknown.

**Summary**

The landmark studies on tularemia by Dr Francis have been recognized by designating the causative organism *Francisella tularensis* rather than *Bacterium tularense*. A review of his original 1925 article clearly demonstrates the lasting value of critical clinical, epidemiologic, and laboratory studies. Except for expansion of knowledge concerning some aspects of the epidemiology and clinical spectrum and advances in treatment and prevention, the 1925 article is as contemporary as the current literature and textbooks.

**References**

1. Buchanan TM, Hook EW III: Tularemia, in Petersdorf RG, Adams RD, Braunwald E, et al (eds): *Harrison's Principles of Internal Medicine*, ed 10. New York, McGraw-Hill Book Co, 1983, pp 977-978.

2. Hornick RB: Tularemia, in Wyngaarden JB, Smith LH Jr (eds): *Cecil Textbook of Medicine*, ed 16. Philadelphia, WB Saunders Co, 1982, pp 1524-1526.

3. Boyce JM: *Francisella tularensis* (tularemia), in Mandell GL, Douglas RG Jr, Bennett JE (eds): *Principles and Practice of Infectious Disease*, ed 1. New York, John Wiley & Sons Inc, 1979, pp 1784-1788.

4. Yow MD: Tularemia, in Feigin RD, Cherry JD (eds): *Textbook of Pediatric Infectious Diseases*. Philadelphia, WB Saunders Co, 1981, pp 1005-1011.

5. McCoy GW, Chapin CW: Further observations on a plague-like disease of rodents with a preliminary note on the causative agent *Bacterium tularense*. *J Infect Dis* 1912;10:61-72.

6. Pearse RA: Insect bites. *Northwest Med* 1911;3:81.

7. Francis E: Tularemia. *JAMA* 1925;84:1243-1250.

8. Francis E: The occurrence of tularemia in nature as a disease of man. *Public Health Rep* 1921;36:1731-1738.

9. Larson CL: Tularemia, in *Tice's Practice of Medicine*. Hagerstown, Md, Harper & Row Publishers Inc, vol 3, pp 663-676.

10. Hopla CE: The ecology of tularemia. *Adv Vet Sci Comp Med* 1974;18:25-53.

11. Tularemia. *MMWR* 1982;31:39-41.

12. Jellison WL, Epler DC, Kunn E, et al: Tularemia in man from a domestic rural water supply. *Public Health Rep* 1950;65:1219-1226.

13. Hughes WT Jr, Etteldorf JN: Oropharyngeal tularemia. *J Ped* 1957;51:363-372.

14. Overholt EL, Tigertt WD, Kadull PJ, et al: An analysis of forty-two cases of laboratory acquired tularemia. *Am J Med* 1961;30:785-806.

15. Dennis JM, Bondreau RP: Pleuropulmonary tularemia: Its roentgen manifestations. *Radiology* 1957;68:25-30.

16. Young LS, Bicknell DS, Archer BG, et al: Tularemic epidemic: Vermont 1968. *N Engl J Med* 1969;280:1253-1260.

17. Alford RH, John JT, Bryant RE: Tularemia treated successfully with gentamicin. *Am Rev Respir Dis* 1972;106:265-268.

18. Sawyer WD, Dangerfield HG, Hogge AL, et al: Antibiotic prophylaxis and therapy in airborne tularemia. *Bacteriol Rev* 1966;30:542-548.

19. Burke DS: Immunization against tularemia: Analysis of the effectiveness of live *Francisella tularensis* vaccine in prevention of laboratory acquired infection. *J Infect Dis* 1977;135:55-60.

## Chapter 21

# Treatment of Pernicious Anemia
# by a Special Diet[*]

George R. Minot, M.D.
and
William P. Murphy, M.D.

Boston

This paper concerns the treatment in a series of forty-five cases of pernicious anemia in which the patients were given a special form of diet. While the problem of diet in the treatment of pernicious anemia is by no means new, in our opinion its possible importance has not heretofore been generally recognized. In 1863, seven years after the publication of Addison's second, but best known, description of the disease now called pernicious anemia, Habershon[1] wrote concerning this condition: "Many patients at an early stage completely recover under the influence of bracing air and a nutrient and stimulating diet." Other early investigators of the disease, as Biermer[2] in 1872, and Pepper,[3] in 1875, appreciated the desirability of prescribing easily digested foods as a form of medication, but no greater emphasis

was placed on the value of diet. Osler,[4] however, in 1885, mentioned that "cases [of pernicious anemia] appear to have got well with change of air and a better diet after resisting all ordinary means."

During the last half century, many clinicians, following the suggestions of the pioneer writers on the subject of pernicious anemia, have advised various kinds of diet as an aid to induce a remission of the disease. More often than not, the recommendations have been of a general sort as might be given for many persons with an impaired condition of the gastrointestinal tract, which always is present in pernicious anemia. Thus, food for the pernicious anemia patient often has been selected because it appeared to be easily digested or because it seemed particularly nutritious and strength-giving. Rarely, diets have been chosen for some assumed direct effect on the blood.

The constant presence of achylia gastrica in pernicious anemia and the frequency of an abnormal bacterial activity within the intestines have been two main reasons for establishing certain forms of dietotherapy in the disease. On these accounts, Fenwick,[5] in 1880, and

[*]This study was aided by a grant from the Proctor Fund of the Harvard Medical School for the Study of Chronic Disease.

[*]From the Medical Clinic of the Peter Bent Brigham Hospital, and the Medical Service of the Collis P. Huntington Memorial Hospital of Harvard University.

1. Habershon, S. O.: On Idiopathic Anemia, Lancet 1: 518, 551 (May) 1863.

2. Biermer: Halt Zunächst einen Vorbrag über eine von ihm öfters beobachtete eigenthümliche Form von progresseiver pernicioser Anämie, welche mit Capillären Blutungen der Haut, Retina, des Gehirns etc., Cor.-Bl. f. schweiz. Aerzte 2: 15 (Jan. 15) 1872.

3. Pepper, W.: Progressive Pernicious Anaemia or Anhaematosis, Am. J. M. Sc. 70: 313 (Oct.) 1875.

4. Osler, William: Pernicious Anemia: A System of Practical Medicine, edited by Pepper, W., assisted by Starr, L., Philadelphia, Lea Brothers Company 3: 898, 1885.

5. Fenwick, S.: On Atrophy of the Stomach in Relation to Pernicious Anemia, Lancet 2: 77 (July 21) 1877.

Naegeli,[6] among others, recommended diets relatively sparing in farinaceous foods and relatively rich in protein. For similar reasons, yet in contrast to the majority, Hunter,[7] in 1890, and others have advised quite the opposite type of diet. Grawitz[8] recommended a diet composed chiefly of fresh vegetables, followed by one with generous amounts of protein. The idea that forced feeding with any sort of food, but especially meats, is valuable to make weak and feeble individuals healthy and strong has caused the frequent use of this form of therapy in pernicious anemia, and Mosenthal[9] has shown that it can restore in these cases a positive nitrogen balance.

Meats and green vegetables, partly because of their iron content, have for a long time been thought to be useful to improve "an anemic state of the blood." Meat apparently has been chosen at times simply because it contained blood, which was supposed to be beneficial as food for persons who had an insufficient blood supply. The scientific foundations of the value of iron-containing foods to affect the blood-forming organs were laid by Menghini[10] in 1746, when he showed that iron could be increased in the blood by feeding such foods to animals. About 200 years later, Gibson and Howard[11] made important observations on the effect of a high iron content of the diet in anemia, and showed that in pernicious anemia it can have a most favorable influence on iron metabolism. They also showed that, in cases constantly losing nitrogen, a positive nitrogen balance could be obtained without forced feeding.

One thus finds that the diet usually advised for the pernicious anemia patient is one containing a relatively high nitrogen-content and often a relatively large number of calories. The recommendations of Smith[12] and of Barker and Sprunt[13] are of this sort and, like some others, the latter wisely recommend that the food be selected with a view of giving an ordinary, well balanced diet to replace a quantitatively deficient and qualitatively ill balanced one, on which these patients are apt to have placed themselves during their illness.

In spite of attention to diet for the anemic patient, the influence of food on blood formation and destruction has received comparatively little consideration, and special sorts of food, because of some particular effect, have seldom been chosen for patients with pernicious anemia.

Complete starvation in man is not considered to cause anemia, but may do so in animals. However, it is known that improper food can cause, and suitable food alleviate, anemia; for example, the "iron starvation anemia" arising in infants who have partaken too long of only a milk diet, and who can be cured by food particularly containing complete proteins and iron. Incomplete diets, particularly those low in protein and relatively rich in concentrated carbohydrate food, can lead to anemia,[14] and even Shakespeare[15] recognized that improper food might impair the state of the blood. Likewise, patients with conditions due to, or associated with, vitamin deficiency experience anemia, and Jencks[16] has noticed that an abundance of vitamins favors blood regeneration. Certain foods, including liver, may benefit patients with sprue. This disease is considered by some partly dependent on a faulty diet, and resembles in numerous ways pernicious anemia, including the fact that the blood picture in the two diseases may be quite similar. Carnivorous animals and thin persons tend to have a greater percentage of hemoglobin in their blood than herbivorous animals and fat persons.[17] This further suggests, as do the observations of Morawitz and Kühl[18] on man, the favorable rôle that animal protein food may play in blood formation, although dehydration may account for the differences observed.

Some of the earlier experimental work concerning the effect of food on blood regeneration is reviewed by Pearce, Krumbhaar and Frazier.[19] Adequate proteins as well as iron are necessary for the formation of hemoglobin. Certain proteins will not suffice, such as gliadin.[20] However, the amino-acid tryptophane may have a special ability to enhance blood formation.[21] The most important recent work concerning the effect of food on blood regeneration has been done by Whipple and Robscheit-Robbins and their associates.[22] Their carefully controlled work on dogs has demonstrated clearly the

6. Naegeli, O.: Blut Krankheiten und Blutdiagnostik, Leipzig, von Veit & Co., 1912.

7. Hunter, W.: Observations on Treatment of Pernicious Anemia Based on a Study of Its Causation, Brit. M. J. 2: 1, 81, 1890.

8. Grawitz, E.: Zur Frage der entwegen en Entstehung schwerer Anämien, Berl. klin. Wchnschr. 1: 641 (June 17) 1901.

9. Mosenthal, H.: The Effect of Forced Feeding on the Nitrogen Equilibrium and the Blood in Pernicious Anemia, Bull. Johns Hopkins Hosp. 29: 129 (June) 1918.

10. Menghini, quoted by Christian, H. A.: A Sketch of the History of the Treatment of Chlorosis with Iron, Medical Library and Historical Journal 1: 176 (July) 1903.

11. Gibson, R. B., and Howard, C. P.: Metabolic Studies in Pernicious Anemia, Arch. Int. Med. 32: 1 (July) 1923.

12. Smith, quoted by Fitch, W. E.: Dietotherapy, ed. 2, New York, D. Appleton & Co. 3: 257, 1922.

13. Barker, L. F., and Sprunt, T. P.: The Treatment of Some Cases of So-Called "Pernicious" Anemia, J. A. M. A. 69: 1919 (Dec. 8) 1917.

14. McCarrison, Robert: Faulty Food in Relation to Gastro-Intestinal Disorder, J. A. M. A. 78: 1 (Jan 7) 1922. Benedict, F. G.; Miles, W. R.; Roth, P., and Smith, H. M.: Human Vitality and Efficiency Under Prolonged Restricted Diet, pub. 280, Carnegie Inst. of Washington, 1919, p. 364.

15. Shakespeare: Henry IV, act 2, scene 3.

16. Jencks, Z.: Studies in the Regeneration of Blood, Am. J. Physiol. 59: 240 (Feb.) 1922.

17. Hammarsten, O.: A Text Book of Physiological Chemistry, trans. by Mandel, J. A., ed. 5, New York, J. J. Wiley and Sons, 1908, p. 244.

18. Morawitz, C., and Kühl, G.: Der Blutumsatz des Normalen unter verschiedenen Bedingungen (Eisen, Aiseu, Fleisch), Klin. Wchnschr. 4: 7, 1925.

19. Pearce, R. M.; Krumbhaar, E. B., and Frazier, C. H.: The Spleen and Anemia, Philadelphia, J. B. Lippincott Company, 1918.

20. Smith, A. H., and Moise, T. S.: Diet and Tissue Growth: The Regeneration of Liver Tissue During Nutrition or Inadequate Diets and Fasting, J. Exper. Med. 40: 209 (Aug.) 1924.

21. Hirasawa, quoted by Wells, H. G.: Chemical Pathology, ed. 5, Philadelphia, W. B. Saunders Company, 1925, p. 334.

22. Whipple, G. H.; Hooper, C. W., and Robscheit, F. S.: Blood Regeneration Following Simple Anemia, Am. J. Physiol. 53: 151, 167 (Sept.) 1920. Whipple, G. H.; Robscheit, F. S., and Hooper, C. W.: Blood Regeneration Following Anaemia, ibid. 53: 236 (Sept.) 1920. Whipple, G. H., and Robscheit-Robbins, F. S.: Favorable Influence of Liver, Heart and Skeletal Muscle in Diet on Blood Regeneration in Anemia, ibid. 72: 408 (May) 1925 (cf. p. 431); Iron Reaction Favorable, Arsenic and Germanium Dioxide Almost Inert, in Severe Anemia, ibid. 72: 419 (May) 1925.

value of certain foods, especially liver, on accelerating blood regeneration following acute hemorrhage and the value of iron added to the diet to decrease the anemia due to chronic blood loss.

McCollum[23] has pointed out that liver and kidneys give an exceptionally high quality protein for a low protein intake and can enhance remarkably the growth of animals. These foods are rich in nucleins, and Calkins, Bullock and Rohdenburg[24] have shown that the products of nuclein hydrolysis can stimulate growth. Whipple[25] has suggested that in pernicious anemia there may be a scarcity of the material from which the stroma of the red blood cells are formed, or that a disease of the stroma-forming cells of the marrow exists. Thus, theoretically perhaps liver and other foods rich in complete proteins may enhance the formation of red blood cells in this disease, especially by supplying material to build their stroma.

Fresh red marrow was first used as a means of treatment for pernicious anemia by Fraser[26] in 1894. He reported beneficial results when a patient ate for some time about 100 Gm. a day. It was then and has since been given apparently on the supposition of some hormone effect. Thus, numerous reports have appeared concerning the use of preparations of small amounts of concentrated bone marrow, but without definite evidence of advantage to the pernicious anemia patient. Reports regarding the effect of eating generously of fresh marrow are few and brief, but suggest that it may be beneficial. The nutritional composition of red bone marrow is similar to that of liver and kidneys. If generous amounts of red marrow and liver can improve the state of the blood in pernicious anemia, may their influence not be due to the same, but unknown, cause?

Various investigators have commented on the blood-destroying properties of certain substances derived from fats and the rôle they may play in pernicious anemia. Stoeltzner[27] recently has reviewed the subject. Also, lipoids have been shown by Baker and Carrel[28] to be a factor in serum that can inhibit growth. Thus, founded on somewhat theoretical grounds, it seemed to us, as it did to Stoeltzner[27] and to Gibson and Howard,[11] that decreasing the amount of fat in the diet of the pernicious anemia patient might have a favorable effect on the state of his blood. Excess of fat in a diet is considered by some to favor putrefaction within the intestine, a condition frequent in pernicious anemia. Hence one might attribute any benefit derived from a low fat content of the diet to alterations in the bacterial flora rather than to some more direct effect on blood formation or destruction.

A further hypothetic reason for decreasing the fat in the diet is that we have noted it is not uncommon for these patients to have consumed throughout life unusually large amounts of food rich in fats. Patients with pernicious anemia also may give a history of partaking for years of some other type of one-sided diet. It is common for them to do so after the definite onset of their illness, when it is not unusual to find that they have a disgust for meat. Pernicious anemia is rare in certain parts of the world where diets are quite different (containing fewer dairy products, less free sugar and muscle meat) from those of the northern parts of Europe and America, in which areas the disease is relatively common. These different facts permit one to speculate on the possible partial rôle that some nutritional excess or deficiency may play in the etiology of the disease. Similar thoughts have occurred to others, including the idea that a vitamin deficiency might be a causative factor, as has been mentioned, for example, by Elders.[29]

Leafy vegetables and fruits usually are considered desirable for anemic patients, especially because of their iron content, and strawberries rich in iron appear beneficial for patients with sprue, a disease, as noted, resembling pernicious anemia. We prefer to add these foods to the pernicious anemia patient's diet not only because they are healthful ones for any person to eat, but also because, as Whipple and Robscheit-Robbins[30] have shown, certain ones have an especially favorable influence on hemoglobin production. It is quite probable, however, that their chief effect is not because of their iron content. It seems that such a factor as the character of the proteins or amino-acids in the diet is of much more importance than the iron content for pernicious anemia patients.

Numerous authorities hold the view that an intestinal bacterial toxemia plays an important etiologic rôle in this disease. One may choose to believe that any benefit these patients derive soon after beginning to take certain foods is to be attributed to changing rapidly the intestinal flora, thus decreasing a bacterial toxemia, rather than considering that the foods influence in some unknown, but more direct, manner the formation or destruction of red blood cells.

Gibson and Howard,[11] taking cognizance of Whipple and Robscheit-Robbins' work and the fact that certain lipoid substances could enhance hemolysis, fed pernicious anemia patients a relatively low caloric diet (from 1,500 to 1,900) "rich in iron [liver (daily), fruits, green vegetables, egg yolk] and low in fat" and adequate in vitamins. A somewhat similar diet but containing a less amount of food rich in purines was recommended by Fenlon[31] in 1921. Gibson and Howard,[11] besides demonstrating the favorable influence of their diet on nitrogen and iron metabolism in pernicious anemia and some other anemias, suggested that it enhanced a remission in pernicious anemia and urged its use.

23. McCollum, E. V.: The Newer Knowledge of Nutrition, New York, the Macmillan Company, 1923.

24. Calkins, G. N., Bullock, F. D., and Rohdenburg, G.: The Effects of Chemicals on the Division Rate of Cells with Especial Reference to Possible Pre-Cancerous Conditions, J. Infect. Dis. 10: 421 (May) 1912.

25. Whipple, G. H.: Pigment Metabolism and Regeneration of Hemoglobin in the Body, Arch. Int. Med. 29: 711 (June) 1922.

26. Fraser, T. R.: Bone Marrow in the Treatment of Pernicious Anemia, Brit. M. J. 1: 1172 (June 2) 1894.

27. Stoeltzner, W.: Ein Vorschlag zur Behandlung der Biermerschen Anämie, München, med. Wchnschr. 68: 1558 (Dec. 2) 1921.

28. Baker, L. E., and Carrel, Alexis: Lipoids as the Growth-Inhibiting Factor in Serum, J. Exper. Med. 42: 143 (July) 1925.

29. Elders, C.: The Form, Course and Prognosis of the Anemia in Indian Sprue and the Etiology of Pernicious Anemia, Nederlandsch. Tidjschr. v. Geneesk. 58: 2267, 1922.

30. Footnote 22, third reference.

31. Fenlon, R. L.: A Diet for Pernicious Anemia, J. Iowa State M. Soc. 11: 50 (Feb.) 1921.

## MATERIAL STUDIED AND OBSERVATIONS

Following the work of Whipple and Robscheit-Robbins, we made a few observations on patients concerning the influence of a diet containing an abundance of liver and muscle meat on blood regeneration. The effect appeared to be quite similar to that which they obtained in dogs. These observations, together with the information given above, led us to investigate the value of a diet with an abundance of food rich in complete proteins and iron—particularly liver—and relatively low in fat, as a means of treatment for pernicious anemia.

Observations set forth below have been made on forty-five patients with typical pernicious anemia first partaking of such a diet when in a relapse and continuing it to date (except temporarily omitted by three), or from six weeks to two and a half year.

The special diet[32] used was made as palatable as possible and for each day was practically as follows:

1. From 120 to 240 Gm., and even sometimes more, of cooked calf's or beef liver. An equal quantity of lamb's kidneys was substituted occasionally.
2. One hundred and twenty grams or more of beef or mutton muscle meat.
3. Not less than 300 Gm. of vegetables containing from 1 to 10 per cent of carbohydrate, especially lettuce and spinach.
4. From 250 to 500 Gm. of fruit, especially peaches, apricots, strawberries, pineapple, oranges and grapefruit.
5. About 40 Gm. of fat derived from butter and cream, allowed in order to make the food attractive. However, animal fats and oils were excluded so far as possible.
6. If desired, an egg and 240 Gm. of milk.
7. In addition to the above mentioned foods, breads especially dry and crusty, potato, and cereals, in order to allow a total intake of between 2,000 and 3,000 calories composed usually of about 340 Gm. of carbohydrate, 135 Gm. of protein, and not more than 70 Gm. of fat. Grossly sweet foods were not given, but sugar was allowed very sparingly.

This diet is rich in iron and purine derivatives, containing about 0.03 Gm. of the former and about 1 Gm. of the latter.

At the time the diet was advised for many of the patients, they were able to take only a small amount of food of any sort. Under these circumstances they were encouraged to take as much as possible of liver and fruits, and at least some vegetables, while other sorts of food were not forced. During the first week of the diet, the intake was often less than a thousand calories. After about this period of time, the patients usually felt distinctly better and their appetite began to improve. Then the food was increased gradually until the complete diet was taken. The patients as a rule did so within two weeks after the diet was begun. In fact, frequently they soon became "ravenously hungry" and often anxious to eat more than the customary allowance of liver and meat.

Twenty-four of the forty-five patients carried out the regimen by weighing portions of liver and meat and estimating the amounts of the rest of their food for at least three weeks, and often for the first six after

commencing the diet. The other patients, like those after leaving the hospital, have taken their diet at home, following out written directions but not weighing any of their food. Our data strongly suggest that the patients who commenced treatment in the hospital and those few able to have a trained nurse at home have improved on the average rather faster and to an even better degree than the others. When the patients had remained much better for many weeks, their diet was sometimes modified particularly by decreasing the amount of liver and fruit.

The therapeutic regimen for these forty-five patients, besides the special diet, included rest, usually at first in bed for twenty-four hours a day. All but three also took each day about 15 cc. of diluted hydrochloric acid (U. S. P.). These three, however, improved at least as much as the majority of the others. None of the patients received any especial treatment shortly before or after the diet was begun except as follows: A man, aged 69, with pronounced spinal cord lesions and advanced arteriosclerosis, was given five transfusions of blood within about six weeks while attempts were made to get him to eat. Now, three months later, he remains the least well of all forty-five, except for one woman who recently has omitted her diet. Blood was transfused to three others at about the time they first took the special diet. The red blood cell count of none was over 1,400,000 per cubic millimeter four days after transfusion.

The forty-five patients represent an essentially consecutive series seen in a relapse, and are all that have taken the special diet except one noted below. The series is not entirely consecutive, because during the time the forty-five cases were seen the following additional ones came under observation:

1. Four patients who had had their disease a long time were exceedingly sick, able to take little or no food, and died within a few weeks after they were seen. They ate no liver or kidneys.
2. Five patients consulting us but once and not taking the special diet. Letters indicate that three improved somewhat and two did not.
3. One patient that was in much better condition soon after taking the diet. This patient is not included in the series of forty-five because of several unusual complications.

Many of the forty-five patients had had definite symptoms due to pernicious anemia for more than two years, and two of them experienced such symptoms ten years before taking the special diet. A number of the cases were observed during a year or more before the diet was begun, others for several weeks, and some for only a few days. Many of the patients had remained in distinctly poor health and were unable to do their usual work for from a few months to more than a year before eating the food especially prescribed. During this time, many received various forms of therapy without distinct benefit, including transfusions of blood.

When the special diet was started, the forty-five patients that have continued to eat this kind of food fell naturally into the three following groups: (1) twelve in their first distinct relapse; (2) seventeen in their second relapse; (3) sixteen having had two or more relapses. It is thus evident that all sorts of variations of the disease occurred among the patients, and that the series was not

---

32. Details concerning this diet with sample menus are given in a paper to be published soon in the Boston Medical and Surgical Journal.

composed chiefly of those in their first relapse, following which considerable "spontaneous" improvement is the rule.

The condition of all forty-five patients became much better rather rapidly soon after commencing the diet. All except one, who has recently omitted her diet, are now at the least in a very fair state of health, and if it were not for disorders in some due to spinal cord lesions, would have an appearance to a layman of being essentially well. However, there are only eleven patients who began the diet a year or more ago, two of whom have taken it for more than two years. Eighteen began taking the diet less than five months ago.

One of the earliest signs of improvement has been a change in the frequency of bowel movements believed to be due particularly to the diet and probably not to diluted hydrochloric acid. Within a few days, those who had had a tendency to diarrhea often began to have one formed stool a day, while, interestingly enough, those who had had normal movements or had been constipated frequently had for several days a few loose stools in each twenty-four hours. The latter patients, then, had a more natural regularity of their bowel movements and a more normal stool than they had had for some time before the diet was taken. The laxative effect of the diet has been observed also to occur in some normal persons.

Clinical improvement has been obvious usually within two weeks. This has been heralded in the peripheral blood before the end of the first week by the beginning of a most definite rise of the reticulocytes (young red blood corpuscles) of from about 1.0 per cent to usually about 8.0 and even to 15.5 per cent of all the red blood cells. This rise occurred in all fifteen patients that have had such counts made every day or so for from one to three weeks before and some weeks after beginning the diet. By the end of the second week, these cells usually had returned close to their normal percentage. Later, when the red blood cell counts were distinctly high, it was frequent to find, as we have noted formerly, an abnormally small number of reticulocytes. Before they began to increase, the icterus index of the blood serum in these fifteen patients started to fall, and soon the yellow tint of the patient's skin disappeared. This index reached normal in from two to four weeks, and often has fallen to below normal even when the red blood cell count had increased to only 2,500,000 per cubic millimeter.[33]

The accompanying chart and table give in a synopsized manner the trends of the state of the blood in the forty-five patients, taking into consideration, on the one hand, the character of the case, and, on the other, the level of the red blood cells when the diet was begun. The data are given for all forty-five patients before and about one month (from four to six weeks) after the diet was started. Although all the patients have been observed repeatedly, data can be given for only thirty-seven at the end of about two months (from eight to eleven weeks) of treatment, and for twenty-seven between four and six months after treatment began, because eight have taken the diet for less than two months, and eighteen for less

than four months. As a measure of the patient's condition, we have chosen to give in the table and chart the red blood cell count rather than the hemoglobin percentage, partly because the latter in pernicious anemia may be at about the same high level (80 per cent) with red blood cell counts of from 2.5 to 4 million per cubic millimeter. It is recognized that figures for both may vary considerably within a few hours. The figure used in synopsizing the data often represents in each instance an average of several counts made within a few days of each other.

Inspection of the chart and table shows the rapidity with which the red blood corpuscles increased, the high level they attained at the end of about one month, two months and from four to six months after the diet was begun, and the rather slight differences that occurred in the bloods in the cases falling into the three groups based on the number of relapses that had occurred. The percentage increase of cells (and the same is true of the hemoglobin) at the end of a month was usually very

*Average Red Blood Corpuscle Count[°]*

| Before Diet Started | | About 1 Month | | About 2 Months | | 4 to 6 Months | |
|---|---|---|---|---|---|---|---|
| Number of Cases | Average R. B. C. Count in Millions | Number of Cases | Average R. B. C. Count in Millions | Number of Cases[†] | Average R. B. C. Count in Millions | Number of Cases[†] | Average R. B. C. Count in Millions |
| 19 | 0.90 | 19 | 3.28 | 15 | 4.08 | 12 | 4.50 |
| 15 | 1.60 | 15 | 3.25 | 13 | 4.09 | 10 | 4.54 |
| 11 | 2.30 | 11 | 3.83 | 9 | 4.41 | 5 | 4.47 |
| 45 | 1.47 | 45 | 3.40 | 37 | 4.16 | 27 | 4.50 |

°The figures represent the count per cubic millimeter before and after starting special diet in three groups of cases of pernicious anemia: (1) with less than 1.2 million; (2) having from 1.2 to 2 million, and (3) having from 2 to 2.75 million before diet was begun. Also, averages for all forty-five cases are shown.

†The differences in the number of cases after about one month is because some have not taken the diet for as long as two, and others as long as four months.

much greater in patients starting the diet when their red blood cell count was less than 1,200,000 per cubic millimeter than in those in whom it was distinctly higher. This occurs in other pernicious anemia patients rapidly restoring their blood. The blood of patients with rather high counts of their red blood corpuscles and prominent signs of injury to the spinal cord responded more slowly perhaps and less well than others, and, as is to be expected, no striking change occurred in very marked symptoms or signs due to spinal cord degeneration.

In pernicious anemia, remissions after two relapses are frequently less marked than previous ones, so that the red blood cell count is apt to be lower in a third or subsequent relapse than in a former one. In spite of the excellent remissions our patients had soon after beginning the diet, the data in the chart show what might be expected; namely, that not only did the third group of patients (those having had more than two relapses) have on the average a slightly lower red blood cell count before the diet was started, but also that afterward their counts were apt to increase more slowly and not become quite so high as in the other two groups. Only four of the patients had red blood cell counts as low as between 3 and 2.5 million per cubic millimeter after taking the diet for about a

---

33. These changes in the blood and numerous others will be presented in a subsequent paper.

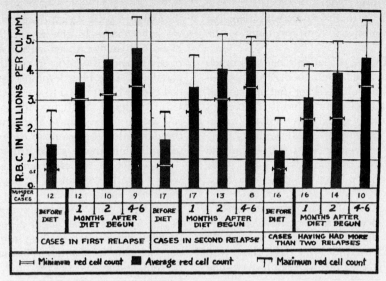

Red blood cell counts in forty-five cases of pernicious anemia before and after beginning special diet. Cases grouped according to the number of relapses the patients had had. One and two months after diet began indicates an approximate amount of time and for any given case is not less and often somewhat more than four or eight weeks. The differences in the total number of cases after about one month are caused by the fact that some patients have had the diet for less than two, and others for less than four, months.

month. The cases of three belong to this third group. Even so, two had 4,000,000 or more red blood cells per cubic millimeter at the end of four months. The other, the patient transfused several times, has now, after three months of dieting, only 2,600,000 per cubic millimeter. However, his hemoglobin has risen from 25 to 70 per cent. The fourth case with a red blood cell count of less than 3,000,000 per cubic millimeter at the end of a month belongs to the second group, and now, two and a half months after the diet was started, shows a red blood cell count of 3,300,000 per cubic millimeter.

The data from which the table and chart were prepared have been analyzed in various ways, and the following statements indicate in a different manner than they do what satisfactory improvement was shown in the patients' blood: Seventy-six per cent of all the patients had 2,000,000 or less red blood corpuscles per cubic millimeter, with their hemoglobin usually 55 per cent or less before beginning the diet. In contrast to this, approximately a month (from four to six weeks) later, 91 per cent had over 3,000,000 and 42 per cent over 3,500,000 red blood cells per cubic millimeter, with corresponding rises in the hemoglobin percentage. After taking the diet for about two months (from eight to eleven weeks), 89 per cent (of the thirty-seven that had taken the diet this length of time) had 3,500,000 or more red blood corpuscles per cubic millimeter, while 73 per cent had 4,000,000 or more. All had a hemoglobin of approximately 80 per cent or over. None of the patients studied after they had eaten the food selected for them for between four and six months had less than 3,500,000 red blood cells per cubic millimeter; 81 per cent had 4,000,000 or more, and the counts of 30 per cent were over 5,000,000 per cubic millimeter. The hemoglobin was 80 per cent or above in all, often 90 per cent, and in several cases reached more than 100 per cent. However, it is to be noted that none of these cases observed between

four and six months after the diet was started had appeared as advanced as several of those in patients that improved the least, but which have not yet had the diet for four months. The observations on the eighteen patients who have been on the diet for more than six months show that their count may fluctuate, though it has remained above 3,200,000 per cubic millimeter, and usually has been over 4,000,000, with the hemoglobin remaining at 80 per cent or more. There are three exceptions to this statement, for three patients had a relapse about eight weeks after changing their diet. One did so a year and another seven months after the special diet was begun. There was a count slightly below 3,000,000 per cubic millimeter in both for two or three weeks. Their red blood cells and hemoglobin then very rapidly increased under rest and on eating an increased amount of liver and fruit. The third patient's red cell count was 4,200,000 per cubic millimeter a month before she changed her diet. She has just resumed the special diet, and her red cell count is 1,900,000 per cubic millimeter and hemoglobin 50 per cent.

## COMMENT

Cases of pernicious anemia undergoing distinct remissions often show rapid and striking improvement, such as occurred in almost all our patients. A considerable number of them have made such remarks as, "I feel better than for several years," "better than for two years," and "stronger than after the two times my blood went low before." Such statements, to be sure, are made by pernicious anemia patients having remissions that have not taken this diet, and there is no case in this series of forty-five that cannot be paralleled by a similar one having a so-called spontaneous remission. However, the records of eleven cases show that the red blood cell count in the remission following the "liver diet" has remained distinctly higher, not only than in a former remission, but also in three cases higher, for at least two months, than in their three previous remissions. It is, thus, again pointed out here that it is rather unusual to find the red blood corpuscle count in a late remission distinctly above the level obtained in several earlier ones. A few of the patients observed for many months before they took the special diet ate, by our advice, relatively small amounts of liver two or three times a week, together with other food of the sort contained in the special diet. Under such a regimen a moderate degree of improvement occurred in some, to be followed later by a relapse of their case. It was rather striking that when the same patients were placed on a diet rich in liver they improved markedly. This suggests, as do similar observations we made some time ago in other cases, that if liver and food like it play a rôle in improving the blood of pernicious anemia, it is desirable for the patients to take such food daily and in large amounts.

The spontaneous remissions of pernicious anemia and the bizarre course it often runs make it notoriously difficult to determine accurately the effect of any procedure on the disease. All sorts of therapeutic procedures have been advised; many because a few cases improved promptly after their trial. Waves of enthusiasm for certain methods have vanished soon when it was shown that the earlier reports of benefit could be attributed readily to the natural course of the disease. There is, however, no doubt, as shown by some of the early and more recent investigators, that a well balanced, nutritious diet sometimes aids to enhance a remission. The patient may be helped by numerous other forms of treatment, such as those to change the intestinal flora, the injection of protein substances, the taking of arsenic, the transfusion of blood, and splenectomy.

At least one remission, as has been noted by Cabot,[34] takes place at some time, but at no regular time, in about 80 per cent of pernicious anemia cases. Precise data are sparse concerning the frequency, degree and rate of remissions in similar groups of cases treated in different ways. Splenectomy has caused quick and marked improvement in 64 per cent of the patients undergoing this operation, while about 15 per cent more have shown some benefit from the procedure.[35] However, the remissions that followed have been of no longer duration than those heretofore reported as of a spontaneous nature. Excluding desperately ill patients, Minot and Lee[36] noted in 1917 that about 35 per cent of forty patients treated in no especial manner had a moderate or better remission soon after they were seen. Following the transfusion of blood into forty-six similar patients, about 50 per cent continued to have definitely improved health for at least many weeks than for some time before the procedure. Not more than 20 per cent of the ninety-six patients of these two groups soon had rapid and marked increase in their red blood cells. An analysis of fifty other cases

observed between 1916 and 1923 in sequence, except for several in a terminal condition, indicates that 45 per cent developed a definite remission soon after we saw them. These patients were treated in various ways by numerous physicians, but did not eat large amounts of liver or similar food. The remissions were seldom of marked degree, with the red blood corpuscles reaching 4,000,000 or more per cubic millimeter.

No entirely satisfactory data have been found concerning the frequency of remissions following the use of a nutritious high caloric diet and such a regimen as that prescribed by Barker and Sprunt. We have treated in this manner twenty-five partially selected cases, from which it appears that distinct remissions may follow such therapy in about 65 per cent of the instances. Even so, apparently the red blood cell counts of patients on such a diet and who were improved distinctly at the end of one or two months averaged less than for all forty-five who have eaten generously of liver for the same amount of time.

The evidence at hand suggests that the dietetic treatment of pernicious anemia is of considerable importance. It has been possible to demonstrate in forty-five cases seen essentially in sequence that following a diet rich in liver and low in fat a distinct remission of the anemia occurred rather promptly. The promptness and rapidity with which the red blood corpuscles and hemoglobin increased, coincident with at least rather marked subjective improvement in the sense of well being and clinical appearance of all the patients and the strikingly better health of many, is at least unusual in pernicious anemia. It is also not customary for the red blood cell counts during remissions of pernicious anemia to be so frequently of the height that occurred in these patients. We are inclined to believe that something contained in the foods rich in complete proteins is particularly responsible for the improvement in the state of the blood. The low fat content of the diet is assumed to have a less important effect than the character and amount of protein, although probably excess of nitrogen per se is unimportant. If liver and similar food is of value, every means must be taken, including the skill of the nurse and cook, to get patients to eat daily as much as possible, preferably 200 Gm. or more. Failure could be attributed to taking too little of such food.

There are no data to indicate whether the remissions in these forty-five cases will last longer than those of others.

It is possible that this series of cases eventually may be proved to be unusual in that there happened to be treated a group that would have taken a turn for the better under other circumstances. Also, time may show that the special diet used, or liver and similar food, is no more advantageous in the treatment of pernicious anemia than any ordinary nutritious diet. Let this be as it may, at the present time it seems to us, as it has to Gibson and Howard, that it is wise to urge pernicious anemia patients to take a diet of the sort described.

34. Cabot, R. C.: Pernicious Anemia, in Osler and McCrae's Modern Medicine, ed. 2, Philadelphia, Lea and Febiger 4, 1915.

35. Krumbhaar, E. B.: Late Results of Splenectomy in Pernicious Anemia. J. A. M. A. 67:723 (Sept. 2) 1916.

36. Minot, G. R., and Lee, R. I.: Treatment of Pernicious Anemia Especially by Transfusion and Splenectomy, Boston M. & S. J. 177:761 (Nov. 29) 1917.

## SUMMARY

The dietetic treatment of pernicious anemia is of more importance than hitherto generally recognized.

Forty-five patients with pernicious anemia observed essentially in sequence are continuing to take a special diet that they have now been living on for from about six weeks to two years but which was temporarily omitted by three. This diet is composed especially of foods rich in complete proteins and iron—particularly liver—and containing an abundance of fruits and fresh vegetables and relatively low in fat.

Following the diet, all the patients showed a prompt, rapid and distinct remission of their anemia, coincident with at least rather marked symptomatic improvement, except for pronounced disorders due to spinal cord degeneration. Improvement was often striking, so that where the red blood cell count averaged for all before starting the diet 1,470,000 per cubic millimeter, one month afterward it averaged 3,400,000; and for the twenty-seven cases observed from four to six months after the diet was begun, the average count was 4,500,000 per cubic millimeter.

Patients having had two or more relapses showed on the average slightly lower red blood corpuscle counts about one and two months after commencing the diet than did those who had started it in their first or second relapse.

Change in the frequency of bowel movements, temporary increase in reticulocytes in the peripheral blood, and decrease of the icterus index of the blood serum were among the earliest signs that heralded the patient's better health.

All the patients had remained to date in a good state of health except three, who discontinued the diet; two rapidly improved on resuming it and the other has just commenced it again. As the diet was advised for most of the patients less than eight months ago, enough time has not yet elapsed to determine whether or not the remissions will last any longer than in other cases.

## SUBSEQUENT OBSERVATIONS

Since the data presented in this paper were compiled, the following additional information has been obtained: The eight patients who had taken the diet for only about one month had red blood cell counts at the end of about two months of between 3,500,000 and 6,000,000, with an average of 4,400,000 per cubic millimeter. One of these had but 2,500,000 at the end of one month and now at the end of three and a half months has 4,500,000 per cubic millimeter.

The ten patients recorded as having taken the diet for only about two months showed in four to six months after starting it as follows: Seven had an average red blood cell count of 5,100,000 per cubic millimeter. One who had had about 5,000,000 had but 3,500,000 per cubic millimeter. Another who had 2,500,000 per cubic millimeter at the end of the second month had the same number two months later, although symptomatically he seemed better. The tenth patient could not obtain the proper diet between the second and fourth month, and had at the latter time 3,000,000 per cubic millimeter.

The patients who had the diet from four to six months, or longer, when the data were compiled, continued in the next two and a half months to have on the average as satisfactory counts, except as noted below. The majority of these have shown higher counts than formerly. Two of the cases have had at three different times red blood cell counts of 6,000,000 or more per cubic millimeter. Two patients who have had the diet for more than six months have recently eaten very little liver, and their counts have fallen in two months from about 4,000,000 to about 3,000,000 per cubic millimeter. The red blood corpuscles of the patient referred to on page 474 as in a relapse increased 3,000,000 per cubic millimeter during the first eight weeks after the diet was resumed.

Information at hand suggests that some cases in which transfusion is done many times before the diet is started may respond but little to it.

Dec 23/30, 1983
(JAMA 1983;250:3336-3338)

# Pernicious Anemia—
# Study and Therapy*

### William H. Crosby, MD

The article by Minot and Murphy[1] had two profound effects on the history of medicine. It presented an effective therapy for a uniformly fatal blood disease and it revolutionized the study of the blood. In 1934, its authors, together with George Whipple, received the Nobel Prize in medicine, the first time it was ever awarded to physicians from the United States.

George Richards Minot, the 40-year-old architect of this research, was chief of the medical service at the Huntington Memorial Hospital, a cancer hospital in Boston. William P. Murphy, aged 34 years, in private practice in Brookline, was a junior associate in medicine at the Peter Bent Brigham Hospital who was invited by Minot to participate.[2] Murphy provided access to the patients with pernicious anemia at the Brigham, supervised their therapy, and performed the essential counting of reticulocytes. Minot had learned years before that a reticulocyte crisis heralds the beginning of a remission in the course of pernicious anemia.[3]

### Gauging Marrow Activity

How did this discovery come about? Several lines of Minot's interest and attributes converged on the research. In the first place, he was compulsive; "his special genius was for taking infinite pains."[2] The medical histories that he elicited from his patients included even the minutiae of their diets. Patients with pernicious anemia, he perceived, did not eat well, perhaps as a consequence of the sore tongue and the dysentery characteristic of the disease. But Minot suspected that inadequate diet might be the cause of the anemia. He stated in his Nobel lecture that this idea had occurred to him as a house officer at the Massachusetts General Hospital in 1912.[4] At that time, his diligence came to the

attention of Roger Lee, an enthusiastic young internist who was breaking ice in clinical research with an investigation of the clotting time of blood. Later, as a junior member of the staff, Minot was asked by Lee to participate in a study of the results of splenectomy in pernicious anemia. Their careful report was read at the 67th Annual Session of the American Medical Association in June 1916.[3] Great pains were taken in the effort to distinguish between beneficial results of the operation and the characteristic course of pernicious anemia in which the inexorable decay of the patient's condition is inexplicably interrupted by spontaneous remissions of variable length and degree. In his study of these remissions, spontaneous and postsplenectomy, Minot measured not only the hemoglobin concentrations but also the reticulocyte count, the latter because of his conviction—ahead of its time—that the reticulocyte count represents activity of the marrow:

The rate and degree of formation of the formed blood elements can be studied clinically in a number of ways. The chief source of these elements is the bone marrow. Thus, in order to gauge the power of regeneration and formation of the formed elements, one must study the activity of the marrow. One must scrutinize, not only the increases of bone marrow activity, but also the intensity and quality of that activity and its possible relation to the therapeutic procedure.

Evidence of increased activity on the part of the marrow in the production of red cells may be shown by an increase of young forms of red corpuscles. The presence of increased numbers of reticulated red cells, especially of a certain type, the presence of blasts, Howell-Jolly bodies, polychromatophilia, and certain types of stippling should be considered in studying the activity of the bone marrow. Variations of size and shape of the red cells may be of significance in certain cases.

The decreased activity in the production of red cells may be evidenced by an absence of the factors indicating activity. A rising red count does not necessarily mean an increased activity of the marrow, for the count may rise as the result of a lessened destruction. Increased activity is entirely consistent with an anemia when formation does not compensate destruction. Likewise, an extreme grade of anemia may be associated

From the Department of Hematology, Walter Reed Army Institute of Research, Washington, DC.

with decreased destruction and caused by decreased formation. . . . It is possible to attribute improvement to an increase in
blood formation as well as to a decrease in blood destruction.
We have, therefore, submitted our cases of pernicious anemia
to a critical study of the effect of splenectomy on the
blood-forming organs with a view of determining if possible the
value of this procedure in altering the activity of the bone
marrow.[3]

The dynamics of pernicious anemia had never been so
carefully scrutinized, and thus the method to be used for
the study of the effects of diet had been locked into place
by Minot ten years before that research was begun.

### Dietary Research

The stimulus to begin came from research performed
on the treatment of induced hemorrhage anemia in
dogs. In the 1926 *JAMA* article, Minot wrote:

Following the work of Whipple and Robscheit-Robbins, we
made a few observations on patients concerning the influence
of a diet containing an abundance of liver and muscle meat on
blood regeneration. The effect appeared to be quite similar to
that which they obtained in dogs. These observations, together
with the information given above, led us to investigate the
value of a diet with an abundance of food rich in complete
proteins and iron—particularly liver— and relatively low in fat
as a means of treatment for pernicious anemia. . . . Whipple
has suggested that in pernicious anemia there may be a scarcity
of the material from which the stroma of the red blood cells
are formed, or that a disease of the stroma-forming cells of the
marrow exists. Thus, theoretically perhaps liver and other
foods rich in complete proteins may enhance the formation of
red blood cells in this disease, especially by supplying material
to build their stroma.[1]

George Whipple and Frieda Robscheit-Robbins (who
unaccountably did not receive the Nobel accolade) had
devised an elegant model to study hemorrhage anemia
in dogs.[5] The animals ate a standard, quasisynthetic diet,
and blood was removed every two weeks in an amount
sufficient to maintain a predetermined level of anemia.
After months of stabilization, one or another material
was added to the diet, and it was then determined how
much more blood must be removed to maintain the level
of anemia. Adding iron worked well to increase the
production of hemoglobin and red cells, and cooked
liver worked even better. It is evident that the dogs had
iron-deficiency anemia, nothing like pernicious anemia,
but both Whipple and Minot suspected that there might
be something else in liver. Their minds were open.

To appreciate the impact on hematology of Minot's
discovery, it is necessary to recall the state of the art
before the Minot era. The first great impetus had been
given to hematology by Ehrlich a hundred years ago,
when he stained the cells on dried blood smears, thereby
permitting a detailed analysis of their microstructure.
Leukocytic disorders were classified and subclassified.
Cells of the marrow disclosed the anatomy of differentiation and maturation, but little more could be achieved,
and hematology stagnated in a period of debate,
sometimes acrimonious, about the relations of these
beautifully tinted corpses. William Castle, MD, describes
this as an era of "dried flower collections" and points out
how important it is that the relevant sections of Osler's
*Principles and Practice of Medicine* in the edition of 1928

differ little from those pages in the first edition published
in 1892 (oral communication, January 1983).

Minot's experience changed hematology from a static
to a dynamic science. It resulted in much more clinical
research, such as Castle's[2] experiments leading to the
discovery of intrinsic factor (see Chapter 26) and Cohn's
successful efforts to concentrate the liver factor. Clinical
research replaced microscopy as the cutting edge of
investigation.

The area of medical science that had burgeoned in
those pre-Minot years was bacteriology and infectious
disease. This beautiful, intricate system of cause and
effect provided the explanation of many forms of illness
as well as a temptation to explain them all by toxic
reactions to subclinical infections and "foci of infection."
The squalor of the bowel and its putrescence became a
focus of medical attention. High colonic enemas were
prescribed for neurasthenia. Colectomy was advocated
for dementia praecox, and pernicious anemia was
believed by many to be a consequence of a toxic injury
to red cells that resulted from intestinal sepsis. This
theory was not to be easily surrendered.

For us, who have seen many terrible diseases come
under control, it is difficult to comprehend the intensity
of celebration that attended the announcement in 1926
of this therapeutic conquest. Francis M. Rackemann,
Minot's cousin, in his biography of George Minot
describes one episode:

In the year following the first announcement of the effect of
liver in pernicious anemia, George Minot's fame had spread
widely. On May 9, 1927, at the Annual Meeting of the
American Medical Association held in Washington, D.C., the
important paper on the morning program of the Section on
Practice of Medicine was the report by Minot and Murphy
entitled "A Diet Rich in Liver in the Treatment of Pernicious
Anemia."[6]
Word about the importance of this paper had spread, and in
the brief interval before it the members crowded in so that
even the big ballroom of the Mayflower Hotel was packed
with men. When the Chairman of the Section, our friend Dr.
Rollin T. Woodyatt, introduced George, the entire audience
rose to its feet and applauded as George walked forward to
the rostrum.
Medical audiences do not do this often, but this time the
admiration for Dr. George Minot and the appreciation of his
achievement were so intense that they had to burst out
spontaneously.[7]

In 1939, Einar Meulengracht, the great Danish physician, reminisced about the reaction in Europe.

We all recall distinctly the profound impression it made when it
became known that a disease with which we had had only the
gravest experience, a disease which sooner or later ended in
death, a disease which—as if to emphasize this human
tragedy—could often be brought into a state of remission only
to make disappointment so much more bitter, that this disease
was now one from which, as if by a miracle, all could
recover.[8]

Actually, the European reaction, although generally
favorable, was, to some extent, a mixed one. That
summer when Soma Weiss, chief of the medical service
at the Peter Bent Brigham Hospital in Boston, went
abroad, he was called on repeatedly to certify that the

work was indeed valid (William Castle, MD, oral communication, January 1983).

There were sceptics and the most famous was Professor Otto Naegeli,[9] the leading European haematologist; he felt it was not a specific therapeutic agent but merely a symptomatic treatment and that, as time went on, there would be more and more reports of failures. He sent a questionnaire to 120 European haematologists asking how many failures they had had; among the eighty who replied, 27 reported successes without any failures and the others reported isolated failures amongst many successes, and reading the article, it is fairly clear that the failures were either not pernicious anemia or had received insufficient treatment. Naegeli's attitude is understandable: he was the leading haematologist, and a very clever and able man; he had written the standard textbook of haematology, a very fine book which can be consulted with profit today, of which the first edition appeared in 1907; he knew that pernicious anaemia showed unaccountable remissions and relapses and that innumerable claims of effective therapeutic agents had been made in the past and after a few years had been forgotten. But Naegeli as a young man had formed a firm conviction that pernicious anaemia was a toxic anaemia; he taught it to his students, it appeared in his textbook and, yet, there was this young man (Minot was just over forty) from America saying something different. It couldn't possibly be right.[10]

On the other hand, some Europeans jumped on the bandwagon. Several Germans published reports of the use of spleen feeding and spleen extract in the treatment of polycythemia[11,12]; the spleen has traditionally been regarded as the foil of the liver.

Years after it was accepted that the Minot experiment had truly established that megaloblastic anemia is caused by deficiency of a dietary factor, some European observers still shook their heads over the reasons for its success. There had been a non sequitur in Minot's reasoning: the correction of Whipple's experimental hemorrhage anemia depended on the iron in liver while Minot's correction of pernicious anemia depended on a vitamin in liver.[13] Again, Minot had made the "false assumption" that the liver would supply good protein to build red cells.[10] Actually, both Minot and Whipple had been commendably modest in explaining results. While contemporaries spoke unhesitatingly of Whipple's iron-rich diet,[14] Whipple himself was cautious. Inorganic iron had not performed as well as liver, for some reason, and in his 1925 article[5] iron is not mentioned; he wrote instead of "evidence that the *body stores in the liver* [his emphasis] parent substances which are used in the construction of hemoglobin and red cells." Minot was certainly aware that Whipple's dogs with microcytic red cells lacked iron for hemoglobin while his patients with macrocytic red cells did not. With no perceivable lack of anything for the synthesis of hemoglobin, he suggested that the lack was of materials for the synthesis of red cell stroma. He noted: "We are inclined to believe that something contained in the foods rich in complete proteins is particularly responsible for the improvement in the state of the blood."[1] Although he noted that the large amounts of liver provided a "complete protein," in his uncertainty he also wrote of the possibility that "liver can improve the state of the blood in pernicious anemia . . . due to . . . [an] unknown cause."[1]

## Toward B[12]

After the discovery in 1943 of folic acid, its abundance in beef liver, and its ability in massive doses to correct the megaloblastic marrow in pernicious anemia, it had been suggested that Minot's success must have depended on the folic acid because the liver did not provide intrinsic factor to permit absorption of vitamin B[12]. At this time, however, in the early 1950s, it was amply demonstrated that large oral doses of cyanocobalamin can consistently correct the avitaminosis, even in the absence of intrinsic factor.[15] Besides, folic acid does not prevent spinal cord lesions. "The unitarian view of the megaloblastic anemias must be abandoned and once again Addisonian pernicious anaemia should stand alone."[10] Castle[2] pointed out later that the 250 g per day of beef liver ingested by Minot's patients provided 250 $\mu$g of B[12], surely a massive allowance for a vitamin of which the daily requirement is but 1 $\mu$g.

In 1950 in England, the toxic theory of pathogenesis of pernicious anemia was still debated seriously.[16] Minot had perceived that this concept was truly believed, and he did not attempt to shoot it down:

Numerous authorities hold the view that an intestinal bacterial toxemia plays an important etiologic rôle in this disease. One may choose to believe that any benefit these patients derive soon after beginning to take certain foods is to be attributed to changing rapidly the intestinal flora, thus decreasing a bacterial toxemia, rather than considering that the foods influence in some unknown, but more direct, manner the formation or destruction of red blood cells.[1]

Minot's[1] modesty carried through to the end of his article:

It is possible that this series of cases eventually may be proved to be unusual in that there happened to be treated a group that would have taken a turn for the better under other circumstances. Also, time may show that the special diet used, or liver and similar food, is no more advantageous in the treatment of pernicious anemia than any ordinary nutritious diet. Let this be as it may, at the present time it seems to us, as it has to Gibson and Howard, that it is wise to urge pernicious anemia patients to take a diet of the sort described. . . .

All the patients have remained to date in a good state of health except three, who discontinued the diet; two rapidly improved on resuming it and the other has just commenced it again. As the diet was advised for most of the patients less than eight months ago, enough time has not yet elapsed to determine whether or not the remissions will last any longer than in other cases.

A last chapter of the relation between George Minot's work and the AMA was written after his death in 1950:

After George died, the officers of the Section on Experimental Medicine and Therapeutics of the American Medical Association established the George Richards Minot Memorial Lectures, with an honorarium made possible by the contributions of his former students. It was very appropriate that the first lecture, given in 1951, was by his loyal associate, Dr. William B. Castle, who described "The Contributions of George Richards Minot to Experimental Medicine" [reference 4]. The second lecture, given in 1952, was by Cyrus C. Strugis [reference 17], and the third in 1953 by Dr. Chester S. Keefer [reference 18], both brilliant disciples of Dr. Minot. George did not know of this "measure of the reverence that thoughtful men hold for the great man and the great physician" — as the editorial [reference 19] in the New England Journal of Medicine expressed it at the time.[8]

### References

1. Minot GR, Murphy WP: Treatment of pernicious anemia by a special diet. *JAMA* 1926;87:470-476.

2. Castle WB: The conquest of pernicious anemia, in Wintrobe MM (ed): *Blood Pure and Eloquent.* New York, McGraw-Hill Book Co, 1980, pp 282-317.

3. Lee RI, Minot GR, Vincent B: Splenectomy in pernicious anemia: Studies on bone marrow stimulation. *JAMA* 1916;67:719-723.

4. Castle WB: The contributions of George Richards Minot to experimental medicine, presented as the first George R. Minot Lecture of the Section on Experimental Medicine and Therapeutics at the Annual Meeting of the American Medical Association, Atlantic City, NJ, June 14, 1951. *N Engl J Med* 1952;247:585-591.

5. Robscheit-Robbins FS, Whipple GH: Blood regeneration in severe anemia: II. Favorable influence of liver, heart and skeletal muscle in diet. *Am J Physiol* 1925;72:408-418.

6. Minot GR, Murphy WP: A diet rich in liver in the treatment of pernicious anemia: Study of 105 cases. *JAMA* 1927;89:759-766.

7. Rackemann FM: *The Inquisitive Physician: The Life and Times of George Richards Minot, AB, MD, DSc.* Cambridge, Mass, Harvard University Press, 1956.

8. Meulengracht E: Some historical aspects of hematology, in *Symposium on Blood.* Madison, University of Wisconsin Press, 1939, pp 3-13.

9. Naegeli O, Bloor HU: Ergebnisse einer Reindfrage über die Erfolge der Lebertherapie bei pernicioser Anämie. *Folia Haematol* 1930;39:527-529.

10. Robb-Smith AHT: The advantages of false assumptions. *Oxford Med School Gazz* 1950;2:53-75.

11. Friedemann V, Deicher H: Orale Milztherapie bei Polycythämie. *Klin Wochnschr* 1929;8:404.

12. Nipperdy W: Ueber die Wirkung von Milzextracten anf das rote Blutbild, insbesonderer bei Hyperglobulia vera. *Dtsch Med Wochnschr* 1928;54:1517-1518, 1929;55:1085-1086.

13. Bodley Scott R: Discussion on the pathogenesis and treatment of the megaloblastic anaemias. *Proc R Soc Med* 1950;43:953-957.

14. Gibson RB, Howard CP: Metabolic studies in pernicious anemia. *Arch Intern Med* 1923;32:1-16.

15. Conley CL, Green TW, Hartmann RC, et al: Prolonged treatment of pernicious anemia with vitamin $B_{12}$. *Am J Med* 1952;13:284-292.

16. Watson GM: Discussion on the pathogenesis and treatment of the megaloblastic anaemias. *Proc R Soc Med* 1950;43:957-960.

17. Sturgis CC: Some aspects of the leukemia problem: The Minot lecture. *JAMA* 1952;150:1551-1556.

18. Keefer CS: Present day treatment of subacute bacterial endocarditis: The Minot lecture. *JAMA* 1953;152:1397-1400.

19. George R. Minot lectureship, editorial. *N Engl J Med* 1952;247:621-622.

# Chapter 22

# The Care of the Patient*

### Francis W. Peabody, M.D.

#### Boston

It is probably fortunate that systems of education are constantly under the fire of general criticism, for if education were left solely in the hands of teachers the chances are good that it would soon deteriorate. Medical education, however, is less likely to suffer from such stagnation, for whenever the lay public stops criticizing the type of modern doctor, the medical profession itself may be counted on to stir up the stagnant pool and cleanse it of its sedimentary deposit. The most common criticism made at present by older practitioners is that young graduates have been taught a great deal about the mechanism of disease, but very little about the practice of medicine—or, to put it more bluntly, they are too "scientific" and do not know how to take care of patients.

One is, of course, somewhat tempted to question how completely fitted for his life work the practitioner of the older generation was when he first entered on it, and how much the haze of time has led him to confuse what he learned in the school of medicine with what he acquired in the harder school of experience. But the indictment is a serious one and it is concurred in by numerous recent graduates, who find that in the actual practice of medicine they encounter many situations which they had not been led to anticipate and which they are not prepared to meet effectively. Where there is so much smoke, there is undoubtedly a good deal of fire, and the problem for teachers and for students is to consider what they can do to extinguish whatever is left of this smoldering distrust.

To begin with, the fact must be accepted that one cannot expect to become a skillful practitioner of medicine in the four or five years allotted to the medical curriculum. Medicine is not a trade to be learned but a profession to be entered. It is an ever widening field that requires continued study and prolonged experience in close contact with the sick. All that the medical school can hope to do is to supply the foundations on which to build. When one considers the amazing progress of science in its relation to medicine during the last thirty years, and the enormous mass of scientific material which must be made available to the modern physician, it is not surprising that the schools have tended to concern themselves more and more with this phase of the educational problem. And while they have been absorbed in the difficult task of digesting and correlating new knowledge, it has been easy to overlook the fact that the application of the principles of science to the diagnosis and treatment of disease is only one limited aspect of medical practice. The practice of medicine in its broadest sense includes the whole relationship of the physician with his patient. It is an art, based to an increasing extent on the medical sciences, but comprising much that still remains outside the realm of any science. The art of medicine and the science of medicine are not antagonistic but supplementary to each other. There is no more contradiction between the science of medicine and the art of medicine than between the science of aeronautics and the art of flying. Good practice presupposes an understanding of the sciences which contribute to the structure of modern medicine, but it is obvious that sound professional training should include a much broader equipment.

The problem that I wish to consider, therefore, is whether this larger view of the profession cannot be approached even under the conditions imposed by the present curriculum of the medical school. Can the practitioner's art be grafted on the main trunk of the fundamental sciences in such a way that there shall arise a symmetrical growth, like an expanding tree, the leaves of which may be for the "healing of the nations"?

One who speaks of the care of patients is naturally thinking about circumstances as they exist in the practice of medicine; but the teacher who is attempting to train medical students is immediately confronted by the fact that, even if he could, he cannot make the conditions under which he has to teach clinical medicine exactly similar to those of actual practice.

The primary difficulty is that instruction has to be carried out largely in the wards and dispensaries of hospitals rather than in the patient's home and the physician's office. Now the essence of the practice of medicine is that it is an intensely personal matter, and one of the chief differences between private practice and

---

*One of a series of talks before the students of the Harvard Medical School on "The Care of the Patient."

hospital practice is that the latter always tends to become impersonal. At first sight this may not appear to be a very vital point, but it is, as a matter of fact, the crux of the whole situation. The treatment of a disease may be entirely impersonal; the care of a patient must be completely personal. The significance of the intimate personal relationship between physician and patient cannot be too strongly emphasized, for in an extraordinarily large number of cases both diagnosis and treatment are directly dependent on it, and the failure of the young physician to establish this relationship accounts for much of his ineffectiveness in the care of patients.

## INSTRUCTION IN TREATMENT OF DISEASE

Hospitals, like other institutions founded with the highest human ideals, are apt to deteriorate into dehumanized machines, and even the physician who has the patient's welfare most at heart finds that pressure of work forces him to give most of his attention to the critically sick and to those whose diseases are a menace to the public health. In such cases he must first treat the specific disease, and there then remains little time in which to cultivate more than a superficial personal contact with the patients. Moreover, the circumstances under which the physician sees the patient are not wholly favorable to the establishment of the intimate personal relationship that exists in private practice, for one of the outstanding features of hospitalization is that it completely removes the patient from his accustomed environment. This may, of course, be entirely desirable, and one of the main reasons for sending a person into the hospital is to get him away from home surroundings, which, be he rich or poor, are often unfavorable to recovery; but at the same time it is equally important for the physician to know the exact character of those surroundings.

Everybody, sick or well, is affected in one way or another, consciously or subconsciously, by the material and spiritual forces that bear on his life, and especially to the sick such forces may act as powerful stimulants or depressants. When the general practitioner goes into the home of a patient, he may know the whole background of the family life from past experience; but even when he comes as a stranger he has every opportunity to find out what manner of man his patient is, and what kind of circumstances make his life. He gets a hint of financial anxiety or of domestic incompatibility; he may find himself confronted by a querulous, exacting, self-centered patient, or by a gentle invalid overawed by a dominating family; and as he appreciates how these circumstances are reacting on the patient he dispenses sympathy, encouragement or discipline. What is spoken of as a "clinical picture" is not just a photograph of a man sick in bed; it is an impressionistic painting of the patient surrounded by his home, his work, his relations, his friends, his joys, sorrows, hopes and fears. Now, all of this background of sickness which bears so strongly on the symptomatology is liable to be lost sight of in the hospital: I say "liable to" because it is not by any means always lost sight of, and because I believe that by making a constant and conscious effort one can almost always bring it out into its proper perspective. The difficulty is that in the hospital one gets into the habit of using the oil immersion

lens instead of the low power, and focuses too intently on the center of the field.

When a patient enters a hospital, one of the first things that commonly happens to him is that he loses his personal identity. He is generally referred to, not as Henry Jones, but as "that case of mitral stenosis in the second bed on the left." There are plenty of reasons why this is so, and the point is, in itself, relatively unimportant; but the trouble is that it leads, more or less directly, to the patient being treated as a case of mitral stenosis, and not as a sick man. The disease is treated, but Henry Jones, lying awake nights while he worries about his wife and children, represents a problem that is much more complex than the pathologic physiology of mitral stenosis, and he is apt to improve very slowly unless a discerning intern happens to discover why it is that even large doses of digitalis fail to slow his heart rate. Henry happens to have heart disease, but he is not disturbed so much by dyspnea as he is by anxiety for the future, and a talk with an understanding physician who tries to make the situation clear to him, and then gets the social service worker to find a suitable occupation, does more to straighten him out than a book full of drugs and diets. Henry has an excellent example of a certain type of heart disease, and he is glad that all the staff find him interesting, for it makes him feel that they will do the best they can to cure him; but just because he is an interesting case he does not cease to be a human being with very human hopes and fears. Sickness produces an abnormally sensitive emotional state in almost every one, and in many cases the emotional state repercusses, as it were, on the organic disease. The pneumonia would probably run its course in a week, regardless of treatment, but the experienced physician knows that by quieting the cough, getting the patient to sleep, and giving a bit of encouragement, he can save his patient's strength and lift him through many distressing hours. The institutional eye tends to become focused on the lung, and it forgets that the lung is only one member of the body.

## PATIENTS WHO HAVE "NOTHING THE MATTER WITH THEM"

But if teachers and students are liable to take a limited point of view even toward interesting cases of organic disease, they fall into much more serious error in their attitude toward a large group of patients who do not show objective, organic pathologic conditions, and who are generally spoken of as having "nothing the matter with them." Up to a certain point, as long as they are regarded as diagnostic problems, they command attention; but as soon as a physician has assured himself that they do not have organic disease, he passes them over lightly.

Take the case of a young woman, for instance, who entered the hospital with a history of nausea and discomfort in the upper part of the abdomen after eating. Mrs. Brown had "suffered many things of many physicians." Each of them gave her a tonic and limited her diet. She stopped eating everything that any of her physicians advised her to omit, and is now living on a little milk and a few crackers; but her symptoms persist.

The history suggests a possible gastric ulcer or gallstones, and with a proper desire to study the case thoroughly, she is given a test meal, gastric analysis and duodenal intubation, and roentgen-ray examinations are made of the gastro-intestinal tract and gallbladder. All of these diagnostic methods give negative results; that is, they do not show evidence of any structural change. The case is immediately much less interesting than if it had turned out to be a gastric ulcer with atypical symptoms. The visiting physician walks by and says "Well, there's nothing the matter with her." The clinical clerk says "I did an awful lot of work on that case and it turned out to be nothing at all." The intern, who wants to clear out the ward so as to make room for some interesting cases, says "Mrs. Brown, you can send for your clothes and go home tomorrow. There really is nothing the matter with you, and fortunately you have not got any of the serious troubles we suspected. We have used all the most modern and scientific methods and we find that there is no reason why you should not eat anything you want to. I'll give you a tonic to take when you go home." Same story, same colored medicine! Mrs. Brown goes home, somewhat better for her rest in new surroundings, thinking that nurses are kind and physicians are pleasant, but that they do not seem to know much about the sort of medicine that will touch her trouble. She takes up her life and the symptoms return—and then she tries chiropractic, or perhaps it is Christian Science.

It is rather fashionable to say that the modern physician has become "too scientific." Now, was it too scientific, with all the stomach tubes and blood counts and roentgen-ray examinations? Not at all. Mrs. Brown's symptoms might have been due to a gastric ulcer or to gallstones, and after such a long course it was only proper to use every method that might help to clear the diagnosis. Was it, perhaps, not scientific enough? The popular conception of a scientist as a man who works in a laboratory and who uses instruments of precision is as inaccurate as it is superficial, for a scientist is known, not by his technical processes, but by his intellectual processes; and the essence of the scientific method of thought is that it proceeds in an orderly manner toward the establishment of a truth. Now the chief criticism to be made of the way Mrs. Brown's case was handled is that the staff was contented with a half truth. The investigation of the patient was decidedly unscientific in that it stopped short of even an attempt to determine the real cause of the symptoms. As soon as organic disease could be excluded the whole problem was given up, but the symptoms persisted. Speaking candidly, the case was a medical failure in spite of the fact that the patient went home with the assurance that there was "nothing the matter" with her.

A good many "Mrs. Browns," male and female, come to hospitals, and a great many more go to private physicians. They are all characterized by the presence of symptoms that cannot be accounted for by organic disease, and they are all liable to be told that they have "nothing the matter" with them. Now my own experience as a hospital physician has been rather long and varied, and I have always found that, from my point of view, hospitals are particularly interesting and cheerful places; but I am fairly certain that, except for a few low grade morons and some poor wretches who want to get in out of the cold, there are not many people who become hospital patients unless there is something the matter with them. And, by the same token, I doubt whether there are many people, except for those stupid creatures who would rather go to the physician than go to the theater, who spend their money on visiting private physicians unless there is something the matter with them. In hospital and in private practice, however, one finds this same type of patient, and many physicians whom I have questioned agree in saying that, excluding cases of acute infection, approximately half of their patients complained of symptoms for which an adequate organic cause could not be discovered. Numerically, then, these patients constitute a large group, and their fees go a long way toward spreading butter on the physician's bread. Medically speaking, they are not serious cases as regards prospective death, but they are often extremely serious as regards prospective life. Their symptoms will rarely prove fatal, but their lives will be long and miserable, and they may end by nearly exhausting their families and friends. Death is not the worst thing in the world, and to help a man to a happy and useful career may be more of a service than the saving of life.

## PHYSIOLOGIC DISTURBANCES FROM EMOTIONAL REACTIONS

What is the matter with all these patients? Technically, most of them come under the broad heading of the "psychoneuroses"; but for practical purposes many of them may be regarded as patients whose subjective symptoms are due to disturbances of the physiologic activity of one or more organs or systems. These symptoms may depend on an increase or a decrease of a normal function, on an abnormality of function, or merely on the subjects becoming conscious of a wholly normal function that normally goes on unnoticed; and this last conception indicates that there is a close relation between the appearance of the symptoms and the threshold of the patient's nervous reactions. The ultimate causes of these disturbances are to be found, not in any gross structural changes in the organs involved, but rather in nervous influences emanating from the emotional or intellectual life, which, directly or indirectly, affect in one way or another organs that are under either voluntary or involuntary control.

Every one has had experiences that have brought home the way in which emotional reactions affect organic functions. Some have been nauseated while anxiously waiting for an important examination to begin, and a few may even have vomited; others have been seized by an attack of diarrhea under the same circumstances. Some have had polyuria before making a speech, and others have felt thumping extrasystoles or a pounding tachycardia before a football game. Some have noticed rapid shallow breathing when listening to a piece of bad news, and others know the type of occipital headache, with pain down the muscles of the back of the neck that comes from nervous anxiety and fatigue.

These are all simple examples of the way that

emotional reactions may upset the normal functioning of an organ. Vomiting and diarrhea are due to abnormalities of the motor function of the gastro-intestinal tract—one to the production of an active reversed peristalsis of the stomach and a relaxation of the cardiac sphincter, the other to hyperperistalsis of the large intestine. The polyuria is caused by vasomotor changes in renal circulation, similar in character to the vasomotor changes that take place in the peripheral vessels in blushing and blanching of the skin, and in addition there are quite possibly associated changes in the rate of blood flow and in blood pressure. Tachycardia and extrasystoles indicate that not only the rate but also the rhythm of the heart is under a nervous control that can be demonstrated in the intact human being as well as in the experimental animal. The ventilatory function of the respiration is extraordinarily subject to nervous influences; so much so, in fact, that the study of the respiration in man is associated with peculiar difficulties. Rate, depth and rhythm or breathing are easily upset by even minor stimuli, and in extreme cases the disturbance in total ventilation is sometimes so great that gaseous exchange becomes affected. Thus, I remember an emotional young woman who developed a respiratory neurosis with deep and rapid breathing, and expired so much carbon dioxide that the symptoms of tetany ensued. The explanation of the occipital headaches and of so many pains in the muscles of the back is not entirely clear, but they appear to be associated with changes in muscular tone or with prolonged states of contraction. There is certainly a very intimate correlation between mental tenseness and muscular tenseness, and whatever methods are used to produce mental relaxation will usually cause muscular relaxation, together with relief of this type of pain. A similar condition is found in the so-called writers' cramp, in which the painful muscles of the hand result, not from manual work, but from mental work.

One might go on much further, but these few illustrations will suffice to recall the infinite number of ways in which physiologic functions may be upset by emotional stimuli, and the manner in which the resulting disturbances of function manifest themselves as symptoms. These symptoms, although obviously not due to anatomic changes, may, nevertheless, be very disturbing and distressing, and there is nothing imaginary about them. Emotional vomiting is just as real as the vomiting due to pyloric obstruction, and so-called "nervous headaches" may be as painful as if they were due to a brain tumor. Moreover, it must be remembered that symptoms based on functional disturbances may be present in a patient who has, at the same time, organic disease, and in such cases the determination of the causes of the different symptoms may be an extremely difficult matter. Every one accepts the relationship between the common functional symptoms and nervous reactions, for convincing evidence is to be found in the fact that under ordinary circumstances the symptoms disappear just as soon as the emotional cause has passed. But what happens if the cause does not pass away? What if, instead of having to face a single three-hour examination, one has to face a life of being constantly on the rack? The emotional stimulus persists, and continues to produce the distur-

bances of function. As with all nervous reactions, the longer the process goes on, or the more frequently it goes on, the easier it is for it to go on. The unusual nervous track becomes an established path. After a time, the symptom and the subjective discomfort that it produces come to occupy the center of the picture, and the causative factors recede into a hazy background. The patient no longer thinks "I cannot stand this life," but he says out loud "I cannot stand this nausea and vomiting. I must go to see a stomach specialist."

Quite possibly the comment on this will be that the symptoms of such "neurotic" patients are well known, and they ought to go to a neurologist or a psychiatrist and not to an internist or a general practitioner. In an era of internal medicine, however, which takes pride in the fact that it concerns itself with the functional capacity of organs rather than with mere structural changes and which has developed so many "functional tests" of kidneys, heart, and liver, is it not rather narrow minded to limit one's interest to those disturbances of function which are based on anatomic abnormalities? There are other reasons, too, why most of these "functional" cases belong to the field of general medicine. In the first place, the differential diagnosis between organic disease and functional disturbance is often extremely difficult, and it needs the broad training in the use of general clinical and laboratory methods which forms the equipment of the internist. Diagnosis is the first step in treatment. In the second place, the patients themselves frequently prefer to go to a medical practitioner rather than to a psychiatrist, and in the long run it is probably better for them to get straightened out without having what they often consider the stigma of having been "nervous" cases. A limited number, it is true, are so refractory or so complex that the aid of the psychiatrist must be sought, but the majority can be helped by the internist without highly specialized psychologic technic, if he will appreciate the significance of functional disturbances and interest himself in their treatment. The physician who does take these cases seriously—one might say scientifically—has the great satisfaction of seeing some of his patients get well, not as the result of drugs, or as the result of the disease having run its course, but as the result of his own individual efforts.

Here, then, is a great group of patients in which it is not the disease but the man or the woman who needs to be treated. In general hospital practice physicians are so busy with the critically sick, and in clinical teaching are so concerned with training students in physical diagnosis and attempting to show them all the types of organic disease, that they do not pay as much attention as they should to the functional disorders. Many a student enters practice having hardly heard of them except in his course in psychiatry, and without the faintest conception of how large a part they will play in his future practice. At best, his method of treatment is apt to be a cheerful reassurance combined with a placebo. The successful diagnosis and treatment of these patients, however, depends almost wholly on the establishment of that intimate personal contact between physician and patient which forms the basis of private practice. Without this, it is quite impossible for the physician to get an idea of the problems and troubles that lie behind so many functional disorders. If students are to obtain any insight into this field of medicine, they must also be given opportunities to build up the same type of personal relationship with their patients.

## STUDENT'S OPPORTUNITY IN THE HOSPITAL

Is there, then, anything inherent in the conditions of clinical teaching in a general hospital that makes this impossible? Can you form a personal relationship in an impersonal institution? Can you accept the fact that your patient is entirely removed from his natural environment and then reconstruct the background of environment from the history, from the family, from a visit to the home or workshop, and from the information obtained by the social service worker? And while you are building up this environmental background, can you enter into the same personal relationship that you ought to have in private practice? If you can do all this, and I know from experience that you can, then the study of medicine in the hospital actually becomes the practice of medicine, and the treatment of disease immediately takes its proper place in the larger problem of the care of the patient.

When a patient goes to a physician he usually has confidence that the physician is the best, or at least the best available person to help him in what is, for the time being, his most important trouble. He relies on him as on a sympathetic adviser and a wise professional counselor. When a patient goes to a hospital he has confidence in the reputation of the institution, but it is hardly necessary to add that he also hopes to come into contact with some individual who personifies the institution and will also take a human interest in him. It is obvious that the first physician to see the patient is in the strategic position—and in hospitals all students can have the satisfaction of being regarded as physicians.

Here, for instance, is a poor fellow who has just been jolted to the hospital in an ambulance. A string of questions about himself and his family have been fired at him, his valuables and even his clothes have been taken away from him, and he is wheeled into the ward on a truck, miserable, scared, defenseless and, in his nakedness, unable to run away. He is lifted into a bed, becomes conscious of the fact that he is the center of interest in the ward, wishes that he had stayed at home among friends, and just as he is beginning to take stock of his surroundings, finds that a thermometer is being stuck under his tongue. It is all strange and new, and he wonders what is going to happen next. The next thing that does happen is that a man in a long white coat sits down by his bedside, and starts to talk to him. Now it happens that according to our system of clinical instruction that man is usually a medical student. Do you see what an opportunity you have? The foundation of your whole relation with that patient is laid in those first few minutes of contact, just as happens in private practice. Here is a worried, lonely, suffering man, and if you begin by approaching him with sympathy, tact, and consideration, you get his confidence and he becomes your patient. Interns and visiting physicians may come and go, and the hierarchy gives them a precedence; but if you make the most of your opportunities he will regard you as his personal physician, and all the rest as mere consultants. Of course, you must not drop him after you have taken the history and made your physical examination. Once your relationship with him has been established, you must foster it by every means. Watch his condition closely and he will see that you are alert professionally. Make time to have little talks with him—and these talks need not always be about his symptoms. Remember that you want to know him as a man, and this means you must know about his family and friends, his work and his play. What kind of a person is he—cheerful, depressed, introspective, careless, conscientious, mentally keen or dull? Look out for all the little incidental things that you can do for his comfort. These, too, are a part of "the care of the patient." Some of them will fall technically in the field of "nursing" but you will always be profoundly grateful for any nursing technic that you have acquired. It is worth your while to get the nurse to teach you the right way to feed a patient, change the bed, or give a bed pan. Do you know the practical tricks that make a dyspneic patient comfortable? Assume some responsibility for these apparently minor points and you will find that it is when you are doing some such friendly service, rather than when you are a formal questioner, that the patient suddenly starts to unburden himself, and a flood of light is thrown on the situation.

Meantime, of course, you will have been active along strictly medical lines, and by the time your clinical and laboratory examinations are completed you will be surprised at how intimately you know your patient, not only as an interesting case but also as a sick human being. And everything you have picked up about him will be of value in the subsequent handling of the situation. Suppose, for instance, you find conclusive evidence that his symptoms are due to organic disease; say, to a gastric ulcer. As soon as you face the problem of laying out his regimen you find that it is one thing to write an examination paper on the treatment of gastric ulcer and quite another thing to treat John Smith who happens to have a gastric ulcer. You want to begin by giving him rest in bed and a special diet for eight weeks. Rest means both nervous and physical rest. Can he get it best at home or in the hospital? What are the conditions at home? If you keep him in the hospital, it is probably good for him to see certain people, and bad for him to see others. He has business problems that must be considered. What kind of a compromise can you make on them? How about the financial implications of eight weeks in bed followed by a period of convalescence? Is it, on the whole, wiser to try a strict regimen for a shorter period, and, if he does not improve, take up the question of operation sooner than is in general advisable? These, and many similar problems arise in the course of the treatment of almost every patient, and they have to be looked at, not from the abstract point of view of the treatment of the disease, but from the concrete point of view of the care of the individual.

Suppose, on the other hand, that all your clinical and laboratory examinations turn out entirely negative as far as revealing any evidence of organic disease is concerned. Then you are in the difficult position of not having discovered the explanation of the patient's symptoms.

You have merely assured yourself that certain conditions are not present. Of course, the first thing you have to consider is whether these symptoms are the result of organic disease in such an early stage that you cannot definitely recognize it. This problem is often extremely perplexing, requiring great clinical experience for its solution, and often you will be forced to fall back on time in which to watch developments. If, however, you finally exclude recognizable organic disease, and the probability of early or very slight organic disease, it becomes necessary to consider whether the symptomatology may be due to a functional disorder which is caused by nervous or emotional influences. You know a good deal about the personal life of your patient by this time, but perhaps there is nothing that stands out as an obvious etiologic factor, and it becomes necessary to sit down for a long intimate talk with him to discover what has remained hidden.

Sometimes it is well to explain to the patient, by obvious examples, how it is that emotional states may bring about symptoms similar to his own, so that he will understand what you are driving at and will cooperate with you. Often the best way is to go back to the very beginning and try to find out the circumstances of the patient's life at the time the symptoms first began. The association between symptoms and cause may have been simpler and more direct at the onset, at least in the patient's mind, for as time goes on, and the symptoms become more pronounced and distressing, there is a natural tendency for the symptoms to occupy so much of the foreground of the picture that the background is completely obliterated. Sorrow, disappointment, anxiety, self-distrust, thwarted ideals or ambitions in social, business or personal life, and particularly what are called maladaptations to these conditions—these are among the commonest and simplest factors that initiate and perpetuate the functional disturbances. Perhaps you will find that the digestive disturbances began at the time the patient was in serious financial difficulties, and they have recurred whenever he is worried about money matters. Or you may find that ten years ago a physician told the patient he had heart disease, cautioning him "not to worry about it." For ten years the patient has never mentioned the subject, but he has avoided every exertion, and has lived with the idea that sudden death was in store for him. You will find that physicians, by wrong diagnoses and ill considered statements, are responsible for many a wrecked life, and you will discover that it is much easier to make a wrong diagnosis than it is to unmake it. Or, again, you may find that the pain in this woman's back made its appearance when she first felt her domestic unhappiness, and that this man's headaches have been associated, not with long hours of work, but with a constant depression due to unfulfilled ambitions. The causes are manifold and the manifestations protean. Sometimes the mechanism of cause and effect is obvious; sometimes it becomes apparent only after a very tangled skein has been unraveled.

If the establishment of an intimate personal relationship is necessary in the diagnosis of functional disturbances, it becomes doubly necessary in their treatment. Unless there is complete confidence in the sympathetic understanding of the physician as well as in his professional skill, very little can be accomplished; but granted that you have been able to get close enough to the patient to discover the cause of the trouble, you will find that a general hospital is not at all an impossible place for the treatment of functional disturbances. The hospital has, indeed, the advantage that the entire reputation of the institution, and all that it represents in the way of facilities for diagnosis and treatment, go to enhance the confidence which the patient has in the individual physician who represents it. This gives the very young physician a hold on his patients that he could scarcely hope to have without its support. Another advantage is that hospital patients are removed from their usual environment, for the treatment of functional disturbances is often easier when patients are away from friends, relatives, home, work and, indeed, everything that is associated with their daily life. It is true that in a public ward one cannot obtain complete isolation in the sense that this is a part of the Weir Mitchell treatment, but the main object is accomplished if one has obtained the psychologic effect of isolation which comes with an entirely new and unaccustomed atmosphere. The conditions, therefore, under which you, as students, come into contact with patients with functional disturbances are not wholly unfavorable, and with very little effort they can be made to simulate closely the conditions in private practice.

## IMPORTANCE OF PERSONAL RELATIONSHIP

It is not my purpose, however, to go into a discussion of the methods of treating functional disturbances, and I have dwelt on the subject only because these cases illustrate so clearly the vital importance of the personal relationship between physician and patient in the practice of medicine. In all your patients whose symptoms are of functional origin, the whole problem of diagnosis and treatment depends on your insight into the patient's character and personal life, and in every case of organic disease there are complex interactions between the pathologic processes and the intellectual processes which you must appreciate and consider if you would be a wise clinician. There are moments, of course, in cases of serious illness when you will think solely of the disease and its treatment; but when the corner is turned and the immediate crisis is passed, you must give your attention to the patient. Disease in man is never exactly the same as disease in an experimental animal, for in man the disease at once affects and is affected by what we call the emotional life. Thus, the physician who attempts to take care of a patient while he neglects this factor is as unscientific as the investigator who neglects to control all the conditions that may affect his experiment. The good physician knows his patients through and through, and his knowledge is bought dearly. Time, sympathy and understanding must be lavishly dispensed, but the reward is to be found in that personal bond which forms the greatest satisfaction of the practice of medicine. One of the essential qualities of the clinician is interest in humanity, for the secret of the care of the patient is in caring for the patient.

Boston City Hospital.

Aug 10, 1984
(*JAMA* 1984;252:819-820)

# Francis Peabody's 'The Care of the Patient'*

Pauline L. Rabin, MD, David Rabin, MD

This classic essay, with its fabric of pristine humanism, its universality, and its timelessness, embodies the noblest aspirations of the medical profession. Peabody gave his address at the Harvard Medical School during a course on the care of the patient. Dr Joseph Pratt[1] was in the audience and subsequently wrote: "After the lecture I talked with Dr. Peabody. His address doubtless made a deep impression on the audience but there was no evidence of unusual approval. In a few minutes the hall was emptied and we were alone." Since that day in 1926, Peabody's words have become a paradigm for all physicians.

## On the Patient as Person

His essay covers three chief topics. The first is the importance of individualizing medical care. Long before the introduction of the SMAC 46 battery, to which so many patients are subjected even before they see their physician, Peabody cautioned the medical profession in the following words: "the essence of the practice of medicine is that it is an intensely personal matter . . . The treatment of a disease may be entirely impersonal; the care of a patient must be completely personal. The significance of the intimate personal relationship between physician and patient cannot be too strongly emphasized, for in an extraordinarily large number of cases both diagnosis and treatment are directly dependent on it . . ." This philosophy was already deeply ingrained in Peabody while still a medical student. In 1906, addressing the Boylston Medical Society on the treatment of diabetes, he said: "We must not forget in treating diabetes that we are treating a man and not a disease."[2]

The following example bears out Peabody's message. A patient with cancer of the breast had great confidence in her oncologist. She was, however, concerned about metastases and was becoming increasingly depressed. Whenever she asked him a question about her illness, he would give her an answer based on statistical results from the literature. The patient inferred from this that to

him she was no more than an impersonal dot in a computer printout. Clearly, statistical information is extremely valuable. The physician, however, should not hide behind numbers to avoid dealing with the patient's underlying anxiety that prompts such questions.

His second concern is a call to awareness about the dehumanizing experience that so often accompanies hospitalization. Peabody displays remarkable insight into the forces that tend to depersonalize the patient who enters a hospital. He emphasizes the difficulties of getting to know the patient as an individual in a hospital setting. These features have been magnified during the past 60 years. As soon as a patient is registered in a medical center today, his entire past record and laboratory data can be obtained by punching the correct code into a computer. This, of course, provides invaluable information. The various teams of consultants and even the patient's personal physician and resident may become so absorbed in receiving the computerized information that they may spend less time with the patient. These realities can be overcome by adherence to Peabody's credo: "What is spoken of as a 'clinical picture' is not just a photograph of a man sick in bed; it is an impressionistic painting of the patient surrounded by his home, his work, his relations, his friends, his joys, sorrows, hopes, and fears. Now, all of this background of sickness which bears so strongly on the symptomatology is liable to be lost sight of in the hospital . . ." These concerns apply equally to current private practice. Peabody was the great champion of the general practitioner who knew the patient and his family intimately. Today, house calls are virtually obsolete and patients may be seen by a succession of specialists, none of whom has a clear picture or understanding of the man or woman who is the patient.

His third topic is the care of patients who have symptoms for which an organic cause cannot be determined. Peabody devotes a considerable segment of his essay to improving the attitudes of physicians to patients who do not show objective, organic pathological conditions and who are generally spoken of as having "nothing the matter with them." Peabody thought that this group of patients constituted up to half of any physician's practice, and this is probably true

From the Departments of Medicine (Dr D. Rabin) and Psychiatry (Dr P. L. Rabin), Vanderbilt University School of Medicine, Nashville, Tenn.
*A commentary on Peabody F: The care of the patient. *JAMA* 1927;88:877-882.

today. It is known that the majority of antidepressants and minor tranquilizers are prescribed by nonpsychiatrists. Peabody advocates an approach that includes a thorough knowledge of psychological factors operative in the patient's life. This can only be obtained by spending time with the person and gaining his confidence about intimate personal history. Rather than communicating to the patient that there is "nothing the matter," one should take the time to explain "how it is that emotional states may bring about symptoms similar to his own." It has been well documented that educating patients about their illness and about psychological issues is an inherent and critical part of all medical treatment. Today, this approach is appreciated as an important adjuvant in the care of the patient, especially those patients with chronic diseases.

## Dr Peabody's Example

When we initially read this article, we were inspired by the clinical sensitivity linked with scientific perspective but were surprised by an omission of a discussion on the role of the physician with terminally ill and dying patients. Jacob Bigelow, addressing a group of medical students in 1858, had described the duties of a physician to encompass diagnosis, treatment, the relief of symptoms, and the provision of safe passage.[3] By "safe passage" is meant the support and ready availability of the physician to his or her patient until death.[4] Although Peabody did not actually discuss the terminally ill in his famous address, he was communicating another important message regarding this subject to his audience by his very presence there. It was known that he was at that time suffering from an inoperable cancer. Yet, he continued to function, teach, and care for his patients as long as he was able. Thus, he was an example of how a person can accept illness and live alongside it with dignity and purpose. Although the quantity of life granted to him was short (he died at the age of 47 years), the quality of his life was enriched by his dedication to his work, his devotion to his family, and the support he received from his friends. Langdon Warner,[5] a lifelong friend, was moved to write his account of those remarkable visits:

You came hesitating, perhaps, and wondering how you could stand it. But you smoked, gossiped and reported the news; discussed a marriage, birth or a death; told your troubles, took some of the invalid's grapes, and left. There had been no sad-eyed bravery about it, no attempt to ignore the obvious. And all this time when our hearts were standing still with the pity of it, his task was gently to show us that there was no need for horror.

There have been dramatic changes in medicine in the nearly 60 years since Peabody died. Much would have delighted and perhaps even amazed him. We suspect, however, that he would have viewed some of the changes with deep apprehension. The cost of medical care now approaches 300 billion dollars annually or 10.5% of the gross national product and, despite this staggering figure, good medical care is not readily available to all citizens (New Republic April 18, 1983, p 19). In 1923, he wrote:

The primary function of a municipal hospital is without question, to provide the best care for the sick poor of the city.

. . . The municipal hospital must be prepared at all times to admit any and every citizen genuinely in need of medical aid. . . . In a municipal institution, even more than in a private institution, there is need for trained social workers. The duty of the city towards the health of its citizens certainly extends beyond the walls of the hospital.[6]

Today, the care of the poor and those without adequate medical insurance is delegated to the already overburdened general hospitals, which are supported by increasingly depleted municipal funds. Some city hospitals, in fact, have been forced to close. The health plight of the poor is becoming critical.

How would this man who chose Boston City Hospital over choice appointments at Johns Hopkins, Yale, and Stanford have viewed the burgeoning hospital-for-profit phenomenon? How would this man who spent the last days of his life completing an essay on the soul of the clinic have reacted to the marketing of health care by enormous corporations?[7] He would surely have been exercised by the growing medical needs of the chronically ill and the aged and by a nursing home population of 1.3 million that is expected to climb to 2 million within a decade. Nor would he have avoided confronting the awesome ethical dilemmas that face physicians engaged in the care of chronically ill, debilitated patients in nursing homes.[8]

In all probability, he would have shared Lewis Thomas' concern about the widening gap between the physician and his patient and might well have commended Thomas'[9] turn of phrase, "Medicine is no longer the laying on of hands, it is more like the reading of signals from machines." He certainly would have agreed also with Thomas' concern for the changing nature of the medical profession today. Writes Thomas, "If I were a medical student or an intern, just getting ready to begin, I would be apprehensive that my real job, caring for sick people, might soon be taken away, leaving me with the quite different occupation of looking after machines." Peabody's scientific contributions were outstanding. Had he lived another few years, it is very possible that he would have shared with his friend Minot the Nobel Prize for the discovery of liver therapy for pernicious anemia (see Chapter 21). Nevertheless, his legacy to medicine is eternal. He was the compleat physician, clinical scientist, teacher, healer, counselor, confidant, and friend to his patients.

## References

1. Pratt JH: The personality of the physician. N Engl J Med 1936;214:364-370.
2. Boylston Medical Society Records, 1899-1908, pp 307-308.
3. Krant J: Dying and Dignity. Springfield, Ill, Charles C Thomas Publisher, 1974, p 60.
4. Bigelow J: Brief Exposition of Rationale Medicine. Boston, Phillips, Sampson and Company, 1858.
5. Warner L, quoted by Peabody FG: Francis Weld Peabody, 1881-1927, a Memoir. Cambridge, Mass, Riverside Press, 1933, pp 69-70.
6. Peabody FW: The function of a municipal hospital. Boston Med Surg J 1923;189:125-129.
7. Peabody FW: The soul of the clinic. JAMA 1928;90:1193-1197.
8. Hilfiker D: Allowing the debilitated to die. N Engl J Med 1983;308:716-719.
9. Thomas L: The Youngest Science. New York, Viking Press Inc, 1983.

Oct 15, 1932
(*JAMA* 1932;99:1323-1329)

## Chapter 23

# Regional Ileitis

## A Pathologic and Clinical Entity

Burrill B. Crohn, M.D.

Leon Ginzburg, M.D.

and

Gordon D. Oppenheimer, M.D.

New York

We propose to describe, in its pathologic and clinical details, a disease of the terminal ileum, affecting mainly young adults, characterized by a subacute or chronic necrotizing and cicatrizing inflammation. The ulceration of the mucosa is accompanied by a disproportionate connective tissue reaction of the remaining walls of the involved intestine, a process which frequently leads to stenosis of the lumen of the intestine, associated with the formation of multiple fistulas.

The disease is clinically featured by symptoms that resemble those of ulcerative colitis, namely, fever, diarrhea and emaciation, leading eventually to an obstruction of the small intestine; the constant occurrence of a mass in the right iliac fossa usually requires surgical intervention (resection). The terminal ileum is alone involved. The process begins abruptly at and involves the ileocecal valve in its maximal intensity, tapering off gradually as it ascends the ileum orally for from 8 to 12 inches (20 to 30 cm.). The familiar fistulas lead usually to segments of the colon, forming small tracts communicating with the lumen of the large intestine; occasionally the abdominal wall, anteriorly, is the site of one or more of these fistulous tracts.

The etiology of the process is unknown; it belongs in none of the categories of recognized granulomatous or accepted inflammatory groups. The course is relatively benign, all the patients who survive operation being alive and well.

From the Mount Sinai Hospital.

Read before the Section on Gastro-Enterology and Proctology at the Eighty-Third Annual Session of the American Medical Association, New Orleans, May 13, 1932.

Such, in essence, is the definition of a disease, the description of which is based on the study, to date, of fourteen cases. These cases have been carefully observed and studied in their clinical course; the pathologic details have resulted from a close inspection of resected specimens from thirteen of fourteen patients operated on by Dr. A. A. Berg.

### RELATIONSHIP OF REGIONAL ILEITIS TO OTHER BENIGN INTESTINAL PROCESSES

There exists in the medical literature a heterogenous group of benign intestinal lesions which have now and then been described under the caption of "benign granulomas." The latter loose term covers a multiplicity of conditions in which both large and small intestines may be involved; it includes all chronic inflammatory lesions of the intestine whose etiology is either unknown or attributable to an unusual physical agent. It represents a hodge-podge or melting-pot in which are thrown all those benign inflammatory intestinal tumors which are neither neoplastic nor due to a specific bacterial agent. Within this group one finds descriptions of foreign body tumors, chronic perforating lesions with gross inflammatory reactions, traumas of the mesentery with intestinal reactions, Hodgkin's granuloma, a late productive reaction to released strangulated hernias of the intestinal wall and numerous other and similar conditions. The so-called benign granulomas all present a tumor-like inflammatory mass which usually simulates carcinoma but which eventually unmasks itself as probably an infectious process of unknown causation. The multiplicity of the possible sites of gastric, intestinal or colonic involvement and the accompanying protean clinical manifestations defeat any effort to include them all in a clear cut clinical entity. The very confusion defies classification.

In this literature, however, there have appeared on occasions references and descriptions that approach the picture that we are about to describe. The entire literature of benign granulomas was reviewed in 1920 by Tietze,[1] who not only described his own cases but covered all previous medical publications. There is nowhere in his encyclopedic article a description which resembles that of regional ileitis. In 1923, Moschcowitz and Wilensky,[2] in describing four cases of benign intestinal granuloma, detailed one case of a disease involving the terminal ileum which closely resembled that in our cases. They grouped it with various other and similar colonic masses as granuloma. Mock[3] in 1931 again described granuloma, but included no example that resembled the cases we have studied.

Just as the generic term of typhus originally included various diseases, from which group eventually typhoid fever, Brill's disease, Rocky Mountain fever, tabardillo and others were split off, so, similarly, do we aim to disintegrate from the general group of varied diseases spoken of as a "benign granuloma" a specific clinical entity with constant and well defined characteristics, which we propose to name "regional ileitis."

### PATHOLOGIC ANATOMY OF THE DISEASE

All the specimens obtained by resection were in patients who had been ill for at least a year. We therefore have no specimen exhibiting the very early phases of the disease. The latter are sometimes encountered at the operating table following an illness of from one to two weeks and diagnosed, as a rule, as acute appendicitis. At this time the terminal ileum is found thickened, soggy and edematous; the serosa is a blotchy red. The mesentery of the terminal ileum is greatly thickened and contains numerous hyperplastic glands. Owing to the possibility of spontaneous resolution, resection has never been performed at this stage, so that we have no knowledge of the intra-intestinal changes present at this time.

The inflammatory process is not, however, a static one, nor is the entire diseased segment affected at one time. The oldest lesions begin apparently at, or just oral to, the ileocecal valve, and the more recent ones are situated proximally. In some of our relatively early cases, we have found isolated lesions separated from the main hypertrophic mass by normal mucosa. These isolated areas are, in our opinion, the earlier and primary lesions of the disease; they consist of oval mucosal ulcerations, about 1 cm. in diameter, located on the mesenteric border of the small bowel and lying in the long axis of the intestine, where a sort of groove is naturally formed by the attachment of the mesentery.

The characteristic, fully developed hypertrophic process is, as a rule, limited to the distal 25 to 35 cm. (10 to 14 inches) of the terminal ileum, including the ileal side of Bauhin's valve and terminating rather abruptly at that point. The most advanced pathologic changes are present at the valve, which in some instances becomes converted into a rigid diaphragm with a small irregular opening. Proximally the severity of the process gradually abates, shading off into normal mucosa. The normal intestinal folds are distorted and broken up by the destructive ulcerative process and rounded and blunted by edema, giving a bullous structure to the mucosal aspect of the intestine, or frequently a cobblestone appearance of the surface of the mucosa may result. A series of small linear ulcerations lying in a groove on the mesenteric side of the bowel is almost always present. Whether these are the remnants of the original ulcerative lesions or whether they are mechanical erosions due to the formation of a *darmstrasse* by the shortening of the fibrotic mesentery, it is impossible to say.

The submucosal and, to a much lesser extent, the muscular layers of the bowel are the seat of marked inflammatory hyperplastic and exudative changes. As a result of these, the wall of the bowel becomes enormously thickened, frequently reaching two or three times its normal density. The lumen of the bowel is greatly encroached on, becomes irregularly distorted and, at times, is only large enough to admit a medium-sized probe. The intestine proximal to the involved segment frequently, but not invariably, becomes greatly dilated and may show superficial irregularly placed tension ulcers. When seen at the operating table, the involved loop is a soggy hoselike mass.

In the older phases of the disease, the exudative reaction is replaced by a fibrostenotic process, and the mucosa appears atrophic with occasional superficial erosions and islands of papillary or polypoid hyperplasia. The serosa loses its gloss and frequently exhibits tubercle-like structures on its surface. The mesentery of the affected segment is greatly thickened and fibrotic, as is the subserosal intestinal fat.

A marked feature is the tendency toward perforation. Free perforation into the peritoneal cavity has not been encountered in this series. The chronic perforation apparently occurs slowly enough to permit of walling off by adhesions to a neighboring viscus, to the parietal peritoneum or to the omentum. There is a marked tendency to the formation of internal fistulas, the sigmoid having been the seat of fistulous involvement four times and the ascending colon and cecum once each. The walled-off abscesses resulting from slow perforation into the peritoneal cavity are, as a rule, considered appendicular in origin. When drained, they give rise to chronic intractable fecal fistulas which defy attempts at simple closure because of the persistence of the underlying inflammatory disease in the bowel. Indirect perforation of the cecum may result from perforation of the ileum into the terminal mesentery with secondary cecal termination of the fistulous tract. Pericecal fibrotic and inflammatory changes which result from the proximity of the ileal focus to the cecum are probably responsible for the roentgenologic changes in the contour of the ascending colon and cecum, such as may be easily confounded

1. Tietze: Ergebn. d. Chir. u. Orthop. **12** : 212, 1920.
2. Moschcowitz, E., and Wilensky, A.: Am. J. M. Sc. **166** : 48, 1923; **173** : 374, 1927.
3. Mock, H. E.: Surg., Gynec. & Obst. **52** : 672, 1931.

with the defect of hyperplastic tuberculosis.

Microscopically, no specific features can be demonstrated. The stained histologic sections showed various degrees of acute, subacute and chronic inflammation, with variations in the predominance of polymorphonuclear, round cell, plasma cell and fibroblastic elements. In the early stages the lesion is a diffuse one, involving mainly the mucosa and submucosa, with the presence of some inflammatory serosal reaction. The mucous membrane shows areas of marked destruction, and at times the glandular structure is almost completely gone, leaving an atrophic layer of epithelium, the result of a regenerative process. In later stages of the disease, the inflammatory reaction is more focal in character. These focal areas of inflammation in the serosa give the appearance, on gross examination, of tubercles.

In some of the cases, the presence of giant cells is quite striking. Special stains have occasionally demonstrated the presence of large pale cells, or groups of cells, probably vegetable in nature, in the vicinity of the giant cells. They could be demonstrated frequently in all the layers of the intestine. These and the giant cells are probably not an essential feature of the pathologic changes in this condition. They are, more likely, accidental findings due to the inclusion of small particles of vegetable matter which have become entrapped in the ulcers, entered the lymphatics and become encapsulated in the process of healing. The resultant foreign body reaction around these nonabsorbable particles results in the presence of the giant cells. To some extent they may be contributory to the marked hypertrophic scarring which occurs. We believe that the attempts, by some authors, to classify this granulomatous condition as an unusual form of tuberculosis were, to a great extent, predicated on the assumption that the giant cells were, necessarily, evidences of tuberculosis.

It is quite likely that in the past this granulomatous condition was confounded with ileocecal tuberculosis, and so missed as a clinical and pathologic entity. The failure of the pathologic reports in our cases to substantiate a suspicion of tuberculosis led us to exercise still greater caution in eliminating a Koch infection as the etiologic agent. With the assistance of Dr. Paul Klemperer in determining moot points, sections from the various cases were again reviewed. No evidences of tuberculosis, syphilis, actinomycosis, Hodgkin's disease or lymphosarcoma were found. Guinea-pig, rabbit and chicken inoculations of triturated material from mesenteric glands and from the intestinal wall proved negative for tuberculosis in five cases. Löwenstein tubercle cultures were also negative in three instances. It is interesting to note that none of these clinical cases presented any evidence of pulmonary tuberculosis; there were no positive Wassermann reactions in this series.

The relation of appendicitis and previous operations to the development of the disease is of some interest. Half of the patients had been subjected to appendectomy before the final resection was performed. In about half of those cases, abnormalities of the terminal ileum were already noted at the time of that operation. In those cases in which there had been no previous appendectomy, the mucosa of the appendix was not involved, as might be expected from the fact that the disease stops on the ileal side of the valve. Inflammation of the outer coats of the appendix, due to the presence of adjacent inflammatory disease, was common.

## THE CLINICAL FEATURES

Etiologically, young adults comprise the largest number of patients. Only two of the patients studied were over 40 years, the average incidence being at 32 years of age; the youngest patient was 17, the oldest 52. Males predominate over females in the proportion of nearly 2:1. There are no known predisposing factors.

Cases of regional ileitis run, in general, a fairly constant and typical clinical course. Most of the patients had been ill for from several months to two years before coming under observation. During this time the outstanding complaints were fever, diarrhea, continuous loss of weight and a progressive anemia. The clinical picture resembles that of a nonspecific ulcerative colitis.

Fever is rarely high, long periods of apyrexia being interspersed with shorter and irregular cycles of moderate temperature. Occasionally, though rarely, the temperature rises above 103 F. Some of the cases run the complete course without fever.

Diarrhea is usually an outstanding feature, though the number of movements and the intensity of the actions never approach those of a true colitis. The average patient has from two to four loose or semisolid daily defecations, sometimes with blood and always with mucus. The stools are rarely mushy or liquid and contain free pus, coagulated lumps of mucus and streaks of blood, but tenesmus is always lacking. There are none of the perianal fistulas, condylomas or perirectal abscesses that characterize the complications of true colitis, for in this disease the rectum and colon are never involved. At times, particularly when the stenotic factor predominates, as in the later periods of the course, constipation rather than diarrhea predominates.

Vomiting characterizes the stenotic type of cases, is never marked or persistent and is usually accompanied by abdominal pain and visible peristalsis.

Pain distributed over the lower abdominal parietes is a common feature of the disease. This pain is dull and cramplike and accompanies, or is followed and relieved by, defecation. It is usually localized to the right lower quadrant and is occasionally referred across the abdomen to the whole lower abdominal region. Occasionally, and not infrequently, when the sigmoid, as is not unusual, becomes adherent to the necrotizing hyperplastic ileum, fistula formation occurs between these two hollow viscera. In these cases the pain is mainly localized over the left lower abdominal quadrants; the mass which is then felt abdominally and per rectum may appear to be an integral disease of the rectosigmoid area.

The general symptoms are those of weakness, usually a rapid and progressive loss of weight, and an anemia which ordinarily is moderate, but which may progress to a severe degree. In the milder cases, however, there may be little or no emaciation and no anemia. The stools contain constantly occult blood. Appetite is poor, particularly during the febrile bouts.

A moderate leukocytosis characterizes some of the cases; in most, the white blood count is normal. Even in the stenotic cases the blood plasm findings that accompany marked obstructions of the upper alimentary tract are rarely seen.

## PHYSICAL EXAMINATION

Certain physical findings characterize this disease, the most constant ones being (1) a mass in the right iliac region, (2) evidences of fistula formation, (3) emaciation and anemia, (4) the scar of a previous appendectomy and (5) evidences of intestinal obstruction.

1. A moderate-sized mass is usually felt in the lower right iliac region or in the lower midabdomen. The mass is usually the size of a small orange, tender, firm, irregular and only slightly movable. This mass is composed of the tremendously hyperplastic ileum, the stenotic inflamed ileocecal junction, which may and often does assume a size of from two to five times that of a normal valve of Bauhin, and frequently an adherent section of the colon or sigmoid to which a fistulous tract has been created. When the sigmoid is adherent and involved, the mass may lie more to the left; when the cecum or ascending colon or hepatic flexure constitutes the distal end of the fistulous tract, the mass may lie more to the right and higher in the abdomen. When the fistulous tract burrows into and through the mesentery, the necrotic process may cause a diffuse mesenteric suppuration which participates in the formation of the mass. The tumor is usually palpable per rectum, though felt only very high with the examining finger.

2. Fistula formation is a constant feature of the disease process. The most common site of adherence is the sigmoid; next in frequency is the cecum and the ascending colon and occasionally the hepatic flexure. As the necrotizing process of the mucosa of the ileum progresses through its several coats, the serosa becomes involved. Any hollow viscus, usually the colon, now becomes adherent to the point of threatened perforation. A slowly progressive perforation is thus walled off, but results in a fistulous tract being formed between the two viscera. In one case the uterus formed the limiting organ of a threatened perforation. In another case, on sigmoidoscopic examination, a nipple-like papillomatous projection was seen high in the rectum, or just above the rectosigmoid angle. This observation was noted at the time, but the proper interpretation was overlooked; it was the colonic end of a perforating fistulous tract. In still another case, the anterior abdominal wall presented a fecal fistula, particularly such as persists after a fruitless appendectomy. These fistulas are usually regarded as cecal in point of origin; they are always, however, communications between the necrotic ileum and the anterior abdominal wall.

3. There are evidences of emaciation and anemia.

4. In at least half of the cases the appendix had been removed at some previous operation. This appendectomy usually antedated by several months or years the present symptoms. In many cases the appendix had been removed several months previous, at which time thickening and tumor-like massive inflammation of the small intestine and mesentery had been noted, though nothing beyond the appendectomy had been attempted. It seemed quite evident that in these cases the lower right abdominal symptoms had resulted in the discovery or in the overlooking of the real pathologic process in the terminal ileum. In all such cases the pathologic report cited "acute and chronic inflammatory changes of the appendix," a report which really whitewashed this organ as a participant in the disease process. In fact, we now know that the process never transcends the limit of Bauhin's valve, and that the appendix is always free from guilt and free from changes.

5. In those cases in which the process has progressed to a stenotic stage, the physical findings are those of intestinal obstruction. Loops of distended intestine may be visible through the emaciated abdominal wall, and puddling is frequently observed in the flat x-ray plates. Visible peristalsis is not uncommon and is accompanied by borborygmus and the passage of gas with evident relief. The visible loops of the distended intestine are usually localized to the lower midabdomen. General distention and ballooning of the whole abdomen are unusual.

## CLINICAL COURSE OF THE DISEASE

There are four various types of clinical course under which most of the cases may be grouped: (1) acute intra-abdominal disease with peritoneal irritation, (2) symptoms of ulcerative enteritis, (3) symptoms of chronic obstruction of the small intestine and (4) persistent and intractable fistulas in the right lower quadrant following previous drainage for ulcer or abdominal abscess.

1. *Signs of Acute Intra-Abdominal Inflammation.—* It is impossible to distinguish these cases preoperatively from those of acute appendicitis. There are generalized colic, pain and tenderness in the right lower quadrant and fever up to 101 or 102 F. The white blood count is elevated. The development of symptoms seems to be somewhat slower than in appendicitis. The presence of a mass even without actual abscess formation is a fairly constant feature. The picture encountered at operation is that of a greatly thickened, red or blotchy terminal ileum, with marked edema of the surrounding tissues and slight exudate of the ileal wall. The mesentery is thickened and edematous, and contains numerous large glands. There is usually clear fluid present in the abdomen. The appendix may appear, and shows evidence of a periappendicitis without mucosal involvement. In some cases an abscess is encountered; in our experience the pus has been thick and grumous, and not as foul smelling as an abscess of appendiceal origin. The future course of these cases cannot be predicted. Some seem to undergo resolution, others to pass into one of the more chronic phases of the disease. Those cases which are drained may develop intractable fistulas.

2. *Symptoms of Ulcerative Enteritis.—*These patients complain of colicky periumbilical or lower abdominal pain. There is a tendency toward looseness of the bowels (from three to five movements a day). The stool is usually liquid or mushy and contains pus, mucus and occult or visible blood. There is no gross melena. A constant fever is present, but the temperature is rarely above 100 F. With the progress of the disease, a marked secondary anemia may develop, reaching as low as 35 per cent hemoglobin. Considerable loss of weight and strength

may occur. In some instances disturbances of general nutrition are slight. This course may continue for as long as a year until exhaustion sets in, or more commonly the cases pass gradually into the stenotic phase of the disease.

3. *Stenotic Phase.*—This is the type most commonly encountered. The symptoms in this stage are those of a subacute or small intestinal obstruction of varying severity. The obstruction, as in most obturating lesions of the small bowel, is not complete. Violent cramps, borborygmus, occasional attacks of vomiting and constipation are present. Visible peristalsis and intestinal erection are common. A palpable mass is practically always present in the lower right quadrant. In this phase of the disease fistulous communications with the colon or sigmoid may lead to the signs and symptoms of colitis, and mask the true nature of the disease. Occasionally the stenotic phase occurs as a primary manifestation of the disease; again, the symptoms may have been present for years (four years in one of our cases).

4. *Persistent Fistulas.*—Even before we had had a resected specimen to confirm our suspicion, we felt that a certain number of the persistent and intractable intestinal fistulas which followed on the drainage of a supposedly appendiceal abscess were in reality due to a nonspecific inflammatory disease involving the terminal ileum. This belief was founded on the following observations: 1. In a number of instances at the time of the second or third operation for closure of the fistulas, the appendix was found intact and not diseased. 2. Removal of the specimens from the sinus tract and from the intestinal end of the fistula failed to reveal any evidence of tuberculosis or other specific disease. 3. The occurrence of ileal without cecal origin of the sinus tract was noted. 4. The tendency of fecal fistulas of simple appendiceal origin is to close spontaneously or to be susceptible of closure by excision of the tract and inversion of the stump. However, in two instances resection of the intestine and fistulous tract revealed the typical pathologic picture of ileitis. We assume, therefore, that fistulas which are of supposedly appendiceal origin, but which have ideal openings and which have resisted simple surgical closure are, in the absence of tuberculosis, to be considered as cases of regional ileitis. One peculiar feature of these fistulas may be remarked: They may develop a few months after the original drainage operation, the wound meanwhile having healed and having remained healed for a few months. An abscess then develops in the wound;

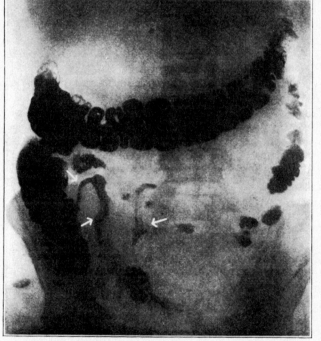

Roentgenogram of the barium meal given by mouth, showing regional ileitis. Note the extent of the strictured area.

when this abscess mass is investigated, a communication with the intestine may be demonstrated.

## ROENTGENOGRAPHIC OBSERVATIONS

Two outstanding facts, one negative and the other positive, are regularly noted. Since the disease simulates regularly the clinical characteristics of ulcerative colitis, the barium enema is first attempted. This procedure results in a negative report. The reason for this is evident in the light of the pathology of the disease. The colon is uniformly free from changes, even though the ileocecal valve is the seat of greatest intensity of the process.

The barium meal, however, when carefully interpreted, gives definite positive findings. These usually consist of distended loops of terminal ileum, in which a fluid level is discernible, and a definite delay in motility of the meal through the distal end of the small intestine. In the four, six and nine hour observations this delayed motility is usually present, though only in the late or stenotic stages is the delay striking. The milder degrees of stasis and puddling in the ileal loops may easily be overlooked by any but a careful roentgenologist. Even when the condition is plainly indicated, the true significance of these reported results may be glossed over by the clinician and an exact diagnosis may thus be missed.

When the ascending colon is the seat of a fistulous communication with the ileum, one may note some stricture deformity of the ascending colon or hepatic flexure, with delayed motility at this point. When the sigmoid is similarly involved in a fistulous tract, a true narrowing and delay at this flexure may simulate carcinoma and so create the necessary indication for operation. Both these areas of stenotic deformity of the large bowel are incidental to only one of the complications of the disease, namely, the formation of fistulous tracts. The entire colon is otherwise exonerated as a primary site of the granulomatous inflammation.

## DIFFERENTIAL DIAGNOSIS

Regional ileitis must be differentiated from several analogous conditions which produce a mass in the right iliac region with diarrhea and fever. The most important differentiation is that of regional ileitis from nonspecific ulcerative colitis. The sigmoidoscopy and the barium enema suffice for the recognition of colitis in the largest percentage of cases. But there are types of colitis which involve only the proximal segments of the colon, and in which the sigmoid and the rectum are free from pathologic changes. While these instances are few and relatively uncommon, they do occur and lead to much confusion; they may be recognized by the deformity and spasm of the cecum and ascending colon when the latter areas are the seat of the segmental phenomena of colitis. Only in severe cases of ulcerative colitis does the process involve the terminal ileum, and then only for a few inches. In regional ileitis, all of the damaged tissue is proximal to the valve. The diagnosis is purely roentgenographic, the clinical differentiation being impossible. Colitis does not cause fistulas except about the anus and rectum; a mass is rarely palpable in colitis.

Ileocecal tuberculosis as a primary process should be easy of differentiation from regional ileitis. We are inclined, however, to agree with Moschcowitz and Wilensky[2] in the skepticism with which they view the actual occurrence of a primary tuberculous process at the ileocecal junction. To repeat their arguments, the latter disease must be rare, for only three cases have been seen at Mount Sinai Hospital in several years. Pathologic examination of all such suspected tuberculous masses has uniformly failed in the demonstration of tubercles or of tubercle bacilli in the sections or smears. Practically all cases mistakenly suspected of, or diagnosed as, ileocecal tuberculosis have been eventually classed as new growth, as appendicitis with abscess or as benign nonspecific granuloma. In all of our first cases of regional ileitis the diagnosis of ileocecal tuberculosis was the unvarying best possibility; operation was undertaken only after the customarily accepted methods of treatment for tuberculosis had been exhausted.

Fibroplastic appendicitis or typhlitis is a disease better known to the surgeons.

Lymphosarcoma, intestinal or mesenteric tuberculosis and Hodgkin's disease simulate regional ileitis in many of its features. The exact differentiation is possible only at the operating table or by the examination of pathologic specimens. Sarcoma of the intestine is usually multiple, causing dilatations at various levels, and involves the jejunum as well as the ileum and not particularly just the terminal 8 to 12 inches of the small intestine. Hodgkin's disease may give its characteristic monocytic blood picture, or a regional lymph node may reveal the true nature of the process.

Actinomycosis of the ileocecal region with fistula formation to the external abdominal wall must always be mentioned in the differentiation from ileitis. The extreme rarity of actinomycosis in this region of the body and in this climate makes this differentiation more theoretical than necessary.

From carcinoma of the terminal ileum or of the ileocecal valve the differentiation cannot be made with any certainty; both conditions call for surgical intervention and both lead to cure by successful and early resections.

## TREATMENT

Medical treatment is purely palliative and supportive. The diseased area cannot be reached by colonic irrigations or enemas, and any attempts by medical means to reach a necrotizing, ulcerating and stenosing inflammation of the terminal ileum is purely and essentially futile.

True, one case, discovered in the course of a cholecystectomy for stones, progressed to spontaneous healing or at least to a cessation of the intestinal symptoms.

But in general, the proper approach to a complete cure is by surgical resection of the diseased segment of the small intestine and of the ileocecal valve with its contiguous cecum. The restitution to complete health in thirteen out of fourteen cases as a result of the radical resection of the pathologic process or of a short-circuiting operation speaks vehemently in favor of surgical methods as the logical successful therapeutic procedure.

In one instance recurrent symptoms were accounted for by the finding of an annular stenosis a short distance proximal to the new anastomosis (ileotransversostomy). Apparently in this case the resection had not been carried out sufficiently oral to the lesion completely to eradicate the disease.

Our experience with short-circuiting anastomoses is limited. In one case a short-circuit ileocolostomy was performed through a segment of ileum that was apparently normal at the time of operation. The pathologic process did not heal; on the contrary, the disease progressed to the proximal loop of the anastomosis. In two cases of intractable fistulas and in one case of inflammatory pelvic mass, ileocolostomy with exclusion has given excellent results. The best operation, as devised by Dr. A. A. Berg, consists of dividing the ileum 3 feet (91 cm.) from the ileocecal junction, closing both ends of the divided ileum and implanting the proximal terminus of the ileum by a side-to-side anastomosis at the transverse colon.

---

## ABSTRACT OF DISCUSSION

DR. J. A. BARGEN, Rochester, Minn.: This presentation would seem timely, for, with improved roentgen technic and more intensive study of intestinal disease, the condition may prove to be less common than it is now supposed to be. Intensive roentgenologic investigation often becomes necessary to determine the nature of disturbances of the ileocecal coil. Undoubtedly some of these cases have been overlooked. In the last few years, several cases annually of this type have come to operation at the Mayo Clinic. Usually the appendix has been removed for complaints similar to those for which the patients presented themselves, that is, recurrent and intermittent attacks of right abdominal pain and discomfort. Some of these conditions were diagnosed preoperatively because of the suggestive roentgenographic and roentgenoscopic signs. The lumen of the intestine in this region is narrowed, and the wall is thickened and shortened. The gross appearance of the removed specimen resembles closely that of the colon in advanced chronic ulcerative colitis. The lesion is inflammatory, containing fibrotic elements and granulation tissue as well as evidence of more acute changes. The evidence points to a regional inflammatory disease perhaps on the basis of localized decrease in resistance to some bacterial invasion. I am wondering whether the designation "terminal" is adequately descriptive. To some it has conveyed the meaning of agonal. Perhaps the modifying adjective "regional" or some other word suggesting its localized nature, instead of the end, would be more suitable. I should like to emphasize that this presentation is an important one, that possibly these cases will be discovered earlier and more frequently in the future, and if so, one instead of two operations may be performed, and that I believe the lesion is infectious.

DR. JULIUS FRIEDENWALD, Baltimore: I am reminded of two

cases quite a number of years back in which this condition was evidently present but which were regarded at the time as instances of carcinoma. Both patients, men, presented almost identical symptoms; the one was 50 and the other 58 years of age. The condition arose in the midst of good health and was associated with rapid loss of flesh, diarrhea, indigestion, slight fever and anemia; it terminated in progressive constipation and in attacks of partial and almost complete obstruction. In both instances an indefinite mass could be detected in the cecal region. At operation an extensive obstructive mass was detected in the terminal ileum. A diagnosis of inoperable carcinoma was made by the surgeon and a lateral anastomosis performed. The patients made a surprisingly rapid recovery and remained well. The recovery could not be explained at the time, but the condition was evidently ileitis, as described by the authors. Since then I have observed a number of instances of a milder type which at operation presented a somewhat similar appearance. In a woman, aged 62, who was operated on about two years ago and who presented symptoms of lower right-sided abdominal pain with loss of flesh and attacks of alternating diarrhea followed by intense constipation, this condition was observed in the terminal ileum in a mild form. The surgeon, not realizing its significance, simply removed a chronically inflamed appendix. Since then the attacks have continued, the distress becoming more marked. The authors have undoubtedly described a clinical entity of great importance, a condition that may occur in so severe a form as to simulate carcinoma or intestinal tuberculosis or, in a milder form, presenting the appearance rather of a chronic appendicitis. The possibility of its occurrence must constantly be borne in mind in the differential diagnosis of chronic abdominal disease.

DR. LOUIS J. HIRSCHMAN, Detroit: I have just such a case under my observation, which presents an interesting phase which has not come under the observation of the authors, at least but rarely, as I recall their paper. This is a youth, aged 18 years, who has been suffering from chronic ulcerative colitis since 9 years of age, half his life. His weight has gone down in the last few months to 78 pounds (35.4 Kg.), so much so that when he was sent to me for surgical relief for his chronic ulcerative colitis, having hemorrhages, I decided on intestinal rest, and enterostomy was performed. A diagnosis of benign papilloma of the ileum was not made. He was sent for relief from the chronic ulcerative colitis. At operation, about 12 inches (30 cm.) of a large, doughy, thickened ileum was discovered. It was resected and ileostomy done, with immediate relief. The appendix also was involved. It was done about eight weeks ago and the patient has gained weight so that he weighs now about 130 pounds (59 Kg.). The interesting point to me is that when the specimen was opened the ileum was almost occluded with granulomas. It was a wonder he had any peristalsis or intestinal movement. I gathered from what the authors said that it is uncommon to have an ulcerative colitis in connection with a granulomatous infection of the terminal ileum. In this case there was no evidence of fistulas in connection with either the terminal ileum or the large intestine and I wondered why, since there is the granulomatous formation they described.

DR. SIDNEY A. PORTIS, Chicago: What were the bacterioscopic observations on the excised portion of the ileum? Did you make any sections of the ileum to find out whether any bacteria were deeply seated in the walls of the ileum?

DR. BURRILL B. CROHN, New York: In a disease of this type, in which an attempt is being made to establish the etiology of the disease, we have naturally taken great pains to exclude every known etiologic factor. Histologic sections were made of the tissues and stained with various types of stains. Cultures were made. Ground material was injected into guinea-pigs and fowl. Various types of laboratory animals were used to eliminate any possible form of tuberculosis. Löwenstein cultures were made. Dr. Klemperer, the pathologist, exhausted all the known possible scientific methods of finding an etiologic factor. I can say that no etiologic factor was found. It is refreshing to address a medical organization of this kind, where one can count on meeting men of large clinical experience and find that Drs. Bargen, Friedenwald and Hirschman have seen cases of this type. I have not had many occasions, in fact this is the first, to read this article. I have spoken extemporaneously at one or two previous meetings and wherever I spoke of this subject, the older clinicians, men with broad experience, surgical or medical, always have said: "We have seen such a thing in past years. We have met with it in surgical experience and didn't know what to do with it." The chairman of the New York Surgical Society, at the time the subject was brought up, said: "I have to operate in such a case and I don't know what to do. I don't know the nature of it." I forgot to mention an important physical sign; namely, the mass that occurs. In these cases a mass develops in the lower abdomen, usually in the right ileac region, consisting of agglutinated coils of ileum massed together. Sometimes the mass will move over from adhesions to the sigmoid and will present more in the left lower abdomen. The mass can usually be felt by rectum. It is a hard mass and a movable mass. It does not feel carcinomatous, though I must say some of the best cases we met had previously been condemned as inoperable carcinomas. In addition to the agglutinated loops of ileum, an inflammatory reaction is set up by the fistulas that travel through the mesentery of the ileum to the loops of the colon. I am thankful for the discussion. I had come to the conclusion that only the abdominal surgeons knew about the condition. I am glad to find that men with older and larger medical experiences have also met with the manifestations of the disease.

DR. FRANK SMITHIES, Chicago: You never found free fluid, did you?

DR. CROHN: Yes, a small amount, not demonstrable by physical signs but a small amount such as one would find in any inflammatory peritoneal lesion—real ascites.

Jan 8, 1984
(*JAMA* 1984;251:80-81)

# Crohn's Disease*

## Joseph B. Kirsner, MD, PhD

'Natura Non Facit Saltus'
*Nature does not proceed by leaps but rather reveals its secrets
slowly, quietly and grudgingly. Notable advances of today have
their background in work often carried out decades before.*
CARL LINNAEUS, *Philosophica Botanica*
Section 777, 1751

Knowledge of the nature of disease, from earliest times, evolved from the careful observation of sickness among individuals. Sir Henry Cohen[1] points out that concepts of illnesses as disease entities first became apparent during the ninth century AD. Increased understanding of human illness has paralleled new developments in science and in medicine[2] and continues today as the observation and the evaluation of the patient's condition become more perceptive and more precise. These circumstances alone, however revealing, sui generis do not always create noteworthy progress. Advances also require men and women of inquiring, critical minds, motivated by Rudyard Kipling's "six honest serving men: who, what, why, how, when and where."

### History

Burrill Crohn, Leon Ginzburg, and Gordon Oppenheimer[3] probably were not the first to observe or describe Crohn's disease. Indeed, medical historians[4] suggest that the initial description may date back to Morgagni (1682-1771), possibly to Carson's "The Iliac Passion,"[5] or even earlier, to the days of Hippocrates and Aretaeus, the Cappodocian. We shall never know, of course, the validity of such assumptions. More suggestive earlier instances of Crohn's disease include the reports of Saunders (1806), Combe and Saunders (1813), Abercrombie (1828), and also Wilks and Moxon (1875), and in the early part of the 20th century, Moynihan (1907), Mayo Robson (1908), Braun (1909), and Tietze (1920).[6] In 1913, Dalziel[7] described a group of 13 patients with findings closely resembling those in the 1932 *JAMA*

article. The important clinical differentiation in the early part of the 20th century was intestinal tuberculosis, which probably often was Crohn's disease. Here also, we are left with intriguing but unresolvable speculation. In 1923, Moschowitz and Wilensky, also from New York's Mount Sinai Hospital, described four patients with nonspecific granulomatous disease of the intestine.[8] Leon Ginzburg's[9] interest in the problem dates to 1925, when he was associated with the noted surgeon, Dr A. A. Berg, whose practice provided the pathological material for the 1932 article. Several years later, Ginzburg and Gordon Oppenheimer, then in surgical pathology at Mount Sinai Hospital, identified a dozen instances of a localized hypertrophic, ulcerative stenosis of the distal 2 or 3 ft of the terminal ileum, "ending rather abruptly at the ileocecal valve." Specific causes such as amebiasis, actinomycosis, and syphilis were eliminated. Intestinal tuberculosis was excluded by bacteriologic and animal studies. In cooperation with the pathologist, Dr William Antopol, the granulomas in the lesions were evaluated as incidental findings.

In 1930, Crohn had under his care two patients with a similar process, also operated on by Dr Berg. At the suggestion of Dr Paul Klemperer, head of the Department of Pathology, the two groups united (Henry Janowitz, MD, written communication, 1982), providing the 14 cases published in the 1932 *JAMA* article, as "terminal ileitis," representing, in the words of Povl Riis, "a nosographic breakthrough" (written communication, 1982). J. A. Bargen suggested the adjective *regional.*[3] The article was credited to the surgical service of Dr A. A. Berg, and, had Berg accepted the invitation to join the alphabetically arranged authorship of the 1932 article, we might today be writing about Berg's disease! Others have claimed priority. In Poland, this entity has been referred to as "Lesniowski-Crohn's disease," and in Scotland, the eponym of "Dalziel's disease" has been recorded.

The paper by Ginzburg and Oppenheimer entitled "Non-Specific Granulomata of the Intestines, Inflammatory Tumors and Strictures of the Bowel," presented at the May 1932 meeting of the American Gastroenterological

---

From the University of Chicago Hospitals and Clinics.
*A commentary on Crohn BB, Ginzburg L, Oppenheimer GD: Regional ileitis: A pathologic and clinical entity. *JAMA* 1932;99:1323-1329.

Association and published in the *Annals of Surgery* in December 1933 (pages 1046 to 1062), contains the first clear reference to what is now known as Crohn's colitis. Early reports include those of Harris and co-workers[10] (1933) ("Chronic Cicatrizing Enteritis") and Bisell[11] (1934) ("Localized Chronic Ulcerative Ileitis"). In other notable articles, Mock (1931) and Colp (1934) chronicled involvement of the colon. Kantor[12] (1934) and Marshak[13] (1951) described the roentgenographic appearance of Crohn's disease in the small bowel and the colon, respectively. An excellent study of the pathology of regional enteritis was reported in 1951.[14] Bryan Brooke[15,16] and W. Trevor Cooke[16] in 1955 were among the first to recognize "right-sided colitis" as Crohn's disease of the colon rather than as ulcerative colitis. But not until the reports by Lockhart-Mummery and Morson[17,18] in 1959 and 1960 was Crohn's disease of the colon generally accepted as a valid entity. The 1954 article by Van Patter and colleagues[19] is noteworthy for its detailed analysis of the natural history of many patients with Crohn's disease. Today, the eponym of "Crohn's disease" is recognized as the most convenient label for an unique inflammatory process involving any part of the gastrointestinal (GI) tract, characterized by chronicity, recurrences, and numerous local and systemic complications. As Brian Brooke, Basil C. Morson, Sidney C. Truelove, and others suggest, the time in 1932 was "right" for the description of this disorder, and, had the Mount Sinai group not done so, others would have reported the condition soon thereafter (written communications, 1982). Crohn and Yarnis[20] wrote in 1957, 25 years later: "From this small beginning we have witnessed the evolution of a Frankenstein monster that, if not threatening to life, frequently results in serious illness, often prolonged and debilitating."

The 1932 *JAMA* article is distinctive for its faithful clinical and anatomic descriptions, although it remained for Hadfield[21] in 1939 to provide the precise histology. As so often characterizes seminal articles in medicine, the article by Crohn and colleagues provided the insight and the clinical guidelines for recognition of this entity. Despite the earlier presumptive instances of Crohn's disease, the 1932 patients probably represented a new disease,[22] then in its early stages of evolution.

### Present and Future

During the past 50 years, the numbers of patients with Crohn's disease have increased steadily, although recent information from Stockholm County[23] and Aberdeen, Scotland, suggests that the peak incidence may have been reached (Ghoran Heller, written communication, 1982). The increased availability of patients for clinical observation and the rapid development of abdominal surgery after World War II provided much pathological material for study. In one literature survey from 1966 to 1981, approximately 4,000 references to Crohn's disease were accumulated. In a second survey of the medical literature, from 1966 to 1982, more than 5,500 references to Crohn's disease were recorded, involving an extraordinary array of scientific disciplines: internal medicine, gastroenterology, microbiology, virology, radiology, pharmacology, psychiatry, nuclear medicine, obstet-

rics and gynecology, pediatrics, dental medicine, surgery, pathology, immunology, epidemiology, genetics, biochemistry, cell biology, "gastrointestinal endocrinology," enzyme histochemistry, and neurophysiology. Although not identifying the cause or causes of Crohn's disease, these studies revealed hitherto unknown fundamental roles for the GI tract in immunologic homeostasis and in other host defense mechanisms and enormously expanded the clinical and the scientific perspectives of gastroenterology.

The prevalence of Crohn's disease, especially in industrialized areas, and its similar clinical, radiological, and pathological features everywhere, despite ethnic, climate, dietary, and sociocultural differences, are intriguing demographic aspects (Ghoran Heller, written communication, 1982).[23] Crohn's disease today differs somewhat from its presentation in 1932. Although still a disease affecting chiefly children and young adults, more patients are in the older age ranges (50 to 80 years). The entire GI tract may be involved from mouth to anus, although not simultaneously, and Crohn's disease of the upper GI tract and of the colon and rectum is more common today. Its familial incidence also has increased, approximately 40% in one series, with the intermingling of ulcerative colitis and Crohn's disease in 25% of affected families.

Crohn's disease occasionally is initially seen with non-GI symptoms, including erythema nodosum and pyoderma gangrenosum, growth retardation, acute arthritis, "scirrhous carcinoma of the stomach or colon," pellagra, gynecologic or urologic complaints, irritable colon, or as an apparent psychiatric disorder (anorexia nervosa). Crohn's disease additionally may involve skin, muscle, bone, urinary bladder, and perhaps the lungs. Its varied systemic complications pose widely ranging clinical problems and pathogenetic challenges. Etiologic suggestions vary from the excessive eating of cornflakes or refined sugars, margarine, bottle feeding of infants instead of breast-feeding, and "hexing" to the swallowing of toothpaste. However, microbial-viral and other environmental agents in genetically vulnerable persons with altered immune responses represent more promising scientific areas for further investigation.[24]

Although the cause and the pathogenesis of Crohn's disease remain elusive, medicine indeed is indebted to Crohn, Ginzburg, and Oppenheimer and to their associates for their insight and their sense of responsibility in describing one of man's more serious illnesses. Their 1932 LANDMARK ARTICLE stimulated worldwide interest in an emerging disease, whose subsequent study has illuminated far more in medicine and in gastroenterology than could have been anticipated 50 years ago.

Dr Burrill B. Crohn died recently at the age of 99 years. Dr Leon Ginzburg is retired and living in New York. At the age of 98 years, Dr Crohn wrote me in December 1982 in his own hand, "All this now is ancient history." Perhaps, but it also is remarkable medical history for its uniquely stimulating influence on medicine.

### References

1. Cohen H: The evolution of the concept of disease. *Proc R Soc Med* 1953;48:159-169.
2. King LS: *Mainstreams of Medicine*. Austin, University of Texas

Press, 1971.

3. Crohn BB, Ginzburg L, Oppenheimer GD: Regional ileitis: A pathologic and clinical entity. *JAMA* 1932;99:1323-1329.

4. Goldstein HI: Regional ileitis. *Rev Gastroenterol* 1947;14:186-188.

5. Carson HW: The iliac passion. *Ann Med Hist* 1931;3:638-694.

6. Warren S, Sommers SC: Cicatrizing enteritis (regional ileitis) as a pathologic entity. *Am J Pathol* 1948;24:475-501.

7. Dalziel TK: Chronic interstitial enteritis. *Br Med J* 1913;2:1068-1070.

8. Shapiro R: Regional ileitis. *Am J Med Sci* 1939;198:269-292.

9. Ginzburg L: The road to regional enteritis. *J Mt Sinai Hosp* 1974;41:272-275.

10. Harris F, Bell G, Brunn H: Chronic cicatrizing enteritis: Regional enteritis (Crohn). *Surg Gynecol Obstet* 1933;57:637-645.

11. Bisell AD: Localised chronic ulcerative ileitis. *Ann Surg* 1934;99:957-966.

12. Kantor JL: Regional (terminal) ileitis. *JAMA* 1934;103:2016-2021.

13. Marshak RH: Granulomatous disease of the intestinal tract (Crohn's disease). *Radiology* 1975;114:3-22.

14. Rappaport H, Burgoyne FH, Smetana HF: The pathology of regional enteritis. *Milit Surgeon* 1951;109:463-492.

15. Brooke BN: Granulomatous disease of the intestine. *Lancet* 1959;2:745-749.

16. Cooke WT, Brooke BN: Nonspecific enterocolitis. *Q J Med* 1955;24:1-22.

17. Lockhart-Mummery HE, Morson BC: Crohn's disease (regional enteritis) of the large intestine and its distinction from ulcerative colitis. *Gut* 1960;1:87-105.

18. Morson BC, Lockhart-Mummery HE: Crohn's disease of the colon. *Gastroenterologia* 1959;92:168-172.

19. Van Patter WN, Bargen JA, Dockerty MB, et al: Regional enteritis. *Gastroenterology* 1954;26:347-450.

20. Crohn BB, Yarnis H: *Regional Ileitis,* ed 2. New York, 1957.

21. Hadfield G: The primary histological lesions of regional ileitis. *Lancet* 1939;2:773-775.

22. Crohn BB: Granulomatous disease of small and large bowel. *NY State J Med* 1972;72:2867-2869.

23. Schachter H, Kirsner JB: *Crohn's Disease of the Gastrointestinal Tract.* New York, John Wiley & Sons Inc, 1980.

24. Kirsner JB, Shorter RG: Recent developments in 'non-specific' inflammatory bowel disease. *N Engl J Med* 1982;306:775-785, 837-848.

Oct 28, 1933
(*JAMA* 1933;101:1371-1374)

## Chapter 24

# Successful Removal of an Entire Lung for Carcinoma of the Bronchus

Evarts A. Graham, M.D. and J. J. Singer, M.D.

St. Louis

Carcinoma of the bronchus in recent years has become a problem of major importance. It is now known that primary carcinoma of the lung, which almost always arises in a bronchus, constitutes between 5 and 10 per cent of all carcinomas.[1] In frequency, therefore, it is comparable with carcinoma of the large intestine, and it is much more frequent than the malignant tumors of some other organs that have received much more comment. The problem of primary carcinoma of the lung is of special importance, since up to the present time at least the prognosis has been almost uniformly bad because of the complete futility of any methods of treatment other than surgical excision. There is no record in the literature of the successful treatment by radiotherapy of a single case in which the pathologic evidence has been incontrovertible and in which a five year interval without recurrence has elapsed between the treatment and the time of reporting the case, despite the fact that many cases have been treated according to the most modern methods of using both x-rays and radium. It would seem, therefore, that unless some entirely new general principle in the treatment of carcinoma is devised, the only method that at present can offer any hope is the wide surgical removal of the tumor and the surrounding tissue.

In a recent extensive review of the literature, Carlson and Ballon[2] of the Barnes Hospital have discussed the reported cases in which surgical removal has been accomplished or attempted. In all, there are apparently six cases in the literature in which a patient has survived the surgical removal of the carcinoma and has been well at the time of the report, a year or more later. Two of these patients were operated on by Sauerbruch,[3] one by Churchill,[4] two by Tudor Edwards[5] and one by Allen and

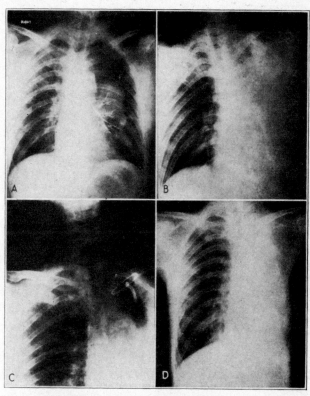

Fig. 1.—Carcinoma obstructing the bronchus of the left upper lobe: *A*, atelectasis of the left upper lobe with the surrounding pneumothorax; *B*, after removal of the entire lung and all but the first two ribs. The air-tight catheter leading to the stump of the bronchus is seen. *C*, drainage of the empyema cavity that was caused by leaving the first two ribs in place. *D*, at time of discharge from the hospital and after the removal of the first two ribs: the empyema cavity is completely obliterated and the wounds are solidly healed; the trachea is in the midline.

Smith.[6] In these reported cases only a limited removal of lung tissue has been performed, amounting, however, in most cases to the removal of one lobe of the lung. In Churchill's case, the lower and middle lobes of the right lung were removed. There have also been six cases

From the Medical and Surgical Chest Service of Barnes Hospital and the Washington University School of Medicine.

1. Junghanns, Herbert: Ztschr. f. Krebsforsch. **28**:573, 1929.
2. Carlson, H. A., and Ballon, H. C.: The Operability of Carcinoma of the Lung, J. Thoracic Surg. **2**:323-348 (April) 1933.
3. Sauerbruch, F.: Chirurgie der Brustorgane **1**:849-850, 1920; Zentralbl. f. Chir. **53**:852 (April 3) 1926.
4. Churchill, E. D.: J. Thoracic Surg. **2**:254-266 (Feb.) 1933.
5. Edwards, A. T.: Brit. M. J. **1**:827 (May 7) 1932.

6. Allen, C. I., and Smith, F. J.: Surg., Gynec. & Obst. **55**:151-161 (Aug.) 1932.

reported in which malignant tumors of the bronchi have been removed by means of the bronchoscope. In practically all the latter cases, however, there is no evidence that survival has extended beyond one year. The case about to be reported is apparently the first one in which an entire lung has been successfully removed for a carcinoma. In fact, it is apparently the first time in which the whole lung has been deliberately removed at one stage. It is possible that Kümmell[7] removed the whole lung for a carcinoma, but the description of the case is so meager that it is difficult to be sure. At any rate, the patient died. There are two instances in which an entire lung has been removed for bronchiectasis, one by Nissen[8] of Berlin and the other by Haight[9] of Ann Arbor, Mich. In both the latter cases, however, the lung was allowed to slough out after ligation of the hilus. It seems particularly

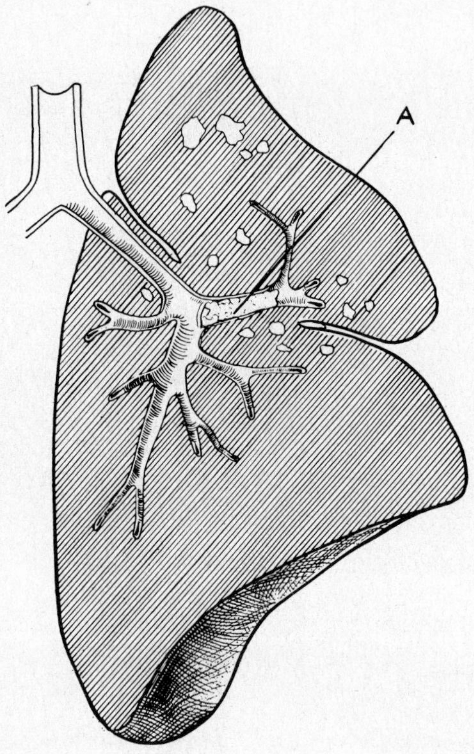

Fig. 2.—Diagram of lung showing (A) location of the tumor in the bronchus of the upper lobe but extending so far medially as to project slightly into the bronchus of the lower lobe. For this reason it was impossible to attempt to save the bronchus of the lower lobe. The location of numerous small abscesses is also seen on the diagram as well as the incomplete interlobar fissure.

important to call attention to the fact that an entire lung has been successfully removed for carcinoma of the bronchus because if this should prove to be a feasible operation in properly selected cases it is probable that many patients would be saved who otherwise would die of carcinoma.

### REPORT OF CASE

J. L. G., a man, aged 48, a physician, admitted to the Barnes Hospital, Feb. 27, 1933, had had repeated attacks of cough and

7. Kümmell: Zentralbl. f. Chir. **38**:427, 1911.
8. Nissen, R.: Zentralbl. f. Chir. **58**:3003 (Nov. 21) 1931.
9. Haight, Cameron: Personal communication to the authors.

fever with pain in the left side of the chest for a period of seven months. Other complaints were loss of weight and general lassitude. In January, 1929, he had a pneumonia of the lower lobe of the right lung (the other lung). The pneumonia in the

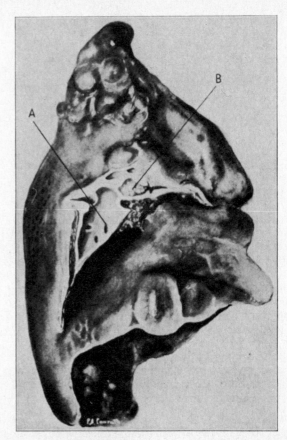

Fig. 3.—Mesial aspect of lung after removal. The main bronchus of the lower lobe (A) has been split open. The tumor (B) is seen projecting from the bronchus of the upper lobe.

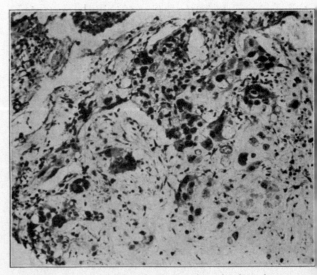

Fig. 4.—Specimen obtained at biopsy through a bronchoscope.

right lung was said to have spread and to have involved the entire lung. After several weeks, however, he stated that he recovered fully from the attack of pneumonia until his symptoms appeared insidiously in the left lung more than three years later.

In July, 1932, he complained of malaise with chilly sensations and a temperature of 104 F. At that time nothing was found on physical examination to explain his symptoms. The leukocytes numbered 17,000. August 11, a roentgen examination revealed a fan-shaped shadow with the base outward in the region of the left axilla. By August 20, his symptoms had subsided and the x-ray shadow had become smaller. October 7, he had a repetition of his former symptoms with a return of the former x-ray shadow. These symptoms subsided in a few days but recurred again about October 20. At this time there was some dullness, and a diagnosis either of interlobar empyema or of lung abscess was made. When an attempt was made to aspirate pus, December 5, a pneumothorax developed, after which a marked improvement in his symptoms was noted, although there was a complaint of some pain in the left side of the chest. Artificial pneumothorax was then continued and the patient showed steady improvement until ten days before his admission to the Barnes Hospital (Feb. 17, 1933), when he had a recurrence of fever and discomfort. At no time was there any actual pain and never any bloody sputum.

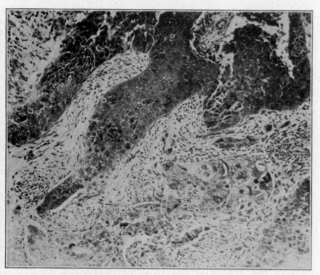

Fig. 5.—Specimen obtained from the tumor after removal of the lung. A careful examination of many slides showed the bronchial cartilage everywhere to be intact.

The patient was of medium build with a suggestion of loss of weight and a rather pale complexion. The left side of the chest moved less than the right, and the breath sounds were diminished or absent on that side. A roentgen examination showed the left upper lobe to be atelectatic with pneumothorax present. The lower lobe seemed to be fully expanded and adherent to the chest wall. The blood examination showed 4,800,000 red cells, 11,500 leukocytes and 85 per cent hemoglobin. Because of the presence of the atelectasis of the upper lobe and in view of the patient's history of an insidious onset, a diagnosis was made of an obstruction of the bronchus of the upper lobe, probably by a tumor. Bronchography with iodized oil substantiated the diagnosis of obstruction of the bronchus of the left upper lobe. A bronchoscopic examination was accordingly advised and performed by Dr. Arbuckle, March 1. At this time tissue was removed which seemed microscopically to be only granulation tissue. The patient's symptoms improved following this examination, because the obstruction of the bronchus had been somewhat relieved. A bronchoscopic examination was repeated on March 14 and again on March 21, and specimens were removed again at both examinations. Both of these specimens revealed a squamous cell carcinoma of the bronchus. The patient was advised to have the left upper lobe

removed because of the presence of the carcinoma obstructing the bronchus of that lobe.

At the operation, however, which was performed, April 5, with intratracheal anesthesia of nitrous oxide and oxygen, it was found that the carcinoma extended so closely to the bronchus of the lower lobe that it was impossible to save the latter bronchus.

Fig. 6.—Section through the wall of the bronchus about 0.5 cm. mesial to the tumor. There is no evidence of carcinoma at this place. Evidently, therefore, the tumor was confined to its original location.

Moreover, there were many nodules in the upper portion of the lower lobe about which uncertainty existed as to whether they were tumor tissue or areas of inflammation. Finally, also the interlobar fissure was not complete. For all these reasons it was decided to remove the entire lung. The adhesions between the lower lobe, chest wall and diaphragm were separated without great difficulty. A small rubber catheter was tied tightly around the hilus as close to the trachea as possible. Crushing clamps were placed on the hilus below the catheter and the lung was cut off with an electric cautery knife. The open end of the left main bronchus was carefully cauterized with the actual cautery as far up as the catheter would permit in order to destroy the

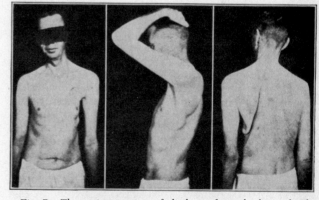

Fig. 7.—The patient at time of discharge from the hospital. The wounds are solidly healed and he has good movement of the left arm.

mucous membrane thoroughly. A transfixing double ligature of number 2 chromic catgut was tied around the stump just distal to the catheter and the latter was then removed. No bleeding occurred. Another transfixing ligature of number 2 chromic catgut was placed where the catheter had been. The stump of the pulmonary artery was then ligated separately with catgut, and seven radon seeds of 1.5 millicuries each were inserted into various parts of the stump. Several enlarged tracheobronchial glands were removed from the mediastinum, and seven ribs, from the third to the ninth, inclusive, were removed from the transverse processes of the spine to the anterior axillary line. The ribs were removed for the purpose of allowing the soft tissues of the chest wall to collapse against the bronchial stump and therefore to obliterate as much as possible the pleural cavity. The first and second ribs were not removed at this time merely because it was desired not to do too much operating at once. Nevertheless, it was felt that there would be some danger of the development of an empyema in the upper part of the pleural cavity because of the failure to obliterate that space. The wound was closed tightly, but provision for drainage was made by the use of an air-tight catheter brought out through a stab wound.

The patient left the operating room in excellent condition but was nevertheless given a transfusion of 500 cc. of blood. The closed drainage yielded about 800 cc. of serosanguineous fluid during each of the first two days. After that period the drainage rapidly diminished and practically ceased on the fifth postoperative day. The catheter was gradually withdrawn. The wound healed by primary intention. There was surprisingly little immediate postoperative reaction of any kind except for a moderate amount of dyspnea on exertion and deep seated pain in the back, which was controlled with opiates. On the ninth postoperative day there was a collection of air and pus in the extreme upper portion of the pleural cavity. The rest of the pleural cavity was completely obliterated by what seemed to be solid healing of the soft tissues of the chest wall against the mediastinal pleura. The small empyema cavity in the upper part of the thorax was drained through a stab wound made posteriorly just below the second rib. It was evident, both from the previous accumulation of air in the unobliterated portion of the cavity and also because the patient was coughing up pus, that there was a small communication between the unobliterated portion of the pleural cavity and the bronchial stump. After about two weeks the drainage tube slipped out of the cavity and was found on the dressings. The wound had healed sufficiently so that it was difficult to replace the catheter. It was therefore decided to reestablish drainage anteriorly in order to have the back free from infection when the first and second ribs should be removed. A small drain, therefore, was placed through the first interspace, anteriorly, for a few days. The patient's temperature and pulse had been normal during the entire time of the drainage of the empyema cavity. May 22, through a posterior incision, the first and second ribs were removed in almost their entire length. There was almost no reaction after this operation. The small remnant of pleural cavity was completely obliterated at once.

The pain in the back subsided and within three weeks the wounds were all solidly healed. The patient's strength gradually increased, his appetite was excellent and he was discharged from the hospital, June 18, looking and feeling better than he had for many months previously. His only complaint was some dyspnea on exertion, but he had been walking about the hospital for two weeks before his discharge. His vital capacity on admission was 3,500 cc.; at his discharge it was 1,650 cc. Also, at the time of discharge an examination of the blood showed 5,100,000 red cells, 8,500 leukocytes and 90 per cent hemoglobin. An electrocardiogram was essentially normal and a roentgen examination showed the left pleural cavity to be completely obliterated. A report received from him, July 25, five weeks after his discharge, stated that he had gained 8 pounds (3.6 Kg.) at home, that he was able to walk about a mile without much dyspnea, that he was driving his automobile and that his strength was rapidly improving. The dyspnea was rapidly becoming less.

## COMMENT

The examination of the lung after its removal was encouraging, because it showed no evidence of any extension of the carcinoma beyond the original site. The whole tumor measured only about 1 cm. in the long diameter, but it was situated almost at the bifurcation of the main bronchus into the bronchus of the upper lobe and that of the lower lobe. The nodules, which had been felt in the lung at operation, were small abscesses that showed no evidence of carcinoma on microscopic examination. Likewise, the enlarged tracheobronchial glands, which had been removed from the mediastinum, showed no evidence of carcinoma. The tumor itself was definitely a squamous cell carcinoma. A feature of it, which is probably important, was that it had not invaded the bronchial cartilage. By analogy with what is well known concerning carcinoma of the larynx, the failure of the tumor to invade the bronchial cartilage in this case would seem to be of excellent prognostic significance.

Several features about this case warrant special comment. In the light of the experience derived from this first case of complete removal of a lung, together with many of the mediastinal tracheobronchial glands, for carcinoma, the operation would seem to be one that is entirely feasible in properly selected cases. Just as experience with carcinoma in other parts of the body has taught that the number of cures is, in general, directly proportional to the extent of radical removal, so it may be inferred, perhaps, that if the entire lung is removed the patient will have less chance of a recurrence than if only one lobe or a smaller portion is removed. In order, however, to have a creditable number of successes, surgeons who are properly qualified by experience in this special field to perform such an operation must receive the patient before extensive metastases have occurred. There is now little excuse for the common failure to diagnose a carcinoma of the bronchus in its early stages. Certainly the majority of such tumors can be diagnosed before demonstrable metastases have occurred.

Another feature of peculiar interest in this case is that, despite the fact that the hilus of the entire lung was suddenly shut off by a tight ligature, none of the signs or symptoms of pulmonary embolism appeared. The sudden obstruction of the pulmonary artery of the left lung by the ligature was analogous to the sudden obstruction of it by an embolus. Nevertheless, not the slightest change in the character of the patient's respiration could be noted immediately following the application of the ligature. Possibly the fact that he was receiving intratracheal anesthesia was of importance.

## SUMMARY

The left lung and many of the tracheobronchial mediastinal glands were removed in a one stage operation because of a carcinoma that originated in the bronchus of the upper lobe but which was so close to the bronchus of the lower lobe that, in order to remove it completely, it was necessary to remove the entire lung. This is apparently the first case in which an entire lung has been removed successfully at one stage.[10]

600 South Kingshighway.

10. A letter from the patient written on Sept. 19, 1933, four and one-half months after the operation, states that his weight has increased by 16 pounds (7.3 Kg.) since leaving the hospital and that he is constantly gaining in strength and energy.

# Evarts A. Graham and the First Pneumonectomy*

Arthur E. Baue, MD

On April 5, 1933, at the Barnes Hospital in St Louis, Evarts A. Graham performed the first successful pneumonectomy for carcinoma of the lung. He was assisted in the operation by Dr William D. Adams. The operation was reported by Dr Graham along with J. J. Singer[1] of the Chest Service of the Barnes Hospital in the Oct 28, 1933, issue of *JAMA* and established treatment by operation for this previously hopeless disease. The patient, Dr James L. Gilmore, a 48-year-old obstetrician from Pittsburgh, survived for a long period and, ironically, outlived Dr Graham, who himself died of lung cancer in 1957.

Dr Gilmore came to St Louis originally for consultation by Dr Graham, believing that he had a lung abscess. Graham told him that it was a lung cancer, and Gilmore went back to Pittsburgh to decide whether to have an operation to remove this portion of his lung. He returned to St Louis a few days later, ready for the operation, and told Graham that while in Pittsburgh, he had had some teeth filled. Graham commented that he "liked an optimistic patient."[2] Gilmore stated some time later, however: "I ought to tell you that I also bought a cemetery lot."[3] The patient brought with him a gynecologist friend from Pittsburgh, Dr Sidney H. Chalfant, who sat in the gallery of the operating room of the Barnes Hospital, watching the proceedings. When the exploration revealed that the cancer was not confined to the upper lobe of the left lung but had its origin close to the main bronchus, Graham looked up to Dr Chalfant, stating: "I'm not going to be able to remove the cancer without removing the whole lung. What do you think about it?" Chalfant asked, "Has it ever been done before?" "No," replied Graham, "but I've done it in animals and I don't see why it couldn't be done in a human. I think I'll go ahead."[2] He did, and history was written.

Before this eventful operation, Dr Graham had made significant contributions in other areas. In 1918, while in the Army and a member of the Empyema Commission, he established the importance of the dynamics of intrapleural pressure and the mediastinum. This led to safe and effective treatment of the problem of acute empyema, and the mortality from this disease dropped from 40% to 3%. In 1922, he conceived the idea of the possibility of visualizing the gallbladder with radio-opaque dye, and in 1924, he reported with Warren Cole[4] in *JAMA* on "Roentgenologic Examinations of the Gallbladder: Preliminary Report of a New Method Utilizing the Intravenous Injection of Tetrabromophenolphthalein." This led to the successful use of oral cholecystography (the Graham-Cole test), an accomplishment that many believed merited a Nobel prize (see Chapter 19).

## Early Treatment of the Lung

Sporadic attempts at pulmonary resection for cancer began in the 1870s. In 1911, Kümmell[5] may have removed the entire lung for cancer, but the case description is unclear on this point, and the patient did not survive the procedure. Before Graham and Singer's report, there were six cases reported in the literature concerning patients who had survived resections of portions of the lung for carcinoma and had lived for some time after the operation. In 1920 and in 1926, Sauerbruch[6] reported performing lobectomies on two such patients in Munich. Another two patients were operated on by Tudor Edwards[7] in England (a left upper lobectomy and a middle lobectomy, each for carcinoma), and a right lower lobectomy in two stages was performed by Allen and Smith[8] in Detroit.

Other surgeons had also attempted resections for carcinoma of the lung, including Heidenhain, Lilienthal, Harrington, Archibald, and Eloesser. These attempts were reviewed in detail in April of 1933 by Carlson and

From the Department of Surgery, Yale University School of Medicine, New Haven, Conn.

*A commentary on Graham EA, Singer JJ: Successful removal of an entire lung for carcinoma of the bronchus. *JAMA* 1933;101:1371-1374.

Ballon,[9] also at the Barnes Hospital. In 1931, Edward D. Churchill[10] of Boston carried out a successful lower and middle lobectomy of the right lung for carcinoma. In his report of April 18, 1932, to the American Association for Thoracic Surgery, Churchill described the tumors of two patients that he had explored but had found to be unresectable. In a third patient, a right lower lobectomy had been performed, but a catheter had been left in the open divided bronchus and the patient had died of pulmonary infection on the third postoperative day. In the fourth patient, use of a preoperative artificial pneumothorax, intratracheal anesthesia, separate ligation of the arteries and veins, and suture closure of the bronchus had allowed for a successful lower and middle lobectomy. In discussing the report at the Association meeting, Graham congratulated Churchill "very much indeed on this brilliant case." Dr Churchill,[10] in closing the discussion, remarked: "The principle that I believe will help us most . . . in lobectomies . . . is a careful implantation of the end of the bronchus into the adjacent lobes. . . . It is important to learn if the main bronchus will stay closed following pneumonectomy."

### Graham's Case

One year later, this question was answered in part in St Louis by Dr Graham. One month after his historic operation, while the patient was still recovering in the hospital, Graham attended the 1933 annual meeting of the American Association for Thoracic Surgery and was the first discussant of a paper by Lilienthal[11] on "Pneumonectomy for Sarcoma of the Lung in a Tuberculous Patient." Lilienthal's patient had died four days after the operation. Graham said:

I was much interested in this case of Dr. Lilienthal because he operated upon his case just a short time before I performed a complete pneumectomy. In my case, however, fortunately the result was successful. I do not call it pneumonectomy as Dr. Lilienthal does because I have the support of the Oxford Dictionary and various other dictionaries to call it pneumectomy instead of pneumonectomy.[11]

(Perhaps because of differences of opinion expressed in the discussion about the proper term for removal of a lung, Graham and Singer[1] did not use any of these terms in their 1933 report.) Graham went on then to describe the patient and the procedure, following which he said: "Apparently this is the first case in which a whole lung has been removed successfully for carcinoma. Moreover it is possible that future experience will determine if better results will follow the removal of the entire lung for carcinoma than merely a single lobe, by analogy with operative results on other organs." Graham's remarks led to discussion of *his* case by Drs Elliot Cutler, Coryllos, Hedblom, and others, and no further discussion of Dr Lilienthal's paper. In closing the discussion, Lilienthal[11] said: "I had hoped to bring out discussion on the matter of operating upon lungs that were tuberculous. I did not present my case merely as one of cancer of the lung." Obviously, Graham's historic operation had captured the mood and thrust of the meeting.

An entire lung had been removed earlier both by Nissen[12] of Berlin and by Haight in Ann Arbor, Mich (oral communication to Graham, 1933), for bronchiectasis.

However, in these two circumstances, the hilus of the lung had been ligated and the lung had been allowed to slough out later. At about the same time that Graham removed the lung in St Louis, Rienhoff in Baltimore performed the first total pneumonectomy to employ the anatomic method of hilar dissection in a patient with a carcinoid tumor. Rienhoff performed two successful pneumonectomies in 1933, one on July 24 on a 3½-year-old child with a carcinoid tumor of the bronchus and the other on Nov 3 on a 24-year-old patient with a malignant tumor. He had produced an artificial pneumothorax two weeks before the operation to collapse the lung to be removed. Intratracheal anesthesia was not used and Rienhoff[13] described the "nuisance of inserting a tube in the trachea." Individual ligation and suture of the pulmonary arteries and veins were carried out and the bronchus was closed by sutures without a thoracoplasty.

### Graham's Success

Thus, many of the pioneering thoracic surgeons of the day were striving to develop a satisfactory operation for cancer of the lung. What was Graham's secret in performing this milestone operation in thoracic surgery and reporting it so promptly? As Graham and Singer[1] indicated in their report, the tumor in the patient seemed to involve the left upper lobe: "The patient was advised to have the left upper lobe removed." Graham thought he was going to perform an operation that, although new, had at least been performed successfully before. He found, however, that during the operation, the tumor "extended so closely to the bronchus of the lower lobe that it was impossible to save the latter bronchus. . . . [I]t was decided to remove the entire lung."[1] This was done by initial mass ligation of the hilus with a catheter. Crushing clamps were then placed on the entire hilus and the lung was excised. The bronchial stump was then suture ligated, as was the pulmonary artery. Radon seeds were inserted (a procedure now once again being used after a lapse of many years), and a thoracoplasty of ribs 3 to 9 was carried out to allow the soft tissues of the chest wall to collapse against the bronchial stump, also decreasing the size of the pleural cavity. The tumor was a squamous cell carcinoma measuring 1 cm with no spread to lymph nodes. Today, this lesion would be classified as a stage I carcinoma or T1 N0 M0.[14] The patient recovered after resolution of a small empyema and bronchopleural fistula. At the time of the report, five months later, the patient was doing well. The patient went on to survive many years.

The key to this operation and its unique contribution was that it was a removal of the entire lung in one stage without preliminary preparation and with suture of the bronchus. The difference from the techniques used today, other than the present use of individual division and closure of the structures of the hilus, the pulmonary arteries, veins, and bronchus, was that Dr Graham believed it necessary to perform a thoracoplasty and collapse the chest wall against the closed bronchus. Both he and others were afraid that a bronchial stump sutured closed would not stay closed. Later it was demonstrated that this was not necessary. Since a transient bronchopleural fistula did indeed develop in Graham's patient, the thoracoplasty may well have saved his life; without it, the fistula may have been large and potentially fatal.

One can only speculate as to whether Graham would have operated on the patient had he known that a total pneumonectomy was required. Fate may have played a role as well as courage, since the authors expressed surprise that nothing untoward had occurred: although "the hilus of the entire lung was suddenly shut off by a tight ligature, none of the signs or symptoms of pulmonary embolism appeared."[1] Graham had previously performed what was called a "cautery pneumonectomy," destroying the tumor and the lung by excavating it out with a large, red-hot soldering iron, followed by x-ray or radium or both on at least seven patients, according to Carlson and Ballon. Although one of these patients had survived for 11 months, most had died within a few days or weeks of operation. He had not described these patients in the medical literature but had published a report in 1923 on cautery pneumonectomy for pulmonary infection in three patients.[15] Early attempts to treat carcinoma of the lung by irradiation, radium, or bronchoscopic removal also had produced dismal results: it was a rare patient who would survive even for a few years after bronchoscopic removal. Early diagnosis was not pursued because treatment was so unsatisfactory. Just as with cancer of the head and neck and the colon and stomach, operative removal of cancer of the lung was considered the only potentially satisfactory treatment. The problem was how to do it safely and successfully.

### Evarts A. Graham

Significant advances in surgery are dependent on a combination of factors: the availability of appropriate technology (in this case, endotracheal positive pressure anesthesia and methods to secure the pulmonary hilus and to close a divided bronchus), trained and experienced surgeons familiar with what has been done and what might be done, the courage to move beyond what is known, and serendipity — the right patient at the right time for an epochal event to occur.

Evarts Graham had a remarkable background and preparation for such a role. During his sophomore year at Princeton, he stated his life's goals: "to do major surgery, to engage in research work, and to have a clinic of young men who would be interested in studying and developing ideas."[16] Graham's father was a professor of surgery in Chicago and Evarts returned to Rush Medical College, from which he was graduated in 1907. This was followed by training in surgery, a prolonged and unique period of work in pathology, physiology, and chemistry, and three years of private practice in Mason City, Iowa. Churchill, speaking at Graham's retirement dinner in 1951, describes this period of Graham's career as his "hegira" — his withdrawal from and return to surgery.[17] The *hegira* refers to Mohammed's flight from Mecca to Medina, a motif of withdrawal and return that can influence a person's development and contributions to society. Thus, Graham's background, his training and hegira, and his intellect all contributed to his immense contributions — in the areas of empyema, cholecystogra-

phy, and pneumonectomy, in the founding of journals and boards, and in the training of surgeons. Thomas Ferguson indicated in his Graham Lecture that Graham considered the first pneumonectomy to be his greatest contribution. Why he valued a technical feat over his other scientific contributions was explained by Ferguson:

When Graham, with his laboratory background, had arrived in St Louis, he was promptly dubbed by detractors as a 'mouse surgeon.' He recognized his technical deficiencies when compared with the meticulous Halstedian surgeons at Barnes Hospital. This is probably the only area in which Graham ever felt the slightest sense of inadequacy, and thus his surgical triumph was all the more dear.[3]

After the pneumonectomy by Graham, other surgeons quickly adopted this procedure and the operation became established as the standard for operative treatment of carcinoma of the lung. A total one-stage removal of the lung with adjacent lymph nodes was believed to represent the best chance for cure of bronchogenic cancer, just as was done with total gastrectomy for carcinoma of the stomach and extended colectomy for carcinoma of the colon. It remained again for Churchill to point out to the surgical community in 1950 that a lobectomy for a bronchogenic carcinoma limited to that lobe was as effective for cure and safer than total pneumonectomy. After Churchill's presentation to the American Association for Thoracic Surgery in Denver, Philip Allison of Oxford, England, stated:

I was about three miles off the coast of America when I heard a sort of Indian warcry to the effect that Churchill was doing lobectomies for bronchial carcinoma. Anybody who has listened carefully to this most clear and precise paper presented by the Boston school of the day must agree that they are in fact still recommending pneumonectomy for carcinoma and that their choice of patients for lobectomy is both reasonable and logical.[18]

Dr Evarts Graham also discussed this paper, stating:

I think, however, that we should distinguish between what might be considered the ideal operation for cancer — and cancer is about the same whether in the lung or elsewhere. . . . It might be far better to take a chance with lobectomy in such a case and make the patient less of a respiratory cripple than he would be by perhaps doing a better theoretical operation — a total pneumonectomy — but leaving him so uncomfortable that life is hardly worthwhile for him.[18]

Thus, the trend returned to a balanced view of selecting the extent of operation based on the location and extent of tumor.

After the operation, Dr Graham continued his illustrious career as the Bixby Professor of Surgery at the Washington University School of Medicine. He was one of the founders of the American Board of Surgery in 1937, Chairman of the Board of Regents of the American College of Surgeons, founder and first editor of the *Journal of Thoracic Surgery,* and member of the first editorial board of the *Archives of Surgery,* and he established a school of surgery in St Louis from which many professors developed and continue to be trained.

At the time of the first pneumonectomy, Evarts Graham was a cigarette smoker, using about half a pack a day. As evidence accumulated for the relationship between cancer of the lung and cigarette smoking, including contributions that he himself made to this area, Dr Graham stopped smoking in 1951. In the same year, he retired. In 1956, he was reported to be working on a technical paper describing the time lag that could occur between the painting of tar on animals and the appearance of cancer and speculated that heavy smokers might get lung cancer years after they quit. Graham said: "I shouldn't be surprised if I died of lung cancer."[2] Early in 1957, after experiencing the symptoms of flu, he was found to have bilateral carcinoma of the lung, of which he died shortly thereafter. One of the last visitors to his bedside during this illness was his grateful patient Dr Gilmore from Pittsburgh. Dr Gilmore was still smoking some 23 years after the original operation, and his cemetery lot was still vacant.[2]

---

Some medical journals relegate case reports to their correspondence section, if they are published at all. Fortunately, this case report was published appropriately in *JAMA,* enabling it to herald the establishment of modern thoracic surgery. Although the credit clearly goes to Graham and Singer, all the pioneers in thoracic surgery shared in this immense accomplishment.

### References

1. Graham EA, Singer JJ: Successful removal of an entire lung for carcinoma of the bronchus. *JAMA* 1933;101:1371-1374.
2. Death of a surgeon. *Time,* 1957, p 42.
3. Ferguson TB: Evarts A. Graham, M.D.: The father of chest surgery. *Outlook Magazine,* Autumn 1981, pp 2-9.
4. Graham EA, Cole WH: Roentgenologic examination of the gallbladder: Preliminary report of a new method utilizing the intravenous injection of tetrabromophenolphthalein. *JAMA* 1924;82:613-614.
5. Kümmell H: Vereinigung nordwestdeutscher Chirurgien: Tagung im Hamburg-Eppendorfer Krankenhaus vom 21. Januar 1911. *Zentralbl Chir* 1911;38:423-432.
6. Sauerbruch F: Die operative Entfernung von Lungengeschwülsten. *Zentralbl Chir* 1926;53:852-858.
7. Edwards AT: The surgical treatment of intrathoracic new growths. *Br Med J* 1932;1:827.
8. Allen CL, Smith FJ: Primary carcinoma of the lung. *Surg Gynecol Obstet* 1932;55:151-161.
9. Carlson HA, Ballon HC: The operability of carcinoma of the lung. *J Thorac Surg* 1932;2:323-348.
10. Churchill ED: The surgical treatment of carcinoma of the lung. *J Thorac Surg* 1932;2:254-266.
11. Lilienthal H: Pneumonectomy for sarcoma of the lung in a tuberculous patient. *J Thorac Surg* 1933;2:600-615.
12. Nissen R: Exstirpation eines ganzen Lungenflugels. *Zentralbl Chir* 1931;58:3003.
13. Rienhoff WF Jr: Pneumonectomy, a preliminary report of operative technique in two successful cases. *Bull Johns Hopkins Hosp* 1933;53:390-393.
14. Baue AE, Matthay RA: Diagnosis and therapy of lung tumors, in Glenn WWL, Baue AE, Geha AS, et al (eds): *Thoracic and Cardiovascular Surgery,* ed 4. New York, Appleton-Century-Crofts, 1982, pp 442-447.
15. Graham EA: Pneumectomy with the cautery: A safer substitute for the ordinary lobectomy in cases of chronic suppuration of the lung. *JAMA* 1923;81:1010-1012.
16. Olch PD: Evarts A. Graham: Pivotal figure in American surgery. *Perspect Biol Med* 1983;26:472-485.
17. Churchill ED: Evarts Graham: Early years and the hegira. *Ann Surg* 1952;136:3-11.
18. Churchill ED, Sweet RH, Soutter L, et al: The surgical management of carcinoma of the lung. *J Thorac Surg* 1950;20:349-365.

Jan 18, 1936
(*JAMA* 1936;106:177-180)

## Chapter 25

# Protamine Insulinate

H. C. Hagedorn, M.D., B. Norman Jensen, M.D.,
N. B. Krarup, M.D., and I. Wodstrup

Copenhagen, Denmark

When treating diabetes with insulin, one has to replace the regulated continuous secretion from the normal pancreas into the portal vein by a few daily injections into the subcutaneous tissue. This method is of course only a poor imitation of nature's own mechanism. Serious disturbances are avoided only because the organism has other means of regulating the blood sugar than to vary the rate of insulin secretion.

This is the reason why treatment with one or two injections daily is found to give fairly good results in many cases. In more severe cases, however, very pronounced oscillations of the blood sugar may occur. During the last few hours before the injection metabolic disturbances develop, which tend to minimize the available deposits of carbohydrate, strongly needed when the blood sugar runs low after the injection.

It is obvious that the insulin hydrochloride will rapidly become absorbed into the blood after the injection.

If the rate of absorption could be retarded, the aforementioned difficulties might possibly become greatly reduced.

In order to obtain such a retardation, different ways have been tried:

1. Injecting the insulin as a suspension or emulsion in oil or similar substances; e. g., Leyton[1] in 1929.

2. Injecting it together with vasoconstrictor substances (experiments in the Deaconess Hospital, Boston[2]).

3. Injecting an insulin compound, sparingly soluble in the tissue fluid.

The third method has been tried through several years in this institute but without success, until experiments made for other purposes indicated that a compound of insulin and nucleic acid had a more acid iso-electric zone than insulin itself. According to this experience it appeared that it might be possible also to combine the insulin with some basic group, so that the combination might get its iso-electric zone nearer to the $p_H$ of the tissue fluid than the insulin hydrochloride.

In a compound of this type the insulin should act as an acid, while in insulin hydrochloride it acts as a base.

### CHEMICAL INVESTIGATIONS

In order to realize this idea, different groups of substances have been tried, kyrin, histones, globins and protamines, but only the last mentioned group has given

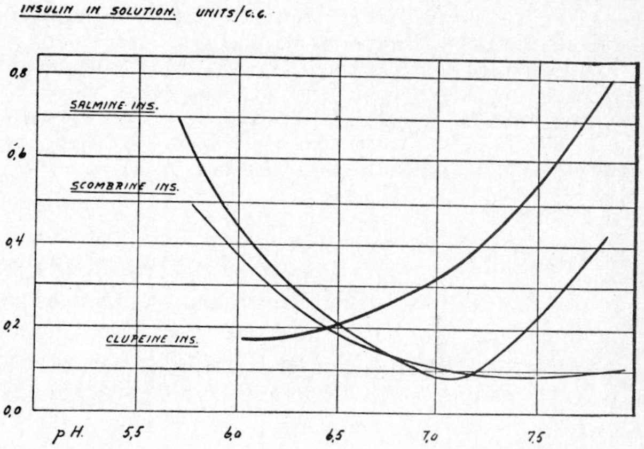

Chart 1.—Solubility of some protamine insulinate compounds in water at different $p_H$.

such solubility results that a clinical experiment has been found justified.

The knowledge of the protamines is rather old. Miescher, as early as 1868, produced salmine. Later on a number of protamines were produced (especially Kossel[3] and his co-workers) and their chemical constitution is now on the whole well known. Their properties as protein precipitants were first observed by Kossel, about 1890.

The protamines are divided into three groups, monoprotamines, diprotamines and triprotamines, according to their contents of one, two or three of the basic constituents lysin, arginine and histidine. A study of compounds between triprotamines and insulin is in progress, but on account of the difficulties in obtaining raw material no

From the Steno Memorial Hospital.

1. Leyton, O.: The Administration of Insulin in Suspension, Lancet 1:756-759 (April 13) 1929.

2. Clausen: Oral communication to the authors.

3. Kossel, Albrecht: The Protamines and Histones, New York, Longmans, Green & Co., 1928.

definite results are available so far. One compound of insulin and diprotamine (cyclopterin) has been investigated and proved to be far more soluble than the monoprotamine compounds, on which, therefore, our work has been concentrated.

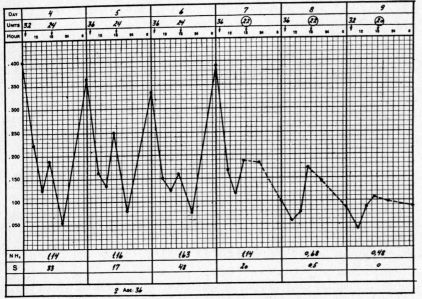

Chart 2.—Transition from a period in which the patient was treated with ordinary insulin to a period in which the patient was treated with protamine insulinate. Protamine insulinate was given on the last three days in the diagram. Explanation of this and the following diagrams: At the top are indicated the days of treatment concerned. Below is the insulin dose in international units. A circle round the figure indicates that protamine insulinate has been used. Under this, an arrow marks the time of the injection. In the coordinate system the blood sugar is given in percentages. A broken line means that protamine insulinate has been used. Below the coordinate system is the ammonia excretion in grams per twenty-four hours; under that the sugar excretion in grams per twenty-four hours and at the bottom the sex and age of the patient.

Chart 1 shows the solubility of compounds of insulin and different monoprotamines prepared from the ripe sperm of the fish in question. The amount of the various protamins that combines with the insulin is about one-tenth the weight of the latter. The insulin used was of purity. As one unit is about 0.04 mg., it appears from the figure that the solubility in water is of the same order of magnitude as that of barium sulfate.

*Solubility of Some Insulin Protamine Compounds in Serum and Serum Dilutions*

|  |  | Insulin in Solution, Units per Cc. | |
| --- | --- | --- | --- |
|  | $p_H$ at Minimum Solubility | Diluted Serum 25% Protein | Undiluted Serum 8% Protein |
| Clupeine | 6.3 | 18 | 55 |
| Scombrine | 7.3 | 17 | 51 |
| Salmine | 7.3 | 14 | 50 |
| New compound from salmo iridius | 7.3 | 6 | 33 |

An experiment carried out on a normal person showed no ill effect after far larger doses of clupeine than would be used by the insulin treatment and therefore a clinical experiment was made on a diabetic patient with the insulin clupeine compound in clear slightly acid solution, but without any effect different from that of ordinary insulin. This negative result is undoubtedly due to the

proteins of the tissue fluid acting as protecting colloids and thus preventing the precipitation. Another experiment was made in which the reaction of the protamine insulinate solution was adjusted before injection to $p_H$ 7.3, whereby the protamine insulinate is precipitated. As the result of the compound being injected as a suspension, the deposit in the subcutaneous tissue consists of a fluid of practically constant insulin concentration, from which the absorption takes place, and a steadily diminishing amount of solid particles. In this way a distinct prolongation of the time of absorption was observed. After having had this experience, we tested the different monoprotamines in the same way.

As a result of these preliminary experiments it was found that the insulin protamine compounds appeared to be more soluble in tissue fluid than in water. In order to investigate this more closely, a series of solubility experiments was carried out on different insulin protamine compounds in serum and serum dilutions.

The solubility in serum has been determined by shaking an exactly known quantity of the recently precipitated protamine insulinate with a suitable volume of human serum for half an hour at 37 C. The mixture was centrifugated and the undissolved part was taken up in a known volume of acidified water. In the acid solution the contents of insulin are determined. The solubility is calculated from the difference between the original and the undissolved quantity, as shown in the table.

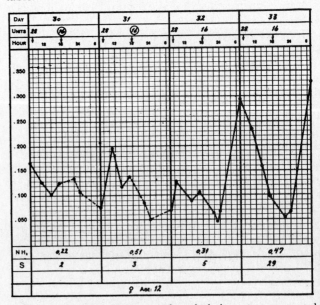

Chart 3.—Transition from a period in which the patient was treated with protamine insulinate to a control period in which the patient was treated with ordinary insulin. Protamine insulinate was given on the first two days shown in the diagram.

As the relative error of the biologic assay is the same whether the quantity of insulin to be estimated is large or small, the experiments are carried out in such a way that the quantity of undissolved precipitate is small, whereby the most exact results are obtained.

Recently a protamine not described before in the literature, prepared from the sperm of Salmo iridius, has been investigated. The insulin compound has shown the hitherto lowest solubility in serum. Therefore we now use this protamine in the clinical experiments.

## CLINICAL INVESTIGATIONS

During more than two years about eighty-five patients have been treated with protamine insulinate in the Steno Memorial Hospital. They have represented all age classes and cases of every degree of gravity, yet most of the cases were severe and several of them presented different complications. In addition to careful examination during their stay in the hospital, the condition of the patients has also been followed after they were dismissed.

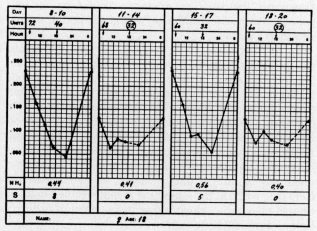

Chart 4.—Four periods in succession. The values represent the average from each period. Protamine insulinate was given in the second and fourth periods.

During their stay in the hospital, generally for about four weeks, the blood sugar was examined as a matter of routine, five times every day: fasting at 7 a. m., at 11 a. m., at 2 p. m., at 5 p. m. and at 10 p. m., the insulin injections generally being given at 8 a. m. and at 6 p. m. By means of numerous controls it has been proved that these five determinations make it possible to form a good picture of the oscillations of the blood sugar during the day. Yet they often have been supplemented with twenty-four hour curves on the basis of blood sugar determinations every two hours. All determinations were made on capillary blood by titration according to the ferricyanide method (Hagedorn-Jensen).

In addition, the daily sugar excretion was regularly determined. As an indicator of fluctuations in the acidosis, the ammonia excretion in the urine was also followed every day.

All together, more than 15,000 blood sugar determinations and 3,000 determinations of sugar and ammonia in the urine form the basis of the present communication.

The patients treated have been on a diet with an average of about 2,300 total calories, individually modi-

fied according to the calculated standard metabolism (Du Bois) of every patient. The diet contains about 100 Gm. of carbohydrate and 70 Gm. of protein. Of the carbohydrates about 40 per cent are given at breakfast (8 a.m.), about 40 per cent at lunch (11:30 a. m.) and about 20 per cent at dinner (5:30 p. m.).

The test of the effect of the protamine insulinate has

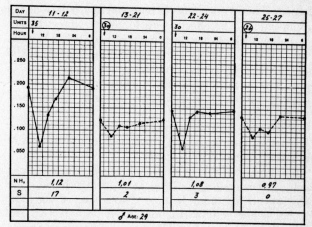

Chart 5.—A mild case, treated with only one injection every twenty-four hours. Four periods in succession. The values represent the average from each period. Protamine insulinate was given in the second and fourth periods.

been made by comparing periods in which the patients were treated with ordinary insulin, with periods in which, under exactly the same conditions otherwise, they were treated with protamine insulinate.

By alternation, control periods were obtained from the patients themselves.

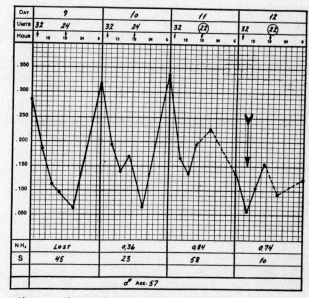

Chart 6.—Showing how an insulin reaction may occur (the fourth day shown in the diagram at 11 a. m.) if the morning dose is not reduced, when protamine insulinate was given the night before.

These investigations have shown that the sharp peak effect, usually seen three or four hours after the injection of ordinary insulin, is largely avoided by the use of protamine insulinate. Furthermore, the effect of protamine insulinate is more prolonged—roughly about twice as long as that of ordinary insulin. Without increasing the number of injections, we can by this means diminish the blood sugar fluctuations, reduce or suppress the glycosuria and reduce the ammonia excretion, and at the same time reduce the risk of the occurrence of hypoglycemia.

We have never observed any ill effects. The injection is painless, there is no local reaction, and protein reactions do not occur. We have never observed any failure of the insulin effect. The effect seems to be the same whether the patients stay in bed or are out of bed. It has been as effective in children as in grown-up persons. The administration as a suspension has never given rise to difficulties or inconvenience. In acute conditions (coma) ordinary insulin is of course to be used, as it works faster.

When the treatment with ordinary insulin gives satisfactory results, the use of protamine insulinate is of no special value.

We have been able to relieve all patients completely of feelings of uneasiness due to acidosis or high blood sugar without giving more than two injections daily. The hypoglycemic insulin reactions have been fewer, and when there has been hypoglycemia the symptoms always have appeared gradually, so that the patient has been well aware of the situation and has been able to provide against it. The treatment by protamine insulinate has proved very adequate and effective with regard to complications. Especially we have noted good results in cases complicated by neuritis and enlargement of the liver in young patients.[4]

In the discharged patients, especially the children, it was found to be easier to maintain the regulation by treatment with protamine insulinate.

In accordance with the more steady course of the blood sugar at night and its more irregular course during the day, the smoother and more protracted effect of protamine insulinate has proved especially useful at night, and we have observed further that, when ordinary insulin is given in the morning after protamine insulinate in the evening, the ordinary insulin will in most cases be much less violent in its effect, because it is given at a moment when the organism is in fairly good balance and the blood sugar fairly low. With ordinary insulin in the morning under these circumstances we can generally avoid the larger fluctuations in the blood sugar throughout the day.

Thus, we have usually obtained the best results by giving the patients ordinary insulin in the morning and protamine insulinate in the evening. Still, there remain some cases in which the result will be the best with protamine insulinate both morning and evening. Then it usually pays to give the injections at equal intervals, say at 8 a. m. and 8 p. m.

Chart 2 is an example among many of the effects of the protamine insulinate when used that way. It shows how under treatment with ordinary insulin the blood sugar fluctuations remain wide, the fasting blood sugar lying between 300 and 400 mg., despite the fact that the evening injection could not be increased without the risk

of hypoglycemia. The ammonia excretion was considerable and there was much glycosuria. On turning to protamine insulinate treatment the situation changed entirely: the blood sugar fluctuations were smoothed out, the fasting blood sugar became normal, the ammonia excretion fell, and the urine became free from sugar, while at the same time the subjective condition of the patient improved considerably. The effect is not always so immediate as in this case. Sometimes it will last a few days (maximum observed five) until the full effect stands out.

Chart 3 shows in exactly the same manner transition from protamine insulinate treatment to treatment with ordinary insulin in a control period. In spite of the doses being exactly the same, the blood sugar fluctuations and glycosuria at once became large when ordinary insulin was given in the evening.

The cases illustrated in charts 2 and 3 were both rather severe, in which of course protamine insulinate is specially indicated. But also in lighter cases it has done good service, as shown in chart 4. This diagram has been drawn on the basis of average calculations of four periods. Protamine insulinate was given in the second and fourth periods.

Furthermore, we have successfully used protamine insulinate in several cases in which it was possible to treat the patient with fairly satisfactory results with one injection of ordinary insulin every twenty-four hours but in which it was found that the subjective condition improved under the protamine insulinate treatment, because this ensures a considerable leveling of the course of the blood sugar curve, eliminating the rapid onset of hypoglycemia (compare chart 5) and the consequent sensations of hunger and weakness so common in the forenoon, while at the same time it combats the tendency toward glycosuria, which is due to the effect of ordinary insulin diminishing so quickly.

In many cases it is possible to do with a smaller dose of protamine insulinate than of ordinary insulin. This is no doubt due to better utilization, which is also well known when one large dose of ordinary insulin is replaced by a number of small doses. In spite of this, it has proved beneficial in certain instances, especially in cases in which only one injection every twenty-four hours is given, to give a rather larger dose of protamine insulinate. In these cases the better utilization of the preparation is balanced by the possibility obtained of satisfying the insulin requirement more completely without risking hypoglycemia.

A single point concerning the dosage is noteworthy. In some cases so great a change will be produced by giving protamine insulinate in the evening that the fasting blood sugar, instead of being for instance 300 to 400 mg., will suddenly drop down to normal or even lower values, in which cases it will often be necessary to reduce the morning dose of ordinary insulin by 10 or 20 per cent.

In the case shown in chart 6 we have purposely omitted this and kept the morning dose unchanged, with the result that a slight insulin reaction occurred, where the arrow is shown on the diagram. In any case this is a matter that requires attention.

A full report of the details of the clinical investigations will be published shortly.

---

4. Hanssen, P.: Enlargement of the Liver in Diabetes Mellitus, to be published.

Jan 20, 1984
(JAMA 1984;251:393-396)

# Protamine Insulin*

## Hagedorn's Pioneering Contribution

Philip Felig, MD

The epoch-making discovery of insulin by Banting and Best led to an appropriate euphoria among physicians treating diabetic patients. Death due to diabetic coma (diabetic ketoacidosis) was largely eliminated. Life expectancy in the child with newly discovered diabetes was increased from two years to 30 years or more, and severely restrictive dietary regimens that bordered on starvation were no longer necessary for the prolongation of the life of the diabetic.[1] Nevertheless, within a few years of the inception of insulin treatment, the limitations in its clinical effectiveness became increasingly apparent.

Improvements in the extraction and commercial preparation of insulin eliminated the impurities that often resulted in localized burning sensations, irritations, and even sterile abscesses at the site of injection. However, as the purity of the preparations increased, the duration of action of the injected hormone decreased.[2] As a consequence, an increasing number of patients required multiple injections through the course of the day and evening to avoid severe symptoms of glycosuria and impending acidosis on arising in the morning. The net effect was often either poor patient compliance and accompanying glycosuria or hyperglycemia alternating with hypoglycemia as a result of the frequent administration of boluses of rapid-acting insulin. By 1928, less than seven years after the introduction of insulin therapy, the need for improvement in insulin delivery was well summarized by Joslin[1]: "How thankful all will be when insulin can be given in such a form (1) that its action will be for twelve hours or more instead of eight hours, and (2) that no sharp peak effect of insulin will occur due to rapid absorption, but that slow absorption will be rule." Eight years later, Hagedorn and co-workers[3] reported that the addition of protamine to insulin notably slowed the absorption and sustained the action of the hormone,

fulfilling the twin desiderata specified by Joslin.

The importance of Hagedorn's discovery of protamine insulin lies not only in providing a means for improving the control of diabetes. Observations with intermediate- and long-acting insulin preparations have enhanced our understanding of normal physiology with respect to insulin secretion as well as action. Furthermore, Hagedorn was among the first to demonstrate that altering drug delivery by developing a controlled release system can notably improve its clinical effectiveness. In this regard, it is noteworthy that new innovations in drug delivery continue to be a major focus of research in therapeutics in general and in diabetes in particular.[4-6]

### Hagedorn: Physician and Scientist

Hans Christian Hagedorn was born in Copenhagen in 1888. The eldest son of a Danish sea captain, he spent much of his boyhood on board ship.[7] In 1912, he received his medical degree from Copenhagen University and, after a year of residency, was a general practitioner for six years in Brande. His interest in the scientific aspects of medicine was already manifest during those years as a general practitioner, as reflected by his development in collaboration with B. W. Jensen of the ferricyanide method for the measurement of blood sugar.[7]

By 1920, Hagedorn decided to return to the University of Copenhagen, where he completed his doctoral thesis (on the differential diagnosis of chronic glycosuria). In 1924, together with Professor A. Krog, a Danish Nobel laureate in physiology who had obtained a license from Toronto University to produce insulin for Scandinavia, Hagedorn established the Nordisk Insulin Laboratories, a nonprofit foundation whose earnings were used to support research. In 1932, Hagedorn became chief physician of the Steno Memorial Hospital, a research hospital adjoining the Nordisk Insulin Laboratories that continues to be a major center for diabetes research.[8]

### Protamine Insulin and Its Successors

Starting in about 1933, Hagedorn initiated a series of experiments designed to modify insulin so as to retard its

From the Department of Medicine, Yale University School of Medicine, New Haven, Conn.

*A commentary on Hagedorn HC, Jensen BN, Krarup NB, et al: Protamine insulate. JAMA 1936;106:177-180.

absorption. Earlier studies by others employing emulsions of insulin in oil and lecithin or combining insulin with a vasoconstrictor (eg, epinephrine or posterior pituitary extract) had failed to give consistent results in prolonging insulin action.[9] As an alternative, Hagedorn conceived the notion that injection of an insoluble precipitate of insulin would provide a subcutaneous reservoir from which absorption would be slower and more sustained than with the standard injection of a solution of the unmodified hormone. To prepare a precipitate of insulin, Hagedorn used the principle that proteins are least soluble at their isoelectric pH. Since the isoelectric point of insulin (approximately 5.2) is well below that of physiological pH, the hormone remains in solution after subcutaneous injection and is rapidly absorbed. Hagedorn reasoned that by combining insulin with a highly basic protein, the isoelectric point of the combined insulin-basic protein complex would be sufficiently close to the pH of body fluids (7.3) so as to yield a precipitate. As the basic proteins he chose the protamines, polypeptides isolated from fish sperm that are rich in histidine, lysine, and arginine. When neutralized in a phosphate buffer at pH 7.3, the protamine derived from *Salmo iridius,* the rainbow trout, was found to be particularly effective in reducing insulin solubility, resulting in a protamine-insulin suspension.

In sustaining the action of insulin, protamine insulin not only improved the management of diabetes but also notably increased patient acceptability of insulin treatment by eliminating the need for multiple injections. Thus, within one year of the introduction of protamine insulin, Joslin[10] noted that the number of diabetic patients treated with insulin in the United States had increased by 70,000. He hailed the discovery of protamine insulin as ushering in a new era in diabetes management, which he appropriately termed "the Hagedorn era."[10,11] Hagedorn's contribution to science and medicine was reflected not only by the importance of his achievements but by his generosity in sharing with other clinical investigators the fruits of his labor. By the fall of 1935, even before his original work had been published, he provided supplies of protamine insulin to the Joslin group[12] and to workers in England[13] and Canada.[2]

Shortly after Hagedorn made his discovery, it was observed that the addition of zinc to the protamine-insulin combination (protamine zinc insulin [PZI]) caused an even further delay in insulin absorption.[14] This formulation, however, resulted in other problems because its absorption was somewhat erratic and its effect often persisted well beyond 24 hours, resulting in hypoglycemia. Furthermore, the rapid onset of insulin action needed to prevent postprandial hyperglycemia in many patients could not be achieved by extemporaneous mixtures of PZI and regular (unmodified) insulin because the excess protamine in PZI formed a complex with the regular insulin when added in the same syringe.

These problems associated with PZI insulin were solved by another major discovery in Hagedorn's laboratory. In 1946, Krayenbuhl and Rosenberg[15] observed that when protamine and insulin are combined in the presence of zinc at physiologic pH in amounts such that neither the protamine nor the insulin is present in excess (a condition that they described as "isophane"), crystals of protamine insulin are produced. This crystalline form of insulin, protamine, and zinc came to be known as Neutral Protein Hagedorn (NPH), or isophane insulin, and is today the most widely-used form of intermediate-acting insulin. Its advantage is not only its shorter duration of action as compared with PZI but its ability to be mixed in the same syringe with regular insulin while maintaining all or most of the rapid effect of the regular insulin (see next section).

## Physiological Lessons From Sustained Insulin Delivery

A major inference from the effectiveness of intermediate- or long-acting insulin in enhancing blood glucose control in diabetes is the importance in normal glucose homeostasis of the ongoing basal secretion of insulin in addition to the bursts of insulin secretion that occur in response to meal ingestion. Normally, the pancreatic beta cells secrete insulin at rates of 0.5 to 0.8 units/hr in the postabsorptive state (eg, during the night) with secretory bursts of 3 to 5 units/hr for one to two hours after meal ingestion. When insulin-dependent (type 1) diabetics are treated with four preprandial doses of rapid-acting insulin without the use of modified (intermediate- or long-acting) insulin, notable fluctuations in blood glucose levels are observed.[16] This failure to normalize glucose homeostasis despite simulation of meal-induced increments in insulin secretion occurs even in the face of optimization of adjunctive measures such as diet and exercise.[16]

The importance of providing basal amounts of insulin in the postabsorptive state, particularly during the night, derives from its action in enhancing the liver's response to subsequent meal ingestion. Thus, when the type 1 diabetic is exposed to an ongoing infusion of insulin at basal rates throughout the night, administration of glucose at 8 AM results in an inhibition of hepatic glucose output comparable to that observed in normal subjects, even in the absence of additional insulin administration.[17] In contrast, when glucose is administered in the morning to a diabetic who has not received insulin in physiologic amounts through the night, hepatic glucose output is not inhibited and the hyperglycemic response to the glucose load is exaggerated.[18] The role of a sustained insulin delivery system is thus not only to normalize the blood glucose level after an overnight fast but also to enhance the responsiveness of target tissues (particularly the liver) to substrate ingestion and the administration of extra insulin at mealtime.

## Shortcomings of Conventional Insulin Therapy

The administration of mixtures of intermediate- or long-acting insulin (either NPH or lente or ultralente insulin) and rapid-acting (regular) insulin provides a means of simulating the basal as well as the meal-associated increments that characterize the normal secretory dynamics of the beta cell. (Delayed action and sustained absorption of insulin are achieved without the use of protamine or other basic proteins in lente or ultralente insulin preparations by suspending the insulin in a sodium acetate rather than sodium phosphate buffer.) Despite the seeming completeness of the replacement therapy afforded by the administration either singly or in various combinations of the variety of insulin preparations available since the advent of the Hagedorn era, for most type 1 diabetic patients, treatment remains less than optimal. Restoration of normal or near-normal blood glucose concentrations as reflected by glycosylated hemoglobin levels occurs in less than 15% of insulin-treated patients.[19] Furthermore, as life expectancy has increased among diabetics, morbidity and mortality caused by microvascular disease (nephropathy and retinopathy) and neuropathy have progressively increased. Whether the development of these diabetic complications is a reflection of the inadequacy of blood glucose control remains a major unresolved question and is the basis of a multicenter clinical trial currently being conducted by the National Institutes of Health.[20]

Irrespective of the role of hyperglycemia in the pathogenesis of diabetic complications, the question may be raised as to why insulin therapy is so rarely successful in restoring normal blood glucose levels in the type 1 diabetic. In this regard it is reasonable to inquire whether insulin is the sole hormonal aberration in type 1 diabetes. For example, glucagon excess had been suggested as a primary event in the pathogenesis of diabetes along with insulin deficiency.[21] The preponderance of evidence, however, indicates that, except in circumstances of acute intermittent stress (eg, sepsis or severe trauma), elevations in the diabetic of levels of plasma glucagon and other counterregulatory hormones (epinephrine, norepinephrine, or growth hormone) are a *consequence* of insulin deficiency rather than a cause of poor diabetic control.[22,23]

The inadequacy of conventionally administered insulin therapy is thus not due to a need to replace or antagonize some other hormone(s) but is primarily related to unresolved problems in patient compliance and drug delivery. Only a relatively small proportion of diabetic patients are sufficiently motivated to take the multiple injections of mixtures of intermediate- and rapid-acting insulin necessary to simulate normal beta cell function. Secondly, even when such motivation is present, the pharmacokinetics of insulin are such as to result often in erratic absorption and unpredictable blood levels. For example, variations in the injection site (abdomen v leg),[24] ambient temperature,[25] and exercise[26,27] may alter insulin absorption. In addition, when mixtures of rapid- (regular) and intermediate-acting (NPH or lente) insulin are employed, contrary to theoretical expectations, some binding of the regular insulin occurs and increases with time.[19] Consequently, unless the mixtures are injected immediately after preparation, there may be some loss in activity of the rapid-acting component. Perhaps the most important factor in the inadequacy of conventional insulin therapy is the lack of a means of altering insulin release from the subcutaneous injection site based on the ambient blood glucose level. As a result, the variations in insulin release that occur in normal humans in response to day-to-day variations in food intake, food absorption, and physical activity are not achieved in the insulin-treated diabetic.

## The Era of Intensive Treatment

In recent years, efforts have been made to improve insulin delivery by simulating the glucose-sensing functions of the beta cell by means of self-monitoring of blood glucose levels by the patient and by improving the pharmacokinetics of insulin absorption by the use of portable infusion pumps. Self-monitoring of blood glucose levels provides a means of tailoring insulin doses to the specific needs of the patient in a manner that is not attainable by means of urine glucose level determination.[28] The use of portable pumps for the continuous subcutaneous infusion of insulin avoids some of the problems in patient compliance and in absorption of insulin encountered with modified insulins or mixtures of modified and regular insulin. The introduction of these techniques of glucose monitoring and insulin administration has, in effect, ushered in a new phase in diabetes management that may be described as the era of intensive therapy.[28,29] These regimens clearly differ from the reliance on urine glucose testing and single daily insulin injections, which have long constituted conventional insulin therapy. The current status of intensive therapy has recently been reviewed[30] and may be summarized as follows: (1) Self-monitoring of blood glucose levels is the cornerstone of intensive therapy. (2) It results in a notable improvement in blood glucose control in many diabetic patients and may be equally effective if insulin is administered by portable infusion pumps or by multiple manual injections. (3) Implementation may be viewed as a therapeutic option for most type 1 diabetics, although specific contraindications have been identified.[30]

## Continuing Problems and Future Solutions

Despite the advantages of intensive insulin therapy, such programs remain less than optimal since they require highly motivated patients and are not universally successful in normalizing blood glucose levels even when appropriately applied.[28,29] To circumvent these problems, current research efforts are being directed at the development of implantable pumps[31,32] and implantable glucose sensors that automatically trigger insulin release on the basis of the ambient blood glucose level.[33] A magnetically controlled implanted polymer system is also being developed.[4,5] In such a system, insulin and magnetic beads are distributed in a polymer matrix that is implanted.[4,5] The insulin is slowly released from the polymer matrix by diffusion to simulate basal secretion.[34] More rapid release (to simulate meal-induced increments) is achieved by the external application of a magnet.[4,5]

An additional unsolved problem concerns the importance of administration of insulin directly into the portal vein rather than via the peripheral circulation. The drainage of the pancreatic vein into the portal vein coupled with the removal by the liver of two thirds of the insulin to which it is exposed on each passage results in portal vein insulin concentrations that are threefold higher than those observed in systemic blood.[35,36] In the 1950s, when the conventional wisdom was that insulin was devoid of direct hepatic effects, Hagedorn[37] was among the first to show an in vivo effect of insulin in stimulating net glucose uptake by the liver. Furthermore,

Hagedorn[37] demonstrated that this effect is enhanced when insulin is administered via the portal rather than peripheral circulation. More recent studies have shown that the liver is more sensitive than peripheral tissues to minor changes in serum insulin[38,39] and is a major site of insulin-mediated glucose disposal.[40] Whether this central role of the liver in insulin action requires that the hormone be administered via the portal system and whether such portal administration of insulin is of importance in preventing the long-term complications of diabetes remain to be established. Thus, despite the advances initiated by Hagedorn's[3] discovery of protamine insulin, optimal drug delivery in the management of type 1 diabetes may be likened to Winston Churchill's perception of Russia: "a riddle wrapped in a mystery inside an enigma."

Jorn Nerup, MD, physician-in-chief at the Steno Memorial Hospital, Copenhagen, provided background information and reprints regarding the accomplishments, life, and times of H. C. Hagedorn, and Hawkins V. Maulding, Jr, PhD, provided useful references.

## References

1. Joslin EP: *The Treatment of Diabetes Mellitus,* ed 4. Philadelphia, Lea & Febiger, 1928, pp 66-68, 80.

2. Campbell WR, Fletcher AA, Kerr RB: Protamine insulin in the treatment of diabetes mellitus. *Am J Med Sci* 1936;192:589-600.

3. Hagedorn HC, Jensen BN, Krarup NB, et al: Protamine insulinate. *JAMA* 1936;106:177-180.

4. Langer RS: New drug delivery systems: What the clinician can expect. *Drug Ther* 1983;13:217-231.

5. New ways with old drugs. *Lancet* 1983;2:259-260.

6. Hager T: New methods of drug delivery: For the future: Polymer-drug systems. *JAMA* 1983;250:145-147.

7. Poulsen JE; *Hans Christian Hagedorn.* Copenhagen, Saertryk fra Dansk medicinhistorisk arbog, 1978.

8. Poulsen JE: *Features of the History of Diabetology.* Copenhagen, Munksgaard, 1982.

9. Krarup NB: *Clinical Investigations Into the Action of Protamine Insulinate.* Copenhagen, GEC Gad, 1935.

10. Joslin EP: *The Treatment of Diabetes Mellitus,* ed 5. Philadelphia, Lea & Febiger, 1937, pp 314-333.

11. Joslin EP, Root HF, Marble A, et al: Protamine insulin. *N Engl J Med* 1936;214:1079-1085.

12. Root HF, White P, Marble A, et al: Clinical experience with protamine insulinate. *JAMA* 1936;106:180-183.

13. Lawrence RD, Archer N: Some experiments with protamine insulinate. *Br Med J* 1936;1:747-749.

14. Scott DA, Fisher AM: The effect of zinc salts on the action of insulin. *J Pharm Exp Ther* 1935;55:206-216.

15. Krayenbuhl C, Rosenberg T: Crystalline protamine insulin. *Rep Steno Memorial Hosp* 1946;1:60-73.

16. Service FJ, Molnar GD, Rosevear JW, et al: Mean amplitude of glycemic excursions: A measure of diabetic instability. *Diabetes* 1970;19:644-655.

17. Sacca L, Hendler R, Sherwin RS: Hyperglycemia inhibits glucose production in man independent of changes in glucoregulatory hormones. *J Clin Endocrinol Metabol* 1978;47:1160-1163.

18. Wahren J, Felig P, Cerasi E, et al: Splanchnic glucose and amino acid metabolism in diabetes mellitus. *J Clin Invest* 1972;51:1870-1878.

19. Galloway JA, Spradlin CT, Jackson RL, et al: Mixtures of intermediate-acting insulin (NPH and lente) with regular insulin: An update, in Skyler JS (ed): *Insulin Update.* Amsterdam, Excerpta Medica, 1982, pp 111-119.

20. Proposed protocol for the clinical trial to assess the relationship between metabolic control and the early vascular complications of insulin-dependent diabetes. *Diabetes* 1982;31:1132-1133.

21. Unger RH: Diabetes and the alpha cell. *Diabetes* 1976;25:136-145.

22. Felig P, Sherwin RS: Glucagon and blood glucose: Insights from artificial pancreas studies. *Ann Intern Med* 1980;92:856-857.

23. Tamberlane WV, Sherwin RS, Koivisto V, et al: Normalization of the growth hormone and catecholamine response to exercise in juvenile onset diabetic subjects treated with a portable insulin infusion pump. *Diabetes* 1979;28:785-788.

24. Koivisto VA, Felig P: Alterations in insulin absorption and in blood glucose control associated with varying insulin injection sites in diabetic patients. *Ann Intern Med* 1980;92:59-61.

25. Koivisto VA, Fortney S, Hendler R, et al: A rise in ambient temperature augments insulin absorption in diabetic patients. *Metabolism* 1981;30:402-405.

26. Koivisto VA, Felig P: Effects of leg exercise on insulin absorption from subcutaneous tissue. *N Engl J Med* 1978;298:79-83.

27. Ferrannini E, Linde B, Faber O: Effect of bicycle exercise on insulin absorption and subcutaneous blood flow in the normal subject. *Clin Physiol* 1982;2:59-64.

28. Felig P, Bergman M: Intensive ambulatory treatment of insulin-dependent diabetes. *Ann Intern Med* 1982;97:225-230.

29. Bergman M, Felig P: Newer approaches to the control of the insulin-dependent diabetic patient. *DM* 1983;29:1-65.

30. Felig P, Bergman M: Insulin pump treatment of diabetes: Decision-making without definitive data. *JAMA* 1983;250:1045-1047.

31. Schade DS, Eaton RP, Edwards WS, et al: A remotely programmable insulin delivery system: Successful short-term implantation in man. *JAMA* 1982;247:1848-1853.

32. Rupp WM, Barbosa JJ, Blackshear PJ, et al: The use of an implantable insulin pump in the treatment of type II diabetes. *N Engl J Med* 1982;307:265-270.

33. Shichiri M, Yamasaki Y, Kawamori R, et al: Wearable artificial endocrine pancreas with needle type glucose sensor. *Lancet* 1982;2:1129-1131.

34. Creque HM, Langer R, Folkman J: One month of sustained release of insulin from a polymer implant. *Diabetes* 1980;29:32-40.

35. Blackard WG, Nelson NC: Portal and peripheral vein immunoreactive insulin concentrations before and after glucose infusion. *Diabetes* 1970;19:302-306.

36. Felig P, Gusberg R, Hendler R, et al: Concentration of glucagon and the insulin: Glucagon ratio in the portal and peripheral circulation. *Proc Soc Exp Biol Med* 1974;147:88-90.

37. Hagedorn HC, Poulsen JE: The direct influence of insulin on the liver in rabbits. *Rep Steno Memorial Hosp* 1956;6:49-64.

38. Felig P, Wahren J: Influence of endogenous insulin secretion on splanchnic glucose and amino acid metabolism in man. *J Clin Invest* 1971;50:1702-1711.

39. Sacca L, Sherwin R, Hendler R, et al: Influence of. continuous physiologic hyperinsulinemia on glucose kinetics and counterregulatory hormones in normal and diabetic humans. *J Clin Invest* 1979;63:849-857.

40. Felig P, Wahren J, Hendler R: Influence of oral glucose ingestion on splanchnic glucose and gluconeogenic substrate metabolism. *Diabetes* 1975;24:468-475.

Oct 31, 1936
(*JAMA* 1936;107:1456-1463)

*Landmark Article*

## Chapter 26

# Observations on the Etiologic Relationship of Achylia Gastrica to Pernicious Anemia

## V. Further Evidence for the Essential Participation of Extrinsic Factor in Hematopoietic Responses to Mixtures of Beef Muscle and Gastric Juice and to Hog Stomach Mucosa

W. B. Castle, M.D.
and
Thomas Hale Ham, M.D.

Boston

Observations on patients with addisonian pernicious anemia have appeared to us to demonstrate that the immediate basis of the anemia is a "conditioned" defect of nutrition. Thus, patients suffering from pernicious anemia are seemingly unable to derive from food some substance essential for normal function of bone marrow. The nutritional defect in such patients is apparently caused by the failure of a reaction which occurs in the normal individual between a substance in the food (extrinsic factor) and a substance in the normal gastric secretion (intrinsic factor). This conclusion is based on the following evidence derived from previous observations[1] on cases of addisonian pernicious anemia:

1. The daily administration of (extrinsic factor) 200 Gm. of beef muscle is without significant effect on blood formation.

2. The daily administration of (intrinsic factor) from 150 to 300 cc. of normal human gastric juice is without significant effect on blood formation.

3. If, however, such amounts of each substance are administered daily in such a way as to permit contact either before or after administration to the patient, clinical improvement and evidence of increased blood formation are usually apparent within ten days and are progressive for the duration of such therapy.

Apparent confirmation of these basic observations has

From the Thorndike Memorial Laboratory, Second and Fourth Medical Services (Harvard), Boston City Hospital, and the Department of Medicine, Harvard Medical School.

The expenses of this investigation were defrayed in part by a grant from the Proctor Fund of Harvard University for the Study of Chronic Disease and by the J. K. Lilly Gift to the Harvard Medical School.

Owing to lack of space, this article has been abbreviated in THE JOURNAL by the omission of a section of the text and corresponding bibliography. The complete paper will appear in the authors' reprints.

The observations on certain patients were made possible through the kind cooperation of members of the staff of the First and Third Medical Services (Tufts) of the Boston City Hospital. We are indebted to Miss Margaret Evans and to Miss Eleanor Fleming for assistance in performing the blood studies.

1. These include:
(*a*) Castle, W. B.: Observations on the Etiologic Relationship of Achylia Gastrica to Pernicious Anemia: I. The Effect of Administration to Patients with Pernicious Anemia of the Contents of the Normal Human Stomach Recovered After the Ingestion of Beef Muscle, Am. J. M. Sc. **178:**748 (Dec.) 1929.
(*b*) Castle, W. B., and Townsend, W. C.: Observations on the Etiologic Relationship of Achylia Gastrica to Pernicious Anemia:

II. The Effect of the Administration to Patients with Pernicious Anemia of Beef Muscle After Incubation with Normal Human Gastric Juice, ibid. **178:**764 (Dec.) 1929.
(*c*) Castle, W. B., Townsend, W. C., and Heath, C. W.: Observations on the Etiologic Relationship of Achylia Gastrica to Pernicious Anemia: III. The Nature of the Reaction Between Normal Human Gastric Juice and Beef Muscle Leading to Clinical Improvement and Increased Blood Formation Similar to the Effect of Liver Feeding, ibid. **180:**305 (Sept.) 1930.
(*d*) Castle, W. B., Heath, C. W., and Strauss, M. B.: Observations on the Etiologic Relationship of Achylia Gastrica to Pernicious Anemia: IV. A Biologic Assay of the Gastric Secretion of Patients with Pernicious Anemia Having Free Hydrochloric Acid and That of Patients Without Anemia or with Hypochromic Anemia Having No Free Hydrochloric Acid, and of the Role of Intestinal Impermeability to Hematopoietic Substances in Pernicious Anemia, ibid. **182:**741 (Dec.) 1931.
(*e*) Strauss, M. B., and Castle, W. B.: The Nature of the Extrinsic Factor of the Deficiency State in Pernicious Anemia and in Related Macrocytic Anemias: Activation of Yeast Derivatives with Normal Human Gastric Juice, New England J. Med. **207:**55 (July 14) 1932.

been obtained by various workers, notably Groen,[2] Hartfall and Witts,[3] Helmer, Fouts and Zerfas,[4] Middleton and Stiehm,[5] Miller and Rhoads,[6] Reimann,[7] Singer,[8] Ungley and James[9] and Wilkinson and Klein,[10] who have agreed with us in supposing the necessity of both an extrinsic and an intrinsic factor for such increased blood production in pernicious anemia. In a recent paper, however, Greenspon[11] has presented the results of experiments from which he has drawn the conclusion that a food (extrinsic) factor is unessential to the production of the positive effects on blood formation in pernicious anemia which we reported from incubated mixtures of beef muscle and gastric juice. He believes that our negative results with normal human gastric juice alone were due to destruction of an "antipernicious anemia principle" by peptic action during the preliminary incubation usually employed. As a corollary, it was inferred by Greenspon that when gastric juice was incubated with beef muscle "the native pepsin in the gastric juice must have been adsorbed by the ground beef" and thus "the beef served to protect the antipernicious anemia principle and not as a substrate for the action of an enzyme-like 'intrinsic factor.'"

Previous evidence exists, however, which would appear to render Greenspon's conclusions unlikely. In our former observations[1b] on patient 11, gastric juice which was not incubated before administration yielded negative results. Middleton and Stiehm[5] and also Groen[2] have obtained similar negative results. Nevertheless, according to Greenspon's theory the activity of such unneutralized gastric juice might have been destroyed by peptic hydrolysis in vivo after administration to the patient. Therefore these observations are not necessarily conclusive. The experiments of Helmer, Fouts and Zerfas[4] can scarcely be so criticized, however, since the gastric juice employed by them was depepsinized and brought to a $p_H$

2. Groen, Juda: Klinisch en experimenteel onderzoek over anaemia perniciosa en voorwaardelijke deficientie, Amsterdam, Scheltema & Kolkema's Boekhandel, 1935.

3. Hartfall, St. J., and Witts, L. J.: The Intrinsic Factor of Castle in Simple Achlorhydric Anaemia, Guy's Hosp. Rep. 83:24 (Jan.) 1933.

4. Helmer, O. M.; Fouts, P. J., and Zerfas, L. G.: Relationship of Intrinsic Factor to Hematopoietic Material in Concentrated Human Gastric Juice, Am. J. M. Sc. 188:184 (Aug.) 1934.

5. Middleton, W. S., and Stiehm, R. H.: The influence of Gastric Juice on Erythropoiesis in Pernicious Anemia, Am. J. M. Sc. 180:809 (Dec.) 1930.

6. Miller, D. K., and Rhoads, C. P.: The Presence in Egg-White and in Rice-Polishings Concentrate Low in Vitamin $B_2$ (G) of an Anti-Pernicious Anemia Principle, New England J. Med. 211:921 (Nov. 15) 1934.

7. Reimann, F.: Zur Frage der Steigerung der antianämischen Wirkung der Leber durch die Einwirkung von Magensaft auf Leber, Klin. Wchnschr. 13:413 (March 17) 1934.

8. Singer, K.: Eiertherapie der perniziösen Anämie, Wien. klin. Wchnschr. 45:1063 (Aug. 26) 1932.

9. Ungley, C. C., and James, G. V.: The Effect of Yeast and Wheat Embryo in Anaemias: II. The Nature of the Haemopoietic Factor in Yeast Effective in Pernicious Anaemia, Quart. J. Med. 27:523 (Oct.) 1934.

10. Wilkinson, J. F., and Klein, L.: The Active Principle in Hog's Stomach Effective in Pernicious Anaemia, Lancet 1:719 (April 2) 1932; The Relationship Between the Antianaemic Principles in Stomach and Liver, ibid. 2:629 (Sept. 16) 1933.

11. Greenspon, E. A.: The Nature of the Antipernicious Anemia Principle in Stomach: I. Method to Improve Stomach Preparations, J. A. M. A. 106:266 (Jan. 25) 1936.

of 4.7 to 5 before administration. In case 8 of their series the daily administration of 150 cc. of such gastric juice was ineffective.

It is thus not certain that Greenspon's experiments throw doubt on the conclusions that we have drawn. Furthermore, for reasons that will be presented later, it seems to us that, unless the necessity for a food factor is conceded, our observations as well as his own do not necessarily disclose the immediate etiologic mechanism in addisonian pernicious anemia. Moreover, without invoking a food factor, it is difficult to find a ready explanation of the etiologic relationship to pernicious anemia of certain other types of macrocytic anemia which likewise respond to the administration of liver or stomach preparations. For these reasons, a repetition of certain of Greenspon's experiments was undertaken as well as a critical analysis of our former observations.

## METHODS

The ten patients included in the present observations were all typical cases of addisonian pernicious anemia. Each had gastric anacidity and an initial red blood cell count of less than 2 million per cubic millimeter. In distinguishing between negative and positive effects on blood formation, use was made of the reticulocyte response that occurs with positive effects on blood formation in suitable patients with pernicious anemia. For this purpose the reticulocyte response was used in all our former observations as well as in Greenspon's[11] experiments. A full discussion of the significance of such reticulocyte responses has recently been published.[12] The methods of blood counting and of reticulocyte staining were those employed in our previous studies. Unless otherwise specified, the normal human gastric juice (150 cc.) was secreted by a healthy fasting individual after the injection of 0.5 mg. of histamine, was then filtered through coarse cloth and placed in the icebox. The patients were maintained on the basal diets used in former observations, which contained no meat, eggs, liver or kidney. Chicken and fish were allowed once or twice a week. In cases 62, 63, 64, 66, 68 and 69 the basal diet was further restricted during the periods of observation and consisted of white bread, rice, macaroni, butter, potato, ice cream, tea, coffee and sugar.

## OBSERVATIONS

*Normal human gastric juice does not contain an "antipernicious anemia principle" effective on oral administration without contact with food (extrinsic) factor.*

As already pointed out, Greenspon[11] does not share this view but considers that gastric juice contains an "antipernicious anemia principle" effective when fed alone. He bases his belief partly on the following direct experimental evidence:

Two normal subjects, after having been given 60 grains (4 Gm.) of calcium carbonate orally as a neutralizing agent, were injected with histamine in order to stimulate the flow of gastric

12. Minot, G. R., and Castle, W. B.: The Interpretation of Reticulocyte Reactions: Their Value in Determining the Potency of Therapeutic Materials, Especially in Pernicious Anaemia, Lancet 2:319 (Aug. 10) 1935.

TABLE 1.—*Negative Results of the Administration to Patients with Pernicious Anemia of Neutralized Gastric Juice (Greenspon), and of Gastric Juice and Beef Muscle Administered Without Opportunity for Contact; Positive Effects of Gastric Juice (Before or After Incubation at 37.5 C. for Two Hours) Administered with Beef Muscle, and of Gastric Juice Administered with Previously Inactivated Hog Stomach Mucosa*

### First Periods.—Daily Administration of Various Substances Except as Indicated Below

Column group descriptions:
- Case 62, 63, 64 — Gastric Juice 250 Cc. Neutralized with Calcium Carbonate (Greenspon)
- Case 65 — Gastric Juice 250 Cc. Incubated 2 Hrs. $p_H$ 1.5, Then to $p_H$ 7.0, with Beef Muscle 200 Gm.
- Case 7a — Hog Stomach Mucosa 200 Gm. Incubated 48 Hrs. $p_H$ 3.0, Then to $p_H$ 5.5
- Case 66 — Gastric Juice 150 Cc. $p_H$ 7.0
- Case 67 — Gastric Juice 150 Cc. Mixed with Boiled Hog Stomach Mucosa 200 Gm. $p_H$ 7.0
- Case 68 — Beef Muscle 300 Gm. and Gastric Juice 150 Cc. $p_H$ 7.0 Respectively, at 8 A.M. on Alternate Days
- Case 69 — Beef Muscle 200 Gm. at 8 A.M.; Gastric Juice 150 Cc. $p_H$ 7.0 at 8 P.M.
- Case 70 — Beef Muscle 200 Gm. at 10 A.M.: Gastric Juice 100 Cc. $p_H$ 7.0 at 4 P.M.

| Days of Treatment | 62 RBC | 62 Ret | 63 RBC | 63 Ret | 64 RBC | 64 Ret | 65 RBC | 65 Ret | 7a RBC | 7a Ret | 66 RBC | 66 Ret | 67 RBC | 67 Ret | 68 RBC | 68 Ret | 69 RBC | 69 Ret | 70 RBC | 70 Ret |
|---|---|---|---|---|---|---|---|---|---|---|---|---|---|---|---|---|---|---|---|---|
| 0 | 1.73 | 2.4 | 1.77 | 1.6 | 0.82 | 0.4 | 0.89 | 1.4 | 1.52 | 0.8 | 1.86 | 1.4 | 0.82 | 1.4 | 1.84 | 1.4 | 1.60 | 3.4 | 1.57 | 0.9 |
| 2 | 1.94 | 1.9 | 1.70 | 1.7 | .... | 1.0 | 0.89 | 1.4 | 1.56 | 2.8 | 1.97 | 1.4 | 0.74 | 1.6 | 1.57 | 1.2 | 1.53 | 3.2 | 1.90 | 3.5 |
| 4 | 1.81 | 0.6 | 1.70 | 1.6 | 0.94 | 0.2 | 0.85 | 3.2 | 1.49 | 2.0 | 1.98 | 3.4 | 0.70 | 1.0 | 1.80 | 0.4 | 1.44 | 2.8 | 1.65 | 2.2 |
| 6 | 1.75 | 0.5 | 1.57 | 0.4 | .... | 0.8 | 1.18 | 13.5 | 1.41 | 2.4 | 1.93 | 2.6 | 0.72 | 3.1 | 1.84 | 1.2 | 1.49 | 3.8 | 1.94 | 3.0 |
| 8 | 1.73 | 0.3 | 1.56 | 0.4 | 0.98 | 0.6 | 1.26 | **14.5** | 1.63 | 2.2 | 2.18 | 2.6 | 0.81 | 13.2 | 1.68 | 1.0 | 1.70 | 4.0 | 1.99 | 2.6 |
| 10 | 1.67 | 0.4 | 1.55 | 1.0 | 0.71 | 2.1 | 1.45 | 12.8 | 1.58 | 1.6 | 1.98 | 0.9 | 1.10 | 29.0 | 1.64 | 1.2 | 1.42 | 2.8 | 2.03 | 4.0 |
| 12 | .... | ..... | .... | ..... | 0.97 | 1.9 | 1.67 | 11.0 | 1.33 | 1.2 | 2.04 | 2.0 | .... | ..... | 1.68 | 1.2 | 1.34 | 1.4 | 2.16 | **9.0** |
| 14 | .... | ..... | .... | ..... | .... | 1.6° | .... | ..... | 1.41 | 0.8 | .... | ..... | .... | ..... | .... | ..... | .... | ..... | 2.45 | 4.6 |

### Second Periods.—Daily Administration of Various Substances Except as Indicated Below

Column group descriptions:
- Case 62 — Gastric Juice 250 Cc. Incubated 1 Hr. $p_H$ 1.5, Then to $p_H$ 7.0, with Beef Muscle 200 Gm.
- Case 63 — Gastric Juice 250 Cc. Incubated 2 Hr. $p_H$ 1.5, Then to $p_H$ 7.0, with Beef Muscle 200 Gm.
- Case 64 — Continued as in First Period
- Case 65 — Gastric Juice 250 Cc. $p_H$ 7.0, with Beef Muscle 200 Gm.
- Case 7a — Liver Extract-Lilly from 600 Gm. Liver
- Case 66 — Gastric Juice 150 Cc. Mixed with Boiled Hog Stomach Mucosa 200 Gm. $p_H$ 7.0
- Case 67 — No Therapy
- Case 68 — Gastric Juice 150 Cc. $p_H$ 7.0 and Beef Muscle 300 Gm. Together on Alternate Days
- Case 69 — Gastric Juice 150 Cc. $p_H$ 7.0 and Beef Muscle 200 Gm. Together

| Days | 62 RBC | 62 Ret | 63 RBC | 63 Ret | 64 RBC | 64 Ret | 65 RBC | 65 Ret | 7a RBC | 7a Ret | 66 RBC | 66 Ret | 67 RBC | 67 Ret | 68 RBC | 68 Ret | 69 RBC | 69 Ret |
|---|---|---|---|---|---|---|---|---|---|---|---|---|---|---|---|---|---|---|
| 2 | 1.72 | 0.6 | 1.47 | 0.6 | 1.28 | 1.9 | 1.74 | 6.4 | 1.07 | 0.6 | 2.04 | 1.0 | 1.31 | 35.9 | 1.53 | 1.6 | 1.46 | 3.0 |
| 4 | 1.73 | 0.2 | 1.34 | 1.2 | 1.39 | 1.0 | 1.52 | 4.4 | 1.17 | 5.4 | 2.04 | 0.2 | 1.35 | 18.2 | 1.35 | 1.0 | 1.43 | 2.8 |
| 6 | 1.84 | 0.9 | 1.44 | 2.1 | .... | 0.8 | 1.74 | 8.7 | .... | 18.2 | 2.13 | 0.2 | 1.45 | 5.4 | 1.52 | 4.0 | 1.47 | 7.1 |
| 8 | 1.74 | 2.9 | 1.43 | 5.6 | 1.42 | 1.1 | 1.88 | 13.9 | 1.97 | 20.4 | 2.07 | 4.2 | 1.69 | 3.1 | 1.53 | 5.0 | 1.55 | 8.4 |
| 10 | 1.94 | 9.3 | 1.61 | 9.5 | 1.09 | 1.5 | 2.32 | 15.9 | 2.31 | 26.0 | 2.17 | 7.5 | 1.85 | 4.3 | 1.30 | 5.9 | 1.52 | 20.6 |
| 12 | .... | ..... | 1.75 | **12.3** | .... | 1.3 | 2.47 | 5.6 | 2.64 | 5.2 | 2.04 | 3.8 | .... | ..... | 1.55 | 6.5 | 1.68 | 13.0 |
| 14 | .... | ..... | 1.95 | 8.4 | 1.10 | 0.8 | .... | ..... | .... | ..... | 2.28 | 2.9 (Nonprotein nitrogen 73.8 mg.) | .... | ..... | .... | ..... | .... | ..... |

### Third Periods.—Daily Administration of Various Substances as Indicated Below

Column group descriptions:
- Case 62 — No Therapy
- Case 63 — Gastric Juice 250 Cc. $p_H$ 7.0, with Beef Muscle 200 Gm.
- Case 64 — Ventriculin 10 Gm.
- Case 68 — No Therapy
- Case 69 — No Therapy

| Days | 62 RBC | 62 Ret | 63 RBC | 63 Ret | 64 RBC | 64 Ret | 65 RBC | 65 Ret | 7a RBC | 7a Ret | 66 RBC | 66 Ret | 67 RBC | 67 Ret | 68 RBC | 68 Ret | 69 RBC | 69 Ret |
|---|---|---|---|---|---|---|---|---|---|---|---|---|---|---|---|---|---|---|
| 2 | 2.33 | **16.1** | 1.80 | 4.4 | .... | 0.9 | .... | ..... | .... | ..... | .... | ..... | .... | ..... | .... | 5.0 | 1.86 | 10.2 |
| 4 | 2.67 | 7.1 | 1.75 | 1.8 | 0.91 | 5.0 | .... | ..... | .... | ..... | .... | ..... | .... | ..... | | | 1.95 | 3.8 |
| 6 | 2.70 | 2.9 | 1.60 | 2.2 | 0.97 | 7.0 | | | | | | | | | 1.47 | **7.4** (Cystitis) | | |
| 8 | .... | ..... | 1.83 | 6.8 | .... | 10.1 | | | | | | | | | | | | |
| 10 | .... | ..... | 1.80 | **14.5** | 0.74 | 14.8 | | | | | | | | | | | | |
| 12 | .... | ..... | 2.07 | 10.6 | .... | 10.4 | | | | | | | | | | | | |
| 14 | .... | ..... | 1.98 | 9.0 | 0.67 | 7.4 | | | | | | | | | | | | |
| 16 | .... | ..... | 2.16 | 3.0 | 0.83 | 5.4 | | | | | | | | | | | | |
| (10 Days Later) | | | | | 1.40 | 5.0 | | | | | | | | | | | | |

°Transfusion of 250 cc. of blood.

juice. By means of a Rehfuss tube the gastric juice was then aspirated and collected in a glass beaker containing ice and surrounded by ice. Care was taken immediately to adjust the reaction of the juice to neutrality and to maintain it so, until it was given to a pernicious anemia patient who had been selected for the testing of this material. The patient was fed about 250 cc. of this cold, neutralized gastric juice each day. It was given in the morning, on an empty stomach, and no food was allowed for the following four hours, in order to avoid the introduction of the so-called extrinsic factor.

In one patient with pernicious anemia and an initial red blood cell level of 2.6 million per cubic millimeter, Greenspon found a reticulocyte peak of 14 per cent on the seventh day of this regimen.

The technic of Greenspon's experiment was exactly followed in observations on patients 62, 63 and 64[13] except that no ice was put into the gastric juice, exactly 250 cc. was administered, and the time interval before food was lengthened to six hours. Patient 66 was given daily 150 cc. of normal human gastric juice neutralized only immediately before administration. No significant effect on reticulocyte or red blood cell production was observed during periods of ten days in patients 62, 63 and 66, and during a period of twenty-eight days in patient 64 (table 1). None of the patients were clinically improved and the condition of patient 64 necessitated a transfusion of 250 cc. of blood on the fourteenth day. Similar negative results from observations with gastric juice neutralized by the method of Greenspon have recently been reported by Flood and West,[14] Hanes, Hansen-Prüss and Edwards,[15] Ungley and Moffett,[16] and Fitz-Hugh and Creskoff.[16a]

The immediately succeeding period of observation in cases 62, 63, 64 and 66 demonstrates the ability of each patient to react positively. Patients 62 and 63 were given a meal containing 200 Gm. of beef muscle simultaneously with 250 cc. of gastric juice unneutralized until immediately before administration at noon each day. Patient 64 responded to the daily administration of 10 Gm. of ventriculin, as did patient 66 to the administration of a mixture of gastric juice and boiled hog stomach mucosa. The details of the blood counts are presented in table 1. A consideration of the nature of the diet given Greenspon's patient suggests the probable explanation for his isolated positive result with neutralized gastric juice fed alone. Since meat,[1b] eggs[8] and whole grain cereals[17] have been shown to yield positive results when administered with gastric juice to patients with pernicious anemia, patients 62, 63, 64 and 66 were given none of these foods in the

special basal diet, specified under methods. Dr. Greenspon has kindly informed us that, on the contrary, the only dietary restriction imposed on his patient was the omission of liver and kidney. The patient may thus have received meat, eggs or whole grain cereals in the hospital diet.

Moreover, if such substances were present in the diet used by Greenspon, the administration of the gastric juice to the fasting patient only four hours before the succeeding meal is not a precaution necessarily adequate to prevent effective contact between gastric juice and food (extrinsic) factor. This is shown by the observations on patient 70. This patient received each morning 200 Gm. of beef muscle. Six hours later he was given 100 cc. of gastric juice collected as usual in our experiments and neutralized only immediately before administration. As will be seen from the data presented in table 1, a reticulocyte peak of 9 per cent resulted on the twelfth day of this regimen. The initial level of the red blood cells was 1.57, and on the fourteenth day the count reached 2.45 million per cubic millimeter. Clinical improvement was obvious. It is therefore clear that effective interaction can occur between extrinsic and intrinsic factors given six hours apart and so may have occurred in the four hour separation of the gastric juice from the next meal employed by Greenspon.

Furthermore, since the gastric juice used in this particular experiment produced positive responses in conjunction with beef muscle, it is clear that the special precautions advocated by Greenspon to prevent peptic activity are not essential to the preservation of the intrinsic factor. Additional evidence for this is obtained in the positive responses occurring with mixtures of gastric juice and extrinsic factor in the final periods in cases 62, 63, 65, 66, 68 and 69 and in the first period in case 67 (table 1). In all these instances gastric juice was collected as in our former observations, with no attempt to maintain its neutrality and so to prevent peptic activity.

*The activity of desiccated hog stomach mucosa is due to the presence of both intrinsic and extrinsic factors.*

We[1c] have observed in a few instances that positive effects on blood formation in pernicious anemia were obtained from the daily administration of as little as 30 Gm. of fresh hog stomach mucosa. Greenspon[11] states that "since Castle's theory is founded on the belief that the addition of beef or some 'other source of extrinsic factor' is necessary for the production of the antipernicious anemia principle, these positive results with gastric mucosa alone require explanation." Now, since the muocsa is obviously not entirely composed of gastric juice, it is clear that something besides intrinsic factor is present in it. If that something else were a source of extrinsic factor, the possibility of an effective interaction occurring could not be excluded. Greenspon's argument that, since gastric mucosa alone is effective, normal human gastric juice alone must also be effective is therefore not logical.

The following observation demonstrates that by a procedure known to destroy intrinsic factor in normal human gastric juice, hog stomach mucosa is rendered inert. To patient 7a was given daily 200 Gm. of hog stomach mucosa which had been incubated in the

13. The observation on Patient 64 was conducted by Dr. C. P. Rhoads of the Rockefeller Hospital, who has kindly allowed us to include his results.

14. Flood, Charles, and West, Randolph: Some Properties of Castle's Intrinsic Factor, Proc. Soc. Exper. Biol. & Med. 34:542 (May) 1936.

15. Hanes, F. M.; Hansen-Prüss, O. C., and Edwards, J. W.: The Feeding of Modified Gastric Juice in Pernicious Anemia, J. A. M. A. 106:2058 (June 13) 1936.

16. Ungley, C. C., and Moffett, Robert: Observations on Castle's Intrinsic Factor in Pernicious Anaemia, Lancet 1:1232 (May 30) 1936.

16a. Fitz-Hugh, Thomas, Jr., and Creskoff, A. J.: Experiments with "Depepsinized" Human Gastric Juice in the Treatment of Pernicious Anemia, Am. J. M. Sc. 192:168 (Aug.) 1936.

17. Castle, W. B.: The Etiology of Pernicious Anemia and Related Macrocytic Anemias, Ann. Int. Med. 7:2 (July) 1933.

presence of hydrochloric acid and native pepsin at $p$H 2.5 to 3.5 for at least forty-eight hours at 37.5 C. No evidence of increased blood formation was observed during a first period of twelve days, although the patient subsequently responded in a second period to the daily oral administration of liver extract-Lilly (N. N. R.) derived from 600 Gm. of liver (table 1).

The following observations show that extrinsic factor is present in hog stomach mucosa. About 5 Kg. of hog stomach was boiled for two hours on a water bath, then cooled, finely minced, and together with the liquor obtained, 2,500 cc. of water, 90 Gm. of pepsin, and sufficient concentrated hydrochloric acid to maintain an acidity of less than $p$H 2.5, was incubated at 37.5 C. for seventy-two hours. At the end of that time the liquefied material was concentrated by vacuum distillation until 100 Gm. was equivalent to 200 Gm. of original mucosa. In this process there were thus employed two procedures known to destroy the activity of hog stomach mucosa;[1c] first, boiling for at least five minutes and, second, digestion with pepsin and hydrochloric acid for forty-eight hours at 37.5 C.

To patient 66 in the second period and to patient 67 in the first period were given daily 100 Gm. of this inactivated hog stomach mucosa concentrate and 150 cc. of gastric juice immediately after admixture and neutralization with concentrated sodium hydroxide. As will be seen in table 1, patient 66 responded moderately with a reticulocyte peak of 7.5 per cent on the tenth day of the regimen. At this time the blood nonprotein nitrogen, which had been slightly elevated throughout, reached 73.8 mg. per hundred cubic centimeters, and the observation was discontinued. Patient 67 responded to a similar regimen with a reticulocyte peak of 35.9 per cent on the twelfth day. From an initial level of 0.82 million the red blood cells increased to 1.85 million per cubic millimeter on the twentieth day. Clinical improvement was correspondingly striking. Hog stomach mucosa therefore contains extrinsic factor and the probable basis for the activity of this material or, as suggested before, of whole hog stomach,[18] depends on the presence of both a thermostable (extrinsic) factor and a thermolabile (intrinsic) factor.

*Incubation of normal human gastric juice for two hours at 37.5 C. inactivates only a portion of the intrinsic factor.*

Greenspon[11] states that the well known hematopoietic activity of ventriculin (desiccated hog stomach) is completely destroyed in the presence of pepsin and hydrochloric acid by incubation at 38 C. for two hours or longer. The reaction of the incubated mixture was acid to congo red. From this observation he infers that in our experiments in which acid and pepsin containing gastric juice was incubated for two hours at 37.5 C. its "antipernicious anemia principle" was similarly destroyed. He presents, however, no direct evidence for this conclusion from observations with incubated gastric juice.

That the incubation of normal human gastric juice under the conditions of former observations[1b] destroys only a portion of its content of intrinsic factor is shown by the positive effects on blood formation in the second period in case 63 and the first period in case 65 (table 1). Two hundred and fifty cubic centimeters of normal human gastric juice containing active pepsin, as shown by Mett's tubes, and having a natural $p$H of about 1.5, was incubated for two hours at 37.5 C. Immediately thereafter the gastric juice was neutralized and given daily to each patient coincidentally with a meal containing 200 Gm. of beef muscle. In case 62 the gastric juice was incubated for only one hour and a similar positive result was observed in the second period.

Since we[19] had previously shown, however, that the incubation of normal human gastric juice for three days at 40 C. completely abolished its content of intrinsic factor, it seemed very likely that some destruction of this component would be produced by incubation for two hours at 37.5 C. Accordingly, in the third period in case 63 and in the second period in case 65 the conditions of the preceding period were exactly reproduced except that the gastric juice was not incubated but was given each day immediately after neutralization and coincidentally with a meal containing 200 Gm. of beef muscle. In the third period in case 63 there was a second reticulocyte response, reaching 14.5 per cent on the tenth day, and in case 65 a second peak of reticulocytes of 15.9 per cent was attained on the tenth day of this regimen. The occurrence of such second rises of reticulocytes indicates that the material given in these periods was more effective than that given in the preceding periods.[12] Greenspon's belief in the destructive action of peptic hydrolysis on an "antipernicious anemia principle" is thus sustained in that a two hour period of incubation is shown to be detrimental to intrinsic factor. However, since removal of pepsin without change in other properties of the gastric juice was not undertaken, our observations clearly do not permit the further definition of the nature of the destructive process as necessarily peptic hydrolysis.

*Beef muscle and gastric juice administered without opportunity for contact are wholly ineffective.*

Since the intrinsic factor of normal human gastric juice is partially destroyed by incubation for two hours at 37.5 C. at $p$H 1.5, the completely negative results of the observations[1b] in the control periods in cases 13, 15 and 17 may be questioned. In these observations such incubated gastric juice was given to the patient each day sufficiently long before the beef muscle as presumably to diminish greatly any opportunity for contact between these substances within the alimentary tract.

A repetition of these observations was undertaken without preliminary incubation of the gastric juice. During the first period in case 69, 200 Gm. of beef muscle was given to the patient at 8 o'clock in the morning. Twelve hours later 150 cc. of gastric juice was neutralized and immediately given. This regimen was

18. (a) Castle, Townsend and Heath.[1c] (b) Sturgis, C. C., and Isaacs, Raphael: Treatment of Pernicious Anemia with Desiccated, Defatted Stomach, Am. J. M. Sc. 180:597 (Nov.) 1930.

19. Castle, W. B.; Townsend, W. C., and Heath, C. W.: Further Observations on the Etiologic Relationship on Achylia Gastrica to Pernicious Anemia, J. Clin. Investigation 9:2 (Aug.) 1930.

repeated daily for twelve days without detectable effect on blood production, as shown in table 1. In the immediately succeeding second period, however, when each day similar quantities of neutral gastric juice and beef muscle were given together, a reticulocyte peak of 20.6 per cent was reached on the tenth day and the red blood cells increased from an initial level of 1.34 to 1.95 million per cubic millimeter on the sixteenth day. In order that the amount of both beef muscle and gastric juice administered in each period of twelve days might be the same, these substances were not given after the twelfth day of the second period.

To patient 68 were given on the odd numbered days of the first period 300 Gm. of beef muscle and on the even numbered days 150 cc. of neutral gastric juice. In all, six administrations of each substance were made on alternate days during the twelve days of this first period. No detectable effect on blood production was observed. During the immediately succeeding period of twelve days, 300 Gm. of beef muscle and 150 cc. of gastric juice neutralized immediately before administration were given together every other day for six such administrations. A moderate effect on blood production occurred. The reticulocytes reached a peak of 7.4 per cent on the sixteenth day and the red blood cells did not increase. This relatively slight effect on reticulocyte production is probably explained by the presence of cystitis with fever complicating the patient's condition and by the fact that since the material was administered only on alternate days the amount given was spread over twice as long a period as in observations in which daily administration was practiced.

The observations on patients 68 and 69 demonstrate that the conclusions reached on the basis of former observations[1b] on patients 13, 15 and 17 were correct; namely, if beef muscle and gastric juice are administered without opportunity for contact, they are not effective. It is obvious, therefore, that the activity of mixtures of beef muscle and gastric juice cannot be due to the simple addition of two subthreshold substances but requires an interaction between them.

*Former experiments apparently demonstrating the absence of extrinsic factor from certain substances are not necessarily valid.*

Observations apparently demonstrating the negative effects of gastric juice incubated with various substances were made in case 5 (cornstarch),[1a] case 19 (washed casein),[1b] case 24 (beef muscle protein),[1e] case 27 (wheat gluten), case 51b (animal nucleic acid), cases 52, 53 and 54 (spleen pulp), cases 58 and 59 (nucleoprotein), and cases 59a, 60 and 61 (yeast nucleic acid).[1e] Since incubation of 250 cc. of gastric juice for two hours at 37.5 C. in the presence of native pepsin and hydrochloric acid at a reaction of $p$H 1.5 detectably diminishes its content of intrinsic factor, the apparently negative results of these former observations need reconsideration.

In table 2 are summarized the amounts of gastric juice, the nature of the substrate, and the reaction and duration of the incubation period in the foregoing cases. Patient 5 was given daily the entire incubated gastric contents of a normal man removed one hour after the ingestion of a meal of 300 Gm. of cornstarch. Since the incubation period in the observation on this patient lasted six hours at a reaction of $p$H 1.5 to 2, the negative result cannot be accepted. It is probable, however, from the nature of the basal diet used in all our observations that refined carbohydrate does not contain extrinsic factor. The negative result of observations on patient 19, who was given daily 50 Gm. of washed casein (A. H. Thomas Company) incubated with 300 cc. of gastric juice from three to five hours at $p$H 2.5-3.5, likewise cannot be accepted because of the prolonged incubation period.

The negative results with spleen pulp and gastric juice in cases 53 and 54 we now believe cannot be accepted, owing to the fact that the observations were made on patients in another city to which the material had to be transported, subject to delay. In former unpublished observations with incubated mixtures of beef muscle and gastric juice known to be fully effective under usual conditions, negative results were obtained when the material was so transported. In the first periods in cases 50 and 51, and in the second period in case 58, positive results were obtained from the daily administration of 50 Gm. or more of spleen pulp or a subfraction after incubation with from 50 to 75 cc. of gastric juice for two hours at $p_H$ 7. Therefore, the negative result in patient 52, who received 100 Gm. of spleen pulp incubated for two hours with 75 cc. of gastric juice at $p_H$ 7, seems to be clear cut. It is thus probable that, as was formerly stated, the divergent results of these observations with spleen pulp are due to variations in the content of extrinsic factor of the spleen.

In cases 24, 27, 52, 58, 59a and 60, the incubation period did not exceed two hours. Assuming the correctness of Greenspon's belief that peptic activity is responsible for the inactivation of gastric juice, the conditions (table 2) of none of these incubation procedures could have been as favorable for destruction of the intrinsic factor as those obtaining during incubation of gastric juice alone for two hours. In the latter case the reaction ($p_H$ 1.5) was almost optimal for peptic hydrolysis and there was no substrate present potentially capable of adsorbing pepsin and so affording protection for the intrinsic factor.

In the observations in cases 52, 59, 59a and 60 in which only 75 cc. of gastric juice was employed, the reaction of the incubated mixture was $p_H$ 6 to 7. In cases 51b and 61 only 50 cc. of gastric juice was incubated for four hours at $p_H$ 7 with the substrates. It is possible that, although incubation of 250 cc. of gastric juice for two hours under optimal conditions for peptic activity only partially destroyed its content of intrinsic factor, the inactivation of a smaller quantity of gastric juice would be sufficiently great to produce the negative results observed. It is also possible that the temperature alone and not the peptic hydrolysis suggested by Greenspon is responsible for the partial inactivation of the intrinsic factor observed. Helmer, Fouts and Zerfas,[4] however, have obtained moderately positive effects from the daily administration of as little as 10 and 25 cc. respectively of gastric juice incubated for four hours at 47 C. with liver extract-Lilly (N. N. R.) derived from 100 Gm. of liver. The daily administration of such an amount of that liver extract alone is essentially ineffective. Because of these facts, it does not seem probable that the reduction of the amounts of gastric juice employed in some of these observations or the incubation in some instances for as long as four hours at $p_H$ 7 could have been responsible for the negative results. Nevertheless, because of the variability of response to oral administration among patients with pernicious anemia, negative results, unless obtained under optimal conditions for interaction between intrinsic and extrinsic factors, cannot be accepted as confidently as positive responses. For this reason the negative observations with washed casein and with certain other substances are being repeated without preliminary incubation.

Unfortunately, criticism may also be justified in respect to the negative results of others who have likewise incubated certain substances for over two hours with acid gastric juice. Thus Diehl and Kühnau[20] and Groen[2] incubated lactoflavin[20a] for three and four hours respectively with gastric juice and obtained no effect on blood production in pernicious anemia. The negative result obtained by Wills and Naish[21] with an extract of egg white incubated with gastric juice for two hours, and confirmed by Groen[2] with egg white after a four hour incubation period, contrasts with the positive result reported by Miller and Rhoads[6] after an incubation period of only one hour. On the other hand, those substances giving negative results in patients with tropical macrocytic anemia may safely be accepted as lacking an extrinsic factor provided the positive effects with other substances are due to the natural presence of intrinsic factor in the gastric juice of these patients.[22] Thus, Wills[23] found that dried yeast, a watery extract of yeast, a vitamin $B_2$ preparation derived from egg white, and a preparation of vitamins $B_1$ and $B_4$ adsorbed on acid clay, in contrast to various preparations of autolyzed yeast (marmite), had no blood-forming activity in tropical macrocytic anemia. In confirmation of this the Lassens[24] found that pressed top yeast and watery extracts of such yeast before or after autoclaving for one hour at 2.5 atmospheres did not lead to increased blood production in pernicious anemia after incubation with gastric juice for two hours.

## COMMENT

When it is shown that for the secretion of the normal stomach to be effective in pernicious anemia a food factor is essential, the demonstration that a disturbance of the stomach is a primary factor in the immediate causation of the disease becomes possible on purely experimental grounds. Whether the fact of failure of the secretion of the stomach in pernicious anemia were known or not, a repetition of the observations which we have conducted with beef muscle and gastric juice would, we believe, lead to the conclusions that we have reached.

Briefly, these experiments have shown that in pernicious anemia the oral administration of either beef muscle or gastric juice alone is without effect. The oral administration of the gastric contents of a normal subject removed after the ingestion of a meal of beef muscle[1a] or the oral administration of mixtures of gastric juice with beef muscle,[1b] eggs,[8] autolyzed yeast,[37] wheat germ,[1e] rice polishings[38] or tomato extract[2] has been shown to produce increased blood formation in pernicious anemia. A

TABLE 2.—*Conditions During the Incubation at 37.5 C. of Mixtures of Normal Human Gastric Juice with Various Substrates Administered with Negative Results to Patients with Pernicious Anemia*

| Case Number and Reference of Previous Report | Gastric Juice, Cc. | Substrate | | Incubation Period | |
|---|---|---|---|---|---|
| | | Nature | Amount, Gm. | Duration, Hours | Reaction, $p_H$ |
| 5 [1a] | 200 | Cornstarch............... | 300 | 6 | 1.5-2.0 |
| 19 [1b] | 300 | Washed casein ......... | 50 | 3-5 | 2.5-3.5 |
| 24 [1c] | 150 | Beef muscle protein .. | * | 2 | 2.0 |
| 27 [1c] | 150 | Wheat gluten flour.... | 100 | 2 | 3.0 |
| 52 [1e] | 75 | Spleen pulp ............. | 100 | 2 | 6.0-7.0 |
| 53 [1e] | 50 | Spleen pulp ............. | 50 | 0 | 7.0 |
| 54 [1e] | 50 | Spleen pulp ............. | 50 | 0 | 7.0 |
| 58 [1c] | 100 | Nucleoprotein .......... | 5 | 2 | 3.5-4.5 |
| 59 [1c] | 75 | Nucleoprotein .......... | 5 | 2 | 6.0 |
| 51b [1c] | 50 | Animal nucleic acid .. | 5 | 4 | 7.0 |
| 59a [1c] | 75 | Yeast nucleic acid..... | 10 | 2 | 6.0 |
| 60 [1c] | 75 | Yeast nucleic acid..... | 10 | 2 | 6.5 |
| 61 [1c] | 50 | Yeast nucleic acid..... | 5 | 4 | 7.0 |

*Derived from 200 Gm. of beef muscle.

similar process would clearly take place in the normal subject in the natural course of the digestion of certain foods.

Our conception of the experimentally demonstrable factors normally involved in the production of the substance that is deficient in the liver of patients with pernicious[35] and related macrocytic anemias[36] is represented by the schematic formula

$$\frac{F \times G}{I} = L.\,E.$$

Here $F$ stands for food (extrinsic) factor, $G$ for gastric (intrinsic) factor and $I$ for intestinal impermeability or any defect causing malabsorption or destruction of those substances or a product of their effective interaction. $L.\,E.$ stands for "liver extract," the independently effective thermostable factor found in mammalian liver, kidney and certain other organs. Probably in none of the anemias referred to is any factor on the left of the equation completely normal, and in every instance there

20. Diehl, F., and Kühnau, J.: Ist Vitamin $B_2$ der therapeutisch wirksame äussere Faktor beim Morbus Biermer? Deutsches Arch. f. klin. Med. 176:149 (Dec. 12) 1933.

20a. We have, however, now entirely confirmed these negative results by giving a mixture of 150 cc. of neutralized gastric juice and 20 mg. of lactoflavin daily for five days without preliminary incubation. We are indebted to Vitab Products, Inc., for supplying the lactoflavin.

21. Wills, Lucy, and Naish, Alice: A Case of Pernicious Anaemia Treated with Vitamin $B_2$ from Egg White, Lancet 1:1286 (June 17) 1933.

22. Strauss and Castle.[1e] Ungley and James.[9]

23. Wills, Lucy: Studies in Pernicious Anaemia of Pregnancy: VI. Tropical Macrocytic Anaemia as a Deficiency Disease, with Special Reference to the Vitamin B Complex, Indian J. M. Research 21:669 (April) 1934.

24. Lassen, H. C. A., and Lassen, H. K.: Yeast or Vitamin $B_2$ as "Extrinsic Factor" in Treatment of Pernicious Anemia, Am. J. M. Sc. 188:461 (Oct.) 1934.

37. Strauss and Castle.[1e] Groen.[2]

38. Strauss and Castle.[1e] Miller and Rhoads.[6]

is a variable participation of defects of one or both of the factors in the numerator[39] or some increase of the denominator value.[40] Any or all such changes from the normal will, however, result in a decrease of "liver extract" which, if sufficiently great, may allow the development of a macrocytic anemia which will respond to the parenteral administration of liver extract derived from the liver of a normal animal.

If the dominant defect is of food (extrinsic) factor, the anemia will respond both to orally administered extrinsic factor and to liver extract (e. g., macrocytic anemia of pregnancy in the tropics[41] and elsewhere[39b] or of certain cases of sprue[36] and idiopathic steatorrhea[42]). The presence of some intrinsic factor in the stomach probably explains the occurrence of "spontaneous" remissions in certain cases of pernicious anemia[43] as well as the usual recovery following delivery of patients with the pernicious anemia of pregnancy.[39b] Likewise the partial success of former methods of treatment with high protein diets in both pernicious anemia[1d] and sprue[36] was probably due to a similar effect. On the other hand, the concept of a defect of an independently active antipernicious anemia principle secreted by the stomach, as proposed by Morris[25] and by Greenspon,[11] does not satisfactorily explain the immediate etiologic mechanism of those instances of macrocytic anemia in which intrinsic factor is demonstrably present in the gastric contents.[36] If the dominant defect is of gastric (intrinsic) factor, the anemia will not respond to orally administered extrinsic factor unless gastric juice is given simultaneously but will respond to liver extract administered orally or parenterally (e. g., addisonian pernicious anemia).

The existence of an essential preliminary reaction between food and gastric juice does not, however, preclude the possibility of defects of other subsequent and essential reactions within or without the alimentary tract. If intestinal impermeability is sufficiently increased, the patient will not respond normally to mixtures of extrinsic and intrinsic factor or to stomach or liver preparations given by mouth but will respond to parenterally administered liver extract (e. g., macrocytic anemia of chronic sprue[36] or of intestinal stenoses or short circuits[44]). In theory at least, failure or inhibition of any essential link in the further metabolism within the body will likewise diminish the supply of liver extract available to the bone marrow.[45] It is certainly clear that infections[12] may have an inhibitory effect on the action of liver extract in pernicious anemia. This concept of the etiologic relationships between pernicious anemia and other types of macrocytic anemia which likewise respond to the parenteral administration of liver extract has been fully discussed elsewhere.[46]

## CONCLUSIONS

The following observations on patients with pernicious anemia fail to sustain the conclusions of Greenspon:

1. Normal human gastric juice does not contain, on oral administration, an "antipernicious anemia principle" effective without contact with food (extrinsic) factor.

2. Hog stomach mucosa contains both a thermostable (extrinsic) factor and a thermolabile (intrinsic) factor presumably responsible for the activity of such mucosa and of whole desiccated hog stomach.

3. Incubation of normal human gastric juice for two hours at 37.5 C. in the presence of native pepsin and hydrochloric acid inactivates only a portion of its content of intrinsic factor.

4. Beef muscle (extrinsic factor) and gastric juice (intrinsic factor) administered without opportunity for contact are not effective in pernicious anemia.

Greenspon's recent experiments have led to the following modified conclusions in respect to former observations:

1. The negative results of the administration of substances after incubation with gastric juice for longer periods than two hours at 37.5 C. at an acid reaction cannot be accepted.

2. Lack of extrinsic factor in substances so incubated with gastric juice is not established by negative results.

3. Preliminary incubations should not be employed in testing the blood-forming activity in pernicious anemia of mixtures of gastric juice and various substrates.

39. (a) Castle, W. B.: The Etiology of Pernicious and Related Macrocytic Anemias, Science 82:159 (Aug. 23) 1935. (b) Strauss, M. B., and Castle, W. B.: Studies of Anemia in Pregnancy: III. The Etiologic Relationship of Gastric Secretory Defects and Dietary Deficiency to the Hypochromic and Macrocytic (Pernicious) Anemias of Pregnancy and the Treatment of These Conditions. Am. J. M. Sc. 185:539 (April) 1933. (c) Goldhamer, S. M.: The Presence of the Intrinsic Factor of Castle in the Gastric Juice of Patients with Pernicious Anemia, Am. J. M. Sc. 191:405 (March) 1936.

40. Castle, Heath and Strauss.[1d] Castle, Rhoads, Lawson and Payne.[36]

41. Wills:[23] Treatment of "Pernicious Anaemia of Pregnancy" and "Tropical Anaemia," with Special Reference to Yeast Extract as a Curative Agent. Brit. M. J. 1:1059 (June 20) 1931.

42. Vaughan, J. M., and Hunter, Donald: The Treatment by Marmite of Megalocytic Hyperchromic Anaemia Occurring in Idiopathic Steatorrhoea (Coeliac Disease), Lancet 1:829 (April 16) 1933.

43. Castle, Heath and Strauss.[1d] Goldhamer.[39c]

44. Castle, Heath and Strauss.[1d] Schlesinger, Annemarie: Nachweis des Antiperniciosa-Prinzips im Magensaft einer Patientin mit perniziös-anämischem Blutbild bei Dünndarmstenose, Klin. Wchnschr. 12:298 (Feb. 25) 1933. Strauss, M. B.: The Role of the Gastro-Intestinal Tract in Conditioning Deficiency Disease: The Significance of Digestion and Absorption in Pernicious Anemia, Pellagra and "Alcoholic" and Other Forms of Polyneuritis, J. A. M. A. 103:1 (July 7) 1934.

45. Castle, Heath and Strauss.[1d] Wintrobe, M. M., and Schumacker H. S. Jr.: The Occurrence of Macrocytic Anemia in Association with Disorder of the Liver. Bull. Johns Hopkins Hosp. 52:387 (June) 1933. Goldhamer. S. M.: Liver Extract Therapy in Cirrhosis of the Liver Relation of Liver Dysfunction to Nonstorage of "Antianemic" Substance in Producing a Blood Picture Resembling Pernicious Anemia in a Patient Secreting Free Hydrochloric Acid, Arch. Int. Med. 53:54 (Jan.) 1934.

46. Castle, Heath and Strauss.[1d] Strauss and Castle.[1e] Castle.[17] Castle.[39] Strauss and Castle.[39b]

Jan 27, 1984
(JAMA 1984;251:522-523)

# An 'Extrinsic Factor'
# and Pernicious Anemia*

Victor Herbert, MD, JD

This classic of lucid exposition brought together the elegant series of prior studies published by Castle and his collaborators beginning in 1929 and demolished the recently expressed opposing view by Greenspon[1] that gastric juice worked alone as a hematopoietic factor. A half century later, this 1936 article remains a model of clear presentation of a series of straightforward observations to draw almost inescapable conclusions.

## Elucidation of Pernicious Anemia

In 1822, Coombe had first described what was almost certainly pernicious anemia in a 47-year-old male patient with a "deadly pale color" who suffered from "a species of dyspepsia . . . probably owing to some disorder of the digestive and assimilative organs."[2]

In 1860, Austin Flint, Sr, "that remarkable American physician and teacher,"[3] aware of the atrophy of the secretory glands of the stomach recently reported by Handfield Jones after microscopic examination of 14 human stomachs, remarked with respect to pernicious anemia:

suspect that in these cases, there exists a degenerative disease of the glandular tubulae of the stomach. . . . Fatal anemia must follow an amount of degenerative disease reducing the amount of gastric juice so far that assimilation of food is rendered wholly inadequate for the wants of the body. I shall be ready to claim the merit of this idea when the difficult and laborious researches of someone [else] have shown it to be correct.[3]

From the Department of Medicine, State University of New York, Downstate Medical Center, Brooklyn; and the Hematology and Nutrition Laboratory, Veterans Administration Medical Center, Bronx, NY.

*A commentary on Castle WB, Ham TH: Observations on the etiologic relationship of achylia gastrica to pernicious anemia: V. Further evidence for the essential participation of extrinsic factor in hematopoietic responses to mixtures of beef muscle and gastric juice and to hog stomach mucosa. *JAMA* 1936;107:1456-1463.

## Castle's Work

Castle was that somebody else. His "difficult and laborious researches" showed the idea to be correct and demonstrated the intertwined relationship of food and gastric juice in the assimilation of an unknown nutrient by humans.[4]

The 1936 Castle and Ham article laid out the sequence of events step by step for health professionals. In 1929, Castle had shown, by eating, himself, 300 g of rare hamburg steak and one hour later recovering an estimated two thirds of the digested material from his stomach, that feeding this recovered mixture of steak and gastric juice by stomach tube to each of ten patients with pernicious anemia produced in eight of the ten a characteristic rise of reticulocytes and progressive increase in RBC count.[5] Conversely, the administration of 200 g of hamburg steak alone was ineffective, as was hamburg steak plus hydrochloric acid or commercial pepsin. He concluded that "the secretions of the normal gastric mucus membrane . . . through their action on food proteins, can produce some substance capable on oral administration of definitely benefiting certain cases of pernicious anemia." His subsequent observations, brought together in the 1936 article, seemingly delineated the fact that an "intrinsic factor" secreted by the gastric tubulae (now known to be secreted by parietal cells) interacted with an "extrinsic factor" (present in beef muscle and now known to be vitamin $B_{12}$) to yield an absorbable hematopoietic factor active in the treatment of pernicious anemia.

Twelve years later, the isolation by others in 1948 of the active principle of liver extract made clear that the role of the gastric intrinsic factor of Castle was to make possible the adequate absorption across the ileum of the "extrinsic factor," vitamin $B_{12}$, so that it could serve its vitamin function.[2-4]

Greenspon had argued that Castle's own data showed

that fresh hog stomach mucosa could produce hematologic response in pernicious anemia; therefore, gastric
juice alone was all that was needed. Others also fell into
the error of not preventing unrecognized dietary intake
of extrinsic factor. Castle and Ham pointed out the
fundamental fallacy of this argument by showing that
hog stomach mucosa contained not only the intrinsic
factor present in gastric juice but also the extrinsic factor
present in beef muscle. The force of Castle and Ham's
procedure was to show that during the preliminary
control period, the same amount of gastric juice and
beef muscle given *separately* caused no reticulocyte
response but did cause one when given *together*.
Castle's work was seminal in developing the concept
that deficiencies of any nutrient could derive from one of
three fundamental inadequacies (ingestion, absorption,
or utilization). Others extended this to note nutrient
deficiency from three increases (requirement, excretion,
or destruction).

### Vitamin B₁₂

In 1926, Minot and Murphy[6] had demonstrated that
pernicious anemia could be cured by feeding large
quantities of liver (see Chapter 21). Castle did not share
the Nobel Prize with Minot and Murphy. The prize was
shared with Whipple,[7] who with Robscheit-Robbins
showed that beef liver enhanced hemoglobin formation
in chronically bled dogs and whose work stimulated
Minot to try liver in pernicious anemia. In 1936, two
years after the Nobel Prize in Medicine had been
awarded for liver treatment of pernicious anemia, it
became apparent that the reason the dogs responded to
liver was the iron content of the liver and not the vitamin
B₁₂ content,[8] for it was iron in which bled dogs (like bled
humans) were deficient and not vitamin B₁₂. The Nobel
Committee thought they saw the recognition of a similar
"essential" for normalizing the bone marrow in dog and
man. The overwhelming importance to hematology of

these quantitative efforts to promote erythropoiesis
suggests that the prize was right even though the
scientific reason was wrong.

The search for the active principle in liver culminated
with the isolation of the pure red vitamin B₁₂ in 1948 by a
pharmaceutical industry research team of Merck scientists[9] working in the United States. The British team at
Glaxo Laboratories in England[10] was preceded in the
publication of the identical discovery by the razor-thin
margin of three weeks. Yet another Nobel Prize (Chemistry, 1964) was to be awarded in the vitamin field, when
Dorothy Hodgkin won that award for her elucidation of
the chemical structure of vitamin B₁₂ by x-ray crystallogra-
phy. Discovery of new and significant details of the role
of digestive tract secretions in vitamin B₁₂ absorption
continues to occupy numerous investigators.[11,12]

---

For a recent scholarly review of the history of
pernicious anemia, one can turn to the excellent monograph by Kass,[2] and for how pernicious anemia yielded
to two Brookline physicians (Minot and Murphy), one
should read Castle's[13] 1975 first-hand account of how
they carried it off while working in medicine in a familiar
pattern of the time: private practice with part-time
appointments for teaching and research in medical
school and hospital.

Another fascinating sidelight in the saga of pernicious
anemia is that vitamin B₁₂ may have been actually isolated
in crystalline form in 1939 — nine years before others[9,14]
made that discovery — by Laland's group in Scandinavia
but Castle and Ham didn't know it until 1960. It seems
that the Laland group had in 1939 placed drops of their
purest liver extract fraction on slides under cover glasses
that were sealed to be left in a drawer at room
temperature. When the slides were examined in 1959,
19 years later, the microscopic field was full of reddish
colored crystals typical of vitamin B₁₂, a color photomi-
crograph of which was published in 1960.[14(p327)]

### References

1. Greenspon EA: The nature of the antipernicious anemia principle
in stomach: I. Methods to improve stomach preparations. *JAMA*
1936;106:266-271.

2. Kass L: *Pernicious Anemia.* Philadelphia, WB Saunders Co, 1978.

3. Castle WB: The Gordon Wilson lecture: A century of curiosity
about pernicious anemia. *Trans Am Clin Climatol Assoc* 1961;73:54-
80.

4. Herbert V: Vitamin B₁₂, in Olson R (ed): *Present Knowledge in
Nutrition,* ed 5. Washington, DC, The Nutrition Foundation, in press.

5. Castle WB, Townsend WC: Observations on the etiologic
relationship of achylia gastrica to pernicious anemia: II. The effect of the
administration to patients with pernicious anemia of beef muscle after
incubation with normal human gastric juice. *JAMA* 1929;178:764-777.

6. Minot GR, Murphy WP: Treatment of pernicious anemia by
special diet. *JAMA* 1926;87:470-476.

7. Whipple GH, Robscheit-Robbins FS: Blood regeneration in severe
anemia: Favorable influence of liver, heart and skeletal muscle in diet.
*Am J Physiol* 1925;72:408-418.

8. Whipple GH, Robscheit-Robbins FS: I. Iron and its utilization in
experimental anemia. *Am J Med Sci* 1936;191:1124.

9. Rickes EL, Brink NG, Koniusczy FR, et al: Crystalline vitamin B₁₂.
*Science* 1948;107:396-397.

10. Smith EL, Parker LFJ: Purification of anti-pernicious anaemia
factor. *Biochem J* 1948;43:viii-ix.

11. Kanazawa S, Herbert V, Herzlich B, et al: Removal of cobalamin
analogue in bile by enterohepatic circulation. *Lancet* 1983;1:707-708.

12. Kanazawa S, Herbert V: Mechanism of enterohepatic circulation
of vitamin B₁₂: Movement of vitamin B₁₂ from bile R-binder to intrinsic
factor due to the action of pancreatic trypsin. *Trans Assoc Am Phy*
1983;96:336-344.

13. Castle WB: Pernicious anemia yields to New England character
in *Proceedings of Brookline Historical Society for 1969-1974.* Brookline
Mass, Brookline Historical Society, 1975, pp 126-131.

14. Jorpes JE, Strandell B: An early attempt at isolating the
antianaemic principle in liver. *Acta Med Scand* 1960;168:325-327.

April 24, 1937
(*JAMA* 1937;108:1407-1408)

## Chapter 27

# The Treatment of Meningococcic Meningitis With Sulfanilamide

## Preliminary Report

Francis F. Schwentker, M.D.

Sidney Gelman, M.D.

and

Perrin H. Long, M.D.

Baltimore

A number of investigators have pointed out the therapeutic value of sulfanilamide (para-amino-benzene-sulfonamide) in infections due to the beta-hemolytic streptococcus. A review of this work will be found in the recent article of Long and Bliss.[1] Buttle and his co-workers[2] and Proom[3] have also demonstrated protective and curative properties for the drug against meningococcic infections in mice. This paper will report the preliminary observations on the use of sulfanilamide in the treatment of ten cases of meningococcic meningitis and one of septicemia only. The ages of the patients ranged from 1 to 34 years. After the first two patients had been treated, the drug was used in every case admitted for meningococcic infection. There was therefore no selection of cases; they ranged in severity from moderate to severe illness.

### METHOD OF TREATMENT

Within the limitations of individual need, all patients were treated in the same manner, by subcutaneous and intraspinal injection of the drug. The solution was prepared in the following manner: A measured volume of sterile physiologic solution of sodium chloride was heated in a flask. When the saline began to boil, the flask was removed from the flame and a weighed amount of sulfanilamide was added in quantity to make an 0.8 per cent solution of the drug. The mixture was cooled to about 37 C. and injected immediately.

After a diagnosis of meningococcic meningitis had been made, sulfanilamide solution was injected intraspinally into the patient in amounts varying from 10 to 30 cc. As a general rule the amount injected was from 5 to 10 cc. less than the volume of spinal fluid removed. A larger amount of the solution was also given subcutaneously, approximately 100 cc. being injected for each 40 pounds (18 kg.) of body weight. Both the intraspinal and subcutaneous treatments were repeated every twelve hours for the first two days and once each day thereafter until definite improvement was evident. In some instances subcutaneous injection of the drug was continued for several days longer than the intraspinal treatment.

### RESULTS

The results are summarized in the accompanying table. Certain interesting facts are evident. In some cases the cell count of the spinal fluid fell rapidly and progressively. In others the count remained elevated for several days, then decreased precipitously. Culture of the spinal fluid of a number of patients was sterile after the first treatment; for others several treatments were required, but in no case was the organism recovered

Read in part before the Medical Society of the County of Kings, Brooklyn, Feb. 16, 1937.

From the Sydenham Hospital, Baltimore City Health Department and the Department of Medicine, Johns Hopkins Hospital.

1. Long, P. H., and Bliss, Eleanor A.: Para-Amino-Benzene-Sulfonamide and Its Derivatives, J. A. M. A. **108**:32 (Jan. 2) 1937.

2. Buttle, G. A. H.; Gray, W. H., and Stephenson, Dora: Protection of Mice Against Streptococcal and Other Infections by Para-Amino-benzenesulfonamide and Related Substances, Lancet **1**:1286 (June 6) 1936.

3. Proom, H.: The Therapeutic Action of Para-Aminobenzenesulfonamide in Meningococcal Infections of Mice, Lancet **1**:16 (Jan. 2) 1937.

| Date | Cell Count | Per Cent of Polymorphonuclears | Globulin | Sugar | Culture | Intraspinally, Cc. | Subcutaneously, Cc. | Comment |
|---|---|---|---|---|---|---|---|---|
| **Case 1.—G. T., Negro man, aged 21** | | | | | | | | |
| 12/31 | 21,000 | .. | 4 plus | ........ | Positive | 30 | 300 | Critically ill, unconscious; smear of spinal fluid showed many organisms; blood culture positive |
| 1/1 | 21,000 | 80 | 4 plus | 0 | 0 | 30 | 300 | |
|  | 20,000 | 80 | 4 plus | 0 | 0 | 30 | 300 | |
| 1/2 | 9,400 | 90 | 3 plus | 0 | 0 | 25 | 300 | |
| 1/3 | 2,400 | 84 | Trace | 3 plus | 0 | 30 | 270 | Constant improvement |
| 1/4 | 1,030 | 90 | Trace | 2 plus | 0 | 30 | 270 | |
| 1/6 | 840 | 90 | Trace | 1 plus | 0 | | | |
| 1/19 | 30 | 0 | 0 | 2 plus | 0 | | | |
| 2/1 | .. | .. | ........ | ........ | ......... | .. | ...... | Discharged well |
| **Case 2.—E. W., white boy, aged 7 years** | | | | | | | | |
| 1/9 | 11,000 | 92 | 1 plus | 1 plus | Positive | 30 | 100 | Moderately ill |
|  | 5,600 | | 1 plus | 1 plus | Positive | 20 | 75 | |
| 1/10 | 2,750 | .. | 1 plus | 1 plus | 0 | 10 | 100 | |
| 1/11 | 880 | 80 | Trace | 1 plus | 0 | 17 | | |
| 1/12 | 60 | 35 | 0 | 2 plus | 0 | 30 | 70 | |
| 1/25 | 8 | 0 | 0 | 2 plus | 0 | | | |
| 2/12 | | | | | | | | Discharged well |
| **Case 3.—L. W., Negro girl, aged 5 years** | | | | | | | | |
| 1/14 | 9,500 | 82 | 2 plus | 0 | Positive | 25 | 200 | Moderately ill; blood culture sterile |
|  | 2,400 | 85 | 1 plus | 0 | Positive | 10 | 190 | |
| 1/15 | 2,500 | 90 | 4 plus | 1 plus | Positive | 15 | 185 | |
|  | 4,800 | 70 | 2 plus | 0 | Positive | 20 | 180 | |
| 1/16 | 3,500 | 90 | 2 plus | 0 | Positive | 30 | 170 | |
| 1/17 | 1,200 | 75 | 1 plus | Trace | 0 | 20 | 180 | |
|  | | | | | | | 200 | |
| 1/18 | 384 | .. | Trace | Trace | 0 | 15 | 185 | |
| 1/19 | ... | .. | ........ | ........ | ......... | .. | 200 | |
| 2/3 | 2 | 20 | 0 | 0 | ......... | .. | ...... | Discharged well |
| **Case 4.—M. A., white boy, aged 2 years** | | | | | | | | |
| 1/17 | 9,400 | 95 | 1 plus | 0 | Positive | 20 | 80 | Semiconscious; quite ill |
| 1/18 | 8,200 | 95 | 1 plus | 1 plus | Positive | 25 | 75 | |
|  | 3,450 | 90 | Trace | 0 | Positive | 10 | 190 | |
| 1/19 | 830 | 80 | Trace | 2 plus | 0 | 20 | 80 | |
| 1/20 | 485 | 40 | Trace | 2 plus | 0 | 30 | 70 | |
| 1/21 | 108 | 25 | Trace | 2 plus | 0 | 15 | 85 | Transient arthritis in right ring finger |
| 1/22 | ... | .. | ........ | ........ | ......... | | 100 | |
| 2/2 | 2 | 0 | 0 | 2 plus | 0 | | | |
| 2/7 | .. | .. | ........ | ........ | ......... | .. | ...... | Discharged well |
| **Case 5.—J. C., Negro man, aged 34** | | | | | | | | |
| 1/22 | 9,000 | 95 | 2 plus | 0 | Positive | 30 | 270 | Severely ill, semiconscious |
| 1/23 | 4,500 | 90 | 1 plus | 0 | Positive | 28 | 272 | |
|  | 2,800 | 80 | 2 plus | 0 | 0 | 20 | 280 | |
| 1/24 | 1,750 | .. | Trace | 0 | 0 | 30 | 270 | |
| 1/25 | 1,775 | 75 | 1 plus | Trace | 0 | 25 | 275 | |
| 1/26 | ...... | .. | ........ | ........ | ......... | .. | 300 | |
| 2/9 | 60 | 0 | Trace | 1 plus | 0 | .. | ...... | Discharged well |
| **Case 6.—C. P., white boy, aged 10 years** | | | | | | | | |
| 1/24 | 9,000 | 92 | Trace | 0 | Positive | 35 | 165 | Moderately ill; blood culture sterile |
|  | 11,000 | .. | Trace | 0 | 0 | 30 | 170 | |
| 1/25 | 17,600 | 95 | 2 plus | 0 | 0 | 25 | 175 | |
|  | 12,200 | 95 | 1 plus | 0 | 0 | 20 | 180 | |

| Date | Cell Count | Per Cent of Polymorphonuclears | Globulin | Sugar | Culture | Intraspinally, Cc. | Subcutaneously, Cc. | Comment |
|---|---|---|---|---|---|---|---|---|
| **Case 6.—C. P., white boy, aged 10 years—Continued** | | | | | | | | |
| 1/26 | 3,650 | 90 | Trace | 0 | ......... | 35 | 175 | |
| 1/27 | ...... | | | | | | 200 | |
| 1/29 | 99 | .. | Trace | 0 | ......... | .. | 200 | Transient arthritis in right wrist |
| 2/11 | 10 | 0 | 0 | Trace | ......... | | ...... | Discharged well |
| **Case 7.—R. B., Negro man, aged 23** | | | | | | | | |
| 1/29 | 11,500 | 93 | 2 plus | 1 plus | Positive | 22 | 200 | Moderately ill, conscious and cooperative; blood culture sterile |
| 1/30 | 12,000 | 95 | 3 plus | 0 | Positive | 30 | 270 | |
|  | 10,100 | 95 | 3 plus | 0 | Positive | 30 | 270 | |
| 1/31 | 14,600 | 95 | 2 plus | Trace | 0 | 25 | 275 | |
|  | 12,000 | 95 | 1 plus | Trace | 0 | 25 | 275 | |
| 2/1 | 4,480 | 95 | 2 plus | Trace | 0 | 20 | 180 | |
|  | | | | | | | 300 | |
| 2/2 | 1,880 | 82 | 1 plus | Trace | 0 | 20 | 280 | |
| 2/3 | ...... | | | | | .. | 300 | |
| 2/9 | 26 | 0 | Trace | 1 plus | 0 | | | |
| 2/17 | 28 | 2 | 0 | Trace | 0 | .. | ...... | Discharged well |
| **Case 8.—W. C., white woman, aged 28** | | | | | | | | |
| 1/30 | 13,400 | 95 | 2 plus | 0 | Positive | 25 | 275 | Severely ill; semiconscious; blood culture sterile |
|  | | | | | | | 300 | |
| 1/31 | 8,900 | 90 | 2 plus | Trace | 0 | 30 | 230 | |
|  | 11,500 | 95 | 1 plus | Trace | 0 | 25 | 275 | |
| 2/1 | 2,600 | .. | 1 plus | Trace | 0 | 20 | 280 | |
|  | | | | | | | 300 | |
| 2/2 | 930 | 82 | 0 | Trace | 0 | 20 | 200 | |
| 2/17 | 11 | 0 | 0 | 1 plus | 0 | .. | ...... | Discharged well |
| **Case 9.—E. M., Negro man, aged 27** | | | | | | | | |
| 1/30 | 9,850 | 95 | 2 plus | 0 | Positive | 25 | 275 | Critically ill; blood culture sterile |
| 1/31 | 22,200 | 95 | 3 plus | 0 | Positive | 30 | 270 | |
|  | 11,000 | 98 | 3 plus | 0 | 0 | 25 | 275 | |
| 2/1 | 3,350 | 95 | Trace | Trace | Positive | 20 | 270 | |
|  | 9,640 | 93 | 2 plus | 0 | 0 | 20 | 280 | |
| 2/2 | 2,240 | 78 | Trace | Trace | 0 | 25 | 270 | Pneumonia |
| 2/4 | 158 | 68 | 1 plus | 2 plus | 0 | .. | 300 | Died |
| **Case 10.—N. A., Negro girl, aged 9 years** | | | | | | | | |
| 2/2 | 7,400 | 94 | 4 plus | 0 | 0 | 20 | 180 | Clinically meningococcic meningitis; moderately ill |
| 2/3 | 20,200 | 95 | 4 plus | Trace | 0 | 20 | 180 | |
|  | 8,200 | 96 | 4 plus | Trace | 0 | 20 | 180 | |
| 2/4 | ...... | .. | ........ | ........ | ......... | .. | 200 | |
| 2/9 | 91 | 0 | Trace | 1 plus | 0 | .. | | |
| 2/19 | 42 | 14 | 0 | 1 plus | ......... | | ...... | Discharged well |
| **Case 11.—C. C., white boy, aged 1 year** | | | | | | | | |
| 1/30 | 6 | 0 | 0 | 1 plus | 0 | .. | 100 | Severely ill; many petechiae; blood culture positive; two siblings died of fulminating meningitis day before |
| 1/31 | ...... | | | | | | 100 | |
|  | | | | | | | 100 | |
| 2/1 | ...... | .. | ........ | ........ | ......... | | 100 | |
| 2/2 | ...... | .. | ........ | ........ | ......... | | 100 | Constant improvement |
| 2/19 | ...... | .. | ........ | ........ | ......... | | ...... | Discharged well |

*Sulfanilamide was used in 0.8 per cent solution in physiologic solution of sodium chloride.

longer than three days after instigation of treatment. The speed of clinical improvement also varied from rapid to a more protracted return to normal. In two patients transient arthritis developed. There was one death. This patient (E. M., patient 9) was desperately ill at the time of admission, showed symptoms of encephalitic involvement and died of pneumonia on the fifth day despite the fact that the spinal fluid had been sterile for three days and the cell count was only 158 on the day of death.

No untoward effects following the use of sulfanilamide have been noted. When given subcutaneously the solution was rapidly absorbed and gave rise to no more tenderness or reaction at the site of injection than that which follows the subcutaneous administration of physiologic solution of sodium chloride. No signs of local or systemic reaction followed intrathecal injection. Although transient methemoglobinemia, sulfhemoglobinemia, mild acidosis and morbilliform rash have each occasionally occurred in patients treated with sulfanilamide for streptococcic infections, none of these conditions have been noted in the patients in this series.

## COMMENT

There are obviously too few cases in this preliminary series to permit any very definite conclusions. The therapeutic response of the patients, however, to treatment with sulfanilamide seems quite comparable to that which usually follows treatment with specific antiserum. The mortality (9 per cent) in such a small series could have no real significance. On the other hand it is so much less than one would expect in cases treated only by repeated subarachnoid drainage that one cannot escape the impression that sulfanilamide has some definite value in the treatment of meningococcic infections. Only with more widespread experience can the decision be reached whether the drug has sufficient therapeutic value to supplant antimeningococcus serum or whether it should be used only as an adjunct to serum treatment. One definite value of sulfanilamide over antimeningococcus serum is the absence of any irritative effect due to foreign protein. Certainly this property of serum, especially when it is injected into the subarachnoid space, gives rise to serious complications.

## CONCLUSIONS

Sulfanilamide has been used in the treatment of ten patients with meningococcic meningitis and of one with septicemia only. The response to treatment was good in all the patients and seemed quite comparable to that caused by the specific antiserum.

Feb 10, 1984
(*JAMA* 1984;251:791-794)

# Sulfonamides and Meningitis*

W. Michael Scheld, MD, Gerald L. Mandell, MD

The article reprinted in this issue of THE JOURNAL[1] was recognized as a landmark study even at the time of its publication in 1937. Schwentker and colleagues reported their preliminary observations on the treatment of 11 patients with invasive meningococcal disease with a new compound, sulfanilamide. The results achieved (ten of 11 survived; 91% survival) were far superior to those obtained with the then-conventional antimeningococcal antisera therapy (survival, 15% to 70%, dependent on age). In addition, there were fewer adverse side effects with sulfanilamide; horse serum injections could be avoided. As a result, sulfonamides became the mainstay of therapy for serious meningococcal disease for more than three decades.

### Presulfonamide Treatment of Meningococcal Meningitis

"Epidemic cerebrospinal fever" (meningococcal meningitis) was described in detail by Gaspard Vieusseux after an outbreak in Geneva in the spring of 1805. The etiologic agent was first isolated from purulent CSF by Weichselbaum in 1887. At the turn of the century in this country, *Neisseria meningitidis* ranked second only to *Mycobacterium tuberculosis* as the cause of meningitis; the disease was occurring in epidemic and sporadic forms with an overall mortality of 70% to 90%.

Soon after the description of the lumbar puncture technique by Quincke in 1891, CSF drainage was introduced for the treatment of meningitis. During the next several decades, various modifications of CSF drainage were employed, including irrigation of the subarachnoid space with Ringer's lactate solution[2] or chemical agents (eg, gentian violet, mercurochrome, and

optochin), air injection through the lumbar needle with exit via the cisterna magna, continuous CSF drainage, and even bilateral carotid injection of an iodine-containing solution. In addition to substantial toxicity, all of these procedures lacked clinical efficacy.[3]

Working in the midst of an epidemic of meningococcal meningitis ($\simeq$6,755 cases; >5,000 deaths) in New York City in 1904-1905, Simon Flexner began an elegant series of experiments at the Rockefeller Institute that eventually demonstrated the protective action of antimeningococcal antiserum. He raised the serum in horses by injecting them with formalin or heat-killed whole organisms and showed that it was efficacious for experimental meningococcal infections in animals, including primates.[4] Antisera therapy proved disappointing after subcutaneous administration to humans and thereafter was given by intraspinal, intracisternal, or intraventricular injection.[5] Since meningococcal meningitis was so prevalent, intrathecal injection of 20 to 30 mL of antiserum (in adults) was administered after the first lumbar puncture yielded cloudy fluid and was continued daily for about four days. This practice was the first important advance in the treatment of meningococcal meningitis. For example, the survival rate increased from 10% to 30% in untreated patients to 69.1% in 1,294 cases treated with antimeningococcal serum in 1913.[6] These excellent results were upheld in a series of studies reported between 1915 and 1922.[7] During the first World War, 2,466 military personnel were admitted to hospitals in this country with meningococcal meningitis; 67% survived.

Direct inoculation of antimeningococcal serum into the CSF by various routes thus became the mainstay of therapy for meningococcal meningitis until the sulfonamide era. During this time, massive epidemics of this disease occurred in the civilian populations of Detroit, Milwaukee, and Indianapolis in 1928-1929. Because of the large number of infant cases, overall mortality remained high (50%) despite antimeningococcal antisera

From the Departments of Internal Medicine (Infectious Diseases) (Drs Scheld and Mandell) and Neurosurgery (Dr Scheld), University of Virginia School of Medicine, Charlottesville.

*A commentary on Schwentker FF, Gelman S, Long PH: The treatment of meningococcic meningitis with sulfanilamide: Preliminary report. *JAMA* 1937;108:1407-1408.

therapy; the mortality rate in infants was 84% in Detroit and 72% in adults older than 40 years. In 1931, Ferry demonstrated the production of exotoxins in filtrates of meningococci; antitoxins were then produced and tested in humans. Despite some favorable responses obtained with intravenous (IV) or intrathecal antitoxin administration,[9] the adjunctive value of this material to standard antimeningococcal antiserum (or later with sulfonamides) was never proved, and this mode of therapy was eventually abandoned.

Thus, in the late 1930s, meningococcal meningitis remained a common disease, capable of explosive and often highly fatal outbreaks. The traditional therapeutic modalities, intrathecal antisera and/or antitoxin, reduced the overall mortality from 70%-90% to 30%-40%, but deaths remained common in infants, young children, and older adults.

### The Early Sulfonamide Era of Meningitis Therapy

Sulfanilamide was actually synthesized in 1908, but many decades passed before the antibacterial properties of this class of drugs were discovered. The first experiments documenting these effects were performed in 1932 in the last month before Hitler's accession to power.

The discovery of the antibacterial activity of sulfachrysoidine (Prontosil) in experimental animal models of infection by Domagk in 1933 while he was working on aniline dyes at Bayer AG in Leverkusen, West Germany, led to substantial alterations in the therapeutic approach and mortality for many infectious diseases. Several other European studies demonstrated antibacterial properties of sulfonamides in experimental animal models of infection and in clinical disease (usually streptococcal) in humans. These early studies by Domagk in laboratory animals and three clinical reports detailing the clinical experience during two years with the use of sulfachrysoidine in human infections appeared in the landmark issue of *Deutsche Medizinische Wochenschrift,* Feb 15, 1935. The first patient treated with a sulfonamide in this country was a 10-year-old girl with *Hemophilus influenzae* meningitis and epiglottitis at the Columbia University Medical Center in 1935. The therapeutic efficacy of sulfanilamide (*p*-aminobenzene sulfonamide) in group A β-hemolytic streptococcal infections in humans, including serious cases of erysipelas, septicemia, infected abortions (septic endometritis), and pelvic peritonitis, was soon demonstrated.[10,11] An event that brought the sulfonamides to the attention of the American public was the treatment of Franklin Roosevelt, Jr (the President's son), at the Massachusetts General Hospital in November 1936. His recovery from a streptococcal sore throat with the use of the German experimental drug "Prontolyn" was reported widely in the press (eg, *New York Times,* Dec 17, 1936), since another president's son, Calvin Coolidge, Jr, had died of streptococcal septicemia 12 years earlier. Sulfonamides became widely available to American physicians soon after these events.

Investigators found that the early administration of sulfonamide prevented septicemia, meningitis, and death after the intraperitoneal injection of meningococci into mice.[12] Some experimental evidence suggested that sulfonamides attained therapeutic concentrations in CSF.[12] These studies in animals and humans suggested a role for sulfanilamide in the treatment of meningitis and led to the report by Schwentker and colleagues[1] in the April 24, 1937, issue of THE JOURNAL.

The report summarizes the results of treatment of 11 cases of meningococcal disease (ten meningitis and one septicemia only) with sulfanilamide. The diagnosis can not be questioned; positive cultures were obtained in all except case 10. Sulfanilamide was administered simultaneously by both the subcutaneous (100 mL/18 kg) and intrathecal ($\simeq$10 to 30 mL) routes. Despite the modest dosages (eg, 8 to 24 mg/day intrathecally), the response to treatment was good, and only one patient (case 9) died, for a mortality of 9%. The one death resulted from pneumonia; since the CSF and blood cultures were sterile at the time of death, this may represent a superinfection. No mention of concurrent antimeningococcal antiserum or antitoxin therapy is made (a shortcoming of the article), but one assumes that sulfanilamide was administered alone. The drug was well tolerated and there were no local systemic reactions to the intrathecal injections. The authors were cautious in their conclusions and suggested that (1) their small series required confirmation in larger numbers of patients, (2) sulfanilamide was more effective than repeated subarachnoid drainage based on retrospective experience, and (3) whether sulfanilamide should replace, or serve as an adjunct to, antimeningococcal serum therapy needed further study. Indeed, these conclusions served as the catalyst for several studies during the next decade and were quickly followed by several other reports in 1937.[3,13]

Thus, the study by Schwentker and colleagues[1] was the first demonstration of cure of meningococcal meningitis by a chemotherapeutic agent. The sulfonamides not only cured meningitis but ushered in the scientific era of medicine. Lewis Thomas, in his beautifully written recent book, *The Youngest Science: Notes of a Medicine Watcher,*[14] describes the major diseases confronting him on the wards of the Boston City Hospital during his internship, including pneumococcal pneumonia, syphilis, tuberculosis, and rheumatic fever. Only a few drugs with any therapeutic benefit (eg, digitalis, morphine, insulin, quinine, and liver extract) were available, and only the administration of specific antipneumococcal antiserum could occasionally reverse an otherwise lethal disease course. Lewis Thomas, as an intern in 1937, observed the dramatic effect of sulfanilamide therapy on the course of pneumococcal and streptococcal septicemia.

For most of the infectious diseases on the wards of the Boston City Hospital in 1937, there was nothing to be done beyond bed rest and good nursing care.

Then came the explosive news of sulfanilamide, and the start of the real revolution in medicine.

I remember the astonishment when the first cases of pneumococcal and streptococcal septicemia were treated in Boston in 1937. The phenomenon was almost beyond belief. Here were moribund patients, who would surely have died without treatment, improving in their appearance within a matter of hours of being given the medicine and feeling entirely well within the next day or so.

The professionals most deeply affected by these extraordinary events were, I think, the interns. The older physicians were equally surprised, but took the news in stride. For an intern, it was the opening of a whole new world. We had been raised to be ready for one kind of profession, and we sensed that the profession itself had changed at the moment of our entry. We knew that other molecular variations of sulfanilamide were on their way from industry, and we heard about the possibility of penicillin and other antibiotics; we became convinced, overnight, that nothing lay beyond reach for the future. Medicine was off and running.

Dr Thomas was personally involved in this chemotherapeutic revolution. Four years later, he coauthored an article, published in THE JOURNAL, detailing the treatment of meningitis with sulfadiazine after investigating a meningococcal epidemic in Halifax, Nova Scotia.[15]

Walsh McDermott shared many of Dr Thomas' experiences; he was an intern at Bellevue Hospital in New York in the early 1930s. Dr McDermott observed the chemotherapeutic revolution after the introduction of the sulfonamides and devoted his professional life to the study of microbial diseases and their profound impact on society at every level. Shortly before his death in October 1981, Dr McDermott began work on a book; the central theme was the influence of antimicrobial therapy, which he likened to a new technology, on society. With the editorial assistance of Dr David Rogers, excerpts of this work were assembled and published after Dr McDermott's death.[16] The article details eloquently the state of medicine before, during, and after the introduction of the sulfonamides; it should be required reading for all students of medicine. The impact of sulfanilamide in the late 1930s was considered by McDermott and Rogers.[16]

Unlike arsphenamine, the new drug was effective against several different microbial species, each the cause of a different and known serious disease. The long-wished-for drug with an action different on microbial cells and body cells was at hand. It was called a "miracle drug" and properly so. In the desperately ill patients the effects produced were no different from those that one might visualize were there to be a true divine intervention. So far as could be determined, nothing like them on such a scale had ever been seen before since the beginning of time.[16]

The social ramifications of this chemotherapeutic revolution and the ensuing changes are considered in detail in Dr McDermott's discussion.[16]

The sulfonamides quickly became the treatment of choice for meningococcal meningitis. By 1941, the concomitant use of antimeningococcal antiserum was no longer recommended.[17] Sulfadiazine was introduced and became preferred owing to fewer side effects when compared with sulfanilamide. The drug was given by various routes (oral, subcutaneous, IV, and intrathecal), and the standard regimen became IV sulfadiazine alone, 400 to 600 mg/kg on the first day with a gradual reduction to 100 to 200 mg/kg four times daily for the balance of the treatment. These doses are much higher than those employed by Schwentker and co-workers,[1] and side effects (including hematuria, drug fever, and skin rash) were more common.[18] Nevertheless, by the mid-1940s, sulfadiazine reduced the mortality of menin-

gococcal meningitis to only 9% to 11%,[18,19] almost identical to the results of Schwentker et al with their 11 patients in 1937. Despite a mortality rate with sulfadiazine therapy of only 3.8% in 14,504 military personnel hospitalized in this country with meningococcal meningitis from 1940 to 1945, this condition still killed more US servicemen during World War II than any other infectious disease. Sulfadiazine remained the agent of choice for the treatment of meningococcal meningitis for another 20 years, and this treatment saved countless patients. The prophylactic benefit of sulfonamides in the prevention of secondary meningococcal meningitis cases was also established by 1943, and sulfadiazine was used liberally for this purpose for more than two decades (see Chapter 33).

### Sulfonamides in the Treatment of Meningococcal Meningitis Today

As noted previously, sulfadiazine was considered the drug of choice for meningococcal meningitis by the early 1940s. Penicillin did not supplant the sulfonamides for the treatment of this condition because little was available and it was thought at that time that the CSF penetration of penicillin was poor. When sufficient amounts of penicillin became available, intrathecal administration of it was discontinued in 1948. Although large doses of parenteral penicillin were found to be equivalent to sulfadiazine in reduction of meningococcal meningitis mortality in 1952,[20] sulfadiazine continued as the preferred drug in the 1960s. Sulfonamides were never as effective against H influenzae or pneumococcal meningitis as they were against meningococcal disease in these early studies. The mortality rate for H influenzae meningitis was approximately 25% to 30% in the early 1940s with combination sulfadiazine–rabbit antisera therapy. This regimen was supplanted by streptomycin and then chloramphenicol by 1947. Penicillin remained the drug of choice for pneumococcal meningitis, but the mortality rate ($\simeq$30%) has not improved since comparatively massive dosages were introduced during 1950 to 1952. In the decade from 1950 to 1961, "triple" therapy was commonly employed in pyogenic meningitis of unknown cause: sulfadiazine (for meningococci), penicillin (for pneumococci), and chloramphenicol (for H influenzae). Nevertheless, it was not the introduction of newer antibiotics (including ampicillin in 1961) but the development of resistance that brought an end to the sulfonamide era of therapy for meningitis.

Some early reports,[21] beginning even before 1948, documented small numbers of sulfonamide-resistant meningococcal isolates. Nevertheless, the important role of sulfadiazine in the treatment of meningococcal disease remained unaltered until the first concentration of cases caused by sulfadiazine-resistant strains was reported from the US Naval Training Center in San Diego during the spring of 1963.[22] Sulfonamide-resistant strains were recognized at Fort Ord in Monterey County, California, shortly thereafter. By 1965, sulfadiazine was largely abandoned for the treatment of meningococcal meningitis. Since that time, sulfadiazine resistance has persisted in this country, although the percentage of resistant strains among serogroup B may be decreasing. The Meningococcal Disease Surveillance Group reported in 1976 the following subgroups among 324 meningococcal isolates: group B, 45%; group C, 32%; group Y, 18%; and group A, 2%. Although only 4% of the group B isolates were sulfonamide resistant, resistance was present in 75% of the group C strains. Similar results were reported by the Centers for Disease Control in this country in 1981, and sulfonamide resistance among meningococci of all major serogroups has emerged as a serious problem worldwide.[23]

Because of these developments, sulfonamides are no longer employed in the routine treatment or prophylaxis of meningococcal meningitis. Penicillin (or ampicillin) remains the drug of choice (see also Chapter 36), with the substitution of chloramphenicol in the penicillin-allergic patient. Several of the newer ''third-generation'' cephalosporins (especially cefotaxime sodium, moxalactam, and ceftriaxone) are exceedingly active against

meningococci in vitro, achieve excellent bactericidal activity in CSF against this organism, and have equal efficacy, when compared (retrospectively) with penicillin, in meningococcal meningitis. The role of these new compounds in meningococcal meningitis remains to be defined. The use of any sulfonamide for treatment of meningococcal disease will be limited in the future, unless resistance of meningococci to $\beta$-lactam antibiotics occurs.

Sulfonamides do remain the drug of choice for one CNS infection: nocardiosis.

Schwentker, Gelman, and Long and other investigators in the late 1930s opened the chemotherapeutic era and with it the scientific approach of modern medicine. They deserve credit for setting the stage for the dramatic decline in death and human suffering caused by infectious diseases that has occurred in the past half century.

## References

1. Schwentker FF, Gelman S, Long PH: The treatment of meningococcic meningitis with sulfanilamide: Preliminary report. *JAMA* 1937;108:1407-1408.

2. Wegeforth P, Ayer JB, Essick CR: The method of obtaining cerebrospinal fluid by puncture of the cisterna magna (cisternal puncture). *Am J Med Sci* 1919;157:789-797.

3. Bell WE, McCormick WF: *Neurologic Infections in Children,* ed 2. Philadelphia, WB Saunders Co, 1981, pp 77-80.

4. Flexner S: Experimental cerebrospinal meningitis and its serum treatment. *JAMA* 1906;47:560-566.

5. Dunn CH: Cerebrospinal meningitis, its etiology, diagnosis, prognosis and treatment. *Am J Dis Child* 1911;1:95-112.

6. Flexner S: The results of serum treatment in 1,300 cases of epidemic meningitis. *J Exp Med* 1913;17:553-576.

7. Blackfan KD: The treatment of meningococcus meningitis. *Medicine* 1922;1:139-212.

8. Daniels WB: Cause of death in meningococci infection: Analysis of 300 fatal cases. *Am J Med* 1950;8:468-473.

9. Hoyne AL: Intravenous treatment of meningococcic meningitis with meningococcus antitoxin. *JAMA* 1936;107:478-481.

10. Colebrook L, Kenny M: Treatment of human puerperal infections, and of experimental infections in mice, with Prontosil. *Lancet* 1936;1:1279-1286.

11. Long PH, Bliss EA: Para-amino-benzene-sulfonamide and its derivatives: Experimental and clinical observations on their use in the treatment of beta-hemolytic streptococci infection: A preliminary report. *JAMA* 1937;108:32-37.

12. Proom H: The therapeutic action of *p*-amino benzenesulfonamide in meningococcal infection of mice. *Lancet* 1937;1:16-18.

13. Carey BW Jr: The use of para-aminobenzene sulfonamide and its

derivatives in the treatment of infections due to the *Streptococcus hemolyticus,* the meningococcus, and the gonococcus: Report of 38 cases. *J Pediatr* 1937;11:202-211.

14. Thomas L: *The Youngest Science: Notes of a Medicine Watcher.* New York, Viking Press Inc, 1983, p 270.

15. Dingle JH, Thomas L, Morton AR: Treatment of meningococcic meningitis and meningococcemia with sulfadiazine. *JAMA* 1941;116:2666-2668.

16. McDermott W, Rogers DE: Social ramifications of control of microbial disease. *Johns Hopkins Med J* 1982;151:302-312.

17. Alexander HE: Treatment of bacterial meningitis. *Bull NY Acad Med* 1941;17:100-115.

18. Goldring D, Hartmann AF, Maxwell R: Diagnosis and management of severe infections in infants and children. A review of experiences since the introduction of sulfonamide therapy: III. Meningococcal infections. *J Pediatr* 1945;26:1-31.

19. Jubb AA: Chemotherapy and serotherapy in cerebrospinal (meningococcal) meningitis: An analysis of 3,206 case reports. *Br Med J* 1943;1:501-504.

20. Lepper MH, Dowling HF, Wehrle PF, et al: Meningococcic meningitis: Treatment with large doses of penicillin compared to treatment with gantrisin. *J Lab Clin Med* 1952;40:891-900.

21. Schoenbach EB, Phair JJ: The sensitivity of meningococci to sulfadiazine. *Am J Hyg* 1948;47:177-186.

22. Millar JW, Siess EE, Feldman HA: In vivo and in vitro resistance to sulfadiazine in strains of *Neisseria meningitidis. JAMA* 1963;186:139-141.

23. Peltola H: Meningococcal disease: Still with us. *Rev Infect Dis* 1983;5:71-92.

July 10, 1937
(*JAMA* 1937;109:128-131)

## Chapter 28

# The Therapy of the Cook County Hospital

### Edited by Bernard Fantus, M.D.

#### Chicago

NOTE.—*In their elaboration, these articles are submitted to the members of the attending staff of the Cook County Hospital by the director of therapeutics, Dr. Bernard Fantus. The views expressed by various members are incorporated in the final draft for publication. The articles will be continued from time to time in these columns. When completed, the series will be published in book form.*—ED.

#### BLOOD PRESERVATION

This preliminary report on the establishment of a "blood bank" at the Cook County Hospital is perhaps justified by the interest displayed in this development, the inquiries received from various parts of the country, and the importance of the promptest and most generous exchange of experience in a new field of life-saving endeavor.

That blood can be preserved for weeks in condition fit for transfusion is now a well established fact, thanks most especially to Yudin's[1] work on cadaver blood. There is, however, something revolting to Anglo-Saxon susceptibilities in the proposal of using cadaver blood and it is not probable, even were this not the case, that enough blood could be secured in this manner to be of great practical importance. The "blood bank" proposition, on the other hand, seems susceptible of extensive development and it is to this, most especially, that we desire to call attention.

The first question that comes to the mind of any one in connection with blood preservation is: Where does one get the blood? At Cook County Hospital we have experienced no difficulty on this score by following simple rules promulgated by the medical staff of the hospital. The necessity for these rules is obvious. Just as one cannot draw money from a bank unless one has deposited some, so the blood preservation department cannot supply blood unless as much comes in as goes out. The term "blood bank" is not a mere metaphor.

#### NOTICE TO MEDICAL STAFF

"Hereafter an effort will be made to preserve by refrigeration blood to be used for blood transfusions. This method should accomplish two things: first, it should make blood available at any time it is needed; second, it should make the process of blood transfusion much more simple.

"It is obvious that one cannot obtain blood unless one has deposited blood. Staff physicians may deposit blood for credit at any time. A record will be kept of all blood credited to each service.

"*Depositing Blood.*—Staff physicians will obtain from the Solutions Laboratory chilled 500 cc. flasks, which will contain 70 cc. of 2.5 per cent sodium citrate solution. These flasks carry two test tubes for the collection of 5 cc. of whole blood in each for the purpose of typing and for the Wassermann test. The blood will be drawn into the flask in the usual manner and taken immediately to the Solutions Laboratory. The date, the name of the donor, his address, his color, the name of the intern and his service should accompany the flask. By means of this system only one donor needs to be bled and he need not be typed, which greatly lessens the trouble occasioned by transfusion.

"*Keeping of the Blood.*—In the laboratory the technician at once files it away in the refrigerator, which must maintain a constant temperature between 4 and 6 C., types it, tests it for sterility and the absence of syphilis, and credits it to the service that furnished the blood.

"*Drawing on the 'Blood Bank.'*—Assuming that a patient needs blood transfusion, the house physician should secure from the patient 5 cc. of blood, type it, and make out a requisition in proper form for the quantity and type of blood needed, which will be delivered to him from the refrigerator. It should be warmed by placing it in a water bath, the temperature of which would not feel too hot for the hand, and used immediately after warming.

"*Cross-Matching Before Injecting.*—The blood thus secured should be cross-matched with the patient's blood by the resident who supervises blood transfusion. Not

1. Yudin, S. S.: Transfusion of Cadaver Blood, J. A. M. A. **106**:997 (March 21) 1936.

nly should the corpuscles to be injected be matched against the patient's serum, but the serum to be injected should be matched against the patient's corpuscles. Owing to the possibility of serious allergic reactions, the blood of a patient allergic to horse serum should not be injected into a patient who recently had a horse serum injection. Repeated transfusions in which the same donor is used may give rise to anaphylactic shock.

*Administration.*—While the hasty injection of blood may produce speedy death from 'speed shock,' the slow injection—literally drop by drop—has no such danger, even in disease conditions of the heart or lungs. Throughout the injection the patient should be carefully observed for any unfavorable reaction. The early and characteristic symptoms are 'uneasiness' in the chest, difficulty in breathing, excruciating pain in the back, and nausea. Failure to recognize these early symptoms may be responsible for a fatal result. Fall in blood pressure and impaired heart action because of insufficient return of venous blood to the right side of the heart with resulting cyanosis, dyspnea and anuria dominate the picture. These symptoms are believed to be due to the liberation of 'histaminoid' bodies from the breaking down of red blood corpuscles, which lead to dilatation of the venous capillaries and spasm of the peripheral arterioles. Embolic closure of the finest pulmonary and renal vessels may also contribute to the clinical picture. It is claimed that the best remedy for this reaction is the immediate infusion of compatible blood.

*Dosage.*—Overloading of the circulation must be avoided. In infants 20 cc. of blood per kilogram of body weight should not be exceeded. In adults, after hemorrhage, the amount of blood required depends on the quantity lost. The loss of from 2,000 to 2,500 cc. of blood may be fatal and the giving of 1,000 cc. of blood may save life in such a case. To increase coagulability of the blood, e. g., in hemophilia, a transfusion of 250 cc. suffices."

## SOURCES OF BLOOD

The main source of blood will no doubt always be the healthy volunteer donor, whose service should be enlisted whenever possible. No matter what type blood the donor furnishes, the blood is sent to the laboratory, where it is exchanged for blood of the type desired. The advantage of the "blood bank" over the previous method is obvious. Only one donor needs to be bled, which dispenses with the commotion occasioned by calling to the hospital a horde of excited relatives before a suitable donor can be found.

A second source of blood is from patients with cardiac decompensation and those with excessive elevation of blood pressure, provided the patient is not suffering from infection, uremia or other toxemia. It should be a rule that practically all patients in need of digitalis should have a preliminary abstraction of blood to unload the heart before stimulating it.

A third source of blood is the antepartum clinic. Here the blood bank function of this project expresses itself most simply. We deposit in a bank money we do not at the moment need, to be able to draw on it when we do need it. In the same way a pregnant woman can easily spare a little blood a week or two before her expected confinement to have it saved for her against the time she may need it during or right after parturition. If she does not need this blood, it should become available for any one who does.

There are some who seem to be in particular need of this antepartum blood. It is the premature child. Some pediatricians seem to be convinced that a premature infant who is not doing well is much benefited by the intramuscular injection every other day of 5 to 10 cc. of blood of a woman who carries a child under her heart.

Now it so happens that the pediatric clinic can furnish blood to the bank also. When a mother brings a sick child to the hospital, it is of great advantage to that child to be given from 10 to 20 cc. of the mother's blood injected intramuscularly—10 cc. in each gluteal region. This will secure passive immunization against measles and most other contagious diseases to which the child may be exposed while in the hospital. In this manner the specter of cross-infection ever present may be largely banished from a children's hospital. There is no reason why a healthy woman might not easily spare, and without greater inconvenience, 120 cc. instead of 20 cc. of blood and have the other 100 cc. preserved in the bank in case her child needs it and, if it does not, she should permit this blood to save the life of some other child.

A patient who is to have an elective surgical operation could do no better than to deposit a week or two before the ordeal a pint of blood in the bank to have it available in case it is needed during or after the operation.

The bank may also function in the way of "lending" blood. Any one who owes his life to blood transfusion clearly owes some blood to some one else who is in great need of this restorative. This is eminently the case with convalescents from infectious diseases. In streptococcic sepsis, for instance, as well as in scarlet fever and probably also in influenza and many other infectious diseases, the blood of the convalescent is curative to the victim of the same kind of infection. It should be the plain duty of the one who has recovered from such a disease to donate some of his blood to save the life of a fellow man in the hour of his desperate need. Surely one whose life has thus been saved owes some of his now curative blood to another victim of the same kind of infection. Opsonic index determinations on the preserved blood might permit one to predict in what kind of infection the convalescent's blood would be particularly serviceable.

## A SERUM CENTER

The limit of blood preservation is lysis of the red blood corpuscles after their death. Obviously the trick of blood preservation is to compel blood corpuscles to enter a "hibernation" stage so that, life processes being at a low ebb, they may continue to live for a much longer time than they otherwise would. The survival period of blood thus preserved seems to be from three to four weeks. It is entirely probable that intensive research, which should at once be undertaken, may extend somewhat this blood corpuscle survival period. But sooner or later hemolysis sets in. With the appearance of the first traces of hemolysis the serum should be separated from the blood and the serum preserved—as it easily can be—for as long a time as may be necessary.

This will not only furnish a liberal supply of the so much needed human convalescent's serum, but also of normal human serum with its natural immunizing and other therapeutic properties. In shock, for instance, when there has been but little or no hemorrhage, compatible human serum should be much more valuable than the 6 per cent acacia solution now advocated for the purpose. In extensive burns in which shock and the loss of blood serum from profuse exudation are the cause of the circulation depression that may be fatal, the intravenous injection of blood serum is much more rational than that of blood, because these patients usually have an excess of red blood corpuscles per cubic millimeter. In certain hemorrhagic conditions, blood serum may furnish the lacking principles, even though in thrombopenic purpura nothing but transfusion of fresh blood may serve the purpose.

## CONTRAINDICATIONS

As blood transfusion is a trying, even dangerous, procedure to the recipient, the indications for it should be drawn strictly and rather narrowly. We have kept statistics for the year preceding inauguration of the blood preservation service and found that death has occurred in about one third of the number of patients in whom transfusion has been done. We hope to better these statistics with the new method. The deaths cannot, of course, be charged to blood transfusion but must be ascribed to the fact that too many antemortem transfusions are being done in this hospital. Unless there is some extraordinary reason for postponing the inevitable end, blood transfusion is not justified in hopeless conditions. The physician's desire to do everything possible for the patient committed to his charge must not lead him to prolong the agony of the dying by major therapeutic efforts.

"In the treatment of sepsis," says Bock,[2] "it is possible to waste more blood than for any other condition. Severe anemia due to sepsis is an indication for blood transfusion, but sepsis per se without evidence of anemia is not." Immunotransfusion is, of course, an entirely different matter.

In leukemia, in the anemia of Hodgkin's disease, and in primary anemias with the exception of pernicious anemia, and then only under special circumstances, blood transfusion is inadvisable. It is also contraindicated by pulmonary edema, myocarditis and nephritis.

## INDICATIONS

Dangerous hemorrhage and shock are the two most important indications for blood transfusion. Transfusions are probably used more in surgical shock than in hemorrhage.

In rapid profuse hemorrhage, a drop in blood pressure soon sets in. It is this drop of pressure that causes the syncope of such hemorrhage. The blood count does not alter to any great extent until sufficient fluids have entered the blood stream to dilute the blood. A person

may suddenly bleed to death and the blood count an hemoglobin percentage remain almost normal. It take from twelve to twenty-four hours for dilution to occur. S a drop in blood pressure and an elevated pulse rate ar the significant factors in the first few hours of sever bleeding.

In case of a slow hemorrhage, on the other hand, th blood pressure may be well maintained, and then a fall i hemoglobin percentage to 50 or below or a rise of th pulse rate to 120 or more indicates that blood transfusio should be undertaken promptly. Blood pressure estima tion furnishes, in slow bleeding, no indications of an value, as the pressure is well maintained by vasoconstric tion until profound sudden shock supervenes on failure o this mechanism.

"Next to ligature," says Bock, "blood transfusion is th most effective means we have to insure cessation o hemorrhage." When the hemorrhage is of the inaccessi ble variety, as well as in hemorrhagic diseases, such a hemophilia and purpura hemorrhagica, small (250 cc. and repeated blood transfusions give better results than large transfusion.

In preparation for surgical procedures, all markedl anemic patients require blood transfusion. Indeed, befor or after any extensive or prolonged operation bloo transfusion is of value. In heroic conditions, massiv blood transfusion is called for. In grave trauma demand ing amputation, 500 cc. of blood given at intervals of ha an hour before, during and after the operation may sav a life. In profuse hematemesis, continuous drip bloo transfusion at the rate of from 90 to 150 cc. an hour ma transform, in two or three days, a patient apparentl moribund into a good surgical risk. Operation performe immediately after such hemorrhage is usually fatal.

In severe cases of pernicious anemia, blood transfusio is indicated during that critical period of a week, more o less, required for liver therapy to become effective.

In jaundiced patients, small blood transfusions before during and after operation will minimize the oozing o blood that may be fatal.

Other indications, such as immunotransfusion and possible food function of blood, require definition bette than we now possess.

## CONCLUSION

This statement of the aims and means of the bloo preservation service is primarily intended to secure th better cooperation of the staff of this hospital.

Dr. Lindon Seed is chairman of a Committee on Bloo Transfusion, which consists of a representative of eac one of the special services at the hospital, and all matter pertaining to this work should be referred to thi committee.

We have had enough experience at Cook Count Hospital to say that the use of properly preserved blood i safe and efficient.

We also know that extensive cooperative investigatio will be required to develop this method as rapidly a seems mandatory to save lives now unnecessarily lost.

It is this need, as well as the desirability of bette financial support for so important a project, that ha dictated this preliminary publication.

---

2. Bock, A. V.: The Use and Abuse of Blood Transfusions, New England J. Med. **215:**421 (Sept. 3) 1936.

Feb 3, 1984
(*JAMA* 1984;251:650-652)

# The Blood Bank

# Concept*

Byron A. Myhre, MD, PhD

### History of Previous Transfusion Therapy

With the usual availability of adequate amounts and types of blood that we encounter today, it is hard to visualize the difficulty that faced physicians wishing to transfuse before World War II. The account by Louis Diamond[1] chronicles how between the years of 1667 and 1937, the major accent in transfusion therapy was direct transfusion from donor to recipient, usually using some type of arteriovenous anastomosis,[2,3] a pump for direct transfusion,[4] multiple syringes,[5] various stopcock-syringe devices,[6] or, occasionally, a paraffin-lined flask[7] to hold the blood temporarily. No anticoagulant was used, the blood was not stored, all transfusions required the immediate availability of the donor, and the donor had to be bled in the proximity of the patient (often in an operating room). For these reasons, almost all transfusions were elective and given for chronic loss or decreased production of red cells rather than for trauma or emergency surgery. Massive transfusions were rarely done. The major aim of transfusion therapy was to bleed the donor in as quick and expeditious a manner as possible and to transfuse the blood immediately into the patient. Direct transfusion persisted for a long time. A perusal of the books by Kilduffe and Debakey[8] or DeGowin and colleagues[9] (although written five to ten years after Dr Fantus' article) shows that even though considerable interest had been generated by the concept of "blood banks," and a chapter in each of their books is devoted to the operation of these entities,

substantial amounts of space are still devoted to the topic of direct transfusion.

Although the first transfusion of blood was given in 1667, only a few transfusions were successful until the early 1900s because of lack of knowledge of the blood groups. Once this fact had been established, the next major stumbling block to transfusions was the necessity of an anticoagulant. The independent discoveries in 1914 by Hustin,[10] Agote,[11] Lewisohn,[12] and Weil[13] (Chapter 11) that sodium citrate would keep blood from clotting and was safe to infuse allowed blood to be drawn, stored, and then transfused. A subsequent discovery showed that if the anticoagulated blood was refrigerated, it would survive longer yet. These changes in blood storage gave the transfusionist much more flexibility but were not seen by most as a great advantage. Most transfusionists had learned the direct technique and were not interested in changing.

Dr Fantus, although not a surgeon himself, was interested in preoperative and postoperative patient care (Charles Schlutz, oral communication, 1982). He developed a number of concepts and devices for patient care that have survived today with modifications. In this instance, the concept advanced by Fantus was that blood could be deposited by donors at their convenience, stored in the anticoagulated state, and then issued when needed just as money is made available from a bank. Therefore, blood would be available at all times and a desired inventory could be established and maintained. This concept completely changed the method of use of blood and even the approach to major surgery and trauma surgery. The precipitous rise in the use of blood and blood products (more than ten million units of red cell products) today is the eventual outgrowth of this simple but profound idea. Surely,

From the Department of Pathology, UCLA School of Medicine, Torrance, Calif.

*A commentary on Fantus B: The therapy of the Cook County Hospital. *JAMA* 1937;109:128-131.

much of the major surgery done today would be impossible if it were necessary to find blood donors for emergencies or to have them waiting outside the operating room door in case of need.

## The Article

The article is somewhat unusual since it is a therapeutic note rather than a scientific communication and, as such, becomes a survey of techniques and clinical practice at the time of its publication. There is no bibliography, and debatable points are not discussed. The procedures used in the blood bank are not listed in detail; however, they have been discussed by Telischi[14] in a fairly recent publication. Many of the statements made by Dr Fantus are still applicable today. Blood was stored at 4 to 6 °C in the refrigerator (now 1 to 6 °C).[15] The anticoagulant used was sodium citrate, even though some hospitals had begun adding glucose to the medium to increase the storage life of the red cells. The recommendation is made that blood should be warmed before use. This was reaffirmed at a later date by Dr Howland[16] and others who found it to be essential in cases of massive transfusion.

It is interesting to read some of the problems addressed by Fantus in his article. The symptoms of a hemolytic transfusion are accurate and are still applicable in most parts today. He urges that the patient should be watched during the transfusion, and this advice is always given in any textbook on transfusion therapy, even if it is not always followed on the wards. Overloading of the patient's circulation is mentioned as a great hazard, and it is still believed to be such.[17] Hemophilia was treated at that time by infusion of small amounts (250 mL) of freshly drawn blood. Although the amount of antihemophilic globulin supplied by this means would be considered entirely inadequate today, the use of labile coagulation factors is routine. The source of donors illustrates the problems that were faced in obtaining blood. The main source used was the volunteer donor — a concept that is still subscribed to today. However, patients with cardiac decompensation or elevated blood pressure or "patients in need of digitalis" would certainly not be acceptable as donors, nor would a pregnant woman two weeks prepartum in a routine situation.

The use of intramuscular blood for pediatric transfusions and for infectious disease prophylaxis is a sign of the times in which the article was written. At that time, intramuscular blood was frequently used and in a few cases, it may have provided some gamma globulin to the child; however, the amount given was very small. The obtaining of extra blood for transfusion from the donors at the same time is a clever, if somewhat sneaky, concept and is one that would not be accepted as well today.

The sending of outdated blood to "serum centers" so that the plasma would not be lost was urged and was carried out in a number of locations. In fact, some of today's community blood banks owe their start to a preexisting serum or plasma center that was expanded.

The statement on autotransfusion still holds today. Most blood bank directors encourage the use of autotransfusions for elective cases if it is at all possible in order to prevent isosensitization and transmitted infectious disease. It is a pity that this means of obtaining blood is not used more than it is.

The "Contraindications" section does contain the rather startling statement that one third of the patients who received blood died before the establishment of the blood bank. Certainly this would indicate that transfusions were being given primarily when the patient was in extremis and not as a routine supportive treatment.

Finally, the head of the Transfusion Committee is mentioned. After this, the concept of the transfusion committee languished, and it is only in the last ten to 15 years that we have once again begun to encourage transfusion committees[18] whose duties are to monitor the use of blood and blood products.

## Transfusion Therapy Since the Article

The concept of the "blood bank" was one of those classic examples of an idea whose time had come. Within several years, hospital and community blood banks were being started all over the nation. Furthermore, with the entrance of the United States into World War II, the American National Red Cross established a nationwide blood program for the war effort[19] and then later extended it to the civilian population. In a parallel manner, many communities started their own blood banks, so a system was developed throughout the country to provide for the constant availability of blood and blood products.

Today, we still use the volunteer donor as the base of our recruitment program. In fact, in some states it is illegal to use paid donors, and if they are used, the Food and Drug Administration requires a label on the blood bag so stating.[20] The volunteer blood donor, however, is still hard to find, and many recruiting strategies have been and are being devised and tried to lure the donor in to give blood. There never seems to be enough blood. If the donor numbers increase, the demand for blood always seems to increase more.

Most blood is now drawn into plastic bags and fractionated into components so that the one donation of blood may provide a number of products to be used for a number of patients. Some of the products now available are red cells, fresh-frozen plasma, platelet concentrates, leukocyte concentrates, washed red cells, cryoprecipitate, and leukocyte poor red cells. This product availability has had an effect in increasing the total number of blood products used for treatment by obtaining several components from each blood donation, but it has not solved the need for more donors. Because of all these factors, the outdating of blood has decreased dramatically.

Outdated blood is only rarely used to make plasma for transfusion. Because of better inventory techniques and anticoagulants that allow a longer shelf life, such as CPD and CPD-A1, the outdating of whole blood and red cells has dropped precipitously, and very little outdates. Therefore, most of the plasma used today is obtained by plasmapheresis at commercial plasma centers. Because of the risk of hepatitis from whole plasma, almost all plasma drawn by these centers is now fractionated into plasma protein fraction or albumin. This chemical fractionation process causes the hepatitis virus to be inactivated and, therefore, the resulting product is much safer.

Currently, there is a considerable amount of interest in the availability of so-called artificial blood, which serves as a red cell substitute. Although the studies on this product present a new and exciting area of research, the presently available substitutes are difficult to store, have not yet been adequately field tested, and only carry oxygen. They do not provide the other components of blood such as platelets and coagulation factors for hemostasis or leukocytes for bacteriolysis. Furthermore, they are rapidly lost from the body. On the other hand, they will provide a good addition to the transfusion armamentarium for the temporary provision of oxygen-carrying capacity until blood can be cross-matched and safely provided. Further time will tell if they can be modified to really replace human blood and decrease the need for most donations.

## References

1. Diamond LK: A history of blood transfusion, in Wintrobe MM: *Blood, Pure and Eloquent.* New York, McGraw-Hill Book Co, 1980, pp 659-688.

2. Bernheim BM: *Blood Transfusion Hemorrhage and the Anaemias.* Philadelphia, JB Lippincott Co, 1917, pp 97-112.

3. Crile GW: *Hemorrhage and Transfusion.* New York, D Appleton & Co, 1909.

4. Feinblatt HM: *Transfusion of Blood.* New York, The Macmillan Co, 1926, pp 105-198.

5. Lindeman E: Blood transfusions without a chill by the syringe-cannula system. *JAMA* 1919;72:1661-1665.

6. Unger LJ: A new method of syringe transfusion. *JAMA* 1915;64:582-584.

7. Kimpton AR, Brown JH: A new and simple method of transfusion. *JAMA* 1913;61:117-118.

8. Kilduffe RA, DeBakey M: *The Blood Bank and the Technique and Therapeutics of Transfusions.* St Louis, CV Mosby Co, 1942.

9. DeGowin EL, Hardin RC, Alsever JB: *Blood Transfusion.* Philadelphia, WB Saunders Co, 1949.

10. Hustin A: Note sur un nouvelle methods du transfusion. *Soc R Sci Med Brux* 1914;72:104.

11. Agote L: Nuevo procedimento para la transfusion del sangre. *An Modelo Clin Med Buenos Ayres,* January 1915, pp 24-30.

12. Lewisohn R: A new and greatly simplified method of blood transfusion. *Med Rec* 1915;87:141.

13. Weil R: Sodium citrate in the transfusion of blood. *JAMA* 1915;64:425-426.

14. Telischi M: Evolution of Cook County Hospital Blood Bank. *Transfusion* 1974;14:623-628.

15. Oberman HA (ed): *Standards for Blood Banks and Transfusion Services,* ed 10. Arlington, Va, American Association of Blood Banks, 1981.

16. Howland WS: Cardiovascular and clotting disturbances during massive blood replacement. *Anesthesiology* 1958;19:140-152.

17. Heustis DW, Bove JR, Busch S: *Practical Blood Transfusion,* ed 3. Boston, Little Brown & Co, 1981, p 260.

18. Guy LR: The regulatory influence of the hospital transfusion committee: Historical perspective, in Wallas CW, Muller VH: *The Hospital Transfusion Committee—A Technical Workshop.* Arlington, Va, American Association of Blood Banks, 1982, pp 1-6.

19. Kendrick DB: *The Blood Program in World War II.* US Army Medical Dept, 1964.

20. *Food and Drugs,* Code of Federal Regulations title 21, part 606. 120 (Labelling), revised April 1, 1978.

Sept 17, 1938
(*JAMA* 1938;111:1068-1073)

## Chapter 29

# Sodium Diphenyl Hydantoinate in the Treatment of Convulsive Disorders

H. Houston Merritt, M.D.

and

Tracy J. Putnam, M.D.

Boston

Good results in the treatment of patients with convulsive seizures have been obtained by a variety of methods, such as medical treatment with bromides or barbituric acid compounds, the ketogenic diet, restriction of fluids, and the surgical excision of scars or irritable cortical foci. In spite of these various therapeutic means there are a great number of patients who are not relieved of their attacks or are helped only temporarily by treatment. The fact that treatment by anticonvulsant drugs is at present the most widely used and on the whole the most effective method of therapy suggested to us the possibility that a direct and systematic experimental search might reveal more potent and less sedative compounds. With this idea in mind we devised an experimental procedure[1] which would produce convulsive seizures in animals at a constant threshold and which would allow for a qualitative and roughly quantitative determination of the relative effectiveness of various drugs. By this method a large number of

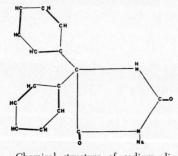

Chemical structure of sodium diphenyl hydantoinate.

chemicals and drugs, selected on theoretic grounds, were studied, and it was found[2] that several heretofore unused chemicals were as effective in protecting animals from the electrically induced convulsions as the drugs commonly used in the treatment of patients with convulsions (bromides, phenobarbital and the like) or even more effective.

One of these chemicals, sodium diphenyl hydantoinate, which was especially effective in protecting animals from electrically induced convulsive seizures with little sedative effect, was subjected to extensive pharmacologic and toxicologic tests by Krayer and by Kamm and Gruzhit.[3] The results of these tests showed that it was well tolerated by the ordinary laboratory animals (cats, dogs, rats) in massive single and long-continued daily doses. It was therefore considered safe to make a trial study of the drug in patients suffering from repeated convulsive seizures.

Sodium diphenyl hydantoinate is somewhat analogous in structure to the barbiturates, being a derivative of glycolyl urea rather than of malonyl urea. It is an odorless white powder with a bitter taste; it is soluble in water, slightly soluble in alcohol and insoluble in benzene and ether. The aqueous solution is alkaline to litmus and shows a $p_H$ of 11.7.

In order to determine the relative effectiveness of this drug on convulsive disorders in human beings, a group of patients was selected who had been having frequent convulsive seizures for many years and who had obtained little or no benefit from the usually accepted treatment, i. e. bromides, phenobarbital, ketogenic diet, restricted fluid intake and the like. The vast majority of these patients would be classified as having severe epilepsy.

Under the auspices of the Harvard Epilepsy Commission.

This study was aided by a grant from Parke, Davis & Co., Detroit.

From the Neurological Unit, Boston City Hospital, and the Department of Neurology, Harvard Medical School.

Read before the Section on Nervous and Mental Diseases at the Eighty-Ninth Annual Session of the American Medical Association, San Francisco, June 17, 1938.

1. Putnam, T. J., and Merritt, H. H.: Experimental Determination of the Anticonvulsant Properties of Some Phenyl Derivatives, Science 85:525-526 (May 28) 1937.

2. Merritt, H. H.; Putnam, T. J., and Schwab, D. H.: A New Series of Anticonvulsant Drugs Tested by Experiments on Animals, Arch Neurol. & Psychiat. 39:1003 (May) 1938.

3. Personal communications to the authors.

At the time of the preparation of this report, the medicine has been administered to 200 patients for a period varying from three weeks to eleven months. The results reported in this study are those in 142 patients with frequent attacks who have received the treatment for a period greater than two months, varying from extremes of eleven and two months, with an average of 4.3 months.

*In Patients with "Grand Mal" Seizures.*—Of the 118 patients with frequent grand mal attacks, complete relief of attacks has been secured in sixty-eight (58 per cent) and a marked reduction in the number of attacks in an additional thirty-two (27 per cent). In eighteen (15 per cent) there was only a moderate degree of improvement or no improvement over the previous status with bromides or phenobarbital therapy.

The results are shown in table 1 and two illustrative case histories are given here:

Case 1.—B. H., highschool boy aged 15, white, with a history of one grand mal attack in infancy, began at the age of 11 years to have mild grand mal attacks with loss of consciousness for from two to four minutes. These attacks occurred three or four times a week for the first year and neither their frequency nor their severity were reduced by treatment with bromides or phenobarbital. At the age of 12 there was a spontaneous remission for one year. The attacks recurred at the age of 13 at daily intervals and were not influenced by phenobarbital or methyl ethyl phenobarbital (mebaral). The physical and mental development was normal and the neurologic examination gave negative results; the blood, urine and cerebrospinal fluid were normal. Roentgenograms of the skull were negative. Electro-encephalography showed evidences of abnormal cortical activity, with frequent short bursts of abnormal waves of the grand mal and psychomotor types described by Gibbs and Lennox.[4]

TABLE 1.—*Effect of Sodium Diphenyl Hydantoinate on Grand Mal Convulsive Seizures in 118 Patients with Frequent Attacks Who Have Been Treated for a Period Greater Than Two Months*

| | | Grand Mal Associated with | | | |
| | Grand Mal Alone | Petit Mal | Equiva-lents | Total | Per Cent |
|---|---|---|---|---|---|
| Frequency of Attacks | | | | | |
| Completely relieved...... | 29 | 35 | 4 | 68 | 58 |
| Greatly decreased......... | 14 | 17 | 1 | 32 | 27 |
| Moderately decreased.... | 6 | 0 | 0 | 6 | 5 |
| No change.................. | 10 | 2 | 0 | 12 | 10 |
| Total...................... | 59 | 54 | 5 | 118 | 100 |

Treatment was started Sept. 15, 1937, with 0.1 Gm. of sodium diphenyl hydantoinate three times a day. There was complete freedom from attacks until May 1, 1938, when attending a dance while visiting friends he forgot to take his medicine and had two grand mal attacks in bed the next day.

Examinations of the blood and urine on several occasions since the start of treatment have shown no abnormalities.

4. Gibbs, F. A.; Gibbs, E. L., and Lennox, W. G.: Cerebral Dysrhythmias of Epilepsy, Arch. Neurol. & Psychiat. **39:**298 (Feb.) 1938.

Case 2.—A. W., a white man, aged 26, suffered from severe grand mal attacks of five years' duration, occurring almost daily with an increase in frequency to two or three attacks daily during the month before entry to the hospital, although the patient was receiving 6 grains (0.4 Gm.) of phenobarbital daily. Examination was negative except for bilateral middle ear deafness and mental deterioration (mental age 9). The blood, urine and spinal fluid were normal. Roentgenograms of the skull were negative. Electro-encephalography showed frequent bursts of abnormal cortical activity of the grand mal type.[4]

Treatment was started Dec. 2, 1937, with 0.1 Gm. of sodium diphenyl hydantoinate three times a day. The patient has been entirely free of attacks since starting treatment.

*In Patients with "Petit Mal" Seizures.*—In seventy-four patients with frequent petit mal attacks, complete relief was obtained in twenty-six (35 per cent) and a marked reduction in the number of attacks in thirty-six (49 per cent). In twelve (16 per cent) there was only slight or no improvement over the status under previous forms of therapy. It will be noted from a study of table 2 that the percentage of relief or great reduction in the petit mal attacks was highest in the patients in whom the petit mal attacks were associated with those of the grand mal type. Two illustrative histories are given here:

Case 3.—D. R., a graduate nurse, aged 22, began to have petit mal attacks two and one-half years before examination. These were characterized by blinking of the eyes and a momentary lapse of consciousness without falling. Attacks occurred from one to three times a day.

The physical and neurologic examinations were negative and the blood, urine and spinal fluid were normal. Roentgenograms of the skull were negative. Electro-encephalograms showed disturbance of the cortical activity typical of petit mal.[4]

Treatment was started Oct. 22, 1937, 0.1 Gm. of sodium diphenyl hydantoinate being administered three times a day, with complete relief of attacks. The patient has attempted to go without the medicine on several occasions since with return of attacks.

Case 4.—H. D., a white youth, aged 19, had been suffering for the past ten years with nocturnal grand mal attacks occurring two or three times a month and petit mal attacks several times a day. Previous treatment with phenobarbital (3 grains [0.2 Gm.] daily) had not reduced the frequency or severity of the attacks. The physical and neurologic examinations were negative. Examination of the blood, urine and spinal fluid was negative.

Treatment with sodium diphenyl hydantoinate 0.2 Gm. at bedtime was started Dec. 10, 1937. Since this date there has been complete relief from the petit mal attacks, but grand mal attacks occurred on December 17 and 28. The dosage of sodium diphenyl hydantoinate was increased to 0.4 Gm. daily on December 29. Grand mal attacks occurred on January 30 and March 20. The dosage was then increased to 0.6 Gm. daily with freedom from all attacks since March 20.

*In "Psychomotor Equivalent" Attacks.*—Of the six patients with psychomotor equivalent attacks there has been complete relief in four (67 per cent) and a very marked reduction in the frequency of attacks in two (33 per cent). The results are shown in table 3 and two illustrative cases are given here.

Case 5.—S. B. R., a white man, aged 54, an insurance salesman, gave a history of attacks of five years' duration, occurring two or three times a day, characterized by a turning of the head to one side, chewing movements of the jaw, mental cloudiness and performance of automatic actions, such as taking off shoes. The patient would not fall but would be unable to answer questions or talk coherently for from thirty to ninety seconds.

The physical and neurologic examinations were negative. The blood, urine and spinal fluid were normal and roentgenograms of the skull were negative. Electro-encephalography showed evidences of abnormal cortical activity typical of those found in patients with psychomotor equivalents.[4]

Previous treatment had consisted of 9 grains (0.6 Gm.) of phenobarbital and 30 grains (2 Gm.) of sodium bromide daily, plus calcium gluconate, with no effect on the severity or frequency of the attacks. The patient was started on treatment with sodium diphenyl hydantoinate Aug. 8, 1937, in doses of from 0.4 to 0.6 Gm. a day. The frequency of attacks has

TABLE 2.—*Effect of Sodium Diphenyl Hydantoinate on Petit Mal Convulsive Seizures in Seventy-Four Patients with Frequent Attacks Who Have Been Treated for a Period Greater Than Two Months*

| Frequency of Attacks | Petit Mal Alone | Petit Mal Associated with Grand Mal | Total | Per Cent |
|---|---|---|---|---|
| Completely relieved...... | 6 | 20 | 26 | 35 |
| Greatly decreased......... | 7 | 29 | 36 | 49 |
| Moderately decreased.... | 1 | 2 | 3 | 4 |
| No change.................. | 6 | 3 | 9 | 12 |
| Total...................... | 20 | 54 | 74 | 100 |

decreased from two or three attacks daily to an average of three attacks a month.

CASE 6.—S. H. R., a man aged 55, an unemployed salesman, had attacks which started at the age of 15 with a transient feeling of nausea and blinking of the eyes. These occurred at irregular intervals for seven years. At the age of 22 he had grand mal attacks at night for a period of eight years, after which the grand mal attacks ceased and the petit mal attacks passed over into psychic equivalents. In these attacks he would perform automatic movements and talk and answer questions, but he would not remember what had happened afterward. These attacks occurred from three to five times a week. An attack would last from one and one-half to three minutes, followed by a period of mental cloudiness for from five to ten minutes.

General physical and neurologic examinations were negative. Electro-encephalography showed evidences of abnormal cortical activity. Previous treatment had been from 1½ to 3 grains (0.1 to 0.2 Gm.) of phenobarbital a day.

The patient was started on treatment March 18, 1938, with 0.4 Gm. of sodium diphenyl hydantoinate a day. There was complete relief from attacks until April 3, when the patient complained of extreme nervousness and shaking of the hands. The dose of medicine was decreased to 0.2 Gm. daily on April 3 with relief of the nervousness but with return of attacks. April 14 the dose was increased to 0.3 Gm. a day with complete relief of attacks since but with the occurrence of anorexia and a feeling of nausea without vomiting. This has been relieved by taking the medicine with his meals. Examinations of blood and urine since treatment was started have shown no abnormality.

## DOSAGE

The dose used for adults varied between 0.2 and 0.6 Gm. a day, depending on the therapeutic effect and toxic reactions. As a rule adult patients were started on a dose of 0.1 Gm. three times a day, increased up to a maximum

TABLE 3.—*Effect of Sodium Diphenyl Hydantoinate on Psychic Equivalent Seizures in Six Patients with Frequent Attacks Who Have Been Treated for a Period Greater Than Two Months*

| Frequency of Attacks | Psychic Equivalents Alone | Psychic Equivalents Associated with Grand Mal | Total | Per Cent |
|---|---|---|---|---|
| Completely relieved...... | 0 | 4 | 4 | 67 |
| Greatly decreased......... | 1 | 1 | 2 | 33 |
| Total...................... | 1 | 5 | 6 | 100 |

of 0.2 Gm. three times a day if therapeutic effects were not obtained. Small children were started on 0.1 Gm. twice a day, increased up to 0.4 or 0.5 Gm. daily until the optimum therapeutic dosage was determined. For convenience the medicine was usually administered at meal time. It was found that gastric symptoms were avoided by the few patients in whom they occurred by taking the medicine along with or after the meal rather than before it. The dose in the seventy-two patients who were relieved of their attacks varied from 0.2 to 0.6 Gm. with an average of 3.6 Gm. Relief was obtained on a dose of 0.3 Gm. a day by forty-two patients. In contrast, the average dose for the forty-five patients in whom the attacks were greatly decreased in frequency was 4.3 Gm. and for the unimproved group the average dose was 4.6 Gm. Although 0.6 Gm. was considered to be the maximum therapeutic dose, the average dose in the group of cases in which treatment was not effective was only 0.46 Gm. This is explained by the fact that many of the patients in the latter group were not able to take larger doses owing to the appearance of minor toxic symptoms, such as tremors, ataxia, diplopia or dizziness.

## TOXIC REACTIONS

The toxic reactions can be divided into two groups:

1. Minor toxic symptoms such as dizziness, ataxia, tremors, blurring of vision, diplopia and slight nausea. This type of reaction occurred in approximately 15 per cent of the patients. They tended to occur between the third and the tenth day of treatment and could be relieved by reducing the dosage. If the reduced dosage was not effective in controlling the seizure, it could in most instances be increased after a few days without the return of symptoms. In a few cases the dose could not be maintained at the optimum level of effectiveness on account of the appearance of these symptoms whenever attempts were made to increase the daily dose to more than 0.4 Gm.

2. More serious toxic reactions in the nature of dermatitis and purpura. Dermatitis occurred in ten cases (5 per cent) but in only one instance was the dermatitis considered to be of a serious nature. This was in a man, aged 55, in whom an exfoliative dermatitis developed forty days after he started the treatment. This medication was immediately discontinued and the dermatitis gradually cleared. A brief abstract of his record is given:

CASE 7.—C. E., a man, aged 55, unmarried, a postoffice employee, was seen in 1933 with a history of grand mal convulsive seizures two or three times a month for two years. Complete physical and neurologic examinations at that time, including roentgenograms of the skull and examination of the spinal fluid, were negative except for a moderate degree of hypertension; the blood pressure was 140 systolic, 106 diastolic. He was discharged to his local physician and treated with phenobarbital and bromides with a temporary decrease in the frequency of the attacks, but they gradually recurred with their former frequency. Sodium diphenyl hydantoinate in a dose of 0.1 Gm. three times a day was started March 7, 1938. The patient's blood pressure at this time was 205 systolic, 130 diastolic. A convulsion occurred March 21 and the dose was increased to 0.1 Gm. four times a day. April 15 a morbilliform rash appeared on the face, trunk and extremities and developed into a brawny red maculopapular rash. There was no fever and, with the exception of a mild degree of itching sensation in the skin, the patient had no symptoms. He was admitted to the hospital, where he remained for approximately three weeks. The rash gradually cleared up, white wash being used to relieve the itching. In the hospital, examinations of the blood and urine were negative. The kidney function test showed a phenol-phthalein excretion of 55 per cent in two hours. With the withdrawal of sodium diphenyl hydantoinate there was immediate return of convulsive seizures. These were controlled with large doses (6 grains [0.4 Gm.] a day) of phenobarbital.

In the remaining nine cases the cutaneous reactions were of erythematous, scarlatiniform or morbilliform nature. This type of reaction usually occurred on the ninth to the tenth day of treatment and was frequently accompanied by fever. The rash disappeared in all patients regardless of whether the treatment was discontinued. In seven of the nine patients the treatment was interrupted by us as soon as a rash was reported. Two patients failed to report the rash and continued to take the medicine throughout the period of duration of the rash. Five of the seven patients in whom the use of the medicine was discontinued during the period of the rash were put back on the treatment after a few days, since the medication had been effective in relieving the attacks. Treatment was discontinued in the two patients who had not been relieved of the attacks. In another patient treatment has not been resumed, although it had been effective, since we desired to observe the patient in the hospital when further treatment was instituted.

Two examples of cutaneous reactions are given:

CASE 8.—G. G., a high school girl aged 13, began to have petit and grand mal attacks at the age of 2½ years. The petit mal attacks occurred several times a day and the grand mal attacks every three or four days. Previous treatment with the ketogenic diet, bromides and phenobarbital were ineffective. The physical and mental development was normal. Physical examination and examinations of the blood, urine and spinal fluid were negative. Roentgenograms of the skull were negative. Treatment with sodium diphenyl hydantoinate 0.1 Gm. three times a day was started Jan. 28, 1938. February 7 (ten days after treatment was started) a generalized scarlatiniform rash appeared accompanied by a fever of 102 F. The treatment was discontinued and the rash and fever disappeared in four days. Treatment was reinstituted four days after the disappearance of the rash in a dose of 0.2 Gm. daily. Grand mal attacks occurred on February 18 and 19. The dosage was increased to 0.3 Gm. daily with no attacks until March 10. On a dosage of 0.4 Gm. a day the patient has been free of attacks since March 10. The blood and urine on several occasions since treatment was started have been normal.

CASE 9.—M. P., a white boy aged 13 years, had had left jacksonian convulsive attacks since the age of 1 year. The third attack at the age of 3 was followed by a left hemiplegia, which has persisted. The frequency of the attacks gradually increased and for the past few years they occurred on the average of five or six times a day. An attack was characterized by convulsive movements of the left arm and leg, lasting from thirty seconds to five minutes without loss of consciousness. Previous treatment had consisted of large doses of phenobarbital, bromides and "donhide," a proprietary preparation containing bromides and extract of scutellaria, without any appreciable effect on the frequency or severity of the attacks. On examination there was a spastic left hemiparesis and a moderate degree of mental retardation.

Treatment with sodium diphenyl hydantoinate 0.1 Gm. three times a day was started Jan. 24, 1938. After five days of treatment there was no change in the frequency of attacks and the dose was increased to 0.5 Gm. daily with complete relief from the attacks. February 2, nine days after the institution of treatment, the patient complained of itching of the legs and hands, and a faint scarlatiniform rash developed over the face and extremities. Treatment was discontinued and there was a prompt return of the attacks. The rash and fever disappeared by February 7 and the sodium diphenyl hydantoinate was started again in doses of 0.1 Gm. daily. This was increased to 0.3 Gm. February 17, and since then attacks have been very mild and very infrequent, permitting the boy to attend school. Frequent examinations of the blood and urine since the treatment was started have shown nothing abnormal.

In one case purpuric lesions developed on the buttocks approximately two months after the treatment was started. The patient had been relieved of his attacks. Since there were no constitutional symptoms and a thorough study of the blood was negative, and since the lesions were beginning to clear before the patient reported them, treatment was not interrupted. A brief abstract of this case is given here:

CASE 10.—K. C., a white man, aged 35, a machinist, had had convulsive seizures three years before entry to the hospital. These occurred occasionally in the day time but were more frequent at night, occurring from seven to eight times each night. They were characterized by an aura of belching and choking sensation and the occurrence of slight convulsive movements of the arm and invariable incontinence of urine. The attacks would last for from thirty to ninety seconds. In addition, the patient had had five grand mal seizures. General physical and neurologic examinations were negative. Studies of the blood and urine were negative and roentgenograms of the skull were negative. Electro-encephalograms showed abnormal waves of the grand mal and psychomotor types.[4] The patient was started on treatment Dec. 7, 1937. For the first three weeks of treatment there was no decrease in the frequency of the attacks, but the urinary incontinence which had previously accompanied the attacks disappeared. After this there was a gradual decrease in the frequency of the attacks so that by the second month of treatment they occurred only two or three times a week and by the tenth week they had disappeared entirely. February 15, approximately eleven weeks after the treatment was started, the patient had some teeth extracted under procaine hydrochloride anesthesia. February 19, large ecchymotic lesions were noticed on the buttocks by the patient's wife. Since the attacks had ceased the patient had discontinued the medicine February 18, but when they began to recur on February 22 he resumed the use of the medicine. The presence of the lesions was not reported to us until March 7, as the patient had attached no significance to them. At that time they were large brownish areas on both buttocks. The hemoglobin content of his blood was 88 per cent, red blood cell count 4,800,000 and white blood cell count 14,200, with 78 per cent polymorphonuclears, 19 per cent small lymphocytes, 2 per cent large lymphocytes, 1 per cent eosinophils. The red blood cells and platelets appeared normal in smear and the platelet count was 322,000 per cubic millimeter. The bleeding time was one and one-half minutes and the tourniquet test was negative. The blood was reexamined carefully ten days later with no change in the red blood count or hemoglobin content. The white blood count was 10,000 with differential count as before; the platelet count was 337,000; bleeding time two minutes, icteric index 5. The patient has been continued on treatment since with no return of attacks. There have been no new lesions, and the lesions on the buttocks have gradually faded. Frequent examinations of the blood and urine have shown no abnormality.

## COMMENT

The results here reported indicate that sodium diphenyl hydantoinate was effective in controlling convulsive seizures in a great majority of a selected group of patients who were not helped by other methods of therapy. It is natural to assume, therefore, that even more satisfactory results could be obtained in patients with a less severe tendency to convulsions.

It must be noted that with a few exceptions the duration of treatment in the majority of the cases was less than six months. It is probable, therefore, that many of the patients in the "completely relieved" group will later be transferred to the other groups, but it is also possible that greater experience with the use of the drug will make it possible to obtain better results in some of the cases in the moderately or greatly improved groups. Whether or not some of the patients will ultimately become refractory to this treatment, as has occurred with other forms of therapy, remains to be seen.

In addition to a relief or a great reduction in the frequency of the attacks, it was frequently noted by the parents of children that they were much better behaved, more amenable to discipline and did better work in school. This improvement must have been due in great part to the freedom from attacks, but it is also possible that the medication produced other changes in the activity of the cerebral cortex. Studies of the cortical activity by means of the electro-encephalogram before and after treatment with sodium diphenyl hydantoinate are being conducted in collaboration with Dr. F. A. Gibbs and will be reported at a later date. The results of this study may conceivably lead to the use of the drug in conditions other than the convulsive state associated with similar cortical dysrhythmias.[4]

Sodium diphenyl hydantoinate has been shown to be a relatively nontoxic drug when given in doses of from 0.2 to 0.6 Gm. a day. There were no fatalities in a group of 200 patients and in only two patients was there a reaction that could be considered as serious in nature—an exfoliative dermatitis in one patient and a nonthrombocytopenic purpura in the second. Frequent studies of the blood and urine failed to reveal any evidence of damage to the hemopoietic system or kidneys in any of the 200 patients. The toxic dermatitis produced by the drug, with the one exception already noted, was of a benign nature and was quite similar to that produced by another hydantoin compound, phenylethyl hydantoin (nirvanol), which was formerly used in the treatment of chorea

minor. Sodium diphenyl hydantoinate is without doubt, however, considerably more toxic than bromides and the barbituric acid compounds. Cutaneous reactions as well as the minor toxic symptoms of tremors, ataxia, diplopia, dizziness and the like are much more frequently encountered. The high degree of alkalinity of the drug sometimes causes a sensation of nausea and discomfort in the abdomen, making it difficult for some patients to take it regularly. It is possible also that a more extensive use of the drug will result in other toxic reactions which we have not as yet encountered in our 200 patients. In spite of these handicaps we feel that sodium diphenyl hydantoinate is a valuable addition to the medical armamentarium in the battle against epilepsy and that it is worth trying with proper precautions in patients who have not responded to the less toxic modes of therapy, such as the bromides, the barbituric acid compounds or the ketogenic diet.

The optimum dosage of the drug must be determined by trial. Children above the age of 6 and adults should be started on a dose of 0.1 Gm. three times a day. Gastric discomfort and nausea can usually be prevented by giving the capsule with or immediately following the meals. If seizures are not controlled by the end of from seven to ten days an additional dose should be given at bedtime. Further increase in the dose, up to a maximum of 0.6 Gm. a day, can be adjusted according to the tolerance of the patient. Infants and children up to the age of 5 years should be started on a dose of from 0.1 to 0.2 Gm. a day, which can be gradually increased to 0.3 to 0.4 Gm. a day if necessary.

The appearance of minor toxic symptoms, such as nervousness, tremors or ataxia, calls for a reduction in the size of the dose. If the reduced dose is ineffective, attempts can be made after from five to ten days to increase it. The use of the drug should be immediately discontinued if more serious toxic symptoms, dermatitis, purpura and the like develop. An exfoliative dermatitis makes further use of the drug absolutely contraindicated. A mild erythematous, morbilliform or scarlatiniform reaction occurring on the eighth to the eleventh day of treatment is not of such serious import, and, if there are definite indications that the drug has been effective in relieving severe attacks, it can be given again in small doses with caution. If no untoward symptoms develop, the dose can be increased gradually every four to six days. On the reappearance of any toxic manifestation, further use of the drug is prohibited.

If patients have been receiving large doses of bromides or phenobarbital, these should be continued along with the sodium diphenyl hydantoinate, the dose of the bromides or phenobarbital being gradually decreased over a period of from four to seven days. This is advisable since the sudden withdrawal of the bromides or phenobarbital may result in the precipitation of a series of attacks before a reservoir of sodium diphenyl hydantoinate has been built up.

Our experience with the drug has not been sufficient to determine all the contraindications for its use. At present we feel that it should not be given to elderly persons with hypertension or other evidences of cardiorenal disease, or to debilitated patients.

## SUMMARY

1. In a previous study it has been shown that sodium diphenyl hydantoinate is effective in preventing electrically induced convulsive seizures in cats. The drug is relatively nontoxic and well tolerated by the usual laboratory animals.

2. A clinical trial of sodium diphenyl hydantoinate was made in 200 patients with frequent convulsive seizures which had not been relieved by the previous modes of therapy.

3. In 142 such patients who have received the treatment for periods varying from two to eleven months, grand mal attacks were relieved in 58 per cent and greatly decreased in frequency in an additional 27 per cent; petit mal attacks were relieved in 35 per cent and greatly decreased in frequency in an additional 49 per cent, and psychic equivalent attacks were relieved in 67 per cent and greatly decreased in frequency in 33 per cent.

4. There were no fatalities. A toxic dermatitis occurred in ten patients (5 per cent), nonthrombocytopenic purpura in one patient and minor (in many instances, transient) toxic reactions, tremors, ataxia, dizziness and the like in approximately 15 per cent.

## CONCLUSIONS

Sodium diphenyl hydantoinate is a valuable addition to the physician's armamentarium in the battle against "epilepsy." Its use should be restricted, for the present, to that group of patients who do not respond to the less toxic forms of therapy previously in common use.

818 Harrison Avenue.

## ABSTRACT OF DISCUSSION

Dr. Eugene Ziskind, Los Angeles: The discovery of this drug is an indication of the mental alertness of these authors, which has been shown in much of their previous experimental work. The discovery is based on attention to a clinical observation with which some physicians may not be acquainted. Drs. Merritt and Putnam observed that whereas phenobarbital controls seizures in a high proportion of cases that is not true of other barbiturates, and so, concentrating on the phenol fraction of the phenobarbital, their investigation led to the trial with these various drugs which showed so definite an effect on the convulsive seizures. In epilepsy, therapy of this type is essential for long periods, often many years. I would be interested in seeing what the incidence of complication is when this drug is used for longer periods. The statistical results so far reported are far in excess of what one would expect as a chance of variation. Dr. Somerfeld and I had occasion to observe that phenobarbital markedly increased the extrapyramidal rigidity in cases of parkinsonism, and we shall be stimulated by this study to investigate also whether or not the response there has been from barbiturates or by the phenol elements. We are also looking forward to an opportunity to use this drug, which appears to be a notable advance in the therapy of convulsive disorders.

Dr. T. J. Putnam, Boston: The results of the use of this drug, as reported by the authors and by Dr. Shurly from Dr. Kimball's clinic, speak for themselves. I should like to emphasize in relation to this project, however, not alone the efficacy of this drug but the fact that, it seems, a new method of studying modes of therapy of convulsions has become available. There probably are several kinds of convulsions. Perhaps there should be several types of medication to control them. This is only one drug found through a preliminary experimental survey. There is reason to believe there are perhaps many others and maybe more effective ones still to be found.

Feb 24, 1984
(JAMA 1984;251:1068-1069)

# Introduction of Phenytoin*

Maurice W. Van Allen, MD

Had the discovery of the anticonvulsant properties of sodium diphenyl hydantoinate been fortuitous, an article first reporting the effectiveness of this drug in man would justify its inclusion as a landmark article in the centennial celebration issues of *JAMA*. This drug, now called *phenytoin* (Dilantin), soon revolutionized the drug treatment of the convulsive disorders when such treatment had been largely limited to the bromides and phenobarbital. Phenytoin remains today a mainstay of therapy in the control of major motor seizures and some other manifestations of epilepsy. Few drugs continue in active use in unmodified form 45 years after the discovery of their usefulness. Few drugs have been as important for the relief of human disability and suffering, and this with an acceptable level of side and toxic effects in most patients.

That phenytoin was chosen by logical inference to be included in a series of drugs actively tested for effectiveness in controlling convulsions is remarkable. And that this effectiveness was identified by testing in animals in a controlled protocol is a landmark for modern clinical pharmacology.

## Work of Merritt and Putnam

The article of our focus in *JAMA* was one in a series by Merritt and Putnam[1] related to this subject. A special article entitled "Experimental Determination of the Anticonvulsant Properties of Some Phenyl Derivatives" appeared in *Science* in May 1937.[2] Here the authors discussed the use of electrical stimulation as "a standard means of producing convulsions in animals," giving credit to Krasnogorosky of Russia and to Spiegel, who had used this method, and to Gibbs and Hoefer for suggesting modifications of the described equipment, which is mentioned in the *JAMA* article. The current flow necessary to produce a convulsion in an animal (cat) was surprisingly constant from day to day. (It is interesting to estimate that this equipment could be duplicated even today for perhaps $75, while a properly elaborate "electronic" stimulator might well cost $1,200.)

In this same article, the authors outlined the rationale for the trial use of phenyl compounds, pointing to similarities to the structure of phenobarbital and to a report that conjugated phenols might be responsible for

suppression of convulsive activity in uremics—"a large number of the less toxic phenol compounds were studied."[3] "The compounds which appear to have the greatest anticonvulsant activity combined with the least relative hypnotic effect of those tested so far are diphenylhydantoin, acetophenone and benzophenone."[2]

Thus, from the beginning of their studies, an effective anticonvulsant drug with minimal soporific side effect was sought—one that might replace phenobarbital.

Merritt and Putnam[4] extended their published observations in a paper presented at the annual meeting of the American Neurological Association in June 1937 with publication the following year in the *Archives of Neurology and Psychiatry*. Sixty-seven chemicals that produced little or no elevation of the convulsive threshold to electrical stimulation were listed. Several more increased the threshold but were not effective in subnarcotic dosages, while diphenylhydantoin was found to be more effective than phenobarbital with less soporific effect in animals. The key article in this series, however, is that reprinted in this issue, "Sodium Diphenyl Hydantoinate in the Treatment of Convulsive Disorders,"[1] which appeared in *JAMA* in September 1938 as a report of the first clinical trial of the drug. Let us note that the results of therapy reported in this article had been presented at a meeting of the Section on Nervous and Mental Diseases of the 89th annual session of the American Medical Association in June 1938. The meetings of this section and those of the American Neurological Association had offered the principal platforms for presentation of clinical neurological material in that decade.

After the authors had established a reproducible way to cause convulsions in cats and had by induction chosen likely drugs for testing in these animals, they found that diphenyl hydantoinate was effective in protecting the cats from electrically induced convulsions without producing disabling sedation or stupor.

We are not told about nor referred specifically to the work of Krayer and Kamna and Gruyhit, who subjected the drug "to extensive pharmacologic and toxicologic tests" in laboratory animals. These investigators apparently found the drug well tolerated. Testing in patients was then appropriate, and this was done by Merritt and Putnam with most gratifying results, as one can gather from their article. Especially important was their finding of the protection of 118 patients with frequent grand mal seizures. Complete relief was experienced by 68 and a marked reduction in seizures by 32 for more than two months of trial. Comparison was made with results in

From the Department of Neurology, College of Medicine, University of Iowa Hopitals, Iowa City.

*A commentary on Merritt HH, Putnam TJ: Sodium diphenyl hydantoinate in the treatment of convulsive disorders. *JAMA* 1938;111:1068-1073.

different expressions of convulsive disorder. The dosage was established at 0.2 to 0.6 g/day, as is used today. A further report appeared in the *American Journal of Psychiatry*[5] in 1940, when the same authors reported that 227 of 267 previously refractory patients had been effectively treated for more than two months to two years.

Dose-related symptoms of dizziness, ataxia, and diplopia were quickly discovered, and toxic symptoms including dermatologic manifestations were recognized and recorded both qualitatively and quantitatively in terms consistent with the current experience.[6] Thoroughness in searching for many kinds of possible toxic reaction is evident, as is honesty and objectivity in reporting their observations. Not much new except for some subtle hematologic changes and disorders of folic acid and calcium metabolism has been added since this first report. The possible teratogenic effects of phenytoin were not discovered until much later.

### Subsequent Developments

Many years passed before satisfactory methods for determination of blood levels of this and other anticonvulsive drugs became generally available. Such laboratory determinations are now mandatory to the satisfactory management of many patients, to the appreciation of individual tolerance and variations in response, to the detection of noncompliance, and to the detection of perplexing drug interactions when more than one anticonvulsant drug is used. That an understanding of the mechanism of action of phenytoin was not grasped by Merritt and Putnam can hardly detract from their contribution, since this understanding is still being sought. As with penicillin in the treatment of pneumonia, it was hardly necessary to employ sophisticated statistical methods to detect the efficacy of the drug.

The foundations for modern epileptology were being laid in this period, much accelerated by the addition of phenytoin to the available treatment modalities. The application of electroencephalography to diagnosis, analysis, and understanding of epilepsy was made possible by technological advances that condensed a laboratory full of equipment to a reasonably sized machine that could be centrally manufactured. An explosion of studies followed in discovering clinical correlations of electrical activity of the brain. A more logical classification of the epilepsies established the basis for appropriate drug therapy in the future.[7]

The problems posed by epilepsy to the armed forces in World War II and to the Veterans Administration later led to active governmental sponsorship of electroencephalography and related studies. The many etiologic and pathogenetic factors of the convulsive disorders and the spectrum of their manifestations make this category of human affliction as complex as that of neoplasia, wherein ignorance of fundamental biologic processes also contributes so heavily to slow progress in treatment.

But not so easily comparable are other factors that continue to hinder even the application of known modalities for better symptomatic management. While recurrent, sudden, short-lived disruptions of neurological function and consciousness afflict almost 1% of the population, the level of expertise in treatment is still well below the "state of the art." The patients are often difficult — denying illness, retreating from public exposure, and reacting to a persistent public prejudice of ancient roots, while subject as well to emotional and behavioral abnormalities secondary to the seizure state or arising from the underlying abnormalities of the brain.

Finally, something should be said about Merritt and Putnam. Merritt[8] wrote an obituary for Putnam, who died in 1975. Only a short paragraph is devoted to their collaborative work on phenytoin and its importance. Putnam left the Boston City Hospital to become professor of neurology and neurosurgery at the College of Physicians and Surgeons and director of the Neurological Institute in 1939 but did not find an environment like that in Boston, and a brilliant career subsequently waned. While the obituaries of Merritt all mention the phenytoin contribution, it is almost secondary in the regard of the authors for the man himself, physician, teacher, and administrator. Dr Merritt died in 1979, having left behind pioneering work on CSF, the *Textbook of Neurology*, a monograph on neurosyphilis, and the editorship of *Archives of Neurology*. He was influential in the formation of the National Institute of Neurological Diseases and Blindness, which he served in various roles for many years as he led the Department of Neurology at Columbia and the Neurological Institute. He was prominent in professional societies at all levels. Perhaps his greatest contribution is reflected in the number of leaders in neurology today who were trained under his aegis.

However, all of these accomplishments cannot overshadow the remarkable boon that phenytoin has been to the all-too-long–suffering epileptic. The interested reader should know that there is now an annual Merritt-Putnam Symposium devoted to epilepsy. In the introduction to the first published symposium, Rowland,[9] a colleague of Merritt, records an excellent perspective on the work discussed herein.

### References

1. Merritt HH, Putnam TJ: Sodium diphenyl hydantoinate in the treatment of convulsive disorders. *JAMA* 1938;111:1068-1073.
2. Putnam TJ, Merritt HH: Experimental determination of the anticonvulsant properties of some phenyl derivatives. *Science* 1937;85:525-526.
3. Harrison TR, Mason MF, Resnik H: Observations on the mechanism of muscular twitchings in uremia. *J Clin Invest* 1936;15:463-464.
4. Merritt HH, Putnam TJ: A new series of anticonvulsant drugs tested by experiments on animals. *Arch Neurol Psychiatry* 1938;39:1003-1015.
5. Merritt HH, Putnam TJ: Further experiences with the use of sodium diphenyl hydantoinate in the treatment of convulsive disorders. *Am J Psychiatry* 1940;96:1023-1027.
6. Merritt HH, Putnam TJ: Sodium diphenyl hydantoinate in the treatment of convulsive seizures: Toxic symptoms and their prevention. *Arch Neurol Psychiatry* 1939;45:1053-1058.
7. Gibbs FA, Gibbs EL, Lennox WG: Cerebral dysrhythmias of epilepsy. *Arch Neurol Psychiatry* 1938;39:298-314.
8. Merritt HH: Tracy Jackson Putnam 1894-1975. *Trans Am Neurol Assoc* 1975;100:271-272.
9. Rowland LP: First annual Merritt-Putnam symposium: Introduction. *Epilepsia* 1982;23(suppl 1):1-4.

Dec 24, 1938
(*JAMA* 1938;111:2377-2384)

## Chapter 30

# An Acute Infection of the Respiratory Tract With Atypical Pneumonia

## A Disease Entity Probably Caused by a Filtrable Virus

Hobart A. Reimann, M.D.

Philadelphia

Infections of the respiratory tract are among the most common afflictions of mankind, and pneumonia, which occasionally accompanies or follows them, is the third most common cause of death in the United States. Any progress made in the knowledge of such infections is therefore urgently needed.

Only recently has the physician been armed with comparatively simple methods for the diagnosis of one of these diseases, epidemic influenza, which is now known to be caused by a filtrable virus. Methods for isolating and identifying the virus of the common cold are still too complicated for the average clinical laboratory in routine diagnosis. The discovery of the causative agent of influenza permits separation of the disease as an entity from the undifferentiated group of infections of the respiratory tract and provides a standard, so to speak, against which other entities may be compared. The discovery also confirmed a long established impression gained on clinical and epidemiologic grounds that influenza is a disease entity caused by a filtrable virus.

From studies already made on the group of acute infections of the respiratory tract other than influenza, it is predictable that it is composed of a number of specific entities probably caused by filtrable viruses which remain to be identified, perhaps by methods similar to those by which the viruses of influenza and the common cold were discovered. Efforts in this direction no doubt will eventually make possible a classification of this important group of infections such as has been made with fruitful

results in the case of pneumonias of bacterial origin.

With these points in mind, I studied a group of seven cases of an unusual form of tracheobronchopneumonia and severe constitutional symptoms which occurred in 1938. The clinical symptoms and signs of the infection were so uniform in these cases and yet so different from those of other common diseases that I was led to regard the disease as an etiologic entity caused by an unknown agent. I have learned from my colleagues that similar cases were encountered by them in New York, Boston, Philadelphia and elsewhere in 1938. The condition was usually called influenza.

### REPORT OF CASES

CASE 1.—H. M., a man aged 44, did not feel well March 3 while in New York. The next day he felt chilly and hot alternately and noticed a slightly sore throat. He went to bed for two days and was thought by his physician to have influenza. There was profuse sweating. He returned to work but on March 7 had a recurrence of chilly sensations and perspiration. Cough with a slight amount of yellowish sputum developed. He then came to Philadelphia, and entered the hospital on March 8, about the fifth day of illness, as a patient of Dr. Guy Nelson.

He was a robust, severely ill man. His face was flushed and his pharynx inflamed. There were occasional periods of coughing, but no sputum was raised. The heart and abdomen were normal. A few rales were present in the interscapular regions. The temperature, pulse rate and respiratory rate are shown in figure 1. The leukocytes numbered 8,000. A diagnosis of tracheobronchitis was made.

During the first week of observation the temperature

From the Jefferson Medical College and Hospital.

remained continuously high, but in contrast the pulse rate was low. There were a frequent hacking cough with scanty mucopurulent sputum, sweating, slight hoarseness, restlessness, abdominal distention, constipation and drowsiness. The patient complained of headache, photophobia and general aching. The breath sounds were suppressed in the base of the left lung posteriorly, where a few rales were heard. The number of leukocytes rose to 11,800. Typhoid was strongly suspected, but no agglutinins for Bacillus typhosus were ever demonstrable, and the bacilli were not found after repeated blood cultures and stool examinations.

About the twelfth day of illness the patient was drowsy, perspired freely and coughed occasionally, and the hoarseness had progressed to aphonia. The abdomen was distended, and

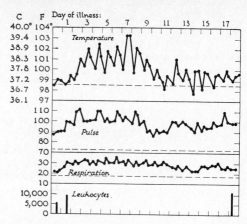

Fig. 2 (case 2).—Clinical course from the first day of illness.

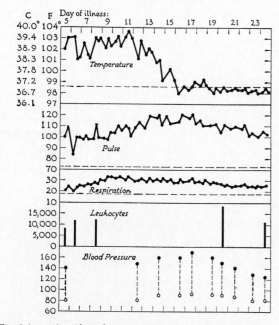

Fig. 1 (case 1).—Clinical course. The pulse rate, respiratory rate and leukocyte count were comparatively low in the first week.

the pulse and respiratory rates were increased (fig. 1). The conjunctivas were injected, the tongue was heavily coated and anorexia was present. Two diarrheal bowel movements occurred. The patient was apprehensive at times, drowsy at others and disoriented, especially at night. With the abdominal distention there was a brief attack of acute pain in the left upper quadrant. The patient was extremely ill, and typhoid was still suspected although no proof was forthcoming. A roentgenogram of the lungs showed a faint increased mottling, especially in the right lung.

For the next few days the temperature declined and the pulse rate rose. Profuse sweating continued. Tachypnea continued, and slight dyspnea and cyanosis developed. Aphonia persisted, and the nasal passages became obstructed by acutely inflamed and swollen mucous membranes. The pharynx was dry and inflamed. Many rales in the base of the left lung and a few in that of the right were now heard. The breath sounds were harsh, but no other abnormal signs except pleural friction were audible in the left axilla. Another roentgenogram, made on the sixteenth day after the temperature reached normal, showed an increased mottled density in both lungs, but particularly on the right side, suggestive of diffuse pneumonia. Garglings of material from the nasopharynx were made at this time and dropped into the nares of ferrets by Drs. Stokes and Francis, but no virus was isolated.

Numerous rales in the base of the left lung and fewer in that of the right persisted with diminishing intensity. Tachycardia and tachypnea persisted for three weeks after the temperature became normal. The patient lost 12 Kg. (27 pounds) in weight.

Two weeks later, because of persistent aphonia, laryngoscopic examination was performed by Dr. Calvin Fox. The epiglottis, arytenoid processes, vestibule of the pharynx and tracheal wall were inflamed. The vocal cords were congested and thick. Roentgenograms made on the twenty-seventh and seventy-second days showed that the mottling had disappeared, but a haziness over the base of the left lung suggested pleural thickening.

*Laboratory Data.*—The leukocyte counts are shown in figure 1. The percentage of polymorphonuclears was found to be increased to 80 or 90 at each examination. Three blood cultures were negative, and agglutinins for Bacillus typhosus, Brucella

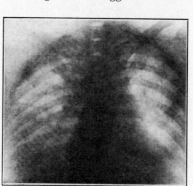

Fig. 3 (case 2).—Appearance on the seventh day of illness. There is a diffuse mottling throughout both lungs, more marked in the right. The interlobar pleura on the right is thickened.

melitensis and Pasteurella tularensis were absent. Numerous examinations of sputum and material obtained by swabbing the throat showed the usual nasopharyngeal flora, with Streptococcus viridans, Streptococcus hemolyticus, diphtheroids, staphylococci, gram-negative cocci and bacilli and on one occasion pneumococcus type XIX. No tubercle bacilli were found. Febrile albuminuria was present. Blood serum obtained on the sixteenth, thirty-third and seventieth days after the onset of illness and tested by Dr. Francis did not contain antibodies for epidemic influenza virus.

*Summary.*—This patient became ill with the symptoms of a sore throat, recovered to some extent but became worse again and exemplified the so-called typhoid state with tracheitis and bronchitis. Although rales were present in the lungs early in the course of the disease, symptoms and signs of massive invasion were delayed until after the temperature had declined, about the twelfth day. The signs persisted long after the fever disappeared. These observations and persistent laryngitis, hoarseness, aphonia, sweating, dyspnea, cyanosis and drowsiness were the main features. The illness lasted sixteen days.

CASE 2.—M. S., a man aged 39, had a herniorrhaphy performed February 25. Convalescence was uneventful until March 11, when he thought he was getting a cold. There was stuffiness of the nose, and pain developed in the left side of the chest. No abnormal signs were present in the lungs. The patient was allowed out of bed, but his discomfort persisted. March 13 he felt generally uneasy, ached all over and felt "grippy." A drenching sweat occurred that night and another on the following night. Fever was noted first March 14 and increased to 38.3 C. (101 F.) the next day, as shown in figure 2. On the third day of fever, sharp pain developed in the lower anterior part of the right axillary region, which was worse on breathing. It became so severe that opiates were required to control it. A few rales were present in this area. The respiratory rate increased to 32. The pharynx was inflamed but was not painful. The leukocytes numbered 9,000.

During the next few days the number of rales increased and the breath sounds were suppressed in the base of the right lung. Occasional pain occurred in the root of the neck on the right side suggestive of the referred pain of diaphragmatic pleurisy. There was no cough and no sputum. Rales appeared in the base of the left lung. Epistaxis occurred on the sixth day. The

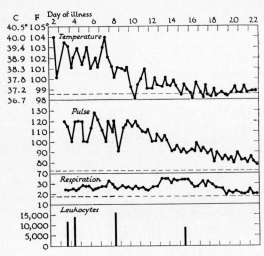

Fig. 4 (case 3).—Clinical course.

abdomen was distended and constipation was present. A roentgenogram of the chest (fig. 3) made on the eighth day showed diffuse increased mottled shadows throughout both lungs, more prominent on the right side, suggestive of diffuse pneumonia (Dr. Karl Kornblum). The interlobar pleura was thickened on the right side, and density at the base suggested a small collection of fluid. At about this time the patient complained of pain and numbness in the right wrist, elbow and shoulder. His legs and teeth ached. There was profuse sweating most of the time. One night his gown was changed fourteen times. Physical signs of fluid appeared in the base of the right lung. Dyspnea and cyanosis appeared and became distressing, but there was no cough or sputum. Nasopharyngeal secretions were obtained about this time by Drs. Kinney and Magill and inoculated intransally into ferrets, but no virus was recovered. A blood culture was sterile. The temperature began to decline after the eighth day, and the patient improved. Dyspnea, cyanosis and sweating diminished. Atropine sulfate controlled the excessive perspiration. A symmetrical patch of hyperesthesia 3 or 4 inches in diameter was noted on the anterior surface of both thighs. The patient began to cough occasionally on the eleventh day and felt that his nose was plugged up again.

A small fleck of blood-tinged tenacious sputum was raised, which contained Streptococcus viridans, Streptococcus hemo-

lyticus, pneumococcus type XIX, diphtheroids and gram-negative cocci.

Thoracentesis was performed, and 300 cc. of bloody, turbid fluid, which was sterile on culture, was obtained. The process was repeated three days later and again on the twenty-second day. Fluid of similar quality and quantity was removed. On the nineteenth day a roentgenogram showed a diminution of the density of the infiltration seen previously. There was an irregular density at the base of the right lung, and there were a few patches of density in the base of the left lung. Low grade fever persisted. Several weeks later a trocar and drain were inserted by Dr. Nassau. The fever increased, and on the fifty-third day the patient suddenly died. Necropsy was not performed.

This patient was observed from the first day of illness; this began as an ordinary infection of the respiratory tract, but profuse perspiration and severe pleuritic pain developed. Evidence of pulmonary invasion appeared about the fourth day and rapidly involved both lungs. Sterile pleural effusion was present. The chief features were the diffuse atypical pneumonia, drenching sweats, dyspnea, cyanosis, severe pleuritic pain and a minimal amount of cough and sputum.

Nasopharyngeal washings were obtained on the eighth day of illness, too late, perhaps, according to the experiences of British investigators,[1] for a virus to be obtained. The blood serum did not contain antibodies for the virus of epidemic influenza.

Experience with these two patients led me to suspect that I was dealing with an unusual form of infection, so that when the next patients were seen, while the first two were still under observation, attempts were made to obtain a virus earlier in the disease. March 20 and March 22, nasopharyngeal washings were obtained at my request from patients 1, 2, 3 and 7 by Drs. Stokes and Kinney of the University of Pennsylvania and Drs. Francis and Magill of the Rockefeller Institute.[2]

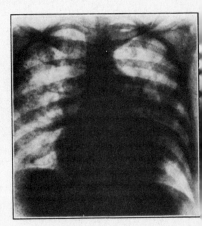

Fig. 5 (case 3).—Appearance on the fifth day of illness. The hilar shadows are increased in density. There is a diffuse mottling in both lungs, with a denser shadow in the middle of the left lung field.

CASE 3.—Mrs. K. A., aged 48, first noticed a "head cold" March 12. Her brother had a similar infection at the same time. The patient, her brother (patient 4), her son (patient 5), a friend (patient 6) and her mother (patient 7), among others, were together at a party March 12. Mrs. K. A. felt unduly warm at the time and had chilly sensations the next day, but disregarded them. During the following days the symptoms of a cold persisted, and March 17 they became worse. March 18, fever

1. Stuart-Harris, C. H.; Andrewes, C. H., and Smith, W., with Chalmers, D. K. M.; Cowen, E. G. H., and Hughes, D. L.: A Study of Epidemic Influenza with Special Reference to the 1936-1937 Epidemic, Medical Research Council, Special Report Series, No. 228, London, His Majesty's Stationery Office, 1938.

2. Drs. Stokes, Kinney, Francis and Magill performed most of the animal and serologic tests.

and coughing began. Chilly sensations recurred, and pain developed in the left side of the chest. The temperature rose to 40 C. (104 F.). The patient was admitted to the hospital on the third day of severe symptoms (fig. 4).

At examination she was restless, apprehensive and overalert. There were slight cyanosis and a hacking, nonproductive cough. The pharynx was slightly inflamed. Marked hyperesthesia was present over both mammary regions. Rales were heard in both interscapular areas and in the bases of both lungs. There was tenderness in the right upper quadrant of the abdomen. The leukocytes numbered 11,800; 81 per cent were polymorphonuclear cells. A blood culture was sterile. Cultures of nasopharyngeal secretions obtained with a throat swab showed Staphylococcus albus and pneumococcus type IV among other forms of bacteria. A roentgenogram revealed an increase in the usual density of the hilus and vascular markings in both lungs. The temperature and pulse rate were high (fig. 4).

The next day more rales were heard in the base of the right lung and the breath sounds had a faintly tubular sound. Nasal washings were made by Dr. Kinney on the fourth day of illness and inoculated intranasally into ferrets. A virus was isolated.

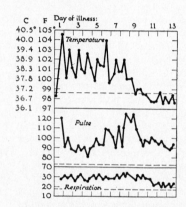

Fig. 6 (case 7).—Clinical course from the first day of illness. Note the low pulse rate.

On the fifth day the patient was severely ill and was stuporous at times. Many rales, egophony, pectoriloquy, weak bronchophony and tubular breathing were now heard in the base of the left lung. There was slight rhythmic flaring of the alae nasi. X-ray examination revealed a diffuse density in the midportion of the left lung (fig. 5) and an increase in the hilar shadows noted two days before which was suggestive of diffuse bilateral pneumonia. During the next few days the patient became considerably worse. On the sixth day, after being urged to raise sputum, she raised the first sample of bloody, tenacious sputum, which contained Streptococcus viridans, Streptococcus hemolyticus, gram-negative cocci and a few type IV pneumococci. Throat washings were obtained at this time by Dr. Magill and inoculated into ferrets. A virus was obtained which was apparently similar to the one obtained by Drs. Stokes and Kinney two days before.

The patient became irrational. Her face was flushed, the mucous membranes were cyanotic and the lining of the mouth, which had felt uncomfortable for several days, was spotted with bright red discrete and confluent macules, some of which contained papules and whitish speckles. Coarse rales were heard in both mammary regions. Pleuritic pain and friction sounds were present in the left axilla. Dyspnea was severe and she appeared to be gravely ill. Oxygen therapy relieved the dyspnea and cyanosis considerably. On the eighth day euphoria and overalertness, with slight mental confusion and disorientation, developed. The skin over the mammary region was hyperesthetic; touching and pinching it caused pain. There was tympany in the left mammary region but no rales were heard. Posteriorly there was dulness in the base of the left lung, with decreased tactile fremitus, loud bronchial breathing, egophony and pectoriloquy. A small area where weak bronchial breathing and rales were heard was found in the right base. The leukocytes numbered 15,800.

On the ninth day muscae volitantes and headache were complained of and the patient became more drowsy. She slept most of the time and appeared to be toxic. Various groups of muscles twitched from time to time. The reflexes were generally hyperactive, especially the patellar reflexes. Encephalitis was suspected, but the spinal fluid was normal in all respects and contained two leukocytes per cubic millimeter.

Gradual improvement then began. Herpes appeared on the lip. A roentgenogram on the thirteenth day showed that the lungs had become relatively clear except for haziness at the base of the left one suggestive of pleural thickening. The number of leukocytes dropped to 9,000.

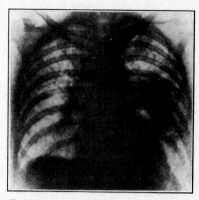

Fig. 7 (case 9).—Appearance on the fourth day. There is a large area of density in the left lung. The left dome of the diaphragm is slightly elevated. The root shadows on the right side are denser than normal.

Improvement was rapid after the sixteenth day, and the patient left the hospital on the twenty-fifth day for further convalescence. She had lost about 7 Kg. (15 pounds) in weight. Rales and friction sounds were still present in the base of the left lung. She was reexamined on the forty-third day. Her temperature was 37.3 C. (99.2 F.) and she felt weak. A roentgenogram showed thickening of the interlobar pleura between the upper and lower lobes of the left lung but no other abnormalities.

*Summary.*—The illness apparently began as a mild infection of the upper part of the respiratory tract, which was followed after several days by severe tracheobronchitis and diffuse pneumonia. In spite of the pulmonary involvement and hacking cough there was practically no sputum. Dyspnea, cyanosis, photophobia, stupor, nervous symptoms and pleuritic pain were conspicuous characteristics. Sweating was not prominent. Rales and roentgenographic evidence of pleural involvement were still present two weeks after the temperature became normal. The type IV pneumococci recovered from the sputum were regarded as commensals without significance.

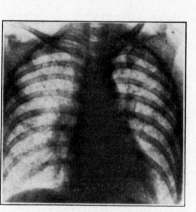

Fig. 8 (case 9).—Appearance on the tenth day. The patch of density in the left lung shown in figure 8 has disappeared, but there is now a diffuse mottling of both lung fields. Plates made on the twenty-third and forty-third days showed progressive diminution of the abnormal densities until the seventieth day, when the lung fields appeared normal.

Nasopharyngeal washings from which an apparent virus was recovered were obtained on the fourth day by Dr. Stokes and on the sixth day by Dr. Francis. Blood serum for tests was obtained on the same days, on the forty-third and on the one hundred and twentieth day but contained no antibodies for the virus of epidemic influenza.

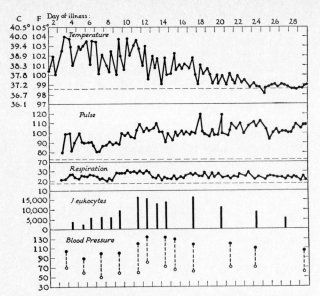

Fig. 9 (case 9).—Clinical course from the second day of illness. Note the low pulse rate and the low leukocyte counts early in the illness. The blood pressure rose during the course.

Patients 4, 5, 6 and 7, as mentioned, had been in contact with patient 3 when they attended a gathering March 12 at which several members of her family and a few friends were present. Mrs. A. (patient 3) and her brother did not feel well at the time. Within the next week Mrs. A.'s son, a friend and her mother became ill.

CASE 4.—Mr. B. (brother), aged 45, became ill about March 12, feeling cold, shivery and "grippy." He kept on working except for one day in spite of his illness, which lasted about two weeks. There was an annoying dry cough but no sputum. He was examined twice about the ninth day of illness by Dr. Burgess Gordon, who noted rales in both interscapular regions on both occasions. The temperature, taken on two occasions, was normal.

CASE 5.—J. A. (son), aged 25, noted dryness of the throat March 14. Two days later the throat was very sore. Rhinitis, malaise and muscle pains were present. It hurt to bend the neck forward. The patient did not go to bed. There was no fever or cough. These symptoms lasted three days and gradually disappeared, so that by the eighth day only soreness of the muscles of the neck was noted.

CASE 6.—Dr. C., aged 57, a friend, had rhinitis and sneezing March 16. He felt hot but did not take his temperature. He continued to work but the next day did not feel well. There were epigastric pain, cough with a small amount of sputum, slight diarrhea and pain. When the temperature rose to 38.3 C. (101 F.) he went to bed. There were headache, anorexia, a disinclination to move and muscle pains "as in influenza." The patient recovered after four days.

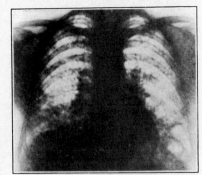

Fig. 10 (case 11).—Appearance on the twenty-first day of illness. There are disseminated nodular areas of density in both lung fields. The shadows in the bases, especially in the right, suggest consolidation.

The symptoms of patients 4, 5 and 6 would generally be regarded as those of a cold and agree with the criteria laid down by Stuart-Harris and his associates[1] for what they call the febrile catarrhs as differentiated from influenza. It would be highly valuable to know whether a single virus caused this "house" epidemic of disease of the respiratory tract, in which patients 3 and 7 had a severe form, and the others had a mild form. The fact that mice inoculated with nasopharyngeal washings from patient 3 and with blood serum from patient 7 seemed to be made ill by a similar filtrable infectious agent lends support to the hypothesis.

Attempts to solve the problem by immunologic methods are under way.

CASE 7.—Mrs. B. (mother), aged 76, noted dryness of the throat and cough about March 16. I saw her March 19, at which time her face was flushed and she appeared to be ill although her temperature was 36.1 C. (97 F.). In the afternoon she became much worse. There was no chill, but the temperature rose to 40.3 C. (104.5 F.) and she was put to bed. She was somnolent and confused, failed to cooperate and was incontinent of feces and urine. She remained at home and was attended by Dr. Burgess Gordon. He found evidence of extensive bronchitis and rales in the base of both lungs. During the next few days high fever persisted, the pulse rate was low and the respiratory rate was 30 per minute, as shown in figure 6. The patient perspired profusely, was cyanotic and coughed but raised no sputum. Pharyngeal exudate was obtained by a swab and inoculated into a mouse. Type IV pneumococci were present. There was constipation, and about the sixth day tympanites, present from the beginning, became severe, tachycardia developed, and the patient appeared to be moribund. She was comatose up to the eight day and confused mentally for a week thereafter. After the eighth day the temperature declined and recovery ensued.

Nasopharyngeal washings were obtained on the fourth and sixth days by Drs. Kinney and Stokes and Magill and Francis, but no virus was obtained. However, blood serum inoculated intracerebrally into white mice by Dr. Francis caused the mice to become ill after twelve or eighteen days. An occasional animal died. The virus apparently died out after the fourth passage.

Patients 8, 9, 10 and 11 were seen in May, June and August and had had no contact with the patients previously described or with any one else with a similar disease. Patient 8 was regarded as having influenza, and in case 9 suspicion of typhoid or psittacosis led to a delay in obtaining nasopharyngeal washings to be examined for a virus until the eighth day.

CASE 8.—Dr. H. C., aged 27, a patient of Dr. George Major of Reading, Pa., had a feeling of malaise, dryness of the throat which developed into a sore throat, hoarseness and cough in the afternoon of May 17. At 9 p. m. a chill occurred, and the temperature then rose to 40 C. (104 F.). The patient had to go to bed, but the next morning there was a remission of symptoms and he resumed his work. He felt fairly well until evening, when fever and malaise returned. For the next few days there were great prostration and weakness and the temperature hovered about 40 C. (104 F.), the pulse rate between 100 and 110, the respiratory rate between 20 and 40 and the leukocyte count between 7,000 and 12,000. The patient was extremely ill, perspired profusely and was greatly distressed by a continuous hacking, unproductive cough. There were photophobia, conjunctival injection and lacrimation. Small amounts of sputum were raised, and numerous cultures of it revealed staphylococci,

Friedländer's bacilli and hemolytic streptococci but no type specific pneumococci. A blood culture was sterile.

I saw the patient on the seventeenth day of illness, at which time there was diffuse pneumonia and restlessness, apprehension, headache, sweating, nasal obstruction, cyanosis, severe dyspnea and cough, which were prominent features. Nasopharyngeal washings were made at this time and sent to Dr. Francis, who inoculated them into ferrets but failed to recover any virus. The blood serum contained no antibodies for the influenza virus.

During the second and third weeks of the illness the temperature declined, but the pulse rate rose to 120 and 130, the respiratory rate to 50 and the leukocyte count to 12,000 and 16,000. The temperature rose again to 38.9 C. (102 F.) on the twenty-second day and followed an irregular course, gradually becoming lower; it remained normal after the forty-first day.

CASE 9.—Miss H. A., aged 38, noted discomfort in the abdomen after a dietary indiscretion June 10. There was no diarrhea or constipation, and the discomfort disappeared after a few days. June 18 she had chilly sensations, and pain developed in both eyes. She was very sleepy June 19 and the ocular pain persisted. June 20 she was awakened by cough, chilliness, pain and soreness under the sternum. The temperature varied between 37.8 C. (100 F.) and 39.4 C. (103 F.). Chilliness recurred several times in the next day or two and was accompanied by sweating, which was perhaps caused partly by the taking of acetylsalicylic acid. Cough was frequent, but no sputum was raised. The patient was admitted to the hospital on the third day of illness.

The voice was slightly hoarse, and the mucous membranes of the eyes, nose and pharynx were reddened. The tongue was heavily coated. No abnormal sounds were heard in the lungs. There was slight abdominal distention. A tender lymph node the size of a hazelnut was palpable under the ramus of the mandible on the right side.

Because of the high fever, relatively slow pulse and leukopenia (4,800 cells), the patient was isolated as presumptively having typhoid.

The chief complaints in the first few days were pain in the eyeballs, photophobia, intense frontal headache and cough. There were hoarseness, congestion of the conjunctival and oral mucous membranes and duskiness of the face. Paroxysms of cough occurred frequently but were not productive. The patient was drowsy at times almost to the point of stupor, apart from the occasional narcosis from codeine given for headache.

No abnormal sounds were heard in the chest until the fourth day, when Dr. Tocantins detected harsh breathing and a few rales in the left infraclavicular region and a few rales in the left scapular region. A roentgenogram made at the bedside revealed a patch of increased density in the periphery of the left lung between the second and fourth ribs, and the left side of the diaphragm was somewhat high, as shown in figure 7. By request a small fleck of sputum was raised; it was raised with difficulty and contained a few indifferent streptococci, Micrococcus catarrhalis and diphtheroids.

When I examined the patient on the seventh day the only abnormal sign I could detect in the chest was diminished breathing in the left scapular area. The patient now had no complaints except headache, photophobia and cough, but she appeared to be gravely ill. On the eighth day a profuse drenching sweat occurred. Rales returned in the left lung, and the inspiratory breath sounds became harsh and sibilant. Sonorous and rasping sounds were heard. Dyspnea was present and cyanosis appeared. A roentgenogram showed that the localized density in the left lung had almost disappeared, but the whole left lung now seemed faintly clouded. The early density may have been caused by atelectasis. By this time it was obvious that the patient did not have typhoid, and the pharyngeal secretions were collected by Dr. Stokes and inocu-

lated into ferrets. A small amount of white creamy sputum raised with difficulty was inoculated intraperitoneally into mice to determine whether the psittacosis virus was present and into guinea pigs to test it for tubercle bacilli. The leukocyte count remained low. On the seventh and eighth days the patient was given a total of 8 Gm. (120 grains) of sulfanilamide. There was no evidence of any effect.

During the next few days the cough was distressing and stupor was present but the patient was lucid on questioning. She lay on her right side to lessen the cough. Cyanosis deepened, and dyspnea was at times distressing. Vomiting occurred several times, there were periods of drenching perspiration, and headache and photophobia persisted. The spleen and liver were not felt. Abdominal distention and constipation were present.

Many rales, suppressed breath sounds and dulness were present in the lower part of the left lung and tympany above; suppressed breath sounds and wheezing were heard in the right side. A roentgenogram made on the tenth day showed a diffused mottling composed of nodular densities in both lung fields (fig. 8).

No unusual events occurred in the following few days except an occasional drenching sweat. Dyspnea and cyanosis persisted and were worse after coughing attacks. No sputum was raised. Oxygen greatly relieved the dyspnea. The temperature, pulse rate, respiratory rate, number of leukocytes and blood pressure during the illness are shown in figure 9. The pulse rate, low in the beginning, rose. The respiratory rate was never rapid. The blood pressure decreased temporarily and then increased. On the seventeenth day friction was palpable and audible in the lower anterior part of the right axillary area, where the patient complained of pain. Evidence of pleuritis disappeared after a few days. Flaring of the alae nasi was noted. In an attempt to get another sample of sputum Dr. Clerf made a laryngoscopic examination. The mucous membranes were found to be markedly congested and covered in places with a thick, white, tenacious exudate. Some of the exudate was obtained, cultured and inoculated into mice. The animals recovered. The leukocyte count rose to 17,000.

The patient improved gradually and the symptoms slowly disappeared, but tachycardia persisted and the tongue was heavily coated. A roentgenogram showed gradual clearing of the density in the lungs. Numerous rales and wheezes persisted. On the twenty-third day another profuse sweat occurred. By the thirtieth day improvement was evident. Many coarse rales were still present in the base of the left lung, but the base of the right lung was almost clear. Tachycardia was present. Bronchoscopic examination by Dr. Clerf revealed inflammation of the whole tracheobronchial tree; it was especially prominent in the lower branch of the left bronchus, which contained thick white exudate. The exudate was again injected into mice. There was a weight loss of 11 Kg. (24 pounds).

When the patient was discharged, forty-three days after the onset of illness, the temperature was normal but the pulse rate hovered between 90 and 110. There were many coarse rales in the lower lobe of the left lung. A roentgenogram showed intensification of the bronchovascular markings, although this was less than before. Density was present in the bases of the lungs, especially in the base of the right lung.

Laboratory Data.—Slight secondary anemia was present. Many stippled erythrocytes were present in the early period. Each examination showed a persistent increase in the proportion of polymorphonuclear cells, the percentage being between 80 and 90. Döhle's bodies were present in the neutrophils. Febrile albuminuria was present. Four blood cultures were sterile. No typhoid bacilli were present in the stool. Agglutinins for B. typhosus, Brucella abortus and Pasteurella tularensis were absent. The sputum was examined and cultured seven times. The usual flora of the nasopharynx were present, streptococci predominating. No tubercle bacilli were found by culture or inoculation of guinea pigs. Psittacosis did not develop in any of the mice inoculated with sputum. The blood serum contained no antibodies against the influenza virus.

*Summary.*—Typhoid with bronchitis was strongly suspected until evidence of pneumonia developed on the fourth day. Psittacosis, tularemic pneumonia and miliary tuberculosis were then suspected until ruled out. A roentgenogram revealed a shadow in the left lung which disappeared a few days later, to be replaced by diffuse shadows in both lungs. Dyspnea, cyanosis, drowsiness, hoarseness, dry cough, abdominal distention, headache, photophobia and pleurisy were prominent symptoms and signs. Visual evidence of laryngitis, tracheitis and bronchitis was obtained. There was a hacking cough and practically no sputum was raised. Pharyngeal washings were obtained on the eighth day of the disease, but no virus was recovered.

CASE 10.—Mrs. T. P., aged 35, a patient of Dr. M. J. Sokoloff, felt tired July 11 and had a shaking chill the next day. Because of fever and malaise she was kept in bed for three days. She improved but on July 15 became worse. There were slight sore throat, conjunctival injection, headache and photophobia. Cough began July 19. It was paroxysmal, dry and racking. Profuse sweats occurred, especially at night. The patient was admitted to the hospital July 21, the tenth day of illness. The temperature was 39.5 C. (103 F.), the pulse rate varied from 100 to 120 and the respiratory rate was about 30 per minute. The tonsils and pharynx were inflamed. There were frequent paroxysms of cough and dyspnea, but no sputum was raised. Cyanosis was present. Signs of atypical pneumonia were present in both lungs. A roentgenogram showed diffuse mottling in both lungs, most dense at the bases. The leukocytes numbered 9,000. Cultures of material obtained from the pharynx showed a mixture of bacteria, chiefly Streptococcus viridans, Micrococcus catarrhalis and gram-negative bacilli. There were no pneumococci. A blood culture was sterile.

The temperature was irregular and gradually declined until the twenty-second day. Cough, cyanosis and sweating persisted, and the patient was gravely ill. Subsequent leukocyte counts varied between 6,000 and 10,000. The temperature rose again on the twenty-third day and followed an irregular course, averaging 37.8 C. (100.4 F.). Dyspnea, cough, sweating and headache were distressing. On the forty-second day the patient became irrational and complained of severe headache, pain and stiffness of the neck. There was occasional vomiting. I saw her at this time. There were photophobia, inflammation of the pharynx and signs of bilateral pneumonia. The reflexes were variable; Kernig's sign, Babinski's sign and ankle clonus could be elicited at times. Encephalitis was suspected, and the spinal fluid was examined. It was under 220 mm. of water pressure and contained 270 cells per cubic millimeter and 74 mg. of protein per hundred cubic centimeters. A portion of it was sent refrigerated to Dr. Francis for inoculation tests. The patient was somewhat relieved after the removal of 10 cc. of spinal fluid, and two days later 10 cc. more was removed. This contained 350 cells per cubic millimeter, 78 per cent of which were polymorphonuclear cells. Neither sample contained bacteria. A portion of the second sample was injected intracerebrally into eight mice and into the footpads of three guinea pigs. No virus was isolated. The spinal fluid when examined again a week later contained 290 cells, 91 per cent of which were polymorphonuclears. The patient's condition was grave, and her state varied between coma and lucidity. The reflexes were variable, the pupils reacted sluggishly to light and slight rigidity of the neck persisted. The temperature rose to 40 C. (104 F.), the pulse rate diminished to 70 or 80 and the respiratory rate was 30 per minute. The patient was incontinent of urine and feces. During the next few days she became worse; strabismus, pupillary dilatation and insomnia were present. The ocular fundi were normal. Death occurred on the fifty-fifth day. Permission for

postmortem examination was not obtained, but a roentgenogram showed a diffuse haziness and fine mottling of both lungs.

The clinical record of the pulmonary infection in this case closely resembles that in the other cases reported, but, as in one of Scadding's cases, death occurred from meningo-encephalitis. Thus the same problem is raised as pertains to the relation of influenza and the encephalitis which occasionally follows it; namely, are the pulmonary and nervous symptoms caused by one agent or by different agents? No virus was recovered from the nasopharyngeal washings or from the spinal fluid.

The following case was studied at the University of Minnesota hospital in 1934, but the report is included here because of its similarity to the cases of 1938:

CASE 11.—A man aged 36 was chilled Oct. 29, 1934. Next day he noted chilly sensations, fever and sweating. On the third day he had a severe chill, sore throat and profuse perspiration, and he went to bed for a day or two. He then returned to work but soon felt chilly and again sought his bed, with a relapse of high fever and generalized aching. He tried to get up but could not because of dyspnea on exertion and severe sharp pain in the left side of the chest. He entered the hospital on the ninth day complaining of difficulty in breathing, sore throat, fever and severe pleuritic pain in the right side. He was slightly cyanotic and had labored breathing and a reddened pharynx. There was slight dulness and a few rales in the lower lobe of the left lung, dulness and bronchial breathing in the base of the right lung and friction sounds in the right axilla. Leukocyte counts varied from 4,000 to 8,000. As the disease progressed there were recurrent attacks of drenching sweats, but there was little or no cough. A few specimens of sputum and material obtained with a swab usually contained bacteria which were predominantly staphylococci. Material aspirated with a needle from the consolidated area of the lung was sterile. The temperature was high, 39.5 C. (103 F.) until the eleventh day, after which it averaged about 38.3 C. (101 F.). It became normal on the twenty-seventh day. The pulse rate varied between 85 and 120 but usually was about 100 per minute. The respiratory rate reached 30 per minute on the twelfth day but was about 22 thereafter in spite of the dyspnea and cyanosis. Blood cultures were sterile. Other serologic tests for typhoid fever, undulant fever and tularemia were negative. A roentgenogram of the patient's chest is shown in figure 10. The tuberculin test was negative during the illness and after recovery. Early in the course of the illness influenza, atypical pneumonia, pulmonary mycotic disease and miliary tuberculosis were suspected. Later in the course, one physician suggested typhoid and bronchitis. The roentgenologist (Dr. L. G. Rigler) made a diagnosis of capillary pneumonia.

The course of the disease was characterized by cyanosis, dyspnea, pain and a sensation of pressure in the chest, especially on exertion, although tachypnea was not prominent. The patient complained of weakness and perspired profusely until the nineteenth day, after which he improved. In a roentgenogram made five months later the shadows shown in figure 10 were present but diminished in density.

In this case there was evidence of early involvement of the upper part of the respiratory tract, soon followed by diffuse patchy bilateral pneumonia with disseminated areas of density and evidences of consolidation in the bases. Severe pleural pain persisted for nearly two weeks. Dyspnea, cyanosis and profuse sweating, but practically no cough or sputum, were prominent features. The leukocytes were not increased in number, and roentgenograms showed slowly resolving bilateral diffuse pneumonia.

## SUMMARY

The strikingly similar clinical features of the cases reported suggest that the condition belongs to a disease group not conforming to influenza or the usual form of the common cold but included in an undifferentiated group of infections of the respiratory tract, often called tracheobronchitis, capillary bronchiolitis or bronchopneumonia.

*Pulmonary Symptoms.*—After several days of mild symptoms of hoarseness and sore throat, the temperature rose in each case, reached high levels, persisted with remissions for the duration of the illness and declined by lysis. In the early period in seven cases the pulse rate was slow in proportion to the fever. The temporary remission of symptoms after the first day or two of illness in cases 1, 3, 6, 8, 9 and 10 suggests that the fever may have been biphasic, a characteristic of many diseases caused by filtrable viruses, but accurate data of the first few days is lacking. The fever curves in cases 2, 7 and 9, observed from the first and second days, were not biphasic. Infection seemed to spread rapidly in some cases and more slowly in others until the trachea, bronchi and eventually the lungs were involved in a diffuse, bilateral process which persisted several weeks and was followed by a residuum which lasted several months. There was involvement of much of the smaller bronchiolar system, as manifested by dyspnea and cyanosis in each case, but evidence of consolidation was never striking. Tachypnea was not prominent. In five cases cough was distressing; it was hacking, paroxysmal or continual, but in no case was more than a slight amount of sputum raised. The respiratory rate was increased somewhat in each case but not to the degree expected from the extent of the pneumonic lesion. Cyanosis and dyspnea were noted in all cases. In cases 2 and 11 cough was minimal in spite of widespread pulmonary invasion. The fact that abnormal signs and roentgenographic shadows persisted so long in some cases suggests that the interstitial tissue was severely injured. Severe pleuritis and friction sounds were present in four of the eight cases of serious involvement, and sterile effusion took place in one.

*Nervous and Other Symptoms.*—Next to the symptoms of tracheobronchitis and pneumonia, sweating and drowsiness were most prominent. Sweating was profuse in six of the cases but not striking in case 3. Headache was present in all, but muscle pains were minimal. Photophobia was distressing in five cases. In cases 3 and 10 nervous symptoms were more severe, with stiffness of the neck, photophobia, intense headache, twitching, somnolence and disturbed reflexes suggestive of meningo-encephalitis, and in case 10 the spinal fluid contained several hundred cells per cubic millimeter.

The only symptoms referable to the gastrointestinal tract were constipation, abdominal distention and a heavily coated tongue, which were present in five cases. Loss of weight was conspicuous in four cases. Early in the course of the disease in several cases constitutional symptoms predominated over those arising from the respiratory tract, as in cases 1, 2 and 9, but later the pneumonia attracted most attention.

The fever lasted from ten to forty-three days in the cases of severe involvement but usually about three weeks. Rales and roentgenographic evidence of pulmonary infiltration persisted in some cases for weeks or months afterward.

The routine laboratory data were not unusual. The urine usually gave evidence of transient febrile nephrosis. Slight secondary anemia developed. The initial leukocyte count was about normal, but initial leukopenia was present in two cases. The count usually increased during the course of the fever. The number of polymorphonuclear cells was usually increased relatively and absolutely. Blood cultures never contained bacteria, and agglutinins for other bacillary diseases were absent.

## THE VIRUS

The failure to isolate a virus in most cases, if one was present, was probably due to the delay before attempts were made or to the weak pathogenicity of the virus for the species of animals which were inoculated. According to British investigators,[1] the probability of obtaining the virus of influenza diminishes rapidly after the third day. These investigators also suggest that when the virus attacks the lungs there is less of it in the upper regions of the respiratory tract.[3] With only two patients of the present series, who had been in close contact, were attempts to obtain a virus made as early as the fourth day of illness. From both patients Dr. Stokes and Dr. Francis obtained an unusual virus, from the nasopharyngeal washings of one and from the blood of the other. It was weakly virulent for mice and caused pneumonia and encephalitis about two weeks after inoculation. It is of interest that a somewhat similar virus was apparently obtained from a series of patients by Francis and Magill.[4] The virus caused meningitis and pneumonitis when inoculated in animals.

Experiments are now under way to determine whether the virus obtained from my patients was (*a*) actually the cause of the disease, (*b*) the cause of encephalitis accompanying an infection of the respiratory tract, (*c*) a commensal unrelated to the disease or (*d*) a virus accidentally encountered in the animals used in the tests. The last possibility is unlikely, since a similar virus was recovered from the same patients by two investigators working in different cities with different lots of animals. The experimental studies will be reported in detail in a later paper.

## DIAGNOSIS

As mentioned, in three of the cases in which the signs of pneumonia were delayed, typhoid with tracheobronchitis was suspected because of the suggestive symptoms, signs and laboratory data. Pulmonary tuberculosis and tularemic pneumonia were suggested in cases 9 and 11, and miliary tuberculosis was suggested in case 10. The clinical descriptions of cases 1, 8, 9 and 11, except for the absence of proof of a biphasic temperature curve, fit well with the clinical description of psittacosis, yet no biologic tests or evidence of contact infection supported this diagnosis. It was more difficult to separate the clinical features from those of influenza or influenzal pneumonia,

---

3. Stuart-Harris and his associates,[1] page 104.

4. Francis, Thomas, and Magill, T. P.: An Unidentified Virus Producing Meningitis and Pneumonitis in Experimental Animals, J. Exper. Med. **68:**147-160 (Aug.) 1938.

which several other physicians believed some of the patients to have, yet it was proved that the virus of influenza was not present. Some of the clinical features were more like those of the "febrile catarrhs" described by British observers[1] than those of influenza, and the task now is to determine whether the disease is one member of the undifferentiated group of febrile catarrhs. It seems likely that the disease as discussed here, particularly in the age group dealt with, represents (a) the severe uncomplicated form of an otherwise mild and commonly encountered infection, (b) the visitation of a special form of virus infection in 1938 or (c) several different infections with clinical characteristics in common.

From London in 1937, Scadding[5] reported under the term disseminated focal pneumonia four cases of an unusual pulmonary infection, two of which were strikingly similar to my case. They were characterized by a gradual onset, malaise, shivering, dyspnea, dry cough, marked sweating, slight leukocytosis and roentgenographic shadows of diffuse pneumonia. The disease lasted three or four weeks, and all patients but one recovered. The patient who died had bulbar encephalitis, which might be significant, considering that there was evidence of encephalitis in two of my patients and that the virus which was recovered from one was pneumonotropic and neurotropic in animals. In Scadding's patient the pulmonary lesion consisted of interstitial inflammation, slight fibrosis of the alveolar walls and edema and hemorrhage in the alveoli, changes which commonly occur with pneumonias caused by filtrable viruses.[6]

5. Scadding, J. G.: Disseminated Focal Pneumonia, Brit. M. J. 2:956-959 (Nov. 13) 1937.

6. Reimann, H. A.: The Pneumonias, Philadelphia, W. B. Saunders Company, 1938, chapter 15.

7. Reimann: The Pneumonias, p. 256.

That it is permissible to group similar diseases together as probable entities on a clinical basis as I have done here has been shown many times in the past. Most of the infectious diseases were delineated long before their causative agents were discovered. The general behavior of the disease in my cases strongly suggests that the infection was caused by a filtrable virus and was not bacterial in origin, as discussed elsewhere.[7] Its similarities to the virus diseases influenza, colds and psittacosis have been mentioned. If the infection described here can eventually be proved to be an etiologic entity, the matter of naming it will arise. To avoid a name too restrictive or too indefinite it would seem best at present to call it a type of infection of the respiratory tract, perhaps type A, or type A virus pneumonia if it can be proved that the virus was the cause.

## CONCLUSION

In a series of eight cases of an unusual, uniform, severe infection of the respiratory tract the disease was not caused by the virus of epidemic influenza or psittacosis, nor was it like other commonly described diseases. I was therefore led to regard it as a separate disease entity pending the outcome of further experimental studies. The infection occurred in adults and began as a mild infection of the respiratory tract; this was followed by severe, diffuse, atypical pneumonia and in two cases by the symptoms of encephalitis. Dyspnea, cyanosis, hoarseness, cough without sputum, drowsiness and profuse sweating were the chief characteristics. The disease lasted several weeks. A filtrable infectious agent recovered from the nasopharynx of one patient and from the blood of another may have been etiologically related to the infection, but the evidence is incomplete. Experiments to clarify this point are under way.

Feb 17, 1984
JAMA 1984;251:945-948)

# The Atypical Pneumonia Syndrome*

Stuart Levin, MD

The 1938 article by Dr H. A. Reimann, a Philadelphia physician from Jefferson Medical College,[1] published in THE JOURNAL, became widely quoted and popularized the term *atypical pneumonia*. Dr Reimann described the presence of a pneumonia syndrome with findings quite different from the lobar consolidation of classic pneumococcal pneumonia and stressed a possible viral etiology. His cases varied from afebrile upper respiratory tract illness to a severe, prolonged pneumonia associated with encephalopathy. Headaches and symptoms of tracheobronchitis often preceded the signs of pneumonia.

Retrospectively, one might question why this article had such a substantial effect in subsequent years. Neither the syndrome nor the name *atypical pneumonia* originated with Dr Reimann. There were many reports from Europe in the early 1920s of an unusual acute pneumonia syndrome of unknown cause. Similar syndromes had been described in army troops, school academies, and colleges in the United States between 1931 and 1936.[2-6] The psittacosis pneumonia pandemic involving many countries in the western world had also been well publicized between 1929 and 1931.[7]

Reimann emphasized the probable viral etiology of the atypical pneumonia syndrome, but the filtrable agent cultured from two of the 11 patients in his original article was never identified and probably was not a true virus. Two different epidemiologic syndromes were included among his 11 patients. Some of his cases were probably *Mycoplasma pneumoniae,* but at least five related cases must have been secondary to a true virus, since the period between the first and the last of these five family-related cases was less than four days. No new management or treatment was suggested, no proved etiologic agent was isolated or classified, and no new diagnostic procedures were described. However, Dr Reimann's publication stimulated significant clinical and laboratory research activity in the ensuing years.

---

From the Section of Infectious Diseases, Department of Internal Medicine and Immunology/Microbiology, Rush Medical College, Chicago.

*A commentary on Reimann HA: An acute infection of the respiratory tract with atypical pneumonia: A disease entity probably caused by a filtrable virus. JAMA 1938;111:2377-2384.

### Historical Setting

In 1900, pneumonia, called by Osler "the captain of the men of death," had been the most common cause of death, annually killing more than 200 people per 100,000 population. By 1940, pneumonia was relegated to third, with approximately 70 deaths per 100,000 population.

At the time Dr Reimann's article was published, pneumonia was classified either descriptively, pathologically, or clinically. Among the common labels were *pneumonitis, abortive, senile, terminal, migratory, lobular, interstitial, capillary, bronchiolitis, contusion, catarrhal, croupous, central, pleural, traumatic, aspiration, silent, terminal, walking, postoperative, alveolitis,* and *adolescent.* Later terms included *viroid* and *nonbacterial.*[8] These terms represent only a small number of the many used to classify pneumonia.

In 1938, the pneumococcus and tuberculous bacillus were the major recognized causes of pneumonia. Common childhood illnesses including measles, chicken pox, pertussis, smallpox, and diphtheria had all been recognized as having a secondary pneumonia, as had the much rarer group of illnesses caused by tularemia, plague, glanders, and anthrax. Reimann differentiated between these rare and potentially fatal pneumonias and the smoldering, subacute, rarely fatal atypical pneumonia syndrome. Psittacosis, Q fever, and lymphocytic choriomeningitis, all considered viral agents at the time, had been proved to be agents of pneumonia. Secondary opportunistic bacterial pneumonia caused by staphylococcus and hemophilus bacteria was also well established. The best-recognized fungal pneumonia was coccidioidomycosis. Pneumonia associated with typhus and Rocky Mountain spotted fever and pneumonia secondary to parasites, such as the lung fluke, *Strongyloides, Ascaris,* and *Amoeba,* were rare but accepted causes of pneumonia in Europe and North America.

### Disputed Terminology— Primary Atypical or Viral Pneumonia

In 1938, an important new concept was the recognition that viruses were important causes of respiratory tract disease. The etiologic agent of human influenza, known to be epidemic in western societies since the 12th century, had been isolated by Smith et al[9] in 1933. Scadding[10,11] and Ramsay[10] then accurately described the roentgenographic and clinical presentations of pneumonia complicating viral influenza. Reimann, using the term *virus* in his article and for many years following, was disturbed that *atypical* had been substituted for *viral* pneumonias by many authors. At that time, many authors had used the label *viral* for all unknown inflammatory syndromes and often compounded this error by substituting *influenza* for *viral* without any supporting data for either. These unfortunate customs have continued up until the present time.

Reimann had also been unhappy with the modifying term *primary*, which had been vigorously adopted by the Commission on Acute Respiratory Diseases.[12,13] However, volunteer studies eventually did prove that *M pneumoniae* was capable of causing a primary pneumonia and did not require special environmental factors or associated infectious agents.[14]

Cole[15] introduced the modifier *atypical* in 1938 to describe all pneumonias that were not classic lobar pneumococcal pneumonia. Although Reimann's article popularized the term *atypical* more than any other article, he disliked this word also and consistently substituted *viral* for *atypical* in subsequent years. According to Reimann, the recognition of viral pneumonia had been delayed because of the high mortality of the well-known bacterial pneumonias, because viral cultures were technically difficult, and because of the lack of appropriate experimental animal models. Accurate pathological description of viral pneumonias was usually obscured by secondary bacterial invasion. Additionally, patients who had mild disease rarely had roentgenograms taken, and physical findings were generally subtle.

The clinical observations of Dr Reimann were immediately confirmed by many others during the next ten years, and there appeared at least 300 English language articles entitled "Atypical or Viral Pneumonia" between the 1938 *JAMA* article and his review in 1947.[16]

### The Next 20 Years

By 1943, several authors had demonstrated cold agglutinins as well as the less common and less helpful streptococcal MG antibody in the serum of some patients with atypical pneumonia.[17,18] These serological tests allowed randomized therapeutic studies with various antibiotics by limiting the study cases to those with positive cold agglutinins. Since each study had a different but unknown ratio of true viral pneumonias to *Mycoplasma* pneumonias, antibiotic responses varied correspondingly and the efficacy of antibiotics like tetracycline remained controversial.[19,20]

In the early 1940s, Eaton and co-workers[21] demonstrated that the sputum from some patients with primary atypical pneumonia could be transmitted and propagated in embryonated eggs. The isolated agent, called "the Eaton agent," could produce pneumonia in cotton rats, and the agent could be neutralized by the convalescent serum of patients recently recovering from primary atypical pneumonia. Unfortunately, contaminating orga-

nisms were often present in experimental animals, the serological techniques were complex, cumbersome, and time consuming, and there was an acknowledged lack of specificity to the cold agglutinin test. These factors led to an inability of other investigators to confirm Eaton's work; thus, the Eaton agent remained a suspected but controversial cause of atypical pneumonia for 20 years.

In 1957, Liu,[22] using an immunofluorescent antibody technique, demonstrated the Eaton agent in the bronchial epithelium of the chick embryo system. In 1959, Marmion and Goodburn[23] found that the Eaton agent was related to pleuropneumonialike organisms (PPLOs) first isolated in 1898 as the cause of epidemic pleural pneumonia of cattle.[23] Stimulated by the studies of Eaton and the Commission on Acute Respiratory Diseases and the suggestions of Marmion and Goodburn, Chanock and colleagues at the National Institutes of Health rapidly showed that the Eaton agent could be grown on cell-free media similar to those used for PPLOs[24] and eventually demonstrated the efficacy of tetracycline therapy.

### The Mycoplasmas

At the time Reimann described the atypical pneumonia syndrome, the mycoplasmas were considered bacteriologic curiosities. Mycoplasma bacteria at 150 to 300 m$\mu$m are smaller than some viruses and are the smallest of free-living organisms. The absence of a cell wall and the presence of a triple-layered unit membrane and a dependence on sterol or cholesterol in the culture media differentiate these organisms from all other bacteria. (A few species of treponemes are the only other known bacteria with a requirement for sterol in the culture media.) Unlike L-forms of walled bacteria, mycoplasma are incapable of reverting to a walled form.[25] The order Mycoplasmatales includes mycoplasma, acholeplasma, spiroplasma, and mycoplasmalike organisms. These tiny bacteria are truly ubiquitous and have been found to colonize or cause disease in humans, birds, insects, and plants, and, as with other prokaryocytes, they themselves are infected with virus agents.[26]

A dozen species of mycoplasma have been isolated from man, but only three have definitely been established as pathogens — *M pneumoniae, Mycoplasma hominis,* and *Ureaplasma urealyticum.* The most commonly invaded organs are the respiratory tree and the urogenital tract. Whether in animals or humans, the entire field of mycoplasmology remains plagued with controversy concerning the etiologic importance of an isolated mycoplasma and its relationship to the particular disease entity being studied. At the present time, examples of this problem include the disputed association of *U urealyticum* with infertility and urethritis and the possible association of *M hominis* with pelvic inflammatory disease, postpartum fever, and pyelonephritis.

### Clinical Disease

*Mycoplasma pneumoniae* causes 20% of all adult pneumonias and more than 50% of all clinically evident pneumonias in such populations as college students and army recruits. Only 3% to 10% of patients newly infected with this organism will display any signs of pneumonia, while in the rest of the symptomatic patients, pharyngitis and tracheobronchitis predominate. The incubation period is approximately seven to 14 days. The disease can be sporadic or epidemic, is not limited to any particular season, and is most common in children and young adults. Intimate contact is usually necessary for organisms to spread from one person to another. Systemic symptoms clear in one to two weeks, cough clears in two to four weeks, but radiological abnormalities may not disappear until one or two months have passed. Small pleural effusions are common, but large effusions are rare. Less common pulmonary complications include pneumatoceles, lung abscesses, hypoxemia, the Swyer-James syndrome, necrotizing pneumonia, and exacerbations of chronic obstructive lung disease.[27] Patients with sickle cell disease or agammaglobulinemia are predisposed to serious complications, including death.[28,29] Immunity to reinfection is often short lived, and cases of repeated infections have been well documented.[30,31]

### The Present Situation

Despite the many advances in diagnostic medicine since 1938, the atypical pneumonia syndrome continues to be a clinical problem for the practicing physician. When a patient is initially seen, sensitive and specific methods are not yet available to differentiate immediately M pneumoniae from other treatable atypical pneumonia syndromes such as psittacosis, Q fever, and Legionella pneumophila, nor do we have methods to differentiate any of these illnesses from the untreatable viral causes of pneumonia. Cultures of M pneumoniae require several weeks to become positive in the few centers with such means of identification. Mycoplasma pneumoniae and L pneumophila are the important causes of pneumonia in which the sputum demonstrates many polymorphonuclear leukocytes but few bacteria. However, there are no means of directly identifying M pneumoniae in the sputum sample. Cold agglutinins develop in only half of patients with pneumonia caused by M pneumoniae, and they appear late in many cases. Diagnostic fourfold or greater antibody rises to specific mycoplasma antigens require two to four weeks and, therefore, are useful only retrospectively. Serological methods, therefore, play only a minor role in the diagnosis of atypical pneumonia at the time therapy is instituted. The clinician still remains dependent on trials of therapy with erythromycin or tetracycline. Erythromycin may be preferable, since it is active against other kinds of atypical pneumonia, including Chlamydia psittaci, Streptococcus pneumoniae, and L pneumophila. Similar to the history of disease caused by M pneumoniae, L pneumophila infections had gone unrecognized for many years, and the agent had been isolated long before its pathogenicity had been established.[32,33]

### Complications

As described by Reimann, CNS syndromes are present in about 5% of patients hospitalized with M pneumoniae pneumonia and include encephalitis, meningitis, cerebellar ataxia, poliomyelitis, facial neuropathy, and cerebral infarction. The presence of M pneumoniae has been identified in the spinal fluid of two patients with a polyneuronitis syndrome associated with an otherwise classic M pneumoniae pneumonia.[34] Other common complications of M pneumoniae include cold agglutinin-induced hemolytic anemia and rashes that range from macular, papular, and vesicular to erythema multiforme and Stevens-Johnson syndrome.[35,36] While the combination of pneumonia and dermatitis has been described with several viruses, including measles and chicken pox, the association of pneumonia with a rash strongly suggests the possibility of M pneumoniae.

Other less commonly reported complications include myocarditis, pericarditis, gastroenteritis, myositis, polyarthritis, and interstitial nephritis.[37-39] Since mycoplasma is a common infectious agent, it is obvious that many clinical syndromes could coincidentally, but incorrectly, be associated with the organism. One good example of this is bullous otitis media, which has long been related to M pneumoniae infections since the early human volunteer studies of the 1960s.[40] However, bullous otitis media seems to be simply otitis media with blisters on the tympanic membrane and is rarely found in naturally occurring M pneumoniae infections.[41]

### Current Areas of Research

The transient immunity of M pneumoniae has been one of the factors that has so far frustrated an effective vaccine, but research continues in this area. The relationship of mycoplasma to chronic rheumatic diseases in man and animals is another area of intense investigation. Current investigators have attempted to elucidate the mechanism of prolonged mucosal surface colonization and the characteristics of membrane adherence. Mycoplasma organisms can have either an immunosuppressive or immunostimulant effect in various experimental animals. The recently described mutagenic properties of these organisms may be related to their ability to attach to lymphocytic surfaces.

### Postscript

It is understandable that new clinical observations do not usually gain the same recognition that important laboratory discoveries receive. Dr Reimann had been a well-known clinician in the Philadelphia area and among his many published contributions were three books titled Pneumonias published in 1938, 1954, and 1971. Dr Reimann crystallized the perception of the medical community concerning a common disease seen by many but recognized by few. The plethora of publications that immediately followed and cited his 1938 article attest to its importance and also accentuate the continuing importance of accurate and perceptive clinical observation and description.

Gordon M. Trenholme and Peter H. Karakusis provided critical review of the article; Debra Pearson and Sandra Blanch provided secretarial and other assistance.

### References

1. Reimann HA: An acute infection of the respiratory tract with atypical pneumonia: A disease entity probably caused by a filtrable virus. JAMA 1938;111:2377-2384.
2. Gallagher JR: Bronchopneumonia in adolescence. Yale J Biol Med 1934;7:23-40.
3. Bowen A: Acute Pulmonary Infections, DeLamer Lectures. Balti-

more, Williams & Wilkins Co, 1927-1928.

4. Cass JW: Question of 'influenza' and atypical pneumonia. *N Engl J Med* 1936;214:187-193.

5. Allen WH: Acute pneumonitis. *Ann Intern Med* 1936;10:441-446.

6. Scadding JG: Disseminated focal pneumonia. *Br Med J* 1937;2:956-959.

7. Bedson SP, Western GT, Simpson L: Observations on the outbreak of psittacosis. *Lancet* 1930;1:235.

8. Reimann HA: *The Pneumonias.* Philadelphia, WB Saunders Co, 1938, p 381.

9. Smith W, Andrewes CH, Laidlaw PP: A virus obtained from influenza patients. *Lancet* 1933;2:66-68.

10. Ramsay H, Scadding JG: Benign broncho-pulmonary inflammations associated with transient radiographic shadows. *Q J Med* 1939;8:79-95.

11. Scadding JG: Lung changes in influenza. *Q J Med* 1937;6:425-465.

12. Primary atypical pneumonias: Etiology unknown — official statement. *War Med* 1942;2:330-333.

13. Commission of Acute Respiratory Diseases: The transmission of primary atypical pneumonia to human volunteers. *Bull Johns Hopkins Hosp* 1946;79:109-124.

14. Chanock RM, Rifkind D, Kravetz HM, et al: Respiratory disease in volunteers infected with Eaton agent: A preliminary report. *Pathology* 1901;47:887-890.

15. Cole RI: *Acute Pulmonary Infections,* DeLamer Lectures. Baltimore, Williams & Wilkins Co, 1927-1928.

16. Reimann HA: The viral pneumonias and pneumonias of probable viral origin. *Medicine* 1947;26:167-219.

17. Peterson OL, Ham TH, Finland M: Cold agglutinins (autohemagglutinins) in primary atypical pneumonias. *Science* 1943;97:167.

18. Thomas L, Mirick GS, Curnen EC, et al: Serological reactions with an indifferent streptococcus in primary atypical pneumonia. *Science* 1943;98:566-568.

19. Meiklejohn G, Shragg RI: Aureomycin in primary atypical pneumonia: A controlled evaluation. *JAMA* 1949;140:391-396.

20. Walker SH: Ineffectiveness of aureomycin in primary atypical pneumonia. *Am J Med* 1953;14:593-602.

21. Eaton MD, Meiklejohn G, Van Herick W: Studies on the etiology of primary atypical pneumonia: A filterable agent transmissible to cotton rats, hamsters, and chick embryos. *J Exp Med* 1944;79:649-667.

22. Liu C: Studies on primary atypical pneumonia: Localization, isolation, and cultivation of a virus in chick embryos. *J Exp Med* 1957;104:455-466.

23. Marmion BP, Goodburn GM: Effect of an organic gold salt in Eaton's primary atypical pneumonia agent and other observations.

*Nature* 1961;189:247-248.

24. Chanock RM, Hayflick L, Barile MF: Growth on artificial medium of an agent associated with atypical pneumonia and its identification a a PPLO. *Proc Natl Acad Sci USA* 1962;48:41-49.

25. Cassell GH, Cole BC: Mycoplasmas as agents of human disease *N Engl J Med* 1981;304:80-89.

26. Cassell GH: The pathogenic potential of mycoplasmas: Myco plasma pneumonias as a model. *Rev Infect Dis* 1982;45:18-33.

27. Westerberg SC, Smith CB, Renzetti AD: Mycoplasma infection in patients with chronic obstructive pulmonary disease. *J Infect Di* 1973;27:491-496.

28. Noriega ER, Simberkoff MS, Gilroy FJ, et al: Life-threatening *Mycoplasma pneumoniae* pneumonia. *JAMA* 1974;229:1471-1472.

29. Foy HM, Ochs H, Davis SD, et al: *Mycoplasma pneumoniae* infections in patients with immunodeficiency syndrome — report of fou cases. *J Infect Dis* 1973;127:388-393.

30. Broome CV, LaVenture M, Kaye HS, et al: An explosive outbreak of *Mycoplasma pneumoniae* infection in a summer camp. *Pediatric* 1980;66:884-888.

31. Foy HM, Kenny GE, Seft R, et al: Second attacks of pneumonia due to *Mycoplasma pneumoniae. J Infect Dis* 1977;135:673-677.

32. McDade JE, Brenner DJ, Bozeman FM: Legionnaire's disease bacterium isolated in 1947. *Ann Intern Med* 1979;90:659-661.

33. Thachter SB, Bennett JV, Tsai TF, et al: An outbreak in 1965 o severe respiratory illness caused by the Legionnaire's disease bacteri um. *J Infect Dis* 1978;138:512-519.

34. Bayer AS, Galpin JE, Theofilopoulos AN, et al: Neurologic diseas associated with *Mycoplasma pneumoniae* pneumonitis. *Ann Intern Med* 1981;94:15-20.

35. Lindstrom FD, Stahl-Furenhed B: Autoimmune haemolytic anaemia complicating *Mycoplasma pneumoniae* infection. *Scand Infect Dis* 1981;13:233-235.

36. Cherry JD, Hurwitz ES, Welliver RC: Mycoplasma *pneumonia* infections and exanthems. *J Pediatr* 1975;87:369-373.

37. Sands MJ, Satz JE, Turner WE, et al: Pericarditis and perimyocar ditis associated with active *Mycoplasma pneumoniae* infection. *An Intern Med* 1977;86:544-548.

38. Pasternack A, Helin H, Vanttinen T, et al: Acute tubulointerstitia nephritis in a patient with *Mycoplasma pneumoniae* infection. *Scand Infect Dis* 1979;11:85-87.

39. Hernandez LA, Urquhart GED, Dick WC: *Mycoplasma pneumo niae* and arthritis in a man. *Br Med J* 1977;2:14-16.

40. Rifkind D, Chanock R, Kravetz H, et al: Ear involvemen (myringitis) and primary atypical pneumonia following inoculation o volunteers with Eaton agent. *Am Rev Respir Dis* 1962;85:479-489.

41. Roberts DB: The etiology of bullous myringitis and the role o mycoplasmas in ear disease: A review. *Pediatrics* 1980;65:761-766.

Feb 25, 1939
(*JAMA* 1939;112:729-731)

## Chapter 31

# Surgical Ligation of a Patent Ductus Arteriosus

## Report of First Successful Case

Robert E. Gross, M.D.

and

John P. Hubbard, M.D.

Boston

The continued patency of a ductus arteriosus for more than the first few years of life has long been known to be a potential source of danger to a patient for two reasons: First, the additional work of the left ventricle in maintaining the peripheral blood pressure in the presence of a large arteriovenous communication may lead eventually to cardiac decompensation of severe degree. Second, the presence of a patent ductus arteriosus makes the possessor peculiarly subject to fatal bacterial endarteritis. While it is true that some persons have been known to live to old age with a patent ductus of Botalli, statistics have shown that the majority die relatively young because of complications arising from this congenital abnormality. Dr. Maude Abbott[1] presented a series of ninety-two cases which came to autopsy in which it was shown that the patient had had a patent ductus arteriosus without any other cardiovascular abnormality. Of these patients, approximately one fourth died of bacterial endarteritis of the pulmonary artery and an additional one half died of slow or rapid cardiac decompensation. The average age of death of patients in this series was 24 years.

The complications arising from the persistence of a patent ductus arteriosus would seem to make surgical ligation of this anomalous vessel a rational procedure, if such a procedure could be completed with promise of a low operative mortality. Dramatic results have previously been obtained in persons with cardiac enlargement and decompensation resulting from a peripheral arteriovenous aneurysm when the short-circuiting vessels have been ligated or excised.[2] On similar theoretical grounds, future cardiac embarrassment should be averted if a shunt between the aorta and the pulmonary artery could be removed. It would also seem plausible to expect that the shutting off of the anomalous stream of blood pouring into the pulmonary artery would lessen the formation of the thickened endothelial plaques within the pulmonary artery, which are so likely to be the seat of later bacterial infection. The surgical approach to the aortic arch and pulmonary conus having been studied previously in animal experimentation,[3] it seemed within reason that a patent ductus could be adequately exposed in man and possibly ligated without undue danger. It was therefore decided to undertake the operation in a child who presented the classic signs of a patent ductus arteriosus. At the age of 7 years she already had cardiac hypertrophy, which developed presumably from the embarrassment resulting from the anomalous communication. It was to be expected, therefore, that she would have increasingly severe disability in the future, aside from the danger of having bacterial endarteritis develop.

From the Surgical and Medical Services of the Children's Hospital and the Departments of Surgery and Pediatrics of the Harvard Medical School.

1. Abbott, Maude E.: Atlas of Congenital Heart Disease, New York, American Heart Association, 1936, pp. 60-61.

2. Holman, Emile: Arteriovenous Aneurysm, New York, Macmillan Company, 1937, pp. 169-178.

3. Gross, R. E.: A Surgical Approach for Ligation of a Patent Ductus Arteriosus, New England J. Med., to be published.

## REPORT OF CASE

*History.*—L. S., a girl aged 7½ years, entered the hospital Aug. 17, 1938, for study of her cardiac condition. The family history was irrelevant. She was born normally at full term. No cyanosis was noted at birth or during the postnatal period. The records of the hospital where she was born give no information about an examination of the heart at that time. At the age of 3 years she was seen in the cardiac clinic of another hospital, where it was found that she had physical signs suggesting congenital malformation of the heart. At this time she had a precordial thrill and a loud murmur. The carotid pulsations were abnormally marked, and pistol shot sounds could be heard over the brachial and femoral arteries. The blood pressure was recorded in both arms as 104 mm. of mercury systolic and 0 diastolic. There was definite cardiac enlargement, as shown by

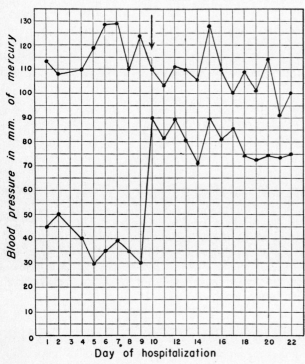

Daily blood pressure readings of the patient with a patent ductus arteriosus before and after operation. Prior to operation the large ductus opening from the aorta produced a low diastolic pressure. Following operative closure of the ductus, the diastolic pressure rose to twice its former level. The average daily diastolic pressure preoperatively was 38 mm. of mercury. The average diastolic pressure postoperatively was 80 mm. of mercury. The arrow points to the time of operation.

teleoroentgenograms. The diagnosis made at that time was "congenital malformation of the heart with a patent ductus arteriosus."

During the next four years she was seen in several different hospitals, where the same diagnosis was made. At no time had cyanosis been observed. Dyspnea developed after moderate exercise, and her physical activities had been limited accordingly. She had never had peripheral edema or other evidence of cardiac decompensation. Frequently the child had been conscious of "something wrong in the chest" and her mother spontaneously offered the information that she had heard a "buzzing noise" in her daughter's chest when standing nearby.

*Physical Examination.*—At the time of admission, the patient was slender and undernourished. The pulsations of the carotid arteries were abnormally forceful. The radial pulse was of the Corrigan type, and a capillary pulsation was readily seen. The veins over the chest were somewhat prominent. There was a precordial bulge. The heart was definitely enlarged by percussion, the enlargement being for the most part to the left. Over the entire precordium there was a prominent coarse thrill which was most intense in the third interspace to the left of the sternum. This thrill was continuous but was accentuated during systole. There was a rough "machinery" murmur heard with maximal intensity over the pulmonic area to the left of the sternum in the second and particularly in the third interspace. It was continuous throughout the cardiac cycle but like the thrill was greatly accentuated during systole. It was transmitted to the left along the third interspace and into the axilla with only slightly diminished intensity. The systolic element was heard faintly over the vessels of the neck and could be heard clearly in the right axilla and over the midthoracic region posteriorly. Blood pressure readings were respectively right arm 115/40, left arm 110/50, right leg 150/55, left leg 140/40 mm. of mercury. There was no clubbing of the fingers and no evidence of peripheral edema. The liver edge was palpable at the costal margin. The examination in other respects was negative.

*Laboratory Data.*—A 7-foot x-ray film of the chest showed the transverse diameter of the heart to be 11.7 cm., compared to an internal diameter of the chest of 20 cm. There appeared to be definite enlargement of the left ventricle. There was questionable prominence of the pulmonary artery. A mottled increased density around the lung hili was interpreted as representing circulatory congestion. Fluoroscopic examination showed a "hilar dance." An electrocardiogram was normal, showing no deviation of the axis. The red blood count was 5,080,000 cells per cubic millimeter and the hemoglobin was 85 per cent (Sahli). Circulation time with dehydrocholic acid was 10 and 8 seconds, respectively, on two tests.

*Operation.*—August 26, operation was undertaken (by R. E. G.) under cyclopropane anesthesia. The approach to the mediastinum was made through the left pleural cavity antero-laterally. Incision was made through the left third interspace, cutting the third costal cartilage, and the third rib was retracted upward. As the left lung was allowed to collapse inferiorly, an excellent view was gained of the lateral aspect of the mediastinum. The parietal pleura covering the aortic arch and left pulmonic artery was then incised and these structures were directly exposed. A large patent ductus arteriosus was found, which was from 7 to 8 mm. in diameter and from 5 to 6 mm. in length. A palpating finger placed on the heart disclosed a continuous and very vibrant thrill over the entire organ, which was increasingly prominent as the finger reached up over the pulmonic artery. A sterile stethoscope was employed and an extremely loud continuous murmur was heard over the entire heart. When the stethoscope was placed on the pulmonary artery there was an almost deafening, continuous roar, sounding much like a large volume of steam escaping in a closed room.

A number 8 braided silk tie was placed around the ductus with an aneurysm needle, and the vessel was temporarily occluded for a three minute observation period. During this time the blood pressure rose from 110/35 to 125/90. Since there was no embarrassment of the circulation, it was decided to ligate the ductus permanently. The ductus was too short to tie double and divide, so that ligation alone was resorted to. When the thread was drawn up tight the thrill completely disappeared. The chest was closed, the lung being reexpanded with positive pressure anesthesia just prior to placing the last stitch in the intercostal muscles.

*Postoperative Course.*—The child underwent the operative

procedure exceedingly well and showed no signs of shock. Prior to operation blood had been taken from a donor in order to have it ready whenever needed, but the patient's condition was so good that it was not given. There was only mild discomfort in the afternoon of the day of operation, and on the following morning the child was allowed to sit up in a chair. By the third day she was walking about the ward. When the skin sutures were removed on the seventh day the wound was well healed, but because of the interest in the case the child was detained in the hospital until the thirteenth day. After the dressing was removed and the chest could be examined adequately the thrill had completely disappeared, there was a faint systolic murmur in the left third interspace which was not transmitted over the precordium, and no murmur could be heard in the axilla, in the neck or over the back. The daily blood pressures which had been taken prior to operation and subsequent thereto showed a striking change in the diastolic levels, as is shown by the accompanying chart. The average of the daily pressures prior to operation had been 114 systolic and 38 diastolic as contrasted with a postoperative daily average of 108 systolic and 80 diastolic.

## SUMMARY

A girl aged 7½ years had a known patency of the ductus arteriosus and beginning cardiac hypertrophy. In the hope of preventing subsequent bacterial endarteritis and with the immediate purpose of reducing the work of the heart caused by the shunt between the aorta and the pulmonary artery, the patent ductus was surgically explored and ligated. The child stood the operative procedure exceedingly well. The most objective finding, which indicated that the serious loss of blood from the aorta into the pulmonic artery had been arrested by operation, was a comparison of the preoperative and postoperative levels of the diastolic blood pressure. Prior to operation the daily blood pressure showed an average diastolic level of 38 mm. of mercury as compared with a postoperative diastolic level of 80 mm. of mercury. This is the first patient in whom a patent ductus arteriosus has been successfully ligated.

March 2, 1984
(*JAMA* 1984;251:1203-1207)

# Patent Ductus Arteriosus*

## The First Successful Ligation

Richard Warren, MD

### THE PROFESSIONAL SETTING

August 1938! Few physicians of today can be fully aware of the forces at play on a surgeon contemplating a new procedure in that year. Even those of us still alive who were active then find it difficult to recreate the setting. I will try to recall some conditions and events.

#### Anesthesia

Intratracheal positive pressure anesthesia had developed to formal acceptance only six years before as the safest way to facilitate intrathoracic procedures. The story of the emergence of that technique paralleled and controlled that of intrathoracic surgery. Rehn's[1] semielective repair of a 1.5-cm stab wound of the right ventricle in 1896, usually cited as the first successful operation on the heart, had been done rapidly while the patient was under ether without positive pressure. The left lung collapsed but the patient survived, the lung presumably expanding satisfactorily postoperatively. A few emergency intrathoracic procedures, such as heart wounds and pulmonary embolectomies, had been successful subsequently, success depending on speed of operation and aspiration of pleural air at the end.

The world's first successful mitral valvotomy, performed by Cutler[2] in 1923, had been via the transventricular approach under intratracheal nasopharyngeal catheter insufflation without provision for positive pressure. A significant part of the recommended technique was the anterior approach, which avoided entering the pleural cavities. The same was true of the early pericardiectomies performed by Churchill[3] in 1929..

The intratracheal tube had been used intermittently in operative procedures since the late 19th century, but more attention had been paid to its role in protecting the airway from blood and secretions during operations on the face and neck than to its use in preventing pulmonary collapse. It was not until the late 1920s that

the demands of surgeons to keep the lung expanded in the open chest forced fast progress in the field. These resulted in the first successful pneumonectomy by Graham and Singer[4] (see Chapter 24) and the four lobectomies by Churchill,[5] both for cancer in 1933.

Souttar[6] in England had been ahead of his time in the use of intratracheal positive pressure anesthesia in 1925 to perform the modern approach to the mitral valve through the left atrium. The 19-year-old patient turned out to have predominant mitral insufficiency, and although she recovered well, the affair was subjected to considerable obloquy. Perhaps that is why the success of this method of anesthesia was brushed aside for years.

#### Preoperative and Postoperative Care

**Blood Replacement.** — The modern era of blood transfusion involving the adequate supplies made possible by blood banking had hardly arrived by 1938. First reports of experience with banks by municipal hospitals (Cook County and Philadelphia General) were just appearing (Fantus,[7] 1937 [see Chapter 28]; Cameron and Ferguson,[8] 1939). This movement was just in time to save the lives of many soldiers in World War II (1939 to 1945).

**Aids to Cardiovascular Diagnosis.** — In 1938, these consisted of the physical examination of the patient, the roentgenogram of the heart and chest, and the ECG. Cardiac catheterization and noninvasive testing were yet to come.

**Postoperative Ambulation.** — In 1938, early ambulation after surgery was still considered a threat to the recently sutured wound. Young men were kept in bed for ten days after simple herniorrhaphy. The policy was even carried into military hospitals during 1939 to 1945. It was only after the war, during which the lessons were provided by the many inevitable exceptions to the policy, that it was abandoned.

**Infection.** — Postoperative pulmonary atelectasis and pneumonitis were common. A rise in temperature on the second and third day was both expected and dreaded. The first effective antibacterial agent, Prontosil (sulfanilamide), was introduced by Domagk[9] in 1935 (see

---

Dr Warren retired from practice, Dedham, Mass.

*A commentary on Gross RE, Hubbard JP: Surgical ligation of a patent ductus arteriosus. *JAMA* 1939;112:729-731.

Chapter 27), but it was not until 1940 that Chain and colleagues[10] applied Fleming's[11] 1929 discovery of penicillin to clinical use. As an example of the hazard from infection posed by surgery, the mortality following simple suture of a perforated peptic ulcer in the late 1930s was 25%. This, as shown by Ulfelder and Allen,[12] was caused primarily by pulmonary infection, not by peritonitis, but as they reported, the advent of the sulfonamides had by 1940 caused a precipitous drop to almost 10%.

**Thromboembolic Disease.** — The decade of the 1930s saw the introduction of the anticoagulants. In 1933, Charles and Scott[13] purified heparin, which had been discovered by McLean[14] in Howell's laboratory at Johns Hopkins Medical School in 1916, and in 1938, Best[15] was first beginning to apply it clinically.

An agent causing hypoprothrombinemia in cattle who ate sweet clover hay was detected by Roderick[16] in 1931 and finally isolated in 1941 by Campbell and Link.[17] By 1938, now known as coumadin, it had not yet been used as an anticoagulant except to poison rats.

The surgical treatment of massive pulmonary embolism by embolectomy had been performed first successfully by Kirschner[18] in 1924. Several successful instances followed in Europe, but as of 1938 none had in the United States. The advent of the clinical use of heparin and its hopeful application to this condition had greatly reduced the attempted number of embolectomies. The story behind the urge of surgeons to make these attempts is important, since it was the desire to bypass the obstructed pulmonary circulation that launched Gibbon[19] on his magnum opus of developing a technique of extracorporeal circulation. This was first successful in animals in 1937 but was not applied to humans until 15 years later, the emphasis for indication now having shifted to intracardiac work (vide infra).

**Fluid and Electrolyte Therapy.** — Knowledge of the disturbances of water and electrolytes in sick children with intestinal obstruction or diarrheal diseases had been accumulating over a 15-year period, much of it contributed by workers at the Children's Hospital of Boston. McIver and Gamble[20] (1928) perceived the water and electrolyte losses resulting from upper intestinal tract obstruction, on which Hartwell and Hoguet[21] had made preliminary observations in the experimental animal as early as 1906. In the early 1930s, Butler and co-workers[22] observed the loss of intracellular water in diarrheal diseases of children in addition to the well-documented (by that time) changes in extracellular water. In 1933, Coller and Maddock[23] had drawn the attention of surgeons to the water requirements attendant on a surgical operation. By 1936,[24] they had begun to outline the maintenance requirements in the surgical patient to be given by the intravenous route, one that was still being approached cautiously because of pyrogenic reactions from the equipment then available. In 1938, the solutions were still prepared in large glass flagons in the hospital supply or operating rooms. The large volumes necessary for the patient with burns were understood after the observations of Underhill and colleagues[25] in 1923, but the identification of the extracellular space as the major site of the fluid loss rather than the exterior via the wound surface had to await the observations of Cope, Graham, and Moore[26,27] (1947 and 1948) after WW II.

**Postoperative Ileus.** — That many patients still suffered this serious complication in the 1930s resulted from the novelty of the nasogastric tube as a preventative. Wangensteen[28] (1933) had demonstrated its effectiveness in recognized intestinal obstruction. Its wider application as a precaution in postoperative patients had not been appreciated, however, and a dynamic ileus subtly, or not so subtly, often abetted pulmonary complications, or even acute dilatation of the stomach with its danger of cataclysmic aspiration of gastric contents.

### PATENT DUCTUS ARTERIOSUS BEFORE AND ON AUG 26, 1938

Surgeons and cardiologists had for some years felt the urge to ligate the patent ductus. The anatomy and pathophysiology were well known. Munro[29] in 1907 wrote that he had for a long time been attempting to interest pediatric specialists in a surgical approach to such a ligation, which he in many autopsy subjects had demonstrated to be possible via a sternal splitting route. "In view of the recent advances in cardiac surgery," he decided to publish his thoughts from experiences with cadavers. The mission to convince pediatric specialists seemed then to have been abandoned possibly because the "advances" had not been as dramatic as Munro suggested. Holman[30] in 1937 wrote that "ever since the suggestion was made in 1907 by John Munro that the patent ductus might be ligated to the benefit of the patient, surgeons have talked hopefully of performing this operation." He warned that "before undertaking such a procedure absolute certainty must be established that no other defects exist." Abbott[31] (1915) advised caution, thinking that circulatory alterations, such as dilatation of the pulmonary artery, that had taken place by the time the distinctive signs appear would be irreversible and ligation "would only introduce a new factor of disturbance."

The first serious attempt at closure was reported in 1938 by Graybiel and colleagues.[32] It was considered an urgent procedure to control the bacterial endarteritis in a 22-year-old woman. The ductus was plicated and the murmur reduced but not obliterated; the patient convalesced reasonably well for four days and then died of "acute gastric dilation." The report of the autopsy was uninformative concerning the completeness of the ligation.

It is diverting to reconstruct the events leading up to the first successful operation. Robert Gross was 33 years old. He had graduated from Harvard Medical School in 1931 and had done his surgical internship at the Children's Hospital in Boston from 1931 to 1933 under Dr William E. Ladd. After that, he took three years of training in pathology, first at the Children's Hospital under Sidney Farber and then under Dr Burt Wolbach at the Peter Bent Brigham Hospital. In 1938, he was chief resident surgeon at the Children's Hospital and had just occupied, in addition, the position of chief resident surgeon at the Peter Bent Brigham Hospital. John Hubbard was 35, a classmate of Gross at medical school, and took his internship in pediatrics at the Children's Hospital in Boston under Kenneth Blackfan. Then, entering pediatric practice as a junior member of the staff of the hospital with a particular interest in cardiology, he became consultant in pediatric cardiology, for which, in those days, there existed no separate department or division.

Hubbard (written communication, 1983) remembers that early in 1938 he was called into consultation by Gross about a child with an acute abdominal condition who showed signs of an incidental patent ductus arteriosus. Having given his blessing to the surgical procedure, he made what he admits was a purposely provocative comment to his surgical colleague: "While you are in the belly why don't you reach up and tie the ductus?" This anecdote undoubtedly had a bearing on subsequent events, and Gross[33] remembers Hubbard's persuading him several times to visit the cardiology clinic to begin thinking about what could be done surgically for some of the patients there. Gross then, with characteristic thoroughness, began to work out in the animal laboratory and autopsy room the technical aspects of a feasible procedure through a left transpleural approach. These details having been completed to his satisfaction and the summer vacation period having arrived, when he felt he would have an unobstructed surgical authority to proceed, he told Hubbard that things were ready. Hubbard began to discuss it with the parents of several suitable patients who were recurrent visitors to the outpatient department. When the parents of one child gave consent, the proposition was taken to the chief of pediatrics.

Dr Blackfan, not being a cardiologist, believed himself unqualified to pass on the decision with final authority and suggested consultation with Dr Paul D. White at the Massachusetts General Hospital. The 7-year-old girl was taken there, and, as Dr Hubbard remembers it, Dr White spoke somewhat as follows: "A brave procedure, and obviously one that has been carefully considered. In my opinion it should proceed as planned."

Dr Gross (written communication, 1983) has been kind enough to provide some background material about his mental processes and conflicts prior to the procedure:

For chest operations on a small child, there was considerable anxiety concerning probably being unable to keep a right lung sufficiently expanded while the left pleural cavity was open. In those days, no intratracheal anesthetic tube for babies or small children had been manufactured (similar to the ones available for use in adults). We thought the whole problem could be surmounted by giving an anesthetic agent through a tightly-fitting face mask. But such a mask had never been manufactured for a small child; we were stumped. Then, one day, the nurse-anesthetist came running to me and called out, "I've solved it!" In those days, anesthesia face masks, available for teenagers and adults, were handled by thorough washing of them in soap and water, then immersing them overnight in a bowl of alcohol. She said, "Recently one of the face masks was forgotten and had been left in the alcohol soak for a couple of weeks—it all shrank!" She showed it to me, and most certainly it would fit tightly to a child's face and make positive pressure anesthesia possible and thus permit lung inflation and expansion quite safe. So for a child, an open chest operation under general anesthesia was going to be possible.

Just about this time, I was told by an elderly staff-member what had happened to a young pediatrician back in 1922-23. In those days, particularly in hot summer months, a considerable number of children or babies entered the hospital with an outright picture of overwhelming meningitis. The young pediatrician in charge of the case inserted a needle into the spinal canal to get fluid for study of cell count and also to make cultures, to establish with certainty the nature of the serious illness. A furor set up by this act of lumbar puncture so riled the authorities that the doctor was dropped from the hospital staff, was cast out by the local medical society, and had revocation of his state license! He was a broken man, went way up north to live on a chicken farm, where he later died. This alarming bit of history haunted me, but I tried to tell myself that such things occurred only in the dim past. Yet, lingering worry made me wonder if it would not be fool-hardy to proceed with any attempt to close off an open ductus.

By August 1938, Dr Hubbard had selected several youngsters, each of whom he was sure had an open ductus. I told him that I would operate on any one of these as a starter, but would do so only if we could schedule a second patient for the following day. I urged this arrangement, feeling that if the first child succumbed, the venture would be severely criticized but could quickly make another attempt and, hopefully, it would succeed.

The result is for all to read in the LANDMARK ARTICLE. No second case on the following day was necessary. It is a pleasure to read the authors' incisive reasoning dealing with the main points that promised to make the closure of this patient's patent ductus a rewarding procedure: (1) that it was unaccompanied by other detectable cardiac anomalies, (2) that the danger of later bacterial endarteritis could hopefully be avoided, (3) that while a small percentage of persons with a tiny ductus can live well into adult life without troubles, most children with a large ductus are headed for an unfortunate outcome, and (4) that closure of the ductal fistula would restore the disordered physiology to normal.

## THE IMPACT

The 1930s were indeed an important decade, and in the field of cardiovascular surgery, Gross and Hubbard's feat was its culmination. It opened our eyes and raised them beyond the horizon. Other events, many of them brewing before 1939, then came thick and fast.

The first event was World War II, without which the advances in blood banking, the concepts of blood replacement in traumatic shock, the disordered physiology of severe burns and their repair, and the first attempts at early skin closure would surely have been slower in arriving. Many of the surgeons joined the armed forces and, by carrying on their clinical and investigative interests, helped with these advances. In the cardiac field, Harken,[34] eg, (1946) in the pursuit of heart wounds and foreign bodies, developed approaches to the heart chambers that were to lead the way to successful attacks by closed methods on acquired diseases of the mitral valve.[35] Those that remained to bear the civilian load and maintain medical education brought other endeavors to fruition.

The most outstanding event in surgery of this period was the contribution of Blalock,[36] who, in 1944, stimulated and backed by Taussig,[36] partially corrected tetraloy of Fallot by subclavian-pulmonary artery anastomosis (see Chapter 38). Early in the 1940s, Cournand and Ranges[37] (1941) developed cardiac catheterization, which, for the first time, gave information on pressures, pulse contours, and gases and later led to angiography of all parts of the vascular system. A major impulse to expansion of this latter field came in 1953 when Morgan and Sturm[38] presented the image intensifier to the medical community.

The next stride in the march of surgical attack on the heart and great vessels came in 1945 from Gross and Hufnagel[39] and simultaneously from Crafoord and Nyhus[40] in Sweden — surgical correction of coarctation of the aorta. And shortly, Gross'[41] momentum and insight carried him to correction of a group of anomalies wherein the great vessels impinge on esophagus and trachea, commonly referred to as a vascular ring. It had been a significant cause of fatal respiratory distress. The next event (1948): Gross and co-workers[42] studied in the animal laboratory and revived arterial grafting in humans as applied to certain aortic coarctations. Their introduction of preserved allografts into the modern era had a wide impact on many branches of surgery in its application to arteries elsewhere in the body and led to the development of other substitutes, an enterprise that still proceeds today.

Awareness of the number of congenital anomalies of the heart and great vessels that might be susceptible to correction now burgeoned. Progress still had to be confined to measures not allowing visualization of the inside of the heart. But the urge to attack atrial septal defects directly rather than by such a limited procedure as invagination of the atrial wall (Murray,[43] 1948) was strong.

In 1953, several important reports appeared. Taking advantage of the work of Bigelow et al[44] and their own experimental work with total-body hypothermia, Swan et al[45] in Denver and Lewis et al[46] in Chicago were successful in repairing simple intracardiac defects under direct vision. Cooling to between 22 and 28 °C was accomplished by cold blankets or ice immersion. Total circulatory occlusion times of up to eight minutes were achieved. Recognizing that racing the clock has never led to optimum technical results, the ingenuity of Gross[47] again came forward with a contribution — the atrial well. This rubber pouch sewn, temporarily, onto the atrium allowed a direct attack for repairing an interatrial defect. Guiding the sutures by palpation with a finger in the atrium was superior to other methods involving nonvisualization, and many successful instances were reported, although with some hazard to the conducting system. Luckily, in the same year (1953), the 16-year effort of the Gibbons[48] to develop a temporary total extracorporeal circulation was marked by successful open repair of an atrial septal defect, and the era of open heart surgery under direct vision was born.

The approach to the patent ductus arteriosus has been standard for 45 years. The only significant modification of the technique of its interruption was division rather than ligation. This has been the preferred practice by all surgeons, but many still use double ligation with a suture between in the very ill infant or the one with an extremely short ductus.

New thoughts about indications have emerged in recent years in connection with the application to premature infants with respiratory distress syndrome, some of whom have a left-to-right ductal shunt after birth. Trials of closure of the ductus by ligation in these infants compared with pharmacologic methods using indomethacin are currently under way.[49] The contribution of Gross and Hubbard was indeed a landmark event not only in revolutionizing the treatment of the condition itself but in opening the door to modern cardiac surgery.

The help of Drs Aldo Castaneda, MD, Robert E. Gross, MD, Francis D. Moore, MD, John P. Hubbard, MD, Samuel H. Kim, MD, and Howard Ulfelder, MD, is gratefully acknowledged.

## References

1. Rehn L: Fall von penetrirender Stichverletzung des nechter entrikel's Herznaht. *Zentralbl Chir* 1896;23:1048-1049.

2. Cutler EC, Levine SA: Cardiotomy and valvulotomy for mitral stenosis: Experimental observations and clinical notes concerning an operated case with recovery. *Boston Med Surg J* 1923;188:1023-1027.

3. Churchill ED: Decortication of the heart (Delorme) for constrictive pericarditis. *Arch Surg* 1929;19:1457-1469.

4. Graham EA, Singer JJ: Successful removal of an entire lung for carcinoma of the bronchus. *JAMA* 1933;101:1371-1374.

5. Churchill ED: Surgical treatment of carcinoma of the lung. *J Thorac Surg* 1933;12:254-266.

6. Souttar HS: Surgical treatment of mitral stenosis. *Br Med J* 1925;2:603-606.

7. Fantus B (ed): The therapy of the Cook County Hospital. *JAMA* 1937;109:128-131.

8. Cameron CS, Ferguson LK: Organization and technique of blood bank at Philadelphia General Hospital: Experiences with 1,000 transfusions. *Surgery* 1939;5:237-248.

9. Domagk G: Ein Beitrag zur Chemotherapie der bakteriellen Infektionen. *Dtsch Med Wochenschr* 1935;61:250-253.

10. Chain E, Florey HW, Gardner AD, et al: Penicillin as a chemotherapeutic agent. *Lancet* 1940;2:226-228.

11. Fleming A: On antibacterial action of cultures of penicillium, with special reference to their use in isolation of B-influenza. *Br J Exp Pathol* 1929;10:226-236.

12. Ulfelder H, Allen AW: Acute perforation of ulcers of the stomach and duodenum. *N Engl J Med* 1942;227:780-784.

13. Charles AF, Scott DA: Studies on heparin: Preparation of heparin. *J Biol Chem* 1933;102:425-429, 437.

14. McLean J: The thromboplastic action of cephalin. *Am J Physiol* 1916;41:250-257.

15. Best CH: Heparin and thrombosis. *Br Med J* 1938;2:977-981.

16. Roderick LM: Problem in coagulation of blood: 'Sweet clover disease of cattle.' *Am J Physiol* 1931;96:413-425.

17. Campbell HA, Link KP: Studies on the hemorrhagic sweet clover disease: The isolation and crystallization of the hemorrhagic agent. *J Biol Chem* 1941;138:21-33.

18. Kirschner M: Ein durch die Trendelenbargsche Operation geheilter Fall von Embolie der Art pulonalis. *Arch Klin Chir* 1924;133:312-359.

19. Gibbon JH: Artificial maintenance of circulation during experimental occlusion of pulmonary artery. *Arch Surg* 1937;34:1105-1131.

20. McIver MA, Gamble JL: Body fluid changes due to upper intestinal obstruction. *JAMA* 1928;91:1589-1594.

21. Hartwell JA, Hoguet JP: Experimental intestinal obstruction in dogs with especial reference to the cause of death and the treatment by large amounts of normal saline solution. *JAMA* 1912;59:82-87.

22. Butler AM, McKhann CF, Gamble JL: Intracellular fluid loss in diarrheal disease. *J Ped* 1933;3:84-92.

23. Coller FA, Maddock WG: Water requirements of surgical patients. *Ann Surg* 1933;98:952-960.

24. Coller FA, Dick VS, Maddock WG: Maintenance of normal water exchange with intravenous fluids. *JAMA* 1936;107:1522-1527.

25. Underhill FP, Carrington GL, Kapsinow R, et al: Blood concentration changes in extensive superficial burns, and their significance for systemic treatment. *Arch Intern Med* 1923;32:31-39.

26. Cope O, Moore FD: The redistribution of body water and the fluid therapy of the burned patient. *Ann Surg* 1947;126:1010-1045.

27. Cope O, Graham JB, Moore FD, et al: The nature of the shift of plasma protein to the extravascular space following thermal trauma. *Ann Surg* 1948;128:1041-1055.

28. Wangensteen OH: Therapeutic considerations in the management of acute intestinal obstruction. *Arch Surg* 1933;26:933-961.

29. Munro JC: Ligation of the ductus arteriosus. *Ann Surg* 1907;46:335-338.

30. Holman E: *Arteriovenous Aneurysm.* New York, Macmillan Publishing Co Inc, 1937, p 122.

31. Abbott ME: Congenital cardiac disease, in Osler W, McCrae T (eds): *Modern Medicine,* ed 2. Philadelphia, Lea & Febiger, 1915, vol 4, p 412.

32. Graybiel A, Strieder JW, Boyer NH: An attempt to obliterate the patent ductus arteriosus in a patient with subacute endarteritis. *Am Heart J* 1938;15:621-624.

33. Gross RE, personal communication.

34. Harken DE: Foreign bodies in, and in relation to, thoracic blood vessels and heart: Techniques for approaching and removing foreign bodies from chambers of the heart. *Surg Gynecol Obstet* 1946;83:117-125.

35. Harken DE, Ellis LB, Ware PE, et al: The surgical treatment of mitral stenosis: Valvuloplasty. *N Engl J Med* 1948;239:801-809.

36. Blalock A, Taussig HR: The surgical treatment of malformations of the heart: In which there is pulmonary stenosis and pulmonary atresia. *JAMA* 1945;128:189-202.

37. Cournand A, Ranges HA: Catheterization of the right ventricle in man. *Proc Soc Exp Biol Med* 1941;46:462-466.

38. Morgan RH, Sturm RE: Roentgen-ray motion pictures by means of screen intensification. *Am J Roentgenol Roentgen Ther* 1953;70:130-146.

39. Gross RE, Hufnagel CA: Coarctation of the aorta: Experimental studies concerning its surgical correction. *N Engl J Med* 1945;233:287-293.

40. Crafoord C, Nyhus G: Congenital coarctation of the aorta and its surgical treatment. *J Thorac Surg* 1945;14:347-361.

41. Gross RE: Surgical relief for tracheal obstruction from vascular ring. *N Engl J Med* 1945;233:586-599.

42. Gross RE, Hurwitt ES, Bill AH, et al: Preliminary observations on use of human arterial grafts in treatment of certain cardiovascular defects. *N Engl J Med* 1948;239:578-579.

43. Murray B: Closure of defects in cardiac septa. *Ann Surg* 1948;128:843-853.

44. Bigelow WG, Callaghan JC, Hopps JA: General hypothermia for experimental intracardiac surgery. *Ann Surg* 1950;132:531-537.

45. Swan H, Zeavin I, Blount SG, et al: Surgery by direct vision of open heart during hypothermia. *JAMA* 1953;153:1081-1085.

46. Lewis FG, Taufic M: Closure of atrial septal defects with the aid of hypothermia: Experimental accomplishments and the report of one successful case. *Surgery* 1953;33:52-59.

47. Gross RE, Watkins E, Pomeranz AA, et al: A method for surgical closure of interauricular septal defects. *Surg Gynecol Obstet* 1953;96:23.

48. Gibbon JH: Application of mechanical heart and lung apparatus to cardiac surgery. *Minn Med* 1954;37:171-180.

49. Castaneda A: Patent ductus arteriosus: A commentary. *Ann Thorac Surg* 1981;51:92-96.

July 8, 1939
(*JAMA* 1939;113:126-127)

## Chapter 32

# An Unusual Case of Intra-group Agglutination

Philip Levine, M.D., Newark, N. J., and Rufus E. Stetson, M.D., New York

This report deals with a rare property in the blood of a patient whose serum showed an iso-agglutinin of moderate activity, which agglutinated about 80 per cent of the bloods of her own group. In view of the fact that this agglutinin tended to disappear after an interval of several months and the fact that this agglutinin gave an equally strong reaction at 37 and 20 C., it would seem to resemble agglutinins resulting from iso-immunization following repeated transfusions. This phenomenon is readily reproduced in some species (cattle, chickens, rabbits), by several repeated transfusions, but in the case of man only two clearcut instances of such iso-immunization to cellular elements are described in the literature.[1] The case to be described differs from these in that the immune iso-agglutinin must have been stimulated by a factor other than repeated transfusion. The nature of this factor becomes evident from a summary of the case history.

### REPORT OF CASE

M. S., a woman aged 25, a secundipara, was registered in the antepartum clinic of Bellevue Hospital July 12, 1937, at which time she showed some pretibial edema and a blood pressure of 130 systolic, 90 diastolic. (The expected date of delivery was in the last week of October.) Two weeks later the blood pressure was 154 systolic, 106 diastolic, and there was a faint trace of albumin in the urine. Hospitalization and rest in bed resulted in subsidence of all symptoms. The fetal heart sounds were not heard, but there were no x-ray signs of fetal death.

Labor pains and vaginal bleeding started on September 8 (the thirty-third week of the gestation), and at midnight September 9 the patient was admitted to the hospital, at which time labor pains lasting one minute occurred every five minutes. There was considerable bleeding before the membranes were ruptured, and a macerated stillborn fetus weighing only 1 pound 5 ounces (595 Gm.) was delivered. After the placenta was expelled, bleeding was finally controlled and the patient (group O) was given her first transfusion of 500 cc. of whole blood from her husband (group O). Ten minutes after she received the blood a chill developed and she complained of pains in her legs and head. About twelve hours later a piece of membrane was passed and this was followed by more bleeding. At 4 p. m. a second transfusion of 750 cc. of whole blood was given, apparently without any reactions. In view of the renewed bleeding, hysterectomy was performed, followed by a third transfusion of 80 cc. of whole blood with no reaction.

Nineteen hours after the first transfusion and eight hours after the hysterectomy the patient voided 8 ounces (240 cc.) of bloody and dusky urine. At this time tests done with a more delicate technic revealed that, although the patient and her husband—the first donor whose blood caused a reaction—were in group O, the patient's serum nevertheless agglutinated distinctly her husband's cells and, indeed, the cells of most group O donors. Subsequently the patient received six more uneventful transfusions from compatible professional donors very carefully selected by the Blood Transfusion Betterment Association.

Subsequent intensive treatment—diathermy over the kidneys, forced fluids by vein, rectum and mouth, the repeated transfusions mentioned and high hot colonic irrigations—resulted in gradual recovery of kidney function.

### COMMENT

The blood was referred to us during the patient's convalescence, October 9, a month after the hysterectomy. Tests previously performed at the Donor Bureau of the Blood Transfusion Betterment Association showed that only eight of fifty group O donors did not react with the patient's serum and hence were compatible. In our series of fifty-four bloods of group O, thirteen failed to react with the patient's serum. Thus, of a total of 104 group O bloods twenty-one were compatible.

From the Department of Laboratories, Newark Beth Israel Hospital, Newark, N. J., and the Blood Transfusion Betterment Association of New York City.

Dr. William E. Studdiford, director, and Dr. John S. Labate, resident, of the Obstetrical and Gynecological Service at Bellevue Hospital, gave the authors permission to study this case.

1. Landsteiner, Karl; Levine, Philip, and Janes, M. L.: Proc. Soc. Exper. Biol. & Med. 25:672 (May) 1928. Neter, Erwin: J. Immunol. 30:255 (March) 1936.

It could be readily shown that these reactions differ from those due to so-called atypical agglutinins occasionally found in the serums of normal persons. The former reactions were just as active at 37 as at 20 C., while reactions of the latter variety as a rule do not occur at 37 C. or else are considerably diminished. In other words, identical results were obtained when tests with serums of the patient were kept either at 20 or at 37 C. or were read after centrifuging and resuspending the sedimented cells.

The reactions were found to be independent of the M, N or P blood factors. Owing to the lack of suitable quantities of the blood, it was not possible to perform absorption experiments in order to supply data on the incidence of the reactions in bloods of groups A, B and AB.

Another specimen drawn two months later, December 3, still exhibited the agglutinin, which however gave far weaker reactions. Here again the reactions at 37 C. were just as intense as those at room temperature or lower. It was not possible to examine the serum of this patient until a year later, when all traces of reactions had disappeared.

In several respects this iso-agglutinin, as already mentioned, resembles the iso-agglutinins described by Landsteiner, Levine and Janes and that of Neter, namely (1) reactions within the same group equally active at room temperature and at 37 C. and (2) the temporary character of the agglutinin. In both of these cases the agglutinin was not demonstrable until an interval of several weeks had elapsed following repeated transfusions. In the present case, however, it is evident that the unusual iso-agglutinin must have been present at the time the patient was given her first transfusion with the blood of her husband, which subsequently was shown to be sensitive. Furthermore, this first transfusion was not uneventful in view of the resulting chills, pains in the legs and intense headache.

It is well established that in instances of iso-immunization in animals the iso-agglutinin serves as a reagent to detect dominant hereditary blood factors in the red blood cells and presumably also in the tissue cells. In view of the fact that this patient harbored a dead fetus for a period of several months, one may assume that the products of the disintegrating fetus were responsible not only for the toxic symptoms of the patient but also for the iso-immunization. Presumably the immunizing property in the blood and/or tissues of the fetus must have been inherited from the father. Since this dominant property was not present in the mother, specific immunization conceivably could occur.

No data are available as to the relationship to one another of the immune iso-agglutinin in the two previously reported cases and in the present case. Judging from the frequency of positive and negative reactions, it is evident that the iso-agglutinin in this case is distinct from the other two; i. e., 20 per cent nonreacting bloods in contrast with 75 per cent in the case of Neter and 60 per cent in that of Landsteiner, Levine and Janes.

Agglutinins of this sort can rarely be investigated thoroughly because of their tendency to diminish in activity and eventually to disappear. Consequently attempts were made to produce a hetero-immune agglutinin of identical or similar specificity by repeated injections of sensitive blood into a series of rabbits. These experiments met with failure, since suitable absorption tests with such serums failed to reveal the presence of the desired agglutinin.

201 Lyons Avenue, Newark—48 East Sixty-Fourth Street, New York.

March 9, 1984
JAMA 1984;251:1318-1320)

# Rh Isoimmunization*

## The Importance of a Critical Case Study

Tibor J. Greenwalt, MD

### Development and Proof of a Hypothesis

The accompanying case report by Levine and Stetson[1] is a fine example of the importance of careful clinical observation. Some may scoff at the publication of case reports, but to the astute scientist, a carefully documented study of an unusual patient represents an experiment of nature that may be the opportunity to explain a long-recorded but unexplained clinical mystery. Some credit must also go to the editorial staff of THE JOURNAL for having published this and a related landmark, "Isoimmunization in Pregnancy: Its Possible Bearing on the Etiology of Erythroblastosis Foetalis," by Levine et al.[2]

A new era in the clarification of the nature of erythroblastosis was opened by the classic observation of Diamond and colleagues[3] that icterus gravis, hydrops fetalis, and anemia of the newborn with erythroblastosis represented different grades of clinical severity of the same unknown underlying process. They did not suspect that the syndrome was a manifestation of hemolytic anemia affecting the fetus.

Ottenberg[4] in 1923 documented the observations of others and his own that leakage of fetal red cells into the mother's circulation might play an immunologic role in the causation of the toxemia of pregnancy. He even stated that "it seems possible that several other unexplained diseases, particularly jaundice of the newborn . . . may be due to the same cause, accidental placental transfusion of incompatible blood." In 1938, Darrow[5] came close to the mark in suggesting that the pathological process was a hemolytic anemia caused by "transfer of immune bodies from an actively immunized mother to the fetus." Having no data to support her hypothesis, she incorrectly selected fetal hemoglobin as the offending antigen.

Landsteiner and Wiener[6] in 1940 reported that they had identified "another individual property of human blood (which may be designated as Rh)" using the sera of some rabbits immunized with the blood of Rhesus monkeys. Wiener and Peters[7] soon demonstrated that this Rh agglutinogen was etiologic in so-called intragroup hemolytic reactions. The fact that the antibody and the agglutinogen described by Landsteiner and Wiener[6] were subsequently shown not to be part of the Rh system does not in any way detract from the importance of their contribution. Serendipity must be given its due.

It didn't take long for Philip Levine and his associates to establish Rh as "the immunizing property in the blood and/or tissues of the fetus," which they correctly surmised in the accompanying report was "inherited from the father" and "not present in the mother." By 1941, Levine and co-workers[8] had collected convincing evidence that the majority of cases of erythroblastosis fetalis resulted from isoimmunization of an Rh-negative mother by the Rh-positive RBCs of the fetus.

### Obvious Benefits

The immediate benefit that occurred was the use of Rh-negative blood to support affected infants and the development of procedures for exchange transfusions. The observation that the anti-Rh antibodies acted best at 37 °C led to improved techniques for crossmatching blood for all transfusions.

### Solution of New Problems

Perhaps more important was the then-puzzling observation that anti-Rh agglutinins were found in the serum samples of less than 50% of Rh-negative mothers who were delivered of newborns with erythroblastosis fetalis. The serologists of those days were schooled in techniques borrowed from the bacteriologists. The antigens (bacterial suspensions) had to be washed carefully and resuspended in saline. Saline suspensions of red cells detected only what we now know to be IgM saline agglutinins, which are seen only during the primary immune response. In 1944, Wiener[9] and Race[10] independently discovered the answer to this puzzling phenome-

From the Hoxworth Blood Center and the Department of Internal Medicine, University of Cincinnati.

*A commentary on Levine P, Stetson RE: An unusual case of intra-group agglutination. *JAMA* 1939;113:126-127.

non. The patients with no anti-Rh saline agglutinins had blocking or incomplete antibodies that attached to the Rh-positive test red cells but were unable to achieve the crosslinking necessary to produce agglutination. Their presence could be detected only by showing that these antibodies would make Rh-positive RBCs less agglutinable or inagglutinable by anti-Rh saline agglutinins.

This form of inhibition test was cumbersome to use. Fortunately, the great interest in these new discoveries soon resulted in simpler and more sensitive methods, which are still in use and widely applied in other immunologic studies. Diamond and Abelson[11] found that a heated slide test using the suspected serum mixed with either oxalated whole blood or a heavy suspension of washed Rh-positive red cells detected the blocking, incomplete antibodies. It was then demonstrated that oxalated plasma and concentrated albumin solutions further enhanced the agglutination of Rh-positive red cells by incomplete anti-Rh antibodies. Shortly, Coombs and colleagues[12] developed the antiglobulin test, which used suitably absorbed rabbit antisera against human globulin to detect incomplete anti-Rh antibodies attached to the surfaces of red cells.

Pickles'[13] observation that Rh-positive RBCs exposed to a filtrate of a broth culture of cholera vibrio became agglutinable by incomplete antibodies led to the use of trypsin and other enzymes in serological procedures. Automation of blood grouping techniques would not have been possible without these observations. The action of trypsin, papain, and other enzymes on the red cell membrane has been an important tool in clarifying the biochemistry of the glycopeptides, which carry the receptors for various blood group antibodies, lectins, and viruses.

### Creation of Greater Complexity

With these new tools available, the serologists responsible for blood transfusions quickly found antibodies that identified additional antigenic determinants (epitopes) believed to be alleles in the Rh/CDE system and added new blood group systems, eg, Kell, Lewis, Duffy, Kidd, and private and public blood group antigens that are possessed only by a very few or lacking only in a very few persons, respectively. A whole genre of blood group specialists developed and formed antibody clubs around the world. These groups continue to share new discoveries, rare sera, and red cells with rare phenotypes, and their expertise helps to make blood transfusions safer from the serological viewpoint and makes it possible to find the rarest of blood donors somewhere if a patient should be in dire need.

These advances in isoimmunohematology have served as the underpinning of our knowledge of the role of antibodies in the warm autoimmune hemolytic anemias and the cold hemolytic syndromes and have stimulated greater interest in the role of complement.

### Increase of Basic Knowledge

The characterization of the warm saline agglutinins observed by Levine and Stetson[1] as 19S IgM molecules and the incomplete blocking antibodies as 7S IgG molecules has resulted in the delineation of the other classes and subclasses of immunoglobulins and, ultimately, greater detailed knowledge of their structure and function. As far as I am aware, the Rh system provided the model for understanding the immunologic differences between the antibodies (19S) produced as part of the primary immune response and the antibodies (7S) produced as part of the secondary immune response.

The discovery of the antiglobulin reaction and its usefulness in detecting antibodies on red cell surfaces has found many applications in clinical medicine and in the research laboratory. Antiglobulin molecules produced in many species to a wide variety of antigens have been purified and labeled with enzymes, ferritin, gold, viruses, and radioisotopes, among others. Without the latter, the development of the solid-phase radioimmunoassay techniques introduced by Berson and Yalow[14] might have been delayed. The use of labeled antiglobulin reagents has helped our understanding of the distribution of antigenic determinants on cellular surfaces and observation of their mobility under varying experimental conditions. This new knowledge served as the basis for the development of the fluid mosaic theory[15] of membrane structure, which represents a major advance in our understanding of what cell membranes do.

The concept of alloimmunization by the transplacental route has led to the clarification of parallel syndromes mediated by the action of maternal antibodies on platelets, resulting in neonatal thrombocytopenia, and or granulocytes, resulting in neonatal granulocytopenia. The interest stimulated in the nature of the fetomaternal barrier has resulted in a much better understanding of certain phenomena and complications related to pregnancy. An interesting sidelight was the accidental discovery made by Grubb[16] of the Gm allotypic markers on the heavy chain of IgG molecule when he observed an unexpected reaction while measuring gamma globulin in sera using the antiglobulin inhibition test with red cells coated with anti-Rh as indicator system. Thus, the great body of information that has developed about gamma globulin and other plasma protein types might not have been disclosed without the previous discovery of the Rh factor.

### Prevention

The ultimate goal of biomedical research is not only the understanding of disease but its prevention and cure. Levine[17] observed that ABO incompatibility tended to protect against Rh alloimmunization; ie, if the fetus is group A and the mother is group O, then Rh alloimmunization is less likely to develop, presumably because the fetal A Rh-positive red cells entering the maternal circulation are destroyed before they can cause immunization. This observation led Stern et al[18] to perform experiments in prisoner volunteers at Joliet, Ill, that demonstrated that Rh-negative persons failed to make Rh antibodies after repeated injections of Rh-positive cells that had been coated by anti-Rh antibodies in vitro. Freda and colleagues[19] and Clarke et al,[20] in New York and Liverpool, England, respectively, demonstrated the effectiveness of giving 7S anti-Rh gamma globulin to prevent isoimmunization. Fortunately, transplacental hemorrhage occurs most frequently intrapartum, and a standard dose of anti-Rh immunoglobulin (300 $\mu$g) protects all but those with massive leaks. More recently, it has been shown that even the few women who have transplacental leaks late in pregnancy can be protected by giving hyperimmune anti-Rh gamma globulin late in pregnancy without any danger to the fetus.

## Appreciation

By training and scientific dedication, Landsteiner, Levine, and Wiener and their associates were prepared to identify the Rh-agglutinogen, but it was their alertness and imagination that made it possible for them to translate chance laboratory observations into the solution of puzzling hemolytic transfusion reactions and the mechanism of hemolytic disease of the newborn. Even the sometimes acrimonious disharmony over the notations to be preferred and the details of the genetics of the Rh system have led to better understanding of the importance of comprehensible notation and the clarification of genetic mechanisms. The important result is that mankind is the benefactor.

I regret that it has not been possible to mention all who contributed significantly to the evolution of this important scientific saga, which is a clear example of the high dividends yielded by the support of clinical and basic scientific research. Those who are interested in further details of the early history of the discovery of the Rh factor and hemolytic disease of the newborn are invited to refer to the excellent monographs by Potter[21] and Pickles,[22] a special issue of *Blood* edited by Hill and Dameshek,[23] and my editorial[24] published on the occasion of the 25th anniversary of the discovery of the Rh factor.

## References

1. Levine P, Stetson RE: An unusual case of intra-group agglutination. *JAMA* 1939;113:126-127.

2. Levine P, Katzin EM, Burnham L: Isoimmunization in pregnancy: Its possible bearing on the etiology of erythroblastosis foetalis. *JAMA* 1941;116:825-827.

3. Diamond LK, Blackfan KD, Baty JM: Erythroblastosis fetalis and its association with universal edema of the fetus, icterus gravis neonatorum, and anemia of the newborn. *J Pediatr* 1932;1:269-309.

4. Ottenberg R: The etiology of eclampsia: Historical and critical notes. *JAMA* 1923;81:295-297.

5. Darrow RR: Icterus gravis (erythroblastosis) neonatorum: An examination of etiologic considerations. *Arch Pathol* 1938;25:378-417.

6. Landsteiner K, Wiener AS: An agglutinable factor in human blood recognized by immune sera for Rhesus blood. *Proc Soc Exp Biol Med* 1940;43:223.

7. Wiener AS, Peters HR: Hemolytic reactions following transfusion of blood of the homologous group with three cases in which the same agglutinogen was responsible. *Ann Intern Med* 1940;13:2306-2322.

8. Levine P, Burnham L, Katzin EM, et al: The role of isoimmunization in the pathogenesis of erythroblastosis fetalis. *Am J Obstet Gynecol* 1941;42:925-937.

9. Wiener AS: A new test (blocking test) for Rh sensitization. *Proc Soc Exp Biol Med* 1944;56:173-176.

10. Race RR: An 'incomplete' antibody in human serum. *Nature* 1944;153:771-772.

11. Diamond LK, Abelson NM: The demonstration of anti-Rh agglutinins: An accurate and rapid slide test. *J Lab Clin Med* 1945;30:204-212.

12. Coombs RRA, Mourant AE, Race RR: Detection of weak and 'incomplete' Rh agglutinins: A new test. *Lancet* 1945;2:15-16.

13. Pickles MM: Effect of cholera filtrate on red cells as demonstrated by incomplete Rh antibodies. *Nature* 1946;158:880.

14. Yalow RS: Radioimmunoassay: A probe for the fine structure of biologic systems. *J Am Med Wom Assoc* 1978;33:243-262.

15. Singer SJ, Nicholson GL: The fluid mosaic model of the structure of cell membranes. *Science* 1972;175:720-731.

16. Grubb R: Agglutination of erythrocytes coated with incomplete anti-Rh by certain rheumatoid arthritic sera and some other sera despite dilution: The existence of human serum groups. *Acta Pathol Microbiol Scand* 1956;39:195-197.

17. Levine P: Serological factors as possible causes of spontaneous abortions. *J Hered* 1943;34:71-80.

18. Stern K, Goodman HS, Berger M: Experimental isoimmunization to hemoantigens in man. *J Immunol* 1961;87:189-198.

19. Freda VJ, Gorman JG, Pollack W: Successful prevention of Rh sensitization in man with an anti-Rh gamma$_2$-globulin antibody preparation. *Transfusion* 1964;4:26-32.

20. Clarke CA, Donohoe WTA, McConnell RB, et al: Further experimental studies on the prevention of Rh hemolytic disease. *Br Med J* 1963;1:979-984.

21. Potter EL: *Rh . . . Its Relation to Congenital Hemolytic Disease and to Intragroup Transfusion Reactions.* Chicago, Year Book Medical Publishers, 1947.

22. Pickles MM: *Haemolytic Disease of the Newborn.* Springfield, Ill, Charles C Thomas Publisher, 1949.

23. Hill JM, Dameshek W (eds): *The Rh Factor in the Clinic and Laboratory,* in *Blood,* Special Issue No. 2. New York, Grune & Stratton, 1948.

24. Greenwalt TJ: The Rh factor after 25 years. *Transfusion* 1965;6:490-491.

# Chapter 33

# Sulfadiazine

## Therapeutic Evaluation and Toxic Effects on Four Hundred and Forty-six Patients

Maxwell Finland, M.D., Elias Strauss, M.D.,
and Osler L. Peterson, M.D.

Boston

Sulfadiazine (2-sulfanilamidopyrimidine), the pyrimidine analogue of sulfapyridine and sulfathiazole, is one of a group of heterocyclic derivatives of sulfanilamide synthesized by Roblin and his co-workers.[1] Laboratory studies on animals indicated that this drug has less toxicity than sulfapyridine and sulfathiazole and is highly effective against experimental infections with common pathogens.[2] Preliminary observations in this clinic[3] and in a number of others in which sulfadiazine was made available[4] indicated that this drug was worthy of extensive trial in the therapy of human bacterial infections. This paper deals mainly with a report of the clinical use of sulfadiazine in 446 adult patients treated at the Boston City Hospital prior to March 1, 1941. The results of laboratory studies will be reviewed briefly.

## ANIMAL EXPERIMENTS

Feinstone and his associates[2] have shown that sulfadiazine is considerably less toxic than sulfapyridine or sulfathiazole both in acute experiments on mice and after prolonged administration in monkeys. In these animals and in rabbits absorption of sulfadiazine after oral administration was rapid, there was little acetylation and the levels of the free drug reached were higher and were maintained longer than after similar doses of sulfapyridine or sulfathiazole. Because of these observations, comparisons of efficacy were difficult to evaluate. When identical doses were used in mice, however, sulfadiazine was found to be considerably more effective than the other drugs in the therapy of experimental infections with pneumococcus, hemolytic streptococcus and Friedländer's bacillus type B and about as effective as sulfathiazole against the staphylococcus. Long[5] has also found sulfadiazine to be effective in mice against infections with these organisms and, in addition, against Escherichia coli, Clostridium welchii and Clostridium septicum infections.

## ABSORPTION, EXCRETION AND DISTRIBUTION IN MAN[6]

In human subjects the maximum blood levels after oral administration of sulfadiazine are uniformly higher and are more sustained than after corresponding doses of the other sulfonamides now in common use. Little of the drug appears in the blood in the conjugated form. Excretion of the drug is somewhat delayed; it is

From the Thorndike Memorial Laboratory, Second and Fourth Medical Services (Harvard), Boston City Hospital, and the Department of Medicine, Harvard Medical School.

This study was carried out with the technical assistance of Mildred W. Barnes and Clare Wilcox, who also assisted in collecting the data. The chemical determinations were made by Elizabeth Shaler Smith and Alice N. Ballou. The visiting and house staffs of the medical services cooperated in this work. The sulfadiazine and specific serums used in this study were supplied by the Lederle Laboratories, Inc.

1. Roblin, R. O., Jr.; Williams, J. H.; Winnek, P. S., and English, J. P.: Chemotherapy: II. Some Sulfanilamide Heterocytes, J. Am. Chem. Soc. **62:**2002, 1940.

2. Feinstone, W. H.; Williams, R. D.; Wolff, R. T.; Huntington, E., and Crossley, M. L.: The Toxicity, Absorption and Chemotherapeutic Activity of 2-Sulfanilamidopyrimidine (Sulfadiazine), Bull. Johns Hopkins Hosp. **67:**427 (Dec.) 1940.

3. Peterson, O. L.; Strauss, Elias; Taylor, F. H. L., and Finland, Maxwell: Absorption, Excretion and Distribution of Sulfadiazine (2-Sulfanilamido-Pyrimidine), Am J. M. Sc. **201:**357 (March) 1941.

4. Plummer, Norman, and Ensworth, H. K.: Absorption and Excretion of Sulfadiazine, Proc. Soc. Exper. Biol. & Med. **45:**734, 1940. Rheinhold, J. G.; Flippin, H. F.; Schwartz, Leon, and Domm, A. H.: The Absorption, Distribution, and Excretion of 2-Sulfanilamido Pyrimidine (Sulfapyrimidine, Sulfadiazine) in Man, Am. J. M. Sc. **201:**106 (Jan.) 1941. Long.[5] Sadusk and Tredway.[6] Bullowa.[10]

5. Long, P. H.: The Clinical Use of Sulfanilamide, Sulfapyridine, Sulfathiazole, Sulfaguanidine and Sulfadiazine in the Prophylaxis and Treatment of Infections. Canad. M. A. J. **44:**217 (March) 1941.

6. Sadusk J. F., Jr., and Tredway, J. B.: Observations on the Absorption, Excretion, Diffusion and Acetylation of Sulfadiazine in Man, Yale J. Biol. & Med. **13:**539 (March) 1941. Peterson, Strauss, Taylor and Finland.[3] Plummer and Ensworth.[4] Rheinhold, Flippin, Schwartz and Domm.[4] Long.[5]

recovered almost entirely in the urine, and about one third of the excreted drug is recovered as the acetylated compound. The appearance of the drug in the cerebrospinal fluid even after intravenous administration of the sodium salt is somewhat delayed, but the drug soon reaches and maintains a level about two thirds of that found in the blood. In other exudates, the concentrations more nearly approximate those of the blood. Neither sulfadiazine nor its sodium salt is absorbed to any significant degree from the rectum.

The drug is distributed in the various organs of the body in about the same manner as is sulfathiazole. In the kidney, however, the concentration of sulfadiazine usual-

TABLE 1.—*Etiologic Factors and Mortality in Pneumonia Treated with Sulfadiazine*

| Etiologic Classification | Number of Patients* | Died* | Per Cent Died |
|---|---|---|---|
| A. Pneumococcic pneumonia | 178 (33) | 19 (8) | 10.7 |
| Type I | 28 (11) | 2 (2) | |
| II | 6 (1) | 0 | |
| III | 33 (6) | 6 (3) | |
| IV | 11 (1) | 2 | |
| V | 12 (2) | 0 | |
| VII | 18 (5) | 6 (3) | |
| VIII | 18 (4) | 0 | |
| Others | 52 (3) | 3 | |
| B. Specific, nonpneumococcic pneumonia | 35 (7) | 7 (2) | 20.0 |
| Staphylococcus aureus, alone | 21 (3) | 4 | |
| With hemolytic streptococcus | 5 (1) | 1 (1) | |
| With influenza bacillus | 3 | 1 | |
| Hemolytic streptococcus | 4 (2) | 0 | |
| Friedländer's bacillus, type A | 2 (1) | 1 (1) | |
| C. Etiology undetermined—"primary" pneumonia | 52 | 3 | 5.8 |
| Lobar pneumonia | 20 | 0 | |
| Atypical pneumonia | 32 | 3 | |
| D. Etiology undetermined—"secondary" pneumonia | 51 | 19 | 37.3 |
| Cerebrovascular accidents | 13 | 8 | |
| Cardiac failure | 29 | 7 | |
| Acute asthma | 4 | 2 | |
| Other serious disease | 5 | 2 | |
| All pneumonias | 316 (40) | 48 (10) | 15.2 |

*Parentheses indicate number of patients with positive blood cultures.

ly is the same as in the blood. In this respect it resembles sulfanilamide and is in contrast to sulfapyridine and sulfathiazole, which are found in the kidney in considerably higher concentrations than in the blood.[7] The solubility of the acetyl sulfadiazine in urine is much higher than that of acetyl derivatives of sulfapyridine and sulfathiazole.[2] The latter condition is of interest in view of the fact that many patients with impaired renal function excrete the free and conjugated sulfadiazine more readily than is usually the case with sulfapyridine or sulfathiazole. This will appear from the data to be presented and was also mentioned by Long.[5]

### IN VITRO STUDIES

It is now recognized that body fluids as well as the

usual laboratory mediums contain substances which inhibit sulfonamide action. Different mediums vary considerably in the degree to which they inhibit the antibacterial action of any given drug.[8] Our studies indicate that, in addition, a given medium may inhibit the activity of different drugs to varying degrees. It is usually not possible to determine to what extent variations in the action of different sulfonamides on any given organism are due to differential inhibition by the mediums or to intrinsic differences in the activity of the drugs, or to both these factors. In certain synthetic mediums of known composition, sulfonamide action is frequently enhanced one hundred fold or more over its effectiveness in the common infusion broths.

Previous experiments with pneumococci have indicated that the blood broth medium used in this laboratory could be used for comparative studies with sulfapyridine and sulfathiazole.[9] In this medium sulfadiazine is much less bacteriostatic than sulfapyridine or sulfathiazole. Similar results with pneumococci were noted by Osgood and Bullowa in cultures taken from bone marrow.[10] In pneumococcidal tests carried out in defibrinated human blood with a technic previously described,[11] however, sulfadiazine was found to be about as effective as sulfathiazole. In all other mediums tested sulfadiazine was less effective against pneumococci than were sulfathiazole and sulfapyridine except in a liver infusion medium,[8] which presumably contains the least inhibitor for all three drugs and in which all these drugs were about equally effective. In this medium a pneumococcus made fast to sulfapyridine and sulfathiazole[9] was also found to be fast to sulfadiazine.

Against Staphylococcus aureus, when a simple liver infusion medium was used,[8] sulfadiazine was somewhat less bacteriostatic than sulfathiazole but considerably more effective than sulfapyridine. In a completely synthetic medium[12] or in a simple medium[13] sulfadiazine was highly bacteriostatic against stock laboratory strains of Friedländer's bacillus types A and B, Flexner dysentery bacillus, Salmonella suipestifer, Salmonella enteritidis, Salmonella paratyphosus A and B, Salmonella aertrycke and Escherichia coli communis. In most of the experiments sulfadiazine had about the same effect as sulfathiazole and in the others it was somewhat less effective in the same concentrations. In urine, also, sulfadiazine is as effective against these organisms as

7. Strauss, Elias; Lowell, F. C.; Taylor, F. H. L., and Finland, Maxwell: Observations on the Absorption, Excretion and Distribution of Sulfanilamide, Sulfapyridine, Sulfathiazole and Sulfamethylthiazole, Ann. Int. Med. 14:1360 (Feb.) 1941. Peterson, Strauss, Taylor and Finland.[3]

8. MacLeod, C. M.: The Inhibition of the Bacteriostatic Action of Sulfonamide Drugs by Substances of Animal and Bacterial Origin, J. Exper. Med. 72:217 (Sept.) 1940.

9. Lowell, F. C.; Strauss, Elias, and Finland, Maxwell: Observations on the Susceptibility of Pneumococci to Sulfapyridine, Sulfathiazole and Sulfamethylthiazole, Ann. Int. Med. 14:1001 (Dec.) 1940.

10. Bullowa, J. G. M.: Personal communication to the authors.

11. Finland, Maxwell, and Brown, J. W.: Immunological Studies in Patients with Pneumococcus Type III Pneumonia Treated with Sulfanilamide, J. Clin. Investigation 18:307 (May) 1939. Spring, W. C.; Lowell, F. C., and Finland, Maxwell: Studies on the Action of Sulfapyridine on Pneumococci, ibid. 19:163 (Jan.) 1940.

12. Fildes, P.: Mechanism of the Antibacterial Action of Mercury, Brit. J. Exper. Path. 21:67, 1940.

13. Sahyun, Melville; Beard, P.; Schultz, E. W.; Snow, J., and Cross, E.: Growth Stimulating Factors for Microorganisms, J. Infect. Dis. 58:28, 1936. MacLeod.[8]

sulfathiazole. As with other sulfonamides,[14] the bacteriostatic and bactericidal action of sulfadiazine is inhibited by para-aminobenzoic acid.

## CLINICAL RESULTS

The laboratory evidence that sulfadiazine has a wide range of effectiveness, the relatively high concentrations of this drug that are so readily maintained in animals and in human beings and its low toxicity which became apparent from the first clinical trials led us to attempt an evaluation of its therapeutic effect in all cases of bacterial infections in which sulfonamides might prove useful. Sulfadiazine was therefore used as the only sulfonamide drug in five of the medical wards beginning November 1 and in three additional wards beginning January 1. Other sulfonamide drugs were used in these wards only while the supply of sulfadiazine was exhausted and in some patients when it became apparent that the response to sulfadiazine was not adequate. As the study progressed, it became necessary, because of the limited supply of the drug available, to exclude from sulfadiazine therapy patients with mild infections when it was felt that an etiologic bacterial incitant would not be identified. The present report includes 446 consecutive patients in whom treatment with sulfadiazine was begun before March 1. Three hundred and sixteen of these patients were treated for pneumonia. The results of treatment in this group will be analyzed in some detail. The remaining patients were treated for a large variety of infections. The clinical results in this group will be summarized briefly and the toxic effects in both groups will be noted.

## RESULTS IN PNEUMONIA

In general, the results of sulfadiazine treatment in pneumonia (tables 1 to 4) compared favorably in every way with those obtained during the previous year with sulfapyridine and sulfathiazole,[15] and the cases were quite comparable as judged by the incidence of various factors which are known to influence the prognosis. Some of the pneumonias occurred as a complication of clinical influenza which occurred in epidemic form during part of this study. In a number of these cases, which will be described in detail elsewhere, the staphylococcus appeared to be the inciting agent in the pulmonary process. Others in which there were pulmonary lesions in which significant pathogens were not obtained on culture are included under the "primary" pneumonias of undetermined etiology.

*Pneumococcic Pneumonias.*—There were 19 deaths among the 178 patients with pneumococcic pneumonia treated with sulfadiazine, a mortality of 10.7 per cent. During the previous season[15] there were 112 deaths among 687 patients treated with sulfapyridine or sulfathiazole with or without specific serums, a mortality of 16.3 per cent. Among the sulfadiazine treated patients 33, or 19 per cent, had positive blood cultures before

treatment and 8 of these bacteremic patients died (26 per cent). More than one lobe was involved in 62, or 35 per cent, of the 178 patients; 59 per cent were over 40 years of age and 26 per cent were more than 60. The incidence of these important prognostic factors in the present series is similar to that found in the pneumococcic pneumonias during the previous year, but the mortality was slightly lower in each of the corresponding groups of sulfadiazine treated patients.

Specific antipneumococcus serums were given to supplement the chemotherapy to 16 of these patients, of whom 6 died. Ten of the recipients of serum, including 5 who died, had positive blood cultures before therapy was started.

Complications in the patients with pneumococcic pneumonias were relatively few. A sterile pleural effusion was demonstrated in 10 patients, conjunctivitis in 1, suppurative otitis media in 4, empyema in 2 and both empyema and fibrinous pericarditis in 1. The latter patient required rib resection for the empyema, while all the others recovered completely without surgical intervention.

Of the fatalities 8 patients were moribund at the time of admission and only 1 of these lived for more than twenty-four hours after the first dose of sulfadiazine. Only 2 other patients may be said to have died of the pneumococcic infection: One was a woman aged 40 who died of vegetative pneumococcic (type VII) endocarditis and old rheumatic heart disease; the other was an alcoholic patient aged 27 with severe leukopenia (1,400 per cu. mm.) and involvement of the entire right lung who had a persistent type VII pneumococcic bacteremia during four days of sulfadiazine therapy. He was then given serum and died the following day. Autopsy revealed abscess formation in the consolidated lung; the cardiac blood was sterile. The 9 other fatalities were of aged patients who died of various untoward events not directly related to the pneumococcic infection and after the latter had apparently been overcome.

The specific antibody response of a number of the patients who recovered was studied and was found to be similar to that of patients who recovered following sulfapyridine therapy.[16]

*Other Specific Pneumonias.*—The 35 pneumonia patients with pathogenic organisms other than pneumococci were, for the most part, severely ill at the time of admission to the hospital. Most of the cases in which the staphylococcus was predominant occurred as a complication of epidemic influenza. Recovery following chemotherapy in some of these cases was prompt and complete. In others, in spite of continued therapy, there was prolonged illness with clinical and roentgen evidence of abscess formation and localized pleural effusion. All except 1 patient recovered completely before discharge from the hospital.

Six of the deaths occurred among the patients with staphylococcic pneumonias. Three of these were of patients with the fulminating type of rapidly spreading

14. Strauss, Elias; Lowell, F. C., and Finland, Maxwell: Observations on the Inhibition of Sulfonamide Action by Para-Aminobenzoic Acid, J. Clin. Investigation 20:187 (March) 1941.

15. Finland, Maxwell; Lowell, F. C., and Strauss, Elias: Treatment of Pneumococcic Pneumonia with Sulfapyridine, Sulfathiazole and Serum, Ann. Int. Med. 14:1184 (Jan.) 1941.

16. Finland, Maxwell; Spring, W. C., Jr., and Lowell, F. C.: Immunological Studies on Patients with Pneumococcic Pneumonia Treated with Sulfapyridine, J. Clin. Investigation 19:179 (Jan.) 1940.

pneumonia complicating influenza, and death occurred within forty-eight hours of admission to the hospital. Culture of the blood of one of these patients taken before treatment yielded hemolytic streptococci but a culture of the sputum showed a predominance of staphylococci. Death occurred after thirty-six hours. At autopsy there was diffuse hemorrhagic pneumonia with ulcerative bronchitis and multiple abscesses. The contents of the abscesses yielded an abundant growth of staphylococci, but the cardiac blood was sterile. The other three deaths were of patients aged 64, 76 and 81 who died fourteen, sixteen and eight days, respectively, after chemotherapy

TABLE 2.—*Mortality in Pneumonia Treated with Sulfadiazine: Effect of Age*

| Age, Years | A No. | A Died | B No. | B Died | C No. | C Died | D No. | D Died | All Patients No. | All Patients Died | All Patients Per Cent |
|---|---|---|---|---|---|---|---|---|---|---|---|
| 3-19 ...... | 12 | 0 | 7 | 1 | 1 | 0 | 1 | 0 | 21 | 1 | 5 |
| 0-29 ...... | 20 | 2 | 5 | 0 | 9 | 0 | 3 | 1 | 37 | 3 | 8 |
| 0-39 ...... | 41 | 0 | 6 | 0 | 8 | 0 | 2 | 1 | 57 | 1 | 2 |
| 0-49 ...... | 31 | 1 | 7 | 3 | 9 | 0 | 4 | 0 | 51 | 4 | 8 |
| 0-59 ...... | 28 | 4 | 2 | 0 | 3 | 0 | 11 | 3 | 44 | 7 | 16 |
| 0-69 ...... | 24 | 4 | 3 | 1 | 10 | 1 | 13 | 4 | 50 | 10 | 20 |
| 0-79 ...... | 17 | 4 | 4 | 1 | 10 | 1 | 13 | 8 | 44 | 14 | 32 |
| 0+ ........ | 5 | 4 | 1 | 1 | 2 | 1 | 4 | 2 | 12 | 8 | 75 |
| Totals .. | 178 | 19 | 35 | 7 | 52 | 3 | 51 | 19 | 316 | 48 | 15.2 |

| Percentage Mortality | A | B | C | D | |
|---|---|---|---|---|---|
| All patients | 10.7 | 20.0 | 5.8 | 37.5 | 15.2 |
| Under 50 ... | 2.9 | 16.0 | 0 | 20.0 | 5.4 |
| Over 50 ..... | 21.6 | 30.0 | 12.0 | 41.5 | 26.0 |

A, B, C, and D refer to groups of patients as listed in table 1.

was started. All were severely ill and showed temporary improvement under therapy. One of these patients died of pulmonary infarcts from thrombophlebitis. One of the others had multiple staphylococcic abscesses in the lung at necropsy.

Fluid was obtained by thoracentesis on 6 of the patients with staphylococcic pneumonia who recovered. The original pleural fluid and subsequent ones of 2 were all sterile. Of the remaining 4, all of whom had pleural exudates which were infected with staphylococci, 2 recovered completely under sulfadiazine therapy and repeated aspirations, while the others underwent surgical drainage by rib resection.

The 4 patients with primary streptococcic pneumonia were all severely ill and 2 had positive blood cultures at the time sulfadiazine treatment was begun. All these patients recovered completely. Two of them, including one with bacteremia, had empyema which cleared up completely with chemotherapy and repeated thoracentesis and did not require surgical intervention.

Two patients with pneumonia of type A Friedländer's bacillus were treated with sulfadiazine. One was a man aged 51 who had a negative blood culture and an atypical pneumonia involving the entire left lung at the time of admission. Chemotherapy was started before the end of the first day and the patient was afebrile and relieved of acute symptoms after sixteen hours. The other patient was a man aged 46 who had been ill six days, had a positive blood culture and a leukocyte count of 2,500 per cubic millimeter at the time sulfadiazine therapy was

started. He died twenty-six hours later in spite of intensive therapy, including intravenous sodium sulfadiazine and specific rabbit antiserum.

*Non-Pneumococcic Pneumonias.*—The mortality in all the 138 cases of pneumonia treated with sulfadiazine in which pneumococci were not obtained (including those in which specific bacteria were involved) was 21 per cent, as compared with 23 per cent in the corresponding group of 95 treated with sulfathiazole during the previous year.[15] In both groups the mortality was higher in the atypical pneumonias (bronchopneumonia) and in those secondary to other serious illness than it was in the lobar pneumonias and in the primary pneumonias, respectively.

*Effect of Age on Mortality* (table 2).—This was most striking in the pneumococcic pneumonias (group A) and in the pneumonias classified as "primary" in which a definite etiologic agent was not identified (group C). Among the latter there were no deaths among 30 patients under 50 years of age, while less than 3 per cent of the 104 patients with pneumococcic pneumonia in this age group died. Among the specific non-pneumococcic pneumonias (group B) and the "secondary" pneumonias (group D) the mortality of patients over 50 was about twice as high as that of those under 50 years of age.

*Dosage of Sulfadiazine Used in the Pneumonias* (table 3).—Most of the patients received an initial dose of 2 or 4 Gm. and then 1 Gm. every four hours until the drug was discontinued—usually three to five days after the fever had entirely subsided. In some of the wards the dosage was reduced to 1 Gm. every six hours after the patient became afebrile. Some of the patients with the severest attacks received an initial dose of 5 Gm. of sodium sulfadiazine either in 100 cc. or more of saline solution intravenously or in a liter of physiologic solution of sodium chloride subcutaneously (as recommended by Taplin[17]). About three fourths of the patients who recovered were treated for six days or less and received

TABLE 3.—*Dosage of Sulfadiazine Used in Treatment of Pneumonia*

| Dose, Gm. | Pneumococcic Pneumonia Recovered Cases | Pneumococcic Pneumonia Fatal Cases | All Pneumonias Recovered Cases | All Pneumonias Fatal Cases |
|---|---|---|---|---|
| 10 or less.............................. | 4 | 7 | 7 | 19 |
| 11-20................................... | 18 | 4 | 36 | 12 |
| 21-30................................... | 54 | 3 | 94 | 7 |
| 31-40................................... | 44 | 2 | 67 | 2 |
| 41-50................................... | 18 | 1 | 29 | 4 |
| 51-75................................... | 18 | 3 | 27 | 4 |
| 76 or more.......................... | 3 | 0 | 8 | 0 |
| Average dose | | | | |
| All cases........................... | 38 | 23 | 37 | 20 |
| Bacteremic ...................... | 44 | 33 | | |
| Nonbacteremic................. | 36 | 17 | | |

less than 40 Gm. of the drug. The average dose among the patients with pneumococcic pneumonias who recovered was 38 Gm. The bacteremic patients received an average of 8 Gm. more than those with negative blood

17. Taplin, G. V.; Jacox, R. F., and Howland, J. W.: The Use of Sodium Sulfapyridine by Hypodermoclysis. J. A. M. A. **114:**1733 (May 4) 1940.

cultures. There was a general tendency, especially in the earlier part of this study, to continue the chemotherapy longer than was indicated. This was definitely attributable to the low toxicity of the drug. It was also noted during the previous year that sulfathiazole treated patients were given the drug an average of one day longer than those who received sulfapyridine. With the latter, nausea and vomiting were more frequent and more severe.

TABLE 4.—*Duration of Acute Illness in Patients with Pneumonia After Sulfadiazine Treatment Was Started*

| Hours from First Dose to Essential Recovery or Death | A Recovered | A Died | B Recovered | B Died | C Recovered | C Died | D Recovered | D Died | All Pneumonias Recovered | All Pneumonias Died |
|---|---|---|---|---|---|---|---|---|---|---|
| 12 or less..... | 38 | 1 | 3 | 0 | 15 | 1 | 9 | 1 | 65 | 3 |
| 13-24.......... | 47 | 6 | 9 | 0 | 14 | 1 | 6 | 1 | 76 | 8 |
| 25-36.......... | 35 | 1 | 4 | 1 | 10 | 1 | 6 | 3 | 55 | 6 |
| 37-48.......... | 15 | 0 | 2 | 3 | 2 | 0 | 4 | 2 | 23 | 5 |
| 49-72.......... | 11 | 1 | 0 | 0 | 5 | 0 | 2 | 1 | 18 | 2 |
| 73 or more .. | 13 | 10 | 10 | 3 | 3 | 0 | 5 | 11 | 31 | 24 |
| Totals...... | 159 | 19 | 28 | 7 | 49 | 3 | 32 | 19 | 268 | 48 |

A, B, C, and D refer to groups of patients listed in table 1.

Sulfathiazole was used instead of sulfadiazine during part of the course in 28 cases of pneumonia. In more than half of these cases the sulfathiazole was used for one or two days to maintain treatment after essential recovery had taken place under sulfadiazine, while the supply of the latter was exhausted. Larger amounts were used mainly in the treatment of febrile complications. In 9 cases of pneumococcic pneumonia an average of 23 Gm. of sulfathiazole was used in addition to 31 Gm. of sulfadiazine. Four patients with staphylococcic pneumonias, including the 2 who had a rib resection for empyema, received an average of 75 Gm. of sulfathiazole in addition to 54 Gm. of sulfadiazine.

*Duration of Acute Illness* (table 4).—Among the 159 patients with pneumococcic pneumonia who recovered following sulfadiazine therapy alone or supplemented with serum (group A), 75 per cent were essentially afebrile and recovered within thirty-six hours after the first dose of the drug. During the previous season[15] about 68 per cent of the patients with corresponding conditions had a similar response to either sulfapyridine or sulfathiazole. Recovery in a large proportion of the patients with specific non-pneumococcic pneumonias (group B) was delayed owing to the presence of febrile complications, as already noted. In about one third of all the fatal cases death occurred within thirty-six hours after treatment was started. In most of the others there was obvious and sometimes striking improvement following sulfadiazine treatment at first, and death occurred several days later as a result of complicating conditions.

RESULTS IN INFECTIONS OTHER THAN PNEUMONIA

Sulfadiazine was used in the treatment of 130 patients with a variety of infections. The diseases treated are listed in table 5 with the average total amount of drug used and an estimation of the curative effect of the drug in each condition. It is possible here to mention only

briefly a few of the salient features concerning each of the groups of cases:

*Acute Infections of the Upper Respiratory Tract.*— The 40 patients included in this group all appeared acutely ill when chemotherapy was started. Many of them had scattered musical and crepitant rales through out the lungs and were suspected of having pneumonia but roentgenograms showed no evidence of pulmonary consolidation. Eighteen of the patients were admitted to the hospital during an epidemic of influenza and had characteristic symptoms of this disease with moderate or severe tracheobronchitis. All these patients recovered rapidly and completely soon after sulfadiazine treatment was started, but it is not possible in most instances to evaluate the role of the drug in the recovery or in the prevention of complications. The 4 patients with sinusitis all had severe symptoms and high fever, and 1 had a positive blood culture for Staphylococcus aureus before therapy. All were noticeably improved and essentially afebrile within fifteen to thirty-six hours after the first dose of sulfadiazine. In 1 of the 2 cases of otitis media

TABLE 5.—*Summary of Results of Sulfadiazine Therapy in Infections Other Than Pneumonia*

| Infection | Number of Cases | Died | ++ | + | ± | 0 | Average Dose Gm |
|---|---|---|---|---|---|---|---|
| Acute infections of upper respiratory tract | | | | | | | |
| Bronchitis.................................... | 3 | 0 | 1 | 2 | 0 | 0 | 20 |
| Pharyngitis and tonsillitis.............. | 13 | 0 | 7 | 6 | 0 | 0 | 19 |
| Sinusitis..................................... | 4 | 0 | 4 | 0 | 0 | 0 | 36 |
| Otitis media................................ | 2 | 0 | 1 | 0 | 1 | 0 | 26 |
| Clinical influenza ........................ | 18 | 0 | 4 | 12 | 2 | 0 | 20 |
| Erysipelas (facial) ........................... | 8 | 0 | 4 | 4 | 0 | 0 | 38 |
| Scarlet fever.................................... | 1 | 0 | 0 | 0 | 1 | 0 | 105 |
| Pyelonephritis and cystitis | | | | | | | |
| Acute ...................................... | 17 | 0 | 11 | 5 | 1 | 0 | 27 |
| Chronic ................................... | 12 | 2 | 1 | 1 | 7 | 3 | 36 |
| Gonococcic arthritis | | | | | | | |
| Acute ...................................... | 4 | 0 | 3 | 0 | 1 | 0 | 72 |
| Subacute or chronic..................... | 5 | 0 | 0 | 1 | 2 | 2 | 87 |
| Meningococcemia with arthritis ........ | 1 | 0 | 1 | 0 | 0 | 0 | 54 |
| Meningococcic meningitis................. | 2 | 1 | 1 | 0 | 1 | 0 | 22 |
| Pneumococcic meningitis................. | 4 | 4 | 0 | 0 | 3 | 1 | 49 |
| Subacute bacterial endocarditis ......... | 5 | 4 | 0 | 0 | 1 | 4 | 90 |
| Chronic pulmonary infections | | | | | | | |
| Pulmonary tuberculosis ................. | 8 | 0 | 0 | 0 | 2 | 6 | 42 |
| Pleurisy with effusion .................. | 3 | 0 | 0 | 0 | 0 | 3 | 32 |
| Nontuberculous (abscess, putrid empyema)............................. | 3 | 0 | 0 | 0 | 1 | 2 | 45 |
| Focal staphylococcic infections.......... | 2 | 1 | 1 | 0 | 1 | 0 | 29 |
| Intestinal and peritoneal infections .... | 3 | 1 | 0 | 1 | 0 | 2 | 84 |
| Miscellaneous febrile diseases............ | 12 | 3 | 0 | 2 | 1 | 9 | 41 |
| Totals ................................. | 130 | 16 | 39 | 34 | 25 | 32 | |

° ++ indicates excellent response apparently in relation to sulfadiazine therapy; +, good recovery, relation to sulfadiazine difficult to evaluate; ± apparent benefit from sulfadiazine with relapse or incomplete recovery; 0, no definite beneficial effect of sulfadiazine discernible.

hemolytic streptococci and staphylococci were cultured from the purulent exudate, which cleared completely in two days. In the other the purulent discharge, from which Staphylococcus aureus was cultured, continued for several days in spite of full doses of sulfadiazine and finally cleared. In the latter case a course of sulfathiazole therapy had previously been given without benefit.

*Erysipelas and Scarlet Fever.*—The results of therapy in 8 patients with facial erysipelas were uniformly good. Four patients had severe attacks of the disease with extensive involvement, edema, high fever and toxemia. All improved definitely within twelve to thirty-six hours after the first dose of sulfadiazine. The other 4 had milder attacks which cleared promptly under treatment. Cultures of the blood of all were negative. One Negro patient with severe scarlet fever and leukopenia (1,700 per cubic millimeter), who failed to improve after four

TABLE 6.—*Toxic Effects of Sulfadiazine Among Four Hundred and Forty-Six Cases*

| Toxic Effect | Number of Cases | Per Cent |
|---|---|---|
| Nausea | 2 | |
| Vomiting, mild | 36 | 9.2 |
| Vomiting, moderate | 3 | |
| Hematuria, gross | 1 | |
| Hematuria, microscopic | 2 | 0.7 |
| Increase in blood nonprotein nitrogen | 5* | 1.1 |
| Leukopenia (drop below 4,000) | 9† | 2.0 |
| Dermititis with or without fever | 9 | |
| Drug fever | 1 | 2.2 |
| Headache | 2 | 0.4 |
| Crystals (? acetylsulfadiazine) in urine | 35 | 7.8 |

*Increases ranged from 15 to 26 mg. per hundred milliliters.

†In 6 of these cases the leukocyte count rose before the drug therapy was discontinued.

Seven cases are listed twice.

days of sulfathiazole treatment, continued to have fever for several days after he was changed to sulfadiazine and then recovered completely.

*Infections of the Urinary Tract.*—There was a striking difference in response between the patients with acute and those with chronic infections of the urinary tract. Among the 17 patients with acute involvement the urinary abnormalities and symptoms cleared completely and cultures became sterile fairly promptly following sulfadiazine treatment. Colon bacillus, alone or with other organisms, was cultured from the urine of most of these patients before treatment, and subsequent urines were sterile. The 12 patients with chronic infections included 3 with Friedländer's bacillus as the predominant organism in the urine (2 of these patients had previously had a nephrectomy), 2 with Flexner dysentery bacilluria and others with a variety of organisms including colon bacilli in cultures of the urine. Only 2 of these 12 patients recovered completely, and both of these had colon bacilli predominantly. Seven others were definitely improved but either had a relapse or continued to have residual symptoms. The patient with Proteus bacillus infection died within thirty-six hours. One other patient died with a complicating diabetic acidosis.

Most of the patients in this group received 6 Gm. daily, but some were given 1 Gm. every six hours during part or all of the course of treatment. Eight of the patients with chronic attacks who failed to show a complete recovery under sulfadiazine had a similar or longer course of sulfathiazole therapy given either before or after the sulfadiazine but with similar lack of success in every instance.

Three of the patients in this group showed abnormal retention of the drug with blood levels above 20 mg. per

hundred cubic centimeters (free and acetylated). In none of them was more than one third of the circulating drug found in the conjugated (acetylated) form. One of these 3 patients had a rise in blood nonprotein nitrogen from 54 to 75 mg. per hundred cubic centimeters during the sulfadiazine therapy, but this dropped slowly to 32 mg. per hundred cubic centimeters within a few days. The patient's urine and symptoms, however, improved steadily during chemotherapy.

*Gonococcic Arthritis With or Without Urethritis.*—The results among patients with these disorders also varied with the chronicity of the disease. Four of the patients had symptoms for less than ten days before sulfadiazine therapy was started, and their disease was classed as acute. All these patients improved rapidly under the treatment. In 1 of them the symptoms recurred one week after discharge from the hospital and shortly after a prostatic massage. Five patients had symptoms for three weeks to several months before admission to the hospital. One of them made a good recovery; the other 4 either failed to improve or improved slowly and then had a relapse of symptoms. Each of these 4 patients also received, either before or after the sulfadiazine, a course of sulfapyridine or sulfathiazole averaging 61 Gm. These drugs likewise failed to bring about a cure.

*Meningococcic Infections.*—Sulfadiazine was used in the treatment of 2 patients with endemic meningococcic meningitis and 1 with meningococcemia and arthritis (without meningitis). One of the meningitis patients was moribund on admission to the hospital and died within twelve hours. The other 2 patients recovered promptly and completely. During the course of the present study, Dingle and Thomas of this laboratory had an opportunity to treat 11 consecutive cases of epidemic type I meningococcic meningitis in Halifax, N. S. They observed an excellent therapeutic response to sulfadiazine in every instance. The details in all 14 cases are reported separately.[18]

*Pneumococcic Meningitis.*—The 4 patients with this disease who were treated with sulfadiazine all had massive infection and bacteremia on admission. One of them died four hours after receiving the first dose of the drug. Two others died after two days of treatment with

TABLE 7.—*Comparative Toxicity of Sulfadiazine and Sulfathiazole in Cases in Which Both Drugs Were Given*

| Toxic Effect from | Number of Cases |
|---|---|
| Sulfadiazine only | 2 |
| Sulfathiazole and sulfadiazine | 11 |
| Sulfathiazole only | 28 |
| Neither drug | 25 |
| Number treated with both drugs | 66 |

the drug and with intravenous specific serum. In the fourth patient the meningitis occurred as a complication of a fractured skull with extensive brain injury. The blood and spinal fluid were rapidly sterilized following treatment with the drug supplemented with intravenous serum, but the patient died during a relapse of the

18. Dingle, J. H.; Thomas, Lewis, and Morton, A. R.: Treatment of Meningococcic Meningitis and Meningococcemia with Sulfadiazine, this issue, p. 2666.

infection five weeks later. Three of these patients received one or more doses of sodium sulfadiazine parenterally.

*Subacute Bacterial Endocarditis.*—The results of therapy with sulfadiazine in 5 cases of this disease were uniformly poor. Negative blood cultures were obtained after treatment in only 1 of these cases. In the others the bacteremia persisted in spite of continued therapy. One of the latter patients is still under treatment and the other 4 have died. The organism was Streptococcus viridans in 4 of the cases and enterococcus in the fifth. In 4 cases, all the other common sulfonamides were used in rotation before and after sulfadiazine, an average of 400 Gm. of these drugs being used—all without demonstrable benefit.

*Chronic Pulmonary Infections.*—Only 3 of the 14 patients in this group showed some improvement under sulfadiazine therapy. This was attributed in each instance to the partial relief of a superimposed acute pulmonary infection. An antipyretic effect such as that noted by Beeson and Janeway[19] in patients treated with sulfapyridine was not observed in any of these patients.

*Focal Staphylococcic Infections.*—In 1 case an infected hydrocele cleared rapidly after the purulent fluid was tapped and sulfadiazine given orally. Culture of the fluid yielded staphylococci as the predominant organisms and also Friedländer's bacilli. In a second case, a staphylococcic pyarthrosis was improved significantly under treatment. Evidences of infection cleared rapidly, but the joint pain persisted.

*Intestinal and Peritoneal Infections.*—One patient with known peptic ulcer had low grade fever and suggestive evidence of a subacute perforation. This patient was afebrile and symptom free during two courses of sulfadiazine therapy, but the ulcer symptoms recurred each time after the drug was stopped. A second patient with a gastrocolic fistula obtained no relief and subsequently was operated on and died. The third patient in this group had chronic ulcerative colitis which was not affected by sulfadiazine given orally and in retention enemas. Salmonella suipestifer was identified in repeated stool cultures from this patient.

*Miscellaneous Diseases.*—In this group are included 4 cases of rheumatic fever, 2 of acute leukemia and 1 each of disseminated lupus erythematosus, S. suipestifer bacteremia (which proved at autopsy to arise from an infected mural thrombus at the site of an old coronary infarct), acute coronary infarction, catarrhal jaundice, infectious mononucleosis and a case of pyrexia of undetermined origin. Definite improvement was noted in only 2 cases: the patient with infectious mononucleosis was afebrile and free of symptoms on the second day of treatment, and one of the patients with acute leukemia showed a definite temporary improvement when a submaxillary abscess cleared under chemotherapy. There was temporary and partial improvement in one case of acute rheumatic fever. The patient who was treated for fever of undetermined origin was the only one of the 446 patients in whom severe renal symptoms (colic and hematuria) developed. This occurred after two and one-half weeks of continued therapy with full doses.

## TOXIC EFFECTS

Toxic symptoms referable to sulfadiazine therapy were comparatively rare and mild. They were noted in 63, or 14.1 per cent, of the 446 patients, excluding those in whom crystals were found in the urine without other abnormalities or symptoms (tables 6 and 7).

*Nausea and Vomiting.*—During sulfadiazine administration nausea and vomiting were noted in 9.2 per cent of the patients, including those in whom this symptom was present before the drug was started. In no instance was this symptom severe. On the other hand, many patients who had been vomiting prior to the sulfadiazine therapy, either as part of their illness or as a result of therapy with other drugs, tolerated the sulfadiazine well.

*In the Urinary Tract.*—Crystals, probably acetylsulfadiazine, were noted in the urine during therapy in 35 patients. These were most frequently of the "sheaves of wheat" type and closely resembled the crystals of acetylsulfathiazole.[20] There were no other urinary abnormalities except in the 3 patients with hematuria. In 2 of the latter a few red blood cells were noted in the urine in the course of therapy, but subsequent specimens of urine taken while the drug was continued were free of blood. In 1 patient ureteral colic and gross hematuria developed followed by anuria on the seventeenth day of therapy. This was promptly relieved by catheterization of the ureters and pelvic lavage. The concentration of sulfadiazine in the blood at the time was 19.8 mg. per hundred cubic centimeters, of which 1.5 mg. was the acetyl derivative. The first urine voided after the catheterization contained 271 mg. per hundred cubic centimeters of sulfadiazine, of which 150 mg. was of the acetyl derivative.

Five patients showed a significant rise in nonprotein nitrogen during sulfadiazine therapy. The concentration of sulfadiazine in the blood of 1 of these patients who was treated for pneumonia rose and reached a level of 44 mg. per hundred cubic centimeters, of which 26 mg. was of the acetyl derivatives. This was the highest percentage of acetylation of sulfadiazine in the blood noted in this study but the patient had no untoward symptoms. There were 16 other patients with elevated levels of nonprotein nitrogen (ranging from 43 to 91 mg. per hundred cubic centimeters of blood) before sulfadiazine therapy was started whose levels dropped 20 to 41 mg. per hundred cubic centimeters during the course of drug therapy.

*Leukopenia.*—Drops in the leukocyte count from high or normal to below 4,000 per cubic millimeter were noted in 9 cases. There was a proportionate drop in the granulocytes. In 6 of the cases the drop occurred during the first four days and the leukocyte count rose again while the drug therapy was continued. In the other 3 the low counts were noted between the eleventh and the sixteenth day of therapy, and the lowest count was 2,000 per cubic millimeter. In these cases the drug was stopped and the leukocyte count promptly rose.

19. Beeson, P. B., and Janeway, C. A.: The Antipyretic Action of Sulfapyridine, Am. J. M. Sc. **200**:632 (Nov.) 1940.

20. Sunderman, F. W., and Pepper, D. S.: Sulfathiazole in Blood and Urine, Am. J. M. Sc. **200**:790 (Dec.) 1940.

There were 8 other patients with initial leukocyte counts below 4,000 before treatment whose counts rose during therapy. One of these had severe alcoholic pneumonia, with bacteremia and infected pleural fluid. His leukocyte count before treatment was 500 per cubic millimeter. This rose gradually under sulfadiazine and serum therapy, and the patient made a complete recovery.

*Dermatitis and Fever.*—Only 1 patient had fever as the only symptom that could be attributed definitely to the drug. A rash was noted on 9 patients. This was morbilliform in each instance, except in 1 patient whose rash was of the "erythema nodosum" type, resembling those often seen in sulfathiazole treated cases. The rash appeared on the fourth day of treatment on 1 patient and after eight to fourteen days of sulfadiazine therapy on the others. In each instance the rash cleared promptly when the drug was stopped. In another patient, readministration of the drug one week later resulted in a recurrence of the rash after twenty-four hours.

*Miscellaneous.*—Headache and slight dizziness were noted during treatment of 2 patients and were relieved when the drug was stopped. Anemia, either of the acute or of the slowly progressive type, resulting from chemotherapy, was not observed in any of these patients. Jaundice did not develop in any patient under treatment. Three patients with clinical and laboratory evidence of impaired hepatic function were treated with full doses of sulfadiazine. In 2 of these patients the hepatic function improved and in the other it remained unchanged during treatment.

*Comparison with Sulfathiazole* (table 7).—Each of 66 patients received a separate course of both sulfathiazole and sulfadiazine. This offered an opportunity for the comparison of the toxic effects of the two drugs in the same patients. Some toxic symptoms, mostly nausea, vomiting, hematuria and dermatitis, were noted in 39 patients while they were receiving sulfathiazole, but only 13 had any untoward effects from sulfadiazine. Twenty-eight patients had symptoms from sulfathiazole and not from sulfadiazine, while the reverse was true in only 2 patients.

### SUMMARY AND CONCLUSIONS

Sulfadiazine was used in the treatment of 446 patients with various infections. It appeared to be highly effective in the treatment of the following diseases: pneumococcic, staphylococcic and streptococcic pneumonias; meningococcic infections; acute infections of the upper respiratory tract including sinusitis; erysipelas; acute infections of the urinary tract, particularly those associated with Escherichia coli bacilluria, and acute gonorrheal arthritis.

No well defined beneficial effects were noted from its use in the treatment of chronic infections of the urinary tract, chronic gonococcic arthritis, subacute bacterial endocarditis or chronic pulmonary infections. However, in all patients with these conditions in whom sulfadiazine therapy was not effective and in whom other sulfonamides were tried, the latter were likewise ineffective.

The results in the cases of pneumococcic pneumonia treated with sulfadiazine are comparable in every respect with the best results obtained in this clinic with the use of either sulfapyridine or sulfathiazole. In all the other conditions the numbers of cases are too few to warrant definite conclusions or comparisons. In general, sulfadiazine appeared to be as effective as sulfapyridine or sulfathiazole in every condition in which it was used.

Toxic effects from sulfadiazine were relatively mild and infrequent. Nausea and vomiting occurred in 9.2 per cent of the cases. Nitrogen retention of moderate degree was noted in 5 cases. Leukopenia occurred early and was transient in some cases. In 3 cases the leukocyte counts dropped between the eleventh and the sixteenth day and returned to normal on cessation of therapy. Morbilliform eruptions were observed in 9 cases and usually appeared on the eighth day or later. In 1 case renal colic, hematuria and anuria were relieved by ureteral catheterization.

A number of patients with definite evidence of renal or hepatic damage were treated with sulfadiazine without further impairment and, in some instances, with actual improvement of function in the course of therapy. Some patients with initial leukopenia showed a rise in the white blood count during sulfadiazine therapy.

Sixty-six patients received both sulfathiazole and sulfadiazine, and toxic effects from sulfathiazole were three times as frequent as they were during sulfadiazine therapy.

Sodium sulfadiazine in physiologic solution of sodium chloride was used for the initial dose in some of the most severe cases. No untoward local or systemic effects were noted from its administration in concentrations of 1 to 5 per cent of the drug intravenously or 0.5 per cent subcutaneously.

# Sulfadiazine*

## A Landmark Study

### Robert G. Petersdorf, MD

### Brief History of the Sulfonamides

Although sulfanilamide was discovered by a German graduate student named Gelmo as early as 1908, the therapeutic potential of the sulfonamides was not appreciated until the demonstration by Domagk that Protonsil protected mice from streptococcal infection. The first patient in whom Protonsil was shown to be effective was an infant with staphylococcal sepsis who was treated in 1933. From that point on, a variety of sulfonamides was described in rapid succession; articles on sulfanilamide, sulfapyridine, sulfathiazole, and sulfamethylthiazole flooded the literature (see Chapter 27). The accompanying article,[1] although not the first clinical description of the sulfonamide drugs, was the most complete dealing with sulfadiazine, an agent that is still with us almost 45 years and many thousands of patients later.

### Content of the Accompanying Article

In brief, Finland and colleagues describe the animal data available for sulfadiazine and compare it with sulfapyridine and sulfathiazole in experimental infections. They summarize its absorption, excretion, and distribution in humans and point out that it is likely to be less nephrotoxic than its immediate forebears, sulfapyridine and sulfathiazole. They point out that the drug behaved differently in different media in vitro, an observation that has become key to all subsequent in vitro studies on sulfonamides and other antibiotics as well.

In vitro studies showed sulfadiazine to be effective against pneumococci, staphylococci, *Klebsiella,* some species of *Shigella* and *Salmonella,* and *Escherichia coli.* Based on this laboratory evidence, sulfadiazine was deployed as the major sulfonamide on the wards of the Boston City Hospital in the winter of 1940-1941, and no

From the School of Medicine, University of California, San Diego; La Jolla.

*A commentary on Finland M, Strauss E, Peterson OL: Sulfadiazine: Therapeutic evaluation and toxic effects on 446 patients. *JAMA* 1941;116:2641-2647.

fewer than 446 patients were treated within a four-month period, 316 of them for pneumonia.

Among the 178 patients with pneumococcal pneumonia treated with sulfadiazine, 10.7% died. This was a somewhat smaller number than the mortality obtained with sulfapyridine the previous year or with serum therapy before that.[2] The results in pneumonia from other bacteria—staphylococci, streptococci, and *Klebsiella*—while far from perfect, were probably as good as could be expected. In fact, most of the antibiotics produced since then have not done much better in these pneumonias because the patients were then, and are now, so desperately ill. They had staphylococcal pneumonia complicating influenza, septic pulmonary infarcts, and Friedlander's pneumonia occurring against a background of severe alcoholism, bacteremia, and leukopenia. As might be expected, sulfadiazine was not as effective in presumptive bacterial pneumonias from which pneumococci were not isolated as it was in pneumococcal pneumonia.

The drug was also used in acute upper respiratory tract infections, where its effectiveness could be assessed only with difficulty; in erysipelas and scarlet fever, where its effect was dramatic; and in urinary tract infections, where it was excellent in acute infections but performed poorly in chronic infections, a response no different than has occurred with dozens of antibiotics that have followed it. Sulfadiazine was also successful in acute gonococcal infection, while failing to cure chronic gonococcal sepsis. Likewise, meningococcal meningitis responded well, but pneumococcal meningitis did not, presumably because levels of the drug in the CSF were not high enough. The drug was ineffective in subacute bacterial endocarditis (SBE)—perhaps because it is bacteriostatic rather than bactericidal—chronic pulmonary infections, deep-seated abdominal infections, rheumatic fever, and fever of unknown origin.

Finally, the study showed that sulfadiazine's toxicity was low and included nausea and vomiting, crystalluria without other serious urinary abnormalities, mild leuko penia, and a rise in the nonprotein nitrogen level. Other side effects included drug fever, rashes, and headache. All in all, the drug was remarkably nontoxic, much less so than sulfathiazole, with which sulfadiazine was compared directly in 66 patients.

## Significance of This Study

I have been reading antimicrobial studies for 30 years, but this one stands out as an example of first-rate clinical research for many reasons. First, this study presents an extraordinary amount of clinical data in seven short pages; it is a paragon of brevity and clarity! Second, it contains an exceptionally large number of patients; 446 were studied in four months, eliminating the vagaries of seasonal variations and other events that are likely to occur when studies drag out over several years, such as the discovery of new diagnostic and therapeutic modalities. Third, the large number of patients studied in a brief time permitted comparison with a similar group of patients studied in previous years with serum therapy or other sulfonamides[2] and also eliminated the need for randomization—for which there really could not be an ethical excuse in patients as ill as these, even in 1940, when this matter did not have as high a priority in clinical research as it does now. Fourth, it makes many pathophysiological observations in addition to describing drug efficacy. For example, the authors point out the adverse prognostic implications of old age, bacteremia, alcoholism, and granulocytopenia on the outcome of pneumococcal pneumonia, irrespective of therapy. We have come to take these "clinical pearls" for granted, forgetting that somebody had to make the observations that extracted the pearls from their oysters. Fifth, the study encompassed the spectrum of infectious disease as it appeared more than 40 years ago and makes us realize that, then as now, we are dealing with pneumonias, upper respiratory tract infections, urinary tract infections, SBE, meningitis, and fevers. Although the hosts were somewhat different, the microorganisms have not changed much; the drugs, of course, have. Sixth, this largely clinical study was accompanied by first-rate laboratory controls. For many years, the Boston City Hospital has had a remarkable clinical microbiology laboratory largely because of the efforts of Maxwell Finland and colleagues. In most patients, a causative organism was identified, its in vitro sensitivity was determined, and the results of treatment were assessed. Finally, this study emphasizes again that all drugs have side effects; fortunately, in the case of the sulfonamides, particularly sulfadiazine, these have remained relatively benign.

## Sulfonamides Today

In contrast to some of the other early antibiotics like bacitracin, tyrothrycin, and neomycin, sulfonamides have remained with us. As a matter of fact, sulfadiazine has had a long, healthy life and is still in use in many parts of the world. The remarkable fact about the accompanying article is that so many of the clinical observations made in it have held up. For example, sulfonamides were as ineffective in SBE in 1940 as they are now. If a meningococcus is sensitive to sulfonamides, there is not a better group of drugs for prophylaxis and even for

therapy. To be sure, penicillin has replaced the sulfonamides in pneumococcal and streptococcal infections, but we need to remember that the drugs will still work in these infections if called on. In most instances, the staphylococcus has escaped from the antimicrobial net of the sulfonamides, but this is also the case for benzyl penicillin and its analogues and for the tetracyclines. The sulfonamides have remained remarkably effective in uncomplicated urinary tract infections, and, in combination with trimethoprim, they have gained a new lease on life against many gram-negative pathogens and *Pneumocystis carinii*.

## Sulfonamides in Urinary Tract Infections

As one who has worked in the field of urinary tract infection, I was amazed by the accurate description of the effect of sulfadiazine in uncomplicated *E coli* infections. The authors showed that among 17 patients with acute urinary tract infections treated with sulfadiazine, both the symptoms and the urinary sediment cleared completely and cultures became sterile. Most of these patients were infected with *E coli*. In contrast, bacteriologic cure was achieved in only two of 12 patients with chronic urinary tract infections, three of which were caused by *Klebsiella*. This clinical observation has been corroborated many times and forms the basis of a study by my colleagues and me done more than 20 years later.[3]

This study proposed a classification of bacteriuria that stratified urinary tract infections into four categories—from acute uncomplicated, generally caused by *E coli* that was sensitive to all antibiotics, including sulfonamides, and that responded well to a conventional course of therapy, to chronic bacteriuria, which was caused by multiply resistant microorganisms and which responded poorly to all antibiotics. This article placed the clinical understanding and prognosis of urinary tract infections on a firmer clinical and microbiological basis. What we did not know is that Finland and his colleagues had been there long before us. Moreover, although today's primary antimicrobial for uncomplicated urinary tract infections is sulfamethoxazole rather than sulfadiazine, the fact remains that a sulfonamide continues to be the first line of defense in uncomplicated urinary tract infections. This observation had its genesis on the wards of the Boston City Hospital and has benefited countless patients since it was first made.

## Why the Accompanying Article Is a Classic

I have already pointed out the virtues of the accompanying article—its brevity and clarity, the large number of patients studied, the high "pearl per page" index, its careful microbiological controls, the astuteness of its clinical observations, and its meticulous attention not only to clinical results but also to adverse side effects. What is more important, however, is that this article set a style for clinical investigation that became the gold standard for how antibiotics should be scrutinized, both in the laboratory and the clinic, before they could be let loose on the profession and the public. Max Finland and his hard-working group of fellows, aided by the indomitable Mildred Barnes and Claire Wilcox, studied literally every new antibiotic as it appeared, each in the same meticulous way. Over the years, they published hundreds of articles. If a new antibiotic did not have the Finland stamp of approval, it had little chance to make it, and for good reason. Considering the many quick and dirty articles that have populated the antibiotic literature over the years, Finland's group served as the beacon of quality that maintained a standard for the whole field.

None of this would have been possible without the indefatigable work habits of Max Finland; he was the driving force. Not only that, he inculcated his standards and his work ethic into two generations of clinical investigators who have carried out the major studies in antimicrobial therapy in this country.

In his review of infectious diseases in the bicentennial volume dealing with the contributions of American Medicine, Beeson[4] fashioned an honor roll of contributors to infectious diseases. Max Finland was in this select group. The accompanying article is important, therefore, not only because it was among the first and is still the best description of the clinical use of sulfadiazine but because it was authored by Max Finland, without whose contributions antimicrobial therapy surely would not be where it is today.

## References

1. Finland M, Strauss E, Peterson OL: Sulfadiazine: Therapeutic evaluation and toxic effects on 446 patients. *JAMA* 1941:116:2641.

2. Finland M, Spring WC Jr, Lowell FC: Specific treatment of the pneumococcic pneumonias: An analysis of the results of serum therapy and chemotherapy at the Boston City Hospital from July 1938 through June 1939. *Ann Intern Med* 1940;13:1567-1593.

3. Lindemeyer RI, Turck M, Petersdorf RG: Factors determining the outcome of chemotherapy in infections of the urinary tract. *Ann Intern Med* 1963;58:201-216.

4. Beeson PB: Infectious diseases (microbiology), in Bowers JC, Purcell EF (eds): *Advances in American Medicine: Essays at the Bicentennial.* New York, The Josiah Macy, Jr, Foundation, 1976, pp 100-156.

May 23, 1942
(*JAMA* 1942;119:331-332)

# Chapter 34

# Diffuse Collagen Disease

## Acute Disseminated Lupus Erythematosus and Diffuse Scleroderma

Paul Klemperer, M.D.

Abou D. Pollack, M.D.

and

George Baehr, M.D.

New York

The thesis of Morgagni that diseases reside in certain organs of the human body has dominated pathologic anatomy and clinical investigation for centuries. Every diagnostic endeavor was directed toward establishing the fundamental organ disease. No doubt, this working hypothesis has been the cornerstone on which rests the edifice of modern medicine.

The great advance of medicine throughout the nineteenth century is essentially founded on the method of correlating observations made in the hospital ward with those at the postmortem table. This clinicopathologic concept was further advanced by the recognition of an interdependence and unity of certain organs to form organ or tissue systems. Diseases of the hemopoietic or of the reticuloendothelial system represent such an extension of the scope of organ pathology. Nevertheless, one cannot justly maintain that an essential site is established in every disease. A number of acute infections and intoxications do not produce characteristic or even significant lesions in any organ. Pathologic anatomy cannot therefore make any fundamental contribution; the exact nature of these maladies will be disclosed only by investigations into etiology and the examination of functional derangements. Another difficulty with the theory of Morgagni arises from the fact that in certain maladies, such as rheumatic fever, apparently unrelated organs are the sites of the morbid process.

Recent anatomic investigations of disseminated lupus erythematosus have offered a similar problem in that conspicuous gross and microscopic changes were observed in various organs such as the heart, kidneys and skin. The question arose as to which of these organ changes were of primary and fundamental significance—in other words, which represented the seat of the disease, in the sense of Morgagni.

For rheumatic fever it has been shown by Klinge[1] that the pathognomonic involvement of the joints and of the heart is initiated by a characteristic alteration of the connective tissue followed by a specific granulomatous phase, the Aschoff nodule. Subsequent detailed investigations by this author and his school have revealed that the morbid process in rheumatic fever is not limited to these sites but affects the connective tissues throughout the body.

The apparently heterogeneous organ lesions in disseminated lupus erythematosus have similarly been shown to be the result of a fundamental alteration of the collagenous tissues. These collagen alterations are in most individual observations more widespread and conspicuous than those in rheumatic fever, affecting with particular frequency the collagen framework of the heart and of small blood vessels and capillaries, especially those of the kidneys. The connective tissue of the mediastinum and of the retroperitoneal space may also be affected by the morbid process. It is reasonable, therefore, to consider these maladies as systemic diseases of the connective tissues. The justification for the concept of a systemic

---

1. Klinge, F.: Ergebn. d. allg. Path. u. path. Anat. **27**:1, 1933.

disease of the connective tissues depends on the actual existence of a connective tissue system.

A system is, in the biologic sense, according to definition, an assemblage of organic structures composed of similar elements and combined for the same general functions. The connective tissue proper can then justly be regarded as a system because it consists throughout the body of an association of similar cellular and fibrillar elements held together by a third component, an amorphous ground or cement substance. The colloidal nature of this ground substance has been stressed by Schade.[2] Obviously these elements are combined not only for the general function of support but also for other fundamental functions. Interposed between the parenchymal cells and the canalicular blood and lymph spaces of the body, the connective tissues not only serve as the site of transfer of metabolites but most actively serve the body economy in other ways; for example, by the regulation of salt and water balance. An understanding of the colloidal nature of the extracellular portion of the connective tissues is necessary to an analysis of these functions. The same knowledge is imperative for an appreciation of the responses of the connective tissues in degeneration and inflammation. Until recently, approach to these morbid processes has been almost entirely in terms of the cellular reaction within the connective tissues. However, the participation of the fibers and ground substance may occasionally overshadow the cellular reaction. For example, in some persons an injury of the connective tissue results in the excessive production of collagenous fibers and ground substance known as keloid.

We first became aware of the disorder of the connective tissue as a system in our studies of disseminated lupus erythematosus.[3] The apparent heterogeneous involvement of various organs in this disease had no logic until it became apparent that the widespread lesions were identical in that they were mere local expressions of a morbid process affecting the entire collagenous tissue system. The most prominent of these alterations is fibrinoid degeneration—a descriptive morphologic term indicating certain well defined optical and tinctorial alterations in the collagenous fibers and ground substance. The straightening and thickening of the collagen fibers, their apparent friability, their intense eosinophilia and refractibility, together with visible increase in the ground substance can be due only to a profound physicochemical aberration of the colloid state of the connective tissues.

A similar widespread alteration of collagen has also been noted in certain cases of diffuse scleroderma.[4] Here, however, the collagen disturbance is manifest not only as fibrinoid degeneration but also as an increase in the bulk and density of the connective tissue. On the other hand, this sclerosing type of lesion has also been observed in

disseminated lupus erythematosus (spleen, pericardium, retroperitoneal tissues). It is evident, then, that fibrinoid degeneration and collagen sclerosis are the morphologic expression of different phases of a disturbed colloidal collagen system.

In these two diseases morphologic alterations may in the individual case be indeed striking. But even here the changes are hardly crucial enough to account for the profound clinical debasement and death of the patient. This is even more impressive in some cases in which the characteristic morphologic indexes of a systemic collagen disturbance are discoverable only after the most minute search. How can one account for such a discrepancy? It is unlikely that other tissue alterations have been overlooked or not comprehended. In the fully developed case the morphologic signs of implication of the collagenous tissues are quite clear. The fact of total involvement of the collagen tissue system is also clear. Can we assume, therefore, that a derangement of the colloidal state of the entire collagenous system exists, though it cannot consistently be revealed by our histologic methods? Such an assumption has already been made by MacCallum[5] in the analysis of a case of acute scleroderma occurring in an 18 year old boy. Furthermore, the spectacular clinical state observed in scleredema adultorum (Buschke) can be accounted for only by a similar assumption. The hardening of the skin in this disease is far out of proportion to the demonstrable histologic alteration. Moreover, the clinical reversibility of the condition lends credence to the view that the alteration is due to a transient colloidal imbalance within the collagenous tissues.

With these considerations in mind, it must become quite clear that one may regard the connective tissues of the body as a whole as a well defined, widely dispersed colloidal system liable to a variety of injuries. We are concerned here only with those processes which affect the system in its entirety. Among these are acute disseminated lupus erythematosus and certain cases of diffuse scleroderma. There are, indeed, other morbid processes which, when analyzed, are also found to affect the connective tissue system. However, to identify this system as the seat of certain diseases is by no means to identify these diseases with one another or even to relate them. This would be an unjustifiable oversimplification.

Klinge[1] has charted most completely the widespread involvement of the connective tissues in rheumatic fever. Here too the seat of the disease is found in the connective tissues of the body as a whole, although those of the heart exhibit the greatest disturbance. There is in rheumatic fever, as in disseminated lupus erythematosus and in diffuse scleroderma, not only widespread involvement of the connective tissues but also similar alteration of the extracellular components of these tissues—fibrinoid degeneration. However, there are such clearcut differences in the localization and evolution of the characteristic lesions in these diseases that they must be strictly separated. Thus the glomerular lesions in disseminated lupus erythematosus and in diffuse scleroderma are never seen in rheumatic fever; the vascular lesions in the latter rarely achieve such intensity as in the former diseases

2. Schade, H.: Die physikalische Chemie in der inneren Medizin, Dresden & Leipzig, Theodor Steinkopff, 1923.

3. Klemperer, Paul, Pollack, A. D., and Baehr, George: Pathology of Disseminated Lupus Erythematosus, Arch. Path. 32:569 (Oct.) 1941.

4. Pollack, A. D.: Visceral and Vascular Lesions in Scleroderma, Arch. Path. 29:859 (June) 1940: article in preparation.

5. MacCallum, W. G.: Tr. A. Am. Physicians 41:190, 1926.

Finally, and most important, the development of a specific granulomatous phase—the Aschoff nodule—occurs neither in disseminated lupus erythematosus nor in diffuse scleroderma.

Roessle[6] and Jaeger[7] have proposed that fibrinoid degeneration of collagen is a characteristic and constant morphologic feature of diseases of allergic or "pathergic" background and have proposed that such diseases (rheumatic fever, periarteritis nodosa and thromboangiitis obliterans) may be considered in a single group designated as the "rhematische formenkreis." Masugi and Yä-Shu,[8] therefore, having found fibrinoid degeneration widespread within the blood vessels in a case of diffuse scleroderma, suggested that this disease also fell into the same category. This, we believe, is both unjust and unwise. In the first place there has been no universal acceptance of the allergic nature of rheumatic fever, the prototype of the group. Secondly, although it has been shown experimentally (Gerlach,[9] Klinge[10]) that hyperergic inflammation is characterized by fibrinoid degeneration of collagen, the converse does not necessarily follow, that widespread fibrinoid degeneration always indicates a state of hypersensitivity. We know that local fibrinoid degeneration of collagen is found in a variety of states not related to hypersensitivity. It is reasonable to assume, therefore, that widespread collagen degeneration may also be the result of causes other than hypersensitivity. In fact, the predominant incidence in females of acute disseminated lupus erythematosus and diffuse scleroderma speaks against hypersensitivity as the sole mechanism.

Until now an inordinate preoccupation with immediate cause has shut the door to an analysis of the fundamental changes within the connective tissues considered as a colloid system. The connective tissues having been established as the seat of certain diseases, it remains for the investigator to explore this system with the methods available to the biophysicist and the chemist.

6. Roessle, R.: Virchows Arch. f. path. Anat. **288**:780, 1933; Klin. Wchnschr. **15**:809, 1936.

7. Jaeger, E.: Virchows Arch. f. path. Anat. **284**:526, 1932.

8. Masugi, M., and Yä-Shu: Virchows Arch. f. path. Anat. **303**:39, 1938.

9. Gerlach, W.: Virchows Arch. f. path. Anat. **247**:294, 1923.

10. Klinge, F.: Beitr. z. path. Anat. u. z. allg. Path. **83**:186, 1929.

March 23/30, 1984
(JAMA 1984;251:1595-1596)

# Diffuse Collagen Disease*

## A Unified Theory

George E. Ehrlich, MD

From the perspective of 1984, the concept of diffuse collagen disease may not seem to be such a major advance. After all, rheumatology and clinical immunology are coming of age and assuming an important place in the spectrum of internal medicine, and the diseases that together form this category—today known as the connective tissue disorders or dyscollagenoses in the United States and systemic connectivitis abroad[1]—provide the backbone of these two new specialties. But the holistic viewpoint that groups rheumatoid arthritis with systemic lupus erythematosus, perhaps with Sjögren's syndrome as a bridge, and encompasses progressive systemic sclerosis, polyarteritis nodosa, and variant forms of vasculitis, polymyositis and dermatomyositis, eosinophilic fasciitis, and some rare or disappearing disorders, including perhaps even rheumatic fever, reflects skills in the laboratory and a respectability that could not be claimed in 1942. Thus, the 47th annual meeting of the American Rheumatism Association, held in San Antonio, Tex, in June 1983, saw 410 papers presented from the platform or in posters. One hundred fifty-two, 37%, dealt with the connective tissue diseases *excluding* rheumatoid arthritis and rheumatic fever. With the addition of rheumatoid arthritis, almost 80% of the program can be accounted for.

### Concept

The concept of a systemic disease involving connective tissue was for its time almost as momentous as the discovery of the Pacific Ocean by "stout Cortez, silent upon a peak in Darien," (wrongly attributed, but the very image of an awe-inspiring experience, alluding to Homer in the original and apt in the current context). As Klemperer and colleagues pointed out in the first sentence of their article, the "thesis of Morgagni that diseases reside in certain organs of the human body has

dominated pathologic anatomy and clinical investigation for centuries." Thus, to suggest a non–organ-directed systemic involvement of certain tissues as a common bond among identifiable disease entities led to a new perception of disease and indirectly prompted research efforts that have made enormous strides toward more basic understandings and better treatment. We have far to go; the solipsism of clinical immunology needs some tempering. (W. Watson Buchanan has pointed out, in a lecture at the aforementioned rheumatologic meeting, that a stroke will spare the paralyzed side from a rheumatoid arthritis that involves the other side, even though, presumably, the same T and B cells live on both sides of the body.)

To recognize the difference that this article made, one has only to return to the few books on rheumatology available at the time. In 1940, just preceding the publication of the accompanying article, Bernard Comroe[2] had published the second edition of his book, *Arthritis and Allied Conditions*. He was able to do this without coauthors. The book devoted most of its attention to rheumatoid arthritis. Lupus erythematosis (sic) is mentioned twice, once in a table of causes of joint pains, and a second time in two sentences of description. Scleroderma is mentioned twice, the second time in a short paragraph that lists only the skin features. Periarteritis nodosa is listed twice, and it is said of it that of the 101 cases reported in medical journals, 26 — *only* 26 — were diagnosed before the death of the patient. Three sentences suffice for dermatomyositis. This book devotes, on the other hand, 24 pages to foci of infection, 14 to splinting, 39 to physical therapy (much of which is still unchanged), 11 to drugs, nine to vaccines, 14 to vitamins, 19 to the newly introduced gold salts, and six to bee venom. The ESR is the only laboratory test deserving of a discussion.

Two editions later, *Arthritis and Allied Conditions,* now edited by Joseph Hollander[3] after the death of Comroe, appeared in 1949, no longer a single-author book. Hollander and his chosen collaborators were "specialists" in rheumatic diseases (the quotation marks were those of the editor, used almost apologetically). The

From the Department of Medicine, New York University School of Medicine, and the Pharmaceuticals Division, Ciba-Geigy Corporation, Summit, NJ.

*A commentary on Klemperer P, Pollack AD, Baehr G: Diffuse collagen disease: Acute disseminated lupus erythematosus and diffuse scleroderma. JAMA 1942;119:331-332.

collagen diseases now merited a section of their own, 35 pages long. It was the first appearance in a textbook of this important concept. It aggrandized serum sickness, polyarteritis nodosa, disseminated lupus erythematosus, rheumatic fever, rheumatoid arthritis, scleroderma, dermatomyositis, and calcinosis under the term. It was suggested that these were diseases of mesenchymal origin and that skeletal and connective tissue were related to the cellular and humoral sources of immunity. Thus, the link that we now take for granted was first forged. It was thought that swollen collagen, the product of fibroblasts, was perhaps responsible for the lesions. The descriptions by Kussmaul and Maier in 1866 of periarteritis nodosa and by Kaposi of 1872 of disseminated lupus erythematosus, drawing on earlier work by Hebra in 1845 and Cazenave in 1851 with discoid lupus erythematosus, were cited approvingly as ancestors of the modern concepts. But these authors, and the discovery in 1890 that serum sickness could result from injection of diphtheria antitoxin, still referred to isolated phenomena, until Klemperer and co-workers produced a unified theory.

Not all concepts were so progressive then. In 1948, another rheumatology text, entitled *Arthritis and Related Conditions,* appeared.[4] It was still capable of speaking admiringly of high carbohydrate intake and overweight in osteoarthritis as responsible for the joint lesion in persons older than 40 years with high blood pressure. It thus cites the important landmarks in rheumatology: Pemberton's regimen of dietary reduction to improve the symptoms of rheumatoid arthritis (1909), the 1910 crusade by Billings to search for and remove focal infections to treat rheumatoid arthritis successfully, and the nonspecific vaccines introduced by Miller and Lust in 1915. But it does credit Forestier, in 1928, with introducing gold therapy. Physical therapy is again prominently mentioned, but systemic lupus erythematosus, polymyositis, dermatomyositis, and progressive systemic sclerosis are nowhere to be found. Periarteritis nodosa is mentioned in passing. The level of understanding of rheumatic diseases is perhaps best gleaned from biased statements concerning certain diseases and race.

## The Klemperer Article

Klemperer and co-workers built their concept on careful collection of clinical material and evaluation of tissues. They had been interested in systemic lupus for some time; Baehr had first published on that subject in 1931 and together with Klemperer in 1935. These articles anticipated their classic study, "Pathology of Disseminated Lupus Erythematosus," published in 1941.[5] They saw alterations of connective tissue, with degeneration and necrosis of collagen, in the various specimens. They recognized some similarities to rheumatic fever, scleroderma, periarteritis nodosa, diffuse and focal glomerulonephritis, and accelerated arteriosclerosis in these tissue findings. Their article in THE JOURNAL finally drew all the threads together and, in less than two pages, legitimized a subspecialty. The editor at the time chose a meritorious lecture on the origin of cancer in man as the lead article of the issue. The article on collagen disease did not merit even second place. But in this placement, THE JOURNAL was only anticipating today's priorities, in which cancer still leads arthritis and related conditions by a wide margin in public attention and apprehension and in appreciation by granting agencies.

Many investigators have had the opportunity to describe a new disease. Few have been privileged to usher in an era.

### References

1. Giordano M: The concept of connective tissue diseases with collagen accumulation. *Conn Tiss Dis* 1982;1:13-18.
2. Comroe BI: *Arthritis and Allied Conditions.* Philadelphia, Lea & Febiger, 1940.
3. Comroe BI, Hollander JL: *Arthritis and Allied Conditions,* ed 4. Philadelphia, Lea & Febiger, 1949.
4. Bach TF: *Arthritis and Related Conditions.* Philadelphia, FA Davis Co, 1948.
5. Klemperer P, Pollack AD, Baehr G: Pathology of disseminated lupus erythematosus. *Arch Pathol Lab Med* 1941;32:569-631.

May 8, 1943
(*JAMA* 1943;122:78-81)

## Chapter 35

# Treatment of Hyperthyroidism With Thiourea and Thiouracil

E. B. Astwood, M.D.

Boston

Two series of chemical compounds have been found to possess the unique property of inhibiting the endocrine function of the thyroid gland. The administration of these agents to experimental animals is followed, after a short latent period, by a lowering of the basal oxygen consumption, a decrease in the rate of growth and development and a diminished food intake—changes which are consistent with a state of hypothyroidism. In certain animal species these changes are accompanied by a hyperplasia of the thyroid gland which is apparently compensatory in nature and mediated by the anterior lobe of the pituitary. It was the object of this investigation to determine whether the endocrine function of the human thyroid gland could be inhibited by these compounds and to obtain information concerning their dosage and toxicity in individuals with normal thyroid glands and in cases of hyperthyroidism.

It was first pointed out by the Mackenzies and McCollum[1] that sulfaguanidine would induce thyroid hyperplasia in rats, an effect not influenced by adding iodide to the diet but one which could be abolished by the administration of effective doses of thyroxin. Similar thyroid changes were observed in rats by Richter and Clisby[2] and by Kennedy[3] as the result of the administration of thiourea derivatives. Further studies on this

This work was done under the auspices of the University Committee on Pharmacotherapy.

From the departments of Medicine and Pharmacology, Harvard Medical School, and the medical clinic of the Peter Bent Brigham Hospital.

The thiouracil was supplied by Dr. R. O. Roblin, American Cyanamid Company, Stamford, Conn., and Dr. B. W. Carey of the Lederle Laboratories, Inc., Pearl River, N. Y.

1. Mackenzie, J. B.; Mackenzie, C. G., and McCollum, E. V.: Effect of Sulfanilylguanidine on the Thyroid of the Rat, Science **94**:518-519 (Nov. 28) 1941.

2. Richter, C. P., and Clisby, K. H.: Graying of Hair Produced by Ingestion of Phenylthiocarbamide, Proc. Soc. Exper. Biol. & Med. **48**:684-687 (Dec.) 1941; Toxic Effects of Bitter Tasting Phenylthiocarbamide, Arch. Path. **33**:46-57 (Jan.) 1942.

3. Kennedy, T. H.: Thioureas as Goitrogenic Substances, Nature **150**:233-234 (Aug. 22) 1942.

phenomenon have demonstrated that the primary action of compounds of these two types is centered on the inhibition of thyroid hormone production.[4]

More than one hundred compounds have been tested[5] in order to select highly active substances of low toxicity for clinical use. Most of the derivatives of thiourea exhibited some activity but varied widely in toxicity, thiourea itself being the least toxic of all. 2-thiouracil was the most highly active compound tested and the minimal lethal dose of this substance in rats was more than 100 times the dose necessary to produce a detectable thyroid

*Doses Administered for Short Periods of Time Without Detectable Toxic Effects and with No Change in the Basal Metabolic Rate*

| Diagnosis | Compound | Daily Dose, Gm. | Duration of Treat-ment, Days | Total Dose, Gm. |
|---|---|---|---|---|
| Cardiac decompensation .. | Thiourea | 2.0 | 17 | 34 |
| Rheumatoid arthritis ....... | Thiourea | 2.0 | 13 | 26 |
| Diabetes mellitus ............ | Thiouracil | 1.0 | 7 | 7 |
| Fever (cause unknown) ... | Thiouracil | 0.4 | 30 | 12 |
| Carcinoma of the thyroid . | Thiouracil | 1.0 | 24 | 24 |
| Hyperthyroidism ............ | Thiourea | 0.5-1.5 | 5 | 5 |
| Hyperthyroidism ............ | Thiouracil | 0.6-1.0 | 10 | 8.4 |
| Hyperthyroidism ............ | Sulfadiazine | 5.0-10.0 | 10 | 56 |

effect. 2-thiouracil, 2-thiobarbituric acid, diethyl thiourea and several derivatives of 2-thiohydantoin were two to five times as active as thiourea but were somewhat more toxic, especially the thiohydantoins.

A second series of active compounds included a

4. Mackenzie, C. G., and Mackenzie, J. B.: Effect of Sulfonamides and Thioureas on the Thyroid Gland and Basal Metabolism, Endocrinology **32**:185-209 (Feb.) 1943. Astwood, E. B.; Sullivan, J.; Bissell, Adele, and Tyslowitz, R.: Action of Certain Sulfonamides and of Thiourea on the Function of the Thyroid Gland of the Rat, Endocrinology **32**:210-235 (Feb.) 1943.

5. Astwood, E. B.: The Chemical Nature of Compounds Which Inhibit the Function of the Thyroid Gland, J. Pharmacol. & Exper. Therapy, to be published.

number of aniline derivatives such as p-aminobenzoic acid, p-aminophenylacetic acid and related compounds and all of the commonly used sulfonamides. This class of substances, with the exception of the highly active sulfadiazine, was considerably less active than the thioureas.

From a clinical point of view thiourea and thiouracil appeared to be the most promising compounds and were therefore used in studies on normal persons and on patients with hyperthyroidism.

The substances under investigation were administered by mouth in the form of tablets or in capsules. The larger quantities were given in divided doses over each twenty-four hours, the smaller in a single dose after the evening meal. Frequent determinations of the basal metabolic rate and serum cholesterol were made.

## PRELIMINARY EXPERIMENTS

Data on the first 8 cases studied are shown in the accompanying table. Four persons exhibiting no evidence of hyperthyroidism were treated; 2 received 2 Gm. of thiourea daily and 2 received 0.4 and 1.0 Gm. of thiouracil, respectively. Treatment was continued for thirteen to thirty days and during this period no change in the basal metabolic rate occurred; the patients exhibited no signs and experienced no symptoms that could be attributed to the drugs.

One patient with advanced cardiac decompensation was treated with 1 Gm. of thiouracil daily for twenty-four days. This patient had a large nodular thyroid gland and a metabolic rate of +20 to +30 per cent under conditions which were not basal. No definite lowering of the metabolic rate occurred during treatment and at operation a carcinoma of the thyroid was found. The remainder of the gland was composed of nodules of colloid filled alveoli with uniformly flat epithelium.

The first 3 cases of hyperthyroidism were treated for short periods of time during the usual preoperative period of rest in bed. Treatment was continued for five, ten and ten days, respectively. These experiments were made before it was recognized from studies on animals that a considerable latent period was to be expected before the metabolic rate would fall. The slight decreases in metabolic rate that occurred during these periods were not greater than may have occurred from rest alone. Microscopic examination of the portions of the thyroids removed at operation did not reveal any changes which could with certainty be attributed to the treatment.

Subsequent studies were confined to the administration of thiourea and thiouracil for periods of three weeks or longer to patients with hyperthyroidism. Three cases which have been observed for a sufficiently long period of time are reported:

CASE 1.—A man aged 58, a janitor, entered the hospital because of increasing weakness, progressive weight loss, nocturia, polyuria and dyspnea of one year's duration. Two months prior to admission these symptoms became accentuated and on consultation at another hospital diabetes mellitus was diagnosed and treatment instituted. Fifteen units of protamine zinc insulin daily and a low carbohydrate diet resulted in a partial control of the glycosuria, but there was no symptomatic improvement and the patient entered this hospital for further investigation. Examination revealed a moderate degree of diffuse enlargement of the thyroid gland, a fine tremor of the hands and a warm moist skin. The basal metabolic rate was +25 to +35 per cent on repeated determinations, the blood cholesterol was 130 mg. per hundred cubic centimeters and the glycosuria persisted in spite of an increase in insulin to 40 units daily.

Details of treatment and subsequent course are shown in chart 1. Thiourea was given orally in 0.5 Gm. doses twice daily for eight days and four times daily for the next thirteen days. The metabolic rate began to fall on the ninth day of treatment and was normal by the sixteenth day. On the tenth day of treatment hypoglycemic symptoms became frequent and on

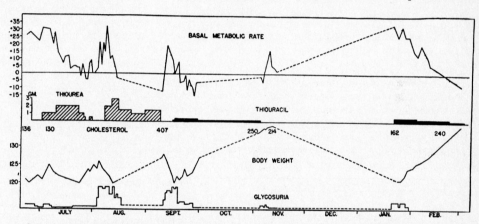

Chart 1.—Changes in the basal metabolic rate, serum cholesterol level, body weight and degree of glycosuria in case 1 during four periods of treatment with thiourea and thiouracil. Insulin was discontinued on July 21. The broken lines represent periods when the patient was not under observation in the hospital.

discontinuation of the insulin the urine sugar remained low, never exceeding a trace. One week after the thiourea was discontinued the metabolic rate again became elevated and the glycosuria returned. Resumption of treatment with thiourea was followed by a prompt return of the metabolic rate to normal and a great decrease in the glycosuria. After a period of three weeks at home and one month after the beginning of the second course of thiourea the patient reentered the hospital for study. At this time there was a maculopapular eruption on the face and on the extensor aspects of the extremities similar to that seen in chronic bromide intoxication. The face appeared to be edematous, the basal metabolic rate was −12 per cent and the blood cholesterol was 407 mg. per hundred cubic centimeters. The drug was discontinued, the rash cleared within four days, the basal metabolic rate rose to a maximum of +19 per cent and glycosuria returned. A third course of treatment was begun, thiouracil being substituted for the thiourea in a dose of 0.4 Gm. daily. After the metabolic rate had fallen and the glycosuria decreased, the dosage was decreased to 0.2 Gm. daily and the patient returned home. After forty days at home he returned in good condition, having regained his normal body weight. The metabolic rate was −2 per cent, the blood cholesterol was 250 mg. per hundred cubic centimeters and there was a trace of sugar in the urine. The thyroid gland was found to be approximately the same size as it had been when treatment was first begun. After he was hospitalized the drug was discontinued. There was a transient and questionably significant elevation of the basal metabolic rate (maximum +16 per cent on one reading), and as the urine remained virtually sugar free the patient was discharged home without treatment. He obtained employment as a locomotive engineer and was able to carry heavy duties for a period of two months. However, weakness gradually returned and with this he noted nervous-

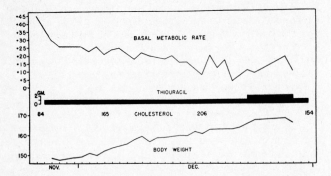

Chart 2.—Effect of a large dose of thiouracil on the basal metabolic rate, serum cholesterol level and body weight in case 2. During the last seven days of treatment symptoms of toxicity developed.

ness, dyspnea, palpitation and pronounced weight loss. When he was hospitalized for the fourth time the metabolic rate was +35 per cent and the thyroid gland was distinctly smaller than it had been previously. Treatment with 0.6 Gm. of thiouracil daily was begun. The metabolic rate fell to +13 per cent in twelve days, when the dosage was reduced to 0.4 Gm. daily. On the thirty-second day the dosage was further reduced to 0.2

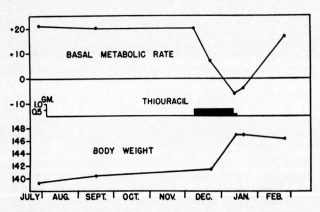

Chart 3.—Decrease in the basal metabolic rate and increase in body weight following the administration of thiouracil in case 3. Five weeks after the drug was discontinued symptoms returned and the metabolic rate became elevated. A second course of treatment was 0.2 Gm. of thiouracil daily during March resulted in a decrease in the basal metabolic rate to +3 per cent and a further increase in the body weight to 152 pounds (69 Kg.)

Gm. daily and on the thirty-ninth day the basal metabolic rate had fallen to −8 per cent. This dosage was continued and the patient returned to work. During this time the thyroid gland slowly increased in size to approximately that noted at the beginning of treatment. The patient has continued to take 0.2 Gm. of thiouracil daily and has remained in good health for a period of two months.

CASE 2.—A man aged 37, a truck driver, first noted symptoms of nervousness, anxiety and tremor following an automobile accident five years before entering the hospital.

After three years of moderate symptoms he began to lose weight and to tire easily. Toxic diffuse goiter was diagnosed on his examination for entry into the army and he was referred to the hospital for treatment. At this time he had lost a total of 35 pounds (16 Kg.) but was not acutely ill. There was moderate exophthalmos and a pronounced stare but minimal lid lag. The skin was warm and moist; the thyroid gland was diffusely enlarged, soft and not nodular. The basal metabolic rate was +45 per cent on the first day and +26 per cent after three days of rest in bed. The serum cholesterol was 84 mg. per hundred cubic centimeters. All other findings were essentially normal. Thiouracil was given in a dose of 0.2 Gm. five times daily for twenty-seven days and then 0.4 Gm. five times daily for six days. Symptomatic improvement became apparent during the second week of treatment, the serum cholesterol increased to 206 mg. per hundred cubic centimeters and although the metabolic rate steadily decreased it did not reach normal levels. The body weight increased 20 pounds (9 Kg.) during four weeks (chart 2). When the dosage of thiouracil was increased to 2 Gm. daily the patient began to suffer vague malaise which he did not admit until subsequently. He was discharged from the hospital on the thirty-fifth day of treatment and was to continue to take 1.0 Gm. of thiouracil daily. Within thirty-six hours of leaving the hospital he returned with a severe pharyngitis and a temperature of 105 F. There proved to be no demonstrable granulocytes in the blood smear and the total white cell count was 1,100. The drug was discontinued and he was treated with sulfathiazole, liver extracts and pentnucleotide. After a severe illness he recovered; granulocytes returned in normal numbers after being absent from the blood smear for seven days. The patient was given 1 cc. of compound solution of iodine daily following this episode but the metabolic rate returned to levels of +30 to +40 per cent three weeks after the thiouracil was discontinued.

CASE 3.—A woman aged 43, a housewife, had been treated for hyperthyroidism for five years. Three years prior to the current episode, subtotal thyroidectomy was performed with subsequent complete relief of symptoms for a period of nine months. Nervousness, irritability and general malaise then returned and continued to be of major concern; treatment with iodine, phenobarbital and estrogens brought no relief. The basal metabolic rate during this period was +20 per cent and the patient was 15 pounds (6.8 Kg.) under her normal weight. The thyroid gland was not palpable, and there was a moderate degree of stare but no exopthalmos. The skin was warm, and the face flushed. Thiouracil was given in a dose of 0.2 Gm. three times daily while the patient continued to work at home. After one week of treatment there was a noticeable improvement in the nervous irritability and the patient noted a general sense of well being. The basal metabolic rate fell in fourteen days to +7 per cent and in thirty-five days to −6 per cent. One week after the drug was discontinued the basal metabolic rate was −4 per cent and in five weeks +17 per cent (fig. 3). Symptoms returned during the fourth week but there was no loss of weight. Thiouracil was resumed in a dose of 0.2 Gm. daily symptoms were again controlled after one week of treatment the metabolic rate returned to normal and the patient has remained well on this treatment for two months.

## COMMENT

These preliminary studies indicate that thiourea and thiouracil may be useful in the control of hyperthyroidism. However, a true evaluation of the merits and dangers of such therapy will require the observation of a large number of cases over a prolonged period of time.

Compounds of the type used in this investigation have never before been administered to human beings except in isolated instances when small single doses were given for studies on intermediary metabolism. Possible toxic reactions of an acute or chronic nature may occur and in the few cases thus far studied one severe and several mild episodes were observed. The occurrence of agranulocytosis (case 2) is a most serious contraindication to any form of drug therapy, and it will be of importance to determine whether this type of reaction to thiouracil represents an idiosyncrasy or whether it is the result of too large a dose. Thiourea is apparently the least toxic substance of the entire series, but for clinical purposes it has the disadvantage of imparting a characteristic odor to the breath, and with some persons it is disagreeable to the taste. The only evidence of toxicity thus far encountered with thiourea was a skin rash in case 1. Thiouracil is apparently free of these disadvantages, and although it is more active it may prove to be more toxic.

There appears to be a variable latent period following the initiation of treatment before the metabolic rate begins to fall, and a similar although somewhat shorter period before clinical improvement is subjectively and objectively apparent. This delay in the effect accords well with the experiments in animals that have been referred to, in which it was noted that the lowering of metabolism coincided in time with a complete or nearly complete loss of detectable colloid from the thyroid gland. If the concept that these drugs prevent the synthesis of thyroid hormone is correct, one might expect that the rate of metabolism would remain nearly constant as long as the store of thyroid hormone in the gland was adequate to supply the organism. When this store nears exhaustion, the decreased rate of thyroid hormone synthesis becomes apparent in the fall of the basal metabolic rate. Support for this explanation is given by the failure of 4 persons with normal thyroid glands to show a decrease in metabolism when the drugs were administered for periods of two to four weeks, while the cases of hyperthyroidism responded within ten to fourteen days. It is known that the store of thyroid hormone in hyperplastic glands is greatly decreased, while that of the normal thyroid is sufficient, if steadily released, to maintain the metabolism of a normal person unchanged for a period of one to three months. As the hyperplastic gland is presumably secreting at an increased rate, one might reasonably expect that its small store of preformed hormone would become exhausted much more rapidly than would that of a normal gland.

Further studies will be necessary in order to determine the optimal therapeutic regimen for long term treatment. Certain cases of hyperthyroidism will probably require treatment over many months or even years, while in other cases the state of hyperthyroidism is apparently temporary and self limited. It may be possible by the use of drugs of this type to maintain such patients in normal health during this period of temporary disturbance.

A rough estimate of the required dosages of thiourea and thiouracil may be formed from the data given. A daily dosage of 0.4 to 0.6 Gm. of thiouracil would appear to have been adequate for the initial treatment of the elevated rate of metabolism in cases 1 and 3, and 0.2 Gm. daily appeared to be an adequate maintenance dose in case 1. Possibly as much as 1.0 Gm. daily is excessive, and from case 2 it is apparent that 2.0 Gm. daily was not more effective than 1 Gm. It may be that this large dose contributed to the severe toxic episode which followed.

Thiourea is about one third as active as thiouracil when tested in rats, and therefore 1 and 2 Gm. daily of the former might be considered an adequate dose for initial therapy, with about 0.5 Gm. daily for maintenance. In case 1 a maintenance dose of 1.5 Gm. daily of thiourea was too large, as symptoms and signs of early myxedema resulted after a period of five weeks and there was evidence of chronic toxicity in the form of a skin rash. A simple chemical method for the determination of the concentration of these substances in the blood might prove to be of value in estimating the proper dose by offering a means of comparison with the more exact determination of dosage requirements that can be made on experimental animals.

In the few cases treated thus far, thyroid enlargement has not been observed with the possible exception of case 1. In this instance there was a distinct decrease in thyroid size when treatment was discontinued and a return of a slight enlargement when treatment was reinstituted. The human thyroid gland usually responds slowly with change in size, and perhaps it was to be expected that little detectable enlargement would occur during a period of only a few months of drug therapy.

These results are considered to be further evidence that thioureylene derivatives inhibit the formation of thyroid hormone and that they may be employed in the treatment of hyperthyroidism.

## SUMMARY

The daily administration of 1 to 2 Gm. of thiourea or of 0.2 to 1 Gm. of thiouracil to hyperthyroid persons resulted in the relief of symptoms and the return to normal of the serum cholesterol and the basal metabolic rate. There were observed a latent period of one to two weeks before these effects occurred, a sustained remission during treatment, and a return of hyperthyroidism when therapy was discontinued.

25 Shattuck Street

April 6, 1984
(JAMA 1984;251:1747-1748)

# An Expeditious Research*

Richard L. Landau, MD

The story of the development of antithyroid drugs, which reached its climax with the publication of "Treatment of Hyperthyroidism With Thiourea and Thiouracil,"[1] is an early example of the sort of research that has transformed clinical science into the most explosive branch of biology. As far as one can tell from the published literature, Astwood, a reproductive endocrinologist, had not directed his research efforts to the control of the thyroid before publication of the articles to be mentioned. One must assume, however, that as a clinician, he dealt with hyperthyroidism and longed for a more effective way of managing the disease. It must have been so, for when he became aware of several available, relatively safe chemical goitrogens, he certainly grasped their potential clinical importance and ran.

### First Goitrogens

In 1941, Julia and C. G. MacKenzie and E. V. McCollum,[2] from the School of Hygiene and Public Health at Johns Hopkins University, wished to make use of the discovery by Marshall that sulfaguanidine reduced the concentration of coliform bacteria in rat feces to see if the antibacterial action would also prevent the bacterial synthesis of essential nutrients. Their careful examination of tissues from these growth-inhibited rats resulted in the discovery that the thyroid glands of treated animals were hypertrophied and hyperemic. The thyroid epithelium was columnar and invaginated, almost obliterating the lumen of the acini, which contained little or no colloid. At about the same time, Richter and Clisby[3] published their observations, in which similar thyroid changes were induced in rats fed phenylthiocarbamide. Soon thereafter, Kennedy[4] reported that the goitrogenic substance in rapeseed was thiourea. By coincidence, these three articles on the goitrogenic activity of several sulfur-containing chemicals appeared within nine months.

We have no way of knowing which of these studies first attracted Astwood's attention. However, at the same time that the MacKenzies[5] and McCollum were extending their studies to explain the goitrogenic activity of sulfaguanidine, Astwood and colleagues[6] were carrying out almost identical experiments. The two groups published simultaneously in February 1943 and reached the same pathogenic conclusions. Both based their protocols and ultimate hypotheses on the earlier work of David Marine and colleagues,[7] who had worked out in considerable detail the importance of pituitary thyrotropin secretion in the regulation of the secretory activity of the thyroid, the goitrogenic influence of iodine deprivation, and the effects of restoring iodide to the diet. It was these studies of Marine that led to the use of iodized salt to prevent endemic goiter in areas where drinking water contained little iodine. The pharmacologic studies of the two groups[5,6] showed that the goitrogenic chemicals induced hyperplastic glands that were indistinguishable histologically from those resulting from iodide deficiency and that the thyroid hyperplasia could be prevented by prior hypophysectomy or the simultaneous administration of thyroid hormone, which would, of course, inactivate the pituitary. Iodide administration did not abolish the goitrogenic activity, and, most important, the basal metabolic rates of rats fed sulfaguanidine or thiourea dropped. From these results, the inescapable conclusion of both groups was that sulfaguanidine and thiourea blocked the synthesis of thyroid hormone, leading to hypothyroidism and, ultimately, a compensatory hyperplasia of the gland caused by increased pituitary thyrotropin secretion. These effects were observed with doses of the drugs that were not otherwise acutely toxic. At this point, the MacKenzies and McCollum stopped.

### Astwood Carries On

Astwood[8] immediately began a systematic investigation of the chemical nature of compounds that inhibit the secretory function of the thyroid gland. He developed a simple bioassay procedure in rats, based on the degree of compensatory thyroid hyperplasia induced by comparative doses of the compounds. Toxicity was also assessed, although the number of rats used in early tests was small indeed by comparison with today's studies. One hundred six chemicals were tested in this series, and the results were reported in 1943. It was shown that substances that had within their structure the grouping NH-CS-NH were the most active if sufficiently water soluble. The inclusion of thiourea in a five- or six-membered heterocyclic structure resulted in a considerable enhancement of activity, as in thiouracil. Subsequently, a more precise and reproducible assay system, based on thyroidal iodine as well as weight, was developed. Twenty-two thiourea derivatives were tested in this assay among a total of 220 substances, including propylthiouracil, today's most widely used antithyroid drug.[9] By this time (1945), as the Astwood group noted, there was confirmation of their results from other investigators, and vigorous competition was leading to the testing of other related compounds in both experimental animals and man. Perhaps it was Astwood's innate belief in Satchel Paige's dictum, "Don't never look back; something may be gaining on you,"[10] that

From the Department of Medicine, Section of Endocrinology, University of Chicago.

*A commentary on Astwood EB: Treatment of hyperthyroidism with thiourea and thiouracil. JAMA 1943;122:78-81.

prompted the early human testing reported in our LANDMARK ARTICLE.

It is remarkable that this report on the first clinical use of thioureas was published just 1½ years after the MacKenzies and McCollum publication and just five months after the publication of the pharmacologic studies in animals. Astwood's survey for the antithyroid activity of 106 compounds[8] had been accepted for publication but hadn't yet appeared. Using today's more formal pharmaceutical development terminology, this would be a phase 1 and phase 2 study. These protocols are now sponsored almost exclusively by the pharmaceutical industry and require three to four times as long to proceed from the initial idea to the first trials in man. Of course, many more toxicity studies in several species must now be satisfactorily completed before the Food and Drug Administration guidelines will permit human trials. In retrospect, I think we must say that Astwood was lucky as well as brilliant.

### New Era in Management

The demonstration that thiourea and thiouracil could effectively control hypersecretion of thyroid hormone opened a new era in the management of Graves' disease and toxic nodular goiter. However, thiourea and thiouracil were too toxic in man to be successful drugs, but as noted, Astwood's group was already searching for more potent and less toxic substituted thiouracils. In the United States today, propylthiouracil and methimazole are the antithyroid agents in general use. Although their toxicity is minimal by comparison with the parent thiourea compound, agranulocytosis is rarely noted and rashes occasionally occur with higher dosages.

Astwood's hope that these thiourea derivatives would provide the definitive treatment of Graves' disease has only been partially fulfilled. With adequate dosage, euthyroidism can always be maintained for as long as the drug is administered. After a year or more of induced euthyroidism, cessation of treatment is followed, more often than not, by recurrence of the thyrotoxicosis. However, if patients with Graves' disease are carefully selected for relatively mild disease in young patients with small goiters, a remission rate as high as 40% has been observed after discontinuation of the drug's use.[11] Taking medications daily for at least a year, with a better than even chance of having the disease recur, is obviously some distance from ideal. For this reason, many physicians prefer surgery or radioactive iodine, both of which have a more certain end point.

In younger patients with Graves' disease (30 to 40 years of age or younger) with severe hyperthyroidism and large goiters, a subtotal thyroidectomy is usually regarded as the treatment of choice. In the hands of a surgeon with substantial experience in thyroid and parathyroid operations, the mortality is negligible and the morbidity slight. In large measure, this is because the thyrotoxic state can be converted to euthyroidism preoperatively, with about two months of treatment with an antithyroid drug, and the gland can be made firmer and less vascular by the simultaneous addition of iodide. With appropriate preoperative management, the once highly-feared thyrotoxic storm is a virtual impossibility.

Radioactive iodine therapy is usually reserved for patients older than 30 or 40 years of age. The primary concern with younger patients is the possibility that ionizing radiation exposure might induce a malignant neoplasm in the damaged thyroid tissue. In very ill patients, it is often judged wise to give an antithyroid drug (with or without potassium iodide) a few days after iodine 131 dosage to ensure control of the thyrotoxicosis as soon as possible. After two to three months, use of antithyroid medication can usually be safely stopped to permit evaluation of the full effect of the radioactive iodine.

From the viewpoint of a consulting endocrinologist, the most frequent error seen in the use of antithyroid drugs by general physicians is underdosage. It is usually wise to initiate therapy with about 600 mg of propylthiouracil or 30 mg of methimazole. The dosage can usually be lowered as the plasma-free thyroxine estimate approaches the normal range. Occasionally more than 600 mg per day of propylthiouracil will be required to control a very active thyroid gland.

---

It is not often that one person or group of scientists can contribute as much to the management of a disease as Astwood and his associates have in this instance. With amazing speed, many potential goitrogens were tested in rats and the more promising compounds were evaluated in patients with Graves' disease. Appropriate dosages were determined, and the place of antithyroid drugs in the management of hyperthyroidism was established just a few years after this first clinical trial. Forty years later, the place of the antithyroid drugs in the management of hyperthyroidism is not too much different from that anticipated by Astwood, although he was a vigorously antisurgical physician. His contribution to the understanding and management of hyperthyroidism, as epitomized in his article, is indeed a milestone.

### References

1. Astwood EB: Treatment of hyperthyroidism with thiourea and thiouracil. *JAMA* 1943;122:78-81.
2. MacKenzie JB, MacKenzie CG, McCollum EV: Effect of sulfanilylguanidine on the thyroid of the rat. *Science* 1941;94:518-519.
3. Richter CP, Clisby KH: Toxic effects of bitter tasting phenylthiocarbamide. *Arch Pathol* 1942;33:46-57.
4. Kennedy TH: Thioureas as goitrogenic substances. *Nature* 1942;150:223-234.
5. MacKenzie CG, MacKenzie JB: Effect of sulfonamides and thioureas on the thyroid gland and basal metabolism. *Endocrinology* 1943;32:185-209.
6. Astwood EB, Sullivan J, Bissell A, et al: Action of certain sulfonamides and of thiourea on the function of the thyroid gland of the rat. *Endocrinology* 1943;32:210-225.
7. Matovinovic J: David Marine (1880-1976): Nestor of thyroidology. *Perspect Biol Med* 1978;21:565-589.
8. Astwood EB: The chemical nature of compounds which inhibit the function of the thyroid gland. *J Pharm Exp Ther* 1943;78:79.
9. Astwood EB, Bissell A, Hughes AM: Further studies on the chemical nature of compounds which inhibit the function of the thyroid gland. *Endocrinology* 1945;37:456-481.
10. Dusseau JL: Mens sana: A page from Paige. *Perspect Biol Med* 1979;23:44-48.
11. Sridama V, Kaplan EL, Reilly M, et al: Long term follow-up of compensated low dose I131 therapy for Graves' disease, abstract 556. Read before the 65th Annual Meeting of the Endocrine Society, San Antonio, Tex, 1983.

Aug 12, 1944
(*JAMA* 1944;125:1011-1017)

## Chapter 36

# Penicillin in the Treatment of Meningitis

Lieutenant Commander David H. Rosenberg (MC), U.S.N.R.

and

Lieutenant P. A. Arling (MC), U.S.N.R.

Great Lakes, Ill.

Reports in the literature pertaining to the clinical effects of penicillin in the treatment of meningitis have in general been confined to observations on small groups of patients or on isolated cases.[1] No definite conclusions may be drawn from them concerning the efficacy of penicillin, the most satisfactory method of treatment or the minimum adequate dosage requirements. However, from in vitro studies demonstrating the pronounced sensitivity of the meningococcus, Streptococcus haemolyticus, pneumococcus and some strains of Streptococcus viridans to the action of penicillin, this agent should prove to be of considerable therapeutic value in the management of such infections, particularly in individuals who are sulfonamide resistant or sulfonamide reactors.

In a preliminary report[2] on 31 patients with cerebrospinal fever, we recorded 30 recoveries following the combined intrathecal and intravenous or intramuscular use of penicillin and concluded that penicillin is a safe, effective and highly potent agent in the treatment of this disease. Since then we have treated 40 additional patients with meningitis without a fatality. We are presenting at this time a report of our observations on this entire group of 71 patients.

Read before the Section on Experimental Medicine and Therapeutics at the Ninety-Fourth Annual Session of the American Medical Association, Chicago, June 14, 1944.

This article has been released for publication by the Division of Publications of the Bureau of Medicine and Surgery of the U. S. Navy. The opinions and views set forth are those of the writers and are not to be considered as reflecting the policies of the Navy Department.

1. Keefer, C. S.; Blake, F. G.; Marshall, E. K., Jr.; Lockwood, J. S. and Wood, W. B., Jr.: Penicillin in the Treatment of Infections, J. A. M. A. **122**:1217 (Aug. 28) 1943. Lyons, C.: Penicillin Therapy of Surgical Infections in the U. S. Army, ibid. **123**:1007 (Dec. 18) 1943. Dawson, M. H., and Hobby, G. L.: The Clinical Use of Penicillin: Observations in 100 Cases, ibid. **124**:611 (March 4) 1944.

2. Rosenberg, D. H., and Arling, P. A.: The Treatment of Cerebrospinal Fever with Penicillin: A Preliminary Report, U. S. Nav. M. Bull., August 1944.

## MATERIAL

*Cerebrospinal Fever.*—Sixty-five patients in this series presented clinical evidence of cerebrospinal fever (table 1). In almost all patients the onset was sudden, with rapidly developing headache, nausea, vomiting and cervical rigidity of eight to forty-eight hours' duration. Twenty-four patients were semicomatose and 21 were comatose. The temperature on admission ranged between 99 (rectal) and 108 F. (rectal); the average for the group was 102.7 F. (rectal). Petechiae were found in 48 instances, and in 4 of these a purpuric rash was also noted. One patient with most extensive purpura presented the clinical picture of the so-called Waterhouse-Friderichsen syndrome. Two other patients who went into shock shortly after admission exhibited widespread petechial eruptions without purpura. Acute arthritis was observed in 15 of the patients on admission. The spinal fluid was turbid in all except 4 patients, and the initial spinal fluid cell count ranged from 21 to 50,100 leukocytes per cubic millimeter. The average cell count for the group was 11,700 per cubic millimeter, 88 per cent being polymorphonuclear leukocytes. In 49 patients meningococci were recovered from the spinal fluid, and in 10 of these the blood cultures were positive. In another patient with clinical evidence of fulminating meningococcemia the blood culture was positive although the spinal fluid was sterile and contained only 66 leukocytes per cubic millimeter. In the 3 other patients with clear spinal fluid on admission, meningococci were found in the spinal fluid on culture. Owing to a lack of serums we were unable to determine the type of meningococci isolated from this group of patients. In 15 patients the clinical picture and spinal fluid findings were characteristic of meningococcic meningitis, but the stained smears and cultures of the spinal fluid revealed no organisms.

*Meningitis Due to Other Bacteria.*—In 3 patients hemolytic streptococci were recovered from the spinal fluid (table 2). In one of these a bacteremia was present and in another bilateral acute otitis media was found

TABLE 1.—*Cerebrospinal Fever*

| | | | | | | | | Spinal Fluid | | | Penicillin (Units) | | I |
| | | | | | | | | | | Per Cent | | Intravenous | |
| | | | | | Semi- | Petech- | Temper- | Blood Cul- | Cul- | Cell | Poly-morpho- | Intra- | and/or | |
| Patient | Age | Duration | Coma | coma | iae | ature | ture | ture | Count | nuclears | thecal | Muscular | Complications |
|---|---|---|---|---|---|---|---|---|---|---|---|---|---|
| 1 | 18 | 25 hr. | + | − | 3+ | 104 | 0 | + | 50,100 | 98 | 125,000 | 860,000 | |
| 2 | 18 | 24 hr. | + | − | 3+ | 104.8 | 0 | + | 15,000 | 92 | 100,000 | 900,000 | Polyarthritis; thrombophlebitis |
| 3 | 25 | 2 days | − | − | 3+ | 101.6 | 0 | + | 8,000 | 98 | 45,000 | 340,000 | |
| 4 | 19 | ? | + | − | 4+ | 108 | + | + | 7,200 | 90 | 55,000 | 380,000 | Hydrocephalus; circulatory failure (autopsy) |
| 5 | 23 | 26 hr. | + | − | 3+ | 103.8 | 0 | 0 | 19,800 | 98 | 15,000 | 400,000 | |
| 6 | 20 | 1 day | − | − | 1+ | 100.8 | 0 | + | 17,500 | 90 | 25,000 | 715,000 | Fibrinous pericarditis; arthritis |
| 7 | 69 | 2 days | − | + | 0 | 104.2 | 0 | 0 | 8,600 | 89 | 25,000 | 280,000 | |
| 8 | 18 | 1½ days | − | + | 3+ | 100.2 | 0 | + | 4,800° | 75 | 15,000 | 260,000 | |
| 9 | 21 | 43 hr. | − | − | 1+ | 102.4 | 0 | + | 11,100 | 100 | 10,000 | 235,000 | |
| 10 | 18 | 1½ days | − | − | 0 | 101.4 | 0 | 0 | 12,800 | 92 | 10,000 | 180,000 | |
| 11 | 18 | 5 days | − | − | 0 | 104 | 0 | 0 | 1,500 | 90 | 10,000 | 80,000 | |
| 12 | 20 | 48 hr. | − | + | 2+ | 99.8 | 0 | 0 | 10,100 | 94 | 10,000 | 110,000 | Transient diplopia, 4th day |
| 13 | 18 | 29 hr. | + | − | 1+ | 105 | 0 | + | 10,400 | 90 | 10,000 | 60,000 | Acute otitis media, 3rd day |
| 14 | 18 | 17 hr. | + | − | 0 | 102.4 | + | + | 21,000 | 94 | 10,000 | 40,000 | Acute tonsillitis |
| 15 | 20 | 2½ days | − | + | 0 | 104.8 | 0 | 0 | 3,800 | 70 | 10,000 | 20,000 | |
| 16 | 18 | 3½ days | − | + | 0 | 105 | 0 | + | 11,500 | 85 | 30,000 | 40,000 | Sixth nerve palsy and paresis |
| 17 | 19 | 1 day | + | − | 3+ | 105.6 | 0 | + | 5,000 | 100 | 10,000 | 40,000 | Epididymitis; arthritis |
| 18 | 28 | 12 hr. | − | + | 2+ | 103 | 0 | 0 | 6,600 | 89 | 10,000 | 20,000 | |
| 19 | 17 | 30 hr. | + | − | 2+ | 102 | 0 | + | 17,300 | 99 | 50,000 | 290,000 | Polyarthritis |
| 20 | 18 | 21 hr. | − | − | 0 | 99.8 | + | + | 14,100 | 96 | 30,000 | 40,000 | |
| 21 | 24 | 20 hr. | − | − | 4+ | 103.8 | + | 0 | 66 | 94 | None | 250,000 | Waterhouse-Friderichsen syndrome |
| 22 | 29 | 40 hr. | − | + | 1+ | 105.2 | 0 | 0 | 5,100 | 90 | 10,000 | 40,000 | |
| 23 | 27 | 34 hr. | − | + | 2+ | 103.4 | 0 | + | 23,500 | 99 | 20,000 | 90,000 | Epididymo-orchitis; diplopia |
| 24 | 20 | 40 hr. | + | − | 3+ | 105 | + | + | 13,100 | 93 | 10,000 | 90,000 | Epididymo-orchitis; arthritis; diplopia |
| 25 | 18 | 24 hr. | − | + | 2+ | 103.2 | 0 | + | 14,800 | 92 | 20,000 | 90,000 | |
| 26 | 20 | 26 hr. | − | + | 1+ | 101 | 0 | + | 11,400 | 95 | 30,000 | 115,000 | |
| 27 | 19 | 22 hr. | + | − | 2+ | 105.2 | 0 | + | 18,700 | 100 | 20,000 | 155,000 | |
| 28 | 18 | 2 days | − | + | 1+ | 104.2 | 0 | 0 | 6,000 | 92 | 10,000 | 100,000 | Arthritis; acute tonsillitis |
| 29 | 18 | 7½ hr. | + | − | 0 | 104.8 | 0 | + | 18,700 | 93 | 10,000 | 100,000 | |
| 30 | 19 | 15 hr. | + | − | 1+ | 102.4 | 0 | 0 | 8,100 | 94 | 10,000 | 90,000 | Polyarthritis |
| 31 | 18 | 1 day | + | − | 3+ | 104.8 | 0 | + | 12,600 | 89 | 40,000 | 200,000 | Epididymitis; polyarthritis |
| 32 | 19 | 1 day | + | − | 1+ | 103.8 | 0 | 0 | 12,100 | 100 | 10,000 | 70,000 | |
| 33 | 29 | 24 hr. | + | − | 3+ | 103.6 | + | + | 22,500 | 96 | 30,000 | 70,000 | Sixth nerve paresis |
| 34 | 17 | 10 hr. | − | + | 4+ | 102 | + | + | 2,000 | 100 | 50,000 | 250,000 | Polyarthritis |
| 35 | 18 | 15 hr. | − | + | 2+ | 105.2 | 0 | + | 12,100 | 94 | 10,000 | 140,000 | Polyarthritis |
| 36 | 19 | 2 days | − | + | 1+ | 102.6 | 0 | 0 | 6,200 | 68 | 10,000 | 40,000 | |
| 37 | 18 | 12 hr. | − | + | 1+ | 104 | 0 | + | 2,500° | 91 | 10,000 | 100,000 | |
| 38 | 22 | 2½ days | + | − | 0 | 101.6 | 0 | + | 31,600 | 95 | 40,000 | 170,000 | Thrombophlebitis |
| 39 | 18 | 24 hr. | − | − | 3+ | 101 | 0 | + | 4,200 | 90 | 20,000 | 100,000 | Acute tonsillitis |
| 40 | 20 | 16 hr. | − | + | 3+ | 101 | 0 | + | 12,500 | 91 | 20,000 | 100,000 | |
| 41 | 17 | 7 hr. | + | − | 0 | 103 | 0 | + | 10,800 | 99 | 20,000 | 100,000 | |
| 42 | 18 | 43 hr. | − | + | 0 | 103.6 | 0 | + | 12,200 | 96 | 20,000 | 50,000 | |
| 43 | 18 | 46 hr. | − | − | 1+ | 101.8 | 0 | 0 | 8,000 | 63 | 10,000 | 40,000 | |
| 44 | 18 | 4 days | − | + | 4+ | 103.8 | 0 | + | 6,400 | 90 | 20,000 | 50,000 | |
| 45 | 32 | 1 day | + | − | 2+ | 99.4 | + | + | 8,600 | 98 | 30,000 | 50,000 | Epididymo-orchitis; arthritis |
| 46 | 18 | 1 day | − | − | 4+ | 102.2 | 0 | + | 7,900 | 94 | 20,000 | 100,000 | Epididymitis, bilateral |
| 47 | 35 | 17 hr. | − | + | 4+ | 100.4 | + | + | 280 | 96 | 50,000 | 200,000 | |
| 48 | 26 | 2 days | − | + | 4+ | 100.2 | + | + | 24,100 | 80 | 40,000 | 200,000 | |
| 49 | 18 | 1 day | − | − | 3+ | 102 | 0 | + | 11,600 | 92 | 20,000 | 200,000 | |
| 50 | 21 | 1 day | + | − | 0 | 102.6 | 0 | + | 21,600 | 96 | 20,000 | 200,000 | Epididymitis |
| 51 | 18 | 1 day | + | − | 3+ | 100.6 | 0 | + | 12,700 | 97 | 20,000 | 200,000 | |
| 52 | 18 | 3 days | − | + | 0 | 102 | 0 | + | 11,400 | 96 | 20,000 | 200,000 | |
| 53 | 18 | 1 day | − | + | 1+ | 102.6 | 0 | + | 12,200 | 95 | 30,000 | 200,000 | |
| 54 | 18 | 4 days | − | − | 0 | 100.8 | 0 | + | 9,300° | 90 | 30,000 | 200,000 | Acute tonsillitis |
| 55 | 18 | 2 days | − | − | 1+ | 101.8 | 0 | 0 | 9,200 | 95 | 10,000 | 200,000 | |
| 56 | 18 | 19 hr. | − | − | 1+ | 102.6 | 0 | + | 3,200 | 98 | 30,000 | 335,000 | Polyarthritis |
| 57 | 18 | 15 hr. | − | + | 1+ | 104 | 0 | + | 11,300 | 97 | 20,000 | 70,000 | |
| 58 | 18 | 8 hr. | − | − | 0 | 103.6 | 0 | + | 255 | 88 | 10,000 | None | |
| 59 | 29 | 1 day | + | − | 2+ | 99.8 | 0 | + | 20,400 | 100 | 50,000 | 50,000 | Polyarthritis |
| 60 | 18 | 2 days | − | − | 0 | 102 | + | + | 2,000 | 96 | 20,000 | 50,000 | |
| 61 | 21 | 1 day | − | − | 3+ | 100.2 | 0 | + | 21 | 0 | 20,000 | 230,000 | Epididymo-orchitis; arthritis |
| 62 | 25 | 1 day | − | + | 3+ | 99 | 0 | + | 10,100 | 92 | 50,000 | 55,000 | Arthritis; epididymitis |
| 63 | 18 | 1 day | − | + | 0 | 100.2 | 0 | 0 | 2,900 | 96 | 10,000 | 50,000 | |
| 64 | 27 | 12 hr. | − | + | 2+ | 103.6 | 0 | + | 6,000 | 87 | 20,000 | 40,000 | Epididymo-orchitis |
| 65 | 23 | 2 days | − | − | 1+ | 99 | 0 | + | 47,100 | 96 | 40,000 | 60,000 | |

°Cell count inaccurate owing to pellicle formation.    In all cases the temperature was taken rectally.    All patients were males.

Two of these patients were semicomatose on admission. The spinal fluid cell counts ranged between 1,000 and 2,290 leukocytes per cubic millimeter.

There were 2 patients with Streptococcus viridans bacteremia and meningitis, both of whom were comatose on admission. Although the initial spinal fluid cell count was 450 leukocytes per cubic millimeter in each instance, in 1 it rose to 25,600 within ten hours.

In 1 patient with acute otitis media complicated by meningitis, pneumococci were cultivated from the spinal fluid. This patient was semicomatose on admission and the maximum temperature was 105.2 F. (rectal). The initial spinal fluid cell count was 1,100 leukocytes per cubic millimeter.

## METHOD OF TREATMENT

Rammelkamp and Keefer[3] have demonstrated that penicillin administered intravenously does not appear in the spinal fluid. Injected intrathecally,[4] penicillin is

Penicillin (10,000 units) was administered intrathecally at twenty-four hour intervals until clinical improvement, sustained fall in temperature and/or a decrease in the meningeal signs were manifest and until the stained smears and cultures of the spinal fluid revealed no organisms. As penicillin was injected intrathecally with each lumbar puncture without awaiting the results of the bacteriologic studies, this plan in effect was tantamount to administering an additional dose of penicillin after the spinal fluid became sterile. We felt that in some instances it was unsafe to withhold treatment pending the results of the spinal fluid cultures. The persistence of coma was regarded as an indication for further intrathecal therapy. In the most severe infections and in those in which coma lasted forty-eight hours or longer, intrathecal penicillin was continued until the spinal fluid was bacteria free on three successive days. It is of paramount importance to drain the spinal canal as completely as is feasible before injecting penicillin. In several instances the spinal fluid

TABLE 2.—*Meningitis Due to Other Bacteria*

| Patient | Age | Duration | Coma | Semi-coma | Temper-ature | Blood Culture | Spinal Fluid Culture | Spinal Fluid Cell Count | Spinal Fluid Per Cent Poly-morpho-nuclears | Penicillin Intra-thecal | Penicillin Intravenous and/or Muscular | Complications |
|---|---|---|---|---|---|---|---|---|---|---|---|---|
| | | | | | | A. Streptococcus Haemolyticus | | | | | | |
| 66 | 27 | 8 days | − | + | 103.8 | + | + | 2,300 | 93 | 20,000 | 400,000 | |
| 67 | 27 | 22 hr. | − | − | 104.4 | 0 | + | 1,700 | 79 | 20,000 | 170,000 | |
| 68 | 25 | 4 days | − | + | 101.4 | 0 | + | 1,000 | 85 | 20,000 | 650,000 | Bilateral acute otitis media |
| | | | | | | B. Streptococcus Viridans | | | | | | |
| 69 | 18 | 3½ days | + | − | 104.6 | + | + | 450 | 85 | 40,000 | 300,000 | Acute pharyngitis |
| | | | | | | | | 25,600 | 95 | | | |
| 70 | 24 | 3 days | + | − | 102 | + | 0 | 450 | 97 | 30,000 | 200,000 | |
| | | | | | | C. Pneumococcus | | | | | | |
| 71 | 35 | 4 days | − | + | 102 | 0 | + | 1,100 | 84 | 30,000 | 800,000 | Acute otitis media |

In all cases the temperature was taken rectally.    All patients were males.

slowly absorbed from the subarachnoid space and may be detected in the spinal fluid thirty-one hours later. It is more rapidly absorbed from the spinal fluid of patients with meningitis but may be found in significant amounts twenty-four hours after injection.

For purposes of investigation our plan of treatment varied somewhat in different patients, particularly from the standpoint of dosage. The most satisfactory method of treatment was found to be the following:

1. The initial diagnostic lumbar puncture was performed in the usual manner and the spinal canal was drained. Ten thousand Oxford units of sodium penicillin, dissolved in 10 cc. of isotonic solution of sodium chloride, was slowly introduced into the subarachnoid space.

was so viscous that aspiration was necessary.

2. Penicillin was also administered either by the continuous intravenous drip method at the rate of 5,000 units per hour or intramuscularly in doses of 15,000 units every three hours, the dose being reduced to 10,000 units every three hours if improvement was satisfactory. Generally, penicillin was given intravenously (40 units per cubic centimeter in a 5 per cent dextrose solution) for the first eight hours and continued intramuscularly thereafter. Patients with the fulminating type of cerebro-spinal fever received penicillin intravenously at the rate of 10,000 units per hour for four hours initially. Owing to a lack of technical facilities the treatment could not be controlled by determinations of the amount of penicillin in the blood and spinal fluid. Instead, frequent clinical observations were made and the temperature, pulse and respirations were recorded every two hours.

In addition to specific therapy, 3,000 cc. of fluid was given daily. To combat shock in patients with fulminating meningococcemia, supportive therapy was given in the form of whole blood, plasma, epinephrine and

3. Rammelkamp, C. H., and Keefer, C. S.: The Absorption, Excretion and Distribution of Penicillin, J. Clin. Investigation **22**:425 (May) 1943.

4. Rammelkamp, C. H., and Keefer, C. S.: The Absorption, Excretion and Toxicity of Penicillin Administered by Intrathecal Injection, Am. J. M. Sc. **205**:342 (March) 1943.

desoxycorticosterone acetate. Oxygen therapy was employed when indicated.

## RESULTS

*Cerebrospinal Fever.*—Sixty-four of the sixty-five patients in this group recovered. The one fatality occurred in a patient who was admitted in a moribund state with clinical and bacteriologic evidence of meningococcemia and with well advanced meningitis. His temperature was 108 F., pulse rate 140 and respiratory rate 66 per minute. He received 12 Gm. of sodium sulfadiazine parenterally in addition to 55,000 units of penicillin intrathecally and 380,000 units intravenously and intramuscularly but died thirty-eight hours after admission. Necropsy disclosed suppurative meningitis, secondary hydrocephalus and edema of the brain and lungs.

In the 64 patients who recovered, progressive improvement was noted soon after penicillin therapy was begun and was generally signalized by the disappearance of the restlessness, stupor and delirium, cessation of vomiting and an abrupt fall in the temperature and pulse rate.

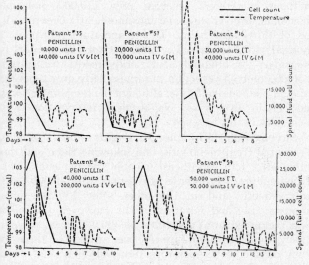

Effect of penicillin on the temperature and spinal fluid cell counts of patients with cerebrospinal fever treated with 10,000, 20,000, 30,000, 40,000 and 50,000 units (total) intrathecally and various amounts intravenously and intramuscularly. Cases representing different grades of severity were selected. In patient 59, fever was prolonged by the presence of arthritis. The increase in the spinal fluid cell count in patients 16, 48 and 49 following the first injection of penicillin intrathecally was noted in 8 other patients. I. T., intrathecal; I. V., intravenous; I. M., intramuscular.

Those who were comatose usually regained consciousness within two to twenty-four hours, but in 5 coma persisted for thirty to forty-eight hours and in 1 for four days. In 22 patients the temperature returned to normal within eight to seventy-two hours. In 16 a low grade intermittent fever (100 to 100.2 F. rectal) remained until the seventh day. In some of the latter patients as well as in those who exhibited a more prolonged febrile course the fever was found to be caused by one or more complications rather than by the meningitis, for the spinal fluid had become sterile and either gave a normal cell count or showed a

residual lymphocytosis. Of the 4 patients whose temperature did not fall abruptly, 3 represented very severe infections and 1 showed signs of acute pericarditis and polyarthritis. Headache disappeared within two to four days and the signs of meningitis subsided completely in two to seven days (average, four days) except in our first 2 patients, who received 100,000 to 125,000 units intrathecally. In the latter the meningeal signs persisted for nine days. Generally there was a prompt reduction in the spinal fluid cell count, as shown in the accompanying chart, and the protein and sugar returned to normal rapidly. In all but the most severe infections this was accompanied by a disappearance of the polymorphonuclear leukocytes within four to seven days. In many a slight lymphocytosis remained until the tenth to the fourteenth day. In a few of our first patients a recurrence of fever was observed on the fourth to the sixth day if intrathecal penicillin was discontinued too soon. This was controlled by an additional dose of penicillin. As a rule the patients were able to be out of bed on the eighth day unless prevented by complications.

The amount of penicillin administered intrathecally to these patients varied with the severity of the meningeal infection. Thus, 42 patients recovered following only one or two injections of penicillin, 10 required three injections and 9 received four to five injections intrathecally. Through a lack of knowledge of the potency and effectiveness of penicillin, the first 2 patients whom we treated received nine and eleven injections respectively, totaling 100,000 to 125,000 units. Another patient with fulminating meningococcemia recovered with intravenous and intramuscular therapy alone, but in this instance the spinal fluid was sterile and showed only 66 leukocytes per cubic millimeter. The first 8 patients whom we treated received an intrathecal dose of 15,000 units dissolved in 15 cc. of isotonic solution of sodium chloride initially, but in view of the symptoms and signs of meningeal irritation resulting therefrom the 10,000 unit dose was employed thereafter. It is noteworthy that the amount of intrathecal penicillin necessary for recovery cannot be correlated with the initial spinal fluid cell count. Instead, it seems to depend on the number, type and virulence of the organisms as well as on the immunologic reaction of the host.

An analysis of the bacteriologic effects of penicillin on the spinal fluid obtained twenty-four hours after an intrathecal injection discloses that of 48 patients with positive cultures on admission in 29 the spinal fluid was sterile after one injection of penicillin, in 8 after two injections, in 3 after three injections and in 4 after four injections. However, in 2 others, both with very severe infections, the spinal fluid was sterile after one injection of penicillin but again showed meningococci twenty-four hours after the second injection. In 1 of these the spinal fluid remained sterile after the third injection and in the other after the fifth injection Further, in 2 patients receiving penicillin every twelve hours the spinal fluid cultures were sterile after the first injection of penicillin, yet the direct smears showed organisms until two and five injections, respectively, were given. These findings suggest that sufficient penicillin is present in the spinal fluid after twelve hours, and occasionally after twenty-four hours, to inhibit the growth of bacteria on the culture medium. It is important, therefore, to correlate the bacteriologic findings with the clinical course and to observe the criteria set forth in our plan of treatment.

The total amount of penicillin administered intravenously and/or intramuscularly varied considerably (20,000 to 900,000 units), the first patients treated receiving the largest amounts. We soon observed that the total dosage could be reduced considerably without risk to the patient. Thus, 55 patients received between 20,000 and 250,000 units of penicillin intravenously and intramuscularly, and 35 of these received 100,000 units or less. One patient, seen several hours after the onset of his illness, recovered without any penicillin intravenously or intramuscularly. Among the patients without bacteremia, no appreciable difference in the outcome and course of the disease was perceptible in the group treated with 20,000 to 50,000 units when compared with those receiving as much as 900,000 units. Nor was there any correlation between the amount of penicillin given by these routes and the amount of intrathecal penicillin required for recovery. Of 10 patients in whom positive blood cultures were found, in 4 the blood was sterile after 40,000 to 50,000 units, in 5 after 70,000 to 125,000 units and in 1 after 250,000 units. In 2 of these the blood was sterile after 105,000 to 110,000 units, but in each penicillin was continued until 200,000 units had been given. As 250,000 units was administered to the patient with the "Waterhouse-Friderichsen syndrome" this dose may represent the maximum amount required to combat the severe forms of meningococcemia unless circulatory failure is too far advanced when the patient is admitted to the hospital.

Acute monarthritis or polyarthritis was present in 15 patients on admission and was uninfluenced by the intravenous and intramuscular administration of as much as 900,000 units of penicillin. In 9 individuals aspiration of the affected knee joints revealed cloudy yellow fluid containing 20,000 to 100,000 polymorphonuclear leukocytes per cubic millimeter. In 8 the aspirated fluid was sterile, while, in the other, meningococci were found on direct smear and on culture. Intra-articular penicillin (10,000 units) was administered to 2 of the patients with sterile synovial fluid, but no beneficial effects were observed. In the patient from whose joint meningococci were recovered, the fluid became sterile after the intra-articular injection of 10,000 units of penicillin on two successive days.

Acute epididymitis, alone or with orchitis, developed in 10 patients. It usually appeared on the sixth to the seventh day of illness, although it was noted as early as the second day and as late as the tenth day. Its occurrence was unrelated to the amount of penicillin administered intravenously and intramuscularly. Three patients were treated with 150,000 to 160,000 units of penicillin over a period of forty-eight hours after the onset of acute epididymo-orchitis, but in none was the period of resolution shortened. In these as in the other 6 patients, spontaneous recovery ensued.

In 3 patients transient diplopia was observed without manifest cranial nerve involvement. Left sixth nerve palsy developed on the second day of admission in 3 of the most severe cases encountered in this series; in 1 of these it was followed twenty-four hours later by paresis of the right sixth nerve. In 2, restoration of function was ultimately complete; in the other, slight diplopia on extreme abduction remained. In 1 patient with fulminating meningococcemia slight transient third nerve paresis was noted. Acute fibrinous pericarditis was found on admission in 1 patient and was unaffected by 715,000 units of penicillin given intravenously and intramuscularly. In 4 patients acute tonsillitis and in another unilateral acute otitis media complicated the convalescence. In 2 instances acute thrombophlebitis of the saphenous vein developed on the fifth and sixteenth days, respectively, and was unrelated to the site of therapy.

*Hemolytic Streptococcus Meningitis.*—All 3 patients with meningitis due to hemolytic streptococci recovered completely following two intrathecal injections of penicillin. The spinal fluid was sterile twenty-four hours after the first injection, and the temperature returned to normal in four to six days. The patient with bacteremia was given 400,000 units intravenously and intramuscularly over a period of fifty-three hours. Blood drawn for culture on the fifth day was sterile. One of the patients without bacteremia received only 170,000 units of penicillin intravenously and intramuscularly over a period of thirty-nine hours. The temperature returned to normal within six days. The other patient with meningitis secondary to bilateral acute otitis media was given 650,000 units of penicillin intramuscularly over a period of eight and one-half days, although the temperature was normal in five days. No surgical intervention was necessary in this instance.

*Streptococcus Viridans Meningitis.*—Both patients recovered from meningitis, one following three and the other after four intrathecal injections of penicillin. The blood cultures were sterile in 1 patient after 40,000 units intravenously and in the other after 130,000 units intravenously and intramuscularly. However, penicillin was continued until 200,000 and 300,000 units, respectively, had been administered over periods of three to four days. The temperature returned to normal after three to five days. No sequelae were demonstrable, though both patients were comatose for twenty-four hours after therapy was begun.

*Pneumococcic Meningitis Secondary to Acute Otitis Media.*—Although there was only 1 patient with pneumococcic meningitis in our series, it is of interest that complete recovery followed three intrathecal injections of penicillin and 800,000 units given intravenously and intramuscularly over a period of ten and one-half days. The spinal fluid cultures remained positive until the third intraspinal injection of penicillin was administered. In view of the presence of acute otitis media and the possibility of bony suppuration in the areas adjacent to the middle ear, intramuscular penicillin was continued until the temperature remained normal for five days. Convalescence progressed uneventfully thereafter without surgical intervention.

### UNTOWARD EFFECTS

In those patients who received penicillin intrathecally every twelve hours, as well as in some individuals who were given intrathecal doses of 15,000 units, more severe and more persistent headache was noted, fever was prolonged and signs of meningitis subsided more slowly. The irritating effect of penicillin on the meninges, when injected intrathecally, was previously demonstrated by Rammelkamp and Keefer[4] and by Pilcher and Meacham.[5] Further, we observed that penicillin produced by different manufacturers caused various degrees of meningeal irritation. Thus, the dark brown product was found to have the greatest irritant effect and caused febrile reactions, whereas the pale yellow product had the least demonstrable irritant effect. It is our belief, therefore, that the dark brown powder should not be used intrathecally. Localized thrombophlebitis developed in 4 patients at the site of the continuous intravenous injections but was of minor significance. In 3 patients with cerebrospinal fever mild transitory urticaria was noted within twenty-four hours after therapy was started. Whether this should be ascribed to the penicillin or to the disease per se cannot be stated. No other local or toxic effects were observed.

## COMMENT

The effectiveness of penicillin in the treatment of meningococcic infections in man is clearly demonstrated by the recovery of 64 out of 65 patients with cerebrospinal fever. That penicillin is also a potent agent in the control of meningitis caused by Streptococcus haemolyticus, Streptococcus viridans and pneumococcus is indicated by the recoveries observed in our small series of 6 patients. Contrary to the reported experiences with other infections, relatively small amounts of intravenous and/or intramuscular penicillin (40,000 to 250,000 units) were required to sterilize the blood stream in our cases of meningococcemia. Further, it was not necessary to continue penicillin for long periods of time, eight to forty-eight hours of therapy being adequate for these patients. It seems logical to assume that, when combined with intrathecal therapy, these data are equally applicable to the treatment of the nonbacteremic cases, the larger doses being employed in the more serious types of infection. On the other hand, in meningitis secondary to otitis media, intravenous or intramuscular penicillin must be continued until all other sources of infection have been adequately controlled. The majority of patients with cerebrospinal fever received only one or two injections of penicillin intrathecally, whereas in the most severe infections as much as five injections were necessary for recovery. It would appear safer, however, to administer a minimum of two intrathecal injections of 10,000 units each to all patients, even though many of the milder or earlier infections may be controlled by a single injection. As 2 patients without bacteremia recovered following only 20,000 units intravenously and 10,000 units intrathecally, and another recovered with intrathecal therapy alone, the question may be raised whether any intravenous or intramuscular penicillin is indicated in the

nonbacteremic cases. Since the clinical picture presented by patients with bacteremia is often indistinguishable from that observed in individuals with negative blood cultures, it is our belief that penicillin should be administered intravenously or intramuscularly to all patients with meningitis. Moreover, it is of the utmost importance to continue penicillin intrathecally until recovery is assured, observing the criteria outlined in our plan of treatment. The findings of Pilcher and Meacham[5] in experimental meningitis support the latter contention.

The failure of penicillin to alter the course of arthritis or pericarditis was not unexpected. Similar failures have been observed with sulfonamide therapy.[6] It is probable that neither of these agents is excreted into these spaces in sufficient amounts, if any, to be effective. The occurrence of epididymitis, with or without orchitis, in 10 patients with cerebrospinal fever is of interest, as it is generally regarded as rare. However, it has been found quite frequently in some epidemics[7] and has also been observed following sulfonamide therapy.

We are fully cognizant of the shortcomings of any therapeutic agent requiring intrathecal administration to achieve its maximum effectiveness. Notwithstanding, it is evident from our experiences that for those patients who develop reactions to the sulfonamides, or in whom sulfonamide therapy is contraindicated for other reasons, for those who are sulfonamide resistant and for those with the fulminating bacteremias wherein a highly potent agent is indicated, penicillin alone may prove life saving. It is not unlikely that, when ultimately prepared in a more concentrated and more highly purified form, free from pyrogens, penicillin may be excreted into the subarachnoid spaces in sufficient amounts following intravenous or intramuscular administration to justify the abandonment of intrathecal therapy. Until then, penicillin should be administered intrathecally as well as intravenously or intramuscularly in the treatment of meningitis.

## SUMMARY AND CONCLUSIONS

1. Penicillin was administered intrathecally and intravenously or intramuscularly to 65 patients with cerebrospinal fever (11 with bacteremia), 3 patients with hemolytic streptococcus meningitis (1 with bacteremia and 1 with acute otitis media), 2 patients with streptococcus viridans bacteremia and meningitis and 1 patient with pneumococcic meningitis secondary to acute otitis media. Seventy of the 71 patients recovered. Except for slight unilateral paresis of the sixth cranial nerve in 1 patient, no sequelae were observed.

2. Although one intrathecal injection of 10,000 units controlled some of the milder or earlier infections, a minimum of two injections is advocated as a precautionary measure. In the severe infections as much as five

5. Pilcher, C., and Meacham, W. F.: The Chemotherapy of Intracranial Infections: III. The Treatment of Experimental Staphylococcic Meningitis with Intrathecal Administration of Penicillin, A. M. A. 123:330 (Oct. 9) 1943.

6. Jaeger, H. W.: Meningococcic Infection of Joints, Rev. chilena de pediat. 14:414 (June) 1943. Rundlett, E.; Gnassi, A. M., and Price, P.: Meningococcic Meningitis: Prognostic Significance of the Spinal Fluid Sugar, J. A. M. A. 119:695 (June 27) 1942.

7. Brinton, D.: Cerebrospinal Fever, Baltimore, Williams & Wilkins Company, 1941, p. 51.

intrathecal injections (50,000 units) were required. Bacteremia was controlled by 40,000 to 130,000 units of penicillin intravenously and intramuscularly in the majority of instances. In a patient with fulminating meningococcemia and "Waterhouse-Friderichsen syndrome," 250,000 units over a period of forty-eight hours was followed by recovery. In meningitis secondary to otitis media more prolonged intravenous or intramuscular therapy is indicated.

3. Intravenous and intramuscular penicillin is ineffective in the treatment of such complications of meningococcemia as acute arthritis, epididymitis, orchitis or pericarditis.

4. Penicillin administered both intrathecally and intravenously or intramuscularly is an effective, highly potent agent in the treatment of meningitis. No significant untoward effects are demonstrable.

ADDENDUM.—Since the preparation of this paper penicillin was administered to 11 other patients with cerebrospinal fever. All of them recovered. For 2 patients who had manifested symptoms of meningitis for one week prior to hospitalization, six intrathecal injections of penicillin (60,000 units) were required.

## ABSTRACT OF DISCUSSION

DR. WALLACE E. HERRELL, Rochester, Minn.: In view of the sensitivity of Neisseria intracellularis to penicillin, it is not surprising that such satisfactory results have been obtained. In 90 per cent of certain cases recovery will follow the use of sulfadiazine or one of the other sulfonamides. Penicillin, however, is an agent which appears relatively free of any serious toxic reactions. When greater supplies of penicillin are available it seems likely that it may be possible, as well as desirable, to treat all of these patients with penicillin without waiting for failures to occur with sulfonamides. This might well result in even greater success than has been attained in the past. It is my opinion that meningitis due to the several organisms isolated in 6 of the 71 cases reported by the authors will be found to respond in a less satisfactory manner to penicillin. It is the experience at the present time that probably no better recovery rates than 60 per cent have been experienced with penicillin. The plan of treatment which has been outlined is an exceedingly satisfactory one. In addition to being administered by the intrathecal route, penicillin also should be given intramuscularly or intravenously in cases of meningitis. It is interesting that Rosenberg and Arling have found that relatively small amounts of penicillin (250,000 units) have been satisfactory. In meningitis due to pneumococci or streptococci I believe that larger amounts of penicillin will be required for the total dose and that the course of treatment will necessarily be somewhat longer. In connection with the arthritis complicating meningococcic meningitis, it is at times difficult to isolate the organism from the joint fluid. Nevertheless I am inclined to believe that there was definitely some beneficial effect. A positive culture was obtained in only 1 of 9 cases of septic arthritis in which cultures were made. Using Fleming's modification of the Wright slide cell technic, my associates and I have made determinations of the concentration of penicillin in the joint fluid of patients receiving this agent. In many instances we have found satisfactory antibacterial amounts of penicillin in the joints. The ratio of blood to joint fluid content is approximately 2 to 1. Urticaria or irritative dermatitis has been observed by us in 2 of 150 cases. I believe this skin reaction will be observed more frequently as more and more penicillin is used. Many people are sensitive to molds and to mold products. One must exercise caution in the presence of irritative dermatitis or severe urticaria. Continuing to force penicillin might result in the development of an exfoliative dermatitis, although at times one may administer penicillin without difficulty to patients who have previously exhibited this reaction.

LIEUTENANT COMMANDER DAVID H. ROSENBERG (MC) U.S.N.R.: Dr. Herrell's comments regarding arthritis are of interest. Our observations were based on the duration of the symptoms and signs of arthritis. It is apparent that the effects of penicillin in these complications should also be studied by assay of the penicillin content of the affected joints.

April 13, 1984
(JAMA 1984;251:1877-1880)

# Penicillin and 'Cerebrospinal Fever'*

### Martin G. Täuber, MD, Merle A. Sande, MD

## Meningitis Before Penicillin

Meningococcal meningitis, or cerebrospinal fever, as the disease was once called, has been registered in the medical literature as a serious health problem for almost 200 years. Since its first description in 1805 by Vieusseaux,[1] many catastrophic epidemic outbreaks and numerous sporadic cases have been recorded. The tendency of the disease to occur in closed populations, where person-to-person spread is favored and high nasopharyngeal carrier rates are observed, has magnified the hysteria over the disease. High attack rates have been observed in military recruit camps, colleges, and similar populations.[2] Before specific anti-infectious treatment became available, the reported mortality from the disease ranged between 30% and 90%, with the highest case fatality rates observed in very young children and in adults older than 40 years.[3]

Treatment before the antibiotic era was based on two principles. Initially, drainage of CSF by repeated lumbar punctures was performed in an attempt to reduce the increased CSF pressure, which was recognized as harmful. Second, serum therapy was instituted during the first part of this century. In 1913, Flexner[4] reported 1,300 cases of cerebrospinal fever, all of which had been treated with intrathecal injections of an "antimeningitis serum" developed by the Rockefeller Institute in New York in 1904. The overall case fatality rate in this series was 30.9%, a substantial improvement compared with historical controls. Although Flexner expressed great hope that the mortality could be reduced further with serum treatment, two large epidemics in the late 1920s showed mortality rates above 50%.[3,5]

The other two major pathogens associated with bacterial meningitis, Streptococcus pneumoniae and Hemophilus influenzae, have not caused epidemics comparable to those seen with Neisseria meningitidis. Before the antibiotic era, the treatment of meningitis caused by these two organisms was similar to that of meningococcal meningitis: extensive drainage of spinal fluid and antiserum. The prognosis of meningitis caused by these organisms was even worse than that of meningococcal meningitis. Of 99 patients with pneumococcal meningitis seen at the Boston City Hospital between 1920 and 1936, not a single patient survived.[6] Fothergill[7] found a 98% mortality in 78 children with H influenzae meningitis before the institution of serum therapy and an 84.6% mortality in 201 children who were treated with serum.

In the late 1930s, the antibacterial properties of sulfonamides and their potential benefit for the treatment of meningitis were discovered. Even though the old, established methods of treatment were not abandoned immediately, the addition of a sulfonamide, usually sulfadiazine, to CSF drainage and antiserum dramatically changed the outcome of the disease. Schwentker and colleagues[8] reported treatment with sulfanilamide of ten cases of meningococcal meningitis and one case of sepsis in 1937, with ten recoveries (see Chapter 27). In 1938, Finland and colleagues[6] reported six survivals in a series of ten patients with pneumococcal meningitis at the Boston City Hospital. Seventy-eight percent of the children with H influenzae meningitis treated after 1937 at Columbia University in New York survived,[9] and in Halifax, Nova Scotia, 75 (92%) of 82 patients with meningococcal meningitis treated with sulfapyridine recovered (see also Chapter 33).[10]

## Impact of Penicillin

In 1941, a group headed by Florey at Oxford University succeeded in producing comparably large amounts of penicillin, an antibacterial agent discovered ten years earlier by Fleming. After initial clinical trials,

From the Department of Medicine, University of California, San Francisco School of Medicine; and the Medical Service, San Francisco General Hospital Medical Center.

*A commentary on Rosenberg DH, Arling PA: Penicillin in the treatment of meningitis. JAMA 1944;125:1011-1017.

the military became the preferential benefactor of this new substance. The second World War, with its increased military activity, concentrated large numbers of susceptible young men in crowded conditions that favored the occurrence of epidemics of meningococcal meningitis, and it is not surprising that the first report of a large series of patients with meningococcal meningitis treated with the new drug came from the US Navy. In a classic article published in THE JOURNAL in 1944, David H. Rosenberg and P. A. Arling[11] reported their results for 71 male patients ranging in age from 17 to 69 years (median age, 18 years) who received penicillin. Sixty-five of these patients had meningococcal disease — 50 proved by culture and 15 diagnosed on clinical grounds — and six had meningitis caused by various streptococci. Only one patient with meningococcal meningitis who was comatose and had extreme hyperthermia (42.2 °C [108 °F], rectal) on admission did not survive. All other patients recovered without major sequelae. Most received penicillin in low doses both intrathecally and intravenously (IV) or intramuscularly (IM). Extensive drainage of CSF before penicillin administration was still considered an important part of therapy.

Despite the excellent survival rate reported by Rosenberg and Arling, penicillin was not immediately accepted as the drug of choice for the treatment of meningococcal meningitis. In another study published in 1944, Meads and colleagues[12] concluded, on the basis of their experience with nine patients treated with intrathecal and systemic calcium penicillin in doses comparable with those used by Rosenberg and Arling, that sulfonamide therapy was superior to penicillin therapy. Even though all nine patients recovered, the authors observed a much slower clinical and bacteriologic response to the penicillin treatment than would have been expected with sulfonamide therapy. In two cases, clinical improvement occurred only after sulfonamides had been added to the penicillin regimen. The authors also considered it to be a major disadvantage that penicillin had to be administered by the intrathecal route and that it did not consistently eliminate the nasopharyngeal carrier state. Their conclusion was that ''if good results are obtained from the treatment of meningococcal meningitis with penicillin, one must suspect that the patient has received sulfonamides before entry.''

Around 1950, the first successful clinical trials using very high doses of systemic penicillin alone were reported. Before that time, the low doses used made intrathecal drug administration essential to achieve effective concentrations in CSF, since penicillin and most other antibiotics were found to cross the blood-CSF barrier poorly. Although the large systemic doses resulted in CSF concentrations sufficient for bactericidal activity, intrathecal administration of penicillin was not completely abandoned for at least another decade, particularly in seriously ill patients.[13] Intrathecal drug instillation is still employed today with aminoglycoside antibiotics for treatment of gram-negative bacillary meningitis in adults because the narrow therapeutic margin of these drugs does not allow use of the high systemic doses necessary to achieve sufficient concentrations in CSF.

While penicillin soon became the drug of choice for

pneumococcal meningitis, the sulfonamides were preferred for meningococcal infections until the mid-1960s, when the increasing emergence of sulfonamide resistance rendered them ineffective for treatment and prophylaxis of meningococcal disease.[14] Today, penicillin remains the drug of choice in nonallergic patients for the treatment of meningococcal and pneumococcal meningitis. Therapy for meningitis caused by *H influenzae* is more complex. During the mid-1960s, ampicillin became the drug of choice for *Hemophilus* infections; however, by 1975, β-lactamase–producing strains of *H influenzae* that were resistant to ampicillin were reported throughout the United States. Today, up to 35% of isolates of both the nonencapsulated and encapsulated strains are ampicillin resistant, and chloramphenicol has again become the drug of choice for initial therapy pending results of sensitivity tests. No clinically significant emergence of meningococci resistant to penicillin has been observed to date. However, a few strains of penicillin-resistant pneumococci have been reported. Although this has been a greater problem in other countries, especially South Africa, isolated outbreaks have occurred in the United States (eg, Denver). This resistance is not due to β-lactamase production and is expressed as either a low (minimal inhibitory concentration [MIC], <0.2 to 1.0 μg/mL)- or high (MIC,>1.0 μg/mL)-level resistance. While it is possible to treat most infections caused by pneumococci with low-level resistance with penicillin, this may not be the case with meningitis in which drug penetration is restricted. Thus, all CSF isolates of pneumococci should be screened for both high- and low-level penicillin resistance.

### Dosage and Distribution

The most remarkable feature in the article by Rosenberg and Arling,[11] when judged from today's perspective, is the dosage and mode of application of penicillin. The treatment regimen, which was slightly modified in some patients, consisted of 10,000 units of penicillin G intrathecally every 24 hours and 5,000 units IV every hour or 15,000 units IM every three hours. In a majority of the patients (42), as few as two intrathecal injections were sufficient to produce a sufficient response (clinical improvement and complete clearance of bacteria from CSF) to allow discontinuance of further intrathecal penicillin administration. Thirty-five patients received a total of less than 100,000 units systemically, another 20 received less than 250,000 units IV or IM, and the remaining 16 received between 250,000 units and 900,000 units of penicillin IV or IM. These doses are minuscule when compared with the massive penicillin doses of 20 to 30 million units daily for ten days as currently recommended.

Although the concentration achieved by the injection of 10,000 units of penicillin into CSF was not determined in Rosenberg and Arling's study, a rough estimate of the penicillin concentrations in CSF of the patients can be calculated. Ten thousand units of penicillin G sodium are equivalent to 6,000 μg, and the total amount of CSF in an adult man is approximately 140 mL. In the ideal case of immediate and equal distribution throughout the entire CSF, this would result in a theoretical peak CSF drug concentration of about 40 $\mu$g/mL. Even though such an ideal distribution certainly does not occur in reality, this calculation demonstrates that most areas of the subarachnoid space can be expected to be bathed with peak concentrations far above the minimal bactericidal concentration (MBC) of penicillin for *N meningitidis*, which is about 0.03 $\mu$g/mL today and was probably even lower in 1944.[14] This is also supported by studies cited in the article by Rosenberg and Arling,[11] which indicated that intrathecally administered penicillin is detectable in the subarachnoid space for many hours. On the other hand, 5,000 units administered hourly IV or IM was probably not in a range to contribute substantially to the amount of drug present in CSF. From data obtained through animal model studies, we know that with inflamed meninges, CSF penicillin concentrations are equal to approximately 5% of steady-state serum levels. The mean serum concentration in humans after the administration of 3 million units of penicillin IV every three hours can be expected to be 20 $\mu$g/mL,[15] with corresponding CSF levels of approximately 1 $\mu$g/mL. Administration of 5,000 units/hr IV would, thus, result in about 200-fold lower serum levels (ie, 0.1 $\mu$g/mL) and CSF concentrations of 0.005 $\mu$g/mL.

These admittedly rough estimates of the drug concentrations in CSF and blood provide a rational explanation of the excellent bacteriologic and clinical response observed by Rosenberg and Arling. Clinical and experimental data indicate that CSF concentrations considerably higher than the MBC of the infecting organism are necessary for optimal bactericidal activity of antibiotics in the treatment of meningitis.[16] Using a rabbit model of pneumococcal meningitis, we have found that the rate of bacterial killing in CSF by penicillin and several other $\beta$-lactams directly correlates with the CSF concentrations of these drugs.[17] All exhibited a maximum reduction of bacterial titers in CSF of about 1 $\log_{10}$ colony-forming units (cfu) per milliliter per hour in concentrations at least 20- to 30-fold higher than their respective MBCs. This requirement is certainly fulfilled in the patients of Rosenberg and Arling, even when their drug levels in CSF are estimated conservatively. In fact, the therapeutic ratio (CSF concentration/MBC) is probably even better in these patients than that achieved with the currently used approach, which results in CSF peak concentrations of about 1 $\mu$g/mL.

Bacterial titers in untreated meningitis are often between $10^6$ and $10^8$ cfu/mL, and maximum rates of bacterial killing of up to 1 $\log_{10}$/hr should, therefore, sterilize the CSF within about half a day. Thus, the findings reported (that 29 of 48 patients with initially positive CSF had negative cultures after 24 hours) can be predicted from extrapolation of the animal experiments. Penicillin concentrations probably do not have to be greater than the MBC throughout the entire treatment period. We recently found in our rabbit model of pneumococcal meningitis that a treatment schedule with dosing every 12 hours, which resulted in drug concentrations in CSF below the MBC for about two thirds of the dosing interval (time between drug administration), was as effective as treatment with four-hour dosing intervals and CSF drug concentrations higher than the MBC for most of the entire treatment period.[18] Cure rates were greater than 90% with both regimens, as long as the single dose was large enough to achieve peak concentrations in CSF at least tenfold greater than the MBC. Penicillin concentrations probably dropped below the MBC of the organism at least in some areas of the CSF during the 24-hour dosing interval in the patients of Rosenberg and Arling. This is particularly likely in the ventricles, where concentrations of drugs administered by lumbar puncture are relatively low, since CSF flows from the ventricles, where it is produced, out into the subarachnoid space. However, as shown by our experiments, this does not have to jeopardize the success of the treatment, as long as peak concentrations are sufficiently high.

## Cure Rates

The excellent cure rate of 98.6% in the series of Rosenberg and Arling is considerably better than in most series reported later, in which mortality ranged from 5% to 10%, and one large series in which a mortality rate of 19% was reported.[19] Studies from before and after the introduction of antibiotics have consistently reported that the mortality rate of meningococcal meningitis is lowest in young adults while it is higher in young children and adults older than 40 years.[18] In this respect, the patient population of Rosenberg and Arling represents a selection of patients with a relatively good prognosis, since most of them were about 20 years old. Also, meningococcal meningitis in general has a better prognosis than meningitis caused by other organisms such as *S pneumoniae*, which in 1978 still showed an overall case fatality rate of 28%.[20] This difference can probably be explained in part by the populations affected by the different organisms. *Hemophilus influenzae* meningitis is almost exclusively a disease of young children, and pneumococcal meningitis is often found in elderly persons who frequently have underlying diseases.[13] In contrast, epidemics of meningococcal meningitis tend to affect healthy young persons, as in the report under discussion.

Meningococcal disease, present in 91% of the patients described by Rosenberg and Arling, has a broad spectrum of clinical manifestations. Wolf and Birbara[21] differentiate four types: (1) a benign course with almost accidentally discovered meningococcal bacteremia, (2) pure meningitis with prominence of the classic signs of meningeal inflammation, (3) septicemic course with generalized symptoms and often profound shock (a clinical picture referred to as Waterhouse-Friderichsen syndrome), and (4) a meningoencephalitic picture in which the patient is comatose and has other neurological signs indicative of parenchymal brain damage. The prognosis is apparently better in patients with "pure" meningitis than in those who show pronounced systemic disease with massive purpuric skin lesions and hypotension. Independent of the infecting organism, the presence of coma at the time of admission is a bad prognostic sign. In the series of Rosenberg and Arling, about one third of the patients were comatose on admission, and only one patient clearly had a septicemic course. The preponderance of cases with a clinical manifestation of meningitis may therefore have contributed to the excellent outcome in this series.

## Toxicity

Drug-related toxicity, which occurs in a small percentage of the patients treated with penicillin, was not a major problem for Rosenberg and Arling. Despite the increased incidence of allergic reactions observed with early preparations of penicillin, no such reactions were noted in this series. This may be explained in part by the fact that most of the patients were treated for relatively short periods and probably were exposed to penicillin for the first time in their lives. On the other hand, Rosenberg and Arling reported increased signs of meningeal irritation in those patients who received intrathecal penicillin more frequently and in higher concentrations than the majority of the patients.

Although the data presented do not allow detailed analysis, it is somewhat surprising that, despite intrathecal penicillin administration and estimated drug concentrations in CSF higher than 10 $\mu$g/mL, no overt neurotoxicity was observed. This form of adverse reaction has become a well-defined clinical syndrome and is related to very high CSF concentrations of penicillin as they can be observed, for instance, in patients with renal failure who receive large doses of the drug.[22] During the uremic state, the excretion of penicillin is competitively inhibited in both the renal tubules and the choroidal plexus by other organic acids that accumulate in the body.[23] With increasing CSF concentrations of penicillin, the most neurotoxic of the $\beta$-lactam antibiotics, some patients will become lethargic and experience multifocal myoclonus and seizures.[22]

---

The article by Rosenberg and Arling represents a landmark in the history of the treatment of meningitis. For the first time, the efficacy of penicillin was demonstrated in a large series of patients with meningococcal meningitis. The excellent results of this study helped bring penicillin forth to play an eminent role thereafter in the treatment of meningitis caused by penicillin-sensitive organisms. On the other hand, as anticipated by the authors in their discussion, the mode of drug administration proved not to be optimal and was refined during the next decade. It was probably because antimicrobial therapy had such a dramatic impact on the outcome of infectious diseases in general and of bacterial meningitis in particular that only in recent years have investigators become concerned with some of the more basic principles of penicillin therapy for meningitis. Several aspects — constant $v$ intermittent drug administration, amount of drug and duration of therapy necessary for maximal cure rates, and complementary treatments aimed at improving the outcome — deserve further investigation even today.

## References

1. Vieusseaux M: Mémoire sur la maladie qui a régné a Genève au printemps de 1805. *J Med Chir Pharamacol* 1806;11:163-182.

2. Feldman HA: Meningococcal infections. *Adv Intern Med* 1972;18:117-140.

3. Norton JF, Gordon JE: Meningococcus meningitis in Detroit in 1928-1929. *J Prev Med* 1930;4:207-214.

4. Flexner S: The results of the serum treatment in 1,300 cases of epidemic meningitis. *J Exp Med* 1913;17:553-576.

5. French MR: Epidemiological study of 383 cases of meningococcus meningitis in the city of Milwaukee, 1927-1928 and 1929. *Am J Public Health* 1931;21:130-138.

6. Finland M, Brown JW, Rauh AE: Treatment of pneumococci meningitis. *N Engl J Med* 1938;218:1033-1044.

7. Fothergill LD: *Hemophilus influenzae* (Pfeiffer bacillus) meningitis and its specific treatment. *N Engl J Med* 1937;216:587-590.

8. Schwentker FF, Gelman S, Long PH: The treatment of meningococcic meningitis with sulfanilamide: Preliminary report. *JAMA* 1937;108:1407-1408.

9. Alexander HE: Treatment of type B *Haemophilus influenzae* meningitis. *J Pediatr* 1944;25:517-532.

10. Dingle JH, Thomas L, Morton AR: Treatment of meningococcic meningitis and meningococcemia with sulfadiazine. *JAMA* 1941;116:2666-2668.

11. Rosenberg DH, Arling PA: Penicillin in the treatment of meningitis. *JAMA* 1944;125:1011-1017.

12. Meads M, Harris W, Samper BA, et al: Treatment of meningococcal meningitis with penicillin. *N Engl J Med* 1944;231:509-517.

13. Schwartz MN, Dodge PR: Bacterial meningitis: A review of selected aspects: I. General clinical features: Special problems and unusual meningeal reactions mimicking bacterial meningitis. *N Engl J Med* 1965;272:779-787.

14. Eickhoff TC, Finland M: Changing susceptibility of meningococci to antimicrobial agents. *N Engl J Med* 1965;272:395-398.

15. Bryan CS, Stone WJ: Comparably massive penicillin G therapy in renal failure. *Ann Intern Med* 1975;82:189-195.

16. Sande MA: Antibiotic therapy of bacterial meningitis: Lessons we've learned. *Am J Med* 1981;71:507-510.

17. Täuber MG, Doroshow CA, Hackbarth CJ, et al: Antibacterial activity of beta-lactam antibiotics in experimental pneumococcal meningitis due to *Streptococcus pneumoniae*. *J Infect Dis* 1984;149:568-574.

18. Täuber MG, Zak O, Scheld WM, et al: Post-antibiotic effect in the treatment of experimental pneumococcal meningitis, abstract 14. Program and abstracts of the 23rd Interscience Conference on Antimicrobial Agents and Chemotherapy, Las Vegas, 1983.

19. Centers for Disease Control: Analysis of endemic meningococcal disease by serogroup and evaluation of chemoprophylaxis. *J Infect Dis* 1976;134:201-204.

20. Centers for Disease Control: Bacterial meningitis and meningococcemia — United States, 1978. *MMWR* 1979;28:277-279.

21. Wolf RE, Birbara CA: Meningococcal infection at an army training center. *Am J Med* 1968;44:243-255.

22. Bloomer HA, Barton LJ, Maddock RK Jr: Penicillin-induced encephalopathy in uremic patients. *JAMA* 1967;200:121-123.

23. Spector R, Snodgrass SR, Levy P: The effect of uremia on penicillin flux between blood and cerebrospinal fluid. *J Lab Clin Med* 1976;87:749-759.

Sept 9, 1944
(*JAMA* 1944;126:63-67)

## Chapter 37

# Penicillin Treatment of Early Syphilis: II

J. F. Mahoney, M.D.

R. C. Arnold, M.D.

Burton L. Sterner, M.D.

Ad Harris
Serologist

and

M. R. Zwally, M.A.
U. S. Public Health Service
Staten Island, N.Y.

In a preliminary report[1] the influence of penicillin therapy on the clinical manifestations and serologic reactions of patients with early syphilis was presented. The report was based on the results of a curtailed period of observation of a group of 4 patients. It is our purpose in the present paper to record the findings of post-treatment observation of the original group for periods in excess of three hundred days. It is also desired to record certain items of information which have resulted from the treatment of an additional 100 patients.

### REVIEW OF ORIGINAL GROUP

Of the group of 4 patients the records of whom formed the basis for the preliminary report,[1] all have been maintained under observation. It will be recalled that these patients displayed dark field positive lesions of early syphilis at the time of treatment. The therapy consisted of an intramuscular injection of 25,000 units of penicillin administered at four hour intervals for forty-eight injections. The total amount of the product utilized was 1,200,000 units and the total time of therapy was about eight days. No other antisyphilitic medication has been employed. The post-treatment observation has consisted of a clinical and serologic examination at

weekly intervals for the first six months and monthly observations thereafter. A spinal fluid examination was carried out at the completion of six months post-treatment observation.

Three members of the original group experienced a rapid healing of penile ulcerations and attained seronegativity within the initial three months of observation. These patients have remained clinically and serologically negative up to the present. The remaining patient has displayed circumstances which warrant discussion.

In this patient the penile lesion healed promptly and the serologic tests were recorded as negative on the 71st day. This situation maintained until the 286th day of observation, at which time strongly positive reactions were recorded in all test procedures. At that time the patient was under treatment for specific urethritis in a distant clinic. After some delay the patient was again made available for study and was found to have a single ulcerative lesion, on an indurated base, located on the inner surface of the lower lip. The regional lymph glands were enlarged and firm. There was no other evidence of involvement of skin or mucous membranes or of general adenopathy. Dark field examination of secretions secured from the lesion, after all precautions had been taken to avoid the contamination of the specimen by mouth spirochetes, was considered to be positive for Treponema pallidum.

Although this patient is being classed as a treatment failure, the probability of reinfection is inescapable. Retreatment with penicillin has been carried out.

Table 1 shows the serologic record of the first patient treated with penicillin for early syphilis. Table 2 shows the complete serologic record of patient 4, including

From the Venereal Disease Research Laboratory and the United States Marine Hospital.

Read in a panel discussion on "Penicillin in the Treatment of Syphilis" before the Section on Dermatology and Syphilology at the Ninety-Fourth Annual Session of the American Medical Association, Chicago, June 15, 1944.

1. Mahoney, J. F.; Arnold, R. C., and Harris, A.: Penicillin Treatment of Early Syphilis: A Preliminary Report, Ven. Dis. Inform. 24:355-357 (Dec.) 1943.

## TABLE 1.—*Results of Serologic Tests in Case 1*

Duration of Disease, Nine Days

| Time After Start of Therapy | Qualitative Methods | | | | | | | | Quantitative Methods | | |
|---|---|---|---|---|---|---|---|---|---|---|---|
| | Super-sensitive Kline Exclusion | Diagnostic Flocculation | | | | | | Complement Fixation, Kolmer Simplified | Diagnostic Flocculation | | Complement Fixation, Kolmer |
| | | Mazzini | Kline Diagnostic | Kahn Standard | Hinton | Eagle | | | Mazzini | Kahn | |
| Days | | | | | | | | | | | |
| 0 | .. | 4 | .. | 4 | Pos | Pos | 4 | 4 4 4 2 1 – | 4 4 4 2 ± – | 4 4 4 4 4 1 |
| 1 | .. | 4 | .. | 4 | Pos | Pos | 4 | 4 4 4 2 1 – | 4 4 4 2 ± – | 4 4 4 4 4 3 |
| 9 | 4 | 4 | 4 | 4 | Pos | Pos | 4 | 4 4 4 4 2 – | 4 4 4 4 1 – | 4 4 4 4 2 – |
| 23 | .. | 4 | .. | 3 | Pos | Pos | 4 | 4 3 2 – – – | 4 4 1 – – – | 4 4 4 3 ± – |
| 30 | 4 | 4 | 3 | 3 | Pos | – | 4 | 4 4 4 2 – – | 4 4 3 1 – – | 4 4 4 2 ± – |
| 37 | 4 | 4 | 1 Dbt | 3 | Dbt | – | 3 | 4 4 2 1 – – | 4 1 – – – – | 3 3 2 ± – – |
| 44 | 3 | 4 | – | 1 Dbt | – | – | 4 | 4 3 2 – – – | 4 ± – – – – | 4 4 3 ± – – |
| 51 | 1 Dbt | 4 | – | – | – | – | 4 | 4 2 – – – – | 1 – – – – – | 4 4 4 1 ± – |
| 58 | 1 Dbt | 4 | – | – | – | – | – | 4 3 – – – – | 1 – – – – – | – – – – – – |
| 65 | 2 | 2 Dbt | – | – | – | – | – | 2 1 – – – – | – – – – – – | – – – – – – |
| 72 | 1 Dbt | 2 Dbt | – | – | – | – | – | 2 1 – – – – | – – – – – – | – – – – – – |
| 80 | – | 2 Dbt | – | – | – | – | – | 2 ± – – – – | ± – – – – – | – – – – – – |
| 86 | – | 2 Dbt | – | – | – | – | – | 2 – – – – – | – – – – – – | – – – – – – |
| 93 | – | 1 Dbt | – | – | – | – | – | 1 – – – – – | | |
| Months | | | | | | | | | | | |
| 4 | – | – | – | – | – | – | – | | | |
| 5 | – | – | – | – | – | – | – | | | |
| 6 | – | 1 Dbt | – | – | – | – | – | | | |
| 7 | – | – | – | – | – | – | – | | | |
| 8 | – | – | – | – | – | – | – | | | |
| 9 | – | – | – | – | – | – | – | | | |
| 11 | – | 1 Dbt | – | – | – | – | – | | | |

## TABLE 2.—*Results of Serologic Tests in Case 4*

Duration of Disease, Eight Days

| Time After Start of Therapy | Qualitative Methods | | | | | | | | Quantitative Methods | | |
|---|---|---|---|---|---|---|---|---|---|---|---|
| | Super-sensitive Kline Exclusion | Diagnostic Flocculation | | | | | | Complement Fixation, Kolmer Simplified | Diagnostic Flocculation | | Complement Fixation, Kolmer |
| | | Mazzini | Kline Diagnostic | Kahn Standard | Hinton | Eagle | | | Mazzini | Kahn | |
| Days | | | | | | | | | | | |
| 0 | .. | 1 Dbt | .. | – | – | – | – | – – – – – – – | – – – – – – – | – – – – – – – |
| 1 | 4 | 4 | ± Dbt | 1 Dbt | – | Pos | – | 2 1 – – – – – | 3 ± – – – – – | ± ± ± – – – – |
| 8 | .. | 4 | .. | 3 | – | Pos | 4 | 3 2 – – – – – | 4 4 ± – – – – | 4 4 4 2 – – – |
| 15 | 4 | 4 | 1 Dbt | 3 | Pos | Pos | ± Dbt | 4 3 2 1 – – – | 4 3 1 – – – – | ± ± ± ± – – – |
| 22 | 4 | 3 | ± Dbt | 3 | Pos | Dbt | ± Dbt | 3 1 – – – – – | 4 1 ± – – – – | ± 1 ± – – – – |
| 30 | 1 Dbt | 2 Dbt | ± Dbt | – | Dbt | – | ± Dbt | 2 1 – – – – – | 1 – – – – – – | ± ± 1 ± – – – |
| 36 | ± Dbt | 2 Dbt | – | – | – | – | – | 2 – – – – – – | ± – – – – – – | – – ± ± ± – – |
| 43 | – | 2 Dbt | – | – | – | – | – | 2 1 – – – – – | ± – – – – – – | – – – – – – – |
| 50 | ± Dbt | 1 Dbt | – | – | – | – | – | 1 – – – – – – | – – – – – – – | – – – – – – – |
| 57 | – | 1 Dbt | – | – | – | – | – | 1 – – – – – – | ± – – – – – – | – – – – – – – |
| 64 | ± Dbt | 1 Dbt | – | – | – | – | – | 1 – – – – – – | – – – – – – – | – – – – – – – |
| 71 | – | – | – | – | – | – | – | – – – – – – – | – – – – – – – | – – – – – – – |
| 86 | – | – | – | – | – | – | – | – – – – – – – | – – – – – – – | – – – – – – – |
| 93 | – | – | – | – | – | – | – | – – – – – – – | – – – – – – – | – – – – – – – |
| Months | | | | | | | | | | | |
| 4 | – | – | – | – | – | – | – | | | |
| 5 | – | – | – | – | – | – | – | | | |
| 6 | ± Dbt | – | – | – | – | – | – | | | |
| 7 | – | 1 Dbt | – | – | .. | – | – | | | |
| 8 | – | – | – | – | .. | .. | – | | | |
| Days | | | | | | | | | | | |
| 286 | 4 | 4 | 2 | 4 | .. | .. | 4 | | | 4 4 4 ± – – – – |
| 295 | 4 | 4 | 4 | 4 | .. | Pos | 4 | 4 4 4 2 1 – – – – | 4 4 1 ± – – – – – | 4 4 4 4 1 – – – |
| 318 | 4 | 4 | 4 | 4 | Pos | Pos | 4 | 4 4 4 4 4 3 1 – – | 4 4 4 4 4 3 – – – | 4 4 4 4 4 ± – – |
| 326 | 4 | 4 | 4 | 4 | Pos | Pos | 4 | 4 4 4 4 4 4 3 1 – | 4 4 4 4 4 4 1 – – | 4 4 4 4 4 4 ± – |

## TABLE 3.—*Results of Serologic Tests in Case 10: Pattern Considered to Be Favorable*
### Duration of Disease, Twenty-One Days

| Time After Start of Therapy | Qualitative Methods | | | | | | | Quantitative Methods | | |
| --- | --- | --- | --- | --- | --- | --- | --- | --- | --- | --- |
| | Supersensitive Kline Exclusion | Diagnostic Flocculation | | | | | Complement Fixation, Kolmer Simplified | Diagnostic Flocculation | | Complement Fixation, Kolmer |
| | | Mazzini | Kline Diagnostic | Kahn Standard | Hinton | Eagle | | Mazzini | Kahn | |
| Days | | | | | | | | | | |
| 0 | ± Dbt | 1 Dbt | — | — | Pos | — | — | 1 1 1 - - - - - - | - - - - - - - - - - | - - - - - - - - - |
| 1 | 1 Dbt | 3 | — | 2 | Pos | — | — | 3 3 2 1 - - - - - | 2 ± - - - - - - - | - - - - - - - - - |
| 3 | 1 Dbt | 3 | — | 2 | Pos | Pos | 3 | 3 3 2 1 - - - - - | 2 ± - - - - - - - | 3 4 4 3 2 ± - - - |
| 8 | 4 | 4 | 4 | 4 | Pos | Pos | 4 | 4 4 3 2 2 1 - - - | 4 4 2 1 ± - - - - | 4 4 4 4 4 - - - - |
| 14 | 4 | 4 | 4 | 4 | Pos | Pos | 4 | 4 4 4 3 2 - - - - | 4 4 2 ± - - - - - | 4 4 4 4 3 ± - - - |
| 20 | 4 | 4 | 1 Dbt | 4 | Pos | Pos | ± Dbt | 4 4 3 2 1 - - - - | 4 3 ± - - - - - - | ± ± 1 1 - - - - - |
| 28 | 2 | 4 | ± Dbt | 3 | Pos | — | ± Dbt | 4 3 2 1 1 - - - - | 4 ± ± - - - - - - | ± ± ± ± - - - - - |
| 35 | 1 Dbt | 2 Dbt | ± Dbt | 1 Dbt | Pos | — | — | 2 2 1 1 - - - - - | 3 ± - - - - - - - | - - - - - - - - - |
| 42 | ± Dbt | 2 Dbt | — | — | Pos | — | ± Dbt | 2 1 1 - - - - - - | 1 - - - - - - - - | ± ± - - - - - - - |
| 48 | ± Dbt | — | — | — | — | — | — | - - - - - - - - - | - - - - - - - - - | - - - - - - - - - |
| 56 | ± Dbt | 1 Dbt | — | — | — | — | -- | 1 - - - - - - - - | - - - - - - - - - | - - ± ± ± - - - - |
| 63 | — | 1 Dbt | — | — | — | — | — | 1 - - - - - - - - | - - - - - - - - - | - - - - - - - - - |
| 70 | — | 1 Dbt | — | — | — | — | — | 1 - - - - - - - - | - - - - - - - - - | - - - - - - - - - |
| 77 | — | 1 Dbt | — | — | — | — | — | 1 - - - - - - - - | - - - - - - - - - | - - - - - - - - - |
| 85 | — | — | — | — | — | — | — | - - - - - - - - - | - - - - - - - - - | - - - - - - - - - |
| 91 | — | — | — | — | — | — | — | - - - - - - - - - | - - - - - - - - - | - - ± ± ± - - - - |
| Months | | | | | | | | | | |
| 4 | — | — | — | — | Dbt | — | — | | | |
| 5 | ± Dbt | — | — | — | — | — | — | | | |
| 6 | — | — | — | — | — | — | — | | | |
| 7 | — | — | — | — | — | — | — | | | |

Pattern showing low reading reactions at the beginning of therapy, with an increase in titer during treatment and a rapid reversal to negative.

## TABLE 4.—*Results of Serologic Tests in Case 35: High Titer Reactions at Onset of Therapy*
### Duration of Disease, Sixty-Nine Days

| Time After Start of Therapy | Qualitative Methods | | | | | | | Quantitative Methods | | |
| --- | --- | --- | --- | --- | --- | --- | --- | --- | --- | --- |
| | Supersensitive Kline Exclusion | Diagnostic Flocculation | | | | | Complement Fixation, Kolmer Simplified | Diagnostic Flocculation | | Complement Fixation, Kolmer |
| | | Mazzini | Kline Diagnostic | Kahn Standard | Hinton | Eagle | | Mazzini | Kahn | |
| Days | | | | | | | | | | |
| −1 | 4 | 4 | 4 | 4 | Pos | Pos | 4 | 4 4 4 4 4 3 1 - - | 3 4 4 4 4 4 1 - - | 4 4 4 4 4 4 4 1 - |
| 1 | 4 | 4 | 4 | 4 | Pos | Pos | 4 | 4 4 4 4 4 3 1 - - | 4 4 4 4 4 3 ± - - | 4 4 4 4 4 4 2 ± - |
| 8 | 4 | 4 | 4 | 4 | Pos | Pos | 4 | 4 4 4 4 2 1 - - - | 4 4 4 4 4 2 - - - | 4 4 4 4 4 4 3 ± - |
| 13 | 4 | 4 | 4 | 4 | Pos | Pos | 4 | 4 4 4 4 1 - - - - | 4 4 4 4 4 3 ± - - | 4 4 4 4 4 4 2 - - |
| 20 | 4 | 4 | 4 | 4 | Pos | Pos | 4 | 4 4 4 4 3 1 - - - | 4 4 4 4 2 1 - - - | 4 4 4 4 4 1 ± - - |
| 27 | 4 | 4 | 4 | 4 | .. | Pos | 4 | 4 4 4 3 ± - - - - | 4 4 3 2 ± - - - - | 4 4 4 4 4 1 ± - - |
| 34 | 4 | 4 | 4 | 4 | Pos | Pos | 4 | 4 4 3 2 - - - - - | 4 3 2 1 - - - - - | 4 4 4 1 - - - - - |
| 41 | 4 | 4 | 2 | 2 | Pos | Pos | 4 | 4 3 2 1 - - - - - | 4 3 ± - - - - - - | 4 4 4 1 - - - - - |
| 49 | 4 | 4 | 4 | 2 | Pos | Dbt | 4 | 4 2 2 1 - - - - - | 4 ± - - - - - - - | 4 4 4 ± - - - - - |
| 56 | 4 | 3 | 2 | ± Dbt | .. | — | 3 | 3 2 1 - - - - - - | 4 ± - - - - - - - | 3 3 1 - - - - - - |
| 63 | 4 | 2 Dbt | 1 Dbt | ± Dbt | — | — | 1 | 2 2 - - - - - - - | 2 - - - - - - - - | 1 ± - - - - - - - |
| 69 | 3 | 2 Dbt | 1 Dbt | — | — | — | 1 | 2 1 - - - - - - - | 1 - - - - - - - - | 1 ± - - - - - - - |
| 91 | 1 Dbt | 1 Dbt | — | — | — | — | — | | | |
| 99 | 2 | 1 Dbt | — | — | Dbt | — | — | | | |
| 112 | 1 Dbt | 1 Dbt | — | — | — | — | ± Dbt | | | |
| 119 | 1 Dbt | 1 Dbt | — | — | — | — | ± Dbt | | | |
| 126 | ± Dbt | — | — | — | — | — | — | | | |
| 153 | ± Dbt | — | — | — | — | — | — | | | |

A representative pattern of patients with secondary syphilis. High titer reactions show a consistent and progressive trend toward reversal to negative.

Duration of Disease, Forty-Six Days

| Time After Start of Therapy Days | Qualitative Methods | | | | | | | Quantitative Methods | | |
| --- | --- | --- | --- | --- | --- | --- | --- | --- | --- | --- |
| | Supersensitive Kline Exclusion | Diagnostic Flocculation | | | | | Complement Fixation, Kolmer Simplified | Diagnostic Flocculation | | Complement Fixation, Kolmer |
| | | Mazzini | Kline Diagnostic | Kahn Standard | Hinton | Eagle | | Mazzini | Kahn | |
| 0 | 4 | 4 | 4 | 4 | Pos | Pos | 4 | 4 4 4 4 4 4 3 - - | 4 4 4 4 4 4 4 ± - | 4 4 4 4 4 4 4 - - |
| 1 | 4 | 4 | 4 | 4 | Pos | Pos | 4 | 4 4 4 4 4 4 3 1 - | 4 4 4 4 4 4 3 ± - | 4 4 4 4 4 4 4 ± - |
| 8 | 4 | 4 | 4 | 4 | Pos | Pos | 4 | 4 4 4 4 4 4 3 - - | 4 4 4 4 4 4 1 - - | 4 4 4 4 4 4 4 3 - |
| 12 | 4 | 4 | 4 | 4 | Pos | Pos | 4 | 4 4 4 4 4 4 2 - - | 4 4 4 4 4 4 1 - - | 4 4 4 4 4 4 1 - - |
| 19 | 4 | 4 | 4 | 4 | Pos | Pos | 4 | 4 4 4 4 4 3 - - - | 4 4 4 4 4 2 ± - - | 4 4 4 4 4 4 2 - - |
| 26 | 4 | 4 | 4 | 4 | Pos | Pos | 4 | 4 4 4 4 4 3 - - - | 4 4 4 4 2 ± - - - | 4 4 4 4 4 3 ± - - |
| 33 | 4 | 4 | 4 | 4 | Dbt | Pos | 4 | 4 4 4 4 4 1 - - - | 4 4 4 1 ± - - - - | 4 4 4 4 4 ± - - - |
| 40 | 4 | 4 | 4 | 4 | Dbt | Pos | 4 | 4 4 4 4 3 1 - - - | 4 4 2 1 - - - - - | 4 4 4 3 ± - - - - |
| 47 | 4 | 4 | 4 | 4 | Dbt | Dbt | 4 | 4 4 4 3 - - - - - | 4 4 3 ± - - - - - | 4 4 1 ± - - - - - |
| 54 | 4 | 3 | 2 | 3 | Dbt | — | 4 | 3 2 2 2 - - - - - | 4 3 1 ± - - - - - | 4 4 3 1 - - - - - |
| 61 | 4 | 4 | 3 | 3 | Dbt | — | 4 | 4 4 4 3 2 - - - - | 4 2 ± - - - - - - | 4 4 4 4 ± - - - - |
| 68 | 4 | 4 | 4 | 3 | Pos | — | 4 | 4 4 4 3 2 - - - - | 4 2 ± - - - - - - | 4 4 4 4 2 ± - - - |
| 75 | 4 | 4 | 4 | 4 | Pos | Pos | 4 | 4 4 4 4 2 - - - - | 4 4 4 3 ± - - - - | 4 4 4 4 2 ± - - - |
| 82 | 4 | 4 | 4 | 4 | Pos | Pos | 4 | 4 4 4 4 4 3 1 - - | 4 4 4 4 4 1 - - - | 4 4 4 4 4 ± - - - |
| 90 | 4 | 4 | 4 | 4 | Pos | Pos | 4 | 4 4 4 4 4 2 1 - - | 4 4 4 4 2 - - - - | 4 4 4 4 4 4 ± - - |
| 96 | 4 | 4 | 4 | 4 | Pos | Pos | 4 | 4 4 4 4 4 4 2 - - | 4 4 4 4 4 2 - - - | 4 4 4 4 4 4 4 3 |
| 105 | 4 | 4 | 4 | 4 | Pos | Pos | 4 | 4 4 4 4 4 3 1 - - | 4 4 4 4 4 2 - - - | 4 4 4 4 4 4 - - - |
| 110 | 4 | 4 | 4 | 4 | Pos | Pos | 4 | 4 4 4 4 4 3 - - - | 4 4 4 4 4 4 ± - - | 4 4 4 4 4 4 ± - - |
| 117 | 4 | 4 | 4 | 4 | Pos | Pos | 4 | 4 4 4 4 4 - - - - | 4 4 4 4 4 - - - - | 4 4 4 4 4 - - - - |
| 124 | 4 | 4 | 4 | 4 | Pos | Pos | 4 | 4 4 4 4 4 1 - - - | 4 4 4 3 1 - - - - | 4 4 4 4 4 3 - - - |
| 131 | 4 | 4 | 4 | 4 | Pos | Pos | 4 | 4 4 4 4 3 - - - - | 4 4 4 2 ± - - - - | 4 4 4 4 2 ± - - - |
| 138 | 4 | 4 | 4 | 4 | Pos | Pos | 4 | 4 4 4 4 1 - - - - | 4 4 4 4 2 - - - - | 4 4 4 4 4 4 1 - - |
| 152 | 4 | 4 | 3 | 4 | Pos | Pos | 4 | 4 2 1 - - - - - - | 4 4 3 - - - - - - | 4 4 3 ± - - - - - |
| 166 | 4 | 2 Dbt | 1 Dbt | 3 | Pos | Pos | 4 | ............. | ............. | 4 4 1 ± - - - - - |
| 188 | 4 | 2 Dbt | 4 | ± Dbt | Pos | Dbt | ± Dbt | ............. | ............. | ± ± - - - - - - - |
| 194 | 4 | 4 | 2 | — | Dbt | Dbt | 4 | ............. | ............. | 4 3 - - - - - - - |
| 201 | 4 | 4 | 2 | 2 | Pos | Dbt | 4 | 4 3 2 2 - - - - - | ............. | 4 3 2 ± - - - - - |
| 208 | 4 | 4 | 3 | 3 | Pos | Pos | 4 | 4 4 3 2 - - - - - | ............. | 4 4 4 3 ± - - - - |

TABLE 6.—*Results of Serologic Tests in Case 68*

Duration of Disease, Thirty Days

| Time After Start of Therapy Days | Qualitative Methods | | | | | | | Quantitative Methods | | |
| --- | --- | --- | --- | --- | --- | --- | --- | --- | --- | --- |
| | Supersensitive Kline Exclusion | Diagnostic Flocculation | | | | | Complement Fixation, Kolmer Simplified | Diagnostic Flocculation | | Complement Fixation, Kolmer |
| | | Mazzini | Kline Diagnostic | Kahn Standard | Hinton | Eagle | | Mazzini | Kahn | |
| 0 | 4 | 4 | 4 | 4 | Pos | Pos | 4 | 4 4 4 4 4 4 3 1 - | ± ± 2 4 2 1 ± - - | 4 4 4 4 4 4 4 ± - |
| 1 | 4 | 4 | 4 | 4 | Pos | Pos | 4 | 4 4 4 4 4 4 2 - - | 2 4 4 4 4 2 - - - | 4 4 4 4 4 4 4 ± - |
| 7 | 4 | 4 | 4 | 4 | Pos | Pos | 4 | 4 4 4 4 4 4 2 1 - | 2 2 2 2 2 2 ± - - | 4 4 4 4 4 4 ± - - |
| 11 | 4 | 4 | 4 | 4 | Pos | Pos | 4 | 4 4 4 4 4 4 2 - - | 2 4 4 4 4 1 ± - - | 4 4 4 4 4 4 4 ± - |
| 18 | 4 | 4 | 4 | 4 | Pos | Pos | 4 | 4 4 4 4 4 3 1 - - | ± 4 4 3 2 ± - - - | 4 4 4 4 4 4 ± - - |
| 25 | 4 | 4 | 2 | 4 | Pos | Pos | 4 | 4 4 4 4 4 2 - - - | 2 4 4 4 3 - - - - | 4 4 4 4 4 4 4 ± - |
| 32 | 4 | 4 | 4 | 4 | Pos | Pos | 4 | 4 4 4 4 4 2 - - - | 4 4 4 4 3 1 - - - | 4 4 4 4 4 4 3 ± - |
| 39 | 4 | 4 | 4 | 4 | Pos | Pos | 4 | 4 4 4 4 4 2 - - - | 2 4 4 4 3 ± - - - | 4 4 4 4 4 4 4 ± ± |
| 46 | 4 | 4 | 4 | 4 | Pos | Pos | 4 | 4 4 4 4 3 1 - - - | 2 4 4 4 2 ± - - - | 4 4 4 4 4 4 4 ± |
| 53 | 4 | 4 | 4 | 4 | Pos | Pos | 4 | 4 4 4 4 2 1 - - - | ± ± ± 1 1 ± ± - - | 4 4 4 4 4 3 - - |
| 60 | 4 | 4 | 4 | 4 | Pos | Pos | 4 | 4 4 4 4 3 2 - - - | 4 4 4 4 2 ± - - - | 4 4 4 4 4 3 - - |
| 66 | 4 | 4 | 4 | 4 | Pos | Pos | 4 | 4 4 4 4 3 2 1 - - | 3 4 4 4 3 ± - - - | 4 4 4 4 4 ± - - |
| 74 | 4 | 4 | 4 | 4 | Pos | Pos | 4 | 4 4 4 4 4 2 - - - | 3 3 4 4 4 ± - - - | 4 4 4 4 4 4 - - |
| 86 | 4 | 4 | 4 | 4 | Dbt | Pos | 4 | 4 4 4 3 2 - - - - | 4 4 4 ± - - - - - | 4 4 4 4 1 - - - |
| 93 | 4 | 4 | 4 | 4 | .. | Pos | 4 | 4 4 4 4 4 3 1 - - | 4 4 4 4 3 ± - - - | 4 4 4 4 4 4 ± - - |
| 109 | 4 | 4 | 4 | 4 | Pos | Pos | 4 | 4 4 4 4 4 3 1 - - | 4 4 4 4 4 2 - - - | 4 4 4 4 4 4 4 ± - |

Pattern displayed by patient with early syphilis in which the therapy failed to influence the serologic picture.

serologic relapse or serologic upstroke accompanying reinfection.

In continuing the general study a series of approximately 100 patients have been treated in essentially the same manner as was employed in the original group. Although the post-treatment period of observation has not been of sufficient duration in a large enough group to warrant the drawing of conclusions, some interesting observations may be presented at this time. These are presented as informative material only and with the understanding that they may or may not be substantiated by more complete data.

The principal clinical features of the study may be summarized in the following manner:

The therapy has consisted of an intramuscular injection of 20,000 units of penicillin administered at three hour intervals, night and day, for sixty injections. The total amount of penicillin employed was 1,200,000 units. No other antisyphilitic medication has been used. All patients have been managed in a uniform manner, and it has not been necessary to decrease dosage or abandon the therapy in any instance. With three exceptions (acute arsenical intoxications) all the patients have displayed lesions characteristic of early syphilis (primary and/or secondary).

Herxheimer-like reactions, or therapeutic shock, of varying degrees of severity were observed during the first day of treatment in 86 patients. Ulcerations and cutaneous lesions manifested a tendency toward prompt recession. All uncomplicated ulcers were completely epithelized at the time of completion of treatment. No severe toxic reactions have been encountered. There were 2 instances of exfoliative dermatitis, 1 mild in character and of short duration, the second more severe and requiring about three weeks for return to normal. The two patients had been treated with the same manufacturer's lot of material. As other irritative qualities were attributed to this particular product, the possibility of impurities being accountable for the skin reaction is present.

Because of the rapid disappearance of lesions the main reliance in evaluating the therapy has been placed on the serologic tests. On the reasonable assumption that the trend of the serologic reactions may be considered as an index to the progress of early syphilis in the human being, the treated patients may be placed into several rather well defined groupings. For a consideration of this phase the records of patients who have had in excess of seventy-five days satisfactory follow-up observation have been selected for scrutiny.

It may be well to state that the serologic routine which has been utilized in this study represents as complete a coverage as is practical: a total of seven accredited methods representing supersensitive and diagnostic flocculation methods, one diagnostic complement fixation technic and three methods with which the reagin content of each positive blood specimen has been quantitated.

On the basis of an arbitrary minimum of seventy-five days of satisfactory post-treatment observation, the records of 52 patients become available for scrutiny. The average duration of observation is one hundred and thirty-five days.

Of this group of 52 patients, 6 with dark field positive lesions were in the seronegative phase of the disease at the time of treatment and passed through the observation period without positive findings being recorded. The records of 25 additional patients display positive serologic reactions in some or all test methods, with a reversal to negative findings during the observation period. The average time for reversal in this group was seventy days. Thus 31 patients may be considered as having responded in a favorable manner up to the present.

In 7 patients there has been a progressive decline in the serologic titer, and although complete reversal in all tests has not been accomplished there has not been a tendency toward a return of the high titer reactions which were recorded at the time of treatment, and it is anticipated that complete reversal will be accomplished with the passage of time. However, there is no assurance of this contingency. There is the possibility that these patients eventually will be added to the favorably reacting groups.

In an additional group of 7 patients the records display an initial post-treatment trend toward seronegativity with subsequent unmistakable evidence of a return to the high titer reactions. These are considered to be instances of serologic relapse.

The remaining 7 patients have displayed serologic patterns which render difficult the making of a favorable or unfavorable classification at this time. Some pessimism is felt as to the effectiveness of the therapy in this group.

If the patients are grouped in accordance with the stage of the disease at the time of treatment, some items of potential interest become discernible. Of the 52 patients 30 may be classed as having dark field positive primary syphilis. Of this number 1 patient, previously mentioned, developed a clinical relapse nine months following treatment. A second patient displayed a well defined serorelapse after an initial favorable serologic trend for one hundred and twelve days after treatment. An additional member of the group experienced a clinical relapse after eighty-four days of practically unchanged high titer positive serologic reactions. Two patients who have displayed a progressive but protracted trend toward reversal cannot be readily classified at this time. The remaining 25 patients are at this time clinically and serologically negative. Therefore there is a possibility of there being twenty-seven satisfactory responses.

Of the 22 patients who displayed evidence of secondary syphilis and who were well into the seropositive phase of the disease at the time of treatment, 11 have progressed to seronegativity or have displayed a consistently satisfactory trend in that direction. Four patients have shown a distinct tendency toward a recurrence of high titer reactions and must be classed as serologic relapses or as treatment failures. Two additional patients are looked on as probable failures and 5 are displaying a serologic trend which, although favorable at the moment, displays a protracted decline which presages an unfavorable outcome.

The remaining tables represent serologic patterns which are considered to be representative of groups of patients.

## COMMENT

The contrast which is displayed in the groups of treated patients rather indicates that (1) very early infections respond in the most favorable manner and (2) the increase in probable failures in patients with secondary syphilis indicates the need of a more vigorous therapy than that used in this study.

In evaluating the effectiveness of arsenic therapy in syphilis and of sulfonamide therapy in gonorrhea, it has been noted that a certain proportion of individuals fail to experience the same curative response which may be demonstrable in the majority of patients. A similar characteristic seems to be emerging in penicillin therapy of syphilis.

A majority of patients with early syphilis appear to respond to treatment in a satisfactory manner, as judged by the clinical course and the trend of the serologic reactions. A small group in the present series (7 definitely and 2 probably) appear to have derived a minimum of permanent benefit and must be considered as treatment failures.

In sulfonamide therapy of gonorrhea, failures of this type are classed as sulfonamide resistant and much has been written in regard to the drug resistance of strains of Neisseria gonorrhoeae. While accepting as possible that strain characteristics may play a role in determining the effectiveness of a therapy, it is felt that certain host factors are largely responsible for determining whether or not an agent, as penicillin, will be effective in infections which are amenable, as a rule, to treatment. It is felt that one of the most important problems in chemotherapy is a delineation of this essential factor and the development of means through which it may be favorably influenced.

In all the patients who have been classed as failures an observation period in excess of eighty-four days was required before an adverse decision as to treatment status was considered warranted. The data in these instances and in those which may occur among patients treated in the future will be scrutinized in an effort to determine a reliable basis for a more prompt decision predicated on clinical response and serologic pattern.

The making available of a pure or reasonably pure penicillin might effect a distinct change in the treatment picture both as to results produced and as to the duration of treatment, dosage and the interval between injections. Equally important will be the development of an assay method which gives assurance that the spirocheticidal activity of a product is consistently proportional to the antibacterial activity on which the present Oxford unit is based.

## CONCLUSION

It is desired to recall that the disease syphilis is one which is characterized by chronicity, with long periods of latency and a distinct tendency to clinical and serologic recurrence. The evaluation of any therapy will require a prolonged trial utilizing a wide variety of treatment schedules and a carefully controlled follow-up system. The combined experience available at this time has served to illuminate only a few of the important aspects. The remainder must await the passage of time.

April 20, 1984
(*JAMA* 1984;251:2011-2012)

# Early Syphilis*

## A Vastly Simplified Therapy

Harry L. Arnold, Jr, MD

### Early Therapy for Syphilis

Paul Ehrlich's dream of the therapia magna sterilisans for early syphilis — destroying the spirochetes en masse with a single intravenous (IV) injection of arsphenamine, the 606th compound he designed and tried for this purpose — seemed in 1912 to have been realized, but it was not. Patients treated in this way relapsed by the hundreds, and dermatologists — practitioners of the specialty that still treated most cases of syphilis in those years because the diagnosis had to be made dermatologically and only confirmed serologically — learned by many failures that (1) heavy metals (mercury or, later, bismuth) had to be alternated with the arsenic and (2) therapy, unless prolonged for a minimum of two or three years, achieved only temporary success.

The complexity of syphilotherapy and its simplification by penicillin are perhaps most dramatically illustrated by the space required to describe the treatment of syphilis in one standard American textbook of dermatology, Andrews' *Diseases of the Skin*. In the second edition of this text, published in 1938,[1] more than 13,000 words were devoted to the treatment of syphilis. In the third edition, written in 1945 and published in 1946,[2] it was accomplished in just under 9,000 words. And in the fourth edition, published in 1954,[3] it was done in an astonishing 168 words — plus 360 on treatment reactions!

Not only was the treatment of syphilis before 1943 hard to learn; it was tedious, expensive, and dangerous, and compliance was difficult to achieve. In a recently published personal reminiscence,[4] I have recounted the elaborate preparations, equipment, and procedures necessary for administering arsphenamine. Everyone knew the treatment schedule urgently needed to be shortened, but it seemed impossible because of the dangerous toxicity of both arsphenamine and neoarsphenamine. The doses could be neither increased nor given more frequently without grave risk of either exfoliative dermatitis or hemorrhagic encephalitis.

The best that it was found possible to do (with arsenic and bismuth) came about after the introduction of oxophenarsine hydrochloride (Mapharsen) in 1938; this remarkable compound was almost identical chemically with Ehrlich's No. 1, atoxyl, which he had abandoned as useless because it was so toxic. When it was tried in very small doses, 30 to 60 mg, it was not as toxic as "old" arsphenamine, and it was even more rapidly effective. When given twice weekly and combined with bismuth, it permitted "intensive" treatment to be completed in two months instead of three years, with serological success — and much later, clinical success in the follow-up — to prove its feasibility.[5]

Central nervous system syphilis was not responsive to such therapy. Only in the earliest acute or subacute forms, such as meningitis 'or meningovascular neurosyphilis or asymptomatic neurosyphilis, did it sometimes suffice. With clinical damage — tabes or paresis — fever therapy was the only effective modality: three weeks of alternate-day fever brought on by either hot baths and blankets, IV typhoid-paratyphoid vaccine, or therapeutic malaria induced by IV injections of blood from a patient with malaria (always induced, never natural). Induced malaria was mysteriously easy to cure; it never became chronic.

In sum, not only was the diagnosis of syphilis the business of physicians skilled and experienced in the mysteries of dermatologic diagnosis, but its treatment was a complicated, prolonged, hazardous process demanding extraordinary knowledge by the physician and exceptionally faithful compliance on the part of the patient. Hospitalization was needed for neurosyphilis. Syphilology was a specialty, occasionally sui generis (as it was for those who entered it from the field of preventive medicine) but most often as a division of dermatology. The practice of dermatology in the 1920s and 1930s was from one fifth to one third syphilology, and few generalists or internists were bold enough to attempt to treat syphilis or even to make the diagnosis, at least in early cases.

### Penicillin

Then came penicillin. Discovered in 1939 by the serendipitous observation that *Staphylococcus aureus* would not grow near the mold *Penicillium notatum* on a culture plate, it was boldly tried against syphilis by J. F. Mahoney, R. C. Arnold (no relation) and A. Harris (a

Dr Arnold is in private practice, Honolulu.
*A commentary on Mahoney JF, Arnold RC, Sterner BL, et al: Penicillin treatment of early syphilis: II. *JAMA* 1944;126:63-67.

serologist) in 1943, first in rabbits and then in four patients in the seropositive primary stage of the disease. In a preliminary report in *Venereal Disease Information*,[6] they made the world aware that aqueous penicillin administered intramuscularly (IM) had apparently cured four patients with seropositive, dark-field–positive primary syphilis. All four chancres healed promptly and the dark-field and serological test results became normal; spinal fluid was normal six months after treatment; three patients remained well, and the fourth, found to be strongly seropositive some nine months later when he came for treatment of gonorrhea in another institution, was also found to have a dark-field–positive chancre in a new site, inside the lower lip. He had presumably been reinfected with syphilis.

To find an antibiotic that could achieve this with eight days of therapy (the total dose was 1,200,000 units, given in 25,000-unit doses IM every four hours) was an extraordinary breakthrough, of course, urgently demanding confirmation and follow-up to establish the correctness and validity of the observations and also, more importantly, to affirm or deny the expectation that such results would prove to be permanent.

For this purpose there was set up in September 1943, under the auspices of the Committee on Medical Research of the Office of Scientific Research and Development and under the direction of the Subcommittee on Venereal Diseases of the National Research Council, a cooperative study on the effect of penicillin on syphilis in humans. Out of that study came, in 1944, three papers on the subject, read before the Section on Dermatology and Syphilology of the American Medical Association at its 94th annual session, June 15, 1944. All three were published in the Sept 9 issue of *JAMA* in the same year.[7-9]

None could have then suspected that the spectacular success of this therapy (with slight subsequent modification) would lead only a decade later into dropping the word *Syphilology* from the title of this section and, shortly afterward, from the names of the American Board of Dermatology and Syphilology and the American Academy of Dermatology and Syphilology as well. Syphilology as a specialty would disappear!

The first of these three initial studies, by the authors of the preliminary report with the addition of a dermatologist, Burton L. Sterner, and a Public Health Service technologist, M. R. Zwally, reported the results of such therapy in approximately 100 additional patients[7] (the second, by Joseph Earl Moore and associates,[8] would report results in 1,418 patients with early syphilis, and the third, by John H. Stokes and associates,[9] would report results in late syphilis).

In this second study by Mahoney et al, treatment was shortened from eight days to 7½ by giving 10,000 Oxford units of sodium penicillin every three hours for the same total dose, 1.2 million units (about 720 mg). Cases with secondary syphilis were included. Of the 100 patients treated, 52 had been observed for at least 75 weeks, and these 52 form the basis of the report reprinted in this issue.

Of these, six had results that were seronegative at the start and remained so. Twenty-five seropositive patients became seronegative within 70 days. In seven, the serological titer declined satisfactorily but did not become negative in all tests, only in the less sensitive ones. However, no doubt was entertained of the success of therapy in these. In only nine patients (seven definitely and two probably) was the outcome judged to be a failure, because of either serological or clinical and serological relapse.

The authors reminded their listeners and readers, with commendable prudence, that the natural history of syphilis is characterized by long periods of latency and a tendency to serological and clinical relapse, and that years would be required for the evaluation of the effectiveness of this or any other form of therapy. They hoped that a purer preparation of penicillin might be more effective and permit a longer period between injections. They could not have foreseen what a boon repository formulations would later prove to be.

But their fondest hopes for the ultimate success of treatment with an antibiotic have certainly been fully realized. They established one of the safest and most effective specific treatments known for any chronic infection. Theirs was a landmark article, and it deserves this recognition.

### References

1. Andrews GC: *Diseases of the Skin for Practitioners and Students,* ed 2. Philadelphia, WB Saunders Co, 1938, pp 485-525.
2. Andrews GC: *Diseases of the Skin for Practitioners and Students,* ed 3. Philadelphia, WB Saunders Co, 1946, pp 468-495.
3. Andrews GC: *Diseases of the Skin for Practitioners and Students,* ed 4. Philadelphia, WB Saunders Co, 1954, pp 409-410.
4. Harry L. Arnold, Jr (contemporaries). *J Am Acad Dermatol* 1983;8:745-752.
5. Massive arsenotherapy for syphilis. *JAMA* 1944;126:554.
6. Mahoney JF, Arnold RC, Harris A: Penicillin treatment of early syphilis: A preliminary report. *Ven Dis Inform* 1943;24:355-357.
7. Mahoney JF, Arnold RC, Sterner BL, et al: Penicillin treatment of early syphilis: II. *JAMA* 1944;126:63-67.
8. Moore JE, Mahoney JF, Schwartz W, et al: The treatment of early syphilis with penicillin: A preliminary report of 1,418 cases. *JAMA* 1944;126:67-73.
9. Stokes JH, Sternberg TH, Schwartz WH, et al: The action of penicillin in late syphilis: Including neurosyphilis, benign late syphilis, and late congenital syphilis: Preliminary report. *JAMA* 1944;126:73-79.

May 19, 1945
(*JAMA* 1945;128:189-202)

## Chapter 38

# The Surgical Treatment of Malformations of the Heart

## In Which There Is Pulmonary Stenosis or Pulmonary Atresia

Alfred Blalock, M.D.

and

Helen B. Taussig, M.D.

Baltimore

Heretofore there has been no satisfactory treatment for pulmonary stenosis and pulmonary atresia. A "blue" baby with a malformed heart was considered beyond the reach of surgical aid. During the past three months we have operated on 3 children with severe degrees of pulmonary stenosis and each of the patients appears to be greatly benefited. In the second and third cases, in which there was deep persistent cyanosis, the cyanosis has greatly diminished or has disappeared and the general condition of the patients is proportionally improved. The results are sufficiently encouraging to warrant an early report.

The operation here reported and the studies leading thereto were undertaken with the conviction that even though the structure of the heart was grossly abnormal, in many instances it might be possible to alter the course of the circulation in such a manner as to lessen the cyanosis and the resultant disability. It is important to emphasize the fact that it is not the cyanosis, per se, which does harm. Nevertheless, since cyanosis is a striking manifestation of the underlying anoxemia and the compensatory polycythemia, a brief discussion of the causes of cyanosis and the factors operative in congenital malformations of the heart is essential in order to understand the principles underlying the present operation.

Cyanosis is due to the presence of reduced hemoglobin in the circulating blood. It is a well established fact that

there must be at least 5 Gm. of reduced hemoglobin per hundred cubic centimeters of circulating blood for cyanosis to become apparent. It has long been recognized that one of the principal factors in the production of cyanosis in malformations of the heart is the direct shunting of venous blood into the systemic circulation. Lundsgaard and Van Slyke[1] in their classic studies on the causes of cyanosis showed that there were four important factors in the production of cyanosis: the height of the hemoglobin, the volume of the venous blood shunted into the systemic circulation, the rate of utilization of oxygen by the peripheral tissues and the extent of the aeration of the blood in the lungs. Their studies demonstrated the great importance of pulmonary factors. The extent of the oxygenation of the blood in the lungs clearly depends on the vital capacity of the individual, the rate of the flow of blood through the lungs, the partial pressure of the oxygen in the inspired air and also on specific pulmonary factors, which these authors designated as the $\alpha$ factor. These investigators showed that in most, if not in all, cases in which there was a pronounced polycythemia, secondary changes occurred in the lungs of such a nature that all of the blood that passed through the lungs was no longer in effective contact with the oxygen in the alveoli. The importance of this factor can be demonstrated by the prolonged inhalation of oxygen. In almost every case in which there is polycythemia, cyanosis can be greatly lessened by the prolonged inhalation of oxygen. The fact that all of the blood which circulated through the lungs is

Read before the Johns Hopkins Medical Society March 12, 1945.

Aided by a grant from the Robert Garrett Memorial Fund for the Surgical Treatment of Children.

From the Departments of Surgery and Pediatrics of the Johns Hopkins University and the Johns Hopkins Hospital and the Cardiac Clinic of the Harriet Lane Home.

1. Lundsgaard, C., and Van Slyke, D. D.: Cyanosis, Medical Monographs, vol. 2, Baltimore, Williams and Wilkins Company, 1923.

not fully oxygenated made it seem improbable that if more blood circulated through the lungs a larger proportion of the blood would be oxygenated. Thus the demonstration of the α factor completely overshadowed another vitally important factor, namely the volume of blood which reaches the lungs for aeration.[1a]

Expressed in the simplest terms, the circulation of the blood through the lungs after birth is essential for life; any one deprived of such circulation dies. Indeed there is a point at which, even though none of the other pulmonary factors are operative in the production of cyanosis and all of the blood that passes through the lungs is fully oxygenated, the volume of blood that reaches the lungs for aeration and hence the volume of oxygenated blood returned to the systemic circulation is insufficient for the maintenance of life. For example, in all cases of pulmonary atresia in which the circulation to the lungs is by way of the ductus arteriosus the closure of the ductus arteriosus renders the condition incompatible with life.

Undoubtedly the importance of the diminution of flow of blood to the lungs has not been fully appreciated, mainly because studies on the nature of cyanosis have been made on older children and young adults, and it is only when this factor is not of vital importance that the individual has survived to that age. All infants with pulmonary atresia with or without a right ventricle and with or without dextroposition of the aorta, in whom the closure of the ductus arteriosus cuts off the circulation to the lungs, die at an early age. In cases of complete pulmonary atresia death occurs before the complete cessation of circulation of blood through the lungs; hence in such cases there is always slight patency of the ductus arteriosus. In cases of a tetralogy of Fallot with an extreme pulmonary stenosis, the ductus arteriosus may become entirely obliterated before death.

There are two different types of congenital malformations which illustrate the importance of the volume of the pulmonary circulation in the production of cyanosis. The first is that of a single ventricle with a rudimentary outlet chamber in which it is common to find that one great vessel is given off from the common ventricle and one from the rudimentary outlet chamber. Usually the vessel which arises from the common ventricle is of normal size and that from the rudimentary outlet chamber is diminutive in size.[2] If the great vessels occupy their normal positions, the aorta arises from the common ventricle and is of large caliber, whereas the pulmonary artery which arises from the rudimentary outlet chamber is of small caliber. Under such circumstances a large volume of blood goes to the systemic circulation and only a small volume of blood goes to the lungs. Consequently a large volume of unoxygenated blood is mixed with a small volume of oxygenated blood and cyanosis is

intense.[3] When, however, the great vessels are transposed and the pulmonary artery is large and the aorta is small, a large volume of blood goes to the lungs for aeration. Under these circumstances a large volume of oxygenated blood is mixed with a relatively small volume of venous blood and cyanosis is minimal or absent, as in the case reported by Glendy and White.[4]

The same phenomenon is also seen in cases of truncus arteriosus. When the pulmonary arteries are given off directly from the aorta there is adequate circulation to the lungs, and cyanosis is minimal or absent. In contrast to this, if the pulmonary artery fails to arise from the heart or connect with the aorta and the circulation to the lungs is by way of the bronchial arteries only a small

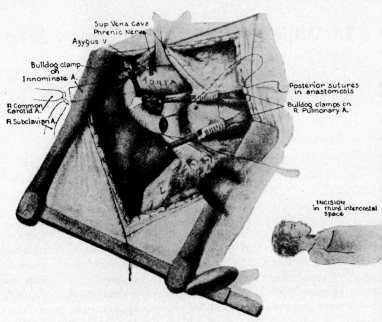

Fig. 1.—General exposure of the operative field on the right side. The end of the innominate artery is being anastomosed to the side of the right pulmonary artery. The posterior row of sutures is complete. The anterior row has not been inserted.

volume of blood reaches the lungs for aeration, and cyanosis is intense.[5]

The importance of adequate circulation to the lungs is further illustrated in the anomalies of the venous return in which all of the pulmonary veins drain into the right auricle; consequently within this chamber there is complete admixture of venous and arterial blood. In such cases a large volume of blood goes to the lungs for aeration and a large volume of oxygenated blood is returned to the right auricle. There is great right-sided cardiac enlargement but no cyanosis until the terminal collapse of the circulation.[6]

These observations clearly indicate that many gross malformations of the heart are compatible with life

1a. The relative importance of this factor and of the α factor will be discussed in a forthcoming paper by Taussig and Blalock.

2. Taussig, H. B.: Clinical Analysis of Congenital Malformations of the Heart, to be published by the Commonwealth Fund, New York.

3. Taussig, H. B.: A Single Ventricle with a Diminutive Outlet Chamber, J. Tech. Meth. & Bull. I. A. M. M. 19:120-127, 1939.

4. Glendy, Margaret M.; Glency, R. E., and White, P. D.: Cor Biatriatum Triloculare, Am. Heart J. 28:395-401, 1944.

5. Taussig, H. B.: Clinical Findings in Cases of Truncus Arteriosus, to be published.

6. Taussig, H. B.: Clinical and Pathological Findings in the Anomaly of Venous Return in Which All of the Pulmonary Veins Drain into the Right Auricle, to be published.

provided there is adequate circulation to the lungs, and furthermore that lack of circulation to the lungs is the primary cause of death in many infants with congenital malformations of the heart. Furthermore, one of us (H. B. T.) has seen several infants with pulmonary stenosis in whom cyanosis was not apparent until the ductus arteriosus closed. In other words, there was no "visible" cyanosis while the circulation to the lungs was adequate. It was an appreciation of these facts (H. B. T.), together with an extensive previous experience with the experimental use of large arteries for the purpose of conducting blood to sites not usually supplied by such vessels, that led to the development of the clinical work recorded in this paper.

The feasibility of anastomosing a systemic artery to one of the pulmonary arteries in experimental animals has been demonstrated by Levy and Blalock.[7] As far as we are aware, this was the first time that both the course and the function of a large artery were altered. Similar experimental alterations were produced subsequently by Eppinger, Burwell and Gross[8] and by Leeds.[9] Blalock and Park[10] have reported the suturing of the severed proximal end of the subclavian artery to the aorta as a means for conducting blood beyond the point of an experimental coarctation of the aorta. In unreported observations by Kieffer and Blalock the divided proximal end of the splenic artery has been connected to the distal end of the divided left renal artery and there has been no evidence of renal failure even though the right kidney was removed. In other words, arterial anastomoses have been performed in animals for the purpose of conducting blood to sites other than those ordinarily supplied by these vessels.

Before undertaking the operations on patients, many experiments were performed in an effort to produce pulmonic stenosis in dogs. This work met with little success. Finally, in an effort to cause a significant decrease in the oxygen saturation of arterial blood, one or more lobes of the lungs were removed from each side of the chest, and the main arteries and veins of these lobes were connected end to end by suture. In other words, bilateral pulmonary arteriovenous fistulas were produced. These procedures resulted in some instances in a pronounced reduction in the oxygen saturation of the arterial blood. As the result of an artificial patent ductus arteriosus made in two such experiments, there was a significant increase in the arterial oxygen saturation. Although this experimentally produced condition is quite different from that seen in patients, it is of interest that the making of an anastomosis between systemic and pulmonary arteries caused an increase in the oxygen

saturation of the arterial blood despite the fact that several lobes of the lungs had been removed.

Since the present operation was devised to compensate for an inadequate flow of blood to the lungs, it seemed desirable that the anastomosis be made in such a manner that the blood from the systemic artery would be able to reach both lungs. It is obvious that the suture anastomosis could not be made to the main pulmonary artery since occlusion of this vessel for more than a few minutes causes death. It appeared, therefore, that the anastomosis should be made just distal to the division of the main pulmonary artery and, furthermore, that the side of the chosen vessel should be used in order that the blood might flow to both lungs.

It was our original idea that the subclavian artery would be the ideal systemic vessel and that after division of this artery its proximal end should be anastomosed to the side of the left pulmonary artery. The fortunate experience to be reported in regard to the second patient has led us to prefer the use of the innominate artery in patients with a severe degree of anoxemia. This patient had a right aortic arch, and the innominate artery was directed to the left side of the chest and neck.

Although there were slight variations in each of the operations, the major features were as follows: Light general anesthesia was produced by the inhalation of ether or cyclopropane. The patient was placed on the table on his back with a slight elevation of that side of the chest which was to be exposed. The patient's arms were strapped in place along his sides. The operation was performed on the right or left side depending on the position of the great vessels and the artery to be used in the anastomosis. The incision was made in the third interspace and extended from the lateral border of the sternum to the axillary line. The pleural cavity was entered and the third and fourth costal cartilages were divided. A rib spreader was introduced and a good exposure of the upper half of the pleural cavity was obtained. This area is shown in figure 1. The right or left pulmonary artery was then exposed and the vessel was dissected from the adjacent tissues for as great a distance as possible. This was more difficult on the right side than on the left and it was necessary to ligate and divide the azygos vein and to retract the superior vena cava medially. Nothing further was done to the pulmonary artery at this time. Attention was then focused on the systemic artery which was to be anastomosed to one of the pulmonary arteries. The subclavian or innominate artery was dissected free of the adjacent tissues and the vessel chosen was occluded temporarily at the point where it arose from the aorta by the use of a bulldog arterial clamp. In cases in which the innominate artery was chosen, its branches (subclavian and common carotid) were ligated at their origins and the innominate artery was cut across just proximal to the ligatures. In the 1 case in which the left subclavian artery was used for the anastomosis to the pulmonary circulation it was necessary to divide the thyrocervical trunk, the vertebral artery and the internal mammary artery in order to gain access to a sufficient length of the vessel. After the removal of some of the adventitia from the systemic vessel the pulmonary artery was further prepared for the anastomosis. A

7. Levy, S. E., and Blalock, A.: Experimental Observations on the Effects of Connecting by Suture the Left Main Pulmonary Artery to the Systemic Circulation. J. Thoracic Surg. 8:525-530. 1939.

8. Eppinger, Eugene C.; Burwell, C. Sidney, and Gross, Robert E.: The Effects of the Patent Ductus Arteriosus on the Circulation, J. Clin. Investigation 20:127-143 (March) 1941.

9. Leeds, S. E.: The Effects of Occlusion of Experimental Chronic Patent Ductus Arteriosus on the Cardiac Output, Pulse and Blood Pressure of Dogs, Am. J. Physiol. 139:451-459 (July) 1943.

10. Blalock, A., and Park, E. A.: The Surgical Treatment of Experimental Coarctation (Atresia) of the Aorta, Ann. Surg. 119:445-456 (March) 1944.

bulldog arterial clamp was placed on the left or right pulmonary artery just distal to the point of division of the main pulmonary artery. A second bulldog arterial clamp was placed on the left or right pulmonary artery just proximal to the point where the vessel gave off a branch to the upper lobe of the lung. A transverse opening was made into the side of the pulmonary artery approximately midway between these two arterial clamps. This opening was of about the same diameter as that of the

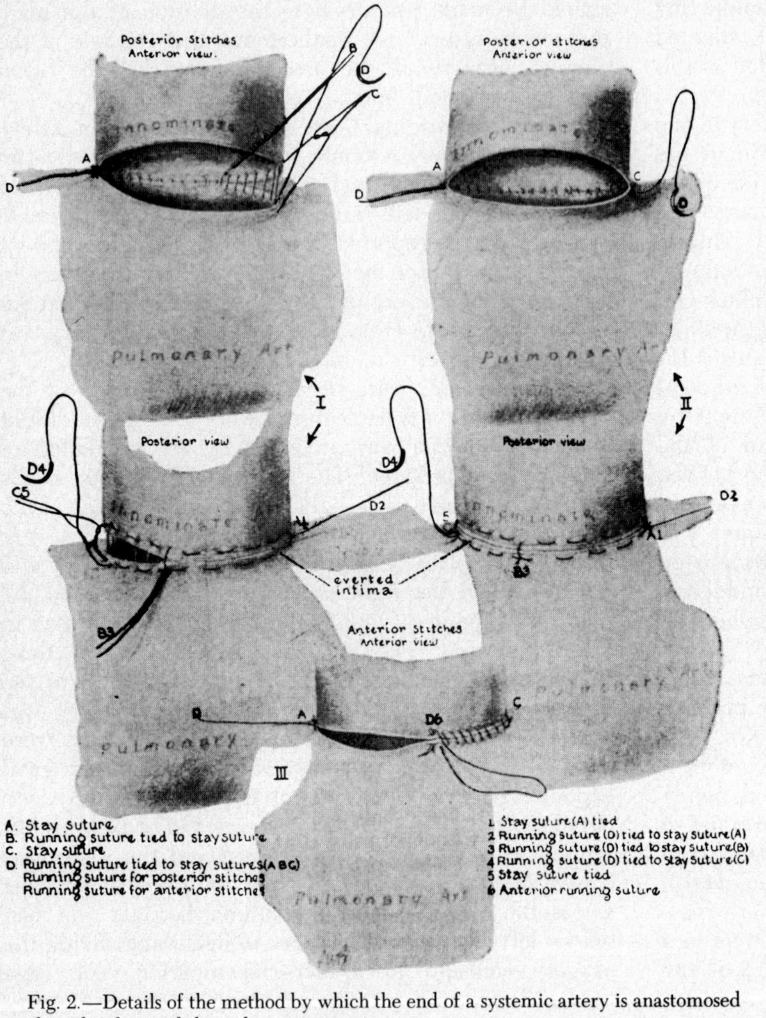

Fig. 2.—Details of the method by which the end of a systemic artery is anastomosed to the side of one of the pulmonary arteries.

end of the systemic vessel which was to be anastomosed to it. It must be emphasized that the pulmonary artery was not occluded until all preparations for the anastomotic procedure had been made.

The anastomosis between the end of the systemic artery and the side of the pulmonary artery was carried out in the following manner: Fine silk on a curved needle was used as suture material. Before placing the posterior row of sutures, a stay suture was placed at one end. This was followed by the insertion of a running suture, which was not drawn taut until the greater part of the posterior row had been placed. The stay suture was then tied and the running suture was in turn tied to the stay suture. The posterior row was completed and was tied to another stay suture. The anterior row consisted of a simple through

and through continuous suture which approximated intima to intima. The anastomosis is shown diagrammatically in figure 2. The bulldog clamps were then removed from the pulmonary artery, and this was followed by removal of the clamp from the systemic vessel. If bleeding from the suture line did not cease spontaneously, it was stopped by the use of additional sutures. The lung was reexpanded and the incision in the chest wall was closed. Two encircling sutures of braided silk were used for approximating the third and fourth ribs. The soft tissues of the chest wall were closed in multiple layers with interrupted silk sutures.

There follows a detailed report of the 3 cases in which such an operation has been performed.

## REPORT OF CASES

CASE 1.[11]—*History*.—E. M. S., a girl, was born prematurely in the obstetric service of the Johns Hopkins Hospital on Aug. 3, 1943. Her birth weight was 1,105 Gm. A systolic murmur was noted shortly after birth. Slight cyanosis was noted on the fourth and fifth days of life; this subsequently disappeared. The baby gained weight slowly and was finally discharged at 4 months of age weighing 2,900 Gm. After discharge the baby was followed in the dispensary. She was at first thought to have a simple interventricular septal defect, because the heart was normal in size and there was no cyanosis.

At 8 months of age the baby had her first attack of cyanosis, which occurred after eating. It was then for the first time that we thought she had a tetralogy of Fallot and not a simple interventricular septal defect. It soon became evident that cyanosis was increasing. It seemed probable that this increase in cyanosis was due to the fact that the ductus arteriosus was undergoing obliteration and thereby lessening the circulation to the lungs. By March 1944 it was obvious that the baby had a serious congenital malformation of the heart. After eating she would become deeply cyanotic, roll up her eyes, lose consciousness and appear extremely ill. Fluoroscopy showed that the heart was slightly enlarged; there was no fulness in the region of the pulmonary conus. In the left anterior oblique position the right ventricle appeared slightly enlarged and the pulmonary window was abnormally clear. The clinical diagnosis was tetralogy of Fallot with a severe degree of pulmonary stenosis.

On June 25, 1944 she was first admitted to the Harriet Lane Home. Physical examination showed that she was poorly nourished and poorly developed. She had a glassy stare. Her lips were cyanotic. The heart was slightly enlarged and there was a harsh systolic murmur best heard along the left sternal border. The liver was at the costal margin. The baby was given oxygen and phenobarbital but remained very irritable and would become intensely cyanotic when taken out of the oxygen tent. During her three weeks' stay in the hospital she gained 200 Gm. and weighed 4.66 Kg. on discharge. She was sent home because it was felt that her condition was hopeless.

She was followed in the cardiac clinic for three months,

11. This case was discussed briefly at the meeting of the Southern Surgical Association, Dec. 5, 1944, in a paper by Dr. Arthur Blakemore.

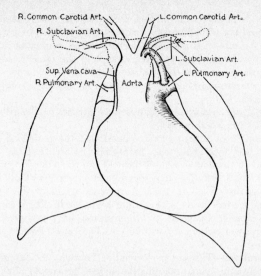

Fig. 3 (case 1).—Procedure used. The end of the left subclavian artery was anastomosed to the side of the left pulmonary artery.

during which time she showed increasing cyanosis and failed to gain weight. She was readmitted on October 17 because of increasing spells of cyanosis, coma and great venous distention of the head and body.

The weight on admission was 4.6 Kg. The venous distention was so great that the possibility of a subdural hydroma or hematoma was considered. Subdural tap was performed, with the removal of 8 cc. of clear fluid from the right side and a small amount of bloody fluid from the left.

The size of the heart as seen in the anteroposterior view was essentially the same as noted previously. There was still a harsh systolic murmur. In the left anterior oblique position the contour of the heart appeared as a little round ball with a narrow aorta and a clear pulmonary window (fig. 4); this, we believe, is characteristic of a very severe tetralogy of Fallot with a functional pulmonary atresia, that is, a pulmonary stenosis which is so extreme that the condition is not long compatible with life.[2] It was questioned at that time whether in addition to the malformation of the heart she suffered from mental retardation.

During the next six weeks she refused most of her feedings; she lost weight and just before operation weighed only 4 Kg. The red blood cell count, which had been 7,000,000 on admission, had fallen to 5,000,000. Cyanosis was proportionally less conspicuous; indeed, at times while lying quietly, cyanosis was not visible. The clinical diagnosis was again tetralogy of Fallot which was so severe that the baby's condition was becoming critical.

*Operation.*—This was performed on November 29. The procedure consisted in the anastomosis of the divided proximal end of the left subclavian artery to the side of the left pulmonary artery, as shown diagrammatically in figure 3. The anesthetic agent was administered by Dr. Merel Harmel.

Under ether and oxygen anesthesia, administered by the open method, an incision was made on the left side of the chest extending from the edge of the sternum to the axillary line. The pleural cavity was entered through the third interspace. The left lung appeared normal. No thrill was felt on palpating the heart and pulmonary artery. The left pulmonary artery was identified and was dissected free of the neighboring tissues. It appeared to be of normal size. The superior pulmonary vein, on the other hand, seemed considerably smaller than normal. The left subclavian artery was identified and was dissected free of the neighboring tissues. In order to secure access to a sufficient length of this vessel it was necessary to ligate and divide the

vertebral artery, the internal mammary artery and the thyro-cervical axis. A bulldog arterial clamp was placed on the subclavian artery at a point just distal to its origin from the aorta. The subclavian artery was ligated distal to the point at which the thyrocervical trunk had been ligated and divided, and the vessel was cut across just proximal to this ligature. Two bulldog clamps were placed on the left pulmonary artery, the first clamp being placed at the origin of the left pulmonary artery and the second clamp being placed just proximal to the point where the pulmonary artery entered the lung. There was ample space between these two clamps for our purpose. A small transverse incision was made in the wall of the pulmonary artery at a point approximately equidistant between the two clamps. By the use of china beaded silk on fine needles an anastomosis was performed between the end of the left subclavian artery and the side of the left pulmonary artery. There was practically no bleeding following the removal of the clamps.

From a technical point of view the anastomosis seemed to be satisfactory. The main cause for concern was the small size of the left subclavian artery. It was somewhat disturbing that one could not feel a thrill in the pulmonary artery. We were confident, however, that the anastomosis was patent. A small quantity of sulfanilamide was placed in the left pleural cavity and the incision in the chest wall was closed. The patient was given 200 cc. of isotonic solution of sodium chloride and 50 cc. of blood during the operative procedure. The operation required slightly less than an hour and a half and the left pulmonary artery was occluded for approximately thirty minutes. The patient's condition at the end of the operation seemed moderately good.

*Postoperative Course.*—This was stormy. The patient's left arm and hand were observed frequently. The radial pulse was not palpable and this extremity was cooler than the opposite one, but it was apparent that the circulation was adequate to maintain life of the part. The child suffered from repeated bilateral pneumothoraces, and frequent aspirations were required. Probably the pneumothorax on the right was due to the use of too great pressure in the reexpansion of the left lung at the completion of the operative procedure. As it was found to be a positive pressure pneumothorax, constant suction was exerted through a needle inserted into the right pleural cavity. Had it not been for the excellent care given by the pediatric house staff, particularly Dr. Kaye, Dr. Whitemore, Dr. Stein-heimer, Dr. Hammond, Dr. Gilger and Dr. Helfrick, in all probability the child's life would not have been saved.

The child's condition began to improve two weeks after operation. Thereafter further aspirations of the pleural cavity were not required. The occasions on which the patient would become cyanotic became less frequent. Otitis media developed and responded to treatment. The systolic murmur became somewhat louder, but a continuous murmur could not be heard in the pulmonary area.

The patient was discharged from the hospital on Jan. 25, 1945, almost two months after the day of operation. Her condition was considerably better than it had been before operation. More recent follow-up studies have shown that she is gaining weight and that she is only occasionally cyanotic. If the cyanosis increases, it may be necessary to perform a similar operation on the opposite side. Roentgenograms of the patient's heart both before and after operation are shown in figure 4.

It is unfortunate that we do not have a quantitative degree of improvement such as might have been afforded by determina-tions of the oxygen saturation of the arterial blood. In view of the small size of the child we did not feel warranted in doing arterial punctures. The clinical improvement, however, has been striking. The baby takes her feedings well, is alert and active and has gained a kilogram in weight (that is, 25 per cent of her former body weight).

CASE 2.—*History.*—B. R., a white girl born July 9, 1933, was first seen at the Harriet Lane Home at 9 years of age, referred by Dr. Dexter Levy of Buffalo. The patient was cyanotic at birth. The birth weight was 6½ pounds (2,955 Gm.). She was breast fed for six months. In infancy she gained extremely slowly. She had erysipelas at 1½ years of age, a septic sore throat at 4½ years of age, chickenpox at 7 years, measles at 8 years and mumps at 9 years.

The patient was first seen in the Harriet Lane Home on Feb. 13, 1943. She was intensely cyanotic, became dyspneic on slight exertion and would constantly squat to get her breath. There was intense cyanosis and clubbing of the fingers and the toes. The buccal mucous membranes were of a deep mulberry color. There was suffusion of the conjunctiva. The chest was barrel shaped. Her heart was within normal limits in size. There was no thrill over the precordium. On auscultation there was a harsh systolic murmur which was maximal low down in the third and fourth interspaces. The murmur was much louder in the recumbent position than in the erect position, and louder when she bent forward than when she tried to sit erect. The murmur was not widely transmitted and was not audible in the back. The second sound at the base was pure. The lungs were clear. The liver was at the costal margin and the spleen was not palpable. The femoral arteries were readily palpable. The extremities, as previously mentioned, showed intense cyanosis and pronounced clubbing. At this time she climbed half a flight of stairs and walked, almost ran, leaning forward, 60 feet to her room, and then fell forward on the bed and lay in a knee-chest position, panting heavily and without speaking for half an hour.

The red blood cell count was 8,700,000; the hemoglobin was 25 Gm.; the hematocrit reading was 78.

The electrocardiogram showed a normal sinus mechanism, PR interval of 0.16 second, normal upright T waves in all four leads, and considerable right axis deviation.

X-ray examination and fluoroscopy showed the heart to be of normal size with a concave curve at the base to the left of the sternum (fig. 6). To the right of the sternum the superior vena cava cast a wide ribbon-like shadow. After the administration of barium, the aorta was seen to indent the esophagus to the left on its right margin. Examination in the left anterior oblique position showed that the right ventricle was not greatly enlarged; indeed, the left ventricle appeared larger than the right ventricle. The esophagus was seen to be indented by the aorta in the left anterior oblique position; in the right anterior oblique position its descent was independent of the aorta. There was no enlargement of the left auricle.

The clinical diagnosis was an extreme tetralogy of Fallot with

previously noted but she was even more severely incapacitated. She could not walk 30 feet without exhaustion, and she panted when she moved from a wheel chair to the examining table. The fluoroscopic findings were essentially the same as noted previously except that the shadows at the hili of the lungs were more conspicuous. There were, however, no pulsations visible in this region.

The patient returned on January 29. Studies on the arterial blood are recorded in table 1.

A sample of venous blood showed that the red blood cell count was 7,500,000, the hemoglobin was 24 Gm., the hematocrit reading was 71 (Wintrobe) and the white blood cell count was 5,200. The electrocardiogram was essentially the same as that taken in 1943. A roentgenogram of the heart showed a small heart with a right aortic arch. The maximal right diameter was 4 cm. and the maximal left was 7 cm. The total transverse diameter was 26 cm. The cardiothoracic ratio was 42.4.

*Operation.*—This was performed on February 3. The procedure consisted in anastomosing the divided proximal end of the

TABLE 1.—*Studies on Arterial Blood (Case 2)*

| Dates | Arterial Oxygen Content, Volumes per Cent | Arterial Oxygen Capacity, Volumes per Cent | Arterial Oxygen Saturation, per Cent | Arterial Carbon Dioxide Content, Volumes per Cent |
|---|---|---|---|---|
| 2/ 1/45 | 11.7 | 32.3 | 36.3 | 34.9 |
| 2/ 3/45 | Innominate artery anastomosed to left pulmonary artery | | | |
| 2/12/45 | 20.3 | 27.5 | 73.8 | 37.8 |
| 3/ 1/45 | 19.8 | 23.9 | 82.8 | 37.2 |

innominate artery to the side of the left pulmonary artery. This is shown diagrammatically in figure 5. The anesthetic agent was administered by Dr. Austin Lamont.

Cyclopropane with a high percentage of oxygen was administered through an endotracheal tube. The incision extended from the left costal margin to the anterior axillary line. The pleural cavity was entered through the third interspace. There were no adhesions between the lung and the chest wall, and the lung looked normal. Although the surgeon had been informed by his pediatric colleague that this patient almost certainly had a right aortic arch, no special thought was given to the fact, and it caused some surprise when it was noted that the aorta was not on the left side. It was fortunate, however, that the incision had been made on the left because this allowed the use of the innominate artery rather than the subclavian artery. There was a very tortuous artery, which was lying anterior to the vertebral column and which appeared to run from the region of the hilus of the lung toward the upper part of the left pleural cavity. Compression of this vessel indicated that the blood was flowing from above downward. It is believed that this vessel was a large accessory bronchial artery. It was estimated that the lumen of this artery was approximately 3 mm. in diameter. Still another abnormal finding was the large size of the posterior portions of the intercostal arteries. It seems likely that these vessels were also supplying blood to the hilus of the lung. The evidence of extensive collateral circulation led us to believe that we were probably dealing with a case of complete pulmonary atresia.

The innominate artery was located and dissected free of the surrounding tissues. The encouragement of the first assistant Dr. William Longmire, played no small part in the continued

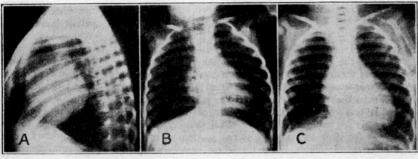

Fig. 4 (case 1).—Appearance before and after operation: *A*, left anterior oblique view before operation; *B*, anteroposterior view before operation; *C*, anteroposterior view after operation.

a right aortic arch.

On Jan. 6, 1945 the patient returned for a check-up and because her parents wished to discuss the possibility of operation. The physical findings were essentially the same as

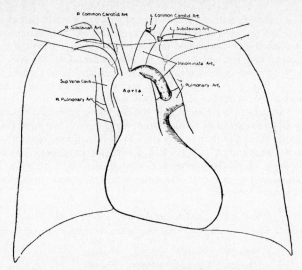

Fig. 5 (case 2).—Procedure used. The patient had a right aortic arch, and the innominate artery was directed to the left. The end of the innominate artery was anastomosed to the side of the left pulmonary artery.

effort to find a large systemic artery. A bulldog arterial clamp was placed on the innominate just distal to its origin from the aorta. The subclavian and common carotid arteries were ligated near their points of origin from the innominate. The innominate artery was divided just proximal to these ligatures. It was estimated that the diameter of the lumen of the innominate artery was approximately 1.3 cm. The left main pulmonary artery was then prepared for the anastomosis. A bulldog clamp was placed just distal to the origin of this vessel from the main pulmonary artery, and a second clamp was placed proximal to its entrance into the lung. A transverse opening was made into the lumen of the vessel midway between the two clamps. A suture anastomosis was performed between the end of the innominate artery and the side of the left pulmonary artery. The length of time that the left pulmonary artery was occluded was fifty to sixty minutes. The bulldog clamps were removed. There was bleeding from one point, which was controlled by an additional suture. An easily palpable thrill was felt in the pulmonary artery both proximal and distal to the anastomosis. The pulmonary artery seemed to be considerably larger than before this new current of systemic blood was admitted to it. The systemic arterial pressure was 110 systolic and 70 diastolic at the time that the arterial clamps were removed. Immediately following the removal of the clamps the systemic pressure declined 30 mm. of mercury. There followed a rise in systolic pressure of 20 mm. of mercury, but the pressure then declined gradually during the next thirty minutes until it reached 60 systolic and 30 diastolic. The pulse rate during this time rose from 72 to 120 per minute.

After the completion of the anastomosis and the removal of the clamps, several grams of sulfanilamide were placed in the pleural cavity. The left lung was partially inflated by the use of positive pressure, and the incision in the chest wall was closed. The patient was given a slow continuous intravenous drip of isotonic solution of sodium chloride during the operation and her condition at the end of the operation appeared to be satisfactory.

The operation required two hours and forty minutes. A considerable part of this time was consumed in studying the tortuous vessel which was seen above the hilus of the lung and also in trying to locate the innominate artery.

The patient awakened from the anesthesia a short time after the closure of the incision. She could move the left arm without difficulty. The left arm and hand were slightly cooler than the

right, but it was evident that the circulation was adequate to maintain life. There was no evidence of a cerebral disturbance as the result of the ligation of the common carotid. No pulse could be felt in the left arm or the left side of the neck and face.

*Postoperative Course.*—This was smooth. There was no vomiting following operation, and fluids were taken by mouth. She was placed in an oxygen tent. The administration of penicillin was started immediately after operation and was continued for nine days. The left pleural cavity was aspirated twenty-four hours after operation; 250 cc. of air and 70 cc. of blood were removed. There were no other thoracenteses. Although a thrill was palpable at the site of the anastomosis immediately on release of the bulldog clamps, no murmur was audible immediately after the chest was closed. By the second evening a faint diastolic murmur was audible over the base and at the apex. By the third postoperative day an extraordinarily loud continuous murmur was audible throughout the chest on both the right and the left side. The oral administration of dicumarol was begun on the fourth postoperative day; 50 to 200 mg. was given daily for several weeks. Prothrombin determinations were performed daily. The dose of dicumarol was such as to keep the clotting time of the patient's blood approximately twice that of the normal control.

Femoral arterial punctures were performed on the ninth and twenty-sixth postoperative days. The results of the analyses are given in table 1. Before operation the red blood cell count was 7,500,000, the hemoglobin 24 Gm. and the hematocrit reading 71. Three days after operation the red blood cell count had decreased to 6,000,000, the hemoglobin to 19 Gm. and the hematocrit reading to 61. By the twenty-first day the red blood cell count was 6,000,000, the hemoglobin was 17.5 Gm. and the hematocrit reading was 55.

A roentgenogram of the heart taken ten days after operation showed that the heart had increased in size; that taken twenty-one days after operation revealed no further increase in

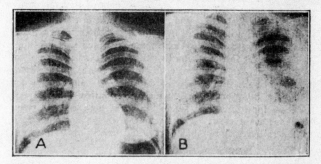

Fig. 6 (case 2).—Heart A, before operation and B, one month after operation.

size. Indeed, the heart was a trifle smaller than on the previous date. Roentgenograms of the heart before and after operation are shown in figure 6. Before operation the cardiothoracic ratio was 42.4 and three weeks after operation it was 44.7. The electrocardiogram showed no change (fig. 7). The stethocardiogram showed a continuous murmur (fig. 8). There was a significant increase in the pulse pressure. The preoperative arterial pressure had been 110 systolic and 90 diastolic. On the thirty-seventh postoperative day the arterial pressure was 98 systolic and 66 diastolic.

An appreciable diminution in the cyanosis of the lips and fingernails was apparent several days after operation. The patient was allowed to walk, beginning two and a half weeks after operation. This exercise resulted in a slight increase in the cyanosis, but it was evident that cyanosis was much less than it had been preoperatively. By the end of the third week she could walk 60 feet in an erect posture without panting, whereas

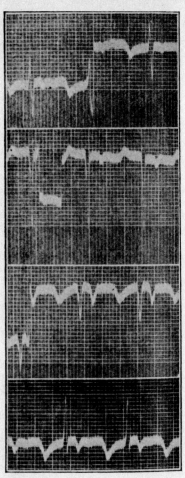

Fig. 7 (case 2).—Electrocardiogram.

before operation, stooping and leaning forward, she could walk only 30 feet and would then stop and pant. There has been a slow but steady recession of the clubbing of the fingers and toes. The patient was discharged from the hospital on the thirty-eighth postoperative day.

CASE 3.—*History.* —M. M., a boy born July 15, 1938, was first seen at the Harriet Lane Home at 8 months of age with the complaint of heart trouble.

The family history is of importance in that the maternal grandfather was known to have heart trouble and had had a heart murmur throughout his life. The mother's brother and sister are both reported to have dextrocardia; both have refused examination.

The past history stated that the patient was a full term baby. The birth weight was 6½ pounds (2,955 Gm.). Development was slow; he held his head up at 5 months and sat alone at 6½ months. At 8 months the patient weighed 13½ pounds (6 Kg.). When lying quietly he showed slight persistent cyanosis, which became intense when he cried. On examination of the heart there was no thrill but a very definite systolic murmur, which was audible all over the precordium and well heard in the back. Fluoroscopy showed that the heart was within normal limits in size. There was a wide shadow above the heart which was interpreted as a large thymus. There was no fulness of the pulmonary conus, and the shadow at the base of the heart was concave. The clinical diagnosis was tetralogy of Fallot.

The patient was followed in the cardiac clinic until January 1940, when the family moved to California. They returned to Baltimore in the fall of 1944 and the patient was again brought to the clinic on September 29. At that time the boy, 6 years of age, was thin and undernourished, intensely cyanotic and dyspneic on slight exertion. The temperature was 99.2 F., weight 34½ pounds (15.6 Kg.), height 42 inches (107 cm.), pulse 140, respirations 20 and blood pressure 90 systolic and 60 diastolic.

There was manifest suffusion of the conjunctiva. The lips were purple and the buccal mucous membranes were a deep mulberry color. The teeth were in bad condition; the tonsils were not unduly enlarged. The chest was barrel shaped. The increase in the size of the heart was in proportion to the growth of the child. There was a systolic thrill at the apex and a harsh systolic murmur, which was maximal along the left sternal border in the third interspace. The second sound at the base of the heart was clear but not accentuated. The lungs were clear.

The liver was at the costal margin; the spleen was not palpable. The femoral arterial pulsations were easily felt. The extremities showed deep cyanosis and pronounced clubbing. Although the patient had learned to walk by November 1944, he was so incapacitated that he was unable to walk and even refused to try to take a few steps. The diagnosis was tetralogy of Fallot with a severe degree of pulmonary stenosis.

The patient was referred to the dental clinic, where several teeth were extracted. Sulfadiazine was given for two days. One month later the patient returned to the cardiac clinic with a rectal temperature of 100.4 F. and with numerous petechiae on his legs, which the mother said were of two days' duration. A blood culture taken at this time was sterile and no further petechiae appeared.

TABLE 2.—*Studies on Arterial Blood (Case 3)*

| Dates | Arterial Oxygen Content, Volumes per Cent | Arterial Oxygen Capacity, Volumes per Cent | Arterial Oxygen Saturation, per Cent | Arterial Carbon Dioxide Content, Volumes per Cent | Comment |
|---|---|---|---|---|---|
| 2/ 8/45 | 7.3 | 31.2 | 23.4 | 27.5 | Patient struggling |
| 2/ 9/45 | 10.7 | 30.2 | 35.5 | 29.3 | Patient quiet |
| 2/10/45 | Innominate artery anastomosed to right pulmonary artery | | | | |
| 2/19/45 | 17.7 | 22.2 | 79.7 | 37.4 | Patient crying |
| 3/ 6/45 | 17.7 | 21.1 | 83.8 | 35.2 | Patient quiet |

The family was desirous of prompt operation and the patient was admitted to the hospital on Feb. 7, 1945. The results of analyses of blood obtained by arterial puncture are shown in table 2. With venous blood the red blood cell count was 10,000,000, the hemoglobin 26 Gm. and the hematocrit reading 81. The patient continued to have a daily elevation of temperature.

An electrocardiogram showed a normal sinus mechanism, a normal PR interval of 16, high P waves in $L_2$, and normal upright T waves in leads 1, 2 and 4, and $T_3$ inverted and an apparent right axis deviation.

X-ray examination (fig. 10) showed that the maximal right diameter of the heart was 2.1 cm., the maximal left 7 cm. and the total transverse diameter 18.8 cm.; the cardiothoracic ratio was 47.5. There was no fulness of the pulmonary conus. Fluoroscopy showed that the aorta descended on the left, and there were no visible pulsations in the lung fields.

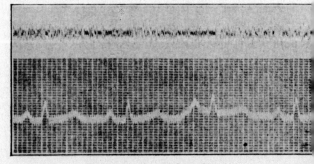

Fig. 8 (case 2).—Stethocardiogram.

*Operation.*—This was performed on February 10. The procedure consisted in anastomosing the divided proximal end of the innominate artery to the side of the right pulmonary artery. This is shown diagrammatically in figure 9. The anesthetic agent was administered by Dr. Merel Harmel.

Anesthesia was produced by cyclopropane with a high concentration of oxygen. It is of interest that the patient's color was much better under anesthesia than it had been previously.

This patient did not have a right aortic arch. In view of the great improvement in the second case we wished to use the innominate artery, and therefore the incision was made on the right side. There were no adhesions between the lung and the chest wall, and the lung appeared normal. The right upper lobe was retracted downward and the azygos vein was visualized. It

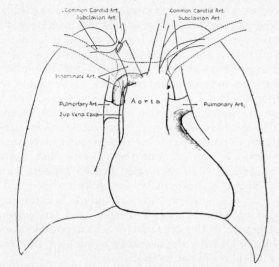

Fig. 9 (case 3).—Procedure used. The end of the innominate artery was anastomosed to the side of the right pulmonary artery.

was doubly ligated and divided. The superior vena cava and phrenic nerve were retracted medially, and the artery to the right upper lobe of the lung was seen. This was followed medially and the main right pulmonary artery was exposed. This exposure was considerably more difficult than that on the left side. Attention was then turned to the innominate artery. By dissecting under and medial to the superior vena cava the innominate artery was exposed and was dissected free of the surrounding tissues. This vessel was occluded temporarily by the use of a lung tourniquet which was equipped with a catheter overlying a piece of braided silk. The subclavian artery and the common carotid artery were ligated just distal to their origins from the innominate artery. The innominate artery was cut across proximal to these ligatures. Two bulldog clamps were placed on the right main pulmonary artery, and a transverse incision was made into the vessel between these clamps. The proximal bulldog clamp was not of sufficient length to secure entire control of the flow of blood. This resulted in a moderate loss of blood, and another clamp was substituted.

With 5-0 silk on a small curved needle an anastomosis was made between the divided proximal end of the innominate artery and the side of the right main pulmonary artery. This anastomosis was more difficult than that in the previous cases because the exposure was less satisfactory. Following the removal of the bulldog clamps from the pulmonary artery there was a rather copious flow of blood from one point along the anterior row of sutures. The clamps were reapplied, and this opening was closed with a mattress suture. Subsequent removal of the clamps did not result in further bleeding. The patient's condition up to the time of this blood loss had been excellent. Occlusion of the right pulmonary artery had not seemed to increase the cyanosis. There was an increase in the cyanosis and a decline in pressure when this loss of blood occurred. It was estimated that at least 250 cc. of blood was lost.

The anastomosis seemed to be a satisfactory one. An easily palpable thrill could be felt in the pulmonary artery both proximal and distal to the anastomosis. It was estimated that the lumen of the innominate artery was slightly less than 1 centimeter in diameter. The right lung was partially inflated

and the incision in the chest wall was closed.

The patient received 500 cc. of a mixture of isotonic solution of sodium chloride and glucose and 200 cc. of plasma during the operative procedure. The operation required a total of three hours, the greater part of this time being consumed in making the anastomosis. It was obvious that a better instrument for occluding the pulmonary artery proximal to the site of the anastomosis is needed. The right pulmonary artery was occluded for approximately ninety minutes.

The patient's condition at the completion of the operation was very good. He was conscious a few minutes after the incision had been closed, was asking for water and was moving his right arm. This arm was slightly cooler than the left. Pulsations could not be felt in the right arm or in the right side of the neck and the face. There was, however, no evidence of cerebral damage, and it was obvious that the circulation of the arm was adequate to maintain life.

*Postoperative Course.*—This was remarkably smooth. The patient was placed in an oxygen tent for several days. The circulation to the right arm remained adequate. Aspiration of the chest was not necessary. Immediately after operation the child's color improved. It was seen on the fourth postoperative day when the administration of oxygen was discontinued that the cyanosis of the lips had disappeared. The cyanosis of the fingertips decreased more slowly. The administration of penicillin was started the day before the operation and was continued for three weeks postoperatively. Dicumarol was given by mouth, beginning on the third postoperative day. The usual daily administration was 25 mg. Prothrombin determinations were performed daily, and the drug was continued for three weeks.

Although a thrill was palpable at the site of the anastomosis after the arterial clamps had been released, no murmur was audible immediately after the chest had been closed. By the first evening a faint murmur was audible, which gradually increased in intensity. By the fourth postoperative day a continuous murmur was audible over the site of the anastomosis and posteriorly throughout both lungs.

The child's compensation has remained excellent. In contrast to a preoperative arterial pressure of 85 systolic and 65 diastolic, the arterial pressure postoperatively was usually 106 systolic and 52 diastolic. The heart increased somewhat in size during the first ten days after operation, but there did not appear to be

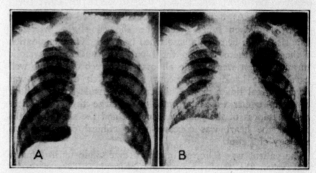

Fig. 10 (case 3).—Heart *A*, before operation and *B*, two weeks after operation.

a further increase in the subsequent two weeks. Roentgenograms of the heart both before and after operation are shown in figure 10.

Arterial punctures were performed on the 9th and 24th postoperative days. The results of the analyses are given in table 2. On comparing the preoperative studies with those performed twenty-four days after operation, samples of venous blood showed that the red blood cell count decreased from 10,000,000 to 6,000,000, the hemoglobin from 26 to 20 Gm. and the hematocrit reading from 81 to 53 (Wintrobe).

The patient had had a preoperative daily elevation of temperature to 100 F., and this continued for three weeks after operation. For this reason he was not allowed out of bed despite his vigorous protests until three and a half weeks after operation. When permitted to do so, the child walked 40 feet with ease. He was then allowed to be up for several hours each day and has walked and played in his room. He did not develop either cyanosis or dyspnea on this activity. The patient was discharged from the hospital on the thirty-eighth postoperative day.

### COMMENT

Each of these 3 patients suffered from such a severe degree of pulmonary stenosis that there was inadequate circulation to the lungs. Although the three operations differed in detail, in each instance the operation greatly increased the volume of blood which reached the lungs.

In the first case the end of the left subclavian artery was anastomosed to the side of the left pulmonary artery. As the baby was small and weak, extensive laboratory studies were not performed. Before operation the baby had been steadily losing ground. She had ceased to be able to sit alone; she had refused her feedings and had lost weight. The red blood cell count had declined from 7,000,000 to 5,000,000; consequently the cyanosis had diminished considerably. After operation her clinical improvement was remarkable. The appetite improved, she gained weight and she is now starting to learn to walk.

The second patient had a right aortic arch; hence it was possible to anastomose the innominate artery to the left pulmonary artery. The patient was deeply cyanotic and severely incapacitated and could not walk 30 feet without panting. Two and a half weeks after operation she walked 60 feet, rested a short time and walked 60 feet back to her room and sat down quietly. The seriousness of her condition and the extent of the improvement are shown by the changes in the oxygen saturation of the arterial blood, which was 36.3 per cent before operation and which rose to 82.8 per cent three weeks subsequently. The red blood cell count dropped from 7,500,000 to 6,000,000, the hemoglobin from 24 Gm. to 17.5 Gm. and the hematocrit reading from 71 to 55.

The success of the second operation led us to perform the same operation in the third case. Since the aorta was in the normal position, in order to use the innominate artery the operation was performed on the right side. The end of the innominate artery was anastomosed to the side of the right pulmonary artery. The patient was younger, and improvement was even more dramatic. Before operation he was intensely cyanotic, the lips were a dark purple, and the child was unable to take even a few steps. The day after operation he lay in an oxygen tent with cherry red lips. When taken out of the tent his color remained good. His disposition has changed from that of a miserable whining child to a happy smiling boy. We were slow to permit him to walk because of a persistent low grade fever, but at the end of the third postoperative week he could walk 40 feet without panting and without becoming cyanotic. The oxygen saturation of the arterial blood rose from 35.5 to 79.7 per cent in nine days, and it

reached a saturation of 83.8 per cent twenty-four days after operation. The red blood cell count fell from 10,000,000 to 6,000,000; the hemoglobin decreased from 26 Gm. to 20 Gm. and the hematocrit reading from 81 to 53.

There are a number of features of the operative procedure which merit discussion. We were fearful that an intensely cyanotic child would not tolerate a long operative procedure in which it was necessary to open the pleural cavity and to occlude temporarily one of the pulmonary arteries. For this reason our first clinical attempt to increase the circulation to the lungs was postponed almost a year after it was decided that the procedure was a sound one, with the hope that some method of administering oxygen in addition to inhalation might prove satisfactory. This seemed particularly important since it was obvious that a new and untried procedure should be performed first on patients with a severe degree of anoxemia whose outlook without aid of some sort was hopeless. Although the use of intravenous oxygen has been reported by Ziegler[12] and may prove to be of benefit in this operation, it was impossible during wartime to procure the necessary equipment. Therefore this method could not be studied.

From our limited experience it appears that this type of patient can tolerate the use of inhalation agents for general anesthesia. We have been fortunate in this respect in that the anesthetic agents were chosen and administered expertly by Dr. Austin Lamont and Dr. Merel Harmel.[13] The first of these 3 patients was only 14 months of age and weighed less than 9 pounds. Ether by the open drip method was used during the major part of the procedure for the reason that a sufficiently small closed system was not available. In the anesthetization of the second and third patients, cyclopropane with a high concentration of oxygen was employed. Fortunately the administration of oxygen apparently increased the oxygen content of the arterial blood and cyanosis was definitely lessened. Although in only 1 patient was there any serious hemorrhage, the precaution was taken of having both blood and plasma readily available. Indeed, a slow continuous drip of plasma is advisable so that at a moment's notice if necessary the patient can be given large quantities of plasma. With these precautions no great difficulty was encountered in spite of the fact that two of the three operations required three hours.

The next question which arose was whether a patient who was already suffering from a severe degree of anoxemia would tolerate the occlusion of one of the main pulmonary arteries for the period during which the anastomosis was being performed. These periods of occlusion were approximately thirty, sixty and ninety minutes in the three operations. It is a remarkable fact that the cyanosis did not appear to be greatly increased during the occlusion period. It may be that the decreased flow of blood to the lungs caused by the congenital deformity rendered it possible for the opposite artery and lung to utilize this reduced volume almost as effectively

12. Ziegler, E. E.: Intravenous Administration of Oxygen, J. Lab. & Clin. Med. 27:223-232 (Nov.) 1941.

13. Drs. Lamont and Harmel will deal with this subject in a subsequent communication.

as could the two lungs. Be that as it may, the 3 children tolerated occlusion of the left or the right main pulmonary artery for periods ranging from approximately thirty to ninety minutes.

Another question which arose was whether ligation and division of the left subclavian artery or the innominate artery would result in serious impairment of the circulation to the arm and the brain. In most instances heretofore these vessels have been occluded because of preexisting disease such as aneurysm, and it is possible under such circumstances that there has been a prolonged stimulus for the formation of collateral arterial pathways. It was gratifying, therefore, to note in our patients that there was little evidence of impairment of circulation to the parts deprived of their major arterial pathway. It is true that the pulse was absent for some time postoperatively and the part was slightly cooler than that of the opposite part of the body, but immediately after operation it was evident that the circulation was adequate to maintain life of the part. It may prove desirable to perform an upper dorsal sympathectomy at the time of operation. This would not add to the gravity of the operative procedure, since one has an excellent exposure of this region in performing the arterial anastomosis. In future cases the circulation of the arm will be studied more carefully.

The operation has not been attempted before on patients and there are many operative as well as clinical features which are still under investigation. The first of these is concerned with the type of anastomosis which is to be performed. This will undoubtedly depend on many factors, especially the age of the patient and the degree of anoxemia. As stated previously, in our patients the anastomosis was performed between the end of the subclavian artery or innominate artery and the side of the left or right pulmonary artery. This type of anastomosis appears to be sound in that it allows the blood to flow from the systemic circulation to both lungs. The fact that the continuous murmur which results from the operation is readily audible on both sides of the chest indicates that the anastomosis does direct blood to both lungs. It was this type of anastomosis which was used by Eppinger, Burwell and Gross[8] in their studies on the cardiac output of dogs with an artificial ductus arteriosus.

The easiest of the end to side arterial anastomoses in this region is that between the end of the left subclavian artery and the side of the left pulmonary artery. On the other hand, the subclavian artery is so small in an infant that the chances of the occurrence of thrombosis at the anastomotic site are great. This is particularly true if the patient has extreme polycythemia. Even though the anastomosis remains patent, the size of the vessel is a limiting factor in the flow of blood to the lungs which may not be sufficient to overcome the high degree of anoxemia from which some of these patients suffer. In an older patient with only a moderate degree of cyanosis the subclavian artery would appear to be the ideal vessel. The left common carotid is somewhat larger than the left subclavian artery, and its employment under some circumstances seems to be warranted. When dealing with the degree of anoxemia which was present in our patients, the innominate artery is much to be preferred to the left subclavian artery or the left common carotid artery. The performance of the anastomosis is not very difficult when the left pulmonary artery can be used. The anastomosis of the innominate artery to the left pulmonary artery is possible only in patients with a right aortic arch and hence an innominate artery on the left. With the innominate artery in its normal position the anastomosis of this vessel to the right pulmonary artery is more difficult because so much of the latter artery lies behind the aorta and the superior vena cava. Improvements in the designs of instruments will facilitate this procedure.

It is important to bear in mind that the degree of impairment in the flow of blood to the lungs varies from patient to patient, and the selection of the vessel to be used depends on the extent of the need of the patient for an increase in the circulation of the lungs. Experimental observations and clinical trial and error will undoubtedly shed additional light on this subject. It is obvious that the vessel chosen and the size of the anastomosis itself should not be larger than is necessary for the relief of anoxemia because of the danger associated with excessive shunting of blood to the lungs.

There are other methods in addition to union of an end of a systemic artery to the side of a pulmonary artery by which an anastomosis between the two circulations may be made. Included among these are (1) anastomosis of the divided proximal end of one of the vessels which arise from the aortic arch (innominate, left common carotid, left subclavian) to the divided distal end of one of the two pulmonary arteries, (2) anastomosis of the divided proximal end of the subclavian artery or the common carotid artery to the divided proximal end of the pulmonary artery to an upper lobe of one of the lungs, (3) anastomosis of the side of the aorta to the side of the left pulmonary artery and (4) anastomosis of the side of the aorta to the side of the left pulmonary artery. These will be considered in the order in which they are enumerated.

The results of the use of the first method, in which the divided proximal end of the left subclavian artery is anastomosed to the divided distal end of the left main pulmonary artery, were reported in 1939 by Levy and Blalock.[7] It was stated that "dogs which have been observed for several months following this procedure appear entirely normal. The left lung was aerated and the respiratory movements were unaltered. The systemic arterial blood pressure was not affected by this operation. The blood pressure in the pulmonary artery only a short distance beyond the anastomosis was less than half of that in the systemic arteries. This was due to the relatively low peripheral resistance in the pulmonary bed. Since only arterial blood entered the left lung, the quantity of oxygen consumed by this lung was very small. However, when anoxemia was caused, a larger quantity of oxygen was taken up by the incompletely oxygenated arterial blood. The left lung appeared pinker than the right on gross examination during life. Microscopic examination revealed no noteworthy alteration in either the left pulmonary artery or lung." Some of these animals have now been observed over periods ranging up to six years. The only disturbing finding has been that a few of the animals at autopsy have shown a thickening of the left pulmonary artery. It was noted by Dr. Arnold Rich that this was found only in instances in which the anastomotic site was partially occluded as a result of thrombosis. The discrepancy in the size of the left subclavian artery and that of the left pulmonary artery may have accounted in part for this finding. Furthermore, this discrepancy in size may be responsible in part for the sudden diminution in the arterial pressure just beyond the point of anastomosis. At any rate, it is improbable that the anastomosis of the subclavian artery to the end of the left pulmonary artery would be the procedure of choice in the treatment of pulmonic stenosis. If this type of anastomosis should be performed, the innominate artery would be a better choice than the subclavian because it is more nearly the size of the pulmonary artery. It may be found that an end to end anastomosis is more apt to remain patent than an end to side one; certainly it is technically easier to perform. If, in the process of performing an anastomosis between the end of the innominate artery and the side of one of the pulmonary arteries, the latter vessel should be torn beyond repair, it should be borne in mind that an anastomosis may still be performed between the end of the innominate and the distal end of the pulmonary artery. Experimental studies are being carried out on the relative virtues of end to end and end to side anastomoses.

A second alternative method consists in anastomosing the proximal end of the divided subclavian or carotid artery to the proximal end of the divided pulmonary artery to one of the upper lobes. Since it is technically easier to perform an end to end than an end to side anastomosis, one may consider the advisability of using this procedure for a patient with only a slight degree of cyanosis. The proximal end of the pulmonary artery is specified because this would conceivably allow blood to gain access to all the lobes except the one supplied by the artery which was used for the anastomosis. This procedure has been performed in the laboratory and is not difficult.

The third possible operative procedure is concerned with an anastomosis of the side of the aorta to the side of the left pulmonary artery. That such a procedure is possible in dogs has been shown by Leeds[9] in his studies on patent ductus arteriosus. We considered the use of this method in our patients but were discouraged by the experience of Blalock and Park[10] in studies on experimental coarctation of the aorta. In these experiments the aorta was divided just distal to the ligamentum arteriosum, the two ends of the aorta were closed, the left subclavian artery was divided at some distance from the arch of the aorta, and the proximal end of the divided subclavian artery was anastomosed to the side of the distal end of the aorta just below the point at which it had been divided. Thus the subclavian artery was used for the conduction of blood beyond the point of division of the aorta. The discouraging feature of these experiments was that in approximately half of the animals the hind legs were paralyzed at the completion of the operative procedure. In 1 dog in which we occluded the aorta for forty minutes for the purpose of making an anastomosis between the side of the aorta and the side of the left

pulmonary artery the hind legs became paralyzed. It is impossible to make an accurate anastomosis between the aorta and the left pulmonary artery without interrupting temporarily the circulation through the two vessels. We were fearful of causing a paralysis of the lower extremities and hence did not use this method with our patients. Another difficulty associated with the use of the aorta is that its walls are thick and rather friable and it is difficult to obtain an accurate approximation of the intimal surfaces.

The fourth method to be considered is that of an anastomosis of the aorta and the main pulmonary artery. It is obvious that occlusion of these vessels for the length of time that is required for an open suture anastomosis would result in death. If such a union was to be secured, it would have to be done by some other method. Fortunately the first portions of the medial walls of the aorta and the pulmonary artery are intimately adherent to each other. The ascending aorta and the main pulmonary artery are contained within the pericardial cavity and are enclosed in a tube of serous pericardium common to the two vessels. We have been able to produce a fistula between the two vessels in dogs by inflicting a stab wound in this region. The knife blade was introduced through the opposite free wall of the pulmonary artery, the walls of the pulmonary artery and aorta which were in intimate contact were pierced, the knife was withdrawn, and the opening in the free side of the pulmonary artery was closed by sutures. The establishment of the fistula required only a few seconds. This method is mentioned because it may be necessary to use the major blood vessels and to employ considerable speed if newborn infants with pulmonary stenosis or atresia are to be saved. It would not be at all surprising if this experimental method should prove to be a useful one in patients.

It remains to be proved whether a communication between the two circulations should be brought about by direct anastomoses between blood vessels such as we have employed or by the use of tubes such as those devised for other purposes by Blakemore, Lord and Stefko.[14] It is our impression that the suture method is preferable when it can be accomplished without undue tension. This method obviates the necessity for leaving a large foreign body in the tissues; furthermore, there is at least a possibility that the opening will increase in size with the growth of the child. Studies on the latter point are in progress. These comments are in no sense a criticism of the Blakemore method, which is of great value in those instances in which part of a blood vessel has been destroyed and the ends cannot be united by direct suture.

One of the possible complications which causes concern is the danger of thrombosis at the anastomotic site. The improvement of our 3 patients indicates that thrombosis has not occurred. Furthermore, in cases 2 and 3 loud continuous murmurs developed after operation. As mentioned previously, partial occlusion of the anastomotic site has been found in some of the dogs in which such anastomoses were performed. Partial occlusion of the

14. Blakemore, A. H.; Lord, J. W., Jr., and Siefko, P. L.: Restoration of Blood Flow in Damaged Arteries: Further Studies on Nonsuture Method of Blood Vessel Anastomosis, Ann. Surg. **117**:481-497, 1943.

opening and emboli in the lungs were found at autopsy in 1 animal in which the end of the subclavian artery had been anastomosed to the side of the left pulmonary artery. This experiment was complicated by the previous creation of bilateral pulmonary arteriovenous fistulas. The sizes of the vessels used and the size of the communication between the two vessels are, of course, of prime importance in the determination of whether or not the opening will remain patent. This consideration is another point in favor of using a large vessel such as the innominate artery. Because of the difference in pressure on the two sides of the anastomotic site between the systemic and pulmonary circulations, it would be more likely that such an anastomosis would remain open than communications of similar size between two systemic arteries or two systemic veins.

As previously stated, most patients with the type of malformation of the heart under consideration have a decided polycythemia and an increased viscosity of the blood. This condition undoubtedly increases the danger of thrombosis. Indeed, cerebral thromboses are of not infrequent occurrence in these patients. Therefore the question arose as to whether these patients should receive heparin shortly after the termination of the operation. After much deliberation it was decided that the possible dangers were greater than the possible advantages. This opinion, however, is subject to change. By way of compromise, it was decided to give dicumarol during the period of convalescence. Therefore, beginning respectively on the fourth and third postoperative days the second and third patients were given dicumarol in small quantities. Prothrombin determinations were made daily and the dose of dicumarol was regulated so as to keep the clotting time approximately double that of the normal control. This medication was continued for a period of approximately three weeks. It is impossible to state whether this therapy has been of importance in the maintenance of the patency of the fistulas.

In order to understand the changes produced by the operation and its application to other malformations, it is essential to understand the nature of this malformation and the course of the circulation. The four features which constitute the tetralogy of Fallot are pulmonary stenosis, dextroposition of the aorta, an interventricular septal defect and right ventricular hypertrophy. The pulmonary stenosis consists in a narrowing of the pulmonary orifice, and it is usual to find that the constriction also involves the pulmonary conus of the right ventricle. Dextroposition of the aorta means that the aorta rises from the left ventricle and partially overrides the right ventricle. Whenever this occurs, the aortic septum cannot meet the ventricular septum; consequently there is a high ventricular septal defect. Such is the nature of an interventricular septal defect in the tetrology of Fallot. The malformation renders it difficult for the blood to be expelled from the right ventricle; hence there is hypertrophy of that chamber. The structure of the heart and the course of the circulation are diagrammatically shown in figure 11.

The degree of incapacity in a tetralogy of Fallot depends on the severity of the pulmonary stenosis and the degree of the overriding of the aorta. It is well known in cases in which the pulmonary stenosis is not extreme that the malformation is compatible with relative longevity. However, with extreme degrees of pulmonary stenosis and greatly diminished circulation to the lungs, the condition causes severe incapacity and death occurs at an early age.

The anastomosis of the innominate artery to the pulmonary artery directs a large volume of blood from the systemic circulation into the pulmonary circulation. By this means the volume of blood which reaches the lungs for aeration is increased; it follows that a greater volume of oxygenated blood is returned by the pulmonary veins to the left auricle and the left ventricle; consequently a greater volume of oxygenated blood is pumped out into the systemic circulation. As some blood from the aorta is diverted to the pulmonary circulation, the volume of blood to the systemic circulation is decreased and less blood is returned to the right auricle and the right ventricle. Thus the volume of blood which is returned to the right ventricle is lessened and that which is returned to the left side of the heart is increased. The alteration in the course of the circulation as influenced by the operation is shown in figure 12.

In short, the operation enables some blood to bypass the obstruction to the pulmonary circulation. Hence the operation should be of value in all malformations in which the primary difficulty is due to lack of adequate circulation of the blood to the lungs; that is, in all cases of the tetralogy of Fallot and complete pulmonary atresia, in cases in which the right ventricle is absent or defective in its development, in cases of truncus arteriosus with bronchial arteries, or even a single ventricle with a rudimentary outlet chamber in which the pulmonary artery is diminutive in size.

Complete pulmonary atresia is, of course, compatible

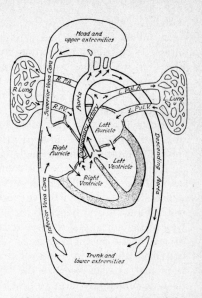

Fig. 11. Diagram of the course of the circulation in the tetralogy of Fallot. In this malformation there is pulmonary stenosis, the aorta is dextroposed and hence receives blood from both ventricles, the ductus arteriosus undergoes normal obliteration and the foramen ovale is closed. The blood from the right auricle flows into the right ventricle; hence part of the blood is pumped through the stenosed pulmonary orifice into the pulmonary artery and part of the blood is pumped directly into the aorta. Only that portion of the blood from the right ventricle which is pumped into the pulmonary artery goes to the lungs for aeration and is returned to the left auricle and the left ventricle. All of the blood from the left ventricle and some of the blood from the right ventricle is pumped out into the aorta to the systemic circulation and is returned by the superior vena cava and the inferior vena cava to the right auricle. There the cycle starts again.

with life only as long as the ductus arteriosus remains open unless the bronchial arteries dilate and establish sufficient collateral circulation for the maintenance of life. This, we believe, happened in case 2, as at operation large aberrant vessels were found in the region of the hilus of the left lung. However, in the great majority of cases of pulmonary atresia the closure of the ductus arteriosus is so rapid that adequate collateral circulation does not develop and consequently the condition is fatal in early infancy. In all such cases the operation, if performed early, may be life saving. The same is true in cases of a defective development of the right ventricle in which all of the blood from the right auricle is directed to the left auricle and hence to the left ventricle and out by way of the aorta, and the only circulation to the lungs is by way of the ductus arteriosus.[15] The operation should be equally valuable in cases of truncus arteriosus with bronchial arteries because the bronchial arteries never become sufficiently large to provide adequate circulation to the lungs.

In every instance there is, of course, an admixture of venous and arterial blood. It would be impossible, therefore, to bring the oxygen saturation of the arterial blood to normal; nevertheless, it is conceivably possible to bring the oxygen saturation of the arterial blood sufficiently high so that there would be no "visible" cyanosis. Certainly in the 2 older children there has been an increase in the oxygen content of the arterial blood, a decrease in the oxygen capacity, an increase in the oxygen saturation of the arterial blood, a decrease in the red blood cell count, a diminution in the hemoglobin and the hematocrit reading, a striking decrease in the patients' disability and a great improvement in the patients' ability to exercise.

In cases of the tetralogy of Fallot the heart is either nomal in size or relatively small. Following the creation of an artificial ductus, the increased volume of blood which reaches the pulmonary circulation undoubtedly increases the work of the left side of the heart. In our patients the heart has definitely increased in size but compensation thus far has remained excellent. Sir Thomas Lewis[16] has emphasized that in cases of coarctation of the aorta prolonged overwork does not cause cardiac failure. Palmer[17] in his studies on cardiac enlargement showed that, in essential hypertension, cardiac enlargement occurs with the gradual rise in blood pressure and that progressive enlargement does not easily occur after the blood pressure level has become stabilized. Therefore it is our hope and expectation that in this operation, although the heart immediately increases in size in response to the altered blood flow, the condition will not lead to progressive cardiac enlargement. It is encouraging that in both cases 2 and 3, although the heart increased in size in the first ten days, there was no further increase in the second ten days.

It is important to emphasize that the operation is not of value to all patients with persistent cyanosis. It is of value only in malformations in which the primary difficulty is lack of circulation to the lungs. The operation would be of no use in cases of complete transposition of the great vessels or in the so-called "tetralogy of Fallot of the Eisenmenger type" and probably not in aortic atresia.

In complete transposition of the great vessels the pulmonary artery arises from the left ventricle and the aorta from the right ventricle. The blood from the left ventricle is pumped out through the pulmonary artery to the lungs and is returned by the pulmonary veins to the left auricle and thence to the left ventricle. The blood from the right side of the heart is pumped out into the aorta to the systemic circulation and is returned by the superior vena cava and the inferior vena cava to the right auricle and the right ventricle. The primary difficulty in this malformation is not in the volume of blood which reaches the lungs but in the mechanism by which the blood which has been oxygenated in the lungs can reach the systemic circulation.

In the Eisenmenger complex cyanosis appears to be due to secondary changes in the alveolar wall or in the pulmonary vascular bed of such a nature as to hinder the aeration of the blood as it passes through the lungs; it is even possible that the high pressure in the lesser circulation may increase the right to left shunt and thereby increase the volume of reduced hemoglobin in the arterial blood. In any event, in this malformation there is no lack of circulation to the lungs and, furthermore, only rarely, if ever, is there deep cyanosis in early childhood.

In aortic atresia[18] not only is there difficulty in pumping blood to the systemic circulation but also the blood which does reach the systemic circulation is pumped through the ductus arteriosus before it has been to the lungs for aeration. Under such circumstances the creation of an additional ductus arteriosus would act to direct a larger volume of blood to the body; but it must be borne in mind that this blood has the same oxygen content as that directed to the lungs.

It is worthy of note in almost all patients with much polycythemia that all of the blood which circulates through the lungs is no longer fully oxygenated. Whether the size of the capillary bed in the lungs varies with the plasma volume and not with the number of red blood cells is not known, but there is clear evidence to show that even in patients in whom the primary difficulty is lack of circulation to the lungs the oxygen saturation of the arterial blood can be appreciably raised by the prolonged inhalation of a high concentration of oxygen. The potency of this factor was demonstrated by the great improvement in the peripheral cyanosis during operation when the patients were receiving oxygen. The importance of the volume of blood which reaches the lungs for aeration is demonstrated in our patients by the extent of the rise in the oxygen saturation of the arterial blood which resulted from the operation; in 1 instance it rose

15. Taussig, H. B.: The Clinical and Pathological Findings in Congenital Malformations of the Heart Due to Defective Development of the Right Ventricle Associated with Tricuspid Atresia or Hypoplasia, Bull. Johns Hopkins Hosp. **59**:435-445, 1936.

16. Lewis, T.: Material Relating to Coarctation of the Aorta of the Adult Type, Heart **16**:205-261, 1933.

17. Palmer, J. H.: The Development of Cardiac Enlargement in Disease of the Heart: A Radiological Study, Medical Research Council Special Report Series, No. 222, 1937.

18. Taussig, H. B.: Clinical and Pathological Findings in Aortic Atresia or Marked Hypoplasia of the Aorta at Its Base, Bull. Johns Hopkins Hospital, to be published.

rom 36.3 to 82.8 per cent and in the other from 35.5 to 83.8 per cent.

It may be that, with prolonged meager flow of blood to the lungs, secondary changes occur so that the pulmonary capillary bed is no longer capable of complete expansion and restoration to normal. Our 6 year old child showed prompter improvement than did the 12 year old girl. Hence the operation may prove less beneficial to older persons than to young children. For this reason the ideal age for operation appears to be after the systemic pressure has risen sufficiently high to permit the continuous flow of blood from the aorta to the pulmonary artery and before the condition has persisted long enough to cause irreversible changes in the lungs. We believe that the optimal age of patients is probably between 4 and 6 years; however, in all cases in which the closure of the ductus arteriosus renders the malformation incompatible with life the operation must be performed in early infancy.

Since the operation should be of value to all patients in whom the primary difficulty is lack of circulation to the lungs, it behooves the clinician to recognize this condition.[19] The two outstanding features, both of which should be present, are (1) roentgenographic evidence that the pulmonary artery is diminutive in size and (2) clinical and roentgenographic evidence of absence of congestion in the lung fields.

The size of the normal pulmonary artery is not difficult to determine by roentgenography. The striking feature in the roentgenogram is the absence of the fulness of the normal pulmonary conus. The shadow at the base of the heart to the left of the sternum is concave and not convex. A concave shadow in this region in patients with persistent cyanosis always means that the pulmonary artery is misplaced, absent or diminutive in size.[2] When the pulmonary artery is absent or diminutive in size, there is the additional finding in the left anterior oblique position of an abnormally clear pulmonary window.[2]

Absence of clinical and x-ray evidence of congestion in the lungs is highly important in reaching a decision. When circulation to the lungs is inadequate, the diminished blood flow to the lungs lessens the chances of congestion in the lungs and congestion rarely occurs.[2] When congestion does occur, it suggests that the circulation to the lungs is adequate or excessive. The operation should never be attempted when x-ray examination shows a prominent pulmonary conus or when there are pulsations at the hili of the lungs. These pulsations should be looked for by careful fluoroscopic examination after one's eyes are fully accommodated.

Virtually the only malformation in which there is absence of the normal shadow cast by the pulmonary artery in the presence of adequate circulation to the lungs is complete transposition of the great vessels. In this condition the pulmonary artery lies behind the aorta; therefore, in the anteroposterior view there is a narrow aortic shadow and a concave curve at the base of the heart to the left of the sternum. In the left anterior oblique position the two vessels lie side by side; hence the shadow cast by the great vessels increases in width[20] and the pulmonary window is not abnormally clear. The condition does not cause pulsation at the hili of the lungs but frequently leads to congestion in the lung fields. These observations, together with evidence of relatively rapid progressive cardiac enlargement,[2] should aid in the establishment of the correct diagnosis.

The operation should be performed on the right or left side, depending on which vessel is to be used and on which side the aorta descends. Furthermore, it is important to bear in mind that the occurrence of a right aortic arch is by no means rare in congenital malformations of the heart which cause persistent cyanosis. Bedford and Parkinson[21]

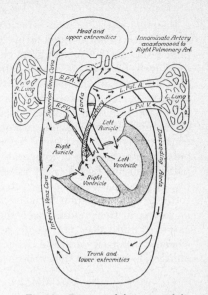

Fig. 12.—Diagram of the course of the circulation in the tetralogy of Fallot after the anastomosis of the innominate artery to the pulmonary artery. Under these circumstances the blood from the right auricle flows into the right ventricle and, as before, part of the blood from the right ventricle is pumped directly into the aorta. Now, in addition to the blood which is pumped through the pulmonary orifice into the pulmonary artery, some of the blood from the aorta is diverted through the anastomosis to the lungs. Thus the volume of blood which reaches the lungs is increased and the volume of oxygenated blood which is returned to the left auricle and the left ventricle is proportionately increased. All of the blood from the left ventricle and also some blood from the right ventricle is pumped into the aorta. Some of the blood from the aorta is directed to the lungs, and the remainder goes to the systemic circulation and is returned by the superior vena cava and the inferior vena cava to the right auricle. Thus the left ventricle receives more blood than before operation and the right side of the heart receives less. The operation has bypassed the obstruction in the circulation of the blood to the lungs.

have shown that the determination of the course of the aorta is not difficult, provided fluoroscopy is carefully performed and the esophagus delineated with a barium opaque mixture. Normally the aortic knob is visible on the left, the esophagus lies in the midline and is indented by the aorta on the left margin, and in the right anterior oblique position the esophagus is seen to be slightly displaced backward by the aorta. In cases of a right aortic arch the aortic knob frequently is hidden within the shadow cast by the superior vena cava. In the anteroposterior view the esophagus is indented on the right and is displaced backward in the left anterior oblique position.

19. The following discussion is based mainly on original unreported observations which are dealt with in detail in chapters II and III of Taussig's forthcoming book on "The Clinical Analysis of Congenital Malformations of the Heart," to be published by the Commonwealth Fund.

20. Taussig, H. B.: Complete Transposition of the Great Vessels, Am. Heart J. **16**:728-733, 1938.

21. Bedford, D. E., and Parkinson, J.: Right-Sided Aortic Arch, Brit. J. Radiol. **9**:776-798, 1936.

It remains to be seen whether these patients will develop heart failure. Even if this occurs, the intervening period appears to be one of great clinical improvement. It may well be that, if more patients with congenital malformations of the heart survive, more will develop subacute bacterial endocarditis. Certain it is that there is nothing in persistent cyanosis which renders an individual immune from subacute bacterial endocarditis. The condition is less frequently encountered in cyanotic persons only because a comparatively small number of patients survive long enough to be liable to contract the disease. The fear of subacute bacterial endocarditis in the future is no justification for allowing a patient to die of anoxemia in the present. Even the possibility of future cardiac failure does not weigh heavily against present extreme incapacity and the danger of early death from anoxemia or cerebral thrombosis.

## SUMMARY

An operation for increasing the flow of blood through the lungs and thereby reducing the cyanosis in patients with congenital malformations of the heart consists in making an anastomosis between a branch of the aorta and one of the pulmonary arteries; in other words, the creation of an artificial ductus arteriosus. Thus far the procedure has been carried out on only 3 children, each of whom had a severe degree of anoxemia. Clinical evidence of improvement has been striking and include a pronounced decrease in the intensity of the cyanosis, decrease in dyspnea and an increase in tolerance t exercise. In the 2 cases in which such laboratory studie were performed there has been a decline in the red bloo cell count, in the hemoglobin and in the hematocri reading, an increase in the oxygen content of the arteria blood, a fall in the oxygen capacity, and most signifi cantly a decided rise in the oxygen saturation of th arterial blood.

The types of abnormalities which should be benefite by this operation are the tetralogy of Fallot, pulmonar atresia with or without dextroposition of the aorta an with or without defective development of the righ ventricle, a truncus arteriosus with bronchial arteries, an a single ventricle with a rudimentary outlet chamber i which the pulmonary artery is diminutive in size. Th operation is indicated only when there is clinical an radiologic evidence of a decrease in the pulmonary bloo flow. The operation is not indicated in cases of complet transposition of the great vessels or in the so-calle "tetralogy of Fallot of the Eisenmenger type," an probably not in aortic atresia. It must be emphasized tha the operation should not be performed when studie reveal a prominent pulmonary conus or pulsations at th hili of the lungs.

April 27, 1984
(JAMA 1984;251:2139-2141)

# The Blalock-Taussig Operation
# and Subsequent Progress*

Dan G. McNamara, MD

In 1945, few would have predicted the sustained worldwide interest in, and profound influence on, the surgical treatment of heart disease that would follow the report of three children operated upon for a cyanotic malformation of the heart. The paper was submitted for publication when the patients were only a few months postoperative, probably leading some critics to question whether the report of success was a little premature. The authors acknowledged and defended the promptness of the report as follows: "The results are sufficiently encouraging to warrant an early report."[1]

The paper was not a hastily assembled report of a new procedure but included, first, a methodical exposition on the prevailing theories of the mechanism of cyanosis in congenital heart disease, then a step-by-step review of how Dr Taussig developed the concept of surgically increasing the volume of blood to the pulmonary circulation in cyanotic malformations with pulmonary stenosis or atresia. Also, the paper described how Dr Blalock,[2] working independently, had already performed in the experimental animal a systemic-to-pulmonary artery anastomosis to achieve an experimental model of pulmonary hypertension. As it turned out, the operation did not create pulmonary hypertension in either the experimental animal or the patient.

The main purpose of the paper was to describe: (1) the clinical course of each of the three patients with tetralogy of Fallot, (2) the futile attempts to treat them medically, (3) the deliberations that preceded the first operation, (4) the technique of the new procedure, (5) early postoperative changes, and (6) anomalies other than tetralogy of Fallot that theoretically could be helped by this operation, as well as those that could not.

From the Cardiology Section, Baylor College of Medicine, and Texas Children's Hospital, Houston.

*A commentary on Blalock A, Taussig HB: The surgical treatment of malformations of the heart: In which there is pulmonary stenosis or pulmonary atresia. JAMA 1945;128:189-202.

### Early Reactions to the Publication

There was immediate worldwide acceptance of the Blalock-Taussig operation as the first effort to treat a child with cyanotic congenital heart disease. Gross[3] had already closed the ductus arteriosus some six years previously (see Chapter 31). Then, a month before the first Blalock-Taussig operation, Crafoord[4] in Sweden excised a coarctation of the aorta, and at about the same time working independently, Gross[5] also excised a coarctation of the aorta in Boston. So, while there were sporadic but widespread attempts at operations on congenital heart defects, the surgical palliation of tetralogy of Fallot offered a new approach to complex anomalies of the heart. While closing a persistent ductus seemed like the obvious and logical thing to do, *creating* a ductus was a new and ingenious concept of indirectly relieving the problem of diminished pulmonary circulation. Furthermore, most patients with isolated patent ductus arteriosus and those with coarctation had a relatively asymptomatic childhood and reached adult life in large numbers, only one fourth of the patients with tetralogy of Fallot reached adolescence, and the patients had severe disabling symptoms from infancy obvious to anyone who saw them.

After the paper appeared, hundreds of cyanotic children, whose parents had either recently or long before already heard the dismal prognosis pronounced, went to Baltimore for the operation. Within the next two years, 500 patients had undergone the Blalock-Taussig operation.

What were the early and late results of the Blalock-Taussig operation? Among 389 survivors of the operation, 97% were improved.[6] There was an early mortality of 16%, and in only 6% of the patients Dr Blalock found at exploratory thoracotomy a malformation that could not be helped by the anastomosis.

In the five-year follow-up, among the patients who had been improved, 67% had maintained their improvement.[6] While the majority of the patients were in improved condition, many of the shunts had closed or become smaller, and 36% required a second operation.[7] This failure of the Blalock-Taussig shunt to remain patent over a long period seems to have served as a stimulus for surgical investigators to learn to repair the intracardiac defect.[8,9]

### New Information Provided by the Paper

The paper provided new information about the potential for surgical treatment of heart disease. Cardiac surgery for acquired as well as congenital heart disease undoubtedly received a great impetus from this published experience, which dispelled some prevailing myths about the limitations of general anesthesia and surgery in general for young and critically ill patients and for operations on the diseased heart.

1. Anesthesia could be given safely to such a patient. In 1945, no equipment for a closed system was available, so drop ether was given! The arterial oxygen saturation proved to be higher with the patient under general anesthesia than when awake, and this explained how these patients could tolerate anesthesia so well.

2. The two- to three-hour operation was tolerated by these three critically ill patients with cyanotic congenital heart disease, and no major problem such as arrhythmia, shock, or brain damage was encountered.

3. The patient could tolerate occlusion of the left or right pulmonary artery long enough for an anastomosis to be performed, periods ranging from 30 to 90 minutes.

4. The arm, deprived permanently of major blood supply by division of the subclavian artery, functioned without ischemic symptoms during the period of postoperative observation. Now, in the 1980s, many years after the early Blalock-Taussig operation, the patient's arm continues to receive adequate perfusion from other vessels, although the arm will be slightly smaller than its mate. Likewise, in two of the first patients, the innominate artery was divided and brought down for the anastomosis without their suffering strokes. (However, use of the innominate artery in subsequent patients resulted in cerebrovascular ischemia in some, and its use was later abandoned.)

5. A popular prevailing theory in the 1940s concerning the mechanisms of arterial hypoxemia in cyanotic congenital heart disease was that polycythemia interfered with gas exchange in the lung.[10] However, Dr Taussig had proposed that it was the reduced volume of blood reaching the pulmonary capillaries in patients with pulmonary stenosis or pulmonary atresia. The clinical features of single ventricle as Dr Taussig described it helped to explain this as follows:

If [in single ventricle] the great vessels occupy their normal positions, the aorta arises from the common ventricle and is of large caliber, whereas the pulmonary artery which arises from the rudimentary outlet chamber is of small caliber. Under such circumstances a large volume of blood goes to the systemic circulation and only a small volume of blood goes to the lungs. Consequently a large volume of unoxygenated blood is mixed with a small volume of oxygenated blood and cyanosis is intense. When, however, the great vessels are transposed and the pulmonary artery is large and the aorta is small, a large volume of blood goes to the lungs for aeration. Under these circumstances a large volume of oxygenated blood is mixed with a relatively small volume of venous blood and cyanosis is minimal or absent . . .'

Her theory was confirmed by the fact that the patient's color and arterial oxygen saturation immediately improved as soon as the surgeon completed the anastomosis, removed the temporary occluding clamps, and allowed blood to flow from the subclavian artery to the pulmonary artery.

6. The operation provided a model and rationale for palliative surgery. Before this report there had been an understandable general apathy among physicians with respect to treatment of the patient with severe cyanotic congenital heart disease, as well as a pessimism about the quality of a prolonged life. The authors, originally armed with only a positive attitude and a conviction that the operation would work, made the following prediction: "even though the structure of the heart was grossly abnormal, it might be possible to alter the course of the circulation in such a manner as to lessen . . . the disability."

Soon other palliative procedures developed. Within a few months the partial occlusion clamp allowed the development of the aorta-to-left pulmonary artery anastomosis by Willis Potts,[11] later, the superior vena cava-to-right pulmonary artery anastomosis by William Glenn,[12] and the Brock[13] pulmonary valvotomy. Many years later, working independently, David Waterston[14] developed the ascending aorta-to-right pulmonary artery anastomosis, and Denton Cooley[15] devised a similar procedure with a different approach.

Palliative procedures were performed for many different types of anomaly in which there was pulmonary stenosis or pulmonary atresia, and ultimately other palliative operations followed for different anomalies: the Blalock-Hanlon[16] creation of atrial septal defect in transposition of the great arteries and the Dammann-Muller[17] banding of the pulmonary artery for ventricular septal defect with pulmonary hypertension.

### The Educational Value of the Paper for Pediatric Cardiologists and Cardiac Surgeons

The report first explains the altered dynamics of some of the complex malformations of the heart in such a way that it not only was (and is) easy to understand but also stirred an interest by physicians to study congenital malformations of the heart. The JAMA article was a good introduction to Dr Taussig's[18] book, Congenital Malformations of the Heart. By the time the book was in print, most of the medical profession knew about the operation, and the book was well received and studied by many disciplines with an interest in cardiology. The book expanded on the clinical features of virtually all of the common malformations, and this led to even wider interest in congenital heart disease and in pediatric cardiology in general. Training programs developed and the Sub-Board of Pediatric Cardiology became a natural consequence. The Board brought structure to the curriculum of those programs and certified qualified persons for the specialty of pediatric cardiology.[19] Today there are more than 600 diplomates of the Sub-Board of Pediatric Cardiology.

Likewise, surgeons developed an interest in congenital

heart disease, an interest that had been started by Gross and Crafoord with treatment of the ductus arteriosus and coarctation but was undoubtedly spurred by the Blalock-Taussig anastomosis. This led to the development of other shunts. The fact that the Blalock-Taussig anastomosis did not last indefinitely further increased the interest in total repair of tetralogy of Fallot and other such malformations. The difficulty in creating an effective Blalock-Taussig shunt in the infant led to development of surgical techniques in the small infant.

The Blalock-Taussig operation was described in minute and careful detail and in easy-to-understand English. For a clear and vivid description of the operation, read the third and fourth pages of the paper beginning with "Although there were slight variations" and ending with "The soft tissues of the chest wall were closed in multiple layers with interrupted silk sutures." Certainly the potential of the operation and the manner in which Dr Blalock was able to teach it created an interest in surgeons furthering their training in cardiovascular disease. Many heads of surgical departments around the country came from Dr Blalock's training program in cardiovascular surgery.

The paper emphasized the value and, in fact, the necessity of teamwork in cardiology between surgeon, cardiologist, and anesthesiologist and the input of the pediatrician, internist, radiologist, and pathologist. Fortuitously, the two investigators ended up in the same institution and became the first team for working on problems of the patient with surgically treatable heart disease. Virtually all of the persons responsible for the care of the three patients described are mentioned by name in the article — the referring physician, the house staff, the anesthesiologist, the surgical assistant, and others.

## Conclusion

Today, intracardiac repair of tetralogy of Fallot is of course preferable to a palliative shunt, and repair can be accomplished with an approximate 5% mortality and a 95% good outlook for an active and productive adult life. But there are still indications for a systemic-to-pulmonary artery shunt.[9] Among all of the other palliative shunts devised, the Blalock-Taussig or its modification is still the first choice among most surgeons. The most recent modification of the Blalock-Taussig shunt by Dr deLaval[20] may be most widely used — the Goretex conduit from the side of the intact subclavian artery to the side of the pulmonary artery. The deLaval modification, like the original Blalock-Taussig anastomosis, does not deform the pulmonary arteries, and the amount of blood flow to the lung is controlled by the size of the subclavian artery and is not likely to be excessive; thus, pulmonary hypertension seldom results and later occlusion for intracardiac repair is easily accomplished.

If THE JOURNAL decides to publish landmark articles for their bicentennial in 2083, I predict that Blalock and Taussig's article will be reprinted there. It is not often that a single, identifiable publication has had such influence on a new discipline of medical science.

## References

1. Blalock A, Taussig HB: The surgical treatment of malformations of the heart: In which there is pulmonary stenosis or pulmonary atresia. JAMA 1945;128:189-202.

2. Levy SE, Blalock A: Experimental observations on the effects of connecting by suture the left main pulmonary artery to the systemic circulation. J Thorac Surg 1939;8:525-530.

3. Gross RE, Hubbard JP: Surgical ligation of a patent ductus arteriosus: Report of first successful case. JAMA 1939;112:729-731.

4. Crafoord C, Nyline G: Congenital coarctation of the aorta and its surgical treatment. J Thorac Surg 1945;14:347.

5. Gross RE, Hussnagel CA: Coarctation of the aorta: Experimental studies regarding its surgical correction. N Engl J Med 1945;233:287.

6. White BD, McNamara DG, Bauersfeld SR, et al: Five-year postoperative results of first 500 patients with Blalock-Taussig anastomosis for pulmonary stenosis or atresia. Circulation 1956;14:512-519.

7. Taussig HB, Crocetti A, Eshaghpour E, et al: Long-time observations on the Blalock-Taussig operation: II. Second operations, frequency and results. Hopkins Med J 1971;129:258-273.

8. Lillihei CS, Cohen M, Warden HE, et al: Direct vision intracardiac surgical correction of the tetralogy of Fallot, pentalogy of Fallot, and pulmonary atresia defects: Report of first ten cases. Ann Surg 1955;142:418-445.

9. Kirklin JW, Blackstone EH, Pacifico AD, et al: Routine primary repair vs two-stage repair of tetralogy of Fallot. Circulation 1979;60:373-385.

10. Lundsgaard C, Van Slyke DD: Cyanosis, Medical Monographs. Baltimore, Williams & Wilkins Co, 1923, vol 2.

11. Potts WJ, Smith S, Gibson S: Anastomosis of the aorta to a pulmonary artery: Certain types in congenital heart disease. JAMA 1946;132:627-631.

12. Glenn WWL, Patine JF: Circulatory bypass of the right heart: I. Preliminary observations on the direct delivery of vena caval blood into the pulmonary arterial circulation — azygous vein-pulmonary artery shunt. Yale J Biol Med 1954;27:147.

13. Brock RC: The surgery of pulmonary stenosis. Br Med J 1949;2:399-406.

14. Waterston DJ: Fallot's tetralogy in children under one year of age. Rozhl Chir 1962;41:181.

15. Cooley DA, Hallman GL: Intrapericardial aorto-right pulmonary artery anastomosis. Surg Gynecol Obstet 1966;122:1084.

16. Blalock A, Hanlon CR: The surgical treatment of complete transposition of the aorta and pulmonary artery. Surg Gynecol Obstet 1950;90:1.

17. Dammann JF, McEachen JA, Thompson WM, et al: The regression of pulmonary vascular disease. Surg Gynecol Obstet 1952;92:213.

18. Taussig HB: Congenital Malformations of the Heart. New York, Commonwealth Foundation, 1947.

19. Adams FH, Blumenthal S, DuShane JW, et al: The review and revision of certification procedures in pediatric cardiology. J Med Educ 1972;47:796-805.

20. deLaval MR, McKay R, Jones M, et al: Modified Blalock-Taussig shunt: Use of subclavian artery orifice as flow regulator in prosthetic systemic pulmonary artery shunts. J Thorac Cardiovasc Surg 1981;81:112-119.

July 20, 1946
(*JAMA* 1946;131:963-967)

# Chapter 39

# Chloroquine for Treatment of Acute Attacks of Vivax Malaria

Major Harry Most
Captain Irving M. London
Captain Charles A. Kane
Captain Paul H. Lavietes
Captain Edmund F. Schroeder
and
Colonel Joseph M. Hayman, Jr.

Medical Corps, Army of the United States

During the recent war an intensive search for new antimalarial drugs was conducted in the course of which thousands of chemical substances were investigated under the auspices of the Office of Scientific Research and Development. Studies were designed to find drugs which might have one or more of the following properties: (*a*) true causal prophylaxis, (*b*) ability to effect complete cure following treatment, (*c*) greater efficacy than quinacrine and quinine in suppression and (*d*) greater efficacy than quinine and quinacrine in the treatment of acute clinical attacks.

The present report is concerned with chloroquine (SN 7618): 7-chloro-4-(4-diethylamino-1-methylbutylamino) quinoline, which is one of a series of new active antimalarial agents. Detailed studies of the antimalarial properties, pharmacology and toxicity of this drug have been carried out by numerous investigators, and undoubtedly the results of these studies will be generally available in the near future.[1] This paper is concerned principally with the clinical application of chloroquine to the treatment of the acute attack of vivax malaria.

## MATERIAL AND METHODS

The observations in this report were made at Moore General Hospital, which was designated by the Surgeon General as a center for the treatment and study of tropical diseases. This study represents the combined efforts of the clinical and of the laboratory staff of the Tropical Disease Section and of an adjunct laboratory ( the United States Public Health Service.

The patients were military personnel who ha acquired vivax infections in the Pacific or Mediterranea theaters of operation. All phases of the disease, fir attacks as well as early and late relapses, were repre sented by significant numbers of men.

All patients with acute clinical attacks of vivax malari were admitted to two special study wards for observatio and treatment with chloroquine. No patient was treate unless his blood smear was positive for malaria parasite and his temperature was over 100 F. No attempt selection of cases was made other than to equalize th groups on various treatment schedules with respect to th geographic area in which the infection was acquired an the active age of the disease. Thus, representative grouȷ of Pacific and Mediterranean infections were obtained well as representative numbers of patients with fir attacks or later relapses. Approximately 50 to 75 patien were included in each of the five treatment plans.

All treatment, for purposes of uniformity, was begu on the morning following the onset of the current attacl

From the Tropical Disease Section of Moore General Hospita Swannanoa, N. C.

1. Activity of a New Antimalarial Agent, Chloroquine (SN-7618 Statement Approved by the Board for Coordination of Malarial Studie J. A. M. A. **130**:1069 (April 20) 1946.

Parasite counts were done twice daily and continued until negative for three consecutive days. Plasma chloroquine levels were obtained frequently during and after treatment to determine the pattern of accumulation, stabilization and disappearance of the drug from the plasma. Temperatures were taken every four hours

TABLE 1.—*Representative Treatment Schedules*

| Plan A: 1.0 Gm. in One Day | |
|---|---|
| Day 1 8 a. m. | 0.4 Gm. |
| 12 noon | 0.3 Gm. |
| 5 p. m. | 0.3 Gm. |
| Total | 1.0 Gm. |
| Plan B: 1.5 Gm. Total During Four Days° | |
| Day 1 8 a. m. | 0.3 Gm. |
| 12 noon | 0.3 Gm. |
| Day 2 8 a. m. | 0.3 Gm. |
| Day 3 8 a. m. | 0.3 Gm. |
| Day 4 8 a. m. | 0.3 Gm. |
| Total | 1.5 Gm. |
| Plan C: 2.0 Gm. Total During Seven Days | |
| Day 1 8 a. m. | 0.4 Gm. |
| 12 noon | 0.2 Gm. |
| 5 p. m. | 0.2 Gm. |
| Day 2 8 a. m. | 0.2 Gm. |
| Day 3 8 a. m. | 0.2 Gm. |
| Day 4 8 a. m. | 0.2 Gm. |
| Day 5 8 a. m. | 0.2 Gm. |
| Day 6 8 a. m. | 0.2 Gm. |
| Day 7 8 a. m. | 0.2 Gm. |
| Total | 2.0 Gm. |

°This schedule is advocated for routine use.

during treatment and every fifteen minutes during a paroxysm. The clinical response was followed during daily rounds. All signs and symptoms possibly related to malaria or chloroquine were recorded in response to daily questioning. In addition, clinical and laboratory observations directed specifically toward recognizing possible toxic manifestations were made and will be referred to subsequently. All drugs were administered by an officer.

Following the completion of treatment and study in the wards, the patients were transferred to a convalescent area on the hospital grounds for observation until relapse or for one hundred and twenty days from the last day of treatment.

During this interval smears were examined twice weekly. In the event of parasitemia the temperature was recorded three times daily and smears were made every day. A temperature rise to over 100 F. by mouth associated with a positive smear was considered a relapse, and the patient was readmitted to a ward for further observation and treatment. Approximately 80 per cent of the relapses were direct admissions from the convalescent area following paroxysms with temperatures of from 103 to 105 F. The other 20 per cent were admitted as a result of temperature observations made during interval parasitemia. Of the latter group at least one half developed paroxysms shortly after admission to the ward. No patient was treated without coincident fever and parasitemia.

## PLANS OF TREATMENT

Protocols for treatment schedules were furnished by the Surgeon General. Following preliminary trials these were revised or extended with regard to the hour of

administration, the total dosage and the duration of treatment with the drug. The various regimens tested included treatment for one, three, four and seven days with total amounts of the drug ranging from 0.8 to 2.0 Gm. The value of each plan was judged by such factors as its efficacy in controlling fever and symptoms, the rate of disappearance of parasites from the blood, the interval prior to relapse and toxicity. Representative treatment schedules which have been found most satisfactory are presented in table 1. (Tablets of 0.1 Gm. and 0.3 Gm. of chloroquine were available and were used singly or in combination to supply the proper individual dose.)

## RESULTS

*Control of Parasites in the Blood.*—The rate of disappearance of parasites from the peripheral blood during the administration of chloroquine and the efficiency of the drug in this respect as compared with quinine and with quinacrine hydrochloride are shown in chart 1.

Within twenty-four hours after the first dose of drug, 38 per cent, 26 per cent and 9 per cent of the patients treated with chloroquine (plans A, B and C), quinacrine (2.8 Gm. in seven days) and quinine (29.0 Gm. in fourteen days) respectively had negative smears. At forty-eight hours the percentages of patients with negative smears in the treatment groups for the three drugs in the same order were 86, 77 and 45. At seventy-two hours, while 96 per cent of the patients treated with either chloroquine or quinacrine had negative smears, only 77 per cent of the patients treated with quinine were parasite free. At ninety-six hours practically all patients in the three groups were negative, although a few treated with quinine continued to have parasitemia for as long as one hundred and thirty-two hours. All the differences

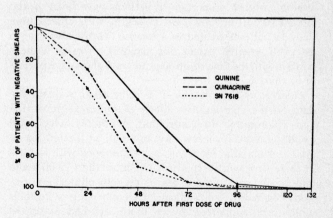

Chart 1.—Comparative rate of disappearance of parasites from the peripheral blood during treatment of attacks of vivax malaria with quinine (172 attacks), quinacrine (397 attacks) and chloroquine (293 attacks).

between the drugs observed in the percentage of negative smears at twenty-four and forty-eight hours are statistically significant. At seventy-two hours the difference between quinine and either quinacrine or chloroquine is significant, while there is no difference between quinacrine and chloroquine. The rate of parasite clearance, particularly during the first forty-eight hours of treatment of the acute attack of vivax malaria with all drugs we have studied is grossly related to the initial parasite density. The distribution of parasite counts at the beginning of treatment in categories of less than 1,000 per cubic millimeter, 1 to 5,000, 5 to 10,000 and above 10,000 are statistically equivalent for the three drugs represented in chart 1. Accordingly, the factor of initial parasite densities does not enter into the differences observed among the three drugs in the rate of parasite clearance.

Thus the peripheral blood becomes free from parasites more rapidly with chloroquine (plans A, B and C) than with either of the other drugs, the difference being more appreciable between chloroquine and quinine than between chloroquine and quinacrine. The superiority of chloroquine was manifest in vivax malaria of Mediterranean or of Pacific origin in first attacks as well as in relapses occurring at any stage of the disease.

*Control of Fever.*—The effectiveness of chloroquine in controlling fever during the treatment of the acute attack of vivax malaria is striking. In a total of 244 patients treated with the drug according to plans A, B and C as previously outlined, only 5 patients, or 2.1 per cent, had fever (temperature of 100 F. or more) the day after treatment was begun or subsequently. In contrast to these observations, treatment with quinine in 184 attacks and with quinacrine in 391 attacks was associated with fever on the second or on a later day in 8.7 and 8.0 per cent respectively of the patients treated. Thus, chloroquine is more effective than quinine or quinacrine in promptly controlling fever during treatment of acute attacks of vivax malaria. This superiority is manifest in infections both of Mediterranean and of Pacific origin regardless of the initial parasite density, and in Pacific infections regardless of whether the attack is the very first or a relapse at any stage of the disease. In delayed primary attacks a higher proportion of patients have fever on the second day after treatment is begun with chloroquine than do patients treated in a relapse. This is also true to an even greater extent for delayed primary attacks treated with quinine or quinacrine, as is shown graphically in chart 2.

*Control of Symptoms.*—It is difficult to evaluate the data on the comparative effects of quinine, quinacrine and chloroquine in controlling symptoms which are usually present for a few days in a patient treated for an attack of malaria. However, our experience with the use of these drugs in the treatment of more than 1,000 acute attacks of vivax malaria leaves us with clinical impressions regarding their efficacy in controlling symptoms which are supported by a more detailed statistical analysis.

Chloroquine is at least as good as quinine or quinacrine in the control of all symptoms and is superior to one or the other in the control of some symptoms.

Headache and backache are relieved more rapidly with chloroquine or quinine than with quinacrine. Quinine is more effective than quinacrine in the control of generalized aching but is not significantly better than chloroquine. Weakness, dizziness and light-headedness disappear more readily with chloroquine or quinacrine than with quinine. Nausea persists longer in patients treated with quinine than in those treated with the other

two. The effect of each of these drugs on the duration of vomiting, abdominal pain and abdominal tenderness is essentially the same.

*Toxicity.*—We have administered chloroquine to 365 patients with acute attacks of vivax malaria in total doses of 0.8 Gm. to 2.0 Gm. over a period of one to seven days. No major toxic manifestations were encountered clinically or in numerous laboratory studies. In no instance was it necessary to interrupt or discontinue treatment. In the therapeutic doses advocated in plans A, B or C chloroquine produced no gastrointestinal symptoms other than occasional mild nausea if the drug was taken by the patient in the fasting state. Dizziness and light headedness that were probably due to chloroquine occurred rarely. Tinnitus which could generally be ascribed to the drug rather than to the malaria itself did not occur. No visual disturbances were observed.

Considerable emphasis was placed on the search for cutaneous symptoms and signs which might be attributed to the toxicity of chloroquine. In consequence of this attention, cutaneous symptoms were elicited only after special questioning, which would rarely have been volunteered by the patients. As similar emphasis was not placed on cutaneous symptoms in patients treated with quinine or quinacrine, it is likely that the figures which follow represent an incidence of cutaneous symptoms in patients treated with chloroquine that is disproportionately high.

Fifty-six, or 20 per cent, of 284 patients treated with chloroquine developed pruritus during the course of treatment. The pruritus was occasionally generalized but more often localized, particularly on the palms and soles. In the majority of cases it was transitory and slight in degree. It occurred

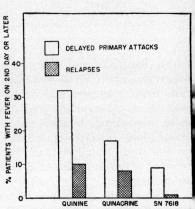

Chart 2.—Comparative efficiency of quinine, quinacrine hydrochloride and chloroquine in controlling fever during treatment of delayed primary attacks and relapses of vivax malaria.

most frequently within the first two days of treatment. Of the 56 patients who developed pruritus during their treatment with chloroquine, 50 had no coincident skin eruptions. Seven patients, or 2.4 per cent of the total number observed, developed erythema, urticaria or a mild papular eruption.

Thus, in the therapeutic doses advocated in plans A, B or C no significant symptoms of toxicity to chloroquine have been found. In comparing chloroquine with quinine or quinacrine one can say that chloroquine does not produce the disturbing symptoms of cinchonism produced by quinine and that it is just as safe as quinacrine. Further, it is preferable to quinacrine hydrochloride for patients with eczematoid dermatitis or atypical lichen planus, in whom the administration of the latter may produce an acute exacerbation of the dermatitis. This statement is based on our experiences in the treatment of this type of patient with chloroquine, which has never caused a flare-up of the underlying dermatitis.

## EFFECT OF DRUGS ON INTERVAL PRIOR TO RELAPSE FOLLOWING TREATMENT

Quinine, quinacrine hydrochloride and chloroquine do not materially influence the ultimate rate of relapse following treatment of the acute attack. Apparently the ultimate rate of relapse in large groups of patients is not affected by the age of the disease, the number of previous attacks, the total amount of drug administered or the duration of treatment. We have treated more than 500

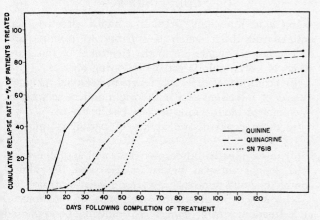

Chart 3.—Cumulative rates of relapse observed during a minimum of one hundred and twenty days following completion of treatment of the acute attack of vivax malaria of Pacific origin with quinine (76 patients), quinacrine hydrochloride (118 patients) and chloroquine (156 patients).

acute attacks of vivax malaria of Pacific and of Mediterranean origin in patients whom we have been able to follow to relapse, or for a minimum of one hundred and twenty days. The rates of relapse following treatment with quinine, quinacrine hydrochloride or chloroquine are from 75 to 85 per cent for infections of Pacific origin and approximately 35 per cent for those of Mediterranean origin. The cumulative rates of relapse following treatment of patients with acute attacks of vivax malaria of Pacific origin with the three drugs are shown in chart 3. At one hundred and twenty days 85 per cent, 80 per cent and 70 per cent of the patients treated with quinine, quinacrine hydrochloride and chloroquine respectively have had relapses.

The interval prior to relapse, however, and the distribution of the relapses which occur during the first two months after treatment are strikingly different for the groups of patients to whom the three drugs have been administered. These differences are presented graphically in chart 4.

During the first month after treatment, 54 per cent of the patients treated with quinine had relapses while 9 per cent had relapses after quinacrine hydrochloride and none had relapses after chloroquine. At forty days, relapses following treatment with chloroquine begin to occur, but these represented less than 1 per cent of the patients treated. In contrast to this small number, 67 per cent and 28 per cent of the patients had relapses at forty days after treatment with quinine and quinacrine hydro-

chloride respectively. At fifty days 72, 40 and 11 per cent of the patients had relapses after quinine, quinacrine hydrochloride and chloroquine respectively. In terms of the total number of relapses which occurred in one hundred and twenty days the percentages of patients who had relapses within fifty days were 85, 50 and 16

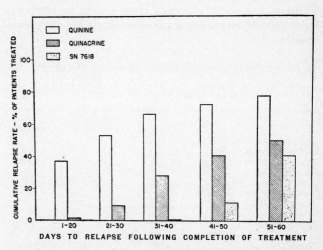

Chart 4.—Comparison of distribution of relapses which occur during the first sixty days after completion of treatment of the acute attack of vivax malaria of Pacific origin with quinine, quinacrine hydrochloride and chloroquine. The rates of relapse shown are cumulative.

respectively for the three drugs in the same order as before. Thus, of the total number of relapses which occur within one hundred and twenty days, more than three fourths will take place in the first fifty days after treatment with quinine, while only one half and one sixth will take place during the same time after treatment with quinacrine hydrochloride and chloroquine respectively. The median interval to relapse following treatment with quinine is twenty-four days, with quinacrine hydrochloride fifty days, and with chloroquine sixty-one days.

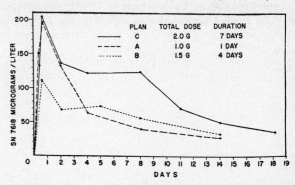

Chart 5.—Average plasma levels of chloroquine for 176 patients during and after treatment under plans A, B and C referred to in the text.

Since none of these drugs produce a complete cure of malaria, the drug of choice on the basis of the interval prior to relapse is the one which gives the longest mean interval, the greatest median interval for a large group of patients and the smallest number of short term relapses.

It is evident from the data presented that chloroquine is superior to both quinine and quinacrine hydrochloride in all these respects. The interval before relapse after treatment with chloroquine will be on the average at least five weeks longer than that after quinine and about two weeks longer than that after quinacrine hydrochloride. Only a negligible number of patients treated with chloroquine will have relapses during the first fifty days after treatment. Thus not only does chloroquine promptly control symptoms, fever and parasitemia, but, in addition, treatment with that drug results in freedom from another attack for a period of approximately two months.

TABLE 2.—*Relative Efficiency of Quinine, Quinacrine Hydrochloride and Chloroquine in Treatment of the Acute Attack of Vivax Malaria*

|  | Quinine | Quinacrine Hydrochloride | Chloroquine |
|---|---|---|---|
| Total amount of drug, Gm. | 29.0 | 2.8 | 1.0, 1.5, 2.0 |
| Duration of treatment, days | 14 | 7 | 1, 4, 7 |
| Rate of parasite clearance | + | +++ | ++++ |
| Control of fever |  |  |  |
| Pacific delayed primary | + | ++ | +++ |
| Pacific or Mediterranean relapses | ++ | ++ | ++++ |
| Interval to relapse |  |  |  |
| Median, days | 24 | 50 | 61 |
| Relapses, first 50 days, % | 85 | 50 | 16 |
| Relapses, total 120 days, % | 90 | 82 | 75 |
| Control of symptoms | ++ | +++ | ++++ |
| Toxicity | +++[c] | +[s] | +[sl] |

Abbreviations: c, cinchonism; s, eczematoid reactions in patients sensitive to quinacrine hydrochloride; s[l], slight, transitory pruritus; rare erythema or urticaria.

## PLASMA LEVELS

Blood was drawn to complete the plasma levels of the patients at such times as to determine the rate of accumulation, stabilization and disappearance of chloroquine from the plasma during and after treatment under various dosage regimens. The values obtained during and after treatment on schedules A, B and C of this report are presented in chart 5.

The minimal plasma concentration of chloroquine that is effective in terminating an acute attack of the disease has been shown to be in the range of 10 micrograms per liter. The levels observed during and after the treatment of patients according to plans A, B or C are well above this range.

No correlation has been found between variations observed in the levels of chloroquine in plasma obtained for persons receiving the same amount of drug and between their interval before relapse or their interval before the first parasitemia after completion of treatment.

## SUMMARY

The data presented in this paper on the relative efficiency of quinine, quinacrine hydrochloride and chloroquine are summarized and presented for ready reference in table 2.

## CONCLUSIONS

1. Chloroquine (SN 7618) is a highly effective, safe antimalarial drug which is superior to quinine and quinacrine hydrochloride in the treatment of the acute attack of vivax malaria for the following reasons:

(*a*) prompter control of fever in delayed primary attacks of infections of Pacific origin and in relapses of infections of Mediterranean or of Pacific origin.

(*b*) more rapid disappearance of parasites from the blood.

(*c*) more effective, prompter control of symptoms.

(*d*) longer interval before relapse and the almost complete abolition of relapses after a short remission.

(*e*) absence of disturbing symptoms of cinchonism, and freedom from danger of inducing eczematoid reactions in patients with eczematoid dermatitis or atypical lichen planus which is due to the administration of quinacrine hydrochloride.

(*f*) ease of administration in short term courses of one or four day schedules of treatment.

2. It is suggested that the acute attack of vivax malaria be treated routinely as follows:

One tablet (0.3 Gm.) of chloroquine is to be administered when the diagnosis of vivax malaria is established by a positive blood smear. This amount of the drug (0.3 Gm.) is to be repeated four hours after the first dose. One tablet (0.3 Gm.) is then to be given on each of the following three mornings. The total dose is five tablets totaling 1.5 Gm. of chloroquine administered during four days.

May 11, 1984
(JAMA 1984;251:2420-2422)

# The Ascent and Decline of Chloroquine*

David J. Wyler, MD

The article by Harry Most and colleagues in a 1946 issue of THE JOURNAL was the first report in the American medical literature on the efficacy of chloroquine (a 4-aminoquinoline) as an antimalarial agent in humans. This study of roughly 300 military personnel who had acquired vivax malaria during World War II demonstrated the superiority of chloroquine over quinacrine (the only synthetic antimalarial compound used clinically at that time) and quinine (an active alkyloid present in cinchona bark extracts, which were used for centuries). The report represented a milestone on the long and winding road toward a highly efficacious and relatively nontoxic synthetic antimalarial agent (reviewed in detail in reference 1) and began a period of about three decades during which the drug served an important role in malaria control programs in endemic areas.

Unfortunately, the days of chloroquine's greatest glory were numbered. In 1961, the first report[2] of chloroquine failure in patients with *Plasmodium falciparum* infection heralded a rapid spread of drug resistance among this species, a development that contributed to the resurgence of worldwide malaria.[3] Fortunately, however, the other three species of *Plasmodium* (*vivax, malariae,* and *ovale*) that infect man have retained their sensitivity to chloroquine. Today and for the forseeable future, the foremost challenge for developing new antimalarials is to keep pace with the rapid evolution of drug resistance in *P falciparum.*

### Then

Empirical treatment of malaria with extracts of the bark of the cinchona tree (indigenous in certain regions of South America) probably dates back several centuries — the first written record of its use appeared in 1633. In 1820, Pelletier and Caventou isolated quinine as one of the active alkaloids in the crude extracts, and the use of quinine became widespread thereafter. In 1891, Ehrlich, observing that plasmodia could be selectively stained with methylene blue, tested this dye and determined that it had weak antiplasmodial activity. Schulemann subsequently determined that side-chain substitutions strikingly enhanced the antiplasmodial potency of the acridine dye. Research efforts directed at synthesizing antimalarial agents gained momentum when quinine became unavailable in Germany in World War I. From these research efforts emerged quinacrine, which in the 1930s replaced quinine as the antimalarial of choice because of its superior efficacy. Its usefulness was, however, limited by toxicity, failure as a causal prophylaxis, and inability to provide radical cure for *P vivax* malaria. And so, research continued.

The synthetic 4-aminoquinoline family, of which chloroquine is a member, had its beginnings in the mid-1930s in Elberfeld, Germany, where H. Andersag, working at Bayer I. G. Farbenindustrie, synthesized Resorchin and Sontochin, chloroquine's ancestors. Bayer, through an international trade agreement, made these compounds available to the United States (Winthrop Chemical Company) and France (Sepia Co), but whereas the French tested Sontochin extensively on patients with vivax malaria in Tunisia, the United States largely disregarded the drugs. This oversight subsequently proved rather unfortunate, since the world supply of quinine was cut off to the Allies after the invasion of Pearl Harbor and a desperate need arose to identify new synthetic antimalarials for troops fighting in endemic areas. To address this need, the Board for the Coordination of Malaria Studies was formed to coordinate research efforts, which included screening more than 16,000 compounds in malarious laboratory animals.

In 1943, after the Allied invasion of North Africa, the US Army in Algiers acquired from the French, who had carried out the field studies, 500 tablets of Sontochin and the clinical data on patients with vivax malaria successfully treated with the drug. Once again, this lead toward an

From the Division of Geographic Medicine, Department of Medicine, Tufts University School of Medicine, Boston.

*A commentary on Most H, London IM, Kane CA, et al: Chloroquine for treatment of acute attacks of vivax malaria. *JAMA* 1946;131:963-967.

| Distribution of Chloroquine-Resistant Strains of *Plasmodium falciparum*\* | | | |
|---|---|---|---|
| **Latin America** | **Asia** | **Africa** | **Oceania** |
| Bolivia | Bangladesh | Burundi | Irian Jaya† |
| Brazil† | Burma | Comoras | Papua |
| Colombia | China | Kenya | New |
| Ecuador | (People's Republic) | Madagascar | Guinea† |
| French Guiana† | Kampuchea | Malawi | Solomon |
| Guyana | India (Assam) | Rwanda | Islands |
| Panama | Indonesia | Tanzania | Vanuatu |
| Peru | Lao People's | Zaire | |
| Surinam† | Democratic | Zambia | |
| Venezuela | Republic | | |
| | Malaysia | | |
| | Nepal | | |
| | Philippines | | |
| | Thailand | | |
| | Vietnam | | |

\*As of December 1983.
†Fansidar resistance also occurs in certain regions.

important class of synthetic antimalarials (the 4-amino-quinolines) was disregarded. In the same year, however, the massive US drug screening program uncovered compound SN (for survey number) 7618 — chloroquine — from among the 25 4-aminoquinoline derivatives synthesized by Winthrop Chemical Company. Thus, despite the initial lack of interest of the United States in the Bayer compounds provided to Winthrop in 1941 and the failure to recognize the importance of the French Sontochin field studies, the story ended happily. Curiously, the Germans had synthesized chloroquine before the war but had themselves disregarded it!

Clinical trials of chloroquine began in early 1944, and by 1946 more than 5,000 persons had been tested. The article by Most et al was the first report of its use for vivax malaria under field conditions and, soon thereafter, reports of its success in falciparum malaria emerged from trials at the 20th Hospital Group of the India-Burma Theater and other Allied military hospitals. The classic pharmacokinetic studies of Berliner and colleagues,[4] wherein they determined that a single 0.3-g (base) dose was sufficient to maintain blood levels adequate for malaria suppression, led to the application of chloroquine as a prophylactic agent. Recommendations for the therapeutic and prophylactic application of chloroquine for malaria were published in THE JOURNAL in 1946 by the Board for Coordination of Malarial Studies.[5]

An important additional development in malaria chemotherapy followed soon thereafter. Inasmuch as chloroquine, quinacrine, and quinine were effective against the intraerythrocytic parasites but not against the latent exoerythrocytic liver forms responsible for relapses in *P vivax* and *P ovale* malaria, the high relapse rates after treatment with these drugs (chart 3 of Most's article) were not surprising. The 8-aminoquinolines were known to be effective as antimalarials since the 1920s, and several such compounds were tested in the massive US drug screening campaign of the 1940s. In 1950, the first report appeared on the efficacy of compound SN 13272 — primaquine — in preventing relapses caused by *P vivax* in humans.[6] Chloroquine and primaquine thus comprised a potent method of treatment and became the mainstays in the therapy for and prevention of clinical malaria.

In the 1950s, the World Health Organization launched a global malaria eradication program that resulted in control of transmission in most temperate regions and some tropical areas as well. The major control modality was DDT spraying around houses, but in some areas this was not a practical control method because of the distinctive behavior of the local mosquito vectors. In such areas, chemoprophylaxis and treatment with chloroquine and other agents played a major role in disease control. Sadly, the eradication program collapsed for several reasons, including development of widespread DDT resistance among mosquito vectors and chloroquine resistance in *P falciparum* strains.

### Now

Chloroquine resistance in *P falciparum* stimulated a return to therapy with quinine. Since this alkaloid is most effective in rapidly lowering the parasitemia but often fails to completely eradicate the parasites, thus allowing for recrudescences, other drugs are being used in combination with quinine, including folate antimetabolites — the sulfonamides and pyrimethamine. A fixed-ratio combination of sulfadoxine (a long-acting sulfonamide) and pyrimethamine, marketed in the United States and elsewhere as Fansidar (Hoffman-LaRoche), has been successfully employed with quinine in treatment, and alone, as prophylaxis in areas wherein chloroquine-resistant strains of *P falciparum* occur (Table). Unfortunately, resistance to the antifolates has recently begun to be identified in Southeast Asia and elsewhere (Table), where quinine in combination with tetracycline is being employed successfully.[7] Since *P falciparum* may gradually also develop resistance to quinine, the longevity of this effective regimen is uncertain.

### The Future

The urgent need for new antimalarials against drug-resistant *P falciparum* remains a stimulus for continued research. By now the US Army has screened more than 250,000 compounds and two new classes of antimalarials have emerged, the quinoline methanols and the phenanthrene methanols.[8] At present, mefloquine (a quinoline methanol) has been subjected to field trials, the results of which indicate that it has great potential in both therapy and chemoprophylaxis.[9,10] Halofantrine (a phenanthrene methanol) is undergoing clinical trials, the results of which have not been published yet. The history of drug resistance in falciparum malaria suggests that these compounds may also enjoy only a short-lived glory and that cross-resistance with related compounds can be expected.

The development by Trager and Jensen[11] in 1976 of techniques for the continuous in vitro cultivation of *P falciparum* has facilitated in vitro drug screening and provided a method of studying the biochemistry of drug resistance. Evidence that ferriprotoporphyrin IX serves as a high-affinity receptor for chloroquine in infected erythrocytes[12] and that this receptor is deficient in red cells infected with chloroquine-resistant strains may provide a basis for novel approaches to the design of new agents. It is disturbing, however, that enthusias and funds for malaria research generally parallel US military involvement in endemic areas and are not sustained at the same level between wars. Furthermore, it is unfortunate that most pharmaceutical companies cannot justify supporting major research efforts directed at developing new antimalarials, since they cannot anticipate substantial financial returns on such investments.

It is encouraging that often the empiricism in medicine compensates where the science may fall short. It was recently discovered that an ancient and traditional Chinese treatment for malaria — extracts of the plant *Artemesia annua* — contains an alkaloid (qinhausu) that is highly active against drug-resistant *P falciparum* and

clinically efficacious.[13] Perhaps once again emerging from the distant past is a potent antimalarial for the future.

---

The reprinting of the article on chloroquine not only celebrates a landmark in modern medical history but also is a testimony to the senior author. Dr Most has been a talented investigator and a charismatic teacher whose dedication to medical problems of the Third World has been an inspiration to many. In addition, his commitment to keeping the medical community aware of the "neglected diseases" of the tropics has been an important service to mankind.

This report was supported in part by a grant from the Rockefeller Foundation.

## References

1. Coatney GR: Pitfalls in a discovery: The chronicle of chloroquine. *Am J Trop Med Hyg* 1963;12:121-128.

2. Moore DV, Lanier JE: Observations on two *Plasmodium falciparum* infections with an abnormal response to chloroquine. *Am J Trop Med Hyg* 1961;10:5-9.

3. Wyler DJ: Malaria-resurgence, resistance, and research. *N Engl J Med* 1983;308:875-878, 934-940.

4. Berliner RW, Earle DP, Taggart JV, et al: Studies on the chemotherapy of human malarias: VI. The physiological disposition, antimalarial activity, and toxicity of several derivatives of 4-aminoquinolines. *J Clin Invest* 1948;27:98-107.

5. Activity of a new antimalarial agent, chloroquine (SN 7618): Statement approved by the Board for Coordination of Malarial Studies. *JAMA* 1946;130:1069-1070.

6. Edgcomb JH, Arnold J, Yount EH, et al: Primaquine, SN 13272, a curative agent in vivax malaria: A preliminary report. *J Natl Malaria Soc* 1950;9:285-292.

7. Reacher M, Campbell C, Freeman J, et al: Drug therapy for *Plasmodium falciparum* malaria resistant to pyrimethamine-sulfadoxine (Fansidar): A study of alternate regimens in Eastern Thailand, 1980. *Lancet* 1981;2:1066-1068.

8. Canfield CJ: Antimalarial amino alcohol alternatives to mefloquine. *Acta Trop* 1980;37:232-237.

9. Doberstyn EB, Phintuyothin P, Noeypatimanondh S, et al: Single-dose therapy of falciparum malaria with mefloquine or pyrimethamine-sulfadoxine. *Bull WHO* 1979;57:275-279.

10. Pearlman EJ, Doberstyn EB, Sudsok S, et al: Chemosuppressive trials in Thailand: IV. The suppression of *Plasmodium falcipum* and *Plasmodium vivax* parasitemias by mefloquine (WR 142,490, a 4-quinolinemethanol). *Am J Trop Med Hyg* 1980;29:1131-1137.

11. Trager W, Jensen JB: Human malaria parasites in continuous culture. *Science* 1976;193:673-675.

12. Chou A, Chevli R, Fitch CD: Ferriprotoporphyrin IX fulfills the criteria for identification as the chloroquine receptor of malaria parasites. *Biochemistry* 1980;19:1543-1549.

13. Jiang JB, Li G, Guo X, et al: Antimalarial activity of mefloquine and qinghaosu. *Lancet* 1982;2:285-288.

Sept 21, 1946
(*JAMA* 1946;132:126-132)

# Chapter 40

# Nitrogen Mustard Therapy

## Use of Methyl-Bis(Beta-Chloroethyl)amine Hydrochloride and Tris(Beta-Chloroethyl)amine Hydrochloride for Hodgkin's Disease, Lymphosarcoma, Leukemia and Certain Allied and Miscellaneous Disorders

Louis S. Goodman, M.D., Salt Lake City

Maxwell M. Wintrobe, M.D., Salt Lake City

William Dameshek, M.D., Boston

Morton J. Goodman, M.D., Portland, Ore.

Major Alfred Gilman

Medical Corps, Army of the United States

and

Margaret T. McLennan, M.D., Salt Lake City

In a recent report the historical aspects of the use of β-chloroethyl amines (halogenated alkyl amines, nitrogen mustards) in the treatment of certain diseases of the blood-forming organs were presented and the chemical, pharmacologic, toxicologic and animal experimental aspects of these compounds reviewed.[1] The interested reader is referred to that report for orientation.

The present preliminary communication concerns the clinical use of halogenated alkyl amines in the treatment of lymphosarcoma, Hodgkin's disease, leukemia and a limited number of allied and miscellaneous disorders. In all, 67 patients have been studied. These include 7 patients[2] treated by L. S. Goodman and Alfred Gilman at the New Haven Hospital; 34 patients treated by M. M. Wintrobe and Margaret T. McLennan at the Salt Lake County General Hospital; 16 patients treated by William Dameshek, Boston, and 10 patients treated by M. J. Goodman, Portland, Ore. The types of diseases treated are shown in the accompanying table. The youngest patient was 3 years of age and the oldest 76. The sexes were approximately equally represented in the series. Twenty-six of the 67 patients are still alive and under observation or therapy.

No attempt will be made at this time to analyze statistically the results obtained or to compare them with those observed after roentgen irradiation. The reasons for this are (1) the small number of patients in the series, (2) the prior use of radiation treatment for most patients, (3) the terminal nature and radiation refractory character of the disease in the majority of cases and (4) the small number of patients in the early stage of their disease. Rather, our purposes in this report are mainly to summarize briefly the clinical experiences obtained and to present the considered opinions of the various investi-

The Jane Coffin Childs Fund for Medical Research, Yale University defrayed part of the expenses of this investigation.

The chemicals employed in this study were generously supplied by Dr. Milton C. Winternitz, Chairman, Committee on the Treatment of Gas Casualties.

Reports of several of the investigations referred to either have not been published or have not been recorded in the open literature. The date given is the year in which the work was carried out.

Dr. L. S. Goodman, Dr. Wintrobe and Dr. McLennan are from the University of Utah School of Medicine; Dr. Dameshek is from Tufts College Medical School; Dr. Morton J. Goodman is from the University of Oregon Medical School, and Major Gilman is from the Medical Research Division, Edgewood Arsenal.

The following physicians have generously cooperated in providing cases for study: Drs. Gustaf E. Lindskog, Grover F. Powers, Francis G. Blake, G. G. Richards, M. J. Taylor and L. A. Wheelwright.

1. Gilman, A., and Philips, F. S.: The Biological Actions and Therapeutic Applications of the B-Chloroethyl Amines and Sulfides, Science 103:409-415, 1946.

2. Gilman, A.; Goodman, L. S.; Philips, F. S., and Dougherty, T. 1943.

gators concerned as to the status and the potential value of the β-chloroethylamines in the syndromes enumerated. In subsequent more complete communications, comparison with the results of radiation therapy will be made and detailed hematologic and pathologic data will be presented.

## CHEMISTRY AND DOSAGE

The chemistry and the pharmacodynamics of the nitrogen mustards and particularly of the two compounds employed in this study have been described recently.[1] The water soluble hydrochloride salts of the tris(β-chloroethyl)amine and methyl-bis(β-chloroethyl)amine were injected intravenously. The doses of the two were the same.

The standard single dose of 0.1 mg. per kilogram of body weight was injected daily or every second day until three to six doses were administered, but the single dose never exceeded 8 mg. This was considered to represent the initial treatment required to induce remissions in suitable cases. In an occasional very ill patient the single dose was reduced to 0.05 mg. per kilogram. Subsequent treatment varied with each patient, depending on the clinical response, the hemopoietic status, the duration and completeness of remission and the like. As a rule an additional dose of nitrogen mustard was not given oftener than every six to eight weeks, and subsequent treatments usually consisted of but two to four doses.

## METHOD AND TECHNIC OF ADMINISTRATION

The nitrogen mustards must be administered only by the intravenous route, great caution being observed to prevent extravasation of the solution. The solution was freshly made by adding 0.9 per cent sterile aqueous sodium chloride solution to sterile glass bottles each containing exactly 10 mg. of the dry salt. Injection was accomplished within five minutes after preparation of the solution, because of the rapid hydrolysis which may occur, with consequent loss of efficacy. In the majority of the 20 patients receiving tris(β-chloroethyl)amine hydrochloride the direct syringe method was employed, the dose being contained in 25 to 50 cc. of saline solution. Pain during injection and subsequent thrombophlebitis of the injected vein were frequent with this technic. In all other cases 10 mg. of the drug was dissolved in 10 cc. of saline solution (1 mg. per cubic centimeter), and the calculated dose was injected into the rubber tubing during the course of an intravenous infusion of glucose or saline solution, special attention being given to assure free and rapid flow of the infusion and rapid injection of the nitrogen mustard solution. Considerable caution was exercised to prevent the solution from touching the skin or mucous membranes of the patient or physician. All patients were hospitalized, no ambulatory therapy being attempted.

## CLINICAL RESULTS AND REPORT OF CASES

*Hodgkin's Disease.*—Twenty-seven patients with this disease, verified pathologically by biopsy, were treated with nitrogen mustard, 22 with methyl-bis(β-chloroethyl)amine hydrochloride and 5 with tris(β-chloroethyl)amine hydrochloride. All but 3 had previously had radiation therapy. The majority were in the advanced or

terminal stage of their illness and also were considered resistant to roentgen irradiation. In nearly every case some benefit was obtained from chemotherapy. Indeed, the clinical results were sometimes dramatic. Whether the halogenated alkyl amines are superior to radiation treatment cannot be stated at this time, but sufficient experience has been obtained to permit the conclusion that remissions may be induced in patients whose disease no longer responds to roentgen irradiation. In fact, in 3 patients sensitivity to irradiation may have been restored after a course of nitrogen mustard. In 1 patient who had Hodgkin's disease for seven years and who was still responsive to radiation therapy a more satisfactory remission was obtained from nitrogen mustard than from any previous course of radiation treatment. In another patient who did not respond adequately either to radiation therapy or to halogenated alkyl amine therapy alone, good results were obtained by combining the two agents.

In addition to rapid partial or complete disappearance of Hodgkin's tumor masses, most patients experienced improvement in appetite, weight, strength and sense of well-being; fever, if present, disappeared. A number of persons were able to return to work. Symptom free

*Distribution by Disease of Cases in Which Nitrogen Mustard Therapy Was Used*

| | |
|---|---|
| Hodgkin's disease | 27 |
| Lymphosarcoma | 13 |
| Chronic myelocytic leukemia | 7 |
| Acute and subacute myeloblastic leukemia | 4 |
| Chronic lymphocytic leukemia | 5 |
| Subacute lymphoblastic leukemia | 3 |
| Miscellaneous diseases° | 8 |
| Total | 67 |

°Melanosarcoma (2), undiagnosed retroperitoneal mass, undiagnosed tumor (probably Hodgkin's disease), reticuloendotheliosis, metastatic mammary carcinoma, metastatic cervical carcinoma and giant follicular lymphoma.

remissions varying from two weeks to at least seven months have been observed.

The following abbreviated case report serves to illustrate a dramatic remission induced by therapy with the tris(β-chloroethyl)amine hydrochloride in a radiation refractory case of terminal Hodgkin's disease.

CASE 1.—L. W., a woman aged 33, a housewife, was first seen in 1941 because of axillary lymphadenopathy, and biopsy revealed Hodgkin's disease. Her father had died of Hodgkin's disease, her mother of polycythemia. In rapid succession nodes appeared in the axillas, the neck and the mediastinum. X-ray therapy was given with initial excellent but with subsequent poorer results. In the summer of 1942 dyspnea and cough developed, and thoracentesis was required for pleural effusion. Complete motor and sensory paralysis of the right arm appeared in the spring of 1943, and the limb gradually increased threefold in size. Cough, weakness and dyspnea became worse, lymph node masses increased, and in the fall of 1943 the patient was bedridden and failed to respond to further x-ray treatment.

On admission to the hospital in December 1943 the patient was extremely ill and very cyanotic, with a shallow dry cough and gasping respiration. The face and neck were greatly swollen and distorted, and the left side of the neck bulged with a hard irregular mass extending into the supraclavicular fossa. There was pitting edema over the upper thorax. Both axillas were occupied by hard irregular masses of nodes, extending on the right side to the lower chest wall. The percussion note was dull to flat over both thoraces, and breath sounds were diminished. The breasts were large and edematous. The right arm was greatly swollen and completely paralyzed. There was no enlargement of the spleen or liver and no inguinal lymphadenopathy.

Roentgen examination disclosed no mediastinal mass, but decided infiltration of the lower two thirds of both lungs was present. Blood values were not remarkable except for a mild eosinophilia and a total absence of lymphocytes. The temperature ranged from 98 to 103 F. and the pulse from 100 to 140.

Treatment consisted of four doses of *tris*(β-chloroethyl)amine hydrochloride, 0.1 mg. per kilogram of body weight every other day, given intravenously by the direct syringe method. Improvement started after the second dose and continued over a period of two weeks. The patient felt much better, the fever and cyanosis disappeared, the dyspnea and cough improved, the lymph node masses shrank 60 to 75 per cent, the breasts became much smaller, the disfiguring edema of the face and

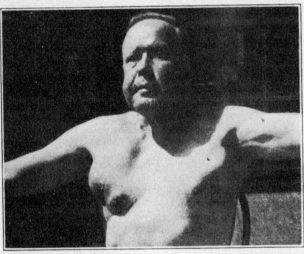

Fig. 1 (case 2).—Appearance in terminal lymphosarcoma in the radiation resistant stage four days after initiation of *tris*(β-chloroethyl)amine hydrochloride therapy. Improvement in well-being, strength, appetite and temperature but no visible change in size of tumor masses.

neck entirely receded, and the hugely swollen right arm returned almost to normal size. Roentgenograms of the chest revealed no change in the pulmonary infiltration. Treatment was well tolerated and only minimal blood changes occurred (a slight reduction in the hemoglobin content and red blood cell count, a moderate decrease in the number of white blood cells).

The dramatic therapeutic remission persisted until it was interrupted at the end of four weeks by a sudden severe attack of pulmonary edema which quickly resulted in death. Postmortem examination was not obtained.

*Lymphosarcoma.*—Thirteen patients with lymphosarcoma were treated with nitrogen mustard, 5 with *tris*(β-chloroethyl)amine hydrochloride and 8 with methyl-*bis*(β-chloroethyl)amine hydrochloride. Most of the cases were terminal. In all but 4, prior radiation therapy had been given. Of the patients who had received such treatment, nearly all had reached the radiation resistant stage of their disease.

The clinical results observed were qualitatively similar to those previously described for Hodgkin's disease but were more frequently unsuccessful. Therapeutic remissions, when obtained, lasted from three weeks to several months; but with each recurrence renewed therapy seemed to be less and less effective, and the remissions became shorter. At least 5 complete failures were encountered without obvious explanation for the lack of satisfactory response. It was impossible to predict beforehand which patients would or would not respond satisfactorily. This was likewise the experience with the nitrogen mustard therapy of experimental lymphosarcoma in mice,[3] in which syndrome it was also observed that the tumor cells became more resistant to the chemicals with successive courses of treatment.

Dramatic results against lymphosarcoma in the terminal stages were observed in several patients near death. In 1 patient, sensitivity to radiation was restored by halogenated alkyl amine therapy. As was also true for Hodgkin's disease, satisfactory responses were obtained even in radiation resistant patients. In addition to definite reduction or complete clinical disappearance of lymphosarcoma masses and the signs and symptoms attributable thereto, the therapeutically induced remissions frequently were associated with an improvement in appetite, strength and weight and with reduction of fever and a sense of well-being.

The following brief case report serves to illustrate the salutary effect of β-chloroethylamine therapy in terminal lymphosarcoma which had become refractory to radiation. The case is of further interest because it is the first in which nitrogen mustard therapy was employed and also because it illustrates the severe toxic effects which excessive dosage produces.

CASE 2.—J. D., a man aged 48, a silversmith, entered the hospital[4] in August 1942 in the terminal stages of lymphosarcoma. He had been seen first in January 1941 complaining of pain and swelling due to a mass on the right side of the neck. Physical examinations and biopsy revealed lymphosarcoma, primary in the tonsil. Radiation therapy was instituted in March 1941 with considerable reduction in the tumor mass. Palliative local resection was performed in June 1941. The patient remained well until December 1941, when masses appeared on both sides of the neck. A second course of x-ray therapy gave relief, but by May 1942 a rapid enlargement and spread of the tumor masses had occurred, the axilla, mediastinum, face and submental region being involved. Additional therapy was given almost continuously, but the masses increased in size.

Physical examination revealed the aforementioned tumor masses (fig. 1), cyanosis, venous dilatation and edema of the face and the upper part of the chest, anisocoria and paresis of the right facial nerve. Chewing and swallowing had become almost impossible, and the axillary nodes prevented adduction of the arms. The spleen and liver were not enlarged. The patient was severely orthopneic, and a tracheotomy set was kept close at hand for immediate use. The results of laboratory examinations were not remarkable, and the blood picture was within normal limits.

Ten consecutive daily doses of *tris*(β-chloroethyl)amine

3. Dougherty, T.; Gilman, A., and Goodman, L. S., 1942. Unpublished observations.

4. Dr. Gustaf E. Lindskog, Department of Surgery, Yale University School of Medicine, gave the authors permission to study and report this case.

hydrochloride were injected intravenously by the direct syringe method, 0.1 mg. per kilogram of body weight per dose. (This dosage, subsequently found to be too large, was arrived at on the basis of results obtained in experimental lymphosarcoma in mice.)[3] On the fourth day of treatment the patient felt better, was able to swallow and could sleep lying down. By the tenth and last day of treatment the cervical masses were no longer palpable, and the axillary masses receded completely four days later (fig. 2). All signs and symptoms due to the disease disappeared.

Tumor masses recurred after one month, and a second course of treatment (three consecutive daily doses) was given. Improvement was transitory and a third course (six consecutive daily doses) was administered three weeks later without sustained benefit. However, at the time of death, three months after the start of therapy and three weeks after the third course of chemotherapy was completed, the tumor masses were relatively small. Death was hastened by the untoward effects of the drug on the bone marrow, especially thrombopenia.

The panmyelopathy caused by the first course of the drug may serve to illustrate the toxic potentialities of the nitrogen mustards.[5] The earliest action was observed on the circulating lymphocytes, which disappeared completely by the time of the fifth daily dose and then slowly returned. The total white blood cell count fell gradually and progressively from the time of the first daily injection until a low of 200 cells per cubic millimeter was reached (despite two blood transfusions) one month after the initiation of therapy, at which time the differential count indicated 52 per cent lymphocytes, 4 per cent monocytes, 12 per cent eosinophils and 32 per cent neutrophilic granulocytes. The total leukocyte count returned to pretreatment values over a three week period. Despite the leukocyte picture, the clinical signs and symptoms of agranulocytosis were absent except for moderate fever. Thrombocytopenia was most pronounced (22,000 platelets per cubic millimeter) at the height of the leukopenia and was accompanied with gingivitis, periodontitis and cutaneous purpura. The platelets rose to normal values over a three week period. At no time was anemia more than moderate. The red blood cell count did not decline until the first course of therapy was completed and the lowest values (red blood cells 3.28 million, hemoglobin 9.9 Gm. per hundred cubic centimeters) occurred simultaneously with those for leukocytes and platelets. Recovery from anemia paralleled that for the other formed blood elements and was hastened by blood transfusions.

An instance of complete failure of halogenated alkyl amine therapy to influence the course of a radiation refractory and terminal case of lymphosarcoma is illustrated in the following brief case report:

CASE 3.—E. W., a woman aged 42, a housewife, was first seen in September 1943, when she complained of severe pruritus, substernal pain, cough and dyspnea. Study disclosed a rapidly growing mediastinal lymphosarcoma, verified pathologically by biopsy (cervical node). Radiation therapy gave temporary relief but finally failed to retard the growth of the mediastinal mass. Observations on final hospital admission in February 1944 included fever, generalized severe pruritus, cough, dyspnea, bilateral pleural effusion, cervical nodes and the intrathoracic mass. The blood picture was not remarkable. Five doses of methyl-bis(β-chloroethyl)amine hydrochloride were given (0.1 mg. per kilogram of body weight per dose, every other day). There was no objective or subjective improvement; the ingravescent course progressed, and death occurred five weeks after the start of nitrogen mustard therapy. Postmortem examination

verified the diagnosis of lymphosarcoma, which was found to involve the lungs, pleura, pericardium, myocardium, diaphragm and ribs.

*Chronic Leukemias.*—Twelve patients with chronic leukemia have been treated with nitrogen mustards, 10 with methyl-bis(β-chloroethyl)amine hydrochloride and 2 with tris(β-chloroethyl)amine hydrochloride. Seven cases were of the chronic myelocytic type, and 4 of chronic lymphocytic leukemia. In 6 terminal or nearly terminal cases the treatment was of no appreciable value. In 6 other patients, however, the results of treatment with the β-chloroethylamines were comparable with those obtained with radiation therapy. In addition, even when concomitant clinical and symptomatic benefits did not occur, nitrogen mustard often caused a reduction in the leukocyte count, a more normal differential formula, improvement in the appearance of the bone marrow and more persistence in the effect of blood transfusion. In 1 patient with chronic lymphocytic leukemia the signs and symptoms of hypermetabolism were considerably relieved. Further experience is needed to determine the status of these agents in chronic leukemias.

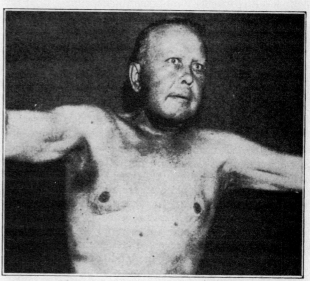

Fig 2. (case 2).—Eight days later and two days after the last dose. Complete disappearance of tumor masses in axillas, neck, jaw and thorax, with decided improvement in the patient's condition.

The following case abstract serves to illustrate the beneficial effect of nitrogen mustard therapy on a patient with chronic myelocytic leukemia:

CASE 4.—B. C., a white man aged 52 with typical chronic myelocytic leukemia of four years' duration, had received radiation therapy at approximately yearly intervals from 1941 to 1944 inclusive, with remission of symptoms following each course of therapy. In May 1945 fatigability had returned, the leukocyte count was 293,000 and the red cell count was 3.11 million per cubic millimeter. The spleen extended 3 cm. below the umbilicus and the liver 5 cm. below the costal margin. Five doses of methyl-bis(β-chloroethyl)amine hydrochloride (0.1 mg. per kilogram per dose) were given over a two week period, and two blood transfusions of 500 cc. each were administered during this same period. Six weeks later the patient had no anemia (hematocrit 50) and the leukocyte count was 25,800 per cubic millimeter. The spleen and liver had decreased appreciably in size. The patient had gained 10 pounds (4.5 Kg.) in

---

5. A complete description of this case has appeared elsewhere.[2]

weight and was able to do light work. Eight weeks later (four months after the start of therapy) the patient was still feeling well, was doing regular work and maintaining the gain in weight but because of a slight anemia (hematocrit 40) and a leukocyte count of 50,400 per cubic millimeter he was hospitalized and given four more doses of the drug. Following this second course of therapy he felt well, the hematocrit again rose and the leukocyte count decreased to 11,300. Two months later he was found to be slightly anemic (hematocrit 37) and the leukocyte count had risen to 103,000. Three more injections of drug were given and again an increased hematocrit and decreased leukocyte count were obtained. At the present time, nine months after the first course of therapy, the patient is in a state of fairly complete remission, both hematologically and clinically.

*Subacute and Acute Leukemias.*—Seven patients with acute or subacute leukemia were treated with nitrogen mustards, 5 with *tris*(β-chloroethyl)amine hydrochloride and 2 with methyl-*bis*(β-chloroethyl)amine hydrochloride. Four cases were myeloblastic in type and 3 were lymphoblastic. The clinical results in most of the cases were not particularly encouraging, but in 3 partial clinical and hematologic remissions were obtained. In 1 patient with subacute lymphoblastic leukemia a brief but definite clinical remission with a decrease in the total leukocyte count and in the size of the spleen occurred, but the ultimate fatal outcome was only briefly postponed. The decrease in thrombocytes caused by halogenated alkyl amines was a complicating factor in the use of this agent in several patients with platelet values which were already quite low. Improvement in the white blood cell count, differential formula or bone marrow picture was not always paralleled by clinical or subjective gain. Indeed, in at least 2 patients there is the possibility that β-chloroethylamine therapy may have accelerated the fatal termination.

The brief case report which follows illustrates the failure of nitrogen mustard therapy in a patient with subacute myeloblastic leukemia:

Case 5.—S. C., a woman aged 66, a housewife, was hospitalized in October 1943 in the terminal phase of subacute myeloblastic leukemia. Symptoms had existed for five months; they were becoming progressively worse and included fatigue, dyspnea, anorexia and dizziness. Examination revealed moderate fever and tachycardia, pallor, cutaneous purpura and ecchymoses. The spleen and liver were not palpable, and there was no lymphadenopathy. Examination of the blood revealed moderately severe anemia (hematocrit 21) with 68,000 leukocytes (89 per cent myeloblasts) and 50,000 platelets per cubic millimeter. Study of the bone marrow revealed almost a "pure culture" of primitive cells (many of them peroxidase positive) and numerous other cells of the granular series.

After several blood transfusions, *tris*(β-chloroethyl)amine hydrochloride 0.1 mg. per kilogram of body weight was given every other day for three doses intravenously by the direct syringe method. Severe nausea, vomiting and weakness resulted. There occurred a rapid fall in the total leukocyte count over a period of one week (to 600 cells per cubic millimeter) with an absolute and relative reduction in primitive cells. But the complete disappearance of platelets and rapid progression of the anemia were concomitant (but not necessarily causally related) features. As the granulocytes and platelets returned during the second week after therapy, more differentiation into myelocytes and metamyelocytes was observed. Although there was a specific effect on proliferating primitive cells, this was short lived and not associated with objective or subjective clinical improvement. The condition of the blood soon deteriorated, cerebral hemorrhage occurred one month after completion of nitrogen mustard therapy, and the patient died shortly thereafter.

Postmortem examination revealed hyperplasia of the bone marrow, diffuse hyperplasia of the lymph nodes of the abdomen and pelvis, multiple punctate cutaneous, pleural and peritoneal hemorrhages and fresh intracranial hemorrhage. The bone marrow was entirely filled with a growth of undifferentiated cells suggesting atypical plasma cells. Similar cells were found in the lymph nodes, spleen, liver, kidney and skin.

*Miscellaneous Neoplasms.*—Eight miscellaneous diseases were treated with halogenated alkyl amines. No observable benefit resulted for 2 patients with melanosarcoma. However, in 1 patient in whom the tumor appeared as a diffuse infiltrating mass in the submaxillary region, chemotherapy with five consecutive daily doses of *tris*(β-chloroethyl)amine hydrochloride resulted in edema around the mass which delineated it from uninvolved tissue and permitted relatively simple enucleation at resection. A patient with a large retroperitoneal mass of unknown etiology failed to respond to treatment with nitrogen mustard. A second patient with an undiagnosed tumor (probably Hodgkin's disease) did not respond to therapy. A patient with reticuloendotheliosis received temporary relief from excruciating pain in the bone, and the leukemoid blood picture improved; but the ingravescent course and the ultimately fatal outcome were not altered. An elderly woman with pleural metastases from a mammary carcinoma which had been resected two years previously required less frequent thoracenteses after chemotherapy with four consecutive daily doses of *tris*(β-chloroethyl)amine hydrochloride, but the causal relationship could not be established with certainty. The clinical course of a patient with carcinoma of the cervix and mediastinal metastases was unaltered by treatment with nitrogen mustard. An elderly woman with giant follicular lymphoma exhibited a moderate reduction in the size of the lymph nodes and spleen after six consecutive daily doses of methyl-*bis*(β-chloroethyl)amine hydrochloride but experienced no corresponding clinical benefit and died three weeks later.

The results of the limited experience here described with neoplasms other than lymphomas and leukemias suggest that the halogenated alkyl amines employed are fairly specific in their tissue affinities, a tentative conclusion supported by animal studies employing experimental virus tumors in fowl,[6] testicular interstitial cell carcinoma in mice, and mammary carcinoma in mice.[3]

### TOXICITY

*Immediate Local and Early Systemic Effects.*—Local extravasation during the injection of solutions of the β-chloroethylamine hydrochlorides resulted immediately in pain and subsequently in tender indurated swellings which resolved slowly. Thrombophlebitis of the injected veins was observed in a number of cases but was probably less prone to occur with methyl-*bis*(β-chloroethyl)amine hydrochloride than with *tris*(β-chloroethyl)amine hydro-

6. Duran-Reynals, F.; Goodman, L. S., and Gilman, A., 1942. Unpublished observations.[2]

chloride. The incidence of thrombophlebitis as well as of pain during administration was decreased by injecting the nitrogen mustard solutions into the lumen of the rubber tubing while an intravenous infusion was flowing rather than into the vein by the direct syringe technic.

Nausea and vomiting were commonly observed after nitrogen mustard therapy, occurring within one to three hours after the injection and subsiding within a few hours. Nausea and vomiting were more apt to follow the first one or two injections in a course. Anorexia was infrequent and transient. Diarrhea was not observed in the patients of this series. Preliminary sedation with a barbiturate and the withholding of food (usually an overnight fast) prior to treatment tended to decrease untoward gastrointestinal symptoms. Febrile response to the therapy was not observed, but 1 patient had a chill shortly after treatment.

*Late Systemic Effects.*—The toxic effects of the halogenated alkyl amines on the blood and bloodforming organs have been carefully investigated in a variety of laboratory animals and in man. As numerous reports[1] are available in this field, it is necessary here only to summarize briefly what may occur during the therapeutic administration of these agents to man. The toxic effects of the β-chloroethylamine hydrochlorides on the hemopoietic tissues are in some respects merely extensions of the therapeutic effects. Although the chemicals seem to have a selective action on primitive cells and abnormal hemopoiesis, in sufficiently large doses the compounds affect all elements of the bone marrow, producing a decided leukopenia and thrombocytopenia and a moderate normochromic anemia. The objective in treatment against lymphomas and leukemia is to keep the dosage within the relatively narrow range of safety, so that maximal salutary clinical results can be obtained with a minimal untoward effect on the formed elements of the blood. The dosage schedules employed were specifically designed to accomplish this end. Nevertheless the leukotoxic action was usually evident. Lymphopenia and neutropenia of moderate degree occurred in most patients within the first week or two after a course of therapy, the lymphopenia sometimes appearing first. Mild reduction in the volume of packed erythrocytes was also observed in a number of patients and reached its peak in about three weeks; but frequently a preexisting anemia improved as a result of the beneficial effect of the nitrogen mustards, for example on myelophthisic anemia.

Detailed and repeated laboratory tests (urine, renal function, liver function, blood chemistry and others) failed to indicate any abnormal or untoward responses to the β-chloroethylamines in the doses employed, other than those previously enumerated.

In the 2 patients who were the first ever treated with *tris*(β-chloroethyl)amine hydrochloride, before optimal dosages could be determined for man, toxic hemopoietic effects were observed in the following sequence: the complete disappearance of circulating lymphocytes, definite leukopenia and granulocytopenia (without mucosal lesions or other signs or symptoms of agranulocytosis except fever), thrombocytopenia of severe grade with purpura, and moderate anemia. Repeated blood transfusions were necessary, and the return of blood values to pretreatment levels required several weeks.

## CLINICAL STATUS OF THE NITROGEN MUSTARDS

The halogenated alkyl amines would appear to be able to produce the same qualitative clinical results in Hodgkin's disease, lymphosarcoma and leukemia as does radiation therapy. In general these chemicals have the same "total" effect on lymphoid cells and those of the bone marrow and on the hyperplasia of the reticulum cells in Hodgkin's disease as does radiation therapy. Whether they have any imperative advantages over the best possible type of radiation therapy remains to be determined. It is fairly certain that the β-chloroethylamines are capable of producing salutary effects and even therapeutic remissions in patients who have become resistant to roentgen irradiation. However, the term "resistant to roentgen irradiation" is variously employed by radiologists, and it was not always ascertainable in the cases herein reported whether the term was truly applicable in the sense that the tumor cells would no longer respond to properly applied radiation.

In 4 patients there was evidence that sensitivity of the tumor tissue to radiation therapy returned after a course of nitrogen mustard therapy. This is not too unexpected, as new generations of tumor cells are involved. In 1 patient who was unresponsive either to radiation or to nitrogen mustard therapy a favorable response was obtained when the two agents were used simultaneously.

Whether the β-chloroethylamines can or should either replace or supplement radiation therapy in any or all categories of cases in which they have been found effective cannot be stated at this time, particularly because the majority of the 67 patients concerned in the report were in the terminal stages of their disease. Nor can it yet be stated whether halogenated alkyl amine treatment may be expected to yield remissions as complete or as lasting as does radiation therapy. The question as to whether the chemicals should be used as agents of choice in "fresh" (i. e. previously untreated) cases also remains unsettled, but there is sufficient evidence to warrant investigation of this problem. Obviously there is as yet no adequate backlog of clinical experience with the nitrogen mustards, such as exists for radiation therapy, to serve as a basis for judging their value in comparison with other therapeutic measures.

As a rule, local and immediate systemic reactions would appear to be less severe after chemotherapy with the β-chloroethylamines than after irradiation, and dermatitis due to the latter is avoided. Certainly therapy should prove to be less expensive, particularly in cases in which ambulatory treatment schedules would be feasible. No costly equipment is required. It must be emphasized, however, that the margin of safety in the use of the nitrogen mustards is quite narrow. The maximal tolerated dose (that which does not cause harmful hemopoietic effects) is usually not much larger than the optimal therapeutic dose. Considerable care must therefore be exercised in the matter of dosage, and repeated examination of the blood is mandatory in all cases as a guide to subsequent therapy.

The answers to numerous other questions which occur to investigator and reader alike cannot even be approximated at present. For example, optimal dosage schedules remain to be determined both for initial therapy and for prophylactic treatment during remissions. Various combinations and schedules of two or more agents (radiation, halogenated alkyl amines, radioactive phosphorus, arsenicals and the like) may prove superior to any one agent alone. The indications and contraindications for the use of nitrogen mustards cannot be stated definitively. Although immediate but transitory side effects may be more prominent with *tris*(β-chloroethyl)amine than with methyl-*bis*(β-chloroethyl)amine, further comparison of the clinical efficacy of these two agents is not as yet possible. Numerous congeners of the two halogenated alkyl amines employed in this study are known, and a number of them are available. It is possible that certain of these congeners may be more selective and potent in action and less toxic than the β-chloroethylamines employed up to the present. Certainly the subject is deserving of investigation.

Encouraging clinical results, sometimes dramatic, have been obtained particularly in Hodgkin's disease and lymphosarcoma and occasionally in chronic leukemia. It is not understood why some patients respond and others do not. Varied results have been seen in acute and subacute leukemia. Giant follicular lymphoma (1 case) did not respond to therapy nor did a small group of miscellaneous disorders including melanosarcoma and reticuloendotheliosis. Like roentgen irradiation, the β-chloroethylamines do not constitute a cure but only offer symptomatic palliative therapy. In our opinion the use of these agents would seem to represent a definite but limited advance in the management of lymphomas and leukemias, though perhaps the clinical implications are less impressive than the heuristic.

## COMMENT

This brief preliminary communication presents the clinical results obtained for 67 patients treated with the nitrogen mustards (halogenated alkyl amine hydrochlorides) for Hodgkin's disease, lymphosarcoma, leukemia and certain related and miscellaneous diseases. Complete reports including pathologic observations and detailed hematologic data will be submitted later.

Salutary results have been obtained particularly in Hodgkin's disease, lymphosarcoma and chronic leukemia. Indeed, in the first two disorders dramatic improvement has been observed. However, some patients fail to benefit from β-chloroethylamine therapy, and the cause of this failure is not known. Varied responses have been observed in acute and subacute leukemias. Diseases other than those of the bloodforming organs would not seem at present to constitute indications for the use of the nitrogen mustards.

In an impressive proportion of terminal and so-called radiation resistant cases, especially of Hodgkin's disease and lymphosarcoma, the β-chloroethylamines have produced clinical remissions lasting from weeks to months. There is evidence to suggest that responsiveness to radiation therapy may occasionally be restored after a course of nitrogen mustard therapy.

The margin of safety in the use of these chemicals is narrow, necessitating the exercise of considerable caution. The blood picture must be carefully followed at frequent intervals as a guide to subsequent dosage. Immediate local or systemic side effects (pain on injection, thrombophlebitis of injected veins, nausea and vomiting, malaise, anorexia and headache) are relatively inconsequential and can sometimes be avoided or mitigated by careful technic. More serious late toxic effects are concerned with the blood-forming organs (leukopenia, granulocytopenia, thrombocytopenia, anemia) and can be largely avoided by adherence to safe dosage schedules.

Optimal dosage schedules—as well as possible combinations of this treatment with radiation or other agents—for initial, continuation or interim prophylactic therapy remain to be determined. It is not known whether the β-chloroethylamines used in this study represent the best compounds of their chemical group.

Although indications and contraindications for the use of the nitrogen mustards remain to be established definitively, it is felt that these agents are deserving of further clinical trial in Hodgkin's disease, lymphosarcoma and leukemia. Like radiation, they do not cure.

Chemicals discovered to be therapeutically active in neoplastic disease deserve close study by clinicians, experimental pathologists, enzymologists and others interested in cancer and in cellular biology. From this point of view the heuristic aspects of the actions of the β-chloroethylamines here reported may eventually prove of greater importance than the chemical results obtained to date.

May 4, 1984
(*JAMA* 1984;251:2262-2263)

# Nitrogen Mustard Therapy*

## A New Era

Emil Freireich, MD, DSc

The beginning of the era of cytotoxic chemotherapy was documented in this signal publication. The title is a concise yet accurate description of the contents of the publication. The trivial name assigned to this chemical — *nitrogen mustard* — persists today, and the association of the chemical with the word *therapy* was virtually clairvoyant.

The authors report a clinical investigation of only 67 patients. Yet they were able to describe the essential activity of this chemical in the effective palliation of a systemic malignant condition that was resistant to all known methods of treatment.

### The Selection of Chemicals for Clinical Trials

The authors point out in this article that the initiation of the first clinical test of chemotherapy early in December 1942 was preceded by extensive investigation of the nature of the interaction of the chemical with other biologic tissues in vitro. These studies included preclinical toxicity study in whole animals and in isolated cells and, ultimately, a therapeutic trial in a preclinical animal tumor model.[1] Of interest is the fact that estimations of dose and of likely spectrum of activity were brilliantly anticipated by the authors based on their knowledge of the chemistry, the pharmacology, and the biology of the drug treatment. This crucial role of the preclinical scientists in the clinical trial was emphasized by Dr Alfred Gilman as an author on this first report of the clinical activity of the drug. I am confident that this collaboration contributed significantly to the continuing collaboration of Dr Louis S. Goodman and Dr Gilman in establishing perhaps the most significant textbook of pharmacology, which has been used by virtually all students of this discipline since 1940. The pattern established in this first successful clinical trial has proved to be an extremely significant model for the discovery of other classes of anticancer drug to the present.

### Initial Clinical Studies: Detection of Significant Antitumor Activity

The article by Goodman et al anteceded the first publication of a prospective randomized formal clinical trial in 1948. Yet the authors properly observed the important distinction between phase I and phase II drug testing. They reported that the nitrogen mustards had a significant effect on the patients with lymphoma and Hodgkin's disease, but they emphasized that the overall impact of these treatment effects on the patient's survival and general well-being required much further study and larger numbers of patients. They were also appropriately conservative about declaring differences between the nitrogen mustards used in the present clinical trial. Thus, this initial report in a small number of patients was sufficient to demonstrate clearly the antitumor activity of this chemical.

This article emphasizes a fact that has been continuously confirmed, the important interaction between the initial phase of clinical testing (ie, the description of the biologic and toxic effects of the drug) and the therapeutic effects. In modern parlance, initial clinical trials referred to as *phase I* drug study are appreciated to have as their primary objective the clear definition of the biologic and toxic effects. In addition, during this phase of study, the proper dose, schedule, and route of administration to achieve reproducible biologic effects are worked out in sequential patients. After the completion of phase I, the evaluation of the drug in a substantial number of patients with a variety of tumor diagnoses is conducted to search for significant therapeutic activity, usually referred to as *phase II*. The primary motivation for separating on an intellectual and a physical basis the first and second phases of drug testing is to avoid false-negative results of clinical trials. That is, the phase I study has the potential for missing significant activity as a result of studying inadequate numbers of patients by inadequate dosage and by the wrong route. However, many authors have emphasized, as these authors have properly recognized, that the initial clinical trial has a clear therapeutic intent.[2] While the authors were conservative about the benefit that the patients obtained, they did emphasize in the case reports the clear evidence of potential therapeutic activity, and they were prepared to conclude that "these agents seemed to represent a definite, but limited advance in the management of lymphomas and leukemias."

Department of Hematology, University of Texas System Cancer Center, M. D. Anderson Hosptial and Tumor Institute, Houston.

*A commentary on Goodman LS, Wintrobe MM, Dameshek W, et al: Nitrogen mustard therapy: Use of methyl-*bis*(β-chloroethyl)amine hydrochloride and *tris*(β-chloroethyl)amine hydrochloride for Hodgkin's disease, lymphosarcoma, leukemia and certain allied and miscellaneous disorders. *JAMA* 1946;132:126-132.

## The Role of Chemotherapy in Cancer Treatment

This article is being republished only 38 years after its initial publication. In that brief interval, the science of chemotherapy for cancer has burgeoned to the extent that there are more than 30 distinctive chemical moieties currently commercially available based on demonstrated, significant therapeutic effects in patients with widespread clinical cancer. It has been estimated that at least 10% of patients with systemic, ie, metastatic, malignant conditions that are uniformly fatal can be cured with chemotherapy.[3] However, there is no doubt that a major fraction of the residual patients have substantial prolongation of life and significant control of morbidity associated with metastatic malignant conditions.

For several tumor types, chemotherapy has become the clear treatment of choice. Particularly for the advanced disseminated lymphomas, for the acute leukemias, and for choriocarcinoma and embryonal testicular neoplasms in males, a high proportion of patients can be cured with primary chemotherapy. In addition, there is a growing use of chemotherapy for patients in whom metastatic cancer has a high risk of developing — so-called adjuvant chemotherapy. This treatment has proved to be of definite value in such diagnoses as breast cancer and in other organ malignant conditions. These statements are simply to underline the enormous intelligence and perception of the authors when they stated that "the heuristic aspects of the actions of the $\beta$-chloroethylamines here reported may eventually prove of greater importance than the clinical results obtained to date." How right they were.

### Clinical Trial Techniques

As emphasized previously, the discovery of the antibiotics and the cytotoxic drugs stimulated the field of clinical trial methodology. Of further importance, this article represented a "cooperative clinical trial" in that the patients were treated in four different institutions. The number of patients being treated at each institution ranged from seven to 34, with a median of 13. The results were presented as in a cooperative trial in that it was not possible from the publication to identify which of the patients were treated where.

Of interest was the fact that the second and third authors, who were the two largest contributors of patients, have subsequently emerged as giants in the field of clinical hematology. Dr Maxwell M. Wintrobe is known not only for his research and teaching of outstanding fellows, but because of his pioneering and significant textbook of clinical hematology, first published in 1942, which, like Goodman and Gilman's textbook of pharmacology, has been the backbone of the teaching of hematology to the entire generation of students to follow, including myself. As with the textbook of pharmacology, this textbook is still in continuous publication, now in its eighth edition, and, like Goodman and Gilman's textbook, it also occupies a place in my office for daily use. Dr William Dameshek emerged as the founding editor of the most important hematology journal, *Blood,* which began publication in 1946 and which he served as the editor-in-chief until 1969. This journal still is the major hematology publication in the United States.

It is a real joy to read this article and to contrast it with modern publications on chemotherapy for cancer. The enormous development of statistics has made a major contribution to clinical research. The clinical trial has converted from a qualitative statement to an objective and quantitative report containing $P$ values, coefficients of variation, sample sizes, staging, randomization, criteria for eligibility, evaluable and inevaluable objective criteria for response, complete remission, partial remission, concepts of curability, long-term survivorship, and the highly technical and advanced methods for estimating toxicity-benefit ratios. The machinery of the modern national cooperative groups involving ten to 30 cooperating academic institutions with patients contributed from hundreds of physicians to give clinical trials with many hundreds of and, occasionally, thousands of patients represent the progeny of this important and signal contribution to the medical literature.

### Chemotherapy and Radiation Therapy

While the authors reported that the effects of nitrogen mustard could be likened to radiation, they recognized that there was an important difference: patients who could not be further treated with radiation or were "radiation resistant" were still able to show dramatic response to the alkylating agents. The similarity of the effect of alkylating agents suggested a "radiomimetic" effect, yet the important observation of the unique activity of the chemicals has been exhaustively confirmed, and the combination of radiation and chemotherapy in many instances has been shown to be truly synergistic and, for the alkylating agents, at the very least, additive in effectiveness. Many modern treatment regimens for lymphoma utilize this important additive property for the treatment of bulky tumors or for the treatment of specific sites of disease such as the central nervous system.

---

This publication, which reports the first significant anticancer activity of a chemical structure, began a new era in cancer treatment. Chemotherapy is one of the proved modalities of cancer treatment along with surgery and radiation. Chemotherapy has greatly stimulated the field of oncology, and medical oncology has become recognized as one of the major subspecialties in the field of internal medicine. In addition, chemotherapy has become a significant component of the modern multimodal approach to cancer treatment, which has enormously improved the outlook for the eventual control of malignant disease.

### References

1. Gilman A: The initial clinical trial of nitrogen mustard. *Am J Surg* 1963;105:574-578.
2. Freireich EJ, Bodey GP: Evaluation of new agents: Planning, execution and evaluation of clinical studies, in Kuemmerle HP (ed): *Anticancer Chemotherapy.* Stuttgart, West Germany, Georg Thieme Verlag, in press.
3. Holland JF, Frei E III (eds): *Cancer Medicine.* Philadelphia, Lea & Febiger, 1982, pp 1309-1319.

Chapter 41

# Considerations in the Preparation and Use of Poliomyelitis Virus Vaccine

Jonas E. Salk, M.D.,

Pittsburgh

In assessing the state of knowledge of any subject at a particular point in time, it is as important to define what is not known as it is to appreciate what is known. It is for this reason that I would like to discuss some of the problems still before us, with respect to vaccination against poliomyelitis, as well as to review knowledge gained in the course of recent work. "Can durable immunity be induced by a noninfectious poliomyelitis vaccine?" is one of the principal questions still to be answered. Since the ultimate answer to this question cannot be obtained until time has passed, we must content ourselves only with an examination of facts now known, from which we can make some tentative interpretations from the trends observed.

The hypothesis that the presence of neutralizing antibody in the circulating blood is an effective barrier in reducing the likelihood of paralysis by the poliomyelitis virus is now well supported by the great volume of indirect, as well as direct, evidence from studies in experimental animals and in man, on passive and active immunization.[1] In this discussion, therefore, I will examine the evidence that exists concerning the creation of

antibody and also the persistence of antibody induced artificially by vaccination.[2] Observations in some, of many more, individuals who were vaccinated one and a half years earlier, and others vaccinated two and a half years earlier, will be shown. I will try to orient my remarks along practical lines but will do so principally by reference to the theoretical and experimental considerations upon which are based the preparation and use of poliomyelitis vaccine.

To begin a discussion such as this, from the practical viewpoint, it would be well to consider first the special attributes required of a poliomyelitis vaccine, as compared to vaccine for any other diseases, since a vaccine for poliomyelitis requires particular attention as regards both safety and effectiveness. We know only too well the uniqueness of paralytic poliomyelitis, among all of the infectious diseases; the unusual combination that exists here is the terror and tragedy inflicted to a degree that is out of all proportion to the frequency of attack. The relative infrequency of severe paralysis under natural circumstances requires, above all else, that the vaccine must be free, insofar as it is possible to create such a

From the Virus Research Laboratory, School of Medicine, University of Pittsburgh.

Read in the Panel Discussion on Prospects for the Control of Poliomyelitis before the Joint Meeting of the Section on Pediatrics and the Section on Preventive and Industrial Medicine and Public Health at the 104th Annual Meeting of the American Medical Association, Atlantic City, June 7, 1955.

Many of the experimental and theoretical considerations discussed in this paper are being elaborated in more detail for publication elsewhere.

This study was aided by a grant from the National Foundation for Infantile Paralysis.

1. Morgan, I. M.: Level of Serum Antibody Associated with Intracerebral Immunity in Monkeys Vaccinated with Lansing Poliomyelitis Virus, J. Immunol. **62:** 301, 1949. Bodian, D.: Sites of Immune Barriers in Poliomyelitis, in Hartman, F. W.; Horsfall, F. L., Jr., and Kidd, J. G.: The Dynamics of Virus and Rickettsial Infections, New York, Blakiston Company, 1954; Experimental Studies on Passive Immunization Against Poliomyelitis; I. Protection with Human Gamma Globulin Against Intramuscular Inoculation, and Combined Passive and Active Immunization, Am. J. Hyg. **54:** 132, 1951. Hammon, W. McD.; Coriell, L. L., and Wehrle, P. F.; Evaluation of Red Cross Gamma Globulin as a Prophylactic Agent for Poliomyelitis: 4. Final Report of Results Based on Clinical Diagnosis, J. A. M. A. **151:** 1272 (April 11) 1953. Howe, H. A.: Studies of Active Immunogenesis in Poliomyelitis: I. Persistence and Recall by Homotypic or Heterotypic Superinfection of Neutralizing Antibody Originally Induced in Chimpanzees by Vaccination or Infection, Am. J. Hyg. **60:** 371, 1954; II. Lack of Immunity in Chimpanzees Receiving Formol-Inactivated Vaccines of Marginal Antigenic Potency, ibid. **60:** 392, 1954. Koprowski, H.: Practical Application of Living Virus Vaccines, in Hartman, F. W.; Horsfall, F. L., Jr., and Kidd, J. G.: The Dynamics of Virus and Rickettsial Infections, New York, Blakiston Company, 1954.

2. Salk, J. E., and others: Studies in Human Subjects on Active Immunization Against Poliomyelitis: I. A Preliminary Report of Experiments in Progress, J. A. M. A. **151:** 1081 (March 28) 1953. Salk, J. E.: Recent Studies on Immunization Against Poliomyelitis, Pediatrics **12:** 471, 1953. Salk, J. E., and others: Studies in Human Subjects on Active Immunization Against Poliomyelitis: II. A Practical Means for Inducing and Maintaining Antibody Formation, Am. J. Pub. Health **44:** 994, 1954. Salk, J. E.: Present Status of the Problem of Vaccination Against Poliomyelitis, ibid. **45:** 285, 1955.

preparation, of the capacity to induce the disease that it is intended to prevent; nor should a vaccine for poliomyelitis cause such side-effects as would make its use undesirable. If either the direct effects associated with its use, or incidental side-effects to any constituent, are of such nature as to make one prefer the chance of escaping the paralytic disease, one would not have a practically useful immunizing agent.

## PRINCIPLES OF VACCINE PREPARATION AND SAFETY TESTING

First, I would like to describe the principles upon which the preparation of poliomyelitis vaccine is based and, particularly, the considerations involved in testing for safety. The objective in the preparation of a

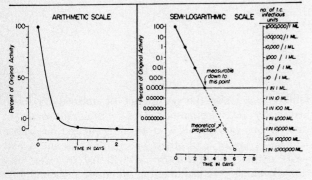

Fig. 1.—Rate of destruction of poliomyelitis virus infectivity at 37 C in presence of 1:4,000 formaldehyde solution (Formalin) at pH 7.

poliomyelitis vaccine cannot include the knowing or willful acceptance of a risk that is tangible, or measurable to any degree. Any risk that is involved, so long as it is recognized, must be corrected, whatever may be its cause; in the preparation of experimental vaccines in our

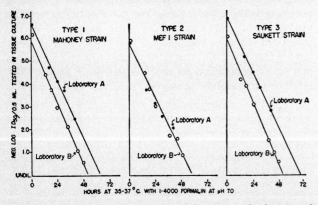

Fig. 2.—Composite of data on rates of destruction of infectivity of types 1, 2, and 3 virus for 13 lots of vaccine prepared by one manufacturer and 20 lots prepared by another. Points indicate mean of virus titers at intervals after addition of formaldehyde solution (Formalin) to warmed fluids.

own laboratory, and on a larger scale for field trial, it was the factor of safety, above all else, that imposed the limitations in the rapidity with which our studies were progressively advanced. To permit the practical application in the field to come close upon the heels of the rapid advances that were being made by investigations in the applied aspects of the problem, rather extensive transformation and expansion of the various facilities necessary

for the availability of vaccine was required.

Although there were no indications either from our own studies in some 15,000 children, or from the much larger experience in the field tests of 1954, that the vaccine preparations employed contained infectious virus, it is understood now generally that certain lots of vaccine used in April, 1955, were associated with subsequent development of paralytic poliomyelitis. This demanded a very intensive reexamination of the theoretical and practical implications of vaccine preparation, testing, and use.

I might say at this point that my own evaluation of the recent reexamination of the manufacturing and testing processes suggested a need for adjusting the techniques employed for large-scale operations so as to approximate that which it was possible to accomplish on an experi-

*Experience of Two Laboratories in Preparation of Vaccine for Field Trial on Production Scale*

| Sequence | Laboratory A° | Laboratory B |
|---|---|---|
| 1 | − | |
| 2 | + | + |
| 3 | + | + |
| 4 | + | − |
| 5 | + | + |
| 6 | + | + |
| 7 | + | + |
| 8 | + | + |
| 9 | + | + |
| 10 | + | + |
| 11 | + | + |
| 12 | + | + |
| 13 | + | + |
| 14 | .. | + |
| 15 | .. | + |
| 16 | .. | + |
| 17 | .. | + |
| 18 | .. | + |
| 19 | .. | + |
| 20 | .. | + |

°Symbols indicate whether finished vaccine met all criteria for safety: −=no, +=yes.

mental basis; the objective is to yield the consistently satisfactory preparations that it has been possible to achieve, not only in the laboratory but even on a large scale. The theoretical considerations that applied originally are still sound and applicable—what is required is closer approximation in practice. I would like to discuss the theoretical considerations first and then to show how the practical problems have been, and are being, met.

It has been realized always that the preparation of a safe poliomyelitis vaccine would, at the beginning at least, require adherence to detail such as is not demanded for the preparation of any other immunizing agent. It was recognized, too, that there must be incorporated into the vaccine preparation process itself a test for safety, which we refer to as "the margin of safety," of such degree that the most sensitive tests upon a sample of each successive batch would be negative for living virus unless something unexpected had occurred, unknowingly, in the process of manufacture, or in subsequent handling, or in testing; it would follow that such would not be expected to occur but rarely. To help in knowing where the difficulty might have occurred in any given instance, tests are needed at various steps in processing, including the final stages. A series of observations, both in our laboratory and in the laboratories of manufacturers of biologicals, indicated that the desirable objective of consistency in reproducibility of vaccine preparation with an adequate margin of safety could be achieved.

In the early phases of our investigations it was necessary, in exploratory experiments, to determine the nature of the reaction between formaldehyde and poliomyelitis virus,[3] using various concentrations of formaldehyde, different temperatures, and different degrees of acidity. The conditions selected for preparation of field test vaccine were those that would lend themselves most readily to large-scale adaptation in a way that would provide the desired margin of safety not only with respect to the destruction of virus infectivity but also with respect to the retention of antigenicity. Such studies furnished the principles upon which a carefully controlled inactivation process could be developed for use in the laboratories of any producer of biological products that could acquire the staff and facilities for making poliomyelitis vaccine.

I can best illustrate what I mean using the accompanying figures, which show the generally expected behavior, based upon experience with experimentally produced

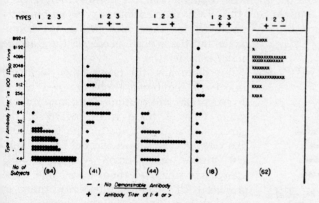

Fig. 3.—Type 1 antibody response to first dose of vaccine in persons with different prevaccination antibody patterns (vaccine lot 309). Different prevaccination antibody patterns are indicated at the top of each column.

vaccine. The left-hand portion of figure 1 shows that within the first 12 hours after the beginning of chemical treatment, 90% of virus infectivity is destroyed; within the subsequent 12 hour period, 90% of the infectivity that still remains is destroyed—or, about 99% of virus infectivity is eliminated within the first 24 hour period; in 48 hours, approximately 99.9% of the original infectious activity is obliterated. To eliminate the last traces of infectivity to a point below which none can be detected requires continuation of treatment for a number of days longer. From the practical viewpoint, the question that had to be answered was, "At what point may it be presumed that virus infectivity is destroyed, either totally or, at least, to a degree beyond which it can no longer be measured and, therefore, can be presumed not to be

3. Salk, J. E., and others: Formaldehyde Treatment and Safety Testing of Experimental Poliomyelitis Vaccines, Am. J. Pub. Health 44: 563, 1954.

harmful to man?" The right-hand portion of figure 1 illustrates further the data depicted on the left, but in another way—that is to say—on a semilogarithmic scale, which allows a more precise examination of the portion of the left-hand curve that is in the range below 1% of remaining infectivity. Here it may be seen that in the course of three days the infectivity for tissue culture of material being converted into vaccine has been so altered that, whereas originally it contained one million tissue

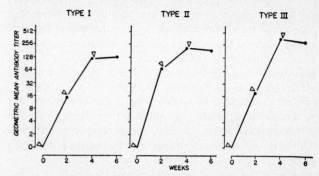

Fig. 4.—Geometric mean titers after each of three doses of reference vaccine "A," 1 ml. given intramuscularly to 20 subjects with no preantibody to any type.

culture infectious units per milliliter, at the end of the first three-day period, there remained but one tissue culture infecting unit per milliliter. If treatment is continued for not less than an additional six days, it is

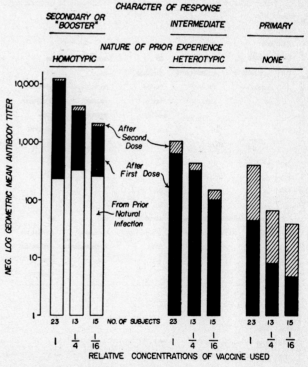

Fig. 5.—Different patterns of antibody response, depending on nature of prior immunologic experience, after two doses of reference vaccine "A" given two weeks apart, with blood drawn two weeks after each dose.

expected that with thorough mixing of virus and formaldehyde, the maintenance of uniform temperature, a reasonably homogeneous population and adequate dispersion, the material treated for a total of nine days or longer should, theoretically, be free of any demonstrable virus—even if all of the fluid being converted into vaccine were tested in tissue culture or even in man. Such experiments were done under the conditions that apply not only in our laboratory but on a large scale in other laboratories in this country and abroad (fig. 2 and table).

The critical factors that influence the slope of the line in the right-hand portion of figure 1 are (1) temperature, (2) formaldehyde concentration, and (3) pH. Since the amount of free formaldehyde will be influenced by such constituents as the protein content, or the concentration of free amino acids, then constancy of composition of the fluid being converted into vaccine is a factor that would affect the rate of reaction. In spite of our ability to control these variables within practicable limits, it is still necessary to ascertain, by suitable tests, that all of the considerations have, in fact, been properly effected. There is one critically important factor that demands close attention and that is the matter of uniform mixing; another is the use of such techniques that reduce, if not eliminate, risk of recontamination with live virus. Failure to mix adequately will introduce such uncontrollable variables as may be described by the term "fractional inactivation," and this may make it appear that resistant particles are present. Another factor is the use of filtration procedures to remove particles that might interfere with inactivation. As has already been mentioned, a check for any deviation from the expected is made by tests upon suitable samples removed at particular stages in the course of processing.

In the critical review that was made recently of the requirement for manufacture, tests were specified at two additional check points in the process, and the volumes of fluid to be tested at each step for each batch were set at fixed quantities. In addition, failure of a batch to be inactivated in the expected time would preclude its being reprocessed, and it is required that such batches be discarded. This is merely in conformity with the present requirement that there be demonstrated an adequate margin of safety for each batch of vaccine. The details that have been spelled out merely define what is meant by adequate margin of safety and in actual practice are further reinforced by requesting compliance with the original requirement that there be satisfactory consecutive experience of each manufacturer in being able to produce vaccine consistently free of living virus, and with the desired margin of safety.

It may be said that the design of the inactivation process, for the experimentally produced vaccine and for larger scale preparations, was intended to provide a quantitative expression of margin of safety. This was based upon the opinion that the testing merely of a sample of the final preparation, as is customarily employed for most biologicals, was inadequate for the special needs of the vaccine under consideration.

But there are still many other technical aspects of the broad problem upon which investigations will continue for a long time to come. One of these is in regard to the particular strains of virus for the most effective vaccine. The strains selected for our very first studies were chosen because, among many from which selections were made, these produced the highest infectivity titers in tissue culture and were also shown to be highly antigenic in monkeys and man. It has now been found that, within broad limits, high infectivity and high antigenic potency are not necessarily associated, and, in fact, they are independent properties. These trends emerge from a series of investigations in which strains are being selected that are among the most potent antigenically, and from among these we will select those that are of low pathogenicity for monkeys when administered by peripheral routes. The principle objective of this phase of our studies is to incorporate in the vaccine a type 1 strain that has the same attributes of high antigenic potency as do the MEF-1 strain of type 2 virus and the Saukett strain of type 3, that appear to be more potent antigenically than does the Mahoney type 1 strain; and while doing so, to select one of low peripheral pathogenicity for monkeys. But the latter is only a secondary consideration, since the first requirement that must be satisfied regardless

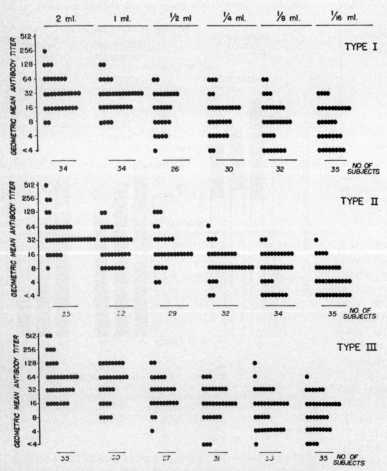

Fig. 6.—Dosage effect: Type 1, 2, and 3 antibody response two weeks after one dose of reference vaccine "A" given intramuscularly to subjects with no demonstrable preantibody to any type.

of strain is that it be rendered noninfectious for man. In studies with laboratory-selected variants that are avirulent, some are very poor antigens whether they are used in their fully infectious form or after inactivation with formaldehyde solution (Formalin). This is something of considerable theoretical and practical interest.

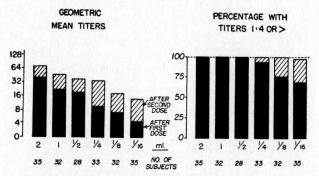

Fig. 7.—Type 2 antibody response two weeks after two doses of reference vaccine "A" given two weeks apart.

## IMMUNOLOGIC FACTORS INFLUENCING VACCINE EFFECTIVENESS

The question of vaccine effectiveness is, of course, secondary to the question of vaccine safety. I would, therefore, like to discuss now the question of vaccine effectiveness. Here we have two distinct issues: (1) the immediate one—the immune response that can be expected after each of the three doses of vaccine, and (2)

one that arises later—regarding the degree of persistence of immunity after the third inoculation. There is the further question of the spacing and frequency, if later inoculations are required.

*Primary Vaccine Response.*—The various factors that influence the primary response to vaccine are illustrated in a series of figures to follow. The first point that I wish to make is that antibody response is influenced by prior immunologic experience. For example, an individual who has not had any prior poliomyelitis virus infection reacts quite differently to vaccination than does an individual who has had an infection with one or more of

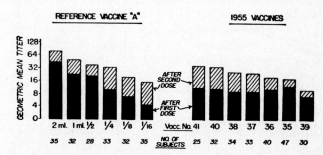

Fig. 9.—Comparison of seven lots of 1955 vaccine with reference vaccine "A." Type 2 response two weeks after two doses given two weeks apart.

these viruses. This is illustrated in figure 3, where it may be seen that the antibody response to the first dose of a relatively poor vaccine was quite different in persons who had no previous immunologic experience as compared with those who had a prior infection with either type 2 or type 3 virus, or both; it is to be expected, of course, that there will be a very different pattern of reactivity if there has been a prior homotypic infection, i. e., type 1 in this instance. It should be clear from these data that, from a practical point of view, it is necessary to know the nature of the antigenic response in persons who have had no prior immunologic experience if one is to make valid comparisons concerning the nature of the influence of vaccine potency, time, and spacing of inoculations, and any other questions that can be answered only by the application of quantitative immunologic methods. It is for this reason that I will confine this presentation, except as necessary, to make a particular point, to data derived in studies in children who had not had any prior experience with any of the poliomyelitis viruses.

Figure 4 illustrates the degree of antibody response after three doses of vaccine given to a group of children who prior to vaccination had no antibody to any of the three types. It is clear from this chart that a substantial response occurred after the first dose of vaccine, a moderate increase occurred after the second dose, but little or no increase occurred after the third dose when the three doses of vaccine, of the potency used here,

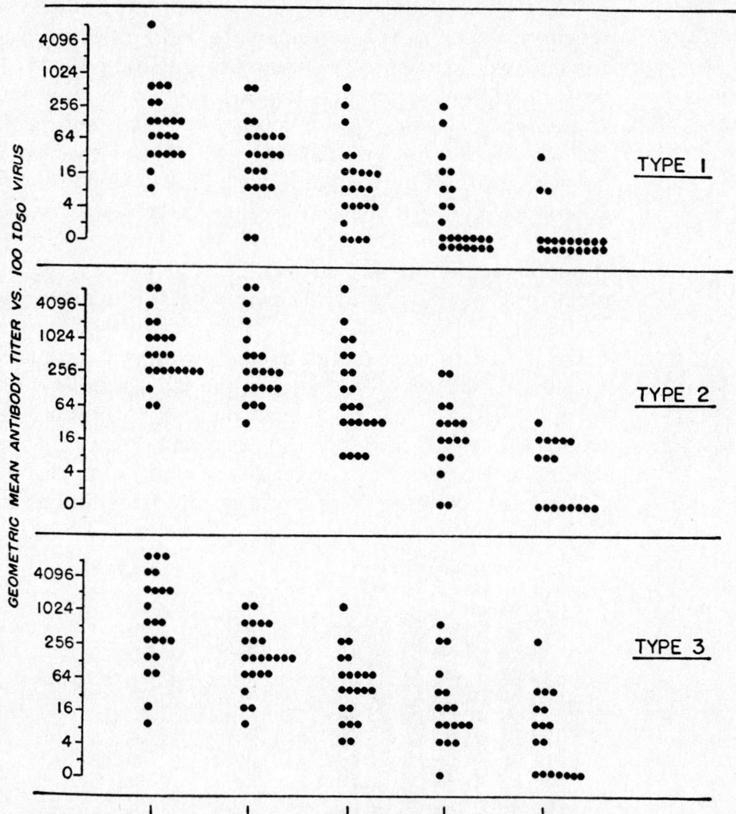

Fig. 8.—Antibody response in groups of monkeys vaccinated with diminishing dilutions of reference vaccine "A" given in three doses intramuscularly, 1 ml. each week one week apart, with blood drawn one week after third dose.

were spaced with an interval of two weeks between each. The reason for the suggestion that the third dose should be postponed is indicated by these data, and the reason for the suggestion that an interval of seven months or more be used will be shown by the results of other experiments referred to later in this discussion.

Additional evidence showing the influence of two other factors; namely, vaccine potency and time for producing the full immunologic effect, superimposed upon the influence of the particular kind of prior immunologic experience, is illustrated in figure 5. This summary reveals that vaccines differing in potency in fourfold and sixteenfold steps elicit different degrees of antibody response. Moreover, a second dose produces substantially more antibody in persons who have had no prior immunologic experience as compared with persons who have had a prior heterotypic experience, or in persons who have had a prior homotypic experience. After the lapse of a suitable period of time after the primary and intermediate types of response, a later inoculation will then evoke titers to levels observed for the booster-type response (fig. 5). But, it is clear that the potency of the vaccine influences the degree of response regardless of the nature of the prior immunologic experience.

So as not to complicate these matters unduly, I would like to mention that the foregoing charts have indicated that persons with no antibody to any of the three types are the ones with whom we need be concerned chiefly; two doses of vaccine, with spacing two weeks or longer, appears to be the most efficient way to administer vaccine for the relatively limited effect that can be induced in the primary stage. Moreover, it is clear that this primary effect is influenced by the potency of the vaccine used. Figure 6 shows in somewhat more detail the influence of vaccine potency in effecting a change in

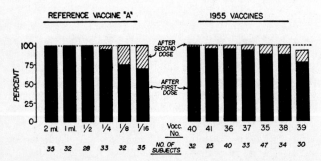

Fig. 10.—Comparison of seven lots of 1955 vaccine with reference vaccine "A." Type 2 response, showing percentage of subjects with demonstrable antibody (1:4 or more) two weeks after each of two doses given two weeks apart.

antibody status in groups of individuals who had no detectable antibody prior to vaccination. It is clear that when the dose given intramuscularly is varied from 2 ml. to 0.06 ml. that there is a spread in the difference in the frequency with which antibody appears and also variation in the degree of the average response. Thus, with a potent vaccine it is possible to induce the formation of antibody in all of groups of the sizes indicated, and with weaker vaccines proportionately lesser effects are

induced. The data for type 2 are illustrated in figure 7 in a somewhat different fashion, showing the geometric mean antibody level after the first and after the second dose of vaccine; in addition there is shown the percentage of individuals who had no antibody to any type before vaccination but, as a result of vaccination, developed a distinctly measurable amount of antibody; comparisons are shown after the first and second dose.

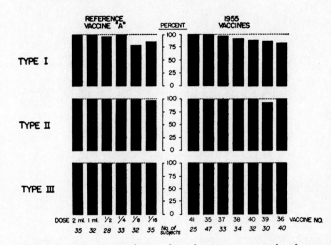

Fig. 11.—Comparison of seven lots of 1955 vaccine with reference vaccine "A," showing percentage of subjects with demonstrable antibody (1:4 or more) two weeks after two doses given two weeks apart.

The data in the foregoing figures were derived in the course of experiments designed to help establish the significance for man of a laboratory test for potency as performed in experimental animals. By varying the dose of reference vaccine "A," in studies both in man (fig. 6) and in laboratory animals (fig. 8), it then becomes possible to establish a basis for the significance of any laboratory test, whether it be done in monkeys, mice, guinea pigs, or any other animal. The underlying principle is the use of a standard reference vaccine for measuring potency in comparison with the unknown to be approved for use in man. To help further in this correlation, a group of seven batches of vaccine, prepared for use in 1955, was also tested in the same way, and the relative activity of these vaccines in children was compared with that of the different quantities of reference vaccine "A." The relative potency of the type 2 component of the commercially prepared material,

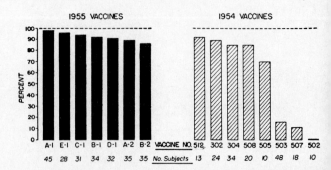

Fig. 12.—Percentage of children with no prior demonstrable antibody to any type who had a type 1 antibody response on the 14th day after first dose of vaccine.

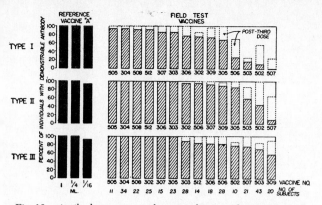

Fig. 13.—Antibody response in human subjects with no antibody for any type prior to vaccination, showing percentage of subjects with demonstrable antibody after two doses given two weeks apart (1954 field trial vaccines).

expressed in terms of geometric mean titer of antibody, is shown in figure 9 and in terms of percentage of individuals who showed a response after the first and after the second dose (fig. 10). Similar data are shown in figure 11 for all three types, in comparison with different quantities of reference vaccine "A."

By means of such quantitative immunologic studies it is now possible, on the basis of a laboratory test performed in any of a variety of ways and in any of a number of animal systems, to predict the probable performance of any vaccine applied in human subjects so long as the vaccine in question is so constituted, and stored, that it will not deteriorate between the time of testing and the time of use. You will recall that in the vaccines prepared a year ago it has been established that the thimerosal (Merthiolate), or a decomposition product thereof, had an adverse effect upon the antigenicity, and particularly upon the type 1 component. The evidence suggests that this factor measurably influenced the response to the vaccines used in the 1954 field studies. This has been corrected by either (1) the elimination of a preservative, or (2) the use of thimerosal with edathamil (ethylenediaminetetraacetic acid), which tends to stabilize the thimerosal, or (3) the use of other preservatives. Any of the preservatives accepted for use must be shown to have no adverse effect upon the stability of the vaccine. That the vaccines used in the field trial were,[4] for the most part, less potent than those now available, is illustrated in figures 12 and 13. Figure 14 illustrates the difference in performance of vaccine with and without thimerosal, and of vaccine with thimerosal and edathamil, as compared with vaccine with no preservative.

*Antibody Response to Vaccine Administered by Different Routes.*—There have been a number of questions concerning antibody response to vaccine given by different routes. I would like to show, in figure 15, the data that are available on antibody response to vaccine given subcutaneously, intramuscularly, and intradermally. It is clear that 1 ml. of vaccine given intramuscularly or subcutaneously elicits about the same order of response;

4. Salk, J. E., and others: Antigenic Activity of Poliomyelitis Vaccines Undergoing Field Test. Am. J. Pub. Health **45**: 151, 1955. Salk, J. E.: Vaccination Against Paralytic Poliomyelitis: Performance and Prospects, ibid. **45**: 575, 1955.

however, there seems always to be a slight advantage, as measured by mean antibody level, following intramuscular injection. When different quantities of vaccine given intramuscularly are compared with 0.1 ml. given intradermally, it would appear that the latter is about equal in effectiveness to 0.25 ml. given intramuscularly. Thus 0.1 ml. intradermally is not as effective, in inducing antibody formation, as is 1 ml. intramuscularly; but, it does appear that this small dose, given intradermally, is somewhat more efficient than a corresponding amount given intramuscularly.

*Optimal Conditions for Eliciting the Booster Effect.*—In the course of our earliest investigations, it became apparent that in man frequent multiple inoculations, given over a period of a few weeks, were an

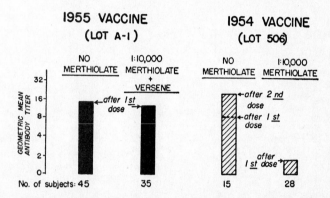

Fig. 14.—Type 1 response to 1955 vaccine (lot A-1) and 1954 vaccine (lot 506). In this instance Versene refers to edathamil (ethylenediaminetetraacetic acid).

inefficient way of administering vaccine. It was apparent, furthermore, that the longer the interval between inoculations the better the effect. This total experience has indicated that 1 ml. of vaccine of reasonable potency, given to subjects who have no antibody to any of the three types, will induce antibody formation in the majority, and a second dose, given two weeks or longer thereafter, will add up this effect; if a number of months is allowed to elapse, the advantage of the third dose will be increased as the time is prolonged, up to approximately seven months, or later, at which time it appears that the height of the hyperreactive state is reached. The evidence indicating the advantage of the relatively long interval between the second and third dose is shown in figure 16, which summarizes data from an experiment in which a sample of vaccine was used that, over the six month period of the study, was deteriorating because of the influence of thimerosal. In spite of this, the advantage of time is evident, but the full effect of the third dose that would have been elicited, had a more potent vaccine been used, is not clear from the mean antibody titers observed. Nevertheless, the trend in favor of the longer interval is evident.

The influence of a more potent vaccine, when used for booster, superimposed upon a more adequate primary stimulus, is shown in figure 17. The degree of response during the primary phase, following the use of vaccine lots 303 and 507 is illustrated, as well as the degree of decline during the 10 months that followed; and then the degree of antibody response to the booster is also shown,

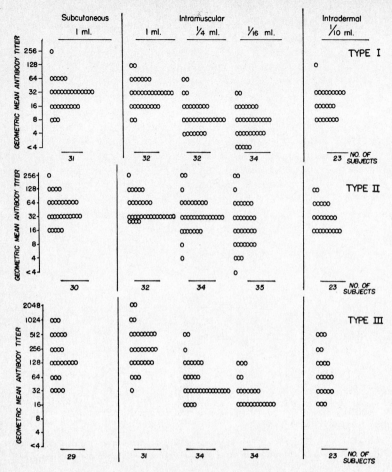

Fig. 15.—Type 1, 2, and 3 antibody response of reference vaccine "A" two weeks after two doses given two weeks apart by different routes of inoculation.

experienced no booster effect to the type 1 component, a rather poor response to type 2, and a more adequate type 3 response. It is clearly evident that there must be a reasonably substantial primary effect for a full secondary, or booster, response. Other data bearing on the question of booster response, when the secondary stimulation is given seven months or longer after the primary, are shown in the next several figures. Here may be seen, in some instances, that even though little or no primary response was elicited, there appears to have been some sensitizing influence as evidenced by the hyperreactive response at the time of the booster.

The general pattern of response, as may be seen in these data, seems to be one in which there is a somewhat more rapid decline in the early postvaccination period followed by a more gradual decline or by a plateau, which suggests that antibody persistence following a course of vaccination of the kind here employed could be expected to persist for a number of years. Figure 18 summarizes observations in 14 individuals who, with exceptions, as noted at the different intervals, were followed for a period of one and one-half years. At that time a fourth inoculation was given to determine the character of the response that would be elicited. It is clear that the decline that occurred in the preceding year was replenished, and then exceeded to a slight degree by the second booster. These individuals will be followed to determine whether or not the rate of decline of antibody following the second booster is the same or, perhaps, more gradual than after the first. However, the magnitude of the level of antibody maintained during the year after the first booster, and the level achieved after the second is considerable, indeed. Several individual examples of persistence after primary, and of booster response,

along with the control representing the response of previously uninoculated children. Persons who initially had vaccine lot 303, and were then given one of the other commercial vaccines for the booster, exhibited marked rises in antibody to all three types. By comparison, individuals who had received primarily vaccine lot 507

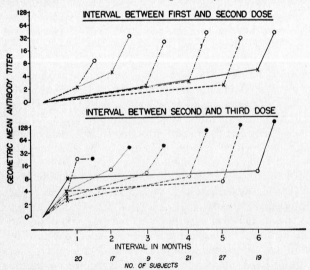

Fig. 16.—Influence of time intervals on type 2 response to second or third doses of vaccine (lot 309) in human subjects with no demonstrable preantibody to any type.

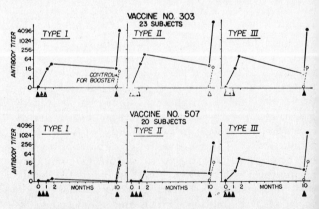

Fig. 17.—Effect of booster dose 10 months after vaccination with two different vaccine lots used in 1954 field trials.

are shown in figures 19 and 20. It is to be noted that vaccine lot 503 was a relatively poor vaccine in comparison with the others used for boosters.

To provide further indications of trend in regard to

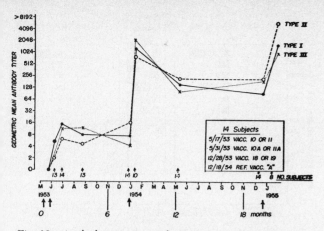

Fig. 18.—Antibody persistence after primary and secondary antigenic stimulation in children with no preantibody to any type who were observed over one and one-half years.

persistence, data are presented in two individuals, of many, from whom blood samples have been tested two and one-half years after primary vaccination. These persons received 0.1 ml. intradermally of each of three virus types on two occasions, in August or September of 1952, and were then reinoculated almost two and one-half years later. The indications are that the relatively low levels of antibody, elicited by the primary immunizing procedure, tended to persist, and when a booster dose was given, even as long as two and one-half years later, a very sharp response was observed. The degree of persistence following the booster is now being followed. These examples of two and one-half year persistence are in persons who had antibody for only one type prior to first vaccination (fig. 21).

*Antibody Response to Vaccination and Infection.*—As a matter of interest, let us compare the levels of antibody observed in vaccinated individuals with those observed in persons who have experienced natural infection. To

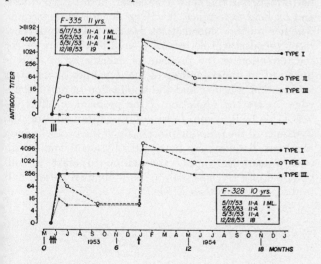

Fig. 19.—Antibody persistence after primary and secondary antigenic stimulation in two children with no preantibody to any type.

illustrate this point, figure 22 shows the prevaccination and postvaccination antibody titers of a group of 61 individuals, for whom we had such data, from among those who had received their initial inoculations with

vaccines lot 303, 305, 306, or 512. In the prebooster period, the type 1 antibody levels of all individuals were below 1:32; 14 days after the booster they all had levels beyond this range, and a high proportion clustering at the level of 1:8,000+. For comparison, there is charted the levels of antibody observed in a group of 56 persons with type 1 paralytic poliomyelitis, and from whom serial bleedings were obtained at approximately weekly intervals while they were hospitalized. The geometric mean level of antibody was 1:128 at the time of hospital admission and shortly after onset of paralysis; there was no serologic evidence of prior infection with any other virus type. The antibody measurement recorded in this figure was the highest observed in the series for each individual; the geometric mean level of the highest titers was slightly less than 1:1024. From other experiences, it is to be expected that these high titers will decline over a period of time and will stabilize at a mean level of approximately 1:128.

It is evident from these data that there occurred, as a result of an infection with paralytic consequences, levels of antibody that in general were higher than that induced by primary vaccination with a killed-virus vaccine. However, it was equally clear that the level of antibody induced with a killed-virus vaccine, when a booster dose was given at a suitable interval, was higher than that induced by the infectious process.

In the right-hand portion of figure 22 are data from another group that is of interest. These data are from a study of 27 children who had been vaccinated either in the spring of 1953 or the spring of 1954, and, in the course of follow-up bleedings, in the winter of 1953 or 1954, respectively, it was evident that these children had experienced a natural infection. This was indicated by the sharp difference in the level of antibody for one type only, when the early and late postvaccination blood samples were compared. In this group of 27 are 2 children who had a type 3 infection, diagnosed serologically; 12 had type 1 infections; 13 had type 2 infections. It is clear that the level of antibody observed in these subjects was, in general, higher than that observed in paralyzed convalescents. It is as if infection, in a previously vaccinated person, elicits a booster-type anti-

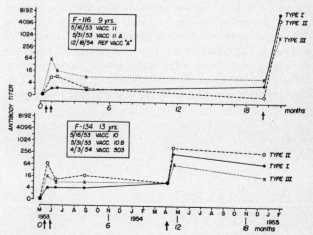

Fig. 20.—Antibody persistence after primary and secondary antigenic stimulation in two children with no preantibody to any type who were observed over one and one-half years.

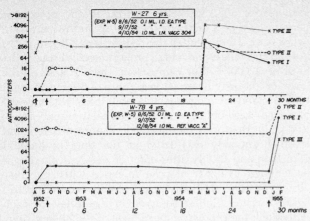

Fig. 21.—Observations over two and one-half years in two children of first group inoculated.

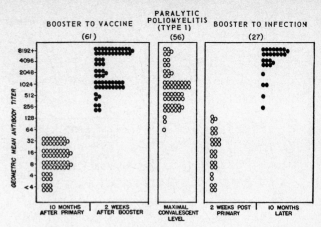

Fig. 22.—Comparison of antibody response to vaccination and to infection.

body response corresponding to the infecting type.

There is a similarity between the levels of antibody following a booster injection, and the postinfection levels in previously vaccinated individuals. The distribution of levels in each appear to be higher than that observed in recently paralyzed convalescents. It would seem from these data, therefore, that the assertion that the levels of antibody following the use of a killed-virus vaccine are lower than those observed in persons who have been infected is, indeed, true. But this is only part of the truth. The whole truth indicates that the level of antibody induced by a properly prepared killed-virus vaccine, properly used, can be higher than that level induced by infection.

COMMENT

It should be clear from all that has been presented that the objective of the immunization process is to effect an immunologic response that will last for a considerable period of time. It appears that this can be accomplished by the introduction of an adequate antigenic mass, the influence of which will be evident after each of the three inoculations. The height of the antibody titer induced by the primary vaccinating doses (two doses spaced two to four weeks apart) is influenced by the intensity of the primary stimulus; i. e., dosage and potency of the vaccine. The height of the antibody titer after the booster dose is influenced by the length of the interval between the primary and secondary injections and by the size and potency of the booster dose. The level of antibody present at any given time after vaccination varies among individuals but is influenced by the total prior immunologic experience as well as by the interval that has elapsed after vaccination. The rate of decline from the different levels achieved after primary and booster doses has been described and in general appears to be more rapid shortly after the postinoculation level; this is followed by a plateau or a very gradual decline. In addition to these effects that are measurable directly, there appears to persist a state of heightened immunologic reactivity that is evident upon reinoculation or upon exposure. This state of hyperreactivity probably does not decline with time. Becuase of it, antibody levels may be further enhanced by revaccination, if need be, or will be augmented in the course of natural exposure.

Although we have said that the ultimate objective of these investigations is to provide the basis for the preparation and the use of a safe and effective vaccine against paralytic poliomyelitis, the orientation of our studies at this time is to determine the degree of completeness with which effectiveness can be demonstrated—first, by means of blood tests, and, ultimately, by performance in the field. Thereafter, both by blood tests and by field experience, it will be possible to determine whether further inoculations beyond the course now recommended will be required—and if so, when. As for the resolution of the problem of vaccine safety, this is linked to an understanding of the dynamics of the virus inactivation reaction and the application of this knowledge. As for the resolution of the problem of effectiveness, this will come from an understanding of the dynamics of the immune process, upon the basis of which recommendations may be made; physicians and health officers can then apply vaccination to elicit its full potential effectiveness both in the individual patient and in the community as a whole.

May 25, 1984
JAMA 1984;251:2710-2712)

# Inactivated Poliomyelitis Vaccination*

## Issues Reconsidered

### E. Russell Alexander, MD

It is difficult to look back at an important scientific contribution and to assess the full significance of the work. It must be evaluated in relation to the time in which it was written. What were its roots? What was the notable contribution of this work? Furthermore, where did it lead us? Only with that precious gift of knowing what really happened can we now look back and assess the broader significance of the contribution. Thus, we can examine the important article, "Considerations in the Preparation and Use of Poliomyelitis Vaccine," by Jonas Salk, published in THE JOURNAL in August 1955.[1]

#### First Polio Vaccine

In that year, there was an urgent problem, and this article represented one important response. Salk had been the first to take advantage of the basic contribution of Enders et al[2] in the propagation of poliovirus in non-neural tissue cultures and produced a formalin-inactivated killed poliovirus vaccine. This was studied in monkeys[3] and then evaluated for antigenic potency in humans.[4,5] This energetic and brilliant series of studies described a very promising vaccine that produced fewer side effects than other bacterial vaccines in use and appeared to confer protection.

Live virus vaccines for smallpox and yellow fever were available, and an inactivated, rather crude, influenza vaccine was being developed (to which Salk also contributed). But an inactivated poliomyelitis vaccine gave promise of tackling an increasing national epidemic, which had devastating neurological sequelae in an unlucky small proportion of those infected. After an unsuccessful attempt to use gamma globulin to control

epidemic poliomyelitis,[6] public health officials were champing at the bit to apply an effective agent. In 1954, with the strong support of the National Foundation for Infantile Paralysis (the March of Dimes) led by the dynamic Basil O'Connor, Salk's inactivated poliomyelitis vaccine was field tested in a massive multicentered study under the direction of a highly respected epidemiologist, Thomas Francis.[7] The field test was a resounding success, and a vaccine plan was developed, consisting of vaccination of elementary schoolchildren, who, in most settings, were at highest risk of severe paralytic disease.

In this era of great expectation, a disaster occurred. A series of lots of vaccine were found to induce paralytic poliomyelitis in a proportion of vaccinees, and the vaccine program was called to an immediate halt. In these lots of vaccine, live virus was found, which had survived the supposed inactivation process with formalin.[8] An intense period of review of the manufacturing processes resulted in solutions to a number of difficult problems.

It became apparent that some incorrect assumptions had been made regarding the dynamics of the inactivation process. In the accompanying article, Salk points out and suggests that the straight line extrapolation of the inactivation curve, although theoretically correct, may not provide the margin of safety necessary when vaccine production is taken from a small research laboratory setting and transferred to large-scale operations in a number of manufacturing units. Salk and Gori[9] discussed this in greater detail in a subsequent article. In reviewing the experience of individual manufacturers of vaccine, it seemed clear that the requirement for consistency of vaccine in successive lots had neither been clearly stated nor invariably followed. This incident, tragic in its consequence of neurological sequelae and death, was not without its positive effect. It began a restructuring of the governmental apparatus to review the safety and efficacy of vaccines by what is now the

From the Operational Research Branch, Division of Sexually Transmitted Diseases, Center for Prevention Services, Centers for Disease Control, Atlanta.

*A commentary on Salk JE: Considerations in the preparation and use of poliomyelitis virus vaccine. JAMA 1955;158:1239-1248.

Food and Drug Administration's Office of Biologics Research and Review. At the time of the incident it was a function of a Division of Biologic Standards within the National Institutes of Health, which did not have the capacity to monitor vaccine manufacture adequately. Salk realized this and also discussed the need for consideration of alternative strains in the vaccine—a suggestion that also was followed. He suggested that a new type I strain might be sought that had greater antibody-inducing capacity (greater protection) with decreased neurovirulence in the monkey model (and presumably in humans).

### After 1955

In the period immediately following this article, 1955 to 1960, inactivated poliomyelitis vaccine was increasingly used in the vaccination of children and adults. Initial vaccines had some problems of marginal potency, as there was an overreaction to the 1955 disaster and some "overcooking" of vaccine as regards inactivation. Vaccines produced during the period 1955 to 1959 were particularly weak in the type I and, to a lesser extent, the type III components.[10] Gradually, between 1959 and 1961, the potency of vaccines increased. None of the vaccines of that era approach the potency of inactivated poliomyelitis vaccines today. What is often overlooked in historical review is how successful these less potent vaccines were. Control of poliomyelitis in the United States was under way before live virus vaccine was introduced in 1961 (see Chapter 45).[11,12]

The discouraging aspect of national poliomyelitis surveillance in the late 1950s was the occurrence of a significant proportion of paralytic poliomyelitis in persons with two, three, or four doses of vaccine. Although this can be expected in a widely distributed vaccine with efficacy less than 100%, the intensity of effort required for adequate control was disheartening to some. What was less apparent at the time was the effectiveness of inactivated vaccine in eradication of poliovirus from segments of intensively vaccinated communities. This was well documented in studies in Des Moines, Iowa,[13] and Providence, RI,[14] in vaccination campaigns following epidemic occurrence.

Oral attenuated live virus vaccines offered a number of attractive benefits that resulted in the conversion of the national vaccine policy to this method. Thus, live vaccines were responsible for the mopping up process. The incidence of paralytic poliomyelitis had decreased from greater than 14,000 cases in 1955, when inactivated poliomyelitis vaccine was introduced, to 829 cases in 1961, when oral vaccines took over.[15] The price paid after elimination was completed by oral vaccines was the continued occurrence of a small number of cases of vaccine-induced disease in vaccinees and their contacts.[16] In addition, there have been failures of oral poliomyelitis vaccine in developing countries for multiple reasons. In both developed and developing countries, interest has been renewed in the place of inactivated poliomyelitis vaccines.

It is at this point that I venture to review the second major contribution of Salk's 1955 article. In consideration of the immunologic factors influencing vaccine effective-

ness, he found that the primary response was related to antigenic mass (less adequately measured in those days than would be true today), that there was some advantage to lengthening the interval for second and third doses, and that, regardless of the apparent decline in the level of circulating antibody, a satisfactory booster effect could be achieved. In this article, Salk began to introduce the concept of "heightened immunologic reactivity," to which he would return in later articles to make the point that such reactivity could protect from death even in marginally adequate vaccines[17] but that the more potent vaccines recently manufactured give greater promise of prevention of serious neurological sequelae after a single dose. This claim has yet to be fully and adequately tested but has not been disproved. However, a considerable problem exists in the ethics of deliberately testing that single-dose hypothesis.

### Current Questions

What is perhaps of greatest interest is the pertinence of the Salk article today. There still remains much to be decided. In developed countries where poliomyelitis is under control, should we evaluate the efficacy and safety of a diphtheria-tetanus-pertussis–inactivated polio vaccine in early infancy, perhaps to be followed by oral poliomyelitis vaccine in later infancy or before school entrance? Would this prevent the rare occurrence of live vaccine–induced disease? These alternatives were carefully considered in 1977 by the Institute of Medicine, and our current primary reliance on oral poliomyelitis vaccine was affirmed.[18] However, we should continue to reexamine the options periodically. In developing countries, is inactivated poliomyelitis vaccine more effective where competing enteric viruses result in less adequate response to oral poliomyelitis vaccination?[19] Alternative strategies with oral vaccination such as the concept of pulse vaccination appear encouraging, but new approaches need to be examined.[20]

In the recent International Symposium on Poliomyelitis Control, held in Washington, DC, in March 1983, we find questions posed that take us back to 1955. The new generation of inactivated poliomyelitis vaccines with high antigenic content is not yet licensed in the United States, nor is it available in large quantities. The results of the small-scale trials of this vaccine and the history of the use of inactivated poliomyelitis vaccine since the 1950s leave no serious doubt as to the ability of this vaccine both to protect the individual from paralytic disease and to control poliomyelitis in the community, providing it is optimally applied. The remaining questions relate to:

- The minimum number of doses required to ensure protection.
- The optimal spacing between doses.
- The lowest age at which the vaccine can be reliably and safely used.
- The ability of the vaccine to suppress the circulation of wild poliovirus in populations living in poor sanitary conditions, particularly when the immunization coverage is low.
- The safety of the vaccine, when applied to a larger number than presently tested, and with adequate

surveillance of side effects.

Laboratory trials of the higher-potency inactivated poliomyelitis vaccine have demonstrated a reliable serological effect after two doses, particularly if the doses can be spaced six months apart. This feature is being exploited in the promotion of a simplified schedule, which requires two encounters only with each child. At each encounter, a dose of diphtheria-pertussis-tetanus combined with inactivated poliomyelitis vaccine is given. BCG is given with the first dose sometime between the ages of 3 and 8 months and measles vaccine with the second dose six months later. The field tests have shown that the serological response to inactivated poliomyelitis vaccine given in this way is good. The protection from pertussis in such a schedule is not ideal, however, and it is hoped that a better schedule can be devised.

We cannot rely completely on the 1955 analyses regarding booster effect. The vaccine product is different, but the general principles are still valid. Therefore, we read this LANDMARK ARTICLE by Jonas Salk not only for historic interest but to help us decide our future course. Few articles maintain such currency.

## References

1. Salk JE: Considerations in the preparation and use of poliomyelitis virus vaccine. *JAMA* 1955;158:1239-1248.

2. Enders JF, Weller TH, Robbins FC: Cultivation of the Lansing strain of poliomyelitis virus in cultures of various human embryonic tissues. *Science* 1949;109:85-87.

3. Salk JE, Lewis LF, Bennett BL, et al: Immunization of monkeys with poliomyelitis viruses grown in cultures of monkey testicular tissue. *Fed Pract* 1952;11:480.

4. Salk JE, Bennett BL, Lewis LF, et al: Studies in human subjects on active immunization against poliomyelitis: I. A preliminary report of experiments in progress. *JAMA* 1953;151:1081-1098.

5. Salk JE, Baseley PL, Bennett BL, et al: Studies in human subjects on active immunization against poliomyelitis: II. A practical means of inducing and maintaining antibody formation. *Am J Public Health* 1954;44:994-1009.

6. Summary of the report of the National Advisory Committee for Evaluation of Gamma Globulin: Evaluation of gamma globulin in prophylaxis of paralytic poliomyelitis in 1953. *JAMA* 1954;154:1086-1090.

7. Francis T Jr, Korn RF, Voight RB, et al: An evaluation of the 1954 poliomyelitis vaccine trials: Summary report. *Am J Public Health* 1955;45:1-63.

8. Nathanson N, Langmuir AD: The Cutter incident: Poliomyelitis following formaldehyde-inactivated poliovirus vaccination in the United States during the spring of 1955: I. Background. *Am J Hygiene* 1963;78:16-81.

9. Salk JE, Gori JB: A review of theoretical, experimental and practical considerations in the use of formaldehyde for the inactivation of poliovirus. *Ann NY Acad Sci* 1960;83:609-637.

10. Murray R: The standardization of potency of poliomyelitis vaccine, in *Poliomyelitis: Fifth International Poliomyelitis Conference, Copenhagen, 1960.* Philadelphia, JB Lippincott Co, 1961, pp 176-185.

11. Salk D: Eradication of poliomyelitis in the United States: II. Experience with killed poliovirus vaccine. *Rev Infect Dis* 1980;2:243-257.

12. Salk J, Salk D: Control of influenza and poliomyelitis with killed virus vaccines. *Science* 1977;195:834-847.

13. Chin TDY, Marine WM, Hall EC, et al: Poliomyelitis in Des Moines, Iowa. *Am J Hygiene* 1961;74:67-94.

14. Marine WM, Chin TDY, Gravelle CR: Limitation of fecal and pharyngeal poliovirus excretion in Salk-vaccinated children: A family study during a type I poliomyelitis epidemic. *Am J Hygiene* 1962;76:173-175.

15. Nathanson N: Eradication of poliomyelitis in the United States. *Rev Infect Dis* 1982;4:940.

16. Moore M, Katsona P, Kaplan JE, et al: Poliomyelitis in the United States, 1969-81. *J Infect Dis* 1982;146:558-563.

17. Salk JE: Persistence of immunity after administration of formalin-treated poliovirus vaccine. *Lancet* 1960;2:715-724.

18. Nightingale EO: Recommendations for a national policy on poliomyelitis vaccination. *N Engl J Med* 1977;297:249-253.

19. Krishnan R, Jadkav M, Selvakimar R, et al: Immune response of infants in tropics to injectable polio vaccine. *Br Med J* 1982;184:164-165.

20. John TJ, Pandian R, Gadomski A, et al: Control of poliomyelitis by pulse immunization in Vellore, India. *Br Med J* 1983;286:31-32.

## Chapter 42

# Successful Homotransplantation of the Human Kidney Between Identical Twins

John P. Merrill, M.D., Joseph E. Murray, M.D., J. Hartwell Harrison, M.D.
and
Warren R. Guild, M.D.

Boston

● A patient whose illness had begun with edema and hypertension was found to have suffered extreme atrophy of both kidneys. Because of the steady worsening of the condition and the appearance of uremia with other unfavorable prognostic signs, transplantation of one kidney from the patient's healthy identical twin brother was undertaken.

Preparations included collection of evidence of monozygosity and experimental transplantation of a skin graft from the twin. During the transfer of the healthy kidney it was totally ischemic for 82 minutes. Evidence of functional activity in the transplanted kidney was obtained.

The hypertension persisted until the patient's diseased kidneys were both removed. The homograft has survived for 11 months, and the marked clinical improvement in the patient has included disappearance of the signs of malignant hypertension.

This report documents the successful transplantation of a human kidney from one identical twin to another. The function of the homograft remains excellent 12 months after the operative procedure. Previous attempts at renal homotransplantation, both clinically and experimentally, have been unsuccessful with one exception. In dizygotic cattle twins, a kidney transplant has survived and functioned for at least nine months. Success in this instance, however, presumably resulted from the production of an acquired mutual tolerance to each other's

tissues by the mingling of fraternal protein in the common placental circulation.[1] Transplantation of the kidney in dogs and other animals rarely maintains function for more than a 10-to-14-day period in spite of vigorous attempts to modify the presumed antibody response that results in rejection of the homograft. Similarly, permanent function has not been maintained in a human renal homograft,[2] although in one such instance adequate renal function in a transplanted kidney has persisted for five and a half months.[3] The ultimate cause for rejection in such cases is in all probability differences in individual tissue specificity. Since, however, skin homografts between identical human twins have survived permanently,[4] it might be expected that renal homotransplantation might also be successful when performed between identical twins. The following case history describes such an event.

### REPORT OF A CASE

A 24-year-old, white, single male was apparently in excellent health until 14 months before his first admission to the Peter

From the medical and surgical services of the Peter Bent Brigham Hospital and Harvard Medical School.

This study was supported in part by grants from the John A. Hartford Foundation, Inc.; the Medical Research and Development Board, Office of the Surgeon General, Department of the Army; the U. S. Public Health Service; and the American Heart Association.

The table and figure 1 have been omitted from THE JOURNAL and will be included in the authors' reprints.

1. Billingham, R. E.: Brent, L., and Medawar, P. B.: Acquired Tolerance of Skin Homografts, Ann. New York Acad. Sc. **59**: 409, 1955.

2. Lawler, R. H., and others: Homotransplantation of the Kidney in the Human: Supplemental Report of a Case, J. A. M. A. **147**: 45 (Sept. 1) 1951. Küss, R.; Teinturier, J., and Milliez, P.: Quelques essais de greffe de rein chez l'homme, Mém. Acad. chir. **77**: 755, 1951. Michon, L., and others: Une tentative de transplantation rénale chez l'homme: aspects médicaux et biologiques, Presse méd. **61**: 1419, 1953.

3. Hume, D. M.; Merrill, J. P.; Miller, B. F., and Thorn, G. W: Experiences with Renal Homotransplantation in the Human: Report of 9 Cases, J. Clin. Invest. **34**: 327, 1955.

4. Brown, J. B.: Homografting of Skin: With Report of Success in Identical Twins, Surgery **1**: 558, 1937.

Bent Brigham Hospital. Except for scarlet fever at age 5 without apparent complications, the history was noncontributory. A few months prior to his discharge from military service, the patient noticed some puffiness about the eyes on awakening in the morning, and on a routine physical examination some elevation of blood pressure was noted. During a five-month study period while at the Boston Public Health Service Hospital, he remained essentially asymptomatic except for epistaxis. Physical examination was negative except for a consistently elevated blood pressure averaging 170/100 mm. Hg. Pertinent laboratory findings included persistent 2 to 3+ proteinuria. The urinary specific gravity was fixed at 1.010 and microscopic hematuria and cylindruria with occasional red blood cell casts were found in all urine specimens. Blood urea nitrogen level ranged between 75 and 100 mg. per 100 cc. Hemoglobin level varied between 7 to 10 gm. per 100 cc. Phenolsulfonphthalein excretion was less than 1% in two hours, and an intravenous pyelogram revealed no dye excretion on either side. X-ray of the chest showed the lungs to be clear and the heart normal in size and shape. After seven transfusions of whole blood he was discharged improved. Five months later he was readmitted again to the Boston Public Health Service Hospital and appeared pale and chronically ill. The blood pressure now varied between 160/80 and 208/120 mm. Hg. The retinal vessels showed narrowing of the arterioles with changes in caliber and occasional arteriovenous compression. He was discharged after a three-day period and readmitted six weeks later because of nausea, vomiting, headache, and general muscular aches. At this time he appeared more seriously ill, and marked pallor of the skin was evident. The blood pressure was 172/90 mm. Hg; retinal vessels showed narrowing and arteriovenous compression; and lungs were clear. The heart appeared to be slightly enlarged to the left. There was a grade 2 blowing systolic murmur over the entire precordium. The remainder of the physical examination was normal. Pertinent laboratory data follow. Hemoglobin was 6.7 gm. per 100 cc. and hematocrit 20%; urine showed 3+ protein, 2+ sugar, and 5-25 red blood cells per high-power field on spun sediment. There were occasional granular and hyaline casts. The blood urea nitrogen was 185 mg. per 100 cc. His course was characterized by persistent nausea and vomiting and on the third hospital day he had a generalized convulsion. In succeeding days he became increasingly drowsy, disoriented, and irritable and had several convulsions. Since the patient had a twin brother, it was suggested by Dr. David C. Miller of the U. S. Public Health Service that the possibility of homotransplantation of a kidney should be considered. For the investigation of this possibility, he was transferred to the Peter Bent Brigham Hospital on Oct. 26, 1954.

On admission the initial blood pressure was 140/90 mm. Hg. The patient appeared thin, pale, drowsy, and extremely disoriented. The remainder of the physical examination and laboratory data were consistent with that outlined above. Urine culture grew out Escherichia coli and enterococci. The patient continued to be restless and unable to tolerate oral feedings and became overtly psychotic. On the fourth hospital day he was treated by external dialysis with the artificial kidney[5] for a four-hour period. A good chemical response was obtained and 36 hours later the patient's sensorium had cleared and he was cooperative and able to take diet and medicaments by mouth.

On the 15th hospital day, full-thickness skin grafts, 2.5 by 2.5 cm., were exchanged between the twins. A control autograft was placed proximally and the homograft was placed 1 cm. distally, allowing a bridge of normal tissue to intervene between the two grafts. On the following day the patient was discharged

feeling well on a diet containing 50 gm. of protein and no added salt. He was followed at weekly intervals in the outpatient clinic, continued to show hypertension, and gradually developed the manifestations of congestive heart failure for which he was digitalized with some improvement. On Dec. 12, 1954, however, he was readmitted to the Peter Bent Brigham Hospital because of marked increase in signs and symptoms of his congestive heart failure. Physical examination at this time revealed a blood pressure of 220/146 mm. Hg. There was 3+ pitting edema of the lower legs up to the knees. Bilateral basal rales were present. The liver edge was tender and was palpated 4 cm. below the right costal margin. There was slight periorbital edema and the optic fundi now showed a 2 diopter papilledema with exudates and hemorrhages. The heart was enlarged to the left with a loud diastolic gallop heard over the entire precordium. A chest film showed marked cardiac enlargement with evidence of fluid at the base of the right side of the chest. During the next three days, 350 cc. of turbid, amber fluid was removed from the right side of the chest and the patient received three units of packed red blood cells. He was started on therapy with parenterally given protoveratrine. On this therapy there was marked clinical improvement.

On Dec. 16, 31 days after the original skin transplant, biopsy study of the homograft was done. In both gross and histological section the transplanted tissue appeared to have survived as normal skin. Because of this evidence of tissue compatibility and ancillary observations suggesting that the twins were monozygotic, on Dec. 23 a normal left kidney was removed from the healthy twin and transplanted to the patient. (Previous hospitalization had disclosed the absence of discoverable disease in the healthy twin and confirmed the presence of two normally functioning kidneys free of infection.)

The postoperative course of the donor was uneventful, and he was discharged on the 14th hospital day. The recipient tolerated the operative procedure well and, soon after the anastomoses were completed, clear urine was noted draining freely from the transplant. Nine days after surgery the intravenous injection of sodium indigotindisulfonate (indigo carmine) showed prompt appearance in good concentration in the urine from the transplanted kidney and no excretion from the patient's own kidneys. During the course of the following month, the homograft appeared to function well and began to hypertrophy. The patient was discharged from the hospital on the 37th postoperative day. He had gained 11 lb. (5 kg.) and was edema free. The blood urea nitrogen was 14 mg. per 100 cc. and the resting blood pressure, 120/60 mm. Hg. The chest was clear and the heart size normal. The serum carbon dioxide combining power was 25 mEq. per liter and the serum concentrations of sodium, chloride, potassium, calcium, and phosphate were all within normal limits. The phenolsulfonphthalein excretion was 18% in 15 minutes and 48% in two hours. Urinalysis at the time of discharge showed a trace of albumin, 4 to 6 white blood cells, and a rare blood cell per high-power field. Urine culture grew out Proteus vulgaris.

After discharge the patient's appetite was good and he had no edema, dyspnea, or orthopnea. Blood pressures ranged from 130/80 to 160/88 mm. Hg. The optic disks were normal, and the retinal vessels became normal, although a few old scars persisted in the optic fundi. Because of continued mild bacilluria and pyuria, the patient was begun on methenamine mandelate (Mandelamine) therapy. An excretory urogram performed two months after the renal homotransplantation showed prompt excretion of the injected dye in good concentration from the transplanted kidney but no detectable excretion by the two diseased kidneys.

Because of persistent mild hypertension, the patient was admitted to the Peter Bent Brigham Hospital for the third time three months after renal homotransplantation. At this time the initial blood pressure was 152/90 mm. Hg. The patient

5. Merrill, J. P., and others: The Use of the Artificial Kidney: I. Technique, J. Clin. Invest. 29: 412, 1950.

appeared healthy and completely asymptomatic. There had been further gain in weight and muscle development. The palpable mass of the homograft in the right lower quadrant had hypertrophied to half again its original size. The electrocardiogram showed disappearance of the changes of left ventricular hypertrophy. The hematocrit was 48%, blood urea nitrogen 14 mg. per 100 cc., and carbon dioxide combining power 23 mM. per liter. On the fifth hospital day a left nephrectomy was performed. The kidney weighed only 49 gm. and was covered by a markedly thickened capsule that was fibrosed and scarred. The cortex was markedly diminished in size and the microscopic section showed the majority of the glomeruli to be completely fibrosed. The renal parenchyma showed diffuse atrophy and fibrosis with disappearance of tubular elements and the appearance was that of diffuse advanced chronic glomerulonephritis. The patient was discharged 12 days after operation feeling entirely well. However, because of the persistence of mild pyuria and mild labile hypertension, he was readmitted for the fourth time on June 14, 1955, five and a half months after renal homotransplantation. On the seventh hospital day the patient underwent an uneventful right nephrectomy. The right kidney weighed only 29 gm. and showed the typical changes of advanced diffuse chronic glomerulonephritis with little functioning parenchyma remaining. On discharge the patient's appetite was good; he had gained more weight and was essentially asymptomatic. At the present time his blood pressure ranges from 125/70 to 146/82 mm. Hg. He weighs 25 lb. (11.3 kg.) more than his initial preoperative weight. He carries on unlimited activity and has no apparent physical disability. The urinary sediment is negative, although his 24-hour protein excretion is 4.5 gm.

## COMMENT

The transplantation of functioning tissue from one individual to another of the same species has, with few exceptions, not been successfully accomplished to date. Successful transplantation has been occasionally reported in the case of embryonic thyroid,[6] parathyroid,[7] and in one instance adrenal[8] tissue. The successful transplantation of bone and blood vessels depends not on their survival as living tissues but on their ability to act as bridges over which recipient tissue may grow. Because of its particular structure and the fact that it is frequently transplanted into an avascular field, corneal transplants in man, however, do survive as living tissues in a large percentage of cases.[9] The immune response leading to the rejection of homografts is incompletely understood. Circulating cytotoxic antibodies cannot be measured in significant amounts. It is probable, however, that antibodies to donor tissue are formed by the recipient and that these are removed by the homograft so rapidly that they cannot be measured in the blood.[10] The fact that an antigen-antibody reaction is responsible for the rejection of homografted tissue and that this response can be modified is suggested by work in which successful skin transplants were made after acquired tolerance to donor tissue resulting from the injection of donor cells into the embryonic recipient.[1] This acquired tolerance by the embryo to foreign cells probably accounts also for the survival of renal homotransplants between dizygotic bovine twins. In the human the role of acquired antibodies is suggested by recent reports of the successful homotransplantation of skin to a recipient with agammaglobulinemia.[11]

Although at the present time permanently successful renal homografts between humans cannot be performed because of this "antigen antibody like" reaction between donor tissue and recipient, skin homografts are known to survive between identical twins.[4] Having established this fact, there were several experimental observations that made the success of a renal homograft seem likely if performed between identical twins and that justified the removal of a normal kidney from a healthy donor.

First, immunologic and genetic similarity accounts for the permanent survival of skin homografts between identical twins.[4] Second, when skin or kidney homografts are carried out between antigenically dissimilar humans, the early function and the histological picture of rejection of each appears similar.[12] Third, skin and kidney homografts possess a common antigen that can sensitize a recipient to a subsequent homograft of either tissue from the same donor.[13] This further suggests that skin and kidney homografts behave similarly. Fourth, we have established to our own satisfaction that renal autografts have normal function indefinitely in animals.[14] This observation is important because, presupposing initial success of the transplant between antigenically similar (identical) twins, a second problem to be weighed was the permanency of such function. There were no reported distances of adequate functional studies in long-term surviving renal autografts.

It thus became imperative to establish beyond a reasonable doubt the fact that the twins were monozygotic (identical). Information that there was a common placenta was obtained from the hospital record of their birth. Blood samples from both twins were tested for all presently known reliable blood groups. These were found to be identical in both instances for each group (table). The two other siblings tested did not match. This was considered good but not indubitable evidence that the twins were identical. The twins and two other siblings were studied by Dr. Arthur G. Steinberg, geneticist of the Children's Medical Center, Boston, who felt that, "On the

6. Sterling, J. A., and Goldsmith, R.: Total Transplantation of the Thyroid Using Vascular Anastomosis: Report of a Successful Result in Chronic Tetany, Surgery 35: 624, 1954.

7. Gaillard, P. J.: Transplantation of Cultivated Parathyroid Gland Tissue in Man, in Preservation and Transplantation of Normal Tissues, Ciba Foundation Symposium, edited by G. E. W. Wolstenholme and M. P. Cameron, London, J. & A. Churchill, Ltd., 1954, pp. 100-109.

8. Broster, L. R., and Gardiner-Hill, H.: A Case of Addison's Disease Successfully Treated by a Graft, Brit. M. J. 2: 570, 1946.

9. Maumenee, A. E.: The Immune Concept: Its Relation to Corneal Homotransplantation, Ann. New York Acad. Sc. 59: 453, 1955.

10. Pressman, D.: Tissue Localizing Antibodies, Ann. New York Acad. Sc. 59: 376, 1955.

11. Good, R. A., and Varco, R. L.: Successful Homograft of Skin in a Child with Agammaglobulinemia: Studies in Agammaglobulinemia, J. A. M. A. 157: 713 (Feb. 26) 1955.

12. Dempster, W. J.: Problems Involved in the Homotransplantation of Tissues, with Particular Reference to Skin, Brit. M. J. 2: 1041, 1951.

13. Simonsen, M., and others: Biological Incompatibility in Kidney Transplantation in Dogs: Experimental and Morphological Investigations, Acta path et microbiol. scandinav. 32: 1, 1953.

14. Murray, J. E.; Lang, S.; Miller, B. F., and Dammin, G.: Long Term Functional Studies on Autotransplanted Kidneys in Dogs unpublished data.

basis of eight blood group systems plus the ability to taste phenylthiocarbamide, the sex similarity, and the a priori probability of dizygotic versus monozygotic twinning, the probability that these boys are identical twins is 0.985. Other data indicating that they are identical are 1) the presence of a single placenta, 2) both twins have the relatively rare Darwin's tubercle on their ears while their sibs do not, 3) the twins have identical eye colors,

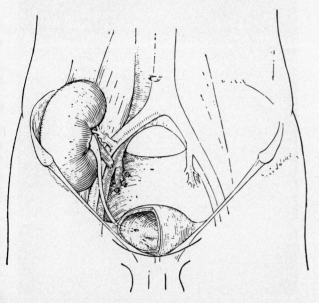

Fig. 2.—Schematic diagram of renal homograft in situ showing vascular anastomoses completed and ureter implanted in bladder. Renal artery end-to-end with hypogastric; renal vein end-to-side with common iliac; ureter mucosa-to-mucosa anastomosis with bladder.

including iris structure and pigment patterns, and their eyes are markedly different from their sibs' eyes in color and in iris structure, 4) there are no data suggesting they are not identical. My conclusion is that the twins are identical." Final decision to operate, however, was based on the most closely applicable evidence for antigenic similarity, that is the survival of transplanted skin between the two twins (fig. 1).

Evaluation of several factors determined the site for transplantation. The natural site for the homograft, the renal fossa, has two disadvantages. First, it requires simultaneous nephrectomy, thus increasing the magnitude of the operation. Secondly, it necessitates a ureteroureteral anastomosis with the possibility of subsequent stricture formation because the length of the transplanted ureter vascularized by the renal pedicle is too short to reach the bladder. The upper thigh, the site of 13 previous homotransplants, was not used because it requires a skin ureterostomy with the possibility of subsequent ascending infection. In addition, it creates a problem in the collection of urine.[3] The site selected, utilizing the iliac vessels for an anastomosis and placing the homograft retroperitoneally within the pelvis, allows implantation of the short ureteral segment directly into the bladder and places the kidney in its natural thermal environment. Furthermore, gravity drainage of the renal pelvis and ureter approaches normal physiological conditions. The observations mentioned above, that renal

autografts in animals maintain normal function indefinitely, appear important because of the previous opinion of other investigators that renal autografts so capable of survival soon develop impaired function manifested by abnormal renal dynamics and electrolyte excretion.[15] We surmised that the permanently successful function observed in our animal experiments resulted from the use of a recipient site that allows direct implantation of the ureter into the bladder, which has a normal thermal environment and which allows gravity drainage. This laboratory technique proved adaptable for use in man, provided that the left kidney was placed into the right iliac area or the right kidney into the left iliac fossa, thus reversing the normal anteroposterior relationship of the artery, vein, and ureter.

With this background, a nephrectomy was begun on the donor simultaneously with the operation on the recipient in an adjacent operating room. Through a right lower quadrant incision, the retroperitoneal area was entered exposing the right iliac vessels in the recipient. The operation was begun at 8:15 a. m., and the vessels were prepared for the anastomoses by 9:50 a. m. The donor kidney was brought into the room at 9:53 a. m. At this time the common iliac artery was occluded for the duration of the anastomosis. An end-to-end anastomosis between the free end of the hypogastric artery and the renal artery was completed at 10:40 a. m., and an end-to-side anastomosis between the renal vein and the

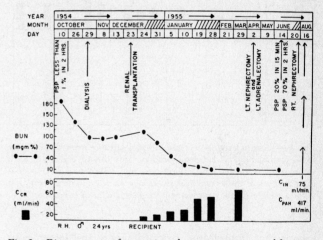

Fig. 3.—Disappearance of azotemia and improvement in renal function after renal homotransplantation. There is a progressive decrease in blood urea nitrogen and an increase in serial creatinine clearances (shown in solid bars at the bottom of the diagram). In October, 1954, there was almost no discernible phenolsulfonphthalein excretion. On June 14, 1955, phenolsulfonphthalein excretion was normal. In August, 1955, filtration rate and renal plasma flow as measured by the clearances of inulin and p-aminohippurate were at near normal values.

common iliac vein was finished at 11:15 a. m. Total ischemia of the donor kidney was one hour and 22 minutes. Both arterial and venous anastomoses were satisfactory, and the entire kidney became turgid and

15. Dempster, W. J., and Joekes, A. M.: Diuresis and Antidiuresis in Kidneys Autotransplanted to the Neck of Dogs, Quart. J. Exper. Physiol. 38: 11, 1953.

pink immediately on release of the arterial clamp. Therefore, a small artery in the renal pedicle that appeared to be an accessory renal artery was ligated rather than anastomosed. The last clamp was removed from the common iliac artery 10 minutes later, and pulsation was noted in the right foot immediately. At this point a suprapubic cystotomy was made in the medial and superior portion of the bladder and a small tunnel dissected in the submucosa. The ureter was let in through the muscular wall of the bladder and through the submucosal tunnel, and a mucosa-to-mucosa suture was carried out (fig. 2). A polyethylene ureteral catheter had been inserted in the ureter to the renal pelvis and carried out through the cystotomy at this time. The incisions in the bladder were then closed after a mushroom catheter had been inserted from a suprapubic site. At this time clear urine was flowing copiously from the ureteral catheter. The kidney now lay rather neatly in its new site

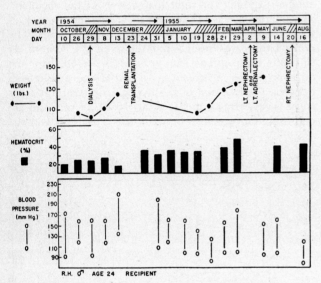

Fig. 4.—There is striking decrease in blood pressure immediately after renal transplantation and some tendency for this to rise again with improved levels after left nephrectomy and return to normal values after removal of the second diseased kidney. Increase in hematocrit and gain in weight reflect improvement in general clinical condition.

except that it projected forward where the lower pole impinged upon the iliac crest. The kidney was fixed by sutures to prevent its rotation, and the overlying oblique muscles and fascia were sutured together over it. The total operating time was three hours and 30 minutes. The postoperative course was smooth, and the incision healed per primam. The ureteral catheter was removed on the ninth postoperative day after evidence of function had been confirmed by the prompt excretion of injected sodium indigotindisulfonate.

The patient's subsequent course was characterized by continued improvement. Renal function improved; and, as it did so, acidosis and nitrogen retention disappeared (fig. 3). There was a marked decrease in blood pressure, and with this decrease the evidence of cardiovascular disease disappeared (fig. 4). Marked cardiomegaly (fig. 5) disappeared, and the abnormalities in the electrocardiogram vanished. The significance of these changes by the

addition of a normally functioning kidney in the presence of two badly damaged kidneys will be discussed in a future publication.[16]

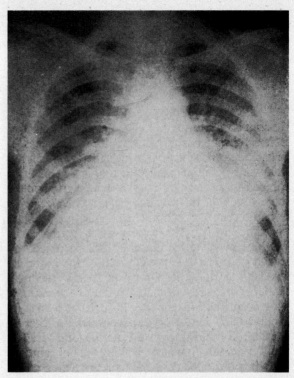

Fig. 5.—Chest film taken nine days before operation shows marked cardiomegaly and pulmonary congestion. Three weeks after operation lung fields were clear and heart size decreased to within normal limits.

During the follow-up visits, however, the patient continued to show evidence of some elevation of blood pressure. This elevation was labile and in some instances directly related to the presence of the examining physician. A persistent tachycardia (pulse rate of 90 to 100 per minute) continued in spite of normal blood

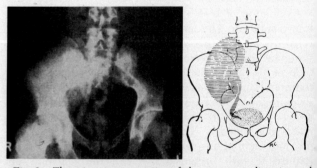

Fig. 6.—There is prompt excretion of the opaque medium in good concentration. Renal pelvis shows no extrarenal dilatation but there is definite dilatation of ureter, attributed to complete denervation of the kidney. No evidence of ureterovesicle obstruction is seen and prompt emptying of ureter into bladder occurs. Bladder is seen to be partially filled on this exposure and more so on subsequent exposures.

16. Merrill, J. P.; Guild, W. R., and Reardan, J. B.: Observations on Renal Hypertension in the Human Following Bilateral Nephrectomy and Successful Renal Homotransplantation: unpublished data.

chemistry and hemoglobin values. The urine continued to show 6 to 8 white blood cells, a rare cast, and 1+ protein. Clean voided urine specimens grew out a variety of organisms, which included P. vulgaris and Esch. coli. In vitro sensitivity tests showed these organisms to be resistant to most of the antibiotics except chloramphenicol. Colony counts varied from 100 colonies per milliliter on a pour plate to 2,000 colonies. After a consideration of the foregoing facts, it was decided to remove the two damaged kidneys for the following reasons. 1. Intravenous pyelography and renal function tests had shown that the renal homograft was functioning well. 2. The data indicated almost total lack of function in the two diseased kidneys. 3. The possibility existed that infection of the graft might occur from the two remaining diseased kidneys. 4. Experimental evidence suggests that a nonfunctioning or infected kidney may ultimately interfere with the function of a normal kidney, particularly with regard to its role in preventing renal hypertension.

After the second nephrectomy the patient's blood pressure stabilized at lower, and almost normal, levels. Frequent urine examinations since that time have shown clearing of the evidence of urinary tract infection. Some proteinuria, however, persists. The renal function of the homograft as measured by the clearance of inulin and p-aminohippurate closely approximates that of its fellow, which remains in the donor twin. Intravenous urography shows prompt excretion of dye in good concentration (fig. 6). The ureter appears somewhat dilated and tortuous, but this appearance might be expected in view of the fact that it lacks innervation.

The survival of the renal homograft for this period of time with continuing good function indicates the complete lack of a rejection response by the host and demonstrates that renal transplantation is a technically feasible procedure. It stresses further that, as indicated in previous studies,[3] total anoxia of the kidney (in this case for a period of one hour and a half) does not mitigate against resumption of adequate function. The implications of the dramatic response in malignant hypertensive disease to the transplantation of a normal kidney should carry considerable weight in future thinking about the renal mechanism in human hypertension. Why one identical twin and not the other should develop glomerulonephritis and whether the kidney of the unaffected twin transplanted into the diseased recipient will be susceptible to further attacks is a question still to be answered. Unanswered also is the question of whether the transplanted kidney in its unusual position with a short and abnormally innervated ureter will escape eventual infection.

## SUMMARY

Homotransplantation of a healthy kidney from one identical twin to another was performed. The homograft has survived for a 12-month period, and renal function is apparently normal despite the fact that both of the recipient's diseased kidneys were removed. A striking sequel to the marked clinical improvement that was observed was the disappearance of the signs of malignant hypertension. Tissue transplantation including that of a functioning kidney appears to be a feasible procedure in identical twins, but to date successful permanently functioning homografts appear to be limited to such individuals.

721 Huntington Ave. (15) (Dr. Merrill).

May 18, 1984
(*JAMA* 1984;251:2572-2573)

# The Landmark Identical Twin Case*

## Thomas E. Starzl, MD, PhD

In the autumn of 1979, the 25th anniversary was observed in Boston of the kidney transplantation that was the subject of the LANDMARK ARTICLE by Merrill and co-workers[1] that is reproduced in this issue. All of the authors of the article were members of the Harvard Medical School Faculty serving at the Peter Bent Brigham Hospital, where research in renal transplantation had been an important activity for several preceding years and where such work has continued to the present time. The decision at these institutions to focus for a historical celebration on the first identical twin transplantation rather than some earlier or subsequent event revealed an in-house perception of the importance of the case that has been shared by outside students of medical history such as Groth[2] of Stockholm.

Of the four authors, Merrill and Guild were internists. The specialty of nephrology was somewhere between nonexistent and fledgling. George Thorn had been given one of the first four artificial kidneys by Wilhelm Kolff, the Dutch physician-inventor. A Brigham version of this machine was built, and with this advantage the first renal dialysis center in the world was born under the direction of Merrill et al.[3] The use of hemodialysis to prepare the identical twin recipient for transplantation foreshadowed this practice for tens of thousands of patients in later years.

The availability of dialysis in the eventuality of poor or absent initial graft function was an obvious factor in the decision to proceed with transplantation. Thus, the Peter Bent Brigham Hospital in 1954 had all the ingredients of a modern nephrology support unit years ahead of its time. In this unit, under Merrill's direction, were trained many of the leaders in nephrology of the next three generations.

### The Twin Transplant

The transplantation was performed two days before Christmas, 1954, by Murray and Harrison, who modified the ectopic extraperitoneal technique originally described by the French surgeons Dubost,[4] Küss,[5] and Servelle[6] and their associates. Merrill had seen the extraperitoneal operation while visiting in France several years previously, as was mentioned by Hume et al[7] in an earlier publication from the Boston group. On Hume's

departure to take over the surgical chair in Richmond, Va, Murray had explored the use of the pelvic position of the transplanted kidney in the dog and had acquired extensive experience with that operation. A brief report of the identical twin case was given by Murray[8] at the American College of Surgeons and published in the *Surgical Forum* of 1955. Murray's legendary contributions to transplantation surgery continued until 1968, when he left this field to return to his first love, plastic surgery.

Living-donor nephrectomy was an unusual operation at that time, and, except for the mother-to-offspring transplantation reported by Michon et al,[9] it had been limited to the removal of "expendable" kidneys excised during creation of ventriculoureteric CSF shunts or for other reasons. No effort was made to preserve the excised identical twin kidney, which functioned promptly even though it underwent 82 minutes of warm ischemia time. Core-cooling techniques with cold solution were not introduced until the next decade. It is possible that some of the abnormalities of renal function reported in the early identical twin recipients could have been late manifestations of ischemic damage.

In addition to the nephrology prototype and the operative procedures, the connection of the Boston activities of late 1954 with many present-day policies is not hard to identify, including the important (and in the identical twin case, crucial) role of tissue matching.

### Tissue Matching, Heterotransplantation, Immunosuppression

In the account by Merrill et al,[1] credit for originally suggesting the transplantation was given to the recipient's physician, Dr David C. Miller of the Public Health Service Hospital, Boston. It had been known for almost two decades that skin grafts between identical twins were not rejected.[10,11] The application of this information in the transplantation of a vital organ was a bold extension of the same principle and one that depended in the absence of immunosuppression on the perfect tissue match that could be obtained only with genetic identity of the donor and recipient. The efforts that were made to be sure of this condition were extraordinary and ultimately included skin grafting. It is no distortion of concept to say that the tissue matching of today between nontwin donors and recipients is an attempt to come as close as possible to the ideal circumstances of the landmark Boston Case.

In their summary, Merrill et al[1] wrote, "Tissue transplantation including that of a functioning kidney appears to be a feasible procedure in identical twins, but to date

From the Department of Surgery, School of Medicine, University of Pittsburgh.

*A commentary on Merrill JP, Murray JE, Harrison JH, et al: Successful homotransplantation of the human kidney between identical twins. *JAMA* 1956;160:277-282.

successful permanently functioning homografts appear to be limited to such individuals." Thus, as an isolated event, this transplantation would have had little significance. The real meaning came from the continuity of effort at the Brigham that had begun earlier with the work of Hufnagel[12] and Hume et al[7] that had as the ultimate objective the transplantation of kidneys from nonidentical donors including cadavers or even animals (heterotransplantation). Renal heterotransplantation was given a surprisingly extensive trial at the beginning of this century, as summarized elsewhere.[2,13] Renal homotransplantation was first attempted by Voronoy[14] of Russia in 1936. The first example of probable extended homograft function was in a patient of Lawler[15,16]; the only other example of prolonged homograft function through 1954 was in a patient of Hume and Merrill[7] whose graft was placed in the thigh with function for five months.

Immunosuppression was to be a necessary condition for the fulfillment of the dreams of early transplanters. The deliberate obtundation of recipient immunologic activity became theoretically feasible with the demonstration that total-body irradiation was immunosuppressive.[17,18] Pharmacologic immunosuppression with steroids[19] and cytotoxic drugs[20,21] provided the basis for the new era of renal transplantation that began in 1962 and 1963. The first demonstration of the possible value of cytotoxic drug therapy in large animals was by a young English surgeon, Roy Calne,[22] who brought his subsequent animal investigations to the Harvard facility.

Within a few years after the watershed identical twin case, Merrill, Murray, and Harrison became responsible for clinical trials with immunosuppression for renal homotransplantation using total-body irradiation[23] and drug therapy.[24] Almost all of these efforts failed, but they paved the way for the "cocktail" therapy with azathioprine and prednisone that opened the modern era of renal transplantation a little more than 20 years ago and that made it possible for the first time to consider the transplantation of extrarenal organs.[13,25]

When great deeds are performed, it is just to honor the heroes and especially those such as the Harvard physicians and surgeons whose efforts were not transient; renal transplantation occupied much of their professional lifetimes, as Moore[26] has emphasized in his history of these events. The personal accolades for the members of the Boston team have been numerous.

---

If gold medals and prizes were awarded to institutions instead of individuals, the Peter Bent Brigham Hospital of 30 years ago would have qualified. The ruling board and administrative structure of that hospital did not falter in their support of the quixotic objective of treating end-stage renal disease despite the long list of tragic failures that resulted from these early efforts, leavened only by occasional encouraging notations such as those in the identical twin case. Those who were there at the time have credited Dr George Thorn, chairman of medicine, and Dr Francis D. Moore, chairman of surgery, with the qualities of leadership, creativity, courage, and unselfishness that made the Peter Bent Brigham Hospital a unique world resource for that moment of history.

This report was supported in part by research grants from the Veterans Administration and grant AM-29961 from the National Institutes of Health, Bethesda, Md.

## References

1. Merrill JP, Murray JE, Harrison JH, et al: Successful homotransplantation of human kidney between identical twins. *JAMA* 1956;160:277-282.

2. Groth CG: Landmarks in clinical renal transplantation. *Surg Gynecol Obstet* 1972;134:323-328.

3. Merrill JP, Smith S III, Callahan EJ III, et al: The use of an artificial kidney: II. Clinical experience. *J Clin Invest* 1950;29:425-438.

4. Dubost C, Oeconomos N, Nenna A, et al: Resultats d'une tentative de greffe renale. *Bull Soc Med Hop Paris* 1951;67:1372-1382.

5. Küss R, Teinturier J, Milliez P: Quelques essais de greffe rein chez l'homme. *Mem Acad Chir* 1951;77:755-764.

6. Servelle M, Soulie P, Rougeulle J, et al: Greffe d'un rein de supplicie a une malade avec rein unique congenital, atteinte de nehprite chronique hypertensive azotemique. *Bull Soc Med Hop Paris* 1951;67:99-104.

7. Hume DM, Merrill JP, Miller BF, et al: Experiences with renal homotransplantation in the human: Report of nine cases. *J Clin Invest* 1955;34:327-382.

8. Murray JE, Merrill JP, Harrison JH: Renal homotransplantation in identical twins. *Surg Forum* 1955;6:432-436.

9. Michon L, Hamburger J, Oeconomos N, et al: Une tentative de transplantation renale chez l'homme. Aspects Medicaux et Biologiques. *Presse Med* 1953;61:1419-1423.

10. Padgett EC: Is iso-skin grafting practicable? *South Med J* 1932;25:895-900.

11. Brown JB: Homografting of skin: With report of success in identical twins. *Surgery* 1937;1:558-563.

12. Hufnagel C, cited by Hume DM, Merrill JP, Miller BF, et al: Experiences with renal homotransplantation in the human: Report of nine cases. *J Clin Invest* 1955;34:327-382.

13. Starzl TE: *Experience in Renal Transplantation*. Philadelphia, WB Saunders Co, 1964.

14. Voronoy U: Sobre el bloqueo del aparato reticuloendotelial del hombre en algunas formas de intoxicacion por el sublimado y sobre la transplantacion del rinon cadaverico como metodo de tratamiento de la anuaria consecutiva a aquella intoxicacion. *Siglo Med* 1936;97:296.

15. Lawler RH, West JW, McNulty PH, et al: Homotransplantation of the kidney in the human. *JAMA* 1950;144:844-845.

16. Lawler RH, West JW, McNulty PH, et al: Homotransplantation of the kidney in the human: Supplemental report of a case. *JAMA* 1951;147:45-46.

17. Dempster WJ, Lennox B, Boog JW: Prolongation of survival of skin homotransplants in the rabbit by irradiation of the host. *Br J Exp Pathol* 1950;31:669-670.

18. Lindley DL, Odell TT Jr, Tausche FG: Implantation of functional erythropoietic elements following total body irradiation. *Proc Soc Exp Biol NY* 1955;90:512-515.

19. Billingham RE, Krohn PL, Medawar PB: Effect of cortisone on survival of skin homografts in rabbits. *Br Med J* 1951;1:1157-1163.

20. Hitchings GH, Elion GB: Activity of heterocyclic derivatives of 6-mercaptopurine and 6-thioguanine in adenocarcinoma 755. *Proc Am Assoc Cancer Res* 1959;3:27.

21. Schwartz R, Dameshek W: Drug-induced immunological tolerance. *Nature* 1959;183:1682-1683.

22. Calne RY: The rejection of renal homograft: Inhibition in dogs by 6-mercaptopurine. *Lancet* 1960;1:417-418.

23. Murray JE, Merrill JP, Dammin GJ, et al: Study of transplantation immunity after total body irradiation: Clinical and experimental investigation. *Surgery* 1960;48:272-284.

24. Murray JE, Merrill JP, Dammin GJ, et al: Kidney transplantation in modified recipients. *Ann Surg* 1962;156:337-355.

25. Starzl TE, Marchioro TL, Waddell WR: The reversal of rejection in human renal homografts with subsequent development of homograft tolerance. *Surg Gynecol Obstet* 1963;117:385-395.

26. Moore FD: *Give and Take: The Development of Tissue Transplantation*. Philadelphia, WB Saunders Co, Garden City, NY, Doubleday & Co, 1964.

March 15, 1958
(*JAMA* 1958;166:1294-1308)

# Chapter 43

# Smoking and Death Rates—Report on Forty-four Months of Follow-up of 187,783 Men

## II. Death Rates by Cause

E. Cuyler Hammond, Sc.D
and
Daniel Horn, Ph.D.,

New York

Between Jan. 1 and May 31, 1952, information was obtained on the smoking habits of 187,783 white men between the ages of 50 and 69 who were then traced through Oct. 31, 1955. During this period of time, 11,870 of the men died. The total experience covered 667,753 man-years. As described in part 1 of this paper,[1] we found that the total death rate (from all causes combined) was much higher among men with a history of regular cigarette smoking than among men who had never smoked cigarettes regularly and that the death rate increased with amount of cigarette smoking. Part 2 of this study is concerned with death rates from specific causes in relation to smoking. Causes of death were ascertained from death certificates, but in every instance that cancer was mentioned we wrote to the doctor, hospital, or tumor registry to obtain more detailed information.

Cause of death as stated on death certificates is subject to error, particularly when the doctor who signs the certificate has little or no opportunity to study the patient before death and no autopsy is performed. We were pleased to find that the diagnosis was confirmed microscopically in 79% of the deaths ascribed to cancer and that in the majority of the remaining 21% the evidence was such as to leave little doubt that death was due to this disease. However, even in microscopically verified cases

The death rates from specific causes have been studied in relation to smoking habits in a group of 187,783 men between the ages of 50 and 69. During the period of the study 11,870 of these men died. For microscopically proved cases of cancer as well as for the total cases reported as cancer it was found that the death rates were higher among regular cigarette smokers than among men who never smoked, that the mortality ratio increased with the number of cigarettes smoked per day, and that the death rates were higher among pipe and cigar smokers than among men who never smoked. A total of 7,316 deaths occurred among regular cigarette smokers, an excess of 2,665 over the 4,651 that would have occurred had the age-specific death rates for smokers been equal to that for nonsmokers. Coronary disease accounted for 52.1% of the excess; lung cancer accounted for 13.5% and cancer of other sites likewise for 13.5%. An extremely high association between cigarette smoking and death rates for men with lung cancer was found in rural areas as well as in large cities. The most important finding of this study was the high degree of association between cigarette smoking and the total death rate.

there is sometimes doubt as to the exact primary site, especially when the disease has already spread widely by the time of first diagnosis. A somewhat analogous situation seems to exist in deaths ascribed to diseases of the heart and circulatory system; that is, many patients suffer from two or more ailments in this class of diseases, and it is sometimes difficult to say which specific conditon was the underlying or principal cause of death. Indeed, the wisdom of attempting to make such a

From the Statistical Research Section of the American Cancer Society.

A summary of this paper was read in the General Scientific Meetings at the 106th Annual Meeting of the American Medical Association, New York, June 4, 1957.

This is the second part of a two-part article appearing in consecutive issues of THE JOURNAL.

TABLE 1.—*Number of Deaths and Death Rates Per 100,000 Man-Years by Cause of Death and by Age at Start of Study for Men Divided into Three Groups by Smoking History*[°]

| Cause of Death | Smoking History | Age Group, Yr. 50-54 No. of Deaths | Death Rate | 55-59 No. of Deaths | Death Rate | 60-64 No. of Deaths | Death Rate | 65-69 No. of Deaths | Death Rate | Observed Vs. Expected[†] No. of Deaths Observed | Expected | Ratio |
|---|---|---|---|---|---|---|---|---|---|---|---|---|
| Total: all causes | None | 218 | 656 | 375 | 1,139 | 438 | 1,575 | 613 | 2,800 | 1,644 | ... | 1.00 |
| | Cigarette | 1,633 | 1,117 | 2,040 | 1,699 | 2,016 | 2,668 | 1,627 | 4,013 | 7,316 | 4,651 | 1.57 |
| | Other | 280 | 691 | 592 | 1,277 | 828 | 1,861 | 1,210 | 3,170 | 2,910 | 2,563 | 1.14 |
| Cancer | None | 35 | 105 | 65 | 197 | 67 | 241 | 91 | 416 | 258 | ... | 1.00 |
| | Cigarette | 276 | 189 | 430 | 358 | 428 | 567 | 326 | 804 | 1,460 | 741 | 1.97 |
| | Other | 42 | 104 | 112 | 242 | 161 | 362 | 216 | 566 | 531 | 400 | 1.33 |
| Heart and circulatory diseases | None | 129 | 388 | 217 | 659 | 285 | 1,025 | 427 | 1,951 | 1,058 | ... | 1.00 |
| | Cigarette | 1,024 | 701 | 1,247 | 1,038 | 1,255 | 1,661 | 1,067 | 2,632 | 4,593 | 2,924 | 1.57 |
| | Other | 167 | 412 | 368 | 794 | 537 | 1,207 | 800 | 2,096 | 1,872 | 1,663 | 1.13 |
| Coronary artery disease | None | 90 | 271 | 142 | 431 | 204 | 733 | 273 | 1,247 | 709 | ... | 1.00 |
| | Cigarette | 765 | 524 | 962 | 801 | 921 | 1,219 | 713 | 1,759 | 3,361 | 1,973 | 1.70 |
| | Other | 113 | 279 | 253 | 546 | 348 | 782 | 513 | 1,344 | 1,227 | 1,112 | 1.10 |
| Other heart diseases | None | 20 | 60 | 37 | 112 | 39 | 140 | 52 | 238 | 148 | ... | 1.00 |
| | Cigarette | 112 | 77 | 131 | 109 | 131 | 173 | 129 | 318 | 503 | 425 | 1.18 |
| | Other | 26 | 64 | 53 | 114 | 78 | 175 | 103 | 270 | 260 | 230 | 1.13 |
| Cerebral vascular lesions | None | 16 | 48 | 31 | 94 | 32 | 115 | 85 | 388 | 164 | ... | 1.00 |
| | Cigarette | 104 | 71 | 123 | 102 | 152 | 201 | 177 | 437 | 556 | 428 | 1.30 |
| | Other | 21 | 52 | 52 | 112 | 96 | 216 | 161 | 422 | 330 | 263 | 1.25 |
| Other circulatory diseases | None | 3 | 9 | 7 | 21 | 10 | 36 | 17 | 78 | 37 | ... | 1.00 |
| | Cigarette | 43 | 29 | 31 | 26 | 51 | 68 | 48 | 118 | 173 | 97 | 1.78 |
| | Other | 7 | 17 | 10 | 22 | 15 | 34 | 23 | 60 | 55 | 59 | 0.93 |
| Pulmonary diseases (except neoplasms) | None | 2 | 6 | 8 | 24 | 7 | 25 | 13 | 59 | 30 | ... | 1.00 |
| | Cigarette | 38 | 26 | 68 | 57 | 71 | 94 | 54 | 133 | 231 | 81 | 2.85 |
| | Other | 5 | 12 | 12 | 26 | 23 | 52 | 37 | 97 | 77 | 48 | 1.60 |
| Other diseases | None | 28 | 84 | 46 | 140 | 49 | 176 | 52 | 238 | 175 | ... | 1.00 |
| | Cigarette | 174 | 119 | 183 | 152 | 188 | 249 | 124 | 306 | 669 | 520 | 1.29 |
| | Other | 37 | 91 | 62 | 134 | 65 | 146 | 112 | 293 | 276 | 268 | 1.03 |
| Gastric ulcer | None | 0 | 0 | 0 | 0 | 0 | 0 | 0 | 0 | 0 | ... | 1.00 |
| | Cigarette | 6 | 4 | 16 | 13 | 13 | 17 | 11 | 27 | 46 | 0 | Inf. |
| | Other | 0 | 0 | 1 | 2 | 2 | 5 | 2 | 5 | 5 | 0 | Inf. |
| Duodenal ulcer | None | 1 | 3 | 4 | 12 | 0 | 0 | 3 | 14 | 8 | ... | 1.00 |
| | Cigarette | 14 | 10 | 11 | 9 | 16 | 21 | 13 | 32 | 54 | 25 | 2.16 |
| | Other | 1 | 3 | 3 | 7 | 5 | 11 | 2 | 5 | 11 | 12 | 0.92 |
| Cirrhosis of liver | None | 3 | 9 | 2 | 6 | 4 | 14 | 6 | 27 | 15 | ... | 1.00 |
| | Cigarette | 30 | 21 | 21 | 18 | 23 | 30 | 9 | 22 | 83 | 43 | 1.93 |
| | Other | 5 | 12 | 7 | 15 | 8 | 18 | 9 | 24 | 29 | 23 | 1.26 |
| Miscellaneous | None | 24 | 72 | 40 | 122 | 45 | 162 | 43 | 196 | 152 | ... | 1.00 |
| | Cigarette | 124 | 85 | 135 | 112 | 136 | 180 | 91 | 224 | 486 | 453 | 1.07 |
| | Other | 31 | 77 | 51 | 110 | 50 | 112 | 99 | 259 | 231 | 233 | 0.99 |
| Accidents, violence, and suicide | None | 24 | 72 | 39 | 119 | 30 | 108 | 30 | 137 | 123 | ... | 1.00 |
| | Cigarette | 121 | 83 | 112 | 93 | 74 | 98 | 56 | 138 | 363 | 385 | 0.94 |
| | Other | 29 | 72 | 38 | 82 | 42 | 94 | 45 | 118 | 154 | 185 | 0.83 |

[°]"None" refers to no history of smoking; "cigarette" refers to regular smoking of cigarettes (including additional cigar or pipe smoking); and "other" refers to occasional smoking, cigar smoking, and pipe smoking but no regular cigarette smoking.

[†]Calculated by applying the age-specific death rates of men who never smoked to the man-years of exposure to risk of men in each of the other groups.

distinction has been questioned.[2]

For these reasons, we first made an analysis classifying the deaths into five broad categories: (1) cancer (International Statistical Classification of Diseases, Injuries and Causes of Death list numbers 140-205), (2) heart and circulatory diseases, including vascular lesions of the central nervous system (international list numbers 330-334 and 400-468), (3) pulmonary diseases, including pulmonary tuberculosis, asthma, influenza, pneumonia, bronchitis, and other pulmonary diseases but excluding neoplasms (international list numbers 001-002, 241, 480-502, and 520-527), (4) all other diseases, and (5) accidents, violence, and suicide (international list numbers E800-E999).

## GENERAL FINDINGS

Table 1 shows the number of deaths and death rates per 100,000 man-years for (1) men who never smoked; (2) men with a history of regular cigarette smoking, many of whom also smoked cigars and pipes; and (3) all other subjects, including pipe smokers, cigar smokers, and occasional smokers who had never smoked cigarettes regularly. Table 2 shows the number of deaths and death rates for men with a history of regular cigarette smoking only who in 1952 were smoking cigarettes regularly in the following amounts: (1) less than one-half pack of cigarettes a day, (2) one-half to one pack of cigarettes a day, and (3) one pack or more of cigarettes a day. On each of these tables is shown the number of deaths which

TABLE 2.—*Number of Deaths and Death Rates Per 100,000 Man-Years by Cause of Death and by Age at Start of Study for Men with History of Regular Cigarette Smoking Only*

| Cause of Death | Packs Per Day | 50-54 No. of Deaths | 50-54 Death Rate | 55-59 No. of Deaths | 55-59 Death Rate | 60-64 No. of Deaths | 60-64 Death Rate | 65-69 No. of Deaths | 65-69 Death Rate | Observed | Expected | Ratio |
|---|---|---|---|---|---|---|---|---|---|---|---|---|
| Total: all causes | <½ | 88 | 937 | 110 | 1,305 | 131 | 2,298 | 141 | 3,849 | 470 | 350 | 1.34 |
| | ½-1 | 443 | 1,128 | 551 | 1,875 | 482 | 2,875 | 357 | 4,441 | 1,833 | 1,081 | 1.70 |
| | 1+ | 421 | 1,408 | 428 | 2,289 | 300 | 3,280 | 177 | 4,714 | 1,326 | 658 | 2.02 |
| Cancer | <½ | 20 | 213 | 33 | 392 | 27 | 474 | 23 | 628 | 103 | 55 | 1.87 |
| | ½-1 | 74 | 189 | 113 | 385 | 79 | 471 | 66 | 821 | 332 | 173 | 1.92 |
| | 1+ | 71 | 238 | 105 | 562 | 85 | 929 | 51 | 1,358 | 312 | 106 | 2.94 |
| Heart and circulatory disease | <½ | 47 | 501 | 58 | 688 | 84 | 1,473 | 93 | 2,539 | 282 | 222 | 1.27 |
| | ½-1 | 278 | 708 | 342 | 1,164 | 318 | 1,897 | 236 | 2,936 | 1,174 | 675 | 1.74 |
| | 1+ | 264 | 883 | 252 | 1,348 | 174 | 1,903 | 102 | 2,716 | 792 | 406 | 1.95 |
| Coronary artery disease | <½ | 35 | 373 | 50 | 593 | 49 | 860 | 58 | 1,583 | 192 | 149 | 1.29 |
| | ½-1 | 213 | 543 | 258 | 878 | 235 | 1,402 | 158 | 1,966 | 864 | 456 | 1.89 |
| | 1+ | 203 | 679 | 199 | 1,065 | 129 | 1,411 | 73 | 1,944 | 604 | 275 | 2.20 |
| Other heart diseases | <½ | 6 | 64 | 4 | 47 | 15 | 263 | 12 | 328 | 37 | 32 | 1.16 |
| | ½-1 | 28 | 71 | 42 | 143 | 31 | 185 | 28 | 348 | 129 | 99 | 1.30 |
| | 1+ | 29 | 97 | 22 | 118 | 19 | 208 | 11 | 293 | 81 | 61 | 1.33 |
| Cerebral vascular lesions | <½ | 3 | 32 | 4 | 47 | 15 | 263 | 19 | 519 | 41 | 33 | 1.24 |
| | ½-1 | 23 | 59 | 36 | 123 | 40 | 239 | 41 | 510 | 140 | 97 | 1.44 |
| | 1+ | 27 | 90 | 24 | 128 | 19 | 208 | 13 | 346 | 83 | 57 | 1.46 |
| Other circulatory diseases | <½ | 3 | 32 | 0 | 0 | 5 | 88 | 4 | 109 | 12 | 7 | 1.71 |
| | ½-1 | 14 | 36 | 6 | 20 | 12 | 72 | 9 | 112 | 41 | 22 | 1.86 |
| | 1+ | 5 | 17 | 7 | 37 | 7 | 77 | 5 | 133 | 24 | 13 | 1.85 |
| Pulmonary diseases (except neoplasms) | <½ | 2 | 21 | 1 | 12 | 5 | 88 | 2 | 55 | 10 | 6 | 1.67 |
| | ½-1 | 9 | 23 | 15 | 51 | 18 | 107 | 15 | 187 | 57 | 19 | 3.00 |
| | 1+ | 12 | 40 | 11 | 59 | 10 | 109 | 7 | 186 | 40 | 11 | 3.64 |
| Other diseases | <½ | 11 | 117 | 12 | 142 | 13 | 228 | 15 | 410 | 51 | 38 | 1.34 |
| | ½-1 | 54 | 138 | 46 | 157 | 48 | 286 | 27 | 336 | 175 | 123 | 1.42 |
| | 1+ | 47 | 157 | 35 | 187 | 21 | 230 | 11 | 293 | 114 | 76 | 1.50 |
| Gastric ulcer | <½ | 0 | 0 | 1 | 12 | 0 | 0 | 2 | 55 | 3 | 0 | Inf. |
| | ½-1 | 1 | 3 | 8 | 27 | 6 | 36 | 2 | 25 | 17 | 0 | Inf. |
| | 1+ | 4 | 13 | 4 | 21 | 1 | 11 | 2 | 53 | 11 | 0 | Inf. |
| Duodenal ulcer | <½ | 0 | 0 | 0 | 0 | 1 | 18 | 2 | 55 | 3 | 2 | 1.50 |
| | ½-1 | 5 | 13 | 2 | 7 | 6 | 36 | 2 | 25 | 15 | 6 | 2.50 |
| | 1+ | 3 | 10 | 3 | 16 | 2 | 22 | 2 | 53 | 10 | 4 | 2.50 |
| Cirrhosis of liver | <½ | 1 | 11 | 2 | 24 | 3 | 53 | 1 | 27 | 7 | 3 | 2.33 |
| | ½-1 | 9 | 23 | 6 | 20 | 1 | 6 | 3 | 37 | 19 | 10 | 1.90 |
| | 1+ | 9 | 30 | 6 | 32 | 2 | 22 | 1 | 27 | 18 | 6 | 3.00 |
| Miscellaneous | <½ | 10 | 107 | 9 | 107 | 9 | 158 | 10 | 273 | 38 | 33 | 1.15 |
| | ½-1 | 39 | 99 | 30 | 102 | 35 | 209 | 20 | 249 | 124 | 107 | 1.16 |
| | 1+ | 31 | 104 | 22 | 118 | 16 | 175 | 6 | 160 | 75 | 67 | 1.12 |
| Accidents; violence, and suicide | <½ | 8 | 85 | 6 | 71 | 2 | 35 | 8 | 218 | 24 | 28 | 0.86 |
| | ½-1 | 28 | 71 | 35 | 119 | 19 | 113 | 13 | 162 | 95 | 92 | 1.03 |
| | 1+ | 27 | 90 | 25 | 134 | 10 | 109 | 6 | 160 | 68 | 59 | 1.15 |

°Calculated by applying the age-specific death rates of men who never smoked to the man-years of exposure to risk of men in each of the other groups.

would have occurred among the men in a particular smoking group if their age-specific death rates had been the same as for men who never smoked. This is designated as the "expected" number of deaths, while the number which actually occurred is designated as the "observed" number. Also shown is the ratio of observed to expected number of deaths (i. e., the mortality ratio). All of the computations were based on rates carried one significant figure beyond what is shown on these tables. The expected number of deaths was then rounded off to the nearest whole number. Significance tests were based upon the chi-square test, with expected values computed from the combined age-specific death rates for the nonsmokers and the smoking group in question. Table 3 shows the observed and expected number of deaths for (1) men with a history of occasional smoking only, (2)

men with a history of pipe smoking only, and (3) men with a history of cigar smoking only.

The death rates from accidents, violence, and suicide were about the same for men with a history of regular cigarette smoking as for men who never smoked (fig. 1). The observed number of deaths from these causes among cigarette smokers was 363, compared with 385 expected deaths, a difference of 22. This difference is not statistically significant ($p=0.22$). We divided this category into two groups of deaths: (1) suicide and (2) accidents and violence. Neither of these two groups showed a statistically significant association with smoking habits.

In contrast, 1,460 men with a history of regular cigarette smoking died of cancer, compared with an expected 741 deaths (had the age-specific death rates due to cancer of these men been the same as those of men

TABLE 3.—*Observed Versus Expected° Number of Deaths by Cause for Men with History of Occasional Smoking Only, Pipe Smoking Only, and Cigar Smoking Only*

| Cause of Death | Occasional Only | | | Pipe Only | | | Cigar Only | | |
|---|---|---|---|---|---|---|---|---|---|
| | Observed | Expected | Ratio | Observed | Expected | Ratio | Observed | Expected | Ratio |
| Total: all causes | 646 | 595 | 1.09 | 774 | 694 | 1.12 | 925 | 761 | 1.22 |
| Cancer | 115 | 93 | 1.24 | 155 | 108 | 1.44 | 160 | 119 | 1.34 |
| Heart and circulatory diseases | 401 | 383 | 1.05 | 485 | 454 | 1.07 | 620 | 492 | 1.26 |
| Coronary artery disease | 259 | 257 | 1.01 | 312 | 302 | 1.03 | 420 | 329 | 1.28 |
| Other heart diseases | 60 | 54 | 1.11 | 70 | 62 | 1.13 | 80 | 68 | 1.18 |
| Cerebral vascular lesions | 72 | 59 | 1.22 | 93 | 73 | 1.27 | 101 | 77 | 1.31 |
| Other circulatory diseases | 10 | 13 | 0.77 | 10 | 17 | 0.59 | 19 | 17 | 1.12 |
| Pulmonary diseases (excluding neoplasms) | 29 | 11 | 2.64 | 23 | 13 | 1.77 | 18 | 14 | 1.29 |
| Other diseases | 67 | 63 | 1.06 | 71 | 71 | 1.00 | 86 | 80 | 1.08 |
| Gastric ulcer | 0 | 0 | ... | 2 | 0 | Inf. | 2 | 0 | Inf. |
| Duodenal ulcer | 3 | 3 | 1.00 | 5 | 3 | 1.67 | 1 | 4 | 0.25 |
| Cirrhosis of liver | 7 | 6 | 1.17 | 5 | 6 | 0.83 | 12 | 7 | 1.71 |
| Miscellaneous | 57 | 55 | 1.04 | 59 | 62 | 0.95 | 71 | 70 | 1.01 |
| Accidents, violence, and suicide | 34 | 44 | 0.77 | 40 | 48 | 0.83 | 41 | 56 | 0.73 |

°Calculated by applying the age-specific death rates of men who never smoked to the man years of exposure to risk of men in each of the other groups.

who never smoked). The mortality ratio was 1.97 (fig. 1). The mortality ratio for cancer increased with the amount of cigarette smoking from 1.87 for men smoking under one-half pack a day to 1.92 for men smoking one-half to one pack a day and to 2.94 for men smoking one pack or more a day (table 2). Both pipe smokers and cigar smokers had higher death rates from cancer than men who never smoked, the mortality ratios being 1.44 and 1.34 respectively (Table 3).

The deaths of 4,593 cigarette smokers were attributed to diseases of the heart and circulatory system, as compared with 2,924 expected deaths, a difference of 1,669. The mortality ratio was 1.57 (fig. 1). The mortality ratio for these causes increased with amount of cigarette smoking from 1.27 for under one-half pack a day to 1.74 for one-half to one pack a day and to 1.95 for one pack or more a day (table 2). For cigar smokers, there were 620 observed deaths from heart and circulatory diseases, compared with 492 expected deaths (mortality ratio, 1.26). This difference is statistically significant (P < 0.001). For pipe smokers, there were 485 observed deaths and 454 expected deaths. This difference is not statistically significant (p=0.25).

Only 338 of the 11,870 deaths were attributed to pulmonary diseases other than lung cancer. These showed a high degree of association with cigarette smoking. A total of 231 deaths of cigarette smokers were attributed to pulmonary diseases, as compared with only 81 expected deaths (mortality ratio, 2.85). For men smoking one or more packs of cigarettes a day, the mortality ratio was 3.64. The death rate from pulmonary diseases was higher for both pipe and cigar smokers than for men who never smoked; but there were not many cases, and these differences were not statistically significant.

Deaths attributed to all other causes combined (including uncertain or unknown cause of death) accounted for less than 10% of the 11,870 deaths. This group, taken as a whole, showed some association with cigarette smoking, as indicated by the mortality ratio 1.29 (see fig. 1). As will be shown later, a few diseases in this category account for most of this relationship.

## CANCER

Malignant neoplasms were mentioned on 2,326 death certificates, and in each instance we wrote to the doctor, hospital, or tumor registry for further information. We sought similar information on 24 cases in which death was attributed to a benign neoplasm. Replies were received for 2,242 (95%) of the cases. Five cases recorded as benign neoplasm on the death certificate were found to be malignant tumors of the brain, and six cases recorded as cancer were found not to be cancer on the basis of further evidence. Making use of this data, we classified 2,249 (18.9%) of the 11,870 deaths in the study as due to cancer and an additional 75 as due to some other cause with cancer present. Of the 2,249 cancers to which death was attributed, 1,780 (79%) were microscopically proved, 381 were not microscopically proved, and 88 may or may not have been microscopically proved (i. e., information from death certificate only).

The general findings for cancer are shown in tables 4, 5, and 6. The following statements can be made for the microscopically proved cases as well as for the total

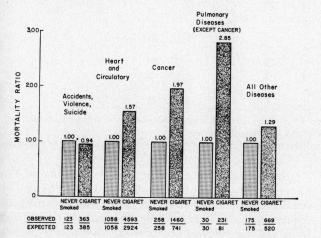

Fig. 1.—Mortality ratios by major causes of death. Ratios for cigarette smokers are compared with those for men who never smoked.

TABLE 4.—*Number of Cancer Deaths and Death Rates Per 100,000 Man-Years by Age at Start of Study for Men Divided into Three Groups by Smoking History*°

| Primary Site of Cancer | Smoking History | 50-54 No. of Deaths | 50-54 Death Rate | 55-59 No. of Deaths | 55-59 Death Rate | 60-64 No. of Deaths | 60-64 Death Rate | 65-69 No. of Deaths | 65-69 Death Rate | Observed | Expected | Ratio |
|---|---|---|---|---|---|---|---|---|---|---|---|---|
| Total: cancer (with or without microscopic proof) | None | 35 | 105 | 65 | 197 | 67 | 241 | 91 | 416 | 258 | ... | 1.00 |
| | Cigarette | 276 | 189 | 430 | 358 | 428 | 567 | 326 | 804 | 1,460 | 741 | 1.97 |
| | Other | 42 | 104 | 112 | 242 | 161 | 362 | 216 | 566 | 531 | 400 | 1.33 |
| Lung | None | 1 | 3 | 3 | 9 | 2 | 7 | 9 | 41 | 15 | ... | 1.00 |
| | Cigarette | 83 | 57 | 141 | 117 | 103 | 136 | 70 | 173 | 397 | 37 | 10.73 |
| | Other | 4 | 10 | 11 | 24 | 8 | 18 | 13 | 34 | 36 | 24 | 1.50 |
| Lip, tongue, mouth, pharynx, larynx, esophagus | None | 1 | 3 | 2 | 6 | 1 | 4 | 2 | 9 | 6 | ... | 1.00 |
| | Cigarette | 16 | 11 | 26 | 22 | 28 | 37 | 21 | 52 | 91 | 18 | 5.06 |
| | Other | 3 | 7 | 7 | 15 | 9 | 20 | 11 | 29 | 30 | 9 | 3.33 |
| Genitourinary system | None | 3 | 9 | 7 | 21 | 14 | 50 | 25 | 114 | 49 | ... | 1.00 |
| | Cigarette | 32 | 22 | 47 | 39 | 69 | 91 | 70 | 173 | 218 | 123 | 1.77 |
| | Other | 4 | 10 | 13 | 28 | 42 | 94 | 52 | 136 | 111 | 80 | 1.39 |
| Digestive system (except esophagus) | None | 16 | 48 | 33 | 100 | 32 | 115 | 36 | 164 | 117 | ... | 1.00 |
| | Cigarette | 85 | 58 | 124 | 103 | 142 | 188 | 115 | 284 | 466 | 344 | 1.35 |
| | Other | 15 | 37 | 53 | 114 | 80 | 180 | 97 | 254 | 245 | 180 | 1.36 |
| Lymphatic and hematopoietic system | None | 7 | 21 | 8 | 24 | 13 | 47 | 8 | 37 | 36 | ... | 1.00 |
| | Cigarette | 30 | 21 | 44 | 37 | 35 | 46 | 26 | 64 | 135 | 110 | 1.23 |
| | Other | 8 | 20 | 13 | 28 | 12 | 27 | 23 | 60 | 56 | 55 | 1.02 |
| Other specific sites | None | 6 | 18 | 12 | 37 | 4 | 14 | 6 | 27 | 28 | ... | 1.00 |
| | Cigarette | 18 | 12 | 36 | 30 | 25 | 33 | 12 | 30 | 91 | 92 | 0.99 |
| | Other | 7 | 17 | 13 | 28 | 13 | 29 | 10 | 26 | 43 | 41 | 1.05 |
| Unknown primary site | None | 1 | 3 | 0 | 0 | 1 | 4 | 5 | 23 | 7 | ... | 1.00 |
| | Cigarette | 12 | 8 | 12 | 10 | 26 | 34 | 12 | 30 | 62 | 16 | 3.88 |
| | Other | 1 | 3 | 2 | 4 | 7 | 16 | 10 | 26 | 20 | 12 | 1.67 |
| Total: cancer (with microscopic proof) | None | 28 | 84 | 56 | 170 | 55 | 198 | 69 | 315 | 208 | ... | 1.00 |
| | Cigarette | 225 | 154 | 363 | 302 | 348 | 461 | 224 | 553 | 1,160 | 605 | 1.92 |
| | Other | 33 | 81 | 98 | 211 | 131 | 294 | 150 | 393 | 412 | 321 | 1.28 |
| Bronchogenic (except adenocarcinoma) | None | 0 | 0 | 1 | 3 | 0 | 0 | 3 | 14 | 4 | ... | 1.00 |
| | Cigarette | 61 | 42 | 102 | 85 | 79 | 105 | 37 | 91 | 279 | 9 | 31.00 |
| | Other | 3 | 7 | 9 | 19 | 6 | 14 | 8 | 21 | 26 | 7 | 3.71 |
| Bronchogenic, adenocarcinoma | None | 1 | 3 | 0 | 0 | 0 | 0 | 1 | 5 | 2 | ... | 1.00 |
| | Cigarette | 7 | 5 | 13 | 11 | 4 | 5 | 2 | 5 | 26 | 6 | 4.33 |
| | Other | 0 | 0 | 2 | 4 | 1 | 2 | 1 | 3 | 4 | 3 | 1.33 |
| Lip, tongue, mouth, pharynx, larynx, esophagus | None | 1 | 3 | 1 | 3 | 0 | 0 | 2 | 9 | 4 | ... | 1.00 |
| | Cigarette | 16 | 11 | 23 | 19 | 25 | 33 | 20 | 49 | 84 | 12 | 7.00 |
| | Other | 3 | 7 | 6 | 13 | 9 | 20 | 8 | 21 | 26 | 6 | 4.33 |
| Genitourinary system | None | 1 | 3 | 7 | 21 | 9 | 32 | 21 | 96 | 38 | ... | 1.00 |
| | Cigarette | 25 | 17 | 37 | 31 | 59 | 78 | 56 | 138 | 177 | 93 | 1.90 |
| | Other | 4 | 10 | 11 | 24 | 22 | 49 | 35 | 92 | 72 | 62 | 1.16 |
| Digestive system (except esophagus) | None | 14 | 42 | 28 | 85 | 29 | 104 | 29 | 133 | 100 | ... | 1.00 |
| | Cigarette | 70 | 48 | 108 | 90 | 113 | 150 | 74 | 183 | 365 | 296 | 1.23 |
| | Other | 9 | 22 | 44 | 95 | 66 | 148 | 65 | 170 | 184 | 154 | 1.19 |
| Lymphatic and hematopoietic system | None | 5 | 15 | 8 | 24 | 11 | 40 | 7 | 32 | 31 | ... | 1.00 |
| | Cigarette | 24 | 16 | 39 | 33 | 30 | 40 | 20 | 49 | 113 | 94 | 1.20 |
| | Other | 7 | 17 | 12 | 26 | 9 | 20 | 20 | 52 | 48 | 47 | 1.02 |
| Other specific sites | None | 6 | 18 | 11 | 33 | 5 | 18 | 5 | 23 | 27 | ... | 1.00 |
| | Cigarette | 15 | 10 | 33 | 28 | 22 | 29 | 9 | 22 | 79 | 89 | 0.89 |
| | Other | 6 | 15 | 12 | 26 | 12 | 27 | 9 | 24 | 39 | 40 | 0.98 |
| Unknown primary site | None | 0 | 0 | 0 | 0 | 1 | 4 | 1 | 5 | 2 | ... | 1.00 |
| | Cigarette | 7 | 5 | 8 | 7 | 16 | 21 | 6 | 15 | 37 | 5 | 7.40 |
| | Other | 1 | 3 | 2 | 4 | 6 | 14 | 4 | 11 | 13 | 3 | 4.33 |

°"None" refers to no history of smoking; "cigarette" refers to regular smoking of cigarettes (including additional cigar or pipe smoking); and "other" refers to occasional smoking, cigar smoking, and pipe smoking but no regular cigarette smoking.

†Calculated by applying the age-specific death rates of men who never smoked to the man-years of exposure to risk of men in each of the other groups.

group: 1. In every age group, the death rates of the men with a history of regular cigarette smoking were higher than the death rates of men who never smoked. 2. The mortality ratio increased with the number of cigarettes smoked per day. 3. The death rates for pipe and cigar smokers were higher, on the average, than the death rates for men who never smoked.

Considering only microscopically proved cases, the mortality ratio was 1.92 for all men with a history of regular cigarette smoking. For men with a history of regular cigarette smoking only, the mortality ratio rose from 1.67 for smokers of under one-half to one pack a day, to 1.82 for smokers of one-half to one pack a day, to 2.86 for smokers of one to two packs a day, and to 3.31

TABLE 5.—*Number of Cancer Deaths and Death Rates Per 100,000 Man-Years by Age at Start of Study for Men with History of Regular Cigarette Smoking Only*

| Primary Site of Cancer | Packs Per Day | 50-54 No. of Deaths | 50-54 Death Rate | 55-59 No. of Deaths | 55-59 Death Rate | 60-64 No. of Deaths | 60-64 Death Rate | 65-69 No. of Deaths | 65-69 Death Rate | Observed | Expected* | Ratio |
|---|---|---|---|---|---|---|---|---|---|---|---|---|
| Total: cancer (with or | <½ | 20 | 213 | 33 | 392 | 27 | 474 | 23 | 628 | 103 | 55 | 1.87 |
| without microscopic | ½-1 | 74 | 189 | 113 | 385 | 79 | 471 | 66 | 821 | 332 | 173 | 1.92 |
| proof) ................ | 1+ | 71 | 238 | 105 | 562 | 85 | 929 | 51 | 1,358 | 312 | 106 | 2.94 |
| Lung ..................... | <½ | 6 | 64 | 6 | 71 | 5 | 88 | 7 | 191 | 24 | 3 | 8.00 |
|  | ½-1 | 16 | 41 | 35 | 119 | 15 | 90 | 18 | 224 | 84 | 8 | 10.50 |
|  | 1+ | 30 | 100 | 45 | 241 | 29 | 317 | 13 | 346 | 117 | 5 | 23.40 |
| Lip, tongue, | <½ | 2 | 21 | 1 | 12 | 2 | 35 | 2 | 55 | 7 | 1 | 7.00 |
| mouth, pharynx, | ½-1 | 4 | 10 | 8 | 27 | 7 | 42 | 5 | 62 | 24 | 4 | 6.00 |
| larynx, esophagus ........... | 1+ | 3 | 10 | 7 | 37 | 5 | 55 | 8 | 213 | 23 | 3 | 7.67 |
| Genitourinary | <½ | 4 | 43 | 5 | 59 | 5 | 88 | 5 | 137 | 19 | 10 | 1.90 |
| system ................. | ½-1 | 7 | 18 | 14 | 48 | 14 | 84 | 14 | 174 | 49 | 27 | 1.81 |
|  | +1 | 10 | 33 | 12 | 64 | 14 | 153 | 11 | 293 | 47 | 16 | 2.94 |
| Digestive system | <½ | 6 | 64 | 10 | 119 | 8 | 140 | 7 | 191 | 31 | 26 | 1.19 |
| (except | ½-1 | 28 | 71 | 32 | 109 | 17 | 101 | 24 | 299 | 101 | 81 | 1.25 |
| esophagus) ............ | 1+ | 14 | 47 | 19 | 102 | 25 | 273 | 13 | 346 | 71 | 50 | 1.42 |
| Lymphatic and | <½ | 2 | 21 | 6 | 71 | 2 | 35 | 1 | 27 | 11 | 8 | 1.38 |
| hematopoietic | ½-1 | 9 | 23 | 10 | 34 | 9 | 54 | 3 | 37 | 31 | 26 | 1.19 |
| system ................. | 1+ | 9 | 30 | 12 | 64 | 4 | 44 | 1 | 27 | 26 | 17 | 1.53 |
| Other specific | <½ | 0 | 0 | 3 | 36 | 2 | 35 | 0 | 0 | 5 | 7 | 0.71 |
| sites ................ | ½-1 | 5 | 13 | 10 | 34 | 8 | 48 | 1 | 12 | 24 | 22 | 1.09 |
|  | 1+ | 1 | 3 | 10 | 54 | 4 | 44 | 3 | 80 | 18 | 15 | 1.20 |
| Unknown primary | <½ | 0 | 0 | 2 | 24 | 3 | 53 | 1 | 27 | 6 | 1 | 6.00 |
| site ................ | ½-1 | 5 | 13 | 4 | 14 | 9 | 54 | 1 | 13 | 19 | 4 | 4.75 |
|  | 1+ | 4 | 13 | 0 | 0 | 4 | 44 | 2 | 53 | 10 | 2 | 5.00 |
| Total: cancer | <½ | 16 | 170 | 25 | 297 | 20 | 351 | 14 | 382 | 75 | 45 | 1.67 |
| (with microscopic | ½-1 | 53 | 135 | 96 | 327 | 65 | 388 | 45 | 560 | 259 | 142 | 1.82 |
| proof) ................ | 1+ | 61 | 204 | 87 | 465 | 71 | 776 | 37 | 985 | 256 | 87 | 2.94 |
| Bronchogenic | <½ | 3 | 32 | 4 | 47 | 2 | 35 | 4 | 109 | 13 | <1 | 16.25 |
| (except | ½-1 | 11 | 28 | 22 | 75 | 10 | 60 | 8 | 100 | 51 | 2 | 25.50 |
| adenocarcinoma) ......... | 1+ | 24 | 80 | 33 | 177 | 24 | 262 | 7 | 186 | 88 | 1 | 88.00 |
| Bronchogenic, | <½ | 0 | 0 | 1 | 12 | 0 | 0 | 0 | 0 | 1 | <1 | 2.00 |
| adenocarcinoma) ......... | ½-1 | 0 | 0 | 4 | 14 | 1 | 6 | 0 | 0 | 5 | 2 | 2.50 |
|  | 1+ | 4 | 13 | 2 | 11 | 1 | 11 | 0 | 0 | 7 | 1 | 7.00 |
| Lip, tongue, | <½ | 2 | 21 | 1 | 12 | 2 | 35 | 2 | 55 | 7 | <1 | 7.78 |
| mouth, pharynx, | ½-1 | 4 | 10 | 6 | 20 | 6 | 36 | 5 | 62 | 21 | 3 | 7.00 |
| larynx, esophagus ........... | 1+ | 3 | 10 | 6 | 32 | 4 | 44 | 8 | 213 | 21 | 2 | 10.50 |
| Genitourinary | <½ | 4 | 43 | 3 | 36 | 4 | 79 | 3 | 82 | 14 | 7 | 2.00 |
| system ................. | ½-1 | 5 | 13 | 12 | 41 | 14 | 84 | 11 | 137 | 42 | 21 | 2.00 |
|  | 1+ | 7 | 23 | 11 | 59 | 14 | 153 | 9 | 240 | 41 | 12 | 3.42 |
| Digestive system | <½ | 6 | 64 | 8 | 95 | 7 | 123 | 4 | 109 | 25 | 22 | 1.14 |
| (except | ½-1 | 21 | 54 | 30 | 102 | 12 | 72 | 17 | 212 | 80 | 70 | 1.14 |
| esophagus) ............ | 1+ | 12 | 40 | 17 | 91 | 19 | 208 | 10 | 266 | 58 | 43 | 1.35 |
| Lymphatic and | <½ | 1 | 11 | 5 | 59 | 2 | 35 | 0 | 0 | 8 | 7 | 1.14 |
| hematopoietic | ½-1 | 6 | 15 | 10 | 34 | 8 | 48 | 2 | 25 | 26 | 22 | 1.18 |
| system ................. | 1+ | 7 | 23 | 9 | 48 | 4 | 44 | 1 | 27 | 21 | 14 | 1.50 |
| Other specific | <½ | 0 | 0 | 2 | 24 | 2 | 35 | 0 | 0 | 4 | 6 | 0.67 |
| sites ................ | ½-1 | 4 | 10 | 9 | 31 | 7 | 42 | 1 | 12 | 21 | 22 | 0.95 |
|  | 1+ | 1 | 3 | 9 | 48 | 3 | 33 | 1 | 27 | 14 | 14 | 1.00 |
| Unknown primary | <½ | 0 | 0 | 1 | 12 | 1 | 18 | 1 | 27 | 3 | <1 | 7.50 |
| site ................ | ½-1 | 2 | 5 | 3 | 10 | 7 | 42 | 1 | 12 | 13 | 1 | 13.00 |
|  | 1+ | 3 | 10 | 0 | 0 | 2 | 22 | 1 | 27 | 6 | <1 | 12.00 |

*Calculated by applying the age-specific death rates of men who never smoked to the man-years of exposure to risk of men in each of the other groups.

for smokers of two packs or more a day. Both for all cases and for microscopically proved cases, the mortality ratios in the last two years of the study (November, 1953, through October, 1955) were in close agreement with the mortality ratios in the earlier part of the study (January, 1952, through October, 1953).

The deaths due to cancer were divided into six groups (see fig. 2) by primary site (plus a seventh group, primary site unknown). Of those with primary site specified, by far the highest association with cigarette smoking was found in primary cancer of the lung, the next highest group being the following sites combined: lip, tongue, floor of mouth, pharynx, larynx, and esophagus. Considering microscopically proved cancer of all specified primary sites other than those just mentioned, the mortality ratio for men with a history of regular cigarette smoking was 1.28, and the mortality ratio for smokers of one pack or more a day was 1.61.

*Lung Cancer.*—Primary cancer of the lung was recorded as the cause of 448 deaths. Only 15 of these men had never smoked, and 8 had smoked only occasionally. Three hundred ninety-seven deaths attributed to lung

TABLE 6.—*Observed Versus Expected° Number of Cancer Deaths by Primary Site for Men with History of Occasional Smoking Only, Pipe Smoking Only, and Cigar Smoking Only*

| Primary Site of Cancer | Occasional Only | | | Pipe Only | | | Cigar Only | | |
|---|---|---|---|---|---|---|---|---|---|
| | Observed | Expected | Ratio | Observed | Expected | Ratio | Observed | Expected | Ratio |
| Total: cancer (with or without microscopic proof) | 115 | 93 | 1.24 | 155 | 108 | 1.44 | 160 | 119 | 1.34 |
| Lung | 8 | 6 | 1.33 | 18 | 7 | 2.57 | 7 | 7 | 1.00 |
| Lip, tongue, mouth, pharynx, larynx, esophagus | 3 | 2 | 1.50 | 9 | 3 | 3.00 | 11 | 3 | 3.67 |
| Genitourinary system | 26 | 18 | 1.44 | 31 | 22 | 1.41 | 27 | 23 | 1.17 |
| Digestive system (except esophagus) | 49 | 42 | 1.17 | 61 | 48 | 1.27 | 80 | 54 | 1.48 |
| Lymphatic and hematopoietic system | 19 | 13 | 1.46 | 17 | 14 | 1.21 | 11 | 16 | 0.69 |
| Other specified sites | 5 | 10 | 0.50 | 16 | 10 | 1.60 | 13 | 13 | 1.00 |
| Unknown primary site | 5 | 3 | 1.67 | 3 | 3 | 1.00 | 11 | 3 | 3.67 |
| Total: cancer (with microscopic proof) | 85 | 75 | 1.13 | 115 | 86 | 1.34 | 129 | 96 | 1.34 |
| Bronchogenic (except adenocarcinoma) | 5 | 2 | 2.50 | 13 | 2 | 6.50 | 6 | 2 | 3.00 |
| Bronchogenic, adenocarcinoma | 1 | <1 | 1.43 | 2 | <1 | 2.50 | 1 | <1 | 1.11 |
| Lip, tongue, mouth, pharynx, Larynx, esophagus | 3 | 1 | 3.00 | 7 | 2 | 3.50 | 10 | 2 | 5.00 |
| Genitourinary system | 19 | 14 | 1.36 | 21 | 18 | 1.17 | 19 | 18 | 1.06 |
| Digestive system (except esophagus) | 35 | 36 | 0.97 | 41 | 41 | 1.00 | 63 | 46 | 1.37 |
| Lymphatic and hematopoietic system | 15 | 11 | 1.36 | 15 | 12 | 1.25 | 10 | 14 | 0.71 |
| Other specified sites | 5 | 10 | 0.50 | 14 | 10 | 1.40 | 12 | 12 | 1.00 |
| Unknown primary site | 2 | <1 | 2.86 | 2 | 1 | 2.00 | 8 | 1 | 8.00 |

°Calculated by applying the age-specific death rates of men who never smoked to the man-years of exposure to risk of men in each of the other groups.

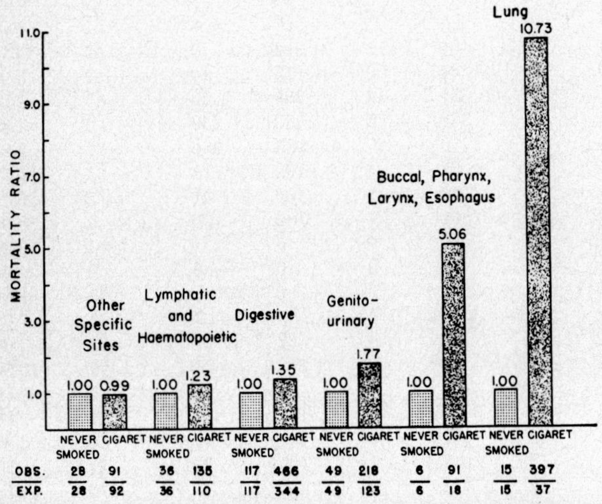

Fig. 2.—Mortality ratios by sites of cancer. Ratios for cigarette smokers are compared with those for men who never smoked.

TABLE 7.—*Number of Deaths and Age-Standardized Death Rates° from Lung Cancer by Smoking Habits*

| Smoking Habits | All Cases | | Well-Established Cases (Excluding Adenocarcinoma) | | Adenocarcinoma | |
|---|---|---|---|---|---|---|
| | No. of Deaths | Death Rate | No. of Deaths | Death Rate | No. of Deaths | Death Rate |
| Never smoked | 15 | 12.8 | 4 | 3.4 | 2 | 1.8 |
| Occasional only | 8 | 19.2 | 5 | 11.9 | 1 | 2.3 |
| Cigars only | 7 | 13.1 | 6 | 11.4 | 1 | 1.7 |
| Pipes only | 18 | 38.5 | 13 | 28.9 | 2 | 4.4 |
| Cigars and pipes | 3 | 7.3 | 2 | 4.9 | 0 | ... |
| Cigarettes and other | 148 | 97.7 | 103 | 67.0 | 12 | 7.3 |
| Cigarettes only | 249 | 127.2 | 162 | 78.6 | 14 | 6.1 |
| Total | 448 | 68.0 | 295 | 44.5 | 32 | 4.7 |
| Current: daily cigarette smoking† | | | | | | |
| <½ pack | 24 | 95.2 | 13 | 51.4 | 1 | 3.3 |
| ½-1 pack | 84 | 107.8 | 50 | 59.3 | 5 | 5.1 |
| 1-2 packs | 90 | 229.2 | 60 | 143.9 | 7 | 11.6 |
| 2+ packs | 27 | 264.2 | 22 | 217.3 | 0 | ... |

°Death rate per 100,000 man-years standardized to the age distribution of the white male population of the United States as of July, 1954.

†History of cigarette smoking only.

cancer occurred among men with a history of regular cigarette smoking, as compared with 37 expected deaths, giving a mortality ratio of 10.73. Only 18 of these deaths occurred among men who smoked pipes only and 7 among men who smoked cigars only. Among men with a history of cigarette smoking only, the death rate increased rapidly with current amount of smoking.

The 448 cases were further classified as follows: 309 microscopically proved cases of bronchogenic carcinomas other than adenocarcinoma, 32 microscopically proved bronchogenic adenocarcinomas, 1 myxofibrosarcoma, 93 cases in which diagnosis was based on x-ray or clinical evidence only, and 13 cases in which the disease may or may not have been microscopically proved (i. e., information from death certificate only).

Adenocarcinoma of the bronchus is considered separately because some investigators[3] have suggested that this form of lung cancer may be less associated with smoking than are other forms. The findings, as shown in

tables 4, 5, and 6, are consistent with this theory, but with only 32 cases we cannot be sure. Nevertheless, this form of bronchogenic carcinoma was highly associated with cigarette smoking. Twenty-six of the 32 deaths occurred among men with a history of regular cigarette smoking, as compared with only six expected deaths. The difference of 20 deaths is statistically significant (p=0.05).

Of the 309 microscopically proved cases (other than adenocarcinoma), 295 were well established as being bronchogenic in origin. The diagnosis in the other 14 was less certain (e. g., diagnosis based on clinical and x-ray findings in the lung with cancer proved by biopsy of a metastatic site). These 14 uncertain cases, in all of which the patients were cigarette smokers, have been excluded from the group which will hereafter be described as well-established cases of bronchogenic carcinoma, excluding adenocarcinoma.

Only four men who never smoked died of well-established bronchogenic carcinoma (excluding adenocarcinoma). Since this is a small number to use as a basis for mortality ratios, we summarized the findings, as shown in table 7, by computing death rates standardized to the age distribution of the white male population of the United States in 1954. Figure 3 shows the age-standardized death rates for well-established cases by type of smoking (classified from lifetime history). The numbers at the bottom of this figure indicate the corresponding number of men who were enrolled in 1952. The rates were low for men who never smoked, occasional smokers, and cigar smokers. Pipe smokers had an appreciably higher rate. The rate for men with a history of regular cigarette smoking only was 23 times as high as the rate for men who never smoked.

Figure 4 shows the rates for men with well-established cases (excluding adenocarcinoma) by amount of cigarette smoking for men with a history of regular cigarette smoking only. The rates increased rapidly with amount of cigarette smoking. The age-standardized death rate for smokers of two or more packs a day was 217.3 per 100,000 per year. In contrast, the age-standardized death rate from microscopically proved cancer, all sites combined, was only 177.4 per 100,000 per year for men who never smoked. In other words, among smokers of two packs of cigarettes a day, the death rate from bronchogenic carcinoma alone is higher than the total death rate due to cancer of men who never smoked.

As shown in figure 4, rates for men who had given up

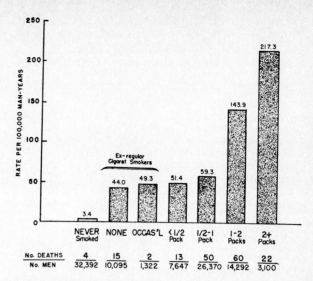

Fig. 4.—Age-standardized death rates due to well-established cases of bronchogenic carcinoma (exclusive of adenocarcinoma) by current amount of cigarette smoking.

smoking less than one pack of cigarettes a day in 1952 was 57.6 per 100,000 per year. Those who had previously smoked at this level but had given up smoking for from 1 to 10 years was 35.5, and the rate for those who had given up smoking for 10 years or longer was only 8.3. The rate for men currently smoking one pack or more of cigarettes a day in 1952 was 157.1 per 100,000 per year. Those who had previously smoked at that level but had given up smoking for from 1 to 10 years was 77.6, and the rate for those who had given up smoking for 10 years or longer was 60.5.

The number of years of cigarette smoking, as well as the amount of smoking, seems to be of importance. The following figures include all deaths from lung cancer. For men with a history of regular cigarette smoking only who were smoking less than one-half pack a day in 1952, the age-standardized death rate was 68 per 100,000 per year

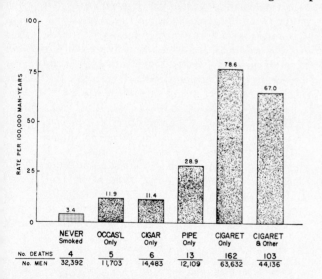

Fig. 3.—Age-standardized death rates due to well-established cases of bronchogenic carcinoma (exclusive of adenocarcinoma) by type of smoking as classified from lifetime history.

cigarette smoking were lower than the rates for men who were smoking cigarettes regularly at the time of questioning in 1952. Figure 5 shows the age-standardized death rates (well-established cases excluding adenocarcinoma) for men with a history of regular cigarette smoking only, who had stopped smoking cigarettes in 1952, by previous daily consumption of cigarettes and by number of years since they had last smoked. The rate for men currently

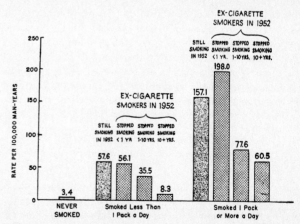

Fig. 5.—Age-standardized death rates due to well-established cases of bronchogenic carcinoma (exclusive of adenocarcinoma). Rates for men who have stopped smoking are compared with those for men who never smoked and those for men still smoking in 1952.

for those who had smoked for less than 35 years and 139 for those who had smoked for 35 years or longer. Among smokers of one-half to one pack a day, the rates were 84 for those who had smoked for less than 35 years and 105

TABLE 8.—*Rates of Death Due to Lung Cancer, by Urban-Rural Classification, Standardized for Age and for Age and Smoking Habits*

| | Cities | | | |
| --- | --- | --- | --- | --- |
| | 50,000+ | 10,000-50,000 | Towns | Rural |
| Men, no. | 45,218 | 43,502 | 50,039 | 46,783 |
| Cigarette smokers, % | 62.5 | 60.1 | 56.9 | 50.4 |
| Total lung cancer cases | | | | |
| Death rate standardized for age | 82 | 68 | 73 | 52 |
| Death rate standardized for age and for smoking habits | 75 | 66 | 73 | 59 |
| Well-established° lung cancer cases | | | | |
| Death rate standardized for age | 56 | 46 | 43 | 34 |
| Death rate standardized for age and for smoking habits | 52 | 44 | 43 | 39 |

°Well-established cases of bronchogenic carcinoma, exclusive of adenocarcinoma.

for those who had smoked for 35 years or longer. For smokers of one to two packs a day, the rates were 93 and 252 respectively. For smokers of two packs or more a day, the rates were 138 and 293 respectively.

As expected, the death rate due to lung cancer (well-established cases exclusive of adenocarcinoma) was found to be higher in urban than in rural areas (table 8). The age-standardized death rate was 34 per 100,000 in rural areas, as compared with 56 per 100,000 in cities of over 50,000 population. However, cigarette smoking is more common among city dwellers than among men in rural areas. Standardized for smoking habits as well as for age, the rate was 39 per 100,000 in rural areas and 52 per 100,000 in cities of over 50,000 population. Thus, when standardized for both factors, the rate was still 25% lower in rural areas than in large cities. This difference may be due to some factor producing lung cancer associated with city life or to better case finding and diagnosis in cities than in rural areas.

The rate of deaths due to lung cancer was low among men who never smoked cigarettes regularly and high among cigarette smokers in large cities, small cities, suburbs and towns, and rural areas (fig. 6). Whatever the urban factor may be, its effect on these rates is small as compared with the effect of cigarettes, as shown by the relative heights of the bars on this chart.

A comparison was made between the findings in the first part of the study (January, 1952, through October, 1953) with the findings in the last two years of the study (November, 1953, through October, 1955). Considering all deaths reported as due to lung cancer, the mortality ratio of men with a history of regular cigarette smoking only was 9.64 in the first part of the study and 14.30 in the second part of the study. For men with a history of regular cigarette smoking only who were currently smoking one pack or more a day, the mortality ratio was 18.00 in the first part of the study and 31.50 in the second part of the study. Corresponding figures for well-established cases exclusive of adenocarcinoma are too unstable to make such a comparison, because of the small number of deaths due to this disease among men who never smoked. However, the rate of deaths due to lung cancer was considerably higher in the last two years than in the earlier part of the study. Trends in the death rates and reasons for these trends were discussed in part 1 of this paper.

*Cancer of the Esophagus, Larynx, Pharynx, Mouth, Tongue, and Lip.*—Tobacco smoke (or saliva and bronchial secretions containing material from tobacco smoke) comes into direct contact with the lips, mouth, tongue, pharynx, larynx, and esophagus. The deaths of 127 subjects were attributed to primary cancer of these sites (table 9). Only six of these men had never smoked, and three were occasional smokers. The other 118 had a history of regular smoking. One hundred fourteen of the 127 cancers were microscopically proved and only 4 of these were in men who never smoked. Considering microscopically proved cases only, the mortality ratio was 7.00 for men with a history of regular cigarette smoking (many of whom smoked pipes and cigars as well as cigarettes), 5.00 for men who smoked only cigars, and 3.50 for men who smoked only pipes. Still considering microscopically proved cases, 52 men had a history of regular cigarette smoking only, 7 had a history of regular pipe smoking only, 10 had a history of regular cigar smoking only, and 38 had a history of two or three types of smoking. The figures suggest that pipe and cigar smoking may be more important than cigarette smoking in relation to cancer of one or more of the sites included in this group, but the number of cases is not sufficient for a reliable evaluation of this point.

Considering microscopically proved cases, out of 34 deaths from cancer of the esophagus only 1 was of a man who had never smoked, of 25 deaths from cancer of the pharynx only 2 were of men who had never smoked, and of 16 deaths from cancer of the tongue only 1 was of a man who had never smoked. No deaths of men who never smoked were reported among 24 cases of cancer of

TABLE 9.—*Number of Deaths from Cancer of Several Selected Sites by Smoking Habits*

| | Total No. of Deaths | Microscopically Proved Cases | | | | | | |
| --- | --- | --- | --- | --- | --- | --- | --- | --- |
| | | | | Type of Smoking | | | | |
| Site of Cancer | | Total | Never Smoked | Occasional Only | Cigarette Only | Pipe Only | Cigar Only | Other° |
| Lip | 1 | 1 | 0 | 0 | 1 | 0 | 0 | 0 |
| Tongue | 17 | 16 | 1 | 1 | 2 | 4 | 0 | 8 |
| Floor of mouth | 6 | 6 | 0 | 0 | 5 | 0 | 1 | 0 |
| Other part of mouth | 8 | 8 | 0 | 1 | 0 | 0 | 3 | 4 |
| Pharynx | 27 | 25 | 2 | 0 | 12 | 1 | 1 | 9 |
| Larynx | 26 | 24 | 0 | 0 | 17 | 0 | 3 | 4 |
| Esophagus | 42 | 34 | 1 | 1 | 15 | 2 | 2 | 13 |
| Total | 127 | 114 | 4 | 3 | 52 | 7 | 10 | 38 |

°Two or three types of smoking.

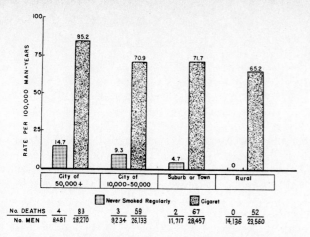

Fig. 6.—Age-standardized death rates due to well-established cases of bronchogenic carcinoma (exclusive of adenocarcinoma) by urban-rural classification. Rates for cigarette smokers are compared with those for men who never smoked regularly.

the larynx, 14 cases of cancer of the mouth, and 1 case of cancer of the lip.

*Cancer of the Genitourinary System.*—Tables 4, 5, and 6 show a summary of the findings for the 368 deaths from cancer of the genitourinary system, 287 of which cases were microscopically proved. The mortality ratios for men with a history of regular cigarette smoking were 1.77 for all cases and 1.90 for microscopically proved cases. For smokers of one pack or more a day of cigarettes, the mortality ratios were 2.94 for all cases and 3.42 for microscopically proved cases. These ratios are significantly greater than 1.00 (p < 0.001 in both instances).

Of these 368 cases, 106 apparently originated in the bladder, 67 in the kidney, 185 in the prostate, and 10 in other parts of the genitourinary system (table 10). We say "apparently" because in many of these cases the tumor involved two or more of these organs, as well as other nearby structures, and the doctor sometimes expressed doubt as to the exact location of the primary lesion.

Among men with a history of regular cigarette smoking, there were 59 deaths from microscopically proved cases of cancer of the bladder, as compared with 27 expected deaths, a difference of 32 deaths and a mortality ratio of 2.17. This difference is statistically significant (p=0.02). In cases of microscopically proved cancer of the prostate, there were 77 deaths among cigarette smokers, compared with 44 expected deaths (mortality ratio, 1.75), and this difference is statistically significant (p=0.05). In cases of microscopically proved cancer of the kidney, there were 35 deaths among cigarette smokers, compared with 22 expected deaths (mortality ratio, 1.58); this difference is not statistically significant (p=0.30).

*Cancer of the Digestive System.*—There were 828 deaths attributed to cancer of the digestive system (exclusive of the 42 cases of cancer of the esophagus), of which 649 cases were microscopically proved. The mortality ratio for men with a history of regular cigarette smoking was 1.35 for all men but 1.23 for men with microscopically proved cases. The sites to which the 828 cases were ascribed were stomach, 240; pancreas, 150; liver, gallbladder, and biliary passages, 70; colon, 226;

rectum, 119; and other and uncertain sites in the digestive system, 23 (table 10).

The most striking association with cigarette smoking was for deaths ascribed to cancer of the liver, the mortality ratio being 4.52 for men with microscopically proved cases. The liver is one of the most frequent sites of metastases, and in many if not most of these cases there was doubt as to the primary site.

There was a negative association between cigarette smoking and deaths ascribed to cancer of the colon (mortality ratio, 0.77), but this was not statistically significant (p=0.43). There was no association between cigarette smoking and cancer of the rectum. The mortality ratio of cigarette smokers was 1.61 for men with cancer of the stomach and 1.50 for men with cancer of the pancreas. In neither case was the difference between observed and expected deaths statistically significant (p=0.12 and p=0.10 respectively).

*Cancer of the Lymphatic and Hematopoietic System.*—There were 227 deaths ascribed to cancer of the lymphatic and hematopoietic system. These included lymphoscarcoma and reticulosarcoma, 66; Hodgkin's disease, 30; multiple myeloma, 32; leukemia, 88; and other, 11 (table 10). Leukemia showed no indication of an association with cigarette smoking. Hodgkin's disease, as

TABLE 10.—*Number of Deaths and Observed Versus Expected° Deaths for Men with History of Regular Cigarette Smoking by Primary Sites of Cancer of Genitourinary, Digestive, and Lymphatic and Hematopoietic Systems*

| Site of Cancer | Total No. of Deaths | Microscopically Proved Cases | | | |
|---|---|---|---|---|---|
| | | | Observed Vs. Expected No. of Deaths | | |
| | | Total | Observed | Expected | Ratio |
| Genitourinary system | 368 | 287 | 177 | 93.4 | 1.90 |
| Bladder | 106 | 90 | 59 | 27.2 | 2.17 |
| Kidney | 67 | 54 | 35 | 22.1 | 1.58 |
| Prostate | 185 | 134 | 77 | 44.1 | 1.75 |
| Other | 10 | 9 | 6 | 0 | ... |
| Digestive system | 828 | 649 | 365 | 296.2 | 1.23 |
| Stomach | 240 | 176 | 107 | 66.5 | 1.61 |
| Pancreas | 150 | 117 | 76 | 50.5 | 1.50 |
| Liver, gallbladder, and biliary passages | 70 | 47 | 33 | 7.3 | 4.52 |
| Colon | 226 | 193 | 84 | 108.4 | 0.77 |
| Rectum | 119 | 104 | 55 | 58.8 | 0.94 |
| Other | 23 | 12 | 10 | 4.4 | ... |
| Lymphatic and hematopoietic system | 227 | 192 | 113 | 93.9 | 1.20 |
| Lymphosarcoma and reticulosarcoma | 66 | 57 | 36 | 20.8 | 1.73 |
| Hodgkin's disease | 30 | 25 | 20 | 7.3 | 2.74 |
| Multiple myeloma | 32 | 28 | 12 | 18.2 | 0.66 |
| Leukemia | 88 | 73 | 39 | 46.0 | 0.85 |
| Other | 11 | 9 | 6 | 1.9 | ... |

°Calculated by applying the age-specific death rates of men who never smoked to the man-years of exposure to risk of the men with a history of regular cigarette smoking.

well as lymphosarcoma and reticulosarcoma, appeared to be associated with cigarette smoking, but in neither was the difference between observed and expected deaths statistically significant. For multiple myeloma, the observed number of deaths among cigarette smokers was smaller than the expected number (12 versus 18), but with so few cases, this difference is not statistically significant.

*Cancer of Other Sites.*—There were 162 deaths from cancer of other specified sites, of which 145 were of patients with microscopically proved cases. Taken as a group, these showed no association with cigarette smoking. The 162 cases consisted of brain, 74; pleura, 6; salivary gland, 9; other respiratory diseases, 7; melanoma, 17; skin, 9; eye, 2; thyroid, 5; bone, 13; adrenal, 4; breast, 5; connective tissue, 5; and other sites, 6. None of these showed a statistically significant degree of association with cigarette smoking habits.

Primary site could not be determined in 89 cases, 52 of which were microscopically proved cancer. These deaths showed a high degree of association with smoking habits.

## HEART AND CIRCULATORY DISEASES

Of the 11,870 deaths in the study, 7,523 (63%) were attributed to diseases of the heart and circulatory system (including vascular lesions of the central nervous system). The International Statistical Classification of Diseases, Injuries, and Causes of Death, Sixth Revision, makes provision for distinguishing between 47 specific disease entities in these general categories (including some rather vaguely described conditions). The only difficulty is that in many instances in this study two or more of these diseases were present and apparently contributed to death.

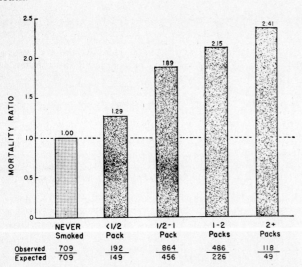

Fig. 7.—Mortality ratios due to coronary artery disease by current amount of cigarette smoking.

Cerebral vascular lesions were recorded as a contributing factor in 135 (36.2%) of the 373 deaths attributed primarily to hypertensive heart disease and in 140 (2.6%) of the 5,297 deaths attributed primarily to coronary artery disease. Coronary artery disease was recorded as a contributing factor in 51 (4.9%) of the 1,050 deaths ascribed to cerebral vascular lesions and 79 (6.7%) of the deaths ascribed primarily to other heart and circulatory diseases. All told, cerebral vascular lesions were recorded in 408 deaths attributed primarily to some other cause, and coronary artery disease was recorded in 384 deaths attributed to some other cause. We attempted to analyze

the data for each of the many combinations, but this turned out to be fruitless. Therefore, we turned to the usual procedure of classifying each death according to the presumed principal underlying cause, regardless of how many other conditions were mentioned.

First, we divided the 7,523 deaths due to heart and circulatory diseases into four groups: coronary artery disease (5,297 deaths), other heart diseases (911 deaths), cerebral vascular lesions (1,050 deaths), and other circulatory diseases (265 deaths). The figures for these are shown on tables 1, 2, and 3. Coronary artery disease and "other circulatory diseases" showed a high degree of association with cigarette smoking; cerebral vascular lesions showed a moderate degree of association with cigarette smoking; and other heart diseases showed a small degree of association with cigarette smoking.

*Coronary Artery Disease.*—Coronary artery disease is of particular importance, because it accounts for a large proportion of all deaths in the United States, the highest rates being among men in the older age groups. In this study, it accounted for 44.6% of all deaths. Therefore, even a moderate percentage increase in deaths from this cause has an appreciable effect on the total death rate.

In all four age groups the death rates from coronary artery disease were far higher among men with a history of regular cigarette smoking than among men who never smoked (see table 1). There were 3,361 deaths from this cause among the cigarette smokers, whereas only 1,973 would have died if their age-specific death rates had been the same as for men who never smoked (p<0.001). As shown by the mortality ratio of 1.70, the death rate from this cause of these cigarette smokers was 70% higher than for a comparable group of men who never smoked. Death rates due to coronary artery disease increased with the amount of cigarette smoking. Among men with a history of regular cigarette smoking only, the mortality ratio rose from 1.29 for men smoking less than one-half pack of cigarettes a day to 1.89 for smokers of one-half to one pack a day, to 2.15 for smokers of one to two packs a day, and to 2.41 for smokers of two packs or more a day (fig. 7).

Men with a history of cigar smoking only also had higher death rates from coronary artery diseases than men who never smoked (observed deaths, 420, expected deaths, 329, ratio, 1.28). This difference is statistically significant (p<0.001). The rates for pipe smokers were about the same as for men who never smoked.

The degree of association with cigarette smoking was higher for deaths specifically described as due to arteriosclerotic heart disease than for deaths described as due to coronary thrombosis, embolism, or occlusion or to myocardial infarction.

Figure 8 shows mortality ratios for men with a history of regular cigarette smoking only, comparing those for men who had stopped smoking with those for men who were smoking regularly in 1952. The mortality ratios of men who had given up smoking for 10 years or longer were much less than those for men who continued to smoke, amount being taken into consideration. The mortality ratios of men who had given up smoking for less than a year were higher than the corresponding ratios for men who were still smoking in 1952. The high ratios for those who had stopped smoking for less than a year may have been due to the inclusion in this group of some men who had recently stopped smoking because of symptoms of heart disease.

The association between cigarette smoking and death rates due to coronary artery disease was about the same in the last two years of the study (November, 1953, through October, 1955) as in the earlier part of the study (January, 1952, through October, 1953). For example, comparing all men with a history of regular cigarette smoking to men who never smoked, the mortality ratio was 1.74 in the first part of the study and 1.68 in the second part of the study. The difference between these two ratios is not statistically significant. The mortality ratio for men with a history of regular cigarette smoking only who smoked one pack or more of cigarettes a day was 2.09 in the first part of the study and 2.27 in the second part of the study.

*Other Heart Diseases.*—Other heart diseases accounted for 911 (7.7%) of the 11,870 deaths in the study. This group consisted of 167 deaths from chronic rheumatic heart disease, 373 from hypertensive heart disease, and 371 from miscellaneous other heart diseases, including many which were described in vague or nonspecific terms. Chronic rheumatic heart disease showed no association with cigarette smoking (mortality ratio 0.98). Hypertensive heart disease showed only a slight degree of association with cigarette smoking (mortality ratio 1.13). This was not statistically significant (p=0.26).

The other deaths ascribed to heart disease showed a statistically significant degree of association with cigarette smoking (mortality ratio 1.39, p=0.05). Some of these cases were probably due to coronary artery disease or to some other circulatory disease. The evidence seems to indicate that coronary artery disease is the only important form of heart disease which is associated with smoking habits.

*Cerebral Vascular Lesions.*—Vascular lesions of the central nervous system were recorded as the underlying cause of 1,050 (8.8%) of the 11,870 deaths. A total of 556 deaths due to this group of diseases occurred among men with a history of regular cigarette smoking, as compared with 428 expected deaths (a difference of 128 deaths and a mortality ratio of 1.30). This difference is statistically significant (p=0.01). The death rate increased with the amount of cigarette smoking, the mortality ratio being 1.46 for men smoking one pack or more of cigarettes a day.

Of the 1,050 deaths in this category, 237 were attributed to cerebral thrombosis or embolism, 749 were attributed to cerebral hemorrhage, and 64 were attributed to other vascular lesions of the central nervous system. Cases described as cerebral thrombosis showed about the same degree of relationship to smoking habits as did cases described as cerebral hemorrhage.

*Other Circulatory Diseases.*—The 265 deaths classified in table 1 under "other circulatory diseases" consisted of 50 attributed to hypertensive disease without mention of heart, 39 attributed to phlebitis and embolism (international list numbers 463-466), 59 attributed to general arteriosclerosis, 90 attributed to aortic aneurysm (nonsyphilitic), and 27 attributed to miscellaneous other circulatory diseases, including aneurysms and thromboangiitis obliterans (5 cases). Hypertensive diseases

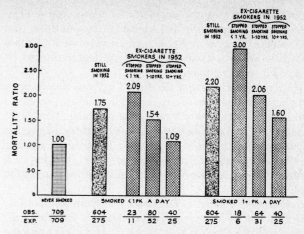

Fig. 8.—Mortality ratios due to coronary artery disease. Rates for men who have stopped smoking are compared with those for men who never smoked and those for men still smoking in 1952.

showed no association with cigarette smoking (mortality ratio 1.00).

General arteriosclerosis and the group including phlebitis and embolism both showed a moderate degree of association with cigarette smoking. However, there were not many cases, and in neither disease was the association statistically significant.

Sixty-eight of the deaths from aortic aneurysm occurred among men with a history of regular cigarette smoking, compared with only 25 expected deaths. This difference of 43 deaths (mortality ratio 2.72) is statistically significant (p=0.005).

In the miscellaneous group (which included other aneurysms, gangrene, and thromboangiitis obliterans), 18 of the deaths occurred among men with a history of regular cigarette smoking, compared with only 4 expected deaths.

## PULMONARY DISEASES

Only 338 deaths were ascribed to pulmonary diseases other than lung cancer. Of these, 124 were attributed to pneumonia and influenza, 41 to pulmonary tuberculosis, 76 to asthma, and 97 to other pulmonary diseases, including bronchitis, abscess of lung, pneumoconiosis, and bronchiectasis (international list numbers 500-502 and 520-527). A total of 231 deaths from all of these causes occurred among men with a history of regular cigarette smoking, compared with 81 expected deaths (a difference of 150 deaths and mortality ratio of 2.85). This difference is statistically significant (p<0.001).

The mortality ratios for men with a history of regular cigarette smoking were as follows: for pneumonia and influenza, the mortality ratio was 3.90 and the difference between observed and expected deaths was statistically significant (p<0.001); for asthma, the mortality ratio was 1.76, but it was not statistically significant (p=0.08); for pulmonary tuberculosis, the mortality ratio was 2.17, and this was not statistically significant (p=0.24); and for other pulmonary diseases, the mortality ratio was 3.62, and this was statistically significant (p=0.005).

## OTHER DISEASES

Only 1,120 (9.4%) of the 11,870 deaths were attributed to diseases other than cancer, cardiac, circulatory, and pulmonary diseases, and accidents, violence, and suicide. These were divided into 101 specific disease entities, plus the category "vague and unknown causes of death." Only three showed a statistically significant degree of association with smoking habits.

*Gastric and Duodenal Ulcers.*—Fifty-one deaths were attributed to gastric ulcers, and all of them occurred among men with a history of regular smoking. They were divided by smoking habits as follows: history of regular cigarette smoking only, 35; history of regular cigarette smoking and also regular pipe or cigar smoking, 11; history of pipe smoking only, 2; history of cigar smoking only, 2; and history of both pipe and cigar smoking but no cigarette smoking, 1. The death rate from gastric ulcer for men with a history of regular cigarette smoking only was about five times as high as the rate for cigar and pipe smokers who never smoked cigarettes regularly.

Gastric ulcers were recorded as a contributing factor in 33 deaths ascribed to some other cause (this in addition to the 51 cases described above). The mortality ratio for cigarette smokers was 3.46 in this group of cases (p=0.08).

Seventy-three deaths were attributed to duodenal ulcers. Fifty-four of them were of men with a history of regular cigarette smoking, compared with 25 expected deaths. This difference of 29 deaths (mortality ratio 2.16) is statistically significant (p=0.05).

Duodenal ulcers were listed as a contributing factor in 46 deaths ascribed to some other cause (this in addition to the 73 cases described above). The mortality ratio for cigarette smokers was 3.67 in this group of cases. This difference is statistically significant (p=0.02).

*Cirrhosis of the Liver.*—Of 127 deaths ascribed to cirrhosis of the liver, 83 occurred among men with a history of cigarette smoking, as compared with 43 expected deaths. This difference of 40 deaths (mortality ratio 1.93) is statistically significant (p=0.05).

*Remainder of Diseases.*—The remaining 869 deaths were attributed to 98 different specific diseases, plus the category "vague and unknown causes." Taking this entire group together, the death rate of the cigarette smokers was slightly higher than that of men who never smoked (mortality ratio 1.07) but the difference was not statistically significant. Diabetes, which accounted for 162 of these deaths, showed no association with smoking habits. No single one of the other 97 specific diseases showed a statistically significant association with smoking habits.

## COMMENT

Other investigations have previously reported an association between smoking habits and many of the diseases for which we found the death rate to be higher among cigarette smokers than among nonsmokers. The literature on this subject is so extensive (particularly in relation to lung cancer) that it is impossible for us to review it in the space available here. However, we must mention that the findings on lung cancer reported by Doll and Hill[4] in their prospective study of British physicians were essentially the same as our findings.

We are fully aware of the fact that cause of death as recorded on death certificates is not always correct. Therefore, it is possible that some of the associations found between smoking habits and certain specific

diseases may have resulted from errors in diagnosis. For example, it is conceivable that the association found between cigarette smoking and death ascribed to pulmonary tuberculosis may have resulted from confusion between tuberculosis and lung cancer. It is also conceivable that the relatively small association found between cigarette smoking and death from cerebral vascular lesions may have resulted from ascribing some deaths to this cause which were actually due to coronary artery disease.

In respect to cancer, we did not depend on death certificate information alone but obtained additional information from the doctor, hospital, or tumor registry. In 79% of the cases classified as cancer in this report, the diagnosis was microscopically confirmed. We found a high degree of association between cigarette smoking and microscopically proved cancer (all sites combined). It is extremely unlikely that this could have been produced by errors in diagnosis. It follows that there must be a high degree of association between cigarette smoking and cancer of one or more primary sites.

The next problem was to determine which specific site or sites of cancer are involved in this relationship. A difficulty arises from the fact that the primary site cannot always be established with certainty. The following relationships were found.

First, lung cancer showed an extremely high degree of association with cigarette smoking. The next highest association with cigarette smoking was for cancer of the following sites combined: lip, tongue, floor of mouth, pharynx, larynx, and esophagus. These are all sites directly exposed to cigarette smoke. Approximately 65% of the association between cigarette smoking and microscopically proved cancer (all sites combined) was accounted for by the association between cigarette smoking and cancer of the sites just mentioned. No site other than those just mentioned showed an extremely high degree of association with cigarette smoking (cancer of the liver being a possible exception).

Second, the degree of association between cigarette smoking and deaths attributed to lung cancer was higher for cancer microscopically proved and with good evidence as to the primary site than for the total group (including cancer not microscopically verified and cases with doubt as to primary site). The same was true for cancer of the genitourinary system.

Third, considering all deaths ascribed to cancer of the gastrointestinal system (except esophagus), there was only a small degree of association with cigarette smoking. In this group of cases, the association was lower for microscopically proved cases than for the total group. Furthermore, there was considerable doubt as to the primary site of many of these cases, particularly those ascribed to the liver.

Considering this evidence, there is no doubt in our minds as to the validity of the association found between cigarette smoking and cancer of the lung and the association found between smoking and cancer of other sites directly exposed to tobacco smoke products. The evidence also suggests that there is a real association between cigarette smoking and cancer of one or more sites in the genitourinary system. Considering the various sites within the genitourinary system, cancer of the bladder showed the highest degree of association with cigarette smoking.

The nature of the evidence is such as to leave doubt as to whether a real association exists between cigarette smoking and cancer of the gastrointestinal system (except esophagus). The apparent association could have arisen through misdiagnosis of primary site in some cases (e. g., primary cancer of the lung with metastasis to the liver being erroneously ascribed to primary cancer of the liver).

In seeking to evaluate the possibilities outlined above, one must keep three things in mind: (1) the likelihood of a physician mistaking one particular disease for another particular disease, (2) the number of deaths ascribed to each of the two diseases involved, and (3) the magnitude of the apparent association between smoking habits and each of the two diseases involved.

One example is sufficient to illustrate the point. Let us consider the hypothesis that the association found between cigarette smoking and death from coronary artery disease resulted from a confusion (in some cases) between coronary artery disease and lung cancer. A total of 5,297 deaths were ascribed to coronary artery disease, and there was a difference of 1,388 between the observed and expected number of deaths among men with a history of regular cigarette smoking. All told, there were only 448 deaths ascribed to lung cancer and most of these were microscopically proved cases. For the hypothesis to be correct, one must assume that at least 1,388 lung

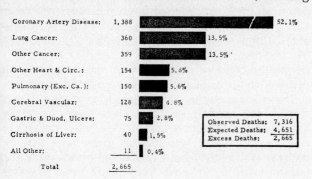

Fig. 9.—Excess deaths among men with a history of regular cigarette smoking.

cancer deaths were missed as such and were diagnosed instead as due to coronary artery disease. We leave it up to the reader to decide the likelihood of this occurring.

The most important finding of this study was the high degree of association between cigarette smoking and the total death rate (fig. 9). Errors in diagnosis, no matter how great, have no effect on this finding. Therefore, if the association found between cigarette smoking and deaths from some particular disease (e. g., cancer of the liver) was due to errors in diagnosis, it only means that the true degree of association between cigarette smoking and death from some other specific disease (e. g., lung cancer) is greater than the figures given in this report appear to indicate.

A total of 7,316 deaths occurred among men with a history of regular cigarette smoking, whereas only 4,651 would have occurred if the age-specific death rates of the smokers had been the same as for men who never smoked (fig. 9). The difference of 2,665 may be considered as

"excess" deaths. Coronary disease accounted for 52.1% of the excess deaths among cigarette smokers; lung cancer accounted for 13.5%; cancer of other sites accounted for 13.5%; other heart and circulatory diseases 5.8%; pulmonary diseases (other than lung cancer) 5.6%; cerebral vascular lesions 4.8%; gastric and duodenal ulcers 2.8%; cirrhosis of the liver 1.5%; and all other diseases combined 0.4%.

## SUMMARY

There is a high degree of association between total death rates and cigarette smoking, a far lower degree of association between total death rates and cigar smoking, and a small degree of association between total death rates and pipe smoking. The available source of information for this study, on diseases involved, was cause of death as recorded on death certificates, supplemented by more detailed medical information in cases in which cancer was mentioned.

The following relationships with cigarette smoking are evident: (1) an extremely high association for a few diseases, such as cancer of the lung, cancer of the larynx, cancer of the esophagus, and gastric ulcers; (2) a very high association for a few diseases, such as pneumonia and influenza, duodenal ulcer, aortic aneurysm, and cancer of the bladder; (3) a high association for a number of diseases, such as coronary artery disease, cirrhosis of the liver, and cancer of several sites; (4) a moderate association for cerebral vascular lesions; and (5) little or no association for a number of diseases, including chronic rheumatic fever, hypertensive heart disease, other hypertensive diseases, nephritis and nephrosis, diabetes, leukemia, cancer of the rectum, cancer of the colon, and cancer of the brain. The relative importance of the association listed above is dependent on the number of deaths attributed to each disease, as well as on their degrees of association with cigarette smoking.

It was found that the death rate of men with lung cancer who had given up cigarette smoking for a year or more before being enrolled in the study was lower than the death rate of men who were smoking cigarettes regularly at that time. An extremely high association between cigarette smoking and death rates for men with this disease was found in rural areas as well as in large cities. If smoking habits are taken into consideration, the lung cancer death rate was somewhat higher in cities than in rural areas.

521 W. 57th St. (19) (Dr. Hammond).

This study was made possible by the cooperation of the subjects, volunteer workers, state health departments, many physicians, and personnel of divisions of the American Cancer Society. Lawrence Garfinkel, M.A., Constance L. Percy, M.S., Leonard Craig, M.A., and Herbert Seidman, M.B.A., assisted in this study.

### References

1. Hammond, E. C., and Horn, D.: Smoking and Death Rates—Report on 44 Months of Follow-up of 187,783 Men: I. Total Mortality, J. A. M. A. **166**:1159-1172.

2. Treloar, A. E.: Enigma of Cause of Death, J. A. M. A. **162**:1376-1379 (Dec. 8) 1956.

3. Graham, E. A.: Cancer of Lung: One Disease? in Cancer of Lung: Evaluation of Problem: Proceedings of Scientific Session, Annual Meeting, Nov. 3-4, 1953, New York, American Cancer Society, Inc., 1954, pp. 205-207.

4. Doll, R., and Hill, A. B.: Lung Cancer and Other Causes of Death in Relation to Smoking: Second Report on Mortality of British Doctors, Brit. M. J. **2**:1071-1081 (Nov. 10) 1956.

June 1, 1984
(*JAMA* 1984;251:2854-2857)

# Smoking and Death Rates*

## Breaking New Ground

### Sir Richard Doll

In 1958, Cuyler Hammond and Daniel Horn[1,2] published two articles in consecutive issues of THE JOURNAL that made outstanding contributions to medical science. The first article described the remarkable enterprise undertaken by the American Cancer Society to determine the effects of smoking and reported the results in terms of the total mortality from all causes associated with different smoking habits.[1] The second, which is reproduced in this issue of THE JOURNAL, described the spectrum of diseases associated with smoking and the extent to which the differences in mortality in the different groups of smokers might actually be due to differences in what they had smoked.[2]

Hammond and Horn's study broke new ground in two ways. First, it showed that it was possible to elicit useful information about personal habits from as many as 200,000 persons, follow them up for several years, and obtain information about their causes of death. Second, it showed that smoking was associated with a much wider variety of ills than had been previously suspected, that the association was, in nearly all cases, much closer for smoking cigarettes than for smoking tobacco in other forms, and that among regular cigarette smokers, smoking might be responsible for anything up to 40% of their total mortality.

The idea that smoking tobacco was deleterious to health and that it could, in some circumstances, lead to cancer and particularly to cancer of the lip and tongue, was already 200 years old when a few articles were published reporting that patients suffering from cancers of the upper respiratory and digestive tracts, including in

particular those suffering from cancer of the lung, were much more likely to have smoked large numbers of cigarettes than patients suffering from other diseases. Some of these articles had been published before or during the war, but it was not until 1950 that a large amount of data was obtained in a sufficiently representative and responsible way to lead more than a handful of people to believe that smoking might actually be responsible for causing a material amount of disease.

These early articles varied greatly in quality, but all shared the characteristic that they were based on information collected retrospectively from patients in hospital and that it was difficult to be sure that the patients with and without cancer (and particularly that control patients suffering from many other diseases) were representative, respectively, of all patients with the disease under study and of the general population of normal persons from whom the patients were drawn. Some other method was, therefore, obviously needed that would both test the predictions that had been made and avoid the possibility of bias that, in the opinion of many at the time, was inherent in the case-control method.

### Large-Scale Cohort Studies

In 1950, when Hammond and Horn's study was first planned, few persons had much experience of applying epidemiological methods to the study of noninfectious diseases, and the large-scale cohort study, which is now so standard, was still in its infancy. Studies of this sort had begun to be used to investigate the causes of miners' pneumoconiosis,[3] and they were adopted more or less simultaneously in the United States and Britain as the natural means of testing the hypothesis that smoking and particularly the smoking of cigarettes, was a major cause of lung cancer in both countries.

To be successful, investigations of this type required

From the Imperial Cancer Research Fund, Cancer Epidemiology and Clinical Trials Unit, University of Oxford, England.

*A commentary on Hammond EC, Horn D: Smoking and death rates—Report on 44 months of follow-up of 187,783 men: II. Death rates by cause. *JAMA* 1958;166:1294-1308.

two things: (1) an ability to collect unbiased information about a sample of individuals with varying personal characteristics that was large enough for there to be a reasonable chance of detecting material differences in disease incidence between different subgroups, within a period that was short enough for the results to be still of interest when they were eventually obtained, and (2) an ability to keep in touch with the individuals concerned closely enough to record accurately the mortality and morbidity from which they suffered.

Hammond and Horn had the imagination to see that both objectives could be achieved by enlisting the support of active members of the American Cancer Society, who needed only to be asked to get questionnaires completed by personal acquaintances whom they knew not to be seriously ill and with whom they expected to keep in touch for several years. They also had the confidence to feel able to handle the mass of data that would be accumulated in the course of a few years and to extract from it the most crucial information without having recourse to the sophisticated computer systems that now make such tasks relatively easy.

The results fulfilled their most extravagant hopes. Detailed data about smoking habits were obtained for 189,854 men aged between 50 and 69 years, follow-up information was obtained annually, and by Oct 31, 1955 (on average, 44 months later), 98.9% had been successfully traced and a copy or abstract of the death certificate obtained for all the 11,870 men who were known to be dead. Thanks, moreover, to the cooperation of hundreds of members of the American medical profession, further information was obtained about the reasons for the diagnosis in 95% of all cases in which cancer was mentioned on the death certificate. By this means, a few deaths were reallocated to other causes, and microscopic confirmation was obtained for 79% of all cases in which death was accepted as due to cancer, while other evidence left little doubt that death was also due to the disease in 17% more. There remained, therefore, only 4% in which the diagnosis of cancer was based on the death certificate diagnosis alone.

The success of this study opened up new vistas for epidemiologists and, although it is still possible to count on the fingers of one hand the studies that have subsequently involved larger numbers of subjects, no one now questions the practicability or value of conducting studies on this scale in appropriate circumstances. Similar studies, although on a somewhat smaller scale, have become routine.

### Special Features of the Study

Three features of Hammond and Horn's study enabled it to make an outstanding contribution to knowledge of the effects of smoking: its large size, the wide geographical area covered, and the care that had been taken to check the diagnosis whenever cancer was mentioned on the death certificate.

This last enabled comparisons to be made between the ''mortality ratios'' (now usually referred to as ''relative risks'') for the well-established and other cases of a particular type of cancer for each particular smoking category (ie, between the ratios of the numbers of

deaths observed and the numbers that would have been expected in men in each category if the men in it had experienced the same age-specific mortality rates as nonsmokers). When these ratios were found to be increased if the data were limited to ''well-established cases'' (as they were for cancers that were closely related to cigarette smoking), it greatly strengthened the grounds for believing that the observed relationship was indeed a real one that would stand the test of time. The histological evidence that had been obtained showed, too, the correctness of the previous suspicion that adenocarcinomas of the lung were much less closely related to smoking than the other histological types.

The second feature of the study, the wide geographical coverage, had been secured by seeking the help of members of the American Cancer Society in 394 counties in nine states, from California through Wisconsin, Minnesota, Michigan, Illinois, and Iowa, to New Jersey, New York, and Pennsylvania. By this means it was not only possible to argue that the results were likely to be representative of the country as a whole, but data could also be obtained to see if there was any evidence that residence in particular parts of the country affected the mortality ratios independently of the effects of smoking.

So far as the individual states were concerned, the ratios for regular cigarette smokers who smoked one pack or more a day varied no more than could be expected by chance (from 1.72 in Wisconsin to 2.21 in California), and the same was true for areas of different densities of population. (In these comparisons, occasional smokers were combined with lifelong nonsmokers to provide more stable rates for comparison.) In this case, the mortality ratios for men who smoked one pack or more a day were actually identical (at 1.82) irrespective of whether men lived in the larger cities or the most rural areas. Some evidence was, however, obtained of a possible effect of urban residence on the mortality rates for lung cancer, which were uniformly higher in both regular cigarette smokers and nonsmokers who lived in large cities than in men with similar smoking habits who lived in rural areas. The differences were small in comparison with those between nonsmokers and regular cigarette smokers in each type of area and set an upper limit to the possible effect of atmospheric pollution, but the lower limit was much less, as the ''urban factor'' could easily have been some aspect of the smoking history that could not be adequately allowed for, such as the age at which the regular smoking of cigarettes had begun.

The first feature of the study, namely, its large size, was, however, the one that enabled it to make the principal contribution for which it is most likely to be remembered in the annals of the history of medicine. With more than 11,000 deaths to analyze, Hammond and Horn were able to examine separately mortality rates from a great variety of diseases, even if they contributed as little as half a percent to the total of all deaths, and to compare, for each of them, the relationship with the different methods of smoking and, among regular cigarette smokers, the relationship with the amount smoked.

## Table 1. — Causes of Death Related to Smoking by Hammond and Horn

| Cause of Death | No. of Deaths | Mortality Ratio | Probability | Current Belief* |
|---|---|---|---|---|
| Cancer† | | | | |
| Lung | 309 | 31.00 | <.001 | Causal |
| Esophagus, larynx, pharynx, mouth, tongue, and lip | 114 | 7.00 | <.001 | Causal |
| Bladder | 90 | 2.17 | .02 | Causal |
| Prostate | 134 | 1.75 | .05 | Unrelated |
| Liver and gallbladder | 47 | 4.52 | <.001 | Uncertain |
| Other Diseases | | | | |
| Coronary artery disease | 5,297 | 1.70 | <.001 | Causal |
| Cerebrovascular disease | 1,050 | 1.30 | .01 | Causal |
| Other heart disease‡ | 371 | 1.39 | .05 | Uncertain |
| Aortic aneurysm | 90 | 2.72 | .005 | Causal |
| Other vascular disease‡ | 27 | 4.50 | <.001 | Many caused |
| Pneumonia and influenza | 124 | 3.90 | .001 | Causal |
| Other pulmonary disease‡ | 97 | 3.62 | <.001 | Most caused |
| Gastric ulcer | 51 | $\alpha$ | <.001 | Causal |
| Duodenal ulcer | 73 | 2.16 | .05 | Causal |
| Cirrhosis of liver | 127 | 1.93 | .05 | Uncertain |

*Belief that smoking contributes to death from the disease not necessarily to its origin.
†Microscopically proved cases only.
‡See original article for description.

## Table 2. — Causes of Death Not Related to Smoking by Hammond and Horn

| Cause of Death | No. of Deaths | Mortality Ratio | Probability | Current Belief* |
|---|---|---|---|---|
| Cancer† | | | | |
| Stomach | 176 | 1.61 | NS | Uncertain |
| Pancreas | 117 | 1.50 | NS | Causal |
| Colon | 193 | 0.77 | NS | Unrelated |
| Rectum | 104 | 0.94 | NS | Unrelated |
| Kidney | 54 | 1.58 | NS | Uncertain |
| Lymphosarcoma and reticulosarcoma | 57 | 1.73 | NS | Unrelated |
| Hodgkin's disease | 25 | 2.74 | NS | Unrelated |
| Multiple myeloma | 28 | 0.66 | NS | Unrelated |
| Leukemia | 73 | 0.85 | NS | Unrelated |
| Other specified sites | 145 | 0.89 | NS | Unrelated |
| Other diseases | | | | |
| Hypertensive heart | 373 | 1.13 | NS | Unrelated |
| Chronic rheumatic heart | 167 | 0.98 | NS | Unrelated |
| Hypertension | 50 | 1.00 | NS | Unrelated |
| Venous thrombosis and embolism | 39 | } ≈1.45 | NS | Unrelated |
| General arteriosclerosis | 59 | } | NS | Uncertain |
| Pulmonary tuberculosis | 41 | 2.17 | NS | Causal |
| Asthma | 76 | 1.76 | NS | Unrelated |
| Other specified diseases | 869 | 1.07 | NS | Unrelated |
| Accidents, other violence | 640 | 0.94 | NS | Unrelated |

*Belief that smoking contributes to death from the disease not necessarily to its origin.
†Microscopically proved cases only.

### Spectrum of Diseases Associated With Smoking

At the time Hammond and Horn's report was published, sufficient evidence already had been obtained for some national committees to feel justified in advising governments that the association between smoking and lung cancer was so strong and consistent and so difficult to explain in any other way that it should be assumed that cigarette smoking was a principal cause of the disease (eg, the Medical Research Council[4]). The situation was very different, however, with regard to other diseases. It is difficult to believe now, but even as late as 1948 there was so little suspicion that smoking was a cause of any notable disease that patients with chronic obstructive lung disease or coronary thrombosis had previously been included in control series in studies of the etiology of lung cancer.[5]

Hammond and Horn's study was so massive that information was obtained about a very large number of diseases for which there had been, hitherto, only a weak suggestion that they might be related to smoking or no evidence at all. For 15 of these diseases (or groups of diseases), they found a statistically significant excess in regular cigarette smokers compared with the numbers that would have been expected from the experience of nonsmokers, while for 19 they found either no excess or one that might easily have occurred by chance. The 15 causes of death that were associated with cigarette smoking included several of the most common causes, and the suggestion that smoking might contribute to causes of death that together accounted for two thirds of all deaths came as a considerable shock. For many persons, the idea that smoking might affect health in so many different ways was, at first, unacceptable, and a variety of biases and confounding factors were suggested as possible alternative explanations for the findings. What was not realized by these critics was that cigarette smoke was not a single chemical that could be expected to have only limited physiological effects but a vehicle for conveying literally thousands of different chemicals into the body that might affect its functioning in a wide variety of ways.

Hammond and Horn's results are summarized in Tables 1 and 2, which show separately those causes of death that they found were significantly associated with cigarette smoking and those that they found were not, and each table compares its findings with current beliefs based on 25 years' further research. From these tables, it is immediately obvious that the great majority of their findings have been fully confirmed. Of the 15 causes of death (or groups of causes) that are listed in Table 1 and were significantly related to cigarette smoking, 11 are now accepted as being due, in part, to this habit, three are still *sub judice,* and only one — prostatic cancer — is now regarded as unrelated to it. Since only 77 deaths were attributed to microscopically proved cancer of the prostate and the excess was only of borderline statistical significance, it is hardly surprising that this one cause should have been classified incorrectly.

Equally impressive are the findings summarized in Table 2. Of the 19 causes of death (or groups of causes) that Hammond and Horn found unrelated to cigarette smoking, ten had mortality ratios of less than 1.25, and all are now considered unrelated. Two — venous thrombosis and embolism and general arteriosclerosis — had a combined mortality ratio of about 1.45 (it is not possible to tell from the text just what the individual ratios were), and the remaining seven causes (or groups of causes) had mortality ratios of 1.50 or more. Three of these are still sub judice (cancers of the stomach and kidney and general arteriosclerosis), while only two are now accepted as causes of death that are due in part to the habit (cancer of the pancreas and pulmonary tuberculosis).

## A Minor Criticism

If Hammond and Horn's article is to be criticized at all, and it would be unrealistic to think that any article covering such a vast and important field would not be open to some criticism, it is that the authors failed to discuss the extent to which the excess mortality observed in the different categories of smoker was actually due to the habit and how far it might be possible to explain it by other factors associated with it, such as alcohol consumption, an extrovert personality, or a modified diet. These possibilities would have opened up a wide field for debate, and the authors were perhaps wise in leaving it for readers to assess them for themselves, or it would have been impossible to keep the article within the limits that would be acceptable to an editor. Even now, alternative explanations for some of the excess rates observed have not been fully disposed of, but the mass of other evidence that has been collected makes it clear that if they do play a part it is one that is synergistic with smoking (as in the case of alcohol) or is relatively small.

## Outstanding Results

Apart from the wide spectrum of disease that was found to be associated with smoking, the four outstanding results of Hammond and Horn's study were the degree to which total mortality among cigarette smokers was increased (by 68% in men who regularly smoked cigarettes only), the much smaller increase in men who regularly smoked only pipes (9%) or cigars (12%), the rapidity with which the rates in smokers fell once smoking had been discontinued but without ever actually reaching the rate in lifelong nonsmokers, and the high proportion of the excess death rate in cigarette smokers that was attributable to coronary thrombosis. All these findings are now acknowledged to be broadly true and have had a profound influence on policies for preventive medicine. One only (the preeminence of coronary thrombosis as a cause of smoking-induced premature deaths) requires any material modification, and that only because the pattern of national mortality has changed, the mortality from coronary thrombosis having dropped and that from cancer of the lung having doubled.

## References

1. Hammond EC, Horn D: Smoking and death rates: Report on 44 months of follow-up of 187,783 men: I. Total mortality. *JAMA* 1958;166:1159-1172.
2. Hammond EC, Horn D: Smoking and death rates: Report on 44 months of follow-up of 187,783 men: II. Death rates by cause. *JAMA* 1958;166:1294-1308.
3. Cochrane AL, Cox JG, Jarman TF: Pulmonary tuberculosis in the Rhondda Fach: An interim report of a survey of a mining community. *Br Med J* 1952;2:843-853.
4. Medical Research Council: Tobacco smoking and cancer of the lung. *Br Med J* 1957;1:1523.
5. Doll R, Hill AB: A study of etiology of carcinoma of the lung. *Br Med J* 1952;2:1271.

July 9, 1960
(*JAMA* 1960;173:1064-1067)

## Chapter 44

# Closed-Chest Cardiac Massage

W. B. Kouwenhoven, Dr. Ing., James R. Jude, M.D.

and

G. Guy Knickerbocker, M.S.E.

Baltimore

When cardiac arrest occurs, either as standstill or as ventricular fibrillation, the circulation must be restored promptly; otherwise anoxia will result in irreversible damage. There are two techniques that may be used to meet the emergency: one is to open the chest and massage the heart directly and the other is to accomplish the same end by a new method of closed-chest cardiac massage. The latter method is described in this communication. The closed-chest alternating current defibrillator[1] that was developed in our laboratories has proved to be an effective and reliable means of arresting ventricular fibrillation. Its counter-shock must be sent through the chest promptly, or else cardiac anoxia will have developed to such a degree that the heart will no longer be able to resume forceable contractions without assistance. Our experience has indicated that external defibrillation is not likely to be followed by the return of spontaneous heart action, unless the counter-shock is applied within less than three minutes after the onset of ventricular fibrillation.

A study was undertaken of means of extending this time limitation without opening the chest. A method was sought that would provide adequate circulation to maintain the tone of the heart and the nourishment of the central nervous system. This method was to be at once readily applicable, safe to use, and requiring a minimum of gadgets.

One of the first attempts at enhancing circulation in the arrested heart was a closed-chest method reported by Boehm[2] in 1878. Working with cats, he grasped the chest in his hands at the area of greatest expansion and applied rhythmic pressure. His results were quite striking in some series of tests. Tournade and co-workers[3] reported that by an abrupt compression of the thorax of a dog in cardiac

Cardiac resuscitation after cardiac arrest or ventricular fibrillation has been limited by the need for open thoracotomy and direct cardiac massage. As a result of exhaustive animal experimentation a method of external transthoracic cardiac massage has been developed. Immediate resuscitative measures can now be initiated to give not only mouth-to-nose artificial respiration but also adequate cardiac massage without thoracotomy. The use of this technique on 20 patients has given an over-all permanent survival rate of 70%. Anyone, anywhere, can now initiate cardiac resuscitative procedures. All that is needed are two hands.

arrest blood pressures of 60 to 100 mm. Hg could be produced. No survival studies were given. Killick and Eve[4] reported that the rocking technique of artificial respiration, by which a patient is tilted about 60 degrees in each direction from the horizontal plane, will produce a change in the blood pressure at the atrium from 38 to 76 mm. Hg. Eve[5] hypothesized that this change will produce sufficient blood flow to nourish the heart and the brain. In 1947 Gurvich and Yuniev[6] found that a capacitor discharge sent through the chest of a dog would be followed by a resumption of the cardiac function if applied not later than one or one and one-half minutes after the onset of induced ventricular fibrillation. They reported that this time limitation might be extended to as long as eight minutes by rhythmical application of pressure on the thorax in the region of the heart. In tests which lasted 10 to 15 minutes 19 animals survived and 17 died. These authors, however, gave no specific information as to the method of application of the pressure. Rainer and Bullough[7] treated cardiac arrest in children by lowering the head about 10 degrees, placing one arm underneath the patient's knees, and flexing the legs and buttocks against the chest. They reported eight successful resuscitations in patients ranging from 8 weeks to 13

---

Lecturer in Surgery (Dr. Kouwenhoven), Resident Surgeon (Dr. Jude), and Assistant in Surgery (Mr. Knickerbocker), Johns Hopkins University School of Medicine.

years in age. Stout[8] in 1957 reported the successful use of this method in one adult.

### EXPERIMENT

With dogs used as the experimental animal, cardiac arrest in the form of ventricular fibrillation was induced. In the initial experiments more than 100 dogs, weighing from 5 to 24 kg. (11 to 52 lb.), were used in testing various methods of moving blood by massaging the intact chest. A safe and effective method of "massaging the heart" without thoracotomy was developed. Adequate circulation for periods as long as 30 minutes was easily maintained with the dog in ventricular fibrillation. A closed-chest defibrillating shock would result in the immediate return of normal sinus rhythm in such animals.

In fig. 1 are shown sections taken from the recording of the variations in blood flow, blood pressure, and electrocardiogram of a dog whose heart was in ventricular fibrillation for eight minutes. Simultaneously recorded on a four-channel recorder were the blood flow in a carotid artery, the instantaneous and average pressures in a femoral artery, and the cardiogram. The tracings in the first column of figure 1 are the normal values of these respective phenomena immediately before fibrillation was induced by a 110-volt shock. The second column shows the build-up of blood flow and pressures that took place when closed-chest cardiac massage was started, one minute after the onset of fibrillation. The third column is a record of what took place about seven mintues later. Note that vigorous fibrillation has been maintained throughout the entire period. The fourth and last column shows the immediate return of normal sinus rhythm when the closed chest defibrillator shock was given. The electrocardiograph was temporarily disconnected when the counter shock was applied.

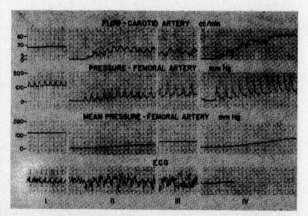

Fig. 1.—Record of blood flow, pressures, and electrocardiogram of dog whose heart was in ventricular fibrillation for eight minutes. I: normal initial values; II: start of closed-chest massage; III: seventh minute of massage; IV: closed-chest defibrillation.

*Method.*—The method of closed-chest cardiac massage developed during these animal studies is simple to apply; it is one that needs no complex equipment. Only the human hand is required. The principle of the method as applied to man is readily seen by consideration of the anatomy of the bony thorax and its contained organs. The heart is limited anteriorly by the sternum and posteriorly by the vertebral bodies. Its lateral movement is restricted by the pericardium. Pressure on the sternum compresses the heart between it and the spine, forcing out blood. Relaxation of the pressure allows the heart to fill. The thoracic cage in unconscious and anesthetized adults is surprisingly mobile. The method of application is shown in figure 2. With the patient in a supine position,

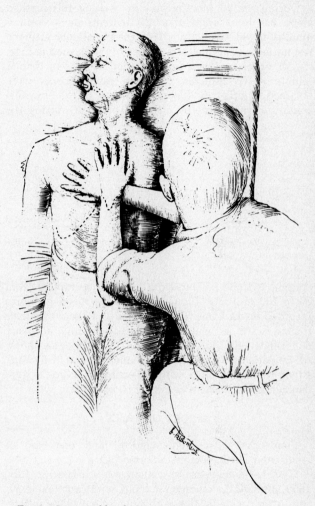

Fig. 2.—Position of hands during massage of adult.

preferably on a rigid support, the heel of one hand with the other on top of it is placed on the sternum just cephalad to the xiphoid. Firm pressure is applied vertically downward about 60 times per mintue. At the end of each pressure stroke the hands are lifted slightly to permit full expansion of the chest. The operator should be so positioned that he can use his body weight in applying the pressure. Sufficient pressure should be used to move the sternum 3 or 4 cm. toward the vertebral column.

Closed-chest cardiac massage provides some ventilation of the lungs, and if there is only one person present in a case of arrest, attention should be concentrated on the massage. If there are two or more persons present, one should massage the heart while the other gives mouth-to-nose respiration.

*Clinical Application.*—About nine months prior to time of writing, at Johns Hopkins Hospital, clinical application of closed-chest cardiac massage was successfully illustrated in a case of cardiac arrest. Initially, it was felt that the method might be useful in treating arrest in children, whose ribs are known to be flexible, but that it would not be effective in adults. This latter assumption was proved to be incorrect, since the chest of an unconscious adult was found to be remarkably flexible.

During the 10 months prior to writing this method alone has been applied on 20 patients aged from 2 months to 80 years. In 13 of these patients artificial respiration was applied simultaneously with the massage; the duration of the massage varied from less than 1 minute to 65 minutes. In seven cases records were obtained of either the blood pressure or of the electrical activity of the heart (by electrocardiogram) during the

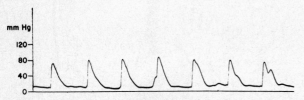

Fig. 3.—Blood pressure produced in an adult by closed-chest cardiac massage.

episode. Systolic pressures during massage ranged from 60 to 100 mm. Hg. Figure 3 shows the blood pressures recorded on an adult. The hearts of 3 of the 20 patients treated were in ventricular fibrillation, and all were defibrillated by a closed-chest A. C. defibrillator shock. All 20 patients were resuscitated and, at time of writing, 14 of them are alive without central nervous system damage and without undergoing thoracotomy.

### REPORT OF CASES

Four cases of cardiac standstill and one case of ventricular fibrillation are reported below.

CASE 1.—A 35-year-old woman was admitted in July, 1959, through the emergency room, with acute cholecystitis. After premedication with 8 mg. of morphine sulfate, 0.4 mg. of atropine, and 100 mg. of pentobarbital (Nembutal), she was taken, one and one-half hours later, to the operating room where anesthesia was induced with thiopental sodium and succinylcholine. Intubation was attempted, but difficulty was encountered, with inability to ventilate the patient. She became pulseless and cyanotic and her respirations disappeared. External cardiac massage was instituted, without artificial respiration. After two minutes a strong transthoracic pulse developed, together with spontaneous shallow respirations. Blood pressure returned to 130/80 mm. Hg and pulse to 100 beats per minute. Intubation proceeded thereafter, with some difficulty but no further cardiac problems. The patient underwent a cholecystectomy for acute hydrops of the gallbladder and had an uneventful recovery. She was discharged five days later without neurological signs or symptoms and has been entirely normal on subsequent follow-up examinations.

CASE 2.—A 9-year-old boy with chronic mastoiditis was admitted and on Nov. 5, 1959, had a mastoidectomy. Postoperatively the patient was very cyanotic. Respirations stopped in the recovery room but a weak heart beat was obtainable. The child was given mouth-to-mouth respiration and cardiac assistance with external cardiac massage for about 30 seconds. He responded to this with good return of all functions and had no further difficulty. On Nov. 17, 1959, the patient was again returned to the operating room for a left mastoidectomy, after preoperative medication with 60 mg. of pentobarbital and 0.25 mg. of scopolamine. The patient was vomiting continuously on arrival in the anesthesia room, and his pulse was irregular. The induction of anesthesia was stormy because of the patient's nausea. He was given open-drop anesthesia with fluothane and intubation was performed with ease. At this point his pulse suddenly disappeared, as did the blood pressure and apical beat. Closed-chest cardiac massage was carried out for one minute and the patient responded with a good return of pulse, blood pressure, and respirations. The operation was canceled, and the patient returned to the ward. He had no further difficulties and no central nervous system damage.

CASE 3.—An 80-year-old woman was admitted with a large tumor of the thyroid and had a tracheostomy with biopsy of the thyroid on Nov. 5, 1959. The diagnosis was papillary adenocarcinoma of the thyroid. She was returned to the operating room three days later for a definitive procedure after premedication with 100 mg. of pentobarbital and 0.5 mg. of atropine. She was given anesthesia with thiopental sodium and fluothane. Succinylcholine in divided doses was also given. Intubation was performed through the tracheostomy. A few minutes thereafter the blood pressure became unobtainable and the administration of fluothane was immediately stopped. There was no apical or peripheral pulse.

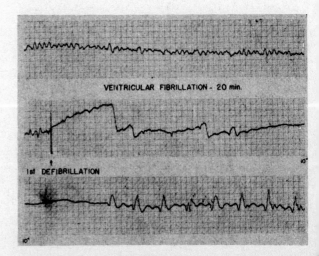

Fig. 4 (case 5).—First defibrillation shock, followed by standstill and return of fibrillation.

External cardiac massage was begun immediately and carried out for a period of two minutes. Mephentermine (Wyamine), 30 mg., and phenylephrine (Neo-Synephrine) hydrochloride, 1 mg., were given intravenously. A good pulse and blood pressure returned about 90 seconds after the beginning of massage. The operation was completed without difficulty and the patient had no sign of central nervous system damage in the postoperative period.

CASE 4.—A 12-year-old boy developed sudden cardiac arrest on Jan. 22, 1960, while undergoing an excision of a verrucus linearis of the scalp. Under thiopental and fluothane anesthesia the patient became anoxic, with an irregular pulse followed by arrest. Local infiltration with epinephrine-saline solution may have contributed. The pupils dilated and the patient was pulseless and without respiration for at least one minute before external massage was begun. After one minute of massage a good pulse and pressure returned. The operation was completed without difficulty. Postoperatively the patient had transitory blindness and bilateral Babinski reflex. Nystagmus was also present. Over 36 hours the neurological findings returned to normal. The remainder of the postoperative course was uneventful.

CASE 5.—A 45-year-old man was brought to the emergency room of the hospital with excruciating substernal chest pains radiating down both arms on Jan. 5, 1960. He was conscious when admitted. While removing his clothing, preparatory to examination, he fell to the floor. His respirations ceased, and there were no heart sounds and no pulse. The house officer immediately began closed-chest cardiac massage. An electrocardiogram was taken and showed the heart to be in ventricular fibrillation. The patient began to breathe spontaneously. Ten minutes after the start of external massage artificial respiration by endotracheal tube was first begun. External heart massage and artificial respiration were continued for 20 minutes, while a closed-chest A. C. defibrillator was being brought to the emergency room.

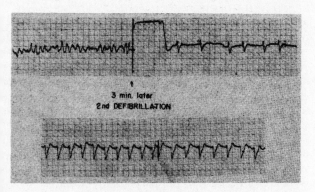

Fig. 5 (case 5).—Second defibrillation shock, followed by natural beats.

Two defibrillator shocks were given; the first (fig. 4) temporarily arrested the fibrillation. After the second shock (fig. 5) the heart resumed natural beats. An electrocardiographic tracing (fig. 6) taken two hours later showed an anterior myocardial infarction. Subsequent tracings confirmed the diagnosis.

The patient had no sign of central nervous system damage, except amnesia for the period of cardiac massage plus two hours. He has followed, without

incident, the usual course of treatment for myocardial infarction.

## SUMMARY

Closed-chest cardiac massage has been proved to be effective in cases of cardiac arrest. It has provided circulation adequate to maintain the heart and the central nervous system, and it has provided an opportunity to bring a defibrillator to the scene if necessary.

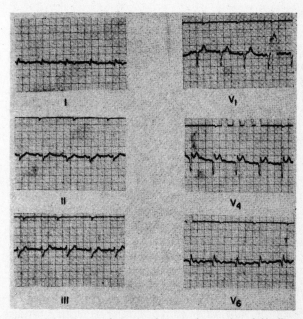

Fig. 6 (case 5).—Cardiogram taken two hours after defibrillation, showing anterior myocardial infarction.

Supportive drug treatment and other measures may be given. The necessity for a thoracotomy is eliminated. The real value of the method lies in the fact that it can be used wherever the emergency arises, whether that is in or out of the hospital.

This study was supported by a grant from the National Heart Institute, National Institutes of Health.

References

1. Kouwenhoven, W. B.; Milnor, W. R.; Knickerbocker, G. G.; and Chestnut, W. R.: Closed Chest Defibrillation of Heart, Surgery 42:550-561 (Sept.) 1957.
2. Boehm, R.: V. Arbeiten aus dem pharmakologischen Institute der Universität Dorpat: 13. Ueber Wiederbelebung nach Vergiftungen und Asphyxie, Arch. exper. Path. u. Pharmakol. 8:68-101, 1878.
3. Tournade, A.; Rocchisani, L.; and Mely, G.: Etude expérimentale des effets circulatoires qu'entrainent la respiration artificielle et la compression saccadée du thorax chez le chien Compt. rend. Soc. de biol. 117:1123-1126, 1934.
4. Killick, E. M., and Eve, F. C.: Physiological Investigation of Rocking Method of Artificial Respiration, Lancet 2:740-741 (Sept. 30) 1933.
5. Eve, F. C.: Artificial Circulation Produced by Rocking: Its Use in Drowning and Anaesthetic Emergencies, Brit. M. J. 2:295-296 (Aug. 23) 1947.
6. Gurvich, H. L., and Yuniev, G. S.: Restoration of Heart Rhythm During Fibrillation by Condenser Discharge, Am. Rev. Soviet Med. 4:252-256 (Feb.) 1947.
7. Rainer, E. H., and Bullough, J.: Respiratory and Cardiac Arrest During Anesthesia in Children, Brit. M. J. 2:1024-1028 (Nov. 2) 1957.
8. Stout, H. A.: Cardiac Arrest: Massage Without Incision, J. Oklahoma M. Assoc. 3:112-114 (March) 1957.

June 15, 1984
(*JAMA* 1984;251:3137-3140)

# Closed-Chest Massage After Twenty-five Years*

Arnold Sladen, MD

*Never in the field of human conflict was so much owed by so many to so few.*

WINSTON S. CHURCHILL

Annually in the United States, approximately 1½ million persons suffer a myocardial infarction.[1] Of these, about 660,000 die. Approximately 60% of these deaths from acute myocardial infarction occur outside the hospital and, in the majority of cases, within the first two hours of the onset of symptoms.[1] In fact, in 25% there are no premonitory signs and death is the first manifestation of coronary artery disease. The primary mechanisms of sudden death are ventricular fibrillation in 62%, ventricular tachycardia in 7%, and severe bradydysrhythmias and asystole in 31%. If there were an easily available technique that could be applied immediately after the onset of "clinical" death and rapidly followed with electrical or chemical therapy or both, it has been estimated that 200,000 to 300,000 persons could be saved annually in the United States alone.

The manuscript entitled "Closed-Chest Cardiac Massage" by W. B. Kouwenhoven, James R. Jude, and G. Guy Knickerbocker published in THE JOURNAL on July 9, 1960, described such a technique and may have resulted in saving more lives than any other medical manuscript during the past century.[2] The publication describes a technique to sustain life when the heart is not beating effectively and without the use of equipment, using skills that require only the two hands and that the lay person easily can apply. Its development depended on the

brilliant observation that the pressure of heavy defibrilla tion electrodes on a dog's chest resulted in a marked rise in femoral arterial pressure.

## History

In 1926, Consolidated Electric Company of New York City, concerned by the increasing number of electric shock accidents and deaths, sought advice from the consultants of the Rockefeller Institute. Five working groups were established, and one chaired by Professo Howell was given the task of studying the effects o electric shock on physiological parameters. Kouwenhov en, professor of engineering, joined Professor Howell a Johns Hopkins University in 1928 and started his studie: on ventricular fibrillation. Howell suggested that he review the work of Provost and Battelli published in 1899, in which it was reported that ventricular fibrillation in the animal heart could be halted by means of an electric countershock applied directly to the surface o the myocardium. Kouwenhoven[3] and his co-worke were able to confirm this earlier study, and Mr Vivier Thomas of the Hopkins Surgical Laboratory built number of open-chest defibrillators, but of course they were not suitable for use in the field since the electrode: were designed for direct application to the surface of the heart.

In 1947, Claude Beck and co-workers[4] at Case Western Reserve University in Cleveland reported the first human case of successful open-chest defibrillation with electrodes applied directly to the surface of the heart. Open-chest defibrillation became the standard technique and was used in conjunction with oper cardiac massage. With the chest open for defibrillation the heart was exposed; the operator could insert a hand squeeze the heart, and provide the essential circulation of blood to the brain and other vital organs.

Open-heart massage was not an innovation, having

From the Division of Critical Care Medicine, Department of Anesthesiology, Monefiore Hospital, University of Pittsburgh School of Medicine.

*A commentary on Kouwenhoven WB, Jude JR, Knickerbocker GG: Closed-chest cardiac massage. *JAMA* 1960;173:1064-1067.

been first described by Niehaus about 1880. The outcome on that occasion was not successful; in fact, it was not until Ingelsrud in 1901 and Starling and Lane in 1902 reported recovery from open-heart massage that this technique was shown to be efficacious in man. Charles White[5] of George Washington University, writing in *Surgery, Gynecology and Obstetrics,* reviewed the available literature in 1906 and observed that there had been 50 reported cases in which open-heart massage had been applied, and ten patients had recovered. It is pertinent that in White's review of the 50 reported cases, 70% of the cardiac arrests were associated with chloroform anesthesia and occurred in the operating room. In this environment, open-heart massage either directly, transdiaphragmatically, or subdiaphragmatically was readily accomplished and in addition was performed by a general surgeon who usually was available immediately and most frequently had experience in abdominal and thoracic procedures. White concluded with two remarks that remain pertinent up to this very day: "It is essential that respiration be invoked by artificial means in conjunction with heart massage," and "the briefer the interval (of arrest) the more rapid the response to heart massage."

Jerome Harold Kay[6] of Johns Hopkins University documented in *Surgery, Gynecology and Obstetrics* in 1951 the experimental results of using a combination of open-chest cardiac massage and direct defibrillation. In 189 canine experiments, cardiac massage for one to two minutes before countershock resulted in successful defibrillation of all the hearts in ventricular fibrillation. In ventricular standstill, one to two minutes of cardiac massage before the injection of cardiac stimulants proved to be efficacious. As a result of these and other publications, emergency thoracotomy and open-heart massage became for many a cavalier maneuver to be used for a person with "cardiac arrest" in the emergency room, general ward, hospital corridor, and even the street. Many of these "arrests" may have been caused by malfunctioning electrocardiograph electrodes or were simple episodes of syncope outdoors. Horken commented that brilliant triumphs in either instance might well have been only the triumph of aggression over wit.

Kouwenhoven and co-workers continued to pursue their studies of the effects of electrical energy on the heart. Because of an increase in the occurrence of electrocution in linesmen, Edison Electric Institute requested that they develop a technique for defibrillation without having to open the chest — closed-chest defibrillation. Initially, they discovered that a brief alternating current of 20 amp across the chest would arrest fibrillation in the canine heart, and, subsequently, with placement of one electrode on the suprasternal notch and the other over the apex of the heart, defibrillation could be effected with only 5 amp.[3]

In 1958, Kouwenhoven and Knickerbocker were proceeding with their studies in closed-chest defibrillation when they observed that there was a rise in intra-arterial pressure when the heavy defibrillator electrodes were applied to the chest wall of the dog with ventricular fibrillation. A relaxation and push caused additional increase in arterial pressure. They considered that the rhythmic application of pressure to the chest wall might cause the heart to empty and provide circulation. These observations and ideas were discussed with the staff of The Johns Hopkins Hospital, but they were assured that pressing on the animal's chest was like pressing on a balloon: "when the pressure was relaxed, the chest expanded and the pressure returned to normal"; the rise was not sufficient indication of circulation.

It is likely that inadequate consideration was given to Kouwenhoven's concepts of the production of an artificial circulation by external cardiac compression, because others previously had condemned this technique. Pike and colleagues[7] commented in the *Journal of Experimental Medicine* in 1908 that they had attempted extrathoracic massage without success. They noted that rhythmic manual compression of the thorax of a cat over the heart gave fairly good results in certain stages of heart stoppage, but the time when massage was effective was much too limited to make the method a sure one. They observed that rhythmic compression of the heart was efficient for three to five minutes after cessation of the external pulse, but they questioned whether, in fact, the loss of pulse was associated with the heart ceasing to beat. When they were sure that the heart had stopped entirely, extrathoracic massage alone had proved useless (artificial ventilation always was started after cardiac arrest was produced). Furthermore, they noted that rhythmic compression of the thorax of a large dog at a rate necessary for resuscitation was exceedingly laborious and often could not be kept up for a sufficiently long time.

### Prefatory Studies and the Article

Jude returned from the National Institutes of Health in 1958, and, despite the comments by the hospital staff that the technique offered no merit, the trio performed additional studies substituting the hand for the electrode and applying rhythmic pressure to the chest wall. Their next step was to attach strain gauges to the ventricle to observe the most effective place on the chest to apply rhythmic compression in order to obtain the maximum rise in blood pressure. Simultaneously, they used flowmeters to study the changes in blood flow with different sites of compression. The optimum site for the application of rhythmic compression proved to be over the lower half of the sternum, over the heart. They believed that pressure on the sternum compressed the heart between it and the spine, forcing out blood, thus providing an effective circulation. Joined by Henry Bahnson, the group found that after 15 to 20 minutes of this rhythmic pressure over the lower half of the sternum, with a force of 100 lb at a rate of 60 per minute, they were still able to defibrillate the dog's fibrillating ventricle, and, most importantly, the CNS seemed unaffected. Kouwenhoven saw this as a technique that would allow life-sustaining maneuvers to be performed on electrocuted linesmen, with ventricular fibrillation, while awaiting the delivery of a defibrillator.

On Feb 15, 1958, Henry Bahnson applied the technique to a 2-year-old child whose heart was in ventricular fibrillation and successfully resuscitated a patient with

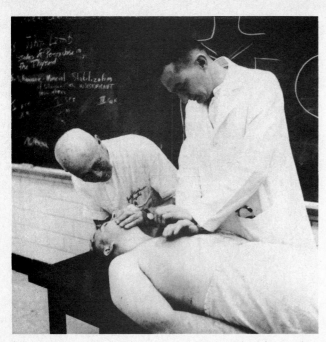

Demonstration of cardiopulmonary resuscitation at the Johns Hopkins Hospital, circa 1960; Dr William B. Kouwenhoven maintaining airway with "chin-lift technique" and Dr. James J. Jude performing "closed-chest massage." "Patient" is third member of research trio, Dr Guy Knickerbocker.

this new combined method — external cardiac compression and closed-chest defibrillation. The following day, Alfred Blalock, professor of surgery at The Johns Hopkins Medical School, directed that external cardiac compression be used for children when necessary. Later in 1958, Jude applied external cardiac compression to an obese patient who experienced ventricular fibrillation while being anesthetized. The resuscitation again was successful, and Blalock gave the technique his "unqualified blessing." Within ten months, 20 persons with cardiac arrest had been resuscitated with external cardiac compression, only three of whom had ventricular fibrillation requiring defibrillation. On the basis of these 20 cases, the manuscript "Closed-Chest Cardiac Massage" by Kouwenhoven and co-workers was submitted. The combination of external cardiac compression and mouth-to-mouth ventilation became known as cardiopulmonary resuscitation (CPR), part of basic cardiac life support.

The new concept of external cardiac compression (in association with artificial ventilation) as the primary step in the management of a patient with cardiac arrest received wide acceptance. In 1961, Jude et al[8] reported on the application of this technique in 118 patients with cardiac arrest at The Johns Hopkins Hospital. Seventy-eight percent had cardiac action restored, but only 60% were returned to prearrest CNS and cardiac status. In 1963, Cotlar and colleagues,[9] writing from Charity Hospital, New Orleans, described a series of 73 patients with cardiac arrests who had been treated with external, internal, or combined cardiac compression. There was a 90% survival in those managed with closed-chest resuscitation, 35% with the combined techniques, and 21% with open massage only. In the same year, Klassen and associates[10] in Montreal described 126 "medical patients, 50% with acute myocardial infarction. Using external cardiac compression, with or without defibrillation, 42 patients were resuscitated and 17 of these survived to be discharged from the hospital. In 1972, report from the same institution documented 1,20 resuscitation efforts with a survival discharge rate o 19%.

### Progress in CPR: Involving the Public

During the 40 years since Kouwenhoven et a published their lifesaving technique, the art and science of medicine have continued to grow. Anesthesia ha become a much safer practice, with minimal morbidit and mortality from anesthetic drugs; cardiac arrests in th operating suite are few and far between. There has bee a greater understanding of the epidemiology of coronar artery disease, myocardial infarction, and sudden death It has been demonstrated that many patients who "di from heart attacks," in fact, do not always demonstrat evidence of acute infarction at autopsy, and death i presumed to be caused by ventricular ectopy, mos usually fibrillation in association with coronary arter disease. Because 60% of deaths from myocardial infarc tion are prehospital and occur within two hours of th onset of symptoms, it is essential that therapy star where the patient is situated and continue all the way t the hospital and until the patient's condition is monitore in a coronary care unit. In 1967, Pantridge,[11] in Belfas initiated a program to deliver ambulances, medica equipment, and operators to out-of-hospital patient with symptoms of acute myocardial infarction an successfully treated a number of patients with ventricula fibrillation in the prehospital setting while, in the Unite States, Grace in New York City pioneered the concept o mobile coronary care units.

Leonard Cobb[12] of Seattle also developed one of th earliest and the best emergency care systems. A essential key in the Seattle system has been th involvement of the general public in the initial manage ment of patients with cardiac arrest. It had becom obvious that with the high incidence of cardiac arrests i the prehospital scene, unless CPR was initiated rapidly the deployment of expensive and elaborate equipmen was useless. To this end, the American Heart Associatio and the American Red Cross developed similar trainin programs based on the Statement of the Ad Ho Committee on Cardiopulmonary Resuscitation of th Division of Medical Sciences, National Academy o Sciences–National Research Council, published in 1966. In the original statement, the teaching of external cardia compression was directed to medical and paramedica personnel only and excluded the lay public. The Ameri can Heart Association Committee on CPR saw th defects in this and developed programs to teach bot mouth-to-mouth ventilation and external cardiac com pression to the lay public.

Parallel with the preparation of written, oral, and visua training material was the need to create a mannequin t train personnel to perform CPR. Asmund S. Laerdal, dollmaker of Stavanger, Norway, had considerable ex perience with the early use of polyvinyl materials t manufacture soft dolls. The Norwegian Society of Anesthesiologists and the Department of Health approached Laerdal to make a mannequin on which to practice mouth-to-mouth breathing, and in 1959 he developed the life-size Resusci-Anne mannequin specifically for this purpose. When Kouwenhoven et al published their manuscript the following year, Laerdal modified his Resusci-Anne so that external cardiac compressions could be included in the skills taught on the mannequin, and so the stage was set to teach CPR to the masses. In Seattle, the fire department accepted the challenge to train the lay public, and, by 1980, 225,000 persons, high school age and older, had been trained in CPR. Now, 35% of resuscitations in Seattle are initiated by bystander CPR. In the period from 1970 to 1978, 1,100 patients resuscitated in the prehospital scene in Seattle were hospitalized and ultimately discharged home.[14] During this period, the annual rate of successful resuscitation and discharge home has continued to rise, based on increased involvement by citizen CPR and more rapid response by trained personnel capable of delivering definitive therapy. When CPR was initiated within four minutes, the survival rate was 43%, whereas at eight minutes, it was, at best, 6%. In 1977, a national survey revealed that 12 million Americans were trained in CPR and 51 million more persons were looking forward to this training. The goal of saving 150,000 to 200,000 lives a year in the United States now is well within the range of possibility within the next few years.[1]

"New CPR," the administration of simultaneous cardiac compression and ventilation at high airway pressures, introduced by Chandra and Weisfeldt, does not challenge the value of closed-chest cardiac massage but only the mechanics of blood flow.[15,16] They postulate that artificial circulation achieved by external cardiac compression is not the simple squeezing of a rubber pump between two rigid structures as proposed by Kouwenhoven but the creation of differences in pressure between vessels inside and outside the thoracic cage, coupled with the role of venous valves, which assist in regulating the direction of flow. Using new CPR, they were able to show an increase in mean systolic radial artery pressure and carotid flow velocity. Criley et al,[17] using intracardiac micromanometers and flow probes in the carotid arteries, observed that conventional external cardiac compression produced a carotid flow of 10% of control, whereas with new CPR, flow doubled to 20% of control while cineangiography revealed that with conventional CPR the heart twisted onto the left hemothorax during sternal compression, resulting in a reduction of forward flow![17]

---

It is almost a quarter of a century since the publication of "Closed-Chest Cardiac Massage" in *JAMA*, and, during this period, thousands and thousands of persons across the whole world have owed their lives to those three men who were able to show that without special equipment, and using only the two hands, anyone with training can save a life. Only a few years before his death, Kouwenhoven, at the age of 83 years, said that the discovery and development of cardiopulmonary resuscitation made the closed-chest defibrillator a useful and effective device for depolarizing fibrillating human hearts. "Many lives have been saved and I thank the Lord for the opportunity that has been granted me."

## References

1. *Advanced Cardiac Life Support.* Dallas, American Heart Association, 1981.

2. Kouwenhoven WB, Jude JR, Knickerbocker GG: Closed-chest cardiac massage. *JAMA* 1960;173:1064-1067.

3. Kouwenhoven WB: The development of the defibrillator. *Ann Intern Med* 1969;71:449-458.

4. Beck CS, Pritchard WH, Feil HS: Ventricular fibrillation of long duration abolished by electric shock. *JAMA* 1947;135:985-986.

5. White CS: The role of heart massage in surgery. *Surg Gynecol Obstet* 1909;9:388-400.

6. Kay JH: The treatment of cardiac arrest: An experimental study. *Surg Gynecol Obstet* 1951;93:682-690.

7. Pike FH, Guthrie CC, Stewart GN: Studies of resuscitation: I. The general conditions affecting resuscitation, and the resuscitation of the blood and of the heart. *J Exp Med* 1908;10:371-418.

8. Jude JR, Kouwenhoven WB, Knickerbocker GG: Cardiac arrest: report of application of external cardiac massage in 118 patients. *JAMA* 1961;178:1063-1070.

9. Cotlar AM, Fleming ID, Thomas PE, et al: Increased survival from cardiac arrest since the introduction of external massage. *Dis Chest* 1963;44:400-407.

10. Klassen GA, Broadhurst C, Peretz DI, et al: Cardiac resuscitation in 126 medical patients using external cardiac massage. *Lancet* 1963;1:1290-1292.

11. Pantridge JF, Gedders JS: A mobile intensive care unit in the management of myocardial infarction. *Lancet* 1967;2:271-273.

12. Cobb LA, Hallstrom AP, Thompson RG, et al: Community resuscitation. *Ann Rev Med* 1980;31:453-462.

13. Cardiopulmonary resuscitation: Statement by the Ad Hoc Committee on Cardiopulmonary Resuscitation of the Division of Medical Sciences, National Academy of Sciences–National Reasearch Council. *JAMA* 1966;198:372-378.

14. Cobb LA, Werner JA, Trobaugh GB: Sudden cardiac death: I. A decade's experience with out-of-hospital resuscitation: *Mod Concepts Cardiovasc Dis* 1980;49:31-36, 37-42.

15. Weisfeldt ML, Chandra N: Physiology of cardiopulmonary resuscitation. *Ann Rev Med* 1981;32:435-442.

16. Chandra N, Rudikoff M, Weisfeldt ML: Simultaneous chest compression and ventilation at high airway pressure during cardiopulmonary resuscitation. *Lancet* 1980;1:175-178.

17. Criley JM, Ung S, Niemann JT: What is the role of newer methods of cardiopulmonary resuscitation? *Cardiovasc Clin* 1983;13:297-307.

Aug 6, 1960
(*JAMA* 1960;173:1521-1526)

# Chapter 45

# Live, Orally Given Poliovirus Vaccine

## Effects of Rapid Mass Immunization on Population Under Conditions of Massive Enteric Infection With Other Viruses

Albert B. Sabin, M.D., Cincinnati, Manuel Ramos-Alvarez, M.D., José Alvarez-Amezquita, M.D.
Mexico, D. F., William Pelon, Ph.D., Richard H. Michaels, M.D., Ilya Spigland, M.D.,
Meinrad A. Koch, M.D., Joan M. Barnes, Ph.D.,
and
Johng S. Rhim, M.D., Cincinnati

I N THE absence of enteric infection with other viruses, the feeding of a single type of live poliovirus vaccine to children who have not previously been infected with the same type of poliovirus usually results in viral multiplication in the intestinal tract, antibody formation, and complete or partial resistance to reinfection. The use of live poliovirus vaccine in areas with climatic and hygienic conditions which permit extensive dissemination of naturally occurring polioviruses and other enteric viruses throughout the year has been complicated by the problem of viral interference,[1] which we have attempted to overcome by the tactics to be described in this communication.

The studies of one of us (M.R.-A.) and associates[2] in Mexico and of Plotkin and Koprowski[3] in the Belgian Congo have shown that vaccination programs in large subtropical or tropical cities that are spread out over a period of many weeks and include only a small fraction of the susceptible population not only fail to immunize a considerable proportion of the vaccinated children but also have little or no influence on the dissemination of the ever-present, naturally occurring paralytogenic strains of poliovirus. Accordingly, it seemed necessary to determine whether at least temporary dominance over the naturally occurring polioviruses and other interfering enteric viruses could be achieved by feeding a mixture of all three types of poliovirus vaccine to almost all susceptible

The phenomenon of viral interference must be taken into account in planning the use of live poliovirus vaccine in areas where conditions favor the extensive dissemination of naturally occurring polioviruses. Experience with feeding a trivalent vaccine to 26,033 children in a tropical city of 100,000 population led to the conclusion that interference was overcome by mass feeding of vaccine to 86% of all children under 11 years within a period of about four days, and that, because dissemination of the poliovirus was self-limited, a second feeding of trivalent vaccine was necessary to achieve immunization of almost all children. Recommendations are here formulated for the eradication of poliomyelitis, but they apply only to subtropical and tropical regions with extensive dissemination of various enteric viruses and not to temperate zones with good sanitation and hygiene during certain periods of the year and under conditions of low or absent dissemination of enteric viruses.

children within a period of a few days. The reason fo using a trivalent mixture instead of feeding the thre types separately at intervals of four to six weeks, which i regarded as optimum during the cold months of the yea in temperate zones, was to implant all three types of th vaccine strains in the largest number of children and the

From the Children's Hospital Research Foundation, University of Cincinnati College of Medicine; Hospital Infantil, Mexico, D. F.; and th Ministry of Health, Mexico.

Read in part before the 73rd annual meeting of the Association of American Physicians, Atlantic City, May 3, 1960.

let nature help in their further dissemination in the community.

## METHODS OF STUDY AND RESULTS

This study was carried out in Toluca, Mexico, in August, 1959. One of us (M.R.-A.) and his associates in Mexico were responsible for the field work and the

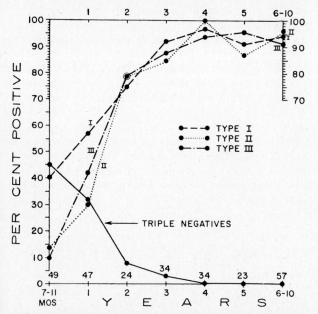

Fig. 1.—Poliovirus antibodies in children in Toluca, Mexico, just before feeding vaccine. Numbers above age groups indicate number of persons in each group tested.

collection of specimens, and all the virological and serologic work was carried out in Cincinnati. Toluca, located at a latitude of about 19 degrees north, has a total population of about 100,000. A serologic survey of the

population just before initiation of the vaccine program indicated that 90 to 100% of the children become immune to all three types of poliovirus during the first 4 years of life (fig. 1). According to available data for the past five years, this city has been paying an average price of 14 paralytic cases per year for this naturally acquired immunity. Twenty cases of paralytic poliomyelitis had already been reported in 1959, when our study began during the second week of August. Rectal swabbings from 1,892 persons—children aged from birth to 10 years and their mothers—obtained at random in different parts of the city within a few days before the vaccination program, were each tested in monkey kidney and human

TABLE 1.—*Proportion of Children of Indicated Age Fed Single Dose of Trivalent Vaccine in Toluca, Mexico, August, 1959*

| Age, Yr. | Persons of Indicated Age, No. | Fed Vaccine, No. | Persons of Indicated Age Vaccinated, % |
|---|---|---|---|
| <1 | 3,195 | 2,965 | 90 |
| 1 | 2,803 | 2,327 | 82 |
| 2 | 3,257 | 2,361 | 71 |
| 3 | 3,329 | 2,453 | 74 |
| 4 | 3,298 | 2,575 | 78 |
| 5 | 2,886 | 2,410 | 83 |
| 6-10 | 11,708 | 10,942 | 93 |
| <1-10 | 30,476 | 26,033 | 86 |
| Total population, all ages | 103,072 | 26,033 | 25 |

epithelioma (HEP 2) tissue cultures as well as in newborn mice. The results, summarized in figure 2, indicate that the special methods used revealed a much higher incidence of natural enteric viral infection than has ever been demonstrated before—beginning during the first days after birth and reaching a peak of 72% during the 1st year of life. Beginning with 1-month-old children, polioviruses were isolated from every age group tested, with a peak rate of 14 to 15% in children between 7

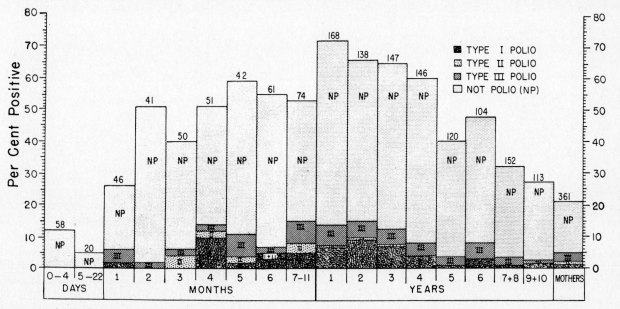

Fig. 2.—Incidence of various types of poliovirus and other enteric viruses (NP) in children from birth to 10 years of age and in their mothers, Toluca, August, 1959, just before feeding vaccine. Numbers above each column indicate number of persons in each age group tested.

months and 2 years of age. The high infection rate among the mothers of these young children was surprising—5% for polioviruses and 16% for other enteric viruses.

It was in this setting that a single dose of trivalent poliovirus vaccine ($10^{5.2}$ to $10^{5.6}$ 50% tissue-culture dose [$TCD_{50}$] of each type) was fed to a total of 26,033 children

TABLE 2.—*Self-Limited Character of Dissemination of Polioviruses After Rapid Mass Oral Administration of Trivalent Vaccine in a Tropical Community*[°]

|  | Before Vaccine Aug., 1959 | 3 Mo. After Vaccine |
|---|---|---|
| Total no. tested | 719 | 417 |
| Incidence of polioviruses (P) | 11.0% | 0.7% |
| Incidence of other enteric viruses (NP) | 50.8% | 50.6% |
| Ratio NP/P | 4.6 | 72.3 |

[°]Carrier rate of polioviruses and other enteric viruses among 1- to 5-year-old children selected at random before and 3 mo. after single dose ($10^{5.2}$-$10^{5.6}$ $TCD_{50}$) of trivalent oral poliovirus vaccine (Sabin) fed within a few days to 86% of children (newborn to 10 years) in Toluca, Mexico.

Carrier rate is based on detection of virus in single rectal swabbing—actual carrier rate is somewhat higher.

in such a community after this rapid and massive artificial seeding over 3,139 rectal swabbings were obtained during the subsequent three months and tested for virus. A total of 2,711 viruses were recovered from the 5,031 prevaccination and postvaccination specimens, and the use of special methods permitted us to classify them rapidly as polioviruses or nonpolioviruses.

The results, shown in figure 3 for a group of 274 children who were tested repeatedly over a period of 3 months and in figure 4 for hundreds of different children randomly chosen before and at monthly intervals after vaccination, indicate the following conclusions. 1. While the total incidence of enteric viruses varied little or not at all during the three months, the polioviruses became dominant during the first three weeks after vaccination, the isolation rates being as high as 40 to 70% in the different age groups. 2. The early dominance of the polioviruses was followed by a quick decline—more rapid in the children over 2 years of age—which by the end of three months reached a point that was markedly lower than before the mass feeding of the live polioviruses vaccine.

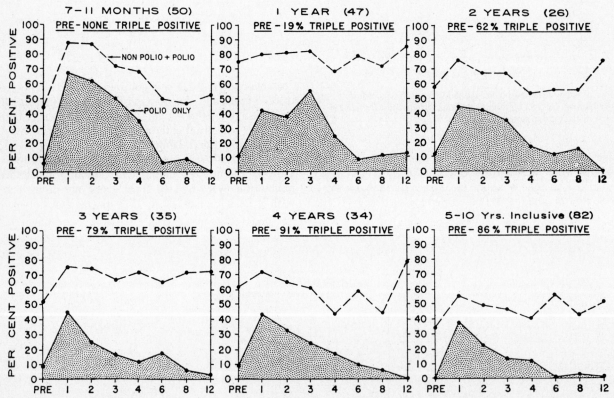

Fig. 3.—Polioviruses and other enteric viruses in group of 274 children tested just before and at weekly intervals after single dose of trivalent orally given poliovirus vaccine, Toluca, August to November, 1959. Number in parenthesis next to each age group indicates number of persons tested.

under 11 years of age—86% of all the children of this age group in Toluca. The actual proportion of children of each age group who received the vaccine is shown in table 1. Only four days were required to feed the vaccine to 97% of the children who received it.

To determine how effectively the attenuated polioviruses competed with the other enteric viruses and how long and extensively polioviruses continue to disseminate

The self-limited character of dissemination of polioviruses after this rapid mass feeding of live polioviruses vaccine, under conditions which favor the continued extensive dissemination of enteric agents, is strikingly brought out in table 2, which shows the results of tests on 1,135 randomly selected 1-to-5-year-old children. The isolation rate of nonpoliomyelitis enteric viruses was about 51% before and also three months after the vaccination program, while the isolation of polioviruses dropped from 11 to 0.7%, a sixteenfold diminution.

The serologic effect of this temporary dominance of

TABLE 3.—*Development of Poliovirus Neutralizing Antibodies During Comparable Ten-Week Period in Two Mexican Cities*[°]

| Type | Toluca—After 1 Dose of Trivalent Vaccine | | Queretaro—No Vaccine | |
|---|---|---|---|---|
| | No.[†] | % | No. | % |
| 1 | 36/53 | 68 | 2/33 | 6 |
| 2 | 64/77 | 82 | 3/33 | 10 |
| 3 | 33/76 | 43 | 5/38 | 13 |

[°]Conversion rates for indicated type are based on simultaneous tests on paired serums from originally negative children.

[†]Children without antibody who were carriers of poliovirus at time first blood specimen was obtained are excluded from this calculation.

conversion rate was 100% in the small number of single-negative, 88% in the double-negative, and 55% in the triple-negative reactors; for type 3 it was 59, 42, and 37%, respectively; while for type 2 there was no difference in the three categories, the conversion rates being 82, 80, and 83%.

An analysis of the data (table 5) on the children from whom rectal swabbings were obtained at weekly intervals indicated two significant facts. 1. Many children who developed antibody did not excrete sufficient virus to be detected in the rectal swabs. 2. Some of the children who had no demonstrable antibody at 10 weeks excreted enough poliovirus to be detected in at least one of the rectal swabbings obtained during the first 4 weeks. When the children in the second category are included, one obtains an estimated total infection rate of 80% for type 1, 87% for type 2, and 47% for type 3 during the first 10 weeks after the single trivalent dose of vaccine. Further

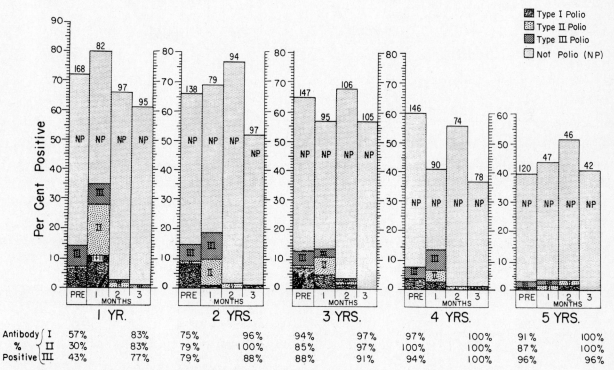

Fig. 4.—Incidence of various types of poliovirus and other enteric viruses (NP) in 1-to-5-year-old children randomly selected just before and at indicated monthly intervals after single dose of trivalent orally given poliovirus vaccine, Toluca, August to November, 1959. Numbers above each column refer to number of children tested during each period.

the polioviruses is shown in table 3, in which the antibody conversion rates during the first 10 weeks after the mass feeding of a single dose of trivalent vaccine in Toluca is compared with the natural antibody conversion rates in the city of Queretaro, which is similar in size, climate, hygienic conditions, and geography, but in which no vaccine was given. The incidence of antibody conversion 10 weeks after the single dose of trivalent vaccine in single-negative, double-negative, and triple-negative children is shown in table 4. The extent of interference resulting from the simultaneous administration of all three types and the dominance of the type 2 strain in this mixture are clearly evident. Thus, for type 1, the

analysis of these data indicates that among the total number infected, antibody was demonstrable at 10 weeks in 86% for type 1, 94% for type 2, and 92% for type 3.

The virological evidence of the marked drop in the dissemination of polioviruses that occurred 8 to 12 weeks after vaccination is supported by the serologic data shown in table 6, which indicate that among the children who failed to develop antibody during the first 10 weeks very few converted during the subsequent 11 weeks. At this point the remaining negative children in the group that were being followed serologically were fed another dose of trivalent vaccine and they then exhibited a further marked immunogenic effect. The total conversion rate

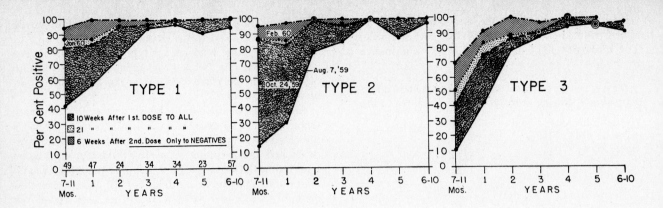

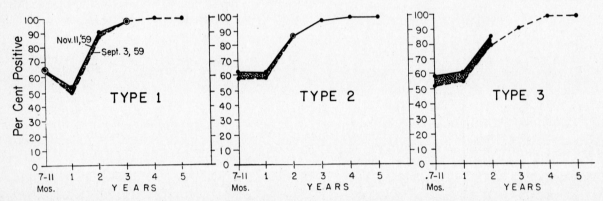

Fig. 5.—Status of poliovirus antibody in two Mexican cities: *top*, Toluca—vaccine given; *bottom*, Queretaro—no vaccine given. Numbers above age groups in left upper diagram indicate number of children tested.

TABLE 4.—*Poliovirus Antibody Conversion Rates in Toluca Among "Single-Negative," "Double-Negative," and "Triple-Negative" Children Ten Weeks After Feeding Single Dose of Trivalent Vaccine*

| Type | Single-Negative | | Double-Negative | | Triple-Negative | | Total | |
|---|---|---|---|---|---|---|---|---|
| | No. Tested | % Converted | No. Tested | % Converted | No. Tested | % Converted | No. Tested | % Converted |
| 1 .......... | 4 | 100 | 16 | 88 | 33 | 55 | 53 | 68 |
| 2 .......... | 17 | 82 | 25 | 80 | 35 | 83 | 77 | 82 |
| 3 .......... | 17 | 59 | 24 | 42 | 35 | 37 | 76 | 43 |

after the two doses of vaccine was 96% for types 1 and 2 and 72% for type 3, despite the interfering effects resulting from the massive infection with other enteric viruses (which was still 55% in January, 1960) and the simultaneous administration of all three types of poliovirus. The lower final conversion rate for type 3 may also be related to the fact that we did not use the pH test for low-avidity antibody, which occurs more commonly after infection with the type 3 virus. It should also be noted that the second feeding was not a mass feeding but involved only 44 children under 4 years of age who were distributed among a large number of families throughout the city. The results might have been even better if nature had been given another chance at dissemination of the polioviruses in the community by feeding all the children under 4 years of age another dose of the vaccine.

TABLE 5.—*Incidence of Virus Recovery from Rectal Swabs in Relation to Development of Antibody—Estimate of Total Infection Rate During Ten-Week Period After Single Oral Dose of Trivalent Vaccine in Toluca*

| Category | Type 1 | | Type 2 | | Type 3 | |
|---|---|---|---|---|---|---|
| | No. | % | No. | % | No. | % |
| Virus In Rectal Swabs Among Those Who | | | | | | |
| Developed antibody.................... | 12/36 | 33 | 52/63 | 82 | 21/33 | 64 |
| Failed to develop antibody............ | 2/17 | 12 | 3/14 | 21 | 2/43 | 5 |
| Estimate of total infection rate.......... | 42/53 | 80 | 67/77 | 87 | 36/76 | 47 |
| Development of antibody among total no. infected (demonstrated + estimated) .......... | 36/42 | 86 | 63/67 | 94 | 33/36 | 92 |

TABLE 6.—*Conversion Rates at Different Times After Feeding Two Doses of Trivalent Poliovirus Vaccine in Toluca*

| | | % Converted at Indicated Time After | | | |
|---|---|---|---|---|---|
| | | First Dose, Mass Feeding | | Second Dose, Negative Only | |
| Type | Children Tested, No. | First 10 Wk. Aug., 1959-Oct., 1959 | Next 11 Wk. Oct., 1959-Jan., 1960 | 6 Wk. Jan., 1960-Feb., 1960 | Both Doses Aug., 1959-Feb., 1960 |
| 1 | 53 | 68 | 7 | 85 | 96 |
| 2 | 77 | 82 | 0 | 73 | 96 |
| 3 | 76 | 43 | 3 | 48 | 72 |

TABLE 7.—*Effectiveness of Aliquots of Same Lots and Same Doses of Vaccine Used in Toluca When Given to Children of Comparable Age During Winter and Spring Months in Northern Climates, Trivalent Versus Monovalent (1-3-2)*

| Investigator, Place, Age of Children, and Time of Year | Method of Administration | No. of Children Without Antibody for Indicated Type | % Developed Antibody for Indicated Type | | |
|---|---|---|---|---|---|
| | | | 1 | 2 | 3 |
| Smorodintsev, Leningrad, U. S. S. R., children's homes, up to 7 yr., May, 1958 | Trivalent, tested 4 mo. later; all together in camp during summer | 29 negative for 1<br>54 negative for 2<br>38 negative for 3 | 82 | 80 | 71 |
| Smorodintsev, Leningrad, children's homes, up to 3 yr., Feb., March, April, 1958 | Monovalent, 4-wk. interval; tested one month after each type | 147 negative for 1<br>68 negative for 2<br>67 negative for 3 | 97 | 100 | 96 |
| Verlinde, Leyden, Holland, individual families, up to 14 yr., May or Dec., 1957 | Monovalent 3-wk. interval | 20 negative for 1<br>18 negative for 2<br>28 negative for 3 | 100 | 90 | 100 |

Figure 5 shows that with these two feedings of vaccine it was possible to achieve an immunogenic effect within a few months and without any cost in paralysis, comparable to that achieved naturally only after four years and at a price of about 56 cases of paralytic poliomyelitis.

The comparable serologic effectiveness of the same lots and doses of vaccine used in trivalent or monovalent form under different conditions in children in northern climates is shown in table 7. It is evident that when the interval between the separate, sequential feedings of the three types was not less than four weeks, the antibody conversion rates were 100% or close to it, while the mixture of all three types yielded conversion rates of only 82, 80, and 71%, respectively, for the three types in a mixed group of single-negative, double-negative, and triple-negative children living under conditions that were conducive to natural spread of the vaccine strains among them. These results, as well as other data collected by Russian investigators in 1959, indicate that the separate sequential administration of the three types of vaccine at intervals of not less than four to six weeks is optimum during the cold or cool months of the year in areas with good sanitation and hygiene.

## CONCLUSIONS

The results obtained in Toluca, Mexico, are of significance for the vast majority of the world population, among whom immunity to poliomyelitis is naturally acquired during the first few years of life at a varying and sometimes considerable price in paralysis. In such areas the feeding of trivalent vaccine on two brief occasions at an interval of six to eight weeks to all children aged under 4 or 5 years, depending on the age incidence of recorded cases of paralytic poliomyelitis or on the result of a serologic survey in the region, constitutes a rational initial approach to the eradication of poliomyelitis. The rapid disappearance of polioviruses from Toluca under the conditions of the present study indicates that the oncoming generations of children will have to be similarly vaccinated at the optimum time during the first 6 months of life, because they will have little or no opportunity for natural acquisition of immunity to poliomyelitis.

This study was aided by a grant from the National Foundation.

Elland and Bethesda Avenues (29) (Dr. Sabin).

## REFERENCES

1. Sabin, A. B.: (*a*) Status of Field Trials with Orally Administered, Live Attenuated Poliovirus Vaccine, J. A. M. A. **171:**863-868 (Oct. 17) 1959. (*b*) Recent Studies and Field Tests with Live Attenuated Poliovirus Vaccine, in Live Poliovirus Vaccines, Papers Presented and Discussions Held at First International Conference on Live Poliovirus Vaccines, scientific publication no. 44, Washington, D. C., Pan American Sanitary Bureau, 1959, p. 14.

2. Ramos Alvarez, M.; Gomez Santos, F.; Rangel Rivera, L.; and Mayes, O.: Viral and Serological Studies in Children Immunized with Live Poliovirus Vaccine—Preliminary Report of Large Trial Conducted in Mexico, in Live Poliovirus Vaccines, Papers Presented and Discussions Held at First International Conference on Live Poliovirus Vaccines, scientific publication no. 44, Washington, D. C., Pan American Sanitary Bureau, 1959, p. 483.

3. Plotkin, S. A., and Koprowski, H.: Epidemiological Studies of Safety and Efficacy of Vaccination with CHAT Strain of Attenuated Poliovirus in Leopoldville, Belgian Congo, in Live Poliovirus Vaccines, Papers Presented and Discussions Held at First International Conference on Live Poliovirus Vaccines, scientific publication no. 44, Washington, D. C., Pan American Sanitary Bureau, 1959, p. 419.

June 8, 1984
(*JAMA* 1984;251:2994-2996)

# Mass Vaccination Against Polio*

Alan R. Hinman, MD

### The Introduction of Oral Vaccine

Although the introduction and immediate widespread use of inactivated polio vaccine (IPV) in 1955 (see Chapter 41) was accompanied by an abrupt decline in the reported number of cases of poliomyelitis in the United States, there was considerable excitement in the late 1950s about the impending availability of attenuated live (oral) poliovirus vaccine (OPV).[1-3] This excitement stemmed both from anticipated advantages of OPV and from some disappointment with the performance of IPV.

The anticipated advantages of OPV included its potential to induce effective and long-lasting protection after only one dose, obviating the need for boosters, its ability to pass to contacts of vaccinees, thereby extending the effects of the vaccine beyond those directly vaccinated, and the fact that the protection induced embraces both infection and disease.

The disappointment with IPV resulted from the fact that, after a record low of 2,499 cases of paralytic poliomyelitis in 1957, a slight increase was noted in 1958 (to 3,697 cases) and, in 1959, the number of cases more than doubled, to 6,289. As pointed out by Langmuir,[4] "this rising trend has appeared in spite of the continued use of Salk vaccine which had accumulated to a total of approximately 300 million doses distributed in the United States by the end of 1959. Clearly the control of poliomyelitis is unfinished business." Although incidence figures indicated that vaccine protected those who were vaccinated, they also indicated that polioviruses continued to circulate in the United States and were capable of causing localized outbreaks in unimmunized or partly immunized persons. The demonstration that circulating antibody titers declined significantly within two to four years after vaccination suggested that repeated, possibly frequent booster doses would be required to maintain immunity. Finally, it was noted that "the fact that 1,500 monkeys must be sacrificed to produce every 1 million doses of killed vaccine has already created great difficulty in supplying sufficient monkeys."[5]

Against this backdrop, major efforts were under way to test several candidate attenuated virus strains in the field. Conferences summarizing the research were held in Washington in 1959 and 1960 (First and Second International Conferences on Live Poliovirus Vaccines)[1,2] and in Copenhagen in 1960 (Fifth International Poliomyelitis Conference).[3] By the time of the Copenhagen conference, live virus vaccines had been administered to more than 60 million children around the world, approximately 80% of them in Russia.

In temperate zone countries, the field trials demonstrated the effectiveness of the oral vaccines in inducing seroconversion and in reducing the incidence of poliomyelitis. However, some of the studies indicated a failure of the vaccine virus to induce satisfactory rates of seroconversion, primarily in tropical climates. The suboptimal response was thought to relate in large measure to interference from other enteroviruses, including wild polioviruses, circulating in the community at the time of vaccination. This raised serious questions about the ability of the oral vaccines to interrupt transmission successfully, particularly when the vaccine was administered over a period of several weeks and included only a fraction of the susceptible population. In addition, the ability of the oral vaccine (or the inactivated vaccine, for that matter) to interrupt transmission of polioviruses in an epidemic situation had not been conclusively demonstrated.

### The Toluca Study

The Toluca study of Sabin and associates[6] represented a daring strategic approach to overcome the effect of interference and to terminate rapidly the circulation of live polioviruses by mass vaccination. The virological and serological studies were carried out in the field on a heroic scale and in a very short time. Rectal swabs were

From the Division of Immunization, Center for Prevention Services, Centers for Disease Control, Atlanta.

*A commentary on Sabin AB, Ramos-Alvarez M, Alvarez-Amezquita J, et al: Live, orally given poliovirus vaccine: Effects of rapid mass immunization on population under conditions of massive enteric infection with other viruses. *JAMA* 1960;173:1521-1526.

obtained from 1,892 persons a few days before the vaccination program began, and 3,139 rectal swabs were obtained during the three months after the vaccination program. The rapidity with which the laboratory work was carried out and the results analyzed deserve mention. The vaccination program took place in August 1959 and the results were presented in Washington in June 1960[2] and published in THE JOURNAL in August 1960.[6] Ten months from field work to presentation and 12 months to publication is a mark that few of us can attain and is a tribute to the dedication and energy of Sabin, the group in the field (led by Ramos Alvarez), and the groups working in the laboratories in Mexico and in the United States.

The prevaccination rectal swabs in Toluca revealed an amazingly high prevalence of enteroviruses in children aged 1 month to 5 years: from 26% to 72%, depending on the age group. Nonpolio enteroviruses made up the vast majority of the viruses recovered, although up to 15% of children in some age groups (7 to 11 months and 2 years) were excreting polioviruses.

During the mass vaccination program, more than 83% of all children younger than 11 years were given a single dose of trivalent vaccine within a four-day period. Serial rectal cultures on a sample of 274 of these children demonstrated that more than 40% were excreting poliovirus one week after vaccination, compared with 11% or fewer before vaccination. Two to three months after vaccination, very few children were excreting polioviruses, although the overall prevalence of enterovirus excretion remained approximately the same, indicating that the "flooding" of the childhood population with vaccine virus in a very short period had successfully interrupted the transmission of wild polioviruses.

What was perhaps most surprising is that this interruption of transmission was accomplished in the face of relatively low seroconversion rates — overall, 68% for type 1, 82% for type 2, and 43% for type 3. Subsequent administration of a second dose of trivalent oral vaccine to a sample of children in whom antibody failed to develop after the first dose indicated further seroconversion with an overall seroconversion rate after two doses of vaccine of 96% for types 1 and 2 and 72% for type 3.

Sabin[7] viewed the combination of a mass vaccination strategy in subtropical and tropical regions along with routine vaccination in temperate regions as a means of eradicating poliomyelitis — a view he still holds.

Shortly after this article appeared, the Sabin strains of attenuated virus were selected in preference to the Cox and Koprowski strains, and, in 1961, monovalent Sabin strains were licensed in the United States. The trivalent vaccine was subsequently licensed in 1963. Oral polio vaccine was rapidly accepted in preference to IPV in most countries of the world and enthusiastically used, usually with dramatic impact on the incidence of poliomyelitis.

## Poliomyelitis in the Tropics

At the time this article appeared, the magnitude of the problem posed by paralytic poliomyelitis in tropical areas was not well appreciated. The predominant view was that paralytic poliomyelitis was a serious problem only in the relatively developed countries where epidemics occur and that in the developing world, where infection was acquired at a very early age, paralytic polio did not pose a great problem. The use of polio lameness surveys, beginning in Ghana in 1974, provided the means of dispelling this misapprehension.[8,9] Surveys of paralysis in children carried out in more than 25 tropical countries have demonstrated a remarkable uniformity in the prevalence of paralysis in youngsters — at a range of two to ten per 1,000 children.[10] This prevalence is comparable with that in developed countries that had suffered epidemic waves of poliomyelitis.

Demonstration of the magnitude of the problem posed by polio in the developing world led to increased efforts in developing strategies to try to contain it. As in the 1950s, recent experience indicates that in some tropical areas, routine administration of OPV to young children has not prevented paralysis to the extent desired nor successfully interrupted the transmission of wild polioviruses. Because of this fact, increased interest is now being paid to the approach advocated by Sabin in 1960.

### Mass Vaccination

The first country to undertake a mass vaccination approach on a nationwide basis was Cuba, which began annual mass vaccination campaigns in 1962 with the result that paralytic poliomyelitis was rapidly eliminated. The success in Cuba was thought by many to be unique, and it is only recently that large countries in South America have undertaken mass vaccination approaches, with dramatic results. The largest experience is that of Brazil, where, beginning in 1980, mass vaccination of children younger than 5 years has been carried out each year in two "national vaccination days" separated by two months. In these programs, more than 95% of eligible children have been vaccinated, and the impact on reported cases of poliomyelitis has been dramatic.[11] Other developing countries, including Chile, Argentina, Mexico, and Dominican Republic, also are using or considering this technique of annual mass vaccination cycles.

### Inactivated v Oral Vaccine Revisited

Appreciation of the extent of the problem posed by paralytic polio in the developing world and of some of the problems in successfully interrupting transmission using OPV has led to renewed interest in the use of IPV in the developing world. After its initial massive utilization, IPV was rapidly displaced by OPV in the United States and in most countries around the world. However, in a limited number of countries where IPV has been used continuously and reached a high proportion of the population, it has successfully eliminated paralytic poliomyelitis and diminished or interrupted the transmission of wild polioviruses. This has been notably true in Sweden, Finland, and the Netherlands. In addition, IPV has not been associated with the rare occurrence of paralysis in vaccines or their contacts, as has OPV. The recent development of techniques to obtain a higher yield of more potent inactivated vaccines that are capable of inducing seroconversion in 75% or more of vaccinees after a single dose (and in 95% or more after two doses administered six months apart) has offered another practical avenue for the possible control of polio in the developing world.[12]

We have thus reached the stage at which debate concerning the relative merits of OPV and IPV is once again engaging a high proportion of public health officials, as demonstrated at an International Symposium on Poliomyelitis Control held in Washington, DC, in March 1983.[13] At this symposium, it was apparent that the two giants in the development of polio vaccines, Salk and Sabin, are continuing intensive work to demonstrate the validity of the positions that they have espoused for years concerning the utility of the vaccines they developed.[7,12] The continued dedication and productivity of these scientists, should be an inspiration to all of us. The article to which this commentary is appended represents but one of the many contributions of Albert Sabin to the health of the world's citizens. It is only to be hoped that the partisan flavor that often arises in discussions of polio vaccines will not cloud the importance of the contributions made by Sabin and Salk nor the fact that two highly effective and safe vaccines are available for the prevention of poliomyelitis. It now remains for us to use them appropriately to eliminate this disease from the face of the earth.

In preparing this article, the author received valuable comments from John P. Fox, MD, Dorothy M. Horstmann, MD, Alexander D. Langmuir, MD, Joseph L. Melnick, PhD, Harry M. Meyer, Jr, MD, Frederick C. Robbins, MD, Albert B. Sabin, MD, and Jonas Salk, MD.

## References

1. *First International Conference on Live Poliovirus Vaccines, Washington, DC, June 1959,* scientific publication 44, Washington, DC, Pan American Health Organization, 1959.

2. *Second International Conference on Live Poliovirus Vaccines, Washington, DC, June 1960,* scientific publication 50, Washington, DC, Pan American Health Organization, 1960.

3. *Poliomyelitis,* papers and discussions presented at the Fifth International Poliomyelitis Conference, Copenhagen, July 1960. Philadelphia, JB Lippincott Co, 1961.

4. Langmuir AD: Inactivated virus vaccines: Protective efficacy, in *Poliomyelitis.* Philadelphia, JB Lippincott Co, 1961, pp 105-113.

5. Smorodintsev AA, Drobyshevskaya AI, Bulychev NP, et al: Immunological and epidemiological effectiveness of live poliomyelitis vaccine, in *Poliomyelitis.* Philadelphia, JB Lippincott Co, 1961, pp 240-256.

6. Sabin AB, Ramos-Alvarez M, Alvarez-Amezquita J, et al: Live orally given poliovirus vaccine: Effects of rapid mass immunization on population under conditions of massive enteric infection with other viruses. *JAMA* 1960;173:1521-1526.

7. Sabin AB: Strategies for elimination of poliomyelitis in different parts of the world with use of oral poliovirus vaccine. *Rev Infect Dis* 1984;6(suppl):S391-396.

8. Nicholas DD, Kratzer JH, Ofosu-Amaah S, et al: Is poliomyelitis a serious problem in developing countries?: The Danfa experience. *Br Med J* 1977;1:1009-1012.

9. Ofosu-Amaah S, Kratzer JH, Nicholas DD: Is poliomyelitis a serious problem in developing couintries?: Lameness in Ghanaian schools. *Br Med J* 1977;1:1012-1014.

10. Bernier RH: Some observations on poliomyelitis lameness surveys. *Rev Infect Dis* 1984;6(suppl):S371-375.

11. Risi JB: Mass vaccination in Brazil. *Rev Infect Dis,* in press.

12. Salk J: One-dose immunization against paralytic poliomyelitis using a noninfectious vaccine. *Rev Infect Dis* 1984;6 Suppl 2:S444-450.

13. Horstmann DM, Robbins FC (eds): International Symposium on Poliomyelitis Control, Pan American Health Organization, Washington, DC, March 14-17, 1983. *Rev Infect Dis* 1984 May-Jun;6 Suppl 2:S301-600.

July 7, 1962
(*JAMA* 1962;181:17-24)

# Chapter 46

# The Battered-Child Syndrome

C. Henry Kempe, M.D., Denver, Frederic N. Silverman, M.D., Cincinnati,
Brandt F. Steele, M.D., William Droegemueller, M.D., and Henry K. Silver, M.D., Denver

The battered-child syndrome, a clinical condition in young children who have received serious physical abuse, is a frequent cause of permanent injury or death. The syndrome should be considered in any child exhibiting evidence of fracture of any bone, subdural hematoma, failure to thrive, soft tissue swellings or skin bruising, in any child who dies suddenly, or where the degree and type of injury is at variance with the history given regarding the occurrence of the trauma. Psychiatric factors are probably of prime importance in the pathogenesis of the disorder, but knowledge of these factors is limited. Physicians have a duty and responsibility to the child to require a full evaluation of the problem and to guarantee that no expected repetition of trauma will be permitted to occur.

THE BATTERED-CHILD SYNDROME is a term used by us to characterize a clinical condition in young children who have received serious physical abuse, generally from a parent or foster parent. The condition has also been described as "unrecognized trauma" by radiologists, orthopedists, pediatricians, and social service workers. It is a significant cause of childhood disability and death. Unfortunately, it is frequently not recognized or, if diagnosed, is inadequately handled by the physician because of hesitation to bring the case to the attention of the proper authorities.

## Incidence

In an attempt to collect data on the incidence of this problem, we undertook a nation-wide survey of hospitals which were asked to indicate the incidence of this syndrome in a one-year period. Among 71 hospitals replying, 302 such cases were reported to have occurred; 33 of the children died; and 85 suffered permanent brain injury. In one-third of the cases proper medical diagnosis was followed by some type of legal action. We also surveyed 77 District Attorneys who reported that they had knowledge of 447 cases in a similar one-year period. Of these, 45 died, and 29 suffered permanent brain damage; court action was initiated in 46% of this group. This condition has been a particularly common problem

Professor and Chairman (Dr. Kempe) and Professor of Pediatrics (Dr. Silver), Department of Pediatrics; Associate Professor of Psychiatry (Dr. Steele), and Assistant Resident in Obstetrics and Gynecology (Dr. Droegemueller), University of Colorado School of Medicine; and Director, Division of Roentgenology, Children's Hospital (Dr. Silverman).

in our hospitals; on a single day, in November, 1961, the Pediatric Service of the Colorado General Hospital was caring for 4 infants suffering from the parent-inflicted battered-child syndrome. Two of the 4 died of their central nervous system trauma; 1 subsequently died suddenly in an unexplained manner 4 weeks after discharge from the hospital while under the care of its parents, while the fourth is still enjoying good health.

## Clinical Manifestations

The clinical manifestations of the battered-child syndrome vary widely from those cases in which the trauma is very mild and is often unsuspected and unrecognized, to those who exhibit the most florid evidence of injury to the soft tissues and skeleton. In the former group, the patients' signs and symptoms may be considered to have resulted from failure to thrive from some other cause or to have been produced by a metabolic disorder, an infectious process, or some other disturbance. In these patients specific findings of trauma such as bruises or characteristic roentgenographic changes as described below may be misinterpreted and their significance not recognized.

The battered-child syndrome may occur at any age, but, in general, the affected children are younger than 3 years. In some instances the clinical manifestations are limited to those resulting from a single episode of trauma, but more often the child's general health is below par, and he shows evidence of neglect including poor skin hygiene, multiple soft tissue injuries, and malnutrition. One often obtains a history of previous episodes suggestive of parental neglect or trauma. A marked discrepancy between clinical findings and historical data as supplied by the parents is a major diagnostic feature of the battered-child syndrome. The fact that no new lesions, either of the soft tissue or of the bone, occur while the child is in the hospital or in a protected environment lends added weight to the diagnosis and tends to exclude many diseases of the skeletal or hemopoietic systems in which lesions may occur spontaneously or after minor trauma. Subdural hematoma, with or without fracture of the skull, is, in our experience, an extremely frequent finding even in the absence of fractures of the long bones. In an occasional case the parent or parent-substitute may also have assaulted the child by administering an overdose of a drug or by exposing the child to natural gas or other toxic substances. The characteristic distribution of these multiple fractures and the observation that the lesions are in different stages of healing are of additional value in making the diagnosis.

In most instances, the diagnostic bone lesions are observed incidental to examination for purposes other than evaluation for possible abuse. Occasionally, examination following known injury discloses signs of other, unsuspected, skeletal involvement. When parental assault is under consideration, radiologic examination of the entire skeleton may provide objective confirmation. Following diagnosis, radiologic examination can document the healing of lesions and reveal the appearance of new lesions if additional trauma has been inflicted.

The radiologic manifestations of trauma to growing skeletal structures are the same whether or not there is a history of injury. Yet there is reluctance on the part of many physicians to accept the radiologic signs as indications of repetitive trauma and possible abuse. This reluctance stems from the emotional unwillingness of the physician to consider abuse as the cause of the child's difficulty and also because of unfamiliarity with certain aspects of fracture healing so that he is unsure of the significance of the lesions that are present. To the informed physician, the bones tell a story the child is too young or too frightened to tell.

### Psychiatric Aspects

Psychiatric knowledge pertaining to the problem of the battered child is meager, and the literature on the subject is almost nonexistent. The type and degree of physical attack varies greatly. At one extreme, there is direct murder of children. This is usually done by a parent or other close relative, and, in these individuals, a frank psychosis is usually readily apparent. At the other extreme are those cases where no overt harm has occurred, and one parent, more often the mother, comes to the psychiatrist for help, filled with anxiety and guilt related to fantasies of hurting the child. Occasionally the disorder has gone beyond the point of fantasy and has resulted in severe slapping or spanking. In such cases the adult is usually responsive to treatment; it is not known whether or not the disturbance in these adults would progress to the point where they would inflict significant trauma on the child.

Between these 2 extremes are a large number of battered children with mild to severe injury which may clear completely or result in permanent damage or even death after repeated attack. Descriptions of such children have been published by numerous investigators including radiologists, orthopedists, and social workers. The latter have reported on their studies of investigations of families in which children have been beaten and of their work in effecting satisfactory placement for the protection of the child. In some of these published reports the parents, or at least the parent who inflicted the abuse, have been found to be of low intelligence. Often, they are described as psychopathic or sociopathic characters. Alcoholism, sexual promiscuity, unstable marriages, and minor criminal activities are reportedly common amongst them. They are immature, impulsive, self-centered, hypertensive, and quick to react with poorly controlled aggression. Data in some cases indicate that such attacking parents had themselves been subject to some degree of attack from their parents in their own childhood.

Beating of children, however, is not confined to people with a psychopathic personality or of borderline socioeconomic status. It also occurs among people with good education and stable financial and social background. However, from the scant data that are available, it would appear that in these cases, too, there is a defect in character structure which allows aggressive impulses to be expressed too freely. There is also some suggestion that the attacking parent was subjected to similar abuse in childhood. It would appear that one of the most important factors to be found in families where parental assault occurs is "to do unto others as you have been done by." This is not surprising; it has long been recognized by psychologists and social anthropologists that patterns of child rearing, both good and bad, are passed from one generation to the next in relatively unchanged form. Psychologically, one could describe this phenomenon as an identification with the aggressive parent, this identification occurring despite strong wishes of the person to be different. Not infrequently the beaten infant is a product of an unwanted pregnancy, a pregnancy which began before marriage, too soon after marriage, or at some other time felt to be extremely inconvenient. Sometimes several children in one family have been beaten; at other times one child is singled out for attack while others are treated quite lovingly. We have also seen instances in which the sex of the child who is severely attacked is related to very specific factors in the context of the abusive parent's neurosis.

It is often difficult to obtain the information that a child has been attacked by its parent. To be sure, some of the extremely sociopathic characters will say, "Yeah, Johnny would not stop crying so I hit him. So what? He cried harder so I hit him harder." Sometimes one spouse will indicate that the other was the attacking person, but more often there is complete denial of any knowledge of injury to the child and the maintenance of an attitude of complete innocence on the part of both parents. Such attitudes are maintained despite the fact that evidence of physical attack is obvious and that the trauma could not have happened in any other way. Denial by the parents of any involvement in the abusive episode may, at times, be a conscious, protective device, but in other instances it may be a denial based upon psychological repression. Thus, one mother who seemed to have been the one who injured her baby had complete amnesia for the episodes in which her aggression burst forth so strikingly.

In addition to the reluctance of the parents to give information regarding the attacks on their children, there is another factor which is of great importance and extreme interest as it relates to the difficulty in delving into the problem of parental neglect and abuse. This is the fact that physicians have great difficulty both in believing that parents could have attacked their children and in undertaking the essential questioning of parents on this subject. Many physicians find it hard to believe that such an attack could have occurred and they attempt to obliterate such suspicions from their minds, even in the face of obvious circumstantial evidence. The reason for this is not clearly understood. One possibility is that the arousal of the physician's antipathy in response to such situations is so great that it is easier for the physician to deny the possibility of such attack than to have to deal with the excessive anger which surges up in him when he realizes the truth of the situation. Furthermore, the physician's training and personality usually makes it quite difficult for him to assume the role of policeman or district attorney and start questioning patients as if he were investigating a crime. The humanitarian-minded physician finds it most difficult to proceed when he is met with protestations of innocence from the aggressive parent, especially when the battered child was brought to him voluntarily.

Although the technique wherein the physician obtains the necessary information in cases of child beating is not adequately solved, certain routes of questioning have been particularly fruitful in some cases. One spouse may be asked about the other spouse in relation to unusual or curious behavior or for direct description of dealings with the baby. Clues to the parents' character and pattern of response may be obtained by asking questions about sources of worry and tension. Revealing answers may be brought out by questions concerning the baby such as, "Does he cry a lot? Is he stubborn? Does he obey well? Does he eat well? Do you have problems in controlling him?" A few general questions concerning the parents' own ideas of how they themselves were brought up may bring forth illuminating answers; interviews with grandparents or other relatives may elicit additional suggestive data. In some cases, psychological tests may disclose strong aggressive tendencies, impulsive behavior, and lack of adequate mechanisms of controlling impulsive behavior. In other cases only prolonged contact in a psychotherapeutic milieu will lead to a complete understanding of the background and circumstances surrounding the parental attack. Observation by nurses or other ancillary personnel of the behavior of the parents in relation to the hospitalized infant is often extremely valuable.

The following 2 condensed case histories depict some of the problems encountered in dealing with the battered-child syndrome.

### Report of Cases

CASE 1.—The patient was brought to the hospital at the age of 3 months because of enlargement of the head, convulsions, and spells of unconsciousness. Examination revealed bilateral subdural hematomas, which were later operated upon with great improvement in physical status. There had been a hospital admission at the age of one month because of a fracture of the right femur, sustained "when the baby turned over in the crib and caught its leg in the slats." There was no history of any head trauma except "when the baby was in the other hospital a child threw a little toy at her and hit her in the head." The father had never been alone with the baby, and the symptoms of difficulty appeared to have begun when the mother had been caring for the baby. Both parents showed concern and requested the best possible care for their infant. The father, a graduate engineer, related instances of impulsive behavior, but these did not appear to be particularly abnormal, and he showed appropriate emotional concern over the baby's appearance and impending operation. The mother, aged 21, a high school graduate, was very warm, friendly, and gave all the appearance of having endeavored to be a good mother.

However, it was noted by both nurses and physicians that she did not react as appropriately or seem as upset about the baby's appearance as did her husband. From interviews with the father and later with the mother, it became apparent that she had occasionally shown very impulsive, angry behavior, sometimes acting rather strangely and doing bizarre things which she could not explain nor remember. This was their first child and had resulted from an unwanted pregnancy which had occurred almost immediately after marriage and before the parents were ready for it. Early in pregnancy the mother had made statements about giving the baby away, but by the time of delivery she was apparently delighted with the baby and seemed to be quite fond of it. After many interviews, it became apparent that the mother had identified herself with her own mother who had also been unhappy with her first pregnancy and had frequently beaten her children. Despite very strong conscious wishes to be a kind, good mother, the mother of our patient was evidently repeating the behavior of her own mother toward herself. Although an admission of guilt was not obtained, it seemed likely that the mother was the one responsible for attacking the child; only after several months of treatment did the amnesia for the aggressive outbursts begin to lift. She responded well to treatment, but for a prolonged period after the infant left the hospital the mother was not allowed alone with her.

CASE 2.—This patient was admitted to the hospital at the age of 13 months with signs of central nervous system damage and was found to have a fractured skull. The parents were questioned closely, but no history of trauma could be elicited. After one week in the hospital no further treatment was deemed necessary, so the infant was discharged home in the care of her mother, only to return a few hours later with hemiparesis, a defect in vision, and a new depressed skull fracture on the other side of the head. There was no satisfactory explanation for the new skull fracture, but the mother denied having been involved in causing the injury, even though the history revealed that the child had changed markedly during the hour when the mother had been alone with her. The parents of this child were a young, middle-class couple who, in less than 2 years of marriage, had been separated, divorced, and remarried. Both felt that the infant had been unwanted and had come too soon in the marriage. The mother gave a history of having had a "nervous breakdown" during her teens. She had received psychiatric assistance because she had been markedly upset early in the pregnancy. Following an uneventful delivery, she had been depressed and had received further psychiatric aid and 4 electroshock treatments. The mother tended to gloss over the unhappiness during the pregnancy and stated that she was quite delighted when the baby was born. It is interesting to note that the baby's first symptoms of difficulty began the first day after its first birthday, suggesting an "anniversary reaction." On psychological and neurological examination, this mother showed definite signs of organic brain damage probably of lifelong duration and possibly related to her own prematurity. Apparently her significant intellectual defects had been camouflaged by an attitude of coy, naïve, cooperative sweetness which distracted attention from her deficits. It was noteworthy that she had managed to complete a year of college work despite a borderline I.Q. It appeared that the impairment in mental functioning was probably the prime factor associated with poor control of aggressive impulses. It is known that some individuals may react with aggressive attack or psychosis when faced with demands beyond their intellectual capacity. This mother was not allowed to have unsupervised care of her child.

Up to the present time, therapeutic experience with the parents of battered children is minimal. Counseling carried on in social agencies has been far from successful

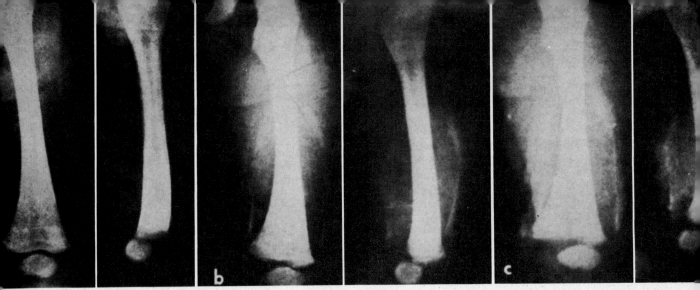

Fig. 1.—Male, 5 months: *a*, Initial films taken 3 to 4 days after onset of knee swelling. Epiphyseal separation shown in lateral projection with small metaphyseal chip shown in frontal projection; *b*, Five days later, there was beginning reparative change; *c*, Twelve days later (16 days after onset), there was extensive reparative change, history of injury unknown, but parents were attempting to teach child to walk at 5 months.

or rewarding. We know of no reports of successful psychotherapy in such cases. In general, psychiatrists feel that treatment of the so-called psychopath or sociopath is rarely successful. Further psychological investigation of the character structure of attacking parents is sorely needed. Hopefully, better understanding of the mechanisms involved in the control and release of aggressive impulses will aid in the earlier diagnosis, prevention of attack, and treatment of parents, as well as give us better ability to predict the likelihood of further attack in the future. At present, there is no safe remedy in the situation except the separation of battered children from their insufficiently protective parents.

### Techniques of Evaluation

A physician needs to have a high initial level of suspicion of the diagnosis of the battered-child syndrome in instances of subdural hematoma, multiple unexplained fractures at different stages of healing, failure to thrive, when soft tissue swellings or skin bruising are present, or in any other situation where the degree and type of injury is at variance with the history given regarding its occurrence or in any child who dies suddenly. Where the problem of parental abuse comes up for consideration, the physician should tell the parents that it is his opinion that the injury should not occur if the child were adequately protected, and he should indicate that he would welcome the parents giving him the full story so that he might be able to give greater assistance to them to prevent similar occurrences from taking place in the future. The idea that they can now help the child by giving a very complete history of circumstances surrounding the injury sometimes helps the parents feel that they are atoning for the wrong that they have done. But in many instances, regardless of the approach used in attempting to elicit a full story of the abusive incident(s), the parents will continue to deny that they were guilty of any wrongdoing. In talking with the parents, the physician may sometimes obtain added information by showing that he understands their problem and that he wishes to be of aid to them as well as to the child. He may help

them reveal the circumstances of the injuries by pointing out reasons that they may use to explain their action. If it is suggested that "new parents sometimes lose their tempers and are a little too forceful in their actions," the parents may grasp such a statement as the excuse for their actions. Interrogation should not be angry or hostile but should be sympathetic and quiet with the physician indicating his assurance that the diagnosis is well established on the basis of objective findings and that all parties, including the parents, have an obligation to avoid a repetition of the circumstances leading to the trauma. The doctor should recognize that bringing the child for medical attention in itself does not necessarily indicate that the parents were innocent of wrongdoing and are showing proper concern; trauma may have been inflicted during times of uncontrollable temporary rage. Regardless of the physician's personal reluctance to become involved, complete investigation is necessary for the child's protection so that a decision can be made as to the necessity of placing the child away from the parents until matters are fully clarified.

Often, the guilty parent is the one who gives the impression of being the more normal. In 2 recent instances young physicians have assumed that the mother was at fault because she was unkempt and depressed while the father, in each case a military man with good grooming and polite manners, turned out to be the psychopathic member of the family. In these instances it became apparent that the mother had good reason to be depressed.

### Radiologic Features

Radiologic examination plays 2 main roles in the problem of child-abuse. Initially, it is a tool for case finding, and, subsequently, it is useful as a guide in management.

The diagnostic signs result from a combination of circumstances: age of the patient, nature of the injury, the time that has elapsed before the examination is carried out, and whether the traumatic episode was repeated or occurred only once.

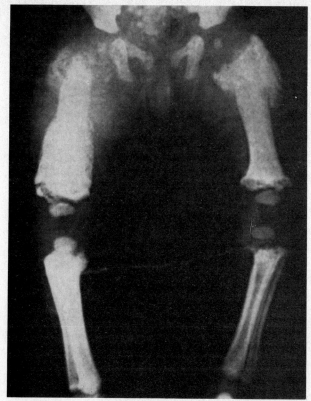

Fig. 2.—Female, 7½ months with a history of recurring abuse, including being shaken while held by legs 4-6 weeks prior to film. Note recent (2-3 weeks) metaphyseal fragmentation, older (4-6 weeks) periosteal reaction, and remote (2-4 months) external cortical thickening. Note also normal osseous structure of uninjured pelvic bones. (By permission of *Amer J. Roentgenol.*)

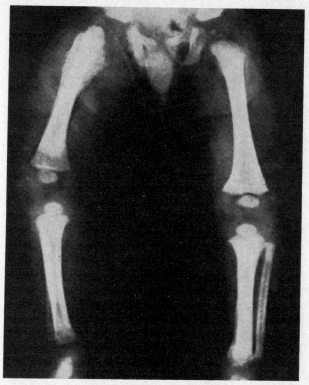

Fig. 3.—Male, 5 months, pulled by legs from collapsing bathinette 6 weeks earlier. Epiphyseal separation, right hip, shown by position of capital ossification center. Healing subperiosteal hematoma adjacent to it. Healing metaphyseal lesions in left knee, healing periosteal reactions (mild) in left tibia. No signs of systemic disease. (By permission of *Amer J Roentgenol.*)

*Age.*—As a general rule, the children are under 3 years of age; most, in fact are infants. In this age group the relative amount of radiolucent cartilage is great; therefore, anatomical disruptions of cartilage without gross deformity are radiologically invisible or difficult to demonstrate (Fig. 1a). Since the periosteum of infants is less securely attached to the underlying bone than in older children and adults, it is more easily and extensively stripped from the shaft by hemorrhage than in older patients. In infancy massive subperiosteal hematomas may follow injury and elevate the active periosteum so that new bone formation can take place around and remote from the parent shaft (Figs. 1c and 2).

*Nature of Injury.*—The ease and frequency with which a child is seized by his arms or legs make injuries to the appendicular skeleton the most common in this syndrome. Even when bony injuries are present elsewhere, e.g., skull, spine, or ribs, signs of injuries to the extremities are usually present. The extremities are the "handles" for rough handling, whether the arm is pulled to bring a reluctant child to his feet or to speed his ascent upstairs or whether the legs are held while swinging the tiny body in a punitive way or in an attempt to enforce corrective measures. The forces applied by an adult hand in grasping and seizing usually involve traction and torsion; these are the forces most likely to produce epiphyseal separations and periosteal shearing (Figs. 1 and 3). Shaft fractures result from direct blows or from bending and compression forces.

*Time After Injury That the X-Ray Examination Is Made.*—This is important in evaluating known or suspected cases of child-abuse. Unless gross fractures, dislocations, or epiphyseal separations were produced, no signs of bone injury are found during the first week after a specific injury. Reparative changes may first become manifest about 12 to 14 days after the injury and can increase over the subsequent weeks depending on the extent of initial injury and the degree of repetition (Fig. 4). Reparative changes are more active in the growing bones of children than in adults and are reflected radiologically in the excessive new bone reaction. Histologically, the reaction has been confused with neoplastic change by those unfamiliar with the vigorous reactions of young growing tissue.

*Repetition of Injury.*—This is probably the most important factor in producing diagnostic radiologic signs of the syndrome. The findings may depend on diminished immobilization of an injured bone leading to recurring macro- and microtrauma in the area of injury and healing, with accompanying excessive local reaction and hemorrhage, and ultimately, exaggerated repair. Secondly, repetitive injury may produce bone lesions in one area at one time, and in another area at another, producing lesions in several areas and in different stages of healing (Fig. 3).

Thus, the classical radiologic features of the battered-child syndrome are usually found in the appendicular skeleton in very young children. There may be irregularities of mineralization in the metaphyses of some of the

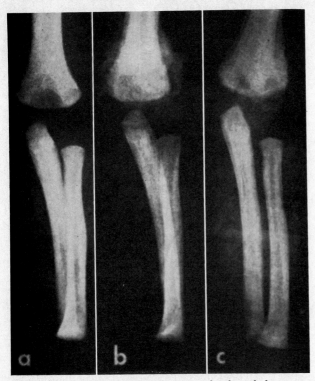

Fig. 4.—Female 7½ months: *a*, Elbow injured 30 hours before, except for thickened cortex from previous healed reactions, no radiologic signs of injury; *b*, Fifteen days after injury, irregular productive reaction, clinically normal joint; *c*, Three weeks after *b*, organization and healing progressing nicely. (By permission of *Amer J Roentgenol.*)

major tubular bones with slight malalignment of the adjacent epiphyseal ossification center. An overt fracture may be present in another bone. Elsewhere, there may be abundant and active but well-calcified subperiosteal reaction with widening from the shaft toward one end of the bone. One or more bones may demonstrate distinctly thickened cortices, residuals of previously healed periosteal reactions. In addition, the radiographic features of a subdural hematoma with or without obvious skull fracture may be present.

*Differential Diagnosis.*—The radiologic features are so distinct that other diseases generally are considered only because of the reluctance to accept the implications of the bony lesions. Unless certain aspects of bone healing are considered, the pertinent findings may be missed. In many cases roentgenographic examination is only undertaken soon after known injury; if a fracture is found, reexamination is done after reduction and immobilization; and, if satisfactory positioning has been obtained, the next examination is usually not carried out for a period of 6 weeks when the cast is removed. Any interval films that may have been taken prior to this time probably would have been unsatisfactory since the fine details of the bony lesions would have been obscured by the cast. If fragmentation and bone production are seen, they are considered to be evidence of repair rather than manifestations of multiple or repetitive trauma. If obvious fracture or the knowledge of injury is absent, the bony changes may be considered to be the result of scurvy, syphilis, infantile cortical hyperostoses, or other conditions. The distribution of lesions in the abused child is unrelated to rates of growth; moreover, an extensive

lesion may be present at the slow-growing end of a bone which otherwise is normally mineralized and shows no evidence of metabolic disorder at its rapidly growing end.

*Scurvy* is commonly suggested as an alternative diagnosis, since it also produces large calcifying subperiosteal hemorrhages due to trauma and local exaggerations most marked in areas of rapid growth. However, scurvy is a systemic disease in which all of the bones show the generalized osteoporosis associated with the disease. The dietary histories of most children with recognized trauma have not been grossly abnormal, and whenever the vitamin C content of the blood has been determined, it has been normal.

In the first months of life *syphilis* can result in metaphyseal and periosteal lesions similar to those under discussion. However, the bone lesions of syphilis tend to be symmetrical and are usually accompanied by other stigmata of the disease. Serological tests should be obtained in questionable cases.

*Osteogenesis imperfecta* also has bony changes which may be confused with those due to trauma, but it too is a generalized disease, and evidence of the disorder should be present in the bones which are not involved in the disruptive-productive reaction. Even when skull fractures are present, the mosaic ossification pattern of the cranial vault, characteristic of osteogenesis imperfecta, is not seen in the battered-child syndrome. Fractures in osteogenesis imperfecta are commonly of the shafts; they usually occur in the metaphyseal regions in the battered-child syndrome. Blue sclerae, skeletal deformities, and a family history of similar abnormalities were absent in reported instances of children with unrecognized trauma.

Productive diaphyseal lesions may occur in *infantile cortical hyperostosis*, but the metaphyseal lesions of unrecognized trauma easily serve to differentiate the 2 conditions. The characteristic mandibular involvement of infantile cortical hyperostosis does not occur following trauma although obvious mandibular fracture may be produced.

Evidence that repetitive unrecognized trauma is the cause of the bony changes found in the battered-child syndrome is, in part, derived from the finding that similar roentgenographic findings are present in *paraplegic patients with sensory deficit* and in patients with *congenital indifference to pain;* in both of whom similar pathogenic mechanisms operate. In paraplegic children unappreciated injuries have resulted in radiologic pictures with irregular metaphyseal rarefactions, exaggerated subperiosteal new bone formation, and ultimate healing with residual external cortical thickening comparable to those in the battered-child syndrome. In paraplegic adults, excessive callus may form as a consequence of the lack of immobilization, and the lesion may be erroneously diagnosed as osteogenic sarcoma. In children with congenital indifference (or insensitivity) to pain, identical radiologic manifestations may be found.

To summarize, the radiologic manifestations of trauma are specific, and the metaphyseal lesions in particular occur in no other disease of which we are aware. The findings permit a radiologic diagnosis even when the clinical history seems to refute the possibility of trauma. Under such circumstances, the history must be reviewed, and the child's environment, carefully investigated.

## Management

The principal concern of the physician should be to make the correct diagnosis so that he can institute proper therapy and make certain that a similar event will not occur again. He should report possible willful trauma to the police department or any special children's protective service that operates in his community. The report that he makes should be restricted to the objective findings which can be verified and, where possible, should be supported by photographs and roentgenograms. For hospitalized patients, the hospital director and the social service department should be notified. In many states the hospital is also required to report any case of possible unexplained injury to the proper authorities. The physician should acquaint himself with the facilities available in private and public agencies that provide protective services for children. These include children's humane societies, divisions of welfare departments, and societies for the prevention of cruelty to children. These, as well as the police department, maintain a close association with the juvenile court. Any of these agencies may be of assistance in bringing the case before the court which alone has the legal power to sustain a dependency petition for temporary or permanent separation of the child from the parents' custody. In addition to the legal investigation, it is usually helpful to have an evaluation of the psychological and social factors in the case; this should be started while the child is still in the hospital. If necessary, a court order should be obtained so that such investigation may be performed.

In many instances the prompt return of the child to the home is contraindicated because of the threat that additional trauma offers to the child's health and life. Temporary placement with relatives or in a well-supervised foster home is often indicated in order to prevent further tragic injury or death to a child who is returned too soon to the original dangerous environment. All too often, despite the apparent cooperativeness of the parents and their apparent desire to have the child with them, the child returns to his home only to be assaulted again and suffer permanent brain damage or death. Therefore, the bias should be in favor of the child's safety; everything should be done to prevent repeated trauma, and the physician should not be satisfied to return the child to an environment where even a moderate risk of repetition exists.

## Summary

The battered-child syndrome, a clinical condition in young children who have received serious physical abuse, is a frequent cause of permanent injury or death. Although the findings are quite variable, the syndrome should be considered in any child exhibiting evidence of possible trauma or neglect (fracture of any bone, subdural hematoma, multiple soft tissue injuries, poor skin hygiene, or malnutrition) or where there is a marked discrepancy between the clinical findings and the historical data as supplied by the parents. In cases where a history of specific injury is not available, or in any child

who dies suddenly, roentgenograms of the entire skeleton should still be obtained in order to ascertain the presence of characteristic multiple bony lesions in various stages of healing.

Psychiatric factors are probably of prime importance in the pathogenesis of the disorder, but our knowledge of these factors is limited. Parents who inflict abuse on their children do not necessarily have psychopathic or sociopathic personalities or come from borderline socioeconomic groups, although most published cases have been in these categories. In most cases some defect in character structure is probably present; often parents may be repeating the type of child care practiced on them in their childhood.

Physicians, because of their own feelings and their difficulty in playing a role that they find hard to assume, may have great reluctance in believing that parents were guilty of abuse. They may also find it difficult to initiate proper investigation so as to assure adequate management of the case. Above all the physician's duty and responsibility to the child requires a full evaluation of the problem and a guarantee that the expected repetition of trauma will not be permitted to occur.

4200 E. 9th Ave., Denver 20 (Dr. Kempe).

## References

1. Snedecor, S. T.; Knapp, R. E.; and Wilson, H. B.: Traumatic Ossifying Periostitis of Newborn, *Surg Gynec Obstet* **61**:385-387, 1935.

2. Caffey, J.: Multiple Fractures in Long Bones of Infants Suffering from Chronic Subdural Hematoma, *Amer J Roentgenol* **56**:163-173 (Aug.) 1946.

3. Snedecor, S. T., and Wilson, H. B.: Some Obstetrical Injuries to Long Bones, *J Bone Joint Surg* **31A**:378-384 (April) 1949.

4. Smith, M. J.: Subdural Hematoma with Multiple Fractures, *Amer J Roentgenol* **63**:342-344 (March) 1950.

5. Frauenberger, G. S., and Lis, E. F.: Multiple Fractures Associated with Subdural Hematoma in Infancy, *Pediatrics* **6**:890-892 (Dec.) 1950.

6. Barmeyer, G. H.; Alderson, L. R.; and Cox, W. B.: Traumatic Periostitis in Young Children, *J Pediatr* **38**:184-190 (Feb.) 1951.

7. Silverman, F.: Roentgen Manifestations of Unrecognized Skeletal Trauma in Infants, *Amer J Roentgenol* **69**:413-426 (March) 1953.

8. Woolley, P. V., Jr., and Evans, W. A., Jr.: Significance of Skeletal Lesions in Infants Resembling Those of Traumatic Origin, *JAMA* **158**:539-543 (June) 1955.

9. Bakwin, H.: Multiple Skeletal Lesions in Young Children Due to Trauma, *J Pediatr* **49**:7-15 (July) 1956.

10. Caffey, J.: Some Traumatic Lesions in Growing Bones Other Than Fractures and Dislocations: Clinical and Radiological Features, *Brit J Radiol* **30**:225-238 (May) 1957.

11. Weston, W. J.: Metaphyseal Fractures in Infancy, *J Bone Joint Surg (Brit)* (no. 4) **39B**:694-700 (Nov.) 1957.

12. Fisher, S. H.: Skeletal Manifestations of Parent-Induced Trauma in Infants and Children, *Southern Med J* **51**:956-960 (Aug.) 1958.

13. Miller, D. S.: Fractures Among Children, *Minnesota Med* **42**:1209-1213 (Sept.) 1959;**42**:1414-1425 (Oct.) 1959.

14. Silver, H. K., and Kempe, C. H.: Problem of Parental Criminal Neglect and Severe Physical Abuse of Children, *J Dis Child* **95**:528, 1959.

15. Altman, D. H., and Smith, R. L.: Unrecognized Trauma in Infants and Children, *J Bone Joint Surg (Amer)* **42A**:407-413 (April) 1960.

16. Elmer, E.: Abused Young Children Seen in Hospitals, *Soc Work* (no. 4) **5**:98-102 (Oct.) 1960.

17. Gwinn, J. L.; Lewin, K. W.; and Peterson, H. G., Jr.: Roentgenographic Manifestations of Unsuspected Trauma in Infancy, *JAMA* **176**:926-929 (June 17) 1961.

18. Boardman, H. E.: Project to Rescue Children from Inflicted Injuries, *Soc Work* (no. 1) **7**:43 (Jan.) 1962.

June 22/29, 1984
(*JAMA* 1984;251:3295-3300)

*Landmark Perspective*

# 'The Battered Child' Revisited*

## Marilyn Heins, MD

The impact of the article "The Battered-Child Syndrome" by Drs Henry Kempe, Frederic Silverman, Brandt Steele, William Droegemueller, and Henry Silver, which appeared in THE JOURNAL on July 7, 1962[1] — and the speed with which this impact was felt throughout the land — were truly astonishing. Within four years of the publication of this LANDMARK ARTICLE, all but one state had adopted child abuse reporting statutes.[2]

Others had suspected the existence of child abuse, and a few previous articles on this subject had been published in the medical literature. Two things made this article different. First, the title. How can a nation ignore an entity called "the battered-child syndrome"? Second, the paper was submitted to the widely circulated *Journal of the American Medical Association* so that the majority of practicing physicians read about child abuse and the press quickly took note.

This perspective will cover four topics: (1) What led to the article? (2) Who was the remarkable man who wrote the article and orchestrated its impact? (3) What was the impact of the article? (4) What is the current status of child abuse and neglect in our country today?

### WHAT LED TO THE ARTICLE?

Violence against infants and children is at least as old as recorded history. Infanticide was an accepted practice for dealing with unwanted children in prehistoric and ancient cultures in the face of scarce resources.[3] Darwin actually postulated that one could correlate the beginning of human civilization with infanticide. "Our early semi-human progenitors would not have practiced infanticide. . . . For the instincts of the lower animals are never so perverted as to lead them regularly to destroy their own offspring."[4]

We know from the Bible that ritual sacrifice of children — or near-misses in the case of Isaac and Moses — was common. In the Judeo-Christian tradition of counteracting infanticide, the customs of circumcision and baptism serve as symbols substituting for the sacrifice of children.[3] After these rituals, infants are provided with both a given name and a family name, which bonds the child to the protecting family that has allowed him life. Early Roman law gave the father the absolute right of life or death over his child, but the Christian church began to preach against infanticide in the fourth century, and Roman laws making infanticide a

capital offense followed. These laws were the beginning of the notion of parens patriae, which defines the right of the state to intervene in the family on behalf of the child. Yet, infanticide, especially of illegitimate children, continued through the 19th century. Abandonment rather than frank murder became the method most often used to get rid of unwanted children. The first foundling home to save the lives of abandoned children was not established until 787 AD.

Concomitant with the Protestant Reformation arose the belief that children should be educated and disciplined in order to create a godly society on earth. Discipline became a sacred duty of families; the Puritans even established the death penalty for disobedient children, although there is no documentation of its use. Calvinist doctrine dictated that children should be whipped regularly to help rid them of innate depravity. Through the 17th century, flogging of children was common; most of these children today would be considered victims of physical abuse.[5]

The 18th century brought enlightenment in the care of children. Locke and Rousseau both held that children were shaped by their experience and were innocent before being corrupted by society. Corporal punishment was no longer considered necessary to ensure salvation. By the 19th century children came to be relatively well treated unless they were poor and forced to work at an early age. In this country, one of the earliest social reforms was directed against the widespread use of child labor, and, when the Children's Bureau was established in 1912 to oversee the health and welfare of children, it was housed in the Department of Labor.

The first recorded case of child abuse in this country occurred in New York in 1874.[3] A church worker calling on an elderly lady in a tenement learned that an 8-year-old child by the name of Mary Ellen, who was in the care of foster parents, was being starved and beaten. The church worker tried to remove Mary Ellen from her home, but appeals to the police and the Department of Charities were futile. She then appealed to Henry Bergh (who had founded the American Society for the Prevention of Cruelty to Animals in 1866). He persuaded the court to accept the case, and Mary Ellen was subsequently removed from the home and placed in an orphanage called "The Sheltering Arms." The foster mother was found guilty of assault and battery and sentenced to prison for a year. Mary Ellen died in 1961 at the age of 96 years after marrying and raising four children.[6] In 1875, the American Society for Prevention of Cruelty to Children was founded, and the establishment

From the University of Arizona College of Medicine, Tucson.
*A commentary on Kempe CH, Silverman FN, Steele BF, et al: The battered-child syndrome. *JAMA* 1962;181:17-24.

of child welfare agencies followed.

With the onset of better economic conditions in our country, children became better cared for. They were clean and well fed; parents had more leisure time to devote to the children. The American childhood seemed idyllic when compared with earlier times and with childhood in other nations. This likely led to a mind-set that held that parental abuse of children was not possible. In such a milieu, how did physicians recognize that children were being abused?

We now know that the first medical article on child abuse was written in Paris in 1860 by Ambroise Tardieu, a professor of legal medicine.[7] He reported on autopsies of 32 children who had died violently, mainly at the hands of their parents. Tardieu's article described the same medical lesions (multiple injuries and traumatic lesions of skin, bone, and brain) and the same demographic and social factors (the perpetrators were generally the parents who had discrepant explanations for the injuries) as Kempe et al described more than 100 years later.

We can gain insight into the progression of medical recognition of abuse by examining the references used in the LANDMARK ARTICLE. The earliest article cited, published in 1935, was entitled "Traumatic Ossifying Periostitis of the Newborn,"[8] an entity attributed to birth trauma. In 1951, the *Journal of Pediatrics* published an article on traumatic periostitis in young children, but no consideration was given to inflicted injury.[9]

In 1946, the father of pediatric radiology, John Caffey, described six cases of multiple fractures in the long bones of infants who had chronic subdural hematomas — signs classic for physical abuse. At one time he postulated that a clotting defect as yet unrecognized was responsible for this entity. Caffey noted that there was no roentgenographic evidence of any underlying pathological bone condition in these children, that subdural hematomas were best explained by trauma, and that the bone lesions were traumatic in nature, adding, "The injuries which caused the fractures in the long bones of these patients were either not observed or were denied when observed. The motive for denial has not been established."[10] According to Dr Frederic Silverman, Dr Caffey believed that these children were victims of inflicted injury but was concerned about legal repercussions. In 1953, Silverman[11] was the first to say that caretakers "may permit trauma and be unaware of it, may recognize trauma but forget or be reluctant to admit it, or may deliberately injure the child and deny it."

In 1956, Caffey[12] further solidified our thinking about child abuse in a speech before the Congress of the British Institute of Radiology urging early diagnosis to save abused children from further injury: "The correct early diagnosis of injury may be the only means by which the abused youngsters can be removed from their traumatic environment and their wrongdoers punished."

Woolley and Evans[13] in 1955 noted the chronic nature of parentally inflicted trauma as well as "instability" in the parents of these children. Subsequently, several articles on what is now called child abuse were published in pediatric, orthopedic, and social work journals. Although we can only speculate on how widely these articles were read, it is clear that child abuse was considered a minor aberration of parenting that rarely was seen and that was likely to be found in children of disadvantaged families. Indeed, a paper on child abuse submitted by Kempe to the Society of Pediatric Research in 1959 was read by title, as it was not considered important enough to be put on the program.

In a letter dated Oct 29, 1983, Dr Kempe wrote:

My involvement in child abuse was at first far from humane; it was, candidly, intellectual, at least at part. Day after day, while making rounds at the University of Colorado Medical School whose Department of Pediatrics I headed since 1956, I was shown children with diagnoses by residents and by consultants and attending physicians which simply were examples of either ignorance or denial. I thought very much the latter. I was shown children who had thrived for seven months and then developed 'spontaneous subdural hematoma.' . . . 'Multiple bruises of unknown etiology' in whom all tests were normal, who had no bleeding disorders and who did not bruise on the ward even when they fell. 'Osteogenesis imperfecta tarda' . . . in kids who had normal bones by x-ray except that they showed on whole body x-ray many healing fractures which could be dated. 'Impetigo' in kids with skin lesions which were clearly cigarette burns. 'Accidental burns of buttocks' in symmetrical form which could only occur from dunking a child who had soiled into a bucket of hot water to punish soiling. In these cases and many others we did often learn from one or both parents, in time and with patient and kindly approaches, that these were all *inflicted* accidents or injuries.

In the fall of 1959, William Droegemueller, MD, currently professor and chairman of obstetrics-gynecology at the University of North Carolina, was a senior medical student at the University of Colorado. He remembers that both Kempe and his colleague, Henry Silver, were young and dynamic role models who inspired a large number of the graduating students to enter pediatrics. Dr Droegemueller wanted to do a research project in this stimulating department but was not interested in the available research possibilities. Dr Silver suggested seeing Dr Kempe, who wanted to determine how widespread was the phenomenon of inflicted injuries in childhood. Together the medical student and Dr Kempe surveyed hospital directors and district attorneys about the incidence of abuse; 71 hospitals and 77 district attorneys responded. When Dr Droegemueller graduated in 1960, he left the data behind in two shoeboxes. Dr Kempe retrieved and collated the information.

Dr Kempe continued,

I have always had a visceral dislike for sloppy thinking in diagnosis and treatment, and I did not sit still for this fairly uniform cover-up which was based for the most part on denial or fear of what the physician's next step should be in getting it all laid out and making a treatment plan. I had seen 'battered children' as a student at San Francisco County Hospital and so had everyone, but not in the private or middle class setting. . . . My teachers said, these terrible events were caused by drunk fathers or inadequate mothers and referred them to Social Services. I was able to enlist Brandt Steele to see these folks as a psychiatrist can. . . . Our social workers and I formed a 'team' to discuss all cases for the week, go over all fractures in the x-ray department in children under 2 as a case finding tool. We finally figured out that 10% of all our ER [emergency room] trauma visits in children were due to child abuse. My own field of smallpox research remained very much an active matter but I wanted a chance to get to all pediatricians. This came when after being a member of the Program Committee of the American Academy of Pediatrics for 5 years, by rotation I became its Chairman for the 1961 meeting in Chicago. One prerogative of that job was the planning of a morning plenary session and on a day when most attended in the ballroom of the Old Palmer house, I wanted a title that would get their attention and named this the 'Battered Child Syndrome.' The presentation went all morning and the room with well over a thousand people was totally quiet. Nobody seemed to leave and after we were done a great many doctors came up and for the next 2 hours talked of cases in their private practice which they had missed. . . . The press and radio picked it up from there.

## WHO WAS THE MAN RESPONSIBLE FOR THE LANDMARK ARTICLE?

Charles Henry Kempe died March 7, 1984. The March issue of the *American Journal of Diseases of Children* is a Festschrift in his honor.

Although Dr Kempe was not the first to recognize child abuse or write about it, he was the first to focus our attention on the problem. Henry Kempe, as he was known, was born in 1922 in Germany and in 1937 went to live in England when his parents went to South America. A year later he was brought to the United States by a refugee organization. He worked his way through the University of California at Berkeley, entering the University of California School of Medicine, where he was classified as an "enemy resident" and placed under curfew so that he could not even go to the library in the evening. However, in a few months he simultaneously became a citizen and a private in the Army when his class was called up for military service, although he was allowed to continue attending medical school. He interned in pediatrics at the University of California Hospital, spent two years in Army service as a biologist, and completed his training in pediatrics at Yale. He returned to the University of California School of Medicine as an assistant professor of pediatrics. In 1956, while still an assistant professor and, only 34 years old, he became professor and chairman of the Department of Pediatrics at the University of Colorado School of Medicine, a job he held until 1973, after which he continued there as a professor of both pediatrics and microbiology.[14] He was married to Dr Ruth Svibergson Kempe, a child psychiatrist, who collaborated with him on several papers and a book on the subject of child abuse.[15] They also collaborated in raising five daughters, two of whom are physicians (a third hopes to enter medical school), and they have six grandchildren. She points out that "the acceptance of an idea requires a lot of hard work and follow up. My husband spoke before innumerable groups of physicians and social workers to convince them of the problem." Until his death, Dr Kempe remained on the faculty of the University of Colorado College of Medicine but lately had worked and written in Honolulu.

Frederic Silverman, the second author of the LANDMARK ARTICLE, is the renowned pediatric radiologist who is currently professor emeritus of pediatrics and radiology at Stanford University School of Medicine. He studied and worked with John Caffey prior to moving to Cincinnati, where he became director of radiology at Children's Hospital. His contributions to the LANDMARK ARTICLE were the roentgenographic findings. Although Dr Silverman's article[11] was actually the first to state that caretakers deliberately inflicted injuries on children, he hastens to add that Dr Kempe deserves all the credit for the LANDMARK ARTICLE and its impact because he coined the term *battered child*.

Brandt Steele, MD, was an associate professor of psychiatry at the University of Colorado School of Medicine at the time the LANDMARK ARTICLE was written.

He is currently professor emeritus of psychiatry there and also a psychiatrist at the C. H. Kempe National Center for the Prevention and Treatment of Child Abuse and Neglect. Although he contributed the psychiatric section of the article and the two case reports, he fully acknowledges the importance of Dr Kempe's contribution. Dr Henry Silver, currently professor of pediatrics at the University of Colorado School of Medicine and its associate dean for admissions, notes that Dr Steele was aware of the dynamics of child abuse and the fact that it could occur in rich as well as poor families before the survey was done. Because Dr Kempe was concerned about the *chronic* nature of abuse after realizing that abused children were brought to the hospital with repeated injuries which sometimes ended fatally, he decided to do the survey. Dr Silver adds, "The article was 99% Henry's baby."

## THE IMPACT OF THE LANDMARK ARTICLE
### Reporting Legislation

Dr Kempe and his medical colleagues were asked to meet with representatives of the Children's Bureau in 1962 to study whether the child abuse problem was of sufficient magnitude to require federal action. A subsequent meeting, which also included lawyers and police officials, led to the drafting of a model reporting law which the Children's Bureau proposed in 1963. By 1964, 20 states had enacted reporting statutes, by 1966, 49 states. Today all 50 states, the District of Columbia, American Samoa, Guam, Puerto Rico, and the Virgin Islands have reporting laws.[2] Reporting—mandated as a result of the LANDMARK ARTICLE—is a mechanism to prevent fatal child abuse or future injuries by setting child protective services in motion.

State reporting statutes are quite similar, but there are minor variations in the purpose clause, reportable circumstances, definition, age limits, and who must report. Early legislation was directed at physicians, and every jurisdiction today requires physicians to report child abuse. Currently, teachers, clergy, social workers, and attorneys are also required to report in some states. Nineteen jurisdictions mandate that "any person" who suspects abuse report it. Immunity from civil or criminal liability is provided for those who report. There is a penalty for failure to report, and physicians have been sued for damages in civil court because they did not report.

Although each jurisdiction defines abuse somewhat differently, almost all statutes now are broadly defined and include neglect as well as physical abuse. The intent of all of the reporting laws is to protect the child rather than punish the perpetrators. Therefore, most states mandate immediate investigation of the report and appropriate action to protect the child, ranging from removal of the child from the home to ongoing social services for the family.

### National and International Impact

After the publication of the LANDMARK ARTICLE, the mass media exploded. Editorials and stories in the popular press abounded, which both fostered and encouraged the legislative action. In 1963, a television episode of "Ben Casey" about child abuse was shown to 200 affiliates. Other series such as "Dr Kildare" and "Slattery's People" followed suit. National magazines used horrifying photographs and graphic titles ("Cry Rises From Beaten Babies," *Life,* 1963, and "The Shocking Price of Parental Anger," *Good Housekeeping,* 1964).[16] Within three years of Kempe's article, 300 scientific articles on child abuse were published. By 1980, an annotated bibliography on child abuse contained 450 pages of references.[17]

The C. Henry Kempe National Center for the Prevention and Treatment of Child Abuse and Neglect was established in Denver in 1972 as an outgrowth of the Child Protection Team Dr Kempe started and directed at the University of Colorado Medical Center. This is a "hands-on" center providing treatment as well as resources for the education of professionals.

Dr Kempe's work culminated in the Federal Child Abuse Prevention and Treatment Act of 1974 (a century after Mary Ellen was removed from her abusive home). This legislation, also known as the Schroeder-Mondale Act, was of historical note as Representative Schroeder was new to Congress and never before had a first termer been named as senior author of a bill. The act established a national center in Washington, DC, with funds for research, demonstration projects, and clearinghouse activities in the field of child abuse and neglect. In 1975, Title XX of the Social Security Act mandated protective services in all the states.

In 1974, Dr Kempe set up a planning meeting for an international organization devoted to the prevention of child abuse. The International Society for the Prevention of Child Abuse and Neglect was established in 1976, at which time Kempe was elected founding president and became editor-in-chief of *Child Abuse and Neglect,* the international journal.

### The Physician and Child Abuse

The physician plays an important role in the recognition and treatment of abuse and neglect. Although physicians have become knowledgeable about abuse and neglect, underreporting by physicians still results from failure to diagnose abuse or ignorance about its seriousness. Some physicians resist reporting because of its potential effect on their relationship with the family or their practice.[18,19] Many also are reluctant to become involved in legal or social bureaucracy.[20] Physicians, as well as the public, are influenced by what Kempe called the "three almost sacred sayings" of our culture. "Spare the rod and spoil the child" highlights our traditional sanction of corporal punishment. "Be it ever so humble, there's no place like home" reminds us of the importance of parents to their children—even flawed parents. "A man's home is his castle" reinforces our sensitivity to the private rights of others, including their right to rear their children without intervention.[21]

Two types of "self-referral" come to the attention of physicians. Some parents have anxiety attacks or other acute psychiatric symptoms, but the real problem is fear they will harm their child. Other parents repeatedly bring a well child to a physician, insisting the child is sick. Indeed, Kempe[22] suggested that if a parent brings a perfectly well baby to the doctor or the emergency room twice in one day, the potential for abuse is high.

In addition to reporting, physicians can play a role in prevention of abuse and neglect by providing advice about childrearing, helping families deal with stress, serving as advocates of children, and becoming an educational resource for the community.[23] Medical schools now include the study of child abuse and neglect in the curriculum, as do residency training programs in relevant specialties such as pediatrics, family practice, emergency medicine, and psychiatry.

The American Medical Association recently has implemented a report of the Council on Scientific Affairs to assume an active leadership role in attacking the problem of child abuse. The AMA will work with state medical societies to facilitate existing programs for the prevention and treatment of child abuse and neglect; to educate physicians about their role in identification, treatment, and prevention; and to disseminate educational materials.

## WHAT IS THE CURRENT STATUS OF CHILD ABUSE AND NEGLECT?

Thanks to the LANDMARK ARTICLE, the public as well as the medical profession became aware that child abuse is a common problem and can occur in families of any socioeconomic status. Health professionals are generally cognizant of the forms abuse takes, the causative factors, and the potentially lethal nature of this "disease" of parenting.

We now understand that physical abuse requires four basic factors: (1) There is a parent with the potential for abuse. Such parents were usually not parented well themselves, often were themselves victims of abuse, are isolated, do not trust others, and have unrealistic expectations of children.[24] (2) There is a child who usually exhibits "some behavior . . . which the parent, correctly or incorrectly, justifiably or unjustifiably, perceives as aversive, and as requiring some intervention to change."[25] (3) There is a stressful situation or incident that serves as a trigger. (4) The family lives in a culture in which corporal punishment is sanctioned or encouraged. In one sense, all parents have the potential to abuse but most of us keep our murderous capabilities in check because we have impulse control, inner resources, and support systems.

### Epidemiology

In 1982, there were 929,310 reports of child abuse and neglect nationwide, representing an increase of 125% since 1976, although the magnitude of the yearly incidence is decreasing (American Humane Association, Child Protection Division, oral communication, Feb 14, 1984). Twenty-six percent of the reports involved abuse, 43% neglect, and 19% combined abuse and neglect. Nearly half of the investigations revealed a need for ongoing protective services. In 40% of the reported cases, no parent or caretaker was employed, and 43% of the families received some sort of public assistance compared with 11% nationwide.[26] Forty-three percent of the reports occurred in single-mother families compared with 14% of all US families, leading to the inescapable conclusion that stress and poverty are related to abuse and neglect.

About 10% of the injuries in children younger than 5

years brought to hospital emergency rooms are inflicted. It is estimated that the incidence of physical abuse is six per thousand live births, with a prevalence of 380 cases per million per year.[27] Estimates vary greatly because not all cases of abuse are reported, the definition of abuse has broadened through the years, and the definition may vary from group to group of professionals.[28] Most health professionals believe that about 1% of the children of America are subjected to abuse and neglect each year.

Reporting cases of abuse has not eliminated the danger to children. Homicide is one of the top five leading causes of death in childhood and accounts for 5% of deaths in children younger than 18 years.[29] In 1979, 1,620 children were murdered, and almost all of the murders in children younger than 3 years were the result of child abuse perpetrated by a parent or caretaker.[30] Abuse is the greatest single cause of death in infants between 6 and 12 months of age.[27]

Physical punishment of children is used by between 84% and 97% of all families.[31] A recent survey of violence in American families revealed that 4% of children, aged 3 to 17 years, had been subjected to severe violence in the survey year, a figure that projects to between 1.2 and 2 million children per year. Neither single-parent homes nor children younger than 3 years were included in this survey, although these two groups are at great risk of violence. Thus, it is likely that even more children are subjected to violence.[32]

It is apparent that the problem of child abuse and neglect has not ended. It represents a significant contribution not only to the morbidity and mortality of childhood but also to crime and violence in our society. We know that abusive parents were likely themselves to have been abused as children. Studies of murderers and others who engaged in violent acts have revealed that these offenders were abused as children.[33]

### Current Problems

Funding for protective services, prevention, and treatment has never been adequate. Now that mandated reporting, central registries, and "hotlines" have added to the protective services case load, the level of funding is dangerously low. Also, concomitant with unemployment and other social ills, recent cutbacks in services at federal, state, and local levels have occurred. In addition, the number of serious cases reported appears to be increasing. Thus, we have a continued increase in reported cases, an increase in severity, and a decrease in services to treat and prevent cases of abuse and neglect.

Reporting is only a part of the solution to the problem of child abuse. Evaluative outcomes of child protection services that follow reporting have been analyzed in numerous studies.[34] There is only modest success in helping abusive parents given the limited resources and current treatment technologies. Self-help programs such as Parents Anonymous may be helpful but are not available in every community.[35] Reporting itself can have a deleterious effect on the family involved, as the investigation is stressful and public knowledge of the problem can add to the isolation.[19]

Personnel turnover in child protection agencies is exceedingly high, and worker "burnout" is common.[34]

Working with abusive families is both exhausting and unfulfilling, as they cannot be helped easily and sometimes not at all.[36] Community resources almost always fall into the "too little, too late" category. There are never enough workers, foster home placements, or temporary shelters. Today, many parents live in isolation far from their extended families, and the number of high-risk groups such as young and single parents is increasing.

Thus, a major issue today is funding for needed family-child social programs as well as proper allocation of resources to manage child abuse and neglect. In addition, we need greater role specificity of the many professionals involved in the multidisciplinary approach to the complex problems of parental failure. Physicians, social workers, law enforcement officers, and lawyers all have a part to play—and all must understand their role and the limitations of that role.[37] We must come to grips with society's conflicts between intervening to protect the child on the one hand and upholding the sanctity of the family and its privacy on the other.[38,39] Volunteer agencies such as churches, parents' groups, and other groups of concerned citizens are vitally needed in this effort to help children. Ongoing review of the legal system and its effectiveness to protect children as well as continued efforts to educate health professionals, educators, and child care workers about child abuse and neglect are also needed.

### Prediction and Prevention

Prevention of child abuse and neglect can be conceptualized on two levels: prediction followed by intervention in high-risk groups and societal changes to promote optimal parenting. Sorting parent-child dyads into high- or low-risk groups is possible,[40,41] although not without risks. No questionnaire instrument or observation is perfect in specificity or sensitivity. Labeling high-risk parents without providing treatment is not only unethical but could serve as a self-fulfilling prophecy. We could, however, provide parenting help not only for those in need of extra services but for all parents who wish help. Examples of parenting services include a perinatal coach who trains parents in communication with their baby or a health visitor who visits the home shortly after birth.[42,43]

Kempe continued in his letter,

The future lies in prevention. We can often identify those 'at risk' even when the child is born. Instead of just labeling those couples we give them extra services to help from the first. This does prevent much abuse and neglect when lay therapists—taken from within the community—and visiting nurses are used. Those families simply feel that our health care system has greatly improved, and I do not feel that it is an invasion of privacy or undemocratic. The child in a non democracy belongs to the State and 'you cannot damage State property.' In a democracy the child belongs to himself or herself, in the care of the parents. If parenting fails, the rest of Society, its citizens, become the other parent.

### Parenting

Parenting itself is an issue. Parental failure not only hurts the child today but also leads to "failure" in the future adult. Kempe suggested,

Certainly, violent families, which may have 'battered wives' as well alcoholic outbursts, etc. all can trigger chaotic lives for spouses who have never had role models of good parenting and, regrettably, they tend to marry each other. Such couples are like two non-swimmers drowning while clutching each other. Parenting can be enhanced by

Family Life Education starting in the primary schools. . . . Family life isn't a bed of roses as so many of our junior high 12 year olds think. Let them have a nursery school experience, housed on school sites, and hear crying, see dirtying, even for a day! This would delay, I feel, early sexual activity with almost planned early pregnancy and immature marriages, often to get away from miserable home lives but with a very naive view of adult parenting and the needs of even one child. It would help young boys to get to know a lot, too. Such programs are under way in Oregon and elsewhere with fine results. If our nation truly believes in the family as a central concept of a free society, then we must help pregnant women as much as the Scandinavians do. Not only do they need practical teaching in 'mothercrafting,' so that 'mothering' can more easily follow, but nutrition advice, avoidance of harmful substances during gestation etc, all are a national priority if we wish to help to enhance parenting. Community support is just not enough now. There ought to be a block party for each baby born in each block to make sure each mother knows that, while she may not have the previous extended family support, she does have caring neighbors. Our department started fostergrandparents long before it became a national program, in 1958 actually, and I will always recall that the loving older folks felt useful, both male and female, and that often they

supported not only the child but also its parents. We simply need to recapture the caring attitudes of our pioneer forefathers! We are, in a way, one big family.

Bronfenbrenner notes that the worth of a society can be judged by the way that society treats its children. Our worth as a nation tomorrow depends on our protection of the children of today — "the concern of one generation for the next."[44] One hundred years elapsed between the case of Mary Ellen and the passage of the Federal Child Abuse Prevention and Treatment Act of 1974. Children to be protected need more than reporting; there must also be sufficient resources both for treatment and for carefully evaluated prevention methodologies. Physicians should lead the way to ensure that another century does not go by before child abuse and neglect become as uncommon as smallpox and polio.

## References

1. Kempe CH, Silverman FN, Steele BF, et al: The battered-child syndrome. *JAMA* 1962;181:17-24.

2. Sloan IJ: *Child Abuse: Governing Law & Legislation,* series 79. New York, Oceana Publications Inc, 1983.

3. Robin M: Sheltering arms: The roots of child protection, in Newberger EH (ed): *Child Abuse.* Boston, Little Brown & Co, 1982, pp 1-21.

4. Bakan D: *Slaughter of the Innocents.* San Francisco, Jossey-Bass Inc, 1971, p xi.

5. De Mause L: The evolution of childhood, in de Mause L (ed): *The History of Childhood.* New York, Harper & Row Publishers Inc, 1974.

6. Steele B: Notes on the history of child abuse. Presented at Children's-Mercy Hospital, Kansas City, Mo, January 1983.

7. Silverman FN: Unrecognized trauma in infants, the battered child syndrome, and the syndrome of Ambroise Tardieu. *Radiology* 1972;104:337-353.

8. Snedecor ST, Knapp RE, Wilson HB: Traumatic ossifying periostitis of the newborn. *Surg Gynecol Obstet* 1935;61:385-387.

9. Barmeyer GH, Alderson LR, Cox WB, et al: Traumatic ossifying periostitis in young children. *J Pediatr* 1951;38:184-190.

10. Caffey J: Multiple fractures in the long bones of infants suffering from chronic subdural hematoma. *AJR* 1946;56:163-173.

11. Silverman FN: The roentgen manifestations of unrecognized skeletal trauma in infants. *AJR* 1953;69:413-426.

12. Caffey J: Some traumatic lesions in growing bones other than fractures and dislocations: Clinical and radiological features. *Br J Radiol* 1957;30:238.

13. Woolley PV Jr, Evans WA Jr: Significance of skeletal lesions in infants resembling those of traumatic origin. *JAMA* 1955;158:539-543.

14. Silver HK: Presentation of the Howland Award: Some observations introducing C. Henry Kempe, MD. *Pediatr Res* 1980;14:1151-1154.

15. Kempe RS, Kempe CH: *Child Abuse.* Cambridge, Mass, Harvard University Press, 1978, pp 1-123.

16. Paulsen M, Parker G, Adelman L: Child abuse reporting laws—some legislative history. *George Washington Law Rev* 1966;34:482-506.

17. *Child Abuse: An Annotated Bibliography.* Metuchen, NJ, Scarecrow Press Inc, 1982.

18. Schmitt BD, Kempe CH: The pediatrician's role in child abuse and neglect. *Curr Prob Ped* 1975;5:3-45.

19. McNeese MC, Hebeler JR: The abused child: A clinical approach to identification and management. *Clin Symposia* 1977;29:35.

20. Sanders RW: Resistance to dealing with parents of battered children. *Pediatrics* 1972;50:853-857.

21. Kempe CH: Paediatric implications of the battered baby syndrome. *Arch Dis Child* 1971;46:28-37.

22. Kempe CH: Child abuse—the pediatrician's role in child advocacy and preventive pediatrics. *AJDC* 1978;132:255-260.

23. Ellerstein NS: The role of the physician, in Ellerstein NS (ed): *Child Abuse and Neglect: A Medical Reference.* New York, John Wiley & Sons Inc, 1981, pp 1-71.

24. Pollock C, Steele B: A therapeutic approach to the parents, in Kempe CH, Helfer RE (eds): *Helping the Battered Child and His Family.* Philadelphia, JB Lippincott Co, 1972, pp 3-21.

25. Kadushin A, Martin JA: *Child Abuse: An Interactional Event.* New York, Columbia University Press, 1981, p 253.

26. *Highlights of Official Child Neglect and Abuse Reporting, Annual Report, 1981.* Denver, American Humane Association, 1983.

27. Schmitt BD, Kempe CH: Child abuse: Management and prevention of the battered child syndrome, in *Folia Traumatologica.* Basel, Switzerland, CIBA-GEIGY, 1975, p 3.

28. Gelles RJ: Child abuse and family violence: Implications for medical professionals, in Newberger EH (ed): *Child Abuse.* Boston, Little Brown & Co, 1982, pp 25-41.

29. Christoffel KK: Homicide in childhood: A public health problem in need of attention. *Am J Public Health* 1984;74:68-70.

30. Jason J: Child homicide spectrum. *AJDC* 1983;137:578-581.

31. Gelles RJ: Violence towards children in the United States, in *American Association for the Advancement of Science, Symposium on Violence at Home and at School, Denver, 1977.* Washington, DC, American Association for the Advancement of Science, 1977.

32. Snyder JC, Hampton R, Newberger EH: Family dysfunction: Violence, neglect, and sexual misuse, in Levine MD, Carey WB, Crocker AC, et al (eds): *Developmental-Behavioral Pediatrics.* Philadelphia, WB Saunders Co, 1983, pp 256-275.

33. Steele BF: Violence in our society. *Pharos* 1970;33:42-48.

34. Kadushin A, Lathrop J: *Child Welfare Services,* ed 3. New York, Macmillan Publishing Co Inc, 1980, pp 156-205.

35. Lieber L, Baker J: Parents anonymous and self-help treatment for child abusing parents: A review and an evaluation. *Child Abuse Neglect* 1977;1:133-148.

36. Cohn AH: Organization and administration of programs to treat child abuse and neglect, in Newberger EH (ed): *Child Abuse.* Boston, Little Brown & Co, 1982, pp 89-101.

37. Giovannoni JM, Becerra RM: *Defining Child Abuse.* New York, The Free Press, 1970.

38. Rosenfeld AA, Newberger EH: Compassion vs control: Conceptual and practical pitfalls in the broadened definition of child abuse. *JAMA* 1977;237:2086-2088.

39. Markham B: Child abuse intervention: Conflicts in current practice and legal theory. *Pediatrics* 1980;65:180-185.

40. Helfer RE: Preventing the abuse and neglect of children: The physician's role. *Pediatr Basics* 1979;23:4-7.

41. Lealman GT, Haigh D, Phillips JM, et al: Prediction and prevention of child abuse—an empty hope? *Lancet* 1983;1:1423-1424.

42. Kempe CH: Approaches to preventing child abuse. *AJDC* 1976;130:941-947.

43. Gray J, Kaplan B: The Lay Health Visitor Program: An 18-month experience, in Kempe CH, Helfer RE (eds): *The Battered Child,* ed 3. University of Chicago Press, 1980, pp 373-378.

44. Bronfenbrenner U: *Two Worlds of Childhood: U.S. and U.S.S.R.* New York, Russell Sage Foundation, 1970, p 1.

April 6, 1964
(*JAMA* 1964;188:22-26)

Landmark Article

## Chapter 47

# Asbestos Exposure and Neoplasia

Irving J. Selikoff, MD, Jacob Churg, MD, and E. Cuyler Hammond, DSc,

New York

Building trades insulation workers have relatively light, intermittent, exposure to asbestos. Of 632 insulation workers, who entered the trade before 1943 and were traced through 1962, forty-five died of cancer of the lung or pleura, whereas only 6.6 such deaths were expected. Three of the pleural tumors were mesotheliomas; there was also one peritoneal mesothelioma. Four mesotheliomas in a total of 255 deaths is an exceedingly high incidence for such a rare tumor. In addition, an unexpectedly large number of men died of cancer of the stomach, colon, or rectum (29 compared with 9.4 expected). Other cancers were not increased; 20.5 were expected, 21 occurred. Twelve men died of asbestosis.

ALTHOUGH PULMONARY CARCINOMA had been observed in the earliest studies of asbestosis, association between the two conditions was first suggested by Lynch and Smith in 1935.[1] Additional reports of such association followed. Perhaps the most striking data was presented in the annual report of the Chief Inspector of Factories of Great Britain for 1955.[2] Every death with asbestosis in the files of the Factory Department, from the first recognition of asbestosis as a disease entity, was studied. Altogether 365 such deaths were recorded (1924-1955). Sixty-five or 17.8% were found to be accompanied by cancer of the lung or pleura. Doll,[3] after reviewing the problem and adding data of his own, concluded that lung cancer was a specific industrial hazard of heavily exposed asbestos workers.

Nevertheless, some investigators have held that, while these observations might be suggestive, they did not establish an increased incidence of carcinoma of the lung in pulmonary asbestosis, and further, that the association was unproved.

The factor of selection was considered a potential

weakness in evaluating reports of autopsy series. It was noted that complicated and unusual cases would be more likely to come to autopsy, thus raising the apparent frequency of associated lung neoplasms.[4] Further, it was argued that autopsy statistics, which dealt with particular groups of those who died, do not reflect total populations of asbestos workers.[5] Additional reservations were based on the frequent absence of data regarding exposure, smoking habits, and personal history, on the size of series, and on inadequate histological verification in some cases.

Within the last few years a number of additional problems connected with asbestos exposure have appeared, making clarification and resolution of the foregoing statistical uncertainty a matter of considerable concern. First, there has been greatly increased use of the various types of asbestos (a five-fold increase in world utilization of this group of minerals, from 500,000 tons to 2,500,000 tons per year in the last 30 years), as well as a greatly increased number and variety of industrial applications of asbestos (over 3,000 such uses now recorded). Second, suspicion has been growing that malignancy associated with asbestos exposure may include neoplasms other than carcinoma of the lung. Thus, a significant relationship has been claimed between diffuse mesothelioma of the pleura and peritoneum and asbestos exposure.[6]

This communication is concerned with investigations undertaken to study the following factors: (1) the incidence of deaths due to pulmonary carcinoma among a group of workers exposed to asbestos under United States industrial conditions in the past several decades, (2) whether or not such individuals would also be found to have an increased risk of other neoplasms, and (3) whether such risks would be present in an industry other than the asbestos-producing or asbestos-products industries, with which most reports in the past have been concerned but which would not necessarily represent the most important areas of asbestos exposure at this time.

From the Division of Thoracic Disease, Department of Medicine, and the Department of Pathology, Mount Sinai Hospital.

Read before a joint meeting of the sections on radiology and diseases of the chest and the American College of Chest Physicians at the 112th Annual Meeting of the American Medical Association, Atlantic City, NJ, June 17, 1963.

Further, it was hoped that study of an industry with asbestos exposure of limited extent and intensity would throw some light on the potential problems associated with minimal exposure to asbestos.

## MATERIALS AND METHODS

Our investigations have been concerned with 1,522 members of the Asbestos Workers Union in the New York metropolitan area, members of New York Local 12 and Newark, NJ, Local 32 of the International Association of Heat and Frost Insulators and Asbestos Workers. As the full title implies, these men are insulation workers. Although the union is considered one of the building-trades unions, its members do insulation work in a variety of industries, including shipbuilding. Called "laggers" in Great Britain, they are often designated "pipe coverers," "insulators," or "asbestos workers" in this country.

The union is one of the oldest in the country. The New York local, as the "Salamander Association of Boiler and Pipe Felters," was the first union of insulation workers in the United States. It amalgamated with other locals as the current Asbestos Workers Union in 1912. The stability of this union has been reflected in the stability of its membership rolls. "Once a pipecoverer, always a pipe-coverer" has been of epidemiological importance to us and has made this group of men particularly suitable for the study of long-term effects of asbestos inhalation. Unlike unskilled workers exposed to asbestos inhalation in poorly paid industries, there is little labor turnover among insulation workers. Accurate employment records are maintained by the union, which has also been concerned with health problems in the industry.

The trade was badly hit during the depression; some men had to drop out and very few were added during the 1930's. By the end of 1942 the union rolls consisted mainly of men with considerable experience, plus a few who joined in 1940, 1941, and 1942. Between 1946 and 1962 union membership increased substantially.

*Source of Data.*—From union records, a list was prepared of every individual who was a member of either of the metropolitan locals on Dec 31, 1942, or who joined between that date and Dec 31, 1962. No one was omitted, whatever his subsequent work history. The 1942 list included 632 men; 890 men joined after 1942.

Personal data were obtained from union records, and the work history of each man was detailed, including withdrawal from employment (war service, other employment, retirement, illness). These data gave the baseline for calculation of the onset and duration of exposure. For members who had died, records of the Health and Welfare Fund provided date and place of death. Copies of death certificates were obtained on all but one of them. Autopsy protocols, histological specimens, and hospital records were obtained and reviewed in those deaths, approximately one half, in which the terminal illness had occurred in a hospital.

*Statistical Analysis.*—Previous studies have suggested that neoplasia associated with asbestosis seldom occurs until 20 years after first exposure to asbestos dust. Therefore, we decided to limit the present analysis to men with such an exposure history. Our complete records cover all members of the union (including active and

Table 1.—Man-Years of Experience of 632 Asbestos Workers Exposed to Asbestos Dust 20 Years or Longer

| Age | Years | | | |
|-----|-------|-------|-------|-------|
| | 1943-1947 | 1948-1952 | 1953-1957 | 1958-1962 |
| 35-39 .............. | 85.0 | 185.0 | 7.0 | 11.0 |
| 40-44 .............. | 230.5 | 486.5 | 291.5 | 70.0 |
| 45-49 .............. | 339.5 | 324.0 | 530.0 | 314.5 |
| 50-54 .............. | 391.5 | 364.0 | 308.0 | 502.5 |
| 55-59 .............. | 382.0 | 390.0 | 316.0 | 268.5 |
| 60-64 .............. | 221.0 | 341.5 | 344.0 | 255.0 |
| 65-69 .............. | 139.0 | 181.0 | 286.0 | 280.0 |
| 70-74 .............. | 83.0 | 115.5 | 137.0 | 197.5 |
| 75-79 .............. | 31.5 | 70.0 | 70.5 | 75.0 |
| 80-84 .............. | 5.5 | 18.5 | 38.5 | 23.5 |
| 85+ .............. | 3.5 | 2.0 | 8.0 | 13.5 |
| Totals ........... | 1,912.0 | 2,478.0 | 2,336.5 | 2,011.0 |

retired members, both dead and alive) during the 20-year period from Jan 1, 1943, through Dec 31, 1962. However, with few exceptions, the only men with a history of 20 years or longer since first exposure to asbestos were the 632 men on the union rolls as of Jan 1, 1943. (The exceptions were a few men who joined the union after Jan 1, 1943, but who had been employed previously as asbestos workers elsewhere.) Of these 632 men, 255 died before Jan 1, 1963.

Of these 632 men, 339 had been exposed to asbestos dust prior to 1924. In other words, as of Jan 1, 1943, 20 years or longer had elapsed since these 339 men were first exposed. The remaining 293 men reached the 20-years-since-first-exposure point at some time after Jan 1, 1943, and before the end of 1962. The 339 men who were first exposed prior to 1924 were counted in each of the 20 years (or up to the time of death of those who died). The 293 who were first exposed in 1924 or later were counted only after they reached the 20-years-since-first-exposure point (those who died being dropped at the time of death). When the statistics were completed, we found that we had records covering a total of 8,737.5 man-years of experience of men with a history of 20 years or longer since first exposure to asbestos dust.

Of the 8,737.5 man-years, 1912.0 were in the five-year period 1943-1947; 2,478.0 were in the period 1948-1952; 2,336.5 were in the period 1953-1957; and 2,011.0 were in the period 1958-1962. Table 1 shows the age distribution of the man-years in each of these five-year periods. Table 2 shows (1) the average age-specific death rates of all US white males during each of these periods, and (2) the average age-specific death rates from cancer of the lung, pleura, mediastinum, and trachea among US white males during each period, as reported by the US National Office of Vital Statistics.

The man-years were then multiplied by the corresponding reported US death rates to ascertain the *expected* number of deaths under the null hypothesis that the death rates of asbestos workers do not differ from death rates of all US white males (both age and date being taken into consideration). The results are summarized in Table 3.

## RESULTS

*Total Deaths.*—During the first five years (1943-1947) only 28 deaths occurred among the asbestos workers,

Table 2.—Total Deaths and Deaths From Cancer of the Lung, Bronchus, Pleura, Mediastinum, and Trachea per 10,000 White Males per Year°

| Age | 1943-1947 Total | 1943-1947 Lung Cancer† | 1948-1952 Total | 1948-1952 Lung Cancer† | 1953-1957 Total | 1953-1957 Lung Cancer† | 1958-1962 Total | 1958-1962 Lung Cancer† |
|---|---|---|---|---|---|---|---|---|
| 35-39 .......... | 36 | .... | 30 | .... | 26 | .... | 25 | 1 |
| 40-44 .......... | 55 | 1 | 48 | 1 | 43 | 1 | 42 | 1 |
| 45-49 .......... | 85 | 2 | 78 | 3 | 72 | 3 | 70 | 3 |
| 50-54 .......... | 133 | 4 | 124 | 5 | 115 | 6 | 116 | 7 |
| 55-59 .......... | 196 | 5 | 189 | 8 | 178 | 10 | 178 | 11 |
| 60-64 .......... | 295 | 7 | 281 | 10 | 276 | 14 | 272 | 17 |
| 65-69 .......... | 435 | 7 | 417 | 11 | 416 | 17 | 418 | 21 |
| 70-74 .......... | 634 | 6 | 605 | 11 | 586 | 16 | 607 | 21 |
| 75-79 .......... | 977 | 6 | 915 | 10 | 878 | 14 | 866 | 17 |
| 80-84 .......... | 1,453 | 5 | 1,353 | 8 | 1,346 | 12 | 1,363 | 15 |
| 85+ ............ | 2,422 | 3 | 2,162 | 7 | 2,017 | 9 | 2,148 | 11 |

°Death rates as reported annually by the US National Office of Vital Statistics. A five-year average is given here for each period. Average for 1958-1962 is a projection of 1958-1960, since 1961-1962 rates are not yet available.

†Death rates include cancer of the lung, bronchus, pleura, mediastinum, and trachea, assigned to international list code No. 47b-f prior to 1949 and to No. 160-164 thereafter.

whereas 39.7 deaths would have occurred had their age-specific death rates been the same as for all US white males during those years (Table 3). In other words, at the start of the study, the asbestos workers had below average death rates. This is by no means surprising. Indeed, such is almost always found in the first few years of a prospective epidemiological study of this type. The explanation is almost certainly as follows: The 632 men in this analysis were actively employed as asbestos workers in 1942. Since disability from illness or other causes precludes employment in a trade of this type, these men were presumably well (or at least not disabled) at the start of the study period. Almost any group so selected as to exclude the ill and disabled has a lower death rate during the ensuing few years than does the general population, since ill and disabled persons have extremely high death rates. A selective effect of this type gradually wears off with time and largely disappears within five to

Table 3.—Observed and Expected Number of Deaths Among 632 Asbestos Workers Exposed to Asbestos Dust 20 Years or Longer

| Cause of Death | Years 1943-1947 | Years 1948-1952 | Years 1953-1957 | Years 1958-1962 | Total, 1943-1962 |
|---|---|---|---|---|---|
| Total, all causes .................... Observed (asbestos workers) | 28 | 54 | 85 | 88 | 255 |
| Expected (US white males) .. | 39.7 | 50.8 | 56.6 | 54.4 | 203.5 |
| Total cancer, all sites ............. Observed (asbestos workers) | 13 | 17 | 26 | 39 | 95 |
| Expected (US white males) .. | 5.7 | 8.1 | 13.0 | 9.7 | 36.5 |
| Cancer of lung and pleura ...... Observed (asbestos workers) | 6 | 8 | 13 | 18 | 45 |
| Expected (US white males) .. | 0.8 | 1.4 | 2.0 | 2.4 | 6.6 |
| Cancer of stomach, colon, and rectum .......................... Observed (asbestos workers) | 4 | 4 | 7 | 14 | 29 |
| Expected (US white males) .. | 2.0 | 2.5 | 2.6 | 2.3 | 9.4 |
| Cancer of all other sites combined .......................... Observed (asbestos workers) | 3 | 5 | 6 | 7 | 21 |
| Expected (US white males) .. | 2.9 | 4.2 | 8.4 | 5.0 | 20.5 |
| Asbestosis ............................. Observed (asbestos workers) | 0 | 1 | 4 | 7 | 12 |

ten years from the time of initial selection.

During the second five-year period (1948-1952) the death rate of the asbestos workers was slightly higher than the death rate of all US white males, ie, 54 observed deaths compared with 50.8 expected deaths. In later periods, the death rate of the asbestos workers was proportionately higher. For the period 1953-1957, there were 85 observed deaths compared with 56.6 expected deaths, and for the period 1958-1962, there were 88 observed deaths compared with only 54.4 expected deaths.

*Cancer of the Lung, Pleura, and Trachea.*—In each of the four five-year periods, far more deaths from cancer of the lung and pleura occurred among the asbestos workers than would have occurred had their death rates from these diseases been the same as for all US white males (Table 3). Altogether 45 of the 632 asbestos workers died of cancer of these sites, whereas only 6.6 such deaths would be expected from general US experience. Of these 45 deaths, 42 were recorded as due to bronchogenic carcinoma and 3 to neoplasms of the pleura. The pleural neoplasms were all recorded as mesotheliomas.

Thus it was found that the death rate from cancer of the bronchus and pleura was 6.8 times as high among these asbestos workers as in the general US white male population (both age and date being taken into consideration).

It may be asked whether the high rate of lung cancer among these asbestos workers could possibly be attributed to an unusually large proportion of cigarette smokers among them. We cannot answer this question directly, since we have not yet been able to ascertain the smoking habits of the men who died. However, the following pieces of evidence indicate that unusual smoking habits cannot account for the high death rate from lung cancer among these workers:

We have interviewed 320 of the 377 surviving members of the 1942 group. Table 4 gives a summary of the smoking habits in this group compared with a sample of men drawn from the general population of 1,121 counties in 25 states.[7] The union sample is somewhat inadequate since it does not include the men who died

Table 4.—Smoking Habits of 320 Asbestos Workers Exposed to Asbestos Dust 20 Years or Longer
Compared With Sample of Men From the General Population[*]

| Age | Never Smoked Regularly | | Smoked Pipe, Cigar, Never Cigarettes | | History of Cigarette Smoking | |
| --- | --- | --- | --- | --- | --- | --- |
| | Asbestos Workers % | General Population, % | Asbestos Workers, % | General Population, % | Asbestos Workers, % | General Population, % |
| 40-49 | 9.3 | 18.8 | 4.6 | 7.5 | 86.1 | 73.7 |
| 50-59 | 14.3 | 19.9 | 6.1 | 9.9 | 79.6 | 70.2 |
| 60-69 | 20.3 | 23.6 | 10.1 | 16.2 | 69.7 | 60.2 |
| 70+ | 25.5 | 37.1 | 11.8 | 23.9 | 62.7 | 39.0 |

[*]Sample of men from general population as reported by Hammond and Garfinkel.[7]

and does not include all of the present living members of the union. Nevertheless, it shows that a substantial proportion of asbestos workers never smoked cigarettes regularly. Certainly the 632 men in our analysis of death rates were not all heavy cigarette smokers.

In the general male population, lung-cancer death rates are about ten times as high among cigarette smokers as among nonsmokers; and the death rate from lung cancer increases greatly with the amount of cigarette smoking.[8] However, a large proportion of all men in the United States have a history of regular cigarette smoking. From data in a prospective study on smoking,[8] it may be estimated that if all men smoked a pack or more of cigarettes a day (ie, if all the nonsmokers, cigar smokers, pipe smokers, and light cigarette smokers had, instead, been heavy cigarette smokers) the lung-cancer death rate would be approximately 3.4 times as high as it is at this time.

From this we may conclude that even if *all* our asbestos workers had smoked a pack or more of cigarettes a day (and, indeed, from our sample we know they did not), and if exposure to asbestos were of no significance, then their lung cancer death rate would have been about 3.4 times as high as the rate in the general US male population. Clearly, the smoking habits of the asbestos workers cannot account for the fact that their lung-cancer death rate was 6.8 times as high as that of white males in the general population.

*Gastrointestinal Cancer.*—Rather to our surprise, the death rate from cancer of the stomach and the death rate from cancer of the colon and rectum were higher among the asbestos workers than would be expected from the rates reported for the US white male population, calculated in the same way as for lung cancer. Twelve deaths from gastric cancer occurred among the asbestos workers, as compared with only 4.3 expected. Seventeen deaths from cancer of the colon and rectum occurred among the asbestos workers, as compared with 5.2 expected.

*Cancer of All Other Sites.*—The combined death rate from cancer of all sites other than lung and pleura, and stomach, colon, and rectum was not increased. Twenty-one such deaths occurred among asbestos workers, as compared with 20.5 expected.

*Asbestosis.*—Of the 255 deaths, 12 were due to asbestosis (pulmonary insufficiency, cor pulmonale). The elapsed time from first asbestos exposure to death from asbestosis averaged 45.8 years, with a range of 32 to 59 years.

## COMMENT

*Carcinoma of the Lung.*—The results with regard to carcinoma of the lung are clear. Industrial exposure to asbestos by insulation workers, as studied here, results in a marked increase in the incidence of cancer of the lung, approximately six to seven times the expected incidence. Altogether, 45 (17.6%) of 255 men with more than 20 years elapsed since the onset of exposure died of cancer of the lung or pleura.

These data do not give the "incidence of cancer of the lung in asbestosis." They relate to the specific conditions of our investigation: to a group of men with only intermittent exposure to materials containing limited amounts (often 2% to 20%) of asbestos under working conditions varying from very dusty, as in extracting old insulation in closed quarters, to those with little dust exposure, as in building construction in open air. Moreover, they relate to the relatively recent past, in a trade with the shorter work week of the strong building trades unions, in an era when industry has been aware of potential asbestos hazard and the working population has had some consciousness of potential risk associated with dust exposure. These data would not necessarily apply to asbestos exposure in other industries, such as the factory production of asbestos products, the asbestos textile industry, etc, where conditions of employment might be quite different. Our results do not contradict the even higher incidence of lung cancer suggested in other studies[3]; they are merely a shade less striking.

*Diffuse Pleural and Peritoneal Malignancy—Mesothelioma.*—Determining the incidence of diffuse pleural mesothelioma is complicated by the insecurity of its histological verification. While some pathologists will so categorize a high proportion of diffuse pleural tumors, in the experience of others it is a very rare tumor and may be mimicked by anaplastic peripheral carcinoma of the lung and diffuse fibrosarcoma of the pleura. It is difficult to evaluate completely the published reports of diffuse pleural mesothelioma in asbestosis in the absence of complete details of each case.

To the present time, there has been no information concerning the *incidence* of diffuse pleural mesothelioma in asbestosis, since the published cases are reported without reference to a total population in which they occur. Nevertheless, the growing number of reports of individual cases suggests that these tumors are perhaps becoming relatively frequent complications of asbestos exposure.

Our observations in this series are similarly suggestive. In three of the 255 deaths among the men who had worked for 20 years or more, the examining pathologist considered the death due to diffuse pleural mesothelioma, and in the two cases in which we have been able to review the histological material, the histological appearance was that often so categorized, and asbestos bodies were present. This incidence of more than 1% of deaths from pleural mesothelioma is strikingly high for a tumor which is generally considered to be extremely rare. In one case in our series pathological examination suggested diffuse peritoneal mesothelioma. This single experience is too fragmentary for evaluation.

*Gastrointestinal Carcinoma.*—Isolated instances of gastrointestinal carcinoma in the presence of asbestosis have been known, but there have been no data to indicate that these were more than coincidental findings. Among the asbestos workers studied here, cancer of the stomach, colon, and rectum was three times as frequent as expected. These data suggest that there may perhaps be an etiological relationship between industrial asbestos exposure and carcinoma of the gastrointestinal tract.

*Environmental Asbestos Exposure.*—The recent demonstration, by South African[6] and British[9] investigators of pleural and peritoneal neoplasms among individuals who had chance environmental exposure to asbestos many years before raises the very important question of possible widespread carcinogenic air pollution. The possibility of environmental exposure has long been known. Soon after the initial clarification of asbestosis as a clinic entity, Haddow[10] demonstrated asbestos bodies in a man not employed in the industry but living next door to an asbestos factory. This finding was later mirrored in the finding of chronic beryllium disease among residents of a community near a beryllium factory.[11] What is new, however, is an appreciation of the potential extent of the problem. Thomson and associates[12] have reported the frequent findings of asbestos bodies in the lungs of urban dwellers. Among 6,312 individuals x-rayed in an area about an asbestos mine in Finland, Kiviluoto[13] found 499 cases of pleural calcification of the type characteristically seen among asbestos workers, without obvious cause. In a comparable area without any asbestos mine, no cases were found among 7,101 persons x-rayed. It should be noted that these were not people who worked in the mine—none did—but, rather, were farmers, housewives, and others who lived in the general location. In one subject who came to autopsy, polarized-light microscopy demonstrated asbestos fibers in the lung. Similarly, the lung of a cow grazing near the mine also showed the presence of asbestos.

A particular variety of environmental exposure may be of even greater concern. Asbestos exposure in industry will not be limited to the particular craft that utilizes the material. The floating fibers do not respect job classifications. Thus, for example, insulation workers undoubtedly share their exposure with their workmates in other trades; intimate contact with asbestos is possible for electricians, plumbers, sheet-metal workers, steamfitters, laborers, carpenters, boiler makers, and foremen; perhaps even the supervising architect should be included.

1 E 100th St, New York 10029 (Dr. Selikoff).

This study was supported by the Health Research Council of the City of New York.

Cooperating in this investigation were the executive officers of the International Association of Heat and Frost Insulators and Asbestos Workers, Washington, DC, and the officers and membership of the New York and Newark, NJ, locals of this Union.

### References

1. Lynch, K.M., and Smith, W.A.: Pulmonary Asbestosis: Carcinoma of Lung in Asbesto-Silicosis, *Amer J Cancer* 24:56-64 (May) 1935.
2. Annual Report of Chief Inspector of Factories for Year 1955, London: Her Majesty's Stationery Office, 1956, cmnd 8, p 206.
3. Doll, R.: Mortality From Lung Cancer in Asbestos Workers, *Brit J Industr Med* 12:81-86, 1955.
4. Bohlig, H., and Jacob, G.: Neue Gesichtspunkte über den Lungenkrebs der Asbestarbeiter, *Deutsch Med Wschr* 81:231-233 (Feb 17) 1956.
5. Braun, D.C., and Truan, T.D.: Epidemiological Study of Lung Cancer in Asbestos Miners, *AMA Arch Industr Health* 17:634-653 (June) 1958.
6. Wagner, J.C.; Sleggs, C.A.; and Marchand, P.: Diffuse Pleural Mesothelioma and Asbestos Exposure in North Western Cape Province, *Brit J Industr Med* 17:260-271, 1960.
7. Hammond, E.C., and Garfinkel, L.: Smoking Habits of Men and Women, *J Nat Cancer Inst* 27:419-442 (Aug) 1961.
8. Hammond, E.C., and Horn, D.: Smoking and Death Rates: Report on Forty-Four Months of Follow-up of 187,783 Men. I. Total Mortality; II. Death Rates by Cause, *JAMA* 166:1159-1172 (March 8); 1294-1308 (March 15) 1958.
9. McCaughey, W.T.E.; Wade, O.L.; and Elmes, P.C.: Exposure to Asbestos Dust and Diffuse Pleural Mesotheliomas, *Brit Med J* 2:1397 (Nov 24) 1962.
10. Haddow, A.C., in Report of Annual Meeting of British Medical Association, Manchester, 1929, *Lancet* 2:230-231 (Aug 3) 1929.
11. Chesner, C.: Chronic Pulmonary Granulomatosis in Residents of Community Near Beryllium Plant: Three Autopsied Cases, *Ann Intern Med* 32:1028-1048 (June) 1950.
12. Thomson, J.G.; Kaschula, R.O.C.; and MacDonald, R.R.: Asbestos as Modern Urban Hazard, *S Afr Med J* 37:77-81 (Jan 19) 1963.
13. Kiviluoto, R.: Pleural Calcification as Roentgenologic Sign of Non-Occupational Endemic Anthophyllite-Asbestosis, *Acta Radiol* Suppl 194, pp 1-67, 1960.

# Asbestos*

## Industrial Asset With a Health Cost

William R. Barclay, MD

Asbestos is a useful, even indispensable component of many materials with which we come into daily contact. It has unique properties of heat resistance and durability and is cheap and abundant. Unfortunately, it is a serious threat to the health of those who handle it carelessly over a long period of time, and its dangers went unrecognized for many years after it was put into widespread use.

The first ill effect to be recognized in asbestos workers was pulmonary fibrosis, termed *asbestosis,* and between 1906 and 1928, sporadic case reports of asbestosis appeared in the medical literature. These reports stimulated the Ministry of Labour in Great Britain to undertake a detailed study of asbestos workers. Merewether and Price[1] reported this study in 1930, and, of 363 asbestos textile workers examined, 26.2% were found to have roentgenographic evidence of pulmonary fibrosis. In 1937, the Public Health Service undertook a similar investigation[2] and demonstrated a dose-response relationship between exposure to airborne particles of asbestos and clinical symptoms of pulmonary damage. From this study, an exposure limit to asbestos fibers for workers in industry was established.

Although pulmonary fibrosis and pleural plaques seen on chest x-ray films came to be recognized as frequently being caused by inhalation of asbestos fibers, they did not necessarily correlate with disability or even with nondisabling symptoms of cough and shortness of breath. Therefore, no great concern was aroused in asbestos workers, the public, industry management, or public health authorities.

In 1935, Lynch and Smith[3] in the United States and Gloyne[4] in England reported cancer of the lung in workers who had died of asbestosis. Other reports linking asbestosis and cancer of the lung appeared, and in 1947, Merewether and Price[5] reported a 17.8%

occurrence of lung cancer in workers who died of asbestosis. In 1955, Doll[6] reported 11 deaths by lung cancer in 113 workers who had been exposed to asbestos for more than 20 years.

Early reports that link exposure to a substance and the occurrence of a disease are often not generally accepted as proof of a cause-and-effect relationship. This is particularly so when a long latent period exists between exposure and the appearance of a disease. A well-designed and carefully executed study was needed to persuade physicians, public health authorities, and industrial management that asbestos was indeed a potent carcinogen. Such a study was reported by Selikoff and co-workers[7] in 1964 and is reprinted in this issue of THE JOURNAL as a LANDMARK ARTICLE.

The Selikoff study showed that workers exposed to asbestos for 20 or more years had a notable increase in the occurrence of cancer of the lung and also increases in mesotheliomas and cancers of the digestive tract. This article is a landmark in the medical literature because it established without any doubt that asbestos is a carcinogen, and it became the basis on which even stricter exposure limits were set for asbestos.

The long latent period between exposure to a carcinogen and the appearance of cancer, and synergism between carcinogens, eg, asbestos and tobacco smoke, create difficult legal, social, and legislative problems. A patient with cancer may have worked over the course of his lifetime in several industries and have been exposed to more than one carcinogen in widely varying concentrations. In addition, the patient may have a long history of smoking cigarettes. Where then should the blame for the cancer be placed? Should one or several employers be forced to pay compensation, or should the patient accept the blame because of having smoked? Asbestos is so widely used and in so many products indispensable to a technologically advanced society that perhaps society as a whole through legislation should accept responsibility for the adverse health effects of asbestos rather than laying the blame on a single industry.

Dr Barclay is editor emeritus of *JAMA.*
*A commentary on Selikoff IJ, Churg J, Hammond EC: Asbestos exposure and neoplasia. *JAMA* 1964;188:22-26.

There is a problem that involves not just asbestos but many substances that are in current use and that physicians suspect are the cause of cancer, sterility, birth defects, hypersensitivity, nerve damage, or target organ damage. The physician's responsibility with respect to exposure hazards is clear: any unusual cluster of cases with similar signs and symptoms should not be regarded as coincidence but be reported and then followed up by public health authorities. Ultimately, when several reports appear in the literature linking a suspect substance and a disease, a definitive study such as that of Selikoff and colleagues must be undertaken so that industry and government have indisputable evidence on which to take action that will limit exposure to a proved hazard without curtailing the use of suspect but relatively nontoxic substances that are of value to society.

## References

1. Merewether ERA, Price CW: *Report on the Effect of Asbestos Dust on the Lungs and Dust Suppression in the Asbestos Industry: Occurrence of Pulmonary Fibrosis and Other Pulmonary Affections in Asbestos Workers.* London, H. M. Stationary Office, 1930.

2. Dressen WC, DallaValle JM, Edwards TJ, et al: A study of asbestosis in the asbestos textile industry. *Public Health Bull,* 1938.

3. Lynch KM, Smith WA: Pulmonary asbestosis: III. Carcinoma of the lung on asbestosis-silicosis. *Am J Cancer* 1935;14:56-64.

4. Gloyne SR: Two cases of squamous carcinoma of the lung occurring in asbestosis. *Tubercle* 1935;17:5-10.

5. Merewether ERA, Price CW: *Annual Report of the Chief Inspector of Factories in England 1947.* London, H. M. Stationary Office, 1947.

6. Doll R: Mortality from lung cancer in asbestos workers. *Br J Ind Med* 1955;12:81-86.

7. Selikoff IJ, Churg J, Hammond EC: Asbestos exposure and neoplasia. *JAMA* 1964;188:22-26.

'eb 15, 1965
*JAMA* 1965;191:541-546)

# Chapter 48

# A "New" Antigen in Leukemia Sera

Baruch S. Blumberg, MD, Harvey J. Alter, MD, and Sam Visnich

The "Australia antigen" is found in the sera of some normal individuals from foreign populations. The total absence of the antigen from the sera of normal United States subjects and its relatively high frequency in acute leukemia suggests that the presence of the antigen may be of value in the diagnosis of early acute leukemia. Whether the antigen results from or precedes the leukemia process remains to be seen.

Patients who receive large numbers of transfusions for anemia and other causes may develop precipitins in their blood. These precipitins may react in agar gel double diffusion experiments with specific human serum lipoprotein found in the blood of other individuals. Since these precipitins were found only in patients who had received transfusions they were thought to be antibodies against serum lipoproteins which developed in the patients as a result of the repeated transfusions. The precipitin is referred to as an isoprecipitin since it develops against a specificity found in an individual from the same species. The antilipoprotein isoprecipitin[1,2] developed in approximately 30% of 47 patients with thalassemia who had received transfusions. Isoprecipitins also developed in a smaller number of transfused patients with other diseases. All precipitins stained with sudan black, a dye specific for lipid. Immunoelectrophoretic and ultracentrifugal studies showed that the protein with which the isoprecipitins reacted was a low density lipoprotein. The reactor specificity associated with the beta lipoprotein is inherited as an autosomal-dominant trait and several lipoprotein specificities have been found.[3-5]

In 1963, sera from patients with hemophilia who had received transfusions were tested for the presence of isoprecipitins using a panel of 24 sera from normal individuals, including sera from foreign populations. Two of the hemophilia sera formed a clearly defined precipi-

tin line with one of the panel sera (from an Australian aborigine), but with none of the others. In contrast to the usual findings the precipitin line stained only faintly with sudan black; it did, however, stain with azo carmine, a general protein stain (Fig 1). Subsequent studies have shown that this protein system differs from that detected with the antilipoprotein antisera. The serum protein with which the hemophilia isoprecipitin reacts has not been fully characterized and has been tentatively called the "Australia antigen." This paper will describe the epidemiologic and immunologic aspects of the Australia antigen-isoprecipitin system.

## MATERIALS AND METHODS

Double diffusion in agar gel was done using a micro-Ouchterlony technique on lantern slides.[5] Each of the two hemophilia sera containing the isoprecipitin was placed in the center well of a seven-hole micro-Ouchterlony pattern. The sera to be tested for presence of Australia antigen were placed in the peripheral wells. When a panel of antigen-containing sera were identified in this manner, they in turn were each placed in the center wells of similar seven-hole Ouchterlony patterns, and the sera of patients who had received transfusions, which were to be tested for the presence of isoprecipitins, were placed in the peripheral wells. In the final testing program two sera-containing Australia antigens which reacted with all the hemophilia antisera first discovered, were selected to screen for the remaining antisera. Two of the strongest hemophilia antisera were used in screening for the sera containing Australia antigen. In screening for antilipoprotein antisera, the sera from patients who had received transfusions were tested using a panel of 24 sera selected from four or more population

From the Institute for Cancer Research, Philadelphia (Dr. Blumberg), and the National Institutes of Health, Bethesda, Md (Dr. Alter and Mr. Visnich).

Reprint requests to 7701 Burholme Ave, Philadelphia 19111 (Dr. Blumberg).

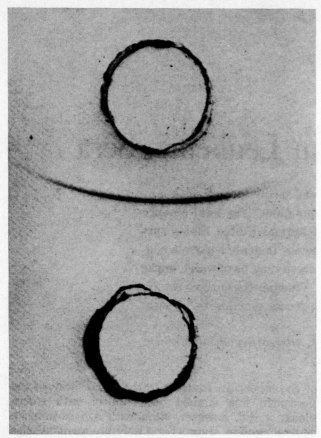

1. Formation of precipitin line between serum from leukemia patient (top well) and hemophilia serum (bottom well).

groups as in previous studies.[2]

Immunoelectrophoresis was done by a modification of the method of Grabar and Williams.[6] The precipitin lines were first stained with sudan black and then with azo carmine.[7] Sera were fractionated by ultracentrifugation in high density salt medium.[8] Fractions with a specific gravity greater and less than 1.063 were prepared.

A total of 28 hemophilia sera were studied. These included samples from patients from Mt. Sinai Hospital, NY, New York Hospital, and the Clinical Center of the National Institutes of Health. They were all United States whites and had all received transfusions many times with fresh frozen plasma and whole blood obtained from the hospital blood banks as well as commercial sources. The

racial makeup of the donors could not be known with certainty, but they probably included United States whites and Negroes. The hemophilia serum used in the immunoelectrophoresis experiments contained antibodies against both lipoproteins and the Australia antigen. It was obtained from a patient (1) who had received more than 900 transfusions.

The sources of some of the normal sera used in the studies are given in the Tables. The sera from patients were obtained at the Clinical Center, National Institutes of Health, New York Hospital, and elsewhere. The calculation of the probability value was done by using two by two tables and Fisher's $\chi$-square method.

### RESULTS

*Frequency of the Isoprecipitin.*—The sera of 107 patients who had received approximately ten or more transfusions, and of 150 normal individuals who had not received transfusions, were tested for the presence of the Australia isoprecipitin (Table 1). Eleven isoprecipitin containing sera were found in the patient group; none was found in the normal population. Of these 11, eight were patients with hemophilia, one had plasma thromboplastin component deficiency disease (PTC), one thalassemia, and one aplastic anemia. The frequency is highest in the hemophilia and related PTC group, and the difference from the other groups combined is statistically significant ($P < 0.001$). It had previously been found that the frequency of antilipoprotein isoprecipitin was very high in thalassemia as opposed to other patient groups.[2] Hemophilia sera containing the Australia isoprecipitin were tested for the presence of antibeta lipoprotein; they were found to have an incidence similar to other patients who did not have thalassemia. Only one of the patients in the latter group had an anti-Australia antigen isoprecipitin.

There were two sera which contained both antilipoprotein and anti-Australia antigen isoprecipitins. This is approximately the number expected by chance.

*Frequency of Antigen.*—A total of 1,704 sera from nonhospitalized and presumably normal subjects were tested for the presence of Australia antigen using at least two, and generally more antisera (Table 2). Reactors were found only in Oceanic, Oriental, and Mediterranean populations, and in one from the American Indian population. No reactors were found among the approximately 700 United States sera tested including cord

Table 1.—Isoprecipitins in Patients Who Had Received Transfusions Which React With the Australia Antigen and With Lipoproteins

| Disease | Antibody to Australia Antigen | | | | Antibody to Lipoprotein | | | |
|---|---|---|---|---|---|---|---|---|
| | Total | Present | Absent | % Present | Total | Present | Absent | % Present |
| Hemophilia | 28 | 8 | 20 | 28.6 | 31 | 3 | 28 | 9.7 |
| PTC° | 2 | 1 | 1 | .... | 2 | 0 | 2 | .... |
| Thalassemia | 48 | 1 | 47 | 2.1 | 47 | 14 | 33 | 29.8 |
| Other Diseases | 29 | 1 | 28 | 3.4 | 33 | 3 | 30 | 9.1 |
| Total | 107 | 11 | 96 | 10.3 | 113 | 20 | 93 | 17.7 |
| Normal controls | 150 | 0 | 150 | 0 | 200 | 0 | 200 | 0 |

°Plasma thromboplastin component deficiency disease.

serum from 18 newborns. The highest frequencies were found in a small group of native Taiwanese and in Australian aborigines. All of these tests were done on stored sera.

Sera from a total of 659 patients with various illnesses were tested against one or more of the antisera as shown in Table 3. Of the ten reactors found, eight had leukemia (including one patient with a diagnosis of both acute lymphocytic leukemia and multiple myeloma, and one patient with a newly described preleukemia syndrome associated with a missing chromosome in marrow cells,[10]) and two had thalassemia. These patients with thalassemia were siblings whose parents were born in Greece. As noted in Table 2, the frequency of reactors in presumably normal Greeks is 4%. The difference between the frequency in leukemia patients and that in all the disease groups combined is statistically significant ($P < 0.001$). All of the patients with the Australia antigen had received transfusions. However, approximately 300 of the patients who did not have the Australia antigen had also received transfusions.

The leukemia sera were studied in greater detail. The antigen was found in all the larger subclassifications with the exception of chronic myelogenous leukemia. The patients with reacting sera were of both sexes, and their ages at the time of the diagnoses varied from 6 to 55 years. Of the ten patients in whom the antigen was found, eight are now dead, including all but one of the eight patients with leukemia, and one of the patients with thalassemia.

A total of 54 patients with acute leukemia were studied. Of these, six had the Australia antigen and were all dead. Of the 49 who did not have the Australia antigen, 19 were dead. The sample size is too small to permit adequate corrections for age, duration and intensity of disease, and other factors, but there does appear to be a gross difference with respect to mortality between these two groups.

*Characteristics of Antibody and Antigen.*—The original isoprecipitin-containing sera and the reacting sera had been found using specimens which had been collected and stored at −20 C for various lengths of time up to three years. Several specimens collected at different times were subsequently obtained from patients who had received transfusions and whose sera contained the isoprecipitins, and from patients with leukemia and normal subjects whose sera contained the Australia antigen. These studies showed that the isoprecipitin was present in sera or plasmas which had been stored at −20 C for up to 27 months. The Australia antigen was present in fresh sera as well as in sera or plasmas stored for up to six years. These studies also indicate that within the limits of observations, the presence of the Australia antigen is essentially an invariant characteristic of the individual; that is, if it is present at one point in time, it is present when tested subsequently.

The isoprecipitin appears to be a 7S γ-globulin.[9] Australia antigen migrates in the beta and slow α-globulin region on immunoelectrophoresis, but can readily be distinguished from the antigen which reacts with the antilipoprotein isoprecipitin found in the serum of patient 2[1] as shown in Fig 2. (The top basin contains the

antilipoprotein antiserum from patient 2,[4] and the second basin serum from hemophilia patient 1. The latter has isoprecipitins directed against both the Australia antigen and lipoprotein. The electrophoresis well contains the serum of a patient with leukemia which reacts with serum from patient 2 and with both of the isoprecipitins in serum from patient 1. Two distinct lines of slightly different mobility were seen between the sera of patients 1 and 3. The lower one, which stains blue with sudan

Table 2.—Australia Antigen in Normal Populations

| Population | No. Tested | Australia Antigen Present | |
|---|---|---|---|
| | | No. | % |
| Aborigines, Australia | 208 | 12 | 6 |
| Chinese, USA and Taiwan | 65 | 0 | 0 |
| Eskimo, Alaska[13] | 24 | 0 | 0 |
| Greeks, Greece[14] | 179 | 8 | 4 |
| Indians, Canada[15] | 78 | 0 | 0 |
| Indians, Mexico | 100 | 1 | 1 |
| Israelis | 96 | 2 | 2 |
| Japanese, USA | 48 | 0 | 0 |
| Koreans | 1 | 1 | |
| Micronesians, Rongelap[16] | 193 | 7 | 4 |
| Negro, USA[17] | 241 | 0 | 0 |
| Newborn children, white | 18 | 0 | 0 |
| Polynesians, Bora Bora | 24 | 1 | 4 |
| Samaritans, Israel[18] | 125 | 2 | 2 |
| Taiwanese | 23 | 3 | 13 |
| Tristan da Cunha Islanders | 42 | 0 | 0 |
| Vietnamese | 24 | 1 | 4 |
| White, USA (NIH° employees) | 215 | 0 | 0 |
| **Total** | **1,704** | **38** | |

°National Institutes of Health.

Table 3.—Australia Antigen in Patients

| Disease | No. Tested | Australia Antigen Present | |
|---|---|---|---|
| | | No. | % |
| Abetalipoproteinemia | 4 | 0 | 0 |
| Amyotrophic lateral sclerosis | 15 | 0 | 0 |
| Anemia | 18 | 0 | 0 |
| Arthritis, various° | 15 | 0 | 0 |
| Cancer (other than leukemia) | 47 | 0 | 0 |
| "Connective tissue" disorders† | 5 | 0 | 0 |
| Diabetes | 96 | 0 | 0 |
| Hemophilia | 24 | 0 | 0 |
| Hypercholesterolemia | 17 | 0 | 0 |
| Leukemia | 70 | 8‡ | 11.4 |
| Acute myelogenous | 17 | 4 | |
| Acute lymphocytic | 38 | 2 | |
| Chronic myelogenous | 10 | 0 | |
| Chronic lymphocytic | 3 | 1 | |
| 45 chromosomes[10] | 2 | 1 | |
| Lupus erythematosis | 69 | 0 | 0 |
| Multiple myeloma and macroglobulinemia | 93 | 1‡ | 1.1 |
| Myasthenia gravis | 11 | 0 | 0 |
| Rheumatic fever | 124 | 0 | 0 |
| Tangiers Island disease | 3 | 0 | 0 |
| Thalassemia | 48 | 2 | 4.2 |
| **Total** | **659** | **10** | |

°Includes eight patients with rheumatoid arthritis, three with psoriatic arthritis, and four with Sjögren's disease.

†Other than lupus erythematosis.

‡One patient had both chronic lymphocytic leukemia and multiple myeloma, and is included in both categories.

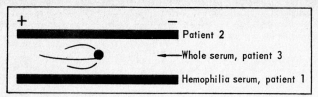

2. Diagram of immunoelectrophoresis experiment: antilipoprotein (patient 2), leukemia (patient 3), and anti-Australia antigen (patient 1).

black, corresponds to the patient 2 lipoprotein line. The upper one, which stains only faintly or not at all with sudan black, does stain with azo carmine. Using the hemophilia serum from patient 1 (see above), two distinct lines with slightly different mobilities can be seen. One of these stains blue with sudan black and corresponds to the lipoprotein antigen which reacts with patient 2. The other, which has a slightly different mobility and a different curvature, does not stain with sudan black, but does stain with azo carmine. In addition, a reaction of nonidentity can be demonstrated by immunodiffusion when the Australia isoprecipitin system is compared with the typical lipoprotein precipitin as shown in Fig 3. (The serum of patient 2 contains an antilipoprotein isoprecipitin. The serum of a patient with thalassemia with an isoprecipitin against Australia antigen is in the top right hand well. The serum of the Australian aborigines has both the specific lipoprotein and the Australian antigen. The patient-2 line stains blue with sudan black and the patient-4 line stains red with azo carmine.) Additional characteristics of the Australia antigen and a method for its partial isolation are described in another paper.[9]

*Specificity.*—To determine if the antisera had different specificities, they were all tested against the same antigen placed in the center well of a seven-hole-

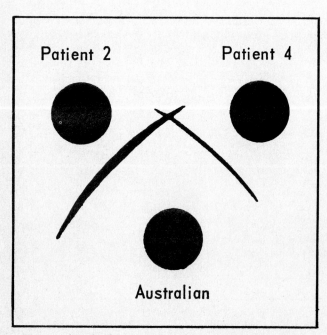

3. Diagram of Ouchterlony experiment showing crossing of antilipoprotein (patient 2) and anti-Australia antigen (patient 4) lines.

Ouchterlony pattern. No crossing of lines were seen between the antisera. Similar experiments were used to compare the Australia antigen found in the presumably normal subjects with that found in the leukemia patients and no differences could be detected. On the basis of these initial experiments, we have not been able to detect any specific differences between the various antisera, nor between the Australia antigen found in normal persons and in leukemia patients.

*Family Studies.*—The studies on normal populations were done on sera collected on field trips for other purposes and stored in the Institutes serum bank. In some cases, family sera were available, and the results were analyzed to determine if there was a family aggregation of Australia antigen. Batsheva Bonné examined 125 sera from Samaritans living near Tel Aviv, Israel[18] (Fig 4). This represented nearly all the members of this highly inbred community. Of these, two siblings who were the offsprings of a consanguineous marriage (both of whose parents were double cousins) were the only individuals with detectable antigen. In the Micronesian population, there was one father and son affected, but in the five other cases the individuals were only remotely related or unrelated. The reactors in the Greek study were not apparently closely related. Of the 47 patients with thalassemia studied, only two were positive, and they were siblings. Their parents and one aunt were not reactors. The two brothers of one of the patients with leukemia with the Australia antigen did not react with the antisera.

#### Comment

A second kind of isoprecipitin system has been revealed by this study. The Australia antigen with which the isoprecipitin reacts differs from the lipoprotein antigens previously described and the distribution of isoprecipitins and reactors in patients and in normal populations is very different from that found for the lipoprotein system.

It has not been firmly established that the isoprecipitin in the hemophilia sera is an antibody nor that the protein with which it reacts is an antigen. However, by analogy with the lipoprotein system, it is probable that this is the case and these terms have been used in describing the system.

In our discussions it has been assumed that the "antibody" is present in the sera of patients with hemophilia and other patients, and the "antigen" in the leukemia and normal sera. This appears likely since the patients with hemophilia and other patients had all received transfusions whereas some of the individuals in whose sera the Australia antigen was found had not. The possibility still remains, however, that the rare normal sera and leukemia sera actually contain an antibody against an antigen present in hemophilia patients. It is hoped that further studies with patients with hemophilia may help resolve this point.

The high incidence of this isoprecipitin in the hemophilia-patient group suggests that either hemophilia per se predisposes to the formation of the isoprecipitin or that the administration of fresh frozen plasma (which distinguishes the treatment of hemophilia and PTC patients from the other individuals who had received transfusions)

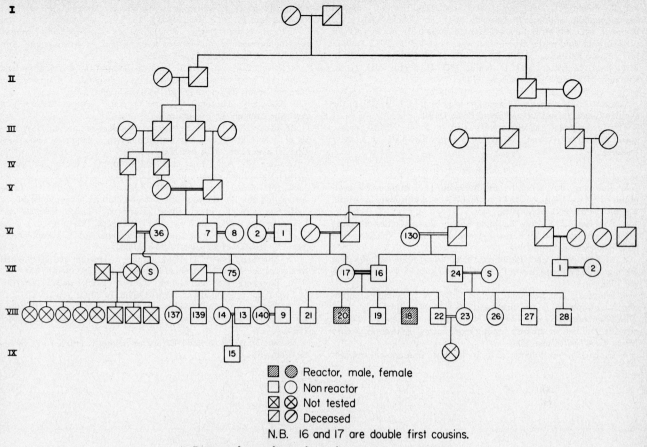

I
II
III
IV
V
VI
VII
VIII
IX

[36] [7] [8] [2] [1] [130]

[S] [75] [17] [16] [24] [S] [1] [2]

[137] [139] [14] [13] [140] [9] [21] [20] [19] [18] [22] [23] [26] [27] [28]

[15]

◪ ◉ Reactor, male, female
□ ○ Non reactor
⊠ ⊗ Not tested
◪ ⊘ Deceased

N.B. 16 and 17 are double first cousins.

4. Portion of a pedigree from the Samaritan community,
representative of nearly all members, showing the presence of
the Australia antigen and the close interrelation of the parents.

particularly predisposes to the formation of the antibody. Preliminary evidence suggests that the Australia antigenic sites may be revealed by a freezing process which leads to the denaturation of lipoprotein. This possibility will be discussed in another paper.[9]

The high incidence of the Australia antigen in the leukemia population as compared with normals or other patient populations suggests either that; (1) persons with the Australia antigen have an increased susceptibility to the development of leukemia, or (2) the antigen itself is a manifestation of the disease process, perhaps secondary to an alteration in some normal serum constituent with a resultant change in antigenic configuration, or (3) the Australia antigen is related to the virus which has been suggested as the cause of leukemia.

The first hypothesis implies that the Australia antigen is present in a patient before he develops signs and symptoms of leukemia. The long-term observations necessary to support this possibility have not yet been made. The Micronesian, Samaritan, and Australian aborigine populations would be suitable for such a study. In the case of the "preleukemic"[10] (Table 4) patient the presence of the Australia antigen predated the development of frank leukemia.

Changes in red blood cell antigens during the course of leukemia lend indirect support to the hypothesis that the Australia antigen results from, rather than precedes the leukemia process. Many authors have demonstrated alterations in red blood cell ABO specificities during the course of leukemia.[11] More recently, it has been shown that there is a loss of I specificity on the red blood cells of certain patients with leukemia.[12] The I antigen is almost universally present in normals and patients with other diseases.

The third hypothesis is being tested in collaboration with workers at the National Institutes of Health.

The total absence of the Australia antigen from normal United States subjects studied and its relatively high frequency in acute leukemia suggests that the presence of the antigen may be of value in the diagnosis of early acute leukemia.

The available data are too few to support a genetic hypothesis, but none of the family studies are inconsistent with simple recessive inheritance of the specificity.

Summary

An isoprecipitin is present in the sera of many patients with hemophilia who have received transfusions. It reacts with a protein (the "Australia antigen") that is found in the sera of some normal individuals from foreign populations but is absent in sera of the United States populations studied. It is found in approximately 10% of patients with leukemia.

R. Rosenfield, MD, and E. Smith, MD, of Mt. Sinai Hospital provided the hemophilia antisera. P. Carbone, MD, E. Cohen, MD, E. J. Freireich, MD, and A. B. Rey, MD, provided the leukemia sera. Other valuable sera used in the experiments were provided by T. D. Dublin, MD, Marion Erlandson, MD, J. Fahey, MD, H. H. Fudenberg, MD, R. Kirk, PhD, L. Laster, MD, L. Rosen, MD, C. Sheba, MD, N. R. Shulman, MD, and A. G. Steinberg, PhD.

Samples of sera on patient 1 were provided by J. M. Hill, MD, of the Wadley Research Institute and Blood Bank, Dallas.

This investigation was supported in part by Public Health Service grants CA-08069-01 and CA-06551-02 from the National Cancer Institute.

### References

1. Blumberg, B.S.; Dray, S.; and Robinson, J.C.: Antigen Polymorphism of a Low-Density Beta-Lipoprotein. Allotypy in Human Serum, *Nature* **194**:656-658 (May) 1962.

2. Blumberg, B. S., et al: Multiple Antigenic Specificities of Serum Lipoproteins Detected With Sera of Transfused Patients, *Vox Sanguinis* **9**:128-145 (March-April) 1964.

3. Allison, A.C., and Blumberg, B.S.: Isoprecipitation Reaction Distinguishing Human Serum Protein Types, *Lancet* **1**:634-637 (March 25) 1961.

4. Blumberg, B.S.; Bernanke, D.; and Allison, A.C.: Human Lipoprotein Polymorphism. *J Clin Invest* **41**:1936-1944 (Oct) 1962.

5. Blumberg, B.S., and Riddell, N.M.: Inherited Antigenic Differences in Human Serum Beta Lipoproteins. Second Antiserum, *J Clin Invest* **42**:867-875 (June) 1963.

6. Grabar, P., and Williams, C.A., Jr.: Methode Immuno-electrophoretique d'analyse de Melanges de Substances Antigeniques. *Biochim Biophys Acta* **17**:67-74 (May) 1955.

7. Uriel, J., and Grabar, P.: *Emploi de colorants dans l'analyse electrophoretique et immuno-electrophoretique en milieu gélifié*, *Ann Inst Pasteur* **90**:427-440 (April) 1956.

8. Havel, R.J.; Eder, H.A.; and Bragdon, J.H.: Distribution and Chemical Composition of Ultracentrifugally Separated Lipoproteins in Human Serum, *J Clin Invest* **34**:1345-1353 (Sept) 1955.

9. Alter, H.J.; Blumberg, B.S.; and Visnich, S.: Further Studies With Australia Antigen: To be published.

10. Freireich, E.J., et al: Refractory Anemia, Granulocytic Hyperplasia of Bone Marrow and Missing Chromosome in Marrow Cells. New Clinical Syndrome? *Clin Res* **12**:284, 1964.

11. Richards, A.G.: Loss of Blood Group B Antigen in Chronic Lymphocytic Leukaemia, *Lancet* **2**:178-179 (July 28) 1962.

12. McGinniss, M.H.; Schmidt, P.J.; and Carbone, P.P.: Close Association of I Blood Group and Disease, *Nature*, to be published.

13. Corcoran, P., et al: Blood Groups of Alaskan Eskimos and Indians, *Amer J Phys Anthrop* **17**:187-193 (Sept) 1959.

14. Barnicot, N.A., et al: Haemoglobin Types in Greek Populations, *Ann Human Genet* **26**:229-236 (Feb) 1963.

15. Blumberg, B.S., et al: Blood Groups of Naskapi and Montagnais Indians of Schefferville, Quebec, *Human Biol* **36**:263 (Sept) 1964.

16. Blumberg, B.S., and Gentile, Z.: Haptoglobins and Transferrins of Two Tropical Populations, *Nature* **189**:897-899 (March 18) 1961.

17. Cooper, A.J., et al: Biochemical Polymorphic Traits in US White and Negro Population, *Amer J Human Genetics* **15**:420-428 (Dec) 1963.

18. Bonné, B.: Samaritans: Demographic Study, *Human Biol* **36**:61-89 (Feb) 1963.

# The Australia Antigen*

Thomas J. Gill III, MD, David E. Jenkins, Jr, MD

The article by Blumberg and associates describing the antigen that was ultimately found to be associated with infection by the hepatitis B virus (HBV)[1] presents a classic example of serendipity in scientific research and the fact that "chance favors the prepared mind." It also presents a fascinating insight into the nature of the scientific process and the way in which important discoveries are made.[2]

The work was careful, logical, and meticulous. It provided solid evidence for the presence of an antigenic system that was later identified as that of the HBV. The initial interpretation of the work was colored by a fortuitous association between the presence of the antigen and patients with leukemia. However, Blumberg and colleagues quickly grasped the true significance of their finding, ie, that the presence of the antigen was associated with blood transfusion and the subsequent development of hepatitis. Their observations became a new paradigm for studies into the pathogenesis of hepatitis and its consequences. The spate of clinical and laboratory investigations that followed this discovery greatly increased our knowledge about viral hepatitis in general and posttransfusion hepatitis in particular. This has revolutionized the practice of blood banking throughout the world. Other studies have clearly established the important interrelationship between hepatitis B, postnecrotic cirrhosis, and hepatocellular carcinoma. Therapeutic means of controlling hepatitis B have also been developed: initially, hepatitis B immune globulin, and more recently, a vaccine for prevention of the disease.

## The Original Observations

Blumberg and colleagues were not searching for a specific marker for hepatitis but rather for a genetic marker that would be useful in population studies, since the major focus of investigation in their laboratory had been population genetics. They were aware that precipitating antibodies developed in the blood of patients who received large numbers of blood transfusions, and they had previously shown that antibodies ("isoprecipitins")

against a serum lipoprotein had developed in approximately 30% of patients with thalassemia who received blood transfusions. It was in further pursuit of this line of study that the discovery of the Australia antigen was made. These investigators had at their disposal only the simplest of the tools of modern immunochemistry — double diffusion in agar ("Ouchterlony plates") and immunoelectrophoresis — and serum resources from their extensive past population studies. Both resources were used perceptively, but some of the epidemiologic data led to the incorrect assumption that the new antigen was associated with leukemia per se and was found in normal serum samples from foreign populations but not from normal subjects in the United States.

In their initial work on the lipoprotein antigen, they demonstrated that serum samples from patients with thalassemia who received multiple transfusions formed precipitates by immunodiffusion against normal sera. These precipitates stained with Sudan black, a dye specific for lipids. In the studies that resulted in the discovery of the Australia antigen, they tested serum samples from patients with hemophilia who had received multiple transfusions against a panel of serum samples from apparently normal persons. Two of the hemophilia samples reacted with one normal sample from an Australian aborigine — hence, the name *Australia antigen*. The key points in the identifying the Australia antigen as different from the previously identified lipoprotein antigen were as follows: (1) The antibody-antigen complex formed by immunodiffusion did not stain with Sudan black but did stain with azocarmine, a general protein stain. (2) Australia antigen gave a reaction of nonidentity with serum lipoprotein antigen by immunodiffusion. (3) The Australia antigen migrated throughout the slow $\alpha$- and $\beta$-globulin regions by immunoelectrophoresis, whereas the serum lipoprotein antigen migrated only in the $\beta$-globulin region. At this point, it was still not unequivocal that these precipitin reactions represented antibody-antigen interactions, although circumstantial evidence favored this interpretation. Nor was it clear whether the serum samples from the patients with hemophilia or the serum from the Australian aborigine contained the antibody. Subsequent studies[3] show that the samples from the hemophiliacs contained the antibody that was characterized as a 7S $\gamma$-globulin.

Their epidemiologic studies provided clear evidence for a relationship between blood transfusion and the serum antibody reacting with Australia antigen. How-

From the Departments of Pathology (Dr Gill) and Pathology and Medicine (Dr Jenkins), University of Pittsburgh School of Medicine, and the Central Blood Bank of Pittsburgh (Dr Jenkins).

*A commentary on Blumberg BS, Alter HJ, Visnich S: A 'new' antigen in leukemia sera. *JAMA* 1965;191:541-546.

ever, the initial epidemiologic studies were misleading in identifying the source of the antigen. In screening 1,704 serum samples from normal populations, Australia antigen was found in samples from Australian aborigines, Greeks, Micronesians, and Taiwanese but not from the US population, which made up approximately 35% of the normal samples studied. This finding was probably due, in retrospect, to the higher prevalence of hepatitis in the other populations studied compared with the US population. In 659 patients with various diseases, the Australia antigen was found in eight (11.4%) of 70 patients with different types of leukemia, two (4.2%) of 48 patients with thalassemia, and one (1.1%) of 93 patients with multiple myeloma or macroglobulinemia. Because of the higher incidence in leukemia, the authors postulated a possible relationship between Australia antigen and this disease. The high frequency of the antigen in patients with leukemia and the always powerful urge to discover a "cancer marker" initially obscured recognition of the strong relationship between Australia antigen positivity and a previous history of blood transfusion. Also overlooked was the prevalence of this antigen in normal persons from populations in which leukemia was not particularly prone to develop but with high endemic rates of infectious diseases.

Epidemiologic studies provided further evidence that Australia antigen was different from the previously described serum lipoprotein antigen because the distributions of the serum samples containing the antibody and those containing the antigen were very different for both antigenic systems in normal populations and in patients with various diseases. Family studies did not provide any clear data for a genetic factor being operative in the Australia antigen system, whereas the serum lipoprotein antigen was inherited as an autosomal dominant trait and had several specificities.[4] In retrospect, the familial aggregations of Australia antigen-positive persons that were found are best explained on the basis of the environmental transmission of an infectious agent.

### The Impact of the Observations

The impact of the discovery of Australia antigen on scientific investigation and medical practice was almost immediate. The work defining the entity was done in 1963-1964, and the classic article describing the Australia antigen was published in 1965.[1] The initial hypothesis derived from the epidemiologic data was that Australia antigen was a marker for leukemia. On the assumption that persons in whom leukemia has a high likelihood of developing would be more likely to have Australia antigen, Blumberg and colleagues studied a group of children with Down's syndrome, since leukemia has a much higher probability of developing in them than in other children. In a group of such patients in a large institution, they found that the Australia antigen was very common (approximately 30%).[3] Then, in early 1966, the test result of a patient with Down's syndrome that had originally been Australia antigen negative became Australia antigen positive when tested for a second time, and a chronic form of anicteric hepatitis developed. This observation provided strong suggestive evidence for a relationship between Australia antigen and hepatitis, so a study employing liver biopsy and serum enzyme measurements in a population of patients with Down's syndrome and in a large normal population was undertaken. It showed that many patients with hepatitis had Australia antigen in their blood early in the course of their disease and that the disease was caused by the transmission of an infectious agent. At approximately the same time, a technician in their laboratory became ill and tested her own serum for Australia antigen. It was positive, and hepatitis developed: thus, she became the first patient whose condition was diagnosed as hepatitis by the Australia antigen test.[2]

By early 1967, Blumberg and associates[2] had established a connection between Australia antigen and hepatitis, and they suggested that the infectious agent was a virus. Shortly thereafter, Okochi and Murakami[5] found that Australia antigen could be transmitted by blood transfusion, that it was associated with the development of hepatitis in some of the patients who had received transfusions, and that antibody to Australia antigen appeared in the serum of these patients. Other investigators[6,7] and further work by Blumberg and colleagues[2] confirmed the relationship between Australia antigen and posttransfusional hepatitis.

The viral etiology of hepatitis, which had eluded detection by conventional virological techniques, was established by electron microscopy[2,8] by the discovery in 1968-1970 of several types of viral particles that reacted with antisera to Australia antigen. The differential presence of hepatitis B surface antigen (HBsAg), antibodies to the surface antigen, and antibodies to hepatitis B core antigen (HBcAg) were used to identify acute and chronic infections and to define the carrier state. The role of antibody-viral antigen complexes in immune complex disease was also recognized. Finally, in 1975, the association between viral hepatitis and primary hepatic carcinoma, which had been suggested by a variety of investigators in Africa,[9] and the importance of the maternal transmission of the virus were established by Blumberg and collaborators[2] and by Ohbayashi and colleagues.[10]

Almost immediately, the efficacy of immune globulin in preventing hepatitis was recognized,[2,5] and the development of a vaccine was undertaken. In 1972, a patent was issued to Blumberg and associates[2] for the production of a vaccine. During the late 1970s, hepatitis B vaccines were found to be highly efficacious in extensive field trials and are now clinically available for immunization of high-risk individuals or populations.

Thus, within two years of the publication of the initial finding of Australia antigen and within four years after the work had actually begun, a unique scientific observation had a profound impact on medical practice and provided a new and incisive insight into a common disease. Within ten years of the initial observation, the major outlines of the nature of the HBV and its wide range of pathological consequences were established. Within 15 years, techniques for passive and active immunization had been developed, offering the prospect for substantial inroads into the control of this disease in the coming years.

## Significance

Hepatitis B virus infection and its consequences are among the major disease problems in the world. For example, it is estimated that more than 200 million persons are clinically infected with HBV.[11] The identification of the HBV and the diagnostic, scientific, and therapeutic consequences of this discovery rank among the major medical advances of this century.

The key aspect of this research was the recognition that posttransfusional hepatitis could be produced by an agent that was shortly identified as the hepatitis B virus. The ability to detect a viral-associated antigen, designated now as hepatitis B surface antigen, led to new methods of diagnosis and of monitoring the course of infection, defined the primary route of infection as being parenteral, and led to the serological definition of acute and chronic infection and the carrier state. With this knowledge as the background, it was posssible to establish a relationship between HBV hepatitis, postnecrotic cirrhosis, and hepatocellular carcinoma. It was then possible to define the second major form of hepatitis, which was caused primarily by transmission by the fecal-oral route, as being a separate disease and caused by another virus, the hepatitis A virus. With the antigens of HBV and hepatitis A virus and the antibodies against them now available, it was possible to diagnose by exclusion a third form of hepatitis, non-A, non-B hepatitis. This is now the most significant form of posttransfusional hepatitis in the United States.[12] Fortunately, it is usually less severe than HBV posttransfusional hepatitis, although it can sometimes progress to chronic active hepatitis. The ability to identify HBV infection by testing for HBsAg made possible the epidemiologic studies that showed that this infection could also be transmitted by intimate contact between sexual partners, by transplacental passage or by contact between an infected mother and her offspring in the perinatal period, and by contact with patients or blood products in a renal dialysis unit. Finally, it made possible the study and definition of the natural history of viral hepatitis.[13] (See Chapter 49.)

This information revolutionized the practice of blood banking and identified the public health problems caused by maternal transmission of the hepatitis virus. The switch from primarily paid blood donors to volunteer blood donors has dramatically reduced the morbidity and mortality from posttransfusion hepatitis. The testing of all blood donors for HBsAg to identify the carriers has virtually eliminated HBV as a cause of posttransfusion hepatitis. Appropriate child care procedures and the use of hepatitis B immune globulin for mothers infected with HBV can substantially reduce the transmission of the infection to the infant.

Understanding the pathogenesis of viral hepatitis and its epidemiology stimulated the development of therapeutic agents. Hepatitis B immune globulin, obtained from persons who have recovered from HBV infections, is quite efficacious in treating short-term exposure to HBV, eg, by inadvertent needle puncture, in providing protection during short-term exposure in a highly endemic area, and in treating infected mothers during the perinatal and postnatal periods.[14] Much longer protection against infection can be conferred by hepatitis B vaccine made from chemically inactivated HBsAg-containing particles from the plasma of chronic carriers.[15,16] The initial studies indicate that the antibody response to the vaccine lasts for more than three years and that a booster injection is probably needed only every five years.[17] Similar attempts are in progress to develop a vaccine to the hepatitis A virus.

---

In a remarkably short time, the serendipitous observation that led to the discovery of Australia antigen, which was made in a pursuit of an entirely different objective, has had a tremendous scientific and clinical impact. The story emphasizes the importance of careful observation and logical follow-up at each step, the power of simple experimental approaches when used imaginatively, and balanced judgment and restraint in interpreting experimental data.

## References

1. Blumberg BS, Alter HJ, Visnich S: A 'new' antigen in leukemia sera. *JAMA* 1965;191:541-546.

2. Blumberg BS: Australia antigen and the biology of hepatitis B. *Science* 1977;197:17-25.

3. Blumberg BS: A serum antigen (Australia antigen) in Down's syndrome, leukemia, and hepatitis. *Ann Intern Med* 1967;66:924-931.

4. Blumberg BS, Riddell NM: Inherited antigenic differences in human serum beta lipoproteins: Second antiserum. *J Clin Invest* 1963;42:867-875.

5. Okochi K, Murakami S: Observation on Australia antigen in Japanese. *Vox Sang* 1968;15:374-385.

6. Prince AM: An antigen detected in the blood during the incubation period of serum hepatitis. *Proc Natl Acad Sci USA* 1968;60:814-821.

7. Gocke DJ, Kavey NB: Hepatitis antigen: Correlation with disease and infectivity of blood-donors. *Lancet* 1969;1:1055-1059.

8. Dane DS, Cameron CH, Briggs M: Virus-like particles in the serum of patients with Australia-antigen–associated hepatitis. *Lancet* 1970;1:695-698.

9. Davies JNP: Hepatic neoplasm, in Gall EZ, Mostofi FK (eds): *The Liver.* Baltimore, Williams & Wilkins Co, 1973, pp 361-369.

10. Ohbayashi A, Okochi K, Mayumi M, et al: Familial clustering of symptomatic carriers of Australia antigen and patients with chronic liver disease or primary liver cancer. *Gastroenterology* 1972;62:618-625.

11. Alter HJ: The evolution, implications, and applications of the hepatitis B vaccine. *JAMA* 1982;247:2272-2275.

12. Aach RD, Kahn RA: Posttransfusion hepatitis: Current perspectives. *Ann Intern Med* 1980;92:539-546.

13. Krugman S, Overby LR, Mushahwar IK, et al: Viral hepatitis, type B: Studies on maternal history and prevention re-examined. *N Engl J Med* 1979;300:101-106.

14. Seeff LB, Wright EC, Zimmerman HJ, et al: Type B hepatitis after needle-stick exposure: Prevention with hepatitis B immune globulin. *Ann Intern Med* 1978;88:285-293.

15. Inactivated hepatitis B virus vaccine. *MMWR* 1982;31:317-328.

16. Szmuness W, Stevens CE, Harley EJ, et al: Hepatitis B vaccine in medical staff of hemodialysis units: Efficacy and subtype cross-protection. *N Engl J Med* 1982;307:1481-1486.

17. Krugman S: The newly licensed hepatitis B vaccine: Characteristics and indications for use. *JAMA* 1982;247:2012-2015.

# Chapter 49

# Infectious Hepatitis

## Evidence for Two Distinctive Clinical, Epidemiological, and Immunological Types of Infection

Saul Krugman, MD, Joan P. Giles, MD, and Jack Hammond, MD

The identification of two types of infectious hepatitis with distinctive clinical, epidemiological, and immunological features provided an explanation for the occurrence of second attacks of the disease. One type resembled classical infectious hepatitis (IH); it was characterized by an incubation period of 30 to 38 days, a relatively short period of abnormal serum transaminase activity (3 to 19 days), a consistently abnormal thymol turbidity, and a high degree of contagion. The other type resembled serum hepatitis (SH); it was characterized by a longer incubation period (41 to 108 days), a longer period of abnormal transaminase activity (35 to 200 days) and a relatively normal thymol turbidity. Contrary to commonly accepted concepts, the SH type was moderately contagious. Patients with IH type were later proved to be immune to the same type. Patients with the SH type were not immune to the IH type infection.

Infectious hepatitis has been recognized as an endemic disease at the Willowbrook State School, Staten Island, NY, since 1953. As a result of this endemic environment, 1,153 cases of infectious hepatitis with jaundice were observed to have been transmitted by natural contact in this institution during the past 12 years. Second attacks with jaundice have occurred in 63 patients or 5.5% of this group. In most instances the second attack of jaundice

From the Department of Pediatrics, New York University School of Medicine, New York (Drs. Krugman and Giles), and Willowbrook State School, Staten Island, NY (Dr. Hammond). Dr. Giles is recipient of the New York City Health Research Council Career Scientist award.

Read in part before the Pan American Health Organization–World Health Organization International Conference on Vaccines Against Viral and Rickettsial Diseases of Man, Washington, DC, Nov 11, 1966, and before the 77th annual meeting of the American Pediatric Society, Atlantic City, NJ, April 27, 1967.

Reprint requests to 550 First Ave, New York 10016 (Dr. Krugman).

occurred within one year but occasionally as late as four and seven years after the first attack. One possible explanation for second attacks would be the existence of multiple types of infectious hepatitis virus, immunologically separate and distinct. Examples of this phenomenon have been observed in enterovirus, adenovirus, and myxovirus infections. The studies reported in this communication provide evidence for the presence of two distinctive clinical, epidemiological, and immunological types of infectious hepatitis.

The nature of the endemic situation at the Willowbrook State School has been described in detail in previous reports.[1-3] Briefly, infectious hepatitis was first noticed among Willowbrook patients as early as 1949. From 1949 to 1963 the patient population increased from a mere 200 to over 6,000. As the population increased and new susceptible children were admitted, hepatitis found a continuous foothold. Attempts to relieve overcrowding have now reduced this population to approximately 5,400 mentally retarded patients, predominantly children, who are distributed among 24 buildings. The constant admission of many susceptible children and the natural transmission of the disease via the intestinal-oral route have been responsible for the continuing endemic situation. Many of the patients are incapable of being toilet trained and prone to put everything that they pick up into their mouths. This intensifies the problem of control. Under the chronic circumstance of multiple and repeated natural exposure, it has been shown that most newly admitted children become infected within the first 6 to 12 months of residence in the institution.

Prior experience indicated that γ-globulin did not prevent hepatitis infection; it attenuated the disease. Eleven separate dosage trials with γ-globulin have been undertaken since 1956 in an attempt to reduce the number of clinical cases of infectious hepatitis in the institution. The direct measurable result of these programs was a reduction of approximately 85% of icteric hepatitis among patients and employees at Willowbrook. With the realization that subclinical cases persisted and were contagious, elimination of the disease could not be accomplished. In the absence of an effective vaccine, the study on the natural history of infectious hepatitis in this institution was therefore considered an important step toward better understanding and future control of this infection. The benefits of such a program to the entire institution were obvious. It remained then to assess the risks and the benefits to the children who would be active participants in the study.

The decision to propose the controlled infection of a small number of newly admitted children was based on the following considerations:

1. It was well recognized that infectious hepatitis was a mild and relatively benign disease in children as compared with adults; most cases were anicteric and asymptomatic. Experience at Willowbrook indicated that the disease observed at this institution was especially mild. Consequently, only the Willowbrook strains of infectious hepatitis virus would be used for the study.

2. The study group would include only children whose parents gave written consent after being informed of the details, potential risks, and potential benefits of the investigation.

3. The study would be carried out in a special isolation unit with special medical and nursing personnel to provide close observation and optimum care. Thus, these children would be protected from other endemic diseases in the institution, such as shigellosis, parasitic infections, respiratory infections, and other infectious diseases. Experience has indicated that the children in the special isolation unit were subjected to *less* risk than the children who were admitted directly to the institutional wards.

4. It is important to emphasize that the studies were to be carried out at the Willowbrook State School because of the local endemic situation, and *not* because the children were mentally retarded.

Observations on approximately 250 children who acquired artificially induced hepatitis in the Willowbrook study since 1956 revealed that the experimental disease was generally milder than the observed natural infection. In fact, many cases would have gone unrecognized if it had not been for careful daily observation and serial biochemical tests of liver function.

The studies were reviewed and sanctioned by the University Committee on Human Experimentation, by the New York State Department of Mental Hygiene, and by the Armed Forces Epidemiological Board. The Willowbrook studies have been conducted in accordance with the World Medical Association's Draft Code of Ethics on Human Experimentation.[4] The guidelines which were adopted for the study at its inception in 1956 conform with the following general principles of the Code of Ethics: (1) that where children are to be the subject of an experiment, the nature, the reason, and risks of it should be fully explained to their parents or lawful guardians, who should have complete freedom to make a decision on behalf of the children; (2) that children in

institutions and not under the care of relatives should not be the subject of human experiment; (3) that the experiment should be conducted only by scientifically qualified persons and under the supervision of a qualified medical man; (4) that during the course of the experiment the subject of it should be free to withdraw from it at any time; (5) that the investigator, or investigating committee, or any scientifically or medically qualified person associated with him or the committee should be free to discontinue the experiment if in his or their judgment it may, if continued, be harmful to the subject of the experiment; (6) that any risk to which the subject of an experiment may be exposed should be carefully assessed in terms of direct benefit to himself or indirect benefit to others, on the assumption that the risks have been explained to, and freely accepted by, the subject of the experiment.

### Materials and Methods

The children in the various study groups were 3 to 10 years of age. They were admitted directly to a special isolation facility capable of housing up to 16 children. The number of children included in each study generally ranged between 6 and 14. They had no contact with the rest of the institution and were cared for by physicians, nurses, and attendants who had minimal contact with other patients and personnel.

*Source of Hepatitis Virus.*—Blood serum from patients in the Willowbrook study provided the source of infectious virus. The material was tested for safety to rule out the presence of adventitious bacterial viral, or mycotic agents. The serum was inoculated into suckling mice and into the following tissue cultures: rhesus monkey kidney, human embryonic lung fibroblasts, and the WISH strain of continuous human amnion cells. No cytopathic changes were seen in tissue cultures and no illness was observed in the animals.

*Biochemical Tests of Liver Function.*—In addition to careful clinical observation for presence of jaundice, hepatomegaly, and other manifestations of hepatitis, tests of the following were performed at periodic intervals: serum bilirubin, thymol turbidity, serum glutamic oxalacetic transaminase (SGOT) and bilirubin in the urine. Blood was obtained before exposure and at weekly intervals or more often thereafter. The following methods were employed: serum bilirubin (Malloy and Evelyn[5]), thymol turbidity (Maclagan[6]) and SGOT (Karmen[7]). A result was considered abnormal if the serum bilirubin value was more than 1.0 mg/100 ml; the thymol turbidity more than 6 units, and for the purpose of the present study if the SGOT was 100 units or more.

*Criteria for Diagnosis of Hepatitis.*—The occurrence of clinical jaundice associated with an abnormal serum bilirubin and an abnormal SGOT was required for a diagnosis of hepatitis with jaundice. The diagnosis of hepatitis without jaundice was reserved for cases in which the serum bilirubin value was less than 1.0 mg/100 ml but in which a crescendo-like rise in SGOT activity exceeded 100 units.

*Definition of Incubation Period.*—The method of determining the incubation period of infectious hepatitis has varied in many studies. Most often, it has been measured as the number of days between exposure and either onset of symptoms or onset of jaundice. It is well known that jaundice may occur as early as two days or as late as two weeks after the first sign of illness. Moreover, experience at Willowbrook indicated that most cases of infectious hepatitis were anicteric and asymptomatic. Consequently, under the conditions of the present study the incubation period was usually defined as the number of days between exposure and first evidence of abnormal serum transaminase activity as indicated by a SGOT level above 100 units.

The evidence for the presence of two types of infectious hepatitis was accumulated from a series of seven separate trials which were carried out during the period from September 1964 to January 1967.

### First Trial

Willowbrook serum pool No. 5 (WSP-5) was used for the first trial. It was prepared from specimens obtained three to seven days before onset of jaundice in 27 Willowbrook study patients. On Sept. 23, 1964, WSP-5 was fed to 11 of 13 newly admitted subjects in a dose of 1.0 ml. Two children served as controls. All subjects were intimately exposed to each other but were isolated from other Willowbrook patients.

*Results.*—As indicated in Fig 1, oral administration of WSP-5 was followed by hepatitis in ten of 11 subjects. The incubation periods ranged between 30 and 36 days in six children and between 51 and 58 days in three; in one child evidence of hepatitis was first detectable on the 125th day. Patient Mac had a spontaneous second attack of hepatitis on the 97th day, 67 days after onset of the first attack. At least one of the two unfed controls may have had possible anicteric hepatitis. Jaundice was observed in six of ten subjects with hepatitis.

### Second Trial

The second trial was undertaken to study the problem of second attacks of hepatitis. On March 26, 1965, WSP-5 was given to ten of 13 subjects who had participated in the first trial six months previously. The dose was 0.25 ml intramuscularly. Three additional subjects were uninoculated controls. All 13 subjects were isolated from other Willowbrook patients from the beginning of the first trial until the termination of the second trial.

*Results.*—As indicated in Fig 1, hepatitis was observed in six of ten subjects who were inoculated with WSP-5. The incubation periods ranged between 38 and 102 days. The occurrence of hepatitis in four subjects (Sch, Mas, Wac, and Mir) represented second attacks.

As indicated in Fig 1, the following differences were apparent when the results of the first two trials were compared: (1) During the first attack of hepatitis in four subjects (Sch, Mas, Wac, and Mir) the incubation period ranged between 35 and 51 days; it was longer during the second attack, ranging between 66 and 82 days. (2) Duration of abnormal SGOT activity was relatively short (5 to 17 days) in most patients during the first trial; it was much longer (17 to 64 days) during the second trial. These findings suggested the possibility that the two attacks of hepatitis were caused by two different viruses.

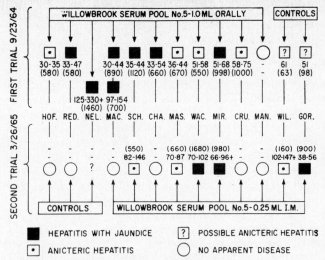

1. *First trial*, occurrence of first attack of hepatitis after subjects were fed Willowbrook serum pool No. 5 (WSP-5). *Second trial*, occurrence of second attacks of hepatitis in same subjects following inoculation of WSP-5 six months later. First number indicates first day SGOT exceeded 100 units/ml; second number, first day SGOT declined to levels below 100 units; numbers in parentheses, peak SGOT levels.

During the course of the first two trials, serial samples of serum were obtained before and after onset of first and second attacks of hepatitis in individual subjects. This material was stored in the deep freeze at −20 C. Serum specimens from subject Mir were selected for special study. It was postulated that blood obtained during the week prior to onset of the first attack of jaundice should contain the virus responsible for the first attack. It was also postulated that blood obtained six months later should contain neutralizing antibody against the virus responsible for the first attack, and consequently, if the

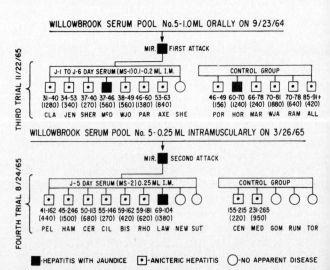

2. *Third trial*, occurrence of hepatitis in subjects who received serum (MS-1) obtained from patient Mir during first trial. Note onset of hepatitis after relatively short incubation period; relatively short period of abnormal transaminase activity; and high attack rate in control group. *Fourth trial*, occurrence of hepatitis in subjects who received serum (MS-2) from patient Mir during second trial. Note longer incubation period, longer period of abnormal transaminase activity, and contact infection in two of five control subjects.

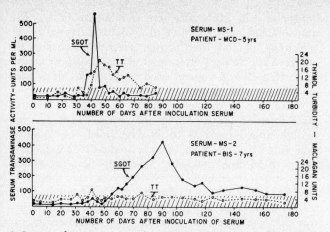

3. Pattern of serum transaminase (SGOT) and thymol turbidity (TT) activity response after inoculation of serum from first attack (MS-1) and second attack (MS-2). Note spiking rise and precipitous fall of SGOT and abnormal TT activity following MS-1 infection. In contrast, note gradual rise and prolongation of SGOT activity and normal TT following MS-2 infection.

second attack serum were infectious, it would suggest the presence of an immunologically distinct type of virus.

The serum specimens obtained from subject Mir prior to the first attack were pooled and designated MS-1. This material was used for the third trial. The serum specimens from the same subject immediately before the second attack were designated MS-2 and were used for the fourth trial.

### Third Trial

Fourteen newly admitted subjects participated in the third trial. On Nov 22, 1965, a pool of MS-1 serum was given intramuscularly to eight subjects; the dose was 0.1 to 0.2 ml. Six subjects were uninoculated controls. All children were intimately exposed to each other during the course of the trial.

*Results.*—The results of the third trial are shown in Fig 2 and Table 1. Hepatitis was observed in seven of eight subjects who were inoculated with MS-1 serum; the incubation periods ranged between 31 and 53 days. A transient jaundice with a slight elevation of serum bilirubin (1.4 mg/100 ml) was present for one day in one patient, subject McD. The remaining six children had anicteric hepatitis. The results of serial biochemical tests of liver function in the seven inoculated children infected with MS-1 serum are listed in Table 1 which shows (1) the spiking rise and precipitous fall in SGOT activity and (2) the presence of abnormal thymol turbidity in all seven patients.

All six subjects in the uninoculated, intimately exposed control group contracted hepatitis 46 to 85 days after the beginning of the third trial. Jaundice was observed in only one of the six control children (Hor). The observation of contact infection after 46 days indicated that hepatitis caused by MS-1 serum had an incubation period of 31 to 38 days.

### Fourth Trial

Fourteen newly admitted children participated in the fourth trial. On Aug 24, 1965, MS-2 serum was given

| Day After Exposure | CLA | | JEN | | SHER | | MCD | | W JO | | PAR | | AXE | |
|---|---|---|---|---|---|---|---|---|---|---|---|---|---|---|
| | TT° | SGOT† | TT | SGOT | TT | SGOT | TT | SGOT | TT | SGOT | TT | SGOT | TT | SGOT |
| 0 | 4 | 34 | 2.5 | 14 | 3 | 19 | <1.2 | 21 | <1.2 | 16 | 4.0 | 26 | 2.5 | 26 |
| 10 | 2.7 | 27 | 1.2 | 20 | 3.2 | 28 | <1.2 | 20 | <1.2 | 16 | 1.8 | 27 | 3 | 27 |
| 16 | 2.5 | 28 | 4 | 34 | 4.2 | 42 | 3.5 | 18 | <1.2 | 21 | 3 | 21 | 2.1 | 27 |
| 22 | 2.7 | 20 | 5.7 | 27 | 8.7 | 42 | 2.1 | 42 | 1.8 | 26 | 2.7 | 20 | 3 | 22 |
| 28 | 6.2 | 84 | <1.2 | 50 | 7.5 | 27 | 1.2 | 16 | 2.1 | 18 | 3 | 16 | 7.5 | 24 |
| 31 | 6.5 | 1,280 | 2.1 | 40 | 4.5 | 20 | 5.7 | 21 | 1.8 | 12 | 5 | 21 | 6 | 16 |
| 34 | ... | ... | 8 | 310 | ... | ... | ... | ... | ... | ... | ... | ... | ... | ... |
| 35 | 12.5 | 120 | 12.5 | 160 | 13.7 | 24 | 3.2 | 24 | 2.1 | 14 | 4.2 | 10 | 6.5 | 20 |
| 37 | 11.2 | 170 | 15.5 | 340 | 6.2 | 270 | 2.1 | 170 | 1.2 | 86 | 2.1 | 17 | ... | ... |
| 40 | 12.5 | 56 | 25 | 138 | 7.5 | 84 | 7.5 | 180 | 3 | 560 | 4.2 | 40 | 5 | 14 |
| 42 | 10 | 39 | 25 | 140 | 8.2 | 40 | 14.8 | 560 | 7.5 | 420 | 7 | 22 | 4.5 | 19 |
| 46 | 6.5 | 48 | 22 | 91 | 10 | 34 | 21 | 75 | 6.7 | 114 | 5 | 128 | 1.2 | 20 |
| 49 | 6.2 | 29 | 27 | 126 | 7.7 | 27 | 18 | 84 | 5.5 | 51 | 3 | 750 | 7 | 21 |
| 51 | ... | ... | ... | ... | ... | ... | ... | ... | ... | ... | 7 | 1,380 | ... | ... |
| 52 | ... | ... | ... | ... | ... | ... | ... | ... | ... | ... | 7.5 | 940 | ... | ... |
| 53 | ... | ... | 21 | 64 | 8.5 | 50 | 17.5 | 39 | 13.4 | 56 | 9.2 | 740 | 11 | 840 |
| 55 | ... | ... | ... | ... | ... | ... | 13 | 48 | ... | ... | 13 | 600 | ... | ... |
| 56 | 8 | 49 | 22.2 | 34 | 8.5 | 41 | ... | ... | 11.7 | 46 | 11 | 480 | 16 | 560 |
| 58 | ... | ... | ... | ... | ... | ... | ... | ... | ... | ... | ... | ... | 15 | 138 |
| 60 | 4.2 | 21 | 17.5 | 44 | 8.7 | 35 | 10.5 | 20 | 11.2 | 44 | 9.5 | 60 | 22 | 106 |
| 63 | 7 | 42 | 16.4 | 57 | 11 | 18 | 11.5 | 42 | 8.7 | 18 | 13 | 34 | 16.5 | 49 |

Table 1.—Serial Liver Function Tests in Seven Children Infected With MS-1 Hepatitis Serum

°Thymol turbidity, units.
†Serum glutamic oxaloacetic transaminase, units/ml.

intramuscularly to nine subjects; the dose was 0.25 ml. The specimen of MS-2 serum was obtained five days before onset of the second attack of jaundice. Five subjects were uninoculated controls. All 14 children were intimately exposed to each other during the course of the trial.

*Results.*—As indicated in Fig 2 and Table 2, hepatitis was observed in seven of nine subjects who were inoculated with MS-2 serum. The incubation periods ranged between 41 and 69 days. Jaundice occurred in one patient, Law, on the 83rd day, 14 days after first evidence of abnormal SGOT activity (> 100 units). The remaining six children had anicteric hepatitis. The results of serial tests of liver function shown in Table 2 reveal a gradual rise and a prolonged persistence of SGOT activity. Thymol turbidity was normal in five of seven subjects.

Anicteric hepatitis was observed in two of the five uninoculated control subjects, 155 and 231 days after the beginning of the fourth trial. Hepatitis occurred in contact Cen, 86 days after onset of the disease in subject Law. Hepatitis in contact Med occurred 76 days after onset of hepatitis in contact Cen.

A comparison of the results of the third and fourth trials revealed the following differences: (1) Incubation period ranged from 31 to 38 days (mean of 35 days) following MS-1 infection, as compared with 41 to 69 days (mean of 54 days) following MS-2 infection. (2) Abnormal serum transaminase activity was relatively short (3 to 19 days) following MS-1 infection and relatively long (35 to 200 days) after MS-2 infection. (3) Thymol turbidity was consistently abnormal after MS-1 infection; it was frequently normal after MS-2 infection. (4) Contagion— MS-1 infection was highly contagious for all six presum-

Table 2.—Serial Liver Function Tests in Seven Children Infected With MS-2 Hepatitis Serum

| Day After Exposure | PEL | | HAM | | CER | | CIL | | BIS | | RHO | | LAW | |
|---|---|---|---|---|---|---|---|---|---|---|---|---|---|---|
| | TT° | SGOT† | TT | SGOT | TT | SGOT | TT | SGOT | TT | SGOT | TT | SGOT | TT | SGOT |
| 0 | 4.9 | 16 | 3 | 16 | 1.2 | 10 | <1.2 | 34 | 3 | 12 | 2.1 | 18 | 1.2 | 8 |
| 6 | 6.7 | <8 | 2 | 16 | 2 | 12 | 1.2 | 30 | 1.2 | 12 | 3 | 21 | 4 | 20 |
| 14 | 7 | 16 | 4.2 | 19 | 4.2 | 12 | 1.5 | 16 | 1.2 | <8 | 2.2 | 10 | 2.2 | 16 |
| 20 | 9.5 | 15 | 7.5 | 34 | 3 | 9 | 1.2 | 26 | 3.7 | 14 | 3 | 18 | 4 | 10 |
| 27 | 5.7 | 20 | 2 | 19 | 1.5 | 8 | <1.2 | 19 | 3.5 | 10 | 3.5 | 18 | 1.5 | 11 |
| 31 | 6.5 | 18 | 3.7 | 20 | 6 | 11 | 1.5 | 18 | 6.2 | 16 | 3.5 | 13 | 3 | 8 |
| 34 | 4.2 | 31 | 3 | 41 | 1.7 | 10 | <1.2 | 16 | 3.2 | 14 | 2.5 | 15 | 2.2 | 4 |
| 37 | 6.7 | 50 | 3 | 52 | 3 | 18 | <1.2 | 28 | 4.7 | 31 | 3.2 | 26 | 3.2 | 21 |
| 41 | 8 | 129 | 6.5 | 54 | 3 | 15 | 1.2 | 33 | 8.2 | 41 | 4.2 | 26 | 2.7 | 12 |
| 45 | 5.5 | 340 | 6.5 | 111 | <1.2 | 30 | <1.2 | 37 | 4 | 32 | 3.2 | 29 | <1.2 | 15 |
| 48 | 7.7 | 410 | 1.5 | 150 | 3 | 89 | <1.2 | 50 | 3.2 | 22 | 2.7 | 25 | 4 | 15 |
| 50 | 7.7 | 350 | 4.2 | 380 | 4 | 152 | <1.2 | 80 | 4.2 | 40 | 2.5 | 31 | 2.5 | 20 |
| 55 | 5.5 | 440 | 2.5 | 950 | 13 | 680 | 1.2 | 180 | 4 | 78 | 2.5 | 60 | 1.2 | 61 |
| 59 | 6.7 | 410 | 8.2 | 1,120 | 20.2 | 420 | <1.2 | 240 | 5 | 119 | 4 | 124 | 2.5 | 56 |
| 62 | 5.5 | 340 | 5.5 | 1,390 | 22 | 200 | 2.5 | 200 | 5 | 112 | 5.2 | 160 | 3.5 | 49 |
| 66 | 6.2 | 420 | 6 | 1,500 | 10.5 | 120 | 3 | 140 | 4.2 | 140 | 3 | 150 | 2.1 | 84 |
| 69 | 7.7 | 340 | 5 | 1,320 | 7.5 | 150 | 3 | 220 | 4.5 | 190 | 3 | 410 | 4.5 | 120 |
| 76 | 5.2 | 250 | 5.2 | 940 | 4.2 | 150 | 3.7 | 270 | 6.7 | 260 | 5.5 | 620 | 10 | 750 |
| 83 | 6.5 | 200 | 2.1 | 760 | 3.2 | 510 | <1.2 | 180 | 3.7 | 320 | 2.1 | 480 | 15 | 1,060 |
| 90 | 8.7 | 410 | 3 | 560 | 6 | 340 | 2.1 | 260 | 5 | 420 | 5 | 580 | 11.5 | 1,250 |
| 97 | 6.5 | 270 | 2.5 | 200 | 6.2 | 200 | 4.2 | 220 | 5.2 | 280 | 4.2 | 400 | 13.7 | 1,380 |
| 104 | 7 | 220 | 5 | 110 | 7.2 | 140 | 2.5 | 166 | 5 | 176 | 6.2 | 620 | 9 | 120 |
| 113 | 6.2 | 188 | 3 | 170 | 10 | 78 | <1.2 | 210 | 4.5 | 142 | 6.7 | 560 | 6.5 | 94 |
| 118 | 6.2 | 176 | 2.5 | 190 | 5.5 | 56 | <1.2 | 184 | 3 | 156 | 4 | 440 | 6 | 42 |
| 126 | 4.5 | 120 | 2.1 | 140 | 5.5 | 14 | 1.8 | 146 | 5.7 | 96 | 7.5 | 132 | ... | ... |
| 132 | 5 | 124 | 2.5 | 144 | 5 | 20 | 2.5 | 180 | 4 | 106 | 3.5 | 112 | 2.1 | 14 |
| 146 | 5 | 124 | 4 | 490 | 3.5 | 34 | 7.5 | 90 | 5 | 124 | 7 | 340 | 3.2 | 20 |
| 150 | ... | ... | <1.2 | 670 | ... | ... | ... | ... | ... | ... | 3 | 132 | ... | ... |
| 155 | 6 | 148 | 4.7 | 420 | 7 | 27 | 5.7 | 84 | 5 | 112 | 6 | 160 | 4 | 22 |
| 162 | 7.5 | 74 | 2.5 | 220 | 5 | 27 | 5.2 | 98 | 4 | 88 | 10 | 160 | 4.5 | 22 |
| 174 | 6.2 | 140 | 3.2 | 170 | 1.2 | 32 | 6 | 94 | 2.7 | 84 | 6.5 | 172 | ... | ... |
| 181 | 5 | 54 | 1.8 | 126 | 2.5 | 14 | 1.8 | 36 | 2.1 | 27 | 4.2 | 84 | ... | ... |
| 189 | 5 | 114 | 2.1 | 118 | ... | ... | ... | ... | 2.1 | 76 | 4.5 | 106 | 4 | 15 |

°Thymol turbidity, units.
†Serum glutamic oxaloacetic transaminase, units/ml.

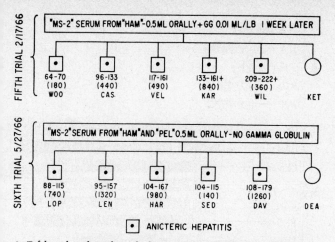

FIFTH TRIAL 2/17/66

"MS-2" SERUM FROM "HAM"-0.5ML ORALLY+GG 0.01 ML/LB I WEEK LATER

| 64-70 (180) WOO | 96-133 (440) CAS. | 117-161 (490) VEL | 133-161+ (840) KAR | 209-222+ (360) WIL | KET |

SIXTH TRIAL 5/27/66

"MS-2" SERUM FROM "HAM" AND "PEL" 0.5 ML ORALLY-NO GAMMA GLOBULIN

| 88-115 (740) LOP | 95-157 (1320) LEN | 104-167 (980) HAR | 104-115 (140) SED | 108-179 (1260) DAV | DEA |

◉ ANICTERIC HEPATITIS

4. *Fifth and sixth trials*, oral administration of MS-2 serum followed by anicteric hepatitis in ten of 12 subjects after long incubation periods. First number indicates first day that SGOT exceeded 100 units/ml; second number, first day the SGOT declined to levels below 100 units; numbers in parentheses, peak SGOT levels.

ably susceptible contacts; MS-2 infection was less contagious, spreading to only two of five presumably susceptible contacts.

The striking contrast in the pattern of SGOT and thymol turbidity response is illustrated in Fig 3. MS-1 infection in subject McD (third trial) is characterized by a spiking rise in SGOT activity followed by a rise in thymol turbidity. In contrast, MS-2 infection in patient Bis (fourth trial) is characterized by a normal thymol turbidity and a gradual, prolonged rise in SGOT activity.

The results of the first and third trials clearly demonstrated that infectious hepatitis virus MS-1 type was infectious by mouth and the disease was highly contagious. The results of the fourth trial indicated that infectious hepatitis MS-2 type was less contagious but it did spread to susceptible contacts. The fifth and sixth trials were designed to test the infectivity of MS-2 serum by mouth. The sera to be tested were obtained from subjects Ham and Pel who had a typical MS-2 type infection (fourth trial).

## Fifth Trial

Nine newly admitted children participated in the fifth trial. On Feb 17, 1966, MS-2 type serum obtained from subject Ham was given to six subjects. The dose was 0.5 ml by mouth; three children were unfed controls. One week later the six children received γ-globulin, 0.01 ml per pound of body weight intramuscularly. The use of γ-globulin was a precautionary measure because of limited experience with MS-2 type of infectious hepatitis virus.

*Results.*—The results of the fifth trial are shown in Fig 4. Anicteric hepatitis was observed in five of six presumably susceptible subjects. The incubation periods ranged between 64 and 209 days. The duration of abnormal SGOT activity was prolonged and the thymol turbidity response was normal in three of five subjects with hepatitis. All children were clinically normal. They were asymptomatic and they gained weight. Hepatitis was not observed in the three children who were unfed controls.

## Sixth Trial

The fifth trial indicated that infectious hepatitis virus MS-2 type was infective by mouth. It was considered important to confirm this observation. Accordingly, on May 27, 1966, MS-2 type serum from subjects Ham and Pel was given to six presumably susceptible newly admitted subjects; the dose was 0.5 ml by mouth. Gamma globulin was not administered.

*Results.*—As indicated in Fig 4, the results of the sixth trial were similar to the fifth trial. Anicteric asymptomatic hepatitis was observed in five of six subjects after prolonged incubation periods ranging between 88 and 108 days. The SGOT activity was prolonged and the thymol turbidity response was compatible with a MS-2 type of infection.

The previous six trials provided evidence for two types of infectious hepatitis with distinctive clinical and epidemiological features. The seventh trial was designed to study the immunological aspects of the disease following MS-1 type infection (third trial) and MS-2 type infection (fourth trial).

**RESULTS OF INOCULATION WITH MS-1 SERUM (11/22/65)**    **RESULTS OF CHALLENGE WITH MS-1 SERUM (3/28/66)**

| SUBJECT | TYPE OF HEPATITIS | ABNORMAL SGOT ACTIVITY PEAK LEVEL UNITS/ML | DURATION DAYS | PEAK THYMOL TURBIDITY UNITS/ML | TYPE OF HEPATITIS |
|---|---|---|---|---|---|
| AXE | ◉ | 840 | 10 | 22.0 | ○ |
| MAR | ◉ | 240 | 12 | 13.5 | ○ |
| McD | ■ | 560 | 9 | 21.0 | ○ |
| JEN | ◉ | 340 | 19 | 27.0 | ○ |
| SHR | ◉ | 270 | 3 | 10.0 | ○ |
| WJA | ◉ | 1880 | 11 | 15.0 | ○ |
| WJO | ◉ | 560 | 11 | 13.4 | ○ |
| SHE | ○ | - | - | - | ○ |

■ HEPATITIS WITH JAUNDICE    ◉ ANICTERIC HEPATITIS    ○ NONE

5. Evidence for homologous immunity following MS-1 hepatitis infection.

**RESULTS OF INOCULATION WITH MS-2 SERUM (8/24/65)**    **RESULTS OF CHALLENGE WITH MS-1 SERUM (3/28/66)**

| SUBJECT | TYPE OF HEPATITIS | ABNORMAL SGOT ACTIVITY PEAK LEVEL UNITS/ML | DURATION DAYS | PEAK THYMOL TURBIDITY UNITS/ML | TYPE OF HEPATITIS | ABNORMAL SGOT ACTIVITY PEAK LEVEL UNITS/ML | DURATION DAYS | PEAK THYMOL TURBIDITY UNITS/ML |
|---|---|---|---|---|---|---|---|---|
| RHO | ◉ | 620 | 122 | 5.5 | ■ | 1500 | 15 | 32.0 |
| PEL | ◉ | 440 | 121 | 8.0 | ◉ | 830 | 15 | 15.5 |
| CER | ◉ | 680 | 63 | 22.0 | ◉ | 510 | 14 | 20.0 |
| BIS | ◉ | 420 | 103 | 5.0 | ○ | - | - | - |
| HAM | ◉ | 1500 | 200 | 7.5 | ◉ | 1360 | 15 | 25.0 |
| MED | ◉ | 950 | 34 | 7.5 | ■ | 1040 | 17 | 40.0 |
| SUT | ○ | - | - | - | ◉ | 380 | 14 | 15.7 |
| GOM | ○ | - | - | - | ■ | 750 | 14 | 21.2 |

■ HEPATITIS WITH JAUNDICE    ◉ ANICTERIC HEPATITIS    ○ NONE

6. Evidence for lack of heterologous immunity following MS-2 hepatitis infection.

## Seventh Trial

The sixteen subjects who participated in the seventh trial included eight children from the third trial and eight children from the fourth trial. The entire group was isolated from other institutional patients during the entire period of the study. On March 28, 1966, four months after the third trial and seven months after the fourth trial, all 16 subjects were inoculated with infectious hepatitis serum, MS-1 type; the dose was 0.2 ml. intramuscularly.

*Results.*—Evidence for homologous immunity following MS-1 infection is presented in Fig 5. The initial inoculation of MS-1 serum on Nov 22, 1965, had been followed by infectious hepatitis in seven of eight subjects; the pattern of serum transaminase and thymol turbidity activity was typical of MS-1 infection. Subsequent challenge with infectious MS-1 serum on March 28, 1966, revealed no evidence of hepatitis with or without jaundice; all eight subjects were immune.

Lack of heterologous immunity in subjects first infected with MS-2 virus is shown in Fig 6. The initial inoculation of MS-2 serum on Aug 24, 1965, was followed by infectious hepatitis in six of eight subjects; the pattern of transaminase and thymol turbidity activity was typical of MS-2 infection. Subsequent challenge with infectious MS-1 serum on March 28, 1966, was followed by hepatitis in all eight subjects. The pattern of the SGOT and thymol turbidity response in this second attack was characteristic for MS-1 type of infection. Thus, inoculation of MS-1 serum was followed by hepatitis in five of six subjects who had a previous infection caused by MS-2 serum (Fig 6). In contrast, the same MS-1 serum produced no evidence of infection in seven subjects who had a previous attack of hepatitis caused by MS-1 serum (Fig 5). These observations indicate that the two types of hepatitis virus are immunologically distinct.

## Comment

The data accumulated during the course of these studies confirm the presence of two types of infectious hepatitis in Willowbrook. In the series of seven trials it has been possible to identify distinctive clinical, epidemiological, and immunological features characteristic of each type of infection. The two types of hepatitis were caused by two different viruses, designated as MS-1 and MS-2. MS-1 virus was derived from the serum of a patient during the first attack of hepatitis; MS-2 virus was derived from the serum of the same patient six months later.

The disease associated with MS-1 virus infection is undoubtedly the classical type of infectious hepatitis, a disease also known under the following aliases: infective hepatitis, IH hepatitis, virus A hepatitis, and in former years, acute catarrhal jaundice and epidemic jaundice. The disease associated with MS-2 virus infection resembles serum hepatitis which has also been referred to as homologous serum jaundice, SH hepatitis, virus B hepatitis, posttransfusion hepatitis, and postvaccinial hepatitis. A comparison of the incubation period, thymol turbidity pattern, and epidemiological and immunological aspects provides evidence supporting the relationship of MS-1 to

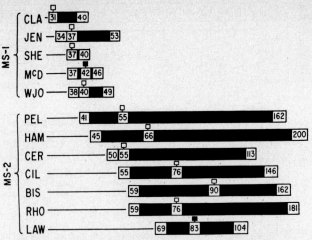

7. Comparison of incubation period and abnormal SGOT activity following MS-1 and MS-2 hepatitis infection. Note relatively long incubation period, more prolonged period of abnormal SGOT activity following MS-2 infection, also delay in onset of jaundice or peak SGOT activity following MS-2 infection. First number indicates time interval in days, from exposure to first increase in SGOT above 100 units; black square, day of onset of jaundice; white square, day of peak transaminase; last number, first day the SGOT declined to levels below 100 units.

infectious hepatitis (IH) and MS-2 to serum hepatitis (SH).

*Incubation Period.*—The incubation period of infectious hepatitis has been reported to range between 15 and 50 days[1,8-11]; the mean is approximately 30 to 35 days. In contrast, the incubation period of serum hepatitis has been observed to be much longer, generally ranging between 43 and 180 days with most cases occurring between 60 and 90 days.[9,11,12] In natural disease, especially infectious hepatitis, the limits of the incubation period are often ill-defined because the precise time of infection is unknown. Incubation periods following MS-1 and MS-2

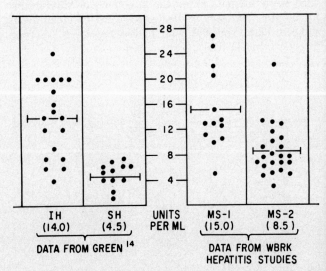

8. Comparison of peak thymol turbidity levels within two weeks after onset of jaundice in 19 patients with infectious hepatitis (IH), 12 patients with serum hepatitis (SH), 13 Willowbrook patients with infectious hepatitis (MS-1 type), and 23 Willowbrook patients with infectious hepatitis (MS-2 type). Note similarity in thymol turbidity response between IH and MS-1 and between SH and MS-2.

types of infection are charted in Fig 7. Two types of incubation period have been recorded: (1) the interval between the time of exposure and first sign of hepatic involvement, as indicated by an increase in SGOT above 100 units/ml; and (2) the interval between time of exposure and peak SGOT or onset of jaundice. Experience at Willowbrook has indicated that onset of jaundice generally occurs at the time of peak transaminase activity. As indicated in Fig 7, the incubation period following MS-1 infection was 31 to 42 days; the mean was 37 days. In contrast, MS-2 infection occurred after an incubation period of 55 to 90 days; the mean was 71 days. The similarity of MS-1 to IH and MS-2 to SH is obvious.

The mode of transmission did not affect the incubation period of MS-1 type of infection; it was essentially the same following oral and parenteral exposure. On the other hand, the incubation period of MS-2 type of infection was longer following oral exposure (sixth trial) than parenteral inoculation (fourth trial).

*Thymol Turbidity Pattern.*—Reports by Neefe[13] and by Green[14] have indicated that the thymol turbidity test is often negative in serum hepatitis. Neefe stated that "In two small but closely comparable groups of patients with induced virus IH hepatitis and virus SH hepatitis, respectively, the responses to the serum colloidal gold and the thymol (turbidity and flocculation) tests were less in degree and duration in the virus SH hepatitis than in the other group." Green described the thymol turbidity pattern in 12 cases of serum hepatitis and 19 cases of infectious hepatitis. His data, charted in Fig 8, support Neefe's observations. As indicated in Fig 8, the thymol turbidity test in serum hepatitis was relatively normal within the first two weeks after onset of jaundice; the mean level was 4.5 Maclagan units/ml. In contrast, it was increased significantly in infectious hepatitis; the mean level was 14.0 units. The data from the Willowbrook studies, charted alongside Green's data in Fig 8, highlight the striking similarity between IH and MS-1 type hepatitis and SH and MS-2 type hepatitis.

*SGOT Activity.*—The striking contrast between the SGOT pattern in MS-1 infection as compared with MS-2 infection is illustrated in Fig 3 and 7. In future studies it will be important to accumulate comparable data for typical cases of infectious hepatitis and serum hepatitis. The spiking rise in SGOT activity and its short duration in MS-1 infection may be indicative of infectious hepatitis. On the other hand, serum hepatitis may be characterized by a gradual rise and a prolongation of SGOT activity.

*Epidemiological Aspects.*—It is well recognized that infectious hepatitis is a contagious disease and that the most common mode of transmission is via the intestinal-oral route. Contact infection usually occurs under conditions which favor crowding and close association. The evidence that MS-1 type of hepatitis was highly contagious was presented in the third trial (Fig 2); all six contacts contracted MS-1 type hepatitis after exposure to children with MS-1 type of infection. This phenomenon is characteristic of IH type of hepatitis.

The most widely accepted concept of the spread of serum hepatitis supports the parenteral mode of transmission of infective blood or blood products. A limited number of trials in volunteers indicated that serum hepatitis virus was not infective by mouth.[11,15] The results of these studies suggested that serum hepatitis was rarely transmitted through personal contact.

The observation that MS-2 type hepatitis was communicable (Fig 2) and infective by mouth (Fig 4) would not be compatible with the prevailing view that serum hepatitis is not contagious after intimate contact. On the other hand, these findings would be compatible with reports by Findlay and Martin,[16] by Freeman,[17] and especially by Mirick and Shank,[18] who described an epidemic of serum hepatitis in 272 persons who had been inoculated with human plasma. The incubation period was long; it ranged from 49 to 125 days (average 79 days). Thirty additional cases of serum hepatitis were observed in uninoculated personnel who had been in intimate contact with plasma-inoculated personnel. The epidemiological aspects of MS-2 hepatitis in Willowbrook are similar to the epidemic of serum hepatitis described by Mirick and Shank.

Although both types of virus were infective by mouth, it was clear that MS-1 was more highly infectious than MS-2. During the course of the first trial (Fig 1) the two viruses were inadvertently fed as components of Willowbrook serum pool No. 5. Of ten subjects who acquired hepatitis, nine had a typical MS-1 or IH type of disease. In one patient, Nel, hepatitis occurred after an incubation period of 125 days; the disease was a typical MS-2 type of infection. It is likely that patient Nel was immune to IH before exposure to the serum pool. In four subjects (Sch, Mas, Wac, and Mir) the phenomenon of interference may have been responsible for the occurrence of only one infection, MS-1 type. In contrast, subject Mac had a double infection caused by MS-1 after 30 days and MS-2 after 97 days. There was no evidence of interference in this patient.

*Immunological Aspects.*—The immunological aspects of MS-1 and IH hepatitis and MS-2 and SH hepatitis are essentially the same. Studies by Neefe and associates[11] and by Havens[10] confirmed the existence of homologous immunity following IH and SH hepatitis. In contrast, there was no evidence of cross immunity between the two types of hepatitis. The same phenomenon has been observed following MS-1 and MS-2 infection (Fig 5 and 6).

*Clinical Aspects.*—It was impossible to differentiate between the two types of hepatitis on the basis of clinical manifestations alone without the aid of serial laboratory determinations. During the course of the seven trials, MS-1 type hepatitis was observed in 29 subjects; ten were jaundiced and 19 were anicteric. MS-2 type hepatitis was observed in 27 subjects; six were icteric and 21 anicteric. Jaundice in both groups was mild, the bilirubin value ranging between 1.0 and 3.0 mg/100 ml; it subsided after one to ten days, average of five days for both groups. There was no correlation between persistence of abnormal enzyme activity and presence of clinical symptoms. The children were asymptomatic and gained weight in spite of a prolonged elevation of SGOT. The weight gain during a 25-week period of observation was 0.9 to 3.6 kg (2 to 8 lb), average 2 kg (4.5 lb), for the MS-1 group.

During a 30-week period of observation, the weight gain in children in the MS-2 group ranged between 1.8 and 3.6 kg (4 and 8 lb), average 2.7 kg (6 lb).

## Conclusions

The evidence presented in the foregoing discussion indicates that the two types of infectious hepatitis in Willowbrook are examples of infectious hepatitis and serum hepatitis with distinctive clinical, epidemiological, and immunological features. This phenomenon is a logical explanation for the occurrence of second attacks of hepatitis in this institution.

This investigation was supported by a contract from the US Army Medical Research and Development Command, Department of the Army, under the sponsorship of the Commission on Viral Infections, Armed Forces Epidemiological Board, Office of the Surgeon General (contract DA-49-193-MD-2331).

Assistance was provided by Alan D. Miller, MD, New York State Commissioner of Mental Hygiene, and the following members of the hepatitis research group: Olive Lattimer, RN, Florence Goodfield, RN, Mrs. Alma Bertolini, and Mrs. Ruth Kirk. Philip A. Brunell, MD, performed the safety tests.

## References

1. Ward, R., et al: Infectious Hepatitis: Studies of Its Natural History and Prevention, *New Eng J Med* 258:407-416 (Feb 27) 1958.

2. Krugman, S., et al: Infectious Hepatitis: Detection of Virus During the Incubation Period and in Clinically Inapparent Infection, *New Eng J Med* 261:729-734 (Oct 8) 1959.

3. Krugman, S.; Ward, R.; and Giles, J.P.: The Natural History of Infectious Hepatitis, *Amer J Med* 32:717-728 (May) 1962.

4. World Medical Association Draft Code of Ethics on Human Experimentation, *Brit M J* 2:1119 (Oct 27) 1962.

5. Malloy, H.T., and Evelyn, K.A.: Determination of Bilirubin With Photoelectric Colorimeter, *J Biol Chem* 119:481-490 (July) 1937.

6. Maclagan, N.F.: Thymol Turbidity Test: New Indicator of Liver Dysfunction, *Brit J Exper Path* 25:234-241 (Dec) 1944.

7. Karmen, A.: Note on Spectrophotometric Assay of Glutamic-Oxalacetic Transaminase in Human Blood Serum, *J Clin Invest* 34:126-133 (Jan) 1955.

8. MacCallum, F.O., and Bradley, W.H.: Transmission of Infective Hepatitis to Human Volunteers: Effect on Rheumatoid Arthritis, *Lancet* 2:228 (Aug 12) 1944.

9. Paul, J.R., et al: Transmission Experiments in Serum Jaundice and Infectious Hepatitis, *JAMA* 128:911-915 (July 28) 1945.

10. Havens, W.P., Jr.: Period of Infectivity of Patients With Experimentally Induced Infectious Hepatitis, *J Exp Med* 83:251-258 (March) 1946.

11. Neefe, J.R.; Gellis, S.S.; and Stokes, J., Jr.: Homologous Serum Hepatitis and Infectious (Epidemic) Hepatitis: Studies in Volunteers Bearing on Immunological and Other Characteristics of Etiological Agents, *Amer J Med* 1:3-22 (July) 1946.

12. MacCallum, F.O., and Bauer, D.J.: Homologous Serum Jaundice: Transmission Experiments With Human Volunteers, *Lancet* 1:622-627 (May 13) 1944.

13. Neefe, J.R.: Recent Advances in Knowledge of "Virus Hepatitis," *Med Clin N Amer* 30:1407-1443 (Nov) 1946.

14. Green, P.: Some Serochemical Differences Between Homologous Serum Hepatitis and Infectious Hepatitis, *Canad Med Assoc* 63:365-368 (Oct) 1950.

15. MacCallum, F.O.: Transmission of Arsenotherapy Jaundice by Blood: Failure With Faeces and Nasopharyngeal Washings, *Lancet* 1:342 (March 17) 1945.

16. Findley, G.M., and Martin, N.H.: Jaundice Following Yellow Fever Immunization, *Lancet* 1:678-680 (May 29) 1943.

17. Freeman, G.: Epidemiology and Incubation Period of Jaundice Following Yellow Fever Vaccination, *Amer J Trop Med* 26:15-32 (Jan) 1946.

18. Mirick, G.S., and Shank, R.E.: An Epidemic of Serum Hepatitis Studies Under Controlled Conditions, *Trans Amer Clin Climat Assoc* 71:176-190, 1959.

19. Havens, W.P., Jr.: Experiment in Cross Immunity Between Infectious Hepatitis and Homologous Serum Jaundice, *Proc Soc Exp Biol Med* 59:148-150 (June) 1945.

July 20, 1984
(*JAMA* 1984;252:402-406)

# Landmarks in Viral Hepatitis*

## Sheila Sherlock, MD, DBE

Epidemic jaundice was mentioned by Hippocrates[1] (460-375 BC) in *De Morbus Internis*. It was recognized as an infectious disease of war, huge epidemics being reported in almost every conflict from the American Civil War to Gallipoli in 1915[2] (Fig 1). The second World War proved no exception, there being 200,000 cases among US troops from 1942 to 1945[3]; five million Germans, civilians and military, are said to have suffered. This led to a great impetus to the understanding and prevention of the disease. In 1865, Virchow[4] had described one patient, suffering from epidemic jaundice, in whom the lower end of the common bile duct was blocked by a plug of mucus. This led to the term *catarrhal jaundice*; the disease was thought to be due to catarrh, with mucus obstructing the bile duct. This caused confusion and limited progess in the understanding of the disease. In the early 1940s, the advent of safe aspiration needle biopsy of the liver at once demonstrated that the lesion in epidemic jaundice was indeed a true inflammation or hepatitis and not obstructive.[5,6]

Between 1939 and 1945, there were large epidemics of syringe transmissions of jaundice in venereal disease clinics, diabetic clinics, and rheumatology clinics. This led MacCallum[7] to suggest that there was a common factor in all these outbreaks, namely, that jaundice may be transmitted from patient to patient by means of syringes and needles that had been inadequately sterilized. In 1942, there was the largest outbreak of serum hepatitis, when jaundice developed in 28,585 young American soldiers inoculated with yellow fever vaccine, 62 of whom died.[8] The cause was presumably a filterable agent that was present in the human serum used in the culture medium for the yellow fever vaccine.

Although studies of natural history had suggested two distinct types of epidemic jaundice, there was still uncertainty concerning the number. This was partly solved by human volunteer studies. One type was produced by fecal material and the other transmitted by serum.[3] The actual distinction of the two types, now designated virus A (formerly infectious) and virus B (formerly serum), was a direct consequence of Saul Krugman's[9] work at the Willowbrook State School. One type resembled classic infectious hepatitis and had an incubation period of 30 to 38 days, a relatively short period of abnormal serum transaminase activity (three to 19 days), and a high degree of contagion. The other type resembled serum hepatitis and had a longer incubation period (41 to 108 days) and a longer period of abnormal transaminase activity (35 to 200 days). This type was only moderately contagious. Patients with the infectious type were immune to the same type, and patients with the serum type were not immune to the infectious type

From the Royal Free Hospital School of Medicine, University of London.

*A commentary accompanying Krugman S, Giles JP, Hammond J: Infectious hepatitis: Evidence for two distinctive clinical, epidemiological, and immunological types of infection. *JAMA* 1967;200:365-373.

Fig 1.—Landmarks in virus hepatitis, from epidemic campaign jaundice to Krugman's MS1 and MS2.

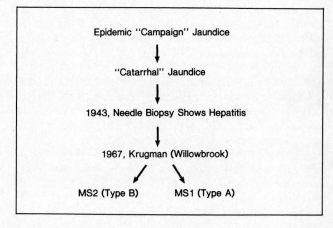

infection. Krugman's pioneer landmark studies at the Willowbrook State School were conducted in accordance with the World Medical Association's draft code of ethics on human experimentation.

### The Nature of the Viruses

**Hepatitis B (SH, MS2).**—The major breakthrough came in 1965, when Baruch S. Blumberg, a geneticist working in Philadelphia, published his classic paper on Australia antigen (Fig 2). (See Chapter 48.) He found in the serum of some patients who had received multiple transfusions an antibody that reacted with an antigen obtained from an Australian aborigine in a simple Ouchterlony immunodiffusion system. This antigen was originally associated with leukemia, and it was only in 1967 that it was associated with virus hepatitis.[10,11] In the next year, this Australia antigen was definitely associated with the posttransfusion serum type of hepatitis now termed *hepatitis B*. In 1976, the Nobel Prize in physiology or medicine was awarded to Baruch S. Blumberg.

Immune electron microscopy was then applied to Australia antigen–positive serum, and virus particles were observed. In 1970, Dane and colleagues[12] described the large spherical particles now known to represent complete hepatitis B virion.

The next major advance came in 1971, when June Almeida and colleagues[13] applied detergent to Dane particles and observed by immunoelectron microscopy that there were two particles, surface and core. The surface particles consisted of both tubules and spheres. The surface particles (HBsAg) in fact represented Australia antigen. They were shown to be uninfectious per se but are of great value in screening the blood of donors and others such as pregnant women, health care workers, drug abusers, and homosexuals likely to be carrying hepatitis and who are at risk of spreading the disease. Hepatitis B surface antigen (HBsAg) also provides material for the hepatitis B vaccine (Fig 3).

The pioneer for introducing a hepatitis B vaccine was again Saul Krugman.[14] Active immunization was induced in children at Willowbrook by inoculation of a boiled, inactivated preparation of a one-in-ten dilution of MS2 serum in distilled water. This was shown to be effective in preventing MS2 hepatitis. The preparation, however, was crude, and protection was not constant. The eventual preparation of a safe, commercially available vaccine was the work of M. R. Hilleman and associates at the Merck Institute of Medical Research. A rather similar vaccine was prepared at the Institut Pasteur in Paris. The source is HBsAg-positive carrier plasma, from which the uninfectious HBsAg particles are extracted. The vaccines are prepared under stringent control, and any infectious agent, even a slow virus, could not survive the various inactivation steps used. The chance of an agent causing acquired immune deficiency syndrome, if it exists, being spread by the vaccine is infinitesmal and has not, to my knowledge, been reported. These hepatitis B vaccines have been shown to be effective in preventing type B hepatitis in homosexuals, renal dialysis staff and patients, neonates born to mothers carrying hepatitis B, and children living in high-risk areas.[15]

The nucleocapsid core of the hepatitis B virion has

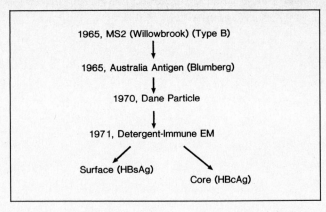

Fig 2.—Landmarks in virus hepatitis, from MS2 to surface and core of hepatitis B virion (Dane particle). EM indicates electron microscopy.

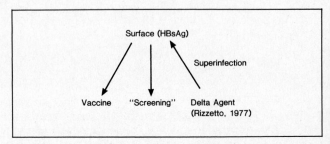

Fig 3.—Hepatitis B surface antigen (HBsAg) is used for vaccine and for "screening" hepatitis B carriers. It may be superinfected with delta agent.

been subjected to even more sophisticated analysis (Fig 4). The core contains an antigen found only in the hepatocyte nucleus. Antibodies to it of both IgM and IgG class can be detected in plasma. The virus-specific IgM-class antibody is relatively short lived and used as a marker for acute hepatitis B infection. It is especially useful at the stage when HBsAg has been cleared from the blood and the IgG HBsAg has not appeared.[16]

In 1972, Magnius and Espmark[17] described a new antigen complex occurring with Australia antigen. This HBeAg is a low molecular weight polypeptide component of the core of the hepatitis B virus, which, like HBsAg, is produced in excess of requirements for the formation of hepatitis B virus (HBV) particles. The "e" antigen and infectious virus particles are secreted from the hepatocyte at the same time. The presence of HBeAg is, therefore, presumed to indicate the presence in plasma of virus particles and the presence of anti-HBe, the absence of virus. Two phases of chronic HBs antigenemia, replicative and nonreplicative, are initially identified by the presence of HBeAg and HBeAb, respectively.

The core of the virion contains DNA. This is circular and double stranded with a gap. DNA polymerase is also found, which apparently repairs the gap. The DNA has been cloned in *Escherichia coli,* with expression of viral antigenic proteins.[18] This has allowed the analysis of hepatitis virus DNA in the blood and liver tissue.[19] Such techniques have confirmed the existence of replicative and nonreplicative phases of chronic HBV infection. Hepatitis B virus DNA may be a more sensitive indicator of the viral replicative phase than the presence of e

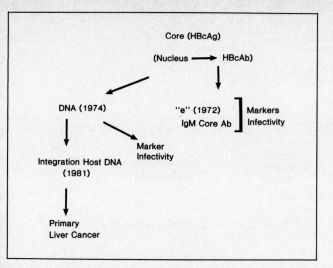

Fig 4.—Hepatitis B core antigen (HBcAg) contains DNA that is marker for infectivity, integrates with host DNA, and is important in etiology of primary liver cancer. "e" antigen is part of core. Serum IgM core antibody marks recent hepatitis B infection.

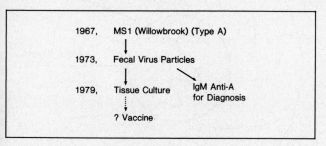

Fig 5.—Landmarks in virus hepatitis A from MS1 to tissue culture and possible vaccine.

antigen in plasma.[20] Virtually all e antigen–positive patients are positive for HBV DNA. Anti-HBe–positive patients are rarely HBV DNA positive. This may explain why anti-HBe patients' blood is rarely incriminated, either in needle-stick incidents or in causing hepatitis in infants of carrier mothers.

**Hepatitis A (MS1).**—The identification of this agent came in 1973, when Feinstone and co-workers,[21] using immunoelectron microscopy, described 27 nm virus–like particles in the feces of volunteers infected with the MS1 strain (Fig 5). These are found at least five days before the elevation of the serum transaminase values and disappear at the time of peak enzyme levels. The patient is thus infectious during the prodromal period but not after the onset of jaundice. The agent has been shown to contain RNA. In 1979, it was grown in tissue culture.[22] This has allowed the preparation of large quantities of viral antigen, so that serological tests for antibody are available. The plasma IgG hepatitis A antibody appears after the acute attack, and its presence simply indicates past exposure to hepatitis A. The wide prevalence of this antibody, in up to 70% of older Americans living in cities, reflects the extent of exposure in early life culminating in mild anicteric disease. The IgM antibody is transient in the plasma, disappearing after about three months. It is, therefore, a useful diagnostic test for acute hepatitis A.

## Further Developments

**Hepatitis B.**—Tissue culture of the HBV has been fraught with difficulty. Certain experimental hepatocellular cancers, particularly the Alexander cell line, can produce HBsAg when transplanted into "nude" (immunodeficient) mice. The latest development has been the successful inoculation of hepatitis B into human hepatocytes in tissue culture, with prolonged excretion of both HBs and HBe.[23]

There is evidence of a strong association between hepatitis B infection and primary liver carcinoma. There is a geographic concentration of hepatitis B viral markers with primary liver cancer, higher in Saharan Africa and Southeast Asia, lower in Japan and India, and still lower around the Mediterranean. The association is least in the United States, the United Kingdom, and Australia.[24] There is a high incidence of hepatitis B viral markers in families of patients with primary liver cancer, especially mothers. It seems likely that 20 to 30 years of hepatitis B viral carriage is necessary for the development of primary liver cancer.

Much more has become known concerning the molecular biology of hepatitis B. Specific probes have been devised to detect HBV DNA sequences in liver and blood. It has been shown that, although in the early stages viral replication is performed using viral DNA, eventually the viral DNA is integrated with that of the host.[25,26] Viral proteins are then coded for by host DNA. This is a necessary preliminary to the development of primary liver cancer. Those who are free of all serum markers of hepatitis B may still have viral DNA integrated in the liver and presumably be at risk of the later development of cancer. This integration makes therapy particularly difficult.[27] Some therapy, with corticosteroids, for example, might even increase integration and thus the risk of the development of a later cancer.

Identification of the patient at risk of having primary liver cancer develop is for the future. It would demand the identification of precancerous (dysplastic) cells in a liver biopsy, but screening procedures that would improve on the diagnostic value of $\alpha$-fetoprotein and better imaging techniques are required. Ultimately, the development of monoclonal antibodies directed against the segment of the viral DNA responsible for carcinogenesis might be useful in diagnosing and localization. Any additional growth impulse, necessary for carcinoma (cocarcinogen) must also be identified. Alcohol may be such a cocarcinogen.

The production of hepatitis B vaccines from carrier plasma is clearly undesirable, and alternative methods of obtaining immunogenic material must be considered (Fig 6). Recombinant monoclonal DNA techniques have allowed the expression of hepatitis B surface antigen in yeast cells and in *E coli*.[28] The antigen closely resembles the HBsAg of human plasma and could be used for a vaccine. The nucleotide sequence of the viral DNA and the organization of the viral genome are known. This has led to the identification of peptides that are immunogenic. Chemically synthesized hepatitis B vaccines are currently under development. It is uncertain whether these vaccines will be protective or whether immunity will persist. One can confidently predict, however, that within ten years the present hepatitis B vaccines will be replaced by those independent of carrier plasma.

**Delta Antigen.**—In 1977, Rizzetto and colleagues,[29] working in Turin, Italy, recognized a new antigen-antibody system in the nuclei of HBsAg-positive patients, and this was called *delta*. This antigen is now known to be a protein with a molecular weight of about 68,000. In serum, delta antigen is a 35- to 37-nm RNA particle coated with HBsAg (Fig 7). It is believed to be a defective virus dependent on HBsAg for its survival. Infection with delta is shown by serum conversion to IgM antidelta or by demonstrating delta antigen in liver biopsy sections.

At first, delta antigen was described in HBsAg carriers from southern Italy, many of them drug abusers, but now it has been found worldwide, preponderantly in HBsAg-positive patients with hemophilia who have received multiple transfusions or in drug abusers.[30]

Simultaneous infection with hepatitis B and delta results in a biphasic hepatitis with two transaminase peaks separated by two to three weeks. Delta antigen is detectable in serum.

Superinfection with delta in an HBsAg-positive carrier patient may be subclinical and marked only by a rise in serum transaminase levels with appearance of IgM antidelta. Alternatively, there may be a clinical and even fulminant viral hepatitis. Delta may eliminate integrated cells containing HBV and so suppress HBV replication and eliminate HBsAg from the serum.

Persistence of delta infection in a HBsAg carrier is usually associated with more severe liver disease, usually chronic active hepatitis and cirrhosis.[31] Vertical spread of delta infection from mother to baby has been recorded.

**Hepatitis A.**—With improving economy and hygiene in the developed countries, virus A hepatitis is disappearing. However, instead of being a mild disease in childhood, often unrecognized, it now affects young adults, often after a visit to a country with less high hygienic standards. In the older person, the attack is more severe and often followed by a prolonged period of relative ill health. A vaccine against hepatitis A would therefore be useful. Preparation would be easier than for hepatitis B, since the agent has been grown in tissue culture. Such a vaccine is currently under development. When available, it would be indicated for use in the military and for those handling feces, such as sewage workers and hospital and laboratory staff. It might be useful to check all those leaving high school for hepatitis A IgG antibody and, if negative, to give hepatitis A vaccination.

**Non-A, Non-B Hepatitis Viruses.**—The identification by serological testing of hepatitis A, B and others such as cytomegalovirus or Epstein-Barr virus did not solve the problem of virus hepatitis. It has become apparent that there are other types with different modes of spread and incubation periods.[32,33] Epidemiologically, there seemed to be at least three types.

The transfusion-associated type accounts for the 7% to 10% of patients receiving transfusion in whom hepatitis develops. It has a long incubation period (about eight weeks), a mild, acute course with continuously fluctuating serum transaminase elevations for many

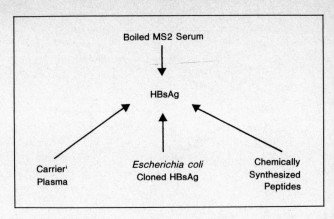

Fig 6.—Methods of obtaining vaccine against hepatitis B.

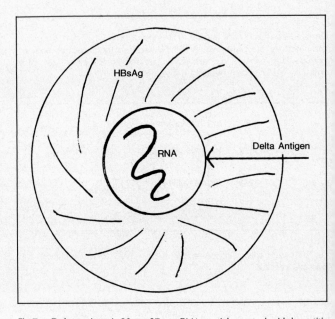

Fig 7.—Delta antigen is 32- to 37-nm RNA particle coated with hepatitis B surface antigen (HBsAg).

months, and a long-term chronicity rate of 50% to 60%. The acute and chronic stages may be virtually asymptomatic, but there is often steady progress toward cirrhosis.

There is also a short-incubation (seven to 16 days) type related to repeated administration of blood and blood products as in hemophiliacs or thalassemics.[34] This has a high chronicity rate.

The third type is the sporadic person-to-person form, which accounts for about 30% to 40% of acute hepatitis in adults in urban areas. It is spread by nonpercutaneous means, presumably enteric. It rarely becomes chronic. The water-borne epidemic form is described from India and is fecal spread. It does not become chronic but may run a fulminant course, particularly in pregnant women.

Transfusion- and blood product–related non-A, non-B hepatitis can be transmitted to chimpanzees and to human volunteers, but specific viral particles, antigen, and antibodies have not been identified. Various explanations have been put forward for the difficulty. The amount of circulating antigen may be small. The absence of a carrier state in some forms with failure to develop antibody has also been evoked. The agent may form complexes with antibody. It has also been speculated that non-A, non-B hepatitis might be attributed to nonimmunologic viruslike agents, such as DNA and RNA, which may be found in blood and plasma derivatives and might end like a virion. Any candidate diagnostic agent for non-A, non-B hepatitis is tested against a panel of infectious sera held at the National Institutes of Health. Failure of the various candidates to react with the sera may indicate that the panel is not representative of non-A, non-B hepatitis as it exists in various parts of the world.

There is no question that non-A, non-B virus hepatitis is being overdiagnosed, but this will continue until virus-specific serological markers become available.

### Summary

Developments in viral hepatitis have been traced from Saul Krugman's distinction of two types, MS1 and MS2 (A and B), and Baruch S. Blumberg's discovery of Australia antigen.

Hepatitis A has been grown in tissue culture, the structure of the virus is known, and the acute disease can be diagnosed. Knowledge of the molecular biology of the more complex hepatitis B virion has allowed the development of an effective vaccine and distinction of replicative and nonreplicative stages of infection. Integration, in the hepatocyte, of hepatitis B viral DNA into host DNA is the precursor of liver cancer. The infection of hepatitis B carriers with another infectious agent, delta, has added a new dimension to the problem. Other unidentified causes of hepatitis have been lumped together as non-A, non-B, and these remain to be defined and accurately diagnosed.

### References

1. Hippocrates: De Morbus Internis in Oeuvres Complètes, vol 7, pp 237-243.

2. Macpherson WG, Herringham WP, Elliot TR, et al (eds): Epidemic catarrhal jaundice, in History of the Great War Based on Official Documents: Medical Services, in Diseases of the War. London, His Majesty's Stationery Office, 1921, vol 1, pp 395-400.

3. Havens WP Jr: Viral hepatitis. Yale J Biol Med 1961-1962;34:314-328.

4. Virchow R: Über das Vorkommen und den Nachweiss des Hepatogenen, insbesondere des Katarrhalischen Icterus. Virchows Arch Pathol Anat Physiol 1865;32:117-125.

5. Krarup NB, Roholm K: Development of cirrhosis of liver after acute hepatitis elucidated by aspiration biopsy. Nord Med 1941;10:1991-2002.

6. Dible JH, McMichael J, Sherlock SPV: Pathology of acute hepatitis: Application biopsy studies of epidemic, arsenotherapy and serum jaundice. Lancet 1943;2:402-408.

7. MacCallum FO: Jaundice in syphilitics. Br J Vener Dis 1943;19:63.

8. Jaundice following yellow fever vaccination, editorial. JAMA 1942;119:110.

9. Krugman S, Giles JP, Hammond J: Infectious hepatitis: Evidence for two distinctive clinical, epidemiological, and immunological types of infection. JAMA 1967;200:365-373.

10. Blumberg BS, Alter HJ, Visnich S: A 'new' antigen in leukemia sera. JAMA 1965;191:541-546.

11. Blumberg BS, Gerstley BJS, Hungerford DA, et al: A serum antigen (Australia antigen) in Down's syndrome, leukemia and hepatitis. Ann Intern Med 1967;66:924-931.

12. Dane DS, Cameron CH, Briggs M: Virus-like particles in serum of patients with Australia-antigen–associated hepatitis. Lancet 1970;1:695-698.

13. Almeida JD, Rubenstein D, Stott EJ: New antigen-antibody system in Australia-antigen–positive hepatitis. Lancet 1971;2:1225-1226.

14. Krugman S, Giles JP, Hammond J: Viral hepatitis, type B (MS-2 strain): Studies on active immunization. JAMA 1971;217:41-45.

15. Krugman S: The newly licensed hepatitis B vaccine: Characteristics and indications for use. JAMA 1982;247:2012-2015.

16. Chau KH, Hargie MP, Decker RH, et al: Serodiagnosis of recent hepatitis B infection by IgM class anti-HBC. Hepatology 1983;3:142-149.

17. Magnius LO, Espmark A: A new antigen complex co-occurring with Australia antigen. Acta Pathol Microbiol Scand B 1972;80:335-337.

18. Burrell CJ, Mackay P, Greenaway PJ: Expression in E coli of HBV sequences cloned in plasmid pBR-322. Nature 1979;279:43-47.

19. Monjardino J, Fowler MJF, Montano L, et al: Analysis of hepatitis virus DNA in the liver and serum of HBe antigen positive chimpanzee carriers. J Med Virol 1982;9:189-199.

20. Sherlock S, Thomas HC: Hepatitis B virus infection: The impact of molecular biology. Hepatology 1983;3:455-456.

21. Feinstone SM, Kapikian AZ, Purcell RH: Hepatitis A: Detection by immune electron microscopy of a virus-like antigen associated with acute illness. Science 1973;182:1026-1028.

22. Provost PJ, Hilleman MR: Propagation of human hepatitis A virus in cell culture in vitro. Proc Soc Exp Biol Med 1979;160:213-221.

23. Guguen C, Thézé N, Brechot C, et al: Prolonged excretion of HBs and HBe antigen by normal adult human hepatocytes in culture with hepatitis B virus, abstracted. Liver 1984;4:68 (abstract).

24. Beasley RP: Hepatitis B virus as the etiologic agent in hepatocellular carcinoma: Epidemiologic considerations. Hepatology 1982;2:215-265.

25. Brechot C, Hadchouel M, Scotto J, et al: State of hepatitis B virus DNA in hepatocytes of patients with HBsAg positive and HBsAg negative liver disease. Proc Natl Acad Sci USA 1981;78:3306-3310.

26. Shafritz DA, Shouval D, Sherman HI, et al: Integration of hepatitis B virus into the genome of liver cells in chronic liver disease and hepatocellular carcinoma: Studies in percutaneous liver biopsies and post mortem tissue specimens. N Engl J Med 1981;305:1067-1073.

27. Bassendine MF, Chadwick RG, Salmeron J, et al: Adenine arabinoside therapy in HBsAg positive chronic liver disease: A controlled study. Gastroenterology 1981;80:1016-1021.

28. Valenzuela P, Gray P, Quiroga M, et al: Nucleotide sequence of the gene coding for the major protein of hepatitis B virus surface antigen. Nature 1979;280:815-819.

29. Rizzetto M, Canese MG, Arico S, et al: Immunofluorescence detection of a new antigen/antibody system (delta/anti-delta) associated with hepatitis B virus in liver and serum HBsAg carriers. Gut 1977;18:997-1003.

30. Redeker AG: Delta agent and hepatitis B. Ann Intern Med 1983;98:542-543.

31. Colombo M, Cambieri R, Grazia Rumi M, et al: Long-term delta superinfection in hepatitis B surface antigen carriers and its relationship to the course of chronic hepatitis. Gastroenterology 1983;85:235-239.

32. Dienstag JL: Non-A, non-B hepatitis: I. Recognition, epidemiology and clinical features. Gastroenterology 1983;85:439-462.

33. Dienstag JL: Non-A, non-B hepatitis: II. Experimental transmission, putative virus agents and markers, and prevention. Gastroenterology 1983;85:743-768.

34. Bamber M, Murray A, Arborgh BAM, et al: Short incubation non-A, non-B hepatitis transmitted by factor concentrates in patients with congenital coagulation disorders. Gut 1981;22:854-859.

Aug 5, 1968
(*JAMA* 1968;205:337-340)

## Chapter 50

# A Definition of
# Irreversible Coma

### Report of the Ad Hoc Committee of the
### Harvard Medical School to
### Examine the Definition of Brain Death

Our primary purpose is to define irreversible coma as a new criterion for death. There are two reasons why there is need for a definition: (1) Improvements in resuscitative and supportive measures have led to increased efforts to save those who are desperately injured. Sometimes these efforts have only partial success so that the result is an individual whose heart continues to beat but whose brain is irreversibly damaged. The burden is great on patients who suffer permanent loss of intellect, on their families, on the hospitals, and on those in need of hospital beds already occupied by these comatose patients. (2) Obsolete criteria for the definition of death can lead to controversy in obtaining organs for transplantation.

Irreversible coma has many causes, but *we are concerned here only with those comatose individuals who have no discernible central nervous system activity.* If the characteristics can be defined in satisfactory terms, translatable into action—and we believe this is possible— then several problems will either disappear or will become more readily soluble.

More than medical problems are present. There are moral, ethical, religious, and legal issues. Adequate definition here will prepare the way for better insight into all of these matters as well as for better law than is currently applicable.

### Characteristics of Irreversible Coma

An organ, brain or other, that no longer functions and has no possibility of functioning again is for all practical purposes dead. Our first problem is to determine the characteristics of a *permanently* nonfunctioning brain.

A patient in this state appears to be in deep coma. The condition can be satisfactorily diagnosed by points 1, 2, and 3 to follow. The electroencephalogram (point 4) provides confirmatory data, and when available it should be utilized. In situations where for one reason or another electroencephalographic monitoring is not available, the absence of cerebral function has to be determined by purely clinical signs, to be described, or by absence of circulation as judged by standstill of blood in the retinal vessels, or by absence of cardiac activity.

1. *Unreceptivity and Unresponsitivity.*—There is a total unawareness to externally applied stimuli and inner need and complete unresponsiveness—our definition of irreversible coma. Even the most intensely painful stimuli evoke no vocal or other response, not even a groan, withdrawal of a limb, or quickening of respiration.

2. *No Movements or Breathing.*—Observations covering a period of at least one hour by physicians is adequate to satisfy the criteria of no spontaneous muscular movements or spontaneous respiration or response to stimuli such as pain, touch, sound, or light. After the patient is on a mechanical respirator, the total absence of spontaneous breathing may be established by turning off the respirator for three minutes and observing whether there is any effort on the part of the subject to breathe spontaneously. (The respirator may be turned off for this time provided that at the start of the trial period the patient's carbon dioxide tension is within the normal range, and provided also that the patient had been breathing room air for at least 10 minutes prior to the trial.)

3. *No reflexes.*—Irreversible coma with abolition of central nervous system activity is evidenced in part by the absence of elicitable reflexes. The pupil will be fixed and dilated and will not respond to a direct source of bright light. Since the establishment of a fixed, dilated

The Ad Hoc Committee includes Henry K. Beecher, MD, *chairman;* Raymond D. Adams, MD; A. Clifford Barger, MD: William J. Curran, LLM, SMHyg; Derek Denny-Brown, MD; Dana L. Farnsworth, MD; Jordi Folch-Pi, MD; Everett I. Mendelsohn, PhD; John P. Merrill, MD; Joseph Murray, MD; Ralph Potter, ThD; Robert Schwab, MD; and William Sweet, MD.

Reprint requests to Massachusetts General Hospital, Boston 02114 (Dr. Henry K. Beecher).

pupil is clear-cut in clinical practice, there should be no uncertainty as to its presence. Ocular movement (to head turning and to irrigation of the ears with ice water) and blinking are absent. There is no evidence of postural activity (decerebrate or other). Swallowing, yawning, vocalization are in abeyance. Corneal and pharyngeal reflexes are absent.

As a rule the stretch of tendon reflexes cannot be elicited; ie, tapping the tendons of the biceps, triceps, and pronator muscles, quadriceps and gastrocnemius muscles with the reflex hammer elicits no contraction of the respective muscles. Plantar or noxious stimulation gives no response.

4. *Flat Electroencephalogram.*—Of great confirmatory value is the flat or isoelectric EEG. We must assume that the electrodes have been properly applied, that the apparatus is functioning normally, and that the personnel in charge is competent. We consider it prudent to have one channel of the apparatus used for an electrocardiogram. This channel will monitor the ECG so that, if it appears in the electroencephalographic leads because of high resistance, it can be readily identified. It also establishes the presence of the active heart in the absence of the EEG. We recommend that another channel be used for a noncephalic lead. This will pick up space-borne or vibration-borne artifacts and identify them. The simplest form of such a monitoring noncephalic electrode has two leads over the dorsum of the hand, preferably the right hand, so the ECG will be minimal or absent. Since one of the requirements of this state is that there be no muscle activity, these two dorsal hand electrodes will not be bothered by muscle artifact. The apparatus should be run at standard gains $10\mu v/mm$, $50\mu v/5$ mm. Also it should be isoelectric at double this standard gain which is $5\mu v/mm$ or $25\mu v/5$ mm. At least ten full minutes of recording are desirable, but twice that would be better.

It is also suggested that the gains at some point be opened to their full amplitude for a brief period (5 to 100 seconds) to see what is going on. Usually in an intensive care unit artifacts will dominate the picture, but these are readily identifiable. There shall be no electroencephalographic response to noise or to pinch.

All of the above tests shall be repeated at least 24 hours later with no change.

The validity of such data as indications of irreversible cerebral damage depends on the exclusion of two conditions: hypothermia (temperature below 90 F [32.2 C] or central nervous system depressants, such as barbiturates.

## Other Procedures

The patient's condition can be determined only by a physician. When the patient is hopelessly damaged as defined above, the family and all colleagues who have participated in major decisions concerning the patient, and all nurses involved, should be so informed. Death is to be declared and *then* the respirator turned off. The decision to do this and the responsibility for it are to be taken by the physician-in-charge, in consultation with one or more physicians who have been directly involved in the case. It is unsound and undesirable to force the family to make the decision.

## Legal Commentary

The legal system of the United States is greatly in need of the kind of analysis and recommendations for medical procedures in cases of irreversible brain damage as described. At present, the law of the United States, in all 50 states and in the federal courts, treats the question of human death as a question of fact to be decided in every case. When any doubt exists, the courts seek medical expert testimony concerning the time of death of the particular individual involved. However, the law makes the assumption that the medical criteria for determining death are settled and not in doubt among physicians. Furthermore, the law assumes that the traditional method among physicians for determination of death is to ascertain the absence of all vital signs. To this extent, *Black's Law Dictionary* (fourth edition, 1951) defines death as

The cessation of life; the ceasing to exist; *defined by physicians* as a total stoppage of the circulation of the blood, and a cessation of the animal and vital functions consequent thereupon, such as respiration, pulsation, etc [italics added].

In the few modern court decisions involving a definition of death, the courts have used the concept of the total cessation of all vital signs. Two cases are worthy of examination. Both involved the issue of which one or two persons died first.

In *Thomas vs Anderson*, (96 Cal App 2d 371, 211 P 2d 478) a California District Court of Appeal in 1950 said, "In the instant case the question as to which of the two men died first was a question of fact for the determination of the trial court . . ."

The appellate court cited and quoted in full the definition of death from *Black's Law Dictionary* and concluded, ". . . death occurs precisely when life ceases and does not occur until the heart stops beating and respiration ends. Death is not a continuous event and is an event that takes place at a precise time."

The other case is *Smith vs Smith* (229 Ark, 579, 317 SW 2d 275) decided in 1958 by the Supreme Court of Arkansas. In this case the two people were husband and wife involved in an auto accident. The husband was found dead at the scene of the accident. The wife was taken to the hospital unconscious. It is alleged that she "remained in coma due to brain injury" and died at the hospital 17 days later. The petitioner in court tried to argue that the two people died simultaneously. The judge writing the opinion said the petition contained a "quite unusual and unique allegation." It was quoted as follows:

That the said Hugh Smith and his wife, Lucy Coleman Smith, were in an automobile accident on the 19th day of April, 1957, said accident being instantly fatal to each of them at the same time, although the doctors maintained a vain hope of survival and made every effort to revive and resuscitate said Lucy Coleman Smith until May 6th, 1957, when it was finally determined by the attending physicians that their hope of resuscitation and possible restoration of human life to the said Lucy Coleman Smith was entirely vain, and

That as a matter of modern medical science, your petitioner alleges and states, and will offer the Court competent proof that the said Hugh Smith, deceased, and said Lucy Coleman Smith, deceased, lost their power to will at the same instant, and that their demise as earthly human beings occurred at the same time in said automobile accident, neither of them ever regaining any consciousness whatsoever.

The court dismissed the petition as a *matter of law*. The court quoted *Black's* definition of death and concluded,

Admittedly, this condition did not exist, and as a matter of fact, it would be too much of a strain of credulity for us to believe any evidence offered to the effect that Mrs. Smith was dead, scientifically or otherwise, unless the conditions set out in the definition existed.

Later in the opinion the court said, "Likewise, we take judicial notice that one breathing, though unconscious, is not dead."

"Judicial notice" of this definition of death means that the court did not consider that definition open to serious controversy; it considered the question as settled in responsible scientific and medical circles. The judge thus makes proof of uncontroverted facts unnecessary so as to prevent prolonging the trial with unnecessary proof and also to prevent fraud being committed upon the court by quasi "scientists" being called into court to controvert settled scientific principles at a price. Here, the Arkansas Supreme Court considered the definition of death to be a settled, scientific, biological fact. It refused to consider the plaintiff's offer of evidence that "modern medical science" might say otherwise. In simplified form, the above is the state of the law in the United States concerning the definition of death.

In this report, however, we suggest that responsible medical opinion is ready to adopt new criteria for pronouncing death to have occurred in an individual sustaining irreversible coma as a result of permanent brain damage. If this position is adopted by the medical community, it can form the basis for change in the current legal concept of death. No statutory change in the law should be necessary since the law treats this question essentially as one of fact to be determined by physicians. The only circumstance in which it would be necessary that legislation be offered in the various states to define "death" by law would be in the event that great controversy were engendered surrounding the subject and physicians were unable to agree on the new medical criteria.

It is recommended as a part of these procedures that judgment of the existence of these criteria is solely a medical issue. It is suggested that the physician in charge of the patient consult with one or more other physicians directly involved in the case before the patient is declared dead on the basis of these criteria. In this way, the responsibility is shared over a wider range of medical opinion, thus providing an important degree of protection against later questions which might be raised about the particular case. It is further suggested that the decision to declare the person dead, and then to turn off the respirator, be made by physicians not involved in any later effort to transplant organs or tissue from the deceased individual. This is advisable in order to avoid any appearance of self-interest by the physicians involved.

It should be emphasized that we recommend the patient be declared dead before any effort is made to take him off a respirator, if he is then on a respirator. This declaration should not be delayed until he has been taken off the respirator and all artificially stimulated signs have ceased. The reason for this recommendation is that in our judgment it will provide a greater degree of legal protection to those involved. Otherwise, the physicians would be turning off the respirator on a person who is, under the present strict, technical application of law, still alive.

## Comment

Irreversible coma can have various causes: cardiac arrest; asphyxia with respiratory arrest; massive brain damage; intracranial lesions, neoplastic or vascular. It can be produced by other encephalopathic states such as the metabolic derangements associated, for example, with uremia. Respiratory failure and impaired circulation underlie all of these conditions. They result in hypoxia and ischemia of the brain.

From ancient times down to the recent past it was clear that, when the respiration and heart stopped, the brain would die in a few minutes; so the obvious criterion of no heart beat as synonymous with death was sufficiently accurate. In those times the heart was considered to be the central organ of the body; it is not surprising that its failure marked the onset of death. This is no longer valid when modern resuscitative and supportive measures are used. These improved activities can now restore "life" as judged by the ancient standards of persistent respiration and continuing heart beat. This can be the case even when there is not the remotest possibility of an individual recovering consciousness following massive brain damage. In other situations "life" can be maintained only by means of artificial respiration and electrical stimulation of the heart beat, or in temporarily by-passing the heart, or, in conjunction with these things, reducing with cold the body's oxygen requirement.

In an address, "The Prolongation of Life," (1957),[1] Pope Pius XII raised many questions; some conclusions stand out: (1) In a deeply unconscious individual vital functions may be maintained over a prolonged period only by extraordinary means. Verification of the moment of death can be determined, if at all, only by a physician. Some have suggested that the moment of death is the moment when irreparable and overwhelming brain damage occurs. Piux XII acknowledged that it is not "within the competence of the Church" to determine this. (2) It is incumbent on the physician to take all reasonable, ordinary means of restoring the spontaneous vital functions and consciousness, and to employ such extraordinary means as are available to him to this end. It is not obligatory, however, to continue to use extraordinary means indefinitely in hopeless cases. "But normally one is held to use only ordinary means—according to circumstances of persons, places, times, and cultures—that is to say, means that do not involve any grave burden for oneself or another." It is the church's view that a time comes when resuscitative efforts should stop and death be unopposed.

## Summary

The neurological impairment to which the terms "brain death syndrome" and "irreversible coma" have become attached indicates diffuse disease. Function is abolished at cerebral, brain-stem, and often spinal levels. This should be evident in all cases from clinical examination alone. Cerebral, cortical, and thalamic involvement are indicated by a complete absence of receptivity of all forms of sensory stimulation and a lack of response to stimuli and to inner need. The term "coma" is used to designate this state of unreceptivity and unresponsivity. But there is always coincident paralysis of brain-stem and basal ganglionic mechanisms as manifested by an abolition of all postural reflexes, including induced decerebrate postures; a complete paralysis of respiration; widely dilated, fixed pupils; paralysis of ocular movements; swallowing; phonation; face and tongue muscles. Involvement of spinal cord, which is less constant, is reflected usually in loss of tendon reflex and all flexor withdrawal or nocifensive reflexes. Of the brain-stem-spinal mechanisms which are conserved for a time, the vasomotor reflexes are the most persistent, and they are responsible in part for the paradoxical state of retained cardiovascular function, which is to some extent independent of nervous control, in the face of widespread disorder of cerebrum, brain stem, and spinal cord.

Neurological assessment gains in reliability if the aforementioned neurological signs persist over a period of time, with the additional safeguards that there is no accompanying hypothermia or evidence of drug intoxication. If either of the latter two conditions exist, interpretation of the neurological state should await the return of body temperature to normal level and elimination of the intoxicating agent. Under any other circumstances, repeated examinations over a period of 24 hours or longer should be required in order to obtain evidence of the irreversibility of the condition.

### Reference

1. Pius XII: The Prolongation of Life, *Pope Speaks* 4:393-398 (No. 4) 1958.

Aug 3, 1984
(JAMA 1984;252:680-682)

# A New Look at Death*

Robert J. Joynt, MD, PhD

Death concerns all of us and is a subject of interest as old as humankind. It is, therefore, surprising that a whole new look at death should have been initiated less than 20 years ago with publication of a report from the Ad Hoc Committee of the Harvard Medical School.[1] Reports from committees are, in many instances, deservedly ignored. It is equally surprising that a set of guidelines set up by one institution should have such wide acceptance. The ad hoc committee was chaired by Henry K. Beecher, MD, an anesthesiologist, and various disciplines were represented: neurology, psychiatry, neurosurgery, electroencephalography, theology, and law.

There were two reasons for the report. First, the benignity of nature is such that the organs of the body, which are normally interdependent, usually die together. Unfortunately, the nervous system may not fit into this scheme. The result is a dead brain or a damaged brain in an otherwise healthy body. While this has always occurred, it has been increasingly more common with advances in therapy, particularly the support of the cardiorespiratory system. Second, the acquisition of living organs from dead patients has become an accepted part of medical practice. At the time of the report in 1968, this mainly centered around the need for kidneys. Thus, the imminence of these two issues led to the report, and, interestingly, there had been almost no discussion of such guidelines before the report.[2] The report had three major effects: it was influential in changing the medical and legal concept of death, it set criteria for determination of brain death, and it introduced controversial terms and concepts, such as irreversible coma, into the field of death determination.

The effect of the report touched almost all branches of medicine, opened up new areas of law, and posed new and difficult problems for the theologians and ethicists. The writings on the determination of death have burgeoned, with a recent citation list containing 177 items for a five-year period.[3] It has made physicians into lawyers, lawyers into physicians, and both into philosophers.

### The Change in the Concept of Death

The ancient and traditional view of death is the stoppage of the heart and the cessation of breathing. This is reflected in the legal definition of death from *Black's Law Dictionary:* "the cessation of life; the ceasing to exist; defined by physicians as a total stoppage of the circulation of the blood, and the cessation of the animal and vital functions consequent thereon, such as respiration, pulsation . . ."[4]

With the gradual acceptance by physicians of the concept of brain death, there was increasing anxiety in the medical profession about the lack of legal acceptance of this condition. Although judicial opinion generally accepted the concept, there were numerous cases citing medical personnel as the proximate cause of death and seeking to dismiss charges against the assailant who was responsible for the final injury.[5] In jurisdictions using common law, the first statute recognizing the concept of brain death was enacted in Kansas in 1970.[6] This statute and many to follow accepted two conditions as criteria for death: the first was the traditional condition, the absence of function of the heart, but the second was the absence of function of the brain. This two-choice model has been criticized, because confusion might arise as to which criterion should be used. Two of the critics proposed a model to rectify this problem.[7] In the model, irreversible cessation of spontaneous brain function is considered death only if irreversible cessation of spontaneous respiratory and circulatory function cannot be determined because of artificial means of support. Several states have statutes using variations of this model.[8]

As state after state recognized brain death, there was

From the Department of Neurology, University of Rochester (NY).

*A commentary on A definition of irreversible coma: Report of the Ad Hoc Committee of the Harvard Medical School To Examine the Definition of Brain Death. *JAMA* 1968;205:337-340.

increasing concern about the lack of uniformity in the wording of statutes dealing with this issue. Walker,[5] in an excellent review, suggests that the nonuniformity might lead to the macabre situation in which a patient transported interstate might be legally dead in one state and not the other. Recognition of this problem led to the effort by many groups to construct a proposal for the legal definition of death and to encourage universal acceptance of such a definition.[8] The American Bar Association, the American Medical Association, and the National Conference of Commissioners on Uniform State Laws all provided model wording for a statute defining death. Other countries have also struggled with the problem and have adopted legal definitions of death. The diversity of proposals led to the formation of the President's Commission for the Study of Ethical Problems in Medicine and Biomedical and Behavioral Research, chaired by Morris B. Abram, JD. The report of the commission that defined death was presented to President Reagan on July 9, 1981.[8] It contained the definition recommended by the commission and also was approved by the three organizations just mentioned, which had previously proposed model legislation. The recommended proposal was as follows:

### Uniform Determination of Death Act

An individual who has sustained either (1) irreversible cessation of circulatory and respiratory functions, or (2) irreversible cessation of all functions of the entire brain, including the brain stem, is dead. A determination of death must be made in accordance with accepted medical standards.

It goes on with this statement: "The Commission recommends the adoption of this statute in all jurisdictions in the United States."

In a preamble to the recommendation, the commission made a number of conclusions, among which was that "death is a unitary phenomenon which can be accurately demonstrated either on the traditional grounds of irreversible cessation of heart and lung functions or on the basis of irreversible loss of all functions of the entire brain." At present, most statutes and most judicial opinions accept the extension of the definition of death originally introduced by the Harvard Medical School committee, although the form of the acceptance varies.

The public acceptance of the concept of brain death varies. It is ingrained in most people's minds that stoppage of the heart is death. All of us have grown up with the movie or television image of the sad shake of the doctor's head after he feels for the lifeless pulse. The frightening specter of being buried alive after premature pronouncement of death has been dreaded for centuries and has not disappeared. In 1980, after a BBC television program entitled "Transplants – Are the Donors Really Dead?" there was a great public furor and a drop-off in the number of kidney donors.[9,10] So, there is still not universal acceptance of the idea of brain death or the means of its determination.

### Criteria for Determination of Death

There were four criteria recommended by the Ad Hoc Committee for the Diagnosis of Irreversible Coma:

unreceptivity and unresponsivity, no movements or breathing, no reflexes, and a flat EEG. The last of these was confirmatory. The first two conditions have remained as fundamental for the diagnosis. The third, no reflexes, has been modified as more and more of these patients have been examined. The last condition, a flat EEG, has been and continues to be a controversial issue.

The clarifying statement from the committee concerning the first condition is "a total unawareness of externally applied stimuli." Refinements in testing methods have not changed this rule.

The second condition of lack of spontaneous respiration is fundamental to the diagnosis but may be difficult to demonstrate. The methods for determining apnea have been argued. The patients, who are on mechanical respirators, must be deprived of respiratory assistance to determine whether they are truly apneic. The time recommended by the ad hoc committee was three minutes without respiratory assistance. However, this committee, as have other groups, placed admonitions regarding carbon dioxide tension of the blood. In order for a suitable impetus to activate the respiratory centers if they are still viable, the arterial $PCO_2$ level must rise above the value necessary to stimulate respiration. If the patient has had low levels of $PaCO_2$, it could take several minutes to achieve a suitable level. Most recent recommendations urge that blood gas monitoring be done so that normal levels of $CO_2$ are present before the period of apnea. Therefore, the original proposal of three minutes without the respirator is of reduced value. However, the committee noted that the carbon dioxide tension should be normal before the test and that the patient should have been breathing room air ten minutes before the test period.

The condition that no reflexes be present has been modified, as muscle stretch reflexes are frequently present when all of the other criteria for brain death have been satisfied.[11] The ad hoc committee report was equivocal on this when it stated, "As a rule the stretch of [sic] tendon reflexes cannot be elicited." In a collaborative study,[12] 71 of 187 patients satisfying the criteria for brain death had active muscle stretch reflexes. Because spinal reflex activity may remain, the emphasis is now on absent cephalic reflexes, which require an intact brain stem. Examples of these are pupillary, corneal, oculocephalic, oculovestibular, snout, gag, and swallowing reflexes. Also, the pupils are not always dilated, but they are fixed to stimulation. In the collaborative study,[12] 44 of 187 patients had small pupils but had all of the other conditions necessary for the diagnosis of brain death.

The flat or isoelectric EEG has been recommended as a confirmatory test by most groups or individuals setting criteria for brain death. Much of the discussion has centered around technical matters of recording,[13] but the major concern has been the reliability of the flat EEG to indicate brain death. It has been accepted that drug intoxication and metabolic disorders may be associated with a flat EEG and that these conditions must be ruled out in making a diagnosis of brain death. However, sporadic reports appear in which a flat EEG is recorded in the absence of these conditions and the patient survives.

In many instances there are technical inadequacies in the recording of the EEG or there is disagreement about the presence or absence of brain waves.[14] The EEG must be used in conjunction with all the other clinical criteria and remains, as the ad hoc committee emphasized, a confirmatory test.

The duration of time for observation has never been settled. In referring to the clinical criteria, the ad hoc committee stated, "All of the above tests shall be repeated at least 24 hours later with no change." With the increasing demand for donor organs, there is greater pressure for organs in the best possible condition. However, all of the criteria for brain death warn against associating the two issues. In the report to the President,[8] the commission reiterated this separation in their conclusion "that any statutory 'definition' should be kept separate and distinct from provisions governing the donation of cadaver organs and from any legal rules on decisions to terminate life-sustaining treatment." In this same report, guidelines were offered for medical consultants by a group of physicians with great experience in this area. They recommended an observation period of six hours if confirmatory tests were available and 12 hours if they were not. For anoxic brain damage, they stated that 24 hours of observation is generally desirable for ascertainment of brain death but that this period may be reduced if a test shows cessation of cerebral blood flow or if an EEG shows electrocerebral silence in an adult patient without drug intoxication, hypothermia, or shock.

### Introduction of Controversial Concepts

The ad hoc committee used the term *irreversible coma* as the new criterion for death. Some authors had used this term as a translation of *coma dépassé,* a term originally introduced in 1959 to designate patients in deep coma.[15] Irreversible coma can exist in cases other than brain death, eg, patients with long-standing coma without structural damage to the brain.[16] The term is also occasionally used for a persistent vegetative state in which the patient has vestiges of neurological function and seems wakeful but is unaware and does not initiate any complex behavior. Therefore, the term introduced by the committee has been criticized for its inexactness, and other terms have been used to describe this clinical condition. These other terms have also been criticized for various reasons. There is also confusion about the terms *brain death* and *cerebral death*. There are, for example, patients with cerebral destruction in whom the brain stem is still active, and patients with cerebral activity without brain-stem function. Many authors have advanced the concept that death of the brain stem is brain death, and clinical signs that indicate this are the only requisite for the determination of death.[9] This view is commonly held in the United Kingdom.

While arguments about these terms may seem like inconsequential carping about technical terms, they have great significance as to how the medical profession and the public view this concept. There are convincing arguments that *brain death* is a confusing term to physicians and that this confusion may be transmitted to the public.[10] It is often thought of as a prelude or a sign of imminent death. While the ad hoc committee may have used an unfortunate term, *irreversible coma,* there was no equivocation about the presence of their clinical criteria and the declaration of death.

---

The Harvard Committee report likely spawned more medicolegal discussion and action than any other publication. Almost every legal entity has had to deal with this new concept of death, and most medical standards for death of the brain originate, with some modifications, from the criteria set forth in this article. The prescience of this committee has become even more obvious as hundreds of clinical observations have borne out the diagnostic value of their clearly stated clinical rules.

### References

1. A definition of irreversible coma: Report of the Ad Hoc Committee of the Harvard Medical School to Examine the Definition of Brain Death. *JAMA* 1968;205:337-340.

2. Silverman D: Cerebral death: The history of the syndrome and its identification. *Ann Intern Med* 1971;74:1003-1005.

3. Brain death criteria, in *National Library of Medicine Literature Search (January 1977 through April 1982),* No. 82-2. Bethesda, Md, National Institutes of Health, National Library of Medicine, 1982.

4. *Black's Law Dictionary,* ed 4. St Paul, West Publishing Co, 1968.

5. Walker AE: *Cerebral Death,* ed 2. Munich, Germany, Urban and Schwarzenberg, 1981.

6. Curran WJ: Legal and medical death: Kansas takes the first step. *N Engl J Med* 1971;284:260-261.

7. Capron AM: The development of law on human death, in Korein J (ed): *Brain Death: Interrelated Medical and Social Issues.* Ann NY Acad Sci 1978;315:45-61.

8. President's Commission for the Study of Ethical Problems in Medicine and Biomedical and Behavioral Research: *Defining Death: Medical, Legal and Ethical Issues in the Determination of Death.* Government Printing Office, 1981.

9. Pallis C: *ABC of Brain Stem Death,* in *Br Med J.* London, Tavistock Square, 1983.

10. Molinari GF: Brain death, irreversible coma, and words doctors use. *Neurology* 1982;32:400-402.

11. Black PM: Brain death: I. *N Engl J Med* 1978;299:338-344.

12. An appraisal of the criteria of cerebral death: A summary statement: A collaborative study. *JAMA* 1976;237:982-986.

13. Silverman D, Saunders MG, Schwab RS, et al: Cerebral death and the electroencephalogram: Report of the Ad Hoc Committee of the American Encephalographic Society of EEG Criteria and Determination of Cerebral Death. *JAMA* 1969;209:1505-1510.

14. Bennett DR: The EEG in the determination of brain death, in Korein J (ed): *Brain Death: Interrelated Medical and Social Issues.* Ann NY Acad Sci 1978;315:45-61, 110-120.

15. Mollaret P, Bertrand I, Mollaret H: Coma dépassé et necroses nerveuses centrales massives. *Rev Neurol* 1959;101:116-139.

16. Korein J: Terminology, definitions, and usage, in Korein J (ed): *Brain Death: Interrelated Medical and Social Issues. Ann NY Acad Sci* 1978;315:6-10.

June 16-19, 1899
(Transactions of the Section on
Obstetrics and Diseases of Women,
American Medical Association, pp 453-470)

July 8, 1983
(*JAMA* 1983;250:222-227)°

# The Gynecologic Consideration
# of the Sexual Act°

## Denslow Lewis, MD

MAN first seeks to live, then he seeks to make others live. The instinct that determines self-preservation is almost equaled in importance and in its control of the individual by the instinct that dictates the perpetuation of the species. Indeed, in certain instances, where there is special individualization, this instinct so far transcends all others that even life itself is worthless without the attainment of the object so ardently desired, ie, without the actual possession of a certain person of the opposite sex.

It is, therefore, proper for medical men in their deliberations to take cognizance of this great factor in human life. They should know its relationship to health and happiness. They should not be deterred from its scientific investigation by false modesty or by the fear of being accused of sensationalism. They should realize its importance as a dominating force in the economy, and they should approach its study from a physiological as well as a pathological standpoint in reference to each sex.

### Description of the Sexual Act

The perpetuation of the species is ensured by the fact that the all-powerful instinct demands the perpetration of the sexual act, which differs in its mechanism according to the individual exigencies of different genera. In the genus *Homo* there is first *libido sexualis,* which is normally followed by erection on the part of the male

and by a relaxation of the vulva and vagina together with increased secretion from neighboring muciparous glands on the part of the female. There is also a turgescence of the female external genitals, accompanied by what may be called an "erection" of the clitoris, which is the analogue of the penis or, as Browning[1] claims, of its glans, corpora cavernosa, and crura. However, the clitoris, on account of its frenum, when erected, points downward. Then follows intromission, which is favored by the shape of the glans penis and the direction of the vestibule. There now occur variable movements with a view of increasing the voluptuous sensation that has been produced by contact. On the part of the male, the movement is chiefly in a to-and-fro direction, accompanied by an increase in erection and in the pleasurable sensation experienced. Finally, the acme of delight is reached and culminates in the orgasm, at which time an emission of semen and the contents of different glands takes place by means of ejaculation. The tendency at this time is toward extreme penetration, so that the ejaculated fluid is brought into direct contact with the os externum.

On the part of the female, the increased secretion of mucus and the relaxation of the vulva and vagina have been a preparation for the reception of the penis. There is normally a participation in the pleasurable sensation and a reciprocity in the movement, which occasions increased and repeated contact. There is alternate contraction and relaxation of the vagina and a variable movement of the pelvis. There is a spasmodic expulsion of mucus, simulating an orgasm, which occurs several times in some women during the act, with a variable and sometimes progressive increase in the voluptuous sensation experienced. In most women, such a pseudoorgasm takes place at least once, usually at the time of ejaculation on the part of the male. It has been claimed that at such times there is a forcible contraction of the sphincter vaginae around the base of the penis.[2]

Following the act, there is normally a feeling of pleasurable lassitude, during which erection subsides and the spasmodic contractions of the vagina cease. The

°This article was originally presented by Denslow Lewis, MD, in June 1899 at the 50th Annual Meeting of the American Medical Association in Columbus, Ohio. It was subsequently published by Henry O. Shepard Co, Chicago, in 1900, and reprinted by M&S Press, Weston, Mass, in 1970. Dr Lewis was professor of gynecology, Chicago Polyclinic, and attending surgeon, Cook County Hospital, Chicago.

This article was brought to the attention of the present Editor of *JAMA* by Marc H. Hollender, MD, who, since chancing upon it 15 years ago, has taken up Dr Denslow Lewis' cause. The details of Dr Lewis' struggle to have this article published in *JAMA* are described in Dr Hollender's account of "A Rejected Landmark Paper on Sexuality" (p 473).

psychic phenomena now differ in the two sexes, as Schopenhauer[3] has well explained. The woman has given the supreme proof of her love. She experiences toward the partner of her embrace an increased affection, dependent, perhaps, on her recognition in him of the potential father of her child. In the man, the case is different. He has first of all obeyed the dominating instinct of his nature. His gratification, especially in case of repetition, becomes not unmixed with disappointment. The male animal, from the nature of things, is normally polygamous. Man is no exception. Often his marriage vows and the restraints imposed by modern civilization fail to prevent extramarital fornication.

It is not my purpose, except incidentally, to refer to the perversions and unnatural practices so ably described by Kraft-Ebing. They exist, however, in our midst, especially among young girls, to a deplorable extent, and they have their effect on women in their marital relationship. I propose to discuss the sexual act from its gynecologic aspect and, after a presentation of the facts as I understand them, to inquire into the etiologic relationship of certain habits, practices, and pathological conditions that interfere with the normal performance and, thus, bring disaster to many a home and disruption to many of our social institutions. The sexual act must be performed with satisfaction to both participants in the conjugal embrace, or there is danger for husband and wife as well as society in general.

### Sexual Education

What are the facts regarding the bride? She too often comes to the marriage bed with inexact ideas of all that pertains to sexual intercourse. Her husband is not usually so ignorant. Not that his parents have told him of the responsibilities and privileges of his new relationship, nor that his physician has instructed him in the proper consideration due a virgin. His experience in sexual matters is a result of intercourse with prostitutes. His knowledge is imperfect and often dangerous. His relations with his bride are sometimes brutal but, it must be added, rarely with design. I have known a hemorrhage started up by the first intercourse, which required ligation of an artery. In this case no harm was intended. The husband simply performed the act as he had been in the habit of doing before his marriage.

Sexual matters should be taught the young at any early age. Girls, especially, should know the usual consequence of sexual intercourse. Their modesty may be shocked but their virtue will be saved. I have twice within a year seen girls aged 13 years well advanced in pregnancy. When a young man is to marry, someone should tell him the difference between a virtuous girl and a streetwalker. He should be aware of the anatomic conditions. He should know that intromission is painful until dilatation of the parts has occurred. He should understand that reciprocity in the mechanism of the act is not to be expected until his wife is accustomed to the marital relationship. He should treat her with the forebearance and consideration that is due the woman he loves, and not as he would treat a woman of the town. As regards the bride, she should be aware of the mechanics of the sexual act. She should realize that at first it is attended with pain and that often

slight hemorrhage may take place. She should be informed that it is a consecration of the·marriage vows and a bond of union between her husband and herself. She should be told that it is right and proper for her to experience pleasure in its performance. It is hardly necessary to give instruction in the danse du ventre as the Arabs do, but it is only fair for the girl to understand that there is no immodesty in her active participation, but on the contrary that such action on her part will increase the interest of the event for both her husband and herself.

### Marital Incompatibility

Now it may happen that six months or a year after marriage the husband may, incidentally perhaps, tell his physician that he is disappointed in his wife. He finds no satisfaction in the performance of the sexual act. This is a serious matter of more importance than many of us imagine. The happiness of that family is at stake. The polygamous nature of the man may assert itself. Gonorrhea or syphilis may be the portion of that young wife. Even the perpetuity of that family is threatened. It needs no statement of mine to inform you how many divorces are obtained on account of marital incompatibility, although that is rarely the ground stated in the bill.

I believe any deviation from the normal standard in the performance of the sexual act should be carefully investigated. Very often there is an error of function that can be remedied. It often happens that the fault is the man's. He fails to appreciate the anatomic and physiological differences of the sexes. He will come home from the club at midnight and find his wife in bed and half asleep. Erection is speedily followed by intromission, and often before the wife is really awake, the orgasm has occurred. What is there to say to such a man? He should be told the physiology of the act. He should be informed regarding libido sexualis. He should understand that he is not the master but the companion of his wife. Her rights should be acknowledged and respected as well as his. Marriage, after all, partakes very much of the nature of a business partnership; every principle of justice and equity demands that there be no tyranny or assumption of superiority in a matter like the sexual act, which is vital to the happiness of each partner. Every egotistic attempt defeats its own end.

The physiology and philosophy of sexual erethism in the female require no detailed description in this connection. Suffice it to say that the clitoris, introitus vaginae, and portio vaginalis are the chief factors in its production. These parts vary, in different individuals, in relative excitability. Moreover, they are not the only factors. The nipples, the tongue, the lips, the neck, indeed, almost the entire body may be judiciously utilized to maintain and increase the libido sexualis. It must be remembered that in the woman, the desire for courtship often exceeds the desire for the sexual act. The preliminaries are, therefore, with her of chief importance and should receive proper consideration in every instance. The secretion from the Bartholin glands and the relaxation of the vulva and vagina are the normal indications for intromission, which should be accomplished without pain. This is always possible by the exercise of due caution and kind consideration, which is no more than the wife has a right to demand.

As regards the movements that by repeated contact produce and intensify the voluptuous sensation experienced, there is much variation in different women. In certain instances, the extreme degree of pleasure is experienced when the penis is in direct contact with the clitoris and introitus vaginae. In these cases deep penetration will be avoided. By judicious maneuvering, titillation of the most sensitive regions by the glans penis will be practiced, and the endeavor will be made to cause repeated orgasms on the part of the woman, very much to her satisfaction. In other cases, there is a variable degree of vaginismus. When this is the case, it is the part of wisdom for the man to be passive.

I recall one case where the woman was older than 40 years and the mother of four children. She never experienced the slightest sensation until one evening her husband came home, very much intoxicated, and attempted the sexual act. Erection was only sufficient to permit intromission. The man could do no more and the woman found herself called on to do all. To her very great surprise, for the first time in her life she felt a pleasurable sensation that gradually increased and culminated in an orgasm. She then realized what it meant to be married.

Taylor[4] tells us that in the East Indies it is the practice of the man to plunge both hands into basins of cold water to prevent orgasm. I am not prepared to recommend this method, nor have I statistics as to its efficacy. At the same time, it is only fair to secure the reciprocity of the woman by all legitimate means, and a little consideration of her interests in the proceedings will inure to the benefit of both parties. No unkind or ill-advised word should be spoken. No diversion from the business at hand should be allowed. By every possible means each party to the act should endeavor to make the enjoyment mutual.

### Sexual Response of Women

Women differ very greatly in relative susceptibility to external influences as a means of influencing *libido sexualis*. In some instances, a caress or a clasp of the hand is sufficient to include mucus secretion and an orgasm. The woman turns pale, her lips quiver, her eyes dilate, she almost faints at the anticipation. During the act, she experiences frequent orgasms, accompanied sometimes by convulsive seizures almost epileptiform in character. The orgasms vary in intensity. There is not always a progressive increase. More often a violent orgasm will be succeeded by others of less intensity. There is great variation even in the same woman at different times, dependent on the degree of excitability and the influence to impressions.

Other women are apparently absolutely devoid of sexual sensation. All efforts to awaken an interest in the act are unavailing. They submit to their husbands because they believe it to be their duty. I have known them to insist on the performance of sexual intercourse because they felt a certain indulgence was incident to the marriage contract and they were anxious to do their part. They would apparently feel that any abstinence on the part of the husband was an evidence of lessening affection, and unquestionably they often believe, in a

very general way, that when gratified at home the husband is likely to resist temptation abroad. The ordinary methods of inducing *libido* fail in these women. They are appreciative of the details of courtship, but there is no evident effect. In some instances, there is a defect in temperament or in the general nervous system or an individual incompatibility that no manipulation or treatment can overcome. In many cases, I am happy to say, observation and the intelligent application of a rational therapeusis permit the woman to return to the normal type, and to take her place, where she by right belongs, as the companion of her husband and as his partner in the conjugal embrace.

There are women for whom the sexual act is not only devoid of pleasure but positively repugnant. In certain instances, these women have been accustomed to find gratification in abnormal practices from their earliest girlhood. It is, I fear, not generally known to what extent these practices exist among young girls. They would look with shame on any familiarity with a boy. They are circumspect in their behavior and modest in their demeanor. The thought of ever allowing a boy to kiss them would not be entertained. They have been warned perhaps against indiscretion, and their regard for conventionality, their natural refinement of character, protects them against all semblance of impropriety. They think no harm can come from any form of intimacy with one of their own sex. With the awakening of sexual appetite there too often develops an objectivation of affection toward a congenial girl friend. No warning has ever been given against the dangers of such an intimacy. The parents look with approval on the growing friendship between their daughter and the daughter of worthy neighbors. They are thankful, perhaps, that their daughter shows no inclination to associate with boys. The young girls, thus thrown together, manifest an increasing affection by the usual tokens. They kiss each other fondly on every occasion. They embrace each other with mutual satisfaction. It is most natural, in the interchange of visits, for them to sleep together. They learn the pleasure of direct contact, and in the course of their fondling they resort to cunnilinguistic practices.

I do not wish to be an alarmist, but I can positively assert the existence of these pernicious practices to an extent that is not imagined by most physicians, simply because they have given the subject no thought. The poor, hard-working girl is not addicted to this vice. The struggle for life exhausts her capabilities. The girl brought up in luxury develops a sexual hyperesthesia that is fostered by the pleasures of modern society. She indulges in these irregular and detrimental practices, perhaps for years, and when she assumes the responsibilities of a wife, the normal sexual act fails to satisfy her.

### Treatment of Sexual Disorders

In the treatment of such a condition, I have often found an overdue hyperemia of the external genitals, which has been relieved by the application of a cocaine solution and the exhibition of saline cathartics. Often the glans clitoris will be especially irritable. On two occasions in my experience it was adherent. When liberated it was possible, by the means indicated, to control the hyperesthesia. In one case, the clitoris was hypertrophied and excessively sensitive. As a last resort, I felt justified in performing an amputation, and the ultimate result of this case was gratifying. Systemic treatment is usually indicated. The patient is apt to be anemic and debilitated, and the tension of the nervous system is often extreme. In certain instances, large doses of bromides are indicated, sometimes combined with *Cannabis indica*. At other times, calomel and salines are given for a time, followed by pyrophosphate of iron. It is sometimes my practice to give strychnia by hypodermic injection, in connection with the remedies mentioned. The result in 15 of the 18 patients thus treated by me was satisfactory. The intense reflux excitability subsided. By moral suasion and by intelligent understanding of the duties of the marital relationship, the patients became, in time, proper wives. Thirteen of these became mothers. Of the three unsuccessful ones, two of the patients never experienced any gratification during the sexual act, but they both became mothers and their family life has been undisturbed. In one instance, the patient, a marked neurotic, finally became insane and is now in an asylum.

Another class of cases consists of women apparently of a phlegmatic temperament. The anerotism is often due to ignorance, and the passion of these women can sometimes be excited by the means already indicated. In a large percentage, there is a preputial adhesion, and a judicious circumcision, together with consistent advice, will often be successful. I have treated 38 cases of this character with reasonably satisfactory result in each instance, in four to an uncomfortable extent, as the husbands testified. In the others, sufficient passion, real or stimulated, was developed to afford the husband a satisfactory sexual life. Thirty-four of these women became pregnant, one of them five times within the past 14 years.

Occasionally, the clitoris, in addition to being adherent, is abnormally small or singularly deficient in excitability. Under these conditions, in addition to the separation of adhesions it is advisable to endeavor to reproduce the normal physiological state. This is accomplished rarely by electricity, but often by the use of an exhaust pump that may be properly designated a "congestor." When this instrument is employed daily for several weeks, it is usual to observe an increase in size of the clitoris and a development of the normal condition of excitability. Systemic treatment, as already outlined, is persisted in at the same time. The value of damiana has never, in my experience, been demonstrated, although it has been given frequently. The value of alcohol as an aphrodisiac is well known and has been repeatedly demonstrated. Any approach to intoxication defeats the end in view. The judicious use of champagne, a glass or two of sherry or port, or a little whiskey and water will often stimulate sexual passion to a sufficient extent. I have used the congestor in 24 cases. Of these, 14 developed a normal sexual appetite, and the others, possibly as a result of instruction, became satisfactory wives, so there was no domestic complaint.

The cases of infection where the inflammatory sequelae make the sexual act painful need only be mentioned.

The extension of infection to the areolar tissue about th vagina and uterus, the occurrence of endometritis o salpingitis, an inflammation of a cervical laceration— these factors often interfere with the normal performanc of intercourse and, when they are removed, the prope marital relationship may be again resumed, often wit increased satisfaction. This observation has especiall been noted in reference to pyosalpinx, ovarian absces and recurrent pelvic peritonitis.

### Anatomic Interference
### With the Sexual Act

Traumatism of the copulative organs may constitute a anatomic interference with the proper performance o the sexual act. A perineal laceration involving the levato ani muscle or the pelvic aponeurosis may preven satisfactory contact with the penis. It is, I hope, a accepted fact among obstetricians that immediate repai of the vaginal and perineal lacerations is to be recom mended, not so much for fear of prolapse and displace ment, but because each wound of the parts may becom an additional door of entrance for pathogenic bacteri An understanding of the mechanics of copulation fur nishes another important indication for the immediat repair of these injuries. It appears also to favor th technique that for years I have taught and practiced namely, the use of sutures within the vagina. Howeve successful may prove the closure of perineal laceration by sutures passed through the skin and encircling th tissues, I contend that in average hands other methods ar preferable. It is certainly a simple procedure, soon afte the delivery of the placenta, to place the patient in th exaggerated lithotomy position, to introduce retractors and to inspect the injury to the posterior vaginal wall an perineum. If it is found that the tear begins high up, th needle is passed at the superior extremity of th laceration beneath the torn surface, and by a series o interrupted sutures the wound is closed. If the injury i extensive, buried sutures are employed or the continuou suture as recommended by Martin of Berlin. In any event, the attempt is made at a reposition of the parts a they were before the accident, and special care is taken t include the torn fibers of the levator ani muscle and th pelvic aponeurosis. I have known husbands to insist o the repair of perineal and vulvar lacerations, and it i perhaps not unreasonable to infer that fear of sepsis wa not their only motive.

In secondary operations, the result, from the standpoin of this consideration, has often been satisfactory. To b sure, in many cases, infection existed and the jus proportion of benefit derived from the operation canno be determined. In several instances of rectocele and cystocele, where inquiry was made, it was acknowledged that the restoration of the parts has resulted in a resumption of normal intercourse with satisfaction t both husband and wife. In eight cases, where the patien was under treatment for indifference to the conjuga embrace, the restoration of the vagina and perineum according to Goldspohn's method, together with other appropriate treatment, resulted successfully. In two other cases, the vagina was restored by suture, within th vagina, of the torn pelvic aponeurosis and levator ani, but constitutional disturbance—Bright's disease and neurasthenia—apparently prevented a successful outcome.

Injury of the cervix, unless infection follows, seems to have no effect on the sexual act. In three instances, where observation was made, in old stellate lacerations, amputation produced no change in sexual appetite. Removal of tubes and ovaries, in my experience, has been without effect except, as is generally known, in cases of pyosalpinx and other inflammatory affections, where the removal of diseased organs freed the patient from pain and improved her general condition, so that an increase in sexual pleasure would accompany the restoration to health.

In one instance, I had occasion to do an abdominal section for the removal of a silver catheter that had perforated the uterus in an attempt at criminal abortion. The uterine wall was closed, the catheter was removed from under the liver, and an ovarian cyst the size of a hen's egg was tied off. Six months later the patient was safely delivered of an infant, and ever since her sexual appetite has been excessive, very much to the discomfiture of her husband who, during a married life of 12 years, was unaccustomed to such demonstrations on the part of his wife.

### Hysterectomy

Removal of the uterus has the same general effects as removal of its adnexa. In case of disease, restoration to health is apt to restore the sexual appetite. Statistics are meager, but as a general proposition, hysterectomy does not destroy sexual appetite nor in any way interfere with sexual intercourse. My own cases of hysterectomy for inversion were performed in elderly or insane women, so that no information could be obtained. In 18 cases of hysterectomy for carcinoma, the marital embrace was resumed without noticeable difference. In three of high amputation for the same cause, the sexual relationship was continued without interruption. These amputations were performed many years ago, before it was generally recognized that hysterectomy is the only proper operation in uterine carcinoma. Two instances of inoperable cases have been observed where the Paquelin cautery was used from time to time. The presence of carcinoma here caused no diminution in sexual desire, even when intercourse was impossible.

Observations have been made of three cases of vesicovaginal fistula, four of urethral caruncle, six of submucous uterine polypi, 18 of hemorrhoids, and two of anal fissure, with negative results regarding interference with copulation or variation in the sexual appetite. Several instances of hemorrhoids are noted where intromission was painful, but where the normal condition returned following the operation. Abscesses of a vulvovaginal gland in three instances made intromission impossible because of pain. In one case of a large cyst of the left vulvovaginal gland, the sexual appetite was markedly increased to the satisfaction of the husband. In two instances of interstitial fibroids, there developed great sexual desire. One of these cases was operated on by enucleation by the late Dr Etheridge two years ago. The sexual desire, unrecognized until the fibroid appeared, has continued. In the other case, the patient has not yet consented to an operation, but here, also, the sexual appetite was not noticed until the tumor developed. It is possible the increased hyperemia of the parts is a factor in the awakening of sexual desire. This statement is made from analogy, for during pregnancy there is often increased desire during the early months unless undue vomiting or other incidents cause decided interference with general health.

### Discussion

**Dr Howard A. Kelly, Baltimore:** With all due respect to Dr Lewis, I am strongly opposed to dwelling on these elementary physiologic facts in a public audience. I am very sorry he has read the paper. I think we can all sum up these matters very safely and be guided by our common sense and experience. The husband should show due respect to the wife and the wife to the husband in the consideration of this subject, and I do not believe in the current teaching of the day, ie, talking freely about these things to children. The child always follows the immediate impulse, and I do not believe in going into details further than necessary in the elementary instruction which the child receives from teachers in botany and the elements of zoology, because I should be very sorry if in this country these matters became as freely talked about as they have been on the other side of the water. I do not believe mutual pleasure in the sexual act has any particular bearing on the happiness of life, that is the lowest possible view of happiness in married life, and I shall never forget the utter disgust which I felt once when a professional friend of mine in Philadelphia told me that he had repaired the perineum of a mistress for the sake of increasing the sexual gratification of her paramour. I do hope we shall not have to go into details in discussing this subject; it is not necessary. Its discussion is attended with more or less filth and we besmirch ourselves by discussing it in public.

**Dr Charles S. Chamberlin, Kinsman, Ohio:** I wish to thank Dr Kelly for his criticism of this paper. I have a little daughter I think very much of, and I should regret to have her taught such things, and when we come to consider some of the points mentioned in the paper, even a little knowledge would be a dangerous thing to children.

**Dr B. Sherwood-Dunn, Boston:** Before this subject is passed I desire to say a few words. I regret that my absence from the room prevented me hearing the first part of Dr Lewis' paper. All that I have heard I endorse and commend, and I am free to say that I believe that if the majority of our essayists had his courage, the result would be a benefit to the profession and to the public at large. There is not a gynecologist in this room, who has been ten years in this specialty, who has not had women consult him, telling him that they did not have the slightest conception of knowledge of the act of menstruation when children or when they arrived at the age, and that when the menses first appeared they resorted to the application of cold water and stopped the flow, thereby laying the foundation for troubles which have followed them from that time forward. Neither is there a gentleman, who has been a long time in practice, that has not met women who have told him that when they got married they did not have the slightest conception as to the sexual act, what it pertained to, or of what it consisted. I consider that state of affairs a disgrace to the motherhood of America. This is due to a great extent to the false modesty that pertains to our American civilization, which descends to a maudlin degree of sentimentality when it excludes a discussion of the physiologic process which is the foundation of the propagation of the race. The question arises, whether the sons and daughters of the household shall receive sufficient physiologic knowledge to protect themselves from error, and as to whether or not they shall produce in the marriage state the best specimens of their species. The degree of false modesty manifested in the consideration of this subject pertains to America alone. For many years past I have written a number of articles along these lines. Last year, before this Section, in Denver, Colorado, we heard from Dr Denslow Lewis a masterly paper on everyday dispensary work, and I think the time has arrived when false modesty should be relegated to its proper sphere in the human household, and we should approach these questions, which are vital to our well-being and the propagation of our race, with some sort of common sense.

**Dr Denslow Lewis,** closing the discussion: I am aware that I have only a minute or two in which to reply to the remarks of Dr Kelly, so I will simply suggest that there is something more in gynecology than suspension of the uterus and catheterism of the ureters. I contend that we, as physicians, and especially as gynecologists, have a duty to perform toward society, which is not fully performed by the use of the knife or the application of a tampon. I contend that gynecologists above all others should take a stand in the community and exert an influence for the public good. In no way can they do this better than by impressing the truth on the public. The age of consent in certain states is 9 years; that means a child can be offered a box of candy, can be seduced, can become a mother, and the man goes free, because at 9 years the age of consent exists. I have seen many pregnant young girls in the Cook County Hospital, Chicago, and in other institutions with which I am connected, and I have talked with them. Often I find that they permitted sexual intercourse without knowing what it was. Unquestion-ably children should be taught, not necessarily in a brutal way, regarding sexual intercourse and reproduction. I think, as I stated in my paper, that while their modesty may be shocked their virtue will be saved. As regard[s] the question of marriage, it is nice to take a high and lofty view; but if some of the gentlemen will study the philosophy of the subject, they will reach the conclusion that the sexual act is the basis of love, otherwise there is only friendship. The affection which draws one man toward a particular woman is a desire for intercourse, or, as Schopenhauer says, it is the genius of the genus, seeking to assert itself.

I announced to the chairman last year, in Denver, that I would read a paper on the subject of the sexual act, giving the results of 21 years of close observation. My connection with several institutions, where I have seen many illegitimate births, has prompted me to study the sociologic aspect of the subject, and I have endeavored to give logical conclusions, believing that they will be of great importance not only to the members of this Section, but to the profession at large. I trust many gentlemen here present may be induced to study the philosophy of gynecology, and may become as expert in this branch of the subject as they now are in its operative technique.

### References

1. Browning WW: *Practice of Obstetrics.* Jewett, p 24.
2. David R: *Historie de la Generation.* p 96.
3. Schopenhauer A: *The Metaphysics of Love.* Dropper & Dachsel, p 71.
4. Taylor RW: *Sexual Disorders of the Male and Female.* p 96.

July 8, 1983
(*JAMA* 1983;250:228-229)

# A Rejected Landmark Paper on Sexuality*

Marc H. Hollender, MD

FIFTY landmark articles, published in THE JOURNAL during its first century, will be republished during this, the centennial, year. Doing so seems most appropriate. But what about the articles that were rejected because they were too far ahead of their time? No matter how careful the scrutiny or how sound the judgment of an editor, it is to be expected that some important articles would be turned down. A notable instance is the preceding article by Denslow Lewis, MD, entitled "The Gynecologic Consideration of the Sexual Act," presented at the annual meeting of the American Medical Association in 1899.

Howard A. Kelly of Johns Hopkins, a discussant of the paper, stated that the discussion of sex "is attended with more or less filth and we besmirch ourselves by discussing it in public," and George H. Simmons, editor of THE JOURNAL, stated that he was opposed to publishing "this class of literature."[1]

At the turn of the century, it was customary for THE JOURNAL to publish all papers presented at the annual meeting. Therefore, the editor's rejection of the article by Lewis was unusual. On principle, Lewis decided to do battle. Clearly, the difficulty he encountered was because he was ahead of his time.

Like the artist Thomas Eakins, who painted the *Gross* (surgical) *Clinic,* Lewis favored realism and focused on an aspect of life that most people chose to avoid. Eakins shocked or horrified his viewers by realistically depicting a surgical procedure; Lewis shocked or horrified his audience by realistically dealing with a tabooed subject.

As might be expected, Lewis encountered formidable opposition. The forces at play are clearly seen in his interchange of letters with the editor of THE JOURNAL. When Lewis wrote Simmons inquiring when his article would be published, he was informed, "I will candidly say that I do not want to publish your paper. There is much in it that I would like to print, but there is more that I believe would be out of place in THE JOURNAL. . . . There

From the Department of Psychiatry, Vanderbilt University School of Medicine, Nashville, Tenn.

*A commentary on Lewis D: The gynecologic consideration of the sexual act. Presented in 1899 at the 50th Annual Meeting of the American Medical Association. Republished in *JAMA* 1983;250:222-227.

is nothing in it that is not true, and possibly it ought to appear in THE JOURNAL, but with my personal views in reference to this class of literature, I hardly think so."[1]

Lewis' rejoinder was as follows: "I wrote my paper after very careful study and close observation during twenty-one years. . . . I know the extent of ignorance and apathy which exists in the profession in regard to sexual matters. I recognize the amount of injury which is done our women by the thoughtlessness of their husbands. I know how young girls are degraded and outraged by the egotism of men. I felt it my duty to try to bring about some amelioration of this unfortunate situation by calling attention to the truth. . . . If you still see fit to decline my paper, kindly inform me. . . . I shall appeal to the Trustees and, if necessary, to the membership at large. . . ."[1]

Following the receipt of this letter, Simmons submitted the paper to the Publication Committee for their decision; only one of the three members favored publication. After conveying this information, Simmons stated, "If you are willing to rewrite the first part of the article, putting the matter in a little more delicate way, I will be willing to publish the article, otherwise I shall be compelled to return it." The offensive paragraphs were marked. Lewis noted that Simmons' proposal would have the following effect: "An elimination of all reference to the physiology of coitus, the psychic phenomena incident thereto, and the importance of a correct education of the young in sexual hygiene takes away my major premise and my deductions are without scientific foundation."[1]

Lewis added the following comments in stating his position: "I feel called upon to awaken an interest in the profession in what I consider to be a most important matter, however it may be regarded. Moreover, I look upon THE JOURNAL as the official organ of the American Medical Association, designed above all things for the publication of its TRANSACTIONS. I consider it unjust to permit the presentation and discussion of a paper, and then refuse to publish it, unless some motion to that effect has prevailed. . . ."[1]

One member of the Publication Committee stated, "I am opposed to the publication of the article in THE JOURNAL, as it will lay the Board of Trustees open to the charge of sending obscene matter through the mail." On this score, Lewis sought the opinion of eminent lawyers, one of whom, Clarence Darrow, stated that "any physician who did not have the courage to deliver such a paper before an association of scientific men, when he believed it was for the purpose of making people better and happier, and who hesitated for fear that some law might be construed to send him to jail, would not be worthy of the profession to which he belongs."

Lewis submitted the favorable opinions of five of the most eminent jurists of Chicago, but this did not suffice. The previously mentioned member of the Publication Committee now demanded a statement from postal officials. To this, Lewis responded, "If the five legal opinions I submit to you are not convincing, no opinion of any postoffice official would influence you." He added: "We should all do what we think is right. I shall do so at the risk of adverse criticism and even misrepresentation and ridicule. I shall succeed in directing attention to the important subject of sex relationship. I shall make the members of the profession think seriously of these matters and good will come of it. What may be thought of me I can not foretell, nor is it of special importance. Many men have suffered for what they believed to be the truth. I have no wish to be a martyr and I regret any sensationalism. Nevertheless, since I am forced to act, as I believe, in the interests of the young girl and the married woman, I shall make the best fight I can. My paper has already been published in the transactions of the Section. You will have difficulty in explaining why it should not also be published in THE JOURNAL."[1]

Finally, Lewis wrote to the President of the AMA stating that he wished to move in General Session that the members "specially instruct" that his paper be published in THE JOURNAL.[2] He then took steps to inform the membership of the issues involved by publishing his article in pamphlet form, together with a statement of the facts regarding the controversy and the legal opinions in reference to obscenity.[2] He requested instructions regarding the distribution of the pamphlets but received no reply. His efforts to distribute them at the annual meeting were met with one obstacle after another, including orders to desist distribution. The President of the AMA, Dr W. W. Keen, stated that he was unalterably opposed to the distribution of the pamphlets, and he alleged that the pamphlets had been given to women and children, an accusation that Lewis denied.[2]

The matter was referred to the General Executive Committee, where the resolution of Dr Lewis was "very fully discussed." The Committee then moved to sustain the action taken by the editor and the trustees. The membership voted in favor of this motion.[3]

From our vantage point, we see that a landmark article was rejected by THE JOURNAL, much as we recognize now that Eakins' Gross Clinic is a great work of art. Those who are ahead of their times must wait for posterity's verdict. Almost a century has passed since Lewis fought to have his article published in THE JOURNAL, and at last it can be said that his efforts were not in vain.

### References

1. Lewis D: The Gynecologic Consideration of the Sexual Act. Chicago, Henry O Shepard Company, 1900 (reprinted, Weston, Mass, M&S Press, with an introduction by M. H. Hollender, 1970).
2. Lewis D: The advocacy of public regarding venereal prophylaxis: A personal experience. Pacific Med J 1906;49:411-421.
3. Association news. JAMA 1900;35:1559-1560.

# Index

# Index